DATE DUE

			PRINTED IN U.S.A.

CLASSICAL AND MEDIEVAL LITERATURE CRITICISM

Guide to Gale Literary Criticism Series

For criticism on	Consult these Gale series
Authors now living or who died after December 31, 1959	*CONTEMPORARY LITERARY CRITICISM (CLC)*
Authors who died between 1900 and 1959	*TWENTIETH-CENTURY LITERARY CRITICISM (TCLC)*
Authors who died between 1800 and 1899	*NINETEENTH-CENTURY LITERATURE CRITICISM (NCLC)*
Authors who died between 1400 and 1799	*LITERATURE CRITICISM FROM 1400 TO 1800 (LC)* *SHAKESPEAREAN CRITICISM (SC)*
Authors who died before 1400	*CLASSICAL AND MEDIEVAL LITERATURE CRITICISM (CMLC)*
Authors of books for children and young adults	*CHILDREN'S LITERATURE REVIEW (CLR)*
Dramatists	*DRAMA CRITICISM (DC)*
Poets	*POETRY CRITICISM (PC)*
Short story writers	*SHORT STORY CRITICISM (SSC)*
Black writers of the past two hundred years	*BLACK LITERATURE CRITICISM (BLC)*
Hispanic writers of the late nineteenth and twentieth centuries	*HISPANIC LITERATURE CRITICISM (HLC)*
Native North American writers and orators of the eighteenth, nineteenth, and twentieth centuries	*NATIVE NORTH AMERICAN LITERATURE (NNAL)*
Major authors from the Renaissance to the present	*WORLD LITERATURE CRITICISM, 1500 TO THE PRESENT (WLC)*

ISSN 0896-0011

Volume 29

CLASSICAL AND MEDIEVAL LITERATURE CRITICISM

Excerpts from Criticism of the Works of World
Authors from Classical Antiquity through the
Fourteenth Century, from the First Appraisals
to Current Evaluations

Jelena O. Krstović
Editor

GALE

DETROIT • LONDON

STAFF

Jelena Krstović, *Editor*
Suzanne Dewsbury, *Associate Editor*
Craig E. Hutchison, *Assistant Editor*
Janet Witalec, *Managing Editor*

Susan M. Trosky, *Permissions Manager*
Kimberly F. Smilay, *Permissions Specialist*
Steve Cusack, Kelly A. Quin, *Permissions Associates*
Sandy Gore, *Permissions Assistant*

Victoria B. Cariappa, *Research Manager*
Tracie A. Richardson, *Research Associate*
Phyllis Blackman, Corrine Stocker, *Research Assistants*

Mary Beth Trimper, *Production Director*
Deborah Milliken, *Production Assistant*

Pamela A. Reed, *Imaging Coordinator*
Randy Bassett, *Image Database Supervisor*
Robert Duncan, Michael Logusz, *Imaging Specialists*
Christine O'Bryan, *Desktop Publisher*

This book is printed on acid-free paper that meets the minimum requirements of American National Standard for Information Sciences—Permanence Paper for Printed Library Materials, ANSI Z39.48-1984.

Library of Congress Catalog Card Number 86-645085
ISBN 0-7876-2408-X
ISSN 0883-9123

Printed in the United States of America
Published simultaneously in the United Kingdom
by Gale Research International Limited
(An affiliated company of Gale Research)
10 9 8 7 6 5 4 3 2 1

Contents

Preface vii

Acknowledgments xi

Preface

Since its inception in 1988, *Classical and Medieval Literature Criticism* has been a valuable resource for students and librarians seeking critical commentary on the writers and works of these periods in world history. Major reviewing sources have assessed *CMLC* as "useful" and "extremely convenient," noting that it "adds to our understanding of the rich legacy left by the ancient period and the Middle Ages," and praising its "general excellence in the presentation of an inherently interesting subject." No other single reference source has surveyed the critical reaction to classical and medieval literature as thoroughly as *CMLC*.

Scope of the Series

CMLC is designed to serve as an introduction for students and advanced readers of the works and authors of antiquity through the fourteenth century. The great poets, prose writers, dramatists, and philosophers of this period form the basis of most humanities curricula, so that virtually every student will encounter many of these works during the course of a high school and college education. By organizing and reprinting an enormous amount of commentary written on classical and medieval authors and works, *CMLC* helps students develop valuable insight into literary history, promotes a better understanding of the texts, and sparks ideas for papers and assignments. Each entry in *CMLC* presents a comprehensive survey of an author's career, an individual work of literature, or a literary topic, and provides the user with a multiplicity of interpretations and assessments. Such variety allows students to pursue their own interests; furthermore, it fosters an awareness that literature is dynamic and responsive to many different opinions.

CMLC continues the survey of criticism of world literature begun by Gale's *Contemporary Literary Criticism (CLC)*, *Twentieth-Century Literary Criticism (TCLC)*, *Nineteenth-Century Literature Criticism (NCLC)*, *Literature Criticism from 1400 to 1800 (LC)*, and *Shakespearean Criticism (SC)*. For additional information about these and Gale's other criticism series, users should consult the Guide to Gale Literary Criticism Series preceding the title page in this volume.

Coverage

Each volume of *CMLC* is carefully compiled to present:

• criticism of authors and works which represent a variety of genres, time periods, and nationalities

• both major and lesser-known writers and works of the period (such as non-Western authors and literature, increasingly read by today's students)

• 4-6 authors or works per volume

• individual entries that survey the critical response to each author, work, or topic, including early criticism, later criticism (to represent any rise or decline in the author's reputation), and current retrospective analyses. The length of each author or work entry also indicates relative importance, reflecting the amount of critical attention the author, work, or topic has received from critics writing in English, and from foreign criticism in translation.

An author may appear more than once in the series if his or her writings have been the subject of a substantial amount of criticism; in these instances, specific works or groups of works by the author will be covered in separate entries. For example, Homer will be represented by three entries, one devoted to the *Iliad,* one to the *Odyssey,* and one to the Homeric Hymns.

Starting with Volume 10, *CMLC* will also occasionally include entries devoted to literary topics. For example, *CMLC*-10 focuses on Arthurian Legend and includes general criticism on that subject as well as individual entries on writers or works central to that topic—Chrétien de Troyes, Gottfried von Strassburg, Layamon, and the Alliterative *Morte Arthure.* Presocratic Philosophy is the focus of *CMLC*-22, which includes general criticism as well as essays on Greek philosophers Anaximander, Heraclitus, Parmenides, and Pythagoras.

Organization of the Book

An author entry consists of the following elements: author heading, biographical and critical introduction, principal English translations or editions, excerpts of criticism (each preceded by a bibliographic citation and an annotation), and a bibliography of further reading.

• The **Author Heading** consists of the author's most commonly used name, followed by birth and death dates. If the entry is devoted to a work, the heading will consist of the most common form of the title in English translation (if applicable), and the original date of composition. Located at the beginning of the introduction are any name or title variations.

• A **Portrait** of the author is included when available. Many entries also feature illustrations of materials pertinent to the author or work, including manuscript pages, book illustrations, and representations of people, places, and events important to a study of the author or work.

• The **Biographical and Critical Introduction** contains background information that concisely introduces the reader to the author, work, or topic.

• The list of **Principal Works** and **English Translations** or **Editions** is chronological by date of first publication and is included as an aid to the student seeking translated versions or editions of these works for study. The list will focus primarily on twentieth-century translations, selecting those works most commonly considered the best by critics.

• **Criticism** is arranged chronologically in each entry to provide a useful perspective on changes in critical evaluation over the years. All titles by the author featured in the critical entry are printed in boldface type to enable the user to ascertain without difficulty the works being discussed. Also for purposes of easier identification, the critic's name and the publication date of the essay are given at the beginning of each piece of criticism. Anonymous criticism is preceded by the title of the journal in which it appeared. Publication information (such as publisher names and book prices) and parenthetical numerical references (such as footnotes or page and line references to specific editions of works) have been deleted at the editors' discretion to provide smoother reading of the text. Many critical entries in *CMLC* also contain translations to aid the users. Footnotes that appear with previously published pieces of criticism are reprinted at the end of each essay or excerpt. In the case of excerpted criticism, only those footnotes that pertain to the excerpted text are included.

• A complete **Bibliographic Citation** provides original publication information for each piece of criticism.

• Critical excerpts are also prefaced by **Annotations** providing the reader with information about both the critic and the criticism, the scope of the excerpt, the growth of critical controversy, or changes in critical trends regarding an author or work. In some cases, these notes include cross-references to excerpts by critics who discuss each other's commentary. Dates in parentheses within the annotation refer to a book publication date when they follow a book title, and to an essay date when they follow a critic's name.

- An annotated bibliography of **Further Reading** appears at the end of each entry and lists additional secondary sources on the author or work. In some cases it includes essays for which the editors could not obtain reprint rights. When applicable, the Further Reading is followed by references to additional entries on the author in other literary reference series published by Gale.

Topic Entries are subdivided into several thematic rubrics in which criticism appears in order of descending scope.

Cumulative Indexes

Each volume of *CMLC* includes a cumulative **author index** listing all authors who have appeared in Gale's Literary Criticism Series, along with cross references to such biographical series as *Contemporary Authors* and *Dictionary of Literary Biography*. For readers' convenience, a complete list of Gale titles included appears on the page prior to the author index. Useful for locating an author within the various series, this index is particularly valuable for those authors who are identified with a certain period but who, because of their death date, are placed in another, or for those authors whose careers span two periods. For example, Geoffrey Chaucer, who is usually considered a medieval author, is found in *Literature Criticism from 1400 to 1800* because he died after 1399.

Beginning with the tenth volume, *CMLC* includes a cumulative index listing all topic entries that have appeared in the Gale Literary Criticism Series *Classical and Medieval Literature Criticism, Contemporary Literary Criticism, Literature Criticism from 1400 to 1800, Nineteenth-Century Literature Criticism,* and *Twentieth-Century Literary Criticism.*

Beginning with the second volume, *CMLC* also includes a cumulative nationality index. Authors and/or works are grouped by nationality, and the volume in which criticism on them may be found is indicated.

Title Index

Each volume of *CMLC* also includes an index listing the titles of all literary works discussed in the series. Foreign language titles that have been translated are followed by the titles of the translations—for example, *Slovo o polku Igorove (The Song of Igor's Campaign)*. Page numbers following these translated titles refer to all pages on which any form of the title, either foreign language or translated, appears. Titles of novels, dramas, nonfiction books, and poetry, short story, or essay collections are printed in italics, while those of all individual poems, short stories, and essays are printed in roman type within quotation marks. In cases where the same title is used by different authors, the author's name or surname is given in parentheses after the title, e.g. *Collected Poems* (Horace) and *Collected Poems* (Sappho).

Critic Index

An index to critics, which cumulates with the second volume, is another useful feature of *CMLC*. Under each critic's name are listed the authors and/or works on whom the critic has written and the volume and page number where criticism may be found.

A Note to the Reader

When writing papers, students who quote directly from any volume in the Literary Criticism Series may use the following general forms to footnote reprinted criticism. The first example pertains to material drawn from a periodical, the second to material reprinted from books.

Rollo May, "The Therapist and the Journey into Hell," *Michigan Quarterly Review,* XXV, No. 4 (Fall 1986), 629-41; excerpted and reprinted in *Classical and Medieval Literature Criticism,* Vol. 3, ed. Jelena O. Krstovic (Detroit: Gale Research, 1989), pp. 154-58.

Dana Ferrin Sutton, *Self and Society in Aristophanes* (University of Press of America, 1980); excerpted and reprinted in *Classical and Medieval Literature Criticism,* Vol. 4, ed. Jelena O. Krstovic (Detroit: Gale Research, 1990), pp. 162-69.

Suggestions Are Welcome

Readers who wish to make suggestions for future volumes, or who have other comments regarding the series, are cordially invited to write or call the editors (1-800-347-GALE).

Acknowledgments

The editors wish to thank the copyright holders of the excerpted criticism included in this volume and the permissions managers of many book and magazine publishing companies for assisting us in securing reproduction rights. We are also grateful to the staffs of the Detroit Public Library, the Library of Congress, the University of Detroit Mercy Library, Wayne State University Purdy/Kresge Library Complex, and the University of Michigan Libraries for making their resources available to us. Following is a list of the copyright holders who have granted us permission to reproduce material in this volume of CLC. Every effort has been made to trace copyright, but if omissions have been made, please let us know.

COPYRIGHTED EXCERPTS IN *CMLC* VOLUME 29, WERE REPRODUCED FROM THE FOLLOWING PERIODICALS:

Allegorica, v. 1, Spring, 1976. Reproduced by permission.—*The American Benedictine Review,* v. 34, December, 1983; v. 36, December, 1985; v. 39, September, 1988; v. 40, September, 1989. Copyright 1983, 1985, 1988, 1989 by The American Benedictine Academy. All reproduced by permission.—*Church History,* v. 39, September, 1970. (c) 1970, The American Society of Church History. Reproduced by permission.—*Collectanea Cisterciensia,* v. 42, 1980. Reproduced by permission.—*Harvard Journal of Asiatic Studies,* v. 43, 1983. Reproduced by permission.—*The Historian,* v. XLI, February, 1979. Reproduced by permission—*The Humanities Association Review,* v. 29, Spring, 1978 for "Homage to Roswitha" by Karl A. Zaenker. Reproduced by permission of the author.—*International Journal of Women's Studies,* v. 2, May/June, 1979. Reproduced by permission.—*The Journal of Theological Studies,* v. XX, 1969. (c) Oxford University Press 1969. Reproduced by permission.—*Monumenta Nipponica: Studies in Japanese Culture,* v. 43, Autumn, 1988. Reproduced by permission.—*The Second Century: A Journal of Early Christian Studies,* v. 2, Winter, 1982. (c) 1982. Reproduced by permission of The Johns Hopkins University Press.—*Vigiliae Christianae,* v. 31, March, 1977. (c) North-Holland Publishing Company 1977. Reproduced by E. J. Brill NV.—

COPYRIGHTED EXCERPTS IN *CMLC* VOLUME 29, WERE REPRODUCED FROM THE FOLLOWING BOOKS:

Bell, David N. From *Archives: D'Histoire Doctrinal et Littéraire du Moyen Age.* Librairie Philosophique J. Vrin, 1978. (c) Librairie Philosophique J. Vrin, 1978. Reproduced by permission.—Brower, Robert H. and Earl Miner. *From Japanese* Court Poetry. Stanford University Press, 1961. Copyright (c) 1961 by the Board of Trustees of Leland Stanford Junior University. Reproduced with the permission of the publishers, Stanford University Press.—Butler, Sister Mary Marguerite. From *Hrotsvitha: The Theatricality of Her Plays.* Philosophical Library 1960. Copyright, 1960, by Philosophical Library. Reproduced by permission of Philosophical Library.—Davis, O.C.S.O, Thomas X. From "Loss of Self in the Degrees of Humility in the Rule of Saint Benedict, Chapter VII" in *Benedictus: Studies in Honor of St. Benedict of Nursis.* Edited by E. Rozanne Elder. Cistercian Publications, 1981. (c) Cistercian Publications, Inc., 1981. Reproduced by permission. Dronke, Peter.—From *Women Writers of the Middle Ages: A Critical Study of Texts from Perpetua († 203) Marguerite Porete († 1310).* Cambridge University Press, 1984. (c) Peter Dronke 1984. Reproduced with the permission of Cambridge University Press and the author.—Gasquet, Cardinal. From an introduction to *The Rule of Saint Benedic..* Translated by Cardinal Gasquet. Cooper Square Publishers, Inc., 1966. Copyright 1966 by Cooper Square Publishers, Inc. Reproduced by permission.— Gilder, Rosamond. From *Enter The Actress: The First Women in the Theatre.* Routledge Copyright, 1931, renewed 1958 by Rosamond Gilder. All rights reserved. Reproduced by permission.—Goodspeed, Edgar J. From *A History of Early Christian Literature.* University of Chivcago, 1942. Copyright 1942 by the University of Chicago. All rights reserved. Reproduced by permission.—Haight, Anne Lyon. From *Hroswitha of Gandersheim: Her Life, Times, and Works, and Comprehensive, Bibliography.* Hroswitha Club, 1965. Copyright (c) 1965 by the Hroswitha Club. Reproduced by permission of the Estate of Anne Lyon Haight.—Hilpisch, O. S. B., Stephanus. From *Benedictinism Through Changing Centuries.* Translated by Leonard J. Doyle. St. John's Abbey Press, 1958. Copyright 1958 by The Order of St. Benedict, Inc.,

St. Benedict of Nursia

c. 480-c. 547

Italian saint and theologian.

INTRODUCTION

Considered the father of Western monasticism, Saint Benedict of Nursia is among the most influential of the early Medieval Christian saints. The founder of the original Benedictine monastery at Monte Cassino, Italy, Benedict is credited with composing the first true text for monastic rule of the Roman Catholic Church. Written during the decline of the Roman Empire and the nascent era of the Medieval papacy in Rome, the *Regula Sancti Benedicti* (c. 540; *Rule of Saint Benedict*) outlines the ideals of life in a religious community of monks. It is known for its emphasis on compassion and spiritual counsel, and for its relative leniency in describing the requirements of monastic life—the precepts of the *Rule* notably contrast with those of the more austere Eastern monasticism and focus on sanctity, virtue, humility, and obedience rather than on material self-denial. Today the *Rule* continues to be embraced by the Western monastic community and remains one of the most enduring and studied documents in Christian literature.

Biographical Information

Most of what is known about Benedict's life comes from the second book of St. Gregory the Great's *Dialogues*, which he devoted entirely to Benedict. According to Gregory, Benedict was born at Nursia, an area in the Sabine hills of central Italy (what is now the province of Umbria) in about 480. Born into a well-to-do family, he was educated at Roman schools in his youth and later, at the age of fourteen, traveled to the imperial capital of Rome to complete his studies. While there, Benedict experienced first-hand the decadence and vice of the waning Roman Empire. Disgusted with what he saw, he left the capital city to join a loosely organized community of religious ascetics at Enfide (now the town of Affile). Finding his life in the Simbrunian hills unsatisfactory, Benedict retreated to a cave some forty miles east of Rome at Subiaco. After three years of living in seclusion, engaged in prayer and introspection broken only by brief contact with a monk named Romanus, he emerged from his cave and accepted the request of the local monks to become abbot of their monastery at Vicovaro. Disharmony and an attempt on his life forced Benedict to return to the cave. Unable to maintain solitude, however, as word of his wisdom and sanctity spread throughout Italy, Benedict, with the assistance of his numerous disciples,

formed a conglomeration of small monastic communities at Subiaco. Still persecuted by his more ambitious underlings, Benedict later traveled south and created his famous hilltop monastery, Monte Cassino, above the city of Cassino in the province of Campagna. He resided at Monte Cassino for the remainder of his life as abbot of the monastery. There he probably wrote the majority of his monastic *Rule* and, according to Gregory, performed many miracles. Among the most famous is one that is said to have occurred during the well-documented visit of the Gothic King Totila to Monte Cassino in 542, for which Benedict reputedly prophesied the King's second sack of Rome and death within the next decade. Benedict is believed to have died at Monte Cassino in about 547. His feast day is celebrated by monks on March 21, the traditionally accepted day of his death, while the Roman Catholic Church has since reserved July 11 as the saint's day.

Major Works

Benedict's only extant literary work is the *Regula Sancti*

Benedicti (Rule of Saint Benedict), his holy rule for monks. A work of somewhat less than 20,000 words composed over several decades, the *Rule* consists of seventy-three chapters and was originally codified in about 540. The *Rule* itself is primarily concerned with the spiritual and material life of cenobites—monks who live together in the community of the monastery and observe strict obedience to their abbot. Loosely structured, the document is generally organized by subject matter. It begins with a prologue—probably written after the rest of the *Rule* was complete—and several chapters which act as a general constitution for the monastery and offer instructions on living a spiritual life. As for political organization, the *Rule* invests supreme authority over the monastery in the abbot, who is in turn accountable only to the word of God and to the *Rule* itself. The balance of the *Rule* details the structure of life at the monastery, including a proper regimen of prayer, study, consumption, and manual labor, as well as correct behavior for monks and punishments for those who fail to meet these requirements. The *Rule* also includes a considerable discussion of the *opus Dei*, or "work of God," the liturgy the monks were to recite daily, which has since been given Benedict's name as the *Cursus S. Benedicti*. Among the most compelling portions of the *Rule* for critics are those dealing with the monks' spiritual instruction, particularly its seventh chapter, entitled "On Humility." In this chapter, Benedict describes twelve degrees of humility, which he arranges using the common Medieval symbol of the ladder of ascent to heaven. For Benedict, each rung of this ladder represents one aspect of the virtue of humility that the monk must embrace, from his initial fear of God to a vow of silence and a continual awareness of his sinful guilt. Only when the monk has accepted these twelve aspects of humility will he reach the goal of union with God, according to Benedict. In addition to many passages aimed at the spiritual edification of monks, Benedict's *Rule* also contains a great many mundane or bureaucratic pronouncements designed to assure that the Benedictine monastery runs smoothly and in accordance with the decree of God.

Textual History

Critics believe that Benedict drew on many sources for his *Rule*. In addition to the *Bible* and the writings of the great Catholic fathers St. Augustine, St. Jerome, St. Basil, and others, the *Rule of Saint Benedict* demonstrates a significant debt to the earlier treatise *Regula magistri*, or *Rule of the Master*, as well as to the thought of Abbot John Cassian of Marseilles. Most critics are careful to point out, however, that the work is not a compilation of previous writings. In its original form, the *Rule* was composed in the *lingua vulgaris*, or vulgar Latin, the vernacular of Benedict's day, and thus departs in many respects from Classical Latin syntax and grammar. The last seven chapters of the work

appear to have been added sometime after Benedict had codified the prior sixty-six, and its prologue was most likely written last. The oldest extant copy is an Old English text that is preserved at the Bodleian Library at Oxford, England, and was probably written by Benedictine monks in Canterbury in the early eighth century. Among the best-preserved manuscripts is a transcription produced one century later at Aachen, Germany. In 1928 Dom Benno Linderbauer produced his critical text of the *Rule* in Latin, the *S. Benedicti Regula monasteriorum*, which was considered standard in the first half of the twentieth century, while the latter half of the century has seen a proliferation of commentaries on and translations of the *Rule*, attesting to its continued significance and interest to the Catholic clergy, laymen, and contemporary scholars.

Critical Reception

Because critics have observed that Benedict borrowed liberally from the *Regula magistri* and various other sources in composing his *Rule*, the question of its originality has been a perennial theme of scholarly inquiry. While arguments on both sides of this question continue to be offered, there is critical consensus that, despite Benedict's considerable debt to prior spiritual literature, his *Rule* reflects a quality of innovation unique in the genre. Benedict himself humbly described the work as "a little rule for beginners," which scholars have since interpreted as a reflection of the deep humility he championed in the document. Overall, commentators have seen the *Rule* as simply a model of monastic behavior and have warned against extrapolating Benedict's words outside of the context of the monastery. Antoine Vergote is representative of many scholars in arguing that the *Rule* does not present "a universal, religious human ideal" and in emphasizing its focus on monastic obedience, humility, and self-discovery as a means of human redemption. More recently, critics have pondered whether the *Rule* should be interpreted literally in modern times; most have observed that Benedict's tendency to embrace the subjective qualities of human nature in the document has contributed to the enduring currency of his *Rule* and to its continued applicability in modern life.

PRINCIPAL WORKS

Regula Sancti Benedicti [*Rule of Saint Benedict*] c. 540

PRINCIPAL ENGLISH TRANSLATIONS

The Rule of Saint Benedict [edited and translated by Justin McCann] 1952

The Rule of Saint Benedict [edited and translated by
  Cardinal Gasquet] 1966
*Households of God: The Rule of Saint Benedict with
  Explanations for Monks and Lay-People Today* [ed-
  ited and translated by David Parry] 1980
Benedict's Rule: A Translation and Commentary [ed-
  ited and translated by Terrence G. Kardong] 1996

CRITICISM

Cuthbert Butler (essay date 1919)

SOURCE: "St. Benedict" and "St. Benedict's Idea" in
*Bendictine Monachism: Studies in Benedictine Life and
Rule*, Longmans, Green and Co., 1919, pp. 1-10; 23-
34.

[*In the following excerpt, Butler surveys St. Benedict's
life and monastic ideals.*]

St Benedict

One morning, in the early spring of the first year of the
century, I was standing at a cave, looking out into the
darkness that still enshrouded the scene. And as I looked
the first streaks of dawn began gradually to lift the
shroud of night and to reveal, first the rugged mountains across the ravine that lay beneath my feet; and
then the cruel naked rocks, with never a tree or shrub
to soften their austerity, surrounding the valley on all
sides; and at last the wild grandeur of the scene in its
solemn simplicity and solitude. And as the features of
the landscape gradually took shape, my thoughts went
back to a youth who just fourteen centuries before had
passed the years of opening manhood in that cave, and
on many such an early spring-day morning, belike in
the first year of the sixth century, looked out on the
same wild, grand, austere scene that was unfolding
itself beneath my eyes. And the thought of that youth,
that boy, arose in my mind—what he could have been
like, who had the courage and the strength to live for
three years in that cave, feeding his young heart on
God alone; what must have been that spirit, what that
soul, that could brave, and endure, three such years of
solitary formation for the work God called him to do.

St Benedict was born somewhere about the third quarter of the fifth century; the year 480, traditionally given
for his birth, is no more than an approximation, but it
may be accepted as representing the date with rough
accuracy. The only fixed chronological point in his life
is the year 542, when he was visited by the Gothic
king Totila at Monte Cassino; it is clear he was then
advanced in years, and it seems he died not long after.
All that we know of the facts of his life is what St
Gregory the Great tells us in the Dialogues, the second
book of which is wholly given up to St Benedict. St

Gregory assures us that his information was derived
from authentic sources, the reminiscences of four of St
Benedict's own disciples whom Gregory had himself
known. The Dialogues is in some ways a trying book
to the modern mind; but the outlines of St Benedict's
life may be traced from it with entire security.[1]

St Benedict was born at Nursia, then a municipal town
and the seat of a bishopric, on the slopes of the Sabine
Apennies: the modern name is Norcia, in the province
of Umbria, not far from Spoleto. St Gregory says he
was born 'liberiore genere,'—of gentle family, we
should say,—words suggesting the wealthy country
gentry of the provinces, but not patrician or senatorial
rank, and thus excluding the late fable that St Benedict
was of the great Anician family. He was in due course
sent to Rome to pursue in the Roman schools the studies of a liberal education; but disgusted and horrified
at the general licentiousness prevailing in Rome, 'he
withdrew the foot he had just placed in the entry to the
world; and despising the pursuit of letters, and abandoning his father's home and property, desiring to
please God alone, he determined to become a monk'
(St Gregory). In accordance with the monastic ideas of
the time, his resolve was to retire to a desert place and
be a hermit. So he fled secretly from Rome and wandered through the hills of Latium, until he came to the
ruins of Nero's palace and the artificial lake at
Sublacum (Subiaco) on the Anio, some dozen miles
beyond Tivoli and thirty miles from Rome; and here he
found the cave that was suited for his purpose.

It has been usual to represent St Benedict as a mere
boy at the time of his retirement from Rome; but those
recent Benedictine writers are almost certainly right
who have maintained that 'puer' means not a child but
a young man;[2] for it seems clear that while in Rome he
was old enough to have been in love (Dialogues, ii, 2).
It is altogether more probable that he was of under-
graduate rather than of school-boy age. The year 500
may be taken as an approximate date for Benedict's
withdrawal from the world and inclusion in the Sacro
Speco at Subiaco.

There in his cave we shall leave him awhile, in order
to take a brief survey of the condition of things social,
civil, and religious in Italy at the time, so as to have an
understanding of the framework in which his life was
set. The picture is one of decay, disorganisation, and
confusion perhaps without parallel in history.[3] The
disintegrating processes that had been at work during
the latter days of the Republic had gone on in ever-
increasing volume during the Empire, and at last assumed vast proportions. Italy had become pauperised
and depopulated: the ceaseless wars at home and abroad
had thinned the population; the formation of huge es-
tates worked by slave labour had crushed out the yeo-
man farmer class; oppressive taxation had ruined the
provincial middle classes; the wholesale employment

of barbarous mercenary soldiers, who in payment for their services often received allotments of the land of Italy, established in the country an element of lawlessness and savagery that was a perpetual menace to the inhabitants. The land was devastated by famines and pestilences, till by the end of the fourth century great tracts had been reduced to deserts, the people had become demoralised and degenerate, agriculture and education had well-nigh died out, and society was corrupt to the core. And then, to complete the ruin, began the long series of invasions of Italy by Teutonic and other barbarians. In 400 came the Visigoths under Alaric and swept over northern Italy; five years later came Radagaisus and his Goths, who were exterminated near Florence; in 408 Alaric returned and this time came to Rome, which he besieged thrice in three successive years, and gave up to plunder and sacking on the third occasion (410), and then penetrated to the southernmost parts of Italy. At the middle of the century the savage Huns, under Attila, the 'Scourge of God,' ravaged the valley of the Po (454), and Gaiseric the Vandal took and sacked Rome (455). A series of minor incursions into Italy, Alans, Herulans, and others from the north, and Vandals by sea from the south, followed in swift succession. Ricimer at the head of the Teutonic mercenaries of the Roman army besieged and sacked Rome (472), and four years later these same mercenaries demanded that one-third of the land of Italy should be given them; on refusal they broke into revolt, seized and plundered Pavia and Ravenna, made their leader Odovacar or Odoacer the ruler of Italy during seventeen years, and from him received the coveted third of Italian land.

In 489 came Theodoric and the Ostrogoths, and there ensued a four years' war between him and Odoacer over the length and breadth of northern Italy, the chief cities being in turn sacked, and other hordes of barbarians pouring into Italy to take part on either side of the fray. In 493 Theodoric slew Odoacer with his own hand and became ruler of Italy, recognised as such by the Byzantine emperor. Under Theodoric and his successor the desolated lands of Italy and the exhausted and decimated population experienced for a generation a respite from the horrors of invasion and war, and a period of recuperation. Theodoric reigned for thirty-three years, till 526. He was a strong and enlightened ruler, and with the assistance of his minister, the Roman Cassiodorus, he set himself to repair the evils that had befallen Italy. His policy is thus characterised by Hodgkin: 'the maintenance of peace and tranquillity, and the safeguarding of all classes of his subjects from oppression and violence at the hands either of lawless men or of the ministers of the law.'[4] As part of this policy, till the last three years of his reign, though an Arian, he gave religious toleration to the Catholics. It is to be noted that the beginnings of St Benedict's monastic institute were made during this brief period of peace and rest for Italy.

And then, soon after Theodoric's death, Justinian conceived the idea of reuniting the Western Empire to the Eastern, and sent his great general Belisarius to wrest, first Africa, and then Italy from the Barbarians and restore them to the Empire. Belisarius landed in Sicily in 535 and passed to Italy the next year. Then began a long period of unparalleled suffering for the whole of the unhappy Peninsula. Naples first was taken, and then Belisarius entered Rome. A twelve months' siege of Rome by the Goths ensued and proved ineffectual. A desultory warfare of four years began, in which the chief cities of Italy—Rimini, Urbino, Orvieto, Milan, Fiesole, Osimo, Ravenna—were in turn besieged; while 100,000 Franks descended into Italy, attacking impartially both Goths and Romans, plundering and sacking indiscriminately, till a pestilence, that carried off a third of their number, compelled them to retire across the Alps. These years, 537-542, were a time of misery for the Italian peoples that baffles description: the entire country went out of cultivation, and famine, starvation, and pestilence raged throughout the land.

At this time Totila became king of the Goths (541), and the war broke out again all over Italy; Florence and Naples and many another city were besieged and taken, and then began Totila's siege of Rome (545). It lasted for a year and more, the inhabitants enduring the extremity of hardship and famine, till in December 546 Totila entered Rome animated with the grim resolve utterly to destroy the city and raze it to the ground. He pulled down great portions of the walls and prepared to fire the public buildings, when he stayed his hand and marched his troops out of Rome, carrying with him all, literally all, of the miserable remnant of the Romans, 'suffering not a single person to remain in Rome but leaving Rome absolutely desolate,' so that 'for forty days or more, no one, either man or beast, remained there.'[5] For six years more was the war continued between the Roman generals and Totila with varying fortunes all over southern Italy, Rome being reoccupied by Belisarius and again besieged by Totila, unsuccessfully in 547, successfully in 549. Then after ravaging Sicily and suffering defeat at the hands of Narses, Belisarius' successor, at Gubbio in Umbria, Totila died in 552. The following year the remnant of the Ostrogothic race in Italy was brought to bay by Narses near Mount Vesuvius and was there annihilated, 553. The very next year the Alamans made an incursion, penetrating as far as Capua, where they also were defeated and almost destroyed by Narses. And then in 568 came the Lombards, who for half a century and more ravaged, harried, devastated the whole Peninsula from sea to sea. But this was after St Benedict. His life tallied almost exactly with the period of Ostrogothic dominion; for he was born but a few years before they came in 489, and he died a few years before their destruction in 553.

If we extend our survey over the rest of the Western Empire we shall see that the calamities of Rome and of

Italy only symbolise those of the provinces. During the two centuries from 400 to 600 covered by the foregoing sketch, what was happening in Italy was happening throughout western Europe. Everywhere was going on the same round of invasions, of internecine warfare between the Teutonic races, of ravages, famines, pestilences, sieges, sackings, burnings, slaughterings—all the horrors of war, utter destruction of the civilisation and institutions of Rome, unspeakable misery and destitution. Gaul, Spain, Britain—it was the story of Italy repeated, for the invasions of Italy were but incidents in the progresses of the various barbaric races through Europe. The Visigoths, and the Huns, and the Vandals in turn swept through Europe in the first half of the fifth century, to say nothing of the lesser peoples that preceded or followed them. At the date of St Benedict's birth the Teutonic settlements may be described thus: Italy formed the kingdom of Odoacer, whom the mixed multitude of revolted Teutonic mercenaries in Roman armies had set up as king; but he was destined to be in a few years overthrown by Theodoric and his Ostrogoths, then occupying what now is Hungary and the lower Danube lands. The Visigothic dominions extended over Spain, except the north-west corner, whither they had driven the Suevi, and over the southern and central parts of Gaul to the Loire. The southeastern parts of Gaul, the country of the Rhone, formed the kingdom of the Burgunds. The north of Gaul and of the Rhineland was held by the various tribes of the Franks, still pagan, like the Angles and Saxons, whose conquest of Britain was in progress. The pagan Alamans held Switzerland and the Black Forest, and had pressed their way almost to the heart of Gaul; while in the great German background hovered the pagan Frisians, Saxons, Thuringians, Lombards, all destined to play their part in the making of Europe. Finally, in northern Africa, the Vandals had established their kingdom, which included Sardinia and Corsica.

In such a time of upheaval and confusion it is needless to say that the bonds of morality were relaxed and society sunk in a deep corruption. The barbarous Teutons had indeed the vices, but had also the virtues, of the savage. Salvian of Marseilles (*cir.* 450) balances the virtues and the vices of all the principal races: 'not one of these tribes is altogether vicious; if they have their vices, they have also virtues.' It is the Romans, the relics of a luxurious and effete civilisation, that are altogether bad. 'You, Romans and Christians and Catholics, are defrauding your brethren, are grinding the faces of the poor, are wallowing in licentiousness and inebriety.' 'Shall we be surprised if God gives all our provinces to the barbarians, in order that through their virtues these lands may be purified from the crimes of the Romans?' In short, the vices of the Romans are the real cause of the downfall of the Empire.[6] The picture is one of deep corruption of life and manners in the Roman world, and it shows forth the degenerate Roman populations as more vicious and more depraved than their wild conquerors.

Nor was the religion of the Western Empire in better plight than the morals. In such a time of relaxed morality and material and social catastrophe no high religious level can be looked for. The Teutonic nations were in St Benedict's time still in great part pagan, and those that had accepted Christianity were Arian; both races of the Goths were Arian, as also the Vandals and Suevi, and later the Lombards. The Franks alone, converted about 500, were Catholic. This meant that in St Benedict's lifetime, in Italy, in southern Gaul and Spain, Arianism was the religion of the dominant races. The Teutonic settlers in all these countries constituted a large proportion of the population, for they were no mere invasions of armies but migrations of nations. Catholicism was buried beneath these populations of heresy.[7] In many parts the Arians carried on long and bitter persecutions of the Catholic Church, and throughout Arianism was held fanatically by the conquering races. Thus the religious map portraying the western Europe of 485 shows it all pagan or of Arian ascendancy, fully Catholic districts being only in the northwest corner of Gaul and in Wales and Ireland.[8]

In St Benedict's Italy the religious situation may be summed up thus: a Catholic substratum of the remains of the old Roman or Italian population, overlaid by numerous settlements of dominant Arian Teutons of many races (like the Protestant Plantation of Ulster, except that during Theodoric's reign there was toleration for the Catholics); and underlayers of still surviving paganism, for paganism lingered long and died hard in Rome itself, and long survived in the remoter districts, as appears from St Benedict's own life.

And so in the year 500 there was a Europe to be reconverted, christianised, civilised anew; law and order to be restored; the fabric of society to be rebuilt; the dignity of labour to be reasserted; agriculture, commerce, education, the arts of peace to be revived; civil and political life to be renewed: in short, a Europe to be remade. And the man marked out by Providence to play in the ultimate event a giant's part in the colossal work of reconstruction, had left the world never to return, and was spending the years of opening manhood in his cave at Subiaco, with none other thought in his mind than 'the desire to please God alone' (St Gregory).

After three years passed in entire solitude in the Sacro Speco, Benedict's existence became gradually known to the shepherds and country folk around; and then disciples began to come and place themselves under his guidance, so that a community of monks grew up, in such numbers that in the course of a few years he was able to establish in the neighbourhood twelve monasteries of twelve monks each, with abbots whom he appointed. At this time, too, Roman nobles, even of patrician rank, began to entrust their sons to his care, to be brought up as monks. Before long the influence he was rapidly and widely gaining stirred up the jealousy and enmity of a neighbouring priest, who manifested it in such wise that Benedict determined to yield to evil and go elsewhere with a selected band of monks, leaving the twelve monasteries at Subiaco in charge of their superiors. The little band travelled southward till it reached the Roman municipal town of Casinum, halfway between Rome and Naples. Behind it rises abruptly from the plain a mountain standing solitary, of considerable height. On the summit was an ancient fane of Apollo, where still lingered on among the mountain folk the relics of their pagan worship. Benedict and his monks climbed the mountain, and cut down the sacred wood, and turned the temple of Apollo into a chapel of St Martin, and established there their monastery, destined to be the one before all others associated with St Benedict's name, ever after looked on as the centre of Benedictine life and spirit, the Holy Mount of the Benedictines, whence flowed over Europe streams of religion and civilisation and culture.

Some year about 525 is a likely date for the foundation of Monte Cassino. The remaining years of his life, perhaps some five-and-twenty, St Benedict passed there, to us at this distance a dim patriarchal figure standing out colossal through the centuries. We catch in St Gregory's pages glimpses of him working in the fields with his monks, or sitting reading at the monastery gate, or spending the hours of the night in prayer, or ruling and guiding his monks. We see him preaching to the half-heathen folk of the country-side, and alleviating the sufferings of the poor in the famines and pestilences of those troublous times, always a centre of beneficent influence to whom men turned naturally in their difficulties. Often must he have watched from his mountain top the Roman and Gothic armies in the plain below, as they marched and countermarched through the land, spreading havoc and desolation around them. He became the most notable personage in the district, the one whom Totila desired to meet in 542, and from whom he received in patience a stern rebuke that made him henceforth less cruel (St Gregory). We read in St Gregory's picture the beautiful story of the last visit of his nun-sister, Scholastica; how when night began to fall and Benedict prepared to say adieu and return to the monastery, Scholastica prayed, and God sent such a storm of rain that her brother had against his will to stay, and so they passed the night together in holy converse on the spiritual life. We read too of the wonderful contemplation St Benedict had from the tower, a contemplation expressed by St Gregory in language so extraordinary that theologians, and among them St Thomas, have discussed whether it was really a foretaste of the Beatific Vision, and Benedict, like Moses and St Paul, for a moment saw the Being of God; an

experience in any case so exalted and so spiritual that it makes good his claim to a place in the ranks of the highest and most gifted of the mystics.

Finally, there is the picture of his death; how being overcome by fever, he caused himself to be carried to the oratory by his monks, and there being fortified for death by the Body and Blood of the Lord, his feeble body supported in the arms of the monks, he stood with hands upraised to heaven and breathed his last breath in words of prayer. And the monks saw a path stretching straight from his cell to heaven, strewn with rich garments and bright with lamps. And One radiant, of venerable aspect, standing above declared: This is the path whereby the beloved of the Lord, Benedict, hath mounted up to heaven.

. . . . .

St Benedict's Idea

In another connexion I have written as follows: 'How far have Benedictine history and work in the world, and, it may be said, Benedictine ideas, gone beyond anything that can have been in St Benedict's mind. How little he thought that his monks were to be apostles, missionaries, civilisers, school-masters, editors of the Fathers. How surprised would he have been at the figure of a medieval mitred abbot, a feudal baron, fulfilling the functions of a great landlord and of a statesman. How bewildering to him would have been the gorgeous church functions and the stately ceremonial that have become one of the most cherished traditions among his sons. How meaningless would the work that has come to be regarded as characteristically Benedictine have seemed in his eyes, and how strange would the adjective "learned," associated as a sort of *constans epitheton* with his name, have sounded in his ears, who (to use St Gregory's quaint phrase) fled from the Roman schools "scienter nescius et sapienter indoctus." What a development, what a transformation is here! Yet, for all that, it is by common consent recognised that, on the whole and in its great currents, Benedictine history has been true to the idea of the Founder, a legitimate development, not a perversion.'[9]

In this passage is applied to Benedictine monachism the principle accepted in regard to all institutions, social, political, religious, that live on and work during long periods of time, that they must needs change and develop and grow, it may be almost out of recognition. It is a sign of life; for to live is to grow and to change, and such changes, however seemingly great, which are but as the vital responses of a living organism to the conditions and needs of its successive environments, are justified as legitimate and true developments of the original idea. Hence to isolate St Benedict's idea, or St Francis' idea, and make it the sole measure of Benedictine or Franciscan history, ruling out whatever was not explicitly present to the Founder's consciousness, would be unhistorical, uncritical, and untrue.

And so, if we now endeavour to bring out into the clear St Benedict's own idea, his reconstruction of monasticism as it shaped itself in his mind, it is not at all with the object of showing that whatever is outside his concept is thereby false to his idea, or that the most literal reproduction of the physical conditions of life in his monastery would be the most faithful presentation of his mind and spirit throughout all ages. Quite otherwise. But, on the other hand, it is true that fidelity to the original type and continuity of principles are the chief tests of the truth of historical developments.[10] And so an examination and appreciation of St Benedict's idea in its simplicity and as it was in his own mind is the necessary prelude to any study of Benedictine monachism, the norm by which must be judged all manifestations of Benedictine life and activities at all times. We have, therefore, at the outset to try to arrive at a correct conception of what St Benedict's idea was.

(1) It is fortunate that he tells us himself quite definitely what he intends to do: 'We are going to establish a School of God's Service, in which we hope we shall establish nothing harsh, nothing burthensome, (Prologue).[11] St Benedict, we have seen, when he first made up his mind to be a monk, acting according to the Egyptian monastic ideals current in western Europe, retired to a desert spot and dwelt in a cave, enduring hunger and thirst, heat and cold, and all the inclemency of the weather. But when he came to write his *Rule* and to legislate for the life of his own monastery of Monte Cassino and any others that might adopt his *Rule,* his ideas had undergone a change, embodied in those words in which he says that in the school of divine service he was founding, he intended to establish 'nothing harsh or burthensome.' These words have very commonly been interpreted as a pious exaggeration or device to encourage his disciples, and as not really meaning what they say; but it is easy to show that they do mean exactly what they say. They are borne out by other passages of the *Rule.* The forty-ninth chapter opens: 'Though we read that a monk's life should at all times have the Lenten observance, yet as few have this courage, we urge them in these days of Lent to wash away the negligences of other times.' Similarly in the fortieth chapter: 'Though we read that wine is not for monks at all, yet as in our days monks cannot be persuaded of this, at any rate let us agree to use it sparingly.' And there are other cases in which what may be called the appeal to monastic tradition in regard to austerity of life is made, only to be set aside, that mitigations may be deliberately adopted.[12] This point will be worked out in some detail in the next chapter; here it will suffice to quote St Benedict's words when summing up in the last chapter of the *Rule:* 'We have written this *Rule* in order that by observing it in

monasteries we may show we have in some measure at any rate integrity of morals and a beginning of the monastic life.'[13] And in concluding he calls his *Rule* 'a very little rule for beginners' (*minima inchoationis regula*).

In this St Benedict is not using the language of feigned humility, but is speaking the very truth, as appears from a comparison of his *Rule* with the records of the monachism of Egypt or of western Europe in his day. However austere may seem in the twentieth century a life according to the letter of *St Benedict's Rule,* in his own day it can have appeared but as an easy form of monastic life, when compared either with the existing monastic rules and accepted traditions on the one hand, or with the ordinary discipline of the Church for the faithful, as in the matter of fasting and penitential code, on the other. Indeed, Dom Morin declares that in these matters St Benedict's régime was no more than was often imposed on Christians living in the world.[14] Thus in his reconstruction of the monastic life St Benedict's idea was to establish a manner of life, self-denying, of course, and hard; but not a life of great austerity. Benedictine life is not, and is not intended to be, what is called a 'penitential life'; and any one who feels called to such a life should go to some other order and not become a Benedictine, for a life such as this is not in accordance with St Benedict's idea.

(2) Another of St Benedict's fundamental ideas appears in the first chapter of the *Rule.* He lays it down that he writes his *Rule* for cenobites (i.e. monks living in community), and for cenobites only. After speaking of other kinds of monks, both good and bad, he says in conclusion: 'Let us proceed to legislate for the strongest and best kind, the cenobites.'[15] He has just given a definition of cenobites; but as this chapter is in large measure based on passages of St Jerome and Cassian (see my edition of the *Regula,* p. 9), it will be helpful to know precisely their idea of cenobites, which St Benedict had before his eyes when framing his own definition. St Jerome only says that cenobites may be called 'men living in common' (*in commune viventes*), or 'dwelling in common' (*qui in commune habitant*) (*Ep.* xxii, 34, 35). Cassian's description is: 'Who live together in a congregation and are governed by the judgement of a single elder.'[16] St Benedict explains cenobites as 'monasterial, serving as Christ's soldiers under a rule or abbot.'[17] He uses the word 'monasterial,' not monastic, as the latter would be applicable to hermits as well as cenobites.[18] 'Monasterial' receives its interpretation in various places in the *Rule;* 'dwelling in cenobia' (c. V), 'persevering in the monastery till death' (Prol. 128); and, as a matter of fact, the whole tenor of the Rule contemplates nothing else than an organised community living a fully common life under rule; common prayer, common work, common meals, common dormitory; a life lived wholly within the precincts of the monastery, the occasions of going forth

being reduced to a minimum, and regarded as definitely undesirable and dangerous (c. IV *fin.*, c. LXVI *fin.*).

St Benedict speaks, indeed, with admiration of the eremitical life (c. I), which then formed an integral part of European monachism, and was commonly regarded not only as the most perfect realisation of the monastic life, but as the goal to be aimed at in practice by those who had the necessary courage and strength in virtue; but he expressly declares that he legislates for cenobites alone. Consequently, when we find instances of eastern or western monks, especially Irish, going forth from their monasteries to lead the eremitical life; or when we see them undertaking pilgrimages or wanderings as a practice of asceticism, as is common now among Buddhist ascetics, such things have great interest for the general history of monasticism: but they have no interest for Benedictine history, and afford no help for the interpretation of St Benedict's idea, which was plainly and only cenobitic. There are other kinds of monks, good and bad; but St Benedict's idea of his own monks was that they were to be cenobites, spending their lives in the monastery, under the conditions of community life.

(3) But St Benedict introduced a modification into the idea of cenobitical life. Up to his time monks, though looked upon as bound, whether by vows or without them, irrevocably to the practice of the monastic life, so that to abandon it was considered an apostasy, still were not tied to a particular monastery or community, but were allowed with little difficulty to pass from one house to another. St Benedict's most special and tangible contribution to the development of monasticism was the introduction of the vow of stability. It will be necessary later on to inquire with some care what was his own full idea of stability. Here it will be enough to say in general that by it he put a stop to such liberty of passage from monastery to monastery, and incorporated the monk by his profession in the community of his own monastery. St Benedict thus bound the monks of a monastery together into a permanent family, united by bonds that lasted for life. This idea that the monks of each Benedictine monastery form a permanent community, distinct from that of every other Benedictine monastery, is among the most characteristic features of Benedictine monachism, and a chief discriminant between it and the later orders. This idea of the 'monastic family,' at any rate in its concrete realisation, was St Benedict's. The great Coptic monasteries of Pachomius and Schenute were far too big to be families; they were rather great agricultural colonies, divided into houses, and organised on the basis of the different trades carried on in them. Concerning the inner life of St Basil's monasteries we have not sufficient information; but neither St Martin's at Tours, where the eighty monks abode in separate caves, nor the huge Celtic monasteries with their hundreds of monks, can

be regarded as embodying the family type so characteristic of Benedictine monachism: nor could they, without the idea enshrined in the Benedictine vow of stability.

(4) In view of current notions concerning religious orders, it is necessary here at the outset to bring out a negative side of St Benedict's idea, and emphasise the fact that he had no thought of instituting an 'order.' There was no such thing in his time as monastic or other orders. St Benedict had no intention that the monasteries wherein his ***Rule*** was followed should form a group apart; nor did they for many centuries, but each Benedictine monastery was a separate entity, autonomous and self-contained, having no organic bond with other monasteries. Among the houses of the Black Monks, pure and simple (that is, outside of the systems of Cluny and Citeaux), each abbey continued to stand in its primitive isolation, until the formation of national chapters at the beginning of the thirteenth century.

Moreover, associated with the modern concept of a religious order is the idea of some special work to be done, some need of the Church to be met; and a man joins the order hoping thereby to be enabled the better to carry out this work to which he feels called. But with the Benedictines it was not so: there was no special form of work which their organisation was designed to undertake. A man became a monk precisely because he felt called to be a monk and for no other purpose or object whatever, nor as a preparation for anything else—except Heaven. The monk's object is to sanctify his soul and serve God by leading a life in community in accordance with the Gospel counsels. Works of various kinds will be given him to do; but these are secondary, and no one of them is part of his essential vocation as a monk. What has been here said may be illustrated and enforced from the earlier pages of Cardinal Gasquet's *Sketch of Monastic History*.[19] The monastic life 'is nothing more than the Christian life of the Gospel counsels conceived in its full simplicity and perfection. It has no determinate object in view beyond this; it has no special systems or methods. The broad law of Christian liberty is its only guide; it is neither strict nor lax; it aims neither at too high things nor is it content with any low standard of conduct; but it adapts itself to the workings of grace in each individual soul, and gains its end when it has brought that individual soul to the highest perfection of which its natural and supernatural gifts render it capable' (p. xiv). Again: 'It is merely a systematised form of a life according to the Gospel counsels, existing for its own sake, as a full expression of the Church's true and perfect life' (p. xi).

(5) Returning to St Benedict's definition of his monastery as 'a school of the service of God,' we ask what was the kind of service that he established? It may be

said to be contained in the three services: Self-discipline, Prayer, Work. Of these three services, self-discipline is, of course, the subjective basis and condition of the others, that which gives its meaning to the whole life; it will be enlarged upon in the two succeeding chapters.

Of the external services St Benedict placed prayer, and in particular common prayer, the celebration in choir of the canonical office, first in order of thought and importance. He calls it 'the duty' or 'the task of our service' (servitutis officium, *vel* pensum, c. XVI, 5; c. L, 8); it so filled his mind that it is the one subject on which he legislates in minute detail, devoting eleven chapters to that ordering of the psalmody and office which after fourteen centuries is still used by his sons: 'the Work of God' is his name for it, and he says that 'nothing is to be set before the Work of God' (nihil operi Dei praeponatur) (c. XLIII). That by 'Work of God' (opus Dei, opus divinum) St Benedict means precisely the public recital of the office, and nothing else, is made clear by an examination of the places where the term occurs in the *Rule*.[20]

The prominence of the opus Dei in St Benedict's mind has been erected into a principle, that the public celebration of the office is the purpose of his institute, and that Benedictines exist for the sake of the choir, 'propter chorum fundati.' I have heard of a Benedictine abbot who expressed this idea so crudely as to say to his monks: 'You have the choir and the refectory; what more do you need?' But the view finds expression also in Abbot Delatte's excellent Commentary on the *Rule,* which I read in general with great agreement: 'The proper and distinctive work of the Benedictine, his portion, his mission, is the liturgy. He makes his profession in order to be one in the Church—the society of divine praise—who glorifies God according to the forms instituted by herself.'[21] This means that the essence of a Benedictine vocation is the celebration of the Liturgy. If that be the case, it is due to St Benedict himself, and must be counted among the innovations he made in the monastic life, for it was not part of the inheritance he received from the earlier monasticism. The public celebration of the canonical office always held a prominent place in cenobitical life of whatever kind; but the idea that it was the essence of the life does not emerge from the records of the Egyptian monks, nor from the writings of St Basil or Cassian. So far as the earlier monachism goes, a much stronger case could be made out for Fr Augustine Baker's contention that private spiritual prayer is the scope of the monastic state.

The 'nihil operi Dei praeponatur,' when taken in its context and in relation to the passage in the Rule of Macarius on which it is based, does not afford ground for thinking St Benedict narrowed the conception of the monastic life in this way. Is it to be supposed that

his idea was: I want to secure the celebration of the divine office, and therefore will I establish a monastery. This no doubt has been true of many a founder of individual monasteries, collegiate chapters and chantries in the middle ages; but can hardly be true of St Benedict. Was not his idea rather: I want to establish a monastery to be a school of God's service, wherein the primary community service shall be the public celebration of the divine office. Consequently I agree with Dom Morin in holding that the 'propter chorum fundati' is an exaggeration.[22] I believe the idea arose at a later date, in the ninth or tenth century, at a time when manual labour had dropped out of the life of the monasteries, and there was a prodigious increase in the church services, masses, offices, additional devotions, so that the monks spent most of their time in church, as will be explained in a later chapter. It was then too that the liturgical pomp and circumstance and the elaboration of ritual underwent a great development; whereas St Benedict's liturgy was doubtless of a severe simplicity that would nowadays appear puritan.

But whatever view be held on this point of Benedictine theory, all will accept what Cardinal Gasquet has written on the actual place the office holds in Benedictine life: 'The central figure of the society (of the monastery) was its divine King. The monastery was a palace, a court, and the divine office was the daily service and formal homage rendered to the divine Majesty. This, the opus Dei, was the crown of the whole structure of the monastic edifice. It was pre-eminently the work of the monk which was to take precedence of every other employment, and to which monastic tradition has ever given a marked solemnity. Day by day, and almost hour by hour, the monk, purified by his vows, enclosed from the world, seeks to renew the wonderful familiarity with his God and Father which our first parents forfeited, but which, through our second Adam, is restored in the Christian Church. In a word, the divine office is the soul of the monastic life' (*Sketch,* xiii). The Declarations of the English Congregation say that 'our primary duty is to carry out on earth what the angels do in heaven,'[23] and to this probably no exception will be taken.

(6) Of the service of Work it will here suffice to say that the work fell under the categories of manual labour and reading, between which were apportioned the hours of the day not spent in the church. The labour was predominantly work in the fields and garden, or the housework in kitchen and elsewhere, necessary for the life of a large community. The reading, it may safely be said, was confined to the Scriptures and the Fathers, and was devotional rather than intellectual in character and scope: 'lectio divina' is St Benedict's way of describing it (c. XLVIII, 3).

A simple life it was, made up of a round of simple duties; and the monks were quite simple men: though no doubt some were of the same station in life as St Benedict himself, the great majority of them were recruited from the Italian peasantry, or from the semi-barbarous Gothic invaders (*Dialogues,* ii, 6). They were not priests, they were not clerics; there were only two or three priests, perhaps only one, in the community, just sufficient to celebrate the Sunday mass and administer the sacraments. The general conditions of life were probably not rougher or harder than would have been the lot of most of them had they remained in the world. The difference lay in the element of religion brought into every detail of their lives. And so they lived together their common life, serving God by the daily round of duties in choir, in farm and garden, in kitchen and bakehouse and workshop—chanting, praying, working, reading, meditating—their lifework and their life-interests being concentrated as far as possible within the precincts of the monastery or its immediate vicinity.

Such were the primitive Benedictines, St Benedict's own monks, such was the mustard seed which has grown into the great and varied and complex tree that will be revealed to us when we come to study St Benedict's institute as it has developed itself in history. Such was St Benedict's own idea of the monasticism which in the maturity of his religious experience and spiritual wisdom he established at Monte Cassino and legislated for in his *Rule.* And this was the community, and these the men, destined by God to play so great a part in repairing the ruin, religious, social, material, in which Europe was lying, and in converting, christianising, and educating the new nations that were to make the new great Christian Commonwealth.

From what has been said the pertinent observation follows, that to set up, as has been done, St Benedict in his cave at Subiaco as the embodiment of the truest Benedictine ideal, and the pattern which it would be well for Benedictines, had they the courage and firmness of mind, to try to imitate, is unhistorical and untrue: no less untrue than it would be to set up St Ignatius at Manresa as the best embodiment of the spirit and life of the Society he founded. Such episodes in the lives of these and other great founders were only periods of formation and preparation for their work of religious creation; and when they came forth from their retirement they did not shape their institutes on the lines they had themselves at first adopted, but in conformity with the lessons they had learned therein in many things they turned their back upon their own early experiences; so that their fully formed and matured idea is to be seen in their rules and in their institutes in the final form in which they left them.

It is impossible to include under any single formula St Benedict's idea, or the Essence of Benedictinism; just as impossible as it is to include under any single formula the Essence of Christianity. All that can be done

is to state various aspects which taken together may afford an adequate conception. The following description gathers up the points that have been brought out in this chapter. St Benedict's idea was to form a community of monks bound to live together until death, under rule, in common life, in the monastery of their profession, as a religious family, leading a life not of marked austerity but devoted to the service of God—'the holy service they have professed,' he calls it;[24] the service consisting in the community act of the celebration of the divine office, and in the discipline of a life of ordered daily manual work and religious reading, according to the Rule and under obedience to the abbot.

It will be of interest in conclusion to confront this account of original Benedictine life with Newman's impressions of it as given in his essay on 'The Mission of St Benedict.' Benedictines have reason to be grateful that one of Newman's knowledge and insight and historical genius should have given them this objective study of their life and spirit. The monks of those days, he writes, 'had a unity of object, of state, and of occupation. Their object was rest and peace; their state was retirement; their occupation was some work that was simple, as opposed to intellectual, viz. prayer, fasting, meditation, study, transcription, manual labour, and other unexciting, soothing employments. . . . The monastic institute, says the biographer of St Maurus, demands *Summa Quies,* the most perfect quietness; and where was quietness to be found, if not in reverting to the original condition of man, as far as the changed circumstances of our race admitted; in having no wants, of which the supply was not close at hand; in the "nil admirari"; in having neither hope nor fear of anything below; in daily prayer, daily bread, and daily work, one day being just like another, except that it was one step nearer than the day before it to that great Day which would swallow up all days, the day of everlasting rest.'[25]

Notes

[1] Modern Lives of St Benedict are Abbot Tosti's *S. Benedetto,* 1892 (translated into English and French), and Dom L'Huillier's *Patriarche S. Benoit,* 1904.

[2] Tosti, Schmidt.

[3] What follows is in large measure based on Hodgkin's *Italy and her Invaders.*

[4] *Op. cit.* iii, 248.

[5] Quoted from Procopius and Marcellinus Comes, contemporary historians, by Hodgkin, iv, 507.

[6] Quoted from Salvian's *de Gubernatione Dei,* by Hodgkin, *op. cit.* i, 918-34. Dill, *Roman Society,* 318-

23, thinks that Salvian's pictures are overdrawn, but he does not question the substantive truth of his thesis of the deep corruption of Roman society. Cf. also Gregorovius, *City of Rome,* i, 252.

[7] See Newman, *Development of Christian Doctrine,* 'The Church of the Fifth and Sixth Centuries,' §I.

[8] See Heussi-Mulert, *Atlas zur Kirchengeschichte,* v.

[9] *Hibbert Journal,* 1906, p. 490.

[10] They are Newman's first two 'Notes of a Genuine Development of an Idea,' in the *Essay on the Development of Christian Doctrine.* The other Notes are: Power of Assimilation, Logical Sequence, Anticipation of its Future, Conservative Action on its Past, Chronic Vigour.

[11] 'Constituenda est ergo nobis dominici schola servitii. In qua institutione nihil asperum, nihil grave nos constituturos speramus' (*Regula,* Prol. 116; the lines added in references to the Rule are those of my 'Editio critica-practica,' Herder, 1912).

[12] See cc. XVIII *fin.,* XLVIII, 16-22.

[13] 'Regulam hanc descripsimus, ut hanc observantes in monasteriis aliquatenus vel honestatem morum aut initium conversationis nos demonstremus habere' (*Reg.* LXXIII).

[14] *L'Idéal Monastique,* iii.

[15] 'His ergo omissis (*scil.* heremitis, sarabaitis, gyrovagis) ad coenobitarum fortissimum genus disponendum veniamus' (*Reg.* 1). 'Fortissimum genus' is difficult to translate. Evidently it does not mean 'most austere,' or 'most strenuous.' It has been translated 'most steadfast,' or 'most valiant,' or even 'best.' This latter is what it really means. On the whole the rendering given above, 'strongest and best,' seems to bring out the meaning.

[16] 'In congregatione pariter consistentes unius senioris iudicio gubernantur' (*Coll.* xviii, 4).

[17] 'Monasteriale, militans sub regula vel abbate' (*Reg.* 1). 'Vel' with St Benedict often is equivalent to 'et' (see my ed. of the *Regula,* p. 197). There were many monasteries without any rule other than the living voice of the abbot, but there were not any with a rule and no abbot, or other superior. At the present day the 'idiorhythmic' monasteries of the Eastern Church are governed by a board of seniors without any personal superior.

[18] 'Monasticus' is from monachus; 'monasterialis' from monasterium. The word is found elsewhere, but it is not common.

[19] Prefixed to reprint of translation of Montalembert's *Monks of the West,* 1895, vol. i.

[20] See my edition, Index, pp. 191 and 203. 'Opus Dei' was used in the same sense at Lerins, as appears in the *Lerins Psalmody* and in the Rules of Caesarius; but in other literature of early monasticism it has a wider meaning and signifies the works of the spiritual and ascetical life (*loc. cit.*).

[21] 'L'oeuvre propre et distinctive du Bénédictin, son lot, sa mission, c'est la liturgie. Il émet profession pour être, dans l'Église, société de louange divine, celui qui glorifie Dieu selon les formes instituées par elle' (p. 153).

[22] *L'Idéal Monastique,* vii.

[23] 'Primarium officium nostrum est in terra praestare quod angeli in caelo.'

[24] 'Servitium sanctum quod professi sunt' (c. v, 4).

[25] *Mission of St Benedict,* 3 (p. 29 in separate reprint).

Cardinal Gasquet (essay date 1929)

SOURCE: An introduction to *The Rule of Saint Benedict,* translated by Cardinal Gasquet, Cooper Square Publishers, Inc., 1966, pp. ix-xxviii.

[*In the following introduction to his 1929 translation of the* Rule of St. Benedict, *Gasquet examines Benedict's religious and monastic ideals and the influence of these in early medieval Europe.*]

The **Rule of St. Benedict** may fitly find a place in any collection of classics. As a code of laws it has undoubtedly influenced Europe; and, indeed, there is probably no other book, save of course the Holy Bible, which with such certainty can be claimed as a chief factor in the work of European civilization. It is undeniable that most of the nations of modern Europe were converted to the Christian faith and tutored in the arts of peace by the influence of the mode of life known as monastic. The men whose names are connected with the beginnings of civilization in the various countries of Europe, and their fellow-labourers, were for the most part trained for their mission under the **Rule of St. Benedict.** Such, for example, was Augustine in England, Boniface in Germany, Ansgar in Scandinavia, Swithbert and Willibrord in the Netherlands, etc.

In view of the facts, therefore, it will hardly be denied that the monastic system, as codified in the **Rule of St. Benedict,** has been proved to possess some strange power of influencing great bodies of men and winning them from the darkness of paganism and the horrors of savagery to the light of Christianity and the blessings of a civilized life. The secret of this fascination is obvious, and the monuments, such as Canterbury and Fulda, Salzburg, and the thousands of Benedictine abbeys which existed, or still exist, in Europe, all testify to the fact that it was the monastic life lived by monk-apostles in the midst of the peoples they hoped to convert, upon which their success mainly depended. The monastic plan was similar to the old Roman plan of civilizing by means of "colonies" planted among the conquered races of the empire. The colonists brought with them the arts, and to some extent the culture, of Imperial Rome, and their mere life lived among the subjugated peoples induced these latter of their own accord to adopt the manners, the language and the law of their conquerors. There was probably no programme, or pretence, but the influence of the life followed by the trained Roman colonist worked its charm without noise or compulsion.

In the same way the monk came with the like lesson of peace and civilization, but with the addition of the all-powerful assistance of religion and the strong attraction which self-sacrifice ever exerts over the minds of the unlettered. Thus Augustine came to England with forty companions, all trained in the "school" of St. Benedict, and in the principles of his *Rule.* They landed in this country and won it to Christ with cross and banner and religious chants. Then they settled down to live their lives of prayer and labour, and whilst their success is written in the annals of our country, we know the names only of a very few of these apostles, and they those only who were called later to form similar centres in other parts. History can tell us nothing of their preaching and teaching. No doubt they did all this; but what we know of their work is that they lived their life according to the *Rule;* they built up other places and formed other colonies, and then they died; and, behold! the peoples among whom they dwelt were Christian.

St. Benedict

St. Benedict, the author of this code of monastic rules, to the influence of which Europe owes so much, was born at Nursia, a city of Umbria, in the year 480. The beginnings of his life witnessed the extinction of the Roman Empire in the West, and the year of his birth saw Odoacer, the first barbarian who had ruled in Italy, in possession of the throne of the Cæsars. All over the Western world the times were difficult and the outlook gloomy, and Italy especially presented a sad spectacle of misery and desolation. At a time when civilization appeared to be upon the very verge of extinction, and the Christian Church seemed to be on the point of losing the foothold it had gained amid the ruins of the Roman Empire, St. Benedict appears as the providen-

tial instrument of regeneration. After experiences gained in the schools of Rome, in his cave amid the solitudes of Subiaco, and as ruler of the monks of Vicovaro, he gathered round him at Subiaco a body of monks whom he distributed in twelve separate colonies and ruled for eighteen years. It was here, probably, that he conceived the lines of his celebrated monastic code, which he compiled finally when, about the year 528, he removed to the spot where now stands the renowned sanctuary of Monte Cassino. He died, according to the tradition of the Benedictine Order, on March 21, 543 A.D.

The Spirit of Monasticism

To understand the position of the **Rule** set forth by St. Benedict, and to comprehend the reason of its success in the Western world generally, it is necessary to know the meaning of monasticism in the early ages of the Church. In comparatively modern times various religious Orders have come into existence in order to meet some accidental needs of the Church, using the religious life as a means to carry out those objects. In the early ages the conception of utility or purpose, other than the perfecting of the individual soul, does not appear to have entered into the ideal of the regular life. It was regarded merely as a systematized form of life on the lines of the Gospel counsels of perfection, to be lived for its own sake and as the full expression of the Church's true and perfect life. Whatever the means, the end to be attained by religious life was the same in all systems or methods of life, namely, the more complete realization of the supernatural end of human existence, and the closer conscious union of the soul with God. This was to be attained by the removal of every hindrance to this elevation of mind, arising from self or external things; and by the practice of the Christian virtues according to the counsels of perfection. Whatever might conduce to the realization of the supernatural and higher life was enjoined and eagerly adopted. To some the practice of a solitary life in the desert appeared the most efficacious means of attaining to this desired elevation of the soul; to others the discipline of severe and sustained bodily labour seemed necessary; to others, again, the practice of astonishing austerities, of self-inflicted punishment, or of long and ever-increasing vocal prayers, seemed the most sure road by which to reach the object in view. In Egypt and the East generally the most characteristic features of the monastic life have been described as "the craving for austerities, individualism and the love of the eremitical life."

The early conception of what was necessary for monastic life was modified to some extent by St. Basil in the latter half of the fourth century. His changes tended to the introduction of community as opposed to the eremitical life and the placing of religious and ascetical exercises under the control of a Superior. From Egypt monachism was introduced into Rome and Italy, and is found already established in Gaul about the time when St. Basil was modifying earlier practices in the East. It is somewhat difficult to say how far the individual rules of Eastern monastic reformers, like St. Basil or St. Pachomius, affected the life of Italian or other European monasteries. That these rules were known is certain, both because Rufinus had translated into Latin that of St. Basil, and St. Jerome that of Pachomius, and because St. Benedict refers in his code to "the Rule of our Holy Father Basil," as well as to the Collations of Cassian and the Lives of the Fathers of the Desert (cap. 73). But those who have best reason to pass a judgment on the matter consider that the influence of the "reforms" of St. Basil, etc., on Western monasteries had been very slight up to the time of St. Benedict, and that, at most, some of the "rules and regulations" had been borrowed in a spirit of eclecticism from the codes of Basil and Pachomius. It seems almost certain, writes a modern authority, that "in Italy, as in Gaul and Ireland, early monachism was thoroughly Egyptian in its ideals and its working."

The Work of St. Benedict

The danger of adopting Eastern ideals by Westerns is obvious. A method of life which may suit the people of Egypt and the East generally, may and probably will be found to be wholly unsuitable for those of Italy and Gaul, and if unsuitable and impracticable, such a method of life must inevitably lead to laxity, and tend to become a hindrance rather than a help to attain the end for which it exists. This was a recognized fact even before the time of St. Benedict. Cassian found it necessary to introduce mitigations into the Egyptian practices to make them possible for European monks, and there is evidence at least of some laxity in the monasteries of Italy in the fifth century. In his *Rule* (cap. 1) St. Benedict speaks with severity of the Sarabites and Gyrovagi, two classes of monks to be found as the result of the system. As the same authority, quoted above, says, "This falling away may no doubt have been largely due to the fact that the monks of Italy and Gaul were trying to live up to an ideal which the climatic and other conditions of the country rendered impossible, or, at any rate, extremely difficult, and to the discouragement and demoralization consequent on an abiding sense of failure."

It was to meet this real danger that St. Benedict wrote his *Rule.* It must be remembered, he had had for three years at Vicovaro personal experience of the existing quasi-Eastern monastic system which had almost ended in the tragedy of his death for endeavouring to insist upon the proper carrying out of the rule which the monks professed to follow. His remedy for the state of general laxity which prevailed amongst those professing to lead the higher life was bold and novel. He did not endeavour to insist upon the discarded austerities and penitential exercises of the East, but sought reformation on new lines. He secured the old ideals of the ascetical life by moderation and common-sense ruling over men given to prayer and labour directed and controlled by obedience to authority. But the life was made possible by sufficient food, ample sleep, proper clothing, regulated prayers, and even personal austerities checked by the will of the abbot. All this was strangely different from the type of monastic observance which had hitherto prevailed not only in the East, but in Italy and Gaul. The ideals, the attainment of those spiritual heights which the soul was competent to gain, were the same, but for the more sure success Benedict's code of laws was characterized by a wide and wise discretion. To secure this end, those who wished to walk in the path of the Gospel counsels were required, as the Prologue of his *Rule* tells us, to promise a life-long obedience. This was a new feature, and was the first introduction of a life-long "profession," or promise of obedience "according to the *Rule,*" and it was with the utmost care made known to the monk who "wished to fight under the law" that "from that day forth it was not lawful for him to withdraw his neck from the yoke of the rule."

The Adoption of the Rule *in the West*

The result of the introduction of this principle was two-fold: on the one hand it established that continuity of family life known as "stability in the community," which has since become characteristic of the monastic life; and on the other it substituted for the personal will of a Superior the code of laws by which his government was to be fashioned. Further, as the *Rule* shows, though St. Benedict required obedience to his code of laws, he never intended to prohibit other customs and practices not at variance with it. In fact, he expressly refers his followers to the Rule of St. Basil and to other authorities for further guidance. That in process of time St. Benedict's legislation should have superseded all others was in the nature of things inevitable. As I have elsewhere said, "The difference of tone and form between his *Rule* and that of others is unmistakable; and however deep and intense the piety which breathes in the *Regula Cœnobialis,* which goes under the name of St. Columban, it is a relief to pass from its crude expositions of monastic discipline to the grave and noble laws of the Roman monk. Under these circumstances it is not wonderful that by the end of the eighth century not merely had *St. Benedict's Rule* superseded all others, but in France the memory of any other code had so completely perished that it could be gravely doubted whether monks of any kind had existed before the time of this great monastic legislator, and whether there could be any other monks but Benedictines."

The Contents of the Rule

The code of monastic laws, as will be seen in the translation here printed, consists of a Prologue or Preface and seventy-three chapters. The Prologue contains many important principles of the spiritual life, and the beginning makes it clear that St. Benedict had before him the Latin translation of St. Basil's *Admonitio ad filium spiritualem.* The ideas, and many of the actual words of the introductory paragraph are evidently taken from these writings of one whom he calls "our Holy Father Basil." In the first chapter of the **Rule** the "Patriarch of Western monachism" divides those wishing to lead the "higher life" into hermits or anchorites, that is, solitaries, and cœnobites, or those living together in communities. It is for this latter class only that his **Rule** is intended, namely, for monks living together in a monastery under an abbot and following a common form of life. Of the actual material buildings we have unfortunately very few details. All that we gather is that they were intended to be placed in the midst of fields, to be enclosed by walls, and ought to contain as far as possible all that the monks could need for their life. The monastery was to be looked on as the "school of divine service" and the "workshop" where the monk was to labour at the *"artes spirituales"*—the spiritual work of his supernatural vocation—by exercising himself in the use of the "Instruments of good works," described in the fourth chapter, which included the commandments of God and the natural virtues. St. Benedict shows himself as above all things practical in his system of spirituality, and he warns his followers that the first work on the road of perfection is the rooting up of their vices and labouring at the exact performance of what God long ago ordered as necessary in the ten commandments for all classes of Christians in common.

According to the **Rule** the monks were to be occupied in manual labour, reading and, above all, in the liturgy of the Church. The former included not merely labour in the fields, but the exercise of any art in which some might be proficient, the result of which might be sold for the benefit of the monastery, or be in any other way useful for the common good. The necessity of supplying books for public and private reading would show that St. Benedict, although he does not expressly mention it, intended monks that were capable of writing and illuminating to be employed in this way, which subsequently proved of the greatest service to European civilization by multiplying in the *scriptoria* of the monastic houses, and thus preserving to our times the literature of classical ages and the works of the early Fathers of the Christian Church. The time devoted to reading—to intellectual studies generally—varied according to the period of the year, but the hours after Vespers, from three to six o'clock, as well as Sundays, were apparently set apart for study (chap. 48); whilst St. Benedict's declaration that every monk must have his *graphium* or style, and his tablets for writing, shows that intellectual work was contemplated by him. The centre of the monastic life, according to the **Rule,** was unquestionably the Liturgy, or as St. Benedict calls it,

the *Opus Dei,* or Divine Office. "Nothing was to be preferred" to this part of the common life of the religious house, and the legislator devotes several chapters of his code to ordering and arranging the Psalmody for his monks.

The monastery properly constituted resembled a self-centred state or city. Surrounded by walls, with its workshops, its farms, its gardens, its mill, etc., it was governed by the various necessary officials under the direction of a Superior. St. Benedict, however, conceived the religious house to resemble rather the family of which the abbot held the place of the father, and a father in whom the members of the family acknowledged, with affectionate respect, the obedience due to our Lord Himself, because, as he says, "he occupies the place of Christ." This father, or abbot, was chosen by the votes of the monks, and the principles which should guide him in ruling his family are amongst the most important and useful laid down by St. Benedict. Though he has the appointment of his officials, and has the right and duty of ruling and watching over each individual member of the religious community, he himself is subject to the provisions of the **Rule,** and is bound to live the common life of the brethren.

The Text of the Rule

It is unnecessary to say much under the present circumstances as to the text of the **Rule of St. Benedict.** There appears never to have been any serious doubt cast upon the fact that the book as we have it now is substantially what came from the pen of the author. In the text of a work so frequently copied as this must have been during the whole of the Middle Ages, and especially in the period from the ninth to the twelfth century, when it was practically the only monastic Rule of the West, it is inevitable that differences should be found to exist. The original, or what was believed to have been the original autograph of St. Benedict, after having been long preserved at Monte Cassino perished in a disastrous fire in the Monastery of Teano, whither it had been taken for safety during the invasion of the Saracens into Italy. It is of interest to Englishmen to know that the oldest MS. at present known is Hatton MS. 42, written in England in the seventh or eighth century; the next oldest being the St. Gall MS., which is probably not older than the beginning of the ninth century. For the benefit of nuns in England who followed the **Rule,** and of others, the work was several times translated into English during the Middle Ages, and for the benefit of the "devout religious women" of his diocese it was "Englished" by Bishop Richard Foxe, and printed by Pynson on January 22, 1516-17. In the seventeenth century another translation was made partly by Father Leander Jones and partly by Father Cuthbert Fursden in their connection with the English Benedictine nuns of Cambrai. This was published first in 1638, and has been more than once since printed.

Upon this the present translation has been based, although it must be confessed that I have found it necessary to take considerable liberties with the work of the seventeenth-century translators.

Justin McCann (essay date 1937)

SOURCE: "The Text-History of the *Rule*" and "The Contents of the *Rule*" in *Saint Benedict,* Sheed and Ward, 1937, pp. 117-46.

[*In the following excerpt, McCann offers a textual history of the* Rule of St. Benedict *and summarizes its principal statements on the structure of Benedictine monastic life.*]

> *Scripsit monachorum regulam discretione*
> *praecipuam, sermone luculentam*
>
> (Dial. II, 36)

There are two standard modern editions of the Latin text of the *Rule,* those of Abbot Butler (2nd ed., 1927) and Dom Benno Linderbauer (1928). Dom Linderbauer's is a critical text with full apparatus; it gives St. Benedict's text as nearly as it can be determined and with none but orthographical changes. For the scholar who desires an exact text and to be fully informed regarding the manuscript evidence, this is the only edition of the *Rule.* Dom Linderbauer published earlier (1922) a philological commentary. The *Rule* is an important monument of Late Latin, and this commentary explains it carefully throughout with reference to the vocabulary, grammar and syntax of that form of the language. Dom Linderbauer's two books are essential for a student of the *Rule.*

Abbot Butler's edition of the text is a 'critico-practical' one. It also is based on a full study of the manuscripts; it contains a valuable introduction, very full indication of sources, select variant readings and important appendices; but the text is a revised one. The more serious irregularities of St. Benedict's Latin, as judged by the standards of normal Latin, are corrected, so that the text may be more serviceable for liturgical use. Since there is no full apparatus, it becomes necessary to turn to Linderbauer's text in order to determine what St. Benedict actually wrote. For the general reader who wishes to understand the *Rule* and to appreciate St. Benedict's use of his sources, this is the best edition.[1] Its text has already been adopted as their official text by several of the Benedictine Congregations and bids fair to obtain general currency as the modern Textus Receptus of the *Rule.*

Both Butler and Linderbauer in their introductions give an account of the history of the text with references to all the pertinent literature, which references need not be repeated here. But we should not fail to mention the name of Ludwig Traube,[2] the greatest of modern palaeographers, whose Text-History of the *Rule* (1st ed., 1898) effected a revolution in the study of the text comparable to the revolution effected by Copernicus in astronomy. Practically all modern work on the text derives from and depends on his. In the preface to his book Traube affirms that the *Rule* is one of the few ancient texts—he ranks it with the Vulgate and the collections of the Canon Law—which have a text-history in the fullest sense of that phrase. The manuscripts are so abundant, the internal and external evidence so copious, that it is possible to trace the history of the *Rule* with much exactitude back to the time of its first writing. The story is a unique one and of great interest; we propose therefore to summarize it here.

To begin with, it is a curious fact but a true one, that the *Rule* though issued in innumerable editions, of greater or less value, was not subjected to an exact critical study until the late nineteenth century. No thorough examination of all the manuscript evidence was made and no scientific interpretation of the conflicting tradition attempted before the year 1880, when Dom Edmund Schmidt of Metten published his *Regula S. Benedicti juxta antiquissimos codices cognita.* Dom Schmidt was in a true sense a pioneer. After him came a series of scholars: Traube, Plenkers, Morin, Butler, Linderbauer, carrying forward the work which he had begun. As a result of their work it is possible now to speak with some certainty of the true text of the *Rule* and of its history. Let us set forth succinctly the results which have been attained.

St. Benedict did not write his *Rule,* so to say, at one sitting; the *Rule* itself falls into independent sections and it bears evident traces of revision and addition. We should regard it, not as a code of law that was first devised as a whole by the legislator and then imposed on his disciples, but as the redaction of rules that had been in practice long before they were codified.[3] It is most probable, for instance, that the long section regarding the Divine Office existed separately as the liturgical regime of St. Benedict's monasteries from the earliest date. So also the section on faults and their punishment, which the Germans call the *Strafkodex,* forms a self-contained unity and probably had had an independent existence. The last seven chapters of the *Rule* would seem to be an addition, and the prologue was probably written last of all. At what date did St. Benedict put together the whole *Rule,* with its prologue and seventy-three chapters, as we have it now? We cannot say, but can only surmise that he did the work at Monte Cassino and towards the end of his life. Abbot Chapman, in his *St. Benedict and the Sixth Century,* argued from the traces of the *Rule* which he considered that he had found in contemporary documents, that the *Rule* was composed about the year 525; but the argument is of uncertain quality and will not bear close examination. To take but one point: he found plain echoes of the **Rule of St. Benedict** in the Rule of St. Caesarius of Arles, of which the probable date is 534, and argued that St. Caesarius had St. Benedict's **Rule** before him when writing his own. But the texts of Caesarius which were available to him were bad ones, containing much interpolation of late date *from the Benedictine Rule.* And as to the genuine resemblances between the two Rules, not due to such interpolation, Dom Morin agrees decisively with Abbot Butler that St. Benedict used St. Caesarius and not vice versa.[4] Which conclusion, if we could rely on the date given for the Rule of St. Caesarius, would manifestly place St. Benedict's work after 534. However, the evidence which we possess does not, in fact, allow us to give a precise date for the composition of the **Rule** and we must be content to suppose that it was written, in the form in which we have it, well on in the first half of the sixth century, without attempting greater exactitude.

St. Gregory describes St. Benedict when he fled from the world as *scienter nescius et sapienter indoctus* (consciously ignorant and wisely unlearned). He had in fact abruptly broken off his schooling, and these words may fairly be interpreted as a graceful apology for the saint's lack of a full literary training. It is quite clear from the pages of the **Rule** itself that St. Benedict subsequently acquired a considerable measure of monastic learning, for the **Rule** contains abundant evidence of wide and fruitful study; but it is clear also from the same **Rule** that he did not take pains to acquire, or at least to use, any very correct literary form. For the **Rule** is written in that Late Latin of his period which departs considerably in grammar and syntax from the standards of classical Latin. A man who can write: *Post quibus lectionibus sequantur ex ordine alii sex psalmi cum antiphonas* and many similar sentences, is not concerned to write correct Latin, but is adapting himself to the usage of his time. In doing so St. Benedict doubtless consulted the convenience of his immediate disciples, but he left behind him a text which inevitably attracted the hand of the corrector. In fact the subsequent history of the **Rule** was largely determined by its original character.

For it would appear that at once, in the next generation after his death, the disciples of St. Benedict began to edit the text of their founder. There survives in some manuscripts a verse prologue to the **Rule** which is of doubtful import but would seem to attach the name of Simplicius, the third abbot of Monte Cassino (about 560), to such an edition, and Traube accepts this as fact. However that may be, a revised edition of the **Rule** *did* appear in the sixth century and had a wide vogue, practically supplanting the original text. This revised edition is represented, for instance by Oxoniensis, the oldest of all extant manuscripts, which was probably written at Canterbury about the year 700. So by that year there were in existence two distinct

forms of text, the original of St. Benedict and the early revised version (also called the 'interpolated text'). In the course of the eighth century there came into existence a third form of text, a mixture of the other two with 'improvements' of its own. This is known as the Textus Receptus, the received test or vulgate of the **Rule.** It was a text from which all difficulties of grammar and syntax had been removed and the whole redressed in a fair Latin. It is sufficiently true to say that some such vulgate text of the **Rule** has been the current text among Benedictines until the present century.

But, meanwhile, what were the fortunes of St. Benedict's original text? Monte Cassino was sacked by the Lombards about the year 581 and the monks fled to Rome, taking with them, says Paul the Deacon, 'the book of the holy rule which the aforesaid father had written, some other books, the weight for bread and the measure for wine, and what furniture they could get away'.[5] It is the conviction of most scholars that Paul in this passage intends not just a copy of the **Rule,** but the autograph itself. This autograph was taken to the Lateran monastery and from that probably passed into the papal library. For, when Paul comes to narrate the history of the restoration of Monte Cassino under Abbot Petronax (717-47) he records that Pope Zachary 'gave him many helps, namely books of Holy Scripture and other things useful for a monastery, and moreover, of his fatherly love granted him the rule which the blessed father Benedict wrote with his own holy hands' (vi. 40). The precious autograph thus returned to Monte Cassino and stayed there until the year 883 when the monastery was attacked by the Saracens and the community fled to Teano near Capua, taking the autograph with them. The monastery of Teano was destroyed by fire in the year 896 and the autograph with it. But the Cassinese monks evidently, and naturally, possessed copies, for there are extant still at Monte Cassino manuscripts of the tenth and later centuries which though by no means free from other influences are judged to derive their descent from this source. Yet, strangely enough, it is not to these Cassinese manuscripts, but to a German manuscript, that we must go for a faithful copy of the autograph.

It happened in this way. The Emperor Charlemagne, as a promoter of learning, set a high value on correct texts. He was anxious also to regulate the monasteries of his empire. In the course of his Italian campaign in the winter of 786-7 he visited Monte Cassino and doubtless there saw the autograph of the **Rule** with his own eyes. Shortly after his return to Aachen, in the summer of 787, he wrote to Abbot Theodemar of Monte Cassino and asked him for a faithful copy of the autograph. Abbot Theodemar sent him the copy with a covering letter written by Paul the Deacon. That letter contains this sentence: 'Behold, according to your order we have transcribed the rule of our blessed father from the very codex which he wrote with his own holy hands and have sent it to you.' That is the first stage: Charlemagne has obtained a copy of the autograph to serve as the standard for the text of the *Rule* in the monasteries of his empire. The next stage was the dissemination of this text among these monasteries. Many copies were made from this standard text and began to supersede that revised text which had hitherto reigned supreme. The royal copy has perished but some of the copies of it remain, and of these copies—grandchildren so to say of the original—one stands out above the rest for its completeness and accuracy and for its precisely-known history. This is Sangallensis 914, transcribed at the beginning of the ninth century for the Abbey of Reichenau. Its history is as follows:

Charlemagne's successor, Louis the Pious, held a synod at Aachen in the year 817 which ordained that the *Rule* of St. Benedict should be observed in all the monasteries of the empire, and made regulations for its exact observance. As part of this monastic policy Louis established the great reforming abbot, St. Benedict of Aniane, in a special monastery near Aachen which should set the standard of observance for all other monasteries. It was provided also that inspectors should visit these monasteries to see that the emperor's wishes were being carried out. In order to comply with these regulations, Haito, abbot of Reichenau and bishop of Basle, sent two young monks of his abbey, by name Grimalt and Tatto, to Aachen to be instructed in the standard observance. The librarian of Reichenau, by name Reginbert, took advantage of their visit to ask the two emissaries to make him an exact transcript of the imperial copy of *St. Benedict's Rule.* Grimalt and Tatto fulfilled his commission with great fidelity. They made a very careful transcript and dispatched the copy to Reichenau with a letter to their 'most excellent and most beloved master, Reginbert' in the course of which they speak thus: 'Behold, we have sent you the rule of the great teacher Saint Benedict, which your heart has always with intense longing desired to have. Our copy lacks nothing, we believe, of the sentences and syllables and even of the letters that were set down by the aforesaid father; for it has been copied from that exemplar which was copied from the very codex which the blessed father took care to write with his own sacred hands for the welfare of many souls.' They add that they have supplied in the margin the readings of other texts corrected by 'modern masters', wishing their abbey to have both the original text and the current revision. Such is the very precise history of Sangallensis 914. It may be observed upon this history that the position of the *Rule* among ancient books is thus a unique one; of no other ancient book have we a copy which is separated from the original by only one intermediary. The text of Sangallensis 914 has been printed in a diplomatic edition by Dom Morin.[6] The manuscript itself bears out the claim made for it by its scribes; it is accepted by the critics as a very faithful copy and as the necessary basis of any edition of the text of the

Rule. But this is not to say that Sangallensis is free from all error; its scribes were very careful, but they were human and have made a few obvious mistakes. Moreover, the manuscript has suffered a little in the course of the centuries. However, Sangallensis 914 does not stand alone; there are other representatives of the Carolingian tradition. And, besides these, there are the Cassinese manuscripts and the ancient representatives of the early revised version. Taking Sangallensis as his basis and using these other manuscripts to control and correct its text, the modern editor is able to reproduce *St. Benedict's Rule,* as he himself wrote it, with reasonable certainty.

. . . . .

Constituenda est ergo nobis dominici scola
servitii

(Reg. Prol.)

'Besides the many marvels which made Benedict famous', says St. Gregory, 'he was eminent also for his teaching. For he wrote a *Rule* for monks which is remarkable for its discretion and lucidity. And if anyone wishes to know his character and life more precisely, he may find in the ordinances of that *Rule* a complete account of his practice, for the holy man cannot have taught otherwise than as he lived' (*ch.* 36). In these words the biographer draws our attention to that which is certainly the most authentic source for our knowledge of the work of St. Benedict.

The famous *Rule for Monks* has come down to us in many ancient manuscripts. The oldest of these, which is preserved in the Bodleian Library at Oxford, was probably written by the Benedictines of Canterbury at the beginning of the eighth century, that is to say about a century after St. Augustine and his companions brought the knowledge of the monastic rule to this island along with the knowledge of the faith, and a century and a half after St. Benedict. The Venerable Bede was then living his life of fruitful monastic and literary labour in his peaceful Northumbrian monastery. Scholars have examined this and many other manuscripts and determined the pure text, over against the interpolated version which seems almost as ancient as the other, so that some have thought that St. Benedict issued two editions of the *Rule.* But, in speaking of this variety of text, we do not wish to give the impression that the variations are very great in number or substance. Only in one passage—the conclusion of the prologue—is there a considerable and substantial difference between the two traditions, and there the 'interpolated text' has abbreviated and not enlarged the original. We have already spoken of the history of the text as written elaborately by the palaeographer Traube and discussed by many scholars. There is no doubt about the authenticity of the *Rule.*

What were St. Benedict's sources? He is familiar of course with the Scriptures and with the writings of those whom he calls the holy Catholic Fathers. He quotes St. Augustine, St. Jerome, St. Cyprian, St. Leo. He displays an extensive acquaintance with monastic literature, including the Rules of St. Basil, St. Pachomius, St. Macarius of Alexandria, St. Orsiesius and other anonymous rules. He knew the lives of Eastern monks and their recorded sayings. But his chief debt is to the writings of Abbot John Cassian of Marseilles, who collected in his *Institutes* and *Conferences* a copious body of monastic theory and practice. St. Benedict used his sources industriously—he is very occasionally content to reproduce them verbally—but the **Rule,** though its composite character is plain, is not, for all that, an unoriginal patchwork. It is a complete whole, a structure with a genuine unity. A considerable portion may be borrowed from earlier writers, but the presiding spirit, the wisdom, sobriety and moderation which run through the whole, these are St. Benedict's own.[7]

When was the **Rule** written? For this, as we have said already, no definite date can be assigned. It is believed—and the belief is very probable—that the saint did not compose his **Rule** at one time or in one effort. Portions of it may have been formulated even at Subiaco. There are sections such as the chapter on the 'Instruments of Good Works', and that on the 'Twelve degrees of Humility', which may very likely have existed independently, as useful summaries for purposes of instruction. Probably also the considerable section which deals with faults and their correction had a similar separate existence. And the liturgical *cursus* was doubtless custom long before it was set down as law. Indeed we must suppose that the whole **Rule** is the result of experience, of the application of old monastic principle and precept to the purpose which St. Benedict sought to realize, conditioned by the circumstances of locality and temperament. The **Rule** was lived before it was codified. It is supposed that the saint drew up the **Rule,** as we now possess it, at Monte Cassino and towards the end of his life, when he was about sixty years old and had had some forty years' practical experience of the life and government of monks. As we have it now it consists of a Prologue and seventy-three chapters. Of these chapters the last seven would appear to be an addition by St. Benedict to his first codification, and it is probable that the Prologue was written last.

The seventy-three chapters of the **Rule** cannot be made to conform to a clear-cut, logical sequence; indeed it would seem at first sight that St. Benedict did not attempt any logical order, but set his chapters down haphazard. However, it will be found that they fall into groups, united by similarity of subject. After the Prologue there come three chapters which characterize the form of life which he is instituting and provide its

main constitution, in the chapter on the abbot, and the chapter on calling the brethren to Council. Then there follow four chapters of fundamental spiritual instruction (4-7). After that we have eleven chapters on the Divine Office (8-18), ending with one on the proper method of assisting at the Office (19) and another on prayer in general (20). After two chapters (21, 22) of particular ordinances (on Deans and Sleep) we have a large section devoted to the methods of correcting faults (23-30), of which the legislator has more to say later (43-6). With Chapter 31 we resume particular ordinances for the life of the monastery (31-42, 47-57). The fifty-eighth chapter begins a section of the **Rule** which deals with admission into the monastery (58-61). Then we have chapters on the priests of the monastery, the order of the community, the appointment of the abbot, of the prior and gate-keeper. The last seven chapters, which are considered to be later than the rest, deal with certain particular points, and the **Rule** ends with an exhortation to zeal.

The abbot is the corner-stone of St. Benedict's monastic edifice. The polity which he creates might be described epigrammatically as 'autocracy tempered by religion', but the epigram would be misleading. A more accurate description would speak of paternal government. Roman law gave the father of a family very large authority over the members of his household. The government of the family was concentrated in his hands, and in the times of the Republic his power was so absolute that he could even inflict the punishment of death. By the imperial legislation, and especially by that of the early Christian emperors, the *patria potestas* was curtailed. Yet it remained considerable. Law and custom gave the father a status and an authority to which there is no parallel in modern times. St. Benedict conceived the abbot as exercising an authority which is similar to that of a Roman father. He has a paramount authority; but he must exercise it according to the law of God and the **Rule,** with the counsel of his monks, with prudence and equity, firmness and discretion, and with a constant sense of his accountability. The officials of the monastery are appointed by him and removed at his pleasure, while his own authority is for life. The whole life of the monastery hinges upon him, and there is no part of its activity but the direction and regulation of it appertains to him, though he may give others a delegated authority. The **Rule** recommends him to summon the community to advise him, but he is not bound by their advice. 'As often as any important business has to be done in the monastery let the abbot call together the whole community and himself set forth the matter. And, having heard the advice of the brethren, let him take counsel with himself and then do what he shall judge to be most expedient' (*ch. 3*). In the same way the *paterfamilias* of a Roman family might summon the members of the family to a *judicium domesticum* before exercising his supreme authority. For less important matters the abbot is advised to seek the advice of the senior monks.

St. Benedict has no qualms about entrusting this absolute power to one man. He is content to remind the abbot constantly of the responsibility of his position, of the account which he will have to render. For the rest this paternal authority seems to him the most natural thing in the world. And indeed it was entirely according to monastic precedent and contemporary secular practice. St. Benedict probably thought very little about the problem of authority, and it is even doubtful whether he was alive to the parallel between the authority of the abbot and the authority of the *paterfamilias*. He accepted the absolute abbot as he accepted many other elements of monastic tradition. Moreover, the secular government of his day was conceived in the same fashion. Therefore his institution would seem to his contemporaries natural and almost inevitable. And if abbot and monks were faithful to their ideals and lived up to the standard which St. Benedict requires of them, if the abbot were always such a wise and prudent ruler as the saint envisages, then certainly the system would be ideal. But, as in secular government, so here, it has been found that absolute authority is dangerous both for ruler and ruled. Benedictinism has in this point modified the **Rule** of its founder. The councils which St. Benedict prescribes now enjoy a legal status, and besides the consultative voice have also in important matters a right of veto.

The provisions of the **Rule** regarding the method of the abbot's appointment have given rise to much discussion, for they contain elements which seem strange to us in our more ordered times, when all is precisely regulated by long custom and definite law. It is quite clear, however, that St. Benedict expected the abbot to be chosen normally by the community and from among the community, as is now the standard practice. But this choice appears to fall short of a definitive election, for he provides for the case where the majority of a lax community might choose a too complaisant abbot, and in such a case he wishes the choice of the 'healthier' minority to prevail, by the intervention of external authority. He says expressly that if the community should even unanimously elect an unworthy abbot, he would wish the bishop of the diocese, or neighbouring abbots, or even devout layfolk to intervene to prevent such a consummation and to 'set a worthy steward over the house of God'. The history of the time—as revealed, for instance, in St. Gregory's correspondence—shows plainly that such a provision was not unnecessary. The lax monks of Vicovaro, who would have poisoned the saint when he tried to reform them, are not by any means a figment of the imagination.[8]

Besides the abbot, the chief officials of the monastery are the prior, deans, cellarer, novice-master, guest-master, infirmarian. St. Benedict would have them appointed

by the abbot, and hold their authority in entire dependence on him. The chapter on the prior—an official whom St. Benedict does not care for—is instructive on this point. The saint speaks with vehemence of the evils that arise when the prior is appointed by external authority. Such a one is tempted to think himself the abbot's equal, for he has been appointed by the same authority, and there ensues a state of rivalry and dissension which is disastrous for the monastery. The saint is prepared to do without a prior altogether, and to entrust the subordinate governance of the monastery to deans. These *decani* had charge of ten monks each, over whom they were to exercise constant supervision under the general control of the abbot. The cellarer—to whom also a whole chapter is devoted—has charge of the material side of the monastery life. St. Benedict requires much of him. 'As cellarer of the monastery let there be chosen out of the community a man who is prudent, of mature character, temperate, not a great eater, not proud, not headstrong, not rough-spoken, not lazy, not wasteful, but a God-fearing man who may be like a father to the whole community' (*ch.* 31). He has to be a prudent manager, but also a kindly, affable man, whose ministration shall be acceptable to his brethren. And he must ever keep a religious sense of his responsibility. So too with regard to the other officials, St. Benedict requires such character and qualities as shall enable them to fulfil their duties to the corporal and spiritual benefit of those under their charge.

After the constitution of the monastery and careful provision for its administration, it is important to consider the sanctions with which the legislator supports his legal structure. The **Rule** is quite full and explicit on this point, devoting as many as twelve chapters to the subject of faults against the monastic discipline and their punishment, besides incidental references to the 'discipline of the **Rule**'. St. Benedict recognizes two main divisions of faults, slight and grave. The second class admits of degrees, running from the faults which submit to treatment up to those which resist all efforts to amend them and are to be cured only by expulsion from the community. We may classify the penalties recognized by St. Benedict as of three kinds, verbal rebuke, corporal punishment, spiritual punishment, with the fourth and extreme measure of expulsion. Verbal rebuke will be the natural preliminary in every case; in most cases it will perhaps suffice, and St. Benedict provides for its threefold application before sterner measures are called into play. Corporal punishment, under which we may include everything from small acts of humiliation to actual bodily stripes, operates throughout the whole range of faults, for its severer forms may be the only way of influencing those upon whom spiritual penalties have no effect. Spiritual punishment is excommunication, that is to say isolation from the life of the community in its common exercises. It may operate in the refectory only, or both in refectory and in oratory. This penalty comes into effect when rebuke has failed and when the offender is amenable to spiritual punishment. Its milder form, excommunication from the common meal, is the penalty for lighter faults, the double excommunication being reserved for grave offences. When all these measures have failed, St. Benedict bids the abbot resort to prayer—'his own prayers and those of all the brethren, that God, who can do all things, may effect the cure of the sick brother'. But if prayer too fails, then the abbot must use the 'knife of amputation' and expel the refractory brother 'lest one diseased sheep contaminate the whole flock'. Boys are to have special treatment, the normal punishments for them being fasting and the rod.

It would probably be a mistake to infer, from the prominence given in the *Rule* to this subject of the punishment of faults, that offences against the monastic discipline were very numerous and that the abbot and his officials were continually occupied in the business of correction. It is true that characters were ruder then and that Christianity and civilization have combined to produce an improvement in social behaviour, perhaps not without some loss of native vigour and spontaneity. There may have been some barbarians in the community at Monte Cassino. But we should remember at the same time that the faults dealt with are offences against monastic discipline, various degrees of disobedience to the law of the monastery, not offences against the law of God, except indirectly. The punishments prescribed are the natural safeguard of the monastic community, if it would preserve itself from dissolution. Therefore we find that St. Benedict is constantly severe on grumblers—he will not have 'murmuring' at any price—and that the worst offender, for whom expulsion is decreed, is one in whom disobedience has passed into absolute and obstinate mutiny.

In the first sentence of the *Rule* the saint speaks of obedience; to obedience he devotes a whole chapter; it is frequently referred to elsewhere; it is part of the vow taken by the novice; it is to be exercised in an heroic degree. There is no mistaking his meaning. He conceived the monk's life as the service of God by obedience to the monastic rule. The monk has to see God's will in the ordinances of his superiors. He has to realize the absolute surrender that is expressed in Our Lord's words: 'I came not to do my own will, but the will of Him that sent Me.' By this surrender and only so shall he achieve sanctity. Such surrender, it may be, is uncongenial to modern notions of the autonomy of the individual, but objection to it is generally based on a fundamental misunderstanding. It must be remembered that it is an obedience freely chosen and accepted, and further, that it is exercised within the ambit of a well-defined spiritual system, and as a means towards a definite spiritual end. It is an instrument which the individual elects to use, not for the destruction of his individual liberty, but for its strengthening, for the development of his spiritual life to a point that it would otherwise be unable to attain.

In fact, the purpose of all the ordinances of the *Rule* is the same, the purification of the soul and the development of its true life. The monk's aim is spiritual perfection. To this prayer and work, obedience, silence, fasting and every element of the monastic code are directed. Of prayer and work sufficient has been said already. Of silence it need only be said that St. Benedict does not seek to impose it in an absolute manner but allows some social intercourse. Of fasting, while recognizing the undoubted austerity of St. Benedict's regime, we may point out that, judged by the standard of contemporary monastic tradition, it is moderate. His regulations as to the normal allowance of food and drink are again austere in our eyes, but generous even to the point of laxity when judged by Eastern standards. A sentence that occurs in the chapter on the measure of drink deserves to be quoted as displaying the prudence and discretion of the saint, and also what seems like gentle himour: 'We do indeed read', he says, referring to the Book of the Sayings of Eastern monks, 'that wine is no drink for monks; but, since, nowadays monks cannot be persuaded of this, let us at least agree upon this, that we drink temperately and not to satiety' (*ch.* 40). And he allows his disciples a sufficient daily measure of wine.

The last considerable section of the *Rule* to claim attention may be said to be the first in order of historical incidence, the section, that is, which deals with the conditions and method of admittance into the monastic community. Four chapters (58-61) deal severally with four classes of postulants: the 58th with the ordinary applicant, the 59th with oblates, the 60th with priests, the 61st with monks. The last two, if they are granted admittance, receive it on simple terms: they accept the life and promise stability in it. The oblates are young boys who are not of an age to make their own profession; they are offered by their parents and this offering is regarded as a valid contract. The custom was common and ordinary then, but it has long fallen into desuetude. There remains the main class of ordinary adult postulants.

Their trial begins at the very gate of the monastery. We read in the life of Paul the Simple that St. Antony kept him waiting several days outside the door of his cell in order to test his resolution. In the same way St. Benedict ordains that no easy admittance shall be granted to the postulant. 'If such a one, therefore, persevere in his knocking, and if it be seen after four or five days that he bears patiently his harsh treatment and the difficulty of admission and persists in his petition, then let admittance be granted to him.' After a few days in the guest-house he enters the novitiate and is put under the care of the novice-master, a senior monk 'skilled in winning souls', who is to 'watch over him with the utmost care and to consider anxiously whether he truly seeks God, and is zealous for the Work of God, for obedience and for humiliations'. The difficulties, the *dura et aspera,* of the monastic life have to be put plainly before him. For twelve months his trial continues, and the **Rule** is formally read to him three times during this period with the monition: 'Behold the law under which you wish to serve; if you can observe it, enter; if you cannot, freely depart.' If he persevere to the end, then he shall be received into the community; but he is told that it is 'decreed by the law of the **Rule** that he is no longer free to leave the monastery or to withdraw his neck from under the yoke of the **Rule,** which it was open to him, during that prolonged deliberation, either to refuse or to accept'. Then St. Benedict proceeds to arrange the ceremony of the profession. The novice has to make a public avowal of his purpose, in the oratory before the community. He makes a formal promise of stability, discipline of life, and obedience. This promise is not oral only; the monk must present a document embodying his promise and, having signed it, place it upon the altar. Then with his brethren he chants three times the sacrificial words of the psalm: *Suscipe me, Domine, secundum eloquium tuum et vivam: et non confundas me ab exspectatione mea* (Ps. cxviii, 16). Finally he begs the prayers of all, and thenceforward is reckoned as a member of the community.

This solemn ceremony, so carefully conceived both spiritually and juridically, with the preliminary year of prudent trial, shows the master-hand, the wisdom and spiritual insight of the Roman and the saint. It has remained through all the centuries the form of the Benedictine initiation, and has served as a type for many subsequent religious foundations. In one respect only has it suffered substantial modification: the Benedictine does not now take *perpetual* vows until he has spent *four* years of life in the monastery, one as a novice and three under temporary vows. The vows themselves deserve special notice.

St. Benedict's ritual for the profession ceremony distinguishes between the novice's verbal promise and the formal document which embodied that promise. At the present day—and such has been the practice for centuries—this document is itself the formula of the vows and the novice pronounces his vows by reciting it. But that was not the ancient practice; there were two distinct things, a short formula of the vows used by the novice and the longer petition embodying the same vows. Moreover, the manner in which the novice makes his promise has changed. Since the eighth century that promise has been made in the form of a direct statement of the vows: 'I promise stability, etc.' But this was probably not the method of the sixth century. Abbot Herwegen[9] has shown good reason for the view that the earliest form of profession followed the method

of that standard contract in the Roman law, the *stipulatio.* This was a contract made by oral question and answer according to fixed verbal forms. (There is a good example of its method in the ritual for Baptism.) Now there is an ancient ritual for the Benedictine profession which is conceived in this manner. It is found in a ninth-century manuscript which derives from the diocese of Albi, and it was in that diocese that the first Benedictine monastery of Gaul was founded, at Altaripa. Traube[10] prints a letter which the founder of the monastery, by name Venerandus, sent to the bishop of Albi about the year 625 along with a copy of the Rule of 'Saint Benedict, Roman abbot' (*sancti Benedicti abbatis Romensis*), bidding him see that the monks of Altaripa followed that Rule without the least deviation. It cannot now be proved that the ritual of which we are speaking goes back to the foundation of Altaripa and the early seventh century, but the supposition is very plausible, both from the use of the ancient technique of the *stipulatio* and from the occurrence of the word *conversatio* in the correct primitive form. Leaving out eight words which Abbot Herwegen regards as a characteristic Frankish addition to the Roman simplicity of the original, we here give this profession ritual:

> *Suscipiendus in oratorio frater coram omnibus sic interrogatur:* Promittis de stabilitate tua et conversatione morum tuorum et obedientia coram Deo et sanctis ejus?
>
> *Ipse novitius respondeat sic:* Promitto.
>
> Credis ut, si aliquando aliter feceris, a Domino putas te damnandum quem irrides?
>
> *Et ipse respondeat:* Credo.

However, this form of profession went out of use at a very early date and the Benedictine has since recited his vows in the form of a direct statement. Following the text of the **Rule** he vows 'stability, conversion of life[11] and obedience'. By the promise of stability he binds himself to permanence in the community of his profession. St. Benedict was keenly alive to the value of stability, which had been impressed upon him by the spectacle of the loose lives led by the roving monks of his time, the Gyrovagues, whom he castigates in his first chapter. He therefore exacts a precise promise of stability from his monks and from stranger monks or priests who wish to join his community. They shall promise to abide steadfastly in the monastery until death. Such was his meaning. In modern Benedictine practice stability in the monastery is generally extended to stability in the community and sometimes even to stability in the congregation. The effect is that a monk, though normally living in the actual monastery in which he pronounces his vows, may dwell in a dependency of that monastery or even in another monastery of the same congregation.

The second vow, *of conversion of life,* is a very general one. We propose to discuss it fully in the next chapter. For the present it will be sufficient to say that the monk in taking it promises to discipline his life according to the monastic programme. It is the most comprehensive of the three vows. Stability and obedience are particular conditions of the cenobitic life as St. Benedict conceived and regulated it; the second vow embraces the whole complex of the precepts and counsels which are involved in the profession of the monastic life.

The third vow, of *obedience,* like the first, emphasizes an element which St. Benedict regarded as essential to his monastic institute, but which had not always been considered necessary to the monk. The hermit has no occasion to exercise obedience, and the depraved Sarabaite will have none of it. 'Their law is their own good pleasure: whatever they think of or choose to do, that they call holy; what they like not, that they regard as unlawful.' Thus it may be said that *stability* and *obedience* represent St. Benedict's criticism of contemporary monachism and are his reaction against its chief faults. They are to be characteristic of his cenobitical institute, to form the *differentia* distinguishing it from other forms of monachism and from degradations of monachism. On the other hand, the vow of *conversion of life* is the general monastic vow.

Notes

[1] That is, for the reader who has Latin. There are several English versions, but I do not know of one that takes account of the latest textual work. I have ventured to make such a version which will be published immediately by Stanbrook Abbey (Worcester).

[2] Traube died in 1907 before he could issue the second edition of his book. The editor of that edition (Plenkers) has no doubt but that Traube would have brought his work to even greater perfection in a new edition, 'doch dessen hat uns der unerbittliche Tod beraubt'.

[3] It is Abbot Chapman's striking thesis that St. Benedict wrote his Rule at the instance of Pope Hormisdas (514-23) to provide a single, clear code for Western monachism. It is a very attractive thesis. He is able to point out very justly that codification was then the order of the day; he shows reason to believe that St. Benedict's phraseology copies the style of the canons; he is right in maintaining that the Rule is a well-ordered code of monastic law and was designed for use in other monasteries. On the other hand, any positive evidence for the thesis is lacking, and the actual history of the slow diffusion of the Rule would seem to conflict with it. It may be, too, that it is something of an anachronism to suppose that the conception of a unitary monachism was then present to the minds of monks or Pope. Certainly Rome attempted no general regulation of the institute until long afterwards. However, the age of Hormisdas is separated as by a gulf from the period which follows. The disastrous Gothic War baulked many projects and interrupted the continuity of ecclesiastical life and culture in Italy in the most decisive fashion. I hesitate, therefore, to dismiss the thesis as no more than a brilliant fancy.

[4] See Morin: *S. Caesarii Arelatensis Episcopi Regula Sanctarum Virginum* (Bonn, 1933), p. 2. Abbot Chapman required an early date for his chief thesis.

[5] *Historia Langobardorum,* IV, 17.

[6] *Regulae S. Benedicti traditio codicum manu scriptorum Casinensium* (Monte Cassino, 1900).

[7] Much was written in the years 1929-31 about a short, anonymous rule which has been generally known as the 'Second Rule of St. Augustine' (Migne, *P.L.,* XXXII, 1499-52) but of which the more correct title is 'Of the Order of the Monastery' (*De Ordine Monasterii*). Dom Lambot first directed attention to it in the *Revue Liturgique et Monastique* (XIV, 1929, pp. 331-57), describing it as a precursor of the Benedictine Rule. It had not previously attracted much notice, and Abbot Chapman dismisses it as an 'abstract of St. Benedict'. Dom Donatien De Bruyne pursued Dom Lambot's work in the *Revue Bénédictine* (XLII, 1930, pp. 316-42), giving an accurate text of the *De Ordine Monasterii* and arguing vigorously for the opinion that it was St. Benedict's first Rule, written by him at Subiaco. The discussion would appear to have been settled decisively by Dom Germain Morin in the same review (XLIII, 1931, pp. 145-52). He puts the document well before St. Benedict, about the year 440, and believes that it was composed in southern Italy under African (Augustinian) influence. He suggests as a possible author an exiled African bishop, by name Gaudiosus, who founded a monastery at Naples about the year 440. The document is of great interest in regard to the monachism of Cassiodorus (see Chapter XII) for in its true text (the Migne text is faulty) it shows the same liturgical horarium as was used by Cassiodorus.

[8] See the letter of Venerandus (p. 231) for an illustration of the jurisdiction which the Rule expects the bishop to exercise in a monastery. The community normally *chooses,* the bishop always *appoints* the abbot. This is implied in St. Benedict's words about the prior.

[9] *Geschichte der benediktinischen Professformel* (1912), pp. 38-9.

[10] *Textgeschichte der Regula S. Benedicti* (1910), p. 88.

[11] The form *conversio morum* is still in use and we translate that.

Stephanus Hilpisch (essay date 1950)

SOURCE: "St. Benedict and His Foundation" in *Benedictinism through Changing Centuries,* translated by Leonard J. Doyle, St. John's Abbey Press, 1958, pp. 11-7.

[*In the following excerpt, originally published in German in 1950, Hilpisch comments on St. Benedict's life and the organization of his monastery at Monte Cassino.*]

Benedictine monachism, customarily called the Benedictine Order in later times, is the oldest monastic community of the Western Church, its origin dating all the way from Christian antiquity. Its founder, teacher and lawgiver, St. Benedict, was born about the year 480 in the Sabine mountains, in the old Italian province of Nursia. His parents belonged to the free, landholding class, and were probably leading a retired life, far removed from the capital of the world empire, in a province whose people were famed for their austerity and tenacity. They were open-minded enough, however, to send their son Benedict to Rome at an early age to pursue his studies. There is proof of his family's Christian spirit in the fact that they offered their daughter Scholastica to God even as a child, by having her join the ranks of the consecrated virgins.

Young Benedict arrived at a Rome that still showed the magnificence and splendor of the old Roma in the architecture of the ancient times, but had started to adorn itself with the glories of the new Christian era. Already prominent were the great basilicas of the Lateran, of the Vatican over the grave of St. Peter, and the one outside the walls over the grave of the Apostle Paul.

Yet the city showed signs of decay. The transfer of the imperial residence to Constantinople had demoted Rome to a provincial capital. Besides, the city bore the marks of plunder by the barbarians, and want and privation had beset the people for some time. In still more deplorable state were the affairs of the Church. After the death of Pope Anastasius II in the year 498, a double election had followed. To the pope lawfully elected and also recognized by King Theodoric the Great, another group opposed the presbyter Laurentius, and now two popes strove for the chair of St. Peter. Passions rose so high that blood was shed in the churches, and it was to be years before peace was restored in the Roman community.

Living in Rome at this time, young Benedict was so depressed by this and other events in his immediate surroundings that he left the city, gave up his studies, and proceeded to Enfide (now Afile), a small place in the Sabine mountains, where he joined a community of ascetics who had their house by the church of St. Peter. The members of this community followed a religious life but were not bound by a rule, and each was free to order his life as he saw fit. We do not know how long Benedict stayed here. He left this community of ascetics, however, and resolved, in spite of his youth, to lead a hermit's life, evidently seeking a stricter form of asceticism.

In the solitude of Subiaco he found a cave where he led a life of renunciation far from the company of men. He had received the monk's garb from the monk Romanus and was thus accepted as a God-seeking servant of Christ. For three years he lived in the cave in complete solitude, devoting himself entirely to prayer and to converse with God.

By and by he became acquainted with other hermits who were joined in a loose union with an abbot at the head. After the abbot's death they begged Benedict to take over their guidance, and he finally agreed, after first declining the invitation. He might even then have been engrossed in plans for the kind of reorganization of monachism that he had probably envisioned during the years of his solitude, which were filled with the reading of holy Scripture, the fathers of the Church, and monastic literature; and it appears that he intended to carry through his plans with these hermits whose life was a combination of the solitary and the community life. He ventured to introduce a stricter order and the regular mode of cenobitic life for the hermits. But they had their own idea of an abbot: they saw him as a teacher and spiritual father, but not as their lord and lawgiver. Benedict's attempt encountered the unanimous and determined opposition of the community, who went so far as to try to remove the innovator by poison.

Benedict left the hermits, deeply disappointed and yet enriched by a new experience. He now knew different forms of contemporary monachism, which, after not quite 200 years of existence, showed obvious signs of decay. About such monastic life he wrote later in his **Rule:** "It is better to pass it over in silence than to speak of it," and again, "Their tonsure marks them as liars before God."

Returning to his cave, he now began to form the monastic life as he had envisioned it, with disciples who had joined him, some from Rome itself. The influx was so great that he was able to erect twelve cells in the valley of the Anio, in each of which a number of monks lived under a superior, while he himself directed the whole community and introduced the young monks to the monastic life. This mode of life corresponded somewhat with the traditions of Pachomius.

Partly because of the enmity of a neighboring priest, the saint after some years left Subiaco and moved with some of the monks to the hill of Monte Cassino that towers over the plains of the Campagna. At the summit of the mountain he built a monastery on the site of an old fort and a former temple. Upon this mount with its wide view, there came into existence the **Rule** in which St. Benedict explained his thoughts about the life of Christian perfection and in which he clearly outlined the practice of the monastic life as he saw it.

Here Benedict espoused with full determination the cenobitic mode of life under an abbot, with an exact, stabilized rule binding all the monks of the monastery. He rejected the free asceticism and was just as much opposed to the tramp monks and the semi-anchorites. In the hermit's life he saw a high ideal, but only for those with a special vocation who had prepared themselves in monastic community life and had proved their aptitude for this extraordinary ascetical form. For the average he regarded the cenobitic life as the only fitting form of monasticism.

To St. Benedict, being a monk means living according to the demands of the gospel, complying with the divine will, participating in the Lord's Passion, and being filled with the Spirit of God. The monastic virtues he considers to be silence, obedience, humility, and brotherly love. The daily life of the monk is characterized by prayer, first by the psalmody rendered in common at night and at the day hours sanctified by the Church's tradition; then by the silent prayer of the heart, as also by reading and manual labor. Thus prayer, work and study are to establish the rhythm of the day and of the year.

The monastery is separated as far as possible from the outside world and takes care of the greater part of its necessities by itself; hence it has landed property, gardens, vineyards, mills and workshops where the necessary things are made. While property for the community is lawful, private property is banned in every way and is viewed by St. Benedict as a particularly detestable evil, endangering brotherly love and contradicting the community spirit exemplified by the pioneer community at Jerusalem.

Leading the monastic community is the abbot, whom the whole community elects and who bears full responsibility for all the monks and the whole monastery. As the representative of Christ he exercises full authority, to which all in obedience submit. He is bound by the **Rule,** but Benedict gives him far-reaching powers to modify certain things according to conditions of time and place, so that a just agreement between constancy and growth may be found.

Even though the abbot makes the final decisions and has full freedom to act, yet he is to appoint experienced brethren as his assistants for the conduct of particular functions; he shall also be assisted by a council composed of older brethren and solicit the opinion of all brethren in important matters. His assistants in the government of the monastery are the prior, the cellarer (under whose care are all material things), the master of novices, the porter, the infirmarian, and the choirmaster. The fundamental principle is that in the house of God all things should be handled wisely and by wise men.

In addition to the oratory and the monks' residence, the monastery shall have a separate house for the reception of guests, a house for the sick brethren, one for the novices, and a room for the library.

Benedict eliminated austerities of the old monastic tradition and espoused a prudent moderation in which his demands were high, but always with regard for the weakness of individuals. He wanted to arrange everything in the monastery as the strong ones desired it, but in such a way as not to discourage the weak. Thus wisdom, kindness, and firmness are joined together in wonderful harmony in the **Rule.**

The saint displays a certain severity only where he treats of private property and of murmuring against authority, for he sees in these a threat to the foundations of the cenobitic life and of true monasticism. But in no way does he intend privation for his monks, nor does he see the ideal in absolute poverty: the monk may have for his use all that is necessary, may ask it of the abbot, and the abbot shall give it to him; yet nobody shall have the right of free disposal or claim anything as his property.

St. Benedict's work was clearly conceived by him as a new formulation of the monastic ideal and a new organization of the monastic life; for he had witnessed more than once in his life a caricature of the true meaning and content of the monastic state. Up to his time Western monachism had not reached any historic importance at all; in fact, there was yet no Western monachism, properly speaking, however numerous the monasteries in the West might be, in Italy, Gaul and Spain. Fundamentally it was Eastern monachism that was practiced in the West, without the prerequisites, however, that were present in the East. There was no rule to expound and regulate the high ideals of monasticism in a manner which would appeal to the people of the West. Lacking, too, were the spiritual transformation of the monk's life, and occupations for the hosts of monks who crowded the monasteries.

St. Benedict brought about a great change and thereby saved the monastic institution from decline and stagnation. The West was far removed from the monachism which Antony and the fathers in the desert lived, which Cassian in his works had proposed as a high aim, and whose embodiment had been the holy monk-bishop, Martin; still greater was the distance from the monachism of St. Basil, who had united asceticism with the heritage of the ancient culture and so led it to a spiritual height.

Without higher culture, without a serious occupation, and without a strict discipline and proper guidance, the monks of the West lived as hermits or wandered about; and where they lived in community, they had no moderate yet rigid rule. Generally, each abbot made statutes for his house as best he could, following old traditions; and there were as many rules as monasteries.

Against these evils St. Benedict set a determined hand. He bound the monk to stability, thus to residence and perseverance in the monastery. By this means he did away with the practice of having monks wander about. This had once been a high religious ideal, on the plea of Christ's homelessness; but when great numbers followed this way of living, it degenerated into lack of discipline. Benedict led the monk to obedience to an authoritative *Rule* and to an abbot and thereby eliminated the state of the semi-anchorite and of the free ascetic, whose only law at that time was free choice. He demanded of the monk a life of virtue, prayer and work, for there were numerous monks who went to ruin in idleness and became harmful to the Church.

His first concern was to establish the individual monastery, to give it vitality and protect it against outside influences that might threaten it; his other concern was the spiritual formation of the monks. He wanted to create a livable rule for the monasteries of the West and also give the abbots of the individual monasteries permanent directions for guiding their monasteries and their monks in a manner pleasing to God. He had no thought of an order, a union of all monasteries under a central authority. What he wanted was monastic life and the existence of the individual monastery.

The basis was not a narrowly circumscribed religious ideal. The whole Christian life in general was demanded, in which man was simply placed before God and assigned to the service of God in prayer, virtue, and sacrifice. Much less had the saint intended a special objective for his foundation. The service of God left the monk free for all manner of tasks without binding him completely to any special one. Any task could be assumed in so far as it did not interfere with the essence of the monk's life. It was the saint's aim to realize in a community the life of the gospel, devotion to God and to His holy service. Of other outside tasks he had no thought. His monks were to praise God in the psalmody, and praise Him moreover by their whole life.

In his monastic *Rule* he happily combined the oldest traditions with new ideas, holding unconditionally to the supernatural, yet with consideration of the pure human element, clinging strictly to the basic essentials with wise consideration of individual weaknesses. Because of its inner strength and balance, the Rule gradually became the common law of Western monks and at length displaced the other monastic rules, not only the Eastern in so far as they had gained a foothold, but also the national, such as the Irish and Visigothic rules. In this diffusion his *Rule* enjoyed the support of the Apostolic See at Rome; St. Gregory the Great himself wrote the life of St. Benedict, in which the knowledge of his personality was spread throughout the Church and words of highest approval were found for his *Rule.*

St. Benedict did not live long enough to see the extensive influence that his *Rule* would exert. We know with certainty only of his first monasteries in the valley of the Anio and at Monte Cassino and the foundation at Terracina which he planned. Venerated as a prophet and wonder-worker filled with the Spirit of God, he died on March 21, probably in the year 547, lifting his hands to heaven in prayer before the altar of his oratory, and found his rest in the sanctuary of St. John the Baptist, which he himself had built.

His monastery at Monte Cassino was not to enjoy a long existence at first. Not quite 30 years after his death it was demolished by the Lombards, and the monks escaped, leaving the Saint's body behind on the mountain. Thus the place of his work was temporarily devastated, but his work was not destroyed; rather, it now found its great historic hour, for soon the diffusion of the *Rule* started throughout and beyond Italy.

Since St. Benedict left the individual monasteries their independence and created no all-embracing organization, the history of Benedictine monachism is above all the history of its monasteries. The individual monasteries became the agents of its development; they determined the direction and the manner in which the saint's work expanded, and in their history one can read of the bloom and decay of Benedictine monachism in the course of time.

Ildephonse Cardinal Schuster (essay date 1951)

SOURCE: "The Liturgical Work of St. Benedict" in *Saint Benedict and His Times,* translated by Gregory J. Roettger, O. S. B., B. Herder Book Co., 1951, pp. 228-36.

[*In the following essay, Schuster details the influential liturgy St. Benedict outlined in his* Rule—*later known as the* Cursus S. Benedicti.]

Besides the Roman rite, the Oriental rite, and the Ambrosian rite, the Middle Ages also recognize a

Cursus S. Benedicti, that is, they give the Patriarch's name to the entire liturgy of the Divine Office which the monks day and night chanted in their monastery churches. This special rite of the *Opus Dei,* as the Patriarch usually calls the Divine Office, is described in the **Rule** in chapters 8-20 and in chapters 43, 47, 52, 58, one of the most complete expositions of the Divine Office left us by the ancients.

As in the rest of the **Rule,** so also with regard to the liturgy, which he bases on the rite of Rome, the man of God follows the more enlightened tradition of the Fathers, but he casts the practices of the various churches together into a harmonious and wisely balanced whole, in accordance with his Roman character. It would suffice to compare the **Cursus S. Benedicti** with the Office of the Oriental monks and with that of the Irish and the Franks, to bring out immediately that a criterion of discretion inspired the Patriarch in composing his monastic **Cursus.**

When we consider that he divides the longer psalms into two sections; that during the short summer nights, in order not to abbreviate unduly the monks' rest, he shortens and cuts down even the Scriptural reading; that for smaller communities he dispenses from the obligation of singing the antiphons; that between Matins and Lauds he prescribes a brief intermission, so that the old men may retire a moment for the necessities of nature: weighing all these criteria of humaneness, it is impossible not to subscribe to the judgment of St. Gregory regarding the **Rule:** " . . . outstanding for its discretion."[1]

When the man of God set his hand to compose his liturgical **Cursus,** he found himself face to face with venerable traditions which he could not disregard. Especially there existed a Roman tradition, to which the Apostolic See attached such importance that it obliged all new bishops to swear to conform to it and to propagate it in their dioceses, so that it might become common among the clergy. The formula of this oath is found in the *Liber diurnus.*[2] The new bishop swears and promises that every day, from cockcrow till morning, he will be present in the church with all his clergy for the daily celebration of the morning Office: *"Vigilias in ecclesia celebrare."*

For this purpose the year is divided into two parts, short nights and long nights, summer and winter. The first section runs from Easter to the autumnal equinox (September 24); during this time only three lessons, three antiphons, and three responsories are sung at the Office. There follows the litany customary at the beginning of Mass. At other times, however, because morning comes later, they will say "four lessons, with their responsories and antiphons." On Sundays throughout the year, on the other hand, "nine lessons, with their responsories and antiphons are recited. . . . The

litanies twice a month at all times." During the sixth century this constituted the entire Office of the cathedral churches in the metropolitan province of the pope.

Besides this primitive Roman *Cursus,* Italian monachism of St. Benedict's time had before it, too, the ascetical traditions of the great Oriental Fathers, those of the monasticism of Jerusalem, of Cassian, of the abbey of Lerins, and of the Ambrosian Church. But there is this difference, namely, that if, confronted by such varied local customs, St. Benedict felt free to choose the best for his monasteries, this liberty did not extend to the practices of the Church of Rome and to the ancient ritual traditions of the Catholic Church, to which, without a doubt, he had to conform.[3]

The daily **Cursus S. Benedicti** comprised, besides the night Office, also the prayers of the seven day hours. In them are sung the Psalter, the collection of odes, namely, the hymns of St. Ambrose; there are read the Scriptures with the comments of the most famous Fathers. The chants are taken from the *Liber antiphonalis* or the *Responsoriale;* their execution demands great musical skill on the part of the chanters and the soloists.

According to the Roman fashion the year is divided into two parts: winter and summer. But since the fasts of summer end with the Ides of September, differing in this detail from the *Liber diurnus,* St. Benedict's winter begins with the Kalends of November and lasts till Easter.

In accord with the *"Cautio episcopi,"* there is a difference between the ferial night Office and that of Sunday. To conform as far as possible to the Roman usage, St. Benedict has the Roman Office of the dawn at cockcrow, which he calls *Matutinarum solemnitas,* preceded by another of monastic devotion, which is known simply as *nocturna laus.*

This night Office, peculiar to the cenobites, begins shortly after midnight and, following the practice of the Egyptian monks, twelve psalms are sung in order, with the concluding alleluia. Contrary to the Roman usage, which reserved the scriptural readings for the morning Office, monastic piety anticipated them and inserted them between the psalms of the *nocturna laus.* Thus the morning Office will not be so long and burdensome and will permit the monks to go to their work in good time.

Now, the Roman morning Office enjoys a venerable tradition, which has determined for each day the psalms and the canticles to be used. St. Benedict follows it faithfully ("as the Roman Church prays"). He could not have acted differently; and that is the reason why even today in the **Cursus S. Benedicti** the psalms of the morning Office do not follow the order of the

Psalter, but are chosen here and there in David's songbook.

As a conclusion to the morning Office, also in the Lateran the custom of Gaul and of Spain was followed, namely, of having the bishop recite the *Pater noster* before dismissing the assembly. St. Benedict introduces this usage into his **Cursus,** reserving the chanting of the closing *Pater* to the abbot, since he holds the place of Christ in the monastery.

On Sundays or feast days the Benedictine rite of the *nocturna laus* is more extended. The Patriarch remains faithful to the Egyptian tradition of twelve psalms each night; but then, after the reading of the scriptural commentary of the Fathers,[4] he introduces, in accord with the custom of Jerusalem and Milan, a special section of chants chosen from the canticles. This extraordinary *nocturna laus* comes to a close with the abbot's chant of the Gospel of the resurrection, preceded by the *Te Deum* and followed by a doxology *post Evangelium,* according to the Ambrosian custom. It is not hard to explain these Milanese elements in the **Cursus S. Benedicti** if we will remember what St. Paulinus says in the life of St. Ambrose, namely, that almost the whole of Italy and the Occident had followed the example of the saint in introducing the night Office into their cathedrals: "At this period for the first time antiphons, hymns, and vigils began to be celebrated in the Church of Milan. Faithfulness to this practice persists until the present day not only in that Church, but throughout almost all the provinces of the West."[5]

Going contrary to Rome, which preserved intact its liturgical traditions—and which for long centuries allowed neither the singing of hymns nor other anticipations of its Office at cockcrow—as St. Benedict had received into his **Cursus** the Ambrosian tradition of hymns, so he also admitted that of the chant of the three canticles which on Sunday precede the solemn Gospel of the resurrection of Christ. At Jerusalem, as we know from the pilgrim Etheria, this chant was executed by the bishop in person, standing directly over the entrance of the cave in which the Savior was buried. St. Benedict prescribes that it be done by the abbot, "while all stand in awe and reverence."

When the reading of the word of God is finished, all must answer "Amen," precisely as is done at Milan when the Eucharist is received. There follows the Oriental Trinitarian hymn: *"Te decet laus . . ."* of the Apostolic Constitutions, which takes the place of the chant *post Evangelium,* according to the Ambrosian usage.

During the day, the hours of Prime, Terce, Sext, None, Vespers, and Compline call the monk to choir and to liturgical prayer. The determination of these hours, which formerly divided the civil day, came from the Christian tradition which grew out of the Jewish practice.[6] According to St. Benedict, who remains indebted to the tradition of Cassian and of Lerins, in each of these hours three psalms are sung, and they terminate with the litany.

But when the monks are engaged in the work of the fields at some distance from the oratory, it is not prescribed that they betake themselves to the choir for the individual hours. In this circumstance they can sing the psalms out in the open, under the vault of heaven and in the sight of God who looks down upon them from His throne. Only let them pray with reverence: they "shall perform the work of God in the place where they are working, bending their knees in reverence before God" (chap. 50).

The Divine Office constitutes for the monk a daily and a personal obligation toward the majesty of God. Hence, also outside the choir, even on a journey, he has to sing the divine praises at the determined times: "Likewise those who have been sent on a journey shall not let the appointed hours pass by . . ." (chap. 50).

The day hours of the Office can indeed be sung by the monks while engaged in work, in the open field. Vespers, on the other hand, like the Office at dawn, enjoys a special solemnity and is celebrated only in church, a few hours before sunset.

Since, then, in the monastery the work must be accomplished by the light of day, because it is not wise to keep the community in the dim light of lanterns, the *vespertina synaxis* of St. Benedict does not at all agree with the *Eucharistia lucernaris,* that is, the chanting of the *Lucernarium,* as practiced at Milan, in Gaul, by Eugippius at Naples. On the other hand, it was not introduced in Rome; and this suffices that St. Benedict should not mention it in the *Regula monasteriorum.* The Ambrosians are accustomed to divide Vespers into several parts, with scriptural readings and distinct orations; but the Vespers of St. Benedict will be adapted to men who are already fatigued after the hard work of the day, who in Lent are still fasting, and at other times have taken their only meal a little before, namely, after None.

The *synaxis vespertina* consists of the daily chant of but four psalms, taken in order from David's songbook. There follows the Ambrosian hymn, *Deus Creator omnium,* with the Magnificat, the Sunday collect sung by the abbot, and the concluding litanies. St. Benedict himself explains what he means by these litanies: ". . . the verse and the petition of the litany, that is, 'Lord, have mercy on us' . . ." (chap. 9). The practice has been preserved in the Ambrosian liturgy, where in the festive Lenten Mass, in the Vespers of the vigil of the greater saints, and in the obsequies of the deceased, these final litanies are sung at the conclusion of the rite.

Differing from the brevity to which they are now reduced in the Benedictine Breviary, these ancient litanies resemble the *Orationes solemnes* of the Roman Missal for Good Friday, where they occur after the afternoon gathering and before the adoration of the wood of the cross. The deacon announces the prayer for the various needs of the Church, for the pope, for the bishop, for the sick, for those imprisoned or condemned to the mines, and people answer: *"Kyrie eleison,"* or *"Domine, miserere."*

St. Benedict carefully distinguished the two parts of the deacon's prayer: " . . . the verse and the petition of the litany, that is, 'Lord, have mercy on us'. . . . "

The Office of *Completoria* seems also to derive from Ambrosian usage, which adds *Completoria* to Vespers. There is question here of three short psalms, always identical, which the monks recited before going to bed, in order to sanctify also the end of the day with prayer and the blessing of the abbot.

Compline is not sung, nor are antiphons interpolated; hence the psalm verses are recited in unison: " . . . three psalms, which are to be said straight through without antiphon" (chap. 17). Compline is treated almost as if it were private prayer; in enumerating the parts of the Divine Office in chapter 15 of the Rule, the Patriarch does not even mention it.

In agreement with the rule of Eugippius, spiritual reading from some work of the holy Fathers or from the Collations of Cassian precedes Compline. Hence arose the medieval custom of abbots granting their monks a light refreshment in the summer shortly before retiring, namely, a bit of watered wine or some fruit to restore them somewhat, and this received the name of "collation."

This, in general, constitutes the **Cursus S. Benedicti,** which together with the **Regula** spread into the entire world and in its turn influenced the Divine Office of the Church universal itself. After St. Benedict has completed his arrangement, he remarks that if his weekly distribution of the Psalter appears unacceptable to some abbot, he should consider himself free, most free, to order it differently, provided always that he remains faithful to the principle of the recitation of the Psalter and Canticles every week, and provided he respects, be it well understood, the liturgical tradition of the Church regarding the Office at dawn *ad galli cantum.*

The holy Patriarch himself reveals to us the measure of his discretion when he notes that the Psalter, which he distributed over the course of a whole week, was formerly recited daily by the ancient Fathers. To whom does he allude? The *Cursus* of Eugippius is exceedingly brief and contains only a few psalms. St. Benedict is aware of that fact, because he consulted Eugippius' rule and used it extensively.

The Ambrosians divided the Psalter into decades, and even to this day employ fifteen days in its recitation. To St. Benedict, however, this distribution does not appeal for his monks; indeed he says outright: "For those monks show themselves too lazy in the service to which they are vowed, who chant less than the Psalter with the customary canticles in the course of a week" (chap. 18). The saint probably was not aware of the fact that the Ambrosians repeat the same psalms in the day hours, so that actually their *Cursus* effectively is much longer than the monastic and runs to about two hundred psalms.

The **Cursus S. Benedicti** represented the true monastic *ratio studiorum* of the Middle Ages. From the moment that in the Benedictine conception the abbey was the "school of the Lord's service," the formative program of this school was supplied by the Divine Office, that is, the *Opus Dei,* as the Patriarch called it. This Divine Office, to which each monk dedicated about ten hours daily, contained everything knowable at that time; for, in a form eminently dramatic, it was at the same time prayer, Scripture study, patristic study, poetry, music, and history of the Church, for the solace of the spirit striving toward heaven.

Standing in choir and assiduously singing the Divine Office, the monk became acquainted with all those varied disciplines. Thanks to this intense higher instruction imparted to Benedictine communities with ability, method and constancy, the Patriarch of Cassino became and remained for more than seven centuries the Master of the Middles Ages.

The celebrated musical *scholae,* the numerous *scriptoria,* the architecture and sacred art, even the various schools of liturgical drama, arose in former times in connection with the *Opus Dei* regulated by St. Benedict, to which he ascribed an absolute primacy when he wrote: "Let nothing, therefore, be put before the Work of God" (chap. 43).

The sacred drama or the *Opus Dei* that is daily celebrated in Benedictine abbeys demands, besides gifts of the spirit, also a true literary and artistic competence. The dispositions of the spirit required for a good understanding of the Divine Office are described in chapters 19 and 20 of the *Regula monasteriorum* and are summed up in the golden principle: " . . . that our mind may be in harmony with our voice," and in the other to which reference has already been made: "Let nothing, therefore, be put before the Work of God."

In order to endow his monks with the suitable cultural preparation for an adequate understanding of the Sacred Scriptures and the songs of David, which go to make up the Divine Office, the Patriarch lays it down that the commentaries on them which are read in public be those "by well known and orthodox Catholic Fathers" (chap. 9). In the last chapter of the **Rule** he returns to recommend the study of the Bible and the holy Fathers (chap. 73). But since, besides these readings in common, some of the monks had need also of private and personal study, St. Benedict sets apart for this purpose not only the interval between the morning Office and Prime, but also three or four hours of the workday and the entire Sunday (chap. 48).

In choir everything—readings, chants, and ceremonies—must be executed to perfection and according to the rules of art. Whoever is not capable of doing these things in a worthy manner is without further ado excluded from performing such a function: "The brethren are not to read or chant in order, but only those who edify their hearers" (chap. 38).

Father Faber has written a most interesting chapter on the ancient Benedictine school of asceticism. More recently, too, the ancient ascetic tradition of monasticism has received attention, and the conclusion is that all those giants of Catholic sanctity, many of whose lives are contained in the nine folio volumes of Mabillon's *Acta Sanctorum Ordinis S. Benedicti* from the sixth to the twelfth centuries, received their formation in the "school of the Lord's service," thanks above all to the daily *Opus Dei* ordered by St. Benedict. This aspect of the doctrinal apostolate of the holy Patriarch by means of the liturgical **Cursus,** which receives its name from him, generally receives little notice from the historians, despite its decisive effect on ecclesiastical culture during the Middle Ages.

We may observe that the numerous Benedictine abbeys of a former age, spread over Europe, differed greatly from one another in spirit, in nationality, in purpose, in the activity developed by them. Yet all the great saints, apostles, bishops, teachers, and other Benedictine abbots of whom history makes mention possessed an identical spirit and a similar *forma mentis,* that which they derived from the same "school of the Lord's service," by virtue of the efficacy of a common and magnificent liturgy which supplied the place of a regular *ratio studiorum.* For this reason the fathers of the Council of Duzia in 874 placed the **Regula monasteriorum** "among the canonical Scriptures and the writings of the Catholic doctors."

Notes

[1] The Ambrosian rite divides and distributes the Psalter into decades, assigning one of them to a night. This division is rather ancient, since it is that followed also by St. Augustine in his *Enarrationes in Psalmos,* as Cassiodorus testifies: *"Uno codice tam diffusa complectens, quae ille [Augustinus] in decadas quindecim mirabiliter explicavit"* (Comment. in Psalt., Praef.)

[2] *"Cautio episcopi,"* no. 82.

[3] An Irishman of the eighth century thus describes the relations between the Roman *Cursus* and that of St. Benedict: *"Est et alius cursus beati Benedicti, qui ipsum singulariter pauco discordante a cursu Romano, in sua Regula repperies scriptum"* (Haddan and Stubb, *Councils and Ecclesiastical Documents,* Oxford, 1869, I, 140).

[4] In ancient times the faithful stood not only during the divine psalmody, but also during the scriptural readings and the sermon. St. Benedict, however, permits the monks to sit at the night Office during the singing of the lessons and the responsories: " . . . *residentibus cunctis disposite et per ordinem in subsellis"* (chap. 11). At Arles St. Caesarius introduced a similar discipline among the faithful "when longer *Passiones* are read or more extended explanations given." In such a case, the weak and others who found it difficult to stand sat on the floor (*PL,* XXXIX, 2315).

[5] *Vita S. Ambrosii,* no. 13.

[6] The *Cursus* of Eugippius and Cassiodorus differed from that of St. Benedict in making no provision for the hour of Prime.

Justin McCann (essay date 1952)

SOURCE: A preface to *The Rule of Saint Benedict,* edited and translated by Justin McCann, The Newman Press, 1952, pp. vii-xxiv.

[*In the following excerpt from his preface to* The Rule of Saint Benedict, *McCann recounts the early history of the* Rule *and discusses issues surrounding its language and textual history.*]

Saint Benedict lived and worked in central Italy in the first half of the sixth century, the approximate date of his death being A.D. 547. His life began and ended with periods of devastating war, during which Italy was gravely disorganized; but at its centre, under the masterful rule of Theodoric (493-526), it knew some thirty years of peace. Yet this period too, though free from the alarms and excursions of war, was not one in which the arts of peace flourished greatly, so that we cannot be surprised that the slender chronicles of the time contain no record of the Saint's life and work. It is not until nearly fifty years after his death that we have any record of him, i.e. until the year 594 and the *Dialogues* of Pope St Gregory the Great. However, this record, when it came, was certainly an appreciative one, and it contains an item which is of particular interest and value to an editor of the *Holy Rule.* Here is the important piece of information that St Gregory gives his deacon:

> I should like, Peter, to tell you much more about this venerable abbot; but I purposely pass over some of his deeds, for I hasten to get on to the lives of others. Yet I would not have you ignorant of this, that Benedict was eminent, not only for the many miracles that made him famous, but also for his teaching. In fact, he wrote a *Rule* for Monks, which is of conspicuous discretion and is written in a lucid style. If anyone wishes to know Benedict's character and life more precisely, he may find a complete account of his principles and practice in the ordinances of that *Rule;* for the Saint cannot have taught otherwise than as he lived (II 36).

Such is the testimony of the greatest of all the disciples of the *Rule*, who introduced it into that monastery of his whence came the apostles of the English people, who commended it regularly in his letters, and whose advocacy it was that set the *Rule* upon the career which resulted in its becoming the monastic code of Western Europe.

1. Date of Composition of the Rule

When did St Benedict compose his *Rule?* He would have felt the need of some code of law from the very beginning, as soon as he had accepted the task of organizing community life, that is to say, at Subiaco and in the earliest years of the sixth century. It is necessary to suppose, for instance, that his first communities had a definite horarium for the Divine Office, for study, and for manual work, that they had officials and a discipline of punishments for breaches of monastic rule, etc. It is probable, therefore, that the corresponding chapters of the *Rule* were established, at least in substance, as early as this. In fact, it seems very reasonable to suppose that St Benedict composed his *Rule,* so to say, "as he went along", adding from year to year the conclusions suggested by experience and by his monastic reading, and in this gradual way constructing finally a complete code of monastic observance. The *Rule* itself contains various indications which support such a theory of progressive composition. Although there is, of course, a fundamental continuity of subject-matter, yet there are not a few chapters which occur in a somewhat haphazard fashion and according to no easily recognizable plan. In contrast with these are several compact groups of chapters, held together in so close and self-contained a manner by their unity of subject, as to suggest strongly that they had previously enjoyed an independent existence. The chief groups of this sort are the eight chapters on faults and their punishment (the *Strafkodex,* as the Germans call it) and

the eleven chapters which determine the substance and ritual of the Divine Office. This latter group of chapters is noteworthy for the abundance of its "vulgarisms", i.e. the forms and usages of popular Latin, a circumstance which would persuade us—a thing otherwise likely—that it is the most primitive portion of the *Rule.* Opposed to these compact groups are the numerous chapters which occur in an accidental fashion and have in some cases the air of postscripts or supplements. There is a postscript of this sort in connexion with the important matter of the abbot and his necessary qualities. The topic is dealt with professedly in the second chapter, but is resumed and supplemented, towards the end of the *Rule,* in the sixty-fourth. There is a specially interesting indication in the sixty-sixth chapter, which ends with a sentence that is plainly a terminal one, marking the final point of one draft of the *Rule.* Then there came a second draft, with seven additional chapters. And so the work was completed. We may guess that this consummation was reached towards the end of the Saint's life, perhaps in the decade 530-40. And then the *Rule* left St Benedict's hands to be launched sooner or later upon the world of western monachism. It was welcomed, for western monachism needed just such a *Rule.* It may perhaps be construed as a proof of the sincerity of the welcome that it took the form, at a very early date, of a comprehensive revision of the *Rule*'s latinity.

2. The Latinity of the Rule

St Benedict's Rule is a Late Latin document. When the Saint wrote it, it was six centuries from Cicero's day, and during those six centuries the Latin spoken by the people of Italy had suffered inevitable changes. Even in the classical period there had been a distinction between literary Latin and the Latin of everyday use, a distinction that was naturally much greater among the uneducated populace. By the time of St Benedict the language of the people of Italy—Vulgar Latin, as it is called—differed widely in vocabulary, grammar, and syntax from Classical Latin. So strong and general was this linguistic movement that it did not stop with the speech of the people but exerted its influence upon the writers of the period, an influence which can be traced quite clearly in the ancient versions of the Scriptures and in the writings of the Fathers of the Church. Even such a practised latinist as St Augustine—not in his formal treatises but in his popular sermons—employs forms and constructions which derive from Vulgar Latin. It was a further step when writers who were addressing themselves to a practical purpose and were not concerned to study literary correctness, admitted not merely the sporadic influence of Vulgar Latin but a generous measure of its characteristic usages. St Benedict was one of those who took that step.

It is not that he was unacquainted with that more regular Latin which is employed by those Fathers of the

Church who were his constant reading. There are, indeed, tracts of his **Rule** in which he writes just such a Latin. Yet it would seem certain that both he himself and his disciples were more at home with the Vulgar Latin of their time. When St Gregory the Great is describing the Saint's flight from the world, he speaks of him as "knowingly ignorant and wisely unlearned". He had, in fact, abruptly broken off his schooling, and we may fairly read into those words a graceful apology for the Saint's lack of a full literary training. So, although in the Prologue and in his doctrinal chapters generally he uses a Latin which has only a small admixture of "vulgarisms", there are other chapters—and especially the chapters that regulate the Divine Office—in which these vulgarisms abound.

The Latin of the **Rule** is, in fact, not a rigidly self-consistent Latin, of uniform texture throughout, but a Latin which, so to say, oscillates between Classical Latin and Vulgar Latin. But that, again, is characteristic of the documents of Late Latin. . . . St Benedict wrote largely in the transitional Latin of his day; six centuries further on and he would doubtless have written in something like modern Italian. We do not condemn and outlaw Italian as nothing more than a corruption of Classical Latin; have we much better right to condemn Late Latin? A classical reader will inevitably not be entirely comfortable with St Benedict's Latin; but I should like to persuade him that Late Latin has an interest and value of its own. If it be too much to expect him to join the philologists and venerate the Rule precisely for its latinity, he may be asked to abstain from too severe reprobation.

It has been said already that the **Rule,** when launched upon the world, was welcomed and yet suffered a revision of its latinity. In some relatively more cultured circle, perhaps of monastic Gaul, the Latin of the **Rule** was taken in hand, revised and amended, and a text produced which had a very wide vogue. Thus, almost at the beginning of its history, the text-tradition of the **Rule** was split into two. The most ancient manuscripts bear unmistakable witness to this phenomenon of the Great Divide. Henceforth there were two quite distinct texts which are known as (1) the pure or authentic text; (2) the interpolated or revised text. I propose now to speak successively of these two texts.

3. *The Authentic Text*

The seventh century saw the propagation of Benedictine monachism in the countries of Western Europe, a movement which gained rapidly in momentum until there existed innumerable monasteries following the **Rule of St Benedict.** For the service of these monasteries there were made many copies of the **Rule,** so that there is scarcely any ancient text—the Scriptures apart—which is represented by such an abundance of manuscripts. From an early date there was formed a sort of vulgate

of the **Rule,** a generally received text, and from the tenth century down to quite recent times this Vulgate Text dominated the monastic scene, being everywhere received without question as the true text.

The first editor to give the text of the **Rule** a full examination in the light of the most ancient manuscripts was Dom Edmund Schmidt of the Abbey of Metten.[1] His examination led him to the discovery that the most ancient manuscripts fell into two distinct classes: that in more than two hundred places one group of manuscripts agreed upon one and the same reading, while the other group with similar unanimity agreed upon a different reading. He discovered, in fact, the phenomenon which we have called the Great Divide. His explanation of this phenomenon was that St Benedict himself had issued two editions of his **Rule.** He recognized that the text which is characterized by vulgar forms and usages was the better text and regarded it as the second edition; but he was disposed to attribute the vulgarisms partly to the copyists. In his manual edition of 1892—of which I have a copy before me—he removes most of these vulgarisms from his text.

A later, and most important, critical student of the text was the palaeographer, Ludwig Traube (d. 1907). Building upon Dom Schmidt's work but carrying through a more searching investigation, he interpreted the relation of the two texts in an altogether different fashion. Dom Schmidt was right in giving the preference to the text characterized by vulgarisms, but wrong in regarding these vulgarisms as interpolations; they were from St Benedict's hand. He was wrong also in conceiving the other text as St Benedict's "first edition". This was the text where the interpolator had been at work. It was a revised and amended text; it was made at a very early date, perhaps as early as the end of St Benedict's century; but it was definitely none of his work. These conclusions of Traube's, based upon a careful confrontation of twenty-five crucial passages, have won general acceptance among scholars.[2]

For our earliest witness to the authentic text we have to go, not to manuscripts of the **Rule** itself, but to the *Regula Magistri,* and to the early commentators, Abbot Smaragdus of St Mihiel and Paul the Deacon of Monte Cassino (both c.800). The earliest extant manuscript of this text is of about the year 820 and is the famous "Sangallensis 914". Alongside Sangallensis are "sister" manuscripts, of like origin and approximately the same date, one at Vienna, two at Munich, one (if not more) at Monte Cassino.[3]

Paul the Deacon tells us, in his *History of the Lombards* (IV 17), that when Monte Cassino was sacked by those invaders (c.580) and the monks fled to Rome, they took with them "the book of the holy rule which the aforesaid father had written", by which Paul means St

Benedict's autograph. When he comes to record the eighth-century restoration of Monte Cassino, he tells us that Pope Zachary presented to Abbot Petronax "the rule which the blessed father Benedict wrote with his own holy hands" (VI 40). In the year 787 Paul was instrumental in sending to the Emperor Charlemagne, at the latter's request, an exact copy of the *Rule,* which he describes (in the covering letter) as having been made "from the very codex which Benedict wrote with his own holy hands".

It cannot be maintained with absolute confidence that Paul the Deacon was right in his belief that Monte Cassino possessed in his time St Benedict's autograph; the possibilities of error in this matter are too many. It would appear safer to regard the Monte Cassino copy as no more than an ancient and important manuscript of the *Rule.* It was the exemplar from which was made Charlemagne's copy (kept at Aachen), and the latter copy (now lost) was the exemplar of Sangallensis 914 and of its sister manuscripts. Among these copies of the Aachen exemplar Sangallensis stands out from the rest for its completeness and for the care taken by its scribes to make their transcript accurate. So, in Sangallensis and its fellows, we have a small group of ninth-century manuscripts which testify to the Authentic Text. It is upon the witness of these manuscripts that the modern editors rely in order to construct their presentation of that text.

4. The Revised Text

At a very early date there appeared in the West a text of the *Rule* in which St Benedict's latinity had been revised and corrected. Our earliest witness to the existence of this Revised Text is the *Regula Donati,* a rule for nuns composed in the middle of the seventh century which embodies some portions of *St Benedict's Rule.* Our earliest manuscript of the same text is Oxoniensis, the most ancient of all extant MSS. of the *Rule,* written in England about the year 700. This revised edition obtained so wide a vogue as practically to supplant the original text in general monastic usage. I have already offered an explanation of the revision and have suggested that the work was perhaps done in Gaul. On the whole it was not done badly; but—as will appear in the Notes—there were some mistakes made, both of omission and of commission.

Yet we should beware of dismissing the Revised Text as of no value. For the Authentic Text—apart from external witnesses—we have a series of manuscripts which derive for the most part from the Aachen exemplar. (It is a matter of dispute whether the important Cassinese manuscript "K" derives from the same source or is an independent witness.) Much turns, therefore, on the accuracy of that exemplar. Scholars are prepared to admit that the Cassinese scribe who copied it may have had difficulty in reading, and may in places

have misread, the ancient manuscript from which he made his copy. And all scribes are fallible. So we may not treat Sangallensis and its fellow-copies of the Aachen exemplar as infallibly right. But, in the Revised Text, despite its revised character, we have an ancient witness to an independent tradition of the text. It is at least possible that this witness may on occasion be able to give us valuable assistance.

The Revised Text, as it appears in the earliest manuscripts, has about it a uniformity and consistency which have persuaded scholars that the revision was a single effort and perhaps the work of a single hand. On the basis of some verses that appear in certain ancient manuscripts, Traube argued that the work was done by Simplicius, third abbot of Monte Cassino, a view which has failed to win acceptance. The interesting suggestion has been advanced that the English St Benet Biscop was the author of the revision. But, although the Venerable Bede portrays St Benet Biscop as a lover of books and an assiduous collector of monastic customs, he is far from portraying him as a scholar or attributing to him any literary activity. However, the suggestion may perhaps be accepted as indicating a likely locality for the revision. St Benet Biscop learnt his monachism in the great monastic centre of Lérins, and it is in just such a centre that the work may very well have been done.[4]

Tatto and Grimalt, monks of Reichenau, who copying the Aachen exemplar produced Sangallensis, besides taking infinite pains to make their copy exact, went to the trouble also of reporting the readings of what they called the "modern masters". In these notes of theirs we have many, though not all, of the characteristic readings of the Revised Text; and we have some readings of later date than the original revision. . . .

5. The Vulgate Text

Charlemagne had hoped, by means of the Aachen exemplar, to provide the monasteries of his empire with a single, and absolutely authentic text of the *Holy Rule.* The hope was not, in fact, fulfilled, for the reason that Vulgar Latin was little at home in transalpine regions. In the Germanic countries, it had no sort of appeal; in Gaul—and in Spain also—the people were engaged in developing Latin on lines of their own. Nevertheless, the dissemination of copies of the Authentic Text did have some effect. The Revised Text, hitherto everywhere current, was in some degree corrected by means of it, so that from the tenth century onwards the monastic world is found to be agreed upon a uniform text of the Rule which may be described as a mixture of the Authentic and Revised texts with some "improvements" of its own. And so, with the production of this Vulgate Text (otherwise known as the *Textus Receptus*), the development terminated. Down to quite recent times, this Vulgate occupied the field unchallenged. If any reader should desire to consult it, he may find it in Abbot Delatte's excellent modern *Commentary* on the **Rule** (Eng. trans. 1921, 1950).

6. Modern Editions of the Rule

The first modern editor to make use of the critical work that has been mentioned was Abbot Cuthbert Butler (Downside, d. 1934) in his *Editio critico-practica* (1912; 2nd, fully-revised, edition 1927; re-impression 1936).

As indicated by the title, and announced in the Proem, the text is one that has been considerably emended, in order to make it more suitable for use in choir. When this emendation consists only in the removal of vulgarisms and their replacement by correct forms, the editor does not consider it necessary to say anything more about it, so that there are chapters where one may walk unawares over a good deal of "made ground". However, for textual matters of greater importance, there are footnotes to the text and (at the end) twenty-two pages of *Lectiones Selectae*. A very valuable, and largely original, aspect of Abbot Butler's edition is his comprehensive indication of St Benedict's sources. Limitations of space having compelled me to forgo any similar indication, I would ask leave to refer the interested reader to the editions of Abbot Butler and Dom Linderbauer.

The second modern editor of the Rule, Dom Benno Linderbauer (Metten, d. 1928), published at Bonn a few months before his death his *S. Benedicti Regula Monasteriorum,* which, though not yet the perfect edition that scholars hope for, is certainly a very useful one. Dom Linderbauer reproduces the Authentic Text with great fidelity and furnishes his text with a convenient *apparatus criticus*. This *apparatus* might with benefit have been fuller, yet is of great value. But this book is not his only service to the **Rule.** Six years previously he published a text accompanied by an elaborate philological commentary, based upon a comprehensive study of Late Latin and its literary remains. This is his *S. Benedicti Regula Monachorum herausgegeben und philologisch erklärt* (Metten, 1922). I had better say at this point that I have used this valuable book assiduously, so that my translation and notes are constantly indebted to Dom Linderbauer's expert knowledge of Late Latin usage.

There have been two recent editions of the **Rule,** neither of which is based upon a fresh survey of the manuscript evidence. The edition of Dom Gregory Arroyo (Silos, 1947) is content to reprint Abbot Butler's text. The other edition (Maredsous, 1946) is by Dom Philibert Schmitz, who agrees closely with Dom Linderbauer but differs from him in this, that he removes the vulgarisms to his footnotes, replacing them

by easier readings. The resulting text is an admirably practical one.

7. The Rule *of the Master*

I may be expected to say something in this Preface about a debate affecting the **Rule** which has been carried on since the year 1938 and is still continuing.[5] The debate revolves around an anonymous monastic rule, of uncertain date, which goes by the name of *Regula Magistri,* "The Rule of the Master". (There is a convenient text in Migne, *P.L.* 88; but a new edition from the manuscripts is much needed.) These are the rival positions of the parties to the debate:

> (1) The *Regula Magistri* is prior to **St Benedict's Rule** and is its source.

> (2) The *Regula Magistri* is posterior to St Benedict's Rule, from which it has borrowed freely.

The *Regula Magistri* gets its current title from the literary technique adopted by its author. His chapter-titles regularly ask a question and the exposition which follows is presented as "the Lord's answer through the Master": *Respondet Dominus per Magistrum.* (Dom Cappuyns shows reason for the belief that the true title of this rule is *Regula Sanctorum Patrum.*) The Rule is nearly three times as long as St Benedict's; but the crucial point is this, that very nearly the whole of **St Benedict's Rule** is embodied in it, either in verbal transcript or by paraphrase and allusion. Every part of the **Rule** is clearly represented save the last seven chapters.

It is only in the last few years, i.e. since 1938, that much notice has been taken of the *Regula Magistri* or much importance attached to it. Before 1938 it was common form among scholars—from the seventeenth-century Maurists to Linderbauer—to dismiss it as a somewhat crude paraphrase of **St Benedict's Rule.** The Maurist editor (Dom Hugh Ménard), noticing the passages borrowed by the author from St Benedict, finds that they contrast strikingly with the "rude and scabrous style" of the remainder of the document. Having studied the *Regula Magistri* a good deal, and having subjected parts of it to the test of translation, I have much sympathy with this judgement. The Master commands, and appears to enjoy displaying, an extensive vocabulary, which includes many unusual words of a semi-barbarous character. This circumstance alone makes him difficult to read; but his syntax often increases the difficulty. And then there is the distinct oddity of many of his regulations.

As has been said already, this debate is not yet concluded. Although, for myself, I believe that the Master's Rule is the work of a later writer, working upon the text of the *Regula Monachorum,* yet I do not wish to press this view upon my readers. What I should like to do is to persuade them that in any case—whatever be the issue of the debate—the Master's Rule has in regard of St Benedict's a twofold value: (1) When the exact relationship of the two Rules to each other has been determined, new light may be thrown upon the early history of **St Benedict's Rule;** (2) and, even now, before that relationship has been determined, the Master's Rule cannot fail to assist us in the interpretation of St Benedict's. I conceive, in fact, that it may be mobilized for our benefit and employed to illustrate and explain some passages of the Benedictine Rule.

Notes

[1] *Regula S. Benedicti juxta antiquissimos codices cognita,* Metten, 1880.

[2] Traube's decisive work was done in his *Textgeschichte der Regula S. Benedicti,* Munich, 1898. There was a second edition in 1910, edited by Plenkers.

[3] An accurate edition of Sangallensis 914, with a careful collation of many Cassinese MSS., was published in 1900 under the title: *Regulae S. Benedicti traditio codicum Casinensium a praestantissimo teste usque repetita, codice Sangallensi* 914. This book was predominantly the work of that accomplished scholar, Dom Germain Morin. I have used it much and found it of the greatest service.

[4] Early in the seventh century the monks of St Columbanus (at Luxeuil and elsewhere) began to make use of St Benedict's Rule. It is possible that we owe the revision to them.

[5] The debate originated in the researches of a French Benedictine, Dom A. Genestout, engaged upon a new edition of the Rule. It has aroused much interest and produced a large crop of articles in various continental Reviews. Among the best of these are the contributions of Abbot Bernard Capelle of Mont César (Louvain). Of great interest are two recent contributions by monks of the same abbey: Dom M. Cappuyns and Dom F. Vandenbroucke. These essays maintain the view that the author of the *Regula Magistri* is none other than Cassiodorus, St Benedict's contemporary, and that Cassiodorus based his work upon a primitive text of the Holy Rule. The present writer entered the lists in 1939 and 1940, with two articles in the *Downside Review.* He has recently surveyed the problem and its significance with an article in the *Ampleforth Journal* for May 1950. Part of what is said here is taken from that article. If any reader should desire to have a bibliography of the debate, I would refer him to Dom Cappuyns's article (already mentioned) in the Mont César periodical *Recherches de Théologie ancienne et médiévale,* xv, 1948, pp. 209-68. In a footnote at the beginning, there is an alphabetical list of every contribution to the debate from its beginning down to the middle of 1948. Since that date there have been further items. Of these I mention only: Dom P. Blanchard, "La Règle du Maître et la Règle de Saint Benoît", *Revue Bénédictine,* 1950, pp. 25-64. It is the conclusion of this closely-reasoned essay that the Rule of the Master belongs to the middle of the seventh century and was probably compiled at Bobbio.

Sighard Kleiner (essay date 1974)

SOURCE: "Foreward," "The Cult of the *Rule,*" and "The *Rule* of Today" in *Serving God First: Insights on "The Rule of St. Benedict,"* translated by James Scharinger, Cistercian Publications, 1985, pp. 3-10.

[*In the following excerpt from his* Dieu premier servi *(Serving God First),* originally published in French in 1974, Kleiner comments on the spiritual importance of the *Rule of St. Benedict* and its enduring role in Christian life.*]*

Serve God First: there is here a norm, a measure, a hierarchy of values. It appears to be beyond question, yet it is not easy. We hear about the human crisis nowadays. A crisis is a reversal of values and criteria. Man has always had the tendency to want to be served first, but the formulation of a theory, a doctrine of self-service, has been reserved to our own day. An immense process of secularization is under way when God, having become an embarassment to man, is sent away to heaven's furthest corner, when indeed, he be not proclaimed dead. The world turns in upon itself and cuts itself off from God. In the past, secondary causes have sometimes been ignored; today the Primary Cause no longer counts. For many, religion has become a holiday ornament or a last resort against tragedy. Nothing remains of it in daily life, clinically purified as it is of the slightest practical faith. Man looks after himself, and religion becomes folklore or a refuge for those in trouble.

Now, religion is specifically the service of God. Serve God? Love God, yes; but serve? The word makes us uneasy. Yet we accept service to our brothers. Brotherhood is the religion of our times. 'Everything for man' is a slogan which pleases businessmen. Yet God, amazingly, has willed to adapt himself to that solidarity limited to man. In his Son, he became our brother. He came not to be served, but to serve. Having entered on an equal footing into human psychology, he made himself the servant of our salvation, our well-being.

He did all this, however, not to put man in God's place, but to introduce God among men, and to make us understand that we cannot establish durable fraternal relationships among ourselves without a Father who makes us brothers, who puts these relationships in order and gives us the Spirit of brotherhood: his Spirit. This Father is the God of justice, of love, of peace. It is through him that we are brothers.

To serve man well, then, we must know how to serve God. Where God is served first, man is served well. In reality, there is nothing more demanding, more absorbing, often more difficult than to serve man as he is. To be able to serve takes a good dose of self-forgetfulness. Jesus Christ teaches us this by making himself the servant of our well-being; in serving us, he did not turn his gaze away from his Father, because in giving himself to us, he served, obeyed, and loved his Father. Serving his brothers was for him the same as serving his Father. Besides, if man were to be served first, a thousand unanswered questions would immediately arise: who ought to be the first served? How and by whom ought man to be served in the first place? Ought the weak to serve the strong? Ought the strong to serve the weak? We are familiar with these questions.

To serve God first is to assure that man will truly be served, not according to beautiful theories which suppose him to be naturally good, or which impose a so-called universal brotherhood among the privileged while sacrificing others, but according to the divine plan whereby God is the Father of all without discrimination.

This is precisely the image which the ***Rule of St Benedict*** suggests. It is a rule of service to God and to one's brothers. From morning until evening, the monk is in service. On entering the monastic life, he learns to recognize 'the duties of his service' (RB 49:5). This is first of all the *Opus Dei* (RB 16:2, 50:4), but also the full ascetical and community life of the monk (RB 49, 71, 72). At the 'school of the Lord's service' (Prol. 45), the monk learns that all the services he renders to his brother end in God, and that the Lord is always therefore served first.

Vigorously trained by the ***Rule*** to seek God in everything he does (RB 58:37), to have God always present (RB 7, 14, 23), to realize that he is continuously seen and observed by God (RB 4:49, 7:13), to think of him and to love him above all things (4:1), the monk lets himself be carried along the way on which he has set out by the ***Rule*** he observes, and so does not turn away from his orientation toward God, who becomes more and more the center of his thoughts.

Is this a diversion of human energies toward a God who has no need of the poor services man may render him, while our neighbor remains in trouble? This objection is justified by certain disorders. Some people accumulate riches very negligibly ordained to the glory of God, while at the same time the poor lack basic necessities. The true service of God, far from neglecting man, sees God in one's neighbor and serves God in him. It would be an illusion to want to go to God without passing through creatures. Christ will not receive us if we have not seen him in the hungry, the thirsty, the pilgrim, the poor, the sick, and the prisoner (cf. Mt 25:35ff.). St Benedict has given his ***Rule*** a strong Christocentric bent. The monk sees Christ in the abbot (RB 2:2, 63:13), and receives Christ in the guest (53:7), the poor, and the pilgrim (53:15); he serves Christ in the sick (36:1). He who serves his brother serves Christ, God. For the person who believes, there is no problem of precedence in this service. To serve God first means that if he does not serve his brother humbly and sincerely, God is not being served. On the other hand, he will not believe that he can create an excuse from serving God by serving men, especially when he chooses by his own whim those whom he claims to help.

The ***Rule of St Benedict*** is imbued with an extraordinary force for normalizing the relations between God and man, and between man and his fellow. It has a rare wholesomeness and capacity for giving man an equilibrium both psychic and physical by re-establishing in him right concepts and by ordering an hierarchy of value in him. There is in it no neurotic affirmation of the rights of man. Where God occupies his true place, everything sorts itself out in the best way for man. The rights of man are assured where the rights of God are respected.

More than ever, people today live in insecurity. The sources of their ideas are troubled. An anguish without outlet seizes them. Strong personalities make fun of this anxiety; others battle against confusion, even against despair. The remedy is simple; for many it seems too simple: we must order our values. Moral and intellectual health are restored only by re-establishing the normal order of things. The first commandment for man is not to have false gods, to give God his place. By that very fact, man finds his own place, and the rest follows. The ***Rule of St Benedict*** possesses this charism of setting a man forcefully and smoothly upon the right track, of assigning him his special place. In this way it renders him happy, balanced, healthy. The logic of the ***Rule*** begins with God, and anyone who seeks God will seek man as well.

This is the orientation of Jesus' life. All of his thoughts, his work, his aspirations were directed to the Father. 'I go to the Father' (Jn 14:12, 28). This is the direction of his life. Everything he did he did to orientate his disciples toward the Father and to give life to the world by rendering to God what is God's. Therein lies the entire theme of the ***Rule:*** 'That in all things God may be glorified' (RB 57:9).

The Cult of the Rule

Some people use the expression the 'cult' of the ***Rule***—what does it mean? First of all, that we have for our ***Rule,*** for that little book crowned with such honor, all the respect due it. Many illustrious men knew it intimately. Is the *Rule* not one of the most celebrated documents of human thought for the person who seeks God? A rule for a holy and christian life for the Church? Finally, a creative force of true culture for Western society? The expression 'cult' of the *Rule* expresses first of all a veneration for its teaching, its orders and directives, and the fidelity of the disciple toward the basic *Rule* (RB 3:7). Does it not teach the monk a simple and sure route to God?

In view of the extraordinary moral authority of the *Rule,* it is necessary to define its limits exactly and measure its meaning. Let us admit at the outset that the cult of the *Rule* could lead us to attribute to it a role which it does not fit, for example, to esteem the letter at the expense of the spirit, or to give a disproportionate importance to details.

First of all, we cannot isolate the *Rule,* putting it, without realizing it, on the same level as the Gospel. The *Rule* has no value except in relation to the Word of God. It leads us to the Gospel (Prol. 21); it is an exposition of its message, a manual, a practical résumé, designed for the use of simple men wanting to be monks. It is, through its institutions, a permanent reference to the Gospel and to its summons to the Lord, which it translates into sound practices, wholly bathed in the humble search for God.

If the *Rule* is a law (RB 58:10), it is one only in order to turn the Gospel to profit (cf. Mt 5:17ff.). For 'the object of the law is Christ' (Rm 10:4). The law of the Gospel binds us to Christ: chains us to make us prisoners of Jesus Christ (cf. Eph 3:1). The yoke of the *Rule* (RB 58:16) has no other function than to submit us to the sweet yoke of Christ (cf. Mt 11:30). It is our *Rule,* the norm of our life. The mentality of St Benedict makes him express himself in the same way when he speaks to us of God's service, of the school to which he sends us for our apprenticeship in that service (cf. Prol. 45) through the imitation of Christ (cf. Prol. 50; 7:34).

The role of the *Rule* as a guide to lead us to the Gospel and to Christ is thus summarily characterized. The *Rule* is a norm which refers us, in accordance with what is said in the decree *Perfectae Caritatis* (cf. no. 2 a), to the supreme norm of all religious life: the imitation of Christ.

In this matter, St Benedict, following his predecessors, set himself a task both delicate and difficult: to gather the marrow of the Gospel and extract from it a concrete way of life for his monks. It was necessary not only that he not betray the Gospel in any way by commentaries which might filter out the divine Word, but he had also to transmit all its fullness, all its depth, so that the teaching of the Gospel 'might be spread like the leaven of divine justice in the hearts of his disciples' (cf. RB 2:5).

The high esteem which the Church has given the *Rule* by irrefutable signs through the centuries testifies to the success of St Benedict. If, along with paternal gentleness, he shows himself very strict in his insistence on the observance of the *Rule* (cf. RB 3:7, 64:20), this apparent severity, far from obscuring the Gospel's primacy of charity, is but a very realistic manifestation of a love which knows how to support human weakness.

In this way, we avoid another possible danger in the 'cult of the *Rule*', that of giving an exaggerated importance to small details. The careful reader of the *Rule* draws from his meditations, the distinct impressions of a perfect and harmonious balance. Each detail remains in its proper place and never in the spotlight. The spirit, with its energetic and clear principles so predominates that no amount of insistence, however strong on particular points, changes St Benedict's intention as to the pastoral aim of the *Rule:* to lead the monk to Christ. The *Rule* fades away as soon as the end is obtained, as John the Baptist made way for Jesus. The ladder of humility is an example of this. The day when the monk, having climbed to the top, arrives at perfect charity, all that had to do with fear, that is to say, with the effort of climbing, will have had its day and can disappear. One can see there the provisional nature of everything that is only a means.

The *Rule* itself therefore has only a relative value. Yet all of its prescriptions do not have the same importance. The novice who still lacks perspective can in his first fervor attach too much importance to rules at the expense of the *Rule*, and may have trouble establishing a hierarchic order in its prescriptions. One day he will understand that certain superior rules take precedence over secondary ones, and he will also understand that it is through fidelity to the *Rule* that a certain number of its prescriptions have fallen into disuse and that, paradoxically, it is the *Rule* itself which has caused the suppression of certain minor usages it mentions. For it is thanks to the discretion, pastoral prudence, a certain pluralism, and above all, the principle according to which means ought to be directed toward the end which individuals, concretely placed in a determined context of time, place, and circumstances, propose to attain, that the *Rule of St Benedict* adapts itself to very different situations. In this it proves itself to be a masterpiece compiled by one of the most remarkable spirits of all humanity, assisted by Divine Wisdom.

In the course of these conferences there will be no dearth of occasions to go back over the values of the *Rule* briefly mentioned here by way of introduction.

The Rule *Today*

Is the Rule still timely? Can St Benedict, the patriarch of Western monks, the fifteenth centenary of whose birth we will soon [1980] be celebrating, still be listened to and understood by people who spontaneously believe that they surpass everything the preceding centuries were able to discover? This author of a famous *Rule* whose style, diction, syntax, and setting take us back to the sixth century, the very thought of which often reflects situations of another age, how can he pretend to be able to tell anything? Could not men of our own times transmit the message to us far better? Why spend time with this document from another era, whose language is, at least at first glance, difficult for modern man to understand?

This book sets out to give good reasons for attaching ourselves to St Benedict. The *Rule* has no need of being reformed or reshaped to be up-to-date; quite simply, we must know how to read it, as an ancient book ought to be read in our day. Holy Scripture is not outdated simply because it is dressed in well-worn garments.

Some may object that the *Rule* is not an historical or didactic book like the Bible, but a law written in a concrete sociological context which no longer exists in our age of technology and urbanization where education is wide-spread and where secularism and existentialism are rife. Who can deny that the human situation in time and space, in relationships to the world and to fellowman and even, phenomenologically speaking, to God, have changed profoundly in fifteen hundred years? The one thing that has not changed essentially is the human person. He remains what he has always been, having come from the hands of his Maker and been deformed by sin. Methods of education may have changed, but the fundamental laws of man's education remain the same. The image of man seen by St Benedict corresponds to the reality of man as truly today as it did in the sixth century. We need only to separate this image from the context of an age now past for it to maintain its vital worth.

This book seeks to show, without apologetics or polemics, the present value of the *Rule of St Benedict* and why it is still up to date. We should remember that the Church to this day places this *Rule* among the books richest in salutary effects, recognizing also that for thousands of monks and nuns and for thousands of the faithful of benedictine spiritual orientation, it ponders the practical and concrete norm of the christian life. Might we not add to these the religious who, more recently, and under different forms have drawn and continue to draw from the pure fountain of the *Rule?* This fact alone proves that the great Legislator is still up to date, as he was during the grand flowering of Christianity and indeed during the ages when the monks, far from the world's hubbub and notice, prepared the coming of better days.

In this precise sense St Benedict is for us, as it were, a contemporary. Under his guidance the person of to-day, often profoundly uprooted and neurotic, can find healing. Fundamentally, St Benedict does nothing but lead us to the living waters of the Word of God by means of a wise pedagogy embracing, without constraint, the entire course of our life.

Antoine Vergote (lecture date 1976)

SOURCE: "A Psychological Approach to Humility in the *Rule of St. Benedict*," *American Benedictine Review,* Vol. 39, No. 4, December, 1988, pp. 404-29.

[*In the following essay, originally delivered as a lecture in 1976, Vergote offers an interpretation of humility in the* Rule of St. Benedict, *tracing the ideals of obedience and self-knowledge expressed in Benedict's text and in the Christian scriptures.*]

I humbly beg you to listen, for you have given me a stiff challenge: I must speak to you about a text which is so familiar to you and about which I know so little. And I must do this before exegetes, historians, philologists and I don't know what.

I must confess the shock I felt on reading a text I had not picked up in thirty years: it really seemed very strange to me. I also gave it to friends of mine, Christian laypeople, and they reacted the same way. We are at a great cultural distance from this text—but doubtless it is not the same for you. We will ask: How has this come about? In this way we may find some indication as to how young people today could accept it and feel about it.

I will divide the conference into four parts:

—First I will try to give an interpretation of the text

—Then I will clarify what I think is the underlying anthropology

—I will add some critical remarks and questions

—And finally I will present some suggestions for a presentation of humility which might be more up-to-date.

I. A Hermeneutic

First I will tell you how I understand this chapter of Benedict on humility. I must begin thus, for I am not part of your monastic tradition. I have tried to understand the text on its own terms, considered as a whole capable of providing some insight.

1. A first question: What is humility (*humilitas*) for St. Benedict? To me, this is clearly explained in the introduction, in the first degree and in the last. Certainly,

anyone who is used to working with clear concepts will experience the great complexity of a text such as this. And I think it is rather evident that in this passage—at least as I perceive things—Benedict presents a new perspective on the monastic life. I say "new," for it seems to me that the vision of Benedict is in opposition to the tendencies of earlier monasticism. (But this would demand a precise historical study, and I can only fall back on some ideas I once gained in a course on religious history.)

Humility is formulated in the paradox of St. Luke: "Whoever exalts himself will be humbled, but he who humbles himself will be exalted." This is a paradox which was also dear to St. Francis and which is stated very forcefully in the antithesis of the "Magnificat." This means that humility is a fundamental Christian attitude: pride rules out all possibility of salvation; salvation is received in faith. Humility is the Christian attitude *par excellence:* it is the attitude of faith. Such seems to me to be the fundamental notion that Benedict is going to push so far in concrete application. One might suggest that the Dutch term *deemoed* (humility-submission) would be better for this central notion. In Dutch I think that *nederigheid* (humility) has a moral and psychological content, while *deemoed* has a more religious meaning. This fundamental religious attitude was already known by the Greeks. You know the saying of the Oracle of Delphi: *gnôthi seauton* ("Know yourself"), which is so frequently interpreted as an invitation to self-knowledge. According to a specialist in the mystery cults, the meaning should rather be: "Know that you are a human being and not a god." In this sense, the word *deemoed* brings us back to our true human position vis-à-vis God. "Know yourself": for the Greeks, the word forms a contrast with *hubris,* that presumption in which a human being poses as God and by that fact breaks the bond with divinity. In Christian revelation, *deemoed* is not only the religious attitude pure and simple; it receives its specific content of faith, of a readiness to listen, of obedience. *Gehoor-zaamheid,* obedience is willing attention to God who reveals himself. This basic notion is still, of course, a general concept open to multiple interpretations, and it is important to see just *how* Benedict has concretely worked out this fundamental Christian notion.

A second point flows from the first and is to be joined to our notion about the meaning of humility: humility brings about a satisfaction of the desire for God. It is the condition of peace, of appeasement: one reaches peace, since one is pacified. This reveals a profound desire. Peace is found in the pacification of the heart of the person who seeks God. In my opinion, we find here a mystical content. Compared to the task of "humbling oneself," peace and humility are for Benedict the positive phase. This is nicely put in RB 7.4 where Benedict uses the classic mystical image of the infant sleeping on its mother's breast. We have here a universal symbol of the desire for God.

In the third place it seems to me that Benedict joins to his fundamental idea a warning against that presumption which is typically religious. One does not find in **Benedict's Rule** the legalistic religious presumption of the Pharisees which is roundly condemned in the Gospel. The presumption which Benedict opposes is rather that mystical effort which relies on its own strength. I think that this is clearly expressed in RB 7.3. At least that is the way I understand this verse: "Lord, my heart is not exalted, my eyes are not lifted up"—and especially, "I have not walked in the ways of the great nor gone after marvels beyond me."[1] In my view, Benedict is here alluding to that which represents for him the preponderant tendency of the monastic movement before his time: the search for extraordinary mystical experiences which characterized many eremitic and cenobitic movements.

In the fourth place, we come to a more concretely developed form of the fundamental concept: Christian humility is understood in a very precise way as being an awareness of sin. This is the point of departure for the ladder of humility given at the first degree and it is also its culmination in degree twelve, where there is an allusion to the Publican in the Gospel. This is why Benedict comes down so hard on the basic Christian attitude: the fear of God. It produces vigilance and wards off forgetfulness. It consists for Benedict in placing oneself under the watchful gaze of the Divine Judge. These texts are saturated with the theme of the fear of divine chastisement. To me this is striking. To be vigilant means to keep oneself from sin, to live under the eyes of God the Judge. Benedict carries this so far—and this is worth noting—that he interprets the words of the Our Father, "may your will be done," in this sense. It is remarkable to see in verses 20-21 how the citation "There are ways which men call right which in the end plunge into the depths of hell" is presented as an interpretation of "may your will be done," which is the text immediately preceding. Likewise, in the twelfth degree (RB 7.64-65), the theme of the fear of judgment returns in force: "He should consider that he is already at the fearful judgment; and constantly repeat in his heart what the Publican in the Gospel said with downcast eyes: 'Lord, I am a sinner, not worthy to look up to heaven.'"

To sum up: to me, the meaning of humility seems to lie in a general religious attitude, specified as an attitude of faith, characterized in Christianity by that receptivity which pays heed to God. The corollary of this is the vigorous warnings against the presumption of a mystical effort which tries to be sufficient unto itself. Taken concretely, this willing listening is also changed into a making present of the Divine Judge. The theme of judgment is connected with that of chastisement.

2. A second point: The *goal* of humility. I use this word purposely, since for Benedict, humility is an attitude that one exercises systematically, something that one pursues. There is here then a goal, an intention. Three elements emerge clearly in the last part of the text. I will compare them rapidly with the perspective of Cassian.

The goal of humility really involves going beyond the constitutive, fundamental attitude, without, however, abandoning the Christian attitude. In other words, the goal is the transformation of motivation. One aims at no longer acting on the basis of the motives that inspire humility. RB 7.69 is very clear on this point: "no more out of fear of hell but for love of Christ." Under Platonic influence, ancient texts often speak of acting for love of the Good. Benedict corrects this to read: "for the love of Christ."

Second goal: The systematic exercise of humility leads to a psychological transformation; a vitally Christian attitude becomes second nature. "Through this love, all that he once performed with dread, he will now begin to observe without effort, as though naturally, from habit" (RB 7.68). Ascetical effort, then, cannot be a permanent attitude; it leads to a psychological transformation of the individual.

In the third place, one can point to the mystical goal such as it is expressed in RB 7.67: "Now, therefore, after ascending all these steps of humility, the monk will quickly arrive at the perfect love of God which casts out fear." I call this the mystical element, the element of covenant with God, mystical unity, love of God.

If now we compare this with Cassian, we note that he sets down three stages in the progress of the monk. The first degree of ascesis is the practical life (*bios praktikos*), which consists essentially in the struggle against the eight capital vices, the renunciation of possessions, even of one's own past. The second degree is that of contemplation, understood in a sense clearly inspired by Platonism. By this, one is raised beyond the creation to the contemplation of Christ, Word of God.

The third degree is that of pure contemplation, which not only surpasses the created realm, but everything that is conceivable; this is an immaterial contemplation without images of any kind (*"Jubilatio sine verbis"* of Augustine). We have here the two characteristic phases of Platonism: action which is in some sense inferior, but which prepares for that which alone has value in itself: namely, contemplation which raises us beyond the visible.

By means of the accent which he puts on the double command of charity, Basil, who is himself also a source

for Benedict, corrects this perspective and gives more importance to action. Benedict, in my view, remains ambivalent. I was struck by reading in the Epilogue (RB 73) that he proposes his **Rule** as something written for beginners, as if he still had nostalgia for the heroes of contemplation. In RB 7, however, it seems that for him perfection clearly lies in the love of Christ. This is precisely the end of the road of practice and ascesis. One sees no more trace of nostalgia for the old monastic ideal of pure contemplation. Likewise, in other passages of the **Rule,** charity receives such a fullness of meaning that it has become Christian perfection. In this way the opposition between action and contemplation inspired by Plato is removed.

3. Third, after discussing the meaning and purpose of humility, I would like now to consider its *object*. Where is the seat of humility? Essentially in the will. This is very clearly stated in RB 5, "On Obedience," as it is in the Prologue, where Benedict says explicitly in verses 2 and 3 that the essence of the monastic life lies in obedience: it is a matter of renouncing one's own will, of entering into the service of Christ the Lord, the true king, to accomplish the will of God to which the will of Christ is equated. In RB 7, humility is very concretely set out as obedience, even if other themes also come into play.

In the first degree of humility, Benedict enumerates different elements. He speaks of the will, but also of concupiscence, of delight, in such a way that one has the impression that the will is only one of the various domains where obedience resides. Desire or pleasure also seem to be its domains. But on the other hand, Benedict also seems to subsume everything under the single concept of the will, which he always relates to the will of God. This is clearly affirmed in RB 7.19-20: "Truly, we are forbidden to do our own will, for Scripture tells us: 'Turn away from your desires.' And in the Prayer too we ask God that his will be done in us." It is, in my opinion, precisely by the emphasis placed on the will and on detachment that humility in Benedict seems to have an ascetic character. And I would add: a character that is singularly religious, moral, and—without necessarily seeing in the word a pejorative connotation—legalistic. Let me explain. RB 7.11 reads as follows: "He must constantly remember everything God has commanded—(the commandments are the expression of the will of God in opposition to our own will: whence the 'legalistic' character)—keeping in mind always that all who despise God will burn in hell for their sins, and all who fear God have everlasting life awaiting them." It is obvious that if one considers the matter from the psychological point of view alone, one would say that the object of humility is the will. But this would be to restrict humility totally to obedience to the superior. The means of such an ascesis would be obedience to the abbot, the Rule, to regulations. These are surely an important element, but it is evident that this ascesis is not simply a moral, psychological and personal ascesis, for self-will is continually set over against the will of God. It is precisely by the juncture of all the human dimensions: desire, pleasure, passion, willing, gathered under the single term "the will set before the will of God," that humility becomes all-encompassing for Benedict. Obviously this seems rather strange when one reads the text for the first time: we are not accustomed to such a large vision of humility.

This description of the object of humility as "self-will set before the will of God" enables us to establish a certain coherence of thought which is not present as such in Benedict. If humility is detachment from self-will, which is also the source of personal initiative, then humility becomes synonymous with obedience in the strict sense. But this meaning is enlarged to include the same dimensions as the word "will." Benedict speaks of detachment in regard to patience, mutual support and finally desire. This is to make humility into a universal virtue identical with detachment from self in all domains.

Because desire is here also placed continually in the presence of the will of God, self-will is only indirectly the object of humility. I can state this in psychological terms: Just as that will is in the strictest sense the energy with which one pursues desire, so too humility resides in desire. But in the last analysis, the will is for Benedict a general manner of situating oneself in regard to the other, in regard to God. Humility is then at the same time a specific virtue and a general disposition. Is that still true in our current way of speaking? In any case, this extension of the term explains the central place it occupies in Benedict's scheme.

4. Why is humility a field for systematic ascetical labor? It is such because it includes the whole complement of human activities under the single aspect of "the (human) will placed before the will of God." Humility is, for Benedict, a task, a labor. It is even the primary task, because human beings, with all that lives in them, are *not* humble. We must state this very clearly: A person has to work at humility very systematically. On their own, people do not obey God; they are sinners. We can say with Paul: The wrath of God has fallen upon him insofar as he is not converted. And this conversion takes place by the labor of humility. I am struck by the comparisons Benedict makes: the monastery is like a workshop, the monastic life is a craft, a spiritual labor. Nor should we forget the instruments of the spiritual art, which the monks must employ without stint and return on Judgment Day in order to receive their reward, once the work is accomplished. And the workshop where one works with diligence and care is the cloister of the monastery and stability in the community. The practical way, so misunderstood by the Platonic tradition, is here restored to full honor:

the work of humility is set side by side with the fields. Characteristically, it is not a question of devoting oneself to it for a determined time, but throughout life. This is a new sign of the importance that Benedict attaches to it.

In other words, we could say that the monastic craft ought to lead to liberation, to that liberty which renders one receptive to the love of Christ. Humility is then the craft of *metanoia,* of conversion, of the systematic reversal of self-will centered on itself. It is a matter of effecting this reversal by systematic effort and of turning the will toward service.

5. Now we can approach the degrees of humility. This will be my last hermeneutical point. I will develop it at some length, since it will furnish us with elements necessary to our discussion.

When one considers for the first time the series of the degrees of humility, and when one attempts to discover some progression, one is a bit surprised. It seems like we have here a literary figure typical for that period: everything is put on a ladder! This continues the Platonic tradition of the climb, with the important difference that here one rises by descending. We can also see this literary figure at work when we are told that the soul and the body are the two sides of this ladder (see RB 7.9)!

Why twelve degrees? After several readings, I discovered beneath the literary figure the intention of an orderly temperament.

To one who begins the ascetical labor, the first degree gives a general principle, a fundamental notion: one must open oneself humbly to God and prepare oneself to do his will. The second degree isolates (this) as a reflexive moment touching the object of this labor of humility: self-will, considered as the source of the personality set before God. Benedict immediately adds to this the matter of desire (RB 7.31). One could transpose and render the two terms by the couplet: the voluntary and the involuntary. One retreats into oneself and says: I will renounce my will.

The third degree is the concretization of this decision, the first application of this renunciation of self-will: obedience to the superior.

The fourth degree is more personal, consisting of an interiorization of humility through patience and endurance. Thus there is a certain graduation from the third to the fourth degree. The object of humility is now seen as the will placed in situations where one spontaneously recoils and revolts. In the obedience of the third degree, ascetic labor was applied to the will as an operative power enabling one to perform a given personal action; here (in the fourth degree), detachment applies to the spontaneous movements of the heart. The target becomes that which Plato calls *thumos* or what psychology calls the *irascible*. This is a violent, aggressive thrust of opposition to injustice, to suffering. This is moreover a normal human reaction; this flight from suffering is inscribed in our very nature. *Thumos* is not desire, but the spontaneous rebellion against all that represents a danger to the subject. With the fourth degree, then, we come to a degree of interior detachment from this spontaneous impulse. At first glance, this might seem like the Stoic ideal of *apatheia*, in the line of an Evagrius or a Cassian. But to arrive at detachment of heart is not necessarily to come to unfeelingness, as the word impassibility might suggest. It is rather to move toward liberty in place of spontaneous passion, to achieve a balance of disposition in one's sentiments—and that is far from unfeelingness.

A balanced disposition, peace of heart, liberty in regard to spontaneous impulse: this ideal proposed by Benedict is evidently not Stoic but very specifically Christian. The whole program of transformation is seen in the light of a direct personal relationship with God. This relationship has two poles, which are presented as a double testing by God: on the one hand, God tries us by suffering, injustice and other kinds of things which detach us from ourselves; on the other hand, we are tested by him in view of the future recompense, as metal is tested by fire. The strength to meet the test is then to be found in obedience to God and in confidence that he will reward, and not, for example, in what we might call mutual toleration. Humanly speaking, we bear with one another so as to arrive at peace, to make peace. We show ourselves tolerant and patient because we know well that if others show themselves unjust, it is because they are reacting with passion without knowing very well what they are doing. When we are tested, we think spontaneously of that mutual tolerance which makes for peace, instead of saying, as Benedict invites us: "God is personally testing me now in order to make me worthy of the reward he has in store for me."

The fifth degree is confession. (This makes one think of confession to laypersons, but I leave that point to historians.) Here one can truly speak of a new step upward: one takes the initiative to enter into "compunction of heart." It seems to me that there is a continual progression in steps three, four and five.

The sixth degree of humility does not offer a new step. It only amounts to a concrete example of the obedience of the third degree and the interior detachment of the fourth degree. It is thus that "A monk is content with the lowest and most menial treatment, and regards himself as a poor and worthless workman in whatever task he is given, saying to himself with the Prophet: 'I am insignificant and ignorant, no better than a beast before you, yet I am with you always.'"

From the psychological point of view, it is interesting to. note that one here sees humility in the context of an inborn impulse to make something of oneself and the desire to find satisfaction in one's work. This represents a fundamental human tendency and one which is healthy and normal, and yet Benedict demands precisely that one also separate oneself from this tendency which promotes the establishment of a positive self-concept!

What is striking once more is the motive given: the conviction of personal unworthiness, an awareness of being a sinner before God. Benedict does not appeal, for example, to a sense of being a link in the chain of service. He means to push us to a conviction of personal unworthiness by means of an explicit detachment from this legitimate tendency to self-esteem. If I had to address myself to young people, I myself would appeal to their sense of solidarity. Each of us is but a small part, a small function, of the whole. We cannot exist except in relation to a group, and each of us ought to be detached from that fundamental aspiration to find for ourselves just that work which gives full personal satisfaction. We must do much work that is not interesting, for, to tell the truth, what is interesting must be the fruit of the collaboration of all. This human realism, this type of "human" humility, is not part of Benedict's way of thinking.

The seventh degree, to my way of thinking, is an extension of the preceding: it sets down in broader terms the mentality recommended by the sixth degree: "A man not only admits with his tongue but is also convinced in his heart that he is inferior to all and of less value."

The eighth degree is very short, and yet . . . perfection consists in following the common rule of the monastery and in doing nothing to contradict it. This is perfect detachment from self-will and from every egotistic tendency.

As for degrees nine, ten and eleven, it is very interesting to note all that can be included under the rubric of humility. Since he has taken as his point of departure and foundation for humility all that comes under the term "will," he can include here considerations about that which one might call the discipline of the word. In place of taciturnity, it would no doubt be better to speak of reserve in speech. All social contact that can be made by means of words also involves detachment from self. Here again the theme is very clear: to avoid sin and not to indulge in heedless behavior.

And so we arrive at the twelfth degree. The last area where humility is applied is the body and the "gaze," which is so important for Benedict: our attitude toward Go who sees us and our attitude toward others. A general evangelical posture of humility is well expressed here, in my opinion: "Do not judge, do not regard your brother with a haughty eye." The theme is specified even more precisely: awareness of being a sinner. "(Let the monk) constantly say in his heart what the Publican in the Gospel said with downcast eyes: 'Lord I am a sinner, not worthy to look up to heaven.'" (RB 7.65)

To sum up, this short analysis uncovers some elements of a progression. Degrees one through five lead to a certain interiorization; degrees six and seven seem to be the application to different tasks imposed by life, the twelfth pertains to one's carriage and manner of looking on others; nine, ten and eleven are on the demands of detachment in word and laughter.

II. Anthropology

It is evident that I will have to deduce an implicit anthropology from all this, one which underlies the text and one which Benedict himself did not consciously construct. But it is nevertheless possible to imagine the notion of humanity that he has, by studying how he conceives his candidate for the monastic life, the goal which he proposes to him, and the means which he recommends to him.

I would make two preliminary remarks. First, there are in Benedict, as it were, two different points of view concerning the spiritual journey: one which looks to the ideal and one which takes into consideration concrete possibilities. Secondly, it is good to recall the historical perspective: each epoch, each cultural period produces a particular human type. We should not overlook this historical relativity: even if there is something eternal in humanity, that eternal is always incarnated in a very definite human type.

What is so striking about Benedict is that his anthropology is clearly turned toward the supernatural. His anthropology is Christian, not psychological or philosophical. Benedict sees humanity from the point of view where he invites the monk to place himself: under the gaze of God, and of a God who is the final judge. In reading and rereading this chapter on humility, I can not help but think each time of that beautiful Byzantine church near Athens (Daphni) in which you always find yourself under the gaze of Christ the Pantocrator, no matter where you stand. This very definite, indeed towering, perspective naturally gives to life a seriousness which goes along with the ever-present alternative: eternal life or damnation. Under the eye of the Pantocrator, the fear of God takes on the heavy flavor of the fear of reprobation. Thus humility is a tool which serves to keep us in this perspective, but also to surpass it so as to arrive at an attitude of perfect liberty which drives out fear. This gives to monastic life, as Benedict sees it, a permanent seriousness.

The second point to be noted is the conviction of being a sinner. Benedict constantly sets before us this alternative: my will or God's will, my will being synonymous with sin and the will of God being the grace which delivers me from sin and judgment. If one pushes this to its extreme limits—which Benedict surely never does, but which it is good to do, so as to understand the impression this text can have for certain people—one arrives at a kind of Lutheranism. I have asked myself whether the Wisdom Literature, which is so pessimistic and which is so willingly cited by Benedict, has not had some influence here. One often feels closer to John the Baptist than to the Gospel: the axe is at the root of the tree! This initial impression, however, will be moderated and surpassed through the systematic exercise of humility.

A third point about this anthropology: Benedict considers humanity from a strictly objective point of view, based on the demands made on us by the will of God. In this sense, the text is not psychological. The human person is presented very objectively as free to choose between God's will and self-will; one is in possession of that freedom of choice which ought, through personal labor and through the craft of the monastic life, to render one free for the will of God which is salvation. Taken literally and without commentary, the text sounds very voluntaristic. It is certainly as voluntaristic as the (system) of Ignatius which was, moreover, very probably inspired by Benedict at Montserrat. But Benedict will moderate this voluntaristic perspective by his recognition of human weakness (that entire domain which does not depend on the "will"). No doubt he is forced into the voluntarist perspective by the context of conversion. Just like Ignatius, the monk is at the beginning of his conversion. Also, Benedict is speaking for a kind of hippie, or semi-barbarian, or at least for people who are making a great step. A line of demarcation is clearly traced: as with Ignatius, one must choose between two allegiances. We have something of this kind in the Prologue: one enters into the service of God, into the army of Christ the Lord, the true king.

When I compare him with earlier ascetic and mystical movements, two more points strike me in Benedict. First, the monk is considered as an eternal beginner. He converts and surely arrives at a kind of perfection, but he is always beginning over. The realistic view that Benedict has toward the candidate prevents him from thinking that the high ideal of former years is realizable for the common run of monks.

In the second place, the true Christian disposition consists very precisely in the concrete disposition of the will detached from itself and rendered totally receptive to God. It is in renouncing a height which no longer appears possible that Benedict arrives at the heart of the Christian attitude: at detachment from the will closed in on itself, a detachment which renders it free for the salvation of God. Even if Benedict reduces the meaning of the term "will of God" to a moral or legal sense, it still seems that for him the heart of Christianity is located in obedience to the will of God, which is the will of salvation. To be converted is in the concrete to let oneself be commandeered, here and now, by the will of God mediated through the abbot, into work, into the rear lines. "You are not attaining to the mystic heights. That is not important. You are weak; we are not up to the standard of the heroes of old; that is of no importance whatsoever, for it is the acceptance of this weakness that leads in the end to truth." The circumstances, then, occasion the limits posed on the ideal and they lead to the essential.

I have asked myself whether the personal spiritual evolution of Benedict might not have been decisive in this matter. This son of a nobleman renounced everything to become a contemplative hermit; he departed for Subiaco where disciples soon came to join him in leading a semi-anchoretic life. After an unfortunate experience of reform in a nearby community and after various other trials, he left to found the cenobium of Monte Cassino. He had learned what is at the heart of the monk. In sum, Benedict travelled the road of Cassian backwards: from contemplation, he returned to ascetic life, in the sense explained above. To be a Christian is to enter into the call of God. His spirituality will be an eminently biblical spirituality, a spirituality of the covenant. The monk perceives the call of God: he must be ready to respond. God is here, he need not be sought. Ascesis is the work of faith. And then there is humility: it is not the means to contemplation, but the labor of faith. The **Rule** is not, then, as is often said, a kind of Christian form of a universal, religious human ideal. Also, it is often said that monasticism is a kind of archetype of culture and religion which one finds in all religions and which Christianity has simply lived out in a Christian fashion. That is not the vision of Benedict. He keeps nothing from this cultural and religious archetype. On the other hand, I do find this ideal in the spirituality of Carmel. Benedict has, so to speak, immediately descended from this ideal to arrive at a very different kind of behavior. To characterize it, I would speak rather of a spirituality of the covenant. One is called by God, one enters into his service, one listens, one hears. It is not necessary to search for God; he is here. That is what gives the **Rule** its extremely concrete character and which doubtless opens it to so many possible implementations.

A final point of anthropology: the realism of the "charity" of Benedict, who takes into consideration human subjectivity with so much wisdom and moderation. In this regard, it is quite instructive to see that the abbot must not load his monks down too heavily with work, and he must see to it that they do not lapse into a depressed sadness. People are weak and they are sinners; the abbot must recognize this in all humility; hence the care in regard to persons that Benedict de-

mands of him, the attention to subjective dispositions, this realism that flowers throughout the Rule. Here again we recognize something fundamentally Christian. It is by basing himself on this very realistic consideration of humanity that Benedict arrives at the essential, at the primacy of charity. Yet, the different motivations do not seem to be perfectly integrated, and it is surprising to see how RB 7 hardly mentions charity at all—in contrast to our spirituality today. In this key chapter on the spiritual art, which is the masterpiece of Benedictine spirituality, charity as such remains in the background.

To sum up in one word: Benedict interiorizes Christian values and does so in the context of a certain pessimistic realism—or better, of a realism which is a bit pessimistic.

III. Some Critical Notes

We are separated from this text by a great psychological and cultural distance. Two points catch our attention: first and foremost, the emphasis placed on sin and judgment; then second, the related interest in subjectivity with the emphasis again on judgment and the inclination to sin. This point of view is the product of a Christian pessimism which proceeds not so much from an awareness of sin as from a whole theological perspective which is expressed in a series of antinomies where everything has its meaning: sin/pardon of God—self will/will of God—fear of judgment of God/love of God, the fruit of humility.

Many influences have worked in the same direction. Certainly the anti-Pelagian influence of Augustine can be felt here: "that which is my will cannot come from God." One conceived of an alternative or opposition: nature/God, my will/will of God. Obviously, this Augustinian influence could combine with Platonic dualism. (I have also been struck by this in John of the Cross, who constantly emphasizes the place of human desire as something sinful in itself, since it is self-will that steals from God that which belongs to him. In him, too, we see what is almost a dualist antinomy: that which is from me cannot be from God.) Probably a certain climate of pessimism inherited from the cultural situation entered into play here: it was an epoch of war, of barbarity, of decadence in monastic morals.

In any case, we find ourselves faced here with an extreme polarization and a theology of liberation which is very specific. In the Johannine opposition of God/world, the world, in the theological sense, is mostly the world judged by God, and liberation clearly means deliverance from sin—so this theology merits its name as a theology of liberation in the strictly limited ancient sense of the word. Ascesis, which is the work of faith, becomes at the same time the work of liberation from sin. To the liberation from sin offered by God there corresponds, in the relationship of faith, the human contribution, which is the task of liberation from self-will, from sin. To put it bluntly, we have here a lack of attention to the creation. That is why I call this theological vision, which is polarized to the extreme on the matter of liberation, a theology of liberation. Protestant as well as Catholic exegetes stress the importance of the first covenant sealed with God with the whole human race as a fundamental covenant, a covenant of creation. Benedict's theological perspective, which is consonant with the entire anthropology of that period, is completely different. For him, the whole weight is placed on redemption, on the intervention of God in history to liberate humanity from sin.

Let us consider for a moment the contribution of "secularization." It has promoted the harmonization of the two poles of creation-theology with liberation-theology. Secularization is bound up with a culture which leads to seeing human beings and the human community, human ethics and history, in non-religious terms. The world is the domain of humanity and it has its own importance. In the concrete, one grants humanity its autonomy, without any intention of denying its relation to God. The use of the same word "autonomy" in the Benedictine perspective would have a completely different connotation: it could only mean opposition over against God, since Benedict always operates within the alternative: "self-will/will of God." It seems to me that today this sharp antinomy has been superseded or at least corrected by the principle of secularization. Not that one could secularize (in a banal sense of the word) Christianity; but we have to take into account a fundamental affirmation of secularization, namely, the recognition of the autonomy, the independent worth of ethics, of social politics, of the great domain of culture. Think of Kant and his ethic. There is a place today for a sexual morality and a morality of justice which, without being religious, pertain to the nature of man and which permit agreement with non-believers. And this principle of secularization can be integrated with a theology of creation, but, on the contrary, it is difficult to assimilate it to a theology of liberation in the restrictive sense in which we have defined that word.

But if, recalling an ancient patristic theme, we recognize the *logoi spermatikoi* at work in creation and the divine Word actively permeating culture, the formation of human conscience, and ethical movements toward human liberty and dignity, we will welcome a theology which is founded on the covenant of creation and which can integrate in its religious perspective the best contribution of secularization. Now the horizon of liberation is enlarged, for it is no longer limited to liberation from sin, but is open to the historical dimension of the manifestation of God as a dynamic element in the history of humanity. One insists less, then, on the fallenness of human nature than on the historical perspective

of humanity as being-in-becoming, which, through research and the development of culture and science, pursues its path toward fulfillment. The goal remains shrouded in mystery, if it remains in a purely worldly perspective. For Christianity as well, the meaning of this immense cultural, social, ethical activity remains wrapped in mystery. We can say that everything leads finally to the Kingdom of God—by what routes remains an enigma. We can, of course, affirm the existence of a goal, but we cannot be sure that this goal coincides exactly with our earthly labors. We can only hope and believe that it does.

Today one also prefers to present the human person in a dynamic perspective as a being-in-becoming, a creator of history, and not only as an individual but also as a member of collective humanity. Human beings create history; they grow throughout the whole development of the cultural history of humanity. Thus, the recognition of human rights mark an important step in human ethical progress. And it is quite evident that Christianity has played an active role in this maturation. Merleau-Ponty affirms this very clearly, at a time when he is otherwise rather critical toward Christianity. Many of the most precious ideas of our thought and of our western philosophy have come from Christianity, he says, and they have become today the common possession of our humanism. The ideas of liberty, of responsibility, of history, of subjectivity have become liberating ideas for all of humanity.

After all this, you see that "liberation" can no longer mean only the my liberation from sin, and from yours and others' as well; liberation through Christ extends to the whole contribution of the manifestation of God and Christians to the development of mankind and to the humanity of human beings. Naturally, this grants Christianity a great deal of significance. It influences and frees people well beyond the frontiers of the Church.

This dimension is obviously absent from Benedict, and it has resulted in a certain shrinkage of perspective which irks me—and many others with me: liberation from sin and the fear of God have stamped humility with a very specific meaning. Later, I believe, monastic spirituality evolved, thanks to study (among other things), and especially when monks entered by their humanistic studies into contact with certain forms of secularization. The horizon was enlarged.

Very recently I have reread certain texts of St. Francis; it appears to me that he has a kind of qualitative bond with the created order. One has the impression of a new interiorization, of a new kind of person at the heart of Christianity: the created order as such has been integrated. Once more this reminds us how our texts, no matter how spiritual they are, are limited by their own proper historical context.

A second point of critical reflection concerns the interest focused on the subject. I perceive in this text—and I am not alone—a strong preoccupation with the self. One struggles to be humble in the eyes of God so as to assure one's personal salvation and in the hope of finding it in God's love already in this world. A great interest in individual ascetic effort corresponds to the strict theology of liberation of which we have spoken and to the whole classic theology of substitutionary satisfaction; this is very much centered on the individual and not on the historic dimension of human life. One systematically humiliates oneself, one strives to see oneself as an unworthy servant, one lowers one's eyes so that others can see one's humility. All this might make us smile if it were not considered in its historic context. It must have had a different meaning for the people whom Benedict addressed, who were a rougher, more violent sort than we. (I think of the violence which Huizinga has described in the late Middle Ages; it is also shown by an episode in which an abbot is stabbed by one of his monks on the stairs leading to the church at the hour of Matins.) The mentality is ruder, more refractory, more "popular." But there is an even more essential difference. Compared to our culture, the disposition of people at that time was of a much more objective sort, and texts such as Benedict's may not have seemed to them as centered on the subject as they seem to us.

We might say the same thing about everything that touches on the mystical. When young people today think of the mystical, they think mostly of their own experience, of a kind of awareness of their own experience. What amazing stuff is written nowadays about religious experience! The expression is also indicative of the orientation of a culture saturated with "subjectivism." The ancients spoke quite otherwise. They are more attentive to objective criteria. In the development of the spiritual life, they hold to objective steps which are described in the symbols and concepts inherited from Platonism. One adapts oneself to the objective model which they represent.

The same holds true in the area of ethics. When the Congregation of the Faith speaks of sexuality, its language is still connected with a terminology drawn from a culture turned toward objective norms. And this is what gives those documents a legalistic character which is so disconcerting to modern people.

After Descartes, philosophy is reflexive. Objectivity takes refuge among the natural sciences, whereas for the ancients, it provided a symbolic system for any subject one discussed. For them the laws of the development of the spiritual life were as objective as the laws of nature are for us. We can never overestimate the cultural and psychological break brought about by "subjectivism." Much more than previously, people today are turned toward themselves, preoccupied with

the self, conscious of their own feelings, their ideals. Romantic literature is typical of this modern culture just as epic literature was characteristic of the other. When we compare the drama of Shakespeare with that of Sophocles we find that the former is already moving toward psychological analysis and self-consciousness. Ancient people were more extroverted in their entire orientation toward the objective order of symbols. We must be alert to this typically modern situation when we present ancient texts such as this chapter on humility. To gaze in the mirror so as to be continually present to myself as "me," this a phenomenon of modern culture. This implies a spontaneous care for the self which is reflected in the language and in the surrounding culture. There is a splitting of the self: one is attentive to oneself in a mirror relation, with all that implies of the anxiety of losing the self and of the desire of being recognized.

This phenomenon is so powerful that we can say, using the fine expression of Max Scheler, that the person who pursues humility invariably misses it. That is obviously in total contradiction to Benedict, for whom humility is precisely the labor of faith. Scheler's formula becomes clear in a culture where to pursue humility can only mean to pursue an ideal of the self, "to decide" to be humble. In a culture so preoccupied with the self, one cannot attain to humility in this fashion; methodical application to humility becomes a technique which invariably leads to self-satisfaction.

We have here what Kierkegaard calls the Catholic type of hypocrisy. For him, hypocrisy is a particular occupational hazard of Catholicism. One must confess that what so often strikes laypeople when they enter into contact with a religious community—and this has posed quite a few problems in teaching and is something that deserves to be discussed frankly—is the lack of spontaneity, the difficulty in contact, the impression that there exists a sort of screen between the partners. Without knowing it, even in an unconscious manner which escapes self-awareness, one is always careful of the impression given. The pursuit of humility can really become the pursuit of a personally fabricated self-image. That also explains why the person who pursues humility in this way can only miss it, according to the saying of Scheler. Like Narcissus, and even unknowingly, one is in love with the ideal self-image. Precisely here lies the hazard to Catholicism underscored by Kierkegaard. I do not wish to tone down his claim by reducing it to a warning against possible deviations. Quite the contrary, this is a fundamental trait of a culture which still runs strong in Catholicism. It is a kind of psychological climate which we must overcome. It comes from our culture. All breathe it, religious and laity, but perhaps it is reinforced by asceticism and in particular by the asceticism of humility. Often religious give the impression that their humility is more narcissistic than that of the laity! I am telling you what I often hear and I think that it is good to know how we are perceived by the laity. I have often noticed that the act of quitting of the habit has revealed narcissistic immaturity clearly enough. Evidently the habit is one of the elements of this image that one is creating for oneself and for others. It is a symbolic way of presenting the self, one that makes the person constantly alert, at least when one is in the midst of brothers and sisters with the same habit.

All this is simply to suggest that a text which, in its own era, was not in the last analysis "subjective" in the sense that we have said, can still become such in our time and be vulnerable to a very "narcissistic" interpretation.

Another characteristic of our culture is that it experiences a sense of guilt more than bygone ages did. I am not talking about awareness of sin but of the feeling of guilt. (It would take too long to go into this question). According to Freud, this is the price we pay for the progress of culture. This feeling of guilt is not morbid, but rather takes the form of a psychological disposition of continual anguish, of an uneasy fear of losing love which is found in all kinds of relationships: husband-wife; subordinate-superior; parent-child; humanity-God.

A first consequence: The text of Benedict on humility, taken literally, without a relativizing interpretation, can easily reinforce the tendency to psychological self-accusation. If today we wish to foster the process of religious conversion desired by Benedict, we surely ought to take the opposite route: not to start with guilt feelings, which still do not mean that one is conscious of being a sinner—that takes a deepening of faith—but to learn first to accept oneself and to trust in God. That is for me the first step on the ladder of humility. You may say that this implies an awareness of one's sin; no doubt, but we should not give that the first place. There is much more need to keep in sight "the goodness of God our Savior and his love for humanity" as St. Paul invites us (Titus 3:4). For many this would be a first liberation from self, a distancing from the preoccupation with one's own innocence, an acceptance of the self in humility. For this is humility: as in married love, to accept being called to be loved by God such as one *is*. This can help us escape from our excessive preoccupation with ourselves.

A second consequence: The text can also give rise to a false interpretation which suggests that the "little child" is ideal, and thus contributes to infantilism. Think of the spirituality of St. Therese of Lísieux; it is a bit ambiguous and psychologically marked by its time and its circumstances. The analysis of self-will, such as we have presented it above, in a dualistic optic of opposition such as presented in the text of Benedict (my will/ the will of God), can lead to this conclusion: I must get rid of my self-will, I must be emptied of myself. In a

dualistic climate, that can be equivalent to infantile resignation, a flight from all responsibility, since all self-affirmation is thought to be a seeking of self. If, on the contrary, one sets oneself from the outset in a triangular relation: God—me—community, the reference to the social dimension opens perspectives. I must take the initiative, I must bear my responsibility, I must have the courage to carry through, even at the expense of my reputation. In these conditions, humility takes on an objective dimension which is oriented toward the task of the group and the progress of the community. One is at the service of humanity. The will of God is the will which builds the Kingdom; not the will defined by the prescription of the law, but the dynamic will which comes to establish the Kingdom with and for humanity. To be detached from self-will is to be engaged in this creative dynamism. Is it not a form of humility to disappear into the function that one carries out, with all the willingness required for this task?

This approach is different from that of Benedict. It is all the more important to see that many candidates for the monastic life are young people who have still not arrived at a real self-affirmation nor at a normal development of their identity. As you know, psychological adolescence is greatly prolonged in our day. Young people mature too quickly and too slowly at the same time. This is a complex situation. It is not because they know too much that the young people mature quicker. On the contrary, the amount of knowledge makes the art of becoming oneself more complex. It is because they are exposed to so many contradictory systems of thought, to multiple influences and models of life, that the modern youth have difficulty acquiring self-identity. They are certainly not psychological adults at 18 or 20 years, even though they have often had much experience.

That can also help us understand how—and this is very surprising to some people—some monks, more than laypeople, can have a sort of delayed adolescence. For them, problems may make their appearance later than for someone who has a home and children and who must struggle to feed and clothe them; such a person comes to a sense of reality and commitment sooner. I have the impression that to the extent that one takes on a kind of premature ascesis of detachment—before self-will and the sense of responsibility have had a chance to develop—one simply risks retarding the crisis of maturity.

IV. A Positive Statement on Humility

My conclusion will be brief.

A first point. The word "humility" rubs us the wrong way and irritates us a bit today. Not because in fact one is not humble, but because of the pejorative connotation attached to the word. Today we prefer the word "authenticity." Without having made a systematic study of the question, I think that today the term connotes a preoccupation with the self which is too narcissistic. It suggests concern about one's virtue, preoccupation with a personal ideal of perfection.[2]

A second connotation of humility is that a person is seeking in religion some consolation for weakness. Nietzsche is the byword for this critical tendency in our culture. He is probably an author most read by those interested in philosophical works, but he is expressing a sentiment which is very much alive and widespread. The charge against our culture, which, as everyone knows, is formed by Christianity, is that we pursue a kind of unconscious cult of weakness along with a compensating search for consolation in religious emotion, a kind of comforting experience. It seems to me that this is the idea which the word "humility" suggests to many, especially when one stresses the search for voluntary humiliation. One gives the impression of cultivating weakness so as to experience an artificial paradise sought in religious intimacy. It is a kind of religious illusion which has its roots in the cult of personal weakness.

On the other hand, I note a clear preference for the word "authenticity," which fits very well with what the ancients called humility. At first sight, the word "authenticity" seems to have a purely humanistic meaning, but it also has ethical value and can serve as a foundation for Christian humility. "Authenticity" is the word which perfectly expresses the intolerance young people today feel toward pride, smugness, pretension. If the young reject humility, it is not because they support pretence. Quite the contrary: in their eyes, one ought to be able to approach a professor man to man, and—at least if one does not seek counsel—in a certain sense equal to equal. A judge ought to be able to "take a glass," but he remains a judge. I call him by his first name, but he remains my boss and I am under his orders. He exercises a function. I believe that this "democratic attitude" which is so dear to the young lies in a rejection of the pretension whereby someone esteems himself more than someone else solely by reason of the function which he exercises.

To be authentic is to be true to oneself, and that means, for the young, not to think oneself better than another and, as a consequence, to have respect and patience for others. This is a humanistic and ethical value, and it could also become a true "face of God." To keep to one's true place, neither more nor less, before God. We find ourselves back at an ancient saying "Know thou thyself": know that you are a responsible person; you are not God. Authenticity bases itself on a totally human simplicity in order to become religious humility.

A second point seems important to me for a contemporary presentation of humility. I will call it a "sense of celebration." What can this expression mean when it is applied to a text? This is what happens when a text frees me from myself, when it removes me from worry about moral application—without making me therefore immoral!—but evokes in me sentiments of wonder and admiration such as happens with many of the psalms. These are texts which teach us to look with joy on the magnificence and splendor of God and the creation. This quality is often lacking in modern texts and melodies which turn people back too much on themselves and come across as too moralizing.

Such a perspective goes along naturally with a theology of creation and one can also develop it on the foundation of an enlarged theology of redemption. We are free from ourselves, for the person who has heard and seen Christ looks on the world differently. This person sees future possibilities, open-ended growth, manifest splendor. Such a person is clothed with a kind of innocence which sometimes bursts forth in a look of knowing admiration.

In my opinion, admiring attention is an attitude of humility, even though the word is not uttered. It breaks open the narcissistic turning back on the self. Such an attitude may seem too emotional at times, but it may also be simply realistic. This is the Gospel ideal: to be an infant, without trying to be—for to seek it would be infantilism. This form of humility is forgetful of self. In this sense, I could be rejoining St. Benedict when he says that one should not seek the mystic heights. Don't seek systematically to be humble; be objective; learn to discover God; learn also to recognize him in others. Get out of yourself and without knowing it humility will be given to you besides.

A final remark: I would like to give a slightly different meaning to the term "the will of God." I would not see it to be primarily an order, a commandment that God addresses to me. I would see it in a more objective way by distancing it from a dualist perspective. That would make it more a will for the salvation of all humanity and also a will for salvation integrated into the created order. To learn to see God as he reveals himself in human work, guiding the development of the Kingdom, this is to plug into the will of God and to become detached from self-will.

I think I can conclude thus: I have then connected humility to obedience (*ob-audire*), to obedience especially as a way of learning to listen to that which speaks of God and appears in humanity and in Christ. This attention oriented toward its object seems to me to be the fundamental obedience of humility. Naturally, it admits of different degrees which extend the readiness to listen to various domains and to the concrete here and now of life. This places it at the extreme opposite pole from any of those utopian dreams which break and sour so many people, and not only in the political and social world but also in religious houses. The dream of a heavenly Jerusalem reminds me of the text of Matthew about the violent who wish to take heaven by force: the dream of a utopian church, of a heavenly Jerusalem that one wants to establish by violence, a dream always aimed toward the future, toward a future to be lived here on earth.

What is fundamental in St. Benedict is that he teaches us to discern here and now, concretely, the actual possibilities of a situation. I find that this is precisely the realism which demands the greatest detachment from self. Here is where I find true humility. Its fundamental meaning lies in being alert to discern the traces of God and in an attentive listening in order to respond to the divine invitation which is offered to me in the reality of each day.

Notes

[1] All English translations of the Latin text of RB used in this article are taken from *RB 1980,* ed. Timothy Fry et al (Collegeville, MN: The Liturgical Press 1981).

[2] The author has indicated in a verbal communication that on the basis of a little poll he took on the meaning people attach to "humility," he found that the word carries a positive sense as well as a negative. For some it conjures up a feeling of respect, as something opposed to pride; for others it has the negative connotations analyzed in the text; for still others, it can bear various meanings.

David N. Bell (essay date 1978)

SOURCE: "The Vision of the World and of the Archetypes in the Latin Spirituality of the Middle Ages" in *Archives: D'Histoire Doctrinal et Littéraire du Moyen Age,* Librarie Philosophique J. Vrin, 1978, pp. 7-31.

[*In the following excerpt, Bell discusses various interpretations of St. Benedict's* visio mundi, *or "vision of the world," as recorded in Gregory the Great's biography of Benedict.*]

Our source for this mysterious vision is Gregory the Great's life of Benedict, which forms the second book of the *Dialogues.* The saint (Gregory tells us) was standing at the window of a tower, and saw, to his wonder, "sicut post ipse narravit, omnis etiam mundus velut sub uno solis radio collectus", and in the splendour of the light, saw too "Germani Capuani episcopi animam in sphaera ignea ab angelis in coelum ferri"[1]. Gregory's explanation of this remarkable experience is neat and simple: "non coelum et terra contracta est, sed videntis animus est dilatatus, qui in Deo raptus videre sine difficultate potuit omne quod infra Deum est"[2]. The ravishing to God of the *mens* of Benedict showed him,

in God's light, how small things really were here below. If we were to accept this explanation and consider it as generally applicable, then any similar *raptus* might in theory be expected to produce the same vision, provided, of course, that a similar *raptus* is possible.

Gregory himself, however, seems to make of Benedict a notable exception to his general rule, for in a clear passage in the *Moralia* he points out that the boundless light of God fills all things with itself and encircles all things (including the human *mens*), but "idcirco mens nostra nequaquam se ad comprehendendam incircumscriptam circumstantiam dilatat, quia eam inopia suae circumscriptionis angustat"[3]. But Benedict seems not to have been constrained by this general principle. Furthermore, if Gregory intends to imply by his description that Benedict saw God face to face, then this makes the saint an even rarer and more remarkable exception, for Gregory is insistent on our inability here below to see God *sicuti est,* and presents an abundance of texts stating this fact[4]. If Benedict, then, *did* see God in this way, his experience was most extraordinary, and we cannot hope to see what he saw. But it is not at all clear that Gregory *did* wish to imply this with regard to Benedict. He certainly does not say directly that this was so, and Thomas Aquinas shows that from Augustinian premises it is impossible that he could have thought so[5]. But Gregory, although deeply devoted to Augustine and deeply influenced by him, does not copy him slavishly, and as Dom Butler says: "If St Augustine's view be accepted, it is clear that St Benedict did not enjoy this supreme vision. But our question is: Did St Gregory believe St Benedict to have had the vision of God's Essence? rather than: Did St Benedict really have it?"[6] Robert Gillet would answer the former question affirmatively, pointing out that "la *lux creatoris* des *Dialogues* semble donc devoir être identifiée avec la nature même de Dieu"[7], and that as a consequence to see one is to see the other. There is no doubt that, as Gillet points out, Gregory's general viewpoint is contrary to this concept, but he is prepared to see exceptions to the general rule in Moses, Paul, and Benedict[8].

A. Schaut, however, is less certain[9]. There is no doubt, he says, that Benedict attained "zur höchsten Höhe der Contemplatio"[10], but must this indicate a vision of the essence of God *sicuti est?* "Auf den ersten Blick", he observes, "sind wir geneigt, die Frage zu bejahen, da Gregor in der Vision von einem *videre Creatorem* spricht. Hätten wir nur diesen Text Gregors vor uns, so müsste die Frage wohl in diesem Sinne entschieden werden, da wir zu wenig Anhaltspunkte hätten, die uns veranlassen könnten, eine gegenteilige Behauptung aufzustellen"[11]. But he considers that the overwhelming weight of the other texts of Gregory gainsays this conclusion, and decides that "eine Gottesschau ist für den noch im Fleische Lebenden nur möglich per aenigma und per speculum; denn im Fleische leben heisst die caligo corruptionis an sich tragen. . . . Von dieser Regel gibt es auch für Jakob, Moses, Job, Isaias und Paulus keine Ausnahme. Ihr Schauen war kein Schauen per speciem"[12]. It is clear, therefore, that there is room for doubt on the question, and I am not sure that we can be certain what Gregory's thought was on this point. That he conceived the vision to be very exalted is not in doubt, but whether he thought of it as a vision of God *sicuti est* is another question. For myself, I am by no means convinced that he did. Certainly (and as Schaut has noted) Gregory speaks of *videre Creatorem* ("quia animae videnti Creatorem angusta est omnis creatura"[13]), but in the very next sentence grows cautious as to how much of this light may be seen. *"Quamlibet etenim parum* de luce Creatoris aspexerit . . ."[14]. Even faith in God is a slight glimpse of his light ("Jede Glaubenserkenntnis ist bereits ein Schauen im Lichte Gottes", Schaut observes, "denn der Glaubensinhalt kommt ja von Gott"[15]), but no-one, I am sure, would conclude from this that "jede Glaubenserkenntnis" is the full Beatific Vision.

The comments of Bernard of Clairvaux on the *Dialogues* passage do not assist us to any great extent[16]. The views of Dom Butler[17], of Mabillon[18], and others are that Bernard understood the description as referring to a face to face vision. Their reasoning appears to be that (a) Bernard says here that this vision really pertains to the *natura angelica,* not the *natura humana*[19]; (b) Bernard says in a number of places that the angels see the face of God[20]; therefore (c) the vision of Benedict is the face to face vision of God *sicuti est*[21]. This argument, however, is not strictly logical, and the conclusion (c) does not necessarily follow from the premises. There is no doubt that angelic consciousness is very remarkable[22], but Gilson is right in expressing doubts that Bernard's account of Benedict's vision provides a rare exception to his general standpoint that the vision *sicuti est* is not permitted us here on earth[23]. Bernard does not actually say in this passage "Benedict saw God face to face" (and Benedict, according to Gregory, never said he did); happy are they, he says, "qui . . . invisibilia Dei non visibilibus rimando perquirunt, sed in ipsis ad liquidum intellecta conspiciunt"[24]. Happy indeed! But this is not necessarily the Beatific Vision. On the other hand, I am not sure that we can be quite as certain as Gilson that the vision *sicuti est* is not in Bernard's mind here, and I do not think we can deny the possibility that Butler and Mabillon (even if not strictly logical) are correct. The account in Bernard, like that in Gregory, is open to different interpretations. Bernard does not seem quite sure what to do with it, and after his brief and ambiguous account hastens on, and turns his attention instead to the safer and standard theme of perceiving God via his creatures[25].

The vision of Benedict, in other words, although unquestionably of a very high level, poses considerable problems as to what precisely to do with it and how exactly to interpret it. In one way this is not particularly surprising, for as Odo Casel pointed out in 1917[26], the actual description of the vision (as distinct from Gregory's interpretation of it) is rather more akin to hellenistic mysticism than to standard Christian spirituality. "Die Seele", he writes, "die ja selbst von Aetherhöhen herabgestiegen ist, die ein Funke des göttlichen Feuers ist, fühlt sich bei Betrachtung der Himmelskörper mächtig angezogen, dorthin zurückzukehren; sie wird emporgetragen unter den Reigen der Sterne und schaut nun von oben in seliger Schau auf die Erde und das Welthall hinab. Sie lässt den Leib unten auf der Erde und vereinigt sich mit der Gottheit"[27]. And he adduces examples for this concept from Stobaios, Philo, Cicero, and Seneca[28]. The vision of the soul of Germanus "in sphaera ignea" also has a hellenistic parallel, for Casel reminds us of the "Kaisarapotheose", a representation of which (at the base of the Antoninus column, for example) Benedict himself might have seen in Rome[29]. And "es ist auffallend", he adds, "dass in dem eigentlichen Bericht über die Vision von der Anschauung Gottes nicht gesprochen wird. Das geschieht in der von Gregor auf Bitten des Petrus beigefügten Erklärung, die eigentlich erst dem Ganzen eine spezifisch christliche Ausdeutung gibt"[30]. The conceptual imagery in which the vision of Benedict is described, therefore, ties it to its times, and since it is much less specifically Christian than much other material, the interpretations placed upon it may vary directly with the ingenuity and imagination of the interpreter. Perhaps because of its somewhat alien nature, the vision of Benedict occupies no major place in the mystical theology of the Middle Ages, and other examples of such hellenistic/Christian visions of the world are extremely difficult to find.

William of St Thierry, for example, conceives of the highest spiritual attainment in this world as being when the *mens* becomes not *Deus,* but *quod Deus est*[31], when it participates as fully as it may in the divine nature, and if the *mens* is thus expanded in God, we might surely expect it to be vouchsafed at least a modicum of the *visio mundi* such as Gregory records. Yet there is no evidence in William of such a vision, and the *unus simul intuitus* we find in one passage of the *Aenigma Fidei* (PL 180.435B) refers not to an experience of Benedict's type, but to the post-mortem experience/vision of the oneness and threeness of the Trinity at the same time. We have here a sound theoretical basis for the vision (if Gregory's explanation is to be believed), but no account of the vision itself.

If, however, we turn to the obscure Cistercian, Hildebrand of Himmerod[32], we find an account of a most interesting experience which presents certain similarities to the vision of Benedict. The author, whose entire published work comprises less than twelve full columns in volume 181 of the *Patrologia Latina,* flourished in the latter part of the thirteenth century, and in his *Libellus de Contemplatione* produced a brief but extremely interesting opuscule. In it, after discussing various matters concerned with the quest for God, and (following Bernard) delineating various types of contemplation, he speaks of the ecstatic *raptus* thus:

> Optimum enim videndi genus erit, ut te viso, nullius eguerim ad omne quod libuerit te contentus. *In te quidquid est a te, videre dabitur per te.* Claritas refulgens in te, resplendebit mihi totum quod es, *et omne quod est ex te.* . . . Quia in lumine tuo videbimus lumen, in tuo lumine, Fili Dei, videbimus lumen Patris Dei; videbimus et lumen Spiritus sancti Dei. Non autem tria videbimus lumina Dei, sed . . . videbimus in tribus discretis personis unum indiscretum lumen Deum. Non solum quippe in tuo lumine deiformiter illuminati, videbimus te divinum increatum lumen; sed etiam videbimus et nunc et tunc, quantum illuminatio vultus tui super nos, et pro quanto nos fecerit, *creata lumina lucentia,* ante Dominum[33].

In this description, Hildebrand clearly conceives the experience to be both the Trinitarian *unus simul intuitus* of William of St Thierry, and the vision of the totality of creation. What he does not make quite clear, however, is whether the "shining created lights" are seen in their earthly manifestations (as in the case of Benedict), or in their archetypal structure as Ideas or Forms[34]. Or, in other words, whether we have a *visio mundi* or a *visio mundi archetypi*. The passage, however, is undeniably of considerable interest.

A brief comment in Bruno the Carthusian is in some ways similar to this description of Hildebrand, but less detailed, and—as in the case of Bernard—difficult to place in the broader scheme of Bruno's thought. The author is speaking of the *invisibilia Dei* of Romans 1.20, and opens his discussion by explaining why the plural number (invisibilia) is used when, as everyone knows, God is *simplex.* "Ideo autem", he observes, "pluralem numerum posuit, quia infirmitas humani intellectus non sufficit considerare in Deo, nisi per interpositiones temporum, quae in eo naturalia *et simul sunt et uno ictu* (si fieri potest) consideranda"[35]. But after this intriguing comment, he slips back—as did Bernard—into a quite unexceptional account of how we can arrive at a partial understanding of the Trinity through consideration of the created order[36]. The vision of the *temporalia* in God is not where his interest lies, and he presents here no philosophical explanation of how and why the vision occurs. Nor is it quite clear whether Bruno is thinking of the manifested world or the archetypal world in this passage. The vision of the latter is of much more frequent occurrence than that of the world of manifestation, and, unlike the difficult

vision of Benedict, occupies an important place in the *via mystica* of the Middle Ages.

Notes

[1] Gregory the Great, *Dialogues* II.35 PL 66.198B. The passage is noted and briefly discussed in C. Butler, *Western Mysticism* (London, 1967³), pp. 86-87. Reference may be made generally to the excellent paper by A. Schaut, "Die Vision des hl. Benedikt" in R. Molitor (ed.), *Vir Dei Benedictus* (Münster i.W., 1947), pp. 207-253. Although much of it is a general study of Gregory's spirituality rather than a specific study of Benedict's vision, it is nevertheless most useful and most informative.

[2] *Dialogues* II.35 PL 66.200B. Cf. his comment in 200A: . . . quia ipsa luce visionis intimae, mentis laxatur sinus, tantumque expanditur in Deo, ut superior existat mundo, etc. On the matter of *dilatare,* see Schaut, *art. cit.,* pp. 227-230.

[3] Gregory the Great, *Moralia in Job* XXIV.VI.12 PL 76.292D. See also the texts referred to in Note 4 *infra.*

[4] A number of the important texts are cited in Butler, *op. cit.,* pp. 87-91, and see also Schaut, *art. cit.,* pp. 218-221.

[5] See Aquinas, *Quodlibetales* i.1 and the *Summa* II/II q. 180 a.5 cited by Schaut, *art. cit.,* pp. 217-218, and Butler, *op. cit.,* p. 92.

[6] Butler, *ibid.*

[7] R. Gillet (ed.), *Grégoire le Grand, Morales sur Job,* Livres I et II (Paris, 1952), p. 35 fn 1. See further Schaut, *art. cit.,* pp. 219-220.

[8] See Gillet, *op. cit.,* p. 35 and p. 36. Gillet also considers that *Moralia* XVIII. liv. 88-89 PL 76.91-93 also indicates the remote possibility of direct face to face vision of God here on earth. That text, however, presents its own difficulties and we cannot discuss them here. In any case, it is not concerned with Benedict.

[9] See his paper cited in Note 1 *supra.*

[10] Schaut, *art. cit.,* p. 252.

[11] *Ibid.,* p. 218.

[12] *Ibid.,* p. 219.

[13] *Dialogues* II.35 PL 66.200A.

[14] *Ibid.*

[15] Schaut, *art. cit.,* p. 222. See also *ibid.,* p. 238.

[16] See Bernard, *Sermones de Diversis,* Sermo IX.1 PL 183.565D-566A.

[17] In his *op. cit.,* pp. 92, 120.

[18] See his comments on *In Cantica,* Sermo XXXI.2, in *S. Bernardi Opera Omnia* (Paris, apud Gaume Fratres, 1839⁴), Vol. IV, cols. 2863-4. Cf. also the editorial foot-note to *Serm. de Div.* IX.1, PL 183.565-6.

[19] *Serm. de Div.* IX.1 col. 566A: "Verum . . . angelicae felicitatis istud est, non fragilitatis humanae". See also *ibid.,* col. 565CD.

[20] Cf. the text of *Serm. de Div.* IX.1 itself: " . . . et quemadmodum creatura coeli, sic et creatura mundi, jam non per speculum et in aenigmate, sed facie ad faciem Deum videbit, et sapientiam ejus ad liquidum contemplabitur in se ipsa, etc." (PL 183.565C). See also *In Ps. Qui habitat,* Sermo XI.6 PL 183.228B: "Ascendunt (i.e. the angels) ad vultum ejus, descendunt ad nutum ejus; quoniam Angelis suis mandavit de te. Nec tamen vel descendendo visione gloriae fraudantur, quia semper vident faciem Patris". And see further *In Festo S. Martini Episc.,* Sermo, sect. 7 PL 183.493C.

[21] Butler's reasoning clearly follows this line—see his *op. cit.,* p. 92.

[22] Cf. the discussion in *In Cantica,* Sermo V PL 183.798D-803B, especially sect. 4 of that sermon (col. 800A-C).

[23] See E. Gilson, *La théologie mystique de S. Bernard* (Paris, 1947), pp. 113-4 n. 1.

[24] *Serm. de Div.* IX.1 PL 183.565D-566A. On the *invisibilia Dei,* see Note 87 *infra.*

[25] So in sect. 2 of the same sermon: "Quaeramus igitur, per ea saltem quae facta sunt, intellectum invisibilium Dei, etc." (col. 566A).

[26] See O. Casel, "Zur Vision des hl. Benedikt (Vita c. 35)" in *Studien und Mitteilungen zur Geschichte des Benediktinerordens* 38 (1917), pp. 345-348. Schaut presents a summary of this paper in his *art. cit.,* pp. 208-209. Casel would appear to have derived his inspiration for this account from Joseph Kroll, *Die Lehren des Hermes Trismegistos* (Münster i. W., 1914), pp. 367-372 "Sternenmystizismus".

[27] Casel, *art. cit.,* p. 345.

[28] See *ibid.,* pp. 345-6. We shall discuss the influence of Macrobius on the matter a little later.

[29] *Ibid.,* p. 347.

[30] *Ibid.*

[31] See especially his *Epistola ad Fratres de Monte Dei* II.15 PL 184.348B, but generally *ibid.,* II.14-16 cols. 347-349. Gilson's comments in his *op. cit.,* pp. 230-232 are useful on this matter of *quod Deus est.*

[32] The Migne Patrology (see PL 181.1691-2) follows Fabricius in attributing the *Libellus de Contemplatione* to the twelfth-century author, Hildebrand the Young. This attribution cannot, however, be sustained, and there can be little doubt that our Hildebrand flourished at the end of the thirteenth century. The arguments for this dating may be found in G. M. Oury, "Le *Libellus de Contemplatione* de Maître Hildebrand", *Revue d'ascétique et de mystique* 43 (1967), pp. 268-9. The ms. of the *Libellus* was found at Himmerod in 1718 by Martène and Durand, and edited in 1733 in their *Veterum Scriptorum et Monumentorum . . . Amplissima Collectio,* Volume IX cols. 1237-1250. It is reproduced in PL 181 cols. 1691-1704 with some inaccuracies and different paragraph enumeration, but for convenience all our citations here will be to the PL version. We cannot be certain that Hildebrand was a monk of Himmerod, but it seems eminently probable, and I know of no other copy of the MS save that at Himmerod used by Dom Martène.

[33] *Lib. de Cont.* 12 PL 181.1700AB. Three points with regard to this text: (a) for PL *nullus,* read *nullius;* (b) *deiformiter:* this has a special significance for Hildebrand, see the *Libellus* sect. 10 col. 1697CD; (c) *ante Dominum: ante* presumably for [*enantios*] (cf. Luke 1.6); i.e. *ante = coram.* The Martène/Durand edition of the text (*Amp. Coll.* IX, col. 1245E) ends "ante te Dominum".

[34] We might note here that Ideas and Forms are not necessarily coterminous in our authors. Achard of St Victor, for example, is quite aware of the distinction made by Seneca in *Epist.* 58.18-21 and reproduces it himself—but not without some confusion. See his *De Unitate et Pluralitate Creaturarum* II.13, in A. Combes, *Un Inédit de saint Anselme?* (Paris, 1944), p. 46 §26. Combes discusses the matter in *ibid.,* pp. 127-130. The *idea* and *eidos* run parallel to the *forma secunda* and *forma tertia* in *De Unitate . . .* II.13, p. 48 §28 Combes (the *forma prima,* of course, being Christ the Logos). See further Combes' comments in *ibid.,* pp. 67-68, 151-160, and the excellent discussion in J. Chatillon, *Théologie, spiritualité, et métaphysique dans l'œuvre oratoire d'Achard de Saint-Victor* (Paris, 1969—hereafter cited as *Achard de S. Victor*), pp. 297-302. The whole of the latter's Chapter XI is here important. Achard's terminology is very wide. Augustine, on the other hand, ends his tractate *De Ideis* (*De Div. Quaest. 83,* qu. 46 PL 40.29-31): "Quas rationes, ut dictum est, sive ideas, sive formas, sive species, sive rationes licet vocare, et multis conceditur appellare quod libet, sed

paucissimis videre quod verum est" (col. 31). Nor does Erigena distinguish in *De Div. Naturae* II.36 PL 122.615D: "Causae itaque primordiales sunt, . . . quas Graeci ideas vocant, hoc est, species vel formas aeternas et incommutabiles rationes . . .". Cf. also *ibid.,* II.2 col. 529AB for the same theme. We shall follow Augustine and Erigena here, and distinguish idea and form only when specifically necessary.

[35] Bruno, *Exp. in Ep. Pauli—in Ep. ad Rom.* I PL 153.24B.

[36] See *ibid.,* col. 24B-D.

André Zegveld (essay date 1981)

SOURCE: "A Guide: *The Rule of St. Benedict,*" *The American Benedictine Review,* Vol. 36, No. 4, December, 1985, pp. 372-93.

[*In the following essay, originally published in 1981, Zegveld presents an overview of the fundamental concerns in the* Rule of St. Benedict *and explores how the* Rule *is to be interpreted and obeyed in the modern era.*]

The Call

In the writings of the New Testament a strong undercurrent of longing for the Kingdom of God makes itself felt, a longing for a new world, a new society entirely penetrated by the spirit of Jesus Christ, a desire for a new heaven and a new earth, in a word, for a life based on the precepts of the Sermon on the Mount. On the other hand, they also present, without any illusions, a clear view of humanity and the world of humanity as they actually exist: laboring with egotism, with the debilitating weight of sin, with the powerful drive of the passions.

Between these two worlds stands Jesus Christ. He combines both by offering to people, as they are, a community with a greater reality. This offer showed itself particularly in his resurrection. All had deserted him, had broken community with him and thus practically rejected what he had offered them. Still, after his death, despite everything, the conviction grew that the offer of a new life continued, that Jesus had forgiven them and that he was alive. Whoever therefore in faith lives in him as the Risen Lord, already lives in this world as in the coming Kingdom of God. Such faith is not an intellectual insight, but a conviction of the heart; in other words, a change of heart, a deep, vital knowledge that one has been accepted and transported purely by grace into the other world. This faith moves a person to give one's life a new direction, to rethink it. This faith calls for conversion.

In an early section of the Acts of the Apostles we find all these elements joined together: after the descent of the Holy Spirit, Peter spoke to the crowd that had gathered; he told them that they had unjustly delivered to death Jesus, a man sent by God, that he had arisen and was still offering himself to them. "When they heard this, they were deeply shaken. They asked Peter and the other apostles, 'What are we to do, brothers?' Peter answered, 'You must reform and be baptized, each one of you, in the name of Jesus Christ, that your sins may be forgiven!" (Acts 2:37f.). On the basis of this repentance, this conversion and this faith, the first assembly in Jerusalem will soon form, and its characteristic feature is *community;* its first reaction to the resurrection of Jesus is one of *sharing:* sharing of prayer, of food, of possessions. It is a community that wants to live out of God in a new manner, as God appeared in Jesus Christ and in his resurrection: a permanent offer of community on the basis of the new commandment, namely, that of an all-forgiving love.

Monastic life has always considered itself as a continuation of this primitive community of Jerusalem, as a radical and charismatic decision for the presence of God as it became apparent in Jesus Christ. It always desired to be a manner of life in which people could realize their pervasive desire to live in union with God. This union with God is sought with such absolute determination that literally everything is sacrificed for it (eremitical desert monasticism); it is also sought, with a like determination, in a quest for fraternal charity (cenobitical monasticism). In either case the monk seeks to become *simple,* wants to concentrate solely on one thing, wants to live a life directed to the one thing that counts: the monk seeks God alone—through the help of others who are of one heart and one soul.

The ***Rule of St. Benedict*** stands in this tradition. It is very definitely a place where these two complementary directions come together. In the ***Rule*** we see God's offer of union, we see the faith that becomes a vocation and stimulates the monk to conversion, to a form of life that is determined by a new consideration of all values.

What position does the ***Rule*** take with regard to this seeking after God, to union with God? I should like to discuss this question under the following four rubrics, and naturally this is no more than an attempt at an answer:

  1. Why do we live according to a Rule?
  2. How does the ***Rule*** present itself?
  3. What are the basic values of the ***Rule?***
  4. What does it mean "to live according to the ***Rule***"?

Why Do We Live according to a Rule?

As has already been said, monks desire to live in the spirit of the Gospel, according to the norms and values of the Gospel. These norms and values are synthesized in the old and the new commandment of love, because God is love. Is, then, a Rule really necessary? Do not all Rules, great and small, yield to this one commandment? To know God and to live with him is a form of love, love on the basis of a knowledge that one has been accepted and is affirmed as a unique person. Now, such a "knowledge in love" in reality cannot be transferred, just as every knowledge of truth is non-transferable. A person may indeed assert something, seek to explain something, repeat the words of the Gospel, paraphrase them, translate them, give a new direction to them—but one cannot be sure that the hearer is affected. A spiritual insight simply cannot be transferred from one person to another, as one might hand over apples to another—or the pox. Something more is needed.

In the first place, then, there is required "illumination," an "interior master," as Augustine would say, who repeats in the heart of each one external words, but in one's own language, so that the person begins to understand and grasp this external word internally. A person must—to use a somewhat lame comparison—always listen with two ears: one ear directed to the outside and one ear to the inside; the first listening to the word that comes from the outside, the second ardently open to the reaction of the heart and to the echo of the word in it.

Many people listen by directing their ears solely to the outside; they are not affected, they do not allow themselves to be affected; they never grow warm, but remain stuck with externals—words, sources, research. Some people speak often and easily, enter readily into conversation; they try to discern what words are expected of them "to remain in the conversation." Others listen by turning their ears inward; they are always affected, but generally it is not clear by what; in most cases this does not lead to commitment. They are lost in a maze of feelings. They dream and become enthusiastic about an entirely different theory, in which another cannot participate.

No, in listening one ear must be directed to the outside and one ear to the inside, both in speaking with others and in speaking to one's own heart: the word for the outside resides in a person's heart and is only there grasped as a "word-for-me": illumination. Still, as has been said, no one can give or transfer this illumination. The "inner master" serenely goes its own way.

What, however, can be transferred is *a form of life.* Hence, in the second place: If you want to lead people to the knowledge of a spiritual truth, offer them a manner of life. People with "insight" hand on how they have lived *in practice.* And they do so with the certainty acquired by experience: If you live this way,

then at a given moment, if you are really listening with both ears, outside and inside, "insight" will surely come, by itself, in its own good time. Forms, life styles, bring their own light with them. In other words, to grow into a definite experience, to enter into a definite experience, always means at the same time to grow into a definite culture, a definite manner of life, definite ways of conduct, rules and arrangements. With a view to a hoped-for experience a person must submit to forms which, at least at first glance, have little to do with the experience that is envisioned. Besides, there is no essential connection between form and experience. It is a matter of trust, because in the realm of the spiritual life other laws apply.

The monk's life is in the first place a life style. Certainly, it is meant to lead to the experience of an all-embracing love, to prayer without ceasing, to a lived experience that God is all in all, to the coming of the Kingdom of God which incarnates itself in a person's life—and all these are synonyms. But none of the monastic writers have ever been able to present an illumination of that kind. What they could hand on is the manner in which they lived, what their life actually looked like. Hence they left their Rules, not as documents of laws, but as the end-result of their spiritual experience and as a concrete example as to how they lived God's Good News. It is as if they said, "Live in the manner here prescribed and you will—if God grants it—arrive at the goal, because the voice of the inner master will be aroused in you. Grow into these forms, and the hoped-for life will grow in you."

Besides, this agrees fully with the pedagogy of Jesus. The Lord wants to lead us to the knowledge of God, to an experience of God's own Spirit, to the point where we shall know God as we are known by him. "Eternal life is this: to know you, the only true God, and him whom you have sent" (Jn 17:3). But this "illumination" is possible only if the person becomes *like* the human Jesus, if he follows after him, and thus begins to live as he lived. By living like him, a person will attain to Jesus' basic attitude in his own soul (Phil 2:5). The great mystics have well recognized this, as for example Hadewijch. She longed to "taste" God, to "savor" him, to become one with him, to see God as God, but she learned that this is possible only by way of imitation, by following him in the way he became man.

Why do we live according to a Rule? In general terms the answer may run as follows: We long to see God, we desire to enter into the kingdom of his presence, we want—"like the angels," the ancients say—to become all eye, to be eye alone for God. That can happen only through our humanity, in concrete human ways, through imitation. Imitation is presumed and handed down as such. It was initiated by Jesus himself, and our ancestors have given form to that imitation. Their Rules are meant to be nothing more than this: the Good News of Jesus, the imitation of the Lord's life style.

How Does the Rule *Present Itself?*

The **Rule of St. Benedict** must be understood in the light of the Rules that preceded it. It intends to be neither more nor less than an incarnation of the great values of the Gospel (cf. Prologue: " . . . by the guidance of the Gospel"). It seeks to define a form of life which, if faithfully followed, leads to a definite experience of God, to a Promised Land, of which again it only makes mention. Hence the two following aspects: The **Rule** considers itself indispensable—and at the same time it regards itself as a point of departure that must be jettisoned.

First, the **Rule** is indispensable. In Chapter 1 St. Benedict says that the cenobites, the monks whom he envisages, are characterized by the fact that they "serve under a Rule and an abbot." It is striking that the **Rule** is mentioned *before* the abbot. In contrast to earlier monasticism, where the abbot regulated the entire life, the superior here becomes the custodian of the **Rule.** Thus the **Rule** becomes a kind of universal point of reference, also, for the authority that is exercised in the community: "In all things, therefore, let all follow the Rule as their guide, and let no one be so rash as to deviate from it" (RB 3). The abbot, too, must act "in observance of the Rule" (RB 3). Furthermore, at the installation the abbot is told to "keep this Rule in all its details" (RB 64). (In the *Rule of the Master* a copy of the Rule is handed to the abbot immediately after the blessing.)

Hence the **Rule** is a kind of universal point of reference. For this reason it is expressly read several times during the course of the novitiate, so that the novices may well know what they are undertaking. For the monk's life is not primarily a seeking after subjective experiences, but the assumption of the yoke of the **Rule:** "Let this Rule be read through to him, and let him be addressed thus, 'Here is the law under which you wish to fight . . . '; let him understand . . . that from that day forward he may not leave the monastery nor withdraw his neck from under the yoke of the Rule" (RB 58).

Because becoming and being a monk means to assume this yoke, Benedict prescribes, "We desire that this Rule be read often in the community, so that none of the brethren may excuse himself on the ground of ignorance" (RB 66). In a word, the **Rule** presents itself as indispensable, as a universal point of departure, as a necessary norm for monks living the cenobitic form of life. According to St. Benedict they distinguish themselves by the fact that they follow a Rule (and not, as with Cassian, by their attitude toward possessions), in contrast to the sarabaites, that "detestable kind of monks

who are . . . as soft . . . as lead; their law is the desire for self-gratification: whatever enters their minds or appeals to them, that they call holy" (RB1).

Still, the **Rule** does not govern the entire spiritual horizon of monks; it is not the last or the only word. Doubtless it considers itself indispensable, but regards itself only as a beginning, in other words, as the indispensable *point of departure*. The **Rule** does not embrace the whole of perfection; it is only a "minimum Rule which we have written for beginners," a starting point for those who strive for perfection (RB 73). It tends to lead the life of the Gospel fully; for this it is a first step on the way (RB Prol.), a way that leads to other, greater incarnations of the Good News: the Desert Masters, the patristic writers and the entire monastic tradition. All this stands between the good Word of God itself and our finite experience, in order to unite the two.

As a point of departure the **Rule** occasionally appears harsh and uncompromising. Still that characteristic is not, at least according to the **Rule,** to be ascribed to itself, but rather to the weakness of those who want to follow it. They have only to endure these hard things; because he who misses the beginning misses everything. The **Rule** is the "narrow" starting point, which obliges the monk always to advance further, so that the heart becomes enlarged, and what at first was confining later becomes progressively easier, because the human heart itself widens. The "narrow" beginning of the Prologue (" . . . do not be at once dismayed and fly from the way of salvation, whose entrance cannot but be narrow") is identical with "the rudiments of the religious life" in the final chapter of the **Rule** (RB 73). For those who have advanced, the **Rule** is only a minimum which leads to what the theologians of the monastic life have demonstrated: the way of unceasing prayer, conformity with Jesus Christ, all-embracing love.

The "fulfillment" of this point of departure consists in faithfulness to this **Rule** by trying to fathom the mystery of God, by drinking again and again at the fountain of the patristic commentators on Sacred Scripture. This means that faithfulness to the **Rule** is possible only by tirelessly drawing on the authentic tradition. It may be remarked in passing that at the present time there exists a tendency of being satisfied with secondary literature and a multiform but superficial kind of piety. If a monk confines himself to that sort of thing, he will necessarily lose in depth and, despite external observance, not be faithful to the **Rule.** There must be an inner conviction not only to live this **Rule,** but also to advance in the direction of greater reverence, more profound silence, more intensive prayer, more perfect conformity. The observance of the **Rule** is only a beginning, the door to something "beyond"—and St. Benedict wants to stress this perspective. Hence a monk must not be satisfied with the *Rule;* he should not concede that the observance of the *Rule* sets a limit to his own religious ambitions. As observance, waiting at table is a form of fraternal love; it leads to that love, makes a beginning of it possible; but it is not the end or goal of fraternal love. Similarly, the Divine Office, as observance, is not the ultimate. It leads to unceasing prayer, and the monk may never dispense himself from striving for that unceasing prayer. Only with a view to the maintenance and deepening of this effort does the *Rule* itself permit changes in its observance (cf. RB 18.40).

Basic Values in the Rule of St. Bendict[1]

What are the basic values, expressed or implied, in the **Rule of St. Benedict?** This much is clear: The *Rule* wants to engender a definite basic *attitude,* a definite *model,* giving life and support to the observances of the monastic life. By the words "basic values" we do not mean the shape that the monastic life assumes (in this sense the Divine Office is not a basic value), but the fundamental attitude from which the life proceeds.

The choice of basic values naturally brings something arbitrary with it. This becomes evident when various attempts in this regard are compared. The result is not always the same, because it is dependent on the usually hidden convictions of the one making the choice. Dom Victor Dammertz distinguishes the following: *ordo, discretio, stabilitas,* humility and peace.[2] Father H. Arts, S.J., comes to a different conclusion; he cites: vocation, listening, definite commitment, concern for humanity, humility and meditation.[3] In his book, *Vie monastique selon St. Benoît,* Dom P. Miquel again has different terms,[4] while the older commentaries of Dom P. Delatte or Dom I. Herwegen present other categories.

We would like to add our own melody to this illustrious choir of learned voices and distinguish four basic values:

—a sense of the subjective;

—an appreciation of horizontal relationships;

—humility;

—"discreet observance," that is, fidelity to the observance, with accommodations.

a) *Sense of the Subjective*

Repeatedly Benedict stresses the interior attitude which should govern the monk's activity. In other words, in the *Rule* the emphasis is not on *what* monks do (must do), but on *how* they do (must do) it.

Here are several examples: In the chapter on the porter in the *Rule of the Master* we find all sorts of prescriptions for those entrusted with the care of the door: They are not only to open and close, they are also to inform the abbot, lock the door whenever they go for reading in the cloister or when the bell rings for Office; besides their duties at the door, they should also perform some other work, care for the horses and dogs, keep the porter's lodge clean and care for the night illumination (RM 95).

Benedict orders things quite differently. True, the porter is to open the door, but not without further ado. He should do so, "with all meekness inspired by the fear of God" and respond to visitors "with the warmth of charity" (RB 66). Benedict really does not say anything more; he is concerned about the interior attitude with which the porter carries out his duties. The personality of the official, a spiritual portrait, is limited, and personal responsibility is stressed. We might almost say: Benedict believes that a good interior attitude by itself leads to the correct fulfillment of a task.

In this connection we may consider Benedict's concept of obedience, particularly in the case where a monk is ordered to do something impossible (RB 68). The *Rule of the Master* simply threatens sanctions for the disobedient monk; besides, it considers obedience purely from the standpoint of the superior (RM 7, 57). St. Benedict insinuates himself, as it were, into the skin of the monk and asks, "*How* shall the monk handle the good of obedience when it becomes difficult for him?" Then he describes both the interior and the exterior attitude, that is, the *manner* in which the monk should receive an order, the *manner* in which he may manifest his own desires, the *manner* in which he ought to treat authority and the bearer of authority. Thus the relationship between abbot and monk is humanized. Doubtless obedience is demanded, but it becomes a common concern (RB 68), and the abbot is asked to see whether, in fact, something is *subjectively* impossible for the monk.

We see a similar sensitivity for the subjective in connection with obedience in Chapter 71. While the *Rule of the Master* lays emphasis on the *objective* content of the order, St. Benedict looks upon obedience as a *subjective* good. In his view obedience is a good not only because *something* is demanded, no matter what it be, but because it is good to be submissive in love to one another, and because it is good to make oneself the servant of all, as Jesus did. The Master's great concern for the maintenance of order here yields to make room for concern for souls.

Hence a sense for the subjective is the first basic value of the **Rule of St. Benedict.** And it is something we must carefully nurture in ourselves. As was said above, the *Rule* presents itself as indispensable. Still it imposes on the monks the obligation to find the motivation for their actions in their own hearts. It emphasizes that external compliance does not suffice; it wants to lead to an inner commitment, so that the monk personally consents to what is done externally; it demands that the monks as persons grow interiorly from what they conceive the **Rule** to be. External observance of the **Rule** does not suffice; monks must give themselves interiorly, embracing the basic attitude that animated Jesus Christ.

If we draw this line farther, we behold in Benedict a great concern for the personality of the monk, also, in its limits, an understanding of the differences in people and a reverence for them. Hence the saying, "Monks as like as peas in a pod," is certainly not Benedictine. This shows itself in Benedict's view of the abbot. In the **Rule** the abbot is more or less a composite of the spiritual Desert tradition, the head of the Christian community and the head of the house according to the law then in vogue. He gives instruction to the community, supplies spiritual guidance and also regulates the material side of life. Contrary to the *Rule of the Master,* Benedict strongly emphasizes the authority of the abbot by leaving many details to his judgment. Father de Vogüé puts it as follows, "The written law must give place to the living authority of the person. The lawgiver draws back and permits the abbot to act."[5]

Two examples: " . . . let the abbot appoint brethren on whose manner of life and character he can rely; and let him, *as he shall judge to be expedient,* consign the various articles to them" (RB 32). And in accommodating clothing to the climate, St. Benedict says, "This is to be taken into consideration by the abbot" (RB 55).

In certain ways Benedict's **Rule** gives more power to the abbot than the *Rule of the Master:* it emphasizes strongly the cases in which the abbot, in accordance with the **Rule,** must use his own judgment. On the other hand, while stressing the autority of the abbot, the **Rule of St. Benedict** becomes more humane. Contrary to the *Rule of the Master,* the abbot is obliged to seek advice: " . . . let the abbot consider prudently" (RB 61) or ask "the counsel of God-fearing brethren" (RB 65). In this light the order in the community receives its significance (RB 63). The *Rule of the Master* abolishes all rank in the monastery. Benedict again introduces an order among the monks, but at the same time warns that "the abbot must not disturb the flock committed to him, nor by arbitrary use of his power ordain anything unjustly" (RB 63). And when Benedict insists that monks do not call one another by their simple names, but use a correct form of address, he at the same time wishes to prevent the abbot, by virtue of his office, from becoming too familiar with his monks, and in this way seeks to prevent him from falling into a domineering attitude, jealousy and injustice (RB 27,

65). For Benedict is always concerned with the monk's salvation, and for that reason the abbot must be careful about it as well as about the quality of the interior life of those committed to his care.

In a word, a care for the subjective is the first basic value of Benedict's **Rule.** Not *what* the monk does is of primary importance, but rather the *manner* in which he does it. Hence the individuality of the monk must be kept in view, considering what is or is not possible for him. This concern must be exercised above all by the abbot and his officials (for example, the cellarer—RB 31). For this reason Benedict's **Rule**—quite unlike that of the Master—emphatically asks that the abbot keep his own weaknesses ever in mind.

b) *An Appreciation of Horizontal Relationships*

The second basic value of Benedict's **Rule** is closely connected with the preceding one: a sense for horizontal relationships, for relationships among the brethren. This becomes very evident when we again compare the **Rule** of Benedict with that of the Master, particularly in the way in which they regard the abbot.

In the *Rule of the Master* a close vertical bond exists between the abbot and the monks. The monastery is a school in which one learns the service of the Lord. In this school the abbot stands forth as "teacher" (*magister et doctor*). He alone is that! In other words, the monastic community is an educational establishment, a pedagogical milieu, which finds its basis in the individual relationship between the abbot as teacher and the monk as "disciple." The community evolves from this relationship: it is a community of individuals who, as it were, accidentally happen to be disciples under the same abbot at a given time. It forms a circle with the abbot at its center. For the monks the abbot symbolizes God's unique Fatherhood.

This central position of the abbot in the *Rule of the Master* manifests itself in the emphasis on obedience toward the abbot as a decisive element in the education to which the monk submits. Poverty on the part of the monk is closely linked to this obedience; for where the monk submits unconditionally to the guidance of a teacher, there also material things may not be excluded from the educational relationship. As a consequence, in the *Rule of the Master* any order or rank among the monks is abolished, apart from competition among individuals striving with one another for perfection under the guidance of the abbot. Of horizontal relationships there is no word.

St. Benedict sees the situation quite differently. First, he emphasizes strongly that, apart from the educational relationship between abbot and monk, there must be another: that of love, a relationship between person and person. The monk must relate to the superior not only by external obedience, but by that which essentially characterizes the human person; and the abbot, in all actions and commands, must constantly keep in mind the personality of the monk. Secondly, Benedict again introduces a definite order among the members of the community, an order that basically is a prolongation of the abbot-teacher and the monk-disciple relationship. Older monks receive the title which traditionally was reserved to the abbot, namely, *nonnus*—reverend father. The younger monks are to obey not only the abbot, but also the elders (RB 71). This mutual obedience is hierarchical in character! The elders are warned—as Benedict also warns the abbot—not to abuse this hierarchical order (RB 70), although all of them share in the educational function of the abbot.

But there is more. Apart from the common educational responsibility, Benedict is interested in mutual relationships. He desires these to be permeated with genuine love. In this connection, Chapter 72, "The Good Zeal of Monks," is important. This chapter is Benedict's original creation. Here, as in the *Rule of the Master,* zeal is stressed. Yet it is not the individual zeal of surpassing one another in the observance of the ***Rule,*** but the zeal—and every monk should possess it—of all in common striving for a common goal, Christ, "and may he bring us all together to life everlasting" (RB 72). The external competition of the *Rule of the Master* becomes interiorized (care for the subjective) and simultaneously joined to the relationships among the monks. Of course, these relationships are organized (RB 63), but again they are viewed as relative (RB 71, 62), as only *one* aspect of the monks' journey to God. This dimension of mutuality, together with the traditional components, belongs to the monastic way of life. One is (or becomes) a monk by showing oneself a person, that is, in love, to other persons as reverent, patient, willing and selfless (RB 72). For Benedict the community is not only an educational milieu in which individuals strive to attain perfection; it is a community of persons who are bound together in love and *in* this common bond follow the Lord. In other words, the community as "a school for the Lord's service" (RB Prol) in its deepest sense is a community in which Christ is recognized as *the* way, *the* truth and *the* life not only in the abbot but in *everyone* of the monks. The entire process of monastic asceticism is colored by this mutual love. Whoever has it possesses everything; whoever (still) does not have it—even though they carry out the observance perfectly—must still begin. For *the* great observance is the observance of love without limits.

c) *Humility*

In all that the monks do, they must keep in mind the subjective and the horizontal elements. But with that, little or nothing is said about what really makes a monk. Here the concept of *humility* becomes important. It is

simply the key word to the entire spirituality of St. Benedict. For this reason Chapter 7 is the chapter richest in content, the chapter that specifically describes the way of the monk. For, as we said above, the ***Rule*** wants to lead the monk by way of the first two basic elements to love without limits (cf. Chap. 7). Now, love is self-abasement. Genuine love is conformity with the Lord in all things, a meeting with the Lord in everyone and everything. From the Gospels we know that the Lord showed his love for us by humbling himself, and in this way he came close to all of us (Phil 2:7-8).

Humility is a word which indicates that the monks oblige themselves by their lives to the following of Christ, and for that reason dedicate themselves to self-abasement. Hence humility signifies obedience, patience, self-denial, selfless submission, economic dependence. Not as if these things were ends in themselves, but because they are prerequisites for genuine love and are its marks. True love is shown essentially by the free acceptance of and assent to the fact that others dispose of our lives. Exactly that was revealed in Christ. He despoiled himself of everything, became a brother to all, allowed others to dispose of him to the extent that he willed to give his life for them.

Benedict sees this love as the basis and final goal of the monk's life. Both externally and internally one must strive to grow in this love. Without such striving one cannot speak of a monk's life. It is identical with "truly seeking God" (RB 58), seeking after the true God. Genuine seeking after the true God is not an intellectual pursuit, not a growth in theological insight. Fundamentally it means not to be scandalized by the manner in which he revealed himself, not to be scandalized by the ways he chooses. Genuine seeking after the true God means not to turn away from the ways in which God manifests himself as the God of humanity. If St. John says that God is love (1 Jn 4:8), in other words, that wherever love happens there God "happens," this must be understood in the light of the pronouncement of Paul which was alluded to before: love is humility, humility is love. Thus love and humility proceed from the same source and they have the same origin, namely, God.

What has been said hitherto may be formulated as follows: St. Benedict intends to further the quality of life. He desires that the monk do everything in the best manner possible and live as a simple, integrated person (first basic value). Further, he wants the monk to function as a community being, equally whole and simple (second basic value). As a dedicated person the monk meets our Lord. Still St. Benedict also understands that a monk can only be such a dedicated person if true love resides in the heart. True love is not feeling, not being overwhelmed by emotion, not a condition of constant ecstasy. True love has something to do with

God, is an expression of God's being. Love is only genuine when it makes the true God externally visible, if it makes him "happen," if it seeks to travel paths he himself trod: humbly, in selfless service of others, with unconcern for self, patiently and simply. For this reason—it is important to understand this—monks must possess humility toward themselves, must be able to love themselves as poor members of the Body of Christ, of that Body through which the genuine love of the true God appeared in human form. True love is something entirely human: to look upon oneself with compassion and to associate with others in a selfless manner, without the common pretenses, such as ideas of grandeur, false modesty or being governed by the passions. St. Benedict desires that the love of 1 Jn 4, Jn 13 and Phil 2 constitute the heart of the monastery and form the basic condition of every individual monk.

d) *"Discreet Observance"—Fidelity to the Observance, with Accommodations*

Finally, "discreet observance" is the fourth basic value in the **Rule of St. Benedict.** In order to show what is meant by these two words, reference may be made to what was said above regarding the way in which the **Rule** presents itself. It was discovered that on the one hand the **Rule** regards itself as indispensable and therefore imposes a certain rigor; but on the other hand it was also seen that the **Rule** is to be transcended and that consequently it is relative. Hence, in the **Rule** we have an emphasis on observances and yet a relativity regarding them. Therefore, as the fourth value we have two contradictory words: discreet "observatism," that is, fidelity to the observance, but with spiritual accommodation.

Stress is laid on the observances; they are emphatically imposed and strictly prescribed, as for example: The extremely severe attitude with regard to "the vice of private property" (RB 34, 54, 55); the strong prohibition of "idle talk" (RB 4, 6, 8); the emphasis on silence at table (RB 38), at night (RB 42) or in the cloister (RB 67). In matters that I might call "the pivots of the monastic life" (contacts with other monks, with the world outside, with possessions) St. Benedict is strict. Here *ordo,* a holy discipline, comes strikingly to the fore. Fear of God, reverent adoration of God's holiness and humility manifest themselves in "faithful service," in an upright, loyal observance.

Thus we come to the eighth degree of humility, where the monk does only what the Rule of the monastery and the example of the seniors prescribe (RB 7). The monk here disregards self, considering solely the practice of the written Rule as it is lived. Thus it becomes possible for the many in the monastery still to observe one and the same order. In this manner the individual monk can be assumed into the community by means of the observances and still be preserved from a competitive spirit and the mania of making an impression by external conduct. Observance and the order it guarantees form the backbone of the community (cf. RB 63).

But that is not all. Observance is to be discreet, that is, it should be seen together with the charism of every individual, because a mutual relationship exists between the form of life that is lived and the love that is sought. Love—also the true love which seeks after the true God—needs a form, namely, observances and interior conversion, because man is composed of body and soul. No one can live by feelings alone; besides, they are too abstract. The interior element—the love that is humility—is sought through externals and by means of externals: dedication to the Work of God, the concrete practice of silence and persistence in holy reading, the practice of personal prayer, seeking for solitude and sobriety. In that manner a person gives himself to God. And so, through these externals, one is formed, liberated, purified and interiorized. Fidelity to externals may prevent a person from going astray internally. Benedict says that a certain severity is necessary in order to preserve the soul and to persist in love (RB Prol). Some severity is also required to keep the community alive. If monks begin to wallow in their own experiences, they separate from one another and splinter the community, for inner experiences cannot be bound together except by means of forms and institutions. If people are intent solely on their own experiences, the important aspect of their life-parameters—the sense for horizontal relationships—gets lost, and the individual withdraws into his own shell. Then personal emotions become the "rule." Anyone who has lived more than three weeks in community knows that no rule ever becomes so hard and binding as that which one has created on the basis of feelings.

Still, with a view to what is "farther" and "beyond," the observance may be surpassed. Here surpassing means nothing else than this: within the framework of the monastic life the wide field of a humble love without limits presents itself. This framework no longer sets any goals to be attained, but offers a springboard to greater divestment of self, to ever more intense prayer, to an evergrowing concern for the welfare of the brethren. And then the God who is love itself will indicate to the monk how to walk; he points to the observances and gives discernment as to what is essential in them.

What Does "According to the Rule*" Mean?*[6]

We might have spoken very optimistically about the power of the **Rule,** about the significant place it occupies in the life of the monk and about its formative character. Yet, in many respects, the **Rule** cannot be followed literally today. And that holds true not only for matters that are clearly of secondary importance, but precisely of such as the **Rule** itself regards as essential. Here are a few examples: no longer is everything subject to the abbot's judgment, but in some cases the decision is left to the community (cf. RB 3); usually the Psalter is no longer recited within a week (RB 18); monks occupy individual cells (RB 22); a great moderation of the fast and abstinence from flesh-meat has come into vogue (cf. RB 41). How are such things to be judged? How can one know whether these changes are in accord with the *Rule* or not?

In a general way two extreme attitudes exist regarding these questions.[7] First there is the concept: the literal observance of the *Rule* leads to important experiences. This implies that one must remain faithful to the letter of the *Rule* in order to follow the path of the spiritual experiences of St. Benedict. Spirit and letter, content and form, cannot be separated. The Divine gives itself only through *these* observances, and becomes palpable, experienced only in the letter. Dom de Vogüé says quite simply, "Apart from the practice of definite observances, the spirit of St. Benedict is only a word." Hence the necessity of abiding by the letter. In other words, observances produce their own light; the monk must abide by them in order later to see the light which is in them.

Opposed to this is the second attitude: St. Benedict was concerned about handing on an inspiration. Benedict did this in forms accommodated to his time—culturally, socially and economically. The forms must be sacrificed in order to liberate the inspiration found in them and to prevent the letter from killing the spirit that wants to incarnate itself in contemporary monachism. When times change (as they have in the past fifteen centuries), a form bound to a particular era may suffocate inspiration. Not even Dom de Vogüé would insist that children be "offered" to the monastery (cf. RB 59). The modern age simply does not tolerate such a practice.

It is obvious that these two concepts are mutually exclusive. Still, both want to remain faithful to the *Rule,* want to embrace the *Rule* as norm and guide of life. An example may illustrate this dilemma—if it is a dilemma. The monk's life seeks to observe solitude in a definite manner. Now, does one arrive at solitude by following the observances with a certain literalness, or do not the forms prescribed by Benedict rather hinder a genuine (experience of) solitude in favor of a pseudo-solitude? Or consider this: St. Benedict wants to lead his monks to a true life of poverty; they are not to possess anything and should be satisfied with the least. Does one attain this by following his rules, or does one not rather become mired in an unreal bourgeois world in which one has everything—without so-called ownership? Or take this case: Is separation from the world really accomplished if monks follow the *Rule* literally? Or does it not rather demand a sincere turning away from the world of the rich, from a bourgeois

mentality, from economic conformism? The problem is clear: Must the *Rule* be accepted as a literal norm, or must one go beyond the *Rule* in order to remain faithful to it? In other words, must monks do what St. Benedict says, or must they do what he would have said in our situation?

Doubtless it was Benedict's intention to create a framework by means of which monks might become free spirits, a framework that clearly should stand at the edge of the social structure. This last observation means that Benedict intended to prescribe a life style in which socially endangered values (reading, prayer, human relationships and so on) would expressly find their place with a view to the spiritual growth of the monks. Thereby the monks are to become free, spiritual persons, free for contact with the living God, free for the joys and the difficulties of life in a group, free with regard to material things. In the *Rule* the following can be discerned: In the first place it assigns a certain priority to the framework (for the sake of freedom, one must accept tradition); then it shows that this alone leads to interior experience; thirdly, it is made clear that only fidelity to the end by way of struggle, sorrow and disappointment leads to final freedom.

But the other side of the coin is just as clear: imitation, of itself, does not mean freedom. Forms can lead a life of their own, which, as it were, bypass the soul of the monk. They may represent mere window dressing. By imposing the old forms one may lead people to bypass life, and that, as the problem of the place of the monastery in today's world shows, has happened in one way or another. While insisting on forms, monks may be shielded against the risk of life and the Holy Spirit. This may lead to a certain superficiality, the result of identifying with a pre-existing scheme of thought and life; it obliges monks to dwell in an oasis not conducive to spiritual growth, where they must maintain the status quo at all costs. And that can never have been the intention of the *Rule*!

So again the question: What does "to live according to the *Rule*" mean? In the following I shall treat, only in passing, five important points that must be borne in mind in any discussion about the relevance of the *Rule,* its letter and its spirit.

In the first place, an enthusiasm, an eagerness, for the monastic life is presupposed. By this I mean to say: Everyone at one time experienced a calling, a vocation, to be a monk, a vocation to live exclusively for God, a vocation to live by prayer both personal *and* communal, a vocation to "leave" (be it a position, the "world," particular relationships and so on), a vocation to live from an interior source. This calling is the true mystery of the monk's life. In the course of the years it may have changed, been buried, covered over, but it is and remains the heart of the monastic life.

I repeat, there must exist *enthusiasm,* a definite commitment, a certain glowing zeal, to progress farther on the way—the way of prayer, of living for God. Hence there must also be a zeal for the great constitutive elements of the monk's life: Sacred Scripture, silence, a degree of solitude, moderation in all things. If this enthusiasm suffers, all these forms degenerate into restraints, limitations of freedom. Every observance becomes a burden; it remains purely external, and the feeling arises, "Is *that* also forbidden?" Our life becomes worldly, and the **Rule** no longer plays a role or at the most is looked upon as an outdated book of etiquette, and the question, "What does it mean 'to live according to the **Rule**'?" becomes irrelevant. In such a situation monks live only according to their transient desires.

Something of this attitude always lurks around the corner as a danger which manifests itself in the *fear* to try new, vitalizing, demanding ways, in a *violent* defense of positions and functions that were once embraced, and in a rigid reference to *tradition.* No; enthusiasm is demanded, above all enthusiasm to walk the way of the life of God--with heart and soul, fearlessly, with imagination and with fidelity.

In the second place, fidelity to the *basic inspiration of the* **Rule** is required. This basic inspiration I presented above in the four basic values: a sense for the subjective, a sense for horizontal relationships, striving for humility and love, discreet observance. Monks must ask themselves sincerely: What role do these basic values play in my life? Am I really concerned about bettering my attitude qualitatively in all that I do? In my concrete decisions, if there is a choice in the work I am to perform, in the relationships I foster within and without the monastery, in my hobbies and so on, does a great concern for the **Rule** play a predominant part, namely, do I see something of the living God in the faces of my community? Or, by defensively and fearfully clinging to the past, do I seek to go my own way and live in my own world? Do I try to serve? Am I available to others? And lastly, regarding the rules that are actually in force in the monastery, do I resist or exercise a minimal and niggardly sort of compliance? Or do I generously follow them, without constantly nibbling away at the edges?

By now this should be clear: before one can ask about concrete points, whether this or that is really in accordance with the **Rule,** the question must be answered by practice in life. Am I faithful in a magnanimous way to the four basic values of the **Rule?** If someone seeks to bypass them, then all the talk about changes in observance, about *aggior-namento* and so on, becomes an unholy, nitpicking attempt at justification through rationalization.

In the third place, it is necessary to have reverence for forms. The monastic life-framework exists to *attract* people, not to *force* them. It is there to lead to an inner experience. The manner in which we treat the framework also characterizes the way we consider our own inner experiences; care for externals reflects our care for the inner element, and the solicitude with which we treat rules and forms gives an idea as to how we regard our vocation. On the other hand, the framework must give witness to an intensive inner life, for without culture there is no soul, and without a soul there is no culture.

Fourthly, and only on the basis of the above three points may one ask, *What is in accordance with the* **Rule** *at the present time?* The **Rule** may never be interpreted in such a way that it disappears. Naturally, it cannot be handled like a yardstick which one applies to life, so that as a result one can say, "This is and that is not in accordance with the **Rule.**" What, then, are we to do? Now, the **Rule** must prove its authenticity; it must be viable. Every interpretation must be able to be lived as a viable witness to the basic values of the monastic life. In other words, every interpretation that actually leads away from humility, discreet observance, a sense for the subjective, and for horizontal relationships, is a false, worthless interpretation *not in accordance with the* **Rule** and consequently untrue. Naturally, interpretations must not be made on an individual basis; the **Rule** is also the bond that binds the monks together. Hence a decision must be made by the community, must be the result of an exchange of views in which everyone is respected by reason of the mystery of one's vocation, by reason of one's relationship to God. Further, this criterion must be observed: Every interpretation that would bypass the vocation of (one of) the members of the community, that would show too little reverence for it, is a worthless interpretation and hence not in accord with the **Rule.** Validity presupposes solidarity. In other words, whether one lives according to the **Rule** (correctly or not) depends also on whether one lives with others regarding the basic values. And that includes the possibility of diversity of views, but always with reverence for one another.

Finally, the fifth point. The **Rule** is *a rule for life.* In a certain sense the **Rule** is in danger of disappearing as a norm of life. And here I return to its absolute and progressive character. It is a **Rule** that wants to urge us "farther," "beyond," to more intensive prayer, more fruitful reading, more eloquent silence, a more humane community. Every interpretation which, from the community standpoint, leads toward that goal is valid. But for that, it is also required that we read the **Rule** by directing one eye to the text and the other to our life, reverently, with a readiness to listen, with a practical sense, and with the desire truly to leave everything in order finally to experience God himself.

Notes

[1] Basic values: in order to limit the notes in this section, the following works of A. de Vogüé are listed and freely cited: *La communauté et l'abbé dans la Règle de Saint Benoît* (Brugge 1966); *La Règle du Maître*, 3 vols. (Paris 1964-65); *La Règle de Saint Benoît,* 7 vols. (Paris 1971-77).

[2] In *Benedictijns Tijdschrift* (1980) pp. 46-47.

[3] *Ibid.,* pp. 53-65.

[4] *La Vie monastique selon Saint Benoît* (Paris 1979) pp. 187-212.

[5] *La Règle de Saint Benoît* I:57.

[6] Cf. A. Zegveld, "Wat wil zeggen: volgens de regel?" in *Monastieke Informatie* 56 (1978) 79-106, translated in *Collectanea Cisterciensia* 41 (1979) 157-76, under the title "Que veut dire: selon la Règle?" What I discussed there is not repeated here.

[7] Here I am reliant on A. de Vogüé, "S. Benoît aujourd'hui. La vie monastique et son aggiornamento" in *Nouveau Revue Theologique* (1978) pp. 720-33; and A. Veilleux, "Le rôle de la sous-culture monastique dans la formation du moines" in NRT (1978) pp. 734-49.

Benedicta Ward (essay date 1981)

SOURCE: "The Miracles of St. Benedict" in *Benedictus: Studies in Honor of St. Benedict of Nursia,* edited by E. Rozanne Elder, Cistercian Publications, 1981, pp. 1-14.

[*In the following essay, Ward investigates accounts and changing conceptions of the miracles associated with St. Benedict.*]

'One day when the brethren of this monastery were quarreling, one of them met St Benedict outside the door and the saint immediately gave him this command: "Go and tell the brethren that they give me no rest. I am leaving this house and let them know that I shall not return until I bring from Aquitaine a man who shall be after my own heart." '[1] The place is the abbey of St Benoît-sur-Loire at Fleury; the man from Aquitaine Odo of Cluny, the reforming abbot called in to deal with that turbulent house; and when the monk met St Benedict in the cloister, the father of monasticism had been dead for about four hundred years. It is a story with many layers of interest, and one which provides an entrance into the later tradition about St

Benedict of Nursia. Here there is a monastery being refounded in France after the Norse invasions, a rough, undisciplined group who, as the writer says, 'had been scattered far and wide through fear of the enemy,' and were 'now united in body but divided in heart. The turbulence of society is reflected in the cloister and the level of comprehension of the monks is further illustrated by the fact that when they were told that St Benedict had left them, 'they did not have recourse to prayers and tears . . . but getting on their horses they rode hither and thither to find him and bring him back by force.' John of Salerno, the writer of this life of Odo of Cluny, scorns such a literal reaction; he is a monk of the spiritualizing tradition of Gregory the Great himself, and he tells the story as a vivid image of the place of St Benedict as the peace-maker within the community of monks, 'those who choose the narrow way . . . so that not living by their own will and obeying their own desires and passions, but walking by anothers judgement and orders, they dwell in monasteries and desire to have an abbot over them.'[2] But the reaction of the monks was not by any means unusual in tenth century Europe; the location of the saints was taken very literally indeed, and the relationship men made with them differed little if at all from their human relationships. If a great lord withdrew his patronage, it was only reasonable to go and force him to return to his duties if you could.

But what was St Benedict, the father of monks, the *advocatus monachorum* to do with Fleury anyway? What has Odo of Cluny to say in the matter? Why start so far away from St Benedict's own monastery in Italy, when he himself seems to have left it so rarely? Cluny, Fleury, Monte Cassino: one of the links between them is undoubtedly the miracles of St Benedict, that tradition of signs and wonders which is there in the first account by Saint Gregory the Great and continues for many centuries elsewhere. I propose to examine briefly some miracles connected with the name of St Benedict in order to see what insight can be gained from such material.

First of all there are the miracles of St Benedict which are related by St Gregory in the second book of the *Dialogues*. These claim to be miracles connected with the life of St Benedict; they are presented as his *res gesta,* what St Benedict did when he was alive. Now there are two aspects for comment here about such an account. The first is the purpose of the account; it was specifically written for the edification and encouragement of the reader; the second is that it is not a biography but a hagiography. These are stories which above all link the saint with the scriptural tradition of sanctity; the miracles validate St Benedict, they place him in the main stream of christian witness: 'I will tell you about the miracles of the venerable man Benedict, *in praise of the Redeemer.*'[3] So we find that St Benedict brings water from the rock, like Moses; he makes iron float like Elisha; he causes Marus to walk on the water like St Peter; ravens who feed him recall the feeding of Elijah in the wilderness; like David, he grieves at the death of an enemy. He possesses, comments Peter, the interlocutor in the *Dialogues,* 'the spirit of all the just'; but St Gregory as the narrator corrects him, 'Benedict' he says 'possessed the spirit of one man only, the Saviour, who fills the hearts of the faithful.'[4] Such miracles are related for a specific purpose; they are not the accidental deeds of a good man, they are the miracles of a saint. They link him with the wonders God showed through his predecessors, as an authentic saint of God, and above all, as St Gregory says, they give to his life the only test of christian sanctity, the likeness to Christ.

The miracles of St Benedict in the *Dialogues* of St Gregory can be discussed in many ways, but this hagiographical dimension is fundamental to them. They are not primarily intended as an account of the actions of the man Benedict (though that is not to say that they weren't). They are about holiness of life in a christian context. They are, for instance, about man restored to his right relationship in control of the natural world—a broken dish mended, a man walking on water, a thunderstorm obedient to a woman's prayers. They are about insight so profound that it pierces the clouds that divide men from one another, so that they are known for what they are, and a servant cannot be mistaken for a king, nor can Exhilaratus take even a sip of wine undetected. It is about that understanding of the vision of God that sees the whole of creation in a ray of the sun. And it is about the battle with the demons, a fight so central to the monastic life that it becomes visible in images and sounds: the demons shout and rage, they even sit on a stone to prevent it from forming part of the house of God; like a dragon coiled round the monastery, the devil lay outside the walls, and the sight of him was shock treatment enough for any monk who turned away in discouragement.

I do not wish to be misunderstood here. I am not saying that these stories are literary fictions of no consequence. I mean that the truth they embody and are designed to convey are more subtle and important than a simplistic reading of the narrative suggests. The images used to denote Christian sanctity are loaded with resonance and meaning and they are equally at the disposal of writer, of observers, and of the saints themselves. This is not an easy point to make clear but it has something to do with the fact that one apprehends realities through the images at ones disposal and not otherwise. We need a way of perceiving in order to see, and especially we need a way of writing in order to convey our understanding. To say that an image is a type, that it is there in similar stories, that it is found in previous accounts, does not mean that it can be dismissed, as if we had found out the writer in the act of copying from his neighbour in class; the reso-

nances, the previous meaning, the allusion, is precisely what the writer wishes us to discover. The images are a lens, a telescope through which we view reality in its long perspective. For instance when the death of St Benedict is described in terms of light, brightness, and a road towards the east, this echoes not only his own vision of 'the whole world gathered in a single ray of light,'[5] it also contains all the echoes of heaven in the Scriptures, and most of all the stories of the resurrection of Christ, as it is meant to do. This man, they tell us, is dead and alive unto God in Christ: 'the tomb of Christ who is risen, the glory of Jesus' resurrection' still exists as the gate and entrance into heaven and the images tell us far more than any amount of argument can.

St Gregory presents St Benedict as the *vir dei,* the man of God before all else. It is an ideal of holiness set in a scriptural pattern and it is presented for edification: imitation of virtues, not amazement at wonders is Gregory's purpose. The miracles of St Benedict are the climax of St Gregory's description of the true christian man, whose virtues have made him so like Christ that the wonders and signs of the life of the new Adam flow again in the world through his life and actions.

Later, the second book of the *Dialogues* became in itself one of the great patterns for accounts of sanctity. Again and again in the Middle Ages saints' lives are modelled on either the *Life of St Benedict,* or the *Life of St Antony,* or the *Life of St Martin.* They become authenticating patterns, just as they themselves found authentication in the scriptures. For instance, when St Anselm strikes water from the rock at Liberi, his biographer has in mind not only Moses but also St Benedict;[6] when iron floats at Monte Cassino, the reference is to both Elijah and to St Benedict.[7] Odo of Cluny delivered from an accident at sea, recalls to his biographer 'what Peter and Paul and then our father Benedict had previously merited.'[8] The curious habit of receiving food from birds afflicted not only Elijah and Benedict but their successors, such as Cuthbert of Lindisfarne. The first account of St Benedict then is no simple record of events, but a highly sophisticated piece of theological writing.

But what became of this image of St Benedict in later accounts of him, above all in stories told after his death? For the Middle Ages had no doubt that a saint continues his work after his death; he is in fact more alive unto God and therefore more powerful and more accessible to men. The long tradition of northern Europe centres on the graves of the dead, on their relics, their dead bodies. Devotion in the early Middle Ages north of the Mediterranean could be called almost exclusively a thaumaturgy of the dead. Now the dead have one advantage over the living which gives them at once a popularity which is unique: they are dead, and they cannot answer back. If you consult a Simon Stylites, or an Antony, or a Macarius, you encounter a living person, whose replies are his own and not shaped by your predilections. You say, 'Father, speak a word to me' and you may be disconcerned, to say the least, by a reply listing your most private and secret faults and suggesting some practical remedies: 'Poemen said to Isaac, "Let go of a small part of your righteousness and in a few days you will be at peace."[9] 'Blessed Symeon said to Batacos, "for what reasons have you come here?" Batacos said, "I hope to transact business and bow before the feet of your holiness." "Wretched man," replied Symeon, "you don't mention that you are really here to act against Gelasios the man of God; go and ask to pardon at once." '[10]

St Benedict himself had not always in his lifetime been a comfort to his petitioners: 'he warned them to curb their sharp tongues and added that he would have them excommunicated if they did not.'[11] But go to the tomb of a dead saint and you have a quite different kind of freedom. You shape your requests, and by and large you hear the reply that your mind and imagination suggests to you. The stories of the posthumous miracles of the saints may reflect some aspects of the original tradition created around the living man, but ninety-nine percent of the time they reflect nothing of the kind. They are the reflection of an age, the record of the needs, sorrows, ambitions and ideals of each generation, each person, who experiences the contact with the dead. As such these collected stories of the miracles of the saints provide historical material of an unparalleled value. It is not the part of a historian, of course, to assess the supernatural value or content of such tales; but what he has to accept is the value given to them by medieval men and the vital role they actually played in their world. Once that is said, there are in these records glimpses of that person who is so rarely heard of as to be virtually unknown and inaudible, the medieval man in the street, or rather, the medieval monk in his cloister, since it was the monks who were the guardians of the relics and the recorders of the miracles. One does not expect to find out anything at all about St Benedict from such records; but one can see in a bewildering kaleidoscope of material what generation after generation made of him.

Let us look at two such records. First there are the *Miracles of St Benedict,* written under that title by Desiderius, abbot of Monte Cassino, in the second half of the eleventh century in Italy at St Benedict's own monastery. The account is in three books, and in form it follows the pattern of the *Dialogues* of St Gregory; there is an interlocutor, Theophilus in place of Peter, who encourages the discourse with his questions and comments. The intention of the writer is similar to that of St Gregory: to show the action of God among contemporaries for the encouragement of faith.[12] As well as the similarity in form and intention between the two

accounts, there are close parallels between the content and even the phrases. The second book of the *Dialogues* provided an exemplar for the work by Desiderius, thus creating a continuity between the early tradition and the later one. But the content is very different when taken as a whole. Few of the stories turn out to be about St Benedict at all: there are far more instances of supernatural rewards and punishments meted out to monks and their neighbours. The monastic practices of fasting, obedience, humility, simplicity, stability, are rewarded; demons are rebuked; and enemies of the monastery receive severe and dramatic punishments for their crimes. In two cases only are there accounts of men cured of illness at the tomb of St Benedict: a boy visiting the abbey with his father is cured of insanity by lying all night before the altar of St Benedict;[13] the nephew of a monk of the house, Theoderic, was paralyzed and cured after praying before the altar of St Benedict and also having had the relics of St Maur placed on his chest.[14] The stories recorded in the last book by Desiderius hardly concern either St Benedict or the monastery, but are set in Rome and are connected with the reforms of Pope Gregory VII. What can be discovered from this account, then, is first, the interest in the tradition of St Benedict by an eleventh century abbot and his desire to show that St Benedict's protection and power are still at work in his monastery; secondly, a shift in interest from St Benedict as the father of monks to St Benedict as the protector of his own monastery at Monte Cassino; thirdly, a curious lack of miracles actually performed by St Benedict in connection with the tomb where St Gregory says he was buried. This is not a collection of posthumous shrine miracles in any ordinary sense of the term, and perhaps this was because the claim of Monte Cassino to exclusive rights in the body of St Benedict had been challenged.

This brings us at once to a very difficult question indeed: where is the body of St Benedict? Monte Cassino assumed that St Benedict was buried there, as St Gregory says, and that he either never went away or if he did at least some of him returned. But the abbey of Fleury claimed, and still claims with startling perseverance, that they once stole the body of the saint and took it to France and kept it there. It is still a debatable question. For the purpose of this paper, it is what each side said and claimed that matters—not, note, what each side really believed, because it would be a mistake to think medieval men, least of all monks, were deceived by their own reasoning. To summarize the rival claims: the body of St Benedict was said to have been stolen from its sepulchre at Monte Cassino by the monk Aigulf sent by Mummoldus, second abbot of Fleury, at the end of the eighth century. Desiderius does not allude to this, either to deny or admit it, nor does he use a quotation from the *Dialogues* of St Gregory which would have fitted the case: 'the holy martyrs can perform outstanding miracles where their bodies rest; but . . . in places where their bodies do not actually lie buried, . . . they must perform still greater miracles.'[15] The theft is, however, mentioned in Paul the Deacon's *History of the Lombards;* and it forms the basis of the *History of the Translation* by Adrevald of Fleury. It was necessary at Fleury to emphasize the point that these were really the relics of St Benedict, and throughout the Fleury collection this recurs: in the story of the translation, the first book by Adrevald, there is a story about *quidam* "someone", who warned the pope in a dream that the relics were being stolen from Italy.[16] The legal question of the ownership of the relics is mentioned in two chapters of Adrevald's first book of miracles, where he describes a request from the pope for their return; Fleury is represented as having no counter-claim, and therefore being ready to surrender the body. Adrevald says it was St Benedict himself who refused to go back—he came to Fleury *propria sponte* and will not leave it unless he chooses to do so.[17] Another vision recorded by Andrew of Fleury at the end of the eleventh century continues the theme of the favour of St Benedict towards Fleury, but here it is also said that St Benedict shares his favours equally with Fleury and Monte Cassino: Richard, abbot of Monte Cassino, is said to have had a vision of St Benedict assuring him that this was so.[18]

The account written by Adrevald is an instance of a theme familiar in the ninth and tenth centuries of *pius furtus.* Adrevald had to show that the relics taken to Fleury were genuine; this meant that he had to show equally clearly that they were stolen. Phrases like 'by divine revelation' or 'St Benedict wills it' are the only justification for keeping what was taken; there is no attempt to show that the relics were in any way the legal property of Fleury. To have the body was all important, and the next most important thing was to show that it worked. It was genuine because it was really taken from its original shrine, and Monte Cassino was shown to admit this even in its counter-claims. It was also genuine because it worked miracles. The remainder of the books of miracles of St Benedict at Fleury are the assertion of just this claim; where the miracle collection is, there is the body—at Fleury and not at Monte Cassino.

At Fleury the tradition of the miracles of St Benedict underwent a further change. The book of miracles of St Benedict at Fleury covers two and a half centuries and comes from the hands of five different writers, each with his own style, interests, and background. They reflect changes in culture, secular as well as monastic, to an amazing degree and, not surprisingly, they say virtually nothing about St Benedict.

The possible qualification to this is that there was an indirect concern at Fleury to present a continuation with the tradition of the miracles of St Benedict as recorded in the *Dialogues* of St Gregory. In the abbey church at Fleury there are carvings on some of the pillars from the twelfth century and earlier. They show scenes from the miracles of St Benedict as recorded by St Gregory: St Benedict fed by a raven, tempted by a devil, holding his **Rule,** and finally shown giving his blessing to the family of the carver, the monk Hugh de St Marie, who was also the writer of the last book of miracles. It is an amazing piece of propaganda by which the standard, authentic miracles of St Benedict are transferred visually to Fleury. Over the lintel of a door a scene is carved of the translation of the relics and the first cures at the shrine, a suggestion of continuity which is permanent and vivid and beyond argument.

Another visual aid at the abbey shows another side of the change in location perhaps even more radically. The carvings say, St Benedict is here; there is an unbroken tradition from his life until this moment and this place. In the excavations under the high altar the first place where the shrine of the supposed relics was placed has been uncovered. Around it, facing towards it, are stone sarcophagi of the ninth century containing the bodies of local magnates, determined to be as close as possible to this great friend of God at the resurrection, when they were certain to need all the help they could get. This practical concern with *Dies illa, dies ira* led these men, who, if the miracle-books are to be believed, were no great friends of the abbey during their lives, to take this final step to secure the saint's intercession in the next world:

> 'what shall I, frail man, be pleading,
> who for me be interceeding
> when the just are mercy needing?'

The coffins provide a very firm statement about the position St Benedict had come to hold in the countryside of the Loire.

St Benedict is seen, therefore, as the intercessor for Fleury and its dependants. The carvings and the coffins tell the same story and the miracles fill in the details. Each writer presents St Benedict in different situations but in each story the image has a remarkable consistency: he is now no longer the father of monks, the abbot of a monastery, but the lord of his domains, the patron of a house and its inmates, responsible for them, as they are also responsible to him. The stories contain a wealth of detail therefore about monks and lay people living near the abbey, and their relationship to it. In the first book of miracles, for instance, written by Adrevald about 878/9, soon after the translation of the relics, the overwhelming impression is of a violent society, of small knights at war with one another, to whom the possessions of the abbey are fair game in a continual struggle for land and loot. In seven instances, the stories show the anger of St Benedict falling upon those who attacked the monastery, in four instances his protection is extended towards its inmates. What is interesting for the historian is to trace the dynamics of power, the aggression and defence pattern in this small part of tenth-century Europe. What is the significance of this anger of a saint? Who sees him as active and what does this mean in society? When Rohan, count of Orleons, for instance, attacks the lands of Fleury in a small piece of ground ajoining his own property, he is acting according to obvious methods for obvious ends; what defense does a monastery have? It needs to protect and consolidate lands just as much as the count, and it has at its disposal a force more potent than any army of knights: when the count falls ill, the abbey, through the writer Adrevald who records the sequence of events, sees the attack and the illness as cause and effect: St Benedict, he says, has acted mysteriously to defend his own and punish aggressors.[19] The relics of the saint are recognized as possessing mysterious but incalculable powers and in each incident where this supernatural sanction is asserted to have acted, the abbey is that much more secure. Imagination can be a more forceful shield than swords. The most notable characteristic of St Benedict at Fleury is that he proves his presence there by miracles; and the social situation in which the abbey exists determines that those miracles shall be above all acts of power and ferocity. Adrevald explicitly compares the relationship between St Benedict and Fleury with the covenant between Jehovah and Israel in which devotion is repaid by protection and the destruction of enemies. It was a covenant of mutual help and dependance, in which the monks were by no means always submissive. The monk Christian, the sacristan, guarded the shrine of the saint with energy, and when some treasures were stolen from it he confronted St Benedict with displeasure: 'Believe me, father Benedict,' he said, 'if you do not see to it that those bracelets are returned to me, I will never light another candle to you.'[20] A strange transformation for Saint Benedict, 'beloved of the Lord.'

After a long gap occasioned by the disturbances of the tenth century and the Norse invasions, Aimon of Fleury wrote two more books of the miracles of St Benedict. Odo of Cluny had taken control of the abbey and under his successor, Abbo, Fleury knew sufficient security for monastic life and learning to emerge. Aimon was a child-oblate, coming from a noble family in the Périgord, and he proved to be an able writer. Beginning in 1000, he records instances of miracles connected with the body of St Benedict at Fleury; again there is the firm assertion that the saint is really there by the proof of his miracles in that place. And what, beyond that central fact, emerges in these stories? In nine instances punishment falls upon the enemies of the abbey; the local knights have by no means learned their lesson, nor have conditions become much more peaceable than when Adrevald wrote; Fleury and its lands are still a focus for hostility and attack, and the assertion of the power of St Benedict must still be made. Rainald, Gerard of Limoges, Herbert of Sully,

Romuald of Chartres, pass through these pages, with their attempts to acquire monastic property and the penalty this brings upon them. The point the writer is making is that St Benedict is *tutor loci,* the protector of that place, a violent saint with unlimited power who will repay attacks on what is his by supernatural retribution. Once the ills that happen to these men have been linked with their inroads on the abbey lands, a powerful piece of propaganda is in existance and it is at least meant as a deterrent. It needed only a few instances of misfortunes to befall those who trespassed against the abbey and its patron for the power of St Benedict to become an established feature of social life in the valley of the Loire. Romuald, a citizen from Chartres, let his pigs root in the part of a forest belonging to Fleury; he resisted the orders of the monks, even appealed to the bishop of Orleans: it was not his fault that the pigs had strayed. But he fell ill with a fever and was dead by daybreak. The monks were not slow to point to this as condemnation by their saint: 'Lo,' they said, 'the decree of the most just Judge has fallen upon him.'[21] So we find the name of St Benedict taken up as a war-cry in local fights: when, for instance, Adhemar of Chabannais fought with a friend of the abbey, Boso of Poitou, Boso's men were quick to use the name of the saint: 'they shouted the name of St Benedict to the heavens; the whole valley echoed with it and the woods threw back the name Benedict.'[22] A woman who lived near the abbey entertained a travelling knight who was ignorant of the powers at her disposal, and when he stole one of her geese she could rest assured in the protection of 'the most holy Benedict who has jurisdiction over this whole countryside.' Needless to say, the knight fell from his horse and sustained lasting injuries, which in turn increased respect for the saint.[23] The monks themselves were particularly alert to the responsibility St Benedict had for them, and when one of them was insulted and called a fool he felt justly aggrieved with his saint: 'Most holy Benedict, my lord, are you then sound asleep that you let one of your sons be insulted thus?'[24]

St Benedict has become in the imagination of local society a power to be reckoned with; a terror to the enemies of the abbey, a strong protector of its monks. It is a further stage in the projection of local needs and values onto the saint. It is a development from the original image of St Benedict at Fleury. There is, however, another element in these stories of Aimon. As well as marauding knights and cunning monks, there are pilgrims—men, women, and children—who come to the shrine to pray to St Benedict and offer gifts, rich gifts very often and eventually enough to rebuild the church. The pilgrims are also presented in the stories as the people of St Benedict; his protective power extends from his own monks to them, and at times his power is displayed in curing their diseases. Moreover, another element in these stories is significant: St Benedict is not the only saint who works miracles now at Fleury; at his side stands St Mary, the lady of Fleury, lending him her assistance in at least half the miracles recorded by Aimon. It is a common phenomenon of the times: St Mary moves into the centre of medieval devotion from this time onwards, and eventually miracles which were once attributed to the prayers of saints such as St Benedict were not only shared with her but transferred totally to her. But here it is of particular interest for Fleury, since it is in contrast to the early exclusive claim that St Benedict alone worked wonders there. Perhaps the suggestion is that his place at Fleury is now well-established and no longer needs quite such exclusive emphasis.

Aimon wished to continue this record but was deflected to writing the *Lives of the Abbots of Fleury*. The work of recording the miracles of St Benedict was taken up by another monk of Fleury, Andrew. He began in 1043 and was still writing in 1056. He was the son of a local noble family and entered Fleury under the abbot Gauzelin. The four books of miracles which he wrote are in a style notably more ornate than that of his predecessors, a symptom of the times as well as a reflection of his own interests. Again, the preponderance of miracles are those of vengeance: knights die suddenly after pillaging the lands of the abbey; serfs become paralyzed when they work on festivals; the serf Stabilis who ran away from the abbey and lived as free man in the town for several years is summoned in a dream by his lord, St Benedict, and returns to his former serfdom.[25] Litigation over monastic property results in punishments by the saint not only of the ones who bring the cases but for the lawyers involved in opposition to the monks. St Benedict is still shown as having a care for his own people, and for the pilgrims: in time of plague, his relics are taken in procession over the countryside as a pledge of his power to deliver his own. Several of the sick are reported as receiving healing by prayer at his shrine. And the stories are no longer confined to Fleury: St Benedict is now venerated in Spain and Aquitaine, and pilgrims come from there to give thanks to him at Fleury, thus continuing to focus veneration for St Benedict there.

The next writer to take up the tale of violence in high places is the monk-poet Ralph of Tortaire, who was born in 1063 and became a monk at Fleury. He recorded eighteen miracles of vengeance, thirteen instances of protection and favour, and three cures at the shrine. Ralph is a lively and enterprising writer, and in his stories there are instances of the power of the saint exercised against animals—dogs, pigs, and peacocks. The increasing interest in miracles connected with the sacraments is illustrated here, too: a dying man is miraculously enabled to recover sufficiently to make his confession, by prayer to St Benedict. Ralph feels compelled, as none of his predecessors did, to explain the miracles of vengeance in theological terms: for our profit, for the chastisement of our souls, for our eternal

benefit, he says; not at all how the earlier writers thought about it. For them punishment had a more practical and immediate value. But the old theme of St Benedict as a stern patron is still prominent: in his first chapter, Ralph ascribes the death of Eudes, the brother of King Henry, to his contempt for the possessions of the abbey.[26] The sick were still cured by the relics of the saint, but equally those who attacked his lands or worked on his feast day or molested his people were punished. Warinus, for instance, a peasant on the lands of the abbey, was attacked by a knight, Hugh Bidulf, and had his arm broken; he complained to St Benedict before his shrine: 'My lord, St Benedict, I am your slave; you are my lord. This arm which is broken then belongs to you. I would not complain if you had broken it yourself, but why should Hugh Bidulf be allowed to do it?'[27] Belinus, another servant of the abbey, turned to the saint in illness saying, 'if foreigners can secure my lord's favour, how much more should he care for me, since he is my lord according to law and they only come here from a far country?'[28] The powers of St Benedict continue, then, into the eleventh century; what has changed is the increase in foreigners, pilgrims, who now seem to have first claim on the saint, so that one of the saint's own people has to remind himself that he also can appeal to him.

The last miracles in the collection were recorded by the monk of Hugh of St Mary, who added eleven miracles in 1118. The collection ends there, either from a break in the manuscript or in reality. There is a marked difference in these stories from their predecessors: apart from the first miracle, which is an account of the deliverance of a captive, they are all cures of pilgrims. They happened at the shrine, and are recorded in detail, with names, dates, diseases, and the manner of the cure. One instance from Hugh's record will show how similar these were to cures at other healing shrines and how different from the usual miracles of St Benedict which were best described thus: 'This punishment was deserved, since he had opposed the friend of Christ with all the pride of his heart, and was laid low because of his sin.'[29]

> A woman from the town, who was called Hosanna, on that same night [the feast of the Annunciation, 25 March 1114] lay prostrate before the altar, holding out her arm and hand which were in need of healing. For a grievous sickness had taken all the strength from both and she could not even flex her fingers. When she had prayed earnestly, she found that she was cured and felt no pain at all.[30]

By 1118 the miracles of St Benedict had achieved their primary purpose of focusing devotion to St Benedict on the place where his body was buried at Fleury. How strong this centralization was can be further illustrated by reference to the veneration of the monks of Cluny for St Benedict. This was primarily focused on his shrine at Fleury. Relations between Cluny and Monte Cassino were, in the eleventh century, cordial: Hugh of Cluny visited Monte Cassino in 1083 and established a confraternity between the two abbeys,[31] Peter Damian visited and admired the life at both monasteries.[32] But nevertheless, the veneration of the Cluniacs for St Benedict's relics was focused on Fleury. The feast of the translation of the body of St Benedict to Fleury was celebrated at Cluny in the eleventh century[33] and Peter the Venerable supplied a new hymn for it in the twelfth, acclaiming the wonders surrounding the body of the Italian saint in his new shrine in Gaul:

> Claris coniubila Gallia cantibus
> Laetaris Benedicti patris ossibus
> Felix quae gremio condita proprio
> Servas membra celebria.
>
> Miris Italiae fulserat actibus
> Gallos irradiat corpore mortuus
> Signis ad tumuim crebrius emicat
> Illustrans patriam novam.[34]

The vital contact between the two monasteries had been made long before, when Odo of Cluny became abbot of Fleury. John of Salerno says, as we have seen, that Odo was called, elected, and pre-ordained to be abbot of Fleury by St Benedict himself. During Odo's abbacy, St Benedict appeared in visions, supporting his reforms, and he appeared also to Odo himself while he was keeping vigil at Fleury 'before the body of the saint.'[35] It also seems from this account of St Odo that the body of St Benedict had been removed from Fleury during the Norse invasions and was restored, amid miracles, at this time. This complete acceptance of Fleury as the miracle-working shrine of St Benedict containing his body by the monks of Cluny is a strong indication of the triumph of the propanganda of Fleury through the records of miracles there.

While these miracles do not add directly to our knowledge of St Benedict, they hold up a mirror to an age with exceptional clarity. They point perhaps towards another fact about the place of the saints in history. We have for some years been demythologizers of the saints; if their legends are found to be unrelated to the facts of an edifying life, we dismiss them from the kalendar and from consideration, even when they are such major figures as St George and St Christopher. But the tradition about St Benedict indicates something further for consideration: the stories told about a saint after his death can have a more creative role in the lives of others than any plain historical facts about his life. Of course, with St Benedict there is always the fact to be borne in mind that his major contribution to civilization is that unique document of the human spirit, **The Rule.** But in addition, the legends, miracles, and stories provide not a dead weight of fanciful but outdated tradition, but a record of a living current of human experience, continually alive and infinitely varied. The texture of life is as varied as we care to make it, and for the monk especially one strand in it can still be the deeds of St Benedict.

Notes

[1] John of Salerno, *Life of St Odo of Cluny, Bibliotheca Cluniacensis,* 51E-2A; ed. Marrier and Duchesne (Paris, 1618).

[2] *Rule of St Benedict,* ch. 5; ed. Justin McCann (London, 1952).

[3] St Gregory the Great, *Dialogues* Bk. 1, p. 70; ed. U. Moricca (Rome, 1934).

[4] Ibid., Bk. 11, p. 93.

[5] Ibid., Bk. 11, p. 129.

[6] Eadmer, *Life of St Anselm* Bk. 11, cap. xxxi; ed. R. W. Southern (Oxford, 1962).

[7] Desiderius, *Dialogi di Miraculis Sancti Benedicti,* Bk. II, cap. 6; ed. G. Schwartz and A. Hofmeister (*MGH* XXXII, 1934).

[8] *Life of St Odo,* 48A.

[9] *Sayings of the Desert Fathers,* trans. Benedicta Ward (Kalamazoo-Oxford, 1975) 157.

[10] Ibid., p. 39.

[11] *Dialogues,* Bk. 11, p. 109.

[12] Desiderius' *Dialogi,* Prologue, p. 1117.

[13] Ibid., p. 1134.

[14] Ibid., p. 1135.

[15] Gregory, *Dialogues,* Bk. II, p. 134.

[16] *Les Miracles de S Benoit écrits par Adrewald, Aimon, André, Raoul Tortaire et Hugues de Sainte Marie,* Cap. 1, Histoire de la Translation de Saint Benoit, viii, pp. 28-9; ed. E de Certain (Paris, 1858).

[17] Ibid., Bk. 1, cap. xvii, pp. 40-46.

[18] Ibid., Bk. VII, cap. xv, pp. 273-4.

[19] Ibid., Bk. 1, cap. xix, p. 46.

[20] Ibid., Bk. 1, cap. xxv, pp. 56-60.

[21] Ibid., Bk. 11, cap. viii, pp. 109-10.

[22] Ibid., Bk. 111, cap. v, pp. 135-42.

[23] Ibid., Bk. 11, cap. xiv, pp. 116-17.

[24] Ibid., Bk. III, cap viii, pp. 148-50.

[25] Ibid., bk. VI, cap ii, pp. 218-20.

[26] Ibid., Bk. VIII, cap. i, pp. 277-78.

[27] Ibid., Bk. VIII, cap. x1vi, pp. 353-54.

[28] Ibid., Bk. VIII, cap. xxxix, pp. 342-44.

[29] Ibid., Bk. IV, cap. iv, pp. 179.

[30] Ibid., Bk. IX, cap. xi, pp. 370-71.

[31] *Chronica Monasterii Casinensis, MGH SS* VII, p. 741.

[32] Peter Damian, 'Sermon for the Vigil of St Benedict,' *PL.* 144.

[33] Udalric, *Consuetudines Cluniacensis,* i, 34; *PL.* 149:637.

[34] Peter the Venerable, *Letters;* ed. G. Constable, (Harvard, 1967), vol. i, p. 320.

[35] *Life of St Odo,* p. 53 D and E.

Thomas X. Davis (essay date 1981)

SOURCE: "Loss of Self in the Degrees of Humility in the *Rule of Saint Benedict,* Chapter VII" in *Benedictus: Studies in Honor of St. Benedict of Nursia,* edited by E. Rozanne Elder, Cistercian Publications, 1981, pp. 23-9.

[*In the following essay, Davis summarizes the twelve degrees of humility in the* Rule of St. Benedict, *focusing on the state of selflessness required to achieve humility and realize the complete love of God.*]

The God-Exemplar

'In overflowing wrath for a moment I hid my face from you, but with everlasting love I will have compassion on you, says the Lord.'[1] In the christian dimension, the loss of self through the attitude of humility has its ancient exemplar in the tender, compassionate, humble love of Yahweh for his people. Such an anthropomorphic revelation of divinity as this culminates in Jesus, the Son of God. Christ, the Revelation of God, styles himself as 'the least' in the kingdom[2] because his love is a *kenosis,* a giving up of self in the lowly death on a cross.[3] Our God is a humble, loving God.

The Self and Its Dynamic

Our existence, the self, is a gift whereby we participate in the life of this humble loving God.[4] With this existence comes the divine command[5] to know oneself, and to develop from an unrealized to a realized identification with the divine. Insight motivates the self from an identification with lower animal impulses, a narcissistic self, a selfish love, i.e., pride, vanity, passions, and other ego-centric desires,[6] towards an identification with a personality formed by relationships with things, other persons, and God. By the gradual purification of these relationships through sincere love as taught in the Gospels, we discover a still greater self that can experience the fruits of true, sincere love, namely, 'powerlessness' and 'nothingness.' An authentic love experience is one of total surrender to another; one gives all and holds nothing back. One's identity will shift; it will no longer be formed by impulses or relationships but it will become an identity formed by union with God.

Union with God through the No-Self

Union with God is the beginning of an encounter we 'know not'; yet it is truly the place where our self belongs. We arrive here by a ruthless campaign against all forms of illusion and the desires that come from self-complacency and spiritual ambition. A total surrender of our life, a holocaust, leads to a discovery within ourselves of a no-self: of deep silence, humble detachment before everything that exists, and before God. Even our prayer is not to be the source of our identity; it can be a net ensnaring us in our own self-regard.[7] Cassian teaches that prayer is not perfect if in it a monk is aware of himself or of the words he is praying.[8] This no-self is monastic purity of heart.

Humility in the Rule of St Benedict

Chapter VII of the **Rule of St Benedict** 'Of Humility' in continuity with christian tradition views humility as a disposition basic to integrating human and divine life: God comes to us, we go to God through the *kenosis* of Christ. The ladder spoken of in the opening words of this chapter, 'a ladder set up by our ascending actions like the one Jacob saw in his vision,'[9] is not then to be taken as suggestive of a method or technique. Rather, the ladder symbolizes our life: resting on a humbled heart, it is raised to heaven by the Lord himself. In other words, a humbled personality provides the disposition needed for removing any duplicity, any complexity; it prepares the self for the manifestation and presence of God.

The Twelve Degrees of Humility

The twelve degrees of humility are paradigmatic of very early christian teaching on contemplative prayer as the no-self. In order to see this connection, let us cite some examples from the early fathers at each of the twelve degrees.

The seventeenth homily attributed to Macarius the Great[10] reveals the need to enter our darkened self and put to death the evil serpent existing deep in the abyss of our soul at the root of our thought. Death, forgetfulness of God, comes from having this serpent digging itself ever deeper into the chambers of our life. The first degree of humility is to flee this forgetfulness by being always mindful of all that God commands and exposing every part of our abyss to his divine presence. Facing squarely a life based on this forgetfulness within brings us a fear and dread of its consequences: negligence, falsity, unfaithfulness here, eternal damnation hereafter. This initial phase of fear and dread is not to be regarded as something pertaining to primitive religion. This fear is an initial means of understanding God's absolute sovereignty over self, a basic experience of the self as 'nothing' in comparison with a Being so totally other. This brings about the realization that self-manipulative control over one's life has to be broken through, if there is to be any attempt to destroy or change the usual mode of living and thinking, of choosing and willing, of awareness and consciousness. Without this breakthrough there is no departure from the world of illusion.

The second degree of humility is 'that a person love not his own will, seek not to fulfill his own desires but carry out in deed that word of the Lord, "I came not to do my own will but to do the will of him who sent me." '[11] This places selfishness opposite selflessness, that loss of self which comes from doing what must be done.[12] The Holy Spirit of repentance, accompanying the experience of God's sovereignty, makes us begin to exercise discernment about our life's activities, with the result that the relationship between body and soul is purified and healed. This discernment restores proper balance between body and soul and orientates the self towards its true identity in the loss of self. The self becomes 'reasonable' in the sense of very early desert spirituality:[13] that is, a person who does what must be done under the influence of the Holy Spirit of God.

Obedience to any superior in imitation of Jesus, the **Rule**'s third degree of humility, integrates the loss of self into the tradition of paschal transfiguration. Such an obedience, by rooting out addiction to desires stemming from the self, brings conscious and unconscious mental activity to peace. It enables the self to die to personal choice and brings the flexibility and readiness to be at the disposal of God.

The real shift of the center of gravity from self to God, causing every component of the self to disappear before the divine, is achieved by embracing patience with a quiet consciousness, *tacita conscientia*, in all the hard, contrary, and even unjust dimensions of life. This,

humility's fourth degree, gives deep inner peace: *apatheia.* It literally allows the self to be supplanted by the sensitiveness of the Good Spirit of God, whose dwelling—the self—needs to be a spacious place free of all anger and sadness, as the *Shepherd of Hermas* teaches.[14]

Integral to patience with a quiet consciousness is a humble manifestation of one's evil thoughts and past secret sins to the abbot. This, for St Benedict, is the fifth degree of humility. The faith experience and the experience of having a life-giving father—the fruits of this degree—remove from self the deep tendency to sin and darkness, illusion, deception, pretence, and vainglory—all of which intercept the workings of divine mercy and distort our relationships. This experience of faith and of a lifegiving merciful father ought not be underestimated in the destruction of selfishness.[15]

Since the self is clever in avoiding the recognition of illusions, especially those cherished about itself, it is possible to grow old in spiritual endeavor without really being humble in self-knowledge. Instead of a gradual discovery of the no-self before God, there emerges from such spiritual discipline a kind of subtle presumption or delicate effrontery in our relationship to one another and to God. By contrast, in the sixth degree of humility, the disciple is asked to be content[16] with what is poor and abject and to see himself a sinful and useless laborer. Macarius' twenty-sixth homily teaches that this attitude is the sign of an authentic Christian.[17]

'Happy the person who thinks himself no better than dirt!'[18] This beatitude of Evagrius is a joyful echo of the seventh degree of humility: to believe with deep, intimate convication, *intimo credat affectu,* that one is lower and more vile than anything else, that one is a worm and not a man[19] . . . just poor mountain dirt![20] Recognition of God comes in direct proportion to the depth of the recesses of self that our inner humbleness can plumb. When the self is without any desires, for the sake of the kingdom of God, it is actually led by a desire so great that it can comprehend no thing. The self becomes a no-self, for nothing can satisfy it save the Divine Presence. No previously determined conditions and limitations are given for this presence.[21] The paradox that no-self is an incomprehensibly great desire means that you are not giving God a name along with the rest of creation,[22] nor equating God with the name given him and thereby making the divine after your own personal image and likeness.

Responding to the Divine Presence as the principal formative influence in our life is the eighth degree of humility: to do only what the example of the seniors and the Rule authorizes. An authentic person cannot interpret his life apart from a wholeness reflected in and integrated by his spiritual and physical environment. For, like a spiritual master, people and things place an unexplicable burden on us and so enable us to know our own nothingness and our need to give and receive, to love and be loved.

The ninth degree of humility is to maintain silence until questioned. Talkativeness can be a subtle means of self-affirmation, self-assertiveness, arrogance, and consequently an indication that a person has not yet come to a proper self-knowledge and sincere compunction. Intelligent silence, that is, an esteem for and correct use of speaking with emphasis on silence and listening, is the matrix of authentic relationships with others and of contemplative prayer.[23]

The growing awareness of our illusory and distorted self through everything that hurts self-esteem reveals to us our inner repulsiveness, fragmentation, wounds. The temptation is to disguise or to flee from these areas by flattery, ostentation, being easily and readily moved to laughter or by a lack of seriousness.[24] Not to give in to this urge to escape is the tenth degree of humility. This painful revelation is the beginning of *penthos:* an abiding and developing sense of separation of self from God. Weeping, the gift of tears, heralds a growth in *apatheia,* that deep inner stillness and peace, the loss of self before the Divine Presence.

The eleventh degree of humility: speaking with few and reasonable words, *pauca et rationabilia,* maintains the self as 'reasonable' in very early desert spirituality.[25] But, in this instance, it guards against levity of mind and ignorance. By a verbal and mental silence, traces of self-will are dissipated and preparation is made to receive with freedom that wisdom and Spirit which cannot be seen, heard, or conceived.[26]

The self's curiosity about things, persons, or events must be eliminated so that it does not turn to them to indulge in some dissolute or disordered passion, emotion, thought, or desire. It also needs to be purified of its mental images, concepts, ideas of God and of every dimension of its relationship with him. This purification produces attitudes and activities of harmony between the inner person and his outward conduct. They produce *hesychia, quies,* serenity, a tranquility of the inner and outer person proper to a complete renunciation of self in an absolute surrender to God. This manifestation of serenity and tranquility in our daily life, a transfiguration coming from the paschal mysteries, is the twelveth degree of humility. A humble quietness is revealed not only in the inner heart but also in the body.

Loss of Self Identified with Pure Prayer

Chapter VII of the **Rule** and Chapter XX, 'Of Reverence in Prayer,' have a remarkable similarity. In Chapter XX, purity of heart, humility, compunction, and tears are equated with the pure prayer, *oratio pura,*

which brings salvation from God. The twelve degrees of Chapter VII see the same elements, purity of heart, humility, compunction, tears, as true selflessness or loss of self. The important conclusion is: pure prayer is identified with loss of self. In this identification, the **Rule** is consistent with the tradition of Evagrius and Cassian.[27]

The experience of selflessness is an experience of darkness, emptiness, nothingness. Because the self is a gift from God, a created participation in his life, this experience of darkness, emptiness, nothingness is likewise an experience of God working in us. *The Letter of Diognetus,* one of the earliest teachings on contemplative and mystic imitation of the powerlessness and long-suffering of God,[28] echos this in posing the question: Who really understood what God is before Jesus Christ came? Or, as Ignatius of Antioch expresses it in the circumstances of his own life: To be near the sword is to be near God.[29]

Love Casts Out Fear

The **Rule of St Benedict** makes available in its teaching of these twelve degrees the contemplative, mystic imitation of God. Fidelity to such an imitation of God and his Son, Jesus the Christ, brings one to that love which casts out fear. The **Rule** expresses this love by the Latin words *charitas Dei,* a phrase which carries the nuance that we identify with the divine love which is God, not that we love God in much the same way as we love another person.

The Man of the Spirit

The last sentence in Chapter VII of the **Rule** testifies that these twelve degrees of selflessness are the working of the Holy Spirit in us.[30] This presence of the Holy Spirit is in accord with the Old and New Testaments. Scripture reveals that the outpouring of the Spirit is the definitive sign that God has visited his people. The place proper for this Spirit is our emptiness, nothingness, no-self.[31] He spans the incomprehensibility both of our void and the total otherness of the divine. His presence means, first of all, that the nothingness, the no-self, of an authentic love experience proper to any complete surrender is far more total, radical and profound when given to God. Secondly, and here is the paradox, this gift to God of being a no-self is precisely the ability to receive the gift of being an authentic person, that is, one living with the life—the Holy Spirit—of God. We imitate Jesus as revealed in the Gospel of Mark: one who dies and gives up his spirit precisely because he was the Son of God.[32]

Notes

[1] Is 54:8.

[2] Mt 11:11.

[3] Ph 2:1-12.

[4] God is to the soul what the soul is to the body. This is a common patristic teaching.

[5] This is the underlying theme of Mt 16:24-26 and other scriptural passages.

[6] I.e., the illusory and/or empirical self.

[7] Thomas Merton, *Mystics and Zen Masters* (New York: Farrar, Straus and Giroux, 1967) pp. 20 ff.

[8] Cassian, *Conferences,* 9:31 ('The First Conference of Abbot Isaac').

[9] *Rule of St Benedict,* Chapter VII.

[10] Macarius the Great, *Homilies,* 17:15.

[11] *Rule of St Benedict,* Chapter VII.

[12] *Necessitas* is the word used in the second degree of humility.

[13] See, for example, *The Letters of St Antony the Great.*

[14] *Shepherd of Hermas,* Fifth Mandate I & II.

[15] Cassian, *Conferences,* No. 18 ('The Conference of Abbot Piamun').

[16] Lk 3:14.

[17] Macarius the Great, *Homilies,* 26:11.

[18] Evagrius Ponticus, *Chapters on Prayer,* No. 121.

[19] Ps 21:7 (Vulgate); 22:6 (Hebrew).

[20] *Life of Pachomius, Vita Prima Graeca,* No. 110.

[21] Refer to the teaching of John of Lycopolis, Rufinus of Aquileia, *Historia Monachorum in Aegypto,* PL 21:395-8.

[22] Gn 2:19-20.

[23] Climacus, *Ladder,* Step 11.

[24] *Apophthegmata, Alphabetical Collection,* John the Dwarf, No. 9; Poemen the Shepherd, No. 137.

[25] *Letters of St Antony the Great; Letters of Ammonas,* Nos. 12 & 13.

[26] 1 Cor 2:9 and teaching of John of Lycopolis, Rufinus of Aquileia, *Historia Monachorum in Aegypto,* PL 21:395-8.

[27] Evagrius Ponticus, *Praktikos,* No. 23; Cassian, *Conferences,* 9:3.

[28] *Letter to Diognetus,* No. 8 ff.

[29] Ignatius of Antioch, *Letter to the Smyrnaeans,* No. 4.

[30] *Rule of St Benedict,* Chapter VII.

[31] Gn 1:2; Is 66:2.

[32] Mk 51:39.

A. W. Richard Sipe (essay date 1983)

SOURCE: "The Psychological Dimensions of the *Rule of St. Benedict,*" *The American Benedictine Review,* Vol. 34, No. 4, December, 1983, pp. 424-35.

[*In the following essay, Sipe endeavors "to extrapolate ten essential psychological features that show [Benedict's] understanding of the human experience" that are addressed by the monastic experience.*]

Benedict of Nursia, born in 480 A.D., wrote a brief rule—an order for a way of life—for monks. In 1980, approximately 30,000 men and women around the world claim this rule as their guide. That one fact alone would be of interest: why do some things endure over long centuries? But it is not simply durability that impresses me as I look into the *Rule* of St. Benedict. Much of the history of religious life in western culture has been influenced in some way by the *Rule.* Bernard of Clairvaux, Bruno of Cologne, Ignatius of Loyola, and even Thomas Aquinas, who grew up in a Benedictine house, are part of its legacy. Reforms, both monastic and ecclesiastical, cultural movements of almost opposing emphasis have been influenced by the *Rule.*

Wherein lies the *Rule's* secret for its endurance and attraction? In examining this document, one would find that it embodies a perception of reality that allows for vitality and that seeks creative expressions. Some say that the vitality and creativity of the *Rule* comes from its inspiration in Scripture, for it is an astute application of the Gospel message in the establishment of a Christian community. But there is also a psychological dimension that ensures the *Rule's* persistence. It lies in Benedict's keen perception of human nature and the human condition. To be sure, this psychological area is an appropriate one for study, as exemplified by the workshops and publications of the Institute for Religion and Human Development, the heir to St. John's University's Institute for Mental Health, in Collegeville, Minnesota. The Mental Health Institute was a unique endeavor that brought together Catholics and Protestants, laity and clergy, psychiatrists and psychoanalysts.

Yet even those at the Institute would admit that the psychological elements to be studied are grounded in the monastic experience.[1] So, before identifying ten such elements, let me review the essential features of that monastic life.

Essential Elements of the Monastic Way of Life

Four elements characterize the Benedictine tradition: adaptability, relatedness, community awareness, and contemplation—all of which are related ultimately to a real awareness of the mystery of life and death.[2]

1. *Adaptability.* The quality of adaptability is embodied in a vague vow, *conversatio morum,* unique to this religious tradition. By promising to change his habits, the monk seeks an ongoing change and development of himself and rejects any spiritual complacency that would hold him back. This quality implies a knowledge of the developmental character of any state in life and the necessity to be willing to give up what is outmoded if one is to grow. Indeed, there are both individual and communal (or social) components of this search for new or better ways to live and serve. The fact that monasticism has survived, is in some measure due to its adaptability.

2. *Relatedness to Time and Place.* Because of this need to adapt to one's circumstances, the monk needs to be aware of his particular time and place—it is an historical realism that allows him to grow. Likewise, the monastic tradition, as contained in the *Rule* of St. Benedict, draws upon its historical ambience and relates to it. Because it is able to relate to it, monastic living is able to contribute in a real way to the culture of its time.

3. *Community Awareness.* Benedictine monasticism is also concerned with the development of a community. Prior to Benedict's establishment of a rule, a person who pursued a religious dedication generally did it alone and practiced it in silence or in some remote area or even atop a pillar.[3] Benedict's concept of community fosters individual dedication within the context of a group: it is based on the admonition of the Gospel to love one's neighbor as oneself. The community ideal is to make love of neighbor a practical reality. In modern terms, the monk is to become an expert in interpersonal relations. The sense of community goes beyond the community's immediate members and even extends its bonds of relatedness to the immediate and more distant historical past.

4. *Contemplation (Intra-personal Integrity).* Contemplation is an essential part of the monastic life; yet it has been miserably misunderstood over the past decades and mistakenly identified with isolation or romanticized with no relation to practical existence. Contemplation as a process has to do essentially with self-discovery. In modern terms, it has to do with intra-personal awareness. Indeed, psychoanalysis and psychotherapy have secularized and popularized this ancient achievement. For Benedictines, it is a process of finding God in oneself and of losing oneself in God. It is more than an exercise, but a real, practical, and personal experience. There is no way of knowing God without knowing oneself: the measure of loving God whom one does not see is the love one has for the neighbor (the community) whom one does see, and the measure of one's love for another is the measure of love which one has for oneself. Especially at the beginning of the monastic experience, Benedict's *Rule* provides a time of quiet work and meditation to allow the novices to examine their deepest motivations and clarify life's goals. Erik Erikson has pointed out that the monastery

> offers methods of making a meditative descent into the inner shafts of mental existence from which the aspirant emerges with the gold of faith or with the gems of wisdom. These shafts, however, are psychological as well as meditative; they lead not only into the depths of adult inner experience, but also downward into the most primitive layers and backwards into our infantile beginnings.[4]

Psychological Elements of the Monastic Way of Life

The monastic regimen—as marked by these four essential elements of adaptability, relatedness, community awareness, and contemplation—reflects Benedict's perception of reality and human existence. His understanding of human life values personal growth, productivity, charity, and humility—the fruits of the four essential elements of the monastic experience. But he recognizes, as other spiritual leaders before him do not, that religious life, one that was completely human, was not one of extremes or severe denials of the self. Instead, he sees the need for balance and integration.

Thus, when Benedict drafted his *Rule* in the sixth century, he intended it as a document that would guide others in their living, in order "to save their souls." His acute perception of what made human life "whole" fills the many concrete precepts of the *Rule.* At the same time, there are psychological underpinnings to the *Rule* that seem to speak even to the modern world. It is a credit to Benedict's genius that he recognized this psychological dimension to human life. In my reading of Benedict's *Rule,* I have tried to extrapolate ten essential psychological features that show his understanding of the human experience that are fulfilled in the monastic experience.

1. *Interiority.* The spirit of interiority infuses the whole *Rule* (=RB); the commitment to this element is expounded unmistakably in chapter six, "On Silence," and chapter seven, "On Humility," which preeminently

lays out the inner quest. Benedict compares the human condition—the present here-and-now life—of the monk with Jacob's ladder (Gen. 28:13): "We may call our body and soul the sides of this ladder, into which our divine vocation has fitted the various steps of humility and discipline as we ascend" (RB 7.9).[5] He then describes a process of progressive interior awareness that will result in an integrated life. These twelve steps lead the aspirant into the depths, a course "tried by fire," that can be countered or matched only by difficult denials and mastery of self.

A modern psychologist might be tempted to dismiss summarily such a process that ends with the subject being "ever mindful of the guilt of his sins" before the judgment seat of God. But the language of sixth century Europe should not blind us to the profound reality that Benedict describes and the masterful observation it represents. The people who complete this process will find themselves beyond fear, free (cleansed), and "in tune" with themselves and their environment: "all that he once performed with dread, he will now begin to observe without effort, as though naturally, from habit. . . . " (RB 7.68) The process of growth that Benedict outlines is based on his observation of the human condition, one that reveals a deep abiding awareness of its external, internal, and transcendental reality.[6] The awareness of guilt restores an essential order within ourselves and our environment that is manifested in meaningful and productive living.

2. *Reverence for Physical Needs.* Benedict's concept of interiority fosters a sense of reverence for human needs—food, sleep, clothing—because the external life has to be ordered realistically, if the interior life is to grow without undue hindrance. The interiority of the **Rule** is not a product of excessive deprivation, aimed at killing human instincts. Order, self-mastery, moderation, faith in the process of personal growth and development characterize the rules that regulate the food, drink, sleep, and clothing of monks. Each person is to receive "as he had need" (RB 34). Infirmities are also to be looked after.

Seven full chapters (RB 35-41) are devoted to the regulation of meals. Those persons who serve food should be given enough help so that they may perform their duty "without distress." Kitchen workers should receive "a drink and some bread over and above the regular portion, so that at mealtime, they may serve their brothers without grumbling or hardship" (RB 35.12-13). Sick brethren should have special food and care (RB 36). The elderly and children should also receive special consideration: e.g., they should eat before regular hours (RB 37). The atmosphere at these meals should be peaceful, free from the concern or burden of socializing: thus, a competent reader reads from Scripture or sacred writings to provide this ambience. His service, too, "because of Holy Communion

and because of the fast may be too hard for him to bear [should be eased] by some diluted wine before he begins to read" (RB 38.10). The amount of food and drink is regulated by chapters thirty-nine and forty. The portions allowed are certainly generous and at least two dishes are provided: "In this way, the person who may not be able to eat one kind of food may partake of the other . . . and if fruit or fresh vegetables are available, a third dish may also be added" (RB 39.3) and an amount of wine is provided daily. The hours of meals are set, but flexible, depending on work, weather and needs of the liturgical season. "Similarly, he [the abbot] should so regulate and arrange all matters that souls may be saved and the brothers may go about their activities without any justifiable grumbling" (RB 41.5).

Benedict's provisions for clothing (RB 55) is a masterpiece of common sense: "The clothing distributed to the brothers should vary according to local conditions and climate" (RB 55.1). Preferably, they should be locally-made, economical, and well-fitting. Discarded clothing should still be good enough to be of use to the poor. Those who go on a journey ought to dress a little better than they usually would at home.

Sleeping arrangements are well-provided for (RB 22), and Benedict's instructions even reveal a sensitivity for those who find it difficult to rise from sleep. Bed linen should be in good supply and on the comfortable side (RB 55). Sleep should be ample, so that they may rise fully refreshed (RB 8), with digestion comfortably completed.

3. *Community Bonding.* The **Rule** is clearly intended for cenobites, "those who belong to a monastery, where they serve under a rule and an abbot" (RB 1). The psychological binding is to a group of people, who share a common space and time. The analogy to "family" is natural. The abbot is the "father" (or "mother") figure who bears the ultimate and awesome responsibility for the functioning and well-being of the monastery (RB 2). Although the image of "shepherd" is also liberally used throughout the **Rule** to describe the role of the abbot, he is ultimately the "father" (parent) to the monks, who are termed "brothers" (RB 64). Although the abbot is to seek counsel from the brethren (RB 3), and even if he appoints assistants to aid in administering affairs, in the end, all must remain under his direction (RB 65): "For the preservation of peace and love we have, therefore, judged it best for the abbot to make all decisions in the conduct of his monastery" (RB 65.11).

Thus, the monastery provides that important psychological factor—a personal structure to which a person can relate. The particular disciplines of monastic living are not as essential (in psychological terms) as the reality of the object relationships that are expected, fostered, relied upon, and enhanced by the members of the community. The **Rule** provides for a well-regulated, ordered, and well-disciplined social organization that can be called a family. Entrance into this close communal bond is first through a period of thoughtful deliberation that ends with a religious ritual marking the reception of the candidate into the community (RB 58). Once a candidate becomes a full member of the community, he is given a particular place or rank within the group (RB 65). The seven chapters on the manner of punishment (RB 23-30) only emphasize the importance of the group's solidarity: excommunication is the severest consequence of aberrant behavior. The order, reverence, mutual concern, and interdependence of its members upon each others talents and material goods as required by the **Rule** cultivates personal identification, a sense of belonging, and deep friendship—in short, it offers a personal bonding, based on authentic object relatedness.

4. *Attention to Learning.* The **Rule** allows a place for learning, education in the more formal sense, in recognizing it as an essential part of human nature. Schools, one of the hallmarks of the Benedictine order, are not a necessary outgrowth of the **Rule,** but this essential psychological orientation toward learning makes schools logical and acceptable. The monastery itself as "a school for the Lord's service" (RB Prologue) is a place and an experience of personal growth and development (we have already commented on the seminal nature of the growth process described in chapter seven of the **Rule**). Chapter four, on the instruments of good works, provides a compendium of tasks to be mastered and attitudes to be actively cultivated.

Learning, reading, and study are woven closely into the fiber of daily existence. Reading, for instance, found its way into the monastic routine: "Reading will always accompany the meals of the brothers" (RB 38.1); as soon as they have risen from supper, "all the monks will sit together immediately. . . . Someone should read from the *Conferences* or *Lives* of the Fathers or at any rate something else that will benefit the hearers" (RB 42.3). Reading is encouraged at midday, and during Lent special attention is given the task of reading (RB 48). Through the daily recitation of psalms in the liturgy of the hours (the Divine Office), a monk grows to know the psalter well: "In the time remaining after Vigils, those who need to learn some of the psalter or readings should study them" (RB 8.3).

A love for learning is presumed by the **Rule.** A monk must know his letters, since his petition for vows is to be written in his own hand (RB 58). When an abbot is to be selected, "goodness of life and wisdom of teaching must be the criteria for choosing the one to be made abbot" (RB 64.2). The final chapter of the **Rule** (RB 73) is a veritable bibliography for monastic study: the books of the Old and New Testament, the teaching of the Holy Fathers (i.e., the Desert Fathers), the holy Catholic Fathers (Fathers of the Church), conferences, Institutes of John Cassian, and Lives of the Fathers, and the *Rule* of St. Basil, among others. Furthermore, this reverence for learning as an integral part of daily living led naturally to the preservation and reproduction of books, secular as well as sacred, in the monastic scriptorium. This psychological stance toward learning, then, as a natural part of daily existence, supports a tendency toward competency and an intellectual orientation that is confirmed by observing the monastic life itself.

5. *Work as Mastery.* The learning that is encouraged is balanced by the practical demands of physical work. This positive attitude toward work is sustained partly by the nature of communal life and common property. Some time is spent each day in maintaining one's environment. Two substantial work periods are prescribed for each day, when the monks "are to return to whatever work is necessary" (RB 48.6). Since "the monastery should, if possible be so constructed that within it all necessities, such as water, mill, and garden are contained, and the various crafts are practiced" (RB 16.6), work is always at hand. No one looks upon work as demeaning or the wages of sin; instead, "when they live by the labor of their hands, as our fathers and the apostles did, then they are really monks" (RB 49.8). Through work, the monks come to understand the meaning of interdependence and mutuality as well as how to develop and share their talents. This pride in the necessity of labor flowered over and over again in the agricultural, artistic, and architectural expressions of significant dimensions wherever the **Rule** was established throughout history.

6. *Service as Meaningful Existence* (Altruism). The idea of service is central to a monk's whole life, for he believes that service makes a difference in the lives of others. In one of the final chapters, the **Rule** encourages a zeal for altruism as inspiration for the monastic life: "No one is to pursue what he judges better for himself, but instead, what he judges better for someone else" (RB 72.7). In fact, the monastic life is wholly dedicated to another's service, that of God. Each member of the community provides a service. The abbot serves the brethren and does not lord it over them (RB 64). The prior (RB 65), the cellarer (RB 31), and the porter (RB 66) see "that no one may be disquieted or distressed in the house of God" (RB 31.19). Service is always directed toward someone else. Honor, empathy, charity, sincerity, and humility should mark the brotherhood and their mutual service. The cellarer is "like a father to the whole community" for he attends guests with reverence (RB 53). All monks should receive the poor with a prompt and gentle response (RB 66). Indeed, Benedict speaks of the "usual measure of our service" (RB 49.5) that is fulfilled in the regular daily observance of the **Rule.**

7. *Order.* Thirteen chapters of the **Rule** are devoted to the regulation of community prayer. Called the *opus Dei* (work of God), the official regimen of prayer set aside specific times of the day—morning, noon, night— around which all other aspects of daily life, work, maintenance, and meals were fit. Even a journey outside the monastery (RB 50) or the inability to return to the oratory for prayers was not in itself enough cause to lay aside this daily order and structure of life. The daily, seasonal, and annual cycle of recitations measured out human life into manageable segments and made synchrony with vital rhythms possible. Since it is a high priority of the **Rule,** order provides a major force for fostering inner regulation in strong personalities and at the same time provides a workable structure for weaker developing ones.

8. *Balance* (Moderation). If any quality of spirit stands out in the Benedictine **Rule,** contrasted to earlier monastic rules or later reforms, it is moderation. Moderation in all things is counseled; excess should be avoided (RB 39). In food and drink, wine should be used sparingly (RB 40), and the hour of meals should be tempered and arranged to avoid complaints among the brethren. The abbot, especially, has responsibility for the tone of life and must practice the moderation the **Rule** seeks. He "must show forethought and consideration in his orders, and whether the task he assigns concerns God or the world, he should be discerning and moderate" (RB 64.11). In correcting vices, he must "use prudence and avoid extremes" (RB 64.12). He must accommodate himself to the character, intelligence, and disposition of many (RB 2) as well as be adaptable and balanced in his judgment. Even prayer, in spite of its premier place in the structure of monastic life, was to be moderated—always "short and pure" (RB 20.4)—and "if anyone finds this distribution of psalms unsatisfactory, he should arrange whatever he judges better" (RB 18.22).

Thus, balance lies at the heart of the **Rule.** It provides structure without rigidity, principle without arrogance, and like tempered steel, it is both strong and flexible. Besides infusing the whole of monastic living with a tone of moderation, it integrates its various parts. Benedict must have understood that balanced living could meet the demands of human nature, resolve the conflicts between the inner and outer realities, and forge a psychic unity and a spiritual integrity.

9. *Security.* The **Rule** also anticipates the need for security in human nature. Several aspects of monastic living engender this sense of security. One of them is the distribution of goods, where each receives according to his particular need (RB 34), so that mutual reliance is cultivated. As a correlative, a monk should not own anything, but hold all things in common with his brothers (RB 33). However important these matters are in the ordinary material disposition of daily life,

they do not comprise in themselves the core of the security described in the **Rule.** Essentially, this security rests upon a commitment to a way of life, formalized in the vow to a monastic way of life (*conversatio morum*) and made permanent in the vow of stability. The monastery is the "house built on rock"; it is the world where the monk lives and perseveres until death (RB Prologue). Cenobites are the "strong kind" of monks (RB 1) and the only ones whom Benedict will consider in his **Rule.** One is not easily admitted to this community, but only after being examined for "perseverance in his stability" (RB 58) and after having studied the **Rule** three times.

In other words, the sense of stability, enduring circumstances, rootedness in interpersonal relationships, with bonds to time, place, and practical realities, are fundamental to personal growth and development as Benedict sees it. Commitment to a community in time and place reflects the inner reality of these permanent bonds and roots that make transformations of external reality a logical consequence. One needs only to look at the cultural, educational, and scientific achievements made by religious communities in Western culture to appreciate the impact—and freedom—of psychological security in coping with life.

10. *Beauty* (Acknowledgment of Legitimate Pleasure). Beauty is an integral part of the **Rule.** The monasteries themselves testify to this.[7] The site of Benedict's first full monastic experiment, Monte Cassino, is only the premier example of this element in monastic life; Mont St. Michel is perhaps the most romantic example of it in practice. To be sure, this last element, the need for legitimate pleasure in forms of beauty, is the most derivative and the least explicit of the elements presented in the **Rule.** Yet, a love for beauty seems to flow naturally from the conditions provided by monastic living. The order and balance in day-to-day living, reverence for learning, and attention to simple human needs, form a psychological synergism easily demonstrable in monastic history. They give rise to a number of expressions. For example, liturgical prayer led to its natural enhancement through psalmody and gesture. The practical necessity of providing permanent, stable housing allowed for architectural achievements. The task of copying manuscripts led to the art of embellishment and illumination. In short, it seems that the monastic spirit cannot be indulged without a natural sublimation into beautiful as well as practical forms.

Thus, the psychology manifested in the Benedictine **Rule** reveals a keen perception of the human condition. Yet my exploration into this psychological dimension of the **Rule** barely touches the wealth of insight embedded in the document. Further analysis of the psychological principles of the **Rule** can profit from inquiry that takes into account the formulations of modern social sciences. Topics such as character formation, narcissism, and object relationships are but a few areas where religious and social scientific perspectives can exchange insight with mutual practical results. Scientific analysis and identification of modern psychological equivalents of the monastic experience do not denigrate the **Rule**'s religious value. If anything, they only deepen our appreciation for the profound religious contribution made by St. Benedict.

Notes

[1] Thomas Merton, *The Silent Life* (New York: Farrar, Straus and Cudahy 1957) p. 81.

[2] A. W. Richard Sipe, "*Memento Mori: Memento Vivere*—In the Rule of St. Benedict," *The American Benedictine Review* 27 (March 1974) 96-107.

[3] Although St. Basil wrote rules for communal monasticism in the fourth century and, in the same century, St. Pachomius established monastic communities in Egypt, neither tradition represents the balance, maturity and integration manifest in Benedict's rule.

[4] Erik H. Erikson, *Young Man Luther* (New York: W. W. Norton 1958) p. 109.

[5] *RB 1980: The Rule of St. Benedict, in Latin and English with Notes,* ed. Timothy Fry (Collegeville, MN: The Liturgical Press 1981).

[6] Thomas Merton, "Final Integration: Toward a 'Monastic Therapy,'" *The Journal of Pastoral Counseling* 4 (1969).

[7] Walter Horn and Ernest Born, *The Plan of St. Gall,* 3 vols. (Berkeley: The University of California Press 1979).

Peter E. Hammett (essay date 1988)

SOURCE: "Care for the Individual in the *Rule of Benedict,*" *The American Benedictine Review,* Vol. 39, No. 3, September, 1988, pp. 277-86.

[*In the following essay, Hammett demonstrates "how a genuine care for the subjective dimensions of the monk's personality" is reflected in the* Rule *of* Benedict.]

We live in a world which places a great deal of emphasis on the subject and on the psychological aspects of the person. Since the Enlightenment, philosophy's turn to the subject and a deepening understanding of the psychological dimensions of the human person have become characteristic of our contemporary Western world-view. The basic thesis of this paper is that this turn to the subject is not incompatible with the empha-

sis which the **Rule of Benedict** (RB) places on living the ideal of monastic life within community. Nor does a psychological emphasis detract from the monk's vow of *conversatio morum.* The following reflections seek to show how a genuine care for the subjective dimensions of the monk's personality is presupposed in the **RB** and how attention to the pyschological can help in living the monastic way of life.

To insure that no misunderstanding occurs, it is necessary to draw a distinction between subjectivity and subjectivism. In his book *The God of Jesus Christ,* Walter Kasper offers a workable distinction, useful for our purposes. He says:

> But subjectivity should not be confused with subjectivism, although this is a mistake constantly made. Subjectivism, which absolutizes the subject's limited position and private interests, is a particularist point of view; modern subjectivity, on the other hand, is a universalist mode of thought, a new approach to the whole of reality.[1]

With this distinction in mind, and avoiding a narcissistic subjectivism, we are concerned here with genuine subjectivity: the subject as intentional being, oriented toward relationship with others and with God, based on a truthful relationship with self. Thus the subject is both unique in individuality and placed in the real, objective world.

Having made this distinction, we can now situate the problematic for study here. Does emphasis on personal growth, with a strong psychological orientation, water down the living of the monastic way of life, ordered as it is to the individual monk achieving the Kingdom precisely through communal living and obedience to an abbot? Does contemporary attention to the rhythms and conflicts of life and developmental stages so turn the monk in on self that living under a Rule and abbot within community becomes secondary to the life project of the individual? Expressed differently, how do we understand and deal creatively with the tension between the individual in unique phases of growth and development (at times manifesting maladaptive behaviors) and the objective demands of the monastic way of life?

The following discussion will be carried out in three sections: 1) care for the subject in Benedict's instructions to the abbot; 2) care for the subject in his understanding of community; 3) Benedict's paschal spirituality, *conversatio morum* and the subjective.

Care for the Subject in Benedict's Instructions to the Abbot

In Chapters 2 and 64 of the **Rule,** Benedict gives lengthy guidelines for the abbot. Within these instructions we can find some insights and principles to speak to the above questions. The abbot will have a variety of characters on his hands: some will be virtuous and eager to grow, some may be stuck in their growth efforts (the stubborn), while others may be questioning and unsettled. He speaks of the abbot as shepherd of a "restive and disobedient flock" with "unhealthy ways" (RB 2.8). The abbot is to "lead his disciples by a twofold teaching: he must point out to them all that is good and holy more by example than by words, proposing the commandments of the Lord to receptive disciples with words, but demonstrating God's instructions to the stubborn and dull by a living example" (RB 2.11, 12). Because these various growth needs of the individual must be responded to, the abbot is told to vary with circumstances. He threatens and coaxes; he is to be stern or devoted and tender, as the situation warrants. The abbot is to be so attuned to various personalities in the community that he will know when to use firm argument and when to appeal for greater virtue. Finally, to indicate that the abbot is dealing with the subjective dispositions of unique individuals, Benedict says that the abbot "must so accommodate himself to each one's character and intelligence" that he will not only lose none of the flock entrusted to him, but "will rejoice in the increase of a good flock" (RB 2.32).

One should complement the above with reference to Benedict's teaching on obedience in Chapter 5 of the **Rule.** To properly do this would entail a detailed study of obedience; a few observations will perhaps indicate the relationship between care for the individual and obedience.

Obedience has as its purpose a responsiveness to the will of God as manifested in the superior's directive, and so, ultimately, to the Kingdom of God itself. Obedience is difficult: it demands putting aside one's own needs, concerns, will and judgments; forsaking the satisfactions of one's whims and appetites (RB 5.12), and responding to the superior's orders willingly and without grumbling in the heart. But Benedict says, in speaking of obedience, that "it is love that impels them to pursue everlasting life; therefore they are eager to take the narrow road . . ." (RB 5.10). This "labor of obedience" (RB Prol. 2) is meant to bring the monk back to God from whom he has strayed through disobedience, and is therefore one way in which the abbot shows his care for the individual. Obedience to Rule and abbot, with a strict penal code, is one objective way of protecting genuine subjectivity from degenerating into subjectivism.

Translating this into the contemporary problematic of subjectivity-subjectivism, we might say that the psychological condition of each monk is indeed relevant to living the monastic way of life. In the spiritual journey to the Kingdom, the monk will have to face vari-

ous inner psychological as well as spiritual conflicts which can produce a seemingly stubborn, dull or restive person. While these states may at times seem to remove the person from fully living the monastic way of life, and so cause worry to the abbot about the objective ordering of the monastery, Benedict seems to presuppose such subjective states as part of the journey. That is why the abbot must be flexible, accommodating himself to the needs of each individual. Obedience to **Rule** and abbot is a specific tool in the hands of the superior by which he continually holds before the monk the objective goal of the Christian and monastic life: fulfillment through sharing in the Kingdom. At the same time, all of the **Rule**'s emphasis on the community at prayer, at meals, at work or holy reading, all of which make up the monastic way of life, must be seen in isolation from the subjective state of the individual monk. There is therefore a tension in the **Rule:** growth into the Kingdom through obedience and common observance and attention to the legitimate subjective needs of the individual monk.

Care for the Subject in Benedict's Understanding of Community

Two passages in the **RB** offer a transition from the abbot to the community's concern for the individual. At the end of the Prologue, Benedict says, "Therefore we intend to establish a school for the Lord's service" (RB Prol. 45). The footnote in the *RB 1980* says that in the Latin, *schola* is not merely a place but a grouping of people who receive instruction, a "vocational corporation."[2] In this *schola* cenobites not only learn to serve but actually do serve Christ the King. As a community, cenobites learn from Christ who teaches his disciples. The monk is therefore one who has chosen a path of lifelong learning and therefore lifelong growing. The cenobite, to continue in this school for the Lord's service, is in constant need of the support of the other students, the community, in the combat that produces personal growth (RB 1.4,5).

The individual is to find in the community the understanding and support needed for growing in the project of the *schola*. The monastery and "stability in the community" (RB 4.78) are the workshop for the growth of the monk. The tools of good works, those elements of the spiritual craft, are for the individual to use to achieve his goal, which is full conformity to the death and resurrection of Christ.

I would suggest that, since the community is meant to give help and guidance to the individual (RB 1.4) in his struggle to grow, the monk needs the community's support in order to use tools of the spiritual craft to the fullest.

Benedict, though, is a realist when it comes to viewing the concrete individual. Some brothers don't live up to the ideal: some waver in living the monastic way of life and some do not use the tools of good works well, while still others may become disobedient. Just as in contemporary monasteries, Benedict's monks came late for meals and prayer. To all of these the abbot responds as a skillful surgeon, showing concern for the faltering. Benedict states that the abbot has "undertaken the care of the sick" (RB 27.6) and so responds to the wayward with "all speed, discernment and diligence," using "*senpectae,* that is, mature and wise brothers" (RB 27.2). Thus, the abbot does not act alone; he relies on the mature wisdom and growth found within the community. The sleepy like to make excuses, so, when arising for the work of God, the brothers will quietly encourage one another (RB 22.8). When making satisfaction "he [the monk] must come before the abbot and community" (RB 46.3) so that they may pray for him. Before a monk is excommunicated, there are two private warnings by seniors (again, the abbot employing wise and tried members of the community), then a public rebuke if necessary (RB 23), presumably to bring positive peer pressure to the troubled monk. There is a strong emphasis on the reality of the spiritually sick, the weak, the faltering and the wavering in the community and also on what the community, guided by the abbot, often represented by *senpectae,* can do for the sick monk. In reality, the monastery is not a house of those who have reached perfection of life and observance. Rather, it is made up of real individuals who, for various subjective reasons, do not live up to the ideal. These people are not dead weight to the community. Benedict quotes the Gospel of Matthew: "It is not the healthy who need a physician, but the sick" (Mt 9:12/RB 27.1). The above examples suggest that the community as a whole (along with the abbot) has functions as physician for the brothers needing care.

In Chapter 28 Benedict legislates for those whose growth seems to be painfully slow and whose stubbornness is severe. Even here we see the solicitude of both abbot and community. The abbot is to come down hard on the brother who has been non-responsive to the healing care shown him. He applies the "ointment of encouragement, the medicine of divine Scripture, and finally the cauterizing iron of excommunication and strokes of the rod" (RB 28.3). After these progressive steps of harshness have failed, the abbot and community seek the better remedy: prayer (RB 28.4). Yes, the ***Rule*** does make explicit that at times the care shown the individual in his stymied growth will be severe. Benedict's realism is again manifest. At times the individual must be made to feel in some dramatic and painful way the need to grow. But note that prayer is the climax and is considered even more radical and powerful than strokes (RB 28.6).

Paschal Spirituality, Conversatio Morum and the Subjective

What are we to make of this care for the monk plagued with failures, waverings and disobedience? What are we to make of the seemingly harsh treatment that the monk receives from the abbot, aimed at having him die to his former ways? Perhaps we can pull these reflections together by understanding *conversatio morum* as living in the rhythm of the paschal mystery. This will enable us to embrace a true subjectivity without the dangers of private interest and subjectivism. According to the ***Rule,*** the paschal mystery is to permeate all of the monk's life and it is to lead into a living love.

To make dying to the old man for a new life in Christ concrete, Benedict says that through humility we willingly suffer now, especially through obedience to superiors. This is a real death to self, for the sake of the reward which lies ahead: eternal glory and exaltation (RB 4.35,41). The monk is therefore to share patiently in the sufferings of Christ through humble obedience, so as to share in his Kingdom (RB Prol. 50). His life is to be a continuous Lent made manifest in the forty days so that a longing for Easter may be his goal (RB 49).

To speak of Benedict's spirituality is to speak of living the paschal mystery of Christ. The passing over of Jesus to the Father through death permeates the ***RB,*** providing the model for the monk's life. So, living the monastic way of life [*conversatio morum*] is the monk's chosen way of living out the paschal mystery, a personal appropriation by the monk of the death and resurrection of Jesus and of the sending of the Spirit. The monastic way of life is ordered to the monk's sharing in the sufferings of Christ and so sharing already in this lifetime the risen life of eternity.

By seeing the monk's vow of *conversatio* as his way of incarnating the paschal mystery in his life, we come to understand what the monk is and what he hopes to become. We see concretely life and fidelity to the Gospel lived in the community of the monastery with its goal being the Kingdom. *Conversatio* is a fitting of the rhythm of the paschal mystery into the fabric of the monk's daily life. Life under a Rule and an abbot, daily dying to the old man, a life surrendered to the common good: this is the monastic way of life and this is the paschal mystery lived concretely in the monastery.

Benedict legislates for this way of life in "this little rule that we have written for beginners" (RB 73.8). Ascetical theology, with its popular notions of religious life as the life of perfection, has tended to lose the journey aspect of life in the Spirit, stressing, instead, the static ideal of perfection. But all life is a journey, a process which takes time. Benedict therefore instructs the monk to persevere until death, indicating that the struggle for both fidelity and virtue continues through life and is a process.

If today we are to confront realistically the many possible detours which the spiritual journey of a monk can take and respond in more than a merely legalistic or psychological way, we must recapture the process of the paschal spirituality of the **RB** and see its union with *conversatio morum. Conversatio* is not something accomplished once and for all in profession. It is a way of life, an attitude lived through daily dying and rising. Being a process, it can go askew at any point in the monk's life.

Coping with Problems

As they journey through life towards the Kingdom, monks today are subject to many problems arising from contemporary life, culture and its demands. There are physical problems associated with aging, sexual frustrations, chemical addictions, stress and burnout from workloads. There are psychological difficulties: loss of a sense of self-worth, feelings of inadequacy and uselessness through being replaced by younger workers. There are social challenges: the tensions of community living, pluralism in community, Church and society, changes in abbatial office and administration in the monastery. Finally, there are spiritual difficulties: loss of religious fervour, feelings of failure in the ideals of spiritual growth that once motivated the monk.

These problems bring an added stress: they indicate that a secure and comfortable way of being self is being left behind with a new self-project being placed before the person. Contemporary studies have indicated that one's bodily death is accepted only after other stages have been gone through. This is not only the case with biological death; it is also the case when one must die psychologically and spiritually to an outgrown mode of being a person (and a Christian monk). This means that transitional moments in life *can* be accompanied by the same reactions one experiences over the approach of biological death, namely: 1) by a rejection of what is taking place; 2) by a deep depression over the loss of what is a known and therefore secure way of being self; 3) by moments of seeming acceptance of the change, followed by 4) anger at self and the whole growth process that is causing so much unrest and turmoil; and, let it be hoped, 5) by a final resignation to the new life which is emerging in a surrender, a "yes" to the love calling one to a fuller life.

All these manifestations of struggle, grief and dying to self, caused by the many problems of life and challenges from society, can manifest themselves in maladaptive behavior. Superiors may tend to view such behaviors as lapses in monastic observance, as breaches of basic commitment. While this is so on the level of observable behavior, it is indeed possible that such behavior is an indication of a deeper struggle, a basic inner warfare in which the monk is being called to die to self and accept graciously the offer of a new and fuller life in Christ. Thus, we are dealing with a spiritual problem which, in reality, is the struggle to make the death and resurrection of Jesus something personal. Ideally, the individual monk and superior can respond to problems, failures, sins or spiritual deadness as a challenge, an offer of grace, an opportunity to grow in the life of the Spirit. When there is a loving concern and understanding on the part of the superior, he can effectively use the many tools which Benedict places at his disposal in order to present to the individual the rhythm of the monastic way of life as a healing power because of its objective: submersion into the paschal mystery of Christ. Used with sensitivity, obedience can and should be very healing.

Some Conclusions

The very rhythm of life, with its stages of growth, transitional moments, and detours in the journey, can and should be seen within the rhythm of the struggle to accept death, a death that can daily issue into new life. When seen in this light, one can understand the moments of personal turmoil, the times of struggle, laxity and failure, not merely as maladaptive behavior or as flights from regular observance, but as intense moments of a deep spiritual struggle to die to a former way of life.

The abbot is called by Benedict to govern the monastery on two levels simultaneously: that of the ideal, to which he witnesses by his very life and teaching, and that of the real, the subjective dispositions of his monks. The ideal level is the **Rule,** the customs of the house and the spiritual program that makes up the monastic way of life. At the same time there is the subjective level, because the community is made up of unique individuals. Each has a personal history, unfinished growth projects, spiritual longings and frustrations, experiences of failure and success. But any possible dichotomy between the ideal and subjective level is eliminated when it is realized that the monastic project succeeds only to the extent that the various subjects who make it up experience healing in their personhood and growth into the death and resurrection of Jesus. This teaching on the care the abbot should have for the subjective disposition of his monks is illustrated in the following, quoted from *The Rule of St. Benedict: A Doctrinal and Spiritual Commentary,* by Adalbert de Vogüé.

> It is enough to note that Benedict's personal contribution denotes not only the extreme interest he brought to the question of the abbot in general,

but also a particular solicitude for the consideration which the superior should have for the different characters of his subjects. . . . This feeling for, and respect of, persons is generally one of Benedict's distinctive traits in comparison to the Master, but it is particularly interesting that he makes it a special duty of the abbot. . . . Superiors [today] are much re-proached for having ignored the graces and perso-nal needs of their subjects. . . . But if the abbot of the monastic tradition is decidedly above the community, this fact, which in no way can be changed, does not prevent an extreme sensibility on the part of the legislator—as we see in Benedict—to the needs and weaknesses of individuals, a sensibility which he seeks in every way to communicate to the abbot.[3]

The community likewise lives the monastic way of life on two levels. The ideal level is the very rhythm of prayer, work, meals, rest, *lectio* and obedience, all of which define the life. But the community is made up of individuals who often struggle, as individuals, to em-body the ideal and give it substance. For this reason, to respond creatively to the psychological and developmen-tal dimensions of the spiritual project does not mean to fall into subjectivism. As the individual achieves ever greater subjective wholeness, that person lives more fully the objective ideal of the monastic way of life, and the community is strengthened as the *schola* which both learns how to and actually does serve the Lord. When an individual falters, wavers or fails in living the monas-tic way of life, the community is only weakened if it fails to be a source of strength, wisdom and prayerful encouragement for the individual monk.

Conversatio morum, living the monastic way of life, is a path of dying to self, so that biological death may one day bring the monk fully into the Kingdom. Benedict seems to instruct the abbot and the commu-nity: dying is a tough project. So, support, sustain, even punish when necessary, but lead and guide one another to new life.

Notes

[1] Walter Kasper, *The God of Jesus Christ* (New York: Crossroad Publishing Co. 1986) p. 18.

[2] Timothy Fry, O.S.B., *RB 1980* (Collegeville, MN: The Liturgical Press 1981) p. 165.

[3] Adalbert de Vogüé, *The Rule of Saint Benedict: A Doctrinal and Spiritual Commentary* (Kalamazoo, MI: Cistercian Publications 1983) p. 72.

Jerome Theisen (essay date 1989)

SOURCE: "Personal Prayer in the *Rule of Benedict,*" *The American Benedictine Review,* Vol. 40, No. 3, September, 1989, pp. 291-303.

[*In the following essay, Theisen focuses on the meth-ods of prayer and sacred reading contained in the* Rule of St. Benedict.]

The monk in Benedict's monastery leads a rather simple and balanced life: public prayer with the community; private reading, study, and prayer; manual labor; pub-lic reading; refection; and sleep. In this paper I pro-pose to look at 1) features of personal or private prayer in the *Rule of Benedict,* 2) notions of listening to the word of God, 3) values of sacred reading, and 4) methods of listening and praying. My purpose is to suggest how people of today can use the Benedictine experience for their prayer life, an experience that has stood the test of time since the appearance of the *Rule of Benedict* in the middle of the sixth century.

Simple and Heartfelt Prayer

Benedict legislates in great detail for the service of public prayer by day and by night, but he devotes only a few paragraphs to the theology and method of prayer.[1] In Chapter 19, which deals directly with common prayer, Benedict provides two principles of prayer: re-membrance of the presence of God and harmony be-tween mind and voice; in other words, paying attention to the divine subject of prayer and the meaning of the psalms.

Benedict broaches the subject of private, individual prayer more explicitly in Chapter 20 which bears the title "Reverence in Prayer." His first reason for rever-ence in prayer seems rather mundane: we customarily approach important and powerful persons with respect and humility. He reasons that a reverent bearing should guide our approach to the very God of the universe.

In recommending this approach to God, however, Benedict uses two phrases that help us understand his notion of prayer. He wants his monks to petition God "with the utmost humility and sincere devotion" (*cum omni humilitate et puritatis devotione*). The word hu-mility is key in the spirituality of Saint Benedict. It describes the disposition of total dependence on God. The monk is taught in Chapter 7 to be empty of pride and self-will, to follow the obedience of Christ, and to regard himself as an unworthy servant. The monk ac-knowledges his sin and his emptiness in the presence of God. With such a disposition the monk is ready to receive the favor of God.

If humility represents the emptiness with which we should come into the presence of God, sincere devo-tion designates the intensity and fullness that should characterize the human heart at prayer. The Latin of verse 2 reads literally: "with the devotion of purity." "Sincere devotion" is a commendable translation but it does not catch all the nuances of the Latin phrase. The word "devotion" depicts the person's dedication to God;

connotations of vows and commitment are also present in the word. "Purity" refers to the simplicity, the straightforwardness, and the single-mindedness of the disposition. The person of pure devotion, having removed outer noise and inner distraction, attends wholeheartedly to the Lord.

Verse 3 of Chapter 20 begins (in Latin) with an indication of what should not characterize our prayer: "many words." Benedict most likely has Jesus' admonition in mind: "In your prayer do not rattle on like the pagans. They think they will win a hearing by the sheer multiplication of words" (Mt 6:7). The multiplication of words creates noisy static that militates against the disposition of simplicity and single-mindedness. It also goes counter to the inner emptiness that is required of the humble heart.

Verse 3 continues with two phrases that more sharply define the kind of disposition that Benedict promotes: "purity of heart and tears of compunction" (*in puritate cordis et compunctione lacrimarum*). Here we meet the word *puritas* once again, this time conjoined to the word "heart." Since genuine prayer comes from the heart, Benedict specifies that the heart must be pure, single-minded, and unclouded. It cannot be a heart that is distracted, heavy, and complicated. The pure of heart are disposed to see God. As one monk has put it: "Blessed are the pure in heart, who have become as little children, for they shall see God in all things."[2]

The prayer that Benedict has in mind is also marked with "tears of compunction" (literally, according to the Latin, "with the compunction of tears"). Compunction refers to the piercing of the heart to make it responsive to God. The monk at prayer experiences a lancing of the heart, effected by God and resulting in a stream of tears. The heart not only experiences sorrow for personal sins but also the pressure and presence of God. Both sorrow for sins and joy in the love of God result in a flow of tears.[3]

Surprisingly, given the traditional command "to pray without ceasing," Benedict directs that prayer should be "short and pure, unless perhaps it is prolonged under the inspiration of divine grace" (RB 20.4). Perhaps he wants this personal prayer to be short because it is nearly impossible to maintain its simplicity and intensity over a long period of time; the type of prayer he has in mind is more like a glance directed to the face of God.

For the third time in this chapter we come across the word "pure," this time in adjectival form. As explained above, the word pure here means simple, without complication, without obstruction, direct, and straightforward.

Benedict advocates brief and direct prayer unless prolonged by God, literally (according to the Latin) "un-

less perhaps it is prolonged by the affection of the inspiration of divine grace" (*ex affectu inspirationis divinae gratiae*). The sense of the passage is that God's favor may very well impart great fervor and thus promote an extension of the time of prayer. The glance may turn into a prolonged contemplation. But Benedict seems to imply that such is not always the case; in fact, that such is the exception rather than the rule.

Another significant reference to private prayer occurs in Chapter 52, "The Oratory of the Monastery." One gets the impression that Benedict's oratory is simple and austere. It is designed for one purpose only—to accommodate the brothers at prayer. It is not a multi-purpose room as many of our churches are today. Benedict's oratory surely has an altar (see RB 58.20, 29; 59.2; 62.6), but it is significant that the place is named, not from the presence of the altar and the Eucharist which must be celebrated there from time to time, but from the divine office which is accomplished there: "The oratory ought to be what it is called . . ." (RB 52.1).

Benedict notes with satisfaction the possibility that a brother will remain in the oratory for private prayer after the completion of the Liturgy of Hours. He also desires that a monk go into the oratory at other times for private prayer. In this context he provides us with more of his thought about the qualities of private prayer. The monk, he says, "may simply go in and pray, not in a loud voice, but with tears and heartfelt devotion." He repeats some terms and ideas from Chapter 20. But some terms are new and here the ideas are expressed differently. The negative in Chapter 20 was "not in many words"; here the negative is expressed with the phrase "not in a loud voice." God does not need the loud voice, of course, and in the oratory the loud voice would disturb others who wish to pray there.

The reference to tears occurs once again. Obviously the ancients were not embarrassed with a flow of tears to express their emotions of sorrow or love; in fact, tears were regarded as a gift of God and a noble way of acquiring purification and virtue.

The new phrase is "heartfelt devotion" (*intentione cordis*). Our English translation is fairly accurate, but it does not contain all the overtones and undertones of the Latin phrase *intentio cordis*. The word "heart" qualifies the word *intentio* which here denotes the heart's attention to God. Michael Casey sums up an analysis of the phrase with these words:

> What he [the monk who follows Benedict's advice] experiences is what constantly takes place beyond the limits of consciousness, the inevitable stretching forth of the human heart toward its God. Prayer for Saint Benedict, therefore, is a matter of concentration of heart: concentration in the sense of an active

effort to restrict other activities, thoughts and desires; concentration in the sense of strengthening one's awareness of the reality of the heart's movement toward God; concentration in the sense of returning to one's centre.[4]

Listening to the Word of God

Benedict begins his **Rule** with the word "listen" (*obsculta*). No better word could characterize the whole monastic enterprise, for the Christian turns to the monastic life precisely so that he or she can hear the word of God. Of course, the word of God is found elsewhere; in fact, the monk generally hears it elsewhere and finds that for him it leads to the monastery, a place steeped in the word. The word is sounded frequently throughout the monastic day: in the public prayer of the community, in the private readings of the Bible, and in the teachings of the abbot. The word is present in abundance, but it bears no fruit if no one is there to listen to it with an attentive heart.

Benedict exhorts the monk to obedience because obedience is closely akin to listening. "The labor of obedience will bring you back to him from whom you had drifted through the sloth of disobedience" (RB Prologue 2). There is no obedience without first listening. Heeding the word of God implies that one first hears the word and is disposed to listen with attention. Heeding the word implies that one overcomes the sloth of disobedience and makes one's journey back to God. Listening with the heart is a way of life.

Benedict does not concern himself with questions about whether or not the word of God is present; he is convinced in faith that it is present. While he does not cite the prologue of John's Gospel, he surely hears its central statement: "The Word became flesh and made his dwelling among us, and we have seen his glory: the glory of an only Son coming from the Father, filled with enduring love" (Jn 1:14). The word of God, therefore, is not in a distant land, unapproachable and impenetrable. The word of God is present in the midst of the monastery, ready to be perceived by those who listen and heed.

Benedict is acquainted with the teaching of the Letter to the Hebrews. Its author draws out the implications of the Word made flesh, extending the Word's presence to our inmost being:

> Indeed, God's word is living and effective, sharper than any two-edged sword. It penetrates and divides soul and spirit, joints and marrow; it judges the reflections and thoughts of the heart. Nothing is concealed from him; all lies bare and exposed to the eyes of him to whom we must render an account. (Heb 4:12-13)

Benedict does not cite this passage from Hebrews, but he must have read it and he perceived the truth of it. He states, for instance, that God sees the heart of the monk who obeys but grumbles (RB 5.18). We have already seen that according to Benedict the public prayer of the community takes place in the presence of the God of the universe. God penetrates the heart; the word of God slices to the center of our being.

Benedict regards the monk as a listener to the word of God. He does not speculate on this human activity as does Father Karl Rahner, an insightful theologian of our day! Rahner, it is well known, defines humans as hearers of the word, persons listening for the word, persons transcendentally oriented to the divine.[5] Benedict is content to remind the monk of the presence of God and to make sure that the word reverberates throughout the monastery on a daily and hourly basis. He assumes quite naturally that it is possible for the monk to perceive the word and to carry it out in practice.

Benedict is not bothered by any doubt about whether there is a dialogue partner in the heavens. Or so it seems in the **Rule** and in the *Dialogues* of Saint Gregory. Benedict assumes the presence of a God, someone who addresses the monk in a direct fashion. Many Christians today, and others throughout history, find this God distant or evanescent; they feel alone and isolated. Such is the experience of some modern monks as well, at least for certain periods of their lives. God seems far away and the monk feels alone. It is at this time that the monk should ponder the two aspects of the divine being: silence and word. At times he will relate to silence, and at times to the word.[6]

Benedict's solution is attention to the word, a listening to the heart of the word in the midst of human life. God is really present in the Sacred Scriptures. The real presence of Jesus is not confined to the sacrament of the altar but extends to the words of the Bible.[7] Benedict does not state the matter in precisely these terms, but he is convinced that Christ is present in the words of prayer; in fact, he also finds Christ in the guest, in the sick, and in the abbot.

What becomes apparent, therefore, is that people are words of God to each other. God speaks forth a word and the universe comes into being. The universe becomes a word of God; human beings become words of God.[8] Benedict does not carry his thinking this far; at least he does not this language. But today we can acknowledge the truth of the ubiquity of the word in our universe. We are words to each other; the world at large is a word to us.

If we are the word of God in our own fashion, we should be extremely sensitive to the intrusion of the divine word around us. Some teachers stress the ubiquity of the word and advise us to read the word everywhere: in a piece of poetry, in a sunset, in human love, in a smile, etc. There is no dearth of words; but there is a lack of attention to the words of every moment and of every experience.

Each monk listens for the word, but the word is not just for the individual; it is for the whole community. In fact, the whole community listens for the word and receives it better when many concentrate on the word. Individual perceptions of the word are corrected by the perceptions of others. Community listening ultimately results in a community commentary on the word.

The word that we hear leads us to a new understanding of ourselves and the world. It leads us to new challenges. Thomas Merton expressed this truth when speaking of the Bible: "We all instinctively know that it is dangerous to become involved in the Bible. The book judges us, or seems to judge us, on terms to which at first we could not possibly agree."[9]

Benedict never offers his monks a vacation from listening to the word of God. The word is always present, and listening for it is always a duty and a pleasure. Monks wait patiently for the word to clarify itself, even though they know that it is never entirely clear. But it is the task of monks and it is the task of people generally to wait in patience for the unfolding of the word of God. The Scriptures are like flowers that open up if people have the patience to stand before them in expectation.

Sacred Reading

It should be apparent that listening is not confined to the Divine Office or to the conferences of the abbot. Listening takes place throughout the day in a great variety of ways. But a primary way of listening in Benedict's monastery is sacred reading. The practice is called *lectio divina.* The full phrase, which occurs only once in the Rule (48.1), is variously translated: divine reading, sacred reading, prayerful reading, spiritual reading. The word *divina* evidently refers to the divine character of the text and the godly practice of sacred reading.

Benedict never explains the method of sacred reading; he does not even devote a chapter to the subject, though the topic comes up most frequently in Chapter 48: "The Daily Manual Labor." He assumes that his monks will involve themselves in this practice for three, four, and even five hours a day.[10] When he sets up the horarium of the monastery, especially the times for manual labor, he makes certain that the monks have ample time for sacred reading. He begins Chapter 48 with the general principle: "Idleness is the enemy of the soul. Therefore, the brothers should have specified periods for manual labor as well as for prayerful reading" (RB 48.1). He then proceeds to set up the schedule of the day, alternating manual labor and sacred reading. The times for both vary according to the season of the year, but in all cases he seems to preserve prime time for *lectio divina;* he is also careful not to prescribe manual labor during the hottest hours of summer.

Benedict even allows a siesta during the summer months, both because of the heat and because of the shorter nights for sleeping. He does not require the siesta, and he allows a brother to read privately at that time if he wishes; but he warns him not to disturb others (RB 48.5). This little admonition gives us a clue to the method of reading in Benedict's time. They normally read aloud and not silently to themselves. This practice should not surprise us, for it was common among the ancients. Even today some people find that they can study a text better if they read it aloud; and English teachers recommend the oral reading of poetry for better enjoyment and understanding.

What did the monks read? The primary book was the Bible, but sacred reading also included commentaries on the Bible, the writings of earlier monastic authors, and the writings of noted Christian authors. They believed that the message of the Sacred Scriptures could be articulated outside the Bible itself. We should not assume, however, that Benedict's monastery, or most monasteries of that time, possessed a large number of volumes. Books were precious and expensive. But since Benedict refers to the reading of various authors such as Saint Basil, his monastery must have owned a representative number of books.

Benedict makes specific mention of the distribution of books at the beginning of Lent: "During this time of Lent each one is to receive a book from the library, and is to read the whole of it straight through. These books are to be distributed at the beginning of Lent" (RB 48.15-16). One author suggests that Benedict is speaking about various sections of the Bible.[11] In any event there is reference to a place where books are kept (*bibliotheca*). The texts are handed out at the beginning of Lent, both to show that monks should be especially observant during this sacred time of the year but also to indicate that sacred reading is an *opus,* i.e., a task, a discipline, and an ascetical work.

During their reading periods the monks could pore over or devote themselves to the psalms (cf. RB 48.13). They not only studied the psalms, which formed the bulk of their Divine Office, they also learned them by heart, both for purposes of recitation in choir and for prayerful recall during the day.

Sunday is a special day of reading for Benedict. One gets the impression that much of the day is devoted to this practice: "On Sunday all are to be engaged in reading except those who have been assigned various duties. If anyone is so remiss and indolent that he is unwilling or unable to study or to read, he is to be given some work in order that he may not be idle" (RB 48.22-23). One might conclude from this passage that some of Benedict's monks were illiterate and therefore had to be given some other task to occupy themselves.

The passage also throws more light on Benedict's method of reading; he uses the words "to study or to read" (*meditare aut legere*). Are these practices entirely separate occupations or are they similar? Benedict seems to find them more similar than not. Both in study and in reading the monk ponders the text, ruminates on it, savors it, even learns it or some of it by heart. The text is not just something to absorb for its informational value; it is designed to lead to prayer. Prayer is a natural outgrowth of the reading of the text. Prayer is the very goal of the reading.

One gets a feel for this prayerful reading in a passage that occurs in Chapter 49, "The Observance of Lent." Benedict wants his monks to live intense and penitential lives during Lent. "This we can do in a fitting manner by refusing to indulge evil habits and by devoting ourselves to prayer with tears, to reading, to compunction of heart and self-denial" (RB 49.4). The four practices are not entirely distinct. It takes self-denial to devote oneself to reading and to prayer. Moreover, prayer with tears and compunction of heart can develop directly out of sacred reading; poring over the sacred words leads one to a prayerful relationship to the presence of God. Reading, therefore, is a discipline of prayer.

It is clear that Benedict does not regard the Divine Office as the only period of prayer in the horarium of his monastery. Prayer continues throughout the day but in different modes and methods: the public prayer of the Divine Office, prayerful reading, the remembrance of God during the hours of manual labor and at all times of the day. The monastic life is structured in such a manner that monks may give themselves over to the ascetical practices of reading and prayer. The monk has space opened up in his life for sacred reading and for prayer and tears. His life is simply given up to prayer.

Methods of Listening and Praying

It remains to review briefly the monastic methods of private prayer and to make some suggestions for all who wish to deepen their prayer today. Monastic methods need not be confined to monasteries; they are adaptable to other circumstances.

Benedict's **Rule** teaches us first of all that we need to make space in the day for sacred reading and private prayer. We need to have leisure for this discipline. If prayerful reading is important, and we are convinced

that it should be a part of every Christian's life, space must be made in the schedule of the day.

Each person should find a suitable place and set aside the same time each day, a period in which he or she is usually not disturbed, e.g., early in the morning, before work, or late in the evening. It is important to view that time as one's own sacred time. One should look forward to it as to a time for listening, as a time to come into contact with one's deepest thoughts and feelings. One can regard this personal time as the day's anchor. All else takes on direction and meaning in terms of this private contact with God.

The time for prayerful reading and listening will automatically bring about a slowing down of one's thoughts and activities. Our life is usually frenetic and we very much need to slow down, to take time for reflection and prayer.

Creating a space in the day for private reading and prayer does not mean that we do not listen for the word at other times. Listening should be our stance throughout the day, for the word comes to us in many ways: through other persons, through our community, through the changes of nature, etc. Of course, we need to listen selectively and with discretion because there is a glut of sounds in our society and we are surely limited in the number of words we can assimilate.

The monastic method teaches us that we do not read the Scriptures only for the information that they provide. Of course, we need to know much about the origin and nature of the Bible (authors, forms of writing, languages, etc.). *Lectio divina* does not disdain a critical approach to the Scriptures; certainly this approach is required of any clear thinker today. But the point of the monastic practice is the reading with the heart as well as with the mind. It is listening with the heart, under the inspiration of the Spirit, and a response in living prayer.

Listening to the word with the mind and the heart opens the person to the influence of the Spirit. God cannot approach us with delight and freedom unless we make ourselves vulnerable to the word. *Lectio divina* and private prayer permit our inner selves to be touched or wounded by the word. It is a word that pierces but also heals. Prayer is basically healing and communion.

In sacred reading we need not go for mileage, trying to cover as many pages as possible in the time allotted. Sacred reading is a slow pondering of the text; perhaps one will cover only a chapter or a few paragraphs of a book. We will have to slow down if we read the Scriptures out loud or if we are careful to savor the text. Sacred reading is rumination and meditation on the text, not a speed reading course.

If we are attentive to the sacred text, even memorizing portions of the Scriptures, especially the psalms, we can repeat words and phrases at other times, at odd moments of the day. The voices we hear in private prayer and reading can resound in our ears during the course of the day, just like a familiar tune keeps running through our mind. Attention to the word in *lectio divina* makes it possible for the prayer to spill over into the rest of the day.

Lectio divina may be regarded as a primer for other forms of prayer. Yes, there are many other forms of prayer: the prayer of quiet, contemplative prayer, public prayer, etc., but *lectio divina* may set the scene for all of them. For example, after reading a chapter or two of Sacred Scripture and a commentary, one may put aside the books and just rest in silence, letting the Spirit lead where the Spirit will. Some may prefer to repeat a mantra or to assume various methods of breathing and sitting in order to deepen the sense of quiet and centeredness. *Lectio divina* may lead us to all forms of quiet prayer.

It should be apparent from these reflections that the monastic methods of private prayer are not confined to monks; they are available to Christians generally. They can be adapted to anyone's disposition and schedule of life. Anyone can progress in the discipline of prayer and sacred reading. Benedict was not writing for spiritual giants but for ordinary Christians who were monks and who wished to seek God in a practical way, especially by a regular round of sound reading and heartfelt prayer. His way of prayer is still a guide for monks and for any Christian believer.

Notes

[1] The edition and English used in this paper is generally Timothy Fry, O.S.B., ed., *RB 1980: The Rule of St. Benedict in Latin and English with Notes* (Collegeville, MN: The Liturgical Press 1981).

[2] William O. Paulsell, ed., *Sermons in a Monastery: Chapter Talks by Matthew Kelty* (Kalamazoo, MI: Cistercian Publications 1983) p. 46. See also Jean Gribomont, O.S.B.: "The habit of recollection and above all purity of heart constitute the most efficacious preparation [for prayer]. 'Meditation,' that is to say the rumination seeping into the memory, fills up the silence and gives work a minimum of spiritual nourishment." "Prayer in Eastern Monasticism and in Saint Benedict," *Word and Spirit* 2 (1981) 8.

[3] See Michael Casey, O.C.S.O., "Intentio cordis (RB 52.4)," *Regulae Benedicti Studia* 6/7 (1981) 119.

[4] *Ibid.*

[5] See his *Foundations of Christian Faith: An Introduction to the Idea of Christianity* (New York: The Seabury Press 1978) Part I: The Hearer of the Message.

[6] See Jean Leclercq, O.S.B., "Silence and Word in the Life of Prayer," *Word and Spirit* 6 (1984) 110.

[7] Cardinal Carlo Martini says: "The Scriptures are a real presence of Jesus." "The School of the Word," *Worship* 61 (1987) 196.

[8] See M. Robert Mulholland, *Shaped by the Word: The Power of Scripture in Spiritual Formation* (Nashville, TN: The Upper Room 1985).

[9] *Opening the Bible* (Collegeville, MN: The Liturgical Press 1976) p. 33.

[10] For various suggestions of time, see Bede Urekew, O.S.B., *Lectio Divina in the Rule of Benedict* (Rome: Private Distribution 1979) p. 585.

[11] See *RB 1980*'s footnote to RB 48.15.

Adalbert de Vogüé (essay date 1991)

SOURCE: "Humility" in *Reading Saint Benedict: Reflections on the "Rule,"* translated by Colette Friedlander, O. C. S. O., Cistercian Publications, 1994, pp. 75-100.

[*In the following essay, originally published in French in 1991, de Vogüé undertakes an exegesis of the seventh chapter of the* Rule of St. Benedict, *which describes a monk's spiritual ascension to heaven upon the ladder of humility. Footnote numbers designate line numbers of the* Rule *throughout this essay.*]

This chapter [the seventh], which is longer and more important than any other, does not simply describe one of the monk's great virtues. Because that virtue, as we have seen, encompasses the other two, the chapter contains the whole of the **Rule**'s spiritual teaching. Moreover, this description of humility is drawn from a passage in Cassian (*Inst.* 4.39) which outlined the monk's journey toward perfection, from initial fear of God to the love which drives away fear. Integrated as they are into the present chapter, this starting point and conclusion really give the treatment found in the Master and Benedict the scope of a synthesis. The image of a twelve-step ladder, which serves as its framework, is presented by our authors in a preamble:

> [1] Brothers, divine Scripture calls to us saying: 'Whoever exalts himself shall be humbled, and whoever humbles himself shall be exalted'. [2] In saying this, it shows us that every exaltation is a kind of pride. [3] The Prophet indicates that he shuns this by saying: 'Lord, my heart is not exalted, and my eyes are not

lifted up. I have not walked in the ways of the great nor gone after marvels beyond me.'⁴ But what would happen 'if I had not a humble spirit, if I had exalted my soul? You would treat me as a child weaned from its mother.'

⁵ Accordingly, brothers, if we want to reach the summit of supreme humility, and if we want to attain speedily that exaltation in heaven to which we climb by the humility of this present life, ⁶ then by our ascending actions we must set up that ladder on which Jacob in a dream saw angels descending and ascending. ⁷ Without doubt, this descent and ascent can signify only, according to us, that exaltation makes us descend and humility makes us ascend. ⁸ As for the ladder erected, it is our life here below. When our hearts have been humbled, the Lord will raise it to heaven. ⁹ We may say that our body and soul are the sides of this ladder. Into these sides, the divine call has fitted the various steps of humility and good conduct that we may ascend them.

The words of Christ which open the chapter can be read three times in the New Testament. Their purpose there is to instil now modesty which makes us agreeable to men (Lk 14:11), now the spirit of service which must impel God's representatives (Mt 23:12), now the attitude appropriate to the sinners we all are before the Lord (Lk 18:14). Quoted here in the form given by Saint Luke, this keyword of the Gospel has two parts, both of which will be briefly commented on by means of texts from the Old Testament. The first, on the humbling of the proud, is paraphrased by the Psalmist: the soul that gives itself over to pride shall be weaned from God (Ps 130:1-2). The second, on the exaltation of the humble, is explained by Jacob's dream: a ladder rises up to heaven (Gn 28:12). In both these Old Testament passages, humility appears under a twofold aspect, interior and exterior. The Psalmist speaks of both 'heart' and 'eyes'; Jacob's ladder has two sides, symbols of body and soul. Benedict and especially the Master note the predominantly interior or bodily aspect of certain steps.

The gospel maxim will therefore be illustrated by the image from Genesis. Giving these scriptural texts their broadest and strongest meaning, our authors draw from them a vision of all of christian life, both here below and in the hereafter. We abase ourselves in this world in order to be exalted in the next. The ladder is a figure of our entire present life, viewed as an ascent towards heaven. This is why the Master very logically concludes his chapter with a description of heaven, while Benedict, wishing to abridge the text, stops at the spiritual summit attained on earth, which is charity.

To ascend to heaven is a uniquely christian ambition. The author of Genesis did not contemplate it: the beings Jacob saw going up and down the ladder were angels, not human beings. In order to give humankind

the unheard of hope of going to God, nothing less was needed than the ascension of the Son of God made man. It is in his wake and by his grace, obtained through his abasement, that we dare to start up the ladder and to aspire to see the transcendent God.

Like the gospel quotation, the image of the ladder is unique to the Master and Benedict. It is not found in the underlying passage from the *Institutes*. Cassian did, to be sure, outline a journey which went from fear to charity by way of outward renunciation and humility, but its ten 'signs' did not constitute a progression. Though carefully ordered—three traits relating to obedience and two to patience, then three concerning self-effacement and two connected with stillness—they were not set out as a methodical and complete agenda, but merely as a list of examples liable to be expanded and ordered differently.

By transposing this description of the humble monk within the framework of his graduated ladder, the Master, followed by Benedict, gave it a progressive and systematic appearance which should probably not be taken too seriously. Like Cassian's signs, to which they correspond, the steps of our Rules are not so much rungs to be climbed one after the other as signs of virtue which can and should appear simultaneously.

In contrast to this central block, made up of steps 2-11, the first step has a clearly initial and basic character. This is because the Master has borrowed it not from the list of the ten signs of humility, but from the preliminary stage constituted, in Cassian's view, by 'fear of the Lord'. Originally external to humility, this religious fear was inserted into it by our Rules, giving the great monastic virtue a primordial orientation towards God. Cassian's signs concerned only humility toward one's neighbor. By adding a first step relative to the Lord and a twelfth which has the same direct connection with the divine Master, our Rules envelop humility towards human beings within a gaze turned towards God.

¹⁰ The first step of humility, then, is that placing the fear of God always before our eyes, we always shun forgetfulness, ¹¹ and constantly remember everything God has commanded, constantly going over in our mind how hell burns all those who despise God on account of their sins, as well as everlasting life prepared for those who fear God. ¹² And guarding himself at every moment from sins and vices of thought or tongue, of hand or foot, of self-will or fleshly desire, ¹³ man must be persuaded that God is looking at him from heaven at every moment, that the deity's glance sees his actions everywhere and that angels report on them at every hour.

Just as Chapter 7 is disproportionate in size, so the first step likewise differs entirely in length from those following it. Together with the twelfth, it amounts to a picture of humility with regard to God which is barely less ample and less detailed than that of humility with regard to human beings contained in the ten intermediate steps.

The details of this great fresco are nearly all drawn from a passage of the 'tools for good works' (4:44-60): awaiting the last things, watching over our own conduct, believing that we are always in God's sight, controlling our thoughts and words, renouncing fleshly desires and self-will—all of these have already been found there as separate items. But the phrase 'fear of God' under which these elements are grouped here echoes Cassian. More specifically, Cassian spoke of the 'fear of the Lord' (*Inst.* 4.39.1) which, according to Scripture, is the beginning of wisdom (Ps 110:10; Pr 9:10). Our authors substitute 'God' for 'the Lord' because they have in mind another expression from the psalms: 'keeping the fear of God before one's eyes' (Ps 35:2).

According to Cassian, this initial fear, in permeating the soul, gives rise to the outer renunciation of all ownership, and the latter leads to the inner renunciation which is humility. These two steps, the first of which corresponds to entering the monastery and the second to monastic life itself, imitate Christ's successive abasements: the deprivation of the Incarnation and the humiliation of the Cross (Ph 2:6-8). Omitting the stage of renouncing the world, which they describe at the end of their Rules, the Master and Benedict bring together fear of God and humility, so that the former becomes the latter's basic element. Instead of leading from the world to the monastery, it emerges as the dominant and constantly fostered feeling which permeates the monk's entire life.

In the conclusion to the chapter, as we shall see, fear will be eliminated by love, which is the summit reached after climbing the twelve steps. When we follow John the Apostle in thus opposing fear and charity, we have in mind its least noble form, the fear of punishment, which impels a slave to obey, as it were, in spite of himself. Here the fear of God (and not of punishment) far transcends this baser feeling. As in the entire Old Testament and in almost all of the New, we are dealing with the religious attitude *par excellence,* consisting in unspeakable respect for the Lord whose word is listened to with veneration and whose law is lovingly observed. The high quality of this feeling is shown by the end to which it leads: we are told that everlasting life is prepared for those who fear God.

Here below, the person who fears God 'guards himself at every moment from sins and vices'. We may remember that the struggle against the vices of body and mind is the monk's great task (1:5), and that the prospect of amending his vices is the great hope offered the abbot (2:40). Guarding oneself against all manner of sin is evoked by a list of the six parts of the human compound in which it must be practised: thoughts, tongue, hands, feet, self-will, and fleshly desires. The Master then goes over these six areas in the light of Scripture. Benedict, aiming as always at brevity, will include only the first and the last two in his scriptural reflections.

Along with the struggle against these various sins and in order that that struggle may be effective, our authors instil the conviction that God, who is everywhere present, sees us always. These two joint themes are characteristic of the Rule of Saint Basil, from which the Master seems to draw his inspiration throughout the first step and in the twelfth. Basil however, is more reserved than our authors on the role of fear in the search for God—seemingly at least, for, as we have seen, the term 'fear' is an ambiguous one.

> [14] This is what the Prophet indicates to us when he shows that God is always present to our thoughts, saying: 'God searches hearts and minds'; [15] again: 'The Lord knows the thoughts of men'. [16] And he says besides: 'From afar you understood my thoughts'. [17] And: 'For the thought of man shall open up to you'. [18] Moreover, that he may take care to avoid perverted thoughts, the virtuous brother must always say in his heart: 'I shall be blameless before him only if I guard myself from my own iniquity'.
>
> [19] As for our own will, we are forbidden to do it when Scripture tells us: 'And turn away from your wishes'.
>
> [20] And in the Prayer we also ask God that his will be done in us. [21] We are thus rightly taught not to do our own will, when we beware of what Scripture says: 'There are ways which seem right to men and whose end plunges into the depths of hell', [22] and also when we dread what is said of the negligent: 'They are corrupt and have become depraved in their wishes'.
>
> [23] In the desires of the flesh, we must believe that God is always present to us, since the Prophet says to the Lord: 'All my desires are before you'. [24] We must then be on guard against any evil desire, because 'death is stationed on the doorstep of pleasure'. [25] For this reason Scripture has given us this precept: 'Pursue not your lusts'.

Cut down to half its original size by Benedict, this scriptural anthology has a double purpose: to show both that God is present to all human action; and that man must guard himself from all sin. The second thesis obviously flows from the first, but the Master nonetheless strove to find distinct proof of it. He did not fully succeed in carrying out this twofold agenda. Granted that his first and last paragraph, devoted to thoughts and fleshly desires, offer biblical texts witnessing both to the presence of God and to the necessity of eliminating sin, his intermediate sections illustrate only one of the themes: that of the divine presence appears alone in the paragraphs on the tongue, hands, and feet (omitted by Benedict), and only the notion of mounting guard against sin is mentioned in connection with self-will.

The case concerning thoughts consists entirely of psalm quotations, arranged first in ascending and then in descending order (ascending: Ps 7:10, 93:11, 138:8; descending: Ps 75:11; 17:24). The passage regarding self-will begins with a saying from Ecclesiasticus (Si 18:30[b]) whose other half is to be found in the next paragraph; then, after the Lord's Prayer (Mt 6:10), the **Rule** quotes another wisdom book (Pr 16:25; cf. Mt 18:6), and finally the Psalter (Ps 13:1). As for fleshly desires, two phrases from the Old Testament (Ps 37:10 and Si 18:30[a]) frame another quotation, which remains anonymous and even implicit: 'Death is stationed on the doorstep of pleasure'. The phrase comes from one of those Passions of roman martyrs of which the Master was so fond, that of Saint Sebastian (*Pass. Seb.* 14).

At the end of the exposition on thoughts, one detail deserves to be noted. The virtuous brother (literally: 'useful', that is, good) must 'always say in his heart' a certain phrase from the psalms, but slightly rearranged. No doubt this precept is not to be taken strictly, as an invitation ceaselessly to repeat a prayer formula. The Master and Benedict do not have in mind here the exercise advocated by Cassian (repeating: 'God, come to my assistance . . . '), by oriental monasticism (the Jesus prayer) and by Hinduism (the mantra), still more since their psalm formula is addressed not to God but to the person who says it. Besides, by offering other words to be said constantly further on (7:65; cf. 7:50 and 52-54) our authors show clearly that they do not have in mind a contemporary practice of perpetual repetition, continued invariably throughout one's life. Yet, such recommendations do put us on the track of the methods of 'meditation' we mentioned. Whatever the formula used and the way it is used, the repetition of a sacred phrase is a device whose value has been tested by several great monastic traditions independently of one another, and can still be of great help to seekers of God today.

> [26] Accordingly, if 'the eyes of the Lord are watching the good and the wicked', [27] if 'the Lord looks down at all times from heaven on the sons of men to see whether there is one who understands and seeks God'; [28] and if every day the angels assigned to guard us report our deeds to the Lord day and night, [29] then, brothers, we must be vigilant every hour lest, as the Prophet says in the psalm, God observe us 'falling' at some time into evil and 'made worthless', [30] and lest, after sparing us in the present

> time because he is good and waits for us to improve, he tell us in the future: 'This you did, and I said nothing'.

This long sentence, which concludes the first step, draws our attention back to the last things. But now we are dealing with an event which has not yet been mentioned—judgment. That is where we run the risk of hearing God say to us: 'This you did, and I said nothing' (Ps 49:21). Here below the Lord observes us in silence, with a continuous gaze which can already tell the good from the wicked (Pr 15:3), the God-seeking from the wayward (Ps 13:2-3). God's goodness, which leads him to await our conversion this way, has already been celebrated in the Prologue (Prol 35-38).

While simply copying what he read in the Master, Benedict has become so thoroughly convinced of it that he will repeat it in a section which is unique to him: the introduction to the chapter on psalmody (19:1-2). In his view, the Office is the time when faith in God's presence and sight reaches its point of incandescence.

> [31] The second step of humility is that we love not our own will nor take pleasure in the satisfaction of our desires, [32] but rather imitate in our actions those words of the Lord saying: 'I have come not to do my own will, but the will of him who sent me'. [33] Scripture also says: 'Will has its punishment and constraint wins a crown'.

This second step introduces us into the middle zone of the ladder, where the Master and Benedict draw their inspiration from Cassian's 'signs of humility'. While recasting these quite thoroughly, the Master has enriched them with scriptural illustrations which make them more attractive: in practising them we do not merely show that we are humble; we also answer God's calls.

This step, closely connected with the following one, presents the negative face of obedience before its positive aspect. It corresponds to Cassian's first 'sign': the mortification of one's will, yet to this it adds desires. In the first step, the two already formed a pair originating in the Bible (Si 18:30; Gal 5:16-17).

As for the two quotations on which this detachment from all personal will is grounded, they are very unequal in weight. The first, which we have already come across (5:13), is nothing less than words spoken by Christ of himself (Jn 6:38). The second, while also presenting itself as 'Scripture', is actually drawn from the legendary Passion of Saint Anastasia, a martyr venerated in Rome (*Pass. Anast.* 17). In reproducing it, Benedict was most likely unaware of its non-biblical origin. This saying, ascribed in the story to a martyr called Irene, adds to the words and example of Christ the witness of a disciple who followed him until death.

> [34] The third step of humility is that, for the love of God, we submit to the superior in all obedience, imitating the Lord of whom the Apostle says: 'Having made himself obedient even to death'.

This third step contrasts by its conciseness with the Master's, from which it is drawn. Benedict has retained only one of his forerunner's seven scriptural quotations, and it is perfectly chosen. In fact, except for one expression, the others have already appeared in both Rules in the chapter on obedience and in the first step of humility. On the contrary, the great pauline phrase which Benedict retains (Ph 2:8) has not yet been quoted, and this evocation of Christ on the cross is extremely valuable. Thanks to it, the doctrine on obedience developed in Chapter 5 and here condensed is enriched with a priceless touch. 'Imitating Christ' was already suggested in the previous step, but it is good to be reminded here that 'doing the will of the Father', as Jesus said in the words of the Gospel quoted there, entailed for him, in the last analysis, 'making himself obedient even to death'.

If we look to the Master's source-text, we find that he had in mind Cassian's third 'sign of humility': the humble monk follows not his own will, but that of the senior who watches over him. On the other hand, it had not occurred to the Master to motivate obedience by the words 'for the love of God'. This motivation is unique to Benedict. The addition is all the more significant because it muddles up the blueprint drawn by Cassian and the Master: only after humility, as we shall see, do we rise to charity. But the consistency of this doctrinal scheme matters less to Benedict than his own conviction, based on the first commandment of Scripture and on daily experience: all christian life, and *a fortiori* all monastic life, is rooted in divine love. Here as elsewhere (68:5; 71:4), he does not hesitate therefore to make divine love the motive behind obedience, even though he gets ahead of himself.

> [35] The fourth step of humility is that in this very practice of obedience, when we are subjected to harsh treatment or contradiction or even to all sorts of injustices, our conscience silently embraces patience [36] and that, holding out, we neither become discouraged nor retreat, as Scripture has it: 'He who perseveres to the end will be saved'. [37] And also: 'Be firm of heart and bear with the Lord'.

> [38] And wishing to show how the faithful must even endure any and every contradiction for the Lord's sake, it puts the following words in the mouth of those who suffer: 'For your sake we are put to death daily. We are regarded as sheep marked for slaughter.' [39] And sure of the divine reward which they expect, they continue, saying joyfully: 'But in all this we overcome because of him who loved us'.

> [40] And elsewhere Scripture also says: 'You have tested us, o God, you have tried us as silver is tried by fire; you have led us into a snare. You have placed affliction on our backs.' [41] And in order to show that we must be under a superior, it continues in these terms: 'You have placed men over our heads'.

> [42] Moreover, they are fulfilling the Lord's command by patience in the midst of hardships and injustices: when struck on one cheek, they turn the other also; to whoever deprives them of their tunic, they also offer their cloak; when pressed into service for one mile, they go two; [43] with the Apostle Paul, they bear with false brothers, as well as with persecution, and when cursed, they answer with blessings.

Cassian's fourth sign consisted in remaining patient in obedience. Then, broadening the theme, the author of the *Institutes* advanced as a fifth sign the peaceful acceptance of wrongs of all kinds, things which can be caused not only by the superior who commands, but also by any member of the community.

These two signs are combined in the present step, the longest of the ten intermediate rungs in our Rule. By comparing it with two parallel passages from the Master, we can see that the latter regards such patience in obedience as an equivalent of martyrdom. In fact, scriptural illustration is drawn from the most heroic texts found in both Testaments.

These quotations go two by two. First the 'perseverance to the end' required by Jesus (Mt 10:22) and the courage to 'bear with the Lord' of which the psalmist spoke (Ps 26:14). Then 'daily death' for God's sake, another psalm image (Ps 43:22) taken up and elaborated on by Saint Paul, who turns it into a victory (Rm 8:36-37). The Psalter also provides the next two quotations, in which the evocation of the 'fire' and 'snare' of trial ends with a remarkably realistic figure of obedience: 'men are placed' by God 'over our heads' (Ps 65:10-11 and 12). We return at last to the Gospel, with several touches from the Sermon on the Mount (Mt 5:39-41), and to Saint Paul, that model of patience with false friends (2 Co 11:26), persecutors, and detractors (1 Co 4:12). In this last group of texts we can clearly make out troubles arising not from superiors, those accredited representatives of God, but from any brothers, as in Cassian's fifth sign.

The spiritual climax of the passage is surely to be found in two sentences from the Letter to the Romans. 'For your sake . . . because of him who loved us': without using the word—which he saves for the end of the chapter—the Master, followed by Benedict, here sketches an attitude very close to charity. The name he gives it—'hope'—marks a progression over the 'fear' of the first step. It is true that fear already included the thought of everlasting life, but now, in the fire of trial, faith in that reward turns into joyful confidence.

Combining the gospel themes of perseverance in persecution and not resisting evil, this fine passage is among those pages of the **Rule** to which we go back most often and most happpily in the course of our monastic life.

> ⁴⁴ The fifth step of humility is that, by humble confession, we do not conceal from our abbot any evil thoughts entering our hearts or any evil deeds committed in secret. ⁴⁵ Scripture exhorts us to do this by saying: 'Make known your way to the Lord and hope in him'. ⁴⁶ It also says: 'Confess to the Lord, for he is good, for his mercy is forever'. ⁴⁷ So too the Prophet: 'To you I have acknowledged my offense, and I have not concealed my injustice. ⁴⁸ I have said: Against myself I will report my injustice before the Lord, and you have forgiven the wickedness of my heart.'

Cassian already required the humble monk to 'hide nothing from his senior, not only about his actions, but also about his thoughts' (second sign). In response, the senior gave a judgment concerning the actions and thoughts confessed, and the brother submitted to it fully (third sign). The confession of the one directed and the director's advice formed a pair which the *Institutes* placed in the first group of signs, the features of obedience.

By displacing this opening of the heart and by modifying its formulation, the Master and Benedict have changed its nature. In their texts it is no longer followed by its natural extension, direction given by the senior. Instead of an act of submission by which the monk prepared to receive his director's instructions, we are now dealing with an act of self-abasement in which he confesses his sins. For the object of the confession no longer consists in actions or thoughts of uncertain quality on which one expects a senior's verdict, but *evil* thoughts and actions already judged to be such by the one confessing them.

This fifth step thus no longer belongs like Cassian's corresponding sign, to the group of demonstrations of obedience, but rather to acts of self-abasement or humility proper, which will include the next three steps. Before putting up with all manner of treatment, acknowledging that we are the least of all people and withdrawing into the background by conforming entirely to accepted custom, we make ourselves known for what we are: sinners in thought and deed.

This 'humble confession' to a superior, who is not necessarily a priest, has no sacramental significance in the ecclesiastical meaning of the term. We are seeking not to obtain absolution but to acquire virtue. Yet, the scriptural illustration shows that the abbot to whom we make our confession holds the place of Christ, here as elsewhere. The three quotations, all drawn from the Psalter (Pss 36:5; 105:1; 31:5) speak unanimously of a confession made 'to the Lord' whose mercy and forgiveness we hope for. In the light of these texts, it appears that, besides the acquisition of humility, our authors have in view the remission of sin, which, for that matter, simply follows from the act of humility performed (cf. Cassian, *Conf.* 20.8.3). Only midway through the **Rule** (46:5-6) will Benedict mention another fruit of secret confession: the healing of the soul's wounds through the spiritual father's care.

> ⁴⁹ The sixth step of humility is that a monk is content with the lowest and most menial treatment, and regards himself as a poor and worthless workman in whatever task he is ordered to do, ⁵⁰ saying to himself with the Prophet: 'I have been reduced to nothing and I have known nothing. I have been as a brutish beast before you and I am with you always.'

Cassian's seventh sign, reproduced almost verbatim by the Master, consisted in accepting the poorest objects (food, clothing, shoes, etc.), without asking any other payment for manual work worth much more. This glaring disproportion between salary and work, which was the common lot of egyptian cenobites, could be interpreted in terms of humility: the monk regarded himself as a 'worthless servant', according to the Gospel (Lk 17:10).

By changing one word, Benedict modifies the significance of the text. Instead of objects 'provided' (*praebentur*), he speaks of things 'ordered' (*iniunguntur*). By this alteration, the sixth step becomes an extension of steps 2-4: we are dealing once more with obedience. As we already knew, the latter must be total (step 3) and bear with any and all injustice (step 4). Benedict now specifies that the monk must accept the lowliest tasks and regard them as too good for him.

The Master's scriptural quotation (Ps 72:22-23) lends itself to the new as well as to the former meaning. Beyond giving the feeling of being reduced to nothing, it superbly expresses the monk's sole desire: to be with God always.

> ⁵¹ The seventh step of humility is that, not content to state with our tongue that we are the last and lowliest of all, we also believe it in the depths of our heart, ⁵² humbling ourselves and saying with the Prophet: 'As for me, I am a worm, not a man, scorned by men and despised by the people. ⁵³ I was

exalted, humbled and overwhelmed with confusion'.
[54] And again: 'It was a good thing for me that you humbled me, in order that I might learn your commandments'.

This step, inseparable from the previous one, reproduces Cassian's eighth sign. The most important change made by the Master and Benedict consists in turning the contrast between the two kinds of behavior ('not . . . but rather') into a progression ('not content . . . also'). In such a perspective, statements of inferiority are acceptable and even useful, although they are not enough. According to Cassian, on the contrary, they are superfluous; the only useful attitude consists in believing oneself to be the least of all. The apt story told by abbot Serapion (*Conf.* 18:11) unmasks the deception to which humble language too often amounts. Instead of words by which we delude both ourselves and others, we must cultivate real feelings, neither paralyzing self-deprecation nor masochistic indulgence in abjection, but an honest and peaceful acknowledgment of the actual deficiencies of which we are presently conscious, as well as all those which might reveal themselves under other circumstances.

The conviction suggested by this step is so strange and exaggerated that some have attempted to justify it by some mystical illumination. Without ruling out such an interpretation, which can readily be illustrated by more than one saint's life, we must note first of all that Cassian's target is a kind of verbalism: one half-heartedly declares oneself the least of all men. In reaction against such superficial words, he suggests interiorizing them. When he talks of judging oneself inferior to everyone else, it is the verbal formulas he reproves: instead of saying this, try instead to believe it. The monk is not being required to give a categorical verdict concerning his place in the human race—God is the sole judge of human worth—but asked to transfer his effort at humility from his mouth to his heart.

Our authors give us to understand that this step is one of 'humility' in a special way. This is implied in the phrase which introduces the quotations: the monk 'humbles himself and says. . . . ' And the same verb 'to humble oneself' comes up twice in the quotations themselves. As for the content of the texts quoted, it is helpful to reflect that the first (Ps 21:7) applies naturally to Christ on the cross, even though our authors do not point this out. The second (Ps 87:16), which follows after it immediately, is likewise a lament of the Psalmist for himself. The third, (Ps 118:71-73), on the contrary, is addressed to God. Like the verse quoted in the previous step, it admirably expresses the undivided love of someone who has no other treasure than the divine will.

[55] The eighth step of humility is that a monk does only what is endorsed by the common rule of the monastery and the example set by his superiors.

Unlike the others, this step is not backed up by any scriptural text, since Benedict omits the two quoted by the Master.

While reproducing Cassian's sixth sign almost exactly, our authors modify it by adding a word: *monasterii*. According to Cassian, the 'common rule' to which the humble monk conforms is the universal custom of egyptian monasticism, deemed to have originated in the days of the apostles. By specifying that they have in mind the common rule *of the monastery,* the Master and Benedict particularize this general norm. Correlatively, those whose example is to be followed are no longer the 'seniors' of monastic tradition, but, according to another meaning of the same word (*maiores*), the 'superiors' of the monastery, as the Master's scriptural illustration clearly shows.

Although our authors thus specify the twofold norm to be followed by bringing it down to the setting of their own community, the spirit of the practice remains unchanged. The point is self-effacement pursued by conforming to the local customs, by making the common observance one's own, by unreservedly embracing a tradition.

[56] The ninth step of humility is that a monk forbids his tongue to speak and, remaining silent, does not speak until asked a question, [57] for Scripture warns that 'in speaking a great deal you will not avoid sin', [58] and that 'a talkative man goes about aimlessly on earth'.

After the steps of humility (2-3), of patience (4) and of self-abasement (5-8), here are three which relate to speech and laughter. They correspond to Cassian's last two signs. Cassian's only sign concerning speech is split by our Rules into two steps: steps 9 and 11, which frame the one on laughter (10).

Cassian simply recommended 'restraining one's tongue'. The Master, followed by Benedict, turns 're-strain' (*cohibeat*) into 'forbid' (*prohibeat*). The mere restraint advocated by the *Institutes* thus becomes genuine mutism, the limit of which is, however, outlined further on in the sentence: we are to remain silent until asked a question. The Master thus refers to the complicated casuistry set out in his second chapter on stillness, a casuistry which he develops yet further in the rest of his ***Rule.*** Benedict neglects these subtle regulations, retaining only the principle set forth here. In so doing, does he still have in mind the specific discipline the Master was aiming at: in the presence of his superiors, abbot, or dean, the monk must wait to be questioned? He may instead be thinking of a general atti_ tude, valid at all times and with regard to anyone; this is how we spontaneously understand the passage.

The first scriptural quotation (Pr 10:19) has already been called on in the treatise on silence (6:4). The second (Ps 139:12) is new. Both recommend that one speak sparingly, less in order to acquire humility than to avoid sin or missteps. We may recognize here one of the themes of the chapter on stillness. Whatever its motivations, silence has been a characteristic trait of monks, whether cenobites or hermits, from the beginning. In order to let the word of God reverberate in them and to answer it by constant prayer, they give up exchanging human words.

> [59] The tenth step of humility is that we are not given to ready laughter, for it is written: 'The fool raises his voice in laughter'.

This tenth step reproduces exactly Cassian's tenth and last sign. As for the scriptural motivation (Si 21:23), it was already found in Saint Basil (*Reg.* 8.29), who added the gospel cursing of those who laugh (Lk 6:21) and the example of Christ himself, whom Scripture depicts several times weeping but never laughing. Such reflections occur quite frequently in the writings of the Fathers. They surprise us and, however pertinent they may be, draw our attention to an aspect of monastic asceticism less prominent today than it was then. Perhaps we are too lenient when it comes to laughter; true joy lies elsewhere.

One of the tools of good works prescribed not speaking words that induce laughter, another not loving boisterous laughter (4:53-54). Here the scriptural quotation reminds us of the second, while the sentence borrowed from Cassian relates rather to the first tool: we must be inclined neither to laugh nor to induce laughter. For others as for ourselves, true joy consists in being mindful of God.

> [60] The eleventh step of humility is that, when a monk speaks, he does so gently and without laughter, humbly and seriously, saying only brief and reasonable words, and avoids raising his voice, [61] as it is written: 'A wise man is known by the brevity of his speech'.

Cassian's ninth sign consisted not only in speaking sparingly, but also in speaking in a low voice. We find this last instruction, reproduced literally, at the end of the present step ('let him avoid raising his voice'). The Master availed himself of the opportunity to specify how monks should speak. The first of his three pairs of remarks renews the condemnation of laughter, the second advocates seriousness (*gravitas*), which goes hand in hand with stillness (cf. 6:3), and the third recommends brevity, as does the text quoted at the end.

Our two Rules couple different adjectives with 'brief' (*pauca*): 'holy' in the Master's, 'reasonable' in Benedict's. By 'holy', the Master meant spiritual and edifying words concerning Scripture and the things of God. Benedict is less ambitious; he requires only 'reasonable' talk. 'Reasonable' is a term he likes to use as an adjective (2:18) and especially as an adverb (31:7, etc.). Here his concern with the good use of speech in ordinary life filters through for the first time. Talking about the ordinary things of life is not simply a necessity, to be reduced to the unavoidable minimum. Such exchanges between brothers must have a certain quality, and they must above all bear the stamp of reason.

The final quotation is not drawn from Scripture, as our Rules seem to suggest, but from a collection of pytha-gorean maxims christianized in the third century: the *Enchiridion* or Manual of Sextus (*Ench.* 145). The author, a philosopher, has been confused with Saint Xystus or Sixtus, pope and martyr (+ 258), to whom the work is ascribed by the monk Rufinus, who translated it into Latin for the roman public around the year 400. Was Benedict aware of the origin of this maxim, which he inherited from the Master? Whether he was or not, he made it his own, as he had earlier the one drawn from the Passion of Anastasia, another roman writing. While sounding like an inspired proverb, this quotation from a philosopher reminds us that for some of its greatest founders, like Augustine, monastic life numbered among its roots the wondrous love of wisdom entertained by some currents of ancient thought.

> [62] The twelfth step of humility is that a monk always manifests in his bearing no less than in his heart his humility to those who see him, [63] in other words, that at the work of God, in the oratory, the monastery, or the garden, on a journey or in the fields, everywhere, whether he sits, walks or stands, his head is always bowed and his eyes cast towards the ground, [64] believing himself always guilty of his sins, he believes that he is already appearing at the fearful judgment, [65] constantly saying in his heart what the publican in the Gospel said with eyes cast down toward the ground: 'Lord, I am not worthy, sinner that I am, to lift my eyes to heaven'. [66] And also with the Prophet: 'I am bowed down and humbled to the utmost'.

As we may remember, this last step is not drawn from Cassian's 'signs of humility'. Like the first, which it resembles by so many of its details, it is a creation of the Master. In these two end-steps, the humble monk is turned towards God. Of course he is first required to 'manifest humility to those who see him', but afterwards there is talk only of gestures and feelings relating to God. It is in thinking of God, and of God alone, that the monk assumes the humble attitude which strikes peoples' eyes.

Heart and body: this couplet already appeared at the beginning of the **Rule** (Prol 40). It recalls those we found at the beginning of this chapter: heart and eyes, soul and body (7:3 and 9). In going from the first term to the second, the Master no doubt had in mind the seventh step, where he moved in the reverse direction, from tongue to heart. But the exteriorization of sorts which he now prescribes must not mislead us: here as elsewhere, what is essential takes place inside. This is evinced by the final words, which the monk must 'constantly repeat to himself in his heart'.

To manifest by all our movements and even by our facial expression that we are standing in the presence of God: Saint Basil regarded this as an excellent way of edifying our brothers when we are too old and tired to do anything else (*Reg.* 86.2). The Master required this same example of the fully active monk; the depiction of this activity goes from the center of the monastery—the divine office and the oratory—to its outskirts. Basil, however, did not indicate the precise attitude described by our Rules: bent head, downcast eyes. On this point, the Master drew only on his own principles, which he states several times in the Rule with various motivations. Here the reason for the bent head is the awareness of sin and the expectation of judgment, which is considered imminent.

This sense of already standing before the judge recalls the conclusion of the first step. There the Master and Benedict spoke of judgment as of a 'future' event. Here the future becomes present: the truth known to us by faith appears as an accomplished fact.

This anticipation results in a new relation to sin. In the first step, the point was to avoid it. At the twelfth, the monk considers no longer the misdeeds he might commit, but those he actually has committed. This time his glance goes backwards, as though life were virtually over and all that remains is to take stock of it.

The first of the two final quotations consists of words we must constantly say, as was already required at another phrase in the first step (7:8). Placed in the mouth of the publican in the Gospel (Lk 18:13), these words are not, however, those that Luke has him speak. The Master and Benedict replace the invocation 'Have mercy on me, a sinner'—used by Eastern Christians in their famous Jesus Prayer—with a phrase that begins with the centurion's 'Lord, I am not worthy' (Mt 8:8) but especially recalls the words of King Manasses: 'I am not worthy to look up to the heights of heaven, so many are my iniquities' (*Or, Man.* 10). Several verses of the *Prayer of Manasses,* a brief apocryphal work, are reproduced elsewhere by the Master (RM 14:34-40). Here the penitent king's confession (cf. 2 Ch 33:12 and 18-19) merges with Luke's description of the publican.

Immediately afterwards, the *Prayer* has Manasses say: 'I am bent under the weight of chains'. These words of the captive king probably suggested the second quotation found in our Rules (Ps 37:9), which begins similarly.

It may seem strange to end an ascent with a confession of sin which began with a resolve to avoid all manner of misdeeds. But Gregory the Great and many other saints observe that purification is accompanied by an ever sharper awareness of one's impurity. And Christ himself justified the publican, the model for those who humble themselves that they may be exalted.

> [67] Therefore, once the monk has climbed all these steps of humility, he will arrive at that love of God which is perfect and which casts out fear. [68] Through it, all that he once performed not without dread, he will now begin to observe effortlessly, as though naturally, from habit, [69] no longer out of fear of hell, but out of love for Christ and good habit and delight in the virtues. [70] May the Lord manifest this state by the Holy Spirit in his workman now purified of vices and sins!

After the final step, which is unique to them, the Master and Benedict revert to Cassian in this conclusion. They borrow nearly their whole first sentence from him, whereas the second is original.

The spiritual ascent which began in fear thus ends with love which casts out fear (1 Jn 4:18). Hinted at briefly in the text of the *Institutes* from which our Rules drew their inspiration, this passage from slavish fear to filial love is extensively analyzed in the eleventh *Conference*. It fits a pattern of ascent outlined by Clement of Alexandria and reproduced by many later authors, particularly by Saint Basil and by Evagrius Ponticus, Cassian's master.

Such perfect charity not only eliminates the fear of punishment, as the Letter of John already stated. According to Cassian, followed by our Rules, it does away with all toil: a person reverts to the state in which he was created and acts well effortlessly by virtue of the nature he has regained. Force of habit has a part to play in this recovery of our primeval sanctity, as the Master and Benedict note on their own part. Benedict sets himself off from his two forerunners by specifying that the object of love is 'Christ', not 'the Good', as we find in more abstract fashion in Cassian and the Master.

This picture of the marvelous effects of charity is less unreal than it appears. It doubtless represents no more than an ideal goal towards which we never cease tending here below. But granted that resistance to good and therefore the toil involved in performing it never disappear entirely before death, it is a fact of experience that love and its trail of virtues are a source of joy. Benedict had already observed this at the end of the Prologue. He now repeats it, following the Master and Cassian.

The last sentence, added by our authors to the text of the *Institutes,* is very important. It adds an important touch which was missing not only from Cassian, but also from all this long chapter of our Rules: the acknowledgment of the work of grace. If this has not yet been mentioned, even in the ample treatment of the first step, it is doubtless in order to give full force to the basic instructions regarding watchfulness without respite and ceaseless effort directed against sin, and to avoid letting the monk rely on a work of grace which, he might assume, can go on without his participation. But now a backward glance reveals this work of the Spirit. When did it begin? Our text does not say. Nothing prevents us from thinking, as faith assures us, that the Lord acted long before this final stage of the ascent; in fact, from its very beginning.

The 'vices and sins' which we avoided at the first step (7:12) are thus eliminated now by the purifying action of the Spirit. For *he* performs the purification, if we refer to the Master's text (that of Benedict, which omits the preposition *ab,* is not quite so clear). And through the Holy Spirit, too, the Lord is the source of charity and of its effects. The Spirit's purifying role emerges from the Old Testament (Ps 50:11-13; Ez 36:25-27) as from the New (1 Co 6:11). His relation to the love poured out in the hearts of Christians appears likewise in Saint Paul (Rm 5:5; 2 Co 6:6).

Benedict ends his chapter and the entire spiritual portion of his Rule with this very fine sentence. The Master continues on at some length, describing the joys of paradise, for the ladder of humility is raised up to heaven and must lead to this eschatological goal. Benedict stops at the earthly summit of charity primarily because, here as elsewhere, he aims at brevity. He may also have been uncomfortable with the very down-to-earth description of the hereafter he found in the Master. Already, at the end of Chapter 4, he had cut a full and very colorful picture of the world to come down to a few words from Saint Paul. The present abridgment is still more radical, and does away completely with that horizon.

Benedict does not, therefore, lead his reader to the 'exaltation in heaven' announced in the preamble to the chapter. The unfolding of charity here below is the only goal he offers in his conclusion. In doing so he reverts to Cassian's presentation, which also stopped at perfect love without dealing with the hereafter. This is true at least of the passage from the *Institutes* which is the source of our Rules, for the first *Conference* deals admirably with the two ends of christian life, earthly and eschatological: purity of heart and the kingdom of heaven.

Cassian's tendency was to insist on the immediate and too often unrecognized goal through which we must pass in order to attain the ultimate end. The same emphasis can be found in Benedict's work. At the end of the Prologue, we may remember, he introduces into the Master's purely eschatological perspective, the hope of an 'inexpressible delight of love' experienced in this very life. Here the omission of the other Rule's depiction of heaven also has the effect, intentional or not, of bringing into sharper focus the wonders of perfect charity here below.

Abbreviations

RB: The Rule of Saint Benedict. Latin-English edition: RB 1980. Collegeville, Minnesota, Liturgical Press, 1980. Critical latin edition by Adalbert de Vogüé and Jean Neufville, *La Règle de saint Benoît,* Sources chretiennes 181-186. Paris: Editions du Cerf, 1971-1972.

RM: *The Rule of the Master.* PL 88. Critical latin edition by A. de Vogüé, *La Règle du Maître,* Sch 105-107. Paris: Cerf 1964-1965. English translation by Luke Eberle OSB, Cistercian Studies 6. Kalamazoo: Cistercian Publications, 1977.

AA: SS *Acta Sanctorum*

ACW: Ancient Christian Writers

CC: Corpus Christianorum. Turnhout, Belgium: Brepols.

CSCO: Corpus Scriptorum Christianorum Orientalium

FCh: Fathers of the Church series.

MGH: *Monumenta Germaniae Historica.*

PL: J. P. Migne, *Patrologia cursus completus . . . series Latina.* 221 volumes.

SCh: Sources chrétiennes. Paris: Les Éditions du Cerf,

Works Cited

Cassian, John (+435)

Conf.: Conferences (*Conlationes*). PL 49; CSEL 13, 17; SCh 42, 54, 64. English translation by Boniface Ramsey OP, *The Conferences of John Cassian,* Cistercian Studies Series 136-138, and in the Nicene and Post Nicene Fathers, Series 2, volume 11.

Inst.: Institutes (*De institutis coenobiorum*). CSEL 13 (1886); SCh 109. Translation

Pass. Anast.: Passion of Saint Anastasia *et al.* H.

Delehaye, *Étude sur le Légendier romain* BHL 1795, 118, 8093,401.

Pass. Seb.: Passion of Saint Sebastian. PL 17. AA SS Jan. 2:629-642.

Sextus (third century): Ench. *Enchiridion* (Sentences), translated by Rufinus. Edited and translated by Henry Chadwick, *The Sentences of Sextus,* Texts and Studies, New Series, 5. Cambridge 1959; and by R.A. Edwards and R.A. Wild, *The Sentences of Sextus.* Chico, California: Scholars Press, 1981.

FURTHER READING

Blecker, Michael Paulin. "Roman Law and 'Consilium' in the *Regula Magistri* and the *Rule* of St Benedict." *Speculum: A Journal of Mediaeval Studies* XLVII, No. 1 (January 1972): 1-28.

Details the influence of Roman law in matters of the *consilium*, or "corporation," on sixth-century monasticism as evidenced in the *Regula magistri,* and subsequently in the *Rule of St. Benedict.*

Chamberlin, John. *The Rule of St. Benedict: The Abingdon Copy.* Toronto: Pontifical Institute of Mediaeval Studies, 1982, 87 p.

Translation of an important tenth century Old English manuscript of the *Rule* preceded by a brief introduction on Benedict's life and the manuscript history of his *Rule.*

Chapman, Dom John. *Saint Benedict and the Sixth Century.* New York: Longmans, Green and Co., 1929, 239 p.

Studies the *Rule of St. Benedict*, its sources, and the social conditions in Europe at the time it was written.

Cusack, Pearse Aidan. "The Temptation of St. Benedict: An Essay at Interpretation through the Literary Sources." *The American Benedictine Review* 27, No. 2 (June 1976): 143-63.

Focues on the symbolism of Benedict's temptation as told in Saint Gregory's *Second Dialogue.*

Hardy, Gilbert G. "Fallenness and Recovery in the Monastic *Rules* of Benedict of Nursia and Dōgen Zenji: Parallels or Contradictions?" *The American Benedictine Review* 38, No. 4 (December 1987): 420-42.

Comparative analysis of the exemplary monastic rules of Christianity and Buddhism. Hardy concludes that "they both presuppose the fallenness of mankind, and they both look toward a state of recovery and peace."

Heufelder, Emmanuel. *The Way to God: According to the Rule of Saint Benedict*, translated by Luke Eberle. Kalamazoo, Mich.: Cistercian Publications, 1983, 299 p.

Translation of the *Rule* with extensive commentary focused on the first twenty chapters of the document.

Hickey, Philip E. "The Theology of Community in the *Rule* of St. Benedict." *The American Benedictine Review* 20, No. 4 (December 1969): 431-71.

Examines Benedict's essential idea of community as presented in his *Rule.*

Kardong, Terrence G. *Benedict's "Rule": A Translation and Commentary.* Collegeville, Minn.: The Liturgical Press, 1996, 641 p.

Translation and extensive interpretation of the *Rule.*

Kilzer, Sister Martha Clare. "The Place of Saint Benedict in the Western Philosophical Tradition." *The American Benedictine Review* 25, No. 2 (June 1974): 174-99

Investigates the philosophical and ascetic undercurrents of Benedict's monastic *Rule.*

Latteur, Emmanuel. "The Twelve Degrees of Humility in St. Benedict's *Rule*: Still Timely?" *The American Benedictine Review* 40, No. 1 (March 1989): 32-51.

Argues the enduring usefulness of Benedict's twelve degrees of humility.

Lawson, Richard H. "Some Prominent Instances of Semantic Variation in the Middle High German Benedictine *Rules.*" *Amsterdamer Beiträge zur älteren Germanistik* 22 (1984): 147-54.

Offers evidence which contradicts the notion that the text of the Latin *Rule* was considered "untouchable" by translators.

Lienhard, Joseph T. "The Study of the Sources of the *Regula Benedicti*: History and Method." *The American Benedictine Review* 31, No. 1 (March 1980): 20-38.

Probes the sources, allusions, and method of composition of the *Rule of St. Benedict.*

Maynard, Theodore. "The Holy Rule." In *Saint Benedict and His Monks,* London: Staples Press Limited, 1954, pp. 70-89.

Describes the character of the *Rule* and its significance to Christian monasticism.

Odermann, Valerian John. "Interpreting the *Rule of Benedict*: Entering a World of Wisdom." *The American Benedictine Review* 35, No. 1 (March 1984): 25-49.

Hermeneutic study of the *Rule* as an example of the biblical genre of "wisdom literature."

Oetgen, Jerome. "The Old English *Rule* of St. Benedict." *The American Benedictine Review* 26, No. 1 (March 1975): 38-53.

Discusses the influence of three Old English versions of the *Rule.*

Parry, David. *Households of God: The "Rule" of St Benedict with Explanations for Monks and Lay-People Today.* Kalamazoo, Mich.: Cistercian Publications, 1980, 199 p.

Translation of and commentary on the *Rule*, which

attempts to reconcile the text with modern spirituality and life.

de Vogüé, Adalbert. *The Rule of Saint Benedict: A Doctrinal and Spiritual Commentary*, translated by John Baptist Hasbrouck. Kalamazoo, Mich.: Cistercian Publications, 1983, 403 p.

Critical exegesis of selected portions of the *Rule of St. Benedict*.

Wathen, Ambrose. "The Exigencies of Benedict's Little *Rule* for Beginners—RB 72." *The American Benedictine Review* 29, No. 1 (March 1978): 41-66.

Looks at "the notion of good zeal in chapter 72" of the *Rule* in order "to comprehend Benedict's final synthetic statement about life together in the monastery."

Hroswitha of Gandersheim

c. 935-c. 1002

(Also known as Hrotsvitha, Hrotsvit, Roswitha.) German dramatist, poet, and historian.

INTRODUCTION

A Benedictine canoness, Hroswitha of Gandersheim is primarily known for her composition of six plays, ostensibly imitations in the style of the Roman playwright Terence, which to a degree bridge the lengthy gap between stage drama of the classical era and the later miracle and morality plays of the High Middle Ages. Without precedent in tenth-century European literature, Hroswitha's dramas exhibit a strongly didactic tone throughout. They explore the theme of chastity as a sanctifying spiritual force and reflect Hroswitha's intention of providing an alternative to the licentious plays of Terence. Though chiefly remembered as a unique and original woman dramatist, Hroswitha also wrote a series of more traditional saintly legends in verse and two historical epics, the first a history of her Abbey at Gandersheim, and the second an account of the life and reign of her contemporary, the Holy Roman Emperor Otto the Great.

Biographical Information

The full extent of what is known about Hroswitha's life comes predominantly from internal evidence—her own literary prefaces and histories. Using these sources, scholars have placed her birth in Saxony, a northern German dukedom, in approximately 935, during an era of learning and enlightenment ushered in by the Christianizing reforms of the emperors Charlemagne and Otto I. In about 955, Hroswitha, almost undoubtedly of aristocratic birth, entered the Benedictine Abbey at Gandersheim, where she was schooled in Scholastic philosophy, mathematics, music, astronomy, scriptures, and the Latin writings of Virgil, Ovid, Terence, and others. As a canoness, Hroswitha was required to take vows of obedience and chastity, but not the typical vow of poverty. Yet within the confines of the religious life, Hroswitha explored a literary path rarely followed by women at the time. Calling herself *Clamor Validus Gandersheimes,* "the strong voice of Gandersheim," she began to compose a series of saints' lives and holy legends in verse. Traditional in form, these poems later gave way to Hroswitha's more original writings, a cycle of six dramas inspired by the style of Terence. Later she turned to the genre of the historical and epic narrative, producing verse accounts of

the reign of Otto the Great and of her cloister at Gandersheim. Remaining at Gandersheim throughout her life, Hroswitha lived to see the end of the tenth century and, evidence suggests, perhaps the early years of the eleventh.

Major Works

Chronologically and generically, Hroswitha's principal writings fall into three categories: eight holy legends and saints' lives in verse, six dramas in the manner of Terence, and two narrative poems. "Maria," the first legend, treats the life of the Virgin Mary and inaugurates the major theme that Hroswitha would explore throughout her career, the virtue of chastity. The second legend, "Ascensio," details the ascension of Christ into heaven. The virtuous eighth-century Frankish knight Gongolf provides the subject of the next legend. Manipulated by the Devil, Gongolf's adulterous wife undertakes a failed attempt to bring about her husband's death. Chastity is the theme of "Pelagius," based upon the life of a tenth-century Spanish saint martyred for his refusal to succumb to the homosexual advances of Abderrahman III, the caliph of Cordoba. Faust-like characters in "Basilius" and "Theophilus," Hroswitha's fifth and sixth legends, make pacts with the Devil, exchanging their immortal souls for worldly gain. In the former, Bishop Basilius intercedes, while in the latter, the Virgin Mary saves the soul of Theophilus. The final two legends are "Dionysius," which describes the martyrdom of the first bishop of Paris, and "Agnes," which glorifies this sainted martyr for preserving her virginity.

Hroswitha's highly original dramas are preceded in the second book of her collected works by a dedication to Gerberga, her Abbess at Gandersheim, and by the prose "Epistola ad quosdam sapientes huius libri fautores," a letter addressed to the "learned patrons" of her book. Comprised of two parts, the first play in the cycle, *Gallicanus,* deals with the conversion and martyrdom of the title character, a pagan Roman general. Promised the hand of Constantia, Emperor Constantine's daughter, Gallicanus instead takes a vow of chastity and devotes the remainder of his life to Christianity. *Dulcitius* takes place during the Diocletian persecutions of Christians and dramatizes the martyrdom of three virgin sisters (Agapes, Chionia, and Hirena) who refuse to give up their faith and their chastity. Sometimes referred to as *Agapes, Chionia, and Hirena,* the play takes as its more commonly used title the name of the pagan executioner who imprisons the girls.

Callimachus (sometimes called *Drusiana and Callimachus*) depicts the sin of a pagan youth who tries to compromise a young virgin, Drusiana. Her prayers for death are granted, and when Callimachus breaks into her tomb and attempts to profane her lifeless body, he is struck dead. *Paphnutius, or the Conversion of Thaïs* and *Abraham* treat themes of fall and redemption. In each play a harlot is converted by a saintly anchorite and subsequently lives an ascetic life. The title character of *Paphnutius,* inspired by a holy vision, converts the courtesan Thaïs, while the eponymous hermit in *Abraham* saves his niece, Mary. *Sapientia,* Hroswitha's final play, deals with the martyrdom of three allegorical virgins—Fides (Faith), Spes (Hope), and Caritas (Charity)—who, like the heroines of *Dulcitius,* willingly face death so that they may enjoy eternal life in heaven.

Later in life, Hroswitha composed two verse epics, *Carmen de gestis Oddonis imperatoris,* "Deeds of the Emperor Otto," (often referred to as the *Gesta Ottonis*), and *Primordia coenobii Gandeshemensis,* "Origins of the Abbey of Gandersheim." In the *Gesta Ottonis* Hroswitha depicts the Holy Roman Emperor Otto the Great as an ideal Christian ruler, a descendant of King David. Among the female characters in the work, Otto's queens Edith and Adelheid appear as paragons of feminine virtue and are described in the superlatives typical of the hagiographic tradition. The *Primordia* presents the history of the Gandersheim Abbey from its founding until the death of Abbess Christina in 918. Replete with hagiographic conventions, like the *Gesta Ottonis,* the poem features legendary characters whose exemplary lives are reminiscent of those of the heroes and heroines of Hroswitha's works.

Textual History

Following her death, Hroswitha's reputation and her writings fell into near total obscurity for almost five centuries, until 1493, when the Renaissance humanist Conrad Celtes discovered manuscripts of her works preserved in the Emmeram-Munich Codex, dating from the early eleventh century. The oldest extant manuscript of Hroswitha's writings, the Codex organizes the totality of her literary output chronologically in three books. Book I includes her eight holy legends and saints' lives, Book II contains her six-play cycle, and Book III her epics *Carmen de gestis Oddonis imperatoris* and *Primordia coenobii Gandeshemensis.* Several minor poems also appear in the Codex. Scholars have discovered corroborative manuscript evidence, particularly of the dramas, from other sources, including a late-twelfth-century copy of the play *Gallicanus,* included as part of the *Alderspach Passionale,* as well as a handful of later manuscripts, some of them translations into European vernacular languages. The standard modern edition of Hros-

witha's collected works is the *Hrotsvithae Opera* (1970), edited by Helena Homeyer.

Critical Reception

Despite centuries of relative neglect, Hroswitha's writings have garnered considerable interest among modern scholars. In the nineteenth century, Hros-witha's position as the sole female dramatist of the tenth century raised the question of authenticity for some critics, including Joseph von Aschenbach, who in 1867 argued that Hroswitha, a historical absurdity, had clearly been concocted by her sixteenth-century editor, Conrad Celtes. Such thinking has been discredited by contemporary scholars, although a related point of contention raised in prior centuries continues to command critical attention: Were Hroswitha's plays performed during her lifetime? While no definitive evidence on the matter exists, critics continue to ask the question, with most acknowledging at the very least that the canoness' dramatic cycle was intended to be read aloud, if not performed on stage. In more recent years, critics have shifted their focus to stylistic, thematic, and cultural issues related to Hroswitha's plays, and, to a lesser degree, to her other works. There have been reevaluations of Hroswitha's supposed indebtedness to the Roman playwright Terence, explorations of her moral and artistic intention in crafting the plays, and studies of the decidedly feminine focus in her dramatic works. The last of these areas has sparked particular interest in late-twentieth-century scholars, who have done much to challenge androcentric interpretations of Hroswitha's dramas and even to uncover certain proto-feminist tendencies in her writing. Commenting on her unique overall importance, Cardinal Gasquet has remarked, "Hroswitha's works have a claim to an eminent place in medieval literature, and do honour to her sex, to the age in which she lived, and to the vocation which she followed."

PRINCIPAL WORKS*

Opera Hrotsvite (poetry, dramas, and history) 1501
Hrotsvithae Opera (poetry, dramas, and history) 1902
Hrotsvithae Opera (poetry, dramas, and history) 1970

*Hroswitha's major collected works include the following poems: "Maria", *Historia ascensionis Domini* ("Ascensio"), *Passio Sancti Gongolfi martyris* ("Gongolf"), *Passio Sancti Pelagii* ("Pelagius"), *Lapsus et conversio Theophili Vicedomini* ("Theopilus"), *Conversio cujusdam juvenis desperati per S. Basilium episcopum* ("Basilius"), *Passio Sancti Dionysii* ("Dionysius"), and *Passio Sanctae Agnetis* ("Agnes"); dramas: *Passio sanctarum virginum Agapis Chioniae et Hirenae, Resuscitatio Drusianae et Calimachi, Lapsus et conversio Mariae neptis Habrahae heremicolae, Conversio Thaidis meretricis,* and *Passio sanctarum virginum Fidei Spei et Karitatis;* and works of history in verse: *Carmen de gestis Oddonis imperatoris* and *Primordia coenobii Gandeshemensis.*

PRINCIPAL ENGLISH TRANSLATIONS*

The Plays of Hroswitha (dramas) 1923

The Plays of Hroswitha von Gandersheim (dramas) 1979

*English titles of Hroswitha's six plays are usually rendered as *Gallicanus, Dulcitius, Callimachus, Abraham, Paphnutius, or the Conversion of Thaïs,* and *Sapientia* in translation.

CRITICISM

Cornelia C. Coulter (essay date 1929)

SOURCE: "The 'Terentian' Comedies of a Tenth-Century Nun," *The Classical Journal,* Vol. XXIV, No. 7, April, 1929, pp. 515-29.

[*In the following essay, Coulter investigates the extent to which Hroswitha's dramas may be called "Terentian," concluding that "Hrotsvitha's independent contribution to mediaeval Latin literature is far more important than her connection with Terence."*]

Modern discussions of mediaeval drama are very likely to include the name of Hrotsvitha and some mention of her debt to Roman comedy. Creizenach, in the early pages of his *Geschichte des Neueren Dramas,* takes up her plays with special interest because they are the one isolated example of the imitation of Terence in the Middle Ages.[1] Chambers, in his account of the influence of classical drama on the interlude, quotes Dr. Ward's statement that Terence "led a charmed life in the darkest ages of learning," mentions Notker Labeo, who at the beginning of the eleventh century wrote that he had been commissioned to turn the *Andria* into German, and then says, "Not long before, Hrotsvitha, a Benedictine nun of Gandersheim in Saxony, had taken Terence as her model for half a dozen plays in Latin prose, designed to glorify chastity and to celebrate the constancy of the martyrs."[2] And the introductory chapter of C. M. Gayley's *Plays of our Forefathers* contains the sentence: "Terence, the dear delight of the mediaeval monastery, was in the tenth <century> pruned of his pagan charm and naughtiness, and planted out in six persimmon comedies by a Saxon nun of Gandersheim, Hrotsvitha,—comedies of tedious saints and hircine sinners and a stuffy Latin style."[3] In view of such statements as these, it may be worth while to examine the plays of Hrotsvitha, to see just how great her indebtedness to Terence was.[4]

A writer of the period in which Hrotsvitha lived could hardly have found a more stimulating environment than the duchy of Saxony.[5] Three famous Ottos of the Saxon line, elected in turn to the headship of the Holy Roman Empire, dreamed of making Germany a world power and reëstablishing the empire of Charlemagne. The marriage of Otto the Great to Adelaide, princess of Burgundy and widow of the king of Italy, broadened the interests of the Saxons and gave a cosmopolitan tone to the capital; scholars from Italy, Ireland, France, and Greece thronged to the imperial court; and monastic and cathedral schools, under the leadership of humanists like Otwin and Bernward, bishops of Hildesheim, amassed libraries, multiplied manuscripts, and handed on to the younger generation the highest ideal of scholarship that they knew.

One of the notable monasteries of this period was Gandersheim, a Benedictine abbey founded about the middle of the ninth century by Duke Luidolf of Saxony and his wife Oda. The duke's own daughter was the first abbess, and for the next two hundred and fifty years most of the abbesses were drawn from the Saxon royal house. The nuns were of gentle birth and delicate breeding. Gerberga, who became abbess some time after 954, was a niece of Otto the Great and a granddaughter of Arnolf, Duke of Bavaria, and during Gerberga's primacy a sister of Otto III took the veil.

About the same time that Gerberga entered the monastery, there came to Gandersheim the lady Hrotsvitha. The first syllable of her name is connected with the modern German *Ruhm,* the second with *geschwind, Schwindsucht,* and the like; and the whole name means "a mighty shout,"—as Hrotsvitha herself suggests when, in the Preface to her plays (p. 113), she speaks of herself as *"Clamor Validus Gandeshemensis"*—a strangely incongruous name for one of her gentle modesty.

All our information about Hrotsvitha comes from dedicatory verses and epistles prefaced to the different sections of her works, and from the internal evidence of the works themselves. From these sources we learn that she was a diligent student, at first under the direction of the nun Rikkardis later as a pupil of Gerberga, who, although Hrotsvitha's junior in age, was her senior in knowledge and passed on to her sister nun the instruction which she herself had received from eminent scholars (*a sapientissimis,* pp. 1 f.), perhaps at the monastery of St. Emmeram in Regensburg. Hrotsvitha does not mention her textbooks, but the content and diction of her works show that she must have read the *Peristephanon,* or *Book of Martyrs,* of Prudentius, and many other legends of the saints; Boethius' *Consolation of Philosophy* and his treatises on arithmetic and music; some writings of the church fathers; and at least Vergil and Terence of pagan authors.[6] A large part of her time must have been given to composition in verse—an exercise to which the deacon Thangmar gave special attention in the training of Bernward[7]—and the proficiency which she gained shows in the lengthy hexameter and elegiac poems that form a large part of her collected works.

She tried her hand at original composition, secretly at first (*clam cunctis et quasi furtim,* p. 1), for fear that critics, recognizing the crudities of her style, might deter her from writing altogether. The compositions of this early period are in both hexameter and elegiac verse, and comprise a life of the Virgin Mary; an account of the Ascension of the Savior; and six saints' legends, including the story of St. Pelagius of Cordoba, which Hrotsvitha got from eye-witnesses, and the martyrdom of St. Agnes, drawn from a biography ascribed to Ambrose. These verses (*carminula,* as the author modestly calls them) were presented to Gerberga with the request that she read and correct them (p. 3):

> Et, cum sis certe vario lassata labore,
>   Ludens dignare hos modulos legere,
> Hanc quoque sordidolam tempta purgare camenam
>   Ac fulcire tui flore magisterii,
> Quo laudem dominae studium supportet alumnae
>   Doctricique piae carmina discipulae.

Encouraged by the approval of the abbess, Hrotsvitha now turned to an entirely new form of composition. Her motives for this departure are interestingly stated in the Preface to Liber Secundus of her works:

> There are many Catholics, and we cannot entirely acquit ourselves of the charge, who, attracted by the polished elegance of the style of pagan writers, prefer their works to the holy scriptures. There are others who, although they are deeply attached to the sacred writings and have no liking for most pagan productions, make an exception in favor of the works of Terence, and fascinated by the charm of the manner, risk being corrupted by the wickedness of the matter. Wherefore I, the strong voice of Gandersheim, have not hesitated to imitate in my writing a poet whose works are so widely read, my object being to glorify, within the limits of my poor talent, the laudable chastity of Christian virgins in that same form of composition which has been used to describe the shameless acts of licentious women . . . If this pious devotion gives satisfaction I shall rejoice; if it does not, either on account of my own worthlessness or of the faults of my unpolished style, I shall still be glad that I made the effort.[8]

Just how extensive her first dramatic attempts were we do not know; but some of her plays must have been circulated among her intimate friends at the monastery and then submitted to certain scholars outside; for an epistle of later date addressed **Ad Quosdam Sapientes Huius Libri Fautores** thanks these scholars most humbly for their commendation of her work (*mei opusculum vilis mulierculae*) and begs them to criticize the compositions which she encloses:

> I have been at pains (she concludes), whenever I have been able to pick up some threads and scraps

torn from the old mantle of philosophy, to weave them into the stuff of my own book, in the hope that my lowly ignorant effort may gain more acceptance through the introduction of something of a nobler strain . . . I hope you will revise it with the same careful attention that you would give to a work of your own, and that when you have succeeded in bringing it up to the proper standard you will return it to me. (St. John, pp. xxviii-xxx.)

Still later she composed in hexameter verse two long poems on contemporary subjects: an account of the deeds of Otto I, and a history of the monastery of Gandersheim down to the year 919. At what date her death occurred we do not know.

For us, by far the most significant portion of Hrotsvitha's work is the dramas, and these are particularly interesting because, standing as they almost certainly do in order of composition, they give clear indications of the development of her technique. There are six plays altogether (Creizenach suggests that she intended them to be, in number as well as in subject-matter, an "Anti-Terenz"),[9] and the material is in every case drawn from legends of the saints.

The first play of the series offers interesting material for comparative study, since it has come down to us in two other mediaeval versions, one of which is practically contemporary with Hrotsvitha herself: a life of St. Constantia (or Constantina) in a Visigothic manuscript of the eleventh century,[10] and the story of St. John and St. Paul, as related in *The Golden Legend* of Jacobus de Voragine (c. 1245).[11] These two versions agree in the main outlines of the story, which runs as follows:

> Constantia, the daughter of the Emperor Constantine, had two provosts, named John and Paul. Gallicanus, the commander of the imperial army, was about to set out against the barbarians, and asked that Constantia be given to him in marriage as a reward. Constantine himself was willing, but knew that his daughter had taken a vow of virginity; she, however, told her father that if Gallicanus gained the victory the marriage might be considered; she asked to have the two daughters of Gallicanus dwell with her, and delivered to him John and Paul to go with him to battle. Gallicanus was besieged by the barbarians, and John and Paul told him, "Make a vow to the God of heaven, and you shall conquer." He did so, and there appeared to him a young man carrying a cross on his shoulder, who said to him, "Take your sword and follow me." The young man led him to the king of the opposing army, whom he slew; and the army straightway surrendered. On returning to Rome, he told the emperor that he had taken a vow of chastity, and asked to be released from his engagement to Constantia. His two daughters were also converted, and he gave all his goods to the poor and served God. Gallicanus suffered martyrdom

under Julian; and John and Paul, who had inherited Constantia's property, were put to death by Julian's emissary Terentianus. Terentianus's son was seized with madness; but when Terentianus confessed his sin and became a Christian, the son was healed.

This story Hrotsvitha reproduces faithfully, the only essential difference between her version and that of the legends being that hers is in dialogue instead of in narrative form. The opening scene presents Constantine in conversation with Gallicanus; Constantine explains the urgent reasons why Gallicanus should take the field against the barbarians; and the general agrees to do the emperor's bidding but asks for the hand of Constantia as a reward; Constantine hesitates but promises to consult his daughter. In the second scene Constantine tells her of Gallicanus' wishes, and she protests that she would rather die than break the vow of virginity that she has taken. He appreciates her feeling, but reminds her of the disaster that may befall the state if he does not grant his general's request. She proposes a plan: that Constantine shall pretend to agree to Gallicanus' conditions and shall persuade Gallicanus to leave his two daughters with Constantia during his absence, Gallicanus himself taking as his companions in the war Constantia's chamberlains, John and Paul. "But if he returns victorious, what shall we do?" asks Constantine. "We must call upon almighty God," says Constantia, "to change Gallicanus's heart." The third scene (a scant dozen lines) shows Gallicanus in anxious consultation with other nobles, wondering what the outcome of Constantine's conference will be. In the fourth, he is summoned into the imperial presence, as follows:

> *Constantinus.* Gallicane!
> *Gallicanus.* Quid dixit?
> *Principes.* Procede, procede; vocat te!
> *G.* Dii propitii, favete!
> *C.* Perge securus, Gallicane, ad bellum;
>   reversurus enim accipies, quod desideras,
>   praemium.
> *G.* Illudisne me?
> *C.* Si illudo.
> *G.* Me felicem, si unum scirem!
> *C.* Quid unum?
> *G.* Eius responsum.
> *C.* Filiae?
> *G.* Ipsius.

So the story proceeds, through a total of twenty-two scenes. The two daughters of Gallicanus are brought to Constantia; Gallicanus, with John and Paul, departs for war; the soldiers arm themselves to meet the foe; there is a spirited battle scene, in which we are at one moment on the Roman side, hearing the defeatist counsel of the tribunes and witnessing Gallicanus' vow, and at the next are in the midst of the panic-stricken enemy, as they drop their arms and sue for mercy.

Gallicanus returns to Rome, performs his devotions at St. Peter's, tells the emperor the story of the battle, and renounces his claim to Constantia. And then suddenly we are in the reign of Julian the Apostate, who is ordering a confiscation of Christian goods. The persecution of John and Paul, the madness and restoration of Terentianus' son, all follow in due course; and the play ends with a prayer of thanksgiving by Terentianus.

The defects of the drama are obvious. There is practically no plot, no entanglement to be resolved; the characters have little individuality; and the interest, instead of being unified, centers on Gallicanus in the first part and on John and Paul in the second. But all these defects were undoubtedly in Hrotsvitha's sources; and if she has followed them with too great fidelity, the fault is surely pardonable in one who was working in an unfamiliar medium and had not yet mastered her craft. And in reshaping the legend of Gallicanus, Hrotsvitha has actually contributed something of her own. Out of the shadowy figure of the emperor's daughter she has made a really appealing character, sweet and docile with her father, gentle and affectionate with her maiden companions; and her description of the "young man of lofty stature, bearing a cross on his shoulders," who appeared to Gallicanus, and of the heavenly host who thronged about him on the right hand and on the left, has an imaginative quality far beyond anything in the legends of the saints.

The plays which follow show a marked advance in technique. *Dulcitius,* the next in order, has only fourteen scenes, as compared with the twenty-two of *Gallicanus; Calimachus* and *Abraham* each have nine. And the structure of these dramas is much firmer. In *Dulcitius,* the Emperor Diocletian reasons with three Christian maidens—Agapes (Love), Chionia (Purity), and Hirena (Peace)—trying to induce them to renounce their faith and wed three young nobles of the court. When they refuse, he orders them thrown into prison, under the custody of Dulcitius; and they are accordingly taken to a cell, in the antechamber of which certain cooking utensils are stored. At night, as they are singing hymns, Dulcitius approaches the cell, intending to embrace the maidens. They pray, "Deus nos tueatur!" Then a great rattling of pots and pans is heard; and the maidens, peering through a crack, see Dulcitius clasping the grimy cooking utensils to his bosom and imprinting kisses upon them. Then, blackened with soot, he returns to his soldiers, who stare at him in consternation and cry, *"Quis hic egreditur? Daemoniacus. Vel magis ipse diabolus. Fugiamus!"* Diocletian orders the maidens put to death; Agapes and Chionia are placed upon a pyre, where, however, neither their hair nor their garments are injured by the flames, and their spirits pass quietly from their bodies. Orders are given for Hirena to be taken to a brothel; but two supernatural beings rescue her from the soldiers and lead her to a hill-top, where an arrow from a soldier's bow ends her life, but only after she has uttered this triumphant hymn:

> Hinc mihi quam maxime gaudendum, tibi vero dolendum, quia pro tui severitate malignitatis in tartara dampnaberis; ego autem, martirii palmam virginitatisque receptura coronam, intrabo aethereum aeterni regis thalamum; cui est honor et gloria in saecula.

Calimachus has more dramatic interest than either of the preceding plays, and shows increased skill in character-drawing. It also approaches more closely than either of its predecessors to the Terentian type of plot, in that the entire action of the play is motivated by the love of Calimachus for Drusiana. In the opening scenes Calimachus, like Chaerea in the *Eunuchus,* tells his friends of his passion, which has not yet been revealed to its object; they declare that his hopes are vain, for Drusiana has been baptized and has devoted herself so completely to the service of God that she will not even visit the couch of her own husband. He nevertheless approaches her and declares his love:

> C. Sermo meus ad te, Drusiana, praecordialis amor.
> D. Quid mecum velis, Calimache, sermonibus agere, vehementer admiror.
> C. Miraris?
> D. Satis.
> C. Primum de amore.
> D. Quid de amore?
> C. Id scilicet, quod te prae omnibus diligo.
> D. Quod ius consanguinitatis, quaeve legalis conditio institutionis compellit te ad mei amorem?
> C. Tui pulchritudo.
> D. Mea pulchritudo?
> C. Immo.
> D. Quid ad te?
> C. Pro dolor! hactenus parum, sed spero, quod attineat postmodum.
> D. Discede, discede, leno nefande; confundor enim diutius tecum verba miscere, quem sentio plenum diabolica deceptione.

When he has withdrawn, Drusiana, overwhelmed at the thought of the ruin which her beauty has wrought, prays for death. Her prayer is answered and she is laid away in the tomb. But even this catastrophe does not release Calimachus from the torture of love; he goes to the tomb and bribes the guard to allow him access to the body. But as Calimachus enters the sepulcher, the guard cries out in terror at a horrible serpent; the guard is killed by the serpent's bite, and Calimachus is miraculously struck dead. In the next scene, Drusiana's husband and St. John, approaching the tomb, hear a voice from heaven promising the resurrection of Drusiana and of one who lies near her; John utters a long prayer, and then in the name of Christ calls upon

Calimachus to rise and confess his sins. The restored and penitent lover now swears devotion to Christ alone, and Drusiana's resurrection follows. The guard is also called back to life; but after a few hasty inquiries about the situation, he declares: "If what you say is true, if Drusiana has raised me from the dead and Calimachus believes in Christ, I scorn life and gladly choose death. I prefer not to live rather than to see so much grace and virtue in them." So the others commit him to the fires of everlasting torment, and end with thanksgiving to God.

Abraham (or *The Fall and Conversion of Mary, Niece of the Hermit Abraham*) has some exquisite touches. In the opening dialogue Abraham tells his fellow-monk Effrem of the little niece (*neptis tenella*), bereft of both father and mother, whom he would like to win to a life of celibacy. Mary is called in, agrees to her uncle's plan for her, and is established in a little cell next to Abraham's own, through the window of which he plans to instruct her in the psalter and other pages of Holy Writ. Some years later Abraham, bowed down with grief, comes to Effrem and tells him a sad tale: a lover in monk's garb has come to Mary's window and persuaded her to flee with him; then, her honor lost, she has in despair given herself up to a life of vanity. Word comes to her uncle that she has taken up her abode in the house of a certain procurer to whom she brings much gain. Then, by a ruse similar to that of Chaerea in the *Eunuchus,* but of course with quite a different purpose, Abraham disguises himself as a soldier, with a cap over his tonsured head, and journeys to the place. Mary shows the supposed stranger gentle reverence, kisses his gray head, and kneels beside him to unfasten his boots. Then he throws off his disguise, and calls upon his adopted child, by the love that he has borne her and all her years of holy living, to repent and turn from her sins. She falls prostrate to the earth; but as he encourages her with the hope of forgiveness, she rises, leaves her ill-gotten gains behind, and goes forth with him, in the early morning light, to return to her little cell.[12]

The two remaining plays must have been the ones that Hrotsvitha had particularly in mind when she spoke so proudly of weaving in "threads from the mantle of Philosophy"; but unfortunately these threads only detract from the dramatic value of the plays. *Pafnutius* deals with the conversion of the courtesan Thais—a theme which was treated in the nineteenth century by Anatole France and, through his story, passed over into modern opera.[13] In a long opening scene, Pafnutius explains to his disciples that, just as the *maior mundus* is composed of four opposing elements, so man, the *minor mundus,* is composed of body and spirit, opposed to one another. He discourses on dialectic, the quadrivium, and the harmony of music; and finally explains that he is sad because of the evil life of Thais; he plans to visit her in the guise of a lover and asks for the prayers of his disciples. The scene which follows bears a general resemblance to the one in which the disguised Abraham visits the prostitute Mary, but is much less moving. Pafnutius convinces Thais of her wrongdoing; she repents and makes a huge bonfire of the "mammon" that she has collected from her lovers. He then conducts her to a monastery, and the abbess places her in a small cell, through the opening of which she may receive food; she shrinks from the darkness and the prospect of filth, but Pafnutius sternly bids her remember the fires of hell. He then tells her to pray, not with words, but with tears, and to say only, *"Qui me plasmasti, miserere mei."* When three years of penance have passed, Pafnutius learns that a disciple of the monk Antonius has had a vision of the marvelous glory in heaven awaiting Thais; he then visits her and predicts her death within fifteen days. He is with her in her last hour, as she prays, *"Qui plasmasti me, miserere mei";* and himself offers a prayer for her departing spirit.

The scene of the last play, *Sapientia,* is laid in Rome in the time of Hadrian, but the principal characters (Wisdom and her three daughters, Faith, Hope, and Charity) are allegorical, and the philosophical element so predominates that there is little of the dramatic left. Sapientia and the three maidens are examined before the emperor; and Sapientia, in giving the ages of the three children (eight, ten, and twelve years), goes through an elaborate discourse on number, based on the *Institutio Arithmetica* of Boëthius. Hadrian orders them all to worship the gods of Rome and, on their refusal, puts them into custody; later, he bids Fides sacrifice to Diana and, when she remains steadfast, has her flogged and burned; Spes meets with a similar fate; Karitas is told merely to say "Magna Diana" but refuses to do even this. She is thrown into a fiery furnace, where, although the flames are so intense that they kill 5,000 men, she is seen walking about uninjured, with three shining ones beside her. She is then beheaded, and Sapientia and other matrons take the three bodies and bury them at the third milestone from the city. Sapientia offers a long prayer and then dies.

Clearly there is little in these six plays which, from our point of view, can justly be called Terentian. A faint hint of Terence's themes may be traced in the importance of the courtesans' rôles in *Abraham* and *Pafnutius,* and in the prominence of the love element in some of the other plays, particularly in *Calimachus,* where passionate love is the dominant force in the action. Even here, however, as she warned us in the Preface, Hrotsvitha has deliberately set herself to supplant Terence, by showing the inferiority of earthly to heavenly love and by leading the two courtesans back to the fold. The disguise-motif, as it appears in *Abraham* and *Pafnutius,* is somewhat like that in the *Eunuchus;* but whereas Chaerea dons the eunuch's

clothes for the purpose of gaining access to the girl with whom he has fallen in love, the two monks in Hrotsvitha's plays disguise themselves as lovers in order to save the souls of the women whom they visit. The humorous element may also be discovered in her plays, in the saucy replies of some of the youthful martyrs to their inquisitors (which, as a recent translator has remarked, strike the same note as speeches of the Christians in *Androcles and the Lion*),[14] in the characterization of the guard in *Calimachus,* who would rather stay dead than see virtue spreading itself, and, most notably, in the encounter of the amorous Dulcitius with the sooty pots and pans.[15] More definitely Terentian are certain tricks of vocabulary and phrasing—the exclamations *hercle, edepol, euax, pro dolor, hem;* and idiomatic expressions like *non flocci facio* and *di te perdant.* Winterfeld, in his edition of Hrotsvitha's works, lists in the notes a few phrases which may even have a more direct connection with passages in Terence's plays—*Gall.* p. 119, *paucis te volo,* for instance, which repeats *And.* 29; *Gall.* p. 122, *illudisne me,* similar to *Ad.* 697, *num ludis tu me?* and *Dulc.* p. 142, *nigellis panniculis obsitum,* like *Eun.* 236, *pannis annisque obsitum.*[16]

But when all this has been said, the connections with Terence remain few in number, and the one outstanding similarity is that in both authors a story is developed by means of *dialogue.* That this dialogue could be acted seems never to have occurred to Hrotsvitha; Terence's plays had long since ceased to be given on the stage and were regularly read in private, or at most recited in the monastic schools. It was as reading-drama that Hrotsvitha thought of Terence's plays, and as reading-drama that she planned her own. If there could be doubt in anyone's mind on this point, an attempt to produce a play like *Gallicanus,* with its lightning changes of scene and its sudden leaps in time, should quickly dispel the doubt.[17]

The form in which Hrotsvitha cast her dramas was probably the nearest approach possible for her to the form of Terence's plays. To her, as to other readers of the Middle Ages, Terence's lines appeared to be prose, but prose of a peculiar elegance; and she therefore chose for her dramas a particularly elaborate form of prose composition, in which short phrases are balanced against one another, with the ends of the clausulae marked by rhyme.[18] Some of the speeches quoted earlier in this paper have shown the peculiar qualities of this *Reimprosa,* but the prayer of Drusiana from *Cali-machus* may be given as a further example:

> Intende, domine, mei timorem; intende, quem patior, dolorem! Quid mihi, quid agendum sit, ignoro: si prodidero, civilis per me fiet discordia; si celavero, insidiis diabolicis sine te refragari nequeo. Iube me in te, Christe, ocius mori, ne fiam in ruinam delicato iuveni!

In actual fact, Hrotsvitha's independent contribution to mediaeval Latin literature is far more important than her connection with Terence. It took real inspiration to see that the saints' legends which she and everyone else up to this time had handled in narrative form could be given as well, or better, in dialogue. And in adapting her material to the dramatic form, after the first awkward attempts in **Gallicanus,** she shows a rare gift for seizing on the great moments of a story and presenting them strikingly.[19] The sympathetic insight into the minds of her characters, and the deftness and sureness of the character-drawing in the best of her plays, are remarkable in one who had spent most of her mature years within convent walls. And whether her plays are to be regarded as an isolated phenomenon, without influence on later Latin literature, or whether, as Professor Coffman suggests, they may conceivably have furnished a hint for the later miracle plays,[20] this gentle nun of Gandersheim, who had the genius and the courage to attempt an entirely new literary type, deserves all honor.

Notes

[1] W. Creizenach, *Geschichte des Neueren Dramas*[2]: Halle, Niemeyer (1911), I, p. 16.

[2] E. K. Chambers, *The Mediaeval Stage:* Oxford, Clarendon Press (1903), II, p. 207.

[3] New York, Duffield (1907), p. 2.

[4] References in this article are to the Teubner text of Hrotsvitha's works, ed. K. Strecker, Leipzig, 1906; there is also an edition by P. Winterfeld in the series *Scriptores Rerum Germanicarum:* Berlin, Weidmann (1902), which is particularly valuable for the literary parallels cited in the notes. An English version has recently been published under the title, *The Plays of Roswitha, translated by Christopher St. John:* London, Chatto and Windus (1923). M. Manitius's *Geschichte der Lateinischen Literatur des Mittelalters:* München, Beck (1911), I, pp. 619-32, gives an admirable summary of the facts of Hrotsvitha's life and a critical estimate of her work. For a full bibliography of recent articles in English, including several translations, see O. R. Kuehne, "Recent Literature Concerning Hrotsvitha," in *Class. Wk.* XX (1927), 149 f.

[5] See the illuminating article by G. R. Coffman, "A New Approach to Mediaeval Latin Drama," in *Mod. Phil.* XXII (1925), 239-71, from which much of the material in this paragraph is drawn.

[6] Cf. Manitius, *Lat. Lit. des Mittelalters,* I, 631 f., and the notes in Winterfeld's edition.

[7] See the section from the life of Bernward paraphrased by Coffman in *Mod. Phil.* XXII (1925), 251.

[8] The quotation is from St. John's translation, pp. xxvi-xxviii.

[9] Creizenach, *op. cit.,* I, p. 17.

[10] C. Narbey, *Supplément aux Acta Sanctorum pour des Vies de Saints de l'Epoche Mérovingienne:* Paris, Welter (1899-1900), II, pp. 131-52. M. Narbey believes that this manuscript is an authentic copy of a life of St. Constantia written by a contemporary, of which we find traces in other saints' legends.

[11] Th. Graesse, *Jacobi a Voragine Legenda Aurea:* Dresden and Leipzig, Arnold (1846), pp. 364-67. The first part of the story is also given in the *Acta Sanctorum* collected by the Bollandists, under date of June 25, and the latter part under June 26.

[12] It is rather striking that this play, which marks the high point of Hrotsvitha's dramatic technique, should also contain the largest number of Vergilian reminiscences. The phrase which Abraham uses in speaking of Mary's age (p. 163, *vitali aura vesceretur*) is a blend of two in the *Aeneid* (I, 387, *auras vitales carpis;* and III, 339, *vescitur aura*); and he uses the words of Aeneas (*Aen.* II, 54) and of the unhappy shepherd of the first *Eclogue* (I, 16) when he tells of the dream that might have warned him of Mary's ruin, *"si mens non fuisset laeva"* (p. 167). He places her on his horse, *"ne itineris asperitas secet teneras plantas"* (p. 176; cf. Gallus's words to Lycoris in *Ecl.* x, 49), and Mary cries out in wondering gratitude, *"O, quem te memorem?"* (p. 176; cf. *Aen.* I, 327). Most of these parallels are noted by Winterfeld.

[13] On the origin and growth of the legend, see O. R. Kuehne, *A Study of the Thais Legend with Special Reference to Hrothsvitha's "Paphnutius":* Philadelphia, privately printed (1922). On p. 76 of this book the author notes several additions and changes made by Hrosvitha in the legend, and on pp. 99 f. he points out that the scholastic discussion at the beginning of the play and the introduction of the abbess in a later scene may have suggested similar features in the novel of Anatole France.

[14] St. John, *op. cit.,* Pref., p. xix.

[15] H. E. Wedeck, "The Humor of a Mediaeval Nun, Hrotsvitha," in *Class. Wk.* XXI (1928), 130 f., comments on several other scenes. Personally, I do not feel that the finespun arguments of *Pafnutius* and *Sapientia* were humorous to the author.

[16] We need to use caution in dealing with these verbal similarities. The phrase *panniculis obsitum* is practically the same as *obsita pannis* in vs. 19 of *The Phoenix,* ascribed to Lactantius, and may have been familiar to Hrotsvitha from other sources than Terence; and

phrases like *memoriae fixum teneo* (p. 118), on which Winterfeld cites *And.* 40, *in memoria habeo,* and *immo aliud* (p. 118; cf. *And.* 30, *immo aliud*) are too common in Latin literature to warrant any certain conclusions. The actual number of citations from Terence in Winterfeld's notes is less than from Boethius, Prudentius, or the Vulgate.

[17] For an emphatic statement of this point of view, see Coffman in *Mod. Phil.* XXII (1925), 262. The fact that some of the plays have been produced in recent years does not invalidate the argument. Cf. St. John, *The Plays of Roswitha,* Pref., p. xxiii, for performances of *Calimachus* and *Pafnutius* in London theaters, and C. J. Kraemer, Jr., in *Class. Wk.* xx (1927), 198, for performances of *Abraham, Calimachus,* and *Dulcitius* at the Lawren Theatre Studio in New York City.

[18] Manitus, *Lat. Lit. des Mittelalters,* I, p. 628, defines it as *"die Form, die im 10. Jahrhundert in der Prosa beliebt wurde, die Reimprosa, wo aufeinanderfolgende Stückchen der Rede miteinander gereimt sind, doch ohne dass Umfang und Rhythmus gleich sein mussten."* C. S. Baldwin, *Mediaeval Rhetoric and Poetic:* New York, Macmillan (1928), p. 144, gives other examples of tenth-century rhymed prose; the extract from a ceremonious letter which he quotes in n. 41 is very similar, in tone and style, to the epistles prefixed to different sections of Hrotsvitha's works. In her plays, the use of balance and rhyme is most marked in passages of a heightened emotional tone, particularly in the prayers. To one familiar with mediaeval hymnody, there is a rather striking similarity between these prayers and the "transitional" sequences of the tenth and eleventh centuries, of which the famous *Victimae Paschali* is the best example; and it seems possible that these passages may have been influenced to some extent by the church liturgy. For a parallel situation at a later date, when the cadences of the collects affected the style of twelfth- and thirteenth-century sermons, cf. Baldwin, *op. cit.,* pp. 223-27.

[19] Cf. Creizenach, *op. cit.,* I, p. 18, *"Besser als die Dramatiker des späteren Mittelalters versteht sie es, aus der überlieferten Begebenheit die Hauptmomente herauszugreifen."*

[20] Coffman in *Mod. Phil.* XXII (1925), 263 f.

Rosamond Gilder (essay date 1931)

SOURCE: "Hrotsvitha, a Tenth-Century Nun: The First Woman Playwright," in *Enter the Actress: The First Women in the Theatre,* Houghton Mifflin Company, 1931, pp. 18-45.

[*In the following essay, Gilder summarizes Hroswitha's place in early medieval drama and evaluates her plays,* *noting particularly her masterful characterization in these works.*]

Although the early Christian Church welcomed to its bosom certain repentant actresses, it was on the whole the mortal enemy of the theatre. The war between Church and stage has been long and bitter, particularly in the early days when the theatre represented the last entrenched camp of paganism, and as such was the subject of virulent attack and condemnation. The Church desired nothing less than the complete annihilation of its enemy, and in this, by the close of the fourth century, it had largely succeeded. It is therefore not a little diverting to find that the first woman of any importance in the history of the theatre in Europe is a Benedictine nun. From the darkest of the dark ages of the theatre, as well as of Western civilisation, the work of only one playwright has come down to us intact. The six plays of Hrotsvitha of Gandersheim stand alone, bridging the gulf between Seneca and the *Representatio Adœ,* between the Latin tragedy of A.D. 65, and the French mystery play of the twelfth century of the Christian era. Whatever plays were written and acted, whatever playwrights, actors, and impresarios flourished during these centuries, Hrotsvitha's comedies alone have survived in their complete and original form. Hrotsvitha the Nun, devout daughter of the Church that sought to destroy the theatre, Hrotsvitha, 'German religious and virgin of the Saxon race,' Hrotsvitha, the 'strong voice of Gandersheim,' confined in a remote convent and following the rules of a strict religious order, is yet the first woman of the theatre, the patron saint of the motley followers of Thalia and Melpomene.

The curious anomaly that has placed this devout and dedicated nun of Europe's darkest period in the hierarchy of notable playwrights of all time, grows only more interesting as it is more closely studied. Every circumstance of time and place, of surrounding atmosphere, of education and of outlook would, at first glance, make such a phenomenon seem impossible, so impossible, indeed, that historians of the drama have almost unanimously dismissed Hrotsvitha as, artistically, a 'sport,' without literary or spiritual issue, and therefore of slight importance. Other scholars, more pedantic than accurate, have classed her plays as forgeries, solving the problem presented in her work by denying that she had ever existed. Unfortunately for those who prefer simple classifications and sweeping statements to the vagaries of actual events, this last assumption is untenable.

The manuscript of Hrotsvitha's collected writings, discovered by Conrad Celtes in the Benedictine monastery of Saint Emmeran, Ratisbon, in 1492 or '93, and now reposing in the Munich Library, is authentically of the tenth century. Celtes published his find in 1501, embellishing the book with woodcuts which have been attributed to Dürer. The most interesting of these pic-

tures is the frontispiece, which shows Hrotsvitha presenting her manuscript to Otto II, with the Abbess
Gerberga leaning protectingly over the kneeling nun.
Not to be overshadowed by his protégée, Celtes included a companion picture of himself, in which he in
turn is shown in the act of presenting the first printed
edition of Hrotsvitha's works to his own liege lord.
The most important modern edition of the plays is that
of Charles Magnin, who, in 1845, published the plays
in the original Latin with a complete French translation
and a biographical and critical study of Hrotsvitha's
works. There are several recent English translations of
the plays, so that Hrotsvitha has at last come into her
own. Her existence has not only been established beyond a doubt, but her curious and delightful contribution to the literature of the theatre has become part of
the heritage of the stage. With the venerable scholar
Henricus Bodo, first commentator on the writings of
the Nun of Gandersheim, we who read her plays for
the first time will be tempted to exclaim, 'Rara avis in
Saxonia visa est!'

In order to appreciate fully the strength of that impulse
for expression in dramatic form which must have impelled Hrotsvitha in her choice of so extraordinary a
medium, we must realise what sort of world surrounded
her and appreciate some of the handicaps with which
she was burdened. She lived at the parting of the ways,
a time of stress and strain between the collapse of the
old order and the birth of the new. Europe, beaten
upon by Northmen, Magyars, and Saracens, had at last
repelled these marauders and won a respite from invasion. The crumbling Roman Empire had fallen apart,
and a Saxon Emperor ruled a turbulent and disorganised
band of feudal barons in the West. With the increasing
power of the Christian Church, the last vestiges of the
theatre in Italy had disappeared. It had split into its
component parts, and bands of mimes, jugglers, dancers, and buffoons earned a precarious livelihood by
travelling from place to place entertaining bored women
and war-worn, brutish lords in the great halls of their
feudal castles. The Roman theatre buildings themselves,
scattered throughout Italy and Southern France, had
been turned into donjon keeps—fortified castles for
the protection of each man against his neighbour. The
old order of the Roman world was destroyed and a
new order had not yet come to take its place.

The Church itself was distracted with schisms and
heresies, and its fight against paganism, in the theatre
and elsewhere, was hardly more bitter than its internal
conflicts. Wars, famines, and plagues completed the
sufferings of the unfortunate lower orders, creating a
universal chaos that has made this period seem to historians the most miserable that has afflicted the Western world. In such troubled and violent times, the convents and monasteries, which were growing up throughout Europe, were almost the only centres of culture
and education that existed. The Christian Church, while

doing its utmost to discredit the iniquitous literature of
the pagans, was at the same time beginning to preserve
it, and to act as guardians of the precious manuscripts
which, in Europe at least, were all that remained as
witness of past intellectual glories.

The fate of the women of the Dark Ages was necessarily harsh. A period which depended almost exclusively
on its fighting men for survival had little interest in the
development of the more peaceful arts and small time
for the amenities of living. A woman at the time when
Hrotsvitha lived was, in the eyes of men, a weak and
foolish creature, useful only for the transmission of
property, and the production of offspring. In the eyes
of the Church, she was something more sinister than
this. The venom with which the Church Fathers attacked the theatre was only surpassed by the vitriolic
intensity with which they damned the female of the
species and all her natural functions. Only one hope of
redemption was held out to the unfortunate creature
who through Eve's original weakness had brought sin
and sorrow into the world. She must renounce this
mundane existence and all its so-called pleasures, and
vow herself to an eternal chastity, a virginity in this
world mitigated by the hope of a spiritual union with
the Beloved Bridegroom in the world to come.

The alternative careers which presented themselves to
a woman such as Hrotsvitha in the year of grace 950,
were strictly limited. She must either consent to be
married off by her nearest male relative to some strong-
armed warrior-baron who would acquire her property
and her person simultaneously, and who would exercise a complete and unquestioned control over her
whole future existence, or she might enter a religious
order, where the questionable privilege of serving an
earthly lord would be exchanged for the sure joys of a
heavenly dedication. More compelling still, the convent gave her an opportunity for immediate intellectual
development, the companionship of men and women
keenly interested in the things of the mind, and the
peaceful security of an ordered existence, nowhere else
to be found. Monastic life, though physically restricting, was along certain lines intellectually liberating,
and offered many of the inducements that college and
a career hold out to the young girl of to-day.

The Abbey of Gandersheim would be particularly attractive to an eager and enterprising mind such as
Hrotsvitha's. It was an oasis in a turbulent world, a
centre of light and learning, of hope and peace, in the
midst of danger and damnation. Founded in 850 by
Ludolph, Duke of Saxony, it had already in Hrotsvitha's
day acquired a unique literary and aristocratic tradition. Its abbesses were drawn from the imperial family
of Saxony and held their fief directly from the King.
They provided men-at-arms for their overlord, struck
coins bearing their own image, and exercised all the
rights and privileges of feudal barons. The close con-

nection between the Imperial Court and the Abbey of Gandersheim brought it into the full current of the intellectual development of the day, and there is little reason to doubt that Hrotsvitha entered it the more eagerly because she knew that there she would be under the guidance of nuns who were as famed for their learning as they were for their piety.

Exactly when Hrotsvitha entered the Abbey of Gandersheim is not known, nor is there any record of her life before she took the veil. The dates of her birth and death, her family name, and all the details of her life are equally obscure, but in the brief forewords with which she enlivens her collected writings, we have a vivid impression of this extraordinary nun whose fate it was to play so unexpected a rôle in the history of the theatre. In thus inaugurating the delightful custom of writing prefaces to her plays, Hrotsvitha has given us what knowledge we have of her personality and her methods of work. She tells us that she was older than the Abbess Gerberga, who was born in 940, and from certain references in the texts of her poems, it is evident that she lived into the first years of the eleventh century, probably entering the convent about 960 when she was in her early twenties. She was undoubtedly of gentle birth, for Gandersheim was an aristocratic institution, welcoming the daughters of barons and lords, and presided over by an imperial princess. Moreover, her plays show familiarity with the amenities of life in the world beyond the cloister, and her education itself in an almost illiterate age attests her social standing. If, as her biographers believe, she was twenty-two or three when she took the veil, she had perhaps already experienced some of the joys and sorrows of that world which she renounced in her vows, but which, as her writings testify, she never entirely forgot.

On entering the convent, Hrotsvitha began her studies under the 'learned and gentle novice-mistress, Rikkarda,' but evidently she soon outstripped her teacher, for it is the Abbess Gerberga herself who introduced her to the classic literature which was to inspire her most famous work. She had other teachers as well, very possibly some learned monks and clerics from neighbouring monasteries; but it was in secret, and in those quiet moments which must have been difficult to secure in the carefully apportioned and supervised routine of a nun's existence, that she began her writing. 'Unknown to all around me,' she explains in the preface [The quotations from Hrotsvitha's prefaces and plays are taken from *The Plays of Roswitha*, translated by Christopher St. John.] to her first poems, 'I have toiled in secret, often destroying what seemed to me ill written, and rewriting it. . . . Up to the present I have not submitted the work to any experts, much as I needed their advice, for fear that the roughness of the style would make them discourage me to such an extent that I might give up writing altogether.' Though young 'both in years and learning,' Hrotsvitha

showed already a notable self-reliance. Even in this preface, her humility, the proper attitude of a woman and a nun, is mitigated by her very just sense of her own deserts: 'Although [Latin] prosody may seem a hard and difficult art for a woman to master, I, without any assistance but that given by the merciful grace of Heaven, have attempted in this book to sing in dactyls.' The grace of Heaven is, of course, an inestimable blessing, and a nun must under all circumstances give credit to God for what there is of good in her work, but Hrotsvitha lets us see between the lines, and there we find a conscientious and hard-working artist who is justly proud of her efforts and of the products of her pen.

Hrotsvitha's first work was a collection of poems in praise of the Virgin Mary and of a number of saints and martyrs of the Faith. Most of the poems are founded on the tales and legends of the Greek Church, the sources of which were at first accepted wholeheartedly by Hrotsvitha, but which were beginning to fall under the ban of certain elements in the Western Church. Hrotsvitha, however, had a sufficiently good opinion of her own work to preserve these poems even when the authenticity of their sources was questioned, proving once again her independence of judgment and decision of character.

The Martyrdom of Saint Pelagius is the most interesting among these early poems because it illustrates the sort of contact with the outside world which was possible even in a convent. This tale was told to Hrotsvitha herself by an eye-witness of the event, a Spaniard who came from the very town where Pelagius met his death. It is not surprising that martyrdoms and miracles, with all the horrors that attend them, should seem subjects of intense interest and importance to the poetess of Gandersheim, when travelling strangers could regale her with first-hand descriptions of such events. It is illuminating also to note in passing that the artistic necessity of contrasting good with bad was already present to the young nun, who did not hesitate to describe the criminal advances that were made to the beautiful young man Pelagius by his Saracen captor. His unwillingness to submit to such 'abominable practices,' or to accept the life of ease which would have accompanied such submission, makes his death all the more edifying. Young as she was when she wrote these poems, Hrotsvitha showed none of that ignorance which later ages have often mistaken for innocence. She knew the ways and the weaknesses of the flesh as well as the strength of the spirit, and no false prudery interfered with her frank descriptions of scenes and events which to a modern mind might seem somewhat Rabelaisian. The mediæval point of view, as shown in its legends as well as its art and literature, had a tendency toward realism of detail rarely equalled even to-day.

The only other poem of particular interest in this first effort of the young poetess, is the *Fall and Conver-*

sion of Theophilus, in which she tells a tale later to become the root legend of Germany's greatest drama. The story of Theophilus is one of the most popular in mediæval literature and concerns the priest who sells his soul to the Devil in order to obtain worldly advancement. Rutebœuf, one of the earliest French dramatists, made use of it in his one extant play, and as the basis of Goethe's *Faust,* it has become a classic of world literature.

With this collection of poems, Hrotsvitha established herself definitely as the poet laureate of Gandersheim. Her superiors were well pleased with her accomplishments, and from this time forward her fame as a scholar and a poet spread among the learned and accomplished prelates and laymen of the Saxon Court. To her was entrusted the task of writing a panegyric to the Ottos, and her *Carmen de gestis Oddonis* is important even to-day as an historic document and is quoted in the Encyclopædia Britannica. It was written at the instigation of the Abbess Gerberga and is dedicated to her by Hrotsvitha in a charming preface in which she describes herself as 'one of the last of the least of those fighting under your ladyship's rule.' Singled out for the honour of recording the deeds and accomplishments of the Imperial House, Hrotsvitha had won for herself a position of distinction. Her fame had spread beyond the convent walls and her audience was no longer restricted to her fellow nuns. The panegyric of the Ottos was read by the Court and commented on by Archbishop William, one of the leading prelates of the day, while the plays are definitely submitted to the judgments of 'certain learned and virtuous men, patrons of the book.'

Her prefaces show that Hrotsvitha thoroughly appreciated the recognition she had won, though she never lost sight of what one might term the religious amenities. Her feminine tact was not blunted by her years of conventual life, and she could turn a complimentary phrase with a skill only comparable to that of the preface writers of a later and more sophisticated age. Her own words alone can do justice to the delicate balance she maintained between justifiable pride and graceful humility, between self-assurance and a disarming modesty. The Preface and Epistle which precede the most interesting of her productions, her six plays, is an excellent example of her style:

'To think that you, who have been nurtured in the most profound philosophical studies, and have attained knowledge in perfection, should have deigned to approve the humble work of an obscure woman!' she exlaims in her epistle to her patrons, and then, mindful of an even higher authority, she adds: 'You have, however, not praised me, but the Giver of grace which works in me, by sending your paternal congratulations and admitting that I possess some little knowledge of those arts, the subtleties of which exceed the grasp of my woman's mind. Until I showed my work to you, I

had not dared to let any one see it except my intimate companions. I came near abandoning this form of writing altogether, for if there were few to whom I could submit my compositions at all, there were fewer still who could point out what needed correction and encourage me to go on. . . . I know that it is as wrong to deny a divine gift as to pretend falsely that we have received it. So I will not deny that through the grace of the Creator I have acquired some knowledge of the arts. He has given me the ability to learn—I am a teachable creature—yet of myself I should know nothing. He has given me a perspicacious mind, but one that lies fallow and idle when it is not cultivated. . . . That my natural gift might not be made void by negligence, I have been at pains, whenever I have been able to pick up some threads and scraps from the old torn mantle of philosophy, to weave them into the stuff of my own book . . . that the creator of genius may be the more honoured since it is generally believed that a woman's intelligence is slower. In the humbler works of my salad days, I gathered up my poor researches in heroic strophes, but here I have sifted them in a series of dramatic scenes and avoided through omission the pernicious voluptuousness of pagan writers.'

So for the greater glory of God, and with much 'sweat and fatigue,' Hrotsvitha fashioned the six plays which have brought her a kind of immortality she may not have foreseen, but which, judging by the glimpses we have of her personality, she would have been far too human not thoroughly to have enjoyed.

In telling us what she does of herself in her prefaces, Hrotsvitha unfortunately stops short of certain vital details. She attributes her interest in the dramatic form to her readings from Terence, but she fails to say what other influences led her to adopt so un-Christian a vehicle for her highly Christian teachings. She speaks of showing her productions to her companions, but does not tell us in so many words whether they performed the plays in the great hall of the Abbey of Gandersheim or possibly even in the church itself, or whether her comedies were purely literary exercises for her own entertainment. In consequence the learned scholars have disagreed violently on these points, in the end leaving the decision open to the reader who cares to study the plays with sympathy and imagination. One of the most careful students of Hrotsvitha's work, Charles Magnin, whose 1845 edition restored some of the invaluable stage directions, omitted by Conrad Celtes in his first transcription of the manuscript, is convinced that Hrotsvitha's plays were acted. The assumption that they were not performed is based largely on the fact that no other plays, religious or secular, have come down to us from tenth-century Europe.

The earliest dramatic dialogue recorded in the theatrical history of the West is the Easter trope, the *Quem*

Quæritis described in the *Concordia Regularis* of Saint Ethelwold, and dated about 965 or 975. This is nothing more than an adaptation of the liturgy, the first step toward the dramatic presentation of religious teaching and far indeed from the elaborate plots and characterisations of Hrotsvitha's comedies. The first authentic mystery play, the anonymous *Representatio Adæ,* did not appear until two hundred years after her day. It has therefore seemed much simpler to many scholars to decide that Hrotsvitha was merely doing an exercise in Latin composition than to believe that she could have been moved to write and probably stage real plays at a time when no one else was doing it. This conclusion overlooks two very important factors, the influence of the Greek Church and the Greek tradition on a remarkably enterprising and independent spirit, and the dramatic viability of the plays themselves.

When Hrotsvitha entered the Abbey of Gandersheim, Otto I was still on the throne, but Otto II was Emperor during most of her lifetime. This Saxon prince was deeply interested in the intellectual development of his country. He turned to the older civilisations and particularly to Constantinople as to the seat of culture and refinement, and the Hellenistic influence was brought to his Court by ambassadors and delegates from the East. In 972, he married Theophano, daughter of the Eastern Emperor Romanus II, and this Greek princess assumed an important position in the social and political life of the Saxon Court. The Abbey of Gandersheim was so intimately connected with the Court that when it was decided that Sophia, eldest daughter of Otto and Theophano, must take the veil, the reluctant princess was sent to Gandersheim. Sophia did not wish to become a nun. She had an eye for more worldly honours and a mind capable of government. When her brother Otto III came to the throne, he summoned her to his side to help him. Later Sophia returned to the fold, became abbess in her turn, and undertook various measures to prove her equality with other princes of the Church.

While Sophia was still a novice and a young nun, the Empress Theophano often visited the Abbey, and Hrotsvitha, accredited bard of the Imperial family, was undoubtedly granted special privileges which brought her into contact with the Greek princesses and their attendant train. From such sources she would have learned at first-hand the fascinating story of the war waged in Constantinople between the Orthodox Church and the theatre. In her remote Saxon convent, where such a thing as a play had never been seen, Hrotsvitha must have listened avidly to the accounts of spectacle-loving Constantinople told by the homesick exiles who had followed their princess into the barbarous North.

The tradition of the Greek Church at this time showed two distinct and contradictory attitudes; that epitomised by Saint Chrysostom, who in the fourth century poured out the vials of his wrath and of his sublime eloquence on all that remotely concerned the stage, and that typified by the writing of Gregory Nazienzen and the Apollinari, who, when Julian the Apostate prohibited the teaching of the Greek classics to the followers of Christ, attempted to preserve the Greek literary forms for their people by rewriting the Old Testament as an Homeric epic, and the New along the lines of the classic drama. Other devout Christians made similar attempts with even less success if we can judge by the fact that, of the large body of these Christianized Greek tragedies, only a few fragments have survived.

In Hrotsvitha's day many must still have been in existence, though it is very doubtful that she ever saw them even in manuscript. We do not even know whether she could read Greek, but her constant use of Greek tales and legends as sources for her plots proves her familiarity with the literature of the Greek Church. Though she could not by any possibility have seen a play acted, the mere existence of these Byzantine dramas was enough to encourage her in her efforts. Her failure to acknowledge in her preface so venerable a precedent as that created by these Christian dramas is easily understood when we glimpse the tangled web of heresies and schisms with which the whole history of the early Church is overlaid. It was safer to recognize the pagan Terence as her prototype than to refer to the Christian sanctions of the theatre, tainted as they were by the black heresy of Arius and the triumphs of the hated Iconoclasts.

Hrotsvitha, however, must in her own mind have found ample justification for looking with tolerance upon the drama. The Empress Theophano could have told her of the astonishing truce that had been called in the age-long battle between Church and stage. One of the most extraordinary incidents in the whole history of the Church is the compromise brought about in the year 990 by Theophylactus, Patriarch of Constantinople, a member of the Empress' own family. This reverend prelate, uncle of Romanus II, Theophano's father, and head of the Orthodox Church, actually introduced the theatre into the bosom of the Church itself, permitting professional actors, actresses, and dancers from the Hippodrome to perform in Saint Sophia, and countenancing all sorts of dramatic amusements, even to the wildest buffooneries. Theophano herself loved the stage. Her father had been a devotee of the Hippodrome, her son Otto III attempted to reëstablish the theatre in Italy, and her influence may in some measure account for the curious turn taken by Hrotsvitha's genius.

It does not require too wild a flight of the imagination, to picture the nuns of Gandersheim eagerly preparing to welcome their royal guest with a form of entertainment particularly dear to her heart and one of which she had been completely deprived since her departure from Constantinople. The Abbess Gerberga would not have been unwilling to show the foreign Empress that Saxony could produce a poet worthy of respect and that the resources of Gandersheim were equal to the task of presenting so sophisticated a form of entertainment as a drama. What more appropriate theme could have been chosen for the diversion of a Greek princess than Hrotsvitha's first play, *Gallicanus,* which sings the praises of Constance, daughter of Constantine, and reflects, in the story of the conversion of Gallicanus, the more famous conversion of Constantine himself, first of Christian Emperors and founder of the Empire in the East.

Hrotsvitha's avowed purpose of glorifying the 'laudable chastity of Christian virgins' is here clothed in a panoply of royal pomp. The scenes laid in the court of Constantine, the crowded battlefields, the streets of Rome, the audience hall of Julian the Apostate, offered ample opportunities for the display of all the beautiful vestments, the colourful copes and chasubles, the treasures of silk, embroidery, and plate with which the sacristy of a wealthy convent would be supplied. Possibly the armour needed for the contending forces of Romans and Scythians was contributed by the knights-at-arms attached to the Abbey. With what ardour the young nuns and novices would have thrown themselves into the task of making costumes and learning their parts! If we judge the tenth century by later mediæval custom, the scenes presented before the audience gathered in the Hall of the Abbey, or, as Philarète Chasle believes, in the nave of the Church itself, would not have been devoid of dignity, even of a certain splendour. Hrotsvitha's first effort in dramaturgy is not as skilful as her later plays, but no one who has accepted Shakespeare's sketchy battle scenes, nor the detached and episodic structure of his chronicle plays, need scorn Hrotsvitha's naïve introduction of two contending armies on one stage, or her shorthand method of deciding the fate of a tremendous encounter in twenty-five lines of dialogue. *Gallicanus,* for all its faults, would have been an effective pageant to unroll before a queen.

Hrotsvitha, in all her plays, follows with pious faith the details of the legends which she dramatises, but her originality is evident in the skill with which she succeeds in infusing personality into the lay figures of her tales. Constantine, whom she makes weak and vacillating in order to bring out the strength and even the holy guile of his daughter Constance; Julian the Apostate, who bids his soldiers remind the Christians of their own teachings about renouncing worldly goods while they are stripping them of all they possess; John and Paul, almoners of Constance, who are not above a little judicious prevarication while they go about the Lord's work—all these have a distinct character of their own. In Constance we see the outlines of a real individual, modelled on the lines of those 'royal personages,' Gerberga, Theophano, and Sophia, whom Hrotsvitha

had the privilege of knowing intimately. Constance, receiving the daughters of Gallicanus and offering a fervent and thoroughly orthodox prayer for their salvation, might be the Abbess herself receiving a distinguished postulant; just as the arguments between John, Paul, and Julian the Apostate reflect the pious and at the same time scholastic disputations so typical of mediæval theology.

Hrotsvitha's plays must necessarily be approached with sympathy and understanding, for they are expressed in an idiom alien to our modern point of view. They are all short—running from five to six hundred lines of concentrated dialogue broken into scenes of varying length by the transcribers of the original manuscript. At first glance, they seem naïve, crude, two-dimensional. Everything appears on one plane with little attempt at rounding out of contours. Especially is this true of *Gallicanus* and of the two martyr plays, *Dulcitius* and *Sapientia.* In them Hrotsvitha has been absorbed in her didactic mission. They are preachments rather than plays, and yet even here her native dramatic instinct has not been completely subdued; a character, a scene, a bit of dialogue comes out with startling clarity. *Dulcitius* is particularly interesting in that it contains the one intentionally comic scene in Hrotsvitha's plays.

The legend turns on the strange hallucination that overcame the Roman Governor, Dulcitius, when he attempted to rape three Christian maidens committed to his tender care. Making his way into the Palace kitchen, where he thinks the prisoners are confined, he embraces the pots and pans under the illusion that he is indulging in a night of love, to the immense amusement of the maidens themselves who watch the proceedings through a keyhole. The dramatic effect of having his would-be victims recount to each other the grotesque antics of the demented Governor, while the sound of crashing pans off stage emphasises the excitement, is excellent. Dulcitius' reappearance, covered with soot and his clothes in rags, making futile attempts to convince his own soldiers of his identity, is cleverly worked out. The scene is obviously meant for visual presentation and is a striking example of Hrotsvitha's eye for stage effects.

In the heroic virgins of *Dulcitius* and the other martyr plays, Hrotsvitha has painted a variety of religious fanatic for whom she had apparently very little sympathy. They have none of the royal dignity of Constance, the wisdom of Sapientia, the charm of Drusiana, Mary, or Thaïs. Whether consciously or not, Hrotsvitha presents the women who have been touched by sin far more sympathetically than she does the immaculate virgins who defy their tormentors and fly straight to heaven in a blaze of unfelt torments and complacent glory. The three martyrs of *Dulcitius* have all the objectionable characteristics of the type, but they are saved from complete smugness by their amusement over the Roman Governor's absurd misadventure. Dulcitius, it is to be remarked, disappears suddenly from the story, the laughter he has provoked making him unsuitable as an instrument for really impressive martyrdom. His successor in the office of executioner dispatches two of the maidens in short order, but with the third, Irena, he argues at length, and is, of course, worsted in dialectics as he is frustrated in his design of humiliating and defiling her.

Hrotsvitha's preoccupation, in all her plays, with the glories of virginity must be taken as the hall-mark of her profession. In a community of dedicated nuns it was natural, indeed inevitable, that this aspect of their tribute to God should be presented in all its beauty and nobility, and that all its ramifications should be of palpitating interest. Undoubtedly also, Hrotsvitha obtained a certain release for her own emotional suppressions by elaborating these pictures of carnal dangers and the pitfalls of the flesh. These scenes, wherein holy virgins, refusing advantageous offers of marriage, are dragged off to brothels to be 'abominably defiled,' or are attacked by brutal soldiers and escape only by miraculous intervention, are the product of a mind that may have denied, but has not forgotten, the 'sinful lusts of the flesh.' Hrotsvitha's plays illustrate very vividly the process of psychic compensation which is so striking a feature of mediæval monastic literature.

In *Dulcitius,* as in her last play, *Sapientia,* Hrotsvitha gives expression to a vein of sadism which is also associated with certain aspects of repression. She positively revels in the lurid and suggestive details of her torture scenes in a way which has led some critics to brand these plays as completely unactable. When we remember the enthusiasm with which such scenes were presented in later mediæval mystery plays, as evidenced by the records, and by such pictures as that of the martyrdom of Saint Apollonia by Jean Fouquet, Hrotsvitha's excursions into the horrific are less surprising. We are to-day more squeamish about physical manifestations of the sort on our stage, but the nuns of Gandersheim were nourished in a sturdier school. They were suckled on tales of torture and martyrdom, and the more boiling oil, fiery furnaces, severed limbs, and bleeding wounds a tale provided, the greater the thrill. Hrotsvitha was not unwilling to write penny-dreadfuls of the sort, nor could a more edifying and intimately comforting spectacle be imagined than that of these pure young girls taunting and defying Emperors and all the strength of embattled masculine paganism while their faith prevented them from feeling the pain and ignomy to which their bodies were subjected. We may turn with repugnance from the scenes in which Sapientia's children are scourged by the centurions, but we should not in our disgust forget that one of the most popular scenes ever presented on the American stage was that of the scourging of Uncle Tom, as well

as, curiously enough, the death and ascension of little Eva, a child almost as objectionable in her way as any of Hrotsvitha's smug young heroines.

Again and again, even in these two martyr-plays, which seem to us the least actable of Hrotsvitha's works, little strokes of dialogue vividly suggest the stage picture, as in the opening of the third scene in *Sapientia,* when Antiochus says to the Christians, 'That is the Emperor you see there, seated on his throne. Be careful what you say to him'; or, in another scene when Sapientia is encouraging her horde of infant martyrs, 'Oh, my dearest little ones, My beloved children! Do not let this narrow prison sadden you.' In a phrase or two, Hrotsvitha sets the stage, and one need only imagine the attending groups of nuns, dressed as courtiers, executioners, Roman matrons, followers, or slaves, rounding out the scenes with the action suggested in the text, to realise that the plays are eminently actable.

Dulcitius is the only play containing obviously comic scenes, yet all of them, even the most terrible, are redeemed from sadness by the faith which animates their author. To understand Hrotsvitha's spirit, it is necessary to remember that Catholicism, even mediæval Catholicism, with all its demonology, its horrors and damnations, was essentially a happy religion. The promise of future blessedness compensated for much present suffering, and the little martyrs could giggle like any other children, though in the presence of an executioner. 'What are you muttering there?' one of the latter exclaims in exasperation. 'Behave yourself and do not laugh!' The constant complaint of their persecutors is that the Christians are laughing at them, making fools of them. Not only do the Christians triumph by their holiness, but they outargue and outwit their tormentors at every turn.

Hrotsvitha makes use of these opportunities to air her own scholarly accomplishments, and we find discourses on mathematics and music interjected into the most unlikely situations. She feels it necessary, however, to make some apology for these excursions into what the Emperor Hadrian in one of her plays brands as 'intricate and unprofitable dissertations.' 'It would be unprofitable,' Hrotsvitha's Sapientia answers, 'if it did not lead us to appreciate the wisdom of our Creator, Who in the beginning created the world out of nothing . . . and then, in time and the age of man, formulated a science which reveals fresh wonders the more we study it.'

The Sapientia who formulates this apologia for the pursuit of knowledge may well be taken as representing the Nun of Gandersheim in her later years. Hrotsvitha's intellectual hunger is so evident, her eagerness to know and learn so palpable, both in her plays and prefaces, that we cannot fail to see in such sentiments as these her own excuses for enthusiasms which in a woman and a nun of the Dark Ages needed some measure of explanation. The stately, nobly born, and extremely intelligent Sapientia is Hrotsvitha in the full flower of her maturity and success, devoting her life to the service of God, and the creations of her genius to his everlasting glory.

A more tender and humanly touching Hrotsvitha is revealed in her fourth play, *Abraham.* It is not a martyr play, nor is it overburdened with too many 'threads and scraps from the torn mantle of philosophy.' In a series of swift and straightforward scenes it tells the story of Mary, niece of the hermit Abraham, who at the tender age of eight dedicates herself to Christ. After many years spent in solitary prayer and meditation under the care of Abraham, she is seduced by a passing stranger. In shame and horror she flees from the hermitage and abandons herself to a life of sin. Abraham follows her, and by his love and his exhortations brings her back to God.

The scenes in the brothel where Abraham, disguised as an ordinary traveller, has gone to find his niece, are handled with extraordinary delicacy and charm. At first Abraham is shown talking to the innkeeper, asking for food and lodging and for the company of the beautiful girl with whom he is 'already in love' from the descriptions he has heard of her. Mary comes in, but does not recognise her spiritual father, who with an effort conquers his emotions and continues to play his part. Hrotsvitha's treatment of this scene is particularly sensitive, and though it is almost impossible to capture the quality of her writing in a few lines, this, and the following recognition scene give some idea of the sincerity and directness of her style, as well as her ability to convey profound feeling in a few lines. The innkeeper greets her boisterously—'Luck comes your way, Mary! Not only do young gallants of your own age flock to your arms, but even the wise and venerable come to you.'

> MARY: It is all one to me. It is my business to love those who love me.
> ABRAHAM: Come nearer, Mary, and give me a kiss.
> MARY: I will give you more than a kiss. I will take your head in my arms and stroke your neck.
> ABRAHAM: Yes, like that!
> MARY: What does this mean? What is this lovely fragrance, so clean, so sweet? It reminds me of the time when I was good.
> ABRAHAM: (*aside*): On with the mask! Chatter, make lewd jests like an idle boy! She must not recognise me or for very shame she will fly from me.
> MARY: Wretch that I am! To what have I fallen! In what pit have I sunk!
> ABRAHAM: You forget where you are! Do men come here to see you cry?

> INNKEEPER: What's the matter, Lady Mary? Why are you in the dumps? You have lived here two years and never before have I seen a tear, never heard a sigh or a word of complaint.
> MARY: Oh, that I had died three years ago before I came to this!
> ABRAHAM: I came here to make love to you, not to weep with you over your sins.
> MARY: A little thing moved me, and I spoke foolishly. It is nothing. Come, let us eat and drink and be merry, for, as you say, this is not the place to think of one's sins.

After eating supper, they go into the bedroom where the scene continues:

> MARY: Look! How do you like this room? A handsome bed, isn't it? Those trappings cost a lot of money. Sit down and I will take off your shoes. You seem tired.
> ABRAHAM: First bolt the door. Some one may come in.
> MARY: Have no fear, I have seen to that.
> ABRAHAM: The time has come for me to show my shaven head and make myself known! Oh, my daughter, oh, Mary, you who are part of my soul! Look at me. Do you not know me? Do you not know the old man who cherished you with a father's love, and wedded you to the Son of the King of Heaven?
> MARY: God, what shall I do! It is my father and master Abraham!
> ABRAHAM: What has come to you daughter!
> MARY: Oh, misery! . . .
> ABRAHAM: Why have you thrown yourself down there? Why do you lie on the ground without moving or speaking? Get up, Mary, get up, my child and listen to me!
> MARY: No, no, I am afraid, I cannot bear your reproaches.
> ABRAHAM: Remember how I love you, and you will not be afraid. . . . The mercy of Heaven is greater than you or your sins. Let your sadness be dispersed by its glorious beams. . . .

And so on, until Mary is convinced of God's love and forgiveness and returns to the desert, riding on Abraham's horse, 'that the stony road should not hurt her delicate feet.'

With *Paphnutius,* the play immediately following *Abraham,* Hrotsvitha handles the same theme, that of the conversion of a harlot, in an entirely different manner. *Paphnutius* is the story of Thaïs, the first dramatic presentation of this old and still popular legend. In it Hrotsvitha shows her increasing ability to differentiate character and the art with which she can develop her material. When the hermit Paphnutius goes to Alexandria in the hope of saving a lost soul by converting the famous courtesan Thaïs to the true faith, he, too, like Abraham, dons worldly attire, and, armed with piety and the necessary gold pieces, ventures into a house of sin in pursuit of his worthy purpose. Both plays are surprisingly, if naïvely, realistic, for both hermits boldly demand the most intimate favours of their would-be converts, and Hrotsvitha does not hesitate to introduce her godly men into the bedchambers of these prostitutes. When Paphnutius demands of Thaïs that she take him into a secret room, she shows him her bedroom. 'How would you like a bedchamber fragrant with perfumes, adorned as for marriage? I have such a room. Look!'

The dramatic effect of both conversions is, of course, greatly heightened by the fact that they occur at the very moment when these erring women are engaged in their evil trade—but, though the scene is the same, the whole treatment is radically different. Abraham is throughout the gentle old man, disguising his emotion with difficulty and finally revealing himself in words of kindness and gentle exhortation. Paphnutius, on the other hand, makes a very creditable lover. Young and handsome, he woos Thaïs in words he must have learned elsewhere than in his desert hermitage, but when he begins to admonish her, all gentleness disappears. Fire and brimstone, terror and grief, are the lot of one as confirmed in evil, as hardened and as profligate as Thaïs the Harlot. Hard as Mary's life of penitence, prayer, and fasting may seem to us, it has not the revolting cruelty of the fate to which Paphnutius condemns the unfortunate Thaïs.

Here again Hrotsvitha's eye for realistic detail spares us no aspect of the plight in which Thaïs found herself when she was condemned to pass what remained of her life walled into a narrow cell which had no opening save one tiny window. She shrinks with fastidious disgust from the filth which, to the mediæval ascetic, was far nearer godliness than the perfumed cleanliness of a decadent Roman civilisation. It is no wonder that the unfortunate penitent died shortly after her release. But Thaïs' end is all the more edifying because of her great penitence—and this picture of physical suffering was no doubt considered highly edifying by Hrotsvitha's contemporaries, whatever it may seem to us to-day. Evidently also Hrotsvitha's surprising excursions into houses of ill fame were forgiven by her spiritual pastors and masters in view of the good work she was accomplishing in these unholy places. As her preface proves, she justified her treatment of such subjects by the moral effects of their teachings, but when we read the plays themselves, we cannot help thinking that Hrotsvitha enjoyed these voyages outside the convent walls, and that in her heart of hearts she loved the sinners she painted far more than she hated their sins.

Hrotsvitha must have found some difficulty in justifying all her expeditions into forbidden territory, for this surprising nun was bold enough to write at least one love-story. In the preface of the plays, she shows herself fully conscious of the dangerous ground she was treading. 'One thing has . . . embarrassed me and often brought a blush to my cheek,' she tells us. 'It is that I have been compelled through the nature of this work to apply my mind and my pen to depicting the dreadful frenzy of those possessed by unlawful love and the insidious sweetness of passion—things which should not even be named among us. Yet if from modesty I had refrained from treating these subjects, I should not have been able to attain my object—to glorify the innocent to the best of my ability. For the more seductive the blandishments of lovers, the more wonderful the divine succour and the greater the merit of those who resist, especially when it is fragile woman who is victorious and strong man who is routed with confusion.'

Safely ensconced behind this laudable and appropriate excuse, Hrotsvitha proceeded to write the first romance of modern literature, her third play, **Callimachus.** The curious external resemblances between **Callimachus** and *Romeo and Juliet* are no less striking than the atmosphere of passionate romanticism which emanates from the whole. The plot concerns the fatal love of Callimachus for Drusiana, wife of Prince Andronicus. Drusiana had dedicated herself to God, renouncing 'even that which is lawful,' her husband's bed, and, rather than break her vows of chastity, she prays for death to deliver her from the tempting importunities of her lover. She dies at once, and is buried, but Callimachus' passion follows her into the grave. The scene at the tomb of Drusiana, when Callimachus, aided by the faithless servant Fortunatus, finds himself in the presence of his dead love, strikingly prefigures the famous climax of Shakespeare's tragedy. The deaths are almost as numerous, too, for both Callimachus and Fortunatus are killed by miraculous intervention. The resurrection of all three, and the repentance and conversion of Callimachus is the religious dénouement needed to justify Hrotsvitha's bold attempt at romantic drama and is of less importance than her obvious preoccupation with her love-story.

Hrotsvitha's characterisations, embryonic as they are, show her originality. Drusiana, unlike the strong-minded saints of the martyr plays, sure of their faith and of their ultimate victory, is conscious of her own weakness in the face of temptation. Touched by the ardour of Callimachus, she is afraid that she will be unable to resist him, and, determined neither to rouse the anger of her husband against him nor fall from the grace she has obtained, she prays for death. In the few lines that are allotted to her, from her first scene with Callimachus, where she attempts, rather pathetically, to put off his advances, to her final act after her resurrection, when she restores to life the villain who betrayed her dead body to her lover, the character of Drusiana is consistently gentle, loving, and tender—as far removed from the colourless heroines of the Latin theatre as it is from the heroic figures of Greek tragedy.

The distracted husband, Andronicus, is also, traditionally speaking, a creation of Hrotsvitha's own imagination. Certainly the husbands and fathers of Latin comedy established no precedent on which to model this forbearing and kindly gentleman. One wonders even more where, among the barons and fighting lords of the Dark Ages, his prototype could have been found. His love for Drusiana never wavers, though she has left his bed, and though he knows that she has died in order to escape the importunities of another man. His devotion and faith are so great that it is he, rather than the Apostle John, who is made the mouthpiece for the moral of the tale. Standing over the dead bodies of Callimachus and the servant, he meditates on the heavenly revelation which he had just received: 'What astonishes me most,' he says, 'is that the Divine Voice should have promised the resurrection of [Callimachus] who planned the crime and not of him who was only an accomplice. Maybe it is because the one, blinded by passion of the flesh, knew not what he did, while the other sinned of deliberate malice.' Hrotsvitha had not forgotten the words of One whose understanding was so great that He could say of a certain sinner, 'Her sins, which are many, are forgiven, for she loved much.'

In the character of Callimachus, Hrotsvitha gives a vivid outline sketch of an experienced worldling, not unlike the dashing Romeo. In the first scenes of the play he talks to his friends, in the tenth-century equivalent of Euphuism, a scholastic splitting of phrases that only half-veils the intensity of his ill-advised passion. His relations with Drusiana show him to be as thoughtless of her happiness and safety as Romeo himself. He pursues her even into the grave, and here we see the Benedictine nun handling with extraordinary delicacy and understanding a situation as bold, one might almost say as lurid, as anything the Elizabethans could have invented. Hrotsvitha was evidently so moved by a strong sympathy for the miseries of frustrated love that she did not hesitate to present it in all its intensity. Callimachus' outburst over the dead body of Drusiana has an authentic ring of passion: 'O Drusiana, Drusiana, I worshipped you with my whole soul! I yearned from my very bowels to embrace you! And you repulsed me, and thwarted my desire. Now you are in my power, now I can wound you with my kisses, and pour out my love upon you.'

Strange words to echo in a convent hall, bringing suddenly to the surface the troubled and violent stream of imprisoned feeling. Hrotsvitha's intense and passionate nature is revealed for a moment only, to be quickly covered by the accustomed mantle of sober piety. But Callimachus' conversion and frenzied repentance is merely another phase of an intense emotional experience.

'I came here for an evil purpose,' he exclaims after his resurrection, 'but the pangs of love consumed me. I was beside myself.' And John answers him: 'What mad folly possessed you, that you should dare think of such a shameful outrage to the chaste dead!' Callimachus can only repeat: 'I was mad! . . . I am overwhelmed by the thought of my abominable crime. I repent with my whole heart and bewail my sin. . . . Oh, hasten then to help a man in dire need—give me some comfort! Help me throw off the grief that crushes me! Show me how a pagan may change into a Christian, a fornicator into a chaste man! Oh, set my feet in the way of truth! Teach me to live mindful of the divine promises.'

His plea is not in vain. For all his black sin, Callimachus is forgiven. The note of peace after the storm rings like the quiet tolling of the Angelus, reminding the nuns of Gandersheim that they have found a refuge from the 'dreadful frenzy of passion.' The Judge who could forgive Callimachus because he loved too greatly could be counted upon to 'search the heart and reins and reward or punish fairly.'

The plays of Hrotsvitha, after long years of neglect, have recently been studied with great interest and attention, and have even been acted in English both in London and New York with varying degrees of artistic success. The impossibility of recapturing an atmosphere as alien to us as that of mediæval Christianity will always make their presentation peculiarly difficult. Few indeed are the playwrights who have actually survived their own day unless, in addition to possessing dramatic gifts, they have been poets of such high order that the hungry generations have listened in awe to their music. Hrotsvitha was not a great poet. She was an acute observer, an avid scholar, an adventurous and enterprising soul. To enjoy her style one must have a taste for the phrase that suggests rather than describes, for a simplicity which is at once naïve and full of wisdom. Like the early painters, her work is stiff, clear-cut, often harsh, and occasionally crude, but none the less vital for all its shortcomings. Her plays are all brief, her characterisations often no more than outline sketches, yet in the quick strokes with which she defines an individual she shows a master's hand. Her comedies have a vivacity, a directness of approach, and, in spite of much that is incredible, an essential veracity which gives them permanent value.

If it is true, as the scholars tell us, that Hrotsvitha had no imitators or successors, she nevertheless foreshadowed a new dramatic dispensation, where love, human and divine, were to reign supreme, and where the romantic ideal of individual freedom was finally to replace the Greek conception of inescapable fatality. Working alone in her remote Saxon convent, where plays and players had never been seen, surrounded by a social order barely emerging from barbarism, this Benedictine nun cherished in secret the wavering flame of a great tradition, pouring into it the new oil of the Christian religion and handing it on, sweetened and strengthened by her care, to later generations of those who know and love the theatre.

Rosemary Sprague (essay date 1955)

SOURCE: "Hroswitha—Tenth-Century Margaret Wester," *The Theatre Annual,* Vol. XIII, 1955, pp. 16-31.

[*In the following essay, Sprague surveys Hroswitha's life and works, focusing on the author's development in her six dramas.*]

From the far away past emerges a picture of a nun, with habit tucked up to her ankles and with manuscript in hand, striding up and down a great hall in a convent directing her sisters in a play she herself has written. This is Sister Hroswitha, the pride of the Benedictine Convent of Gandersheim, Saxony, who wrote, as far as can be ascertained, the very first plays in the Western world after the collapse of the Roman Empire. She is not the figment of some pseudo-historian's imagination. There is incontrovertible proof of her existence in the *History of Gandersheim* compiled by Henricus Bodo in 1025[1], and in Munich there is a manuscript codex which proves that she not only wrote plays, six of them, but also wrote seven poems in leonine hexameters on the lives of assorted saints and an epic on the career of Emperor Otto the Great.

Because the religious life has always made great virtue of anonymity, it is almost impossible to document anything about Hroswitha with certainty. Calendar addicts, with their passion for statistics, have tried in vain to date her. She was born, they think, in A.D. 932 or 933—perhaps. She was probably professed in 959. To say which one of her literary efforts was created first would be no more than a guess for their standard of performance is uniform. It may be that the epic on Emperor Otto was completed in time for the coronation of his son and successor in 968 or perhaps its creation occupied Hroswitha until her death in 982. Or did she live, as some authorities maintain, to what then would have been an incredibly old age and die in 1002?

Considerable annoyance has been levelled against Hroswitha's first editor, Dr. Conrad Celtes, who discovered what was believed to be the unique copy of her writings and published it in 1501.[2] The avid calendar addicts have felt that since Celtes was, after all, four hundred years closer in time to the lady than we of the Twentieth Century, he might have made a little more effort to compile a proper biography. But in our age of personal curiosity, called psychological interest, Celtes' disinterest in the nun's private life is rather refreshing. He and the members of his literary fraternity, the "Rheinische Sodalitat," were far more excited over

presenting a Latin writer of German birth than they were about her vital statistics. For just as these men considered the German Holy Roman Empire a continuation of the Imperial Rome of the Caesars, so they definitely considered Hroswitha's literary efforts a continuation of the classic tradition. In her honor, they composed epigrams to demonstrate the rare scholastic excitement which possessed them:

> Those gifts her native generation granted to
>   few of her sex,
> Hroswitha did reveal in virginal genius!
>
> Why should we not praise the writings of this
>   German maid,
> Who, were she Greek, would by now have
>   been made a goddess?
>
> How much the righteous deities of Heaven
>   favor the Germans
> You may discern from this learned virgin.
>
> You Greek, you Italian,
> What do you think of this German maid?[3]

It can be readily seen that the Rheinische Sodalitat did not agree that "scholarship" knows nothing of geographical boundaries. Yet, for all his patriotic fervor, Celtes did not answer the question: How did Hroswitha happen to write plays? Homilies, tracts, catechisms, even devotional poems, would seem to be more likely literary areas for a nun to employ her facile pen. Whatever possessed her to enter the theatre?

It was axiomatic long before Marx and Freud that the best way to approach an author is through his works, but, at first glance, Hroswitha's *Opera* are unrewarding as biographical sources. Their implications, however, are quite another matter. The introduction to the long pseudo-Vergilian epic on the life of Emperor Otto the Great states that Hroswitha was given the task of writing it as an act of obedience by Abbess Gerberga of the Gandersheim Convent. The Abbess was a cousin of the Emperor, therefore it can be assumed that the royal family knew of the undertaking, may even have commissioned it. Here is further proof that Hroswitha's contemporaries considered her as the continuer of the classic epic tradition. The poems on the lives of Saints Agnes, Pelagius, and Gongolfus tell little more, though Gongolfus, the patron saint of henpecked husbands, was, perhaps, an unexpected subject. But the four remaining poems on the Birth of the Blessed Virgin, the Conversion of Theophilus, and the lives of Saints Basil and Dionysius, and the six plays—***Gallicanus, Dulcitius, Callimachus, Abraham, Paphnutius, Sapientia***—shed considerable light on the author and her background.

Without exception these poems and plays find their sources in that vast quantity of extra-canonical Biblical literature, decreed by Rome to be lacking in authenticity if not downright heretical. Certainly it was extra-curricular reading in a tenth-century German convent, and Hroswitha admits it:

> Now, if it be objected that some parts of my work are taken from apocryphal sources, this was not a fault caused by wanton presumption, but a mistake due to ignorance, for, when I laid the foundations, I was not aware that these were doubtful matters on which I had begun to labor. . . . But, when I recognised this, I was loth to destroy, because that which seems to be falsehood may haply prove to be truth.
>
> [*Praefatio 1*][4]

An astounding statement from a supposedly loyal daughter of Rome!

The questions occur at once: How did she get hold of these doubtful materials? How did she dare defend herself for using them? The answers are quite simple. Although Rome condemned the apocryphal acts and gospels, they were read and venerated by the Catholic Church of the East which was already straining away from the mother church. The saints of Hroswitha are the saints of the hagiography of the church of the Byzantine Empire and it was from this church that she derived the inspiration for her plays.

The intimate connection between tenth-century Germany and Byzantium is not always considered by historians. They place the time of Hroswitha's entrance into Gandersheim in the Dark Ages and let it go at that, failing to note that, although the rest of Europe was in turmoil with the influence of Christianity at its lowest ebb owing to the intrigues among several rival popes, Germany was enjoying a period of comparative peace and prosperity. She alone among the nations had the leisure and inclination for cultural pursuits. Emperor Otto (936-973) was a strong ruler; his wife was Adelheid of Burgundy, a brilliant, exceedingly well-educated woman whose long residence in Italy prior to her marriage had brought her into contact with Byzantine culture. As Holy Roman Empress, she naturally had great influence, and when it came time for her son, the future Otto II, to marry, she masterfully arranged an alliance with Princess Theophano, sister of Basil II, the Macedonian Emperor.

It was through Theophano that the great culture of Byzantium came directly into Germany. She was a granddaughter of Constantine VII, the author of the *Liber de Cerimoniis,* whose devotion to the hippodrome and the theatre has gone down in history as without precedent, even for an *aficionado* in that pleasure-loving city. Theophano had witnessed the attack launched on the theatre by the Church and had watched the efforts of Constantine to reconcile the theatre-mad city and the censuring ecclesiastics by bringing drama into the

churches and substituting religious pageants for pagan spectacles. The theatre, then, which in the West had degenerated into mere exhibitions by strolling mountebanks, was an integral part of Theophano's life. It is, therefore, only reasonable to assume that with her wealth and power and ability she would try to adapt some of the glittering shows of Byzantium to her new life.

And this is where Hroswitha enters the scene. After a few years at Gandersheim as a student, Princess Sophia, daughter of Theophano and Otto II, took the veil there. Bodo records that Theophano visited the convent frequently on holy days and that Dowager Empress Adelheid came there to spend the last years of her life. Abbess Gerberga, as has already been noted, was the Emperor's cousin. Hroswitha, then, was in daily contact with one or another of the imperial family which was so profoundly Byzantine in its cultural outlook and personal tastes. This fact is corroborated in the first *Praefatio,* in which the nun tells how her first instruction in the writer's art came from the illustrious Abbess Gerberga, who, "With great condescension, explicated certain writers to me, of which she had been taught by men of great learning."

It might be noted here that if Hroswitha received *explications de texte* from Gerberga her residence at Gandersheim must have considerably antedated her profession, for once Gerberga became abbess she would have had no time for teaching. In other words, Hroswitha must also have been a student there.

What sort of education would she have received? Within its medieval limitations, excellent. In addition to the elementary lessons in deportment, table manners, embroidery, and elegant conversation, the girls were taught the trivium—grammar, logic, and rhetoric. Classes were conducted in Latin and private tutors were available for instruction in Greek. Those who survived this lower division were permitted to follow the quadrivium—arithmetic, music, geometry, and astronomy. Hroswitha would have received additional instruction in philosophy and theology and would have been steeped in Holy Writ. And since, to use Allardyce Nicoll's exquisite phrase, "A good latinity was next to godliness," she read the Latin poets and the plays of Publius Terentius Afer as examples of stylistic excellence.

What was Hroswitha's milieu at Gandersheim? Very different from the usual conception of convent life. Abbess Gerberga directed an enormous estate and had a seat in the German Imperial Diet. As her vote was greatly sought after, she would travel, pay visits, receive important political figures and hold feasts in their honor. She could attend classes at St. Emmeran's Monastery at nearby Ratisbon, where the monks were renowned for their learning, and invite the reverend fathers to hold similar classes for her nuns at

Gandersheim. It is not at all a stretch of the imagination to identify these monks as the "men of great learning" mentioned by Hroswitha in her third *Praefatio* nor to say further that one of them was doubtless the scholarly Bishop William of Mainz, the Emperor's brother. It is not at all fantastic to postulate that the "writers" or books which Gerberga explicated were loaned or given to the Abbess by Empress Theophano and put into the hands of the brilliant Sister Hroswitha to use as background material for the literary career which she had definitely decided to follow:

> I did not wish the small talent entrusted to me to rust through neglect, lying idle and buried in the depths of a sluggish heart, but rather that it might be beaten out by the hammer of constant devotion and give forth a little tinkle of divine praise.

> *[Praefatio 1]*

With an abbess sympathetic to secular learning, an empress addicted to the theatre, and the pageant atmosphere of an imperial court, it is easy to see what gradually moved Hroswitha toward playwriting. The spark which ignited her inspiration is told in the second *Praefatio:*

> Many Catholics are found doing that which we cannot wholly disavow ourselves; namely, to prefer because of the eloquence of its cultivated speech, the vanity of heathen literature to the edification of Holy Scripture. There are others, moreover, who, while they do cling to the sacred pages, nevertheless read too often the works of Terence, and, while being delighted with the sweetness of his diction, are defiled with the acquaintance of unholy things. Therefore I, the "Loud Cry of Gandersheim" [her literal translation of the name Hroswitha] would celebrate, insofar as my poor talents permit, the praiseworthy chastity of dedicated virgins, in the same manner in which he wrote of the shameful abominations of wanton women!

The influence of Terence on Hroswitha has been the subject of much discussion, so there is no need to repeat it here. Suffice it to say that Terence's plots, revolving around dissipated young men about town, wily thieving slaves, foolish elderly senators, beautiful courtesans, and boastful soldiers might very well have brought a blush to Hroswitha's cheek. Those authorities who maintain that she was also conversant with Plautus leave us to infer that his plays rendered her speechless. While recognizing that, even in the cloister, there must be an occasional change from the stately tread of the *Acta Sanctorum,* she became deeply concerned at the sight of religious, dedicated to God, filling their eyes and minds with such irreligious literature. In addition to her own concern, she would have felt the added impetus of the Church's attitude, for Empress Theophano would certainly have told her how actors in Byzantium burlesqued and made mock of Christian ceremonies

and sacraments, and how playwrights vied with one another to produce yet more ribald blasphemies. Thus it was that Hroswitha determined something must be done, and decided to write some plays herself. They were to be written in the best and most polished Latin at her command and treat of subjects fit to be heard within convent walls.

Gallicanus

Her first play, **Gallicanus,** was a most ambitious maiden effort. Her hero was an actual historical personage, one of Emperor Constantine's greatest generals. As the play opens, he is about to depart for the Scythian front. He asks the Emperor for the Princess Constantia's hand in marriage should he return victorious. The Emperor, though aware that his daughter has taken the vow of chastity, is constrained to agree. He reckons without Constantia's resourcefulness. She not only prays for Gallicanus in a prayer of remarkable eloquence, considering the amount of theology the playwright manages to condense into one paragraph, but also sends her two spiritual advisors, John and Paul, to the front in order to give tangible assistance to her earnest desire.

The play proceeds with a blithe disregard of all unities, and soon the opposing forces meet in battle. Gallicanus's troops are yielding under the Scythian attack. "What will happen?" he cries, "My soldiers despise me and yield." At this crucial moment, John calls to him over the battle's din, "Vow to the God of Heaven that you will become a Christian and you shall conquer." Without an instant's hesitation Gallicanus answers, "I do so vow. May my deeds seal it!" Immediately the Scythians surrender and Gallicanus wins the day.

He returns to Rome to give his account of the battle to the Emperor. He takes it to the darkest hour:

> *Emperor.* And how did you escape?
> *Gallicanus.* My dear companions, John and Paul, persuaded me to make a vow to my Creator . . . and as I opened my mouth to pray, I felt the aid of Heaven. . . . There came to me a youth, bearing a cross on his shoulder, who bade me follow him with drawn sword.
>
> *Emperor.* Whoever he was, he was sent straight from Heaven.
> *Gallicanus.* I complied, and straightway on my right hand and left there stood armed warriors.
> *Emperor.* The hosts of Heaven!
> *Gallicanus.* I doubt it not, and straightway following that youth, I walked unafraid into the midst of the foe.

The hero then makes the astounding announcement that, at his baptism following the victory, he had taken a vow of chastity. The Emperor now acquaints him with Constantia's vow, to which he replies amiably, "I pray she may abide in the same."

The question naturally arises why, since the battlefield conversion would make a most exciting moment, did Hroswitha fail to stage it. The answer is that Hroswitha was following her source. In all accounts of Gallicanus he is represented as telling the story to the Emperor, and, while as a playwright the unities might mean little to her, as a nun she must hesitate to deviate from a saint's legend.

Emperor and Gallicanus go into the palace to greet Constantia, who, surprised and pleased at the General's change of heart, invites him to live with them. But he draws the line at that. He states, "No temptation is greater to be withstood than the lust of the eyes, and it would not be good for me to see this maid too often, whom, as you know, I love better than my parents or my life or my very soul." He then bids them farewell and goes off to live as a hermit. Hroswitha's permitting a glimpse of the depth and reality of the soldier's love is a masterly touch. This fleeting worldly note prevents a scene, filled with expressions of noble virtue, from degenerating into one of mere platitudes. It also indicates a delightful feminine sympathy for the man. Nevertheless, Constantia is not permitted to waver for one moment. She is, throughout, as the author intended, a model to those vacillating sisters in religion who just might be persuaded to delight in Terence, over and above the stern voice of duty.

Gallicanus, Part II

Hroswitha takes up the action again in **Gallicanus, Part II.** Thirty years have passed and Rome is now under the rule of Julian the Apostate who is clearing the Empire of Christians. As Hroswitha never had a course in playwriting, she permits the first victim of the persecution to be none other than her former hero, Gallicanus. In the second scene he is removed from the stage. The Emperor says, "Oh worthy deed!" and turns next to John and Paul. He asks these advisors to serve him but they refuse. He reminds them that he, too, was once high up in the Church but that he quickly discovered that there was no profit in the Christian religion so returned to the old gods of Rome. "Devil's disciple," Paul mutters, under his breath, then says aloud, "You have left all true religion and follow the superstition of idolatry." Julian offers both high rank; they spurn him. He gives them ten days in which to change their minds, but Paul says proudly, "Do what you have already decided to do," and the Emperor sentences them both to death.

Hroswitha, however, refuses to end her play so somberly. The soldier chosen to execute John and Paul has a son. The boy becomes possessed of the devil and the father is convinced that he is being punished for executing the saints. He wails, "I, miserable wretch that I am, obeyed the behest of the ungodly Emperor Julian," and he begs the Christians for help, professing his belief and penitently asking to be baptized. At that very moment the boy is cured and the curtain falls on a scene of pious rejoicing.

Judged even by later miracle plays, neither part of **Gallicanus** can be termed a drama. The characters are mere figureheads and are manoeuvred in episodic pageant fashion to suit the author's expositions of theology. Yet, it is impossible to read them without being forcibly struck by the nun's own reverence. Her belief is so great that even palpable absurdities become unimportant and a twentieth-century reader, almost in spite of himself, willingly suspends his own belief.

Dulcitius

The second play, **Dulcitius,** finds Hroswitha writing in a slightly different vein. Three sisters—Irene, Agape, and Chionia—are condemned to death by Emperor Diocletian who turns them over to Prefect Dulcitius for execution. Dulcitius, however, being a lecherous old pagan, has other ideas. Upon attempting to make love to the sisters, he is suddenly stricken with madness and rushes around the kitchen embracing the pots and pans in the belief that he has caught them. Shades of the bemused old gentleman of Terence! Here, however, not a wily slave confounds the lecher but the power of God. The audience is regaled with the sight of a Roman senator, covered with pot blacking and pitch, being refused admission to the imperial palace. "What goes on here?" Dulcitius wails, "Am I not arrayed in Splendid robes? Am I not gorgeous from head to foot? And yet the porter scorns me as a horrible monster." The maiden Agape comments, "It is most fitting he should appear in body as he is in his mind, possessed of the devil." Finally, furious at his lack of success, Dulcitius commands that the sisters be put to torture and then burned at the stake.

The three sisters are heroines quite foreign to the classic tradition. Their characters are far removed from the meek, subservient Pamphilias and Glyceriums of Terence, for the girls have a courage and independence born of virtue and they are completely fearless. Hroswitha doubtlessly intended them as examples of what women could become if they were wholly, militantly Christian. While their nobility may seem a trifle implausible now, perhaps that is an adverse commentary on our own times rather than any criticism of Hroswitha. The sisters did not seem implausible to the contemporary audience which is the important thing. The scenes of Dulcitius' madness were intended for comic relief, and a good actor, even a nun with dramatic flair, could make considerable of them. Pots and pans occupy only a brief space in the action, however.

It is as though the playwright suddenly recollected herself, for the action soon returns to proceed on its way to martyrdom and glory.

Callimachus

In her third play, *Callimachus,* Hroswitha treads on shakier ground. She calls it, "The hateful madness of unlawful lovers, even such things as may not be heard among us" [*Praefatio II*]. *Callimachus* deals with the affection of a young man for a married woman. Today's audience does not consider this subject taboo but Hroswitha and her audience did.

Callimachus is a bachelor of Edessa, frantically in love with Drusiana, a respectable matron, who is shocked by his importunities and repulses him emphatically:

> *Drusiana.* I wonder, young man, that you speak thus to me. By what right of kinship or legal bond do you love me?
>
> *Callimachus.* Your beauty!
>
> *Drusiana.* My beauty? Go away, you wicked seducer. I'm ashamed to listen to you.
>
> *Callimachus.* You doubtless blush to confess what affection my love arouses in you.
>
> *Drusiana.* Nothing but indignation.

Callimachus finally goes away, vowing revenge, and Drusiana prays for death, lest she not only fall into sin herself but also tempt another to sin.

Her prayer is answered. She is laid in her tomb by her husband but even this does not bring Callimachus to his senses. He bribes the servant, Fortunatus, to admit him to the sepulcher and there falls on his knees beside the bier crying, "Oh! Drusiana, Drusiana, I adored you with all my heart. You rejected me in life, but now—now I have you in my power!" Thought naturally turns to *Romeo and Juliet,* but Hroswitha sees to it that her Callimachus is no Romeo—he receives his just deserts. A serpent glides into the tomb and he and the untrustworthy Fortunatus lie dead.

The scene then shifts to a street in Edessa. Andronicus, husband of Drusiana, and St. John the Evangelist are on their way to the bier to pray when they are confronted by a Youth of Flaming Aspect (a typical description of a Byzantine Angelic Messenger). He bids them hurry so that St. John may raise Drusiana and her unfortunate lover. They obey, and St. John with delightful practicality, first disposes of the snake: "We do not want him harmed again by the bite of a serpent," he says, and then he raises Callimachus. The young man, wholly repentant, confesses his sin and receives absolution. Then the Saint raises Drusiana, who also forgives her onetime lover. But Fortunatus, when raised, refuses to repent: "I'd rather be dead than see such virtue triumph in them," he says surlily. Ret-

ribution is swift. Fortunatus's serpent bites swell up and he falls to the ground in agony.

Once the miraculous aspect is accepted, *Callimachus* emerges as a tightly knit drama with a quite powerful final scene. The character of Callimachus is certainly modelled on the young Athenians whom Terence loved so well, and Fortunatus is similar to the wily slaves. But Drusiana is entirely new. Like Caesar's wife, she is above reproach, but Hroswitha has given her the added virtue of true Christianity which raises her sense of honor above mere ethics, something Terence could never have understood. And neither could he have understood a woman who preferred death to temptation, for his ladies were invariably accommodating. In this respect Hroswitha's heroines mark the beginning of a new tradition in the theatre.

Abraham

The chief interest in the brief play *Abraham* lies in its resemblance to *Paphnutius* which followed and excelled it. Two hermits, Abraham and Ephraim, find themselves with Abraham's twelve-year-old niece in their custody. They do not know what to do about her, and the only thing that occurs to them is to have her take a vow of perpetual poverty, chastity, and good works. At this early age such a promise is easily given, but once in her teens Mary decides she has had enough of it and runs away with a renegade monk. She disappears completely for two years and then Abraham receives word that she is living at Assos and is a notorious harlot. He disguises himself as a profligate man about town (Hroswitha demanded much of her actors, considering they were nuns) and goes to Mary. His disguise admits him, but once in her presence, he casts aside his gaudy cloak and pleads with her to return to the desert with him:

> *Abraham.* Why did you forsake me? Why didn't you tell me you had fallen into weakness, so that I might have helped you and prayed for you?
>
> *Mary.* After I fell, I thought I dare not approach you, holy man that you are.
>
> *Abraham.* But who is sinless, but the Virgin's Son? . . . To err is human, but to continue in sin is damnable. He is not blamed who falls, but he who fails to rise again quickly.

Little by little he persuades her until she finally throws aside the jewels her lovers have given her and returns with her uncle to the hermitage.

In this scene, remarkable for its contemporary tone, Hroswitha shows consummate tact. She recognized that the play must consider Mary's sin, and that Abraham's comments must not leave even the most innocent novice in doubt, but she does not gloat over it. Her sole concern is that Mary repent, and Mary does. Her reason for writing the play is to demonstrate the great compassion of Almighty God, and although vice is treated realistically, neither underplayed nor avoided, her treatment has the delicacy which only a wholly immaculate mind can bestow. Taste is a much overused word, a too often ridiculed commodity, but Hroswitha's taste in this and similar situations is dependably excellent.

Paphnutius, or, The Conversion of Thaïs

The fifth play, **Paphnutius, or, the Conversion of Thaïs,** is Hroswitha's masterpiece. Almost everyone is familiar with Anatole France's novel, *Thaïs,* in which Massenet found the inspiration for his opera, but comparatively few people are aware that France was inspired to write his version of her story by a marionette performance of **Paphnutius.** Of course, in the Hroswitha treatment Paphnutius remains a saint throughout. He is a learned medieval doctor who, as the play opens, is discussing philosophy with a group of his disciples— a scene similar to many in which Hroswitha herself must frequently have taken part. The disciples are quite confused (another touch of realism) and Paphnutius admits that such abstruse doctrines are difficult to understand. Shortly he falls into deep melancholy, and when asked what is troubling him, he says that he is gravely concerned over the soul of the notorious courtesan, Thaïs. The disciples agree that she is in need of the Saint's concern "for she is not unknown to any man." Paphnutius accepts their statement, without inquiring as to the source of their information, and, after a little more conversation, he announces that he will go to Thaïs and exhort her to repentance.

Forthwith he goes to her and she receives him with, "I do not withdraw my presence nor refuse my company to any man," but when he asks to speak with her in strictest privacy, she answers, with a sudden flash of truth, "There is no place so hid, so secret, that the recess of it is not known to God." Rejoicing that she is at least aware of the Almighty, Paphnutius begins his exhortation. At first Thaïs listens with amusement, then she becomes angry, but gradually she is moved to sorrow. Finally she calls in her lovers and throws all the gifts they have given her onto a huge bonfire. Then she meekly takes the hand Paphnutius offers her and lets him lead her into a life of penance.

He brings her to a convent, and tells the Abbess that she is to be confined to a narrow cell, without doors or windows beyond a small opening to receive her daily ration of food. The Abbess, shaking her head, says, "I fear her tender spirit can ill endure such affliction." Paphnutius replies, "So grievous a sin must expect a stern remedy." The cell is prepared and when Thaïs is told that it will be her abode for the rest of her life she cries in horror, "How narrow, how dark, how com-

fortless!" Adamant, Paphnutius tells her that she must say nothing, even in prayer, except, "Thou Who hast created me, have mercy on me." Finally she enters the cell, and the door is sealed.

The entire scene is very moving. Its insight into the frame of mind of a woman, accustomed to every luxury, who has chosen in the name of religion to exist on less than the barest decencies, is remarkable. Lest her capitulation seems to come too quickly, it must be remembered that tenth-century audiences saw nothing unusual in instant conversions; if the penance imposed seems impossibly severe, the hidden austerities of religious life of the time must not be forgotten—the hair shirt, the discipline, the hours of kneeling with outstretched arms in imitation of the Cross. In an age when asceticism was a virtue to be practiced rather than endured and martyrdom was eagerly sought, Thaïs's compliance would have been held highly virtuous and commendable.

Three years pass and Paphnutius receives word that Thaïs is dying. He goes to her at once and tells her that because of her penance she is surely pardoned. This scene is brief and poignant with a heartbreaking moment at the end when Thaïs begs him not to let her die alone. Here Hroswitha reaches her highest stature as a playwright. The character of the erring Thaïs is beautifully and sympathetically realized; Paphnutius is excellent both in his character of stern moral censor and in his great compassion in the final scene. Were this the only extant play of hers, Hroswitha would still be a playwright with whom to reckon; several centuries elapsed before anything of equal beauty and significance appeared on the Western stage.

Sapientia

After **Paphnutius** the final play, **Sapientia,** is an anticlimax. Sapientia and her daughters, Faith, Hope, and Charity, come to Rome to convert Emperor Hadrian. The Emperor arrests and tries them in a scene filled with philosophical discussion, most of it drawn from the Roman philosopher, Boethius—a rather strange digression considering Hroswitha's usual directness. The mother and daughters refuse to recant and the girls are put to torture. Sapientia stands by, encouraging them, praying that they may be taken at once to Heaven. Stunned by such resignation, Hadrian releases her, but, after one more prayer, she dies and joins her daughters in death. It is a most extraordinary play, highly stylized, with none of the exaltation of **Gallicanus** and none of the humanity of **Paphnutius.** It is possible that **Sapientia** may have been an early work which Hroswitha revised for some special occasion at Gandersheim for a courtly audience which delighted in lengthy philosophical debate.

A great deal of ink has been spilled in an attempt to determine whether or not Hroswitha's plays were performed. This is rather foolish, for from what is known of Gandersheim and its patrons the plays must certainly have been performed. Objections are raised on the grounds that they would be impossible to stage, but the objectors forget that a medieval audience was accustomed to viewing contending armies, seraphic messengers, diabolic tempters, sacrifices, tortures, and heavenly ascents, separately or simultaneously as the action demanded. And would it not be difficult to imagine so devoted a theatregoer as Empress Theophano failing to see that they were performed once she knew of their existence? What of Hroswitha herself? Had she not written the plays to compete with Terence and what better competition could she provide than an actual performance?

Attempts have been made to assess the Hroswitha influence on the theatre. For many years it was customary to treat her as an isolated playwright whose **Opera** disappeared into oblivion until their recovery by Celtes. Recent discoveries, however, are rapidly modifying this view. The entire script of **Gallicanus,** without Hroswitha's name appended, has been found in the twelfth-century manuscript, Aldersbach Confessional, and there are other references to indicate that she was not unknown in Europe. The new viewpoint has been further strengthened by the discovery of a second Hroswitha codex at Cologne in 1922. It is entirely possible that the tenth-century nun, who is now the object of much scholarly interest, will eventually be linked to later continental miracle plays, and ultimately to the great miracle cycles of England.

So let us enjoy the portrait we have of her as it has emerged from this short survey of her life, her works, and her times. She was a brilliant, well-educated woman, a dedicated religious who retained the sense of urbanity and courtesy of the knightly society into which she had been born; a lady accustomed to royalty, to intellectual conversation, and one who had a considerable knowledge of the world and its ways; a scholar of sufficient wit and perception to see the possibilities for drama in books her church might adjudge unsound, and with the courage to use them as the sources for six plays, which, in any age or society, would bear the stamp of authentic genius. We may not be able to share her religious exaltation, but if we can comprehend it that will be enough. Certainly we must appreciate her single-handed efforts to Christianize the stage of her own time for the benefit of the stage that followed, and, perhaps, even comprehend the excitement of the French critic, Philatre Charles, who, after reading her plays, was moved to exclaim:

A passionate soul, a superior spirit,
Who thought to imitate Terence, but who
    announced Racine![5]

Notes

[1] See Charles Magnin, Théatre de Hrotsvitha (Paris 1845) for various references to Bodo in this article. No copy of the original was procurable.

[2] *Ibid.,* p. xviii.

[3] E. H. Zevdel, "Reception of Hroswitha by the German Humanists after 1493," *Journal of English and Germanic Philology* (July 1945), pp. 239-249.

[4] Quotations from the works of Hroswitha have all been translated by the author from the text of *Hrotsvithae Opera,* ed., Karolus Strecker (Leipzig 1906).

[5] For quotation in French see Vignon Retif de la Bretonne, *Poesies Latine de Rosvith, avec un traduction libre en vers français* (Paris 1854), p. 10.

Sister Mary Marguerite Butler (essay date 1960)

SOURCE: "Hrotsvitha of Gandersheim," in *Hrotsvitha: The Theatricality of Her Plays,* Philosophical Library, 1960, pp. 62-84.

[*In the following excerpt, Butler presents an overview of Hroswitha's life and early writings, then outlines the significant sources, style, influences, and intent of her dramatic works.*]

The Woman and Nun

Most theatre historians admit that there is scant documentary evidence about Hrotsvitha's chronology and background. Three sources will be related here as representative of typical available data.

Magnin, relying on the *Hildesheim Chronicles, Monumenta Germaniae Historica,* and on the *Anti-quitates Gandersheimenses* of Leuckfeld volubly states:

> Hrotsvitha informs us that she was born a long time after the death of Otto the Illustrious, Duke of Saxony, father of Henry the Fowler, which event [the death of Otto] occurred on November 30, 912. In another source (the preface of her poetic works) she says she was a little older than the daughter of Henry, Duke of Bavaria, Gerberga II, the abbess of Gandersheim [consecrated] in 959, who was born, according to all indications, about the year 940. From these two events, it may be deduced that Hrotsvitha was born between 912 and 940, and much nearer the second date than the first, consequently, about 930 or 935. The date of her death is even more uncertain. One fact alone is beyond doubt—that her writing career extended beyond the year 968; since the fragment which still exists of the Panegyric to the Ottos, contains the events of that year and since subsequent to its completion, Hrotsvitha composed another poem to recognize the foundation of the monastery at Gandersheim. Casimir Oudin says she died in the year 1001; she was in her sixty-seventh year, if we are right in our preceding calculations.

Oudin bases his statement on the fact that Hrotsvitha wrote about the first three Ottos. True, the first book of poems, the only extant one, finished with the death of Otto I, but the very title of this work (*Panegyris Oddonum*), proves that we have only the first part. The second dedication addressed to Otto II, king of the Romans, probably served as the preface to the second book, devoted to the deeds of this prince. Let us add to this that in the *Hildesheim Chronicles* it states that Hrotsvitha had honored the three Ottos. If this were true, it would mean that Hrotsvitha was still living in the year 1002, which, incidentally, would only be most probable.[1]

Algermissen states more succinctly:

> Neither her birth year nor the year of her death is historically documented; since the earliest year of her birth which could possibly be recognized is 932, and the earliest year of her death, 1003, therefore, she lived to be approximately seventy years old.[2]

St. John explicitly believes that Hrotsvitha's references to certain historical events and personages in her writings prove that she was born after 912 and before 940 and that she entered the cloister when about twenty-three years old.[3]

Aside from these express statements, there is the evidence within the works themselves. In speaking of Gerberga II, Hrotsvitha describes her as *aetate minor* though *scientia provectior*.[4] Blashfield places Gerberga's birth as approximately 940, alleging she was the daughter of Henry, Duke of Bavaria, who was married to Judith in 938.[5] This fortifies the preceding evidence that Hrotsvitha was born about 935.

Frequent references to contemporaries give further credence to the above-mentioned dates. Hrotsvitha refers to her tyrocinium as an author under *sapientissimae atque benignissimae Rikkardis magistrae* (*ca.* 950-970) and to Gerberga (955-1001) *cuius nunc subdor dominio abbatissae*.[6] She venerates the martyr of Cordova, Pelagius (d. *ca.* 921), in a tribute, the subject matter of which was told to her by an eyewitness. She defers to the Archbishop Willigis (975-1011) to whom Gerberga presumed to show Hrotsvitha's "unpolished lines."[7] She asserts her interest in the contemporary educational scene by including in *Pafnutius* and *Sapientia* impressive dialogue based on the trivium and quadrivium. She presents to Otto II (973-983) an account of the deeds of his illustrious father, saying, "If I were not urged by this dread command, under no circumstances should I have such self-assurance as to presume to offer to thy scrutiny this little book with its obvious lack of polish."[8] Such are the data which justify the statement that the brilliance of Hrotsvitha spanned the Ottonian Renaissance.

It has already been noted that the fourth abbess of Gandersheim, the first to assume ruling power over the monastery after the death of the last of Duke Liudolf's daughters, was a religious named Hrotsvitha, for "which learned lady," Blashfield says, "our more famous playwright [the second Hroswitha] of the same name is often mistaken; a pardonable confusion since the abbess was also an author and continued the literary traditions of the convent."[9]

Magnin, quoting from the Hildesheim sources, says that "some claim this Hrotsvitha, the fourth abbess of Gandersheim, came from the second branch of the ducal family of Saxony, and was the daughter of Duke Otto the Illustrious, the second son of Liudolf and father of Henry the Fowler."[10]

Whatever her family heritage, the first Hrotsvitha apparently had connections with a royal family. Algermissen supports this statement in his discussion of the Gandersheim foundation when he says "the nuns who entered the foundation convent were from noble families of the neighborhood."[11] "The fourth abbess," according to Algermissen, "was probably the aunt of our poetess; she was elected by the community in 916 and was installed by Bishop Walbert of Hildesheim (903-919)."[12]

It seems likely, therefore, that Hrotsvitha, the poetess, was of the same royal family as Hrotsvitha, the abbess. It has not been uncommon from the very earliest days for families to perpetuate the names of respected members through their use in succeeding generations. For example, Gerberga II, the ruling abbess of the monastery (955-1001) during the second Hrotsvitha's lifetime, was the daughter of Duke Henry and granddaughter of Otto the Illustrious, brother of the first Gerberga. It would not be an improbable assumption to assert that the younger Hrotsvitha honored in her name the memory of the abbess Hrotsvitha and might have been a relative.[13]

Little or no data are available about Hrotsvitha's immediate family either from historians or through allusions in her own writings. Numerous and unsubstantiated are the conjectures concerning her birthplace and parentage. Algermissen states that due to the conditions of the time, there are only two facts of which we can be certain, namely, that she was from the Eastphalian area of Lower Saxony and that she entered the *Kanonissenstift* of Gandersheim which was, at that time, the most famous monastery in the area. Since reliable sources have affirmed that this was a canoness convent, we have concluded that Hrotsvitha lived under the canoness rule rather than that of the stricter Benedictines Regular, and that her life was essentially freer, admitting of such privileges which afforded the canonesses contact with members of the court and with those who attended the monastery school.

However, regardless of the paucity of documented facts, a careful reading of the prefaces which she composed for each of her individual works, as well as an analysis of the content and style of her writing, reveals the character of the woman, her great stature as a religious, and her status as a writer.[14]

Of her character and experience before her entrance into Gandersheim much is inferred from her writings, for in them she shows an intimate knowledge of the world and its human conflicts. The fact that she does not suppress this knowledge, but uses it to advantage as a nun and as a littérateur, marks her as a person of integrity and courage.

She is conscious of her talents; and we do not object when she acknowledges the praise of critics to whom she submitted her works, undoubtedly, at the command of her superiors. Following the **"Prefatio"** there is an **"Epistola Eiusdem ad Quosdam Sapientes Huius Libri Fautores,"** a letter to certain learned patrons of this book, in which she says in part:

> You have not praised me but the Giver of the grace which works in me. . . . I rejoice from the depths of my soul that God through whose grace alone I am what I am, should be praised in me, but I am afraid of being thought greater than I am. I know that it is as wrong to deny a divine gift as to pretend falsely that we have received it. So I will not deny that through the grace of the Creator I have acquired some knowledge of the arts. He has given me ability to learn—I am a teachable creature—yet of myself I should know nothing.[15]

Hrotsvitha in any era would have emerged as a woman of stature—noble in origin, learned in mind, great in heart, gentle in word—an honor to womanhood.

Concerning Hrotsvitha, the nun, her prefaces again are the definitive source from which her virtues may be divined. She exhibits sincere humility and industry when she says, "It must be remembered that when I began it [her writing], I was far from possessing the necessary qualifications, being young in both years and learning." Then she relates how she toiled secretly, writing, and rewriting, fearing to submit what she had done lest experts might discourage her because of the "crudity" of her style. She acknowledges the training of her novice mistress, Rikkarda—"most learned and gentle," and the "kind favor and encouragement of a royal personage, Gerberga. . . . "[16]

She again reveals her humility and her ready obedience, when she writes about the deeds of Otto in poetic form, as she had been requested to do by her superiors, regardless of the difficulty of the task. She begins the **"Prefatio"** to this work by addressing Gerberga thus:

> Illustrious Abbess, venerated no less for uprightness and honesty than for the high distinction of a royal and noble race, Hrotsvitha of Gandersheim, the last of the least of those fighting under your ladyship's rule, desires to give you all that a servant owes her mistress. O my lady, bright with the varied jewels of spiritual wisdom, your maternal kindness will not let you hesitate to read what, as you know, was written at your command! It was you who gave me the task of chronicling in verse the deeds of the Emperor, and you know that it was impossible to collect them together from hearsay. You can imagine the difficulties which my ignorance put in my way while I was engaged in this work. . . . At present I am defenseless at every point, because I am not supported by any authority. I also fear I shall be accused of temerity in presuming to describe in my humble uncultured way matters which ought to be set forth with all the elegance of great learning. Yet if my work is examined by one who knows how to appraise things fairly, he will pardon me the more readily because of the weakness of my sex and my inferior knowledge, especially as I did not undertake this little work of my own presumption, but at your command.[17]

It was mentioned earlier that Goetting did not see mere coincidence in the fact that Hrotsvitha concluded her *Primordia* with the death of Christine. The subsequent history of the monastery reveals many administrative complications which resulted in the embarrassing Hildesheim controversy. Algermissen observes that her name does not appear among the nuns involved in the famous quarrel. Thus, Hrotsvitha, the nun, manifests her loyalty to her community.

The Poet

It has been shown that Gandersheim reached its highest point as a center of learning during the reign of the Abbess Gerberga II, which was simultaneous with that rich cultural period of German history known as the Ottonian Renaissance. Since this was also the time of Hrotsvitha's literary endeavors, it seems that she is a figure of far greater importance than literary and theatre historians are wont to recognize.

To her credit are the following works, divided conveniently into three books. *Liber Primus* contains a prose introduction, a verse dedication to the Abbess Gerberga, eight legends—**"Maria," "Ascensio," "Gongolfus," "Pelagius," "Theophilus," "Basilius," "Dionysius," "Agnes,"** and a prose conclusion. In *Liber Secundus* are found a prose introduction, the **"Epistola eiusdem ad quosdam sapientes huius libri fautores,"** six dramas—*Gallicanus I and II, Dulcitius, Calimachus, Abraham, Pafnutius, Sapientia,* and a poem of thirty-five lines on a **"Vision of St. John."** *Liber Tertius* includes a prose introduction, verse dedications to Otto I and to Otto II, *Gesta Ottonis,* a verse introduction, and the *Primordia Coenobii Gandeshemensis.*

In evaluating these works and in an attempt to place them chronologically, Eckenstein says:

Each kind of work has merits of its own and deserves attention. But while Hrotsvitha as a legend writer ranks with other writers of the age, and as an historical writer is classed by the historian Giesebrecht with Widukind and Ruotger, as a writer of Latin drama she stands entirely alone. . . . The first of her two sets of legends was put together and dedicated to Gerberg [*sic*] as abbess, that is after the year 959; she wrote and submitted part if not the whole of her history of Otto the Great to Wilhelm, Archbishop of Mainz, before the year 968, in which the prelate died. How the composition of her dramas is related in point of time to that of the legends and the historical poems cannot be definitely decided; probably the dramas were written in the middle period of Hrotsvitha's life. For the legends bear marks of being the outcome of early effort, while the historical poems, especially the one which tells of the early history of Gandersheim, were written in the full consciousness of power.[18]

Goetting claims that in the ***Primordia,*** as well as in the ***Gesta Ottonis,*** Hrotsvitha is not objective in her writing; that she omits certain historical facts.[19] These observations are true, but it should be noted also that she was writing not only at the command of her superiors who were descendants of the royal founders, but without any objective chronicles for her source material, circumstances which certainly must have affected her writing.

In the preface which introductes the legendary poems, Hrotsvitha expresses the diffidence which she felt when she first began to write:

> Unknown to others and secretly, so to speak, I worked by myself; sometimes I composed, sometimes I destroyed what I had written to the best of my abilities and yet badly. . . . Writing verse appears a difficult and arduous task especially for one of my sex, but trusting to the help of divine grace more than to my own powers, I have fitted the stories of this book to dactylic measures as best I could, for fear that the abilities that have been implanted in me should be dulled and wasted by neglect.[20]

Actually, Hrotsvitha showed considerable skill in her use of the leonine hexameter, a form of verse popular with writers at that time. On the whole, her poetry is characterized by dignity and simplicity, and attests to her facile and sensitive powers of expression.

Hrotsvitha is rightly considered among the first of women poets after Sappho. She is rightly called the first woman dramatist, the only recorded playwright between the Romans and the writers of the medieval church drama of the twelfth century. Algermissen claims, "The first Christian poetess of lower Saxony and of our diocese, she was also the first German poetess. She was the first dramatic writer of the Chris-

tian world whose works represent an attempt to write Christian drama."[21]

Frequently, the dramas are classified as prose. However, since Hrotsvitha was instinctively a poet, there is a natural poetic quality evident in her dialogue. Fife calls attention to the "rhymed prose of her dialogue" which he terms "an undulating prose with its suggestion of a liturgical recitative, with a peculiar charm."[22]

Baldwin gives several examples of the use of tenth-century rhymed prose; and with reference to Hrotsvitha he says:

> the use of rhyme and balance is most marked in passages of heightened emotional tone, particularly in the prayers. To one familiar with medieval hymnody, there is a rather striking similarity between these prayers and the 'transitional' sequences of the tenth and eleventh centuries, of which the most famous 'Victimae Paschali,' is the best example; and it seems possible that these passages may have been influenced to some extent by the church liturgy.[23]

Chasles says that, at first sight, one believes he is reading prose. All editors of Hrotsvitha's dramas have reproduced them in this manner without rhyme or rhythm. If one rereads the lines carefully, Chasles continues, one will be struck by the constant recurrence of assonance and incomplete rhymes which cut the sentence, sometimes in two, and sometimes in three unequal parts. The variety and irregularity of the dialogue suspends in vain this symmetrical movement. The rhyme reappears with tenacity. . . .

Chasles believes this love of the same sound offers a curious singularity and raises the question of the origin of the rhyme of the moderns:

> One feels the balance and the soft cadence of the verse. It is, in effect, modern verse. One has only, to convince oneself, to follow step by step, the Latin of Hrotsvitha and trace verse by verse, the French verse of an equal number of feet and rhymes under the Latin lines. . . .

> Evidently, the religious has written in verse without knowing it.[26]

All of her works were written in the same poetic manner. And thus, Chasles affirms, here is a religious writer, creative and imitative of the time in which she lived, who passed on her impressions clearly. If she held to antiquity by her studies, to the middle ages by the form of style and depth of ideas, she touched, by essential points, the development of the poetry of a new people. Thus, a place is assured Hrotsvitha in the literature of the moderns, for here was a poet who believed she imitated Terence and who announced Racine.[27]

Such is the accolade Chasles accords Hrotsvitha, and in the same tradition, Magnin speaks of "this celebrated monastery which has been for Germany an intellectual oasis springing forth in the barbarian steppes,"[28] and to which Hrotsvitha brought literary immortality because in her poetical works are the origins of some of the great dramatic masterpieces of the centuries.

The Dramatist

Hrotsvitha's dramas have usually been treated in the light of literary and theatre history. It has been alleged that she lived in an age for which there are no established scientific data to prove the existence of a living theatre; thus, she had no immediate master. Drama was considered an alien literary form, one frowned upon by the Church and certainly not to be encouraged among scholars, much less in a woman, and far less in a nun. And so, literary and theatre historians have passed lightly over eight centuries, from the fourth to the twelfth, merely mentioning Hrotsvitha as the author of six short dramas; then they leave her in isolation with no link to the past nor impression upon the future.

Such casual treatment, based upon insufficient evidence, gives cause for serious concern. Research has proved, as shown above, that during these centuries, theatre existed in fluctuating emphasis in classical, mimetic, and liturgical forms; that the Church was, in turn, a friend and a foe to the theatre; that Hrotsvitha did not live in a vast dramatic wasteland since within her plays there can be discerned vestiges of the three forms of theatre existing during her day.

Her works were developed, of necessity, within the framework of medieval life. Realizing the impact of social, political, and religious institutions on the culture of the time, considerable space in this study has been devoted to the fusion of Graeco-Roman and Christian cultures; to the rise and significance of monasticism in general, and to Gandersheim in particular; to the tracing of the Carolingian and Saxon dynasties and Hrotsvitha's flowering within the latter; and to the waning relationship between Crown and Church and its repercussions on religious communities.

According to the Benedictine *Annales,* the rigidity and asceticism of the lives of the Regulars would have precluded the worldly contacts and freedom which, as a canoness, Hrotsvitha enjoyed. For this reason it seemed necessary to investigate as fully as possible the character of the canoness convent in order to understand the free and artistic climate within which she was inspired to write in the dramatic form, and to describe in detail the cloister-arcade which served as a background for much of the canoness' activity.

These data—a living tenth-century theatre, the cultural renaissance of the day, the canoness character, the natural cloister-stage—should not only clarify the problem under consideration, namely, the theatricality of Hrotsvitha's dramatic works, but should also justify the legitimacy of the problem and lend affirmative support to it. The remainder of the chapter will concern itself with Hrotsvitha's place as a dramatist. It will point out the rationale she used for selecting plot material; it will trace the development of the art form which she designed for the presentation of this material; finally, it will identify the dramatic influences which are evident in her plays.

Blashfield, quoting Magnin, says, "Hrotsvitha, like all playwrights, 'elle prenait son bien ou elle le trouvait,' and her goods were the legends of the saints"[29]—the *Acta Sanctorum,* the *Apocryphal Gospels,* and the Christian legends of Greece. Hrotsvitha knew her authors and she knew her countrymen.

Köpke assures us that the library at Gandersheim contained not only the writings of Terence, but also the works of the outstanding Latin poets, historians, and essayists, as well as the writings of the Church Fathers.[30] Whether or not Hrotsvitha had access to the Greek legends in their original form is a matter of controversy. Ebert, in examining the sources of Hrotsvitha's dramas, contends that she read her Greek authors in Latin translations.[31] Barack, pointing to her use of words notably of Greek derivation, would argue her familiarity with that language.[32]

Regardless of the form of language in which Hrotsvitha found her sources, she apparently had the ability to use them in their entirety. As a member of the Gandersheim community, she had the accumulated wisdom of the ages at her disposal. She brought to this storehouse of knowledge a facility for learning, a creative flair, and a discerning eye. This combination impelled her to take material "wherever she found it," and to apply to it an artistic form which would appeal to a wide audience ("plures catholici"), an audience whose personal welfare was of vital concern to her.

The "plures catholici" of her day comprised almost all of the population. They were, for the most part, men and women of blunt candor, childlike in their needs and desires, whose entire way of life was oriented to the spiritual. The stories of the saints of the desert, of the early Christian martyrs, and of the miraculous conversion of the cruel pagan persecutors excited the imagination of the medieval mind just as the stories of the heroes and gods of the ancients exacted the homage of the pagan mind.

However, there is no need to appeal to secondary sources for a rationale to support Hrotsvitha's choice of subject matter and form. She supplies an authentic purpose in her own words:

There are many Christians, from whom we cannot claim to be excepted, who because of the charm of finished diction prefer heathen literature with its hollowness to our religious books; there are others who hold by the scripture and despise what is heathen, and yet eagerly peruse the poetic creations of Terence; while delighting in his flow of language, they are all polluted by the godless contents of his works. Therefore I 'the well-known mouthpiece of Gandersheim' have not hesitated in taking this poet's style as a model, and while others honour him by perusing his dramas, I have attempted, in the very way in which he treats of unchaste love among evil women, to celebrate according to my ability the praise-worthy chasteness of godlike maidens.

In doing so, I have often hesitated with a blush on my cheeks through modesty, because the nature of the work obliged me to concentrate my attention on and apply my mind to the wicked passion of illicit love and to the tempting talk of the amorous, against which we at other times close our ears. But if I had hesitated on account of my blushes I could not have carried out my purpose, or have set forth the praise of innocence to the fullness of my ability. For in proportion as the blandishments of lovers are enticing, so much greater is the glory of our helper in heaven, so much more glorious the triumph of those who prevail, especially where woman's weak-ness triumphs and man's shameless strength is made to succumb. . . . If anyone is pleased with my work I shall rejoice, but if on account of my unpolished language it pleases no one, what I have done yet remains a satisfaction to myself, for while in other writings I have worked, however insufficiently, only in heroic strophe, here I have combined this with dramatic form, while avoiding the dangerous allurements of the heathen.[33]

Many writers have paraphrased this quotation and many have fallen into the oft-repeated error of interpreting it from a contemporary point of view. Eckenstein, avoiding this fallacy, in a few brief paragraphs, has penetrated the essence of this rationale as stated by Hrots-vitha:

The keynote of her dramas one and all is to insist on the beauties of a steadfast adherence to chastity as opposed to the frenzy and the vagaries of passion. In doing so she is giving expression to the ideas of contemporary Christian teaching, which saw in passion, not the inborn force that can be applied to good or evil purpose, not the storage of strength which works for social advantage or disadvantage, but simply a tendency in human nature which manifests itself in lack of self-restraint, and the disturbing element which interferes with the attainment of calmness and candour. . . . For the nun does not disparage marriage, far from it; nor does she inculcate a doctrine of general celibacy. It is not a question with her of giving up a lesser joy for a greater, but simply of the way to remain true to the higher standard, which in accordance with the teaching of her age she identified with a life of chastity. Her position may appear untenable; con-

fusion of thought is a reproach which a later age readily casts on an earlier. But underneath what may seem unreasonable there is the aspiration for self-control. It is this aspiration which gives a wide and an abiding interest to her plays. For she is not hampered by narrowness of thought or by pettiness of spirit. . . . In the plays we find ourselves in a variety of surroundings and in contact with a wide range of personalities. The transition period from heathendom to Christianity supplies in most cases the mental and moral conflicts round which centres the interest of these plays.[34]

To see how she presented this material in a variety of moods—tragic, comic, heroic, romantic, and didactic—one needs only to examine the arguments contained in the title-prologue of each.

In *Gallicanus,* Part I, a woman's strategy results in the winning of a battle, the conversion of a would-be suitor, and his subsequent vow of celibacy. Part II retails his exile and martyrdom under Julian, the Apostate. John and Paul, who befriend him, also suffer death under the same tyrant and are thereby instrumental in converting their executioners.

In *Dulcitius,* the supernatural elements confound Dulcitius to his ridicule, and Sisinnius to his terror, when the virginity of the three maidens, Agape, Chionia, and Irena is preserved contrary to the merciless orders of Diocletian.

Calimachus' illicit and unwelcome love for Drusiana leads him to the brink of hell, when the intervention of John the Apostle restores him to life and grace.

Because of the prayerful influence of the holy monk, Abraham, Mary, his niece, turns from a life of sin and elects a life of penance and solitude.

The Thais legend lives again in *Pafnutius.* At the exhortation of this saintly hermit, the courtesan, Thais, renounces unlawful wordly pleasures for eternal joys.

The three Greek virgins, Faith, Hope, and Charity, through the sustaining strength and wisdom of their mother, Sapientia, endure a cruel and prolonged martyrdom at the hands of Hadrian.

Thus, Hrotsvitha selected her material on the basis of accessibility of sources, appeal to the contemporary mind, and antidotal force. In her zealous apostolate for the Church, although she complains of some little embarrassment in writing on such subjects, she nevertheless felt compelled to use the "manner" of Terence as well as the "matter," thus, her use of the dramatic form.

Zeydel chides the six reputable German scholars who authored *Das deutsche Drama*[35] for their neglect of

Hrotsvitha as a figure to be reckoned with in a consideration of the dramatic form:

> Far from beginning their work with Hrotsvitha, although her plays may well represent a clear-cut and acceptable basis for our knowledge of literature in the dramatic form during the tenth century, these scholars first devote over one hundred large pages to a discussion of the liturgical drama of the period from the twelfth to the fifteenth century growing out of the Easter and Christmas services of the Church, and their *ex post facto* deductions therefrom. Then finally, on page 109, in the opening portion of their chapter on the neo-Latin plays of the sixteenth century, written by Rudolf Wolkan, a short section is allotted to Hrotsvitha. The obvious reason for briefly disposing of her dramas thus belatedly derives from the feeling that, written in Latin and the side-tracked work of a recluse, these plays attained no significance until their publication by Conrad Celtes in 1501.[36]

Zeydel[37] further reports that the German humanists, Tritheim, Pirckheimer, and Dalberg, categorized the form used by Hrotsvitha as a later comedy of manners. Blashfield[38] supports this opinion but Magnin[39] reserves judgment on this point. However, he too, reproves Hrotsvithan scholars because they lack the courage to give this unique nun-dramatist her rightful place in the historical stream of drama.[40] Among literary historians, it is generally agreed that her plays are not liturgical in character, nor are they forerunners of the mystery, miracle, or morality plays. The majority of writers dismiss them as "pious exercises—intentionally didactic."

This art form as Hrotsvitha conceived it—a blend of religion, humor, and didacticism—was ideally suited to the Teutonic temperament. Blashfield notes this when she says:

> Hrotsvitha's work is of the new, the modern epoch, for it shows the form the Latin drama assumes in Teutonic hands. . . . It is a rough new wine of a younger race, of a more child-like faith, that Hrotsvitha pours into the old amphora, and the shapely vessel is fractured by the stir and ferment of the spirit within.[41]

Unlike the impatient audience of Terence, "the practical Teuton wanted plenty of time to be edified as well as delighted; he liked to be sermonized."[42] At the same time he wanted to give full vent to his imagination, and his main concern was with "the thought conveyed by the diction, not the elegance of style."[43] The scenes might take place in the palace of a pagan Emperor, on the battlefield, or in the desert cell of a hermit, but the language was the same—that of educated tenth-century Saxony. Magnin, in speaking of Hrotsvitha's language says:

> Strange thing! the language of the lover of the tenth century is as refined, as quintessential, as affected as that of the sixteenth and seventeenth centuries . . . only, in the poet of the Court of Elizabeth, the young lover is lost in the conceits of the Italian manner, while in Hrotsvitha, he exhausts himself in academic subtleties and distinctions of the doctrine of the Universals.[44]

This affectation of speech was as typical of the tenth century as euphemism was of the Elizabethan age. Blashfield, too, points out in the dialogue examples of "medieval courtesies" and of the "vernacular of the schoolmen of the tenth century."[45]

In her first work, *Gallicanus,* Hrotsvitha occasionally used narration to advance the plot. According to Creizenach:

> It took real inspiration to see that saints' legends which she and everyone else up to this time had handled in narrative form could be given as well, or better, in dialogue. And in adapting her material to the dramatic form, after the first awkward attempts, she shows a rare gift for seizing on the great moments of a story and presenting them strikingly.[46]

Thus in her later plays "she arranges the dialogue in such a manner that the advancing plot is completely absorbed within it."[47]

The strongest arguments offered to justify the inclusion of Hrotsvitha's works in dramatic anthology is the fact that her characters are authentic tenth-century Saxons. They are flesh and blood, three-dimensional, recognizable, not merely the personifications of vice and virtue.

Blashfield calls attention to male characters who are "the forerunners of the lovers, villains, and traitors of the Elizabethan drama," whose like, she says, "do not exist in the comedy of the ancients;" nor would we find "their counterparts among the cheats and rogues of Terence and Plautus."[48] Because of their modern blend of feminine dignity and dauntless spirit, the women characters are far removed from the soft, sweet, pagan heroines; they are "inhabitants of a different moral planet,"[49] representative of the mind which had not yet released itself from the chains of tradition, but which had gone far beyond to the freedom of inquiry. Hrotsvitha's characters, as it were, stood upon the crest of the millennium.

Blashfield, like many of the critics, accuses Hrotsvitha of violating the dramatic unities.[50] It is strange that so many theatre historians refer to this "famous neo-classic superstition." As for "unity of time," it finds support only in one brief passage of the *Poetics.* "Unity of place" is a deduction drawn by critics from the "unity of time." Should proponents of the "Three Unities" attempt to evaluate a Greek tragedy or even a later Greek comedy against this literary tradition, they would find more exception than adherence to the rule.[51] This study contends that Hrotsvitha does not violate the "one and only dramatic unity enjoined by Aristotle, the 'unity of action.'"[52]

Creizenach is one of the most vehement of the critics in his rejection of the dramas on this point. He claims that Hrotsvitha disregarded the limitations of stage presentation—"the distances, the spatial and temporal areas, in such a manner that her pieces would have been impossible upon the ancient stage."[53] This is not an acceptable thesis. The spatial and temporal disparities argued above do not present a problem in the actual staging of the plays. The scenes change in somewhat the same manner as the Elizabethan play of five centuries later. The opening lines of each scene set the time and place and create the mood; the closing lines provide the "curtain" as in the plays of both Terence and Shakespeare.

Throughout each play there is a "unity of action," which, according to Aristotle, is an "organic unity, an inward principle revealing itself in the form of an outward whole,"[54]—a dramatically constructed plot with a beginning, a middle, and an end representing a coherent organism and producing the pleasure proper to it.[55] Clearly, this absolves Hrotsvitha from the perennial accusation that she "violates the three unities," and it supports the conclusion that it is her expert and intuitively dramatic handling of material that merits for her a place among the playwrights.

Finally, there are strong evidences of three contemporary dramatic streams within Hrotsvitha's writings—the literary tradition of classical antiquity, the mimetic influence, and the liturgical form—and the traces of their concomitant theatrical characteristics.

Numerous are the comments—from derogatory to laudatory—regarding these traces of classic authors:

> Terence, the dear delight of the medieval monastery, was in the tenth century pruned of his pagan charm and naughtiness, and planted out in six persimmon comedies by a Saxon nun of Gandersheim, Hrotsvitha,—comedies of tedious saints and hircine sinners and a stuffy Latin style.[56]

> A woman of the darkest of the dark ages, she pored over the pagan poets, and knew her Terence as well as she did Boëthius, or the New Testament.[57]

> But though she might say of Terence as Dante did of Virgil, 'Tu duca, tu maestro, e tu signore,' she was moved by the greater master; indeed her convent-garden is fragrant with many grafts from

antique groves, and the spiritual spouse of Christ was a child of the pagan poets as well.[58]

> The fact that a nun was well aware and able not only to read and understand the poets, Horace, Ovid, Virgil, Plautus, and Terence but also set out to oppose these pagan authors and their works with a Christian work of art, was bound to attract the attention of everyone.[59]

The mimetic influence is strongly supported by Hermann Reich, a classical philologist, who edited Paul von Winterfeld's *Deutsche Dichter des lateinischen Mittelalters*:

> Reich believes that Hrotsvitha's age was 'völlig dramenlos' and that although her dramas fairly cry for performance and she herself, with the blood of the theatre in her veins, would have welcomed their production, her superiors would have vetoed any suggestion to have such sacred materials presented by profane jugglers and mimes, the only possible media of representation before spectators of that time. But both von Winterfeld and Reich are convinced that as a writer Hrotsvitha is strongly under the influence of the contemporary mimes, and that her plays according to von Winterfeld are 'bühnensicher'.[60]

The scholar, Wilhelm Scherer, not only admits the influence of the mimes on Hrotsvitha's plays but goes so far as to suggest the possibility of their performance by the mimes of her day.[61]

Zeydel contributes to the plausible existence of the third dramatic stream in Hrotsvitha's work. He affirms that if the nun-dramatist knew Notker's sequences and, as von Winterfeld believes, wrote her own, she would forge a link between her work and the liturgical drama.[62] That Hrotsvitha knew Notker is implied in Reich when he cites several instances which show similarities of style—devotion to detail, homely humor, terseness, anecdotal interspersions, insight into human behavior, and mystical elements.[63] These, as will be demonstrated, Hrotsvitha used in her dramas—some profusely, some sparingly. In addition, this study will identify passages which seem to contain the language of the liturgy.

Before proceeding with an examination of the text within the boundaries of these three influences—the classical, mimetic, and liturgical—some statement should be given summarizing the implications concerning Hrotsvitha's intention in writing in the dramatic form. Were the plays merely literary exercises intended for reading or were they genuine dramatic pieces intended for performance?

Whatever their subsequent disposition—reading or acting—one thing is clearly perceived, namely, Hrotsvitha's seriousness of purpose in writing them. "It is my object," she said, "to glorify virtue in the same medium as is used to glorify vice."[64] Again, "Modesty cannot deter me from using my pen to glorify the innocent to the best of my ability."[65] And again, "I strive only to use what talent I have for the glory of Him Who gave it me. Nor is my self-love so great that I would, to avoid criticism, abstain from proclaiming wherever possible the virtue of Christ working in His saints."[66]

Here are the words—strong and courageous—of a reformer. It is unthinkable that such clarity and singleness of purpose would be permitted to wither within a cloister cell. Hrotsvitha must have sought some means—quick and sure—to communicate her message. She found it in theatrical expression. Even though Reich believes that "Hrotsvitha's age was 'völlig dramenlos,'" here we have a playwright, a play, and an audience. Reich declares that her superiors would have vetoed any suggestion to use the mimes as actors. This is tantamount to declaring that the only legitimate theatre in existence during the tenth century was the theatre of the mimes. Since we know there was more than one type of theatre in existence, the problem of securing actors would not have been a serious one. Furthermore, it would have been highly inconsistent for her religious superiors to have spurred her efforts in the writing of this dramatic form and to have denied performance.

Further indications that the plays were meant to be acted, lie in the social structure of the day. The general public patronized the mimic shows and the liturgical dramas, leaving the more sophisticated plays of Terence to the educated class and to the nobility—either for viewing or reading. It was this group, the Terence admirers, that Hrotsvitha wished to reach. These people were frequently guests of the monastery. For their anticipated pleasure and subsequent edification, Hrotsvitha had no hesitancy in giving them the bitter pill of censure under the sweet cloak of drama, using the natural stage settings of the cloister and the natural talents of the canonesses.

Finally, the plays, in the words Zeydel, "fairly cry for performance."[67] The use of several dramatic devices within the dialogue—stichomythia, didascalia, oculia, and others—inherently require acting for effectiveness. Although, to the present, it has been impossible to marshal conclusive evidence for or against actual presentation, it should not prevent the acknowledgment that the plays themselves, the "spectacle-demanding" populace, and the talent and urgency of Hrotsvitha attest this intention.

Notes

[1] C. Magnin, *Théâtre de Hrotsvitha* (Paris: 1845), pp. xx-xxii. "Hrotsvitha nous apprend elle même qu'elle

vint au monde longtemps après la mort d'Othon l'Illustre, duc de Saxe, père de Henri l'Oiseleur, arrivée le 30 novembre 912. Ailleurs (préface de ses légendes en vers), elle se dit un peu plus âgée que la fille de Henri, duc de Bavière, Gerberge II, sacrée abbesse de Gandersheim l'an 959, et née, suivant toutes les apparences, vers l'an 940. Il résulte de ces deux indices combinés, que Hrotsvitha a dû naître entre les années 912 et 940, et beaucoup plus près de la seconde date que de la première, par conséquent, vers 930 ou 935. La date de sa mort est encore plus incertaine. Un seul point est hors de doute, c'est qu'elle poussa sa carrière fort au delà de l'an 968, puisque le fragment que nous reste du *Panégyrigue des Othons* comprend les événements de cette année, et que postérieurement à ce poeme, Hrothsvitha en composa un autre sur la fondation du monastère de Gandersheim. Casimir Oudin dit qu'elle mourut l'an 1001; elle aurait eu soixante-sept ans, si nous ne nous sommes pas trompés dans nos précédents calculs. Oudin fonde son opinion sur ce que Hrotsvitha a célébré les trois premiers Othons. Il est vrai que le premier livre du poëme, le suel qui subsiste, finit à la mort d'Othon Ier; mais le titre même de l'ouvrage (*Panegyris Oddonum*), prouve que nous n'en possédons que la première partie. La seconde dédicace addressée à Othon, roi des Romains, qui devint bientôt Othon II, formait probablement le préambule du second livre, consacré aux actions de ce prince. Ajoutons qu'on lit dans une chronique des évêques d'Hildesheim, que Hrotsvitha a célébré les trois Othons. De ce dernier fait, s'il était bien établi, il résulterait que notre auteur aurait vécu au delà de l'an 1002, ce qui n'aurait, d'ailleurs, rien que de très-vraisemblable."

[2] K. Algermissen, "Die Gestalt Mariens," *Unsere Diözese,* XXIII (1954), 139. "Als frühestes Jahr ihrer Geburt kann wohl 932, als frühestes Jahr ihres Todes 1003 angesehen werden. Sie ist also gut 70 Jahre alt geworden."

[3] C. St. John, *The Plays of Roswitha* (London: 1923), p. x.

[4] K. Strecker, *Hrotsvithae Opera* (Leipzig: 1906), p. 2, fol. 2^r, 11. 3-4.

[5] Evangeline W. Blashfield, *Portraits and Backgrounds* (New York: Charles Scribner's Sons, 1917), p. 12.

[6] Strecker, p. 1, fol. 2^r, 11. 28-29; p. 2, fol. 2^r, 11. 2-3.

[7] *Ibid.,* p. 222, fol. 131^v, 1.21.

[8] *Ibid.,* p. 224, fol. 133^r, vss. 11-14.

[9] Blashfield, p. 25.

[10] Magnin, p. xiii. "Suivant les uns, Hrotsvitha l'abbesse

sortait de la seconde branche de la famille ducale de Saxe, et était fille du duc Othon l'Illustre, second fils de Ludolfe et père de l'empereur Henry l'Oiseleur."

[11] Algermissen, "Die Gestalt," p. 139.

[12] *Ibid.,* p. 141. "Die vierte Äbtissin, Hrotsvitha, vermutlich eine Tante unserer Dichterin, war 919 vom Konvent gewählt und vom Hildesheimer Bischof Walbert (903-919) eingesegnet."

[13] When Hrotsvitha said of herself, "I, the strong [or loud] voice of Gandersheim," she provided a fertile source of comment for writers who have attributed many and varied meanings to her statement. Algermissen explains that her name signifies "strong storm . . . it actually is a compound of *Hroud* (sound) and *souid* (strong or clear), and according to the original, the spelling of her name should have been "Hroudsouid," ("Die Gestalt," 139). This is undoubtedly the simplest and most nearly correct interpretation for "Ego, clamor validus." Cf. p. 192, n. 91.

[14] Algermissen, "Die Gestalt," p. 139.

[15] Strecker, p. 114, fol. 79[r], 1. 32; p. 115, 11. 1-2, 16-19; fol. 79[v], 11. 20-23. "Vestra admiratione dignum duxistis et largitorem in me operantis gratiae. . . . Deum namque, cuius solummodo gratia sum id, quod sum, in me laudari cordetenus gaudeo; sed maior, quam sim, videri timeo, quia utrumque nefas esse non ambigo, et gratuitum dei donum negare, et non acceptum accepisse simulare. Unde non denego praestante gratia creatoris per dynamin me artes scire, quia sum animal capax disciplinae, sed per energian fateor omnino nescire."

[16] *Ibid.,* p. 1, fol. 1[v], 11. 18-21; fol. 2[r], 11. 23, 28-29; p. 2, fol. 2[r], 1. 2. " . . . quanto in ipsa inceptione minus ulla proprii vigoris fulciebar sufficientia; quia nec matura adhuc aetate vigens nec scientia fui proficiens, . . . pro rusticitate, . . . sapientissimae atque benignissimae Rikkardis magistrae, . . . prona favente clementia regiae indolis Gerbergae."

[17] *Ibid.,* p. 221, fol. 131[r], 11. 1-15; p. 222, fol. 131[v], 11. 5-14. Gerbergae, illustri abbatissae, cui pro sui eminentia probitatis haut minor obsequela venerationis, quam pro insigni regalis stemmate generositatis, Hrotsvit Gandeshemensis, ultima ultimarum sub huiusmodi personae dominio militantium, quod famula herae. O mea domna, quae rutilanti spiritalis varietate sapientiae prae lucetis, non pigescat vestri almitiem perlustrare, quod vestra confectum si ignoratis ex iussione. Id quidem oneris mihi inposuistis, ut gesta caesaris augusti, quae nec auditu unquam affatim valui colligere, metrica percurrerem ratione. In huius sudore progressionis quantum meae inscitiae obstiturit difficultatis, ipsa conicere potestis, quia haec eadem nec prius scripta repperi, nec ab aliquo digestim sufficienterque dicta elicere quivi. . . . Nunc autem omne latus tanto magis caret defensione,

quanto minus ulla fulcitur auctoritate; unde etiam verior me temeritatis argui tendiculasque multorum non devitare convicii, eo quod pomposis facetae urbanitatis exponenda eloquentiis praesumpserim dehonestare inculti vilitate sermonis. Si tamen sanae mentis examen accesserit, quae res recte pensare non nescit, quanto sexus fragilior scientiaque minor, tanto venia erit facilior; praesertim cum si meae praesumptionis, sed vestrum causa iussionis huius stamen opusculi coeperim ordiri."

[18] L. Eckenstein, *Women in Monasticism* (Cambridge: 1896), pp. 160-161.

[19] H. Goetting, "Die Anfänge des Reichsstifts Gandersheim," *Braunschweigisches Jahrbuch,* XXXI (1950), 10.

[20] Strecker, p. 1, fol. 2[r], 11. 23-25; p. 2, fol. 2[r], 11. 6-12. "Unde clam cunctis et quasi furtim, nunc in componendis sola desudando, nunc male composita destruendo. . . . Quamvis etiam metrica modulatio femineae fragilitati difficilis videatur et ardua, solo tamen semper miserentis supernae gratiae auxilio, non propriis viribus, confisa, huius carmina opusculi dactilicis modulis succinere apposui, ne crediti talentum ingenioli sub obscuro torpens pectoris (antro) rubigine exterminaretur neglegentiae."

[21] Algermissen, "Die Gestalt," p. 139 "Die erste christliche Dichterin Niedersachsens und unserer Hildesheimer Diözese ist zugleich die erste deutsche Dichterin. Sie ist die erste dramatische Dichterin der ganzen christlichen Welt, deren Dramen den ersten Versuch einer christlichen Dramatik überhaupt bedeuten."

[22] Robert H. Fife, *Roswitha of Gandersheim,* (New York: Columbia University Press, 1947), pp. 6-7.

[23] Charles S. Baldwin, *Medieval Rhetoric and Poetic* (New York: Macmillan, 1928), p. 144.

[24] P. Chasles, *Le Moyen Age* (Paris: 1876), p. 297.

[25] Strecker, "Abraham," vi, 171, 27.

[26] Chasles, pp. 305-306. " . . . le balancement et la molle cadence de ces vers, ce sont en effet des vers modernes. On n'a, pour s'en convaincre, qu'à suivre pas à pas le latin de Hrotsvita et à calquer, vers pour vers, des lignes françaises d'un nombre égal de pieds et de rimes sous ses lignes latines: . . . Peut-on nommer cela de la prose? Evidemment la religieuse a écrit en vers sans le savoir."

[27] *Ibid.,* pp. 307-308.

[28] Magnin, pp. vi-vii. "Ce célèbre monastère a été pour

l'Allemagne une sorte d'oasis intellectuelle, jetée au milieu des steppes de la barbarie."

[29] Blashfield, p. 30.

[30] Ernst Rudolf Köpke, *Die älteste deutsche Dichterin* (Berlin: E. S. Mittler und Sohn, 1869), p. 28.

[31] A. Ebert, "Hrotsvith Opera," *Allgemeine Geschichte der Literatur des Abendlandes,* III (1887), 285-290.

[32] K. A. Barack, *Die Werke der Hrotsvitha* (Nurnberg: Bauer und Raspe, 1858), p. 54.

[33] Strecker, p. 113, fol. 78[r], 11. 1-25; p. 114, fol. 78[v], 11. 11-18. "Plures inveniuntur catholici, cuius nos penitus expurgare nequimus facti, qui pro cultioris facundia sermonis gentilium vanitatem librorum utilitati praeferunt sacrarum scripturarum. Sunt etiam alii, sacris inhaerentes paginis, qui licet alia gentilium spernant, Terrentii tamen fingmenta frequentius lectitant et, dum dulcedine sermonis delectantur, nefandarum notitia rerum maculantur. Unde ego, Clamor Validus Gandeshemensis, non recusavi illum imitari dictando, dum alii colunt legendo, quo eodem dictationis genere, quo turpia lascivarum incesta feminarum recitabantur, laudabilis sacrarum castimonia virginum iuxta mei facultatem ingenioli celebraretur. Hoc tamen facit non raro verecundari gravique rubore perfundi, quod, huiusmodi specie dictationis cogente detestabilem inlicite amantium dementiam et male dulcia colloquia eorum, quae nec nostro auditui permittuntur accom-modari, dictando mente tractavi et stili officio designavi. Sed (si) haec erubescendo neglegerem, nec proposito satisfacerem nec innocentium laudem adeo plene iuxta meum posse exponerem, quia, quanto blanditiae amantium promptiores ad illiciendum, tanto et superni adiutoris gloria sublimior et triumphantium victoria probatur gloriosior, praesertim cum feminea fragilitas vinceret et virilis robur confusioni subiaceret. . . . Si enim alicui placet mea devotio, gaudebo; si autem vel pro mei abiectione vel pro vitiosi sermonis rusticitate placet nulli, memet ipsam tamen iuvat, quod feci, quia, dum proprii vilitatem laboris, in aliis meae inscientiae opusculis heroico ligatam strophio, in hoc dramatica vinctam serie colo, perniciosas gentilium delicias abstinendo devito." (Translation from Eckenstein, pp. 168-169.)

[34] Eckenstein, pp. 169-170.

[35] E. Zeydel "Were Hrotsvitha's Dramas Performed?" *Speculum,* XX (1943), 447, n. 1.

[36] *Ibid., "Das deutsche Drama* in Verbindung mit Julius Bab, Albert Ludwig, Friedrich Michael, Max J. Wolff und Rudolf Wolkan herausgegeben von Robert F. Arnold. Munich, 1925."

[37] *Ibid.*

[38] Blashfield, pp. 20-23. "Hrotsvitha's comedies are, in spite of their archaic subject matter, comedies of manners. . . . It is no longer a comedy of movement and manners like that of Plautus, nor of situations and poetic declamation like the work of Terence. It seeks to become ethical like the drama of Greece."

[39] Magnin, p. lii. "S'il est vrai, comme on l'a dit souvent, que la comédie soit l'expression de la société, la comparison que nous sommes à portée de faire entre les deux pièces de Hrothsvita, le colloque d'Érasme et le drame de Decker nous offrirait un moyen sûr et piquant d'apprécier la valeur morale des trois époques."

[40] *Ibid.,* p. lv. "Ces six drames sont un dernier rayon de l'antiquité classique, une imitation prémédités et assez peu reconnaissable, j'en conviens; des comédies´ de Térence, sur lesquels le christianisme et la barbarie ont déposé leur double empreinte; mais c'est précisément par ce qu'ils ont de chrétien et même de barbare, c'est-à-dire, par ce que leur physionomie nous offre de moderne, que ces drames m'ont paru mériter d'être recueillis à part et traduits avec soin, pour prendre rang à la suite du théâtre ancien, et à la tête des collections théâtrales de toutes les nations de l'Europe."

[41] Blashfield, pp. 20-21.

[42] *Ibid.,* p. 21.

[43] *Ibid.*

[44] Magnin, p. xlvii. "Chose étrange! la langue de l'amour au Xe siècle est aussi raffinée, aussi quintessenciée, aussi précieuse qu' aux XVI et XVIIes siècles . . . dans le poète de la cour d'Élizabeth, le jeune amoureux se perd en *concetti* à la mode italienne, tandis que, dans Hrotsvitha, il s'epuise, suivant le goût de l'époque, en arguties scolastiques et en distinctions tirées de la doctrine des *universaux.*"

[45] Blashfield, p. 23.

[46] Wilhelm Creizenach, *Geschichte des neueren Dramas* (Halle: Niemeyer, 1911), I, 19.

[47] *Ibid.*

[48] Blashfield, pp. 23-23.

[49] *Ibid.,* p. 24.

[50] *Ibid.,* pp. 25 and 33.

[51] S. H. Butcher, *Aristotle's Theory of Poetry* (New York: 1951), p. 291. "In the *Eumenides,* months or years elapse between the opening of the play and the

next scene. The *Trachiniae* of Sophocles and the *Supplices* of Euripides afford other and striking instances of the violation of the so-called rule. In the *Agamemnon,* even if a definite interval of days cannot be assumed between the fire-signals announcing the fall of Troy and the return of Agamemnon, at any rate, the conditions of time are disregarded and the march of events is imaginatively accelerated."

[52] *Ibid.,* pp. 288-289.

[53] Creizenach, p. 18.

[54] Butcher, pp. 31-35.

[55] *Ibid.,* pp. 187-188.

[56] C. M. Gayley, *Plays of Our Forefathers* (New York: Duffield, 1907), p. 2.

[57] Blashfield, p. 9.

[58] *Ibid.,* p. 27.

[59] Algermissen, "Die Gestalt," p. 142. "Dass eine Klosterfrau die römischen Dichter Horaz, Ovid, Vergil, Plautus and Terenz nicht nur las und verstand, dass sie auch daranging, jenen heidnischen Dichtern und ihren Werken ein christliches Dichtungswerk entgegenzustellen, musste aller Augen auf sich lenken."

[60] E. Zeydel, "Were Hrotsvitha's Dramas Performed?" *Speculum,* XX (1943), 445.

[61] *Geschichte der deutschen Literatur* (Berlin: Weidmann, 1899), pp. 57-59.

[62] Zeydel, "Hrotsvitha's Dramas," p. 445.

[63] Winterfeld-Reich, *Deutsche Dichter des lateinischen Mittelalters in deutschen Versen* (Munich: 1913), p. 449. "Man denke an Notker und Hrotsvit. Notkers beste Kraft liegt in seinem echt schwäbischen, an G. Keller gemahnenden Humor, mit dem er alles zu vergolden weiss: die Fabel vom kranken Löwen und das Lügenmärchen vom Wunschbock, das noch heute an des Bodensees Ufern lebendig ist, wie die Anekdoten vom Kaiser Karl, dessen überragende Grösse sich im Andenken der Nachwelt nicht schöner abbilden konnte, als es in Notkers Geiste geschehen ist, alles umfassend, das Grösste wie das Kleinste. Der treue Lehrer seiner Schüler, an denen er hängt, auch wenn sie es ihm nimmer danken, dessen Briefe an Mörikes 'Musterkärtchen' erinnern, und der geniale Schöpfer der Sequenz, der die geistliche Lyrik auf Jahrhunderte in neue Bahnen wies, dessen Grösse es ist, dass er im Göttlichen stets das Reinmenschliche zu sehen weiss, dass er das göttliche Geheimnis dem Herzen nahe zu bringen versteht, er ist in seiner liebevoll sinnigen Art

Schwabe durch und durch. Ganz anders die Nonne von Gandersheim. Herbe und verschlossen ist sie, trotz Annette von Droste-Hülshoff, und verbirgt die tief innerliche Weichheit ihres Wesens, dass sie nur hier und da, wo sie von ihrem lieben Gandersheim redet oder liebevoll verweilt bei der Charakteristik ihrer heiligen Jungfrauen, die ihr Schwester, Kind und heiliges Vorbild zugleich sind, unerwartet und schier elementar durchbricht. Ist Notkers Kennzeichen die Lust am Fabulieren, die liebevoll das Bild aus tausend kleinen, feinen Einzelzügen zusammenstrichelt, die ihn in den Sequenzen befähigt, das ganze Lied auf ein Bild zu stellen, daraus aber auch alles hervorzuholen, was darin liegt, so liebt sie es, kurz und knapp, mit wenigen Worten ihr Bild zu umreissen, und führt in ihren Dramen, worin ein geistvoller Erklärer Nordseeluft zu spüren gemeint hat, mit sicherer Hand die Fäden der Handlung: man denkt unwillkürlich an Hebbel. Freilich muss man dabei nicht Massstäbe anlegen, die für ihre Zeit und deren so ganz eigen geartete Kunst nicht passen; doch darüber wird später zu reden sein."

[64] St. John, p. xxvi.

[65] *Ibid.,* p. xxvii.

[66] *Ibid.*

[67] Zeydel, "Hrotsvitha's Dramas," p. 450.

Anne Lyon Haight (essay date 1965)

SOURCE: "Hroswitha of Gandersheim: Her Life, Her Times, Her Works" in *Hroswitha of Gandersheim: Her Life, Times, and Works, and Comprehensive Bibliography,* The Hroswitha Club, 1965, pp. 3-34.

[*In the following essay, Haight surveys the life and writings of Hroswitha, terming her "the most remarkable woman of her time."*]

The most remarkable woman of her time was Hroswitha, the tenth-century canoness of the Benedictine monastery of Gandersheim, Saxony. She was the earliest poet known in Germany and the first dramatist after the fall of the ancient stage of classical times.

In 1494 Conrad Celtes, the Renaissance humanist and first poet laureate of Germany, found an early and incomplete manuscript (*Munich Codex*) of the work of this "German Sappho," as he called her, in the monastery of Saint Emmeram at Regensburg. He published it in 1501, but unfortunately changed the order of her works and made "corrections." It had been lying forgotten for almost six hundred years and her name had slipped into obscurity.

Her writings, as far as they are known, include eight sacred legends in verse, six dramas in rhymed prose, two historical poems, three prose prefaces, several dedications, and finally a poem which compresses *The Revelation* [*Vision*] *of St. John* into thirty-five lines. His Eminence Cardinal Gasquet said of her: "Hroswitha's works have a claim to an eminent place in medieval literature, and do honour to her sex, to the age in which she lived, and to the vocation which she followed."

All we know of this gifted poet is what she tells us in her writings, and what the historians have pieced together by aligning their contents with the scant annals of her time. It has been deduced that she was born about 935, for she says in a preface that her Abbess, the Princess Gerberga, whose known date of birth was 940, was younger than she. The date of her death is also uncertain, but has been placed about 1001-1002.

The tenth century has been called the Dark Ages, but due to the Carolingian renaissance, Germany had become a country of enlightenment and learning. Although it was only at the end of the eighth century that the tribes accepted Christianity—Saxony being the last to do so—thus submitting to Charlemagne's grim threat of acceptance or death, the chieftains, within a few decades, were forgetting paganism and were building churches and endowing monasteries under native bishops.

At the end of the ninth century twenty cloisters were recorded in Saxony, eleven of them nunneries—containing both Benedictine straight nuns and canonesses. One of the first was Gandersheim, the Abbey of Hroswitha, who was to record its history later in her historical poem ***Primordia Coenobii Gandeshemensis.*** It was established first at Brunshausen on the River Gande; later Bishop Altfrid laid the cornerstone of Gandersheim at a more advantageous site about twenty miles from the present city of Hildesheim. The monastery was consecrated on All Saints' Day in 881. Thankmar wrote about the canonesses being moved at that time from Brunshausen to Gandersheim, although some of the nuns were presumed to have remained behind for a time.

The monastery was founded by Duke Liudolf at the request of his Frankish wife Oda and her mother Aeda. Hroswitha says in her ***Primordia*** that Liudolf was, from his earliest years, in the service of the great Louis I, King of the Franks, and was elevated by him to distinguished honors. Aeda, who was deeply religious, had been visited by a vision of Saint John the Baptist who informed her that her famous progeny would someday establish a cloister for saintly maidens. Consequently, Liudolf and Oda made a pilgrimage to Rome to acquire sacred relics and receive the blessing of Pope Sergius II. They petitioned the Frankish King Louis (Ludovic the German, grandson of Charlemagne) for an introduction to the Pope, fitted out a large traveling retinue, and prepared valuable presents. Much impressed with the Duke and his Lady (Hroswitha recounts), the Pope gave them the bones "of two mighty shepherds, Anastasius, the most holy bishop of his throne, and his co-apostle, the sacred Innocent." The holy relics were carried in triumph to Saxony, and Anastasius and Innocent became the patron saints of Gandersheim. The monastery became one of the richest and most distinguished of the convents founded by Liudolf, whose descendants formed the dynasty that ruled Germany in Hroswitha's time. His son Otto the Illustrious lived to see the monastery completed.

Members of the families of the great Saxon patrons often entered their religious establishments, and the first three Abbesses of Gandersheim were daughters of Liudolf and Oda. Hathmodo, the eldest, was born in 840 and was consecrated in 852 at the age of twelve. Goetting, in his *Die Anfaenge,* says that she was sent to be educated in the convent of Herford, which was from the beginning closely connected with the Kloster Corvey, where her brother Agius was a monk. Herford became the model for the many Saxon *Kanonissenstifte,* founded later. Agius also tells about Herford in his *Vita.*

Hathmodo was followed as Abbess at Gandersheim by her sisters Gerberga I and by Christine, who died in 919. They in turn were followed by Hroswitha I [Hroswitha I, the fourth Abbess of Gandersheim, ruled from 919 to 926. It is not known if she was related in any way to the canoness Hroswitha who is the subject of this book.] and Wendelgard, and it was not until Princess Gerberga II became Abbess in 959 that a member of the royal family ruled again. Gerberga II, the friend and teacher of Hroswitha, was the daughter of Henry, Duke of Bavaria, the niece of Otto I, Henry's brother, and the granddaughter of the great Saxon king, Henry the Fowler, who ruled from 919 to 936. Having won leadership by checking the raids of the wild Hungarians and driving back the heathen Slavs, Henry, the Duke of Bavaria, was given the crown and sceptre by Eberhard, Duke of the Franks, after the death of his brother Conrad, King of Germany.

Otto I, following in his father Henry's footsteps, defeated their enemies once and for all, quelled civil war, conquered northern Italy, and was crowned King of the Lombards in Pavia, the capital, where in 951 he married Adelaide, widow of the Italian King Lothar II (his first wife Edith of England had died a few years before). The following year Otto I received the Imperial Crown from Pope John XII in appreciation for restoring law and order in Italy, and became the founder of the Holy Roman Empire of the German people. Under him the arts flourished and books were penned. He was a great statesman, a patron of learning, and a benefactor of the church, although he deposed Pope John XII for treachery.

Hroswitha wrote the **Gesta Ottonis,** a history of his reign. In Celtes' 1501 publication of her works, Albrecht Dürer pictured her kneeling before the Emperor to present her book while the Abbess Gerberga II looked on. It was during this reign, when Wendelgard was Abbess, that Hroswitha entered the monastery. If the conjecture is correct that it was in 955, it was the year in which Otto II was born. Later Hroswitha and Otto II were to become great friends.

Otto II, who was also crowned Holy Roman Emperor to rule jointly with his father, married Theophano, daughter of the Byzantine Emperor Romanus II. She had great influence and introduced many refinements from the court at Constantinople, such as the wearing of silks and the taking of baths, as well as Greek art and customs. After the death of Otto II in 983, Theophano ruled for Otto III as co-regent with the boy's grandmother, Adelaide.

It is interesting to note the various foreign influences introduced into the monastery during the reign of the three Ottos through their conquests and their marriages. Archbishop Bruno of Cologne brought many scholars to Gandersheim, where they contributed to the atmosphere of learning and literary activity which surrounded Hroswitha. She tells of her association with the scholars, churchmen, and royal personages who came and went, for the court and monastery were closely allied. We know that Greek was taught to the Abbess Gerberga and her sister Hedwig, and it is possible that Hroswitha learned the language as well, for she used Greek sources for some of her stories.

Gandersheim was a free Abbey, which means that the Abbess was directly responsible to the King rather than to the church. However, in 947 Otto I freed the Abbey from royal rule and gave the Abbess supreme authority. She had her court of law, sent her men-at-arms to battle, coined her own money (some of which is still extant), and had a right to a seat in the Imperial Diet. Goetting, Algermissen, and other historians of the ninth- and tenth-century cloisters refer to Gandersheim as containing Benedictine straight nuns as well as can-onesses. The discipline of the latter order was not as strict; the canonesses were only required to take vows of chastity and obedience, and not that of poverty. This gave them freedom to be a part of the world, and yet protected from it by the sacred veil of virginity. The canonesses were allowed to receive guests, to go and come with permission, to own books, to own property, and were permitted to have servants, although they lived a communal life and took part in the daily recitation of the Divine Office.

We learn from the *Catholic Encyclopedia* that "towards the end of the eighth century the title of canoness is found for the first time, and was given to those communities of women, who while they professed a common life, yet did not carry out to the full extent the original rule of Saint Anthony of Hippo written in 423." Conrad Celtes and other biographers have called Hroswitha a "nun" as the term was broadly used in the Middle Ages to denote one who lived in a nunnery, regardless of which vows she had taken. The priest Eberhard referred to Gandersheim and neighboring convents in his chronicle of 1215 as "Kanonissenkonvent, Kanonissenkloster and Kanonissenstift." These convents were renowned for their learning and for the excellence of their dedicated teachers.

Nothing is known of Hroswitha's background except that she must have been of noble birth: the canoness convents only accepted novices from noble families. It is not known if she was related to Hroswitha I, the fourth Abbess of Gandersheim, who ruled from 919 to 926. Hroswitha's name has been spelled in many different ways, but she called herself "Clamor Validus Gandersheimensis," the strong voice of Gandersheim, and she mentioned her own name six times in her writings. Dr. Kurt Kronenberg says that the reason her name and works may have remained unknown for so many years was because before the twelfth century it was not the custom to record the names of any except highly placed persons, such as royalty and church dignitaries; although Hroswitha was a great scholar who made Gandersheim famous, she was only a canoness.

She probably entered the cloister when very young, as her skill in Latin points to many years of training under teachers well versed in Latin prosody. Her knowledge of classical and religious literature is evidence that Gandersheim had a rich collection of manuscripts, and the library must have been the center of her intellectual life in the cloister. Dr. Robert Fife said: "Judged by any standard Hroswitha's range of reading was wide and diversified and must have included Virgil's *Aeneid,* and possibly the *Georgics,* the *Eclogues,* Ovid's *Metamorphoses* and Terence's comedies, which she informs us influenced the writing of her plays. She probably read the writers of the early Christian centuries like Prudentius and Venantius Fortunatus. Above all, she seems to be indebted to the great Roman philosopher and statesman of the sixth century, Boethius, whose adherence to Christianity is much doubted by modern historians, but whom Hroswitha's contemporaries revered as a martyr to the Faith. She certainly had some introduction into Scholastic philosophy, mathematics, astronomy and especially music, of which she has shown technical knowledge. But what her young imagination seized upon most avidly was the Apocryphal stories of Christ and the Apostles and above all, the legends of the Saints, familiar reading in the churches and the cloisters of the Middle Ages." The legends, reflecting the triumphs in purity of many martyrs through their faith, filled her with religious ecstasy which is echoed in her solemn and impassioned verse. To her, chastity was the crown of the holy life.

Except for a few intercalated stanzas, Hroswitha's poetry is all in the heroic measures of the classical world, the dactylic hexameter, or in the elegiac verse, composed of two-lined strophes alternately dactylic hexameter and pentameter. She took her patterns from Virgil and the classical authors, but used the rhymed modification that was popular among early medieval writers.

There is no doubt that Hroswitha wrote the eight legends in verse first. The first five were written with a preface and a dedication to Gerberga II, and the last three carried an additional dedication. This modest poet tells in her self-revealing preface, as translated by Sister M. Gonsalva Wiegand, O.S.F.:

> This little volume, adorned with but slight charm of style, but nevertheless labored upon, with no little effort, I offer for the criticism of those kindly and learned minds who take pleasure, not in exposing to ridicule a writer's faults but rather in correcting them. For I admit that I have made many errors not only in prosody but also in literary composition, and that there is much to be discovered in this collection which is deserving of severe censure. But by admitting my shortcomings I may expect a ready pardon, and a kindly correction of my errors.

> Moreover, if the objection is made that, according to the judgment of some, portions of this work have been borrowed from Apocryphal sources, to this I would answer that I have erred through ignorance and not through reprehensible presumption. For when I started to weave the thread of this collection, I was not aware of the fact that the authenticity of the material upon which I planned to work was questionable. When I discovered the real state of affairs, I declined to discard my subject matter, on the plea that what appears to be false, may eventually be proved to be true.

> Under such conditions, my need of the assistance of many in defending this little work now completed is in exact proportion to my lack of native ability for the task at its inception. For as I was both young in years and not much advanced in learning, I did not have the courage to make known my intention by consulting any of the learned, for fear that they would put a stop to my work because of its crudeness of style.

> Unknown to others and secretly, so to speak, I worked alone. Sometimes I composed with great effort, again I destroyed what I had poorly written; and thus I strove according to my ability, scarcely adequate though that was, none the less to complete a composition from the thoughts in the writing with which I had become acquainted within the confines of our monastery at Gandersheim: first through the

> instructive guidance of our learned and kindly teacher Rikkardis, and of others who taught in her stead; and then through the gracious considerations of the royal Gerberga, under whose rule as Abbess I am living at present. Though she is younger in years than I am, yet, as befits a niece of the Emperor, she is farther advanced in learning, and she it was who right kindly instructed me in those various authors whom she herself studied under the guidance of learned teachers.

> Even though the art of prosody may seem difficult and arduous for one of my feeble sex, nevertheless, relying in my own strength, I have attempted to sing the songs of this little collection in the dactylic strains, solicitous that the slight talent of ability given me by Heaven should not lie idle in the dark recesses of the mind and thus be destroyed by the rust of neglect, I submitted it under the mallet of ready devotion, so that thus it might sound some little cord of Divine praise. Thus, though I had not the opportunity to achieve any other gain through use of that talent, it might at least be transformed into an instrument of value at the end.

> Wherefore, gentle reader, whosoever thou mayest be, if thou art truly wise before God, do not hesitate to lend the assistance of thy correcting power to the poor page which lacks the skill of a master hand. If, however, thou findest something which is worthy of approval, give credit to God for this success and at the same time ascribe all the blemishes to my lack of care.

> Let this be done, not in a spirit of censure, but of kindliness; for the keen edge of censure is blunted when it encounters the humility of self-depreciation.

Then Hroswitha addresses her Abbess.

> Dedication to Gerberga: Hail, illustrious offspring of a royal race! Gerberga, renowned for thy character and thy learning. Fostering Mistress, do thou accept with kindly mien these little verses which I offer for thy correction, and do thou graciously direct the crude measures of her whom thine excellent precepts instruct. And when thou art indeed wearied with thy manifold labors, do thou deign to recreate thyself in the conning of these measures, and attempt to purify the unlovely muse and to uphold her by the prestige of thine office.

> Thus may the zeal of the pupil enhance the praise of the mistress, and the poems of the devoted disciple, the praise of the teacher.

The Eight Sacred Legends

Hroswitha used poetic freedom in the psychological treatment of her characters and their actions. Her writings are varied in subject and are filled with miracles.

The first poem, *Maria,* she tells us, was taken from the *Apocryphal Gospel of Saint James* and is in honor of the Virgin Mary. After an impassioned appeal to the "Illustrious Mother of the King, the resplendent Star of the Sea," Hroswitha tells with humble piety of the miraculous birth of the Virgin, her marriage, the Birth of the Christ-child, and their flight into Egypt. This is followed by a short but tender narrative of *The Ascension of our Lord,* translated, she says, by John the Bishop from Greek into Latin. She ends with the appeal, "May he whoever reads these lines, say with a pitying heart: Gentle King, have mercy on poor Hroswitha and spare her, and grant that she may with grace from Heaven continue to sing Thy Divine praises, who in verse has set forth Thy Marvels."

Her third legend, drawn from the store of marvelous narratives from which *The Acts of the Saints* were assembled, tells of Gongolf, a Frankish leader in the Merovingian age in France, who won all hearts by his beauty and godliness. His beautiful but faithless wife plotted against him with a lover of low descent who murdered the saint, and the guilty ones fled. However, divine justice follows swiftly. By heaven's decree the murderer "poured out bowels and heart, so lately puffed with pride and sin," and when the wicked consort vents her scorn upon the pilgrims at the wonder-working tomb of the martyr, she is condemned to bring forth loathsome sounds "so that she, who had refused to maintain due chastity, was a source of uncontrolled ridicule to all."

It will be seen that some of those whom Hroswitha calls "saints" are not saints of the Church, but saints in the sense used by Saint Paul in his Epistle to the Romans, in which he calls all Christians "Saints."

The next poem deals with a more recent martyr, the Spanish youth Pelagius, who fell victim to a lecherous Moorish despot. Hroswitha said that she had heard the story from a visitor from Cordova who had been an eyewitness, hence the realistic description. When the Christian youth repelled the Mohammedan ruler, he was condemned to death; his execution was attended by a series of miracles. Pelagius was hurled by a catapult high over the walls of the city, and fell upon the rocks unharmed. He was then beheaded, "while his soul soars aloft to realms of celestial glory where no words of piety can describe the gleam of his laurel crown, coruscant with the chastity which he had so well maintained."

The Fall and Conversion of Theophilus is the last poem in this group. It is based on the old Greek story of a bond with the Devil whereby earthly joys are given in return for eternal damnation. Theophilus was the first of the medieval figures to become the hero of this theme—one which was repeated in succeeding years down to Goethe's *Faust.* Jealousy and ambition drove

him to accept the aid of the Evil One, but God did not desert the recreant soul in whose heart good blazed into penitence. The Holy Virgin yielded to his prayers and forced the Devil to return the contract. Hroswitha's penetration of the agonies he suffered in his final ascent to sanctity is most touching.

Hroswitha dedicated the last three of the eight poems to her beloved Abbess: "Behold, I bring to thee, Gerberga, my Lady, new verses, thus adding songs to the songs I have been commissioned to write; and how a wretched sinner won loving forgiveness, I joyfully sing in dactylic strains; do not choose to spurn these, even though they be exceedingly crude, but do thou praise with gentle heart the works of God."

The first poem in this group, *Basilius,* has again the Faustian theme of the conflict between good and evil. A rich man of Caesarea, wishing to save the soul of his only daughter whom he loved with deep affection, "planned to associate her with the holy maidens who were consecrated to Christ by the sacred veil of virginity and protected in the narrow enclosure of the monastery." However, her servant conceived a passion for her and appealed to the Devil, who planted a reciprocal passion in the breast of the innocent maiden. Hroswitha understands well the human frailties of the world and unravels the plot with great dexterity, and good triumphs over evil.

The seventh legend was altered from an old *Vita* and tells the vivid story of Dionysius of Athens, said to have been converted by Saint Paul and "subsequently chosen bishop of a Christian flock." The Pope sent him to Paris to convert the Gauls and a struggle ensued between paganism and Christianity, "but the fierce deceit of the ancient serpent raged thereupon in indignation that he should now lose so many souls which he had previously been holding captive in the bitter snares of error." Consequently Dionysius was beheaded. "Then the headless trunk of the dead pontiff raised itself in calm beauty, and lifting its own head in its strong arms—and passing over the tedious distance of two miles—it came to a spot fit for the preservation of that body."

In the last of the poems, Agnes, "a virgin who, desiring to despise the empty vanities of a perishable world and the luxury of the frail flesh," suffered martyrdom in defense of her virginity. Hroswitha tells in a most worldly fashion of how Agnes, having refused the offer of marriage from a pagan youth, was "deprived of her garments and with body entirely exposed to be dragged in the midst of a great concourse of people that had gathered, and to be shut up in the dark den of a brothel, in which wanton youths, maddened with passion, delighted in association with evil women. But Christ bringing consolation to His own spouse, did not suffer her to be touched by any one of these revelers. For when she was thus exposed—immediately the luxuriant hair, which hung in loose tresses—grew longer, and in its descent reached the tender soles of her feet so that her entire body was covered." She was condemned to be burned, but when the flames failed to burn her, she was slain with a sword, and an angel bore her soul aloft with celestial splendor, while she waved farewell to her parents.

In a brief note placed between the legends and the plays, Hroswitha speaks of her sources: "I found all the material I have used in this book in various ancient works by authors of reputation, with the exception of the story of the martyrdom of St. Pelagius, which has been told here in verse. The details of this were supplied to me by an inhabitant of the town where the Saint was put to death. This truthful stranger assured me that he had not only seen Pelagius, whom he described as the most beautiful of men, face to face, but had been a witness of his end. If anything has crept into my other compositions, the accuracy of which can be challenged, it is not my fault, unless it be a fault to have reproduced the statements of unreliable authorities."

The Six Rhymed Dramas

Hroswitha's six short dramas in rhymed prose are considered her most important and original contribution to literature. They are certainly the best known of her works, as they have been produced on the stage from time to time with success. They have been proved theatrically practical, the dialogue is lively and at times stirring, and the structure has continuity. It is not known if the plays were ever produced during the lifetime of Hroswitha, but she must have written them with that purpose in mind, as a few stage directions are found attached to *Gallicanus* and *Calimachus* in the *Munich Codex*. These were later omitted by Celtes in the first printed edition of her works in 1501. As silence was required during mealtime in the refectory, when sacred scriptures, legends, and the early classics were read aloud, it is quite possible that the plays were read, as well. Thus, they may have become familiar to the canonesses.

Sister Mary Marguerite Butler says: "There are strong evidences of three contemporary dramatic streams within Hroswitha's writings—the literary tradition of classical antiquity, the mimetic influence, and the liturgical form—and the traces of their concomitant theatrical characteristics." Hroswitha followed the structure of the plays of the pagan poet Terence, but, as a devout Christian, wrote from an entirely different point of view. She showed great skill in the development of her characters.

In the plays, Hroswitha treated sensual passion in an even more realistic manner than in her first poems, but with the same delicacy of feeling and sincere simplicity. Although she believed that chastity was the crowning glory of a perfect life, she did not condemn marriage; in speaking of Henry the Fowler she says: "With him ruled his illustrious wife, Mathilda, who now, in all the realm none will be found to surpass in exalted holiness. Their union the triune God blessed with three sons." Hroswitha even shows a certain amount of sympathy for those who err, and treats her characters as human beings with all their faults and virtues, but inspired by a spark of sacred fire. She could not resist pointing a moral in each play.

Protestations of modesty and excuses for lack of skill were customary in the writings of Hroswitha's day. There is no doubt but that she was genuinely modest about her work, and always gave credit to her teachers and especially gave thanks repeatedly "for any talent I may have—given me by the merciful grace of Heaven in which I have trusted, rather than to my own strength." However, it may be seen in the following prefaces that with increasing experience she gained confidence in herself, had a surer touch, and explained her purpose very clearly.

The plays and prefaces are in the translation of Christopher St. John (pseudonym for Christabel Marshall), *The Plays of Hroswitha,* London, 1923:

> Preface to the Plays of Hroswitha, German Religious and Virgin of the Saxon Race:
>
> There are many Catholics, and we cannot entirely acquit ourselves of the charge, who, attracted by the polished elegance of the style of pagan writers, prefer their works to the holy scriptures. There are others who, although they are deeply attached to the sacred writings and have no liking for most pagan productions, make an exception in favor of the works of Terence, and, fascinated by the charm of the manner, risk being corrupted by the wickedness of the matter. Wherefore I, the strong voice of Gandersheim, have not hesitated to imitate in my writings a poet whose works are so widely read, my object being to glorify within the limits of my poor talent, the laudable chastity of Christian virgins in that self-same form of composition which has been used to describe the shameless acts of licentious women. One thing has all the same embarrassed me and often brought a blush to my cheek. It is that I have been compelled through the nature of this work to apply my mind and my pen to depicting the dreadful frenzy of those possessed by unlawful love, and the insidious sweetness of passion-things which should not even be named among us. Yet, if from modesty, I had refrained from treating these subjects, I should not have been able to attain my object—to glorify the innocent to the best of my ability. For the more seductive the blandishments of lovers, the more wonderful the divine succor, and the greater the merit of those who resist, especially when it is fragile woman

who is victorious and strong man who is routed with confusion.

I have no doubt that many will say that my poor work is much inferior to that of the author whom I have taken as my model, that it is on a much humbler scale, and indeed altogether different.

Well, I do not deny this. None can justly accuse me of wishing to place myself on a level with those who by the sublimity of their genius have so far outstripped me. No, I am not so arrogant as to compare myself even with the least among the scholars of the ancient world. I strive only, although my power is not equal to my desire, to use what talent I have for the glory of Him Who gave it to me. Nor is my self-love so great that I would, to avoid criticism, abstain from proclaiming wherever possible the virtues of Christ working in His saints. If this pious devotion gives satisfaction I shall rejoice, if it does not, either on account of my own worthlessness or of the faults of my unpolished style, I shall still be glad that I made the effort.

In the humbler works of my salad days I gathered up my poor researches in heroic strophes, but here I have sifted them into a series of dramatic scenes and avoided through omission the pernicious voluptuousness of pagan writers.

The Abbess Gerberga took great pride in the writings of her friend and pupil, Hroswitha, and brought them to the attention of the scholars who visited the monastery, especially to the Archbishop William of Mainz, the illegitimate son of Otto I, and to her sympathetic young friend, Otto II. (Later Hroswitha was to write the life of the Ottos at the request of Gerberga.)

The second preface is addressed to her readers, **"Epistle of the Same to Certain Learned Patrons of this Book"**:

To you, learned and virtuous men, who do not envy the success of others, but on the contrary rejoice in it as becomes the truly great, Hroswitha, poor humble sinner, sends wishes for your health in this life and your joy in eternity.

I cannot praise you enough for your humility or pay an adequate tribute to your kindness and affection. To think that you, who have been nurtured in the most profound philosophical studies, and have attained knowledge in perfection, should have deigned to approve the humble work of an obscure woman! You have, however, not praised me but the Giver of the grace which works in me, by sending me your paternal congratulations and admitting that I possess some little knowledge of those arts the subtleties of which exceed the grasp of my woman's mind. Until I showed my work to you I had not dared to let anyone see it except my intimate com-

panions. I came near abandoning this form of writing altogether, for if there were few to whom I could submit my compositions at all there were fewer still who could point out what needs correction and encourage me to go on. But now, reassured by your verdict (is it not said that the testimony of three witnesses is "equivalent to the truth?"), I feel that I have enough confidence to apply myself to writing, if God grants me the power, and that I need not fear the criticism of the learned whoever they may be. Still, I am torn by conflicting feelings. I rejoice from the depths of my soul that God through Whose grace alone I am what I am should be praised in me, but I am afraid of being thought greater than I am. I know that it is as wrong to deny a divine gift as to pretend falsely that we have received it. So I will not deny that through the grace of the Creator I have acquired some knowledge of the arts. He has given me the ability to learn—I am a teachable creature—yet of myself I should know nothing. He has given me a perspicacious mind, but one that lies fallow and idle when it is not cultivated. That my natural gifts might not be made void by negligence I have been at pains, whenever I have been able to pick up some threads and scraps torn from the old mantle of philosophy, to weave them into the stuff of my own book, in the hope that my lowly ignorant effort may gain more acceptance through the introduction of something of a nobler strain, and that the Creator of genius may be the more honored since it is generally believed that a woman's intelligence is slower. Such has been my motive in writing, the sole reason for the sweat and fatigue which my labors have cost me. At least I do not pretend to have knowledge where I am ignorant. On the contrary, my best claim to indulgence is that I know how much I do not know.

Impelled by your kindly interest and your express wish I come bowing low like a reed, to submit this little work to your judgment. I wrote it indeed with that idea in my mind, although doubt as to its merits had made me withhold it until now. I hope you will revise it with the same careful attention that you would give to a work of your own, and that when you have succeeded in bringing it up to the proper standard you will return it to me, that I may learn what are its worst faults.

The Arguments to the Plays

Sister Mary Marguerite Butler has pointed to the variety of moods—tragic, comic, heroic, romantic, and didactic—to be found in the "Arguments" written by Hroswitha for each play. However, short additional notes have been included here with the hope of further clarifying the plots of these extraordinary dramas.

Argument to the play **Gallicanus:** The conversion of Gallicanus, Commander-in-Chief. On the eve of his departure for a campaign against the Scythians,

Gallicanus is bethrothed to the Emperor Constantine's daughter, Constance, a consecrated Virgin.

When threatened with defeat in battle, Gallicanus is converted by John and Paul, Grand Almoners to Constance. He is immediately baptized and takes a vow of celibacy.

Later he is exiled by order of Julian the Apostate, and receives the crown of martyrdom. John and Paul are put to death by the same prince and buried secretly in their own house. Not long after, the son of their executioner becomes possessed by a devil. He is cured after confessing the crime committed by his father. He bears witness to the merits of the martyrs, and is baptized, together with his father.

NOTE: Constance was a thoughtful young princess, for as a consecreted virgin she knew that she would never marry Gallicanus, but as his going to battle depended upon her consent, and as she realized that the success of the campaign rested upon him, she consented, prayed, and played for time. In the absence of the General she converted his two daughters to Christianity, and relied upon the strategy of John and Paul to convert Gallicanus, which was accomplished amid miraculous manifestations from heaven, and the day was saved.

Argument to the play **Dulcitius:** The martyrdom of the holy virgins Agape, Chionia, and Irena. The Governor Dulcitius seeks them out in the silence of the night with criminal intent, but hardly has he entered their dwelling than he becomes the victim of a delusion, under which he mistakes for the objects of his passion the saucepans and frying-pans in the kitchen. These he embraces and covers with kisses until his face and clothes are black with soot and dirt. Later, by order of Diocletian, he hands the maidens over to the care of Sisinnius, who is charged with their punishment. Sisinnius in his turn is made the sport of the most strange delusions, but at length succeeds in getting Agape and Chionia burnt, Irena shot to death with arrows.

NOTE: The plays of Hroswitha have been called comedies, but it seems that the only real comedy, in the modern sense of the word, is that of **Dulcitius,** where humor and gravity are strangely combined and the situations are truly ludicrous. In this play, fragile woman is victorious and strong man is routed with confusion, for the predicament of Dulcitius when he emerged from his encounter with the pots and pans was most humiliating. When the Christian maidens refused to worship the Roman gods and marry pagans they were sentenced to be burned. However, Agape appealed for divine aid saying: "O Lord, we know Thy power! It would not be anything strange or new if the fire forgot its nature and obeyed thee. But we are weary of this world, and we implore thee to break the bonds that chain our souls, and to let our bodies be consumed that we may rejoice

with thee in heaven." The soldiers exclaimed: "O most wonderful! Their spirits have left their bodies, but there is no sign of any hurt."

Argument to the play **Calimachus:** The resurrection of Drusiana and Calimachus.

Calimachus cherishes a guilty passion for Drusiana, not only while she is alive but after she has died in the Lord. He dies from the bite of a serpent but, thanks to the prayers of St. John the Apostle, he is restored to life, together with Drusiana, and is born again in Christ.

NOTE: With the connivance of an unscrupulous servant, Calimachus visited the tomb where he found Drusiana's body looking more beautiful than in life. When about to embrace her, he was miraculously saved from the sacrilege by a serpent. It is an extraordinary plot to have been chosen from a classical source by a cloistered canoness, but it is delicately and skillfully handled.

Argument to the play **Abraham:** The fall and repentance of Mary, the niece of the hermit Abraham, who, after she had spent twenty years in the religious life as a solitary, abandons it in despair, and returning to the world, does not shrink from becoming a harlot. But two years later Abraham, in the disguise of a lover, seeks her out and reclaims her. For twenty years she does penance for her sins with many tears, fastings, vigils, and prayers.

NOTE: Mary only abandoned her religious life after being seduced by a false monk. The scene between Abraham and Mary in the brothel is compassionate and dramatic, and the play has been considered a masterpiece. When Mary hears her uncle's pleas to return to a life of virtue she cries that everything is over for her, but he assures her that "it is human to sin"—"but it is devilish to continue to sin." When she returns to the desert she prays for the men who are tempted to sin through her.

Argument to the play **Paphnutius:** The conversion of Thaïs by the hermit Paphnutius. Obedient to a vision, he leaves the desert and, disguised as a lover, seeks out Thaïs in Alexandria. She is moved to repent by his exhortations and, renouncing her evil life, consents to be enclosed in a narrow cell, where she does penance for three years. Paphnutius learns from a vision granted to St. Anthony's disciple Paul that her humility has won her a place among the blessed in Paradise. He brings her out of her cell and stays by her side until her soul has left her body.

NOTE: The story is preceded by a learned philosophical discourse between Paphnutius and his disciples. He explains in terms of music the "harmonious arrangement"—"between the mortal body and the spiritual soul." He also gives a technical explanation of the three kinds of music: human, celestial, and from instruments as belonging to "one of the branches of the Quadrivium."

> Argument to the play *Sapientia:* The martyrdom of the holy virgins Faith, Hope, and Charity, who are put to the torture by the Emperor Hadrian and slain in the presence of their mother, Sapientia, she encouraging them by her admonitions to bear their sufferings. After their death the holy mother recovers the bodies of her children, embalms them in spices, and buries them with honor about five miles outside the city of Rome.

> Forty days later the spirit of Sapientia takes its flight to heaven while she is still praying by her children's grave.

NOTE: This play has been considered by dramatists the least successful, and is historically incorrect, as Hadrian was known to be tolerant toward Christians. When the Emperor asks Sapientia the ages of her children, she replies with a numerical discourse on the science of numbers, hoping to confound him, but failing. Christopher St. John thinks that Hroswitha introduced the scientific discussion to impress "the learned men to whom she submitted her work," because it throws an interesting light on the studies pursued in a monastery in the tenth century.

The Achievements of Otto

Hroswitha's two historical epics, the ***Carmen de Gestis Oddonis,*** also called ***Gesta Ottonis*** or ***Panegyric Oddonum,*** and the ***Primordia Coenobii Gandeshemensis,*** are closely allied. They were both translated with their prefaces by Sister Mary Bernardine Bergman, A.B., A.M., from the German text of the Teubner edition of Karl Strecker, ***Hrotsvithae Opera,*** with such minor changes as she has noted in her introduction; it is the only text in English.

The ***Gesta Ottonis*** starts with the "just and wise reign of Henry the Fowler, first King of Saxony," but is primarily a panegyric of the deeds of the Emperor Otto I, called the Great, and Otto II, who ruled jointly with his father from the age of six. Sister Mary Marguerite Butler says that the *Hildesheim Chronical* states that Hroswitha originally honored the three Ottos, and that the very title of this book, ***Panegyric Oddonum,*** known as the ***Gesta Ottonis,*** proves that we have only the first part; she thinks that the second dedication, addressed to Otto II, probably served as the preface to a second book, which is lost. The epic consists of 1517 verses, of which 676 lines are unfortunately missing. The ***Gesta Ottonis*** ends with the marriage of Liudolf, Duke of Swabia, when Otto I was at the height of his power;

this topic Hroswitha feared to treat because "I am withheld by my womanly nature—hence I, hindered by the weightiness of these great themes, proceed no further, but prudently make an end."

The ***Gesta Ottonis*** is prized by historians, who have found it a valuable account of the period although it is at times inaccurate because of omissions and alterations made for diplomatic reasons. Hroswitha found the writing of political facts very difficult, as will be seen in the address to Gerberga and in the dedications to Otto I and Otto II, which precede the poem. It was hard to write the truth about living people, especially during civil war when the members of the Saxon royal family were literally at sword's point. The most treacherous offenders against Otto I were Prince Liudolf, who plotted against his father, and Duke Henry of Bavaria, brother of the King and father of Abbess Gerberga, who had requested Hroswitha to write the ***Gesta Ottonis.*** This created a delicate situation because of Hroswitha's close association with the family, so she tactfully blamed their misdeeds on "the wicked cunning of the ancient foe" who "disturbed our placid existence by his ancient wiles"—"which always seeks to pervert feeble hearts, did not cease, but after the deed of ill urged the addition of a worse crime. The Enemy is said to have entered the breasts of certain men with such frenzy of destructive poison that they desired to inflict death upon the faithful King and to appoint his brother as ruler over the nation—but the Paschal Lamb, who gave Himself in death as a chosen holocaust to His Father for our redemption, permitted not the commission of that hideous crime. But presently, he exposed their plan to all men, and thus happily the blood of the innocent King was saved, and those who were found guilty of the accursed crime were condemned to bitter punishment in proportion of the measure of their guilt."

With all this and more to contend with, it is no wonder that she cries, "I do not think it fitting for a frail woman abiding in the enclosure of a peaceful monastery to speak of war, with which she ought not even to be acquainted. These matters should be reserved for the toil of qualified men, to whom wisdom of mind has granted the ability to express all things wisely in eloquent terms."

Hroswitha's dedication to Gerberga, therefore, should be read with an understanding of the political and personal considerations that influenced it:

> To Gerberga, renowned Abbess, esteemed no less for her integrity than for her illustrious descent from a royal race. I, Hrotsvit of Gandersheim, the lowest of the lowly of those serving under the sway of her ladyship, wish to offer all that a servant owes to her mistress.

O my mistress, thou who enlightenest by the radiant diversity of thy spiritual wisdom, may it not irk thy kindliness to examine carefully what thou knowest has been written at thy bidding.

Thou hast indeed imposed upon me the difficult task of narrating in verse the achievements of an august emperor, which thou art well aware was impossible to gather abundantly from hearsay. Thou canst surmise what great difficulties my ignorance puts in my way while engaged in this work. There are things of which I could find no written record, nor could I elicit information from anyone sufficiently reliable. I was like a stranger wandering without a guide through the depth of an unknown forest where every path was covered over and mantled with heavy snow. In vain he tries to follow the directions of those who are showing the way only by a nod. Now he wanders through pathless ways, now by chance he comes upon the trail of the right path, until at length, when he has traversed half of the thick-treed domain, he attains the place of long-sought rest. There staying his step, he dares not proceed farther, until either he is led on by someone overtaking him or follows the footsteps of one who has preceded him. In like manner, I, bidden to undertake a complete chronicle of illustrious achievements, have gone on my way stumbling and hesitating, so great was the difficulty of finding a path in the forest of these royal deeds.

And so, wearied by my endeavor, I have lapsed into silence as I pause in a convenient resting place. Without guidance I propose to go no further. If, however, I be encouraged by the eloquent treatises of the learned (either already written or in the near future to be written) I might perhaps discover the means of veiling to some degree my homely simplicity.

Now, however, in proportion as I am unsupported by any authority, I am defenseless at every point. I fear, too, that I shall be accused of temerity and that I shall encounter the reproaches of many, because I have dared to disgrace by my uncultured style matters that should be set forth with the festal eloquence of choice expression. Yet, if a person of good judgment, who knows how to appraise things fairly, examines my work, he will pardon me the more readily because of the weakness of my sex and the inferiority of my knowledge, especially since I undertook this little work not of my own presumption, but at thy bidding.

Why, then, should I fear the criticism of others, since, if I have erred somewhat, I become responsible only to your judgment? O, why can I not escape reproofs for these works about which I was anxious to be silent? If, because of its crudeness, I should wish the work to be shown to none, should I not deserve the blame of all? To your decision, however, and that of your most intimate friend, Archbishop William, to whom you have bidden me

present this testimony of my simplicity, I submit the work to be appraised for its worth and its imperfections.

The following is Hroswitha's dedication to Otto I; the remarks above concerning the author's relationship to the various members of the royal family should be borne in mind.

Otto, mighty sovereign of the empire of the Caesars, who, renowned because thou wieldest a sceptre of imperial majesty by the indulgent kindliness of the Eternal King, surpassest in integrity all foregoing emperors, many nations dwelling far and wide reverence thee; the Roman Empire, too, bestows upon thee manifold honors! Do not reject the small offerings of this poem, but may this proffered tribute of praises which the least of the flock of Gandersheim accords thee be pleasing. The kind solicitude of thy forbears has assembled it, and the constant desire of rendering service owes it to thee. Many, perchance, have written and many hereafter will produce masterful memorials of thy achievements. But none of these has provided a model for me, nor have monographs, hitherto written, taught me what I should set down. But devotedness of heart alone is the reason for this undertaking, and this urged me to dare the formidable task. Yet, I am fearful that by verse I may be heedlessly tracing spurious deeds of thine and not disclosing authentic ones. But no baneful presumption of mind has urged me in this matter, nor have I voluntarily played falsely by a disdain of the truth as a whole. But, that the account, as I have written it, is true, those who furnished the material for me themselves declared. Let not, therefore, the benignity of august majesty despise that which a lowly suppliant, devoted of heart, has achieved. And, although hereafter many books may be written praising thee duly, and may be esteemed fittingly acceptable to thee, yet, let this little book which has clearly been written from no earlier copy be not the last in order of regard. And, although thou holdest the honor of Caesar's emperorship, disdain not to be called by the name of King, until, the fame of a royal life having been written, the imperial splendor of the second realm may be declared in an orderly fashion and in becoming language.

Hroswitha's dedication to his son, Otto II, then follows:

Otto, resplendent ornament of the Roman Empire, bright scion of the august and revered Otto, for whom the mighty King throned on high and his Eternal Son destined an empire strong in the zenith of its power: spurn not the poor composition of a poor nun! Thou, thyself, if thou deign to remember, hast lately ordered it to be presented to thy keen gaze; and when thou perceivest that it is marred with many blemishes, be then the more inclined to favor a speedy pardon, the more I am but obeying thy behest in presenting it to thee. If I were not urged by thy dread command, under no circumstance, should I have such self-assurance as to presume to offer to thy scrutiny this little book with its obvious lack of polish.

Thou, who by the decree of God art associated with thy father in his court and art ready to obey his paternal admonitions, holdest harmoniously a like distinction of imperial rule, bearing the kingly sceptre in thy youthful hands. But, since I know that thou art loftily considered like to Solomon, son of the celebrated King David, who, in his father's presence and at his revered command, received the paternal kingdom amid desired peace, I hope that in accord with his example thou wilt be content. Though Solomon, as king resided in a proud citadel, wisely establishing the decrees of sacred laws and penetrating with profound mind into the secrets of nature, yet occasionally he was disposed to relax his mind with trivial investigations. But he did not loathe duly to settle, with the determination of a just and speedy decision, the quarrel of the two women, ordering the child to be restored to its true mother.

Therefore, as a suppliant indeed, I request that thou, our Solomon, though the administration of a harassing empire occupy thee, deign to read now, for amusement, the recent account of thine own poor nun; that thus all crudeness of utterance, in this treatise on thy imperial name, may presently disappear from the badly arranged words, and that enhanced by thy revered title, they may be guarded from the breath of well-merited contempt.

The writing of the *Primordia Coenobii Gandeshemensis* was a labor of love for Hroswitha, as it recounts the founding of Gandersheim in 856 by Duke Liudolf, his wife Oda, who lived there beloved by all to the age of 107, and her mother Aeda. Hroswitha tells of the completion of the monastery by Liudolf's son, Otto the Illustrious, and the reign of his daughters, who were the first three Abbesses. The subject was close to her heart and she wove many spiritual legends into the history with skill and charm, and the miracles which occurred during the building were all very real to her. They were written in much the same manner that Wagner used to weave the legend of Lohengrin around the historic figure of Henry the Fowler, father of Otto I.

If it is true that Hroswitha was born about 935 and entered the cloister about 955, she would have been sixty-five years of age when she died, having spent forty-five wonderful years in study and creative writing.

Otto III, a strong Grecophile, died unmarried in Rome. He, the Abbess Gerberga, and Hroswitha probably all died within a few months of each other during 1001-

1002, and it must have been a great sorrow to the bereaved. Otto II had given his five-year-old daughter Sophia to Gerberga to be educated at Gandersheim, so now after some years as a canoness she was consecrated Abbess. This marked the end of an era; the rule of the three Ottos was over, and jealous disputes arose among the clergy of the diocese. The literary prestige of the monastery declined, and it was two hundred years after "the strong voice of Gandersheim" was stilled before another medieval dramatist appeared.

Marianna da Vinci Nichols (essay date 1976)

SOURCE: "*Callimachus,* A Play by Hrotswitha," *Allegorica,* Vol. 1, No. 1, Spring, 1976, pp. 7-11.

[*In the following introduction to her co-translation of* Callimachus, *Nichols explores the classical sources and romantic / Christian theme of the play.*]

Hrotswitha was a canoness at the Abbey of Gandersheim in Saxony during the tenth century. She wrote two epics, a number of shorter works, and six plays modelled after Terence's to replace his for readers who were "fascinated by the charm of [his] manner [and] risked being corrupted by the wickedness of [his] matter," as she says in her Preface to the plays.

Callimachus is her most romantic drama. At first reading it seems to be a play that loses its sense of direction. It begins with friends drinking in a tavern and ends with resurrections at Drusiana's tomb. Its opening style is literal and jocular: its closing tone is symbolic and reverent. The problem Hrotswitha seems to set for herself with this play is to reconcile apparent contradictions. And she does so, in a manner that is not only dramatically coherent but ·is also a commentary on her relation to Terence. The action starts in a world Terence might have created: the setting is urbane, the characterizations secular, the plot a solution to a love problem. And then the play moves with a kind of inevitability into the Christian world that Hrotswitha lived daily, one which rejected the Terentian idea that the social good is a moral equivalent of the private good.

Several actions in *Callimachus* tell us that while she was writing, Hrotswitha had in mind Terence's play *The Eunuch* in which violent rape has the shock value of Callimachus's attempted necrophilia. In *The Eunuch,* however, the tricks of the slave Parmeno and the disguise of the lover Chaerea seem to be simple necessities to resolve the comic plot and, like all the play's intrigues, are in themselves morally neutral. Their final aims are in any case cancelled out by last act discoveries about true parentage and true citizenship that remove all obstacles to the lovers' marriage and therefore guarantee social continuity. To Hrotswitha, however, intrigues are deceitful and deceit is always reprehensible for it reveals the immoral nature of a pagan sensibility. She therefore has her pagan lover Callimachus allude twice to the most famous scene[1] in Terence's play—the one in which Chaerea is inspired by a picture of Jove descending upon Danae as a shower of gold to take Pamphila by force. Callimachus argues to his friend (sc. ii) that the gods invent plans worse than his intention to seduce a married woman openly. Later, he threatens Drusiana that he will use any means he can to trap her into surrender. According to Chaerea, his rape has the authority of the highest god, a most successful lover. Jupiter behaves in the Greek and Roman mythological traditions much as men do. The moral question is presented in Terence's plays as it is in the Euripidean tragedies which inspired his models in New Comedy, but the answer is never simply given by theology, as in Hrotswitha. To her, tricks and stratagems can only be the inspiration of the devil, the sole instigator of men's sexual impulses whose only possible outcome is evil. Many classical writers were "moralized" in medieval times to make them agree with Christian dogma and ideals. Hrotswitha, nevertheless, does not add on a moral didactically as a closing preachment on the wages of sin. Instead, the drama itself moves toward a statement of belief, and the affirmation of a Christian ethic develops organically out of the central action—the hero's initiation into the spiritual life.

The classical spirit of sensuality that opens the play can lead only downward toward vice and perversity until, and unless, it is redeemed by a saving spirit of grace. The worldliness of a Roman pagan, mellow or corrupt according to the point of view, gives way in Hrotswitha's play to the other-worldliness of a new Christianity. The hero, epitomizing the ephemeral values of a hedonistic actual society, transcends his own nature, as it were, and becomes an exemplar of the greater values in an eternal, divine society. The rival worlds of Eros and Christ are unified here, as they were in history, by a new understanding of the word *love.*

From the viewpoint of plot and action, the force behind Callimachus's transformation is his passion for the chaste Drusiana. The very extremity of necrophilia to which he is driven is a necessary condition for the later exaltation he is to reach, both in terms of the psychology of character and in terms of dramatic development. A more temperate affection would neither have motivated his fervent wish for change, nor have justified the long celebration of triumphant spirituality in the last third of the play.

Callimachus's lust, like his love, is intensely felt and openly expressed. Drusiana's emotions, on the contrary, are more hidden, perhaps even from herself since her plea for death suggests that her fears are greater

and more complex than she realizes. Still, her vow to remain chaste is unwavering—nor ought we probe too deeply into her psychology. Steadfastness makes it possible for her to assume a Beatrice-like role as her lover's guide to Paradise. Like Dante, Hrotswitha is giving an almost neo-Platonic significance to beauty by implying that its powers of attraction are valuable as they may lead to an apprehension of absolute good. If Drusiana suffers for impulses she cannot understand, we are limited by Hrotswitha's portrayal to noticing that her confusion, like Callimachus's torments, are believable because they are essentially human.

Probably the most literary figure in the play is the slave Fortunatus. Like all clever underlings in drama, from Terence's Parmeno to Shakespeare's Iago, he lives by his wits and they remain unregenerate to the end. Hrotswitha's belief in the imperturbable force of right is strong indeed. She knows that this satanic opportunist, licensed not only to steal scenes but to undermine what sounds to him like cant by dying in a rage, will damn himself. But we cannot speak of Fortunatus as a symbol of evil. He, and Drusiana too, are conceived of as static and unchanging: they end as they began, simple patterns of good and evil. Of all the characters, only St. John stands for more than himself. As a typological descendant of John the Baptist, he dramatizes an important link, new to church canon in Hrotswitha's time, between the meaning of baptism and the doctrinal significance of Christ's rebirth. And of all the characters, only Callimachus is dynamic: he becomes heroic when he confirms his understanding of resurrection by choosing to be baptised. In its entirety, the resurrection sequence at Drusiana's tomb is reminiscent of an epic hero's rebirth since that usually comes about through the agency of a special, or magical, or wise figure like St. John, and is always a signal that an heroic lesson has been learned.

The meaning of love, then, is the hero's lesson, the story's romantic theme, the mainspring of the plot, and a key to the play's unity of mundane and celestial realities. We might also expect these multiple aspects of love to motivate the carefully structured miracles; and they do. At the close of the first part of the play (sc. 1-14), God's love, expressed as pity, answers Drusiana's plea for death. In the second part (v - viii), Callimachus at the nadir of depravity is punished by a Snake, the serpentine antithesis of love—a *demon ex machina.* In the long final section (ix), the play's upward movement is accentuated by successive resurrections, demonstrating another attribute of heavenly love. We may see Callimachus's redemption as a reminder that Christ's death brought universal redemption, just as we see Drusiana's rebirth as an illustration of the final reward of the just. As theatrical solutions to problems of character and action, these miracles are apt. Each, however, is also conceived dramatically as a visible expression of each character's will. Fortunatus chooses death as fully as Callimachus chooses life. Hrotswitha's use of Christian symbolism is often casual—as though she expected her audience to make ready associations between, say, an action and its Biblical parallel. God (Christ) announcing the coming resurrection to Andronicus and Saint John is probably a simple variation on the Gospel's angel announcing Christ's resurrection to the women at his tomb. But at a deeper level, Hrotswitha's symbolism is linked to humanistic values of self-determination.

Translating the play brings one up sharply against layers of association in the language that take us backward from Hrotswitha to the classics, and forward from her time to ours. To take an isolated case, Drusiana turns on Callimachus during their first meeting and calls him a "leno." The word is taken by Hrotswitha from Terence and in his context it needs to be translated as "pimp." In the argument between Hrotswitha's lovers, "pimp" makes no sense, for her meaning seems to be something like "buyer and seller of souls." To us such a phrase might evoke the image of Gogol's enterprising landowner in *Dead Souls,* one wholly at variance with the medieval Latinist's idea of "a dealer in slaves." Similar problems occur in Callimachus's conversation with his friends. Read with a Terentian eye, the men comment as town gallants; yet become responsible advisors when they warn Callimachus against "any behavior that might lead him to evil." Clearly, Hrotswitha sees the concept of friendship as demanding and serious. The implications of these linguistic differences interest us as revelations of how Hrotswitha interpreted Terence, of how she understood the early Christian era she uses as a setting, and of how she reflected life in her own century. They are more important still for their advice to us about how to read Hrotswitha.

Hrotswitha's Latin is so deceptively simple and straightforward that the translator is tempted to use the spoken language of our day, perhaps even slang. But such language diminishes the serious import of the speeches and jars with the rhetoric of prayer or conversion. Unable to find a modern, colloquial English flexible enough to move with equal ease between high and low styles, the translator goes back with renewed respect to Tillyard's translation[2] which kept the solemn English rhythms of the King James Bible. Since Helene Homeyer's[3] definitive Latin text appeared in 1970, however, an entirely new translation has become necessary. Making the play readable in English meant expanding Hrotswitha's extremely compressed Latin. A character often required a full line of speech rather than a sharp, monosyllabic "yes" or "no" when the context called for an expression of his emotions. In turn, expansion of this sort led to the inclusion of stage directions. Often these are derived from the text itself and thus are justifiable as part of the translation. At other times they are more interpretive. They are, in any

case, always included within brackets so that the reader will have no trouble distinguishing them from the text proper. Whether the production takes place in the reader's mind, or in a formal stage presentation, there is clearly a need to visualize the scene and to hear the characters speak.

Notes

[1] It is often referred to in subsequent writings. St. Augustine, for one, discusses it in *The City of God.*

[2] H. J. W. Tillyard, *Plays of Roswitha* (London, 1923).

[3] Helen Homeyer, *Hrotsvithae Opera* (Schöningh, Munich, Paderborn, Vienna, 1970).

Karl A. Zaenker (essay date 1978)

SOURCE: "Homage to Roswitha," *The Humanities Association Review,* Vol. 29, No. 2, Spring, 1978, pp. 117-34.

[*In the following essay, Zaenker traces the literary influence and reception of Hroswitha's dramas in the contemporary era.*]

One could think of two immediate reasons why it appears timely to pay homage to Roswitha von Gandersheim, that mysterious Saxon poetess of the tenth century, and concern ourselves with her work and the impact it has had on European literature over the past centuries. On the one hand we could commemorate the 1000th anniversary of Roswitha's death which might well be any of these years. It is very convenient that the uncertain dates of her life offer us some leeway here. In fact, German literary circles bestowed on her two commemorative years in this century: in 1926 her 1000th birthday was celebrated, rightly or rather wrongly, and in 1973 the 1000th year of her death was commemorated through performances of her plays, learned speeches, and postage stamps. However, these dates are arbitrary and it would be more exact to say that Roswitha was born some time before 940 and died some time after 973. Whether she lived to see the new millenium or whether she died exactly a thousand years ago we shall probably never know.[1]

A second reason for our homage to Roswitha lies in the fact that Roswitha has been hailed not only as the first woman playwright in the Christian world, but also as the "first emancipated woman."[2] Such statements have clearly to be taken with a grain of salt. And yet it is undeniable that Roswitha in her literary works champions the cause of women—as she sees it—and portrays constellations where—in the words on her own preface to her plays—"it is fragile woman who is victorious and strong man who is routed with confusion."[3]

This theme strikes us as rather topical today in the wake of feminist movements and as popular as it must have been a thousand years ago, at least in a women's cloister.

Why is it then that her work is not more widely known and read in Canada, why does it not appear more often in University curricula? Among possible explanations there are three major ones: first, the language problem. Roswitha wrote in that kind of medieval Latin which was spoken by a cultivated few in tenth-century Europe; in fact, one reason for her literary production was to further the knowledge of good Latin. This language hurdle would nowadays relegate the study of Roswitha's works to seminars on Medieval Latin Literature, unless, of course, one resorts to modern translations. A second impediment to a more widespread knowledge of her work may lie in the fact that it does not allow itself to be pigeon-holed into one genre, nor can it be claimed by one discipline or one department. Roswitha wrote eight legends, rhymed and in metric form (leonine hexameters), six theatre plays in rhymed prose and also two historical works, again in rhymed meter. This diversity of form and of subject would thus make Roswitha's work a possible object for historical science, religious studies, history of theatre, of Latin literature and of literature in general: obviously an ideal field for comparative or interdisciplinary studies. Third and last, the access to Roswitha's work is made difficult for modern readers by the great shift in values that has taken place over the last thousand years. To be sure, this presents a stumbling block in approaching any older literature, but the *Weltanschauung* of a tenth-century Benedictine nun or rather canoness is definitely worlds apart from ours.

It might be of some interest then to find out what in Roswitha's work, her dramatic work in particular, appealed to people in different times and cultures. By going through the history of its rediscoveries, translations, and adaptations we should be better equipped to answer the question why the work of this exceptional woman survived at all and what it can mean even to contemporary writers. Admittedly, such an excursion into the field of "Wirkungsgeschichte," of literary reception, can only be rather sketchy. We shall concentrate on four stages in the history of Roswitha's literary afterlife: her first rediscovery by German humanists around 1500, her second rediscovery by the literary pope of German Enlightenment, Johann Christoph Gottsched, her impact on Anatole France in the nineteenth century and finally her resurrection on stage brought about by the East German playwright Peter Hacks in 1974.

Nearly all of our scarce information about Roswitha's life comes from her own prefaces and explanations to her works. From them we learn her name (which she spells in the Old Saxon form as Hrotsvit); we learn from them her approximate birthdate (somewhat earlier than that of her abbess Gerberga, born in 940), and also her status. The fact that she was a canoness, a *Stiftsdame* rather than a simple Benedictine nun, makes some difference. Instead of the three monastic vows of chastity, poverty and obedience, a canoness would have to take only those of chastity and obedience. We can also assume that Roswitha was of noble descent to be allowed entry in the illustrious convent of Gandersheim and that she was able to maintain contacts with the outside world of nobility and learned men. In fact, Roswitha did send some of her works, probably the first four plays, to some unnamed learned patrons for advice and critique, as she inserts after the fourth play a thank-you note to these patrons in which she declares:

> To think that you, who have been nurtured in the most profound philosophical studies and have attained knowledge in perfection, should have deigned to approve the humble work of an obscure woman . . . by sending me your paternal congratulations and admitting that I possess some little knowledge of those arts the subtleties of which exceed the grasp of my woman's mind. (p. xxviii)

We would be happy to possess such letters of support by Roswitha's critics and find out more clearly what "those subtle arts" might be. Probably Roswitha has those arts in mind when, in that same letter, she expresses concern about the intellectual or rather spiritual merits of her plays:

> I have been at pains, whenever I have been able to pick up some threads and scraps torn from the old mantle of philosophy, to weave them into the stuff of my own book, in the hope that my lowly ignorant effort may gain more acceptance through the introduction of something of a nobler strain, and that God, the Creator of genius, may be the more honoured since it is generally believed that a woman's intelligence is slower. (pp. xxix-xxx)

As one can see, Roswitha uses the anti-feminist stereotypes of her time to great advantage. I believe she quotes such clichés with an ironic smile. In fact, Roswitha received a thorough training in the seven liberal arts for which she gives credit to her two abbesses, mainly to Gerberga, Mother Superior of the convent of Gandersheim and niece of the Emperor Otto the Great. In her desire to appear learned, to incorporate "scraps of philosophy" into her plays, Roswitha sometimes goes too far for modern tastes. To give but two examples: the conversion play **Paphnutius** opens on a drawn-out dialogue between the venerable hermit Paphnutius and his disciples on the nature of music and harmony until finally Paphnutius announces his plan to disguise as a lover and convert the ill-reputed courtesan Thais. Or, to give a second example, when in Roswitha's last play **Sapientia** the evil emperor Hadrian inquires about the age of the three accused Christian virgins, their mother Sapientia dumbfounds him with an intricate mathematical puzzle followed by a lecture on even, augmented and divisible numbers. To the modern reader, such an excursus into arithmetics does not make the Christian martyrs more psychologically credible and one might nearly side with Hadrian's exasperated decision to have them executed. However, it should not be overlooked that in the context of these plays even such learned digressions have a structural and at the same time spiritual value. For instance, in **Paphnutius** the pernicious activity of the harlot Thais represents a breach of the harmonious arrangement of the world, a dissonance in the pre-established *harmonia mundi:* hence the lecture on music. Similarly, in the mathematical excursus in **Sapientia,** the Christians show themselves thoroughly familiar with God's creation which, according to the Bible, is organized in measure, number and weight. Besides, this scene adds a little touch of that peculiar martyr's humour; it shows to good effect the intellectual supremacy of the victim who plays dialectic catch with her executioner.

There can be no doubt that in Roswitha's plays the message, namely the praise of steadfast Christian chastity in face of temptation and martyrdom, is of foremost importance. But that does not mean that the medium, the dramatic form, is neglected. On the contrary, the authoress comes across as a gifted dramatist who can write lively dialogues and present dramatic development in short contrasting scenes. To be sure, one can easily find flaws in the construction of some of her plays, **Gallicanus** for instance, especially when measured by the hallowed yardstick of the Aristotelian unities. The dialogue, however, makes it always abundantly clear where and when a scene is supposed to take place, so there can be no confusion in the reader. Or should one say in the audience?

The question has to be asked whether these plays were meant for theatrical performances or whether they were just written for reading purposes. The Roswitha criticism over the last hundred years has been divided over this issue. It has been generally believed that there was no theatre to speak of between roughly the end of the West Roman Empire in the fifth century and the beginnings of Christian liturgical plays some five hundred years later. The Church frowned upon actors and would not permit any theatrical performances because of their alleged immorality. Would this not have applied to Roswitha's works, some of which take place in a bawdy-house and depict "those possessed by unlawful love," to use Roswitha's own words? The strongest arguments for the case that her plays were not staged or meant to be, are first, that she does not mention any performance in her prefaces at all; second, that the original manuscripts present the text written in a continuous fashion without subdividing the action into specific scenes or acts; and third, that there are no stage directions in the text.[4]

So it is quite possible that Roswitha's plays were never put on stage until the turn of the twentieth century, nearly a thousand years after they were conceived. Such performances, mostly sponsored by various University or Church groups, received highly favourable critiques in both Europe and North America. The style chosen for performances had to be non-realistic, stressing the symbolic and didactic nature of the plays. Thereby it comes close to that of Brecht's "epic theatre," as Bert Nagel rightly points out (*Hrotsvit von Gandersheim,* p. 79), especially to Brecht's early *Lehrtheater,* in which likewise an exemplary action is shown in order to propagate a message—even though a very different one. It makes sense that Roswitha's plays have finally found an audience, as small as it may be, since the fundamental reorientation in dramatic techniques and theories in the twentieth century has made people more receptive to the frail beauty of medieval theatre.

It is very unlikely that Roswitha's plays had any lasting impact in her time and the immediate centuries thereafter, if one judges by the fact that they have been preserved in only one complete manuscript originally kept in the monastery of Emmeram. When in 1493 Konrad Celtis discovered this Emmeram codex and made its text available in his printed edition of Ros-witha's works in 1501, he caused a literary sensation, mainly because nobody had been aware of Roswitha's existence. The impression which this discovery made on Celtis and his humanistic contemporaries is vividly reflected in their correspondence and in Celtis' preface to his edition. In it he included fifteen Latin and Greek epigrams by several of his fellow poets or connoisseurs of literature who celebrate Roswitha as the worthy successor of Greek and Latin poetry or even, as in Willibald Pirckheimer's epigram, as the eleventh Muse (the Greek poetess Sappho being the tenth). The shock and delight of finding an accomplished Latin poet in the so-called "dark" tenth century after nearly six hundred years is expressed by Celtis as follows: "incredible dictu, quanto stupore et gaudio correptus fuerim, dum mulierem Germanam post sec centos annos . . . Latina oratione et versu loquentem legissem."[5]

Here we have the compound which constitutes Roswitha's glory in Germany around 1500: she is a Latin author, she is German, and she is a woman. Three more examples of this appreciation shall suffice. Johannes Werner of Nuremberg praises her in these words:

> Hroswitha germanis nunc maxima gloria terris,
> Carminibus lacios nectere docta modos,
> Nec minus et voces describit culta solutas,
> Libera therencii cornica facta sequens.[6]

Another panegyric, this one by the famous Abbot of Sponheim, Johannes Trithemius, goes even further:

Cur non laudemus germanae scripta puellae,
Quae si graeca esset iam dea certa foret.[7]

And finally the voice of a woman, Charitas Pirckheimer, abbess of a monastery in Nuremberg and sister of the above-mentioned Willibald, who in a letter to Celtis thanks him for not disdaining to edit the works of a woman.

Plane non possum non fateri fecisse vos contra consuetudinem multorum eruditorum vel forte potius superborum, qui abusive nituntur omnia verba, facta ac dictamina mulierum in tantum parvipendere.[8]

Roswitha could not have agreed more with these words.

After such enthusiastic outpourings it may come as a surprise that the Roswitha-wave which swept Germany around 1500 did not leave a more durable imprint on its literary history. Gottsched, in the middle of the eighteenth century, notes that the works of Roswitha are virtually unknown to men of letters, and this in spite of a second edition of her works in 1707 entirely based on Konrad Celtis' text. Probably the political turmoils of the sixteenth and seventeenth centuries prevented her fame from lasting, a fate she shared with other humanistic writers and achievements.

Gottsched's second discovery of Roswitha is certainly less spectacular than the first one by Celtis, but both authors and their attitudes with regard to Roswitha resemble each other greatly. Both lived in an era which thought itself so much more enlightened than the preceding one that it made a cult out of this idea: Celtis regarded the "dark Middle Ages" with typical humanistic contempt, whereas Gottsched voiced the dislike felt by the early German Enlightenment for what they considered metaphysical Baroque bombast. Both Celtis and Gottsched were highly respected authors as well as book-collectors, University professors, editors and public relations men. Celtis in his preface to his Roswitha-edition describes the painful travels which he undertook all across Germany in search of manuscripts. Gottsched, on the other hand, points out that over the past sixteen years he had been collecting, copying or buying books and manuscripts containing German plays in order to establish a comprehensive library of drama. For both Celtis and Gottsched, their occupation with Roswitha's work was part of a larger case for which Roswitha was a most welcome crown-witness. Celtis had used Roswitha to prove that on German, "barbarian," soil a Latin genius could flourish. For Gottsched, on the other hand, the fact that Roswitha wrote in Latin was not a strong point in her favour. After all, Gottsched's critical anthology of German drama entitled *Nöthiger Vorrath zur Geschichte der deutschen dramatischen Dichtkunst*[9] had sprung from a patriotic impulse, namely to defend the quality and originality of German letters against the attacks of

their detractors—notably against the challenge by an unnamed French writer who, according to Gottsched's *Vorrede,* had claimed that the Germans have always been devoid of any poetic genius: "Nommez moi un Esprit créateur sur votre Parnasse; c'est à dire, nommez moi un Poète Allemand, qui ait tiré de son propre fonds un ouvrage de quelque réputation. Je vous en défie!"

Gottsched takes up this challenge and tries to prove that as far as theatre is concerned the Germans are second to none in European literature, with the exception of the French classics. To be sure, Gottsched proves his case more by quantity than by quality: his collection of titles reached a final number of twelve hundred. Roswitha, in spite of her being a Latin author, is a trump card in Gottsched's author's file and he plays it triumphantly by saying: "*wir fordern billig alle europäischen Völker auf, nur etwas dergleichen, aus eben dem Jahrhunderte, in ihren Ländern zu zeigen.*" Or, in his second volume of 1765, Gottsched flashes the same card again: "*Die scharfsinnige Klosterjungfrau Rhoswitha ist es, auf welche wir Deutsche gegen alle auswärtige Völker stolzieren können.*"[10]

Clearly, Gottsched, the stern censor of the theatre, is not entirely happy with Roswitha's plays, their disregard for the three unities, their mixture of comical and serious events which does not allow him to classify them neatly as comedy or tragedy. After pointing out these flaws, however, Gottsched comes gallantly to her rescue by saying that Roswitha deserves our indulgence because she lived in an unenlightened world, because she had to write in Latin, and because she is a woman.

In his first volume Gottsched just gives the plot of Roswitha's six plays with a few comments added, but the response by his readers was so great that eight years later in his *Nachlese* Gottsched offered a translation of the greater part of **Gallicanus** as a sample. This is in effect the second German translation of any of her plays that we know of. Two hundred and fifty years earlier, Celtis' edition of Roswitha's works inspired the Heidelberg professor Adam Wernher von Themar to translate the conversion play **Abraham,** no doubt the most homogeneous of her works. This first translation seems not to have reached any sizable audience, however, and up to the present day it has never appeared in print.[11] Obviously, the humanists were in no need of a German translation and Themar could not have hoped to reach with it the uneducated masses. I suppose his **Abraham** is a translation exercise as practised by professors and students in the humanistic era. Gottsched, on the other hand, tried to popularize Roswitha's plays by his own translation, but nobody followed in his steps. The young generation of "Stürmer und Dränger" was clearly not attracted to Gottsched's theories and writings; they considered him a living anachronism and searched for stronger inspiration. The encounter between the two generations is vividly portrayed in a scene in Goethe's autobiography *Dichtung und Wahrheit:* the young student Goethe makes a social call on the aging professor Gottsched who calls for his Baroque wig before discoursing on philosophical matters.[12] It took nearly another hundred years for scholars and theatre lovers to renew Gottsched's initiative and provide the first satisfying and accessible editions and translations of Roswitha's works.

At this point, a few remarks on the difficulties in translating Roswitha's style should be added. As mentioned before, her plays are written in rhymed prose; longer narrative or hymnic passages alternate with terse one- or two-syllable question-and-answer exchanges which give such theatrical liveliness to some of the dialogues. The translator is faced with the problem of either trying to keep the rhyme at the expense of meaning or opting in favour of an unrhymed prose rendition. Most translators in German, French and English follow this latter practice. The extreme opposite direction was taken in the German translation of Jacob Bendixen, who forced Roswitha's freely flowing speech into the straight-jacket of *Knittelvers*, a monotonously alternating four-footed verse.[13] The other characteristic feature of Roswitha's Latin (and, incidentally, also of her stylistic model, Terence), namely the occasional abruptness or terseness in the dialogue, is in most translations glossed over. To be sure, a synthetic language such as Latin with its brevity in verbal and nominal forms and its wealth of significant one-word expressions is hard to imitate in our analytical West European languages. But even so, often the translators do not strive to come close to the original, they try to bridge the gaps of silence that seem, to our taste, to separate rather than link speakers in a dialogue. One example of this, the brief, two-syllable reply of the Emperor in *Gallicanus,* "gaudeo," becomes in the English translation of St. John, "I am rejoiced to hear it," in the French by Magnin "Je m'en réjouis," and in Gottsched's version "Das stimmet mich froh." Such stylistic changes together with certain interferences by the translators, such as the subdivision into acts and scenes and the addition of stage remarks, lead away from the original but, on the other hand, make the access to Roswitha's plays easier for modern readers and modern audiences.

When we earlier said that nobody followed in Gottsched's steps, this was only half-true. In fact, his boastful rebuke of some French critics produced some results where he would have least expected them: some eighty years later, a Paris theatre historian, Charles Magnin, produced the first critical edition of Roswitha's plays and had it printed parallel to his own translation into French.[14] Magnin used not only Konrad Celtis' edition but also the Emmeram codex itself as well as all available critical literature on Roswitha, including Gottsched's treatise. Magnin's work with its combination of erudition and enthusiasm set the stage, literally speaking, for the popularization of Roswitha's plays and started a great number of articles and further translations, both in France and Germany. In his introduction to his edition, Magnin propounded two theories which, romantic and unproven as they are, were of some consequence, as we shall see. Magnin believed that Roswitha enacted her dramas herself together with her sisters for the edification of other clerics and guests of their convent, and secondly, he claimed that Roswitha in her depiction of erotic passions and worldly entanglements shows herself suspiciously well-informed of the ways of the world. "La vie de cette femme illustre avant son entrée à Gandersheim nous est absolument inconnue. Cependent, elle montre dans ses ecrits trop de connaissance du monde et des passions, pour que nous puissions supposer qu'elle leur soit demeuree entierement etrangere" (p. xxii).

Before completing his Roswitha-edition, Charles Magnin had distinguished himself already in a study on the history of puppet theatre. Puppet theatres were highly popular in Europe in the eighteenth and nineteenth centuries, and such a successful theatre run by a certain M. Signoret charmed a generation later, in the 1880s, the Parisian population. Among them was the novelist Anatole France, who wrote two critiques of this puppet theatre in the daily newspaper *Le Temps.* France was well familiar with both major works of Charles Magnin, "le savant historien des marionnettes," as he calls him, and he combined his own likings for puppets as well as for Roswitha's theatre in his two articles. In the first one, he urges the puppeteer, M. Signoret, to try his hand on a play by Roswitha, preferably the conversion play *Paphnutius.*[16] Indeed, his suggestion was taken up by Signoret and one year later, in his second article entitled "Hrotswitha aux marionnettes," (*Le Temps,* 7 April 1889) France reports on a successful performance of Roswitha's other conversion play *Abraham,* which is very similar to *Paphnutius.* It is a curious idea to think that Roswitha's plays were premiered on stage by puppets, but this is historically true, unless, of course, one shares with Anatole France the belief that nine hundred years earlier Roswitha herself had already performed her plays with her sisters.

In the same year, 1889, Anatole France completed *Thais* which became probably his best-known novel, not on its merits alone, but also through the subsequent opera by Massenet (1894) of which the libretto is based on France's novel. It is not possible here to attempt an exhaustive analysis of *Thais* but it is useful to note how France is indebted to Roswitha and how he acknowledges his gratitude. In standard works on the great French novelist, Roswitha's influence on the composition of *Thais* is not rated very high; the general study by Reino Virtanen, for example, does not even mention Roswitha at all.[16] Other works concede that France was inspired to write his novel by the legend of *Paphnutius* which, after all, is also contained in standard collections of legends such as the *Golden Legend* by Jacobus de Voragine. The legend relates how the holy hermit Paphnutius, disguised as a worldly lover, seeks out the infamous courtesan Thais in her domicile and converts her on the spot. Thais burns her possessions and follows Paphnutius to a nunnery where she repents her sins in severest seclusion until after some years she dies a blessed death supported by the prayer of Paphnutius.

A few passages in the *Thais* novel prove that France did indeed use Roswitha's play as a major source, to the point of even quoting verbatim from Magnin's translation.[17] His main intention in telling this story is, however, diametrically opposed to that of Roswitha, as a glance at the structure may indicate: in Roswitha's play, Paphnutius descends to the depths of Thais' abjection and lifts her up with himself to eternal glory. In France's novel, the movement of the two protagonists runs irrevocably in opposite directions; to quote France's own words: "J'ai voulu que Paphnuce perdit son âme en voulant sauver celle de Thais."[18] The saint loses his soul while the sinner whom he wants to save becomes a saint. Paphnuce in Anatole France's novel is revealed as a fraud who cheats himself, whose rigorous asceticism and alleged holiness spring from repressed sensuality, from egomania, from blindness towards the beauty of the world and fanatical deafness when confronted with other and possibly more enlightened ideas. Thais, the courtesan, on the other hand, represents beauty and grace and shows even in her moral depravity an innocence of heart and longing for purity which make her redemption the more credible. These characterizations are naturally worlds apart from the idealized, one-dimensional figures in Roswitha's play. The change of heart in Roswitha's courtesan is simply brought about by the Grace of God which needs no explanation. France, on the other hand, goes to great pains in order to justify on psychological grounds the conversion of Thais and the fall of Paphnuce; e.g., he provides both characters with a past, Thais with indelible Christian childhood memories and Paphnuce with the haunting memory of his yearning for Thais' love as a young man. In other words, France introduces into the legend with its typecast characters and its simple power of faith large doses of ironical skepticism and psychological construction.

Anatole France, then, has considerably enlarged the scope of Roswitha's little play. Among the characters whom he introduces is the venerable Albine, abbess of the convent to which Paphnuce takes Thais. It is true that such a figure occurs in one scene of Roswitha's **Paphnutius,** but there she has no name or individualizing characteristics. One striking detail in this connection has, to my knowledge, not received any attention at all in interpretations of France's *Thais*. When

the courtesan is ready to be taken away from this world to lead a life of repentance in a nunnery, Paphnuce explains his plan for her salvation in the following words:

> Or, je te conduirai aujourd'hui même dans ce monastère, ma Thaïs, et bientôt unie à ces saintes filles, tu partageras leurs célestes entretiens. Elles t'attendent comme une soeur. Au seuil du couvent, leur mère, la pieuse Albine, te donnera le baiser de paix et dira: "Ma fille, sois la bienvenue!" La courtisane poussa un cri d'admiration:—Albine! une fille des Césars! La petite nièce de l'empereur Carus!—Elle-même! Albine qui, née dans la pourpre, revêtit la bure et, fille des maîtres du monde, s'éleva au rang de servante de Jésus-Christ. Elle sera ta mère. Thaïs se leva et dit:—Mène-moi donc à la maison d'Albine.

Why should it be so important that the abbess Albine is of royal blood, a grand-niece of the Emperor? One might say, there is a certain snob-appeal which persuades the spoiled courtesan to go. In my view, however, the reason is more than just that. For a solution we have to consider the final scene of the novel where a renegade Paphnuce returns to the nunnery lusting after Thais, only to find her dying. The abbess Albine gives him an account of the life that Thais led in her convent, or rather this account is given to us readers since Paphnuce in his blind desire does not listen. Albine reports that, after a period of seclusion, Thais joined the community of sisters and that together with them she was allowed to use her former talents as an actress in order to play Biblical scenes about brave women and wise virgins for the edification of everyone.

> Quand je vis qu'elle était attachée à Dieu par la foi, l'espérance et l'amour, je ne craignis pas d'employer son art et même sa beauté à l'édification des ses soeurs. Je l'invitais à représenter devant nous les actions des femmes fortes et des vierges sages de l'Écriture. Elle imitait Esther, Débora, Judith, Marie, soeur de Lazare, et Marie, mère de Jésus.

> Je sais, vénérable père, que ton austérité s'alarme à l'idée de ces spectacles. Mais tu aurais été touché toi-même, si tu l'avais vue dans ces pieuses scènes, répandre des pleurs véritables et tendre au ciel ses bras comme des palmes. (p. 345)

There is no doubt in my mind that with this scene Anatole France alludes to Magnin's and his own theory of canoness Roswitha and her sisters performing in the convent of Gandersheim under the benign eyes of their abbess Gerberga, of royal blood, niece of the Emperor Otto. Moreover, had not Roswitha sought refuge in the peace of the cloister after a passionate worldly life, as both Magnin and France had suggested? The figures of Thais, the holy courtesan, and Roswitha, the reformed child of this world, merge in this final scene of *Thais*.

In his article "Hroswitha aux marionnettes" France had declared emphatically that only puppets in their "divine innocence" or else "those Saxon nuns of the time of Otto" could possibly perform a conversion play such as **Paphnutius.** According to Kleist's essay "Über das Marionettentheater," the state of grace, of perfect harmony within oneself and one's movements is impeded by self-reflection; it exists in perfection either in the puppet devoid of any consciousness or in God with his infinite consciousness for which mankind strives:

> . . . so findet sich auch, wenn die Erkenntnis gleichsam durch ein Unendliches gegangen ist, die Grazie wieder ein; so daß sie, zu gleicher Zeit, in demjenigen menschlichen Körperbau am reinsten erscheint, der entweder gar keins, oder ein unendliches Bewußtsein hat, d.h. in dem Gliedermann [in der Marionette], oder in dem Gott.!

In attributing this final stage to Roswitha, as Anatole France has done, he pays her the ultimate homage. One might call it "the apotheosis" of Roswitha.

Our survey has come close to its end: with the opening of the twentieth century the medieval woman playwright has finally established a niche of her own in the literary establishment. She has found theatre audiences and readers in various parts of the world, clubs have been formed in her name (the best known of them in New York in 1944), and an open air theatre festival takes place every summer in front of the Romanesque cathedral of Gandersheim where Roswitha is supposed to have started out, no doubt on a far smaller budget, a thousand years ago. The Roswitha scholarship of the twentieth century deserves study of its own which cannot possibly be attempted here.

In its stead I would like to show in one example the impact of Roswitha's work on contemporary German theatre.[21] The example is an extreme one, admittedly; no other notable playwrights have expressed their interest in their medieval forerunner as explicitly as Peter Hacks in his 1974 play, *Rosie traümt.* Nonetheless his play is also a significant offshoot of the renewed preoccupation with Roswitha's theatrical work which was ostensibly rekindled by the "Roswitha-year" of 1973. Hacks subtitles his play "Legende in fünf Aufzügen nach Hrosvith von Gandersheim."[22]

To the German theatre-goers in East and West Peter Hacks is one of the best-known contemporary playwrights. Ever since Hacks left West Germany in 1955 and chose East Berlin as his further residence, he has made it clear that a Marxist author like himself has a particular role to fulfil, that he should further the cause of socialism by his plays. And yet Hacks has not always shown himself to be a yes-man vis-à-vis the East German brand of Marxism. In fact, he constantly stresses the importance of criticizing wrong aspects of his own society, which in some of his earlier plays promptly caused their temporary withdrawal from the major stages in East Germany. In the last decade, Hacks has turned away from dealing with contemporary matters and has written several historical and mythological plays as well as adapting classical ones for the modern stage. *Rosie traümt* is one in this stream.

Why would a dyed-in-the-wool Marxist writer choose of all things the works of a medieval nun as basis for his own script? In trying to answer this question, I will have to describe first what material Hacks takes from Roswitha's works and what he does with it. The underlying structure of *Rosie traümt* is that of Roswitha's **Gallicanus,** the legend of the Roman Caesar who before going into battle asks his superior, the Emperor, for the hand of his daughter Constantia. Constantia has secretly vowed to live her life in a state of Christian virginity, but she accepts the proposal *pro forma.* Fortunately for her, Gallicanus can win his battle only through divine intervention, which prompts him to convert to Christianity, he gives up his marriage plans and retreats into a solitary life where he later dies a martyr's death. This is the kind of plot that legends are made of: straightforward and to the point (in this case, the glorification of virginity and *contemptus mundi* attitude). Hacks' modern legend is more complicated and the point is not at all clearly visible. He has tried to blend scenes and figures from just about all of Roswitha's plays as well as of some of her legends proper. His additions to the cast include not only the Virgin Mary and the Devil, but also Roswitha herself, Rosie for short, who takes over the original role of Constantia trying to convert Gallicanus. Rosie is portrayed as a "Jesus freak," a candy-eating teenage girl with higher pretensions, namely the totally unrealistic desire to bring about the reign of Jesus on earth. She is always willing to perform a few miracles for the good cause, thereby changing, for example, the outcome of the battle or the heart of the courtesan Thais. Since she can't have her way in establishing Christ's Kingdom on Earth, she is finally granted a swift martyr's death in which she is even joined, out of a whim, by Gallican, and in the final scene we find both of them reunited in Heaven, a happy ending of some sort.

It is obvious that Hacks had the stage effect foremost in his mind when he selected various passages from Roswitha's plays to serve as nuclei for scenes in his own play. In the course of such transplants, the original significance is naturally altered drastically, as one could only show in a detailed comparison. Suffice it to say that Hacks purges Roswitha's dramas of their religious or even allegorical meaning, the *sensus spiritualis;* what is divine for her is comical in his rendition (e.g., miracles). He brings out the comical potential of some of Roswitha's scenes (e.g., in **Dulcitius**) or turns originally serious scenes into farcical ones, such as the conversion of Thais. In short, Hacks transforms Roswitha's plays into parody or travesty.

Here and there, however, Hacks adds to the entertainment value of his comedy his own hidden meaning (his *sensus spiritualis,* as it were): a political one. When looking into hidden political meanings, we have to guard against jumping to quick conclusions from quotations taken out of context. Take, for instance, the resigned remark of Hacks's Thais: "Mit den Mannern in Sirnium steht es wie mit den Bananen in Sirnium: man bekommt nur entweder unreife oder verdorbene." ("Here in Sirnium, it is the same with men as it is with bananas: the only ones you can get here are either unripe or rotten.") Does this imply that Hacks criticizes the availability of tropical fruit in the GDR (which is, indeed, a sore point) or is he just keeping his audience amused? Hacks in a recent interview praised the alertness of his East Berlin public who, in his words, "know how to read a metaphor."[23] We on the other side of the Iron Curtain may completely misread the author's veiled intent.

On the other hand, Hacks himself sets us on the track for a political interpretation of his play in a short essay attached to the play, "Zehn Zeilen uber *Rosie traumt*" (pp. 122-30). In it he states that he unseated Roswitha from the divine author's chair and moved her over to the ultra-Left. Furthermore, when he calls his Rosie an adherent of the *"apostolic"* movement, he puts in a pun by labelling her an "APO-girl." The German noun APO, however, an abbreviation for "Ausserparlamentarische Opposition," is a term commonly used for the young revolutionary opposition in West Germany in pre-Baader-Meinhof times. We begin to understand Hacks' intention a little better. He plays on the parallel in the socio-historical situations between the late Roman Empire and the modern decline of capitalism as diagnosed by a Marxist. There, some revolutionary people lived and died for a new faith promising paradise, here for a new ideology promising something akin to paradise on earth, the classless society.

A thinly-veiled stereotyped Communist message, one may think, but what about the final scene of the play, the "Postlude to Heaven"? Paradise turns out to be a bitter disappointment for Rosie: the heavenly music of the spheres that she had longed to hear all her life is dull, unpleasant people like her executioner have also found their way in, and bureaucracy seems to reign supreme. She addresses herself to a lady who happens to be passing by, none other than the Holy Virgin herself in the habit of an abbess, and learns from her that Jesus does not exist anymore; he has been eaten up by the bishops, and whether or not God exists nobody really knows. The Virgin answers Rosie's final question whether she herself believes in God in these elusive words: "Well, my child, I think one ought to believe if one still can. But don't you want to follow me?"

Are we then justified in assuming that this disappointing paradise is a discreet allusion to the stage of "realer Sozialismus," which the GDR claims to have reached, and that it is, in the author's opinion, far from being the perfect final stage of Marxist society? Or worse even, that the author is not very sure whether his society is moving in that direction at all? A West German critic of the journal "Theater heute" pointed this out and noted the disillusionment and air of resignation in Hacks' play,[24] whereas, interestingly enough, an East German colleague of his regretted that the play does not impart any moral whatsoever.[25]

In my view, the interpretation of the West German critic is better, and I would like to support it with another argument. In the very first scene of his play, Hacks builds into his text a rather strained play on words to express this very banal phrase: "If I, Augustus, were not the Emperor myself, you would deserve to be Augustus." In the German version: "Du verdientest / Wär nicht August August, August zu sein." Hacks is obviously quoting the title of the famous play *August August, August* by the dissident Czech playwright Pavel Kohout, written in 1967. Instead of staging his play in the mock-heroic world of emperors and kings, as Hacks does, Kohout uses the circus world as a setting, his "August" being the underdog clown. What Kohout's play has in common with that of Hacks is that it also deals with the difficulty of realizing one's dream which, in his play, is brutally crushed in the end.[26] This, of course, has strong political overtones as well, which explains why Kohout's works are taboo in the GDR. Hacks scratches this taboo a little in his oblique reference to Kohout's work and from it, I presume, he takes up the dream metaphor in his title "Rosie traümt." It is true that, in contrast to the tragic ending of Kohout's play, Hacks treats us to a pseudo-happy end in Paradise where dreams supposedly come true. But rather than raising our spirits, the ending of his play has a more paralyzing, depressing effect. *Rosie traümt* is, in my view, an East German counterpart of the Czech play. As we have seen, however, Hacks is more willing to compromise and to veil his disenchantment with his own society. Writing for the theatre in the GDR has been compared to a tight-rope act without a net, but I do not think we should fear that Peter Hacks might fall and become a martyr of his faith. That would sound too much like a twentieth century version of a legend written by the medieval playwright Roswitha.

Returning to our initial question why the work of this exceptional woman has survived, we have seen that there are many answers. Whether later generations were fascinated by her elegant style, her theatrical talent, the romantic potential of her subjects, or by her feminist stand, it is evident that it is not only her work that has attracted a considerable amount of attention but also the legends and speculations which evolved around her person. Thus, it is no coincidence that the two works last considered, those of Anatole France and Peter Hacks, incorporate not only material and motives from Roswitha's theatre but also the figure of the authoress herself as well as that of her preceptor, the abbess Gerberga. It is furthermore no coincidence that these two "productive" receptions of Roswitha's work (in contrast to the more academic reproductions, translations and adaptations) operate predominantly with the stylistic elements of irony and parody, thinly veiled in France's *Thaïs* and an openly declared principle in Hacks's *Rosie traümt*. This artistic procedure has not failed to irritate the more traditionally-minded, orthodox admirers of Roswitha's work and its original message. However, according to Dürrenmatt's lucid observation, the modern playwright cannot but reduce and parody traditional subjects and characters if he wishes to make them meaningful for his own purpose. Only through such an act will he regain his artistic freedom.

> Aus diesem Grunde muss denn auch der Kunstler die Gestalten, die er trifft, auf die er überall stösst, reduzieren, will er sie wieder zu Stoffen machen, hoffend, dass es ihm gelinge: Er parodiert sie, das heisst, er stellt sie im bewussten Gegensatz zu dem dar, was sie geworden sind. Damit aber, durch diesen Akt der Parodie, gewinnt er wieder seine Freiheit und damit den Stoff.[27]

To be considered worthy of a parody after a thousand years is certainly a measure of Roswitha's literary success.

Notes

[1] See the comprehensive study by Bert Nagel, *Hrotsvit von Gandersheim* (Stuttgart: Metzler, 1965).

[2] Hermann Reich, ed., *Deutsche Dichter des lateinischen Mittelalters,* 4th ed. (Munich, 1922), p. 110. Quoted after Bert Nagel, "Ego, Clamor Validus Gandeshemensis," *Germanisch-Romanische Monatsschrift,* 23 (1973), 451.

[3] *The Plays of Roswitha,* trans. by Christopher St. John (1923; rpt. New York: Blom, 1966), p. xxvii. This text is used for all English translations of Roswitha. The Latin text used is the edition by Helene Homeyer, *Hrotsvithae Opera* (Paderborn: F. Schöningh, 1970), p. 234 ". . . praesertim cum feminea fragilitas vinceret et virilis robur confusioni subiaceret."

[4] See on this topic Edwin H. Zeydel, "Were Hrotsvitha's dramas performed during her lifetime?" *Speculum,* 20 (1945), 443-56. This question is emphatically but not convincingly answered in the positive by Mary M. Butler, *Hrotsvitha: the theatricality of her plays* (New York: Philosophical Library, 1960).

[5] *Der Briefwechsel des Konrad Celtis,* ed. Hans Rupprich (Munich: C. H. Beck, 1934), p. 464.

[6] Quoted from Edwin H. Zeydel, "The Reception of Hrotsvitha by the German Humanists after 1493," *Journal of English Germanic Philology,* 44 (1945), 245. In Zeydel's English translation, this epigram reads: "Hrotsvitha is now the greatest glory to German lands, learned in weaving Latian melodies in songs. No less refined does she write in prose, following the free comic works of Terence."

[7] Ibid., 244. In Zeydel's rendering: "Why should we not praise the writings of the German maid, who, were she Greek, would long be a goddess without any doubt."

[8] *Der Briefwechsel des Konrad Celtis,* P. 478: "You have acted against the practice of many learned or rather arrogant men who wrongly look down on anything said, written or composed by women" (my own translation).

[9] *Nöthiger Vorrath zur Geschichte der deutschen Dramatischen Dichtkunst,* oder Verzeichniss aller Deutschen Trauer- Lust- und Sing-Spiele, die im Druck erschienen, von 1490 bis zur Hälfte des jetzigen Jahrhunderts, gesammlet und ans Licht gestellet, von Johann Christoph Gottscheden (Leipzig: Johann Michael Teubner, 1757).

[10] *Des nöthigen Vorraths zur Geschichte der deutschen Dramatischen Dichtkunst Zweyter Teil, oder Nachlese* . . . (Leipzig: Teubner, 1765), p. 6.

[11] The only known copy is that of the University Library Heidelberg, Cod. Pal. Germ. 298, fol. 101-122.

[12] *Goethes Werke,* Vol. IX, Ed. Erich Trunz (Hamburg: Ch. Wegner, 1959), pp. 267-68.

[13] The Bendixen translation of 1850 is used again in Hrotsvit von Gandersheim, *Sämtliche Dichtungen* (Munich: Winkler, 1966).

[14] *Théâtre de Hrotsvitha,* ed. Charles Magnin (Paris: Duprat, 1845).

[15] Anatole France, "Les marionnettes de M. Signoret," *Le Temps,* 10 June 1888.

[16] Reino Virtanen, *Anatole France* (New York: Twayne Publishers, 1968).

[17] See Raoul Gout, "Anatole France et le Théâtre de Hrotsvitha," *Mercure de France,* 229 (1931), 595-611.

[18] Quoted after Edwin P. Dargan, *Anatole France* (New York: Oxford University Press, 1937), p. 455.

[19] Anatole France, *Thais* (Paris: Calmann-Lévy, n.d.), pp. 214-15.

[20] Heinrich von Kleist, *Werke,* ed. Erich Schmidt (Leipzig: Bibliograph. Institut, n.d.), vol. IV, p. 141.

[21] For a general discussion on this topic as well as performance records of Roswitha's plays, see Bert Nagel, *Hrotsvit von Gandersheim,* pp. 76-81.

[22] Peter Hacks, *Das Jahrmarktsfest zu Plundersweilern. Rosie träumt* (Berlin: Aufbau-Verlag, 1976).

[23] Reinhart Baumgart, "Das Lahand ist still—noch!" *Die Zeit* (Overseas Edition), 25 Nov. 1977, p. 4, col. 4.

[24] Urs Allemann, "Die poetischen Rückzugsgefechte des Peter Hacks," *Theater heute,* May 1976, 34-36.

[25] Karl-Heinz Müller, *Rosie träumt,* von Peter Hacks," *Theatre der Zeit,* 31, No. 3 (1976), 14-15.

[26] Pavel Kohout, "August August, August," *So eine Leibe, Reise um die Erde in 80 Tagen. August August, August* (Luzern: Bucher, 1971), pp. 66: "Ein Traum soll ein Traum bleiben, August. Sonst bringst du ihn um. Verstehst du das?" There is not yet an English translation of Kohout's play.

[27] Friedrich Dürrenmatt, *Theaterprobleme* (Zurich: Arche, 1955), p. 55.

Dennis M. Kratz (essay date 1978)

SOURCE: "The Nun's Epic: Hroswitha on Christian Heroism" in *Wege der Worte: Festschrift für Wolfgang Fleischhauer,* edited by Donald C. Riechel, Böhlau Verlag, 1978, pp. 132-42.

[In the following essay, Kratz examines Hroswitha's Latin epic Gesta Ottonis, *concluding that it is "among the most successful attempts in the history of Latin literature to adapt the epic genre for the expression of a Christian definition of heroic excellence."]*

Best known for the comedies which she wrote in order to provide her Benedictine sisters a Christian alternative to the comedies of Terence, Hroswitha of Gandersheim stands as a unique figure in the history not only of Latin drama but of epic as well. Her *Gesta Ottonis* and *Primordia Coenobii Gandeshemensis* are the only Latin epics we possess which were composed by a woman.[1] While the latter poem is not without merit, the *Gesta Ottonis,* to which this essay is devoted, is in many respects Hroswitha's finest literary achievement; and the fact that its author is a woman is a far from inconsequential element of its success. For Hroswitha's consciousness of the epic genre as a "masculine" domain provided her with the justification, if not the inspiration, for a departure from tradition which helps raise her narrative above any other tenth century attempt at Christian epic.

Hroswitha turned to epic at the culmination of her literary career. She had already composed eight verse legends and six comedies when, in 967, she began the *Gesta Ottonis.* The narrative is ordered chronologically. Hroswitha begins by praising Otto's parents, Henry and Mathilda. After mentioning each of their three sons—Otto, Henry, and Bruno—she focuses attention on Otto by describing his marriage to Edith, daughter of King Edward. At this point in the narrative, his father dies, and Otto assumes the throne. Almost immediately war breaks out, led by a certain Everhard. Although Otto puts down this rebellion, Everhard soon leads another; and he persuades Otto's brother Henry to join him. After a pitched battle, Otto again is victorious. A third rebellion, in which Henry again participates, ends in an abortive attempt to assassinate Otto on Easter; however, Otto forgives the now repentant Henry. Hroswitha then lauds Otto's rule; but this passage is followed by the report of Edith's death.

The second half of the *Gesta Ottonis* revolves around the conflict between Otto and Berengar II, who had usurped the Italian throne after the death of King Lothair. Lothair's wife, Adelaide, imprisoned by Berengar, escapes and is rescued by Otto. After marrying her, Otto then sets about conquering Italy. He sends his son Liudolf to win over the Italians as allies, then enters Italy himself along with an army, and captures Pavia without opposition from Berengar, who has retreated to a fortified sanctuary. After putting Liudolf in charge of Saxony, Otto devotes his full attention to subduing Italy and soon captures Berengar. He allows Berengar to retain his authority, on condition of obedience to himself; but when Berengar immediately rebels, Otto is compelled to fight again. At this point the text, lamentably, breaks off. Its last extant passages mention a final mission by Liudolf to Italy in 957 and various events from the years 962 through 967.

The narrative seems at first glance straightforward and unexceptional.[2] But Hroswitha has made the *Gesta Ottonis* more than a simple chronicle of events; for underlying her descriptive account of Otto's accomplishments we can discern a prescriptive definition of the qualities which the truly Christian ruler must exhibit. Otto, central figure in the epic, is in fact Hroswitha's model of Christian heroic virtue.

The key to the poem's underlying meaning—and to Hroswitha's artistry—is the comparison of Otto with the Biblical king David which serves as one of the unifying themes in the epic. This theme begins before the narrative itself; for in the second of two verse prefaces to her poem, Hroswitha twice likens Otto's son to the Biblical king Solomon. The first passage urges the younger Otto to follow the example of Solomon in accepting the responsibility of kingship (Prologue 2: 19-23):

> Sed quia te memini sublimiter assimilari
> Nato famosi regis David Salomoni,
> Qui genitore suo praesente iubenteque sancto,
> Optata regnum suscepit pace paternum,
> Ipsius exemplo te contentum fore spero.[3]

In the second passage, Hroswitha addresses Otto II as "our Solomon" (31: *nostrum Salomonem),* as she asks him to receive her unworthy tribute to his father (Prologue 2: 31-38). These comparisons of Otto II to Solomon in the second prologue serve as an introduction to a major theme of the epic—the comparison of Otto I to David, the father of Solomon. Hroswitha first applies this image to Otto while describing his coronation as Emperor (136-140):

> Insuper e tantis ipsum sacra dextra potentis
> Protegit insidiis occulta fraude paratis
> Et tam magnificis ornat persaepe triumphis,
> Ut credas regem David regnare fidelem
> Iam nunc antiquis fulgentem rite triumphis.

Hroswitha's poem, we should note, provides the first literary mention of Otto bearing the title of Emperor. Moreover, David was the name given to Charlemagne by the members of his court circle, a fact which may have influenced Hroswitha; for Otto, like Charlemagne, was attempting to renew a Christian Empire in the West.[4]

Hroswitha employs the David/Otto theme to help portray the necessary qualities of the Christian hero. The first requirement, as articulated in the passage quoted above, is a special relationship with God, Who responds to the hero's fidelity (139: *David . . . fidelem)* by placing him under His divine protection against the power of evil (137: *protegit insidiis occulta fraude paratis*). This divine protection gives to the Christian hero a strength surpassing that of his enemies. Hroswitha is here making use of the common emphasis by Christian writers on David as a *figura* of strength, much as Solomon represented wisdom. She goes on to stress this facet of her comparison, stating (141-145) that Otto not only preserved the territories which he inherited but even extended the boundaries of the Empire. The passage continues (146-152):

> Ad bellum certe quoties processerat ipse,
> Non fuit populus, quamvis virtute superbus,
> Laedere qui posset vel exsuperare valeret
> Ipsum caelestis fultum solamine regis;
> Eius nec cessit telis exercitus ullis,
> Ni sua spernendo forsan regalia iussa
> Illic pugnaret, quo rex idem prohiberet.

In this passage, Hroswitha states clearly that Otto's might derives from God's favor (149: *ipsum caelestis fultum solamine regis*); and she contrasts this strength with the haughtiness (147: *populus . . . superbus*) of his enemies.

The negative corollary of the power which emanates from God is *fraus,* or treachery inspired by the devil. Hroswitha alludes to this concept in the same passage in which she first associates Otto I with David (137: *insidiis occulta fraude paratis*). In describing Everhard's rebellion, the first discord to trouble Otto's reign, Hroswitha establishes *fraus* as her symbol for the sinfulness which provokes men to the disruption of political harmony (163-167):

> O quam tranquillum ridens deduceret aevum
> Fortunata satis nostrae res publica gentis,
> Quae nimis imperio regis regitur sapientis
> Si non antiqui male calliditas inimici
> Turbaret nostrum secreta fraude serenum!

The outbreak of a second insurrection led by Everhard is likewise attributed to the power of *fraus* (202-205):

> His bene dispositis regis iussu sapientis,
> Protulit antiqui rursum mala fraus inimici
> Inventum sceleris primo mage deterioris,
> Cunctis horrendum saeclis meritoque
>   stupendum.

Fraus underlies as well the plot to assassinate Otto on Easter Sunday (318). Berengar too is closely associated with the symbolic image of *fraus.* Hroswitha sees this power at work when he treacherously rebels against Otto despite his sworn promise to respect the Emperor's authority (727-731).

We have already observed that Hroswitha contrasts his enemies' *superbia* and *fraus* with Otto's own David-like reliance on God; and she devotes the rest of the epic to defining more precisely Otto's heroic excellence. One of three specific elements comprising that definition is wisdom, or *sapientia.* On four occasions, Hroswitha speaks of Otto's wisdom. The last mention makes reference to his habit of acting wisely (701: *rex, qui semper fecit sapienter*). The third combines the themes of wisdom and strength (378-385):

> Avaresque per hunc saevi saepissimi victi
> Post haec Ottonis regnum regis spatiosum
> Non laedunt telis consueto more cruentis
> Tangere nec contingentes audent nationes,
> Ex terrore ducis tanti nimium tremefacti;
> Hic quia, prudentis functus valetudine mentis,
> His hominum monstris bellis obstans iteratis
> Ad nos pergendi calles secluserat omnes.

Significantly, each of the first two appearances of this theme, which occur in passages which we have already discussed (163-167, 202-205), sets Otto's wisdom in contrast to *fraus*. Moreover, Hroswitha has foreshadowed the appearance of the *sapientia* theme with her mention of Solomon in the second prologue. We have made note of the general association of Solomon with wisdom, an association which Hroswitha echoes by describing him as *prudenter legum condens decreta* (25) and *penetrans animo rerum secreta profundo* (26).

The second, and most emphasized, element of Hroswitha's definition of heroism is *pietas*. The scene in which she introduces this concept into the epic centers on the battle in which Otto defeats the army of Everhard and Henry. Although Hroswitha does not describe any of the fighting, she does not completely pass over the events of the battle. Instead, she redirects our attention by repeating the comparison of Otto with David (251-256):

> Hoc dico solum (recte quod dicere possum);
> Qui solus semper fecit miranda potenter
> Quique, David regem toties de fraude fidelem
> Eripiens Sauli, sceptrum regni dedit ipsi,
> Hunc pariter regem David pietate sequentem
> Protexit de millenis persaepe periclis.

This passage repays careful analysis. In it, Hroswitha asserts that Otto, like David, is under God's special favor through his fidelity, and therefore protected from the dangers of *fraus*. Key words—*fraus, fidelem, protexit*—are repeated from the first David/Otto comparison (136-140). Moreover, in the last two lines, Hroswitha calls this special relationship *pietas,* and says specifically that the model for Otto's *pietas* is David (255: *David pietate sequentem*).

By so carefully establishing a Biblical model for Otto's *pietas,* Hroswitha adds a second level to her portrait of the Christian hero. Inevitably the application of the epithet *pius* to an epic hero calls to mind Aeneas. Hroswitha's use of David as the exemplar of *pietas* gives her later use of *pius* both Classical and Christian echoes. We recall again that Otto viewed himself as a continuator of the line of Roman emperors; but also, like Charlemagne, saw himself as superior to his Roman predecessor because of his Christianity.

As the battle rages, Hroswitha's attention continues on Otto's reactions, rather than the fighting, and she uses the opportunity to strengthen his association with the Biblical king. Of particular importance is this speech in which Otto bitterly mourns the death of so many brave men (266-275):

> At si forte suos, pugna crescente sinistra,
> Audivit socios letali vulnere laesos,
> Praedicti regis lacrimans mox utitur orsis,
> Quae maerens dixit, tristi cum pectore sensit
> Ictibus angelici populum gladii periturum:
> "En, qui peccavi, dixit, facinusque peregi,

> Hinc ego vindictae dignus sum denique tantae!
> Hi quid fecerunt, damnum qui tale tulerunt?
> Iam nunc, Christe, tuis parcens miserere
>   redemptis,
> Ne premat insontes iusto plus vis inimica!"

Otto's words are modelled on the lament uttered by David when God sent a pestilence upon Israel (II Regum xxiv. 17):

> dixitque David ad Dominum cum vidisset
>   angelum caedentem populum:
> ego cum qui peccavi ego inique egi.
> isti qui oves sunt quid fecerunt?
> vertatur obsecro manus tua contra me
>   et contra domum patris mei.

Among the verbal imitations, Otto's adaptions of David's *ego cum qui peccavi, ego inique egi,* and *quid fecerunt* are unmistakable. Immediately after this speech, Hroswitha again makes note of Otto's *pietas*. In this instance, it prompts God to grant him the hoped-for victory (276-279):

> Has igitur preculas miserans divina potestas
> Parcebat regis solita pietate ministris.
> Et dedit optatum miserans ex hoste
>   triumphum,
> Iusto praedictos comites examine perdens.

At the conclusion of the battle, Hroswitha compares Otto's sadness even at the death of his foes to the reaction of David when he learned that Saul was dead (292-296):

> Denique dum pugnae sensit discrimina tantae,
> Haut gaudens inimicorum de morte suorum,
> Sed plus tantorum maerens de caede virorum,
> Sumpsit non modicum, Davidis more,
>   lamentum,
> Qui super occasum doluit regem pie Saulum.

Here again Hroswitha uses literary evocation (295-296: *Davidis more . . . pie*) to conjoin the theme of Otto's *pietas* with that of David as the model of his heroic virtues.

This entire scene (202-315) stands at the artistic center of Hroswitha's epic. In it, as we have shown, she meticulously establishes David as the *exemplar virtutis* for Otto. She does so at the expense of the battle description which we would expect in an epic poem. It is important to note that she begins the scene by stating her aversion to treating such subject matter; for that passage (237-249), as we will see, establishes even more firmly the centrality of the scene which we have been discussing.

Having now established *pietas* and wisdom as two elements in her portrait of the Christian hero, Hroswitha completes her triad of heroic virtues by emphasizing, in later episodes, Otto's mercy (*clementia*) toward his enemies. For example, his *pietas* leads Otto (363: *victus pietate benigna*) to forgive his brother Henry; and his mercy extends even to the treacherous Berengar (701-707). In this instance, Hroswitha combines the theme of Otto's *clementia* with his wisdom (701: *rex qui semper fecit sapienter*).

We can see, then, that Hroswitha's portrait of the Christian hero, as it is presented in the **Gesta Ottonis,** follows an orderly development. Like David, he must be faithful to God, Who will then grant him protection against treachery inspired by the devil. It is from this divine protection that his might derives. The Christian hero takes no pleasure from his military victories; for he mourns the death of allies and enemies alike. In the aftermath of victory, he is merciful and forgiving. In all his actions, he displays wisdom; and this complex of three interconnected virtues—*pietas, clementia, sapientia*—comprises Hroswitha's definition of Christian heroism.

Hroswitha's emphasis on these three virtues, along with military strength, as the qualities of an idealized Christian ruler is, of course, far from unique. It is impossible even to isolate the specific influence on her thought because the basic political conception, which has its Christian roots in the writings of Augustine, pervades the Ottonian literature.[5] In addition, the emphasis on *clementia* and *pietas* as virtues of a Roman emperor can be traced back to Augustus.[6] With regard to the epic tradition, the importance of *pietas* in Vergil's portrait of Aeneas can hardly be overemphasized. Moreover, to combine *fortitudo* with *sapientia* in the description of a hero was a commonplace of Latin epic poetry.[7] Indeed, similar language in the description of the idealized Christian ruler can be discerned in other Ottonian literature, most dramatically the *Modus Ottinc.*[8]

Hroswitha alone, however, among tenth century poets was able to use the Latin epic genre as a vehicle for the expression of this Christian concept of heroic excellence; and her success stands out even more clearly when we compare the **Gesta Ottonis** with two other attempts at Christian historical epic, the *Annales* of the so-called "Saxon Poet" (which she probably had read) and the *Gesta Berengarii* (which she probably had not).

The *Annales,*[9] which recounts in five books the events of 771-814, was composed around 888 by a Saxon monk from Corvey. As a historical source, it has little value, since it is largely drawn from prose sources, particularly the so-called *Annales Einhardi.* As literature, the work has attracted little attention. A recent study, however, has put forth the suggestion that the poet's ambitious goal was to create an *enkomion* to Charlemagne, in the form of a heroic epic, which would play a part in Carolingian Europe analogous to that of the *Aeneid* in Roman culture.[10]

If the Saxon Poet's goal was the creation of a new *Aeneid,* he failed. The *Annales* is, for the most part, an uninspired recitation of events, with sporadic imitation of epic themes and language. Of some interest, however, is his attempt to enhance Charlemagne's reputation by comparing him with great heroic figures of the past. The one most extensive comparison is that between Charlemagne and David (IV.323-333). Although this association is not developed as a continuing theme in the poem, it does reappear briefly in another long passage devoted to placing Charlemagne's greatness in historical perspective (V.645-686). Among the great historical leaders cited are Constantine and Theodosius, with whom Charlemagne is said to share "Davidic virtue" (V.661-662):

> Illic Daviticae pollet virtutis honore
> Cum Constantino atque Theodosio.

While these instances may have served as one of the models for Hroswitha's use of the David/Otto comparison, the distinction between the two poets' use of the comparison should be noted. Put briefly, Hroswitha succeeded in integrating the image of David into the larger fabric of her epic poem; and the Saxon Poet did not.

A very different work, the *Gesta Berengarii* was composed in the first quarter of the tenth century by an anonymous Italian poet. Its author was a learned man, who was familiar with a wide range of Latin literature.[11] The poem reveals his close familiarity with both classical epic (the *Aeneid, Thebaid,* and *Ilias Latina*) and patristic epic (the *Carmen Paschale* of Sedulius and Prudentius' *Psychomachia*). Its subject is the life of Berengar, who was the grandfather of the treacherous Berengar in Hroswitha's epic, from the time he assumes the kingship over Italy until his coronation as Emperor in 915. The greater part of the narrative, which is divided into four books, concerns Berengar's conquest of his arch-enemy Wido of Spoleto.

The poet views his poem as a Christian continuation of the Latin epic genre. In a 32-line prologue he expressly states his intention to imitate, though not rival Homer and Vergil (Prologue I.1-4):

> Non hederam sperare vales laurumve, libelle,
> Que largita suis tempora prisca viris.
> Contulit hec magno labyrinthea fabula
> Homero.
> Aeneisque tibi, docte poeta Maro.

In the beginning of the narrative itself, the poet returns to the question of his relation to Classical epic. Using language which reflects a familiarity with Sedulius' discussion of the same issue in the *Carmen Paschale*,[12] he defends his poem on the grounds that, if the Greeks and Romans praised their epic heroes, it is proper for him to adopt their literary genre to praise a Christian ruler (I.1-51). Moreover, he concludes the *Gesta Berengarii* as he began, by declaring his reverence for Homer and Vergil (IV.200-202):

> Quando brevi tantos cludo sermone triumphos?
> Doctiloquum, credo, labor iste gravaret
>   Homerum,
> Officio et genuit tali quem Mantua dignum.

The extent to which the poet imitates Classical epic is in fact impressive. He might well have mentioned Statius, along with Homer and Vergil, as a model, since he has reproduced more than 100 lines from the *Thebaid* in the *Gesta Berengarii*. The *Ilias Latina* provides 28 borrowed lines; the *Aeneid*, 14. In the characterization of the two adversaries we can recognize most clearly the poet's desire to recreate a Classical epic. Adopting the *furor/ pietas* dichotomy of the *Aeneid*, he contrasts the madness of Wido with Berengar's piety. The model for Wido is Turnus; for Berengar, Aeneas. Like Aeneas, Berengar exhibits both *pietas* and warlike prowess. For most of the epic, the emphasis is on the latter virtue. Berengar does, to be sure, make a speech (I.107-123) in which he both justifies his war against Wido and professes his dislike for killing. Once in a battle, however, Berengar displays little reticence. He is a cruel and implacable fighter, who shows no mercy to his foes (II.259-262):

> . . . Secreta tibi committere nullus
> Audebit, Thirrene, dehinc, quod apertus
>   habunde
> Hac illacque flues. Sint hec monimenta,
>   minorem
> Te frustra voluisse meis illudere telis!

The mocking tone of speech such as this, uttered by Berengar to a man whose skull he has just split in two, reminds one more of Tydeus than a Christian ruler.

In the final two books, the theme of Berengar's *pietas* becomes more important; but the transition from battlefield to church is too abrupt, and the poet's attempt to fuse piety with ferocity into a portrait of a "holy warrior" does not succeed. Rather, there is an unresolved tension in the characterization of Berengar. The Christian elements are not harmonized with the pervasive influence of Classical epic. That influence is particularly noticeable in the poet's fondness for extended battle scenes, and his descriptions of his hero's *aristeiai*. Consequently, Berengar seems not an integrated portrait of Christian heroism, but an amalgamation of pagan and Christian values.

Hroswitha, on the other hand, avoids the problems which, unresolved, mar the *Gesta Berengarii*. Of cru-

cial importance, as has been demonstrated, is her choice of David, not Aeneas, as the paradigm for Otto's *pietas*. Equally important, however, is her conscious decision to omit scenes of battle from her epic. The interconnection between the two decisions has already been suggested. At the point in her narrative where a battle scene is expected, she substitutes in its place the speech by Otto in which he uses David's very words to lament the death of so many soldiers.

Aware of her departure from epic tradition, Hroswitha both provides a justification for it and underscores its importance (237-249):

> Non me plus licito tantae sophiae fore iacto,
> Ut sperem plene verbis edicere posse,
> Quanta gratiolae Christus virtute supernae
> Saepius hunc ipsum regem digne benedictum
> Fecit multiplices salvum percurrere fraudes
> Necnon insidias hostili parte paratas;
> Sed nec hoc fragilis fas esse reor mulieris
> Inter coenobii positae secreta quieti,
> Ut bellum dictet, quod nec cognoscere debet.
> Haec perfectorum sunt conservanda virorum
> Sudori, quis posse dedit sapientia patris
> Omnia compositis sapienter dicere verbis,
> Principium qui cunctarum, finis quoque,
>   rerum.

We have earlier alluded to the importance of this passage. In it, Hroswitha first argues that she lacks the ability (237: *sophiae*) to cope with so demanding a subject. She then declares that it is unseemly, moreover, for a woman (243: *fragilis . . . mulieris*)—and particularly a nun—to speak of war. The description of fighting is better left to men (246-7: *virorum sudori*) who have the talent (248: *sapienter dicere*) which Hroswitha lacks.

We observe in this passage the common *topos* of "the poet's incompetence" given a second aspect; for Hroswitha has added the difficulty which the material presents to a woman poet. The phrase *perfectorum sunt conservanda virorum sudori* contains a double antithesis—between Hroswitha and accomplished poets, between Hroswitha and men.

Throughout the **Gesta Ottonis,** she has threaded the twin *topoi* of her humility before the theme of Otto's greatness and her inability, as a woman, to deal adequately with so masculine a subject as war. Like the Otto/David comparison, they serve to unify the epic. For example, the same *topoi* of humility (*vili . . . sermone*) and womanhood (*femineo prohibebor sexu*) appear at the conclusion of the epic (1485-1488):

> Nunc scribenda quidem constant, quae fecerit
>   idem
> Augustus solium retinens in vertice rerum.

Tangere quae vereor, quia femineo prohibebor
Sexu, nec vili debent sermone revolvi.

Both passages from the epic itself are foreshadowed by Hroswitha in her prose preface to the **Gesta Ottonis** (4 . . . 9):

> In huius sudore progressionis quantum meae
> inscitiae obstiterit difficultatis . . . quanto
> sexus fragilior scientiaque minor, tanto
> venia erit facilior . . .

We see in this passage Hroswitha's emphasis on her ignorance (*inscitiae . . . minor scientia*) and womanhood (*sexus fragilior*) as together rendering her incapable of coping with her subject. The two passages in the narrative not only repeat the conjoining of the two ideas, but also contain echoes of its language.

Protestations of inadequacy are, of course, not uncommon in Latin literature. They occur with particular frequency, as Janson has shown, in prose prefaces.[13] Hroswitha's *excusatio,* then, makes use of a long-standing rhetorical tradition. But, as with her use of the David theme, she has adapted a common *topos* with great originality to her own purposes. In using the *excusatio* to introduce the subsidiary theme of a woman's aversion to describing battles, she sets the stage for her most striking departure from epic tradition. In the place of a battle, she has the pivotal scene—which includes the use by Otto of David's very words—in the establishment of the Biblical exemplar for Otto's *pietas.*

It is a mistake, we must conclude, to take literally Hroswitha's rhetorical protestations of a *tenuis Musa.* Her narrative artistry, far from being meager, is strikingly apparent not only in her adaptation of traditional themes but also in her skillful interweaving of disparate threads into a complete fabric. The key to her achievement is her use of David (rather than Aeneas, as in the *Gesta Berengarii*) as the exemplar for the conception of *pietas* which underlies her definition of heroism. Unlike the Saxon Poet, who makes a similar comparison between David and Charlemagne, Hroswitha successfully integrates the David theme into the overall design of her narrative. The key to this successful integration derives from her innovative conjoining of a traditional *excusatio* and her own declaration that a woman ought not to describe battles. At the point in the narrative where a battle description would be appropriate, Hroswitha inserts instead an extended and forceful comparison with David.

Earlier in her career, we recall, Hroswitha had attempted to compose Christian comedies; and her reputation long has rested on the **Dulcitius** and its companion pieces. But whatever her achievement as a dramatist, her **Gesta Ottonis** stands among the most successful attempts in the history of Latin literature to adapt the epic genre

for the expression of a Christian definition of heroic excellence.

Notes

[1] With the possible exception of the Vergilian cento composed *ca.* 360 by Faltonia Proba. She refers to an epic poem which she had written concerning Constantius' war against Magnentius, but it has not survived.

[2] Cf. F. J.E. Raby, Secular Latin Poetry I[2] (Oxford, 1957): " . . . there is nothing remarkable about their [referring to both epics] construction or the material with which they deal . . ." Two recent studies which express a more sympathetic view are H. Homeyer, "Imitatio und Aemulatio in Werk Hrotsvithas v. G." Studi Medievali S 3. ix (1969), pp. 966-979; and Marianne Schuetze-Pflugk, *Herrscher- und Maertyrerauffassung bei Hrotsvit v. G.* (Wiesbaden, 1972), esp. pp. 62-101. See also the valuable remarks of C. Erdmann, "Das ottonische Reich als Imperium Romanum," Dt. Archv. für Erf. des MA. 6 (1943), pp. 412-441.

[3] Text: H. Homeyer, Hrotsvithae Opera (Paderborn, 1970).

[4] For the iconography of David, see Hugo Steger, David: Rex et Propheta (Nuremberg, 1961).

[5] See Erich Auerbach, Literary Language and its Public in Late Latin Antiquity and in the Middle Ages, transl. Ralph Manheim (London, 1965), pp. 156-179; Werner Braun, Studien zum Ruodlieb (Berlin, 1962), pp. 18-27; Ludwig Zoepf, Das Heiligenleben im 10. Jahrhundert (Leipzig, 1908), passim.

[6] Res Gestae Divi Augusti, ed P. A. Brunt and J. M. Moore (Oxford, 1967), 34.2.

[7] See E. R. Curtius, European Literature and the Latin Middle Ages, transl. Willard R. Trask (New York, 1953), pp. 173-182.

[8] Karl Strecker, Die Cambridger Lieder (Berlin, 1955), pp. 33-36.

[9] Text: Monumenta Germaniae Historica, Poetae Latini Aevi Carolini, Vol. IV. Part 1, ed. P. Winterfeld (Berlin, 1894), pp. 7-71.

[10] See J. Bohne. Der Poeta Saxo in der historiographischen Tradition des 8.-10. Jahrhunderts (Frankfurt am Main, 1965), pp. 13-86.

[11] Text: MGH, PLAC, IV.1, pp. 355-405.

[12] Cf. Sedulius Carmen Paschale I.1-81. Text: Sedulii

Opera Omnia, ed. Johannes Huemer, Corpus Scriptorum Ecclesiasticorum Latinorum, Vol. 10.

[13] On prefaces, see T. Janson, Latin Prose Prefaces: Studies in Literary Conventions (Stockholm, 1964). On "protestations of inadequacy", see also E. R. Curtius, European Literature and the Latin Middle Ages, tr. W. Trask (New York, 1953), pp. 410-415.

A. Daniel Frankforter (essay date 1979)

SOURCE: "Hroswitha of Gandersheim and the Destiny of Women," *The Historian,* Vol. XLI, No. 3, February, 1979, pp. 295-314.

[In the following essay, Frankforter studies Hroswitha's dramatic exploration of the sources and models of spiritual strength available to women in Medieval society.]

There is a substantial fund of medieval literature which is relevant to the study of the roles, models, and ideals which medieval European society endorsed for women. Most of it was written by men whose educations and vocations gave them a limited capacity for the appreciation of women,[1] and it suggests that the medieval world was often rather harsh in its criticism of females. The version of the Christian faith which dominated the West during the Middle Ages promoted ascetic attitudes which were frequently pessimistic about feminine potentials,[2] and feudal society produced few women whose achievements in positions of power and respect could give the lie to the prevalent misogynic prejudices of their contemporaries. In most cases women found that their social roles were defined for them by the kinds of relationships which they established with men.[3] Women could be wives and could expect in the marital situation to be required to submit to husbands who were to be honored as their natural masters. Women could be whores and could obtain a certain power by surrendering to the weakness of their female flesh and making themselves into fatal traps for the sexually vulnerable male. Or women could be career virgins who overcame the inadequacies of their flesh by refusing to practice the sexuality or cultivate the beauty which marked them as women. The reward for their strenuous renunciation of their feminine natures was often the acquisition of a remarkable degree of independence from male control and the opportunity to play a kind of man's role in society.[4]

Male intellectuals had no difficulty in accounting for what appeared to be a natural and universal order of masculine dominance. There was an ancient school of Biblical exegesis which taught that woman had been created subservient to man and had condemned herself to a position of permanent earthly subordination by her betrayal of her husband in the garden of Eden.[5] There

was also a secular tradition deriving from Greek science which explained woman's secondary social role as the inevitable result of her supposed biological inferiority.[6] On the issues of feminine moral and physical inadequacies, religion and science found themselves in felicitous agreement with social custom, and it must, therefore, have been difficult for the citizens of medieval Europe, male and female, to see injustice in the inequality of opportunity and appreciation accorded the sexes.

One wonders how a medieval woman coped with this situation. How did an intelligent, perceptive female deal with an education and a society which frequently must have served to undercut her self-confidence and her self-respect? Few documents have as yet come to light which provide an opportunity for the exploration of this question. There was not a large number of medieval female authors, and of those women whose works do survive few have been identified who addressed themselves to the topic of the roles which they perceived for women in their world.[7]

The period of the "Ottonian Renaissance" produced a rare exception, a woman who created a body of literature which dealt directly and indirectly with the subject of feminine options in medieval society.[8] Apart from the facts that she called herself Hroswitha and that she was a resident of the Saxon cloister of Gandersheim almost nothing is known about her personal history. On the basis of her works it can be inferred that she lived approximately from 935 to 1002,[9] and her presence in the elite house at Gandersheim argues for the assumption that she was of noble birth. But her family has yet to be identified, and the source of her excellent education remains obscure.[10]

During the course of her career Hroswitha experimented with three different kinds of literature. Her earliest works are contained in a collection of eight poems which narrate saints' legends and apocryphal accounts of the life of Mary and the ascension of Christ.[11] After the composition of the eight legends Hroswitha turned her attention to a cycle of six plays which she says she designed to counter the influence of Terence's popular pagan comedies.[12] They are the earliest extant attempts at the creation of a Christian theater and the only dramas known to have been written in the period between the decline of Rome and the appearance of the mystery plays of the twelfth century.[13] Hroswitha's last works, poems on the reign of Otto I and the background of the cloister at Gandersheim,[14] are also noteworthy for their originality; they may qualify Hroswitha for acclamation as the first woman in the West to try her hand at the writing of history.[15]

Despite the unusual nature of Hroswitha's achievements, interest in her compositions seems to have faded after her death, and it was not until the humanist Conrad

Celtes edited and published all but one of her extant works in the early sixteenth century[16] that Hroswitha succeeded in attracting much scholarly attention.[17] The fact that she was a woman who wrote dramas at a time when dramas were not supposed to have been written and women not equipped with educations adequate to achieve what she achieved made it difficult to place her work in a context which would facilitate its interpretation.[18] All too frequently, therefore, she has been treated as a phenomenon of the period of her "rediscovery," the sixteenth century,[19] or as simply another medieval "monk" who wrote about saints and martyrs. All too infrequently has serious attention been given to the significance of her feminine gender and her interest in women as her subjects.[20]

Women are primary figures in three of Hroswitha's legends; they are the subjects of all six of her plays;[21] the history of Gandersheim quite naturally centers on the careers of women; and the poem dedicated to the reign of Otto I devotes a surprising amount of space to the story of the women associated with the imperial family.[22]

Hroswitha's references to her female characters and to her own feminine nature are often seemingly as unsympathetic as those of many a medieval male observer. Hroswitha seems to have believed that in the strengths of both mind and body women were clearly inferior to men. Given the nature of her education in early Christian theology and her experience in participating in the liturgy of her cloister, it would have been difficult for her to think otherwise.[23] In the preface to her saints' legends she confessed that poetry might be considered a difficult art for someone of her sex,[24] but she excused her attempts at it by asserting that even slight talents ought not to be wasted when God's grace can give them a worth which excels their inherent limitations. In a letter which she wrote to introduce her six plays to a group of male scholars who had encouraged her work, she engaged in an orgy of self-abnegation. She expressed amazement that these men should deign to pay any attention to the little works of a worthless, weak woman.[25] She admitted that she had some knowledge but claimed that the real subtleties of art eluded her feminine abilities.[26] In conclusion she suggested that if her work had any excellence, God had provided it so that His power might be all the more clearly manifested by the weakness of the vehicle which it employed, for, as she recalled, it is generally believed that a woman's understanding is slower than a man's.[27] In the prologue to the poem on the reign of Otto I, she begged mercy from potential critics and asked them to remember the weakness of her sex.[28] During the course of the narration she refused to discuss topics such as war which she claimed were beyond the ability of fragile women,[29] and she ultimately laid down her pen with the declaration that her female nature was not equal to the task of memorializing Otto's great achievements.[30]

Much of this might be dismissed merely as a polite artifice of self-effacement, but Hroswitha is elsewhere not above an occasional remark disparaging the supposedly characteristic limitations of other members of her sex. In her history of Gandersheim she reported that Queen Aeda was so startled by a vision of John the Baptist that she fainted "according to the custom of women."[31] Later in the same poem she recorded that the nuns of Gandersheim were moved to boundless grief at the news of Duke Otto's death because of the deficiencies of their female minds.[32] In the legend of St. Basilius she described a courageous girl as one who put aside her feminine weakness and took on manly fortitude.[33]

Hroswitha seems to have believed that there was a hierarchical structure in nature and society, and in that structure women were created inferior to men.[34] It was only right, therefore, that they should behave toward men with a degree of deference and submissiveness. But that did not rob women of all independent value or worthwhile uniqueness. Given God's ability—one might almost say His tendency—to manifest His infinite power through the weaker members of the human community,[35] the mental and physical inadequacies of women might possibly give them a kind of spiritual advantage. The very real strengths of men constituted temptations to sins of ambition and arrogance which were much less likely to confront women who were inevitably conscious of their innate humility. The natural humility of women made them excellent instruments for the manifestation of divine grace, and when the power of God did work through a human female channel, the earthly distinctions of strength and wit which normally divided the sexes became petty and irrelevant.

This is an idea which Hroswitha intentionally developed in her six plays, but it appears also at relevant points in her other works. In the preface to her plays Hroswitha acknowledged at least two motives which governed her dramatic compositions. The first was the hope that her Christian work might somehow counter the dangerous influence of Terence's pagan plays.[36] The second was the desire to respond to Terence's slanderous treatment of women. Terence's stories celebrated the shameful and impure deeds of wanton women. Hroswitha dedicated her works to the glorification of heroines of chastity,[37] and she pointed out the lesson she wished to teach by warning her reader in advance that her study of good women served to reveal the way in which God's grace enabled the weakness of women to confound the strength of men.[38]

Hroswitha seemed to accept male dominance as a fact of life, and she did not suggest alternatives to traditions which limited women to the three common social roles of virgin, wife, or whore. But as a woman Hroswitha was sensitive to shades of distinction within these categories, and she had well-defined opinions about the spiritual potentials and options of the women who occupied them. In her works Hroswitha examined each of the traditional feminine roles, and in each role she described a woman's progress toward integrity and self-respect.

The obvious model for all women was, of course, the Virgin Mary. Hroswitha was profuse in her praise of the Virgin,[39] and she dedicated the first and longest of her saints' legends to a narration of Mary's early career.[40] Mary was, however, something of an anomaly,[41] and Hroswitha could not present her simply as a literal role model for ordinary women. Hroswitha saw combined in the conditions of Mary's life the two laudible feminine vocations which she recognized: virginity and motherhood. Divine grace made it possible miraculously for Mary to fulfill both roles simultaneously and thus to be the perfect woman,[42] but this option was available to no other earthly female. In this sinful world women had to choose between the two types of fulfillment available to them and be content with a partial completion of their natures.

There was not the slightest question in Hroswitha's mind about the identity of the superior choice. Virginity was the highest of human conditions. Virgins were destined to receive special "crowns"[43] in heaven; they were to have a song of praise to God which only they could sing;[44] they were to stand in the most intimate of relationships with Christ, relationships which were so close that they could be described by marital metaphors. They were literally to be the spouses of Christ who were to enter his "bridal chamber"[45] and share his embraces.[46] So like marriage was their bond with him that the mother of a virgin might speak of herself as the "mother-in-law"[47] of Christ.

Hroswitha was aware of a number of different problems which might confront the woman who made this noblest of choices and sought to preserve her virginity. In her first play, the *Gallicanus*, she dealt with a situation which must have formed part of the experience of many an aristocratic female. The *Gallicanus* is a play about the Emperor Constantine's daughter, Constantia, and her effort to win acceptance for her personal decision to serve God as a virgin. As a good Christian, Constantia's father, Constantine, was in favor of her choice of vocations, but he was not entirely free to assist her. The daughters of feudal noblemen were sometimes needed for bestowal in marriage as pledges and bonds for important family alliances, and their personal preference for the cloister may often have come into open conflict with their duty to their families. So it was with Constantia whose desire to maintain the virgin state was a luxury her father could ill afford. The support of his most powerful general, Gallicanus, was needed in order to win a war against the Scythians—a war which was crucial to the health of the empire—and for his loyal service Gallicanus

wanted the reward of Constantia's hand in marriage. Constantia refused even to consider the possibility of marriage,[48] but she was clever enough to avoid a confrontation. She bent her principles enough to allow Gallicanus to believe that she would marry him when he returned victorious from the war, and in the interim she worked with God for his conversion to Christianity and chastity—terms which Hroswitha considered to be virtually synonymous. Constantia's faith was bountifully rewarded. In the heat of battle Gallicanus was converted; he renounced his earthly loves, embraced the life of a hermit, and ultimately made the supreme Christian sacrifice of martyrdom. Constantia's decision to maintain her virginity not only made her a heroine of the faith; it redirected, purified, and saved the man who had sought to exercise his baser nature through her.

Real human males were not all as responsive to religious stimuli as Gallicanus, however, and Hroswitha believed that occasionally God intervened rather violently to remove suitors who refused to honor a virgin's choice of vocation. In her history of Gandersheim Hroswitha told the story of the Abbess Gerberga I (d. 896) who had been betrothed in her youth to a certain Bernard.[49] Bernard insisted upon having her in marriage even though she plainly stated her preference for the cloister, and since Bernard remained intractable, God found it necessary to cause him to fall in battle to prevent him from working his impious assault on her purity.[50] Hroswitha considered the repudiation of sex to be such a laudable vow that she believed that God was not beyond doing drastic favors for married ladies who wished to escape their legal husbands and enter the cloister. In the history of Gandersheim she suggested that God probably caused Duke Liudulf to die at an early age so that his wife Oda could sever her ties with the world and embrace the monastic life.[51] One hopes that Liudulf received suitable consolation in heaven.

Hroswitha was enough of a realist to understand that not every woman who preferred to preserve her virginity would find an easy way to attain her goal. Sometimes the protection of virginity might require life-and-death struggles against overwhelming odds. Hroswitha was confident, however, that in each such situation the congruence between the woman's desire and the will of God would provide her with miraculous ability to stand against all the powers of this world and, when necessary, would inspire in her the courage to embrace martyrdom. A woman by herself was a weak thing, but a woman who was with God was an invincible force. The model for Hroswitha's virgin heroines is St. Agnes whose story she tells in the last of her eight saints' legends. Agnes was a young citizen of pagan Rome who confessed Christianity and aspired to the condition of "angelic virginity."[52] Unfortunately for her resolution she was an attractive girl of noble birth who inspired an infatuation in the son of the prefect of the city. When she spurned the boy in no uncertain terms, he fell ill from despondency, and his father resolved to force her to give up her Christian goals. The prefect had her thrown into a bordello, but the grace of God surrounded her with a holy light which intimidated any youth who approached her.[53] After working a series of miracles which converted both the prefect and his son, she was granted the release of martyrdom and ascended to heaven as a kind of inspiration for determined Christian women.[54]

In her plays the **Sapientia** and the **Dulcitius** Hroswitha narrated tales about two trios of young virgins who emulated Agnes's example. In the **Sapientia** three sisters goaded their male captors into doing their worst and joyfully embraced martyrdom after they had demonstrated the invincibility of their chastity. It could not have escaped Hroswitha's attention, however, that occasionally a virgin's defenses might be penetrated against her will, and in the **Dulcitius** she hinted at a saving technicality in cases of rape. The three ladies of the **Dulcitius** were prisoners and had the bad luck to inspire the passions of their pagan captor who, for convenience of access, had them locked up in his pantry. When he attempted to assault them, God inspired a delusion in him, and he mistook the soot-blackened kettles of the kitchen for the objects of his lust. The three seemingly defenseless women thus made a fool of a powerful man and hastened eagerly toward their rewards as virgin martyrs. When the last and youngest girl was brought out for execution, her tormentor, who had finally grasped the nature of her values, attempted to intimidate her with a fate worse than death. If she refused to deny her faith, he threatened to confine her in a whorehouse where her body would be defiled and she would be barred eternally from the heavenly company of the virgins. She responded to his ultimatum by asserting that it was better to injure the body than to corrupt the soul and proposed a theory of technical virginity which was based on the idea that it was not the act of sex, but the sensation of pleasure, which stained one with sin. So long as the soul did not consent to the rape of the flesh, the physical condition of the body was irrelevant.[55] Frigidity was a final and unconquerable defense of chastity.

The vocation of the Christian virgin was Hroswitha's own, and she could easily describe the strengths of resolve, faith, and determination which went into its maintenance. She had a great deal more difficulty, however, in understanding the mind of the woman who chose the other acceptable Christian alternative and willingly surrendered virginity for motherhood. From time to time Hroswitha put very harsh condemnations of marriage into the mouths of her virgin heroines. The Virgin Mary rejected marriage as a condition which polluted the spirit with foul desires and made it an unfit temple for God.[56] In the "Basilius" legend a girl

who begged her father to allow her to marry was warned that the pleasure which she sought in this world would bring her eternal punishment in the next.[57] St. Agnes asserted that the chaste soul could acknowledge only Christ as its spouse, and the man who offered her marriage found himself regarded as the next thing to a demon.[58] In the **Gallicanus** the princess Constantia claimed that she would "rather die" than marry.[59] In the **Dulcitius** the three virgin heroines rejected offers of marriage as invitations to corrupt their integrity.[60] In Hroswitha's mind there often appeared to be no middle ground between virginity and illicit love where honor might be found for marriage.[61]

Marriage was, however, a vocation for women that was acceptable to the church, and it was the condition in which the noble patrons of the cloister of Gandersheim lived. Hroswitha was required, therefore, to find some dignity in it, and in the final analysis she gave her approval to two kinds of marriage: those which were conducted as merely legal unions in which the parties lived as man and wife without sexual relations, and those which were established as a necessary means for the production of children.[62] In the play the **Sapientia** the Emperor Hadrian is startled to learn that one of the effects of the conversion of Roman women to Christianity is that they refuse any longer to eat or sleep with their husbands.[63] Drusiana, the heroine of the **Callimachus,** and her husband are described as faithful practitioners of sexless Christian marriage. Such disciplines were, however, virtuosi achievements for ascetic athletes and were dangerous to recommend for general practice.[64]

Most women found themselves in marriages which involved sexual unions, and Hroswitha could speak with respect of their vocations. The queens and princesses of the royal family were described as honorable consorts who enjoyed sweet and loving relationships with their husbands.[65] But as good and religious women Hroswitha seems to have believed that even they were eager, when the opportunity arose, to renounce the role of wife for the spiritually superior profession of the nun.[66] In her works of fiction, where she was somewhat insulated from the dangers of offending the persons whose deeds she memorialized in her historical poems, she clearly stated her belief that in heaven virgins were destined eternally to take precedence over married women. In the play the **Sapientia** Hroswitha produced her clearest analysis of the vocation of Christian motherhood. **Sapientia** was the mother of three young girls who shared her enthusiasm for the Christian faith and for the rewards of martyrdom. As they waited in prison for their final trials, the mother told her daughters what she hoped to achieve through them. She told them that she had raised and nourished them so that she might present them to a heavenly husband and win for herself the honor of being the "mother-in-law of the eternal king."[67] The virginity of her daughters was to be a crown for her in heaven, and their martyrdoms were to redound to her glory.[68] They were the "hope" of her womb,[69] and their special relationship to Christ in heaven would give them the opportunity to plead for her.[70] In her final prayer for herself before her own death, she hoped only to be able to hear her daughters in heaven, for she acknowledged the fact that she would never be able to "sing the song of virginity" and join them in their close association with Christ.[71] Hroswitha's view of marriage seemed to be much like that of St. Jerome: it was an institution which redeemed itself in part by the production of virgins, but it was in itself a rather base condition.[72]

Beyond the nun and the mother Hroswitha recognized one other major vocation for a woman—that of the whore. It is an alternative which she noted with understandable horror, but with surprising sympathy. She narrated the careers of prostitutes in two of her plays, the ***Abraham*** and the ***Paphnutius.*** In both dramas the fallen women become models of triumphant Christian faith by means of strenuous acts of self-renunciation— a scenario which is common enough in medieval literature, but which Hroswitha developed with unusual sensitivity and psychological insight. The ***Abraham*** deals with a young girl who attempted to live the ascetic life of a desert anchorite but who was seduced by the devil into surrendering her virginity and into despairing of her salvation. Thinking herself to be eternally damned she left her hermitage and took up residence in a tavern as a prostitute. Her spiritual mentor sought her out, convinced her that sincere repentance would restore her to God's favor, and led her back to the desert to resume her holy life. In the ***Paphnutius*** Hroswitha told the tale of Thais, the supreme whore of Alexandria, who was a much worse sinner than the poor little fallen nun of the ***Abraham.*** Unlike the nun of the ***Abraham*** Thais was not deceived into her sin but chose her way of life in full knowledge of its opposition to the will of God.[73] Even Thais, however, was not beyond redemption. When her spiritual advisor touched her conscience, her woman's nature proved strong enough to renounce all the vanities of the world and to undertake exhausting penances. She had a few last-minute qualms when she contemplated the unhygienic potential of her future situation,[74] but she allowed herself to be walled up in a tiny cell where for three years she performed remarkable feats of self-mortification before proceeding to an honored place in heaven.

In retrospect Hroswitha's women appear to be strong, courageous, and resourceful people. The weakness, cowardice, and intellectual torpidity which Hroswitha identified as the general features of her sex[75] are conspicuous by their absence from the personalities of her heroines. In the course of her work Hroswitha focused attention on about twenty women, and in contrast to the numerous men whom she described, only one of

them was a contemptible creature.[76] Almost all of Hroswitha's women were able by wit, courage, and faith to win out over the physical power of men,[77] the temptations of this world, and the failures of their own pasts. Almost all of them turned out to be instruments of grace for their own salvation and for that of the men who surrounded them. They enjoyed no unusual advantages. They were simply women who occupied the normal roles which society defined for females, but they were women who found in these roles a power and influence over themselves and others which far exceeded normal expectations. Evidently there were feminine attributes which could form bases for strong personalities and influential careers even for women who were trapped in stereotyped social roles. In the powers of mind and body women might well be weaker than men, but their earthly weaknesses could become a source of spiritual strength.[78]

Hroswitha understood the Christian religion to be a faith which offered the fellowship of God to those who severed their ties with the perverted flesh. Salvation was not earned by ascetic exercises; it was a gift of grace.[79] But the reception of salvation always involved a turning away from this world and a focusing of affections on the spiritual realm; it always entailed a repudiation of the transient pleasures of sex which seem to have symbolized for Hroswitha the very essence of human sin.[80]

Contrary to what many other medieval scholars may have thought,[81] Hroswitha seems to have believed that women have an important spiritual advantage over men in the struggle to maintain the crucial Christian virtue of chastity. Hroswitha's female characters are noteworthy for their lack of sexual passion. Only three of them demonstrate any difficulty in struggling with the impulses of the body. Two of the three, the virgin in the "Basilius" legend and the young anchorite of the ***Abraham*** play, are temporarily betrayed by their naiveté into the snares of the devil, and the third woman, St. Gongolf's wife, is an unnatural creature whose pride drives her to persist furiously in her sins even after she has had numerous miraculous demonstrations of her husband's sanctity. Hroswitha's virgin martyrs deal with threats to their chastity which arise outside themselves. Rarely is there a suggestion that they faced difficult internal battles with the impulses of their flesh.[82] Even the prostitutes, Mary and Thais, conduct their professions with a kind of cold detachment which suggests that they are only doing their jobs and not seeking fulfillment for raging erotic impulses.

In most instances lust appears to be a characteristically male problem. The servant in the "Basilius" legend is so overwhelmed by desire for his master's daughter that he sells his soul to the devil in order to get her. St. Agnes's suitor sickens and takes to his bed from the effects of his frustrated passions. The villain of the

Callimachus is so completely mastered by his baser impulses that he breaks into his beloved's tomb in order to use her corpse for the satiation of his desires. Thais has such power over males that even men of character and substance lose their wits and brawl over her until her doorstep runs red with the blood of their battles.[83] The devil was at the root of all these disorders, but he seems often to have found it easier to work his assaults on chastity through men than through women.

Perhaps Hroswitha wished to imply that men, who enjoyed a greater measure of the powers of this world than women did, were subjected by their stronger flesh to more violent sexual impulses. Their strength of flesh in and of itself constituted a vulnerability of spirit which placed them in great danger and which created a serious problem for the women who aroused them. For better or for worse most males needed females in order to indulge their sinful impulses,[84] and the struggle for the soul's salvation could often degenerate into a battle between the sexes. It was of crucial importance, therefore, how women handled their sexuality. If they restrained its use, they could purify and ennoble men; if they indulged it, they could become a trap for innumerable male souls.[85] If they abandoned chaste conduct, they became the most effective tools the devil could employ; if they guarded their virginity—unto martyrdom if necessary—they became powerful instruments of divine grace in the struggle against sin.

In the natural order of creation men led and cared for the "weaker vessels"[86] who were their women. The weakness of female nature, which consisted in being closer to the animal world than was male nature, gave women, in the opinion of some, the greater capacity for sex and made them a source of huge potential danger to themselves and men. Patristic literature provided Hroswitha with many versions of this argument—which she seems to have accepted as self-evident. But in her dramatic representation of the sexuality of her feminine protagonists, women are most often portrayed as passive potentials for danger to members of the male sex, not as possessors of an independent drive which sought its own destructive fulfillment. Hroswitha seems to have accepted the common opinion that a woman's innate sexual abilities were greater than a man's—Thais seems to have single-handedly undermined the condition of most of the men in Alexandria. But Hroswitha represented a woman's internal fight for salvation as a struggle, not with the active impulses of her own nature but with the strengths of the men who attempt to sin through her. Feminine weakness is vulnerability to guilty exploitation, but, in so far as it entails a lack of drive and initiative, it constitutes a kind of protection against sin. Male strength, if misdirected, is not always virtue; female weakness, if properly utilized, is not always vice. Under the dispensation of grace made necessary by human sin, God reveals apparent strengths to be weaknesses and works through the lowly for the salvation of the mighty. Hroswitha of Gandersheim accepted the secondary role which her society accorded women, but she seems to have seen in the Christian dynamics of sin and salvation a destiny which gave women great worth and a basis for self-respect. For all their apparent weaknesses women were not mere adjuncts to men; they had their own superb and unique opportunities to serve as channels of divine grace. The decisions which women freely made about themselves were of more than personal importance. It was a woman's destiny to be the center of the battle between the realms of the flesh and the spirit, and it lay within a woman's power to have considerable influence on the outcome of the fight for the salvation of her race.

Notes

[1] Recent enthusiasm for the study of the history of feminism has produced much interest in the attitudes of men toward women in the ancient and medieval worlds. Useful surveys of theses and sources can be found in Marie-Louise Portmann, *Die Darstellung der Frau in der Geschichtsschreibung des früheren Mittelalters* (Diss. phil.) (Basel: Basler Beiträge, Bd. 60, 1958); Derrick Sherwin Bailey, *The Man-Woman Relation in Christian Thought* (London: Longmans, 1959); K. E. Børreson, *Subordination et Équivalence: Nature et rôle de la femme d'après Augustin et Thomas d'Aquin* (Oslo: Universitetsforlaget, 1968); and Vern L. Bullough, *The Subordinate Sex: A History of Attitudes toward Women* (Urbana: University of Illinois Press, 1973).

[2] A suggestive theory concerning the history of a Christian tradition of ambivalence toward women has recently been advanced by George H. Tavard, *Women in Christian Tradition* (London: University of Notre Dame Press, 1973). There is a growing body of literature on this subject. See, for example, Derrick Sherwin Bailey, *Sexual Relation in Christian Thought* (New York: Harper and Brothers, 1959); Vern L. Bullough, *Sexual Variance in Society and History* (New York: John Wiley and Sons, 1976); Jeffrey B. Russell, *Witchcraft in the Middle Ages* (Ithaca, N.Y.: Cornell University Press, 1972); H. R. Hays, *The Dangerous Sex: The Myth of Feminine Evil* (New York: Putnam's Sons, 1964); Henry C. Lea, *History of Sacerdotal Celibacy,* 4th rev. ed. (Secaucus, N.J.: University Books, 1966); C. S. Lewis, *The Allegory of Love* (New York: Oxford University Press, 1958); William E. Phipps, *Was Jesus Married?* (New York: Harper and Row, 1970); and Sarah B. Pomeroy, *Goddesses, Whores, Wives, and Slaves* (New York: Schocken Books, 1975).

[3] Rosemary R. Ruether, "Misogynism and Virginal Feminism in the Fathers of the Church," in *Religion and Sexism,* ed. Rosemary R. Ruether (New York: Simon and Schuster, 1974), 163-64.

[4] Women who manifested the virtues of courage, strength, and self-control seem to have been praised often by their medieval biographers for their success in abandoning their female natures and acquiring male characteristics. For an example of a woman's adoption of this pro-male convention, see Anna Comnena's description of her mother in *Alexiad* 15.2. Similar phenomena are discussed in R. A. Baer, Jr., *Philo's Use of the Categories Male and Female* (Leiden: Brill, 1970); Henry Stanley Bennett, *The Pastons and Their England* (Cambridge: University Press, 1951); and Renate Bridenthal and Claudia Koonz, eds., *Becoming Visible: Women in European History* (Boston: Houghton Mifflin Co., 1977).

[5] Saint Paul claimed that the male was created to be "the image and glory of God; but woman is the glory of man" (1 Cor. 11: 7, RSV), and the Pastoral Epistles argued that woman's primordial sinfulness condemned her to subordination to man (1 Tim. 2: 11-15)—a theme which Tertullian *(De Cultu Feminarum)* and other church fathers found useful for polemical purposes.

[6] Plato, *Timaeus* 90, suggested that the difference between the sexes could be explained by assuming that nature created women from the reincarnated souls of inferior men. Aristotle, *Generation of Animals* 4.6.775lb15, suggested that females could be understood as "deformities" which occur as a regular part of nature.

[7] The number of female commentators on the feminine situation has on occasion been seriously underestimated. In her popular work, *The Second Sex* (New York: Alfred Knopf. 1968), 105, Simone de Beauvoir erroneously claimed that prior to the fifteenth century and Christine de Pisan no woman could be seen "to take up her pen in defense of her sex."

[8] It is immediately apparent to anyone who reads Hroswitha's works that there are many references in them to women and much, therefore, which might be learned indirectly about their condition in Hroswitha's world. But the author feels that one can go beyond this and assume that at least in the case of Hroswitha's plays Hroswitha intended to describe directly feminine roles relevant to her society. This theory was presented to the Ohio Conference on Medieval Studies, October 1975, in a paper entitled "The Drama of Salvation: Sex Roles in the Plays of Hroswitha of Gandersheim."

[9] In the *Primordia,* her history of Gandersheim, Hroswitha states that she was born well after the death of Duke Otto (912), and in the preface to her legends she says that she was a little older than her abbess, Gerberga II (940-1001). Her extant works do not deal with events later than the death of Otto I (973), but there is a second dedication of the *Gesta Ottonis* which honors Otto II and which may have served as an introduction to an intended, but uncompleted or now lost, continuation of the poem. The chronicle of the bishops of Hildesheim infers that she survived to write in honor of all three Ottos and thus supports the assumption that she lived at least into the early eleventh century. For a discussion of the problem of Hroswitha's dates, see Sister Mary Bernardine Bergman, *Hrosvithae Liber Tertius* (Covington, Ky.: The Sisters of St. Benedict, 1943).

[10] Hroswitha sends her works for approval to a number of learned men who seem to have encouraged her studies, but she says little about her teachers. In the preface to her first works, her saints' legends, she notes her scholarly indebtedness to her novice mistress, Riccarda, to Riccarda's unnamed successors, and to her younger contemporary and friend, the Abbess Gerberga II.

[11] The legends bear the titles "The History of the Nativity and the Laudible Conversation of the Virgin Mother of God which I have found under the Name of St. James, the Brother of the Lord" (hereafter cited as the "Maria"), "Of the ascension of the Lord, the Narration which Bishop John Translated from Greek into Latin," "The Passion of the Martyr St. Gongolf," "The Passion of St. Pelagius, the Most Precious Martyr who was Crowned with Martyrdom in Cordoba in our Times," "The Fall and Conversion of the Vicar Theophilus," "Basilius," "The Passion of the Distinguished Martyr St. Dionysius," and "The Passion of the Virgin and Martyr St. Agnes."

Hroswitha's poems are not very unusual products for their day, but they have attracted some interest in that one of them, the "Pelagius," supposedly derives from an eyewitness account of the martyr's death and another, the "Theophilus," introduces the "Faustian" theme of a compact with the devil which was later to play a significant role in the literature of Hroswitha's homeland.

[12] The plays are the *Gallicanus* (parts 1 and 2), the *Dulcitius,* the *Callimachus,* the *Abraham,* the *Paphnutius,* and the *Sapientia.*

In the preface to the plays Hroswitha speaks of the spiritual dangers which confront those who read Terence and of her intention to oppose the lascivious impression made by his work by using the dramatic idiom to praise the virtues of female virgins and martyrs. Her actual reliance on Terence appears to have been slight. See Cornelia C. Coulter, "The 'Terentian' Comedies of a Tenth-Century Nun," *Classical Journal* 24 (1929): 515-29.

[13] Mary Marguerite Butler, *Hrotsvitha: The Theatricality of Her Plays* (New York: Philosophical Library, 1960), and Edwin H. Zeydel, "Were Hroswitha's Dra-

mas Performed during Her Lifetime?" *Speculum* 20, no. 4 (1945): 443-56, marshal evidence bearing on the problem of deciding whether Hroswitha ought to be interpreted as an author who stands in the tradition of drama prepared for reading or for actual performance.

[14] Hroswitha may also have composed a no-longer-extant essay on the lives of Popes Anastasius and Innocent whose relics were preserved at Gandersheim, or the vague reference to this "work" which appears in a sixteenth-century source may simply be a misleading citation of the *Primordia* in which these two saints are mentioned.

[15] Georgina Buckler, *Anna Comnena* (Oxford: Clarendon Press, 1929), 4, claims that Anna Comnena, author of the *Alexiad,* deserves the title of "first woman historian of the western world." The *Alexiad* is an indisputably greater achievement than Hroswitha's modest "family history"—as the *Gesta Ottonis* has been characterized by Sister Mary Gonsalva Wiegand, *The Non-Dramatic Works of Hroswitha* (St. Meinrad, Indiana: Abbey Press, 1937), xx. But Hroswitha's ventures precede Anna's by a century and a half, and they deserve some recognition.

[16] In 1501 Celtes published an edition of the manuscript from the cloister of St. Emmeran in Regensburg—now preserved in the Bayerische Staatsbibliothek in Munich (clm 14485)—which is the major extant medieval record of her work. It contains all her compositions except for the *Primordia,* the medieval copy of which disappeared in the sixteenth century. The St. Emmeran document appears to be a tenth-century product of Gandersheim and probably preserves the order in which Hroswitha expected her works to be read. Very few other medieval copies of her writings have survived. The Munich Staatsbibliothek contains (clm 2552) a twelfth-century copy of the *Gallicanus* which may derive from the St. Emmeran document. Late twelfth-century versions of the *Gallicanus, Dulcitius, Callimachus,* and *Abraham* were identified in the collection of the Historisches Archiv in Cologne (W 101) in 1922. They may derive from an original text which was superior to the St. Emmeran manuscript. Twelfth- or thirteenth-century fragments of the Mary legend and the *Sapientia,* which belong to the St. Emmeran tradition, have been discovered in Austria in the Klagenfurt Studienbibliothek (ms. 44).

Evidence of medieval interest in Hroswitha is quite sparse, but enough traces survive in the form of the few scattered manuscripts to indicate that she was not completely forgotten by those who followed her. See Boris Jarcho, "Zu Hrotsvithas Werkungskreis," *Speculum* 2 (1927): 343-44; and Edwin H. Zeydel, "Knowledge of Hrotsvitha's Works Prior to 1500," *Modern Language Notes* 59 (1944): 382-85.

[17] Two organizations have been created to promote the study of Hroswitha's works—one in London (founded in 1926) and one in New York (1944)—and a sizable bibliography of modern commentaries on her writings now exists. Surveys of much of the literature and the major disputes in the interpretation of Hroswitha's work will be found in Ann Lyon Haight, *Hroswitha of Gandersheim: Her Life, Her Times, Her Works, and a Comprehensive Bibliography* (New York: Hroswitha Club, 1965); and Bert Nagel, *Hrotsvit von Gandersheim* (Stuttgart: J. B. Metzler, 1965).

[18] Hroswitha constituted such a challenge to common prejudices concerning medieval women that in the mid-nineteenth century an effort was made to argue her out of existence. Joseph von Aschbach, "Roswitha und Conrad Celtes," *Kaiserlichen Akademie der Wissenschaften, Sitzungsberichte* 56 (Vienna, 1867), maintained that she was a historical absurdity and an impossibility. He claimed that her Latin was too good and her knowledge of the world too extensive for a woman of her supposed generation and vocation, and he suggested that her works were forgeries created by Conrad Celtes, her reputed "discoverer," which he foisted off on his fellow humanists as a kind of elaborate scholarly joke. Aschbach's thesis met early opposition from Rudolf Köpke, "Hrotsvit von Gandersheim," *Ottonishe Studien* 2 (Berlin, 1869), but it was a long time before the Hroswitha manuscripts received an adequate evaluation by paleographers which put their authenticity beyond doubt. See the complaint of Edwin Zeydel, "The Authenticity of Hrotswitha's Works," *Modern Language Notes* 61 (1946): 50-55.

[19] Rudolf Wolkan *et al., Das deutsche Drama* (Munich, 1925).

[20] In 1908 Bernarda Trümper published a book dealing with Hroswitha's women, *Hrotsvithas Frauengestalten* (Münster, 1908), but later scholars have tended to interpret Hroswitha's legends and dramas as studies of concepts of martyrdom and chastity for which questions of sexual differentiation are of secondary importance. Hugo Kuhn, *Dichtung und Welt im Mittelalter* (Stuttgart: J. B. Metzler, 1959), 94-100, suggests that an elaborate structure of major and minor themes can be seen linking Hroswitha's plays and paralleling the internal organization of her legends. Kuhn sees her work as a study of the eternal conflict between the world and the Christian faith which is as real for men as it is for women. Men play a larger role in the legends and women in the dramas, but both the legends and the dramas are part of one scheme designed to illustrate Christian faith in its struggle with a hostile world. Marianne Schütze-Pflugk, *Herrscher- und Märtyrer-Auffassung bei Hrotsvit von Gandersheim* (Wiesbaden: Steiner Verlag, 1972), links Hroswitha's works together as studies of concepts of Christian heroism, of which she identifies three types: "Glaubens-

und Keuschheitshelden," "Glaubenshelden," and "Märtyrer als Mann des Hofes und des Hochadels."

But dissatisfaction with many of the proposed schemes for uncovering a structure in Hroswitha's poetic program has moved Dietlind Heinze, *Die Praefatio zu den 'Draman' Hrotsvits von Gandersheim—ein Programm?"* (Karlsruhe: O. Berenz, 1973), to deny that even the plays, which on the surface appear to be the most coordinated of Hroswitha's works, follow any "Theorie" or "Schema" (72). It is probably unreasonable to hope that all of Hroswitha's compositions can be demonstrated to be parts of one consistently executed plan, but certain significant correlations and enduring attitudes do seem to appear if her writings are approached not just as explorations of the concepts of chastity and martyrdom but as statements by a woman about the different spiritual situations of men and women in her society.

[21] Kuhn (99): "Die Legendenreihe handelt ausser in Anfang und Schluss (1 und 8) durchweg von Männer [note, however, that the third legend, the "Gongolf," features a woman who is central to the fate of the man whose martyrdom is being narrated], während das Dramenbuch (trotz der hierin irreführenden Titel) durchweg Frauen und mit ihnen das Thema der *virginitas* in den Mittelpunkt stellt [note, however, that virginity is also the central theme of the "male" legend of the "Pelagius" and a virtue endorsed for both sexes; see "Maria," 395-400]."

[22] Otto's crucial struggles with the Magyars are dismissed in twenty-two lines, while fifty-five are given to narrating the death of his wife, Edith. Over two hundred lines of the fifteen-hundred-line poem are used to describe the escape of Queen Adelaide from Berengar and her subsequent marriage to Otto. The episode concerning Adelaide's flight is one of the most completely developed in the whole poem.

[23] Helene Homeyer, *Hrotsvithae Opera* (Munich: Ferdinand Schöningh, 1970), 13-14, points out the importance of the effect of the church's liturgy on Hroswitha's works: "In den Legenden und Dramen, in denen die Jungfräulichkeit verherrlicht wird, sind 'Entlehnungen' aus der Liturgie des Weihnachts- und Osterfestkreises und der Marienfeste besonders zahlreich. Anderes stammt aus den rituellen Gebeten, die das klösterliche Leben begleiteten: so spielt z. B. der Gedanke an die Schwachheit des weiblichen Geschlechts eine Rolle (Sap. III 3 u. ö.) . . . ," etc.

[24] "Quamvis etiam metrica modulatio femineae fragilitati difficilis videatur et ardua, solo tamen semper miserentis supernae gratiae auxilio, non propriis viribus, confisa. . . . " (8) The edition of Hroswitha's works employed throughout the paper is Homeyer's *(ibid.),* and when translations occur, they are the author's own.

[25] "mei opusculum vilis mulierculae vestra admiratione dignum duxistis." (3)

[26] "arbitrantes mihi inesse aliquantulam scientiam artium, quarum subtilitas longe praeterit mei muliebre ingenium." (3)

[27] "tanto amplius in me iure laudaretur, quanto muliebris sensus tardior esse creditur." (9)

[28] "Si tamen sanae mentis examen accesserit, quae res recte pensare non nescit, quanto sexus fragilior scientiaque minor, tanto venia erit facilior. . . . " (9)

[29]

   "Sed nec hoc fragilis fas esse reor mulieris
   Inter coenobii positae secreta quieti,
   Ut bellum dictet, quod nec cognoscere debet."
                    (243-45)

[30]

   "Nunc scribenda quidem constant, quae fecerat idem
   Augustus solium retinens in vertice rerum.
   Tangere quae vereor, quia femineo prohibebor
   Sexu, nec vili debent sermone revolvi. . . . "
                   (1485-88)

Marianne Schütze-Pflugk (62) suggests that Hroswitha's feminine reserve could sometimes serve as a useful excuse for not discussing potentially delicate events: "Es leuchtet ein, dass z. B. die politischen Konflikte innerhalb der Ottonischen Familie ein peinliches Thema darstellen für eine Kanonisse, deren Äbtissin die Tochter des rebellischen Königsbruders Heinrich und die Schwester der ebenso rebellischen Heinrich des Zänkers war."

[31]

   "Quem matrona videns nec mortalem fore credens,
   Obstupuit mentis iuxta morem muliebris,
   Procumbens subito magno terrore coacta."
                   (49-51)

[32]

   "Quae, pro defectu mentis solito muliebris
   Vivere spernentes citiusque mori cupientes,
   In lacrimando modum voluerunt ponere nullum."
                   (544-46)

[33]

   "Illaque, mollitiem iam deponens muliebrem
   Et sumens vires prudenti corde viriles. . . . "
                   (168-69)

[34] Not all women were created equal, however, for the hierarchy of worth extended through the class of wom-

Hroswitha presenting her book to Emperor Otto I. From the first edition (1501) of her works. Drawing attributed to Albrecht Dürer.

ankind and explained the superiority of women of royal birth to those of commoner origins. As Bert Nagel (46) observes, "Dass die jüngere Gerberg II, infolge ihrer königlichen Abkunft höhere gelehrte Bildung besitzt, erscheint ihr ganz natürlich. Die ständische Rangordnung der Welt erachtet sie als richtig und gottgewollt."

[35] Hroswitha introduces this theme in the letter to her patrons which preceded the plays. It is not directly stated, but the drift of her thought seems to be that her literary achievements as a woman redound all the more to God's glory because His power is revealed all the more clearly in the fact that He has been able to use a weak feminine instrument for worthy spiritual purposes.

[36] "Plures inveniuntur catholici, cuius nos penitus expurgare nequimus facti, qui pro cultioris facundia sermonis gentilium vanitatem librorum utilitati praeferunt sacrarum scripturarum. Sunt etiam alii, sacris inhaerentes paginis, frequentius lectitant et, dum dulcedine sermonis delectantur, nefandarum notitia rerum maculantur." (1-2)

[37] "quo eodem dictationis genere, quo turpia lascivarum incesta feminarum recitabantur, laudabilis sacrarum castimonia virginium iuxta mei facultatem ingenioli celebraretur." (3)

[38] "praesertim cum feminea fragilitas vinceret et virilis robur confusioni subiaceret." (5) Paul von Winterfeld, *Deutsche Dichter des Lateinischen Mittelalters* (Munich: C. H. Beck, 1913), 110, saw this statement as a basis for according Hroswitha the honor of recognition as a precursor of modern feminism.

> Vor allem aber muss Hrotsvit den emporstrebenden Frauen unserer eigenen Zeit, unseren Gymnasiastinnen, Studentinnen, Lehrerinnen, Dichterinnen als die grosse, um Jahrhunderte voraus geeilte Standartenträgerin erscheinen. Hrotsvit es sich selbst deutlich bewusst, mit ihren Schöpfungen für das Recht der Frauen zu streiten und nach Ruhm und Ehre der Männer zu ringen. Ihre Dramen sind in dieser Hinsicht fast soziale Tendenzstücke. Überall bleibt in ihnen die Frau Siegerin im Kampf gegen männliche Gewalt und Brutalität. . . . So wäre diese Nonne wohl die rechte Patronin der modernen, neuen Zoelen zugewendeten Frau, die ja wie sie oft der fraulichen Krone des Lebens, der Liebe, entsagen muss, wenn sie auf Stolz und Ehre hält.

[39] Hroswitha's Virgin remains quite "female" in her relationship to the male Trinity. She is the vehicle of the incarnation, and Hroswitha has Christ accord her recognition as the only person who could have served in that capacity ("Ascension of the Lord," 82-83: "Inveni solam prae cunctis te quia castam condignamque meum corpus generasse sacratum"). But Mary claims no powers of her own. Salvation is the result of Christ's

sacrifice on the cross, not of the incarnation, and Mary is more the beloved mother of God than she is the queen of heaven.

[40] The "Maria"—with 900 lines—is two to three times as long as all but one of the other seven legends. Its nearest contender is the "Gongolf" at 580 lines. The others range from the "Ascension" at 150 to the "Agnes" at 459.

[41] Hroswitha gives her a rather anomalous birth which hints at the conditions of her own son's conception. Mary's parents, Joachim and Anna, are represented as having separated in chagrin over their sterility. After months of absence from each other's company angels bring them the news that God will grant them a child. Joachim hastens home from the desert, and Anna goes out to meet him with the news, "quaeque fui sterilis, concepi gaudi prolis" (261), and nine months later ("noveno . . . mense," 264) Mary is born.

[42] Mary's lifestyle realizes the condition which St. Augustine imagined to have been Eve's potential before the fall (*City of God*, xiv).

[43] "Maria," 394; *Sapientia*, v, 29; etc.

[44] *Sapientia*, ix, 8.

[45] *I.e.,* "thalamus": "Agnes," 107, and *Gallicanus* I, v, 2.

[46] The metaphor is developed with particular vividness in the Agnes legend (41-110) where the saint compares her earthly and heavenly suitors.

[47] *I.e.,* "socrus": *Sapientia,* iv, 3.

[48] She and her father have a brief, but pointed, conversation on the subject of matrimony:

> Constantinus: Desiderat te sponsam habitum ire.
> Constantia: Me?
> Constantinus: Te.
> Constantia: Malim mori.
> Constantinus: Prescivi.
>
>   (I, ii, 3)

[49] *Primordia,* 315-60.

[50] Marianne Schütze-Pflugk, 43, has a somewhat more mundane theory concerning the vacillations in Gerberga's career: "Die Darstellung der Äbtissin Gerberga beschränkt sich zum grossen Teil auf die Geschichte ihres verlöbnisses mit Bernhard. Während die Wahrscheinlichkeit dafür spricht, dass der Tod ihrer Schwester und das Streben der liudolfingischen Familie, das Eigenstift durch den Primat der eigenen Töchter

fast in Händen zu halten, die Gründe für den Bruch mit Bernhard bilden, lässt Hrotsvit Gerberga längst vorher heimlich mit Christus verlobt sein, *omnino sponsum spernens animo moriturum. (Primordia* 323)"

51 *Primordia,* 296-300.

52

"Si velit angelicae pro virginitatis honore
Ipsius astrigera sponsi caelestis in aula." (4-5)

53 "Sicque locus scelerum domus efficitur precularum." (253)

54 The heroine of Hroswitha's first play, the *Gallicanus,* sets the stage for her own struggle by praying to Christ in the name of St. Agnes: "Amator virginitatis et inspirator castitatis, Christe, qui me precibus martiris tuae Agnetis a lepra pariter corpis et ab errore eripiens gentilitatis invitasti ad virgineum tui genitricis thalamum in quo tu manifestus es verus deus retro exordium natur a deo patre, idenque verus homo ex matre natus in tempore. . . . " (I,v, 2)

55

Hirena: Melius est, ut corpus quibuscumque
iniuriis maculetur, quam anima idolis
polluatur.

Sisinnius: Si socia eris meretricum, non
poteris polluta intra contubernium computari
virginum.

Hirena: Voluptas parit poenam, necessitas
autem coronam; nec dicitur reatus, nisi quod
consentit animus.

—xii, 3

Similar ideas are to be discovered in the writings of early church fathers: *e.g.,* Basilius of Ancyra (d. *ca.* 366), *De Virginitate:* "Were such virgins assaulted and raped, their souls will remain virginal, for, experiencing the death of the flesh, they remain uncorrupted, whatever they might have to submit to." Quoted from André Vaillant's edition, *De Virginitate de St. Vasile; texte vieux slave, traduction française* (Paris, 1943), and translated into English by Tavard, *Women,* 61.

56 "Maria," 391-93:

"Nam Deus in templo gaudet requiescere
mundo
Mentibus et sobriis, nec delectatur in illis,
Crimine quos magno maculat lasciva libido."

57 "Basilius," 136-37:

"Congaude iam nunc servo miserae tibi caro;
At post aeternis poenis maerens capieris!"

58 "Agnes," 23-24 and 61-62:

"qui, genitus sacra de virgine, solus
Sponsus castarum necnon decus est animarum.

. . . . .

O fili montis merito dampnande perennis,
O fomes sceleris, contemptor et omnipotentis."

59 I, ii, 3: "Malim mori."

60 I, 2: "nec ad corruptionem integritatis ullis rebus compelli poterimus."

61 Heinze, *Die Praefatio,* 53. Reuther, "Misogynism," 165, catalogues passages from Augustine (*De Bono Conj.* 3. 15; *De Bono Viduit.* 8 and 11) and Jerome (*Epistola* 107. 13) which argue that the marital act is "intrinsically debasing to a woman." Schütze-Pflugk, 20-21, suggests that Hroswitha can conceive of sexual affection only as a "Raserei"—not a natural impulse of the human spirit but a drive which is imposed on it from without by Satan. Those who fall in love are "Liebeskranken" who are to be described as "*stultus, infelix, miser,* und *misellus*" (27).

62 I Tim. 2:15 (RSV): "Yet woman will be saved through bearing children, if she continues in faith and love and holiness, with modesty."

63 i, v: "nam nostrae conjuges fastidiendo nos contempnunt adeo, ut dedignatur nobiscum comedere, quanto minus dormire."

64 The early church seems to have generally discouraged this kind of behavior, and at a later period St. Bernard certainly had a very dubious opinion of it: "To be always with a woman and not to have intercourse with her is more difficult than to raise the dead. You cannot do the less difficult; do you think I will believe that you can do what is more difficult?" Quoted in R. W. Southern, *Western Society and the Church in the Middle Ages* (London, 1970), 314.

65 For example, *Gesta Ottonis,* 66-124; *Primordia,* 305-14.

66 The case of Countess Oda (*Primordia,* 296-300) has already been mentioned (note 51).

67 iv, 3: "Ad hoc vos materno lacte affluenter alui, ad hoc delicate nutrivi, ut vos caelesti, non terreno, sponso traderme, quo vestri causa socrus aeterni regis dici meruissem."

68 iv, 4: "Hoc exopto, ut vestra virginitater coroner, ut vestro martirio glorificer."

[69] v, 29: "spes uteri mei unica."

[70] vii, 2: "Vale, proles dulcissima; et, cum Christo iungaris in caelo, memento matris, iam patrona effecta te parientis."

[71] ix, 8: "quamvis non possum canticum virginitatis dicere, te tamen cum illis merear aeternaliter laudare."

[72] Jerome, *Epistola* xxii, 20.

[73] The hermit who engineers her salvation is shocked beyond belief to learn in conversation with her that she sins not in ignorance of God but in full acceptance of the fact of his existence: "O Christe, quam miranda tuae circa nos benignitatis patientia, qui te scientes vides peccare et tamen tardas perdere!" (iii, 5)

Some of the earlier forms of the Thais legend contained excuses for Thais's conduct in that they had her mother bear responsibility for placing her in a brothel, but Hroswitha heightens the sense of Thais's sin by omitting reference to mitigating circumstances. For a study of the legend and Hroswitha's narration of it, see Oswald R. Kuehne, *A Study of the Thais Legend* (Philadelphia: University of Pennsylvania Press, 1922).

[74] vii, 12: "Quid inoportunius quidve poterit esse incommodius, quam quod in uno eodemque loco diversa corporis necessaria supplere debebo. Nec dubium, quin ocius fiat inhabitabilis prae nimietate foetoris."

[75] Preface to the legends, 8; letter of recommendation for the plays, 3, 9; prologue to the history of Otto's reign, 9; etc.

[76] She is the adulterous wife of St. Gongolf, the only one of Hroswitha's female sinners to die unrepentant.

[77] Hroswitha's examples of cases where weak women triumph over strong men are not confined to what one might interpret as the wish fulfillments of her works of fiction. In the *Gesta Ottonis* (558-587) she described Queen Adelaide's flight from Berengar as an example of a situation in which God's grace enabled a lone woman to frustrate all the earthly powers which lay at the disposal of males.

[78] William Hudson, "Roswitha of Gandersheim," *English Historical Review* 3 (July 1888): 445: "In Hroswitha's hands Christianity is throughout represented by the purity and gentleness of women while paganism is embodied by what she describes as 'the vigour of men' *(virile robur)."*

[79] Paphnutius gives the repentent Thais a kind of miniature lecture on free grace. When she shows a reluctance to leave her cell and expresses the fear that she has not yet done enough penance to merit God's grace, he calms her fears by telling her, "Gratuitum dei donum non pensat humanum meritum, quia, si meritis tribueretur, gratia non diceretur" (xii, 5). For a discussion of Hroswitha's theology of grace and its possible sympathies with Gottschalk's theories of double predestination, see Erich Michalka, *Studien über Intention und Gestaltung in den dramatischen Werken Hrotsvits von Gandersheim* (Heidelberg: Ruprecht-Karl-Universität, 1968), 114-18 and 189.

[80] Alice Kemp Welch, "A Tenth-Century Dramatist, Roswitha the Nun," in her *Of Six Mediaeval Women* (London: Macmillan and Co, 1913), 20: "The subject which dominates her horizon is that of Chastity. Treated by her with didactic intent, this really resolves itself into a conflict between Christianity and Paganism—in other words, between Chastity and Passion—in which Christianity triumphs through the virtue of Woman."

[81] Eleanor Commo McLaughlin, "Equality of Souls, Inequality of Sexes: Woman in Medieval Theology," in *Religion, ed.* Ruether, 225: "Medieval medical theory assumed that the sexual needs of the woman were as great if not greater than those of the man."

[82] There may be a slight reference to such a problem in the opening lines of the legend of St. Agnes:

"Virgo, quae, vanas mundi pompas ruituri
Et luxus fragilis cupiens contempnere carnis."

[83] I, 26: "Deinde, inito certamine, nunc ora naresque pugnis frangendo, nunc armis vicissim eiciendo, decurrentis illuvie sanguinis madefaciunt limina lupanaris."

[84] Hroswitha was aware of the homosexual alternative. Her legend of St. Pelagius tells the story of a youth who chose martyrdom over the affections of a pagan king.

[85] The careers of the prostitutes in the *Abraham* and the *Paphnutius* are lamented not just for the degradation of the women involved but for the large company of men who found ruin through the two sinful females. The repentent anchorite of the *Abraham* spends the remainder of her life in an attempt to become an example of virtue for the conversion of the men who earned perdition through her (ix, 4). The context for the interpretation of Thais's story is established by the opening scene of the *Paphnutius,* a lecture on the principles of divine harmony which are established in the universe and disrupted by human sinners. Thais is a powerful source of disorder in the creation, and she is explicitly blamed not only for her own damnation, but for the ruin of many others: "quae non solum sese perditioni dedit, sed etiam perplures secum ad interitum trahere consuevit" (ix, 2).

[86] 1 Pet. 3: 7.

A. Daniel Frankforter (essay date 1979)

SOURCE: "Sexism and the Search for the Thematic Structure of the Plays of Hroswitha of Gandersheim," in *International Journal of Women's Studies*, Vol. 2, No. 3, May / June, 1979, pp. 221-32.

[*In the following essay, Frankforter discusses Hroswitha's six plays, arguing that they should be viewed as works focusing on women as Christian heroes rather than as imperfectly realized dramas primarily about their male characters.*]

I

The writing of history has long been an activity controlled by males. Most of the honored commentators who have shaped the western historical tradition have been extraordinary men who have concentrated their professional attentions on others like themselves. As a consequence, the historical method, which was pioneered by their work, often predisposes later scholars, male and female, to approach the writing of history with a set of male presuppositons. Historians are accustomed to searching their data for evidence of the effectiveness of dominant men, and they are often content to stop their unraveling of chains of causality when they trace the roots of an event to the will or program of a powerful individual. The models of power which are used to define significant action seem most frequently to be derived from studies of the careers of men. It has been easy, therefore (until recently) to assume that history is what men make it—and that only men make history.

A sexist bias of this sort seems to have pervaded and confused studies of the work of a most remarkable medieval intellectual: Hroswitha of Gandersheim. Ever since the period of their rediscovery in the sixteenth century by the humanist Conrad Celtes, Hroswitha's six plays have constituted an enigma for students of European literature. Written at the end of the tenth century, they survive as the only evidence of western attempts to write drama in the long period between the fall of the Roman Empire and the invention of the mystery and morality plays of the High Middle Ages.

No accurate record of dates for the span of Hroswitha's life has been preserved, but inferences drawn from her works suggest that she witnessed most of the tenth century. She says in the **Primordia,** her history of the cloister in which she lived at Gandersheim, that she was born after the death of Duke Otto of Saxony in 912. She admits in the preface to her collections of saints' legends to being older than her abbess, Gerberga II (940-1001). Her chief historical work, a poem on the reign of Otto the Great, does not discuss events after the death of Otto in 973, but a chronicle of the bishops of Hildesheim seems to imply that she wrote in the service of Otto's son and grandson and survived into the early eleventh century.[1]

It was Hroswitha's good fortune, therefore, to be a party to the splendid revival of arts and literature which accompanied the foundation of the Holy Roman Empire. The collapse of the old Roman Empire in the fifth century had thrust Europe into a "Dark Age" in which political confusion, economic decline, and isolation combined to retard cultural development. Charlemagne's success in imposing feudal order on most of the continent in the early ninth century made possible a "Carolingian Renaissance" which secured the foundations of western literacy. Europe divided into "French" and "German" spheres of influence in the generations after Charlemagne, and, although there were serious disruptions occasioned by Viking and Magyar invasions, it found a new footing for itself as the locus of an independent civilization.

The northern German dukedom of Saxony which was Hroswitha's home had not been a part of the old Roman Empire. Charlemagne spent thirty years in the process of its conquest and pacification. But it was not until the generation of his great-great-grandson, Henry the Fowler (919-936), that Saxony succumbed to the institutions of civilized life. The ducal government of Saxony actively promoted the establishment of monasteries as centers for the conversion and education of its people. As the dukes of Saxony rose to prominence as a dynasty of German kings and emperors in the tenth and eleventh centuries, the cloisters of Saxony became famous centers of learning. Henry's son, Otto the Great, consolidated and expanded German territory, established close ties with the splendid Byzantine Empire of Constantinople, extended a protective arm over Italy and the papacy, and inaugurated a new phase in German-Christian civilization.

The Holy Roman Empire founded by Otto the Great was home to several traditions which might have affected the intellectual development of Hroswitha of Gandersheim. Hroswitha's own connection, if any, with the imperial family is unknown, but she was a close friend and client of several royal ladies who had taken the veil. The Byzantine princess, Theophano, wife of Otto II, was probably an occasional visitor at Gandersheim and a possible avenue of access to the Christian Greek literature of the east. Otto's involvement in the affairs of the papacy and Italy helped make ancient Latin materials accessible to German scholars. And Hroswitha was in correspondence, as the prefaces to her works testify, with a vital circle of northern European scholars who were products of the reformed monasteries of the Carolingian Renaissance. But none of these possible influences is a sufficient explanation of the uniqueness of Hroswitha's work.

II

During the course of her career Hroswitha tried her hand at three kinds of literature. Her earliest compositions form a collection of eight rather traditional saints' lives and holy legends. Later in life she experimented with more objectively historical narratives: accounts of the history of her cloister at Gandersheim and a record of the reign of Otto the Great. Her modest experiment in writing a description of Otto's deeds, a foray into the genre of contemporary history, deserves more recognition than it has received. Her achievements in this field predate by a century those of the Byzantine princess, Anna Comnena, who is usually accorded the honor of being the world's first woman historian. No modern commentator has failed, however, to be impressed by the originality of her six remaining compositions, a cycle of plays in the style of Terence.

Hroswitha acknowledges no model for her plays other than Terence. Her contemporaries seem not to have shared her interest in him and not to have been stimulated to imitate her work in his genre. Hroswitha revived a long dead art for her own use, but failed to become a bridge between the ancient and medieval phases in the history of theater. Her compositions thus seem shockingly out of context. One does not anticipate this much originality from an obscure scholar of the "Ottonian Renaissance." And one does not expect such an independent mind to have been nurtured in a medieval female.

Hroswitha's work and gender constitute an anomaly which has been troublesome to scholars. Nothing like her dramas precedes her, and for all their uniqueness her achievements seem not to have invited emulation by later medieval generations.[2] Her writings survive in a very slender manuscript tradition which serves largely to confound modern preconceptions about the nature of tenth century literature.[3] Thus when the first of the modern text critics turned his attentions to her in the nineteenth century, his first impulse was to preserve standard academic preconceptions by denying the possibility of her existence. At the time it was widely assumed that early medieval intellectuals were severely limited in their ability to deal with, and their interests in, the literature of classical antiquity. And it was felt to be highly improbable that a tenth century scholar who could imitate the Latin of Terence would also be female. In 1867 Joseph von Aschbach[4] advanced the thesis that Hroswitha was a historical absurdity and, therefore, an impossibility. He argued that enough was known about the general level of intellectual attainments in the tenth century to establish *prima facie* that a woman of Hroswitha's literary education and sophisticated taste could not have existed. He suggested that she be explained out of existence as the creation of her sixteenth century editor, Conrad Celtes. Von Aschbach found it much easier to assume that a sixteenth century

male could forge plays in the style of Terence as an elaborate scholarly joke than that a tenth century nun could produce them as serious works of art. Rudolf Kopke early opposed von Aschbach's thesis,[5] but it was not until the twentieth century that paleographers put to rest doubts about Hroswitha's historical authenticity.[6]

Von Aschbach's arguments are heavy-handed examples of scholarly sexist bias when compared with more recent attempts to interpret Hroswitha's plays. Modern commentators have been less preoccupied with the question of the authenticity of Hroswitha's work than its intent, and in this inquiry as well as the former, a male bias has established the context for discussion.

Nothing, beyond what she herself revealed in the preface to her plays, is known of Hroswitha's intent in reviving the genre of drama: "my aim [is] to celebrate within the limits of my meager ability, the honorable chastity of holy virgins [and to use in this task] the same literary mode which has been employed [by Terence] to recount the shameful, impure deeds of wanton women."[7] It is uncertain from this brief statement whether Hroswitha thought of her works as having a unifying theme, and it cannot be determined whether she intended them for performance or simply for use as classroom reading texts which would replace the rhetorically useful, but morally dangerous, Terentian pieces.

Preoccupation with the question of Hroswitha's intent in writing the plays for performance or for study has tended to focus scholarly attention on the few which are most amenable to contemporary tastes in drama and to obscure the fact that all six seem originally to have been published as a set. The only complete medieval edition of the plays is contained in the St. Emmeran manuscript[8] which may have originated at Gandersheim during Hroswitha's lifetime and which may reflect her understanding of the order in which the plays ought to be read. It is possible that Hroswitha simply wrote six unrelated Christian plays to replace the six independent pagan comedies of Terence. The preface she gave her work suggests, however, that she considered her plays to have a common theme (i.e., "the honorable chastity of holy virgins"), and it is likely that this theme is explored differently in each play and that the collection of six constitutes an integrated cycle.

The problem of identifying a thematic structure in Hroswitha's plays has attracted much scholarly attention and has generated some extremely complex theories. Erich Michalka has suggested a Gottschalkean theology of grace as the primary theme explored in all the plays.[9] Marianne Schutze-Pflugk sees the plays as explorations of three kinds of hero images: "Heroes of faith and chastity," "heroes of faith," and "martyrs of the courts and aristocracy."[10] Dietlind Heinze has called into question the likelihood of any one unifying theme in Hroswitha's work.[11] Hugo Kuhn has developed a very elaborate thesis which purports to identify a structure of major and minor themes linking Hroswitha's six plays with her eight legends.[12]

Kuhn's theory is the only one which sees much significance in Hroswitha's claim that her plays are about women. But Kuhn minimizes the importance of his own observation and ends by positing an excessively conjectural context for Hroswitha's work which gives precedence to the things she wrote about men. Kuhn admits that the plays do focus on the careers of heroines, but he insists that they need to be read in the larger and prior context of the legends which deal with the histories of men.[13] He feels that Hroswitha's primary intent was to explore the Christian's struggle to maintain virtue in a hostile and sinful world, and he suggests that the themes of the eight legends provide the key for understanding the thematic structure of the six plays. The eight legends do not, however, yield without violence to the form of Kuhn's themes,[14] and the cycle of six plays proves to be redundant and incomplete when interpreted as a realization of Kuhn's reconstruction of Hroswitha's original program.

Kuhn suggests that a structure of major and minor themes links Hroswitha's six "female" plays and parallels the internal organization of her eight "male" legends. He claims that the major theme of each of the plays is introduced as the minor theme of the one which precedes it. In the *Gallicanus* the major theme is the preservation of a woman's virginity by means of the miraculous conversion of her powerful suitor, and the minor theme is the praise of martydom. The *Dulcitius* has martyrdom as its primary subject and as its minor interest a depiction of the state of those who are totally obsessed by carnal passion. The third play, the *Calimachus,* concerns a man who is completely debased by the flesh and introduces as its secondary theme the topic of the conversion of sinners. The fourth play, the *Abraham,* and the fifth paly, the *Paphnutius,* both deal with the conversion of sinners, and Kuhn claims that they mark the culmination of Hroswitha's thematic program. The *Sapientia,* the last play in the series, is dismissed as a reprise of some of the ideas explored in the earlier works.

There are problems with Kuhn's thesis. It opposes Hroswitha's own claim that her plays are about women by locating the themes of some of the plays in the destinies of their male characters (e.g., the *Calimachus*). It cannot distinguish between the themes of the "identical" plays, the *Abraham* and the *Paphnutius.* And it cannot account for the *Sapientia* at the end of the series, a play which Kuhn dismisses as a needless iteration of themes developed earlier.

It is possible that the arduous struggle of modern commentators to unravel Hroswitha's dramatic program is due less to the complexity of Hroswitha's texts than to the sexist biases of their interpreters. The male orientation of most medieval literature seems to predispose historians to read Hroswitha as if she were engaged in the kind of project which might just as well have recommended itself to a monk of her generation. Her sex is assumed to have little or no significance by those who have sought to identify her motives and concerns. Her choice of women as the chief characters of her plays is not seen as crucial to their interpretation. When viewed from an asexual (or male) perspective, she appears to be a rather average medieval theologian exploring standard concepts of sin and salvation illustrated in the lives of martyrs and virgins. As such there is nothing very extraordinary or original in what she is seen to say. She emerges as a minor eulogist of ordinary Christian heroes. But if the modern preoccupation with assumedly traditional medieval virgin and martyr images is abandoned and the plays are viewed as what Hroswitha forthrightly says they are (i.e., commentaries on women), a logical and fully realized thematic structure clearly and easily emerges. In the preface to the plays Hroswitha announces her intent not simply to write in the style of Terence, but to use that style to undo the harm which he has done to the reputation of women. He has used drama to publicize the deeds of notorious females; Hroswitha will use the same literary vehicle to explore the dimensions of female virtue. What emerges from the six plays, when read in her order, is a systematic exploration of each of the opportunities for female integrity possible in the social roles permitted women in Hroswitha's world.

III

Each of Hroswitha's heroines is a distinctive creature, and each one of them enjoys a unique destiny. Together their careers mesh to provide a description of female options in the three life styles (virgin, whore, or mother) which were popularly accorded medieval women. If, as seems likely, the St. Emmeran manuscript reflects the order in which she published the plays, Hroswitha analyzed the feminine condition in six logically successive and increasingly complex stages: 1) the young girl who chooses virginity over marriage; 2) the virgin whose desire to remain unmarried is not accepted by those in power over her; 3) the woman who marries but emulates the life of a nun in her marriage; 4) the nun who falls into sin and loses her faith, her religious profession, and her virginity; 5) the whore who willingly adopts a life of vice and wantonness; and 6) the woman who surrenders her virginity for the vocation of Christian motherhood.

Hroswitha's first play concerns the successful attempt of the Emperor Constantine's daughter, Constantia, to avoid an offer of marriage from her father's general, Gallicanus. Constantia has secretly vowed to serve God as a virgin and professes that she would rather die than marry (I,ii,3). Her father concurs in her decision, but Gallicanus's request for her hand puts everyone in a difficult position. Gallicanus is her father's most powerful general, and his support is needed in a great war against the Sythians which will complete the stabilization of Roman world power. If Constantia persists in her determination not to marry, her father may lose Gallicanus's support and the security of his empire. Many medieval women, who found themselves used as prizes and pledges in the political programs of their families, could have sympathized with Constantia's dilemma. How does one handle a situation in which one's personal vocational desires and one's obligations to society come into conflict? By a combination of her own wit and God's grace Constantia devises a clever, if somewhat dishonest, plan. She allows Gallicanus to think that she will marry him, after he returns from the war with the Sythians, and trusts in the interim to God to convert Gallicanus to Christianity and away from the earthly delights of the marriage bed. As a vehicle for God's action she sends her two chaplains, John and Paul, with Gallicanus on his campaign, and she undertakes to convert his two daughters during his absence. All turns out as she desires. The battle against the Sythians goes badly until Gallicanus is enlightened by grace and converts to the Christian religion. He returns to Rome prepared to renounce the woman he loves so that he might please "the Virgin's son" (I,xii,10). Constantia offers him the hope that someday they might enter heaven's eternal joy together, and years later during the reign of Julian the Apostate Gallicanus, now a holy hermit, receives the reward of martydom. Constantia's success in reconciling her beloved to her preference for virginity has as its fortunate outcome his salvation, that of his daughters and all those who observed their pious examples.

Not all women could be as fortunate as Constantia in reconciling their preferences for holy virginity with the pressures of their society, and Hroswitha's second play, the *Dulcitius,* explores a situation in which the desire of three girls to maintain their virginity is forcefully opposed. The play concerns the ladies Agape, Chronia, and Irene, whom the Emperor Diocletian would like to provide with honorable marriages to leading members of his court. They refuse marriage as a "corruption of integrity" (i, 2), and they are turned over to a judge named Dulcitius. Dulcitius falls in love with them and locks them up in his pantry so that he can visit them at his convenience and force his attentions on them. God intervenes to protect the girls and causes Dulcitius to mistake the filthy pots and pans of the kitchen for the objects of his desire. He makes love to the kettles and then convered with soot goes forth to be ridiculed and baited by his men. When he comes to his senses, he attempts revenge on the girls by ordering them stripped in public. But divine grace bonds their clothing to their bodies so that the soldiers who attempt to tear it off sweat and strain in vain. Diocletian then turns the women over to another official, Sisinnius, who is ordered to force them to deny their faith or to execute them. The two older girls, Agape and Chronia, eagerly accept all the tortures which Sisinnius provides and enjoy glorious martyrdoms. Since physical threats have failed to have any effect on them, Sisinnius decides to apply psychological pressure to their youngest sibling, his last remaining victim. He warns Irene that if she does not see things his way, he will lock her up in a brothel where she will be violated and prevented for all eternity from joining the company of her sisters among the heavenly virgins. Irene responds by informing him that is is "better to injure the body than to pollute the soul with idolatry" (xii, 3), and then she proposes a rather curious theory of technical virginity. She claims that "pleasure merits punishment, but compulsion (earns) a reward, and one is not accused of crime unless one's soul consents" (xii, 3). Sissinius thus learns that true virginity of spirit lies beyond mere physical compulsion, and in frustration he grants her the martyrdom she desires.

Irene's concept of the virginity of the spirit sets the stage for Hroswitha's third play, the *Calimachus,* which describes the situation of women who choose to follow the ascetic disciplines of holy virgins within the institution of marriage—a custom which may have been not uncommon during the early Christian centuries. Wives who desire to adopt lives of sexlessness may find it necessary to cope with a variety of different responses from the males of their acquaintance, and Hroswitha's heroine, Drusiana, handles two extreme, but natural, situations. She is fortunate in having a Christian husband, Andronicus, who is willing to join her in the renunciation of the pleasures of the flesh, but one could not expect every husband to be a saint like Andronicus. Therefore, Hroswitha explores the alternative possiblity of resistance to Drusiana's decision by providing her with an aspirant lover whose frantic assaults on her virtue stem from the extremes of frustrated male lust. Callimachus, the lover, is totally obsessed by his desire for Drusiana and devotes all his strength and cunning to an effort to trap her. Drusiana is aware that his plots place her in great moral danger and that they are likely at the very least to occasion a scandal which will disrupt the peace of her community. She, therefore, beseeches God to grant her an escape from an impossible situation by allowing her to die. Her prayer receives an affirmative answer, but even death does not remove her from danger. Callimachus is so frenzied by lust that he forces his way into her tomb to launch a post-mortem assault on her chastity. God does not abandon Drusiana. Before the necrophile can achieve his objective, he is struck down, and one might assume that his death brings the play to an adequate conclusion. But at this point Andronicus and his friend John arrive at the tomb with the news that Christ wishes Callimachus to be raised from the dead and given an opportunity to repent. Callimachus returns to life sobered by his experiences, and he freely renounces the passion which had inspired him to attempt unthinkable crimes. Drusiana's firm resolve has helped to effect his conversion, and the play ends with a reminder that while lust is a horrible emotion, it is not the worst of human sins. Even those who fall prey to it are not necessarily placed forever beyond the possiblitiy of forgiveness and redemption—provided they repent their evil ways in time and die with a virgin's heart.

This theme of the forgiveness of the sins of the flesh provides the context for Hroswitha's fourth play, the *Abraham,* which deals with the painful subject of the girl who vows her virginity to God but subsequently fails to maintain her purity. The young woman in question is Mary, a dependent of a holy hermit, Abraham, who instructs her from infancy in the religious disciplines of the desert anchorites. She spends ten years in a small cell near his ardently imitating his ascetic example. But when she attains womanhood, the devil comes to her disguised as a monk, and he tricks her into abandoning her cell and surrendering her virginity. When she realizes what has happened, she despairs of her salvation and flees the desert. Her uncle Abraham resolves to do whatever he must in order to restore her to her monastic vocation, but it takes several years to locate Mary. Finally the news reaches Abraham that she is employed as a prostitute by a tavern keeper and that she has earned considerable popularity in her trade. Disguised as a soldier Abraham sets out for the brothel, and he obtains an opportunity for private conversation with Mary by pretending to her manager that he wishes to buy her services. Once alone with her he reveals his true identity, and she is overcome by a sense of shame. She confesses that she did not come to him for help for fear of offending his purity by her sin. He reminds her that no human being is beyond sin or in a position to condemn others, and as for her future, she is to contemplate the fact that "it is human to sin, [but] it is demonic to remain in sin" (vii, 6). Mary despairs of ever receiving God's forgiveness, but Abraham talks her into returning with him to the desert. Once back in her cell she becomes a model of repentence, and her example serves to turn many others from their evil ways. Hroswitha ends the play by marveling that the power of God's grace can return even a sinner like Mary to the path of virtue.

But Mary was not the worst of sinners. She had made a bad mistake which had led her to a life of vice, but it was a life to which she felt condemned by despair—not one which she freely chose for herself. Hroswitha knew that there was a deeper level at which the relationship between sin and grace in a woman's life could be explored. Not all bad women became bad by accident or through uncontrollable circumstances. Some had no excuse at all for their decisions to enter and persist in their vices. There were prostitutes who knew

what they were doing and who liked their work. Such a woman was the famous Thais, the arch-whore of Alexandria, whose story Hroswitha tells in her fifth play the *Paphnutius.* Thais was such a phenomenally sexy woman that all the men of the city, old and young, wise and foolish, were caught in her snare. They fought in the streets over her, and her doorstep ran with the blood of their battles. So great was the corruption and disorder which this one sinful woman introduced into God's universe that the holy hermit Paphnutius felt obligated to leave his desert retreat and to do something about her. Armed with his prayers he enters the city and is conducted to her home by a troop of young men he meets in the streets. He asks her for a private conference, and she takes him to her bedroom. But that does not content him. He inquires if she does not have an even more secret retreat, and she admits that there is a room in her house known only to God. Her reference to God gives Paphnutius the opening he needs to discourse on spiritual subjects. He finds to his distress that she is indeed the worst of sinners: she sins not in ignorance, but in full knowledge of God's will and the consequences of her acts. He breaks down and weeps over her, and his concern for her succeeds in awakening her conscience. She determines to abandon her sins, burns all her ill-gotten wealth, and publically repudiates her lovers. She follows Paphnutius into the desert, and he has her walled up in a tiny cell where for three years she does penance—wallowing in her own filth as she once wallowed in her sins. At the end of this period God sends a vision to one of the desert monks which suggests that she has been forgiven. Paphnutius, therefore, orders her released from confinement, but she is loath to leave her cell for fear that she has not yet done enough penance to earn God's grace. Paphnutius reminds her that divine grace is a gift which cannot be earned. As he succinctly puts it, "if it were to be imparted according to [our] merits, it could not be called grace" (xii, 5). Thais dies in her nunnery shortly after her liberation, and although there is no reference to her joining the company of heavenly virgins, Hroswitha promises her an equally glorious future. Visions depict her among "white flocks" of heaven enjoying the reward of a glorious bed guarded by four virgins. It is clear that even the most sinful of women need not despair of her ability to repent and share in the delights of the blessed.

Hroswitha's sixth and last play, the *Sapientia,* takes up what seems to have been for her the most difficult topic of all: the spiritual destiny of the Christian woman who chooses the life of a wife and a mother. Hroswitha comes very close to equating virtue with virginity, and she occasionally infers that the exercise of religion and the practice of sex are incompatible. For her, Christ is the "Virgin's son," who takes a special delight in the company of virgins and reserves to them the highest places in heaven. It seemed self-evident to Hroswitha that the best of all feminine vocations was that of the nun, but she knew that the church blessed marriage and recognized it as an honorable alternative to virginity. Try as she might, however, Hroswitha could not bring herself to accord a married woman spiritual equality with a virgin. But she did attempt in her last play, the ***Sapientia,*** to describe a model of feminine heroism based, not on the repudiation of sex, but on its legitimate use.

The ***Sapientia*** opens with the Emperor Hadrian receiving a report which charges Sapientia and her three daughters with threatening the stability of the state. Hadrian at first scoffs at the idea that a few women could cause any significant trouble, but he becomes alarmed when he learns that Sapientia is converting large numbers to Christianity and, as a result of her teaching, many wives have begun to refuse to sleep with their husbands. Sapientia is brought in for examination, and although Hadrian is most gallant and courteous, she treats the pagan emperor with contempt. She and her daughters are, therefore, locked up for three days to think things over. During their imprisonment, Sapientia has an opportunity to explain to her daughters why she decided to have children: "for this I abundantly fed you with mother's milk, for this I carefully nourished [you], that I might deliver you to a celestial, not an earthly, husband and that I might through your merits be proclaimed the mother-in-law of the eternal king" (iv, 3). "I wish for this: to be crowned by your virginity and to be glorified by your martyrdom." (iv, 4)

When the girls return to Hadrian, they are eager for the trials for which their mother has prepared them, and one by one they receive martyrdom after manifesting numerous miracles of faith. When the last and youngest daughter is brought forth, Sapientia greets her as "the one hope of my womb" (iv, 29), and she sends her on her way to die reminding her of the "crown of unimpaired virginity" which she will soon wear in heaven. In her last speech to her daughter, Sapientia's thoughts seem to be primarily for herself. She says: "Go sweetest child; and when you are joined with Christ in heaven, remember [your] mother, [and be] a patroness of the one who bore you." (vii, 2) The girl dies as valiantly as her sisters, and the play closes as a chorus of Roman matrons assist Sapientia in burying her daughters. In a final prayer before her own death Sapientia reminds God that in sacrificing her children she has forsaken all earthly bonds and although she will not be able to "sing the song of virginity" (ix, 8) with her daughters in heaven, still she deserves an honored place among the company of the saved. It seems that Hroswitha wishes to imply that a mother's salvation derives in part from the virtues of her children. The merit of their virginity and faith can serve to cancel some of the effect of the "impairment" which she acquired in giving them birth. But there

still remains a distinction of precedence in heaven between the virgins and all other women.

IV

With the ***Sapientia*** Hroswitha brought the project which she announced in her preface to a conclusion. Terence wrote six plays in which he celebrated the folly of base women. Hroswitha has redressed the balance by writing six plays in which she has demonstrated the strength and wisdom of women in the exercise of Christian virtues. There are superficial resemblances of theme or situation among some of the dramas, but these are of little consequence. Each play is a distinct work which treats its own separate subject, and each play makes a unique contribution to the structure of a cycle. As a cycle the plays reflect Hroswitha's concern, not with generalized, asexual Christian heroism, but with the unique challenges confronting women in the very circumscribing world of the tenth century.

The discovery of this thematic plan in Hroswitha's six dramas is more surprising in what it reveals about the biases of modern scholarship than in what it depicts as the condition of medieval women. Hroswitha does not rise far above the limits of her own education in her analysis of the condition of her sex. Her understanding of the Christian faith as a war with the flesh is completely consistent with the ascetic worldview of traditional medieval monasticism. Virginity is a condition which she, along with most of the fathers of the church, accepts as self-evidently superior for members of both sexes. Christ is the chaste son of the Virgin, and his life is the ultimate model for all human lives. Those who sink into whoredom and fornication are automatically ranked with the enemies of God. But Hroswitha's Christianity is a theology of grace and forgiveness. The situation of the sinner is not hopeless; the pressures of the flesh are never overwhelming once the soul is stirred by a concern for its own purity. Hroswitha's uniqueness lies not in the articulation of these thoughts, but in her decision to illustrate them in the lives of six kinds of heroic women. Medieval literature is filled with tales of male champions of the faith or women who emulate the examples of males in making similar witnesses of martyrdom. Hroswitha's originality lay in attempting to discuss women as Christian heroes within their normal social roles as women. Many saints legends would read much the same if narrated about heroes or heroines. Hroswitha's plays would be ludicrous if converted into dramas about men.

Modern comentators have been disturbingly slow to recognize this. No one today would be surprised to find a female playwrite choosing the lives of women as the theme for her work. But few historians have shown much sensitivity to the possibility that a medieval woman could have found dignity and significance in the lives of her female compatriots. Hroswitha plainly announces her intent to write about women, but historians have persistently explored the actions of her male characters for clues to the thematic structure of her plays. The result has been the "discovery" of numerous problems, imperfections, and redundancies in her dramatic program. Bert Nagel, for instance, has found the **Abraham** and the **Paphnutius** to be such similar plays that he can account for them only by theorizing that Hroswitha paused between their compositions and wrote the second as a review of the first in preparation for completing the cycle.[15] The two plays are similar, however, only in the situation of their leading males, the holy men who visit prostitutes in order to covert them. The women who receive their attentions are significantly different. Mary, the woman of the **Abraham,** falls into sin unwittingly and remains in it through motives of despair. Thais, the woman of the **Paphnutius,** embraces sin willingly and in full knowledge of its consequences. Hroswitha makes her intention to demonstrate Thais's culpability clear by omitting from her version of Thais's legend the stories which credit Thais's sin to abuses inflicted on her in childhood. Thais is to have no excuse beyond her own will for her immoral career. Her play is not a repetition of Mary's play, for her life, although it comes to the same conclusion by similar means, is not a repetition of Mary's life.

Many of the problems which have preoccupied students of Hroswitha's plays have been suggested not by insufficiencies in her thought or texts, but by imperfections in the perspectives or assumptions which commentators bring to the interpretation of her work. The study of a figure like Hroswitha has value, therefore, on at least two levels. It has something noteworthy to reveal about the lives and intellectual attainments of medieval women. And it also has something to teach about the critical process itself. It becomes a source for discovering and analyzing sexist attitudes which bias apparently objective research, and it offers useful perspectives on the present which encourage the development of more accurate perceptions in the writing of history.

Notes

[1] M. B. Bergman, *Hrosvithae Liber Tertius* (Covington, Ky.: The Sisters of St. Benedict, 1943).

[2] See, Boris Jarcho, "Zu Hrotsvithas Werkungskreis," *Speculum,* 2 (1927), 343-44; and Edwin H. Zeydal, "Knowledge of Hrotsvitha's Works Prior to 1500," *Modern Language Notes,* 54 (1944), 382-385.

[3] The bulk of Hroswitha's work survives in one medieval manuscript from the cloister of St. Emmeran in Regensburg (Bayerische Staatsbibliothek clm 14485). An excellent modern edition of the Latin texts has been published by Helene Homeyer, *Hrotsvithae Opera* (Munich: Ferdinand Schoning, 1970). A rather free English translation of the plays will be found under the name Christopher St. John (Cristabel Marshall), *The Plays of Hroswitha* (New York: Benjamin Blom, 1923).

[4] Joseph von Aschbach, "Roswitha und Conrad Celtes," *Kaiserlichen Adademie der Wissenschraften, Sitzungsberichte,* 56 (Vienna, 1867).

[5] Rudolf Kopke, "Hrotsvit von Gandersheim," *Ottonishe Studien,* 2 (Berlin, 1869).

[6] Edwin Zeydel, "The Authenticity of Hrotswitha's Works," *Modern Langueage Notes,* 61 (1946), 50-55.

[7] Latin text has been omitted. Translations are mine.

[8] Bayerische Staatsbibliothek clm 14485.

[9] Erich Michalka, *Studien uber Intention und Gestaltung in den dramatischen Werken Hrotsvits von Gandersheim* (Heidelberg: Ruprecht-Carl-Universitat, 1968), pp. 114-18, 189.

[10] Marrianne Schutze-Pflugk, *Herrscher-und Martyrer-Auffassung bei Hrotsvit von Gandersheim* (Wiesbaden: Steiner Verlag, 1972).

[11] Dietlend Heinze, *Die Praefatio zu den 'Dramen' Hrotsvits von Gandersheim—ein Programm?* (Karlsruhe: O. Berenz, 1973).

[12] Hugo Kuhn, *Dichtung und Welt im Mittelalter* (Stuttgart: J. B. Metzler, 1959), pp. 94-100.

[13] Ibid., p. 99.

[14] The "male" legend of "Gongolf" features a woman who is central to the fate of the male subject. Kuhn identifies virginity as Hroswitha's "female" theme, but the struggle for its maintenance is the crux of many of her stories about men. It is a virtue which she advocates equally for both sexes.

[15] Bert Nagel, *Hrotsvit von Gandersheim* (Stuttgart: J. B. Metzler, 1965), p. 64 ff.

Peter Dronke (essay date 1984)

SOURCE: "Hrotsvitha" in *Women Writers of the Middle Ages: A Critical Study of Texts from Perpetua († 203) to Marguerite Porete († 1310),* Cambridge University Press, pp. 55-83.

[In the following essay, Dronke undertakes an overall evaluation of Hroswitha's writings, examining her life and relation to the court of Emperor Otto I; her literary intentions and possibly self-conscious pose as a

humble and unassuming woman writer; the thematic structure of her collected writings; her artistic limitations; and her influence in the Middle Ages.]

Hrotsvitha wrote more prolifically than Dhuoda, and planned her major work on a larger scale. Like Dhuoda, she clung to prefaces and preliminaries, dedications and elaborate articulations; but, having far greater literary ambitions than her predecessor, she carried out such manoeuvres with the utmost self-consciousness and craft.

There exists much scholarly writing on Hrotsvitha,[1] yet in it her life and work tend to be misrepresented. Discussion of Hrotsvitha has seldom wholly escaped the assumptions that her existence was 'cloistered' and that her talent was naïve. The stereotype still most widely encountered is that of a woman (usually thought of as a nun) immured in her convent, who unaccountably took it into her head to read the plays of Terence and to 'imitate' them by writing edifying Christian counterparts. It is considered scholarly to add that Hrotsvitha could not have intended her own plays for performance—at most, for reading aloud at mealtimes in the convent refectory.[2]

Specialists, admittedly, have meanwhile recognized how different Gandersheim was from a convent in the usual sense. Founded in 852 by Duke Liudolf, the great-grandfather of Emperor Otto I, Gandersheim was from its beginnings a high aristocratic, then royal and imperial, foundation. Its abbesses were members of the reigning family. When Otto I, in 947, invested the abbess of Gandersheim with supreme authority, she became the ruler of a small autonomous princedom. The situation is well sketched in Ferruccio Bertini's recent study:

> Thus the convent had its own courts, an army of its own, was empowered to mint its own coinage, had its own representative at the imperial Assembly, and enjoyed the direct protection of the Papal See without any interference from bishops.[3]

At least in Hrotsvitha's lifetime, that is, Gandersheim was a small, proudly independent principality ruled by women. Such independence will also have suited the Ottonian dynasty politically, since it gave the unmarried women of royal blood a certain power and intellectual scope, and lessened the danger of their marrying princes outside the family, who might loom as rivals for the throne. All who belonged to Gandersheim (except for the servants) were of noble birth, some taking vows as nuns, others remaining canonesses. It is almost certain that Hrotsvitha, born *ca.* 935, was one of the canonesses. It seems likely, too, that she was related to the earlier abbess of Gandersheim, Hrotsvitha I (919-26), and hence was at least a distant relative of the royal house.[4]

The nuns and canonesses at Gandersheim shared certain intellectual aspirations, which were essentially those that had been realized by Radegunde, Agnes and their circle at Poitiers. The intellectual ideal, which implied cultivation of the mind, the study of major authors both pagan and Christian, and literary exchanges with learned men, was combined with a social ideal, a gracefulness of behaviour towards others, in which an aristocratic habit of *gentilezza* blended with Christian love of one's neighbour. These intellectual and social impulses culminated in the spiritual—the attempt to lead a life serenely dedicated to Christ. While the nuns at Gandersheim, however, accepted strict monastic vows, the canonesses kept a number of significant personal freedoms: they could retain their private fortune, have their own servants and buy their own books, they could entertain guests, and come and go without special difficulty. If they chose to leave Gandersheim permanently, in order to marry, no stigma was attached.

Hrotsvitha's abbess, and (we can safely say, despite her many formulaic self-deprecations) close friend, Gerberga II, was the emperor's niece. Born *ca.* 940, and schooled at St Emmeram in Regensburg, she was still young when she came to rule Gandersheim in 959. As abbess she maintained close relations with the imperial court, and especially with the emperor's younger brother, Bruno, the court's chancellor and chaplain, whom Bezzola has called 'the soul of the Ottonian intellectual Renaissance'.[5]

We do not know how old Hrotsvitha was when she entered Gandersheim. It is possible that she spent some of her youth at the Ottonian court rather than in a convent. One detail here seems to me particularly suggestive. In 952, Otto I had invited Rather, the most widely-read scholar and most brilliant prose-writer of the age, to his court: Rather, exiled from his see at Verona because of quarrels and intrigues, arrived virtually as a refugee. Ostensibly he came to give Bruno some advanced literary teaching; but the fact that Rather cultivated a distinctive style of rhymed prose, which has notable parallels in Hrotsvitha,[6] makes it tempting to suppose that, in Rather's years with Otto, Hrotsvitha too received instruction from him, and then tried to model some of her mannerisms on his. Especially her longest and most complicated sentences, often filled with coinages and new formations as well as rhymes, have to me a markedly Ratherian ring.

There are other good reasons for supposing that Hrotsvitha was at the court at an early age. In the passage of transition that links her series of poetic legends to her series of plays, she distinguishes between the various written sources that she used and the one piece for which she was able to rely on an eye-witness account:

> the order of events leading to Pelagius' martyrdom was told me by a certain man, a native of the city

[Cordova] where Pelagius suffered, who assured me that he had seen that fairest of men and had true knowledge of the outcome of the matter.[7]

This native of Cordova can only have been a member of one of Abd ar-Rāhman III's two embassies to Otto the Great (950 and 955/6). While it cannot be ruled out that one of the ambassadorial party spent some time at Gandersheim, it is far more probable that Hrotsvitha met her witness at the court itself.[8] She must indeed have spoken with him sufficiently long and often to receive not only the account of Pelagius but some detailed related information about the life of Christians in Cordova under Moslem rule.[9]

At all events from the 960s onwards, especially through Gerberga, Hrotsvitha's links with the Ottonian court were far-reaching. And here I believe one should formulate and advance a hypothesis which, strangely, scholars have not hitherto entertained. Ruotger's biography of the emperor's brother, Bruno, mentions not only Bruno's relations with Gandersheim, the foundation ruled by his niece, but also, among Bruno's wide reading, singles out his enthusiasm for 'the unseemly jests and mimetic matter (*scurrilia et mimica*) that, in comedies and tragedies, are presented by various personages: while some people react to these noisily, shaking with endless laughter, he always used to read them frequently and seriously; he set least store by the content, and most by what was exemplary in the style'.[10] The reference (as a passage in Thietmar of Merseburg's *Chronicon*, II 16, confirms) is clearly to Roman comedies and tragedies, and the *scurrilia* alluded to must be first and foremost those of Terence. That these were performed 'a personis variis' is presumably not a mere antiquarian aside. The biographer's contrast between using this material for an occasion of riotous merriment and using it for earnest stylistic study (as he claims of Bruno, and Hrotsvitha affirms of herself), suggests that both possibilities were familiar in his world, and that Bruno's interest—amazing if not scandalous in a holy man—was too well known for even the author of a *Vita* to ignore. The hypothesis I would propose, then, is that when Hrotsvitha prefaces her plays with an 'Epistola ad quosdam sapientes huius libri fautores', Bruno must have been a leading figure among those 'wise . . . favourers'. Hrotsvitha is overjoyed, that is, to have found favour, not in some monastery or other (as has generally been alleged), but at the court itself.

If this is correct, then it does not seem too bold to suggest that at the Ottonian court, with the encouragement of Bruno and others—including quite possibly Rather of Verona, and another spirited writer, Liutprand, likewise a keen Terentian, who often visited the court and served Otto as ambassador and chronicler—the plays of Terence were read aloud with distribution of parts; and that then, after Hrotsvitha had sent Bruno and his circle five of her own plays (the two on *Galli-*

canus; Agape, Chionia and Hirena; Drusiana and Calimachus; and *Mary the Niece of Abraham*), they showed their appreciation by having these too read publicly in a similar fashion. Hrotsvitha's *Epistola* would represent her delighted reaction at this: it made her feel unafraid to complete her dramatic series, with her two longer, more 'philosophical' plays, *The Conversion of Thais* and *The Passion of the Holy Maidens.*[11]

The question, what precise form a tenth-century reading might have taken, is difficult for want of documentation, and has in the past caused the most heated division of scholars into romantics and sceptics. There is indeed no direct evidence that such a reading, even with the apportioning of rôles to different readers, would have been at all like a fully-fledged performance, with the element of impersonation dominating. The chief relevant indirect evidence is the fragmentary poetic altercation between Terence and his critic,[12] copied probably at Reims in Hrotsvitha's lifetime, but itself somewhat older (perhaps early ninth century). There the indications of movement ('Now Terence comes out, hearing this, and says . . . '),[13] of impersonation ('persona delusoris'), and even of asides ('persona secum'), make clear that the *Altercation* was to be performed, and almost certainly performed as prelude to a play by Terence. For how could the *persona* Terence have answered the mocking challenge of the *persona delusoris,* that his compositions were worthless and outworn, save by having a piece of his own presented for the audience to judge? Yet even here (as with the twelfth-century reference to an 'acted reading (*scenica lectio*)' of Terence)[14] this does not, I think, warrant an inference to a fully *staged* performance.

On the other hand, the difference between a lifelessly academic reading of a work and one clarified and pointed by looks, gestures and movements, depends chiefly on the inclinations and skills of those taking part. These must have varied in the Middle Ages, whenever a group of people tried out a new piece, whether spoken or sung, with the text in front of them—just as at the concert performance of an opera, or the first public reading of a play today, there will always be some who cling stiffly to their script or score, and others who are able from the outset to enter into the spirit of the work. And there is no reason to suppose that the Ottonian court had only untalented, statuesque readers.

As regards movement, at least a few reasonable conjectures may also be made from internal evidence in Hrotsvitha's texts. When for instance (*Drusiana and Calimachus* VIII) St John goes to Drusiana's tomb with Andronicus, the heroine's husband, God appears to them in the semblance of a most fair young man:

Andronicus: I am trembling![15]
John: Lord Jesus, why have you deigned to appear

to your servants in such a place as this?

The Lord: I have appeared so as to waken Drusiana and him who lies beside her tomb, for in them my name shall be glorified.

Andronicus: How suddenly he was taken back to heaven!

Even in the most unadorned public reading, these last words of Andronicus would be hard to fathom unless the fair young man were *seen* to vanish before the eyes of the audience. One need not suppose anything elaborate: he could quietly ascend steps to an upper gallery, or even make a simple exit behind the readers. But for Andronicus to speak his sentence while the reader of the Lord's part was still glued to the spot would have been fatuous then, just as it would be now.

More problematic is the 'mime-like' element in such a famous scene as the delusion of Dulcitius, when he embraces the sooty pots and pans in the prison kitchen, convinced that he is enjoying the bodies of the three Christian maidens. The idea of having the girls peeping through the cracks in the wall, filled with mirth at the villain's bewitchment, is Hrotsvitha's own. There is no hint of this in her hagiographic source, nor is it a kind of humour she could have learnt from Terence's text. It is the broader, visual humour of *scurrilia,* performed in such a way as to make people 'shake with endless laughter', in Ruotger's words, that Hrotsvitha must have witnessed at least now and then. This does not necessarily imply that, when her own scene was read aloud, it too was fully mimed; but we can be sure that she would not have shaped her scene in this particular way if she had never herself watched a mime.

At the Ottonian court, too, she will have witnessed many ceremonies that involved elaborate rôle-playing. This, it is well known, was taken to extravagant lengths by Otto III in his years in Rome (996-1002), the young dreamer who played out the life of a Roman emperor in all its grandeur, conjuring up endless imperial offices, rituals and charades.[16] But already with Otto the Great and his son Otto II one has the sense that for them the *imperium* they strove to realize implied replaying a Roman emperor and court, though in a Christian mode. Something of this emerges in the resplendent Ottonian miniatures that survive: men and women are portrayed with grave refinement; the high and low—kings and shepherds—are subtly differentiated in their looks; gestures are stylized and hieratic; costumes and settings often deliberately classicizing. Each episode in the illustrations is solemnly set in its own space, which tends to be demarcated by pillars or curtains. It is a consciously exquisite, even precious, world—like that of Hrotsvitha's plays and poems, with which the work of the Ottonian painters has close affinity. In her dramas especially, Hrotsvitha, like the Ottonian family, wanted to replay the Roman world in a Christian mode. She was not cut off from the imperial *renovatio*

by belonging to Gandersheim: on the contrary, this put her in a position to play a key part among the élite who shaped that *renovatio.* Two of her poems, on the exploits of Otto and on the origins of Gandersheim, are indeed overtly celebrations of the dynasty. But in her poetic legends and plays, too, Hrotsvitha was aware of helping to refashion, for the Ottonians, a culture worthy of the rôle they had chosen—worthy of Charlemagne, of Constantine, and of the myth of Rome.

The double cycle, of poetic legends and plays, gradually became in Hrotsvitha's conception a single *magnum opus,* with vast and elaborate internal symmetries. This was shown in a superb essay by Hugo Kuhn.[17] Readers familiar with Kuhn's argument will see at once how much the following suggestions about Hrotsvitha's larger design owe to him, though I also propose certain qualifications and developments of Kuhn's ideas, and do not re-examine every parallel that he indicated.

Let us consider the two cycles side by side:

LEGENDS	PLAYS
Maria/Ascension	*Gallicanus I-II*
Gongolf	*Agape, Chionia and Hirena*
Pelagius	*Drusiana and Calimachus*
Theophilus	*Mary the Niece of Abraham*
Basilius	*The Conversion of Thais*
Dionysius	*The Passion of the Holy Maidens*
Agnes	*Apocalypse*

If we look at them from the vantage of works completed rather than of works in the making, certain parallelisms are at once evident, others become apparent only gradually.

The fifth composition in each cycle is a thematic *reprise* of the fourth: the story of Thais is a variation on that of Abraham's niece Mary,[18] just as the story of Basil (or better, of Proterius' slave) is a variation on that of Theophilus. Central to the series of plays as to that of legends is the treatment of two women and two men, each of whom sinks to the depths by renouncing God, and rises again at last, through repentance, to win heavenly bliss. This theme, with its deep optimism, meant so much to Hrotsvitha that she illustrated it, with the help of deliberate echoes and analogies, in four different ways.

The next parallels that emerge distinctly are those at the beginning of each cycle. It is not hard to see that the first two legends (the life of the Virgin and the ascension of Christ) form a diptych, as do the two **Gallicanus** plays. In each case a long composition is followed by a briefer coda. Like Gallicanus in the sequel to his play, Mary continues as an important figure in the tale of Christ's ascent—indeed his speech of farewell to her, promising her own assumption into heaven, is central to the second piece. There is also a clear thematic parallel between **Maria** and **Gallicanus I**—each concerns the conflict between virginity and marriage, and shows the conflict resolved—though I find it harder to see one between the sequels.

Gongolf and **Agape, Chionia and Hirena** stand out in each series by their remarkable conjunction of tragic and burlesque elements. Each unfolds a story that ends in the hero's or heroine's death by martyrdom, yet the most memorable moments in each, poetically and dramatically, are filled with comedy and farce. Hrotsvitha's full title for the legend tells us that Gongolf's story is the **Passio Sancti Gongolfi Martiris;** but he is the martyr of marriage—he dies not at the hands of a pagan executioner, but through a plot hatched by his own wanton wife. At the close of this *Passio* the high-spirited tone of many of the earlier episodes becomes outright fabliau, though Hrotsvitha, while heightening the ribaldry in her source, conveys it by means of elaborate, mock-decorous circumlocutions. Gongolf's wife scoffs at the idea that her late husband has become a saint:[19]

> 'Miracles occur at Gongolf's tomb?—
>   only the way that signs and miracles
>   occur out of the back of my behind!'
> Thus spoke she,[20] and a wondrous sign
>   followed her words,
>   one congruent with that corporeal part:
> thence she brought forth a sound of sordid
>   music
>   such as my little tongue is ashamed to tell.
> And after this, whenever she formed a word,
>   as often did she sound that graceless note.

In the play of the martyrdom of Agape and her sisters, the villains at each turn are made to look absurd. Always they lose their dignity, routed by the beneficent 'sorcery (*maleficia*)' of the Christian God. It is this that makes Dulcitius deflower pots and pans instead of maidens, that makes the clothes stick to the girls' bodies as they are about to be stripped naked, or that sends the youngest, Hirena, to a mountain-top, made magically inaccessible, instead of to the brothel planned for her. The illusions that seem 'malefic' to the pagans are in fact innocent, and always in a comic mode. I shall return to this point later.

The story of Pelagius and the drama of Drusiana and Calimachus again show a link in theme: both treat of an illicit love. The Caliph's attempt to seduce the beautiful Christian boy (*Pel.* 227-70) is portrayed with insight and daring realism; his words to the reluctant Pelagius—'o lascive puer, iactas te posse licenter /

spernere . . . ' 21—are worthy of the epigrams in the Greek Anthology. So too, Hrotsvitha's presentation of Calimachus, about to violate the dead Drusiana in her tomb—'I had been happy had I never learnt that her body was still perfect'—shows an imaginative penetration that has no counterpart in her source.

After the 'double bill' in each cycle—the tales of rejecting God and rediscovering him—come two treatments of martyrdom in a serious mode: the legend of Dionysius and the play of Sapientia's three daughters. These too show parallels of theme: the martyred ones are sages—Dionysius, the great philosopher and mystagogue, and Sapientia, the mother who even by her name embodies wisdom, who taunts her judge, the Emperor Hadrian, with the enigmas of Boethian mathematics.

The concluding parallel that Kuhn suggested is in my view correct, though still deeply problematic. The legends conclude with the story of Agnes, the virgin martyr who died refusing marriage, and whose steadfastness led to the conversion of her wooer and his father. Thus this tale both closes the first cycle—reverting to the theme of virginity and marriage in the life of Mary—and foreshadows the first play, where the chaste Constantia's refusal to consummate her marriage brings about Gallicanus' conversion. But what of the counterpiece—if such it is—at the end of the plays, thirty-five hexameters depicting scenes from the Apocalypse? Kuhn noted perceptively how the first line—'The virgin John saw heaven laid open (*Iohannes caelum virgo vidit patefactum*)'—brought once more the virginity-motif that is sounded at the opening and close of both series (from Mary to Agnes, from Gallicanus to John), making each series truly cyclic. He added that, while the first and last protagonist in the legends is a woman, and in the plays a man, all the intervening legends have heroes, but all the other plays have heroines.[22] He also suggested that the scenes from the end of time so swiftly evoked here are a meaningful conclusion to the twofold cycle, which had begun with the nativities of Mary and Christ, and with Christ's promise, at the ascension, that he would protect his own till the end of time. Christ coming again, to bind the dragon and open the book of life, is the fulfilment of the cycle of events that began with Mary's birth; and Hrotsvitha, in her own invocation to Mary before she begins to tell of that birth, looks forward to the apocalyptic moment, when she, 'joining the hosts of virgins, may achieve the praise of the crimson-clad Lamb perpetually' (**Maria** 43-4).

What remains unexplained is the use to which this brief hexameter composition was put. Those, like Homeyer, who have reflected on it, can think of these verses only as a group of *tituli*—inscriptions to be placed under book-illuminations or frescoes in a church.[23] Indeed the wording resembles that of *tituli*: 'Here the angel, seeking someone worthy, finds nobody . . . Behold, the secrets of the book lie open . . . Behold, heaven's habitants are silent as at noon. Here he stood with a censer before the holy altar . . . '

Yet the paradox is that these thirty-five lines, which in a sense fit so well thematically as a conclusion to the double cycle of legends and of dramas, could not serve as their conclusion if they were planned for an illustrated sacred text or for a church wall, and not as directly related to the plays. In that case their position after the plays in the manuscript would be fortuitous, and, if we nonetheless accept the idea that Hrotsvitha planned a double cycle, with many precise symmetries between the legends and dramas and between the structures of each cycle, we should also have to say that the second cycle is incomplete—that a final play on the theme of virginity and marriage, or perhaps on the end of time, is lost, or else was planned but never written.

Or is it possible that the apocalyptic verses *were* performed? In principle there is nothing implausible about this. From the decade 965-75—a time when Hrotsvitha was at the height of her powers—we have the first surviving detailed instructions, set down at Winchester, about how the resurrection-ceremony, *Quem quaeritis,* should be mimed.[24] We also know that the Sibyl's evocation of the fifteen Signs of Judgment—a piece that in length and form (twenty-seven hexameters) as well as content is very close to Hrotsvitha's apocalyptic poem—was performed, both at the climax of the *Ordo prophetarum* and independently, at least from the tenth century onwards.[25] Yet the wording of Hrotsvitha's composition suggests something for which I know no precise parallel in tenth- or eleventh-century sacred performances: a reader who, with expressions such as 'here' and 'behold' (*hic, ecce*), is pointing to and explaining events which, if they were enacted, must have been so silently. If that was the conclusion of Hrotsvitha's dramatic cycle—and it is a big 'if'—does it imply that in the plays themselves there was, after all, more movement than the minimal amount which I believe is all that our other evidence would lead us to suppose? Hrotsvitha's *Apocalypse* raises problems which, in our present state of knowledge, remain unanswerable.

How did Hrotsvitha arrive at her notion of structural and thematic parallels? It is tempting to think of possible iconographic inspiration. The great bronze door of Bernward of Hildesheim, with its subtle parallelisms, was not completed till 1015, a date at which almost certainly Hrotsvitha was no longer alive.[26] Perhaps the likeliest place at which she could have seen paintings or sculptures ordered in series was if she was ever with the court during one of its sojourns in the palace at Ingelheim. This palace had a cycle of reliefs of heroes that began with Cyrus, Romulus and Remus, Hannibal, and Alexander, and went on to Constantine, Theodoric, Charles Martel, Pippin, and Charlemagne.

To what extent the cycle showed parallelism is not clear from the description in Ermoldus Nigellus' poem,[27] though the juxtaposition of ancient pagan hero-rulers with the Christian ones, who founded the empire that the Ottonians inherited, must have struck the eye. The church next to the imperial palace had two series of frescoes, twelve Old Testament scenes (from the creation of Adam to Solomon) on the left wall, twelve New Testament ones (from Annunciation to Ascension) on the right. But while there was symmetry, there seems to have been no interrelation, such as could have been achieved by use of *figura*.

In short, Hrotsvitha's scheme for her legends and plays almost certainly went well beyond any visual patternings that she might have beheld. In the harmonies of theme and structure that she succeeded in establishing, she achieved the boldest and most elaborate compositional design in Carolingian or Ottonian literature and art, at least as far as the surviving monuments can show.

It is important to add that the unity Hrotsvitha envisioned comprises the legends and plays, culminating (as on balance I incline to believe) in the apocalyptic verses—but not her other works. Between the legends and plays comes her brief transitional note, headed 'Explicit liber primus, incipit secundus'. The editors, from Winterfeld onwards, have given the erroneous impression that the **Gesta Ottonis** constituted Book III of Hrotsvitha's work, and scholars have often referred to this poem as 'the third book'. But neither is it called 'liber tertius' in the manuscript nor has it thematically any link with the double cycle: its links are, if anything, with the poem on Gandersheim, which likewise sets narrative in the service of dynastic commemoration.

At what stage in her writing Hrotsvitha began to think out a sweeping overall design for her legends and plays, and when she committed herself to that design decisively, can no longer be fully ascertained. From the close of **Theophilus,** and the new dedication to Gerberga preceding **Basilius,** it is evident that Hrots-vitha had first submitted to Gerberga the group of poems from **Maria** to **Theophilus,** and added the rest later. So when writing **Theophilus,** it seems, she had not yet thought of returning to the motif of renouncing God with a second tale. From the epistle to her favourers it looks as if there may have been a comparable break (what Kuhn called a 'Schaffenspause') in her playwriting, after the drama of Abraham's niece, when once more she felt uncertain whether or not to go on. Yet the notion of a larger design must have been in Hrotsvitha's mind before she determined on her second *reprise,* with **The Conversion of Thais.** Beyond this we are reduced to conjecture.

What we can still trace with some precision, however, especially in Hrotsvitha's Prefaces, is her growing—

and changing—awareness of herself as artist. These Prefaces are written in the most artificial prose of which Hrotsvitha felt capable—yet paradoxically they are also full of self-revelations, at least between the lines. If we can look beyond Hrotsvitha's overwrought façades, beyond her topoi of humility that become almost presumptuous through sheer over-insistence, we can discover what was really on her mind.

In the discussion that follows, I shall quote from the Prefaces and the Epistle substantially, in translation. With the first Preface, it seemed relatively easy to give at least some impression of Hrotsvitha's mode of rhyming as well as an accurate picture of what she says; with the others, conveying her convolutions and nuances of expression was so demanding that rhyme-effects would only have diminished precision, and hence were not attempted.

The Preface to the series of legends begins:[28]

> This small book, adorned with little grace of beauty but elaborated with no little loving care, I offer to the benevolent gaze   of all who are wise   for correction, or at least to those   who take no delight in belittling one who errs,   but rather in the correcting of the errors.

> I confess, indeed, to more than average erring—not only in discerning   the length of syllables, but also in the forging   of poetic style—and many things in this series of poems should go in hiding, as deserving blame; yet forgiveness is easily given to one who admits her errors, and faults merit the correction that's their due.

> But if it is objected that certain things in this work are drawn from writings that some hold apocryphal, there's no blame here for sinister presumption, only an ignorant assumption: for, when I began to weave the thread of this chain, I did not know that things I resolved to work on were held up to doubt. And when I came to know it, I refused to undo the work   —since what seems falsity may perhaps prove truth.

> This being so, I am the more in need of many champions for my finished work, inasmuch as, at its inception, I could rely on too little strength of my own: I was not yet mature enough in years, or advanced enough in knowledge. But I did not dare to lay bare   my impulse and intention to any of the wise   by asking for advice,   lest I be forbidden to write because of my clownishness. So in complete secrecy,   as it were furtively,   now toiling at my compositions alone,   now destroying work that was badly done,   I tried as best I might to produce   a text of even the slightest use,   based on passages in writings I had gathered to store   on the threshing-floor   of our Gandersheim foundation.

There follows a tribute to the guidance of Rikkardis, and of Gerberga, who, 'though younger than I, was more advanced in learning, as behoved an emperor's niece'. Hrotsvitha continues:

> Though metrical composition seems difficult and arduous for women, frail as we are, I, relying only on the help of the ever-merciful grace on high, never on my own strength, decided to harmonize the songs in this trifling work in dactylic measures. The talent of a little imagination, entrusted to me, was not to lie sluggish in the heart's dark cavern and be destroyed by the rust of negligence,   but rather, struck by the hammer of unfailing diligence, was to echo some small ringing note of divine praise, whereby, if no chance came to win more, by commerce with it,   it could still be transformed into an instrument of some—however paltry—profit.

The Preface concludes by asking the indulgence of the reader, who should ascribe to God whatever in the work might perchance prove well-composed.

It was one of the much-worn topoi of prefaces and dedications, from the first century onwards, to offer one's work to a reader, or readers, for improvement, asking that they correct the imperfections which remained.[29] Hrotsvitha, playing upon such a device, makes many asseverations of her inadequacy—yet each is immediately in some way qualified, the rhymes pointing her dialectic of balance and antithesis.

If there are errors of prosody and style, there should also be easy pardon for them, as she admits them freely; if she has erred in her choice of subject-matter, drawing on apocryphal texts, is not the concept 'apocryphal' itself something relative? Or perhaps Hrotsvitha is saying: Can legends not be true in their own way, in that they ring true imaginatively? (As we shall see, she reverted to this troubling question several times.) There is a particular double edge to Hrotsvitha's next 'modest proposal'. She was only a beginner when she started her poems, too timid to ask advice from experts at the time; yet the reason she was too timid, it at once emerges, was because she feared experts might hinder her from composing—and she was determined, come what might, to compose. Her writing secretly was grounded as much in inner resolution as in fear.

Whenever Hrotsvitha alludes (as she often does) to womanly weakness, she is saying something rich in ambiguities. Here the suggestion that writing in classical metres is especially hard for women, because they are frail, is deliberately preposterous, and is said tongue in cheek. At the same time, there is a sly recognition that the 'dactylic measure', the hexameter, was generally deemed the heroic metre *par excellence,* and that the heroic was a masculine prerogative. (This also suggests at least one reason why Hrotsvitha later dwelt so often on the heroism of women.)

Once more the feigned doubt has its answer ready: writing hexameters seems hard for fragile women—yet (relying on God's help) I chose to write them nonetheless. The reason that Hrotsvitha alleges again plays upon a topos: one writes so as not to be accused of idleness. She gives the thought a subtle, individual modulation by her use of the image of the talent. Here she does not quite claim *ingenium*—an imaginative gift, or imaginative genius—as she was to do in her later Prefaces: only *ingeniolum,* a 'little genius'. Yet this too is a 'talent' in the biblical sense, a coin that must not be buried but be used with profit. She sustains the metaphor: the coin-talent can be hammered and sound forth in praise of God. Even if it acquires no wordly surplus-value, it is not valueless: it can be made into an instrument, on which divine jubilations can be played.

Thus in this Preface each admission of weakness is inseparable from an impulse of self-assurance, or self-reassurance. Partly Hrotsvitha *is* diffident about her venture, partly she pretends to be. It is the wavering between real and pretended diffidence that reveals to us the Hrotsvitha beyond the topoi, the woman who says, in effect: 'Some of my legends are apocryphal? But there's no absolute certainty in such matters . . . I didn't ask the advice of sages? No, I was too shy—and I was so determined to write anyway, that I did so secretly. Hexameters are too hard for weak women to compose? Perhaps, but, weak as I was, I still decided to.'

This preface is followed by a verse dedication to Ger-berga, more conventional in tone: the abbess of royal race is to correct and polish Hrotsvitha's graceless compositions. That this here is formula rather than reality is indicated, I think, by the next lines:

> When you are weary, after your varied
> labours,
>   deign to read these songs by way of play.[30]

If reading Hrotsvitha's verses is to be relaxing (*ludens*) for Gerberga, the task of refining them (*purgare*) cannot be meant too strenuously.

Certain moments in the course of the legends should perhaps also be noted for the self-awareness they display. The heading of the first, *Maria,* contains a strong hint of self-justification: it is 'the story . . . of the immaculate mother of God, which I found in written form under the name of St James (*quam scriptam repperi sub nomine Sancti Iacobi*), the brother of the Lord'. After completing the poem, Hrotsvitha had been told that this text was not by St James at all. Yet her rejoinder in the Preface implies that, even if the ascription to James seems to be *falsitas,* it may nonetheless emerge (through the rediscovery of other early docu-

ments?) that this text contained truth. Possibly Hrotsvitha's wording here in the heading even suggests an implicit challenge: how do such ascriptions, if they are incorrect, arise?

A further, almost defiant, allusion to the question of apocrypha comes within the poem—in a passage that Hrotsvitha left unchanged, or perhaps even deliberately added, when she felt it necessary to defend her choice of subject-matter. She does not need, she says, to dwell on Joseph's suspicion of Mary, or on his dream, for these things are known to all from the Gospels, and they surpass her own frail powers to tell: 'I shall base my composition only on those things which are held to be too rarely told in church' (*Maria* 541-2). Hrotsvitha uses the generalized passive construction (*Rarius in templo quae creduntur fore dicta*)—but who else thought the apocrypha were too much neglected in church? Does not the impersonal *creduntur* conceal a very personal *credo?*

The Marian diptych closes (*Ascensio* 147ff) with Hrotsvitha expressing her conviction that poetry is for her a means of winning bliss in heaven. Whoever reads these verses should call down God's mercy on her, so that she may continue celestially, in divine songs, the songs she has composed about God's awesome deeds ("tua facta stupenda'). A similar phrase ('facta dei') occurs in the renewed dedication to Gerberga before ***Basilius,*** and here it is a sign of greater confidence than before. Offering Gerberga her 'new little verses', Hrotsvitha says:

> Do not despise them, even though they're full
> of faults,
>   but, with your gentle heart, praise the deeds
>   of God.[31]

Does the last line imply that it is one of God's deeds to have made Hrotsvitha a poet, or that her poems themselves are 'facta dei', in that they are designed as a means of giving glory to God? On either interpretation, Hrotsvitha's growing sense of a divine calling to compose poetry is unmistakable.

It emerges, too, in the Prelude of ***Basilius*** itself: now Hrotsvitha insists that the matter of her story, the illustration of forgiveness and of the generosity of divine compassion, is so important that she summons her reader to 'peruse these little verses with submissive heart'—

> And let him not scorn the frail sex of the
> woman of no importance
>   who played these melodies on a frail reed
>   pipe,
> but rather let him praise Christ's heavenly
> mercy:
>   he does not want to destroy sinners . . . [32]

The sinner recovering from his or her total rejection of God is, as we have noted, the major theme that Hrotsvitha chose to portray in four different plots in the legends and dramas.

In her brief transitional note between the two series, Hrotsvitha reverts once more to the question of sources and their reliability:

> All the subject-matter of this little work [the plays], as of the preceding one, I have taken from ancient books transmitted under the names of certain authors (*sub certis auctorum nominibus conscriptis*), except for the passion of St Pelagius [for which, as she had told, she relied on a firsthand report] . . . So if in either book I have included anything false in my composing, I have not misled of my own account, but only by incautiously imitating misleading sources.[33]

If the texts used by Hrotsvitha reached her as the works 'of certain authors', much depended on whether the ascriptions were correct: if so, then the texts were indeed by witnesses in a position to know. But were the ascriptions 'certain' in the sense of admitting no doubt? Or could some of the texts Hrotsvitha used be imaginative reconstructions, or fabrications, of more recent date and authorship? Abelard, as is well known, set a cat among the pigeons when he questioned the status of the sources concerning Dionysius—the same sources for the most part as Hrotsvitha used.[34] Had she too a suspicion that for instance Hilduin, writing the life of Dionysius only a century before her own birth, was perhaps not the best authority on things said to have occurred at the time of Christ's death? At all events Hrotsvitha's levelheaded and decisive contrast between the eye-witness account from Cordova, of which she had no doubt, and the written sources, where she cannot vouch for greater veracity than that of the materials available to her, is subtle and acute.

Where the use of apocrypha posed problems for the legends, the use of Terence did so for the dramas. This comes out in Hrotsvitha's astonishing tactics in her Preface to the plays, where she says little of what she really means and means almost nothing of what she says.—

> Many Catholics can be found who prefer the vanity of pagan books to the utility of holy Scripture, because of the pagans' greater eloquence and grace of style—nor can I clear myself wholly of having such a preference. There are others again who cling to the sacred page and who, though they spurn other works by pagan authors, still rather often tend to read the fictive creations of Terence; and while they take delight in the mellifluence of the style, they become tainted by coming to know an impious subject-matter.

> So I, the 'Mighty Voice of Gandersheim', have not demurred at imitating Terence in composing, while others cultivate him in their reading—so that, in the same genre of composition in which the shameless unchaste actions of sensual women were portrayed, the laudable chastity of holy maidens might be celebrated, inasmuch as my little imaginative gift has power to do so.

> Not rarely does it cause embarrassment, and suffuse me with a deep blush, that, compelled by the nature of this mode of composing, I have had to ponder while writing and to set down with my pen the loathsome lunacy of the love-struck and their wickedly sweet conversations, which our ears are not allowed even to entertain. Yet had I passed such matters over bashfully, I could never have done justice to my plan: I should not even have set forth the praise of the innocent as fully as I was able; for, the more seductive the caresses with which the love-maddened ones allure, the more sublime the glory of the helper on high, the more glorious the victory of those shown triumphing, especially when womanly frailty emerges victorious and virile force, confounded, is laid low.

> I do not doubt that some will raise the objection with me, that the poorness of this composition is far inferior to the writing of him whom I resolved to imitate—more limited, and altogether unlike him. I admit it; yet I would explain to objectors that they cannot rightfully reproach me on the ground that I was trying perversely to compete with those who have far outstripped my want of art in loftier knowledge. I am not of such boastfulness as to presume to compare myself with even the least of their pupils. I aspire only to this, that, though I can by no means do so fittingly, still with submissive devotedness of spirit I might redirect the gift of genius I have received back to the Giver. I am not so filled with self-love, then, that—in order to avoid human reproach—I would cease to proclaim the power of Christ, manifest in the saints, in whatever way he himself empowers me.

> If my labour of love gives pleasure to anyone, I'll be glad; but if, because of my worthlessness or the boorishness of my flawed style, it pleases no one, what I have created still gives delight to me—because, while in the other little works that spring from my ignorance, I gathered my poor efforts bound in a chaplet of heroic verse, here I have plaited them in a dramatic chain, avoiding the baleful delights of the pagans by keeping them at arm's length.

It has not I think been pointed out before that none of what Hrotsvitha claims, ostensibly solemnly, at the opening of this Preface can conceivably be literally true. In the fourth century there were, to be sure, some Christian men of letters who preferred reading pagan authors, because of their more elegant style, to reading the Bible—Augustine's and Jerome's admissions of weakness in this matter are especially well known. And it is possible that a handful of the most literate people at Otto's court once again made such a stylistic comparison and came down in favour of pagans—Bruno perhaps, or Rather or Liutprand,[35] and (as she concedes, with feigned reluctance, in a knowing aside) Hrotsvitha herself. But that 'many Catholics (*plures . . . catholici*)' showed this preference in Hrotsvitha's time, or had the knowledge to discriminate among styles in this way, is at least a wild exaggeration, and almost certainly a joke. The joking becomes patent, and more outrageous, in the next sentence: could anyone seriously imagine readers who, out of sheer devoutness, spurn for instance Vergil and Cicero, but still cling to Terence because he is so great a stylist? This may indeed be a teasing allusion to Chancellor Bruno's fondness for Terence, a mischievous hyperbole, pretending that this was his exclusive taste, his addiction. But the sentence can no more be taken straight than if we were to read, in a history of modern literature, that twentieth-century England was full of High Anglicans who rejected all non-sacred writing, yet who could never stop themselves from reading Congreve.

Those who read Terence (naturally only for his style!), Hrotsvitha adds, become corrupted. The question that occurs irresistibly—was she then *not* corrupted by reading Terence?—is the one that, by this mock-serious statement, she wittily passes by.

Or we might say, she redirects the question: *she* reads Terence in order to save those *litterati,* those delicate stylists who are so easily corruptible, from themselves! With her ironically placed Latin equivalent for her name—*Clamor Validus* = Old Saxon *Hrôthsuith*[36]— she even intimates that writing chaste, Christian plays in the Terentian genre, and thereby redeeming the genre, was a kind of prophetic mission she took on. Hers is the 'mighty voice': the expression 'ego Clamor Validus' can hardly help carrying a reminiscence of John the Baptist's 'ego vox clamantis'. At the same time, *clamor* can have an objective as well as subjective force: then her Latinization of the name would suggest something more like 'the big noise of Gandersheim', and be a self-mocking recognition that the spreading rumour of her composing was making her known as a prodigy— or a freak. Once more the diminutive *ingeniolum* comes—her 'little genius' will celebrate chaste maidens, where Terence's great genius had turned to lascivious women. It sounds irreproachable—until we recall that at the centre of her dramatic series are two plays which are not about chaste maidens at all, but which have two zestfully lascivious heroines.

Yet at once Hrotsvitha concedes this: she had to portray sexual love and love-talk, however embarrassing to do so, for the sake of her greater aim—to show the workings of redemption. In order to value chastity, one must first know what love-madness is, and not be so shocked by the very idea that one fails to understand it. Only by showing love, 'wickedly sweet', in all its attractiveness, and lovers in all their lunacy, will the heroic nature of repentance become clear. Hrotsvitha's word-plays here—'amantium dementiam . . . male dulcia . . . amentium'—are characteristic of a pagan way of talking about love. These are Plautine, Terentian and Ovidian turns of phrase,[37] that were still to have a long fortune after Hrotsvitha, and ones that she uses lightly, hardly with prophetic fervour. Yet here, arguing that sin must be shown in all its seductiveness in order to show the sublimity of recovering from it, she is fashioning her own counterpart to the ancient paradox of human love:[38] to experience love's blissful sweetness, the lover must know its bitter sorrow first. She is also touching seriously on that process of redemption which she depicts in her central pair of legends and of plays: the ultimate victory of virtue is a triumph of God, but Hrotsvitha also sees it 'especially (*praesertim*)' as a feminist triumph. Weak women show their power, strong men go under.

Mary and Thais show their strength by renouncing their lives as courtesans (lives in which, Hrotsvitha makes clear, they both enjoyed themselves immensely). Does Hrotsvitha herself, another weak woman, display a power comparable with theirs by renouncing the philosophy of Terence's plays, replacing it by celebrations of Christian mercy? Or is her power merely an arrogant pretence—like that of Terence's Delusor in the *Altercation*—as if she could vanquish a great ancient author? This is the objection to which she next turns.

Again her extravagant protestations of modesty have a twinkle about them. Of course she does not write as well as Terence, she assures—yet even in saying that her plays are 'altogether unlike' his (*penitusque dissimilis*), is she not also making an implicit claim for their originality? And when she goes on to affirm, I am not competing with those (living scholars) who are far wiser than I, does she not equally mean, I am attempting something they have not attempted? Theirs is the 'loftier knowledge (*scientia sublimior*)' of theology, ethics, sciences—yet they never thought of composing in the Terentian mode.

The pair of justifications that follow ('Nec enim tantae sum iactantiae . . . Ideoque non sum adeo amatrix mei . . . ') likewise contain both an affirmative and a negative element. Anticipating criticisms that she is boastful, or full of self-love, she both abases herself and insists that her *ingenium* (now no longer diminutive) must—like the talent in the parable—be moved serviceably towards the God who gave it to her, and, even, that her *ingenium* is itself a proclamation of Christ's power, one that no censure of human beings ought to silence.

With the last sally in the Preface, an impish sense of self-possession gains the ascendant. Hrotsvitha says in effect: you can take my work or leave it—I'm glad if you like it, and if you don't, at least I've given myself some pleasure. Yet the sentence continues craftily, with 'because': 'memet ipsam tamen iuvat quod feci, quia . . .' The reason Hrotsvitha alleges that her work helps, or delights, her (even if it's no good as literature) is because writing it was for her an effective antidote against pagan delights! In this last sentence the wit directed, not against pagan delights but against Christian hypocrisies, is devastating. It is (to resume my analogy) as if the High Anglican who disapproved of secular writing wrote his own plays, ones that kept Congreve constantly in view, and then answered charges of inconsistency by saying: 'But I write them as my protection against Congreve!'

Admittedly, Hrotsvitha claimed she had gone to Terence for style and form, changing the content completely. And yet it is not hard to see that this is disingenuous. Her stylistic debt to Terence is not in fact large. She copies a number of Terentian mannerisms and phrases (exclamations such as 'Pro Juppiter!', 'Ridiculum!', 'Eccam!', 'Atat!' are obvious examples).[39] She likewise imitates certain techniques: the use of rapid exchanges and repartee, or the device of bringing on characters in the first scene of a play to provide needed background information. Yet Hrotsvitha does not imitate Terence metrically, and her diction owes more to Vergil and Prudentius than to him.[40] Where her debt to Terence is far-reaching is not in style but in subject-matter.

For Terence, like Hrotsvitha, had presented with imaginative sympathy a number of young women who were innocent victims.[41] The girls in the *Andria, Eunuchus* or *Adelphoi* do not speak, yet in each case they are the focal point of the play's plot. Always the victimized girl triumphs at the close: she wins her freedom, wins her love-match. In the *Andria* and *Eunuchus* the girls, like Hrotsvitha's heroines, are even hedged by 'miracles'—wondrous revelations that lead to the discovery of their true identity and their distinguished birth. In the *Adelphoi* we see a young girl being rescued, like Hrotsvitha's Mary, from a brothel. In the Terentian plays, as in Hrotsvitha's, we often witness trickery, deception and disguise employed in a good cause, in order to confound the men who think themselves mighty—the blustering, boastful or tyrannic ones. As in Hrotsvitha's scenes of confrontation and martyrdom, there are continual threats of whipping and torture, which hardly ever have any effect: in Terence as in Hrotsvitha, there is a hair's breadth between the comic and the horrible. Terence's emotional gamut—the spheres of tenderness, of trickery, and of blustering force nimbly defeated—is (if we leave the specifically Christian motifs out of account) humanly close to Hrotsvitha's.

I am certain that Hrotsvitha was fully aware of this, and that she couched her elusive defence for having turned to Terence in a deliberately misleading way. To carry off the coup she intended, she created her own weapon of literary coquetry. Her shape-shifting, her 'weak little woman' pose, her headily exaggerated modesty-topoi, her diminutives, her graceful to-and-fro of affirmation and negation, can all be seen as in the service of that coquetry: all are witty, skilled means of commanding recognition and respect for her way of looking.

Hrotsvitha was aware of double standards throughout the world of her experience. First and foremost, a different range of expectations for men and women, and for their capacities. Here her coquetry takes the form of comically stressing women's weakness, never minimizing it, yet always pointing it in such a way as to foil expectations and paradoxically show women's strength.

She is equally conscious of other anomalies: between the values of Terence and those of hagiographic writers; between the counsels of perfection of the Christian life and the lapses from it in the world of court and Church; between the demands of entertainment and those of edification. I am not suggesting that her wit resolved these anomalies in complete relativism (such as we might ascribe, far later, to someone like Jean de Meun). Hrotsvitha is indeed committed to the Christian life, the hagiographic goal and the didactic aim; at the same time, she never for one moment ignores their profane and wicked counterparts. Her art is, while pursuing the first, to keep the second constantly in view—to allow for confrontations that can range from violent clashes for the sake of an ideal (the pagan persecutors versus the martyr-heroines) to humorous recognitions of real frailty (as when St Gongolf, with his magic fountain, out-tricks—rather than punishes—his unfaithful wife). And wherever Hrotsvitha dwells most ardently on the 'higher' values, she cannot help hearing echoes of the 'lower': in this sense both Terence and the Christian antidote delight her simultaneously.

Even her frequent condemnations of lasciviousness in the poems and plays are not incompatible with her fascination with it. Hrotsvitha is well aware that the one sheep which is lost and found again is more interesting than the ninety-nine which have no need of penance ('quanto extitit foedior, tanto appareat nitidior'), and that it gives more delight ('magis delectatur').[42] Chastity becomes an absorbing theme for her as much for its penumbra of wantonness as for its own radiance. The many scholars who have seen Hrotsvitha's aim only in terms of a 'straight' didactic and ascetic intention have not read her Prefaces or her writings sensitively.

The Preface to the plays is followed by the letter to her wise *fautores*.[43] In her relief and joyful gratitude that her work has found a welcoming echo among them, Hrotsvitha's euphuism and overacted womanly submissiveness at first seem boundless:

> I can scarcely marvel sufficiently at the magnitude of your praiseworthy condescension,[44] nor can I fittingly requite, with recompense of condign thanks, the plenitude of your magnificent benignity and charity towards my inadequacy: for, even though you are nurtured above all in spiritual study and are of surpassing excellence in knowledge, you have thought the paltry work of me, a worthless little woman, worthy of your admiration, and, rejoicing with brotherly affection, have praised in me the Giver of operative grace: you think to find in me some little knowledge of the arts, the subtlety of which far exceeds my womanly genius.

> In a word, hitherto I hardly dared to show the clownishness of my little composition[45] even to a few people, and if at all, then only to intimate friends. So the task of composing something further of this nature almost ceased.

Now, however, Hrotsvitha says she has found the confidence she needed to continue, to complete the greater design she had projected, for (playfully she gives her patrons a biblical *auctoritas,* from Deuteronomy 19: 15) 'what is confirmed by three witnesses is true'. In what follows, Hrotsvitha makes her most serious analysis of her calling as poet: she is convinced there is a divine element in human creativity:

> In the midst of this I am torn between diverse impulses—joy and fear: indeed I feel joy deep in my heart that God, through whose grace I am what I am, is praised in me; yet I am afraid to seem greater than I am—I have no doubt that both denying the spontaneously given gift of God and pretending to have received what was not received are equally wrongful.

She is genuinely awestruck by the burden that such a gift imposes; yet she is also unafraid to adapt to herself the words that Paul had used (1 Corinthians 15: 10): 'by the grace of God I am what I am'. Hrotsvitha's *fautores* (unlike her editors) will have recognized her Pauline citation and been aware of its context—a mingled pride and humility close to Hrotsvitha's, as Paul passes from 'I am the least of the apostles, I who am not worthy to be called an apostle' to 'but I laboured more abundantly than all the apostles—not I, however, but the grace of God with me'.

A moment later, with renewed excessive declarations of her own inadequacy, her sense of humour returns irrepressibly:

> Hence I do not deny that through the Creator's grace I have knowledge of the arts potentially (*per dyna-*

min), since I am a living being with the capacity to learn; yet I confess I am utterly ignorant in actuality (*per energian*). I realize that a penetrating imaginative insight was divinely conferred on me, yet when the loving care of my teachers (*magistrorum*)[46] ended, it remained uncultivated.

Hrotsvitha 'demonstrates' her ignorance by using deliberately recherché language—the Greek philosophical expressions *per dynamin . . . per energian*—that she will have drawn from a letter by St Jerome.[47] Here we are not far from the games-playing of Wolfram von Eschenbach two and a half centuries later—Wolfram who, after claiming that he can neither read nor write, proceeds to record the names of the planets in Arabic![48]

Again there is much in the thoughts that follow that is not what it seems:

> Therefore, lest God's gift be annulled in me through my own negligence, I have tried to tear some threads, or even shreds, of cloth, snatching them from Philosophia's robe, to interweave them with the present work, so that the wretchedness of my ignorance be illuminated by the intermingling of nobler stuff, and that the bestower of genius be praised rightfully, and the more copiously in that women's understanding is held to be more retarded.

Hrotsvitha is indicating that, encouraged by the reception of her earlier plays (presumably those from ***Gallicanus*** to ***Mary the Niece of Abraham,*** which survive as a group in the twelfth-century Cologne manuscript), she felt emboldened to try to give her last ones a further, philosophical dimension, with the help especially of Boethian materials. Yet the way she says this is characteristically double-edged. She knew well enough that in Boethius' *Consolation of Philosophy* those who tore shreds from Philosophia's dress were blindly skirmishing sects of pseudo-philosophers, men who thereby degraded Philosophia, grabbing at her dress as if she were a *meretrix.*[49] It is another expression of mock-humility to suggest that she, in her use of Boethius, had done no more than that. But her follow-up—that through the borrowed shreds in the fabric of her work God will be magnified the more, 'in that women's understanding is held to be more retarded'—alludes not only to the common masculine stereotype of women, but indirectly, with telling irony, to Philosophia herself (who in Hrotsvitha's time was mostly identified with Sapientia—divine Wisdom). In the very moment she plays upon the chimera of women's intellectual inferiority, Hrotsvitha reminds her sages that philosophers have always been inspired by Philosophia, she who could be called 'womanly understanding' incarnate.

At the close Hrotsvitha, with the established gesture of submissiveness, asks her patrons to correct and im-

prove her work. Yet even here she slips in a remarkable phrase—'it behoves you to examine and emend
[my little book] with no less affectionate solicitude
than if it were a product of your own labour'—that
deliberately leaves the reader guessing whether it is
meant to be charming or challenging. If Hrotsvitha's
fautores still had any illusions about women's weakness, reading this letter of hers must have been a chas-
tening experience.

There is one other Preface by Hrotsvitha, accompanying the **Gesta Ottonis,** which Gerberga had charged
her to write. The **Gesta,** composed *ca.* 965 and concluded before 968, are generally held to be later than
both the legends and the plays. If this is correct, we
can say that by the time she was thirty Hrotsvitha had
completed her *magnum opus,* her twofold cycle, and
that she had won full recognition by her *fautores* at the
imperial court. Thus it is not surprising that Hrotsvitha
was then asked, as the price of her reputation, to do
something expected in many ages of court poets, or
poets laureate: to celebrate her sovereign in the epic
manner. The commission, her Preface tells, was given
her directly by Gerberga, Otto's niece; but in some
dedicatory verses to Otto II, still only of schoolboy age
when the poem was completed, Hrotsvitha recalls that
he too had asked her for it personally: 'if you deign to
remember, you yourself, your eyes sparkling, recently
bade that the text be presented to you'. In a verse
Prologue to his father, Otto I, we see Hrotsvitha's
characteristic ambiguity, half-concealing both humility
and pride:

> Even though many books praising you fittingly may
> be written after this, books that will deservedly give
> pleasure, yet let this little book not be the last in
> rank, for it was clearly written first, without a
> model.[50]

Hrotsvitha's play on the close of the parable—the last
shall be first—here implies a shrewd claim to originality: her work is the lowliest, and yet, in another sense,
it takes precedence over all others.

Nonetheless Hrotsvitha was not entirely happy in her
commission, or in her rôle as imperial panegyrist.
Unlike the Archpoet, who, two centuries later, was
asked in vain for an epic on the *gesta* of Frederick
Barbarossa, she at least tried to do as she was bidden.
Yet she felt—in this instance quite genuinely—unsure
of herself. Principally because, for the first time in her
composing, she had to work without the help of written sources,[51] or indeed, for many major episodes,
without detailed firsthand reports, such as she had had
for **Pelagius.** Amid the flourishes that open her Preface for Gerberga, Hrotsvitha is plaintive about the situation in which she had been placed, as well as wonder-
fully perceptive about the problems involved in composing official *gesta:*[52]

My sovereign lady, you that shed light with the
sparkling iridescence[53] of your spiritual wisdom, may
it not irk[54] your benignity to look through what, you
are not unaware, has been fashioned at your command. Indeed it was you who imposed this burden,
that I set forth the deeds of great Caesar in poetic
form—deeds that I could not assemble comprehen-
sively enough, even orally. You can ima-gine how
much difficulty I in my ignorance encountered in the
toil of this process of composition, for neither did I
find these matters previously written down, nor could
I elicit an account of them from anyone in a well-
ordered and sufficiently full way.

I journeyed like one who, not knowing the route, is
about to travel through a vast unknown ravine, where
every path lies concealed, covered by thick snow:
led on by no guide, only by signals of direction
received beforehand, such a one would now stray
onto by-paths, now unexpectedly hit the right path
again, until at last, having reached the midpoint of
the densely crowding trees, he would choose a spot
for his longed-for rest, and there, staying his step,
would not dare continue, until another came across
him and could guide him, or he found a previous
traveller's footprints he could follow. No otherwise
did I, commanded to penetrate the vast region of
glorious events, traverse the manifold paths of the
royal deeds faltering and wavering, very ill at ease,
and, utterly exhausted by them, sink to rest in silence
in a suitable spot; nor do I undertake to climb the
pinnacle of imperial excellence without guidance.

Here too Hrotsvitha's diffidence has as its obverse her
positive sense of doing something wholly new. Yet the
last clause, where she is overtly claiming she is too
lowly to celebrate, unaided, Otto's deeds as emperor,
after his coronation at Rome in 962, is in effect more
of a *recusatio,* comparable to the Archpoet's when he
was asked to magnify his emperor's deeds.[55] She has,
she implies, written the 'epic' composition that was
demanded (though indeed she kept it relatively brief);
and she is not prepared to go on, unless she were provided with a coherent written prose account from which
to work. In the poem itself, typically, it is always
'womanly weakness' that is offered as pretext: Hrotsvitha refuses to attempt battle-scenes, because a frail
woman cannot hope to do them justice, especially not
one who leads as sheltered a life as she (**Gesta** 237ff).
And at the close (1487ff) Hrotsvitha revels in a mock-
solemn device of *praecisio:* she has sung the deeds of
Otto as king, but she is afraid to touch his deeds as
emperor, 'for I am forbidden by my womanly nature'.
Yet at once Hrotsvitha goes on to tell all the things she
is 'forbidden' to write about: how Otto was able to
defeat and banish King Berengarius and his odious
queen, Willa, to depose one pope and install another in
Rome, and to arrange for the imperial coronation of
his son. Perhaps this close gives the best pointer to
what did not come fully alive in the course of the
poem: Hrotsvitha's *ingeniolum* was too mercurial, too

much accustomed to mingling the comic and the serious, to adapt well to the kind of panegyric expected from a poet laureate. Like the Archpoet, she could not keep a straight face quite so long.

Finally, I should like to suggest that other aspects of Hrotsvitha's self-awareness become clear if we scan her writings for what I would call indirectly autobiographic moments. This is perhaps a precarious undertaking, yet at times it too can lead to illuminating insights. I shall illustrate by looking closely at three moments: two are chosen from Hrotsvitha's best-known plays, and one from the poem on the origins of Gandersheim, which is virtually unknown save to a few specialists.

Hrotsvitha's play about Agape, Chionia and Hirena (generally, but erroneously, called **Dulcitius**) draws on a strange source, a late Roman *Passion of St Anastasia*, which troubled its twentieth-century editor, the great Bollandist Delehaye, because of the amount of 'fantasy' and 'audacious fiction' that had contaminated what was doubtless a 'good' original.[56] The very features that disquieted Delehaye were those that attracted Hrotsvitha: in fact, she chose to focus on these and ignore all else, discarding even the figure of St Anastasia, the protagonist in the source. Hrotsvitha selected, and brought to life, especially the three sisters (whom her source introduced only as minor characters, protégées of Anastasia) and the villain-buffoons, Dulcitius and Sisinnius, who are mocked and confounded by those girls.

The implicit self-references in the play can, I submit, be perceived by way of a series of verbal echoes that link it with Hrotsvitha's Preface and Epistle at the opening of the dramatic cycle. There Hrotsvitha tried to excuse her concern with the deeds 'of lascivious women (*lascivarum . . . feminarum*)'; she admitted to blushing with shame ('verecundari gravique rubore perfundi . . . erubescendo') when she turned to such matters as lasciviousness, and yet, she stresses, she was trying to show how 'womanly frailty emerges victorious and virile force, confounded, is laid low (*femi-nea fragilitas vinceret et virilis robur confusioni subia-ceret*)'. And in the epistle she speaks of her work as that 'of a worthless little woman (*vilis mulierculae*)'. All these thoughts return, with identical or very similar expressions, in a different modulation in the play of the three maidens. For the Emperor Diocletian, these maidens are 'viles mulierculae' (IX); for the deluded villains, the prison governor Dulcitius and Count Sisin-nius, they are 'lascivae puellae' (VII, IX). And at the close it is the men—Sisinnius and his soldiery—whom Hirena provokes to blush ('erubesce . . . erubesce'), as their show of might is set at naught by a *tenella virgun-cula*.

Hrotsvitha lays special stress on the strength-in-weakness of the youngest of the three girls, Hirena. At the opening, the Emperor expects her to be more amenable than her sisters, because of her youth; instead, punning on her own name ('Peace'), she cries out: 'You'll find the third rebellious and utterly resistant!' She, the littlest, argues the most ferociously and magniloquently ('Conquiniscant idolis, qui velint incurrere iram celsitonantis!'),[57] and at the close she launches her supreme defiance against pagan 'virile force':

> Unhappy man, blush—blush, Sisinnius, and groan at being vanquished ignominiously: for you could not defeat a tender little girl's youth without a panoply of arms . . . You shall be damned in Tartarus; but I, about to receive the palm of martyrdom and the crown of virginity, shall enter the ethereal bed-chamber of the eternal King.[58]

Thus Hirena, like Hrotsvitha the author, turns the language of the aggressive male world to her advantage.

The pagan men continually ascribe their powerlessness against the Christian girls to the girls' witchcraft (*maleficia*). Thus the soldiers lament (XIV): 'We are all "illuded" in wondrous ways (*Miris modis omnes illudimur*)'. In that notion of illusion, too, there may be a poetic connotation relevant to Hrotsvitha herself. The worthless little women, whose defeat of male strength the men see as wantonness and evil illusion, are seen by Hrotsvitha as the blessed, innocent ones, whose illuding is divine grace, and whose 'lasciviousness' is satisfied in the bed-chamber of the divine lover. And here the implicit parallel between the innocent virgin-fighter, Peace, and Hrotsvitha the dramatist, emerges in its full complexity: Hrotsvitha designates herself a *vilis muliercula* as regards her writing; she knows she could be censured as *lasciva* for her fascination with Terence and for some of her own choices of subject-matter; yet she also knows that the intention of her *lascivia* is a blessed one, a celebration of the girls' divine love-union, not of earthly delights—a voluptuousness through chastity. But like the girls, she too 'illudes in wondrous ways', by means of her art: in place of *maleficia,* she achieves the innocent magic of dramatic fiction, and her power in this she, like the heroines in the play, attributes to God's grace. Like Hirena, she stresses (in her Preface to the legends) how young she was when, by beginning to write, she in her own way issued a challenge to the masculine world of her time.[59] But it is precisely the young, fragile girl, Hirena-Hrotsvitha, who, with the help of grace, can conquer the frightening world of men, whether that means the real court of Emperor Otto or the imagined one of Emperor Diocletian. There—in the real as in the imagined court—she can win a moral victory over the mighty pagan (Sisinnius or Terence), she can substitute for the pagan's sexual ruses (the humiliation of the girl-victim, her being sent to a brothel) the 'ethereal bed-chamber' of the Song of Songs.

From Hrotsvitha's play **Mary the Niece of Abraham** I would single out a moment that is filled with borrowed language and literary allusion and is at the same time one of the most moving and personal in all her work. Abraham, who came to the brothel disguised as a lover, so as to rescue his fallen niece, Mary, has persuaded her to repent and return to the desert with him. With a phrase that is close to the lyrical *albas,* where lovers part at dawn, he says to her: 'Dawn grows bright; light is coming; let us leave.'[60] (Where secret lovers in the lyrics must sorrowfully go their separate ways, here the pair, bound by a different love, depart serenely together.) Submissively Mary says she will walk behind him; but Abraham rejoins:

> Not so: I shall walk, but set you on the horse, lest the roughness of the way should cut your tender feet (*secet teneras plantas*).

She answers:

> Oh what name can I give you (*O quem te memorem*)? What reward of thanks can I offer you, you who do not force me by terror, even though I deserve no pity . . .

Into this exchange Hrotsvitha has set a key-phrase from Vergil's *Eclogues* and another from the *Aeneid.*[61] She could be sure that some of her first audience—Gerberga and Bruno among the imperial family, and the finest scholars who had come to the Ottonian court—knew Vergil well enough to recall the original contexts and perceive the full symbolic value of their use here. In the tenth Eclogue, Gallus laments that his beloved Lycoris had (like Mary) become wanton—she had followed the soldiers to the Rhine, far from her home; yet, still in love with Lycoris, he feels nothing but compassion, and imagines how harsh the journey along the Rhine will be for her, 'cutting her tender feet'; for Gallus (like Abraham) is one in whose thoughts 'Love conquers everything.' Hrotsvitha has transformed Gallus' fantasy, his sublimation of sensual obsession, into Abraham's fatherly tenderness. And Mary answers, overcome, in the words Aeneas had used to Venus, as she appeared to him disguised ('O quam te memorem?'). Like Aeneas, Mary has at this moment the sense of a superhuman destiny revealing itself to her in human semblance: the journey back into the wilderness with Abraham ('asperitas itineris') is her life.

As Hrotsvitha tried to 'redeem' Terentian episodes—the girls who are victimized, the brothel-scenes—so here she is 'redeeming' Vergilian language. For her it is no longer Gallus' erotic reverie, or the appearance of a pagan goddess to Aeneas: she has taken the language and transmuted it in her own design. We might say that, in the whole process by which Abraham rescues Mary, Hrotsvitha identified imaginatively with both

parts. As Mary left her monastic cell to go and live in Alexandria, Hrotsvitha is in fantasy a Mary, who had deliberately decided to dwell in the *lupanar* of Terence's world. While (as her Preface hints) many churchmen of her time will have found that decision shocking, she was exhilarated and happy in the Terentian world, just as Mary is in her house of sin. She is fond of Terence, as Mary is of the innkeeper for whom she works, the host who, amazed to see her weeping suddenly, says 'Haven't you lived here for two years, and never a moan or a sad word escaped you?' At the same time, Hrotsvitha sees herself in imagination as someone stronger—as an Abraham who temporarily pretends to be of that wanton world, but who has not really succumbed to it. Like Abraham, she enters the world of wantonness in order to challenge it, or at least to redeem from it what she—or Abraham—holds most dear.

The last of Hrotsvitha's extant works, the poem on the origins of Gandersheim, composed in 973 or slightly later, is the only one without a Preface. Perhaps there was a Preface, which has been lost (the poem no longer exists in manuscripts; its text survived only in the *editio princeps*); yet it is also possible that Hrotsvitha had now gained sufficient reassurance and recognition to be able to open with tranquil directness:

> Behold, my spirit, lowly and submissive,
> breaks forth to tell the origins of blissful
>   Gandersheim.

The site for Gandersheim came to be chosen, Hrotsvitha relates, because of an inexplicable repeated apparition of lights in the depths of a forest, an apparition that was held to be a sign from heaven:[62]

> As the report of many well-informed people
>   tells,
> near our foundation there was then a small
>   forest, circled
> by shadowing hills—that circle us even today.
> There in that wood was set a little farm
> where Liudolf's swineherds used to lodge
> in the farmer's fenced enclosure, letting their
>   weary
> bodies sink into rest in the hours of the night,
> while the swine in their charge were pasturing.
> Here, once upon a time, two days before the
>   high
> feast of All Saints was to be celebrated,
> the swineherds saw many bright lamps in the
>   wood,
> blazing in the dark of the night.
> Perceiving this, awestruck, they wondered
> what the new vision of sparkling light could
>   mean,
> that cleft night's blackness with strange
>   radiance.

Trembling, they told the owner of the
      homestead,
pointing to the place the light had flooded.
He, eager to verify what he had heard,
determined the next night to stay awake,
joining the men in the open, beyond the
      eaves:
he would not shut his eyes, heavy with sleep's
      persuasion,
till they had seen the lit lanterns glint again.
They saw them, vanquishing the first in
      number,
in the same spot as before, though earlier.
Scarcely had Phoebus shed his first beams
      from heaven
when this sign of happy omen, so serene,
was made known, with jocund Rumour telling
      all.
Nor could it be kept hidden from great Duke
      Liudolf—
swiftly it reached his ears.
And he himself, on holy Halloween,
went with a crowd to keep vigil in that forest,
keenly scanning to see if the apparition
would again betoken something heavenly.
At once, as thick night covered the land with
      mist,
all around, circling the wooded valley
where the surpassing noble temple was to be
      built,
many lights were beheld, set in harmonious
      order:
they cleft the tree-shadows, and the dark night
      too,
with their radiantly penetrating gleam.
All affirmed that this spot should be made
      holy,
in the service of him who had filled it with
      such light.

While there are parallels to wondrous visions of light
in hagiography,[63] I think there can be little doubt that
the primary inspiration for this episode lies in the
Gospel account of the birth of Christ. Hrotsvitha, telling of the swineherds, assuredly has in mind the shepherds (Luke 2: 8ff) who kept the night vigil guarding
their flocks, when a divine radiance flashed round about
them, filling them with fear. This fear turned to joy
when the radiance was revealed as a divine omen, the
shepherds then telling it to the people all around (2:
18). That the supernatural light is seen first by the
lowly and only then by kings (the Magi of Matthew 2)
is not stated in the Gospels, yet this was the clear
implication of the 'synoptic' account, which became
the basis for Christmas homilies.

As *in illo tempore,* in the Christmas night, the harbinger of the divine event was beheld first by shepherds,
so with the gleams of light in the darkness that beto-

kened the birth of Gandersheim. The foundation that
was destined to have such regal splendour is first seen
augured by the humblest folk, and it is their telling
what they see that makes the fulfilment of the lights
possible.

Yet the Gandersheim of 852 is the same place, Hrotsvitha insists, as the Gandersheim of her own day. Still
there is a dark forest, and shadowing hills. Can there
still be lights in that forest, heralding a special divine
grace? The secret answer lies, I believe, in Hrotsvitha's
conception of her own rôle. She constantly affirms
herself to be the lowliest, 'last of the last (*ultima
ultimarum*)'[64] of those who dwell at Gandersheim; yet
may it not be because of this that she, like the swineherds, is the first to be blessed by descrying new lights?
Gradually the greater world learns of what the lowly
one has seen—it reaches the ears of Otto, as the first
apparition of lights reached those of his ancestor
Liudolf. Then the great themselves begin to watch, and
the lights appear 'set in harmonious order': an implicit—even if not fully conscious—equivalent to that
ordo, that symmetrical twofold cycle, which Hrotsvitha
came to present. The lights, that is, were once symbols
of Gandersheim the foundation, but they are also—at
least potentially—symbols of the chronicler of
Gandersheim, Hrotsvitha herself. She is the *vilis muliercula* who, in a special, divinely granted way, receives
illumination.

Deep within, Hrotsvitha was certain she had been
blessed with this illumination—or better, she became
increasingly certain of this as her writing progressed.
So in a sense, despite all her protestations, she is not
humble—except in the way of the poet who says 'Not
I, not I, but the wind that blows through me'.[65] Her
insistences on her frailty, lowly submissiveness, and
incompetence all contain an element of deliberate over-
acting: they can be seen as so many ironic glances at
the double standards of the world she knew, and especially of the powerful male-dominated world. So, too,
her constant use of diminutives is more than a stylistic
mannerism. They reveal an aspect of her thought: they
are self-assured, even self-assertive, by being self-deprecating. When she speaks of her *ingeniolum,* or of the
gratiola she receives, she is saying in effect, these may
be of little moment in the world of warriors, sovereigns and popes, yet she is also hinting that she *has*
imaginative genius (*ingenium*) and does receive true
grace for writing.

The evaluation of that writing poses many problems. It
has sparkling moments, and profound ones; it can be
cherished for the complex—and I think attractive—
personality it reveals. One can admire both Hrotsvitha's
many-sided resourcefulness and the high aspirations
revealed by the design of her double cycle of legends
and plays. Yet technically that design remained imperfect. This is chiefly because Hrotsvitha never came to

feel wholly at ease in the classical metres (as the finest Carolingian poets had done); nor, on the other hand, did she take experiment a step further and transform classical verse into a medium wholly her own (as the author of *Ruodlieb* was to do some decades later). The hexameters cited in translation from the ***Primordia coenobii Gandesheimensis*** are among the freshest, most unforced in her writing; yet even here a slight stiffness of movement and somewhat repetitive wording suggest that in quantitative measures Hrotsvitha never reached the flexibility and vivacity of expression that came to her so readily in her rhymed prose, and especially in dialogues.

Hrotsvitha's finest qualities and her limitations are comparable to those encountered among the painters who were her contemporaries. We might say, especially with her poetry in ancient forms, that she tried to press too much of her own thoughts and feelings into frames as classically elegant, and as confining, as those used by the Ottonian miniaturists, where, for all the finesse, something a little aloof and rigid tends to remain.

She began her twofold cycle with Marian legends and ended it with an apocalyptic tableau. It is worth recalling that in the seventh century an unpredictable artist, whose stylistic sources are still in many aspects enigmatic,[66] had painted at Castelseprio a double series of frescoes—Marian and apocalyptic. It is this artist's immediacy, his fluid and dynamic qualities, that neither Hrotsvitha nor the illuminators of her time recaptured. True, they did not aim to—but that does not prevent one from sometimes longing for it.

Hrotsvitha remained, by and large, without influence in the later Middle Ages. Yet some of her plays were copied several times in the eleventh and twelfth centuries,[67] and once ***Gallicanus*** was even furnished with stage-directions. Hrotsvitha's distinctive literary coquetry, however, has parallels in the eleventh century, among some of the women poets to whom we shall now turn: Constance's way with Ovid's *Heroides,* for instance,[68] comes very close to Hrotsvitha's with Terence. And one intriguing possibility of Hrotsvitha's direct influence must at least be broached. The unique comprehensive manuscript of her writings, copied in the late tenth or early eleventh century, was preserved at St Emmeram in Regensburg, where Gerberga had been educated. Did the learned young women at Regensburg who, in the later eleventh century, wrote verses of love, flirtation and teasing wit,[69] ever look at Hrotsvitha's writings? Was their particular brand of coquetry learnt as well as cultivated spontaneously? Did they find their oscillations between deference and proud assurance wholly for themselves—or (as I suspect) with a little help from the *ingeniolum* of their supersubtle predecessor?

Notes

[1] See especially B. Nagel, *Hrotsvit von Gandersheim,* and, for more recent work, the fine survey by D. Schaller, 'Hrotsvit' pp. 105-14. Since Schaller's essay, the most important work has been that of two Italian scholars: G. Vinay, *Alto medioevo latino* pp. 483-554, and F. Bertini, *Il 'teatro' di Rosvita.*

[2] This claim is based on the closing lines of the legend *Theophilus,* which Homeyer (*Opera* p. 152), following Lehmann (*Erforschung des Mittelalters* III (Stuttgart 1960) 126), sees as a 'grace after meals (*Tischsegen*)'. While the legends could indeed have been read aloud at meals, both in the refectory at Gandersheim and elsewhere, I do not think this can be safely inferred from the *Theophilus* lines. In these, Hrotsvitha plays on the language of a *Tischsegen,* but even more on the much-cherished metaphorics of 'spiritual food' (see esp. K. Lange, 'Geistliche Speise', *ZfdA* XCV (1966) 81-122). That is, when Hrotsvitha bids Christ to 'benignly consecrate the dishes of the table I have proffered, making these banquets wholesome for those who taste them' (*Theophilus* 452-3), the primary meaning of the dishes and the banquets is the metaphorical one: they are Hrotsvitha's compositions.

[3] Bertini p. 9.

[4] That she should have the same name as Hrotsvitha I by pure coincidence, or by adoption, seems less probable. It may also be significant that she concludes her last poem, on the 'primordia Gandesheimensis . . . coenobii', with the reign of Hrotsvitha I's predecessor, Cristina (896-919), the youngest daughter of the founders, Liudolf and Oda: a certain reticence to go on to celebrate her own namesake would be understandable if she was also a kinswoman.

[5] R. R. Bezzola, *Les origines* I 248.

[6] On Hrotsvitha's rhymed prose, the discussion in K. Polheim, *Die lateinische Reimprosa* (1925), remains, in its wealth of detail, unsuperseded. There are many extensive, though unsystematic, uses of rhymed prose in earlier centuries—in Apuleius, in Augustine (especially the homilies), in Venantius Fortunatus' *Vita Radegundis,* in the sermons of Hrabanus Maurus, and in the brilliant homily of Scotus Eriugena on the Prologue of John (cf. *Jean Scot Erigène et l'histoire de la philosophie,* ed. R. Roques (Centre National de Recherche Scientifique, Paris 1977), pp. 243-52). Yet no one before Hrotsvitha employed rhymed prose so elaborately and consistently, and with such lavish use of 'rich' rhymes as well as assonances. It is in this last point that the link with Rather is particularly interesting. Compare, for example, in his *Excerptum ex dialogo confessionali* (P.L. 136, 397 C-398 C, line-arrangement P.D.):

Confiteor etiam ipsi   Domino Deo omnipotenti, quod his et plus his omnibus voluptatum foedatus flagitiis, et contagionibus fuscatus omnimodis, semper sine ulla mentis sinceritate,   corporis et sanguinis sacramentum Domini,   fateor, percipi indigne . . .

Praeter haec peccavi iocando, equitando,   ambulando, stando, sedendo sive iacendo, et in his et in aliis omnibus vitiis . . .

On rhymed prose in Rather's letters, see F. Weigle, 'Die Briefe Rathers von Verona, *DA* I (1937) 147-94; some letters—notably *Epp.* 1-6, 19, 20-3—have consistent rhyme throughout ('völlig durchgereimt', p. 187). On Hrotsvitha's having received tuition from men (*magistri*) as well as women teachers, see n 46 below.

[7] *Opera* p. 227. Cf. E. Cerulli, *Studia Islamica* XXXII (1970) 69-76.

[8] In view of Hrotsvitha's precise wording, it is out of the question that she received the information 'through the mediation of her abbess'—as Homeyer (*Opera*, p. 124) thought possible; it is also highly unlikely that Hrotsvitha had, as Homeyer claims, 'not the oral report alone' but written information on the background of the events: this would make nonsense of Hrotsvitha's levelheaded and decisive contrast between oral and written sources.

[9] Unfortunately Hrotsvitha's informant seems not to have explained to her the precise nature of Islamic religious observance, for when she touches on this in her poem she merely adopts Christian caricatures (e.g. making the Moslems into idol-worshippers), such as she would have found in polemic writings, or indeed could have picked up by hearsay in northern Europe, without the help of a Cordovan.

[10] *Ruotgeri Vita S. Brunonis* 8, in *Lebensbeschreibungen einiger Bischöfe des 10.-12. Jahrhunderts,* ed. I. Ott, tr. H. Kallfelz (Darmstadt 1973) p. 190.

[11] Despite the long customary tradition of naming several of Hrotsvitha's plays after men and not women characters (*Dulcitius; Calimachus; Abraham; Pafnutius*), I believe it is important, because of Hrotsvitha's emphasis on feminine protagonists, to return to her own nomenclature. Her second, third, fourth and fifth plays are entitled, respectively, *Passio sanctarum virginum Agapis Chioniae et Hirenae; Resuscitatio Drusianae et Calimachi; Lapsus et conversio Mariae neptis Habrahae heremicolae;* and *Conversio Thaidis meretricis;* the last play, commonly known as *Sapientia,* is entitled *Passio sanctarum virginum Fidei Spei et Karitatis.*

[12] Ed. K. Strecker, MGH *Poetae* IV 1088-90; the text is also in Winterfeld pp. xx-xxiii.

[13] *'Nunc Terentius exit foras audiens haec et ait.'*

[14] Cit. W. Creizenach, *Geschichte des neueren Dramas* (3 vols., Halle ²1911-23), I 3. The passage occurs in the Prologue of a Life of St Mary of Cappadocia, written *ca.* 1180 by a monk Reinerus, at St Laurent in Liège (ed. B. Pez, *Thesaurus Anecdotorum Novissimus* (Augsburg 1721) IV iii, 83ff). Reiner (p. 85) claims that 'Frater etenim quidam pueris sive adolescentibus Terentium legebat. Sed scenica lectio plus obesse quam prodesse auditoribus infirmis solet.' In delirium (*extasis*), the master receives a warning threat from St Laurence, 'quod ludicris sordidaretur, dum comico uteretur'. This last phrase in particular suggests that the *scenica lectio* was no dispassionate textual study, but that the possibilities of *ludicra* were indeed exploited.

[15] Bertini p. 108 (Homeyer, following Winterfeld, emends 'Expaveo' to 'Expavete').

[16] See esp. the fine study by E.-R. Labande, 'Mirabilia mundi: Essai sur la personnalité d'Otton III', *CCM* VI (1963) 297-313, 455-76.

[17] *Dichtung* pp. 91-104.

[18] The two plays, however, are very different in characterization and tone. The holy man of the desert, shown as gently doting and fatherly in the first play, is a relentless, tormenting crusader in the second. Where Mary, the first heroine, is converted lovingly, Thais is humiliated and crushed. The second play is also distinguished by its didactic opening, Pafnutius teaching his disciples the theory of musical harmony; this at first sight irrelevant prelude serves to enrich the close with the theme of cosmic harmony ('caeli concentus', XII 6), extending to the Neoplatonic 'return' of souls ('felici reditu ad te reverti . . . repetere principium sui originis', XIII 2-3—cf. Boethius *Cons.* III m. 9, 20-1).

[19] *Gong.* 570ff (*Opera* p. 122). In the Merovingian *Vita Gangulfi Martyris Varennensis* (ed. W. Levison, *Script. Rer. Merov.,* MGH, VII 142ff), Gongolf's wife speaks her mocking vow on a Friday, and thereafter every Friday must fart as many times as the words she speaks (p. 167).

[20] 'Dixerat'—Hrotsvitha here parodies epic style (cf. e.g. *Aen.* IV 331).

[21] 'Oh wanton boy, with impunity you make a boast of spurning . . . ' (cf. e.g. *Anth. Graeca* XII 22).

[22] *Dichtung* pp. 98f.

[23] *Opera* p. 376.

[24] See esp. O. B. Hardison Jr, *Christian Rite and Chris-*

tian Drama in the Middle Ages (Baltimore 1965) pp. 192ff; J. Drumbl, *Quem quaeritis* (Roma 1981) pp. 82ff.

[25] See P. Aebischer, 'Le "Cant de la Sibil la" . . . ', in his *Neuf études sur le théâtre médiéval* (Genève 1972), esp. pp. 23f.

[26] While we do not know the date of her death, there is no record of Hrotsvitha later than 973. It is ironic to recall that in 1007 Gandersheim, after sixty years of full independence under the rule of its abbesses, was made—despite fierce resistance—a dependency of the diocese of Hildesheim.

[27] *In honorem Hludowici* (Ermold le Noir, ed. and tr. E. Faral (Paris [2]1964)) 2062-3.

[28] *Opera* pp. 37-9.

[29] Cf. T. Janson, *Latin Prose Prefaces* p. 141.

[30] *1. Dedicatio* 7-8 (*Opera* p. 40).

[31] *2. Dedicatio* 5-6 (*Opera* p. 176).

[32] *Basilius* 9-13 (*Opera* p. 177).

[33] *Opera* p. 227.

[34] Cf. E. Jeauneau, '"Pierre Abélard à Saint-Denis"', in *Abélard en son temps: Actes du colloque international* . . . (Paris 1981) pp. 161-73.

[35] A detailed study of the presence of classical authors in the works of Rather and Liutprand would be rewarding. Whilst for Rather's letters there is a fine 'Verzeichnis der Zitate' in F. Weigle's edition (MGH, pp. 205-9), there is nothing comparable for Liutprand, though the recent edition of his works (in A. Bauer and R. Rau, *Quellen zur Geschichte der sächs. Kaiserzeit* (Darmstadt 1971)) has a number of valuable parallels in the notes, signalling, *inter alia,* the Terentian adaptations in the *Legatio.*

[36] Cf. J. Grimm, A. Schmeller, *Lateinische Gedichte des X. und XI. Jh.* (Göttingen 1838), p. ix.

[37] It is not likely that Hrotsvitha had read Plautus (though see also n 57 below); but her play on Terence's phrase, *Andria* 218—*amentium, haud amantium*—is deliberate, and should be noted in the editions.

[38] I have gathered a range of classical and medieval examples in *Medium Aevum XXXIII* (1964) 50.

[39] Cf. *Opera* p. 496.

[40] Cf. *Opera* pp. 494ff; some interesting new parallels

between Hrotsvitha and earlier poets (including Lucan, Ovid, Venantius Fortunatus, and several Carolingians) are suggested in Schaller, 'Hrotsvit.'

[41] This point was well observed by Vinay p. 511.

[42] *Lapsus et conversio Mariae* (= *Abraham*) IX 5.

[43] *Opera* pp. 235-7.

[44] The word is 'humilitas' (glossed by Winterfeld, p. 346, as 'Herablassung'). It is the earliest recorded instance of this 'courtly' sense, which was to become widespread in vernacular love-poetry (see the excursus 'The Concept *umiltà*' in my *Medieval Latin* I 158-62).

[45] 'Dictatiuncula' appears to be attested before Hrotsvitha only in Jerome, *Contra Vig.* 3 (P.L. 23, 341-2), in a context of violent polemic about clerical chastity. Hrotsvitha will have known the passage, and sensed the mock-modesty of Jerome's diminutives, 'dictatiuncula' and 'lucubratiuncula' (*ibid.*).

[46] This key-word, 'magistrorum', must on no account be emended to 'magistrarum' (K. Strecker *Hrotsvithae Opera* (Leipzig [2]1930) *ad loc.*), or translated 'Lehrerinnen' (Homeyer *ad loc.*). Even if in this context we construe it as being of common rather than masc. gender, it is surely a testimony not to be rejected that Hrotsvitha had received tuition from men as well as women teachers. This point of text and translation is a small but revealing instance of how the 'cloistered nun' image could blind even distinguished specialists.

[47] Jerome to Paulinus of Nola, *Ep.* 53, 2-3 (not only the occurrence of the two Greek words but also the context makes Hrotsvitha's knowledge of this passage likely).

[48] *Parzival* 115, 21-34; 782, 5-12.

[49] *Cons.* I pr. I, 5 ('Eandem tamen vestem violentorum quorundam sciderant manus, et particulas quas quisque potuit abstulerant').

[50] *Prologus* 26-9 (*Opera* pp. 387f).

[51] I suggest there is no good reason for disbelieving Hrotsvitha's central statement in her letter to Gerberga, that she had no written sources for the *Gesta Ottonis.* Homeyer (*Opera* p. 390) argues that 'for the events in a time-span of over forty years she could not have relied on oral tradition alone; the correct chronological ordering of the events suggests that she used a chronicle', even if this was complemented by oral reports. In my view this, apart from doing violence to Hrotsvitha's explicit testimony, underestimates her powers of organizing material independently. It also takes no account of the possibility of her presence at

court. Insofar, for instance, as some passages in the *Gesta* are paralleled in the works of Liutprand, the reason for this could be personal acquaintance rather than literary borrowing.

[52] *Opera* pp. 385-6.

[53] 'Varietate': cf. Ps. 44: 10.

[54] 'Pigescat': the frequentative *pigescere* appears to be unrecorded elsewhere.

[55] *Archicancellarie, vir discrete mentis* (*Die Gedichte des Archipoeta,* ed. H. Watenphul and H. Krefeld (Heidelberg 1958) IV). As E. H. Zeydel ('Knowledge of Hrotswitha's Works' p. 383) pointed out, a note in the Chronicle of the Bishops of Hildesheim states that Hrotsvitha wrote a poem about all the deeds of the three Ottonian emperors (*Scriptorum Brunsvicensia . . . illustrantium,* ed. G. W. Leibniz (Hanover 1710) II 787: 'scripsit . . . trium Imperatorum Ottonum res gestas omnes'). Yet this chronicle is not from the eleventh century, as Zeydel claimed: its entries go as late as 1573 (*ibid.* II 806); thus there is no compelling reason to trust this detail and postulate a continuation of the *Gesta Ottonis* that has not survived. Again, the testimony might tempt one to speculate about Hrotsvitha's possible authorship of the lyrical sequence, 'Modus Ottinc' (*Carmina Cantabrigiensia,* ed. K. Strecker, MGH, no. II), which in fact dwells on all three Ottos; on the other hand, it is far too brief a composition to be said to cover 'res gestas omnes'.

[56] H. Delehaye, *Etude sur le légendier romain* (Bruxelles 1936), pp. 163, 168f.

[57] *Passio . . . Agapis* (= *Dulcitius*) I 6; cf. also *Passio . . . Fidei* (= *Sapientia*) V 17. The word *conquiniscere* (to crouch, cower, or bow the head) occurs twice in Plautus, once in Priscian, citing verses from the oldest *fabula atellana,* and once in an epitome of Julius Valerius on Alexander; it does not seem to be attested elsewhere (see *TLL,* s.v.). In terms of transmission of texts, it is clearly likelier that Hrotsvitha had seen Priscian or the Alexander epitome than Plautus—but much that regards the sources of her diction still awaits detailed investigation.

[58] *Passio . . . Agapis* XIV 3 (*Opera* p. 277).

[59] *Praef.* 5 (*quia nec matura adhuc aetate vigens, / nec scientia fui proficiens*).

[60] *Lapsus* (= *Abraham*) VII 15ff. Did Hrotsvitha get her unusual expression for 'dawn' (*matuta*) from Odo of Cluny's *Occupatio,* where it occurs twice (see *NG,* s.v.), rather than from Prudentius (*Symm.* II 562) or Ovid (*Fasti* VI 479)? The occurrence in Lucretius (V 656), cited by Homeyer along with Prudentius, should be discounted.

[61] *Ecl.* x 49 (first noted by Vinay, p. 551); *Aen.* I 327.

[62] *Primordia* 185-226 (*Opera* pp. 457-8).

[63] Cf. Homeyer, *Opera* p. 457.

[64] *Gesta Ottonis, Praef.* I (*Opera* p. 385).

[65] D. H. Lawrence, 'Song of a man who has come through' (*Collected Poems,* 1932).

[66] Cf. esp. M. Schapiro, *Late Antique, Early Christian and Medieval Art* (New York 1979) pp. 67-142.

[67] H. Menhardt, 'Eine unbekannte Hrotsvitha-hs.' 233-6; B. Jarcho, *Speculum* II (1927) 343f; Zeydel pp. 382-5.

[68] See below, pp. 85ff.

[69] See below, pp. 91ff, and my discussion of the new edition of the *Carmina Ratisponensia,* ed. A. Paravicini (Heidelberg 1979), in *Sandalion* V (1982) 109-17.

Abbreviations

CCM: Cahiers de civilisation médiévale

DA: Deutsches Archiv für Erforschung des Mittelalters

NG: F. Blatt, *Novum Glossarium Mediae Latinitatis* (København 1957ff)

ZfdA: Zeitschrift für Deutsches Altertum

Peter R. Schroeder (essay date 1989)

SOURCE: "Hroswitha and the Feminization of Drama" in *Women in Theatre,* edited by James Redmond, Cambridge University Press, 1989, pp. 49-58.

[In the following essay, Schroeder observes proto-feminist themes in Hroswitha's plays, especially "the thematic pattern of feminine weakness overcoming masculine strength."]

Most non-specialists who think about Hroswitha at all tend to think of her largely as a freak of literary history, a kind of duck-billed platypus standing outside the normal flow of evolution—in this case, the evolution of Christian drama in the Middle Ages. Yet our perception of her as a sideshow exhibit—the tenth-century nun who wrote religious plays in imitation of Terence—can prove an obstacle when we come to examine her actual accomplishment: the mere existence of Hroswitha's plays seems odd enough to keep us from finding out if they are anything more than oddities. This paper, ignoring literary history, will take Hroswitha for granted as a phenomenon and focus instead on how, in both her plays and her prefatory comments to the plays, she exploits her own feminine self-consciousness for dramatic and ironic ends.

In the preface and dedicatory epistle to her plays, Hroswitha seems to present herself as an earnestly naive, self-deprecating, artistically insecure but dutifully pious female. She claims that her work, which she calls 'the little work of a weak little woman' ('opusculum vilis mulierculae'), scarcely merits the praise it has received; all credit, rather, is due the giver of the grace which works in her, since her apparent knowledge surpasses her 'muliebre ingenium', her womanly wit.[1] What she has done comes from God, though it would be wrong to deny that with God's help she has acquired a bit of knowledge, since she is a creature capable of learning ('quia sum animal capax disciplinae', p. 236). Indeed, in a sense her works testify more strikingly to God's grace than they would had she been a man, since women are believed to be more intellectually sluggish than men ('quanto muliebris sensus tardior esse creditur', p. 236). The plays themselves, she claims, show how 'feminine fragility conquers and overcomes with confusion the strength of men' (p. 234). These comments suggest that she is acutely conscious of her own position as a woman writer and of her theme as, essentially, a woman's theme.

Though some have taken Hroswitha's demure disclaimers at face value, the tone of the prefatory material is almost certainly ironic. Peter Dronke goes so far as to say that in the preface 'she says little of what she really means, and means almost nothing of what she says'.[2] But while we sense that what Dronke calls her 'weak little woman pose' is indeed a pose, masking considerable self-assurance, her irony is somewhat more complex than would be the case if, for example, Margaret Thatcher were to use a similar ploy to announce a new plan to stamp out the Trades Union Council. Hroswitha's irony is both verbal and dramatic; if on one level she 'means almost nothing of what she says', on another she is forcing us to re-evaluate the very words she is using: seeming weakness becomes strength, as seeming strength reveals its underlying weakness. In this her preface adumbrates, and is illuminated by, the recurrent, ironic overturning of established values in the plays themselves.

Thus, as Dronke shows (particularly in his analysis of *Dulcitius*), the thematic pattern of feminine weakness overcoming masculine strength—the Christian virgins, for example, dismaying their powerful and pompous pagan oppressors—is prefigured in the preface by Hroswitha's own confrontation with Terence.[3] Terence, like the Roman oppressors, is powerful, male, and pagan; Hroswitha is a weak little ill-educated Christian woman.

It is interesting how she emphasizes the comparative *weakness* of her own language ('vilitas dictationis', p. 234); all she really has in her favor is a devotion to Christ. Her relationship to Terence encapsulates the same cluster of oppositions which she says her plays exemplify: female-male, Christian-pagan, weakness-strength. And just as her characters, with God's help, succeed against seemingly overwhelming odds, so, by implication, Hroswitha herself manages the unlikely feat of writing plays worthy of comparison with those of her classical predecessor. In her plays, as Dronke says, 'the ultimate victory is a victory of God, but Hroswitha sees it "especially" ('praesertim') as a feminist triumph. Weak women show their power, strong men go under.'[4] Hroswitha seems to see herself participating in an analogous triumph.

Yet in a sense this identification of weakness and femininity is something of a sleight-of-hand trick by Hroswitha. The pervasive pattern is indeed seeming weakness conquering seeming strength, but in only two of the plays—*Dulcitius* and *Sapientia,* the two dramas of virginal martyrdom—do we find the weak, the feminine, and the Christian explicitly united. The others are dramas of conversion in which, I would argue, we are induced to see *fragilitas* as metaphorically feminine even when it manifests itself in men. At the outset of *Gallicanus,* for example, Gallicanus, the leader of the Roman troops, is pagan, masculine, and apparently powerful, yet he is victorious in battle only when, his defeat seemingly assured, he surrenders himself to the True God and his foes, the Scythians, collapse like a punctured tire. Worldly power has given way to worldly weakness (he gives up his position, gives away his wealth, and goes off to become the disciple of a holy man), paganism has given way to Christianity, but his feminization is by association only, as if the offstage prayers of Constantia, Artemia, and Attica had, in a sense, contributed to unmanning him. Returning from his paradoxical victory, he dramatizes this spiritual feminization by renouncing his earlier desire to marry Constantia, Constantine's daughter, and instead embracing her own vows of chastity. In *Callimachus,* Callimachus undergoes an analogous conversion. Appalled by Callimachus' lustful advances, Drusiana—another chaste Christian—altruistically dies in order to spare him the shame of being exposed, and in so doing lays the foundation for his own quasi-posthumous transformation into a chaste Christian. Again the male character triumphs spiritually after losing his worldly power; again the agent of conversion is a woman; again the conversion itself is represented as the substitution of the values embodied in the virtuous woman (chastity, renunciation of the world) for the lust and worldly power more native to the man.

Hroswitha's two remaining plays, *Abraham* and *Pafnutius,* differ from the others in that their central figures are sympathetic, Christian, unworldly men—earnest grizzled hermits—who undertake the salvation of fallen women. Abraham and Pafnutius may be outsiders to the 'masculine' world of the lovers, but they are, ineluctably, men—men, moreover, who from the outset are steadfast in their piety. In a worldly sense they are weak, and their weakness ends up defeating the more obviously powerful worldly lures that have seduced Thaia and Maris, but in what way do these plays illustrate Hroswitha's stated theme of 'feminine fragility' overthrowing the 'strength of men'? The possible answers to this question, though they may be tenuous, nonetheless cast some light on a non-obvious 'feminine' quality in Hroswitha's dramas generally.

On one level, of course, the two hermits can be seen as agents for restoring Thais and Maria to their true natures—the native purity which they have lost as a result of mingling with the world of men. Both women are depicted as essentially good. Maria has endured an oppressively pious upbringing by the holy Abraham and has fallen only after being seduced by a lecher disguised as a monk. Thais professes an unquestioning belief in God; as she burns her ill-gotten treasures she tells her lovers that for the first time in her life she is sane—a sanity misinterpreted as lunacy by those still enamored of the luxury which she is so spectacularly relinquishing. By accepting the false (and, implicitly, masculine) values of the world and the flesh, both heroines have been, in a sense, turncoats to their sex, and the old hermits are vehicles for their refeminization. We might thus regard the triumph in these plays as the triumph of Thais and Maria over a kind of abstracted Idea of the Male—an Idea subsuming, for Hroswitha, sex, glitter, and general spiritual perversion.

But Abraham and Pafnutius are also representative of another quality, so pervasive in Hroswitha's plays that we take it for granted, as a given: the extraordinary subordination of institutionalized rules to a kind of spiritual spontaneity. Her plays are set in the days of the early church not simply to provide her with the opportunity to meet Terence on something like his own ground, nor because that period provided the richest source of hagiographical material; her non-dramatic works show that she could come much closer to contemporaneity. Primitive Christianity seems to appeal to her in large part because she can depict it as a golden age of religious individualism, without ecclesiastical structures or hierarchy, without regulations or rituals (apart from baptism). The abbess in **Pafnutius** is the only real representative of a Christian institution, and she speaks of her 'exiguatatem habitationis' (p. 342), emphasizing her lack of pomp or the trappings of power. When the converted Gallicanus returns triumphantly to Rome he bypasses the pagan shrines and goes instead 'ad domum sancti Petri' (p. 253); this may be a kind of kenning for a church, but it has a decidedly domestic and personal flavor. He then, as we have noted, relinquishes all his earlier institutional ties. Constantine,

in the same play, must have posed a problem for Hroswitha: he is at the same time Christian and emperor. But, as we shall see later, he lacks the trappings of power or pomp that Hroswitha gives to her pagan emperors. He pleads rather than commands; his worries—in the face of possible disaster for the Empire—seem largely personal; he makes no effort to impose religious conformity on his pagan general. Conversion, it seems, must come from within; God is available to the willing individual without the need for any formal mediation.

This non-institutionalized view of religion is connected, as well, with Hroswitha's almost proto-Abelardan ethic of intentionality. When, in *Dulcitius,* Sissinius threatens to punish Irena by hauling her off to a brothel, Irena points out that it is better for the body to be besmirched than to worship idols, and that in order to sin it is necessary that the soul consent. When Abraham, casting around for some way to retrieve his fallen niece, tells his fellow hermit Effrem of his plan to seek her out disguised as a potential lover, Effrem asks him what he'll do if meat and wine—which Abraham has vowed to avoid—are put before him. 'I shall by no means refuse, that I may remain unknown', says Abraham, and Effrem assures him that God knows what is in our hearts and understands our intentions ('qua intentione unaquaeque res geratur, intellegit', p. 311). In spite of her surface depravity, Thais is redeemed by her belief in God. And the notion that good intentions count for more than pedantic adherence to rules is applied by Hroswitha, in her preface, to herself: in order to carry out her intentions, Hroswitha admits that it has been necessary for her to write about things 'which are not permitted us to hear', but had she not done so she could not have accomplished her purpose. Although we are right to distrust general claims about what is 'characteristically feminine', I think that, in these plays, we almost subliminally perceive this preference for the relational and the spontaneous over the regulated and the institutionalized as in some sense a 'feminine' characteristic. It certainly forms a fourth element in Hroswitha's central set of oppositions: it is the powerful pagan males who seem obsessed with enforcing their rules, and the weak Christian women whose role, as often as not, is to subvert those rules and institutions. In this sense Abraham and Pafnutius take their place on the feminine side of the opposition.

Now that I've stretched the concept of the feminine beyond what the normal elasticity of the term may be able to tolerate, I'd like to examine in some detail the ironic inversion of expectations in **Sapientia,** the most straightforwardly 'feminist' of Hroswitha's plays and the play in which her central oppositions are most clearly exemplified. **Sapientia** begins with a dialogue between the emperor Hadrian and his flattering lackey Antiochus, who immediately establishes his institutional loyalty and identity ('My Lord Emperor, what desire has your servant but to see you powerful and prosperous? What ambition apart from the welfare and peace and greatness of the state you rule?') and emphasizes his alacrity in calling attention to any dangers which might threaten the state. Hadrian wonders what new dangers have appeared:

> *Hadrian.* Come, if you have discovered some new danger, make it known to me.
>
> *Antiochus.* A certain alien woman has recently come   to this city with her three children.
>
> *Hadrian.* Of what sex are the children?
>
> *Antiochus.* They are all girls.
>
> *Hadrian.* And you think that a handful of women threaten danger to the state?
>
> (p. 358; ***Plays,*** pp. 133-4)

As readers or audience we surely share Hadrian's surprise at the bizarre disproportion between Antiochus's fawning buildup and the nature of the threat itself, a disproportion that emphasizes Hroswitha's central contrast between worldly power (male, pagan, institutionalized) and seeming weakness (female, Christian, relational). Hadrian's response also echoes the pet word, 'muliercula', by which Hroswitha refers to herself in her preface: 'tantillarum . . . muliercularum aliquid', some very small little women, a double diminutive. The danger to the Roman state comes not simply from females, but from females shrunk to an extreme of insignificance.

Antiochus goes on to justify his fears: this woman is disrupting the concord ('concordiam') of the state with the dissonance ('dissonantia') of her religious practice. And her disruption has been effective: 'Our wives hate us and scorn us to such an extent that they will not deign to eat with us, still less share our beds.' The institutional harmony of the state is being subverted by the sort of threat that Hadrian's pomp and power are completely unsuited to deal with: this one intrusive woman is infecting all the women of Rome, and the result is marital discord. The largely impersonal institution of the state, Hroswitha implies, rests on the largely relational institution of marriage; women, by exercising their power over the latter, can help bring down the former. Christianity is presented as a feminine attack on the male power structure.

The play thus establishes its polarities at the outset, and establishes as well the ironic technique by which Hroswitha undermines our obvious expectations. The first part of the play, in fact, involves a kind of demolition, one after another, of Hadrian's misconceptions about women. He begins by assuming they are weak, but finds that Rome is being threatened by a feminist conspiracy. He goes on to assume that they are easily manipulated. When Sapientia and her daughters are brought before Hadrian, the emperor decides to persuade rather than threaten, and Antiochus agrees: 'the

frail sex is easily moved by flattery' ('fragilitas sexus feminea facilius potest blandimentis molliri', p. 359). But as we have seen, Hroswitha has a tendency to use 'fragilitas' ironically, and the women turn out to be triumphantly impervious to flattery. Indeed, Hadrian is far more swayed by Sapientia's fair appearance than Sapientia is swayed by his 'fair speeches'; she seems to have a principled contempt for rhetoric as opposed to truth. But Hadrian, a slow learner, persists in his misconceptions and continues to chat up Sapientia in a greasily avuncular way: what are your children's names? How old are they?

This last question opens the floodgates for Sapientia's brain-teasing response, a long passage of complex numerical gibberish that leaves Hadrian totally mystified. Charity, she begins, 'has lived a diminished evenly even number of years; Hope a number also diminished, but unevenly even; and Faith an augmented number, unevenly even'. When Hadrian says that this answer leaves him in ignorance, Sapientia continues: 'Every number is said to be "diminished" the parts of which when added together give a sum which is less than the number of which they are parts. Such a number is 8. For the half of 8 is 4, the quarter of 8 is 2, and the eighth of 8 is 1; and these added together give 7.' And so on and so on. It has been common to regard this speech as an unfortunate bit of showing off on Hroswitha's part—Christopher St John, in the 1923 translation of the plays from which I have just quoted, apologizes in a footnote: 'It has been my duty to preserve this rather tiresome numerical discourse, which no doubt Roswitha introduced to impress the "learned men" to whom she submitted her work' (***Plays,*** pp. 139-40). But a reader more charitably willing to admit that Hroswitha may have known what she was doing can find the passage both amusing and dramatically relevant. Essentially, it strikes me as another undercutting of Hadrian's smug assumptions about women: not only are they weak, harmless, and easily swayed by flattery, they are also stupid and ignorant. But Sapientia's speech leaves Hadrian gasping: 'Your answer leaves me in ignorance.' 'I am not familiar with these terms.' 'Little did I think that a simple question about the age of these children could give rise to such an intricate and unprofitable dissertation.' Sapientia is indeed showing off, but her speech has a double purpose within the play itself: to point Sapientia's own moral—that the exposition reveals God's wisdom in giving human beings the ingenuity to figure out such mathematical formulations—and to point as well the implicit moral that men would be better off not underestimating women. I suspect, in fact, that Hroswitha may have been laughing at the Christopher St Johns among her own circle of learned men.

But Hadrian is too dense to draw the second moral; like the tormentors in ***Dulcitius*** he is an obdurate buffoon unable to recognize that he is supporting a lost cause. And, like most self-important buffoons, he proves particularly vulnerable to mockery. When, unable to move Sapientia, he turns to bullying her daughters, they jeer at him for his foolishness. This serves to enrage Hadrian, and Antiochus calls them crazy for their insolence. In this he echoes Thais' inversion of seeming lunacy and seeming sanity in **Pafnutius;** it is in fact Hadrian and Antiochus, clinging in spite of everything to their own misguided notion of what works, who emerge as the true lunatics. Their tortures prove no more effective than their blandishments; Faith frisks on a heated gridiron and swims in boiling pitch before joyfully allowing herself to be decapitated; Hope, threatened by scourging, tells Hadrian that the more cruelty he shows 'the greater will be your humiliation'; Charity, the youngest of the lot, continues to make fun of Antio-chus' stupidity ('Although I am small, my reason is big enough to put you to shame', p. 371) and mocks the disparity between Hadrian's professions of power and his actual helplessness ('A mighty man! he cannot conquer a child of eight without calling fire to help him!'). After that helplessness has been dramatized by the death of five thousand of Hadrian's men in the fire intended for Hope, she too is beheaded; the play ends with Sapientia, surrounded by matrons, burying her dead daughters and praying for her own death. But, as Hroswitha shows, for this sisterhood of Christians death is victory, and the victory of God is at the same time clearly a 'feminist triumph'.

Sapientia, generally thought to be the last play Hroswitha wrote, is the play which articulates most explicitly her proto-feminist themes: all the women are good, Christian, seemingly weak but really strong, seemingly defeated but really victorious, anti-institutional; all the men are the reverse. The very starkness of the opposition helps us see how, in a play like **Gallicanus,** she can *implicitly* feminize a story in which the moral division between men and women is much less clearcut, and in which the apparently central characters are at the same time powerful men (or men, at least, who hold positions of institutional power) and sympathetic Christians. I'll conclude, then, by looking at the beginning of **Gallicanus** to see how she deals with the character of Constantine, whose dual role as emperor and Christian makes him a particularly interesting challenge.

In the speech with which he opens the play, Constantine sounds, at least, every inch the emperor. Like Julian, Diocletian, and Hadrian—his pagan counterparts—he establishes his role rhetorically, by giving orders: his general, Gallicanus, must hasten off to subdue the Scythians. But Gallicanus balks. Hesitantly, afraid of Constantine's anger, he says that if he is successful in his campaign he wants to marry the

emperor's daughter, Constantia. Constantine's answer seems to surprise everyone. He isn't angry—the expected and appropriate imperial response—but says instead that he must first seek his daughter's consent. That is, instead of answering as emperor—his public persona—he answers as father; but as father he once again subverts expectations. Summoned, Constantia approaches with apparent submissiveness:

> *Constantia.* I am here, my lord. Command me.
>
> *Constantine.* I am in great distress of mind. My heart is heavy.
>
> *Constantia.* As I came in I saw that you were sad, and without knowing the reason I was troubled.
>
> *Constantine.* It is on your account.
>
> *Constantia.* On my account?
>
> *Constantine.* Yes.
>
> *Constantia.* You frighten me. What is it, my lord?
>
> *Constantine.* The fear of grieving you ties my tongue.
>
> > (p. 246; *Plays,* p. 6)

In spite of Constantia's continued filial honorifics, these few lines in effect succeed in reversing the relationship between the characters: she arrives expecting to be commanded, but quickly discovers that in fact her father is an inarticulate suppliant. Constantine himself is quite conscious of his problem in reconciling his imperial role with his role as father and Christian: 'For if, as is my duty as your father, I permit you to be faithful to your vow, as a sovereign I shall suffer for it. Yet were I to oppose your resolution—which God forbid—I should deserve eternal punishment' (p. 247).

It is at this point that Constantia comes to the rescue with her own plan: let Gallicanus believe that she agrees to the match, then trust to God to get them out of the dilemma should he happen to defeat the Scythians. Her suggestion is doubly interesting in light of Hroswitha's general thematic patterns. Unable himself to make a wise decision, Constantine has given the real power to direct events to his daughter: his apparent authority is a kind of façade. And Constantia's trickily expedient solution (tell Gallicanus what he wants to hear and worry about the consequences later) contrasts with Constantine's rather blinkered adherence to rules (a vow is a vow; one's word is one's word). We have noted already how Hroswitha seems willing to subordinate rules to intentions, cavalierly disregarding regulations if the cause is good. Moreover, Constantine's faith in God seems mediated by his faith in his daughter, who needs to remind him that God can resolve the apparent impasse he is confronting.

One effect of these opening scenes, then, is to make us redefine our sense of Constantine's character and role. His initial appearance of power ('Go get those Scy-thians!') has dissolved like a soap bubble in the face of Gallicanus' haggling and Constantia's real authority. In contrast to the Hadrian of *Sapientia,* Constantine shows himself a good Christian in part by showing himself an ineffective emperor—ineffective, that is, according to normal, 'masculine' managerial standards. The opening of *Gallicanus,* like the opening of *Sapi-entia,* also forces us to re-evaluate the relative importance of the two levels of action, the public and the private. In both plays, the emperors, victims in a sense of their masculine fondness for the institutional, initially misperceive what's going on: Hadrian can't accept that a few women pose a threat to the state, while Constantine thinks that his important conflict is with the Scythians, the external enemy. But where Hadrian fails to learn from the instructive women, and preserves to the end his illusion, or delusion, of being in control, Constantine is touchingly eager to relinquish real authority to his daughter (and, incidentally, to God), and to acknowledge the primacy of the domestic over the political. Ironically, Constantine, whom critics tend to treat with dismissive contempt for his 'weakness', in fact proves far more effective than the 'strong' Hadrian.[5] The feminist-Christian conspiracy, a menace to Hadrian's state, is the salvation of Constantine's.

Hroswitha, then, has reconciled the apparent conflict between Constantine's conflicting roles (powerful emperor and sympathetic Christian) by showing that the imperial role is an empty shell: the 'real' Constantine is the concerned father and worried Christian eager to seek guidance from his wiser and more faithful daughter. He is thus, I would claim, feminized. Not only does he acknowledge the power of women to control events; he also fits into the feminine side of the equation so explicitly delineated in *Sapientia,* and takes his place among those virtuous men whose virtue comes from their rejection of the characteristic set of 'masculine' values (love of power, love of sex, love of rules). The pattern of seeming (and feminine) weakness conquering seeming (and masculine) strength thus encompasses Constantine as it does Sapientia and as, indeed, it does Hroswitha herself.

Notes

[1] *Hrotsvithae Opera,* ed. H. Homeyer (Paderborn: Ferdinand Schöningh, 1970), p. 235. Unattributed parenthetical citations are to this edition. References to *Plays* indicate the translation is from *The Plays of Roswitha,* trans. Christopher St John (New York: Benjamin Blom, 1966).

[2] Peter Dronke, *Women Writers of the Middle Ages* (Cambridge University Press, 1984), p. 69. It will be obvious that I agree almost wholly with Dronke's discussion. It should be noted, though, that in this paper I use the more commonly recognizable titles for Hroswitha's plays rather than the fuller and more authentic titles used by Dronke.

[3] Ibid., pp. 78-9.

[4] Ibid., p. 71.

[5] For an example of such dismissive contempt in a recent critic, see A. D. Frankforter, 'Hroswitha of Gandersheim and the Destiny of Women', *The Historian,* 41 (1979), 295-314.

FURTHER READING

Allen, Philip Schuyler. "The Mediaeval Mimus." *Modern Philology* VIII, No. 1 (July 1910): 17-60.
    Includes discussion of some of the Roman sources of Hroswitha's dramas and poetry.

Carter, Barbara Barclay. "Roswitha of Gandersheim." *The Dublin Review,* No. 385 (April 1933): 284-95.
    Short survey of Hroswitha's life and principal dramas.

Coffman, George R. "A New Approach to Medieval Latin Drama." *Modern Philology* XXII, No. 3 (February 1925): 239-71.
    Contains a brief look at Hroswitha's poetry and her relationship to Gandersheim Abbey.

Dale, Darley. "Roswitha, Nun and Dramatist." *The American Catholic Quarterly Review* XXXIX (January-October 1914): 442-57.
    Surveys Hroswitha's dramas, with emphasis on *Gallicanus, Abraham,* and *Sapientia.*

DeLuca, Kenneth. "Hrotsvit's 'Imitation' of Terence." *Classical Folia* XXVIII, No. 1 (1974): 89-102.
    Contrasts Hroswitha's dramas with those of her primary classical influence, Terence.

Eckenstein, Lina. "The Nun Hrotsvith and Her Writings." In *Woman under Monasticism: Chapters on Saint-Lore and Convent Life between A.D. 500 and A.D. 1500,* pp. 160-83. Cambridge: Cambridge University Press, 1896.
    Overview of Hroswitha's writings that emphasizes the uniqueness of her dramatic works.

Heard, John. "Hrotsvitha: The Nun of Gandersheim." *Poet Lore* XLII, No. 4 (Spring 1935): 291-98.
    Brief introduction to Hroswitha's writings that laments scholars' relative disregarding of her works for centuries.

Hudson, William Henry. "Hrosvitha of Ganderseheim." *The English Historical Review* III (1888): 431-57.

Discusses the authenticity of Hroswitha's writings, and the evidence related to her life. Includes a detailed examination of *Dulcitus* and *Abraham.*

Kemp-Welch, Alice. "A Tenth-Century Dramatist: Roswitha the Nun." *The Nineteenth-Century and after* XIX-XX, No. 393 (November 1909): 814-26.

Discusses Hroswitha's dramas in relation to life during the reign of Emperor Otto the Great and in the convent at Gandersheim.

Petroff, Elizabeth Alvilda. "Eloquence and Heroic Virginity in Hrotsvit's Verse Legends." In *Body and Soul: Essays on Medieval Women and Mysticism,* pp. 83-96. New York: Oxford University Press, 1994.

Studies Hroswitha's virgin hero-martyrs.

Roberts, Arthur J. "Did Hrotswitha Imitate Terence?" *Modern Language Notes* XVI, No. 8 (December 1901): pp. 478-81.

Classifies Hroswitha's dramas as "inexplicable, but still significant" and as considerably different from those of the Roman playwright Terence.

Sticca, Sandro. "Hrotswitha's *Dulcitius* and Christian Symbolism." *Mediaeval Studies* XXXII (1970): 108-27.

Focuses on infernal symbolism in Hroswitha's *Dulcitius,* a work often considered somewhat farcical.

Waddell, Helen. "The Tenth Century." In *The Wandering Scholars.* Boston: Houghton Mifflin Company, 1927, pp. 64-82.

Mentions Hroswitha's *Callimachus* as part of a broader study of tenth-century European literature.

Wilson, Katharina M. "The Old Hungarian Translation of Hrotsvit's *Dulcitius:* History and Analysis." *Tulsa Studies in Women's Literature* I, No. 2 (Fall 1982): 177-87.

Examines an early-sixteenth-century Hungarian translation of *Dulcitius,* regarding it as a link "between classical drama and medieval morality plays."

——. "Hrotsvit and the Sounds of Harmony and Discord." *Germanic Notes* 14, No. 4 (1983): 54-56.

Considers Hroswitha's use of musical metaphors, particularly of "the contrast of God-inspired harmo-nious sounds and Devil-inspired cacophony," in her writings.

——. "Hrotsvit and the Tube; John Kennedy Toole and the Problem of Bad TV Programming." *Germanic Notes* 15, No. 1 (1984): 4-5.

Observes the thematic link between Hroswitha's plan to replace Terentian drama with her own, and the crusade of Ignatius—hero of John Kennedy Toole's novel *A Confederacy of Dunces*—against the medium of television.

——. "Antonomasia as a Means of Character-Definition in the Works of Hrotsvit of Gandersheim." *Rhetorica* II, No. 1 (Spring 1984): 45-53.

Concentrates on Hroswitha's use of antonomasia—the rhetorical reference to characters or objects by means of epithets—for laudatory, identificatory, vituperative, and didactic purposes.

——. "Hrotsvit's *Abraham:* The Lesson in Etymology." *Germanic Notes* 16, No. 1 (1985): 2-4.

Explores the thematic implications of Abraham's lesson in etymology, presented to his fallen niece Mary, the theme of which is that "the individual, being given the name of an illustrious model [in this case that of the Virgin Mary], bears the responsibility of trying to emulate that model."

——. "Figmenta vs. Veritas: Dame Alice and the Medieval Literary Depiction of Women by Women." *Tulsa Studies in Women's Literature* 4, No. 1 (Spring 1985): 17-32.

Mentions Hroswitha as part of an informal movement by medieval woman writers "to combat the demon-strably noxious effects of the negative literary depiction of women" by challenging certain stereotypes in their writings.

——. *Hrotsvit of Gandersheim: The Ethics of Authorial Stance.* Leiden, The Netherlands: E. J. Brill, 1988, 176 p.

Endeavors "to explore [Hroswitha's] opus from her own perspective: in the light of her literary training, her utilization of poetic and rhetorical ornaments, formal, generic precepts, and in the way she herself viewed her writing."

Zeydel, Edwin H. "Knowledge of Hrotsvitha's Works Prior to 1500." *Modern Language Notes* LIX, No. 6 (June 1944): 382-85.

Challenges the idea that Hroswitha's works were all but unknown between the time of her death in about 1000 and their rediscovery by Conrad Celtes in 1493.

——. "Ekkehard's Influence upon Hrotsvitha: A Study in Literary Integrity." *Modern Language Quarterly* VI (1945): 333-39.

Designates Ekkehard's *Waltharilied* as an important influence for Hroswitha's *Gesta Ottonis.*

——. "Were Hrotsvitha's Dramas Performed during Her Lifetime?" *Speculum* XX, No. 1 (January 1945): 443-56.

Argues that Hroswitha's plays were likely performed and read aloud by her contemporaries.

——. "On the Two Minor Poems in the Hrotsvitha Codex." *Modern Language Notes* LX, No. 6 (June 1945): 373-76.

Briefly investigates two largely ignored short poems by Hroswitha.

——. "The Authenticity of Hrotsvitha's Works." *Modern Language Notes* LXI, No. 1 (January 1946): 50-55.

Recounts the nineteenth-century controversy over the authenticity of Hroswitha's works and calls for further study to finally settle the question.

——. "'Ego Clamor Validus'—Hrotsvitha." *Modern Language Notes* XLI, No. 4 (April 1946): 281-83.
Presents a small piece of textual evidence that tends to support the authenticity of Hroswitha's works.

Kokinshu

(Also called *Kokin Wakashu*.) Japanese poetry.

INTRODUCTION

Considered the epitome of Japanese poetry for a thousand years, the *Kokinshu* (which loosely translates as "A Collection of Old and New Poems") is an anthology of poems, or *waka*, from the Heian dynasty, which marked the end of Chinese poetry's domination in Japan. Decreed by order of Emperor Daigo and completed between 905 and 917, the *Kokinshu* consists of 1,111 poems, almost all of which are in the form of the *tanka,* or short, 31-syllable poem, composed by 127 poets, selected by Ki no Tsurayuki, Ki no Tomonori, Oshikochi no Mitsune, and Mibu no Tadamine. The poems chosen include selections from the ninth century as well as contemporaneous works, arranged thematically and not in chronological order. They are organized into twenty books with emphasis on the seasons and love. Care was taken in deciding the order of the poems, with sometimes obvious progressions based on the changing seasons, and sometimes subtle transitions based on mood or theme, resulting, as critics have often noted, in a work greater than the sum of its parts. This structure was highly influential on succeeding Japanese poetry and continues to have an impact even to the present day. The *Kokinshu* also contains two prefaces, one in Chinese and one in Japanese. These are significant for the critical theory they advance regarding the nature of quality poetry. The first of a long series of imperially-commissioned Japanese poetry anthologies, the *Kokinshu* is unrivaled in its importance and influence.

In the ninth century the Japanese language was out of favor for use in poetry. Japanese poets composed their verses in Chinese, with Japanese compositions viewed as trivial. A new pride in their own nation led Japanese poets to return to the use of their native language in their literary works, although these still remained modeled on Chinese court poetry. Japanese poets displayed their works at new competitions and contests, and other poems were used in public celebrations, inscribed on large portable screens. Ki no Tsurayuki received an imperial commission to act as supervisor of the compilation of what would be the *Kokinshu.* The most important and most copied of all the poets whose works are represented in the *Kokinshu,* Tsurayuki is also the author of its Japanese preface. Tsurayuki was joined by three other poets of minor-court rank— Ki no Tomonori, Oshikochi no Mitsune, and Mibu no

Tadamine—in selecting the best examples of Japanese poetry and arranging them in the best fashion. The four compilers chose some 243 poems of their own and many anonymous poems. Among the other significant poets included are Ono no Komachi, Ariwara no Narihira, and Oshikochi no Mitsune. The Chinese preface is attributed to Ki no Yoshimochi. In the prefaces, the compilers announce that Japanese poetry has its seeds in the human heart and proceed to describe the glorious history of Japanese poetry, bemoan its impoverished state in the previous hundred years, describe its six styles, and humbly offer their collection to readers. The emphasis placed on human feelings as subject matter contrasts with popular poems of battles, mythical gods, and didactic works.

As is the case with all translations, particularly of poetry, disagreements abound among scholars as to which version of the *Kokinshu* is superior. Some favor a gloss of the Japanese, paraphrasing meaning and neglecting the poetics entirely. This extreme choice is not typically made in the case of the *Kokinshu,* and the translations are rendered in verse. Some translators lean more toward expressing their feelings based on what the original verse spontaneously evokes in them, using the preface's reference to the human heart as support for their interpretation of the original poets' meanings. Other translators favor literal description with additional explanation in footnotes, arguing that the text is more than a thousand years old and commentary is essential to understanding the original authors' intentions.

Critics have long recognized that the chief merit of the *Kokinshu* is not to be found in its individual poems but in the book as a whole. A particular *tanka* on love, while fine in and of itself, becomes something richer when it is read as an element of a progression of poems on a love affair, as seen through the words of several different poets. While there is agreement that some poems are outstanding, critics agree that it is the interesting contexts, progressions, and balance that give the *Kokinshu* its reputation for greatness. Helen Craig McCullough has stated that in following their guidelines, the compilers used "such specific tactics as association by season or other kinds of chronology, by author, by event, by locale, by imagery, by content, by theme, and especially by diction in the broadest sense." Critics have also extolled the compilers' overcoming the challenge of creating an anthology of short verse that does not become wearisome or boring to its readers. Additionally, Robert H. Brower and Earl Miner have praised the contributors to the *Kokinshu* for their use of new words and new imagery. Scholars agree that the *Kokinshu* more than fulfilled its purpose of serving as a reference book for future generations of poets: McCullough has stressed that the *Kokinshu* is "an assertion of national pride and confidence."

PRINCIPAL ENGLISH TRANSLATIONS

Early Japanese Poets: Complete Translation of the Kokinshiu [translated by T. Wakameda] 1922

The Kokin Waka-Shu: The 10ᵗʰ-Century Anthology Edited by the Imperial Edict [translated by H. H. Honda] 1970

Kokinshu: A Collection of Poems Ancient and Modern [translated by Laurel Rasplica Rodd with Mary Catherine Henkenius] 1984

Kokin Wakashu: The First Imperial Anthology of Japanese Poetry [translated by Helen Craig McCullough] 1985

CRITICISM

Ichiro Kobayashi (essay date 1921)

SOURCE: An introduction to *Early Japanese Poets: Complete Translation of the "Kokinshu,"* by T. Wakameda, The Eastern Press Ltd., 1922, pp. xi-xvi.

[*In his introduction (written in 1921) to the Wakameda translation of the* Kokinshu, *Kobayashi advances several reasons why shorter Japanese poems, such as those found in the* Kokinshu, *became far more popular than longer forms of verse.*]

The *Kokinshiu or Poems Ancient and Modern* was published as is seen in its Preface, in the fifth year of Yengi in the reign of the Emperor Daigo, viz., in the year 905 A.D., and fifteen years after the founding of Oxford University. This collection of one thousand poems was selected from those which had been composed during a period of two hundred years after the beginning of the Nara period, with the intention of showing models to those who wished to compose verses. It was edited by order of the Emperor Daigo, the Editors being four of the greatest poets of that day. They were Ki no Tsurayuki, Ki no Tomonori, Ochikochi no Mitsune and Mibu no Tadamine. This was the first time that Japanese poems were edited by order of an emperor; and in the course of three hundred years from this time down to the first stage of the Kamakura period such work was often undertaken. Of all these four

poets, the most excellent was Ochikochi no Mitsune, but the most learned and highest in position was Ki no Tsurayuki. He became chief Editor and wrote the Preface to this collection. In addition, another Preface was written in Chinese by Ki no Yoshimochi, but being nothing but a translation of Tsurayuki's Preface, it was not important.

The first collection of typical poems in Japan is the *Manyoshui*, which appeared towards the close of the Nara period; and the **Kokinshiu** is the second in age. The *Manyoshui* exhibits the features of the verse in the Nara period whilst the characteristics of the poetry in the Heian period are clearly shown in the **Kokinshiu.** Most of the *Manyoshui* poems are simple in diction and express the thoughts direct from both heart and mind, while the **Kokinshiu** poems are generally elegant and graceful in thought. Though the **Kokinshiu** contains some of the poems composed in the Nara period, yet they do not signify the features of that day. This is not surprising for the **Kokinshiu** was originally intended to show models to those who wished to compose verses. There have been many changes in the methods of composing Japanese poetry since these days; but generally speaking, the **Kokinshiu** had been looked upon as a model collection of poems for hundreds of years. Therefore it is most important for those who wish to know Japanese poetry.

The Emperor Daigo was an excellent versifier—nay, and many other Japanese Emperors excelled in poetry. Before founding the capital at Kashiwara, the first Emperor Jimmu subjugated the natives in the neighbourhood: on that occasion he himself composed a song with which he encouraged his men. This poem is mentioned in the ancient history of Japan and handed down to posterity. (It may be called an old song, for it was composed in 662 B.C.) Many of the other emperors, the princes and the court officials composed poetry. And there were some peasants and huntsmen who were fond of composing verse. In such ancient days, of course, they used no special art in making poems, but sang what they actually thought. So these poems have little or no poetical merit, but the elegancy of national spirits can be traced up to such an ancient age. In days of yore, there was little strict distinction between the high and low. Some emperors were of so plebeian taste that when they went out hunting they often talked in verse with peasants. When Chinese learning was imported in abundance and people imitated Chinese institutions troublesome ceremonies arose by degrees and the distinction between the high and low began to assert itself. In the Heian period the emperors and court officials were called "kumo-no-uwabito" or "men above clouds." This was contrary to the intrinsic national traits of Japan, which were simplicity and homeliness, with both of which the emperors treated their people generally. These good qualities later revived among the samurai: the so-called spirit of the samurai was merely the revival of the national traits of the Japanese nation. It will be most interesting to study these national traits by means of Japanese poetry.

The art of composing poetry gradually made progress age after age, until at last many true poets appeared in the Nara period. While the capital of Nara was growing prosperous, art and literature were making great progress; whilst amidst the beautiful fields and mountains splendid edifices arose and the sound of music heard, and those who viewed the moon and blossom and composed poems became more numerous than before.

Japan is a land of scenic beauty. Among the rest, the mountains and rivers at Nara and in its vicinity are like pictures: the sky is blue and clear, the air gentle, the blossoms beautiful, and the birds sing merrily. The Japanese people who dwelt in this atmosphere were specially familiar with nature. They did not look on nature as an external world, but as their intimate friend. It seemed to them as if rivers and mountains had souls of their own, and these souls had communion with them. No wonder that poetry made progress among these people. If we turn over the pages of the *Manyoshiu,* we shall find many valuable poems even in the minor poets, not to speak of Kakinomoto no Hitomaro, Yamabe no Akahito, Yamakami no Okura and Otomo no Yakamochi.

The most notable poems in the *Manyoshiu* are the longer poems. The versification of old days had no definite rules, and the length of a poem was not limited. But towards the Nara period poetry was divided into two classes, longer and shorter poems. The shorter poem consists of thirty-one syllables, while the longer poem consists of stanzas with twelve syllables. A shorter poem will be sufficient to express a bit of thought, but many words will be needed to convey complicated thoughts. So Hitomaro and many other poets spent their energy chiefly on the longer poem. Of course, they composed many excellent shorter poems, but if the longer poems were withdrawn from the *Manyoshiu,* it would lose nine-tenths of its merit. Notwithstanding, in the Heian period the longer poem was completely neglected and all poets paid their full attention to the shorter poem. And the word *uta* has come to mean the shorter poem. It was many, many years after that Kamo no Mabuchi appeared and took pains to revive the longer poem.

There are many reasons for the decay of the longer poem and the shorter poem alone flourished. The first reason is that those who composed poems had become devoid of ideas. It was in the reign of the Emperor Kammu, who was a very able man, that the capital was transferred from Nara to Kyoto. He adopted various methods to make more flourishing the intercourse with China and develop the resources of the eastern part of Japan. It was probably with this object that he transferred the capital to Kyoto. And whenever he had time to spare, the Emperor would go out hunting with his attendants and range over hill and dale. In a word, he was a very plebeian and gallant monarch. However, as some mediocre rulers followed him, the excellent enterprises on the part of the Emperor Kammu ceased, and the Fujiwara family assumed the reins of government. No one, however capable he might be, was appointed to a high office unless he was of the Fujiwara family. They took pains only to increase the prosperity of their family and took negative measures in all other ways. As things went on in this state for a considerable length of time, nobody thought of promoting the national prosperity; and there were few spirited and ambitious men. An indolent atmosphere reigned over all Kyoto. All the rulers grew too self-interested to think of the welfare of the people, who groaned only under the pressure of life and had no time to think of other things. Thus poetry was appreciated only by the court officials, few of whom had great thoughts. So it naturally followed that there was no need of composing long poems. In order to express what they thought the shorter poem was sufficient; for there was no great thinker or poet who wanted a longer form of poetry in which to convey his thoughts.

The second reason is that stress began to be laid on the art of composing poetry. As we have just stated, the Fujiwara family, who had become politically powerful, became luxurious too. They gave little heed to the affairs of state, but whiled away their days, giving banquets in pretence of moon or flower viewing. Their adherents were always present at these feasts and bent upon humouring them. The most refined amusement in such a sumptuous life was verse composing; and they often held *uta-awase or poetical competitions.* At this meeting the verse-composers were divided into two parties, and composed poems on a given theme. These poems were judged by an umpire. When one of these bards turned out the victor, his or her fame was known throughout the court and could often rise to a higher position or rank. These competitions were so intense that some of the competitors actually died from despair. In such ages, it is natural, poetry became rhetorically excellent rather than in thought. And it is inevitable in such an age that the manners between men and women at Court became corrupt, and that they openly talked of intrigues or amours. Lovers composed poems and thus expressed their hearts to each other; and they took great pains to compose verse, for change frequently arose in their love-relation according to the adroitness or clumsiness of the poems. As stress was chiefly laid on art, it would be difficult to adorn a long poem with exquisite epithets. Thus the shorter form of poetry had come in vogue.

The third reason is that Chinese literature had come to be studied. Chinese books had been imported in the

Nara period and became to be read by degrees. And in the Heian period greater grew the number of those who wrote in Chinese prose and verse. Though none of them equalled the Chinese writers, yet those who composed Chinese poems and writings were greatly respected. Consequently, smaller became the number of those who took pains to compose the longer verse.

The fourth reason is that prose had made progress. Japanese prose in the Nara period, compared with poetry, was in a crude condition; but, as Chinese literature was more studied, the more smooth and correct prose became. Poetry became a means of expressing a bit of thought.

For these reasons the longer form of verse had gone downhill. None of the longer poems in the **Kokinshiu** are excellent. This phenomenon was surely a hitch in the development of Japanese poetry; but the shorter verse had made great progress, that is to say, various complicated thoughts are contained in only thirty-one syllables. Few of the *Manyoshiu* poems equal in this point.

The **Kokinshiu** consists of twenty volumes or parts. Of these volumes, six are the *Poems of the Four Seasons* and five the *Poems of Love*. These eleven are thought the most important in the collection. The **Kokinshiu** is a small collection of one thousand poems; but those who study this book minutely will find various suggestions as regards the transition of Japanese thoughts.

Jin'ichi Konishi (essay date 1958)

SOURCE: "Association and Progression: Principles of Integration in Anthologies and Sequences of Japanese Court Poetry, A.D. 900-1350," translated by Robert H. Brower and Earl Miner, *Harvard Journal of Asiatic Studies,* Vol. 21, December, 1958, pp. 67-127.

[*In the following excerpt, Konishi demonstrates that poems in the* Shinkokinshu *were inspired by and developed from poetry in the* Kokinshu.]

. . . The meaning of the title, *Shinkokinshū,* is "New Anthology of Poems Ancient and Modern"—in other words, the "New *Kokinshū.*" In giving their anthology this name, the compilers were consciously expressing a neoclassical ideal and were specifying the source of their inspiration—the *Kokinshū,* or "Anthology of Poems Ancient and Modern," the first collection of Japanese poetry compiled by imperial command early in the tenth century. The *Kokinshū* remained, despite fundamental changes in poetic theory and practice, the almost universally accepted standard of propriety in poetic diction and, to a lesser extent, technique, throughout the history of the Japanese classical tradition. In choosing the name for their anthology, and in raising the image of the older collection through echoings, the

compilers of the *Shinkokinshū* were giving expression to their ideal of recreating in their own age—an age, significantly, of political and social decline for the court aristocracy—the poetic achievement and, by implication, the social brilliance of that more happy period of the *Kokinshū*. We may demonstrate the ways in which these overtones are conveyed by comparing poems 10 through 15 in the *Shinkokinshū* (which have been already quoted above) with poems 17 through 22 in the first book of the *Kokinshū,* a book which is also naturally devoted to spring.

KKS I: 17

. . . Be kind to us,
And do not burn today the withered fields
  Of ancient Kasuga,
For like the young grass sprouting underneath,
She hides there, and I there by her side.

Anonymous

KKS I: 18

. . . O guardian of the fields
Of Tobuhi in ancient Kasuga,
  Come out and look
And tell how many days I still must wait
Until the joyous time to pick young shoots.

Anonymous

KKS I: 19

. . . Deep in the mountains,
Even the snow that fell upon the pines
  Has not begun to melt,
But in the Capital, the fields are thronged
With courtiers gaily picking the young shoots.

Anonymous

KKS I: 20

. . . Today the rains of spring
Spring on us with the suddenness
  Of a far bent bow—
If only they will fall once more tomorrow
So we may soon go out to pick young greens!

Anonymous

KKS I: 21

. . . It was for you
That I went out to the fields of spring
  To pick young shoots,
Though all the while the falling snow
Piled without surcease upon my sleeves.

Emperor Kōkō
(830-887)

KKS I: 22

> . . . Do those girls set forth
> On an excursion for young shoots,
>   That they so gaily wave
> Their white linen sleeves in beckoning
> Towards the fields of ancient Kasuga?
>   Ki no Tsurayuki (d.?945)

A comparison of these six poems with poems 10 through 15 of the *Shinkokinshū* will show that such complexes of images as "picking young shoots in the fields of ancient Kasuga" appear in both sets. It was perhaps inevitable, given the popularity of such images and the annual observance of this social rite, that there should be poems on young shoots in both anthologies. However, the number of poems in each anthology is the same and, what is more important, the same kind of progression is followed in each case. The first poem in each group (*KKS* I: 17 and *SKKS* I: 10) is not properly speaking on the topic of young shoots at all. Each poem is rather an introduction to the series, each prepares the way for those that follow by treating only the young *grass* which had begun to spring up on the fields of Kasuga. The next three poems in each case develop the progress of the actual picking; and the fifth poem in each sequence (*KKS* I: 21 and *SKKS* I: 14) treats the topic in terms of a speaker who has gone out and gathered greens and then makes a present of them to someone who did not go. Finally, the speaker of the sixth poem in each set is a person who, for some reason, did not or could not go on the outing himself.[6]

This evidence seems convincing enough to show that the compilers of the *Shinkokinshū* were consciously attempting to raise the image of the **Kokinshū** at this point in their anthology, and at times this echoing becomes very complex. We must recognize, for example, that Ki no Tsurayuki in the last poem of the group in the **Kokinshū** (*KKS* I: 22) has in turn raised the image of an earlier age with his "fields of ancient Kasuga" and his use of such an old poetic technique as the "pillow word" (*makurakotoba*), or conventional attribute, in the phrase *shirotae no sode,* or "white linen sleeves." This setting and this technique evoke the life and the poetry of the seventh and eighth rather than the late ninth and early tenth centuries when Tsurayuki lived. Thus the reappearance of the "fields of ancient Kasuga" in the *Shinkokinshū,* in a context which echoes by other means the corresponding poems of the **Kokinshū,** means that the readers of the thirteenth century were reminded of the age of the **Kokinshū,** but that this allusion itself alludes to an even more remote and romantic era. Tsurayuki's former evocation of the past mingles with the new evocation, harmonizing three ages of past and present. The identity of the poets within the sequences is also important. The "anonymous" poems, as well as the one by Em-

peror Kōkō, in the **Kokinshū** set are old, in the sense that they employ techniques more "primitive" than those employed in the tenth century—these poems are mostly in the declarative mode characteristic of Japanese poetry of a hundred years or more before the generation of Tsurayuki. The correspondence is not exact, but the poems in the *Shinkokinshū* on the topic of "young shoots" are also for the most part by poets who lived from several hundred years to a generation or two before the time when this anthology was compiled. The fourth and sixth poems in the set (*SKKS* I: 13 and 15) do not fit this rather loose definition, however, and perhaps indeed we are straining a point here. We shall content ourselves, therefore, with simply mentioning the facts and suggesting the possibility that this kind of echoing (which occurs beyond question elsewhere in the anthology) might have been consciously, if imperfectly, attempted in this group of *Shinkokinshū* poems as well.

Despite these astonishing similarities, however, we must be fully aware of the differences which exist between the two sets of poems in the older and the newer collection. The principles of association and progression are already evident in the **Kokinshū,** for example, but not in as thorough or consistent a way as in the *Shinkokinshū.* Thus the first poem in the **Kokinshū** set on "young shoots" (*KKS* I: 17) is principally concerned with the burning of withered fields at winter's end, and may be said to be somewhat too remote from the designated topic. Again, the third poem (*KKS* I: 19) treats the topic in such a way that the courtiers are represented to be already out on their excursion, whereas in the fourth poem (*KKS* I: 20) the young shoots are not yet ready to pick. In other words, these poems are not arranged according to a logically developed time sequence. But in the *Shinkokinshū,* the six poems are all (except the first) clearly on the topic of "young shoots," and the time progression is completely logical and in harmony with the external world. In brief, the poems in the *Shinkokinshū* are far more carefully and consistently arranged than those of the **Kokinshū.** The compilers of the later anthology certainly used the earlier one as their model and their guide, but there is a further significance in the title "New **Kokinshū**": the compilers were not satisfied with mere slavish imitation of their ideal; instead, while following the general outlines laid down in the **Kokinshū,** they obviously attempted to create something "new" and something better than the anthology to which they looked for inspiration.

The "newness" is evident not only in the much greater care taken with the associations and the progression from poem to poem; it is perhaps nowhere more clear than in the appearance in this set of *Shinkokinshū* poems of a personality which is hardly realized at all in the **Kokinshū** group. This is the figure of the "man of elegance," who appears most conspicuously in the second and third poems of the *Shinkokinshū* set (*SKKS* I:

11-12). The notion of "elegance" was perhaps the dominant ideal of both art and life among the aristocrats of Japan in the Heian period (794-1185), and it certainly was already widespread by the time of the **Kokinshū** It was, however, only a century or two later that the concept became realized to such an extent that it was translatable, so to speak, into the terms of poetry. It is not surprising, therefore, that the ideal should be more vividly realized in the *Shinkokinshū*.[7] Like most aristocratic ideals, this one was at once amateurish and esoteric, a glorification of the dilettante with social and philosophical overtones; it is very like Renaissance European ideals of the courtier. Such a man would rope off his fields so that he and his friends might indulge in the elegant, if primitivistic and romantic, activity of picking spring greens, undisturbed by the unwelcome intrusions of the inelegant commoners. Therefore, although this group of poems in the *Shinkokinshū* echoes the similar group in the older anthology, it does so with a difference—an elegance that the compilers have invited us to contrast with that of the anthology on which they patterned theirs but which they were obviously determined to surpass.

Such subtleties in the association and progression of the seasonal poems of the *Shinkokinshū* perhaps make *Tristram Shandy, Ulysses,* or Ezra Pound's *Cantos* seem less uniquely Western or strangely modern than they often seem to be. These same subtle techniques of association and progression are employed in other sections of this anthology such as the love poems (Books XI-XV) or the travel poems (X). There is no need to analyze these sequences to show how they employ the same techniques as the seasonal poems, but they are worth examination for what they show of new techniques.

The love poems are of particular interest in that they are organized in accordance with a kind of time progression which is based entirely upon human concerns and which is more dramatic than that of the seasonal poems; and the poems on travel illustrate still another kind of progression. We shall begin with the love poems, taking as our initial example the first four poems in Book XI.

SKKS XI: 990

  . . . Can it be that I
Shall never see at closer range
  The pure white snow
That glimmers in far Kazuraki
On the peak of Mount Takama?

                      Anonymous

SKKS XI: 991

  . . . Only in story
Had I heard of the waterfalls

Of beauteous Yoshino,
Until this day when my own sleeves
Are moistened with their spray.

                      Anonymous

SKKS XI: 992

  . . . My love is like
The smouldering fires they tend
  Beside their huts
   To frighten deer from ripened grain
   In the fields of distant hills.
         Kakinomoto Hitomaro (fl. c. 680-700)

SKKS XI: 993

  . . . Must I go on,
My love shut up within my breast
  Never to show forth
As do the ears of grain at Wasada
In Furu, land as ancient as the gods?
         Kakinomoto Hitomaro

It may seem surprising that a volume of love poems should begin with what is apparently a seasonal poem on a winter topic. But when this first poem is read in the context of the following verses, its use of the allegorical mode becomes obvious: the speaker of the poem is a man, and the white snow on the peak is his beloved. The poem tells us, further, that although the speaker has seen this woman at a distance, and has fallen in love, he has not yet met her, and we assume that she on her part is unaware of his tender feelings. Such a one-sided beginning was the rule in affairs of the heart at the Japanese court and became a fixed convention in the literary treatment of first love. Each of the poems quoted is, in fact, a variation upon the fixed topic of "love before the first meeting." All of the poems in Books XI and XII of the *Shinkokinshū* are on this, or virtually identical topics, which required a more or less uniform treatment and tone. This shared topic gives these poems a thematic unity. At the beginning of Book XIII, however, there is a progression in the dramatic development of the human relationship, as can be seen in the first poem of this book:

SKKS XIII: 1149

  . . . Since it can scarcely be
That you will remember this road of love
  To the end of our life's journey,
I wish that death would take me now
On this day of new-found happiness.
        The Mother of Gidō Sanshi (fl. c. 980)

This poem was composed on a topic which a Japanese would probably have called "love after the first meeting"—the affair has begun and is in its happy early stages. At the same time, there is foreboding in the poem. Whether or not it was always true in life, it was conventional in the literary treatment of love in this period that the affair should gradually cool and the man become less and less attentive and regular in his visits. At the Japanese court, where polygamy was the norm, it was the common thing for a court noble to keep two or three mistresses or concubines in addition to his consort or lawful wife, and he might also carry on a number of secret affairs as well. These secondary relationships might be formed and broken by the man with more or less casualness, and it was of course the woman who suffered most from the consequences of such an affair. The customs of the day demanded that high-born ladies live in guarded palaces, hidden from the eyes of all men except their husbands or enterprising lovers, and they could seldom leave their cloistered apartments. A woman might be abandoned at any time by her fickle lover, and while he might move on to new and fairer flowers, she must continue her secluded and now empty life until perhaps discovered by some other man, whereupon a new affair might begin its inevitable course.

Such, at least, was the conventional treatment of love in Japanese literature, and it is therefore natural that it should be reflected in the dramatic progression of the love poems in the *Shinkokinshū*. The last half of Book XIV and all of Book XV in fact are devoted to poems which express the woman's suffering as her lover's visits become less frequent. Book XV begins with the following famous poem.

SKKS XV: 1336

. . . The white sleeves covering us,
Glistening with dew and sparkling with our
      tears,
   Are parted by the dawn,
And as we dress, shake in the autumn wind
Which blows its pale color through our
      hearts.[8]

Fujiwara Teika (1162-1241)

We may assume that the parting treated in this poem involves a temporary separation, and that the lover will return. At the same time, the autumn wind is a conventional symbol in Chinese and Japanese poetry for the death of love, and the chill which it blows into the heart is a foreboding of the doom of eternal separation. This theme is developed through Book XV with increasing intensity, and the last poem is an expression of bitter resentment and despair at the lover's infidelity.

The arrangement of the love poems in the *Shinkokinshū* thus follows dramatically the progression of a typical love affair from the first glimpse of the beloved through the successive stages of a passionate courtship, marriage or liaison, disenchantment, separation, and final

despair and loneliness. This provides a clearly defined plot structure which would be inappropriate or impossible for poems on subjects other than love. There are types of association and progression in the poems on travel in Book X, for example, which follow quite different principles, and it is to these poems that we now turn.

Although the poems in Book X do not appear to be arranged according to any common topical element, this is not by any means to say that the arrangement is haphazard, for instead of the time progression of the seasonal poems or the plot development of the love poems, the sequence of the poems on travel appears to have been designed to show—incredible as it may seem—the historical development of Japanese poetry through the centuries. That is to say, close study reveals that the poems are arranged in several large groups which represent in chronological sequence the four major periods in classical poetry down to the age of the *Shinkokinshū*. Specifically, of the total of ninety-four poems in Book X, the first six (*SKKS* X: 896-901) are by poets of the so-called "Man'yō period" (c. A. D. 500-750), the early great age of literary Japanese poetry. Following this group is a single anonymous verse which might be called transitional in that it is in a style characteristic of the late eighth and early ninth centuries, the age between the two great periods of the *Man'yōōshu* on the one hand and the **Kokinshū** on the other. The next group of five poems (*SKKS* X: 903-907) is from the age of the **Kokinshū** proper, and this is followed by a sequence of twenty-four poems which range in date from the mid-tenth to the late eleventh centuries; in other words, they belong to the period spanned by six imperial anthologies, beginning with the second anthology, the *Gosenshū* (c. 951), and ending with the seventh, the *Senzaishū* (c. 1188). The last fifty-eight poems (*SKKS* X: 932-989) are contemporary, which is to say they are by poets of the late twelfth and early thirteenth centuries, the age of the *Shinkokinshū* itself.

There is no doubt that the audience of the *Shinkokinshū* period who read through this volume was aware of this chronological sequence by literary periods, and that this sequence contributed to their pleasure. But there are also in this volume other techniques of association and progression which involve topics, treatment, and imagery. The twelve poems with which the volume begins illustrate these more detailed techniques.

SKKS X: 896

. . . If I abandon my village
Of Asuka, where birds are said to soar,
   For a new capital,
Will it be that I shall nevermore
See you present by my side?

Empress Gemmyō (661-721)

SKKS X: 897

  . . . Longing for my love,
I gaze forth across the pines
  Of Waka's forest,
And see that over the strand of Shiohi
The cranes fly off with mournful cries.
                Emperor Shōmu (701-756)

SKKS X: 898

  . . . Come along, lads!
Let us quickly make our way home
  Towards the Rising Sun—
The pines on the shore at Mitsu in ōtomo
Must wait impatiently for our return.
            Yamanoe Okura (?660-?733)

SKKS X: 899

  . . . As I come rowing
Over the long sea-path from wilds
  Distant as the sky,
Through the Straits of Akashi
The Isles of Yamato come into view.
         Kakinomoto Hitomaro (fl. c. 680-700)

SKKS X: 900

  . . . Because I come
From parting with the wife I love,
  The leaves of rough bamboo
Seem to fill these mountain depths
With their mournful rustling sound.[9]
              Kakinomoto Hitomaro

SKKS X: 901

  . . . Having come this far,
I ask, "Where is Tsukushi now?"
  It seems to lie
Back to the West beyond those hills
Where the white clouds trail away.
             Ōtomo Tabito (665-731)

SKKS X: 902

  . . . Do you walk
Alone along the narrow path
  Across the peaks,
Your robe not yet dried out
From its drenching in the morning mists?
                Anonymous

SKKS: X: 903

  . . . How can the smoke
That rises from the Peak of Asama
  In this country of Shinano

Fail to strike the people far and near
With amazement at the sight?
           Ariwara Narihira (825-880)

SKKS X: 904

  . . . Not in a reality
As real as these hills of Utsu
  That rise in Suruga,
Nor even in the unreal world of dreams,
Can I meet face to face with her I love.[10]
             Ariwara Narihira

SKKS X: 905

  . . . The evening wind
Binds with cold the roadside grass
  That pillows me—
If only I might ask for shelter in that house
That sounds with mallets fulling cloth.
          Ki no Tsurayuki (d.?945)

SKKS X: 906

  . . . I hope this day
That I shall cross the distant bridge
  That hangs across
The gulf between those mountain peaks
Now draped in streamers of white clouds.
             Ki no Tsurayuki

SKKS X: 907

  . . . Am I then doomed
To pass my life in low estate,
  While you rise high
To lofty peaks concealed by clouds
Like Mount Saya on my Eastern way?
         Mibu no Tadamine (fl. c. 877-922)

Although it may not be immediately apparent, the first six of these poems share a common topic which is more specific than mere "travel"—a topic which might be paraphrased as "longing for absent loved ones." At the same time, these six poems are linked still more closely through associations of images from poem to poem, just as in the spring poems which we have already examined. To begin with, the phrase "soaring bird" in the first poem is a pillow-word associated in this case with the place name Asuka. So dulled had this and other such phrases become through long usage that by the thirteenth century they had lost most of their imagistic freshness, and the technique of the pillow-word appears in the poetic practice of the time largely as a neoclassical device for creating a heightened solemnity of tone. But such an expression, no matter how dulled by familiarity, is potentially an image; and when we read the second poem, with its image of cranes flying across the bay, the "soaring bird" of the first poem springs to renewed poetic life, and at the same time provides the association that links the two poems.

The image of the pine forest in the second poem leads us smoothly to the pine-fringed beach in the third, and, further, the movement suggested by the "soaring bird" in the first, and the flight of the cranes in the second poem, provides the impetus to "carry" the reader across the sea to China, which is the setting of the third poem. We should note, too, that in the first three poems we have progressed from an inland setting to the seacoast, and then across the sea. Our direction is at the same time reversed, however, for the movement back to the shores of Japan already begins in this third poem. The overt link between the third and fourth poems is the appearance in each of a poetic term for Japan—the Rising Sun in the third, and Yamato in the fourth—but there is also the imagery of a ship and the sea which, while only implied in the situation of the third poem, is raised in the fourth with its image of rowing. In addition, such images as "strand" (*kata*), "beach" (*hama*) and "straits" (*to*) in the second, third and fourth poems are related in terms of what might be called a category of "sea phenomena."[11]

The change in the situation of the speaker from sea to land is foreshadowed in the fourth poem, with its image of the "isles of Yamato." We may imagine that the speaker of this poem sees from his boat the outlines of the mountains of Japan against the sky, and that there is in this poem submerged or implied imagery of mountains. This provides a link with the fifth poem, where mountains are specifically mentioned. The mountain image of course recurs in the sixth poem, and provides the association between this and the preceding one.

The next seven poems (*SKKS* X: 901-907) are all obviously associated through the imagery of mountains, except for the tenth, which to the Western reader must appear to lack the requisite imagery. However, if the Japanese text is compared with that of the preceding poem (*SKKS* X: 904), it will be seen that the verb *utsu* "to full cloth" in the tenth poem is homophonous with the place name Utsu, the mountainous region of Suruga province mentioned in the ninth poem. In the context of the arrangement of poems in the *Shinkokinshū*, therefore, the verb *utsu* in the tenth poem is a "pivot word" (*kakekotoba*): it carries two meanings, one of which is applicable to the part of the poem which precedes it, and the second to the part that follows. Consequently, the house in the tenth verse is really "that house *in Utsu* that sounds with mallets fulling cloth," and the place name thus suggested also raises the image of the mountains with which the place is associated.

There are also other, less sustained patterns of images by which the association from poem to poem is strengthened. The image of clouds (*kumo*) in the sixth, and

mist (*kiri*) in the seventh poem are words which were traditionally associated by the Japanese poets as members of the same "category of phenomena." This kind of association was particularly important in the technique and practice of the *renga*, or "linked verse," which began to flourish some hundred years or so after the *Shinkokinshū* was compiled, and names came to be given by the *renga* poets to the different categories which they recognized. Therefore, to borrow a term from the technical vocabulary of this later poetic genre, the images of clouds, dew, and the like are "rising phenomena" (*sobikimono*)—moisture or vapor which rises into the air and dissipates itself. Once this category is recognized, the association between the "mist" of the seventh poem and the "smoke" (*keburi*) of the eighth can be accepted, since smoke, like clouds and mist, is a "rising phenomenon."

There is a further link between the seventh and eighth poems. This association is not immediately apparent because it involves a conventional symbolic value attached to a given expression but one which had not been evoked by the poet for the immediate purposes of this particular poem. Specifically, the image of the wet robe (*nurenishi koromo*) in the seventh poem is frequently used as a conventional symbol for the indignation of a lover falsely accused of infidelity. Such is not its function in this poem, but looked at in connection with the verb *mitogamu* "to regard with amazement" in the eighth poem, its symbolic meaning is inevitably raised for an instant, because the verb *mitogamu* is a traditional *engo* or word association for the "wet robe" in its metaphorical sense. This kind of association is quite different from that of the related images of mountains, clouds, fog and the like which we find in this group of poems, for the symbol of the indignant lover has no function either in the poem in which it is used or in the developing pattern of associations in this sequence of poems. As a purely mechanical device for linking the two poems, however, it must be recognized, and although we moderns may find such a technique rather forced, the audience of the thirteenth century probably felt it to be very clever and interesting.

The eighth and ninth poems share the central term, "people/person" (*hito*), although the association is not close because of the great difference in relationship between the people mentioned and the speaker of each poem; the "people" in the eighth poem are strangers, whereas the "person" in the ninth is the speaker's beloved. A much closer association is found in the use in each verse of a famous mountain—the Peak of Asama in the eighth and the hills of Utsu in the ninth poem. These and other names of famous mountains, rivers, and the like came through tradition to possess a quasi-imagistic status, and were bound to evoke in the minds of poet and audience similar associations of romantic beauty. It will be noted further that in each of these poems the name of a province is mentioned—Shinano in the first, and Suruga in the second—and this provides an additional association of related categories.

The ninth and tenth poems are associated, as we have said, through the device of the pivot-word on Utsu/ *utsu;* there is an additional link in the conventional word-association of "dream" (*yume*) in the ninth and "pillow" (*makura*) in the tenth. The same device links the tenth and eleventh verses, where the word-association is found in "wind" (*kaze*) and "streamers" (*tana-biku,* lit., "to trail"). The association between this latter pair of poems, however, is one of total situations as well as discrete elements, and there is a progression from the one to the other in this respect. The time of the tenth poem is evening, and the speaker has lain down upon the ground to spend the cold night under the open sky; in the eleventh poem, it is early morning, and by accepting the speaker as the same person in both cases, we imagine the traveler rising from his bed of grass and gazing out across the mountains in contemplation of the day's journey that lies ahead.

The images of clouds and mountains provide the principal points of detailed association between the eleventh and twelfth poems. It should be pointed out finally, however, that the ninth through the twelfth poems are associated in terms of shared rhetorical techniques as well as those other elements which have been discussed. That is to say, the first two lines in the ninth poem are a "preface" (*jo* or *jokotoba*) for the word *utsutsu* "in reality," and serve to anticipate this word through the identity of sound in the first two syllables of the latter and in the place name, "Utsu," in the "preface." The tenth poem is related on the same basis of rhetorical technique. *Kusamakura,* "pillow of grass," suggests the latent meaning in the *yū* ("to bind up"— the grass for a pillow) of *yūkaze,* "evening wind."

The third line of the eleventh poem is a pillow-word, which is similar in technique and feeling to the preface, though more conventional and usually shorter. Like the preface, it is characteristic of early Japanese poetry, and in the context of this sequence of poems it sustains both the romantic atmosphere of association with a bygone age and the effect of unity achieved through the use of similar rhetorical devices in successive poems. We discover another preface in the first two lines of the twelfth poem, where the word *sayaka* in the third line is "introduced" through the identity of sound in its first two syllables and in the place name "Saya."

The foregoing analyses of sequences from the seasonal, love, and travel poems will serve to show that although the overall unifying principles of progression may differ in the individual books of the *Shinkokinshū,* depending upon the subjects of the poems and the appropriateness to these of different types of organization, the association in detail of images and rhetorical tech-

niques is a constant principle which governs the choice and arrangement of all the poems in the anthology. The labor involved in such a careful and painstaking attempt to achieve an overall unity of structure and harmony of detail among disparate elements must have been prodigious. Such effort would not have been expended unless association and progression answered to the desire of the age for techniques which would create long lyric sequences from the individual poems written by the poets of the age or inherited from a valued literary tradition. The problem of the motivation behind this desire can best be solved by showing how this literary principle was developed and gradually refined in the earlier imperial anthologies before the *Shinkokinshū,* and by tracing it to its ultimate origins.

III *Integration in the Imperial Anthologies Preceding the* Shinkokinshū

With its status as the first and most influential of the imperial anthologies, the **Kokinshū** is clearly the place to begin. To facilitate comparison, we shall again begin by quoting the first few poems from the first book— "Spring"—to see how it exemplifies association and progression.

KKS I: 1

. . . The Old Year not yet gone,
The longed for spring has come at last
  Yet brought confusion—
For are we now to say "last year,"
Or should we rather say "this year?"
          Ariwara Motokata (888-953)

KKS I: 2

. . . Will the wind
That gently blows on this first day of spring
  Melt perhaps the ice
To which was changed the water of the stream
That wet my sleeves in summer when I drank?
          Ki no Tsurayuki (d.?945)

KKS I: 3

. . . Where does it rise,
The haze that is the sign of spring?
  In lovely Yoshino,
Yes, here upon the hills of Yoshino,
The winter snows still fall.
          Anonymous

KKS I: 4

. . . Amidst the snow
The long-awaited spring has come—
  Will they melt today,

Those tears shed by the warbler crying
And turned to ice in winter's cold?
                          Empress Takako (fl. 858-882)

KKS I: 5

  . . . Although the warbler,
Who is the harbinger of spring,
  Has already come
And perches singing in the plum tree
Amongst the branches, the snow still falls.
                          Anonymous

As these first poems indicate, the seasonal poems in the *Kokinshū* set the pattern for a progressive topical development based on the passage of time. In the first two books of the anthology, the spring topics follow one another in harmony with external nature from the beginning of the season (poems 1-16), through "picking young shoots" (17-22); "new growth in the fields and hills" (23-27); "spring birds" (28-31); "plum blossoms" (32-48); "blossoming cherries" (49-68); "falling cherry blossoms" (69-118); "wisteria in bloom" (119-120); "blooming of the yellow mountain rose" (121-125); and the "passing of spring" (126-134). The same kind of arrangement is also to be found in the poems on summer in Book III, autumn in books IV and V, and winter in Book VI.

An examination of the love poems, which are found in Books XI through XV of the *Kokinshū*, also yields similar results: the poems are arranged by similar topics in accordance with the development of an affair from "love yet undeclared" (469-551), through such phases as courtship (552-615), love after the first meeting (616-704), the lover's growing coolness (705-746), and the ending of the affair in bitterness and misery (747-828). It would be possible to divide these larger topical categories into several lesser ones, but what has been said is probably sufficient to show that the love poems in the *Kokinshū* are arranged in a kind of dramatic plot structure very much like that later realized in the *Shinkokinshū*.

At the same time, although there appears on the surface to be no marked difference between the *Kokinshū* and the *Shinkokinshū*, at least as far as the seasonal and love poems are concerned, there are two important points to be made. The first is that a smooth association and transition from poem to poem in terms of images, rhetoric, and the like is not nearly so carefully contrived in the *Kokinshū*. One example of this lack of attention to such matters is to be found in the first two in the series of spring poems which have just been quoted. Because these poems are both on the same topic—the arrival of spring—they can hardly fail to have at least that much in common, and we therefore cannot say that they are completely unrelated. Nevertheless, if it had been the intention of the compliers to

provide a really smooth and harmonious shift from the first poem to the second, with its images of "sleeves," "water," "wind" and the like, it would have been possible to find without great difficulty a more suitable poem to use in place of the first one. The fact that this was not done leads us to conclude that the compilers of the *Kokinshū* were not in this case very deeply concerned with a harmonious association of images from the first poem to the second. The same observation holds true for the relationship between the second and third poems, and could be made repeatedly concerning given sequences of poems throughout the anthology. On the other hand, the succession of images from the third through the fifth poems ("haze," "mountains," and "snow" in poem 3; "snow," "warbler," and "plum" in poem 5) is relatively smooth, so that we cannot say that no effort at all was made to produce this effect of harmony. In other words, although a progression in terms of a logical sequence of topics was consciously carried out in the *Kokinshū*, the association of images from poem to poem was attempted only spasmodically, and no effort was made to give unity to entire books of poems through the consistent application of this principle.

The second point that must be brought out is that even development in a progressive sequence according to poetic topics is actually to be found only in the seasonal poems (Books I-VI) and the love poems (Books XI-XV) in the *Kokinshū*. In the other volumes of the anthology, whether for example those devoted to congratulatory poems (Book VII), those to poems on parting (Book VIII), or those to travel poems (Book IV), there is no evidence at all of any attempt to arrange the poems according to any set pattern of topical development. The reason for the relative lack of attention given to these books by the compilers may perhaps be that they were considered of secondary importance. It should be pointed out in this connection that the arrangement of the twenty books of the *Kokinshū* reflects a clear distinction between different grades of what may be called "formal" and "informal" poetry. Formal poetry was intended for the eyes or the ears of a relatively large audience, and required a greater degree of technical polish; informal poetry was, ostensibly at least, a mode of private communication between a poet and his mistress or friends, and might be written with less complex techniques. In the *Kokinshū*, the first ten books are devoted to formal, and the second ten to informal poetry; and within these two major categories the seasonal poems appear to have been considered the most important variety of formal, and the love poems the most important variety of informal verse. Less care was expended for the arrangement of poems on other subjects and no attempt was made to arrange them according to a topical progression or time sequence.[12] It is true that a few scattered groups of poems in these "secondary volumes" show evidence of some attempt to achieve an associational progression of related images, but it is clear that no great store was set by the result. In other words, the principles of association and progression so carefully followed throughout the *Shin-kokinshū* are only partially and rather carelessly applied in the **Kokinshū**. At the same time, however, the earliest attempt to apply these principles to an anthology of Japanese poetry, albeit in a rather rudimentary fashion, can be traced to this first imperial collection.

A study of the topical arrangement of poems in the six imperial anthologies that fall between the **Kokinshū** and the *Shinkokinshū* reveals a situation very similar to that which we have found in the **Kokinshū**. That is, a topical progression according to the passage of time is limited to the seasonal and love poems in these collections, and no attempt is made to give any such overall unity to the other volumes or the anthology as a whole. On the other hand, we observe an increasing concern with the problem of achieving a smooth transition from poem to poem through associations of images, rhetorical techniques, and the like. Such an attempt, while by no means so overriding a consideration as it was to become in the *Shinkokinshū*, is made with increasing seriousness and consistency in each successive anthology—the later the collection, the more conspicuous this phenomenon becomes. The first six poems in the *Senzaishū* (1188), the seventh imperial anthology and immediate predecessor of the *Shinkokinshū*, will illustrate the point.

SZS I: 1

. . . As I gaze far out,
I see that spring has come this morning,
  For today the haze
Begins to rise across the moor
Of Ashita and its morning fields.
          Minamoto Shunrai (d. 1129)

SZS I: 2

. . . At Mount Mimuro
Has spring now at last arrived
  Deep in the valleys?
The water melting underneath the snow
Taps impatiently against the rocks.
          Minamoto Kuninobu (1069-1111)

SZS I: 3

. . . Even to Yoshino
The spring has come where winter drifts
  Blocked up the path
Leading steeply to my mountain village,
And no visitor's footprint marked the snow.
          Lady Taiken Mon in Horikawa
                        (fl. c. 1130-1145)

SZS I: 4

. . . I hated them,
For they would block the visitor's path
  To my mountain village,
But still their melting fills me with regret,
These snowdrifts of the year just past.
          Ōe no Masafusa (1041-1111)

SZS I: 5

. . . Now that spring begins,
From underneath the snowdrifts
  Streams of water flow,
And the warbler in the valley
This moment breaks into his song.
          Fujiwara Akitsuna (1029-1103)

SZS I: 6

. . . Is it because
The warbler knows that spring has come
  To this mountain village,
That even before the haze appears
He sings atop my brushwood fence?
          Minamoto Takakuni (1004-1077)

Topically, these poems seem to follow a regular progression from what might be called the "onset of spring" into "early spring," and the association of images seems to develop smoothly from poem to poem as the setting shifts from the plains to the mountains and from poem country to an isolated village. On closer examination, however, it may strike us that the position of the fifth poem is somehow wrong. First, the subject of this poem is the first day of spring, whereas in the fourth poem we have already moved beyond this point in the time progression. Second, and more important than this, the description of streams of water from melting snow in mountain valleys is very similar in the second and fifth poems. Therefore from both considerations—time sequence of topics, and close association of imagery—the most logical position for poem 5 would seem to be between the second and third poems. On the other hand, we can find some justification for the placing of this fifth poem in the order to which the compiler assigned it: its imagery of mountains and snow associates it with poem 4, and it introduces the warbler, which becomes the principal image in poem 6. No doubt it was these considerations which led to placing this poem in the position in which we find it today, but it must still be admitted that the topical sequence and progression of images is somewhat rough at this point.

In a situation of this kind, the compilers of the *Shinkokinshū* would have laid primary emphasis upon smoothness of association and progression, and would even have chosen a less "outstanding" poem in place of this fifth one if thereby a more felicitous progression could have been effected. However, when the *Senzaishū* was compiled, the principles of association and progression had not yet been accepted by the poetic elite to be more important even than high quality in each individual poem, and the compiler would not have felt free to reject a good poem simply because another one, less good, would make for a smoother sequence of images. Thus, although the same kinds of principles are followed in the arrangement of poems in both the *Senzaishū* and the *Shinkokinshū,* these principles are applied with much greater consistency and thoroughness in the *Shinkokinshū;* in many instances they outweigh even those considerations of high individual quality which down to this time had been the principal standard for the inclusion of poems in an imperial anthology.

IV. *The Origins and Development of Association and Progression*

Since, as we have seen, the principles of association and progression are found as early as the first imperial anthology of Japanese poetry, the **Kokinshū,** we may ask whether the compilers of this collection did not themselves borrow these principles from some earlier poetic source or develop them by analogy with other art forms. All available evidence suggests that the **Kokinshū** was indeed the first such anthology, for neither in the *Man'yōōshū* nor in the anthologies of China do we find any such arrangement of poems. We do discover in the field of painting, however, conventions which are very similar in effect. By this we mean the techniques employed in the horizontal picture scroll (*emakimono*), in which a given subject is developed continuously from scene to scene in chronological sequence. Sometimes, to be sure, narrative or descriptive passages were inserted at various points to explain the incidents depicted in the scrolls, but frequently the events were portrayed entirely through a continuous series of pictures. In either case, one of the outstanding characteristics of this art form was the continuity of the total sequence. Even though the flow might be sometimes broken by written passages, most of the individual scenes were not set off by frames or other devices, but blended into one continuous linear progression; clouds, mountains, or other natural scenery and even scattered human figures provided a unifying thread connecting the more concentrated scenes of separate incidents in the narrative.

The similarity between the chronological development of scenes in the picture scrolls and the temporal progression in the **Kokinshū** and other imperial anthologies is obvious, but a further analogy suggests itself between the continuous flow of scenery and figures in the scrolls and the association of images and rhetorical devices that link the separate poems in the anthologies. It is tempting to conjecture that a familiarity with the conventions of the picture scroll may have suggested

to the compilers of the **Kokinshū** the desirability of applying these techniques to an anthology of poems. The great age of the picture scrolls, especially those which treat secular subjects, extended from the eleventh through the sixteenth century, however; and since almost no examples survive from an earlier period, we do not know the extent to which such scrolls may have existed and been appreciated by the court nobility of the early tenth century, when the **Kokinshū** was compiled. At the same time, one famous example, the *Kako Genzai Ingakyō,* or "Sutra on Causality Between Past and Present," has come down from the eighth century. This religious scroll is different from the later genre of the *emakimono* in that it is divided horizontally into a continuous written text along the bottom half and a continuous series of pictures illustrating episodes from the text along the top. However, although it is regarded as a somewhat crude ancestor of the great lay scrolls of subsequent centuries, this illustrated sutra shows in its graphic portion the basic narrative conventions of the form: a given number of episodes in the legendary life of the Buddha depicted in a continuous series of pictures in chronological sequence. There is little doubt that the secular *emakimono* developed from such illustrated religious texts as this, and even though the first lay scrolls may have been painted somewhat later than the **Kokinshū** age, numerous illustrated Buddhist scriptures, no longer extant, were undoubtedly available to the aristocracy of the time. Through familiarity with such scrolls, the compilers of the **Kokinshū** may have become accustomed to the convention of narration through a chronological sequence of tableaux which, though separate, are depicted in a single continuum.

Whether or not the poets of the tenth century derived the notions of progression and association from the *emakimono,* their application of these techniques to a series of poems was quite original and unprecedented. Furthermore, as we have seen, it was primarily the techniques of progression through time that were used in the arrangement of the seasonal poems and the love poems in the **Kokinshū**—the various techniques of association through images and rhetoric had apparently not yet been developed to the point of consistent application. Consequently, the consistency as well as the increasing variety and complexity with which the techniques of progression are combined with techniques of association in the *Shinkokinshū* leads us to look to other sources outside the successive imperial anthologies for elements that contributed to this process of refinement.

It is probable that the increasing attention given to the linking of successive poems in the imperial anthologies through image and other associations reflects a growing concern with such matters in other kinds of sequences than those of the great collections. The genre which immediately suggests itself is the *hyakushuuta,* or "hundred-poem sequence," a series of *tanka* composed on a given number of topics by an individual poet. This genre was a formal one, in that it was intended to be read and appreciated by an audience of peers, and it shows in its most usual form the influence of the imperial anthologies in the sequence and kind of topics. But the important characteristic of the hundred-poem sequence was that it was composed and judged as a single artistic unit: praise or criticism was accorded a given sequence not on the basis of the merits of the individual poems, but in terms of the overall effect of harmony, beauty, variety, and smoothness conveyed by the sequence as a whole.

The practice of composing hundred-poem sequences certainly existed by the middle of the tenth century, and we find in the personal collections of the poet Minamoto Shigeyuki (fl. c. 970-1000) and Sone no Yoshitada (fl. c. 985) examples of the genre.[13] However it was not until the twelfth and thirteenth centuries that the hundred-poem sequence became really popular among the aristocracy, and the beginning of this later vogue may be traced to the so-called *Horikawa Hyakushu,* or "Hundred-Poem Sequences Submitted by Command of the Ex-Emperor Horikawa," which were composed between 1099 and 1103 by sixteen of the most prominent poets.[14]

The first poet to apply the techniques of association of images in the hundred-poem sequence may well have been Sone no Yoshitada, for in both of his two surviving sequences we find such techniques. Yoshitada was, however, a poet who was unappreciated and even scorned in his own day, and perhaps because the other poets of his time had not yet come to appreciate the esthetic possibilities of association, we do not find it employed in other hundred-poem sequences until the end of the twelfth century. The reappearance of the technique in this later period was probably not due to a "discovery" and imitation of Yoshitada's technique, but rather to the elaboration of topics and categories in certain kinds of sequences.

The most usual kind of hundred-poem sequence was a kind of miniature imperial anthology in its arrangement and distribution of topics: ordinarily it began with twenty poems on spring, followed by ten on summer, twenty on autumn, ten on winter, twenty on love, and twenty on so-called miscellaneous topics. Towards the end of the twelfth century, however, sets of poems with much more detailed topical divisions began to be composed. We find, for example, a sequence composed in 1200 by the Ex-Emperor Go-Toba (1180-1239) which consists of five poems each on the following specific rather than the usual more general topics: haze, the warbler, cherry blossoms (spring); the *hototogisu,* early summer rain (summer); flowers and plants, the moon, autumn foliage (autumn); snow, ice (winter); Shintō, Buddhism, dawn, dusk, mountain roads, the seaside, the Imperial Palace, entertainments, annual observances,

and felicitations (miscellaneous).[15] All of these specific topics are, it will be noted, either images in themselves, or require, as in the case of "annual observances," that a common imagery of setting be conventionally used in their treatment. A natural and almost inevitable result is that every poem in each group of five would be associated with the other members of the group through the same or related images. Such sequences as this appear to have enjoyed a kind of vogue from the end of the twelfth through the beginning of the thirteenth century, and many examples of them have been preserved.[16] Although they represent only one of several possible methods of organizing and classifying the necessary hundred poems, it may still be conjectured that they influenced other varieties, and that the result was a re-emergence of those techniques of imagistic association that were at first perhaps unconsciously, but later consciously, employed.

Such an assumption is borne out by a study of the hundred-poem sequences of the late twelfth and thirteenth centuries classified according to the usual more general categories of spring, summer, autumn, and so on. For although practice varies with individual poets, we find that in most cases the same poet has composed some sequences in which no attempt at association is made and others in which the poems are linked through deliberate associations of imagery.[17] There is, however, one significant exception—the work of the Ex-Emperor Go-Toba. In all of his extant sequences, each successive poem is linked with the preceding one through association of images.[18] This fact seems of particular importance because of Go-Toba's relation to the *Shinkokinshū:* although this anthology was nominally compiled by a group of five courtiers headed by Fujiwara Teika, their function was in reality only that of assistants or advisers to Go-Toba, and it was the Ex-Emperor himself who was the chief compiler and had the final say in the selection or rejection of poems. Therefore we may conclude that the application of techniques of association in such thorough fashion in the *Shinkokinshū* was a reflection of Go-Toba's own taste and preference for these techniques.[19]

In addition to the techniques of association, there was another feature of the hundred-poem sequences which probably exerted a considerable influence upon the way in which the progression was handled in the imperial anthologies, and again particularly in the *Shinkokinshū.* Because the hundred-poem sequence was intended to be appreciated as a single artistic whole, the overall effect of harmony and balance, variety, and contrast was therefore of greatest importance. In producing the desired impression, a conscious effort was made to vary the pace and avoid monotony within the progression by creating a certain number of high and low points. The high points were individual poems which were striking or remarkable for technical or other reasons, and the effect of such poems might be considered to last longer in the minds of the audience if they were placed next to more mediocre poems which would create no strong impression. In other words, the poet would deliberately include a certain number of bland or "easy" poems at crucial points in his sequence so as to enhance the effect of the more interesting ones and create a general impression of sinuous, undulating flow. By analogy with a piece of woven material, the "easy" verses were called *ji no uta* or "background poems," and the more striking ones were known as *mon no uta* or "design poems": just as the effect of beauty in a piece of material is made more striking when a pattern is contrasted against a plain or neutral background, so with a sequence of poems.

Just when this esthetic principle began to be consciously applied to the hundred-poem sequence is not certain, but we find the term *ji no uta,* or "background poem," employed without definition in one of the poetical treatises of the Ex-Emperor Go-Toba. This is probably some indication that the principle had been current for some time, and that the terms "design poem" and "background poem" were assumed by Go-Toba to be meaningful to his readers. Therefore, although Go-Toba's treatise was presumably written some years after the *Shinkokinshū* was compiled, it is perfectly reasonable to assume that the principle had been known and more or less generally accepted before this anthology was completed.[20] At any rate, such an assumption is helpful in explaining the apparent anomaly of finding in the *Shinkokinshū* a number of poems which could only have been considered bland or mediocre by the prevailing standards of the age. In other words, the inclusion of a number of such poems in this collection was not simply the result of a dearth of suitable materials, nor was it simply an inevitable result of placing paramount importance on the achievement of a smooth transition from poem to poem. On the contrary, the technique appears to have been deliberately used in order to create variety, contrast, and alterations of pace within the progression, and, on the model of the hundred-poem sequences, to apply the principle of "design" and "background" even at the expense of uniformly high quality in an imperial anthology.

Unfortunately, there are no extant treatises on poetics in which the theory of design and background in sequences of Japanese poems is discussed, and there remains the question of how such a concept came to suggest itself to the poets of the twelfth and thirteenth centuries and why it was accepted as a valid esthetic principle. The answer probably lies in part at least in a natural response to the problem of monotony or sameness inevitably posed by a series of *tanka* intended to be read as a single unit. On the other hand, it may be suggested that a considerable influence in shaping the principle was exerted by the theory and practice of a very different literary genre, the formal prose essay. This esteemed prose genre was highly complex, first

because all formal essays and official documents had to be composed in Chinese, and secondly because the proper style of composition required the mastery of numerous rules and techniques. Nevertheless, like the French of English courts of law or the Latin of the humanists, the Chinese language was the only medium considered proper for official documents, both secular and religious, from the eighth to the middle of the nineteenth century in Japan; and this difficult medium had to be learned by court officials and priests—in other words, by the same group who composed hundred-poem sequences and compiled imperial anthologies.

During the four hundred years from the tenth to the thirteenth centuries, it was the official written style of the T'ang dynasty (618-907) in China which was followed as the model for Japanese state papers. This style was particularly complex, and both in China and Japan a number of handbooks were compiled as aids to composition and study. Though none of these has survived in China, at least one Japanese copy of a late ninth or early tenth-century Chinese rule book exists, and a number of manuals written by Japanese were in existence by the twelfth century, of which the *Sakumon Daitai,* or *Essentials for Composing Formal Prose,* by Nakamikado Munetada (1061-1141) is a typical example.[21] The most striking aspect of the practice of the formal essay, and that which seems to relate it to the integration of poetic sequences, was the combination of two distinct kinds of style in a single essay. The first of these consisted of a rhetorically ornate, rhymed, parallel prose, which was reserved for the most important sections of the essay, while the second style, used in the less important passages, was what might be called ordinary prose, in that meter, rhyme, antithesis, and the like were not used. Both styles were employed alternately in the same essay, and a conscious effort was made to distribute the passages in ordinary prose in such a way as to enhance the impression created by the more elegant and ornate sections.

Obviously this practice of alternation of styles resembles very closely the effect of background and design aimed at in the hundred-poem sequences and finally in the imperial anthologies, and it is quite possible that in the techniques of the formal essay we have the original concept which was gradually adapted to the poetic sequences. It should also be pointed out that the Japanese literati became more than ever scrupulous about strict adherence to the rules of formal essay-writing just at the time—around the beginning of the twelfth century—when the hundred-poem sequences began to come into vogue. The lack of a written poetics for the sequences makes it impossible to state categorically that the inclusion of mediocre verses in the earlier ones was not due simply to lack of talent on the part of the poet. However, the historical facts as they have been described indicate that this is highly unlikely, and it would appear, rather, that the most probable historical development was an introduction of the technique of "design" and "background" through the stylistics of the Chinese essay, followed by a conscious adaptation of this esthetic to the hundred-poem sequence, and finally its application to an imperial anthology like the *Shinkokinshū*.

The notion of improving the overall quality of an anthology of poems by including the bad along with the good may seem doubtful practice to the Westerner—surely the consistent application of absolute standards of quality should yield better results. But the integrated beauty of the *Shinkokinshū* speaks for itself, and to the Japanese of the thirteenth century, a long tradition of Buddhist teaching had made clear that absolute standards were an illusion. The central concept of the Tendai sect—the sect whose teachings were most influential among the early medieval aristocracy—was that no phenomenon exists independently in and of itself, but only in complex relation to all other phenomena. This was true of abstract values as well as of anything else; "good" and "bad" did not exist as absolutes, but only in terms of specific situations, and a "bad" act might be "good" if it proved to be a cause that brought the individual closer to final enlightenment. This does not mean that such a general philosophical outlook was a direct cause for the development of the particular literary practice we have been considering. But it helps explain how the medieval Japanese poets could accept without any sense of anomaly the notion that a "bad" poem could be "good" in a given context if its effect was to enhance the overall effect of the interrelated parts of a poetic sequence. . . .

Notes

. . . [6]While it might be thought that the compilers of the *Shinkokinshū* may have had in mind as a pattern one of the similar sequences to be found in all of the six anthologies that intervene between the *Kokinshū* and this eighth anthology, examination shows that either the number of poems is different, or where, as in the *Gosenshū*, the number is the same, the images and patterns of progression differ from those in the *Kokinshū* and *Shinkokinshū* .

[7] The Japanese esthetic ideal, modeled in considerable measure on similar Chinese concepts, came to have an importance in Japan comparable to that of the Confucian ethical ideal in China. The elegant Japanese courtier was artistically and aristocratically conceived: he was expected to have achieved a good hand with the brush, compose poetry, perform reasonably well on one or two instruments, appreciate a beautiful woman, and hold his wine like a gentleman. The hero of *The Tale of Genji* is an embodiment of this and other ideals. In his *Japan: A Short Cultural History* (rev. ed., New

York, 1943), Sir George Sansom has defined the tastes of Heian courtiers and the artistic accomplishments of this "almost entirely aesthetic" culture (pp. 235-41), and in his latest work, *A History of Japan to 1334* (Stanford, 1958), a very interesting chapter—aptly entitled "The Rule of Taste"—is devoted to an analysis of these aspects of Heian court life (pp. 178-96).

[8] The reference to sleeves in this poem suggests not only tears but the custom of lovers, lying together under cover of their removed garments.

[9] Like many of the other poems from the Nara period taken into the *Shinkokinshū,* this one has been altered somewhat to fit new tastes or because the readers of a later age had difficulty in parsing the Chinese characters used in varying ways in the *Man'yōōshū*. Cf. *MYS* II: 133. With the next poem in the text, cf. *MYS* IV: 574.

[10] This poem is the tenth and the preceding one the eighth poem in the *Ise Monogatari*, the famous collection of tales combining poems with prose contexts and attributed to Narihira. See the *Kōchū Nihon Bungaku Taikei* (Tokyo, 1936), II, 40 and 41.

[11] Such categories as "falling phenomena" to designate rain, snow, and the like were identified by later *renga* poets. But we see here a technique which implies these categories and indeed which led to the use and naming of them by *renga* poets. This is one of the respects in which the practice of integrating *tanka* influenced the formation and practice of the *renga*. See also the discussion which follows in the text and section V. below.

[12] Professor Konishi has discussed the arrangement of poems in the *Kokinshū* in his edition, *Kokinwakashū,* for the *Shinchū Kokubungaku Sōsho*, XLIV (Tokyo, 1949), 30-31. The distinction between formal and informal poetry is related to, but different from, that between public and private poetry. All public poetry (e. g., Pope's *Dunciad*) is formal, but not all formal poetry is public (e. g., Donne's "Good-Morrow"). All informal poetry (e. g., Swift's "bagatelles" to Sheridan and others or Dryden's verse letter to Etherege) is private, but not all private poetry (Donne's poem) is informal. The distinctions are largely those of subject, tone, technique, and esthetic distance. Poems on public and social themes tend to disappear from Japanese poetry after the Nara period, except for semi-ritualistic poems on such "congratulatory" occasions as the New Year or those addressed to Emperors on their accession. From about the ninth through the eleventh centuries, the Japanese developed and esteemed a wide range of private poetry, both formal and informal. Gradually formal poetry rises in estimation to the point of almost excluding informal poetry as a valued art; and by the latter eleventh or twelfth century, most of the poetry

thought worthy of preservation in official anthologies and family collections is formal private poetry.

[13] Shigeyuki's one sequence, composed by command of the Crown Prince Norihira (950-1011; reigned 967-969 as Emperor Reizei), is printed in *Shink Gunsho Ruijū* (Tokyo, 1928), XI, 507-509. Yoshitada's two sequences may be found in *Kōchū Kokka Taikei* (Tokyo, 1929; hereafter *Kokka Taikei*), XIII, 53-71.

[14] Printed in *Shinkō Gunsho Ruijū*, VIII, 65-107.

[15] *Kokka Taikei*, X, 56-64.

[16] See, for example, the seventeen sequences by six major poets of the late twelfth and early thirteenth century in *Kokka Taikei*, X, 507-514 (Fujiwara Shunzei); 543-550, 625-632, 655-663, 670-673, 679-686, 716-724, 746-758 (Priest Jien); and XI, 7-15, 15-20, 35-43 (Fujiwara Yoshitsune); 309-316 (Priest Saigyō); 381-388, 447-455, 660-669 (Fujiwara Teika); 754-762, 814-822 (Fujiwara Ietaka).

[17] Two sequences by Priest Jien (1155-?1225) may serve as illustrations. In a hundred-poem sequence composed in 1187 there is no attempt to employ association, while in another, composed in 1190, association is employed to integrate the sequence. See *Kokka Taikei*, X, 612-625 and 670-679, respectively.

[18] Go-Toba's personal collection, printed in *Kokka Taikei,* X, 25-180, contains three sequences of 100 poems, one sequence of 500 poems (a kind of grandiose version of the *hyakushuuta*), and seven sequences of thirty poems (an abbreviated version of the *hyakushuuta*).

[19] For a detailed discussion of Go-Toba's dominant role in the compilation of the *Shinkokinshū,* see Kojima Yoshio, *Shinkokinwakashū no Kenkyū,* II (Tokyo, 1946), 1-48.

[20] See the *Go-Toba-In Kuden* in Sasaki Nobutsuna, ed., *Nihon Kagaku Taikei,* III (Tokyo, 1941), 3. Go-Toba uses the term in criticizing the hundred-poem sequences of Fujiwara Yoshitsune (1169-1206), which, he says, give the impression of containing too few "background poems." Since Yoshitsune is referred to in this passage as the "late Regent," we assume that the treatise was written some years after his death, which, it will be noted, took place the year after the *Shinkokinshū* was first compiled.

[21] An early thirteenth-century Japanese manuscript of a Chinese rule book entitled *Fu P'u,* or *Rules of Composition,* is in the private collection of Mr. Gotō Keita of Tokyo. Two unpublished manuscripts of the *Sakumon Daitai*—not to be confused with the fourteenth-century work of the same title in *Shinkō Gunsho Ruijū,* VI,

488-504—are in the Higashiyama Library of the Imperial Palace at Kyoto. . . .

E. B. Ceadel (essay date 1959)

SOURCE: "The Two Prefaces of *The Kokinshu,*" *Asia Major,* Vol. VII, No. 1 & 2, 1959, pp. 40-51.

[*In the following excerpt, Ceadel contends that the Chinese preface to the* Kokinshu *predates the Japanese one, and offers internal evidence from the prefaces themselves to support his claim.*]

The Japanese poetic anthology the **Kokin wakashū,** from which Dr. Waley translated thirty-five poems in his book *Japanese Poetry, the "Uta"* (Oxford, 1919) was compiled as a result of an Imperial order of 905 A.D. by Ki no Tomonori, Ki no Tsurayuki, Ōshikōchi no Mitsune, and Mibu no Tadamine. Of these four poets, Ki no Tsurayuki undoubtedly took the largest part in the compilation, as may be judged from the fact that out of the 1,111 poems in the collection as many as 102 are his own poems, compared with 60 by Mitsune, 45 by Tomonori and 38 by Tadamine.

Ki no Tsurayuki holds a significant place in early Japanese literature as an advocate of the claims of the native Japanese language to be treated as a literary language in its own right, and his prose writings[2] did much to advance those claims: as a poet he was an eager protagonist of the revival then taking place in the prestige and popularity of Japanese *tanka* poetry, which had rapidly declined from its fine achievements of the seventh and eighth centuries in the *Manyōshū* and had been in the ninth century almost entirely eclipsed by Chinese poetry written in imitation of Six Dynasties and T'ang models.

The **Kokinshū** has two prefaces. One, in Japanese, was composed by Ki no Tsurayuki[3] himself; the other, in Chinese, was composed by Ki no Yoshimochie[4], a scholar well versed in the Chinese classics. The Japanese preface is famous and has been highly praised by both Japanese and Western writers.[5] The Chinese preface, however, has received little notice:[6] some modern Japanese editions of the **Kokinshū** do not even include it,[7] and only the most recent commentaries annotate it.[8]

The two prefaces may be said to be two different versions of the same material: in spite of divergences between them, their subject-matter is basically the same. The problem therefore arises of the relationship between them. Since it is hard to believe that at the time of the presentation of the anthology to the Emperor the preface was simultaneously submitted in two forms, one Japanese and the other Chinese, it can only be concluded that one of the two was the original and that the other was for some reason derived from it or substituted for it later.

The problem of the relationship thus divides into two. Firstly, which of the two was the original, the Japanese or the Chinese? and secondly, why, and in what circumstances, was the second preface derived from or substituted for the original one?

For almost a thousand years Japanese scholars have debated these two linked questions. Controversy has been extensive, all kinds of theories have been evolved, and a whole mass has been written on the subject. A volume could be filled just with a historical account of the controversy.

The view that the Japanese preface was the original is the traditional one and has been widely held by scholars up to the end of the nineteenth century and by several modern scholars.[9] Many reasons have been offered to support this view, among which the following are perhaps the most pertinent:

(1) A number of early works, such as the *Eiga monogatari* (which was written not long after 1092), quote from the Japanese preface as if it were the one and only preface.[10]

(2) Several early manuscripts contain the Japanese preface at the beginning and either omit the Chinese preface or place it at the end of the text.[11]

(3) Since the *Kokinshū* was commissioned by the Emperor as a token of the revival of Japanese *waka* poetry after the "dark age" in which it had been overwhelmed during the ninth century by Chinese poetry, it is claimed that a Chinese preface would have been highly inappropriate and that therefore the Japanese preface was the true and original preface. This view was expressed as early as the beginning of the thirteenth century by the emperor Juntoku in his treatise *Yakumo mishō,*[12] and again about a hundred years later by Kitabatake Chikafusa in his *Kokinshūjo chū .*[13]

(4) Such of the subsequent imperial anthologies compiled in the next three centuries as have a preface have a Japanese, not a Chinese, one.[14] This, it is argued, shows that the first of the series, the *Kokinshū* itself, must have possessed a Japanese preface to set the precedent of Japanese prefaces for the later imperial anthologies.

The contrary view, that the Chinese preface was the original, has been held from early times by various writers and has been supported by a number of modern scholars.[15] The following are some of the reasons adduced in favour of this view:

(1) The poet and scholar Fujiwara no Kintō (966-1041) in his collection *Wakan rōeishū,* compiled just after 1000 A.D., quoted[16] the Chinese preface as if it were the one and only preface. In addition, a few parts of a commentary by Kintō are preserved embedded in a later commentary by Kenshō. Those parts of Kintō's commentary quote 18 passages[17] from the preface, of which number 13 are quotations from the Chinese preface while the other 5 are quotations of single words or names which occur in both prefaces. Since Kintō wrote only about a century later than the *Kokinshū,* this is important evidence.

(2) Another poet and scholar, Fujiwara no Akihira, a slightly younger contemporary of Kintō, included the Chinese preface in his collection of Chinese writings composed in Japan, the *Honchō monzui.*[18]

(3) Up to the time of the compilation of the *Kokinshū,* a Chinese preface for a Japanese work had been the rule. From the *Kojiki* onwards, where a work had been provided with a preface, that preface had been in Chinese;[19] this was because the preface had been recognized in T'ang China as a separate and important genre of literature, and had been adopted as such in Japanese literature also, still in its Chinese form.

With such conflicting arguments available to support the claims of both the prefaces to be the original, impartial critics have found it difficult to choose between them, and the regular judgment of almost all Japanese works of reference has been that it is impossible to establish for certain which of the two prefaces was written first.

Now it will be observed that all the evidence outlined above is external evidence, and it must be admitted that on the basis of external evidence no definite solution of this problem is possible. But there is plentiful internal evidence in the two prefaces themselves, which is sufficient to prove (incontestably, I believe) which of the prefaces was written first.

For the internal evidence to be displayed at length would require a much more detailed treatment of the material than is possible in this article,[20] but an outline of the method used may be given here, with some examples. The key to the internal evidence lies in the fact that both the prefaces contain numerous passages which, in vocabulary and ideas, are identical or almost identical with passages in the prefaces of certain Chinese poetic anthologies and works of literary criticism. This crucial point was not fully noticed by Japanese scholars until recently:[21] the failure to notice it is not entirely surprising because, as already mentioned, Yoshimochi's preface (in which the parallels with the Chinese prefaces are naturally much more easily recognizable) has received little attention from scholars and because the specialists in Japanese literature who studied Tsura-yuki's preface were unlikely to be familiar with these Chinese prefaces.

It is chiefly due to two scholars, Ōta Hyōzaburō[22] and Ozawa Masao[23], that most of the parallels between the *Kokinshū* prefaces and the prefaces of the Chinese texts have now been published in Japan. The main[24] Chinese texts which contain these passages which are identical or almost identical with those in the ***Kokinshū*** prefaces are:

(1) the "Great preface"[25] of the *Shih-ching:* this preface, ascribed to Wei Hung of the first century A.D., was perhaps the beginning of literary theory in China and greatly influenced later literary criticism.

(2) Hsiao T'ung's preface[26] to his *Wên-hsüan,* a classified anthology of Chinese literature, compiled at the beginning of the sixth century; the preface contains an account of his literary principles and is a valuable document.

(3) Chung Hung's preface to his *Shih-p'in,* a work of about the same date as the *Wên-hsüan;* the *Shih-p'in* is the earliest methodical attempt in China at the critical assessment of poetry.

The parallels between passages in these important Chinese works of literary criticism and passages in the *Kokinshū* prefaces are so extensive that coincidence can be immediately ruled out. Since the Chinese works are all earlier in date, it must be recognized that the *Kokinshū* prefaces have a large proportion (probably not less than half) of their material, both in vocabulary and ideas, deliberately borrowed from these Chinese sources. This fact has to be taken as the starting point in considering the relationship between the two prefaces of the *Kokinshū;* it is necessary to realize that the author of the preface which was written first must have been the person who was responsible for this extensive borrowing from Chinese sources. Which of the authors concerned would have been the one more likely to borrow thus? Ki no Tsurayuki, the opponent of Chinese influence and the exponent of the independent use of the Japanese language for literary purposes, or Ki no Yoshimochi, a well-known scholar of Chinese literature, writing a preface in Chinese? Undoubtedly it would seem in these circumstances to be probable that Ki no Yoshimochi would be the one to base his preface on Chinese sources, and accordingly that the Chinese preface came first.

But this is only a subjective argument, and objective proof is available. This is provided by undertaking a series of comparisons between, on the one hand, passages in the Chinese sources, and, on the other hand, the corresponding passages, in Chinese and Japanese, in the two versions of the *Kokinshū* preface. . . .

The divergences of the Chinese preface from the original Chinese sources are not extensive, and in most cases both the vocabulary and ideas are little altered beyond what is necessary to change the subject-matter from Chinese to Japanese poetry: the faithfulness, for example, with which almost the whole of the "Great preface" of the *Shih-ching* is copied in the Chinese preface is noteworthy. On the other hand the Japanese preface makes freer changes in its handling both of vocabulary and of the relative order of sections. Thus of the six sections in the quotation from the "Great preface", the Japanese preface omits one and transfers two others to a much later position, while it also places in the middle of the quotation a quite separate passage which the Chinese preface took from the *Wên-hsüan* preface. Such changes can only be explained if it is realized that Tsurayuki was basing himself on Yoshimochi's text without realizing that it had been so carefully constructed from quotations from Chinese sources. A good example is the section in the above passage derived from the *Shih-p'in* preface, which the Chinese preface follows fairly closely. Tsurayuki's version accepts "the nightingales singing among the blossoms" but replaces "the cicadas chirruping in the trees" by "the frogs living in the water". It is easy to follow the transition from the Chinese source to the Chinese preface and then to the Japanese preface: but if it is thought that Tsurayuki's preface came first, that he took this section direct from the *Shih-p'in* preface, and that the Chinese preface was copied from the Japanese preface (and not from the Chinese source), why did Yoshimochi alter "the frogs living in the water" back into "the cicadas chirruping in the trees"—since the Japanese version is so different from the *Shih-p'in* original that that source is unrecognizable from the Japanese text itself.

The conclusion is therefore inescapable that Ki no Yoshimochi's Chinese preface was the first to be written and that it was very carefully modelled on a number of Chinese sources. Yoshimochi had methodically studied these prefaces of Chinese poetic anthologies and other works of Chinese literary criticism and had constructed his preface to the *Kokinshū* by an amalgamation of numerous quotations from these sources, skilfully interwoven. Such patchwork construction might be expected to give a motley and inferior result, but this is not so. The adaptation of earlier material was a normal practice in much of Chinese literature,[27] and Yoshimochi had the additional justification that most of the vocabulary and ideas of poetic criticism had to be taken in any case from Chinese, since very little had been written on this subject before in Japan, and the little that had been written in Japan had concerned Chinese, rather than Japanese, poetry.

The Chinese preface is in fact a work of importance, deserving fuller recognition than it has yet received. Its layout and sequence of thought are logical and complete; as mentioned below, it gives more details about the early history of *waka* poetry than does the Japanese preface; and it is perhaps the first extant attempt to apply the Chinese techniques of literary criticism to a specific work of Japanese literature. (The Japanese work *Bunkyō hifuron* written about 820 by Kōbō Daishi, was indeed an earlier treatise on literary criticism, but was of a more general nature.[28]) Georges Bonneau, who in 1935 published the only edition of the Chinese preface to have appeared in the West, committed a serious error of judgment in writing[29] concerning it, "Rien de plus terne, rien de moins digne du *Kokinshû* que cette prose maladroite, mal composée et mal écrite . . . Sensibilité nulle, transitions chaotiques, images inharmoniques . . ."

Attention may now be turned to the second problem of the relationship of the two prefaces—why, and in what circumstances, was the Japanese preface derived from the Chinese preface? Although several theories have been proposed by Japanese scholars to explain why a Chinese preface should have been derived from a Japanese preface assumed as the original, I know of only two theories to explain why the Japanese preface should be derived from the original Chinese preface.

The first theory, mentioned by Fujiwara no Kiyosuke in his *Fukuro sōshi*[30] written about 1160, was that Tsurayuki asked Yoshimochi to write a rough draft of a preface in Chinese so that he, Tsurayuki, could base his own, official, Japanese preface upon it. On this theory the Chinese preface, although anterior, is merely an unimportant outline draft which has only happened to survive by accident.

The second theory, first advanced,[31] as far as I can trace, by the Tokugawa period scholar Ōkuni Takamasa (1792-1871), also known as Nonoguchi Takamasa, was that the Emperor permitted, or even ordered, Tsurayuki to make a Japanese translation of the Chinese preface, as a result of suggestions made to him after the Chinese preface had been submitted, that it would be appropriate to have a Japanese version also of a preface of an anthology celebrating the revival of Japanese *waka* poetry.

Apart from these two theories no other reasonable suggestions have been put forward, and none other in fact seems possible. In support of each of these two theories various arguments have been adduced by Japanese scholars on the basis of external evidence, but as in the question of the relative order of the prefaces, external evidence is insufficient to settle the matter. Internal evidence, however, may again be produced with decisive effect:[32] this evidence is extremely interesting, and its implications do not appear to have been previously noticed. The whole argument cannot be unfolded in a small space, but the key to it is contained in the fact that there are upwards of a score of small but nevertheless significant places where there is a definite difference of opinion between the two prefaces. One of these may be quoted as an example: it is

the passage assessing the qualities of the Rokkasen, the "Six Great Poets". Yoshimochi's Chinese preface speaks with uniform praise of all six, and possibly the name "Rokkasen" originates from his preface. But it may be deduced that Tsurayuki approved wholeheartedly of only three of them, Henjō, Ariwara no Narihira, and Ono no Komachi, since he included as many as 17, 30 and 18 respectively of their poems in the *Kokinshū*: in the case of the other three, Bunya no Yasuhide, Kisen and Ōtomo no Kuronushi, only 4, 1 and 2 respectively of their poems were selected by him in the *Kokinshū.*[33]

In case it is objected that it is unsafe to postulate Tsurayuki's opinions of poets by the number of their poems he chose, confirmation is available from Tsurayuki's treatment of the comments in the Chinese preface. In the case of Henjō, Ariwara no Narihira and Ono no Komachi, Yoshimochi's favourable assessments are faithfully rendered: but his assessments of the other three are toned down or omitted by Tsurayuki in his Japanese version. Thus Yoshimochi's comment on Kisen, "his words are beautiful" is altered by Tsurayuki to *kotoba kasuka ni shite,* "his words are vague" and Yoshimochi's praise of tomo no Kuronushi, "he had a great deal of remarkable inspiration" is cut out entirely in Tsurayuki's preface.

The existence of cleavages of opinion such as this completely disposes of the theory that the Chinese preface was a rough draft on which Tsurayuki based his own preface. If this had been the case, and the Chinese preface had been a private draft, Tsurayuki would have been able to depart from it freely whenever he wished, especially when he disagreed with it. For instance, in the example just quoted, he could have entirely disregarded Yoshimochi's selection of six poets and the title of "Rokkasen" which he had used, and he could have made his own selection and given them his own title. It may well be conjectured that had Tsurayuki been free to construct his preface as he wished, it would have been absolutely different. The fact that Tsurayuki followed the Chinese preface so closely, only daring for the most part to make slight and inconspicuous changes, can only be explained on the assumption that the Chinese preface had already been imperially commissioned and officially recognized, and that Tsurayuki had been allowed, or ordered, by the Emperor to prepare a Japanese version. In such circumstances it would have been impossible for Tsurayuki to have departed to any noticeable degree from the framework of the Chinese preface: to have done so would have been an affront to the Emperor (as well as a public slight to Yoshimochi).

The only major divergence[34] Tsurayuki permitted himself was to add some fairly long sentences in semi-poetic vein illustrating the themes and diction of Japanese poetry: this addition he probably felt defensible on the ground that it would have been impossible for Yoshimochi to have handled this in Chinese. Apart from allowing himself this one piece of licence, Tsurayuki must have felt highly constricted by the limitation imposed on him, and many of the faults[35] that can be seen in his Japanese preface are the direct result of this limitation. In the first place, as he was not a scholar of Chinese literature himself and was an opponent of the influence that this literature had in Japan, he must have had difficulty in understanding Yoshimochi's Chinese and the allusions involved. It is hard to escape the conclusion that in some passages he actually misunderstood and mistranslated Yoshimochi's preface.[36]

Another problem for Tsurayuki was the Chinese way of thought visible in much of the expression (which was of course appropriate enough in the Chinese preface); some of these Chinese ideas and attitudes were quietly omitted or altered by him, but he dared not go too far in so doing, and there are several passages in the Japanese preface where Chinese ideas still remain, even though in Japanese garb.

The Chinese preface provides a short but nevertheless full and systematic account of the earlier history of Japanese poetry, including three references to the decline of *waka* after the *Manyōshū*. Tsurayuki was such an eager exponent of the revival of *waka* which the **Kokinshū** heralded that he could not bring himself even to mention its earlier decline, and he omitted these three passages. In addition, he was such an advocate of *tanka* poetry that he failed to mention in his preface the other types, *sedōka*, *kompon*, and *nagauta* (with accompanying *kaeshiuta*) to which Yoshimochi had referred. The result of these and other minor changes made by Tsurayuki in the passages dealing with the early history of Japanese poetry is that the well-ordered account of the Chinese preface is badly distorted and confused in the Japanese preface.

The same thing is true in reference to the make-up of the whole preface. Whereas the Chinese preface is clear, complete, logical and well-arranged, the Japanese preface, in consequence of the cumulative effect of the changes (small in themselves) which Tsurayuki made, appears in some places muddled and difficult to follow. This defect was partly Tsurayuki's fault, partly the inevitable consequence of the limitations within which he had to work.

The Japanese preface, therefore, stands revealed as possessing little real originality in its subject-matter and as having a number of defects in its structure. It may be asked whether the high opinions which have been held of it are still tenable. The answer would appear to be that without question it may still be regarded as an outstanding landmark in Japanese literary history and an achievement of Tsurayuki's skill as a writer. Not only is it probably the earliest extant ex-

ample of a long passage of polished, fluent prose in the Japanese language: it is also the first known attempt to introduce literary criticism into Japanese instead of leaving it in Chinese.

Notes

[1] The substance of this article was communicated as a paper to the XXIIIrd International Congress of Orientalists at Cambridge on 24th August 1954. Some of the arguments used by me have since been independently put forward by Ozawa Masao, "*Kokinshū* ryōjo sengo oyobi kana jo sakusha kō", *Kokugo to kokubungaku* 392 (1956) 10-22.

[2] The prose writings of Tsurayuki (?868-946) include the Japanese preface of the *Kokinshū* (as the *Kokin wakashū* is by abbreviation commonly known), the *Tosa nikki* and the *Ōigawa gyōkō waka no jo*: for the last-mentioned, see "The ōi River Poems and Preface", *A.M.* (*N.S.*), iii, 1 (1952), 65-106. Tsurayuki's prose was much superior to Tadamine's, see "Tadamine's Preface to the ōi River Poems", *BSOAS*, xviii, 2 (1956), 342.

[3] Tsurayuki's authorship of the Japanese preface, although not indicated in the MSS., may be regarded as certain, and has scarcely been challenged except by Yamada Yoshio, who in "*Kokin wakashū* no kana no jo no ron", *Bungaku*, iv, 1 (1936), 1-23, pointed out certain defects in the Japanese preface. He suggested that these were so serious as to be unworthy of Tsurayuki and considered that it must be the work of a later writer. These defects, however, have a different explanation, see below. The genuineness of the Japanese preface is vouched for by the similarity of its style to Tsurayuki's preface to the Ōi River poems in 907, and to his *Tosa nikki*.

[4] Yoshimochi (866-919), son of Ki no Hasco, was a scholar of Chinese literature as well as a Japanese *tanka* poet (one poem of his, 251, was included in the *Kokinshū*). He had by 905 reached a high rank at court, and his qualifications made him a suitable person to be chosen to write the Chinese preface. Yoshimochi's authorship of the Chinese preface is given in some MSS. of the *Kokinshū* and in *Honchō monzui*, compiled by Fujiwara no Akihira in the middle of the eleventh century, and there is no reason to question it. . . . The theory of Ueda Akinari (1734-1809), to be found in Fujii Otoo (ed.) *Akinari ibun* (1919), 529-30, restated by Yoshida Kōichi, *Kokugo to Kokubungaku* 217 (1942), 60-81, that Tsurayuki was the author of both prefaces is disproved by the comparatively small but nevertheless highly significant differences between the two versions.

[5] Thus W. G. Aston, *A History of Japanese Literature*, London (1898), 63, wrote "it has to this day a reputa-

tion in Japan as the *ne plus ultra* of elegance in style".

[6] Aston (*op. cit.*) and M. Revon, *Anthologie de la littérature japonaise,* Paris (1910), make no mention of the Chinese preface.

[7] *E.g.,* Nakamura Shūkō, *Kokinshūshōkai,* 1908. Several editions merely print it on the last page but do not otherwise refer to it.

[8] Good notes are provided by Kubota Utsubo, *Kokin wakashū hyōshaku* (1937).

[9] See Hisamatsu Senichi, *Nihon bungaku hyōronshi, Kodai chūsei hen* (1936), 159-164, Sasaki Nobutsuna, *Kaitei Nihon kagakushi* (1942), 10-11, and Kyūsojin Hitaku, "*Kokin wakashū* ryōjo no ron", *Kokugo kokubun,* viii, 8 (1938), 78-105, "*Kokin wakashū* ryōjo seiritsu nendaikō, *Teikoku gakushiin kiji,* ii, 1 (1943), 57-98.

[10] There are two references in *Eiga monogatari: Kōchū Nihon bungaku taikei* (1927-8), xi, 13, line 4, *tadashi Kokin ni wa Tsurayuki jo ito okashiu tsukurite,* and xi, 753, line 11, *suginishi koto wo ushinawaji ima yori no koto wo mo chirasaji to aru Kokin no jo;* the latter is not a word for word quotation, but a paraphrase of *inishie no koto wo mo wasureji . . . ima mo misonawashi nochi no yo ni mo tsutaware* in the Japanese preface.

[11] This is not a compelling argument since other early manuscripts have only the Chinese preface. In any case, in spite of the excellent work *Kokinshū no dempon no kenkyū* (1954), by Nishishita Kyōichi, the relative value of the manuscripts has not been finally determined.

[12] *Yakumo mishō* (originally called *Yakumoshō*), c. 1, in *Ressei zenshū* ii, (1915), 159.

[13] *Zoku gunsho ruijū,* c. 452, vol. 16, ii, 539.

[14] The prefaces of the fourth anthology, *Goshūishū,* and the seventh anthology, *Senzaishū,* are in Japanese. For a convenient reference list of these anthologies, see E. O. Reischauer and J. K. Yamagiwa, *Translations from early Japanese literature,* Cambridge, Mass., 1951, 131-3.

[15] See Yamada Yoshio, *op. cit.,* Nishishita Ky ichi, "Yamada hakushi no *Kokinshū* jo ni kansuru shinsetsu ni taishite hiken wo nobu", *Kokugo to kokubungaku,* 145 (1936), 1-16, Kaneko Mottomi, *Kokin wakashū hyōshaku* (1927), 31-38, Igarashi Chikara, *Heianchō bungakushi,* i (*Nihon bungaku zenshi,* iii), 1937, 324-356, Yoshida K ichi, "*Kokinshū* ry jo no sakusha seiritsu nendai ni tsuite no saigimmi", *Kokugo to kokubungaku,* 245 (1944), 8-20, Konishi Jinichi, *Kokin wakashū* (*Shinchū kokubungaku sōsho*), 1949, 47, Imai Takuji, "*Kokin wakashū* ryōjo no kenkyū", *Atomi gakuen kiyō,*

1 (1954), 11-70, Saeki Umetomo, *Kokin wakashū* (*Nihon koten bungaku taikei*), 1958, 56-60. Even though the above writers agree on the priority of the Chinese preface, they differ greatly in their interpretation of the second half of the problem—why and in what circumstances the Japanese preface was derived from it.

[16] *Kodai kayōshū* (Yūhōdō bunko), 270.

[17] See Yamada Yoshio, *op. cit.,* 5.

[18] See Kakimura Shigematsu (editor), *Honchō monzui chūshaku,* Kyoto (1922), ii, 577-592.

[19] For possible exceptions see Kyūsojin Hitaku, *Teikoku gakushiin kiji,* ii, 1 (1943), 68-73.

[20] I hope at a later time to publish an edition of the two prefaces, with a study of their relationship and literary significance.

[21] The debt of the *Kokinshū* prefaces to the preface of the *Shih-p'in* was pointed out as early as 1909 by Nonoguchi Seiichi, "*Kokin wakashū* jo to *Shihin*", *Kokugakuin zasshi,* xv, 579-586, and again in 1928 by Tsuchida Kyōson, *Bungaku no hassei,* 325-334, but the full significance of this fact was not then appreciated.

[22] He gave a general survey of the influence of Chinese poetic theory on Japanese poetry including the *Kokinshū* preface in "Nihon kagaku ni okeru Shina shiron no eikyō", *Kokugo to kokubungaku,* 168 (1938), 121-142, and in "Rikuchō shiron to *Kokinshū* jo", *Nihon Chūgoku gakkai hō,* ii (1950) 118-128, he gave detailed parallels with the preface and other parts of the *Shih-p'in.*

[23] He outlined the general influence of Chinese poetic theory in "Heianchō waka wa rikuchō shi wo dō ukeireta ka", *Bungaku,* xxi, 9 (1953), 64-70, and gave parallels with the *Wên-hsüan* preface in "*Kokinshū* no jo to *Monzen* no jo", *Kokugo kokubungaku hō,* 5 (1955), 1-9, with the "Great preface" of the *Shi-ching* in "*Kokinshū* no jo to *Shi* no daijo", *Heian bungaku kenkyū,* 18 (1956), 8-17, and in "*Kokinshū* jo no rikugi ni tsuite no kenky", *Nihon gakushiin kiyō,* xiv, 1 (1956), 27-63, with the *Shih-p'in* in "*Kokinshū* jo to *Shihin*", *Heian bungaku kenky ,* 19 (1956), 6-13, and with other sources in "*Kokinshū* jo ni tsuite", *Kokubungaku kaishaku to kyōzai no kenkyū,* ii, 7 (1957), 16-23.

[24] Apart from the sources pointed out by Ōta and Ozawa, parallels with passages in the writings of Po Chü-i have been given by Kaneko Hikojirō, *Heian jidai bungaku to Haku shi monjū* (1948), 180-209. Parallels with Liu Hsieh's *Wên-hsin tiao-lung* have been given by Ōta Hyōzaburō, *Kokugo to kokubungaku,* 168 (1938), 121-142.

[25] English version by J. Legge, *The Chinese Classics,* vol. iv, i (The She-King), London, 1871, Prolegomena 34-36.

[26] French version by G. Margouliès, *Le fou dans le Wen-siuan, étude et textes,* Paris, 1925, 22-30 (supplement to *Le Kou-wen chinois*).

[27] This is well illustrated by the way in which phrases from the "Great preface" of the *Shih-ching* reappear in the prefaces of the *Wên-hsüan* and *Shih-p'in* themselves.

[28] See the excellent edition by Konishi Jinichi, *Bunkyō hifuron kō,* 3 vols., 1948-53.

[29] *Le Kokinshû, supplément au Volume Premier, Préface chinoise de Ki no Yoshimochi,* Paris, 1935, 12.

[30] This is the second of the views reported in *Fukuro sōshi,* c. 2, *Zoku gunsho ruijū,* c. 462, vol. 16, ii, 778, lower column line 3 (*aru setsu . . . unnun*).

[31] Quoted in Kaneko, *op. cit.,* 35.

[32] It will be realized that all the internal evidence which shows how Tsurayuki based his preface on Yoshimochi's is also additional proof of the prior composition of the latter.

[33] The smallness of these figures can hardly be explained by a hypothesis that few or none other of their poems still survived, for Yoshimochi could not have based his critical assessments of the three poets on such exiguous material.

[34] Less important additions by Tsurayuki include a number of flattering references to the Emperor, presumably to indicate gratitude for his encouragement of the revival of Japanese poetry.

[35] These are the faults that made Yamada Yoshio doubt whether Tsurayuki could really be the author.

[36] It is true that Tsurayuki wrote the short Chinese preface to his *Shinsen wakashū* of 935, but its Chinese style is not impressive. As it is so much later in date, it cannot be used to prove that he had a good knowledge of Chinese when he wrote his preface to the *Kokinshū.*

Robert H. Brower and Earl Miner (essay date 1961)

SOURCE: "Poetic Practice" and "Consolidations, New Developments, and Decline" in *Japanese Court Poetry,* Stanford University Press, 1961, pp. 198-220.

[*In the following excerpt, Brower and Miner discuss the diction, rhetorical techniques, syntax, subjects, themes, and tone of the* Kokinshu.]

. . . Poetic Language and Imagery

The different conventional modes illustrate the complex adjustment of personal response to social environment which is basic to the age. One will fail to understand either the good or the inferior poetry of the period unless one realizes that it produced poem after poem which was at once personal and conventional—or that the great poems of the age are not the songs of Romantic poets singing in the wilderness of their own originality but a personal lyricism in a social context. By comparison with Western poetry, this description is perhaps appropriate for the whole history of Japanese poetry down to modern times, but the particular combination was never more acutely a determinant than in the early classical period. Combined with the intensifying of technique within a narrowed range, the blend of personal lyricism and a social milieu makes it extremely difficult to isolate such aspects of poetic practice as diction, rhetoric, imagery, tone, theme, and styles. But in so far as they are separable, we shall deal with them in turn.

Some separate discussion of the diction of poetry in the early classical period is necessary, if only because the language of serious poetry for centuries afterward is almost wholly founded upon the precedent of the **Kokinshū** and the imperial anthologies that directly followed it. Like the *Man'yōōshū,* the **Kokinshū** has a relatively limited vocabulary, something over 2,000 words, of which rather more than a hundred are not to be found in the *Man'yōōshū.* While this lexicon is probably no larger than that of Anglo-Saxon poetry or Renaissance sonnets (*The Cid* has about 1,200 words), it must be remembered that it was developed for an almost restrictedly lyrical form, in a language whose agglutinative inflections often require extensive paraphrase in English, and whose words came to be a vehicle of connotations as much as denotation. And in order to maintain the native rhythms in a purity of style, it excluded all Chinese loan-words—words that were sometimes dormant, sometimes active in the minds of many writers as they composed Japanese poems, just as Latin lay in the minds of our poets till the end of the last century.

The poets were highly conscious of language as one of the determinants of their art. Often, indeed, a poem achieves its significance not by a strikingly new observation, but by the purity, the beauty, or the splendor of its diction, rendering translation even more difficult than usual. Although appropriate diction is but one of Narihira's many accomplishments, it is the language in cadences of Virgilian resonance more than anything else which makes his art so appealing. He and Komachi often fill the third and fifth lines with liquid, inflected adjectives or verbs that develop the sounds of preceding words with a perfected lyricism. The following poem by Narihira, for example, is one that will never have a wide appreciation among foreign readers, but its pure diction and lovely rhythms will always appeal to the Japanese. The major pause at the end of the third line anticipates the strong conclusion, in which the "o" and "k" sounds of the preceding line are given a new direction; the first and fourth lines have slightly longer pauses and their grammatical structure is similar, except that each of the two nouns in the fourth line has one more syllable than the corresponding noun in the first line (*KKS, I*: 53).

> . . . If cherry flowers
> Had never come into this world,
>   The hearts of men
> Would have kept their tranquil freedom
> Even at the brilliant height of spring.

Such purity of language can only be achieved by poets with a strongly decorous concept of diction. If Chaucer is to our poets "the well of English undefiled," the poets of the **Kokinshū** are even more the source of pure poetic language to the rest of the Court tradition. Even the assured language of Narihira and Komachi was refined, especially by the choices exercised by compilers like Tsurayuki and by the judges at poetry contests, who often came to rule out diction that was not to be found in the first three imperial anthologies. No doubt there is something alien in this reverence for linguistic precedent from which the modern Western sensibility shrinks instinctively. We remember the glorious coinages and free-wheeling indifference to usual meanings and grammatical functions of a Rabelais or a Shakespeare, and feel there is something stultifying about a determined poetic diction. But surely it is a matter of degree. The example of refinement in diction from Ronsard or Dryden onward reminds us of similar tendencies in the West. And if we are to condemn the Japanese poets for restricting themselves to purity of aristocratic diction, what must we say of Wordsworth and his efforts to employ the speech of rural folk or of Burns and his Scots? As always, it is not the ideal that is so important, but the practice, and when a Pope, a Gray, a Wordsworth—or a Narihira, a Tsurayuki, or a Tomonori—achieves a diction that is pure by whatever legitimate standard and able to express the important interests of the age, it is folly to complain. Only in later centuries, when all experiment ceased, when the diction of the **Kokinshū** was no longer expressive of the interests of the age, ought we to condemn the standard of precedent in language.

Both the new words that appear in the **Kokinshū** and the words retained from the preceding age are those which do express the interests of the age. They are words that name the things the poets enjoyed seeing or experiencing, or their actions, or their attitudes toward their world. There were, it seems, three standards for admission of words to the poetic vocabulary. They had to be purely Japanese, since Chinese loan-words disrupt the sinuous fluidity of the verse and make poetry sound like prose. A "new" word had also to be one of common knowledge or sufficiently similar to other accepted words so as not to cause shock. And finally, a word had to have a degree of elegance about it—in sound, in connotation, and in propriety. Very good poems might be written in unusual diction, but although their quality was recognized, they were placed in the category of "unconventional poems" (*haikaiuta*). Experimentation with diction which was inadmissible by such standards of elegant good taste was disastrous for a poet. When, for example, the official reader at the poetry contest at the Teiji Palace began to recite one of the poems on the *hototogisu*—

> . . . Across the fields,
> The Morning Fields of Kataoka,
>   Reverberates—

the company roared so with laughter at "reverberate" for this bird's song that the reader was unable to finish his recitation.

The new words that appear in the **Kokinshū** naturally had their effect upon the imagery of the poetry. Some are images for natural phenomena that have now gained poetic attention. "Autumn mist" (*akigiri*), "spaces between the rocks" (*iwama*), "robe of haze" (*kasumi no koromo*), "cricket" (*kirigirisu*), "moonlight" (*tsukikage*), "patches where the snow has melted" (*yukima*), and "the whole night" (*yomosugara*) are but a few. "Threads" (*itosuji*), "transferred scent" (*utsurika*), and "summer clothes" (*natsugoromo*) are among the new images that come from the daily life of the Court. Since such images as these are highly typical of the poetry of the age, we find it possible to draw several inferences that seem to us pertinent for the poetic practice and the underlying assumptions of the age. The new imagery from daily life is the imagery specifically of Court life, or, like the "jeweled seaweed," it has an elegance which precludes Okura's homely image of the destitute man's kettle filled only with a spider web. Poetry is, as in the preceding period, an art form developed and determined in style by the Court, but the Court poets no longer bother to project their feelings outside or "below" their own refined world.

The natural images that make their first appearance in the **Kokinshū** are even more significant. On the whole, they are finer or smaller and represent more detailed observation than is characteristic of the earlier age. They confirm the impression one has from the poetry as a whole that the poets stood, as it were, closer to the objects they describe and saw them in greater detail. It does not seem difficult to explain why the poets of this period drew into closer contact with their environment and observed it more intimately. The subjective cast of their art required that the observing sensibility deal with objects easily grasped as wholes, rather than sublime sights soaring above comprehension. When we come upon such a new image as "a robe of haze," we see the poet attributing a subjective quality of beauty and intimacy to natural phenomena; or again, the new words for night and the increased use of old images of night suggest the nocturnal activities of the courtiers in that most subjective of all normal human experience, love. A poem by Ariwara Yukihira (818-93) exemplifies this new subjectivizing of nature (*KKS*, I: 23).

> . . . The robe of haze
> Now worn by Spring must indeed be
>   woven
>   Of threads of gossamer,
> For the slightest breath of the mountain
>   wind
> Seems to rend it into shreds.

Along with these developments, comparable new imagistic techniques appear that suggest the increased subjectivity of the age. The evidence available to the senses often is treated as if it were contradictory, as in Takamura's poem on the similarity of the appearance of snow and plum blossoms. Often, too, the senses are divided—hearing from sight or sight from smell—in highly subjective ways. Ariwara Motokata (888-953), for example, found no visible evidence that spring had come to the mountains, but his sense of smell declared it must be so (*KKS*, II: 103).

> . . . Far, far away,
> Those mountain slopes where the mist
>   Rises with the spring,
> But the soft approaches of the breeze
> Are laden with the fragrance of the
>   flowers.

More often than in the earlier period, the imagery of the poetry of the age appeals to this less measurable, more subjective sense of smell. It is also characteristic that many of the images of sight represent visual confusions (of snow and plum blossoms, for example), or something only half seen or even beyond sight, as in the famous anonymous poem on dawn at Akashi Bay (*KKS*, IX: 409).

> . . . Dimly, dimly
> In the morning mist that lies
>   Over Akashi Bay,
> My longings follow with the ship
> That vanishes behind the distant isle.

Not only is the ship just faintly seen, but it is watched for subjective reasons—it carries away the person whom the speaker loves. Perhaps the ultimate in such indirect technique is the poem by Lady Ise (fl. ca.

935) on the cherry trees of her native village (*SIS*, I: 49).

> . . . How I long to hear
> Whether the flowers have yet fallen—
>   If only there were someone
> Come fresh from my native village
> To tell me of the cherry blossoms there.

The cherry trees do have a real existence, but their reality is most important for its impingement upon the poetic sensibility, and there is no person at all to tell her of them. Yet this is only half the story. The headnote says that the poem was written on looking at "a scene of people going flower-viewing, painted on a folding screen at the palace." Lady Ise and other members of Court are assembled to see and appreciate the screen, and in this social context and from the stimulus of a work of art her memories and feelings are stirred for the distant, less elegant, quasi-pastoral scene of her province. One does not question the sincerity or the beauty of the poem, but it is a new thing for poets to be impelled to reverie by art.

There are other indications of the subjective handling of imagery. No small number of the new words in the **Kokinshū** are adjectives like "thin-hearted" or "lonely" (*kokorobososhi*), which often express attitudes and emotions, not imagistic qualities of objects. These new adjectives and pre-existing ones are, in addition, more often used to give the imagery a stronger coloring of human emotion than in the earlier period. Moreover, the imagery is often so directed toward generalization, though not abstraction, that it loses its imagistic concreteness. Narihira's lament "Composed When I Was Weak with Illness" (*KKS*, XVI: 861) does not have a single image that can be apprehended by the senses.

> . . . Though formerly I heard
> About the road that all must travel
>   At the inevitable end,
> I never thought, or felt, today
> Would bring that far tomorrow.

"Road" may be visualized, but here it is of course a metaphor for death. The poem is a complete generalization, and as such carries the subjective tendencies of the age further than most poems. It is indeed one of the most perfect lyrics in Japanese and it is deservedly well known, but its techniques have the stamp of its age so markedly that such poems would not be written again for centuries, when the effect of unimagistic writing was to be far different. . . . If it is an extraordinary example in quality as well as technique, it is nonetheless typical of an age in which reality exists not in the rapport of poet and nature, but in the significance of the external world to the consciousness of the poet.

Rhetoric and Syntax

Poetic rhetoric is inextricably bound up with other aspects of poetry, since it involves the techniques for handling imagery and diction to express meaning. It is all the more important for an age like the early classical, in which aristocratic standards of decorous, elegant, and spirited writing make the manner of expression of paramount importance. One of the most striking and characteristic rhetorical techniques of the age is the pun and, with it, the closely related technique of the pivot-word (kakekotoba)—which we will remember is the use of a sequence of sounds in two senses, often through differing divisions and through the voicing or unvoicing of certain sounds. Poems employing this technique run the gamut in quality from the poems on the names of things with their topics buried in wordplay, to some of the most consummate and moving poetry of the age. Ono no Komachi was by all odds pre-eminent among the poets of the age in her ability to use words and sounds meaningfully in different senses, with the result that her poems have a breathless intensity seldom equaled in Japanese poetry. Following is a prose rendering of one of her most famous poems (*KKS*, XV: 797).

> . . . A thing which fades without its color visible
> is the flower of the heart of a man of the middle of
> the world (i.e., of this world).

About all the prose rendering shows is one aspect of the structure, although in reverse. The "of" phrases represent the four possessive particles (*no*) of lines three and four. With the particles functioning in Japanese order, Komachi orders her poetic materials by limiting the range of attention ever more narrowly and climactically as she ferrets out the changeful culprit—world, middle, man, heart, flower—and having found it exclaims, *ni zo,* "in it!" The climax of discovery is only partially a triumph for the speaker, since happiness is forestalled by the sense of misery she feels to be inflicted upon her by her lover's faithlessness. This is to say that the subject of the poem is love, which is treated with a generalization of its nature from the vantage point of the speaker's unhappy experience.

The subject of love emerges by implication from the diction (*hito,* "person," "lover"; *kokoro,* "heart," "mind," both with traditional connotations of love), but it is primarily the rhetoric that develops the implications into active meanings. The first, second, and fifth lines are made to begin with words bound together by the technique of association (engo). Color-fades-flower is clearly a cluster of similar concepts, even in English, and it functions in the poem to provide a strand of subdued imagery by the association of the concepts, even though their immediate contexts would, in English poetry, forestall any connection. The effect of the association and of the words connoting

love in the fourth line is to show that neither *iro, utsurou,* nor *hana* ("color," "fades," "flower") is purely imagistic. The imagistic strand takes on a metaphorical character as vehicles whose tenor concerns love. The implied meaning of "fade" is therefore "grows untrue," "changes for the worse"; and "flower" becomes a symbol for the attractive yet transient nature of man's affection for women: the association shows that it is the flower of the heart of man which fades. Of the three associated words, however, it is the first whose function is the most significant. *Iro* is used in richly different senses. It refers most limitedly to the color that fades, the color of the symbolic flower of man's heart. Since the fading is metaphorical and the flower symbolic, it should be clear that color, too, must be taken in more complex senses. By perfectly normal usage in classical Japanese, *iro* may mean coloring in the sense of passion, so anticipating the fourth line in suggesting that the subject dealt with is love and, in particular, that the situation behind the outburst is a love affair now grown one-sided. *Iro* may also mean face or appearance, which is opposed in the poem to *kokoro,* the inner mind, the actual state of the man's feelings.

The complexity of Komachi's rhetoric can be appreciated by anyone who seeks to break the poem into divisions. Syntactically there are pauses at the ends of lines one and two, but they are bound together into a unit integrated by the association of words (*iro, utsurou*) in parallel positions and by the logic of the poem, since they tell what will be defined in the next three lines. Lines three to five are bound tightly together by the sequence of possessive particles leading to conceptually ever narrower elements. They are also joined less obviously to the first two lines. The crucial first word of the poem is played off against three words in the last three lines. It associates with *hana* ("flower"), as we have seen. In its secondary meaning of passion it combines by traditional connotation with *hito* ("person") to mean the man beloved by the speaker. And in its tertiary meaning it plays as appearance in contrast to the inner reality (*kokoro*).

Another rhetorical technique fuses the whole poem, a harmony and yet a reversal of states of mind for which the only English term is irony. The poem is ironic because what ought to change in a lover or any living thing, its appearance, remains constant; whereas that which should be so essentially the nature of the thing as its inner being has faithlessly altered. The irony is presented by a woman of intense passion, suffering from anger and fired by pride. Such motives lead her in her suffering to discover the cause—the faithless lover who protests a fidelity that he uses to mask his indifference—and lead her to a further ironic discovery that only appearances are real, that the vowed-for reality is only sham. Surely only Komachi would write a poem unifying all of these meanings into one outburst of passion:

Find mutability
In that being which alters without fading
    In its outward hue—
In the color, looks, and the deceptive flower
Of the heart of what this world calls man!

From such a building on the multiple meanings of
one sound sequence (*iro*), it is not a far cry to Komachi's extraordinary dexterity in the use of pivot-
words. The most complex of her poems employing
the technique, which is to say the most complex of all
poems employing it, is one in which she moves from
emotional calm to frenzied passion within the com-
pass of five lines (*KKS*, XIX: 1030). It might be read
at first to mean:

    . . . On a moonless night when we have no chance
    to meet (because you cannot see the way to my
    house, I sleep, but) I awake longing for you so much
    that my breast excitedly heaves and my heart burns
    within me.

This reading conveys the play upon *tsuki*, "moon" and
"chance," and something of the excitement of the poem.
But the poem also has the most remarkably sustained
and powerful imagery fused in its four word-plays in
pivot-words. We must redefine the word clusters, for
they have two simultaneously apprehended meanings,
in order to understand the poem fully. (The italics indicate sounds with double meanings.)

    . . . On such a night as this
    When the lack of moonlight shades your way
        to me,
        I wake from sleep my passion blazing,
    My breast a fire raging, exploding flame
    While within me my heart chars.

We should also note in passing the superb emotional
paradox that the darkness of the night is the cause of
the searing flames. The technique of kakekotoba is
here perfected art: not only does it enable Komachi to
transcend the tanka form by creating, as it were, four
new words, but the double meaning is also a tonal
vehicle expressive of the most intense experience of
the inner depths of the heart.

It will be recalled that in the preceding age the pivot-
word was normally the technique of juncture in poems
with prefaces (jo). We have been able to find very few
unequivocal examples from the early classical period
of this older rhetorical use of pivot-words. One of them
is a poem very much in the older manner by Sone no
Yoshitada, in which the juncture is a pivot-word in the
fourth line (*GSIS*, I: 42).

    . . . Spring seems to have come
    Within the short space of a single night,
        Short as a single joint

Of the roots of the reeds that sprout
Luxuriantly in the Inlet of Mishima.

Hitoyo no hodo ni means both "in the interval of a
single joint" and "in the interval of a single night."
The old-fashioned flavor of the poem lies in the weakness, the obviousness, of the metaphorical relation
between the sprouting reeds and spring. There is a
relation, but the last two lines of the Japanese (the first
two of the translation) represent a single statement
separable from the rest. In the characteristic poems of
this period, the pivot-word functions not so much for
juncture as to give increased complexity to what is
already a poetic unit.

Another example of a poem employing a preface joined
by a pivot-word to the statement will perhaps suggest
why the technique was altered in this age. The poem
(anonymous, *KKS*, V: 286) ought to be compared with
Hitomaro's envoy to his poem on the death of Prince
Takechi (*MYS*, II: 201), which it so much resembles.
The italicized words are the pivot-words at the juncture. (Hitomaro's poem is first.)

    . . . Just as the waters
    Pent-up by walls in Haniyasu Pool
        Do not know where to flow,
    So now the courtiers of the Prince
    Are trapped with no direction to their
        lives.

    . . . Wretched my plight,
    So like the drifting maple leaves
        Scattered in their fall
    Before the gusts of autumn wind
    And impotent to fix a course.

Hitomaro's world is the public world of city construction
and Court business. The **Kokinshū** poet talks of himself
and finds that the external world is relevant to the speaker
only in terms of his personal response. Hitomaro's technique is therefore not unlike an epic simile that refers to
what all men know, whereas the **Kokinshū** poet tends to
assimilate the metaphorical vehicle into the emotional
tenor. The result, for the poetry of this period, is that
most of the metaphors are fused with other elements of
the poem, not isolated by division into preface and statement. The typical poem of the age employs a simile, a
metaphor, or an allegory in which the poem is not divided, in which the immediacy of subjective response to
a stimulus is more instantaneous.

Two possibilities of the use of the old rhetorical techniques in fresh ways are shown by Tsurayuki. In a
poem very greatly admired by later poets, he employs
a jo in his first three and a half lines (*KKS*, VIII: 404).

    . . . Like my cupped hands
    Spilling drops back into the mountain pool

And clouding its pure waters
Before the satisfaction of my thirst,
So have I had to part from you too soon.

The preface extends through the word *akade* ("not satisfying"), which is employed as a pivot for what goes before and what follows. The old technique, the country setting, and the dipping hands to scoop up water all suggest an older, pastoral scene of somewhat rustic simplicity. If the parting is to be considered one from a woman loved, as some commentators have suggested, the element of pastoralism is considerably strengthened. Tsurayuki has employed a venerable technique which itself helps raise the image of a simpler past.

An even finer poem to our minds employs a pillow-word (makurakotoba) for somewhat similar effect. The quasi-pastoral element is made clear by comparison of the subject of the poem with its headnote: "Composed and Presented in Obedience to the Imperial Command" (*KKS*, I: 22).

> . . . Do those girls set out
> On some excursion for young shoots,
>   That they so gaily beckon,
> Waving their white linen sleeves
> Toward the green fields of ancient
>   Kasuga?

The italicized phrase represents a complex of techniques that distinguishes this poem from the two preceding poems. *Shirotae no* is a pillow-word for *sode*, "sleeves." But Tsurayuki uses the original meaning of the expression, "white hempen," in a literal way, while at the same time keeping the elegant amplification of the pillow-word associations. His phrase therefore means, "girls waving to each other their white-hempen sleeves." But the syllables *furihaete* also have a separate, pivotal significance: "deliberately," "on purpose." The effect of this, along with *hito* ("persons") in the last line, is to separate the poetic speaker from the girls. He wonders why they set out in just the way they do (a very male point of view toward the mysterious antics of young ladies), and wishes they would invite him to participate.

The first words of the poem help us to understand still more. Kasuga is just outside the ancient capital of Nara, not in the Heian capital at Kyoto where the poet is. The word perhaps carries something of the associations of its written characters meaning "spring day," but these overtones are minor compared to the fact that the place name tells us that the poet has created an entirely fictional situation. He represents himself as an observer of the old capital at Nara in its former days. The quasi-pillow-word function of *shirotae no* now appears in its full significance, to help convey the feeling of the past; and its literal meaning suggests (in a

way that does not in the least destroy the poem's elegance) that the girls are perhaps of a lower social class. What we really have is a pastoral poem that creates an idyllic past.

One dimension of the poem remains. The poem was composed at imperial command and is therefore formal, although not precisely public in our sense. Tsurayuki's idyllic re-creation of the past is both a reminder to the emperor of the romantic of the nation's past and, since the vehicle is pastoralism, a suggestion that today all are sophisticated and advanced enough to feel that slightest degree of condescension which lingers in our appreciation for the pastoral. The essential appeal of the poem lies in contrasts of speaker and girls, of past and present, and of two capitals, and in tone it has the charm of a painting by Watteau or Sir Joshua Reynolds. The gentle calm of the poem is accentuated by a quality of the distant and unknown which Tsurayuki's pillow-word has conveyed. How complex the art is can be gauged by its subjectivity. Tsurayuki is the man who presents the poem, the poet who composed it, and, by virtue of a fictional pose, the observer of the past.

Along with the pivot-word, there are some other techniques new to this period or redefinitions of old techniques which characterize the poetic interests of the age. As Tsurayuki's poem shows, pillow-words were still used, but to somewhat different effect. The technique itself suggested the traditional and elegant to the poets of the period. Sometimes the use of pillow-words seems to achieve no more than the appearance of elegance, but there usually appears to be an attempt to relate the literal meaning of the expression (and literal meanings were often made for old pillow-words by "folk etymology") to the poem by means of metaphor. This tendency can be seen most clearly in poems in which new pillow-words seem to be employed, as in the complaint of an anonymous woman to a faithless man whose higher rank enabled him to play a wide field in his amours (*KKS*, XV: 754).

> . . . Have I been forgot
> Because I am one who does not count
>   To such a one as you,
> Who may choose from women as countless
> As the gaps of weaving in a flower basket?

The first line of the original (and the last of the translation) is a pillow-word for *me*. It is typical of the age that *me*—which means both "eyes" and "interstices in the weaving"—functions (with *narabu hito*) by a word play to mean "women ranged before the eye." Perhaps the comparison of number develops into a metaphor—all these flowering beauties are in his basket, but the speaker has been left behind, no longer worth picking. In any case, the pillow-word has been given a personal significance, a role in a private poem that is more characteristic of this than of the preceding age.

Besides these redefinitions of old techniques, some more-or-less new techniques characterize much of the poetry of the period—association (engo), simile, and allegory. Association is a variety of word play which in some ways resembles the pivot-word, since it functions by giving two readings to a single sound sequence; but it differs in that a word later in the poem is given a meaning different from its immediate context by association with, or echo of, an earlier word. We shall render a poem by Tadamine, italicizing the associated phrases (*KKS,* VI: 328).

> . . . The *white snow* falls
> Ever deeper on the mountain village—
>   To what loneliness
> Must even the *thoughts* of that man *fade*
> Who dwells amid the drifts that bury all.

Omoikiyu means "become nothing under the pressure of sad thoughts," but the element *kiyu* is a verb, meaning "fade" or "melt," which associates in both meanings with the "white snow" mentioned at the beginning of the poem: snow melts (*kiyu*), but only after it has buried everything under white drifts that cause the sharp outlines of the landscape to fade away (*kiyu*). Although this association acts as an ingenious method of binding the poem together, it represents more than ingenuity alone. The juxtaposition of *omoi* ("think") and *kiyu* shows both that the villager suffers a growing loss of identity and sense of isolation and that he knows the snow will melt and bring a desired springtime. The result is an irony of pathos: the snow will melt, but not until the villager has "faded away" because of loneliness. In this poem, in Komachi's poem on the faithless hearts of men, and in other fine poems, association is a characteristically Japanese means to a significant literary end.

The problem of the new technique of similes in the poetry of the period is an extremely intractable one. The agglutinative inflections, the fluid syntax, the attributive verbs, and the elusive particles—not to mention such techniques as that of the preface—often force the translator to use awkward similes where the Japanese poet is happily taking a more graceful path. There are some "signs" of similes resembling our "like" and "as": a verb or adjective with an attributive inflection followed by *gotoku* or *goto,* or a noun followed by the possessive particle *no* and *gotoku* or *goto,* or sometimes even by the particle alone, is an explicit comparison. Many other poems suggest comparisons by means of other constructions in which the technique of comparison is fairly obvious, but without a sign for the simile. If we may call these "implied similes" and add to them overt similes, we are ready to discuss this use of metaphor in the period.

Like the pillow-words, and like similes in Western rhetoric, the comparisons in this period are employed for amplification—by comparison something is made lovelier, dearer, and so on. The analogy with the pillow-word is useful, because the similes almost always observe the pillow-word order of preceding what they amplify, as if Burns had said, "Like a red, red rose is my luve." An anonymous bit of advice on love illustrates the technique (*KKS,* XIII: 652).

> . . . If you choose to love,
> Feel it only in deep reaches of the heart;
>   Never let it show
> Where its color will catch all people's eyes
> *Like robes dyed purple with the violet*
>   *grass.*

Lines three and four of the Japanese use the simile of clothes dyed a bright purple to convey the care that is necessary in matters of the heart. Another poem with an implied simile is Lady Ise's composed "At a Time When She Was Unhappy in Love." It is superior both in technique and in a convincing passion which finds expression only by her comparing herself to the fields she sees being burned over to increase the yield the next year (*KKS,* XV: 791).

> . . . If only the resemblance
> Of my fleshly body to the fields
>   Withered dry by winter
> Meant that the way we both are seared by
>   fire
> Would bring me also the awaited spring.

Once the comparison is established by the particle *to,* the metaphor is extended throughout the poem, almost to the point of becoming allegory.

As we remarked in the preceding chapter, allegory worthy of the name is exceptional in the early literary period, but from the generation of Ōtomo Yakamochi on, the increasingly private nature of poetry led to allegory as an elegant and useful vehicle for poems of private discourse. The human mind takes as much pleasure in saying things indirectly as in saying things well, and we may suppose that this was one of the pleasures of allegory in private exchanges. In addition, the fear of exposure in the hazards of love affairs at the Heian Court led lovers to explore the benefits of ambiguous allegory—a fact that explains why some of the poems in the private anthologies are extremely difficult to understand. A further pleasure to be gained from allegory was one that comes from indirect reference to something intimately private—the sharing of knowledge about the significance of a certain place, for example, is a satisfaction all lovers know. Fortunately, the headnotes and various words often suggest allegory in poems whose hidden meanings might otherwise escape us. Such words as "person" (*hito*), the "heart" (*kokoro*) of something, "thought" (*omoi*), and various adjectives indicating sadness often give us the key to unlock a love allegory. This private allegory is often untranslatable, even when we possess its key, because the significance given objects is too wholly personal. But it may readily be found by leafing through the sections on love in such an anthology of the period as the **Kokinshū**, paying special attention to those poems with headnotes like "Sent to ——."

Private allegory may also be found in poems on other subjects. What appears on the surface to be description, for example, may turn out to be allegory. A postscript tells us that an anonymous poem is not purely descriptive, but a woman's lament for the loss of her husband (*KKS*, IX: 412).

> . . . How they cry
> As they wing off to the north!
>   It seems the geese
> Have lost one from the number
> Which flew here with them in the fall.

The woman had taken a trip with her husband to the provinces, where he died, leaving her to return to the capital alone and to symbolize her grief in the crying of the geese.

Allegory is also to be found among the formal poems of the period, which, like informal poems, tend to be descriptive in appearance. The rarity of description employed as an end in itself shows that the complex minds of these poets tended to disdain poetry that only re-created a scene. For them, the external world held its prime significance only insofar as it was shaped by the human sensibility. Eight such apparently descriptive poems were "Written on a folding screen placed behind the seat of Lord Fujiwara Sadakuni, Colonel of the Right, when his sister The Lady of the Bedchamber gave a celebration in honor of his fortieth birthday." Two of the poems are on spring, one on summer, three on autumn, and two on winter—all by the most eminent poets of the day. The most famous is one by Mitsune (*KKS*, VII: 360):

> . . . With the autumn wind
> Blowing through the ageless pines
>   Of auspicious Suminoe
> Are mingled the elated voices
> Of the white waves out to sea.

The waves represent the guests; the inlet of Suminoe carries connotations of the shrine of the god of Sumiyoshi (literally, "auspicious" or "good life") there; pines are a symbol of longevity; and the autumn wind is a symbol of advancing but kindly age. So tonally apt are the images-become-metaphor that for centuries the poem was a model of its kind.

Rhetoric, imagery, and even the structure of Court poetry are closely related to the syntax employed. Narihira's poem on the seemingly changed moon . . . shows in its opening lines how similar syntactical forms might suggest parallelisms of thought and imagery, and Komachi's long series of possessives in her poem on the changeful heart of man . . . shows how the syntax orders the structure into progressive units. The crucial poetic role of syntax is of course not limited to this period of Japanese Court poetry, nor even to Japanese poetry as a whole, but the characteristic features of its syntax tell us a great deal about the special nature of the poetry of the early classical period. Japanese scholars have shown that whereas the tanka in the *Man-'yōōshū* normally employ a syntax demanding pauses after the second and fourth lines, the syntax of tanka poetry in the early classical period normally involves caesuras after the first and third lines. The fact is not to be disputed, but no one seems to know quite how to account for it. Whatever the explanation, the effect is certainly pleasing and the fact of importance to the practice of poetry. Such organization lends the tanka a structural pattern of three units of increasing length. The first line presents a short movement of five syllables; the next two a larger movement of twelve; and the last one a still longer movement of fourteen. The pattern is by no means inviolable, but it seems to provide a familiar structure, to arouse expectations that in English poetry are provided by the latent metrical pattern or by the division of sonnets into patterns determined by rhyme schemes.

The tripartite rhythm of lengthening units is usually played off against other syntactical qualities. Sometimes a poet calls attention to the division with a pivot-word—the effect is at once to intensify the sharpness of the caesura with increased attention and to smooth it over by double or overlapping syntax. . . . More typically, the divisions are harmonized by making the poem consist of a single, complete, and naturally ordered sentence. By comparison with the frequently stiffened syntax of the early literary period with its recurrent parallelism, or with the fragmented syntax of mid-classical poetry, the poets of this age employed a purer, simpler, more lyrical syntax. Such purity combines with the tendency to use highly inflected verbs and adjectives, which often fill the entire third or fifth line, to produce poems whose sounds and cadences are of uncommon beauty. When such sounds and cadences are in addition made the vehicle of rich meaning, the result is a kind of perfection for which there is no comparison. In certain respects it is not so much Narihira's richness of meaning as his aural, syntactic perfection that makes him by far the most difficult of the Court poets to render without feeling one has the words right and everything else wrong.

It is just at this point—when syntax merges with sound, language, imagery, and rhetoric—that the true genius of the period seems to us to lie. In subsequent poetry, the unity of the poem is more intellectual, more artful, and often, to speak the truth, more significant. But except for some sporadic examples, Japanese Court poetry was never again to achieve the beauteous integrity of early classical poetry. It is such excellence of a craft of beauty which shows how positive the ideals of elegance, refinement, decorum, and courtliness truly were, for all of the somewhat negative connotations such terms have in our post-Romantic day. To give point to such generalizations, we may inspect in greater detail a poem long famous for its beauty of sound, imagery, and atmosphere (*KKS,* IX: 409).

> . . . Dimly, dimly
> In the morning mist that lies
>   Over Akashi Bay,
> My longings follow with the ship
> That vanishes behind the distant isle.

Part of the magic of the poem is attributable to its mystery—the pallor of dawn, the mists, the isle-hidden ship, and the relationship of the person on the ship to the speaker of the poem. But the poem's real beauty is so much a part of the language that it can more readily be declared than explained. Only in Japanese might one play upon a place name: Akashi is the name of the bay, but is also used to mean "dawned." The assonance of *Akashi/asagiri,* with *asagiri* picking up the *r* sound of *ura;* the rising excitement of the fourth line, with its combination of "island"-"hide"-"go" into a single verb modifying "ship" in the next line; and the perfect assonance of the last line, picking up and redefining the five *o* sounds of the first; all of this in a single lovely sentence with the usual caesuras is felt either deeply or not at all.

The pure lyricism of this anonymous poem is characteristic of the greater poetry of the age as well, although the great poets achieve their stature by adding thought and feeling of a higher order. In a technical sense, the higher order of poetic expression normally was achieved by means of the rhetorical devices, the wit, the complex tones, and the metaphysical interests of the age. But whether great or mediocre, the poetry of the early classical period possesses some quality that sets it off from all other periods. Against the repose of early literary poetry, the profundity of mid-classical poetry, and the intensity of late classical poetry, we would set the essential assurance of this age. During this period the Court was at its zenith. There was no need to look to the future with dread nor to the past with anything more than the slight nostalgia of Tsurayuki's dream of a rather simpler bygone day. The assurance might well have vanished had the courtiers been aware of their favored historical position. As it was, it would be the lot of later poets to look back with grief over their present to the earlier day as a norm of value, a day when, as Tsurayuki said in his Preface to the *Kokinshū,* all living beings seemed inclined to song, a day when the duties of military officers were to wait upon the emperor and to write poetry, not to cast the nation into civil strife.

The rhetoric of poetry—in the larger sense of its normative syntax and the disposition of elements—is the readiest indication of the poetic character of the age, whether we consider the pivot-word, the highly inflected verbs, the reasoning conceits, or syntactic integrity as particular signs. It was rhetoric in this sense that gave the age its means both of achieving aims of beauty and value and of exploring the subjective reaches of human experience. It is no accident that the greatest single Japanese literary work, the *Tale of Genji,* should have been written in this period, for it reflects the temper of the age by exploring—in a prose studded with poems and itself a marvel of lyric beauty—the same subjective complexities as the poetry, so creating a literary kind without comparison until the modern novel. The rhetoric of poetry in the first classical period is, therefore, the true vehicle of its thought and its greatness. It enabled poets to find a way to transcend the brevity of the tanka form and to convey subjective experience. The difference between this age and its predecessor can almost be represented in the older use of parallelism, a technique admirably suited for lyric narrative and public poetry, and the new use of the pivot-word, a technique ideal for short poems that explore the manifold richnesses of the human sensibility.

Subjects, Themes, and Tones

In the early classical period, the important subjects, the predications about them (themes), and the attitudes toward them (tones) are, in general, of a narrower range than those of the early literary period, and of a greater complexity within the narrowed limits. As we have seen, poetry is almost entirely private, the triumph of lyricism is absolute, and the mind of the poet rules over reality, with the result that we can diagram the subjects of poetry in this age into a few divisions.

A. NATURE AND "THE WORLD"

B. HUMAN AFFAIRS

1. Parting and travel; Love; Death

2. Beauty; Reality and Appearance; Truth

3. Formal subjects (Congratulations, etc.)

C. TIME

In B, we have three groups of subjects, treating different aspects of human experience. The first of these consists of personal experiences, the second of experience of the outer world and its significance, and the third of social or ritual experience. One of the surprises of this literary period is that poems with the single subjects of nature are all but impossible to find. Time and again one comes upon poems that seem merely to describe, only to have closer examination show that they are allegories, or descriptions of screens, or intended to convey some metaphysical truth. And what is true of nature is true of "the world" (*yo no naka*); it, too, functions as a substantive means for a differing thematic end. We have, therefore, placed nature and "the world" above the three areas of experience that are usually the avenue to the expression of these themes. We have also separated time from other subjects, since it is the ground and being of almost all the literature of the age. The poets often wrote of time, but it is less a subject than a condition of reality that involves poet and subject matter, poet and other men, theme, and attitude.

The point upon which all these subjects converge is the subjective consciousness of the poet, and the proper mode of poetry was therefore lyricism. To say this is hardly to announce a discovery—but rather to make explicit in modern Western terms what is implicit in every sentence of Tsurayuki's Preface to the **Kokinshū.** In prose as lyrical—as marked by such contemporary techniques of comparisons, pivot-words, and even pillow-words—as the poetry he describes, Tsurayuki makes it clear that the response of Japanese poets to their subject matter is lyrical and subjective: "The poetry of Japan has its roots in the human heart."

The readiest way to show the force of generalizations about the subjects of poetry in the period is to examine poems with various subjects, themes, and tones, and of varying quality. The first, by Kiyowara Fukayabu, is one of the most purely descriptive poems we have been able to find. There is no surviving evidence to show that it contains an allegory or refers to some screen or picture. It is a poem about nature, specifically, "On Autumn" (*GSS,* VI: 322).

> . . . On the autumn sea,
> The waves rise and fall, each in turn
>   Washing the reflection
> Of the floating moon—yet its appearance
> Remains unaltered by the lapping waves.

The subject here is patently an event in autumn, and the imagery conveys it in lovely detail. The point, however, is one that the perceiving sensibility gives the scene: considering what is happening, the moon should change and does not. The poet chooses to focus upon the "color" (*iro*) of the moon, and as we have seen, *iro* means "appearance" and "form" as well as "color." The basic theme, then, is appearance and reality, with the "appearance" of such a flickering, altering thing as the reflection of the moon (itself inconstant) on waves in constant motion proving to be more

steadfast than the "reality" of its being subjected to forces of change. The poem is more charming than profound, but we would mistake Fukayabu's intent and the character of the age if we failed to see the way in which his sensibility has shaped the subject into an intellectual theme.

The relation of nature to the perceiving sensibility is even clearer in Ono no Komachi's famous poem on growing old (*KKS,* II: 113).

> . . . The color of these flowers
> No longer has allure, and I am left
>   To ponder unavailingly
> The desire that my beauty once aroused
> Before it fell in this long rain of time.

The "color of flowers" (*hana no iro*) is clearly a symbol for "my physical being" (*wa ga mi*), and the natural imagery is sustained to the end by pivot-words. *Furu* means both to "grow old" and to "fall" as rain. *Nagame* means to "gaze" or to "think abstractedly," and "long rain." By establishing a symbol and developing it at length by means of pivot-words, Komachi has managed to suggest—in the very act of statement—the relation between nature and herself. Her view of nature and her attitude of what might be called passionately resigned despair are part of one brilliant poetic whole.

A poem by Narihira shows how "the world" might be brought into the subjective lyricism of the age (*KKS,* XIII: 646).

> . . . Through the blackest shadow
> Of the darkness of the heart I wander
>   In bewilderment—
> You people of this twilight world,
> Explain: is my love reality or dream?

It is extremely difficult to convey the force of *kokoro no yami* without destroying the imagery. The term, "darkness of the heart," anticipates the juxtaposition of *yume utsutsu,* "dream, reality," in the fourth line. A love affair seems to give rise to mixed emotions, while the experience is so intense that the speaker has lost his ability to distinguish appearance from truth. Such generalization of his experience into quasi-philosophical terms is appropriate to the appeal he makes to the people about him, asking them to help him resolve his confusion. The appeal is all the more subtle for Narihira's address, *yohito,* which means "you, I, everyone." Although he asks for advice, he points out that the people about him—who might very well censure him for the "darkness of his heart"—are as much in the psychological and moral dark as he. As a result, his bewilderment over appearance and reality is all the greater, and his love is shown to be even more intense than the imagery originally had suggested. The reference to the world about him is, then, only a means of conveying the depth of his subjective experience.

Death and love are perhaps the two most fertile subjects for lyric poetry. To take a poem with imagery somewhat like that in Narihira's poem, Izumi Shikibu's verses supposedly composed on her deathbed give us an idea of the handling of this subject (*SIS*, XX: 1342).

> . . . I now must set
> "Out of darkness on yet a darker path"—
>   O blest moon,
> Hovering upon the mountain rim,
> Shine clearly on the way I take ahead.

This is clearly an allegory, and the personal relevance is unmistakable. It is interesting to notice the way in which natural imagery of darkness, mountain, and moon are applied to her situation. We have placed the second line of the translation in quotation marks because Izumi Shikibu echoes the *Lotus Sûtra* (VII): "Long night adds its curse to our lot: Out of darkness we enter into darkness" (Arthur Waley's translation). Since the poem was "Sent to His Eminence Shōkū," his priestly teaching is symbolized by the moon, and *michi* ("the way") also has religious overtones. The poem is both a prayer and a message, a literal statement of the need for light and an allegory for the need of enlightenment. And once more it is the mind of the poetic speaker which unifies the diverse elements into a whole.

Mitsune's poem "Composed While He Watched the Snow Falling" (*KKS*, VI: 329) is somewhat similar in imagery, but different in approach. He chooses to generalize about life and death by means of description.

> . . . How sad this road
> Covered over with the obscuring snow,
>   Where not a person passes,
> Where not a trace remains to mark the
>   course
> Of travel through a world of fading hopes.

The last two lines of the Japanese grow increasingly subjective. *Atohaka mo naku* ("without an after-trace") must also be parsed *haka mo naku* ("unstable," "transitory"). *Omoikiyu* means "become nothing under the pressure of sad thoughts," and as we know *kiyu* ("fade" or "melt") is the familiar association for *yuki* ("snow") in the first line. What seems mere description is really an allegory for the speaker's life, and it would not violate the spirit of the poem to any great degree if the first line of the translation were extended to read, "How sad this road, my life."

One more poem seems to us worth quoting for what it shows of this creation of theme and tone by subjective handling of materials, not so much for the poem's quality as for the way it illustrates a variety of treat-

ments characteristic of this age and foreshadows the direction poetry would take in the next period. The priest Sosei (fl. ca. 890) purports to convey a personal experience which shows how much the speaker appreciates the beauty of chrysanthemums (*KKS*, V: 273).

> . . . In what seemed a moment,
> As I gazed on the dew-laden chrysan-
>   themums
>   By the mountain path,
> How many ages passed by in that instant
> When my clothes were soaked and dried?

On face value the poem baldly presents a rhapsody over flowers, but Sosei had other business in mind than passing himself off as such a bewildered person. Behind this poem lies the Taoist legend of the woodcutter who saw some immortals playing chess in the mountains one day. He decided to watch the game a little while, and as at last he turned to depart, he discovered he had watched them so long that the shaft of his axe had rotted away. By echoing this legend, Sosei's hyperbole loses its extravagance. The headnote tells us still more: "On the appearance of a person making his way through the chrysanthemums to arrive at the palace of an immortal." In other words, the poem is written about a picture, and the words are represented as those of the man in the picture. This, too, has the effect of making hyperbole rather more acceptable. Sosei has managed to render a simple affirmation into art, but to leave behind the opinion that he, too, is a great lover of chrysanthemums— as well as a very clever man. This effect is pleasing, even if the play of an instant and several centuries is not a wholly moving treatment of the subject of time. The true center of the poem is an attitude rendered through complexly related allusions.

In our comments on these poems, we have not sought to convey the variety of tones in the poetry of the period, because the dominant attitude is the highly subjective response which we have seen expressed in different ways. Irony, humor, remorse, affirmation, regret—and a great range of other personal attitudes— are expressed in the poetry of the age, but all are part, as it were, of an overriding expression of personality, and the particular emotion is apt to be involved with the general subjective attitude. Such subjectivity in a social milieu helps determine the particular poetic cast of the age. The proliferation of these dual qualities makes the inferior poems of the age almost indistinguishable from each other. The best poets grew in the same environment and created highly individual poems in varying personal styles. . . .

Notes

Japanese Scholarship

No serious study of any aspect of Japanese literature

can be undertaken without reliance upon the many excellent standard editions of texts, literary histories, and critical writings of Japanese scholars. We wish to list here with a few words of comment the principal Japanese works we have drawn upon, together with certain translations and other works in Western languages from which we have quoted or which we believe to be of special interest to our readers. We have not attempted to give a bibliography *in extenso* of works on Japanese Court poetry. Representative bibliographies of important editions, compilations, monographs, and periodical articles may be found in such works as Asō Isoji, ed., *Kokubungaku Shomoku Kaidai* (Tokyo: Shibundō, 1957), a useful annotated bibliography of works on Japanese literature; and at the end of the chapters on waka in Hisamatsu Sen'ichi, ed., *Nihon Bungakushi* (6 vols. Tokyo: Shibundō, 1955-60), which is the most recent and up-to-date of several important histories of Japanese literature. New and important editions, textual and historical studies, and essays on many aspects of our subject continue to appear in great numbers. The Western student will find that among these abundant studies, some are more useful for his particular purposes than others, and perhaps a brief account of the history and concerns of Japanese literary scholarship relating to Court poetry is in order.

If scholarship is the effort to preserve literature and to render it intelligible to successive ages, then Japanese scholarship may be said to have an ancient and all but continuous history. The first collections of poetry were made some thirteen centuries ago; prose glosses and commentaries are but slightly younger. If by criticism we mean theories of poetry, canons of style, and literary judgments, Japanese criticism has a history dating back to the oldest extant anthologies. To a degree unknown in the West, the creators, readers, and critics of Court poetry were the same men and women. With the decline of the Court and of Court poetry in the late fourteenth century, there was for a time a parallel falling-off in scholarship and criticism as well. Rigid orthodoxy, haughty claims to poetic prestige by certain families, and futile conceptions of poetry as family property led the latter-day descendants of the great Court poets to preserve the great achievements of the past as secret—and lifeless—family treasures rather than to make them live anew. Consequently, in the later centuries of the feudal period the creative work of scholarship and criticism was carried on largely outside the Court, among the classes of warriors, priests, and commoners—the classes that produced the important poets of the renga and the greatest of the *Kokugakusha* or National Scholars of the seventeenth, eighteenth, and nineteenth centuries. The National Scholars began the monumental task of reconstructing, re-evaluating, and re-interpreting the literary heritage of the Court, beginning with the earliest chronicles of the eighth century; if it is true that their nationalistic and sometimes naïve predilections led them to some

strange conclusions, it is also true that the best modern editions and detailed commentaries of such great collections of Court poetry as the *Man'yōōshū* the *Kokinshū,* and the *Shinkokinshū* are based solidly upon their accomplishment.

At the same time, many of the National Scholars, and certain influential poets and critics of the early years of this century, have been hostile to the reactionary schools of Court poets surviving in their day, criticizing them sharply for clinging to their secret traditions without showing any signs of poetic creativity. As the Court nobility gradually lost prestige and power, most scholars assigned the sophisticated decadence they saw in their own day to what had in reality been a vital culture centuries before: looking at the corpse, they could not imagine the life it had once possessed. Such a prejudice on the part of many National Scholars combined with their nationalistic, anti-Chinese views to encourage them in their efforts to glorify the remote past before the great age of the Court and the New Learning from China—to seek in the age of primitive song and a naïvely construed *Man'yōōshū* the true, unadulterated products of Japanese literary and moral greatness. Their attitudes have survived in different forms and among various groups down to the present day; they were particularly widespread during the years of this century prior to World War II, partly owing to the Japanese experience of modern nationalism and partly because confirmation for these views was easily found in certain Western Romantic and post-Romantic ideals of primitivism, simple directness, and artless realism.

This is not to suggest that the Japanese have failed to appreciate their own best poetry. Such historical considerations help explain, however, why only the three greatest anthologies—the *Man'yōōshū,* the *Kokinshū,* and the *Shinkokinshū*—have been studied in detail by any appreciable number of Japanese scholars, why it is that there are as yet scarcely any reliable exegetical commentaries on the other imperial anthologies or on most of the private collections of the poets. Moreover, the historic concern of Japanese literary scholars with certain limited aspects and segments of the Court tradition helps explain why such an important literary phenomenon as the integration of anthologies and sequences by the principles of association and progression has only recently been rediscovered and remains as yet almost wholly unknown to students of literature.

But if the coverage of the whole range of Court poetry by modern Japanese literary scholarship has varied in range and depth, its volume has been immense and its achievements impressive. The greatest accomplishments—apart from the exegesis of texts—have been in the related fields of philological, textual, and historical studies, concerns that stem directly from the interests of the National Scholars. Virtually all of the major works of the "classical" past have been subjected to intense scrutiny: their authenticity, age, and authorship have been sharply questioned and vigorously debated; their original form, relation to other works, and growth as texts have been established with increasing precision; their linguistic and orthographic peculiarities have been isolated and explained. The increased technical skill shown in these studies derives in part from the influence of Western methods of textual criticism, in part from the experience of generations of Japanese scholars.

In addition to these concerns there is an admirable tradition of what might be called intuitive or taste criticism that derives from the diaries, miscellanies, and critical writings of the Court. Finally, there is a line of theoretical inquiry pursued by some of the most distinguished modern scholars—an effort to establish the meaning and essential character of such esthetic concepts as beauty and form, or to determine what is characteristically medieval about medieval literature—which owes a great deal of its nature and method to German conceptualist scholarship of the last century.

As for our own use of Japanese materials, since our overriding concern has been with the poetry itself, we have used secondary materials (apart from reference works) to a far lesser extent than editions of the great anthologies, private collections, records of poetry contests, and the critical writings of the Court poets, although we have of course been careful to consult the best literary histories and summaries of recent scholarship, drawing from them much valuable historical and factual information. Owing to the nature of our study, we have had least occasion to use the more theoretical writings of Japanese scholars. We do not question the value of such studies, but we have usually found them too remote from the problems of practical criticism that have claimed our attention. To say this is only to emphasize that we have used a modified form of Western literary criticism in our study—a method which has been largely untried as yet by scholars of Japanese literature in Japan. In a sense, then, we have relied continuously upon Japanese scholarship, without following it in some of its most characteristic methods and emphases. Our results have been closer to evaluations by Japanese of their poetry than might have been expected, although we have often appreciated the great writers for rather different reasons, even as some poems seem more or less significant to us than to the Japanese. . . .

Principles and Forms of Citation Used in This Book

Our general method of citation is set forth in the note on p. 5, but certain refinements and exceptions may be noted here.

1. References to such collections as *Kōchū Kokka Taikei* (*K. Taikei*), *Nihon Kagaku Taikei* (*NKGT*), and *Katsu-*

ranomiyabon Sōsho (*Katsura Series*) include the title of the particular work quoted from, unless it is clear from the context. Thus "*Samboku Kikashū* in *K. Taikei*, XIII, 633" means that the poem in question is in the *Samboku Kikashū* (the personal collection of Minamoto Shunrai) and is printed in *Kōchū Kokka Taikei*, Vol. XIII, p. 633. "*Shinsen Zuinō* in *NKGT*, I, 116" means that the prose passage quoted or referred to is in the *Shinsen Zuinō* (a poetic treatise by Fujiwara Kintō), and is printed in *Nihon Kagaku Taikei*, Vol. I, p. 116.

2. References to *Zoku Kokka Taikan* (*ZKT*) give the number of the poem as indexed in that work. Thus: *ZKT*: 15,364.

3. The poems and songs quoted from works other than the *Man'yōōshū* in Chapter 3 are numbered as in Tsuchihashi and Konishi, *Kodai Kayōshū* (*Anthology of Ancient Song*), not as indexed in *Kokka Taikan*. Poems from the *Ise Monogatari* are numbered as indexed in *Kokka Taikan*.

4. A list of all abbreviations used in the text is given below; imperial anthologies that are described in the Appendix, but from which we have not chosen poems, are not included.

Before listing the primary and secondary sources that we found especially useful or from which we have quoted, we should describe a few principles of bibliographical citation that we have adopted.

1. A work is published in Tokyo unless another place of publication is given.

2. Both Japanese and Western surnames precede given names.

3. Articles, reference works, and non-literary histories are not listed unless they are of unusual importance or we have quoted from them.

4. Translations from Japanese into Western languages are not given unless we have quoted from them, or they possess historical or literary significance for Court poetry.

Bibliographical information for these works is supplied under the appropriate categories below.

SOURCES

One work is of such importance as an index for the *Man'yōōshū* and the twenty-one imperial anthologies that it must be given special notice here: Matsushita Daizaburō and Watanabe Fumio, *Kokka Taikan* (*The Great Canon of Japanese Poetry*). 2 vols. Kyōbunsha, 1903, and often reprinted.

The reader should note that descriptions of the *Man-'yōōshū* and the twenty-one imperial anthologies can be found in the Appendix, pp. 481-87.

PRIMARY SOURCES

I. Collections and Indexes

A few major collections and indexes constitute the materials we have used most intensively. As we have noted, the two volumes of *Kokka Taikan* are indispensable as an index for the *Man'yōōshū* and the imperial anthologies, but they contain other materials as well. Vol. I prints texts not only of these collections, but also of the poems in the *Kojiki,* the *Nihongi,* and the other chronicles and belletristic historical writings of the Court period, and of the poems in the principal diaries, miscellanies, travel accounts, and novels of the Heian period. The poems are printed and numbered in the order in which they appear in the original works. Vol. II consists of an index by lines, arranged in the order of the Japanese syllabary, to the poems in Vol. I. At the time the work was first compiled (1903), some of the materials indexed were not available in the best texts, and we have therefore in some instances (as with the *Kojiki* and the *Nihongi*) referred to better editions, provided we knew them to be easily available to specialists.

As a working text, Vol. I of *Kokka Taikan* is useful. Although the poems are printed in triple columns in rather fine print, this very feature is an advantage for sequential reading of the poems in the imperial collections and for the study of their techniques of integration; and although individual poems must be checked against more recent and reliable editions, the student will in general find that the more he studies Court poetry the more he will use this convenient work.

A second index also deserves special comment: Matsushita Daizaburō, *Zoku Kokka Taikan (The Great Canon of Japanese Poetry Continued).* 2 vols. Kigensha, 1925-26. Intended as a supplement to *Kokka Taikan,* this work collects the poems from the personal collections of more than one hundred important Court poets as well as poems found in certain unofficial anthologies and records of poetry contests. Unfortunately, the numbering system differs from the one in *Kokka Taikan:* the poems are numbered sequentially from the beginning to the end of the index rather than in separate series for each work. Since a total of 41,076 poems are printed, and the manner in which the numbers are indicated is somewhat confusing, the index is extremely cumbersome to use. It is not commonly cited by Japanese scholars, and although we have used it as a working text, we have for the most part not cited it.

Of the special collections devoted to the waka, the most important is: *Kōchū Kokka Taikei (The Great Compendium of Japanese Poetry, Collated and Anno-*

tated). 28 vols. Kokumin Tosho Kabushiki Kaisha, 1927-31. In this work, Vols. I-XIV are devoted to the period covered by our study. A brief summary of their contents is as follows:

Vol. I: collection of ancient songs and poems, including the songs in the *Kojiki* and the *Nihongi, kagura, saibara, Azumaasobiuta,* and *rōei.*

Vol. II: the *Man'yōōshū.*

Vols. III-VIII: the twenty-one imperial anthologies.

Vol. IX: unofficial anthologies and records of *utaawase.*

Vols. X-XIV: personal collections of important poets of the early and mid-classical periods.

In addition, Vol. XXIII contains a rather sketchy and incomplete index of poets, which nonetheless provides some useful biographical information; and Vols. XXIV-XXVIII are a complete index to the poems. Although "collated and annotated," the texts are not wholly reliable, and the annotations are skimpy and occasionally inaccurate. We have, however, used the work constantly; not only does its format make it convenient to use, but more important, apart from the *Kokinshū* and *Shinkokinshū,* it contains the best available annotated texts of the imperial anthologies. In citing poems from personal collections and the like, we have used *Kokka Taikei* in preference to *Zoku Kokka Taikan.*

In the *Shinkō Gunsho Ruijū,* or *Classified Series of Collected Texts, Newly Collated* (24 vols.; Naigai Sho-seki Kabushiki Kaisha, 1928-37), a modern edition of the older *Gunsho Ruijū,* Vols. VII-XIII are devoted to the waka. These volumes contain more than 400 separate items: private anthologies, personal collections of the poets, texts of utaawase, critical and polemical writings, and the like. Originally compiled by the great National Scholar Hanawa Hokiichi (1745-1822), a num-ber of the items were copied from poor texts, and some are of doubtful authenticity, but as our citations in the text show, the collection is very valuable and we have used it extensively. The same may be said of the continuation, *Zoku Gunsho Ruijū* (19 vols.; Keizai Zasshisha, 1902-12), of which Vols. XIV-XVII contain some 200 items.

Representative of the exciting new materials currently appearing in Japan is the *Katsuranomiyabon Sōsho* (18 vols. to date; Yōtokusha, 1949-60). These materials were formerly in the library of the now defunct Katsura family of Princes of the Blood descended from Emperor Ōgimachi (1517-93), and are in the possession of the Imperial Household. When complete, the series will comprise more than a hundred items, largely waka, renga, and fiction. The manuscripts are mostly seventeenth and eighteenth century copies of much older works, but they are said to be unusually reliable, and many of them are unique copies of materials formerly treasured in the Imperial Family and noble houses and since destroyed or lost. We have found such personal collections as that of the "Yamada Priest" (II, 83-88) and the *Daini Takatō Shū* (II, 253-311) of extraordinary value for the evidence they give of survivals, cross-currents, and pre-figurings within the great periods of Japanese Court poetry.

The most important collection of critical and polemical writings and guides to composition by the Court poets is: Sasaki Nobutsuna, ed. *Nihon Kagaku Taikei*, or *Great Compendium of Japanese Poetic Writings* (6 vols.; Bummeisha, 1935; recently reprinted; supplement by the Kazama Shobō). Vols. I-V cover the period of our study; they contain more than eighty items, of which a few are variants of the same texts. Valuable introductions to the individual works are provided in the prefaces to each volume, but there are no exegetical notes, and many of the texts are extremely difficult. We have, however, studied the most important of these works with the help of Professor Konishi, and have cited them extensively in Chapters 5-7.

Some of the other large series of classical texts contain good annotated editions of the most important anthologies and private collections, although different collections tend to duplicate the same items. The older *Kōchū Nihon Bungaku Taikei* (25 vols.; Kokumin Tosho Kabushiki Kaisha, 1925-28) contains in Vols. II and III texts of the principal diaries and *utamonogatari* of the Court period, and in Vol. XXV a useful index to all the Japanese poems that appear in the various prose works in the series. The more recent *Nihon Koten Zensho* (83 vols. to date; Asahi Shimbunsha, 1946-60) and the monumental *Nihon Koten Bungaku Taikei* (51 vols. to date; Iwanami Shoten, 1957-61) are collections of poetry and prose from earliest times to the mid-nineteenth century. They contain a number of items important to the study of Court poetry—editions of the *Man'yōōshū, Kokinshū,* and *Shinkokinshū,* personal collections of certain major poets, diaries, *utamonogatari,* and records of utaawase. The separate volumes of these and similar series are edited by different people, and their quality tends to vary; but with respect to the *Man'yōōshū,* for example, the *Nihon Koten Bungaku Taikei* edition (as yet incomplete, edited by the eminent scholar Takagi Ichinosuke and others) offers unquestionably the best text of the *Man'yōōshū* produced to date, and also has excellent exegetical notes embodying the results of the latest scholarship. We have used the published volumes of this edition intensively in our study, and have listed it separately below along with additional works of this and other similar series that have been particularly helpful to us.

2. Single Works

(a) Primitive Period

We have used as our basic text for this period: Tsu-

chihashi Yutaka and Konishi Jin'ichi, eds. *Kodai Kayō, shū.* Iwanami Shoten, 1957. In *Nihon Koten Bun-gaku Taikei.* This is the most recent and authoritative edition and is provided with excellent notes and commentary.

(b) Early Literary Period

The following excellent annotated editions of the *Man'yōōshū* have been used:

Kubota Utsubo, ed. *Man'yōōshū Hyōshaku.* 12 vols. Tōkyōdō, 1950-52.

Takagi Ichinosuke, Gomi Tomohide, and Ōno Susumu, eds. *Man'yōōshū.* 3 vols. to date. Iwanami Shoten, 1957-60. In *Nihon Koten Bungaku Taikei.*

Takeda Yukichi, ed. *Man'yōōshū Zenchūshaku.* 16 vols. Kaiz sha, 1948-51.

Tsuchiya Fumiaki, ed. *Man'yōōshū Shichū.* 20 vols. Chikuma Shobō, 1956.

We are also indebted to the monumental study and exegesis of the poems of Hitomaro: Saitō Mokichi. *Kakinomoto Hitomaro.* 5 vols. Iwanami Shoten, 1934-40.

(c) Early Classical Period

Four annotated editions of the *Kokinshū,* particularly the detailed exegeses of Kaneko and Kubota, have been especially helpful:

Kaneko Genshin, ed. *Kokinwakashū Hyōshaku.* Meiji Shoin, 1927.

Konishi Jin'ichi, ed. *Kokinwakashū.* Dai Nihon Yū, benkai Kōdansha, 1949. In *Shinchū Kokubungaku Sōsho.*

Kubota Utsubo, ed. *Kokinwakashū Hyōshaku.* 2 vols. 11th printing. Tōkyōdō, 1957. Rev. ed. 3 vols. Tōkyōdō, 1960.

Saeki Umetomo, ed. *Kokinwakashū.* Iwanami Shoten, 1958. In *Nihon Koten Bungaku Taikei.*

. . . . .

Hagitani Boku, ed. *Tosa Nikki.* Asahi Shimbunsha, 1950. In *Nihon Koten Zensho.* An excellent exegetical edition of Tsurayuki's travel diary.

Minegishi Yoshiaki, ed. *Utaawaseshū.* Asahi Shimbunsha, 1947. In *Nihon Koten Zensho.* A valuable collection of the records of important poetry competitions with helpful notes.

Miyoshi Eiji, ed. *Kōhon Shūishō to Sono Kenkyū.* Sanseidō, 1944. A detailed study of the text of Kintō's *Draft of the Shūishū.*

Yamagishi Tokuhei, ed. *Hachidaishūshō.* 3 vols. Yū seidō, 1960. A modern edition, with biographical and other indexes, of Kitamura Kigin's (1624-1705) *Notes on the Collections of Eight Eras.* Kigin's annotations on the poems of the first eight imperial anthologies are so brief and sometimes misleading that the text is of limited value to the novice, but the indexes are very useful.

(d) Mid-Classical Period

We are indebted to the exegeses in three annotated editions of the *Shinkokinshū,* particularly to the detailed commentaries of Kubota and of Shionio and Ōmachi.

Hisamatsu Sen'ichi, Yamazaki Toshio, and Gotō Shigeo, eds. *Shinkokinwakashū.* Iwanami Shoten, 1958. In *Nihon Koten Bungaku Taikei.*

Kubota Utsubo, ed. *Shinkokinwakashū Hyōshaku.* 2 vols. 9th printing. Tōkyōdō, 1946-47. The student should take special note that only the poems the editor attributes to the generation of the compilers are included in this edition.

Shionoi Masao and Ōmachi Yoshie, eds. *Shinkokinwakashū Shōkai.* Meiji Shoin, 1925.

. . . . .

Itō Yoshio, ed. *Sankashū.* Asahi Shimbunsha, 1947. In *Nihon Koten Zensho.* An annotated edition of the priest Saigyō's personal collection.

———. *Saigyō Hōshi Zenkashū.* Ōokayama Shoten, 1935. The complete poems of Saigyō.

Matsuda Takeo. *Kin'yōshūno Kenkyū.* Yamada Shoten, 1956. An important detailed study of the history and structure of the *Kin'yōshū.* (See the note on the principles of association and progression in the integration of anthologies and sequences above.)

Nose Asaji. *Roppyakuban Utaawase, Kenjō Chinjō.* Bungakusha, 1935. A good edition of the records of an important poetry competition, together with the official protest against the decisions of the judge, Fujiwara Shunzei, by the Rokujō poet, the priest Kenjō.

Sasaki Nobutsuna, ed. *Chūko Sanjo Kajinshū.* Asahi Shimbunsha, 1948. In *Nihon Koten Zensho.* An edition of the personal collections of some important women poets.

Saitō Mokichi, ed. *Kinkaiwakashū.* Asahi Shimbunsha, 1950. An annotated edition of Minamoto Sanetomo's personal collection.

Sekine Yoshiko, ed. *Samboku Kikashū no Kenkyū to Kōhon.* Meiji Tosho Shuppan Kabushiki Kaisha, 1952. A detailed textual study of Minamoto Shunrai's personal collection.

(e) Late Classical Period

Apart from the texts in the series and collections cited above, there are no important modern editions of materials from this period.

SECONDARY SOURCES

1. General

Hisamatsu Sen'ichi. *Nihon Bungaku Hyōronshi.* 5 vols. Shibundō, 1936-50. The standard history of Japanese critical concepts.

———, ed. *Nihon Bungakushi.* 6 vols. Shibundō, 1955-59. The most up-to-date detailed history of Japanese literature. Compiled from the work of many contributors, the individual chapters vary greatly in quality. Contains useful summaries of recent historical scholarship and bibliographies.

Konishi Jin'ichi. *Nihon Bungakushi.* Kōbundō, 1953. A highly stimulating essay on Japanese literature that contains much new information.

Minegishi Yoshiaki. *Karonshi Gaisetsu.* Shun'yōdō, 1933. A useful short history of Japanese poetic theory and criticism.

Ōta Mizuho. *Nihon Wakashi Ron.* 2 vols. Iwanami Shoten, 1949-54. A history of Japanese poetry from the theoretical point of view.

Takano Tatsuyuki. *Nihon Kayōshi.* Rev. ed. Shunjusha, 1938. A detailed history of Japanese song and its performance by a distinguished authority.

Tsugita Jun. *Kokubungakushi Shinkō.* 2 vols. Meiji Shoin, 1932-36. The most useful of the older, shorter histories of Japanese literature.

2. Special Studies

Doki Zemmaro. *Kyōgoku Tamekane.* Seikō Shobō, 1947. A short biography of the important late classical poet.

Fujioka Sakutarō. *Kamakura-Muromachi Jidai Bungakushi.* Kunimoto Shuppansha, 1935. A history of Japanese literature in the Kamakura and Muromachi periods.

―――. *Kokubungaku Zenshi: Heianchōhen.* Iwanami Shoten, 1923. A history of Japanese literature in the Heian period.

Igarashi Tsutomu. *Heianchō Bungakushi.* 2 vols. Tō, kyōdō, 1937, 1939. A detailed history of Heian literature.

Inoue Toyoshi. *Gyokuyō to Fūga.* Kōbundō, 1955. A very brief study of late classical poetry, but one of the few works on the subject.

Ishida Yoshisada. *Fujiwara Teika no Kenkyū.* Bungadō, 1957. A detailed biography of the great mid-classical poet Fujiwara Teika.

―――. *Tonna, Keiun.* Sanseidō, 1943. Short biographies of two conservative late classical poets.

Kaneko Hikojirō. *Heian Jidai Bungaku to Hakushi Monjū.* Baif kan, 1943. An important, detailed study of the influence of the Chinese poet Po Chü-i on Japanese literature in the Heian period.

Kazamaki Keijirō. *Shinkokin Jidai.* Hanawa Shobō, 1955. A valuable compilation of articles on the poetry, poets, and ethos of the age of the *Shinkokinshū* previously published elsewhere.

Kojima Yoshio. *Shinkokinwakashū no Kenkyū.* 2 vols. Hoshino Shoten, 1944, 1946. A detailed study of the history of the text of the *Shinkokinshū* and the circumstances of its compilation.

Konishi Jin'ichi. "Chūsei ni okeru Hyōgensha to Kyō, jusha," *Bungaku,* XXI (1953). An important article on the relation between poet and audience in the classical periods.

―――. "Chūseibi no Hi-Nihonteki Seikaku," *Bungaku,* XXI (1953). On the importance of Chinese concepts to the formation of the medieval esthetic.

―――. "*Gyokuyōshū* Jidai to Sōshi," in Jōkō Kan'ichi, ed., *Chūsei Bungaku no Sekai.* Iwanami Shoten, 1960. On the influence of Sung poetry in the late classical period.

―――. "'Hie' to 'Yase,'" *Bungaku Gogaku,* No. 10 (1958). On the concepts of "coolness" and "slenderness" in the poetic of the renga and their relation to the ideals of mid-classical poetry.

―――. "Kokinshūteki Hyōgen no Seiritsu," *Nihon Gakushiin Kiyō,* VII, No. 3 (1949). A valuable article on the importance of Chinese poetry of the late Six Dynasties in the formation of the esthetic of the early classical period.

―――. "Michi no Keisei to Kairitsuteki Sekai," *Kokugakuin Zasshi,* LVII (1954). On the development of the concept of poetry and the other arts as a "way of life" in the medieval period.

―――. "New Approaches to the Study of the *Nō* Drama," *Tōkyō Kyōiku Daigaku Bungakubu Kiyō,* V (1960). An article (in English) showing, among other things, the influence of the poetic ideals of Fujiwara Teika on the theories of the *Nō* dramatist Zeami.

―――. "Shunzei no Yūgentei to Shikan," *Bungaku,* XX (1952).

―――. "Ushintei Shiken," *Nihon Gakushiin Kiyō,* IX (1951).

―――. "Yōembi," *Kokugo Kokubun,* XXII (1953). These last three articles are important studies of the major esthetic ideals of the mid-classical poets Shunzei and Teika.

Kyūsōjin Noboru. *Kenjō, Jakuren.* Sanseidō, 1942. Short biographies of two important mid-classical poets.

Man'yōōshū Taisei. 22 vols. Heibonsha, 1953-56. A valuable compilation of articles by many scholars on various aspects of the poetry and life of the age of the *Man'yōōshū.* Includes a reprint of the important index to the *Man'yōōshū* originally published in 4 vols. by Masamune Atsuo, *Man'yōōshū Sōsakuin* (Hakusuisha, 1929-31).

Minegishi Yoshiaki. *Utaawase no Kenkyū.* Sanseidō, 1954. A convenient survey of the history and extant texts of the poetry competitions.

Minemura Fumito. "Yūgembi no Keisei Katei," *Tōkyō Ky iku Daigaku Bungakubu Kiy ,* I (1955). A study of the development of the ideal of mystery and depth in mid-classical poetry.

Murayama Shūichi. *Fujiwara Teika.* Sekishoin, 1956. A biography of Teika.

Nose Asaji. *Yūgen Ron.* Kawade Shobō, 1944. An important monograph on the history of the concept of yūgen.

Omodaka Hisataka. *Man'yōō Kajin no Tanjō.* Heibonsha, 1956. Essays on the poets of the *Man-'yōōshū.*

Ōnishi Yoshinori. *Yūgen to Aware.* Iwanami Shoten, 1939. A study of two important esthetic ideals of classical literature.

Orikuchi Shinobu. *Kodai Kenkyū*, II: *Kokubungakuhen.* Ōokayama Shoten, 1929. A study of the origins of Japanese literature in folk custom and religion by a controversial scholar and poet.

Sasaki Harutsuna. *Eifuku Mon'in.* Seikatsusha, 1943. A brief sketch of the life of ex-Empress Eifuku together with her collected poems.

Sasaki Nobutsuna. *Jōdai Bungakushi.* 2 vols. Tōkyōdō, 1936. A detailed history of the literature of the primitive and early literary periods.

Takagi Ichinosuke. *Yoshino no Ayu.* Iwanami Shoten, 1941. Valuable essays on the social origins and literary characteristics of poetry in the primitive and early literary periods.

Takeda Yukichi. *Jōdai Kokubungaku no Kenkyū.* Hakubunkan, 1921. A short but distinguished study of early Japanese literature.

Taniyama Shigeru. *Yūgen no Kenkyū.* Kyōiku Tosho Kabushiki Kaisha, 1943. A monograph on the esthetic of *yūgen,* most notable for its chronology of the life of Fujiwara Shunzei.

Yamada Yoshio. *Renga Gaisetsu.* Iwanami Shoten, 1937. The most important single work on the renga.

Yoshizawa Yoshinori. *Kamakura Bungakushi.* Tōkyōdō, 1935. A useful history of Kamakura literature.

TRANSLATIONS, WORKS QUOTED, AND OTHER WORKS IN WESTERN LANGUAGES

For detailed bibliographies of translations from Japanese literature into Western languages see:

Borton, Hugh, *et al. A Selected List of Books and Articles on Japan in English, French and German.* Rev. ed. Cambridge, Mass.: Harvard University Press, 1954.

Japan P.E.N. Club. *Japanese Literature in European Languages.* No pub.,? 1957.

. . . . .

Aston, W. G. *Japanese Literature.* 2d ed. London: William Heinemann, 1899. A typical "Victorian" treatment of Japanese literature.

———. *Nihongi, Chronicles of Japan from Earliest Times to A.D. 697.* 2 vols. *Transactions and Proceedings of the Japan Society, London,* Supplement I, 1896. A pioneer translation, still a standard work.

Benl, Oscar. *Die Entwicklung der japanischen Poetik bis zum 16. Jahrhundert. Universität Hamburg, Abhandlungen,* LVI, No. 31 (1951). A study of Japanese critical and esthetic concepts based on the work of Hisamatsu and other Japanese scholars.

Bonneau, Georges. *Le Monument poétique de Heian: le Kokinshū.* 3 vols. Paris: Librairie Orientaliste Paul Guenther, 1933-35. Translations, of high quality, of the prefaces and famous poems of the *Kokinshū,* together with a romanized text of the complete collection.

Chamberlain, B. H. *Japanese Poetry.* London: John Murray, 1910. A typical "Victorian" treatment of Japanese poetry, but a pioneer work.

———. *Translation of "Ko-Ji-Ki" or "Records of Ancient Matters."* 2d ed., with annotations by W. G. Aston. Kobe: J. L. Thompson, 1932. Still a standard work.

Jenyns, Soame. *A Further Selection from the Three Hundred Poems of the T'ang Dynasty.* London: John Murray, 1944.

Keene, Donald, ed. *Anthology of Japanese Literature.* New York: Grove Press, 1955. The best anthology in English of older Japanese literature; contains fine translations of waka and of the first 50 stanzas of the renga "Three Poets at Minase."

———. *Japanese Literature: An Introduction for Western Readers.* London: John Murray, 1953. Stimulating essays on important aspects of Japanese literature, including poetry, by a recognized Western authority.

Lattimore, Richmond. *The Iliad of Homer.* Chicago: University of Chicago Press, 1951.

———. *The Odes of Pindar.* Chicago: University of Chicago Press, 1947.

MacCauley, Clay, trans. *Hyakunin-Isshu and Nori no Hatsune.* Yokohama: Kelly and Walsh, 1917. Perhaps the best of several translations of the popular short anthology, *Single Poems by One Hundred Poets,* attributed to Fujiwara Teika. Miyamori, Asataro. *Masterpieces of Japanese Poetry, Ancient and Modern.* Maruzen Co. Ltd., 1936. Contains many poems by Court poets, often with helpful notes.

Nippon Gakujutsu Shinkōkai. *The Man'yōoshū: One Thousand Poems.* Iwanami Shoten, 1940. Good translations of a generous selection of poems.

Philippi, D. L. "Four Song Dramas from the *Kojiki,"* *Orient/West,* Vol. V, No. 1 (1960).

————. "Ancient Japanese Tales of Supernatural Marriage," *Orient/West,* Vol. V, No. 3 (1960).

Pierson, E. J. *The Manyôśû,* 10 vols. to date. Leyden: E. J. Brill, 1929-58. The published portion of a projected complete translation of the *Man'yōōshū* "from the linguistic point of view" and with some strange characteristics.

Reischauer, Edwin O., and Joseph K. Yamagiwa. *Translations from Early Japanese Literature.* Cambridge, Mass.: Harvard University Press, 1951. Translations of important works of the Court period with many helpful notes and appendixes.

Sadler, A. L. *The Heike Monogatari.* 2 vols. *Transactions of the Asiatic Society of Japan,* XLVI, 2 (1918) and XLIX, 1 (1921).

Sansom, George. *A History of Japan to 1334.* Stanford: Stanford University Press, 1958. This and the author's other distinguished historical writings that deal with the period covered by our study have been indispensable to us. Our terminal date (1350) practically coincides with that of this volume.

————. *A History of Japan, 1334-1615.* Stanford: Stanford University Press, 1961.

————. *An Historical Grammar of Japanese.* Oxford: Clarendon Press, 1928. A valuable study, particularly helpful to the student.

————. *Japan: A Short Cultural History.* Rev. ed. New York: D. Appleton-Century, 1943.

Seidensticker, Edward G. "On Trying to Translate Japanese," *Encounter,* XI (1958).

Tsunoda, Ryusaku, Wm. Theodore de Bary, and Donald Keene, eds. *Sources of the Japanese Tradition.* New York: Columbia University Press, 1958. A valuable compilation of translations, with excellent introductions, from important source materials in religion, philosophy, esthetics, and political and social thought.

Waley, Arthur. *Japanese Poetry: The "Uta."* Oxford: Clarendon Press, 1919. Line-by-line translations from the *Man'yōōshū* and early imperial anthologies with notes on grammar.

————. *The Tale of Genji.* One vol. ed. Boston and New York: Houghton Mifflin, 1935. A beautiful translation of Japan's greatest novel by the distinguished translator from the Chinese and Japanese.

Yasuda, Kenneth. *Minase Sangin Hyakuin: A Poem of One Hundred Links Composed by Three Poets at Minase.* Kogakusha, 1956. A complete translation, with an introduction, of the best known of the renga.

Yokoyama, Masako. "The Inflections of 8th Century Japanese," *Language,* XXVI (1950), Supplement. A valuable descriptive study.

Yoshida Kaneyoshi [Kenkō]. "The *Tsuredzuregusa* of Yoshida no Kaneyoshi." Trans. George Sansom. *Transactions of the Asiatic Society of Japan,* XXXIX (1911). A complete translation of an important classic.

John Timothy Wixted (essay date 1983)

SOURCE: "The *Kokinshu* Prefaces: Another Perspective," *Harvard Journal of Asiatic Studies,* Vol. 43, No. 1, 1983, pp. 215-38.

[*In the following essay, Wixted explains how the prefaces to the* Kokinshu, *while largely modeled on those of earlier Chinese works, affirm a new value attributed to Japanese poetry.*]

Literary anthologies are compiled for a variety of ends.[1] They can be made for pragmatic / didactic purposes, as was the *Shih ching* (*Classic of Songs*); for the sheer diversionary pleasure of the material, as was the *Yü-t'ai hsin-yung* (*New Songs from the Jade Tower*); or for a more complex mix of motives. The compilation of the most famous Chinese anthology, the *Wen hsüan* (*Literary Selections*), was prompted by considerations that were literary as well as didactic and pragmatic. The first imperially commissioned anthology of Japanese verse, the ***Kokinshū*** (***Kokin waka shū***) (***A Collection of Poems Ancient and Modern***), also served more than one end, the most important doubtless being that it marked, in the minds of its compilers, a coming of age of Japanese poetry.

Making an anthology is perforce a critical act, an implicit assertion of value: underscoring what is to be learned from the past, determining what styles of writing are to be emulated, or setting a standard of what is to be deemed literary. Many of the most famous anthologies in China and Japan are accompanied by critical pronouncements in the form of a preface which serves to explain or justify the compilation. The preface to an anthology is implicitly part of a discourse with previous critical statements.[2] As such, it is more likely to be counterstatement, the assertion of something new, the promise of a new program (even if it is one rejecting what has become new), than simply the restatement of earlier assertions. The thoughts expressed therein are less likely to be carefully developed ideas intended to be taken as ends in themselves than they are to be rhetorical vehicles. What is significant is the intended shift in direction. This is not to deny the importance of the restatement of earlier-held notions; such restatement can serve as a crucial means of legitimizing one's stand. But the restatement of earlier ideas inevitably transforms them by putting them in a new context.

This article will focus on the two prefaces to the **Kokinshū** (completed between A.D. 905 and 917), the one in Chinese, the *manajo* attributed to Ki no Yoshimochi, the other in Japanese, the *kanajo*, by Ki no Tsurayuki. The **Kokinshū** appears in the wake of a more than century-long vogue during which Japanese who were à la mode wrote poetry in Chinese. Several anthologies of Chinese verse written by Japanese had appeared in the previous two centuries, the most famous being the *Kaifūsō* (comp. 751), but only one major anthology of Japanese verse had been compiled, and it was written in a Japanese that appeared quite different from that of the **Kokinshū**[3] The prefaces to the **Kokinshū** stress the importance of Japanese poetry. In all likelihood the very fact that the value of Japanese poetry is strongly asserted reflects a distrust of that value—at least a distrust of the acceptance of that value at the time.

Like most critical tracts, the prefaces to the **Kokinshū** have a Janus-faced quality to them. On the one hand, they look to the past, to China, for arguments to justify and give authority to their position. At the same time, while marking an important transition point, they usher in a new age of literature written in Japanese by Japanese. Only one face of the **Kokinshū** prefaces, however, came to be viewed, for the prefaces themselves became the *terminus a quo* for most later Japanese discussion of poetics. The context of the original discourse was generally ignored.

It is the aim of this article to point out features of the **Kokinshū** prefaces that were devised in implicit interaction with earlier Chinese critical theory; to clarify the background of the discourse used by the authors of the prefaces; and, in the process, to note both the changed thrust of the resultant critical configuration, and at least one feature unique to it. Considerable light can be thrown on the Japanese poetic tradition by examining this topic.

Three main points are developed in this article. Chinese critical theory was modified by early Japanese critics in such a way that the expressive function of literature was stressed. Chinese critical discourse, sometimes in truncated form, was used to give intellectual legitimization to the unprecedented undertaking of an anthology of poetry in Japanese being compiled by imperial commission. At the same time, much of the critical vocabulary and imagery used to characterize Japanese poets, unlike the theory that was propounded, was decidedly non-Chinese in cast.

In examining the Chinese sources for and influences on the **Kokinshū** prefaces, one must look to the corpus of Chinese critical opinion familiar to a ninth-century Japanese educated in Chinese. Such works would include the following:

The "Ta hsü" ("Major Preface") to the *Shih ching*, formerly attributed to Pu Shang (507-400 B.C.), but in more likelihood written by Wei Hung (dates uncertain) in the first century A.D.[4]

The "[*Tien-lun*] Lun-wen" ("Essay on Literature [in *Classical Treatises*]"), written by Ts'ao P'i (187-226) early in the third century.[5]

The "Wen fu" ("Rhymeprose on Literature") by Lu Chi (261-303), composed nearly a century later.[6]

The *Shih-p'in* (*Poetry Gradings*) by Chung Hung (469-518). Its three prefaces offer comments on literary theory and outline the history of Chinese poetry; the body contains characterizations and evaluations of more than 120 earlier poets, ranking them according to categories roughly equivalent to A, A-/B+, and B gradings.[7]

The preface to the *Wen hsüan* by Hsiao T'ung (501-31).[8] It is clear that this anthology was popular in Japan.[9] It contains all of the above-mentioned works on criticism, except the *Shih-p'in*.

The preface to the *Yü-t'ai hsin-yung*, written by Hsü Ling (507-83).[10]

One is tempted to add to this list the greatest work of Chinese criticism, one (like the last three mentioned works) written in the sixth century, the *Wen-hsin tiaolung* (*The Heart of Literature: Elaborations*) by Liu Hsieh (465?-523?).[11] However, that work seems to have been overlooked in Japan, just as it was in China for over eight hundred years, even though short passages from it do appear in the *Bunkyō hifuron* (*A Literary Mirror: Discussions of Its Secret Store*) by Kūkai (774-835).[12]

Critical concepts introduced in the **Kokinshū** prefaces become clearer when explicated in terms of antecedent Chinese models. The *manajo* opens as follows:

> Japanese verse takes root in the soil of one's heart and blossoms forth in the forest of words. While a man is in the world, he cannot be inactive. His thoughts and concerns easily shift, his joy and sor-row change in turn. Emotion is born of intent, song takes shape in words. Therefore, when a person is pleased, his voice is happy, and when frustrated, his sighs are sad. He is able to set forth his feelings, to express his indignation. To move heaven and earth, to affect the gods and demons, to transform human relations, or to harmonize husband and wife, there is nothing more suitable than Japanese verse.[13]

Poetry is said to find its origin in the heart. The source for this statement is the "Yüeh chi" ("Record of Music") chapter of the *Li chi* (*Record of Rites*):

> Emotion stirs within, then takes form in sound. . . . Poetry gives words to one's intent. Songs give music to one's voice. Dance gives movement to one's manner, and all three originate from the heart.[14]

In the "Major Preface" to the *Shih ching,* poetry is described in similar terms:

> Poetry is the outcome of intent. In the mind it is intent; expressed in words, it becomes poetry. Emotion stirs within and forms into words. As the words are inadequate, one sighs them. As the sighing is inadequate, one sings aloud. As the singing is inadequate, without knowing it, the hands start to dance, and the feet beat in time.[15]

The *manajo* passage combines elements that are pragmatic (the poet can "move heaven and earth, affect the gods and demons, transform human relations, and harmonize husband and wife"), as well as expressive (he "sets forth his feelings" and "expresses his excitement"). What is stated as simple fact by Yoshimochi concerning the pragmatic end of literature is presented in a more carefully argued form in the "Major Preface" to the *Shih ching*. There, as noted above, emotion is said to be expressed in sound: in sighing, humming, and the dancing of hands and feet. Wei Hung develops his argument from this point:

> When sounds are accomplished with artistry, they become a theme. The theme heard in a well-ordered time is one of contentment, whereby joy is expressed at the government being in harmony. The theme heard in a disordered time is one of resentment. . . . The theme heard in a state of ruin is mournful. . . . Therefore, to give proper recognition to success and failure, to move the powers of Heaven and Earth, to promote responses amongst ghosts and supernatural spirits, there is nothing like poetry.[16]

Here the implication is that a poet responding to external stimuli cannot but reflect those stimuli; he cannot but reflect the environment in his poetry. (It was for this reason that the *Shih ching* is said to have been collected, as a record or mirroring of the feelings and concerns of the people.)[17] A good environment produces songs of contentment, just as elsewhere in early Chinese critical theory it is stated that the music of a disordered state expresses disaffection and anger.[18]

The further implication, unstated in the "Major Preface," but found in the *I ching* (*Classic of Change*) and beautifully elaborated in the opening chapter of *Wen-hsin tiao-lung,* "Yüan tao" ("On Tracing the *Tao*"), is that patterned words, i.e., poetry or literature, are a manifestation or correlate of a cosmic *tao* (or Way), a correlate that acts in sympathetic harmony, or mutual resonance, with the cosmos.[19] Hence the "Major Preface" states that there is nothing like poetry to give proper recognition to success and failure, to move the powers of heaven and earth, and to promote responses among ghosts and supernatural spirits.

Chung Hung in the opening section of the *Shih-p'in* presents a similar formula:

> Life-breath[20] moves the external world, and the external world moves us. Our sensibilities, once stirred, manifest themselves in dance and song. This manifestation illumines heaven, earth, and man and makes resplendent the whole of creation.

That is to say, poetry, the extension of song and dance, is a cosmic correlate that reflects and adumbrates the manifold glory of the cosmos. He continues:

> Heavenly and earthly spirits depend on it to receive oblation, and ghosts of darkness depend on it for secular reports.

Poetry is said to be an instrument whereby man communes with his two complements in the universe, heaven and earth. He does this by deferentially reflecting their manifold interworkings in his poetry; in so doing, he communicates with the supernatural, just as in the "Great Preface" eulogies are said to be a "means whereby successes are reported to supernatural intelligences."[21] To this, Chung Hung then adds:

> For moving heaven and earth and for stirring ghosts and spirits, there is nothing better than poetry.[22]

Heaven and earth, and the spirits, each in turn, react to literary patternings in sympathetic harmony.

These sources—the "Yüeh chi," the "Major Preface," the *I ching,* and the *Shih-p'in*—form the background to Ki no Yoshimochi's statement:

> To move heaven and earth, to affect the gods and demons, to transform human relations, or to harmonize husband and wife, there is nothing more suitable than Japanese verse.

Interestingly enough, of the functions of poetry that he enumerates, the latter pair, the transforming of human relationships and the harmonizing of husband and wife, are more indebted to the didactic/pragmatic attitude toward literature found in Confucius' *Analects* than to the "Major Preface."[23] Ki no Tsurayuki in his *kana* version of the preface adds an interesting twist to the formula:

> It is poetry which, without effort, moves heaven and earth, stirs the feelings of the invisible gods

and spirits, smooths the relations of men and women, and calms the hearts of fierce warriors.[24]

The concept that poetry is able to calm fierce warriors' hearts, one should add, is quite un-Chinese.

E. B. Ceadel argues that the Chinese preface to the *Kokinshū* was written before and served as the basis for the Japanese preface.[25] Pointing to several passages from Chinese critical sources that appear in the *Kokinshū* prefaces, with but slight modification in the Chinese version and with greater change in the Japanese text, he argues that Tsurayuki wrote the *kana* version by modifying the *manajo* text (the latter being the mediator of Chinese critical principles). This view is open to question. Tsurayuki himself wrote a Chinese preface of his own to the *Shinsen wakashū* (*An Anthology of Japanese Poems, Newly Selected*). Although he was not the master in the writing of Chinese prose that Yoshimochi was, it is likely that they were both familiar with the same Chinese sources.[26] Moreover, there is one passage in particular that appears in the Japanese preface to the *Kokinshū* (with no counterpart in the Chinese preface) and seems clearly indebted to a Chinese model. I refer to the listing (virtually a litany, in a nonreligious sense) of circumstances under which the anthology's poets are said to have expressed themselves; the opening paragraph in the following passage from the *kanajo* has its equivalent in the *manajo*,[27] but not the listing the follows:

> Whenever there were blossoms at dawn in spring or moonlit autumn nights, the generations of sovereigns of old summoned their attendants to compose poetry inspired by these beauties. Sometimes the poet wandered through untraveled places to use the image of the blossoms; sometimes he went to dark unknown wilderness lands to write of the moon. The sovereigns surely read these and distinguished the wise from the foolish.

> Not only at such times, but on other occasions as well:
>   the poet might make comparison to pebbles,
>   or appeal to his lord by referring to Tsukuba Mountain;
>   joy overflowing, his heart might be filled with delight;
>   he could compare his smoldering love to the smoke rising from Fuji,
>   turn his thoughts to friends when he heard the voice of the pining cricket,
>   think of the pines of Takasago and Suminoe as having grown up with him,
>   recall the olden days of Otoko Mountain,
>   or protest the swift passage of the maiden flowers' beauty;
>   seeing the blossoms fall on a spring morn, hearing the leaves fall on an autumn

> evening, he sighed to see the drifts of snow and ripples in the mirror
>   increase with each passing year;
>   he was startled to realize the brevity of his life when he saw the dew on the
>   grass or the foam on the waters;
>   he who had prospered yesterday lost his influence;
>   falling in the world, he became estranged from those he had loved;
>   he might invoke the waves on Matsuyama, dip water from the meadow spring,
>   gaze upon the underleaves of the autumn bush clover,
>   count the flutterings of the wings of the snipe at dawn,
>   or bemoan the sad lengths of the black bamboo;
>   alluding to the Yoshino River, he complained of the ways of the world of love;
>   or he might hear that there was no smoke rising from Mount Fuji,
>   or that the Nagara bridge had been rebuilt.
> At such times, it was only through poetry that his heart was soothed.

Each of the circumstances mentioned above (indicated by a new line in the indented run-on passage) refers to a specific poem or group of poems in the *Kokinshū*. There is no such listing by Yoshimochi in the Chinese preface.

Chung Hung in the *Shih-p'in,* after making a somewhat different prefatory statement, had provided a similar listing of circumstances prompting poetic expression:

> Vernal breezes and springtime birds, the autumn moon and cicadas in the fall, summer clouds and sultry rains, the winter moon and fierce cold—these are what in the four seasons inspire poetry. At an agreeable banquet, through poetry one can make friendship dearer. When parting, one can put one's chagrin into verse.

> When a Ch'u official is banished;
> When a Han consort must leave the palace;
> When white bones are strewn across the northern plain,
>   And souls go chasing tumbleweed;
> When arms are borne in frontier camps,
>   And a savage spirit overflows the border;
> When the frontier traveler has but thin clothing,
>   And in the widow's chambers all tears are spent;
> When, divested of the ornaments of office, one leaves the court,

Gone, no thought of return;
When by raising an eyebrow a woman wins
    imperial favor,
And with a second glance topples the state.

These situations all stir the heart and move the soul.
If not expressed in poetry, how can such sentiments
be presented? If not expanded in song, how can
these emotions be vented?[28]

Although Chung Hung's work was not an anthology, the situations he describes (each beginning with an indented line and concluded by a colon) refer to a specific poet or group of poems that he treats in his critical scheme.[29] What makes this so unmistakably the source of Tsurayuki's list is the latter's tag at the end: "At such times, it was only through poetry that his heart was soothed." He speaks of the same expressive catharsis referred to by Chung Hung at the end of his listing.

Both **Kokinshū** prefaces contain an important passage from the "Major Preface" to the *Shih ching* which is incomprehensible without discussion of early Chinese critical theory. The excerpt is only slightly reworded in the Japanese preface (with sample poems appended), while being cited virtually verbatim in the Chinese preface:

> Japanese verse embodies six principles. The first is the Suasive (*feng*) [principle of the Airs (*feng*) (of the States) section of the *Shih ching*], the second is Description (*fu*), the third is Comparison (*pi*), the fourth is Evocative Image (*hsing*), and the fifth and sixth are the principles exemplified in the Elegantia (*ya*) and Eulogia (*sung*) [sections of the *Shih ching*].

Of the six terms,[30] three refer to aspects or principles of poetry. *Hsing, pi,* and *fu*—Evocative Image, Comparison, and Description—are best thought of as specifying three rhetorical modes. Chung Hung in his work expounds succinctly on them:

> Poetry has three aspects: Evocative Image (*hsing*), Comparison (*pi*), and Description (*fu*). When meaning lingers on, though writing has come to an end, this is an Evocative Image. When an object is used to express a sentiment, this is Comparison. And when affairs are recorded directly, the objective world being put into words, this is Description. If one expands these three aspects and uses them judiciously, backing them up with lively force and lending them beauty of coloration so that those who read a work find it inexhaustible and those who hear it are moved, this is the perfect poetry.

> If only Comparison and Evocative Image are used, writing will suffer from density of thought; and when ideas are dense, expression stumbles. If only Description is employed, writing will suffer from superficiality; and when thought is superficial, language becomes diffuse. Further, if one carelessly drifts back and forth among these, his writing will be without anchoring and will suffer from prolixity.[31]

The other three terms—*feng, ya,* and *sung,* here translated as the Suasive principle of the "Airs of the States" section and the principles exemplified in the "Elegantia" and "Eulogia" sections of the *Shih ching*—had a different import before the writing of the "Major Preface" and are sometimes understood differently by later Chinese critics as well. These terms first appear in the *Chou li* (*Rites of Chou*) in reference to music, where they differentiate melodic tempos, and by extension, poetic rhythms.[32] In the "Major Preface," however, they are used to stress primarily the pragmatic, and secondarily the mimetic, functions of literature. The aim of the Suasive is oblique criticism: "The one who speaks out does so without incriminating himself, and the one who is criticized hears enough to be warned." The Elegantia songs serve the mimetic and didactic purposes of "tell[ing] of the causes for the decay or the rise of the royal government." The Eulogia are also mimetic and pragmatic, for they "are descriptions of flourishing virtue and are the means whereby successes are reported to supernatural intelligences."[33]

If these latter three terms are taken in their original sense of melodic tempos and hence poetic rhythms, all six terms form a nuclear technical vocabulary for poetry—one according with a technical orientation that is objective (or work oriented). Three of the terms, in any case, are so oriented. Alternatively, the other three can be seen to serve more pragmatic / didatic ends—a preferable view, for that is how they were traditionally understood.

An attempt at the application of these critical terms was made by Yoshimochi and Tsurayuki. Variously interpreted and inconsistently applied by Chinese commentators to the *Shih ching*,[34] the terms had become in China a sacrosanct formula invoked for the purposes of legitimizing one's critical stand. Yoshimochi and Tsurayuki employed them in much the same way.

There is another theme in the **Kokinshū** prefaces that deserves attention because of its Chinese model: the view that one gains immortality through literature. As Yoshimochi writes:

> The vulgar contend for profit and fame, and have no need to compose Japanese verse. How sad! How sad! Although one may be honored by being both a minister and general, and though his wealth may be a bounty of gold and coin, still, before his bones can rot in the dirt, his fame has already disappeared from the world. Only composers of Japanese verse are recognized by posterity.

The same theme is developed by Tsurayuki in his preface.[35]

The celebrated *locus classicus* in Chinese criticism for discussion of the gaining of immortality through writing is the "Essay on Literature" by Ts'ao P'i, in which he says:

> Our life must have an end and all our glory, all our joy will end with it. Life and glory last only for a limited time, unlike literature (*wen-chang*) which endures for ever. That is why ancient authors devoted themselves, body and soul, to ink and brush and set forth their ideas in books. They had no need to have their biographies written by good historians or to depend upon the power and influence of the rich and mighty: their fame transmitted itself to posterity.[36]

There are other areas in which comparison between the *Kokinshū* prefaces and antecedent Chinese critical works is fruitful. One is the general structuring of the works. In the prefaces by Yoshimochi and Tsurayuki, as well as in those by Chung Hung, a few general formulations of critical theory are stated, a history of antecedent poetry is outlined, and each (including Chung Hung's first preface) ends with a beautifully worded but rather forced encomium for the reigning Chinese or Japanese sovereign.

Another interesting similarity lies in the nature of the critiques of individual poets. In the *Kokinshū* prefaces, as in Chung Hung's work, writers are given a pedigree that is strained and formulaic: "The poetry of Ono no Komachi is of the school of Princess Sot riō of antiquity,"[37] or "The poetry of tomo no Kuronushi follows that of the Illustrious Sarumaru."[38] This is like Chung Hung's saying that "Hsieh Ling-yün's poetic origins go back to Ts'ao Chih,"[39] or "T'ao Ch'ien's poetry derives from that of Ying Chü."[40]

Furthermore, in both of the *Kokinshū* prefaces and in Chung Hung's *Shih-p'in,* a writer's style is often first described in a terse phrase that may be followed by a concrete analogy meant to sum up the writer's work. For example, Ono no Komachi's poetry is first said to be "seductive and spiritless";[41] to this is added the analogy that it "is like a sick woman wearing cosmetics." The form of Ōtomo no Kuronushi's poetry is said to be "extremely rustic"; it is "like a field hand resting before flowers."[42] And of Fun'ya no Yasuhide it is said, he "used words skillfully, but the expression does not suit the content. His poetry is like a tradesman attired in elegant robes."[43] Compare Chung Hung's description of Fan Yün and Ch'iu Ch'ih: "Fan Yün's poems are bracingly nimble and smooth-turning, like a flowing breeze swirling snow. Ch'iu Ch'ih's poems are quilted patches charmingly bright, like fallen petals lying on the grass."[44]

Another area of similarity between these works is the authors' penchant for setting up a hierarchy of greats.

Thus, Tsurayuki calls Hitomaro the "sage of poetry," which is like Chung Hung's terming Ts'ao Chih and Liu Chen "the sages of literature."[45]

Women writers fare poorly in these critical treatises. Speaking of Li Ling and Lady Pan, Chung Hung states that "together they spanned roughly a century; but discounting the [one as a] woman, there was only one poet for the period."[46] When Yoshimochi describes the decline of earlier Japanese poetry, he states pejoratively, "it became half the handmaid of women, and was embarrassing to present before gentlemen." And Tsurayuki says of Ono no Komachi, "Her poetry is like a noble lady who is suffering from a sickness, but the weakness is natural to a woman's poetry."

It had been common in the Chinese critical tradition to make the "fruit" (or substance) of literature stand in opposition to its "flower" (or beauty of expression).[47] Yoshimochi adopted the terminology whole, using it to decry the decline of poetry after Hitomaro, "who was unrivalled in ancient and modern times":

> Then, when the times shifted into decline and men revered the lustful, frivolous words arose like clouds, and a current of ostentatiousness bubbled up like a spring. The fruit had all fallen and only the flower bloomed.

The idea of decline (especially in recent times) from some antique ideal is a pervasive one in Chinese thought. It had been used by Chung Hung,[48] and is echoed in the *Kokinshū* prefaces. In the following passage, Tsurayuki uses somewhat different language to couch the thought expressed above by Yoshimochi:

> Nowadays because people are concerned with gorgeous appearances and their hearts admire ostentation, poems poor in content and related only to the circumstances of their composition have appeared.

The critical orientations of the *Kokinshū* prefaces differ in emphasis. Yoshimochi's Chinese preface is more explicitly pragmatic than is Tsurayuki's *kana* piece. Both prefaces supply a similar listing of the pragmatic functions of poetry (those of moving heaven and earth, transforming human relations, etc.), and both prefaces state that it is through poetry that the feelings of sovereign and subject can be seen, the qualities of virtue and stupidity distinguished, and so forth. But Yoshimochi has an additional passage unparalleled in the Japanese preface. He says approvingly of the poems of high antiquity: "They had yet to become amusements of the eye and ear, serving only as sources of moral edification."

More significantly, there is no counterpart in the Chinese preface to Tsurayuki's list of the circumstances which give occasion to the writing of poetry in general and which, in fact, gave rise to specific **Kokinshū** poems. The expressive orientation of the Japanese preface is explicit here;[49] when Tsurayuki delineates pragmatic ends, he does so more to illustrate poetry's hallowed origins than to prescribe its goals.

Both authors supply additional kindred statements about the expressive nature of poetry. Yoshimochi says of Japanese verse:

> It is like an oriole in spring warbling among the flowers, or like a cicada in autumn humming high up in a tree. Though they are neither harassed nor disturbed, each one puts forth its song. That all things have a song is a principle of nature.

And there are the similar opening words of Tsurayuki's preface:

> The seeds of Japanese poetry lie in the human heart and grow into leaves of ten thousand words. Many things happen to the people of this world, and all that they think and feel is given expression in description of things they see and hear. When we hear the warbling of the mountain thrush in the blossoms or the voice of the frog in the water, we know every living being has its song.

But the expressive orientation of Tsurayuki's view is underscored by other passages of a sort which do not appear in the Chinese preface. After ascribing the beginning of thirty-one syllable verse to Susanoo no mikoto, he remarks:

> Since then many poems have been composed when people were attracted by the blossoms or admired the birds, when they were moved by the haze or regretted the swift passage of the dew, and both inspiration and forms of expression have become diverse.

And Tsurayuki says of the poems being anthologized:

> We have chosen poems on wearing garlands of plum blossoms, poems on hearing the nightingale, on breaking off branches of autumn leaves, on seeing the snow. We have also chosen poems on wishing one's lord the lifespan of the crane and tortoise, on congratulating someone, on yearning for one's wife when one sees the autumn bush clover or the grasses of summer, on offering prayer strips on Ausaka Hill, on seeing someone off on a journey, and on miscellaneous topics that cannot be categorized by season.

What one should note in reference to these two passages, as well as the important list cited earlier, is that the writing of poetry is linked to an occasion. This suggests much about Japanese attitudes toward the social function of poetry. An occasion which initially may have prompted poetry of an expressive nature became a *de rigueur* demand for versification serving the more pragmatic end of social display. Notwithstanding the development of this tendency in the Japanese poetic tradition, it is important to keep in mind that Tsurayuki's words came to be taken as the classic statement legitimizing the expressive nature of poetry. The earliest critical statement written in Japanese, the *kanajo* later served as the revered source for this view of poetry.

If Tsurayuki's approach is more obviously expressive, Yoshimochi's is more subtly or circuitously so. One can point to the fact that Yoshimochi makes more references to the pragmatic ends (including the didactic) of literature, or that he offers no counterpart to Tsurayuki's list of occasions that prompt poetic expression, but Yoshimochi, like Tsurayuki, was writing a statement to introduce and justify an anthology of poetry written in Japanese.

A preface like the *manajo*, written in Chinese out of regard for the custom in Japan of writing prefaces to important works in that language, could scarcely avoid the accrued referential baggage of classical Chinese. Its argument is couched in terms of Chinese cultural values; Yoshimochi says all of the right things about the nature and function of poetry, as he understood the Chinese critical tradition. But for which poets does he express the highest admiration in his preface? They are Hitomaro and Akahito, authors said to be without peer in all poetic history. Their work scarcely embodies the pragmatic ends of literature repeatedly paid lip service in the *manajo*.

And what of Yoshimochi's discussion of poets of modern times? He echoes a Chinese view of history: alas! poetry has fallen from an earlier ideal state. Yoshimochi enumerates poets' strengths and weaknesses in pithy fashion, but, interestingly enough, not in terms of the abstract normative statements about the nature and functions of poetry made elsewhere in the preface. Bunrin, Ono no Komachi, and Ōtomo no Kuronushi, he says, are among the few poets who understand the poetry of the past. They may not be perfect, but they are acceptable.

Although Yoshimochi earnestly repeats Chinese views (be they of literature or of the nature of things), in the final analysis the message behind his words is that Japanese poetry not only has its sages, but a few greats as well. All of them partake in the immortality that goes with outstanding writing. Ultimately, the Chinese preface is an exercise in verbal bowing to venerable Chinese concepts, and a polite statement of collective self-deprecation for imperfect, yet immortal, Japanese verse. The message is clear: "Only composers of Japanese verse are recognized by posterity. . . . Alas! Hitomaro has died! But is not the art of Japanese verse contained here?"

In terms of critical theory, it is the expressive elements of literature that are stressed in Japan, the pragmatic / didactic elements being given a place that is definitely secondary. Chinese theorists of the third through sixth centuries who were seriously interested in literature, such as Ts'ao P'i, Lu Chi, Chung Hung, and Liu Hsieh, were far more concerned with grounding that interest in a theoretical framework that encompassed the universe and legitimized a pursuit that still seemed to serious-minded men perilously close to being frivolous. The backdrop to all Chinese consideration of literature, from earliest times until today, has been the primacy of its pragmatic ends.[50] In contrast, the *Kokinshū* prefaces, especially the Japanese preface, while paying homage to pragmatic ends, pointed the direction to a more expressively oriented literature. These in turn became the classic earliest source for later Japanese views of poetry. With such a venerable authority as the Japanese preface behind them—its recondite Chinese references misunderstood or ignored—later Japanese writers and theorists (unlike their Chinese counterparts) were spared having to concern themselves with justifying the expressive / lyrical function of literature. This has had profound implication for the later course of Japanese literature.

Notwithstanding their borrowings from Chinese models, the *Kokinshū* prefaces have a remarkable integrity of their own. The creative part of the Japanese transformation of the Chinese critical tradition, however, lies in the area of a different sensibility, a different way of looking at the world, which is reflected in the ways critical views are expressed in concrete language.

One example is the analogies devised by Yoshimochi and Tsurayuki to embody, as it were, the work of the writers they were commenting upon. It is curious how little overlap there is with the Chinese tradition in this regard. Chung Hung, for example, quotes with approval the characterization of two writers: "Hsieh Lingyün's poetry is like lotus flowers coming out of the water; Yen Yenchih's is like a mix of colors with inlays of gold."[51] Yoshimochi, on the other hand, could say of Ōtomo no Kuronushi's poetry that it "is like a field hand resting before flowers." And Tsurayuki said of the same poet's songs: "they are like a mountaineer with a bundle of firewood on his back resting in the shade of the blossoms."[52] There are simply no similar analogies used in earlier Chinese criticism. And few Chinese metaphors characterizing writing are adopted by the Japanese, even in the Chinese-language preface by Yoshimochi.[53] The same difference in sensibility is apparent in the lists of contrastive examples used by Tsurayuki and Chung Hung to make concrete the circumstances or occasions that prompt poetic composition.

In sum, one can say there is no new critical theory in the *Kokinshū* prefaces; it is all based on Chinese mod-

els, but with an emphasis that highlights the expressive function of literature. At the same time, the concrete vocabulary of the applied criticism in the prefaces evidences a sensibility that is not subject to Chinese models. Chinese critical discourse is used in the prefaces to legitimize the compilation of the anthology in intellectual terms. The need to affirm the value of poetry written in Japanese is underscored by its repeated assertion; such affirmation forms the main rhetorical thrust of the prefaces.

Notes

[1] Discussion of critical theory here follows the terminology devised by M. H. Abrams to distinguish orientations of literary theory. The expressive, pragmatic, mimetic, and objective refer respectively to theories concerned with the artist, the audience, the subject (or universe), and the work itself; see *The Mirror and the Lamp: Romantic Theory and the Critical Tradition* (1953; rpt. Oxford: Oxford Univ. Press, 1976), pp. 3-29. (The didactic, although subsumed under the pragmatic, is noted so as to stress that area of pragmatic concern.)

Concerning anthologies in China, see Adele Austin Rickett, "The Anthologist as Literary Critic in China," *Literature East & West,* 19 (1975), 146-65.

[2] The ideas expressed in the remainder of this paragraph are developed from ones voiced in another context by Prof. Stephen Owen of Harvard University, when acting as discussant at the ACLS-sponsored conference, "Theories of the Arts in China," in York, Maine, 10 June 1979.

[3] The *Man'yōōshū* itself an anthology of anthologies, had been compiled in the latter half of the eighth century; but the *Kokinshū* was the first of twenty-one imperially commissioned anthologies of Japanese poetry. Being in *hiragana* (and using *kanji* mostly for their *kun* readings), *Kokinshū* poems were written in a vernacular that was quite different from that of the *man'yōōgana* (i.e., Chinese characters used partly for their meaning and partly to transcribe Japanese sounds) employed in the earlier work.

[4] For text and complete translation, see James Legge, *The She King, or the Book of Poetry,* in *The Chinese Classics,* rev. ed. (1893-95; rpt. Taipei: Wen-hsing shu-tien, 1966), IV, 34-37. Text also found in *Wen hsüan* (Hu K'o-chia edition, 1809; rpt. Taipei: Cheng-chung shu-chü, 1971), 45.20b-22a. An additional complete translation appears in Ferenc Tökei, *Naissance de l'élégie chinoise: K'iu Yuan et son époque* (Paris: Gallimard, 1967), pp. 85-87. Important partial translations include those by Donald Gibbs, "M. H. Abrams' Four Artistic Co-ordinates Applied to Literary Theory in Early China," *Comparative Literature Today: Theory*

and Practice (Procedings of the 7th Congress of the International Comparative Literature Association, Montreal and Ottawa, 1973) (Budapest: Akadémiai Kiadó, 1979), pp. 675-79; and James J. Y. Liu, *Chinese Theories of Literature* (Chicago: Univ. of Chicago Press, 1975), pp. 64, 69, 111-12, 119-20.

For a succinct discussion of this and the following critical works listed here, see James Robert Hightower, "Literary Criticism Through the Six Dynasties," Chap. 6, *Topics in Chinese Literature,* rev. ed. (Cambridge: Harvard Univ. Press, 1962), pp. 42-48.

Full citation of relevant Western-language studies of early Chinese poetics (which often, in turn, cite important Chinese- and Japanese-language studies) is provided here for the convenience of interested readers.

[5] For text, see *Wen hsüan* 52.6a-8a. Note that although composition of the "Major Preface" postdated the compilation of the *Shih ching* by several centuries, it served as an important explanation and justification of the anthology. The preface appears in three complete English translations: Donald Holzman, "Literary Criticism in China in the Early Third Century A.D.," *Asiatische Studien/Études Asiatiques,* 28.2 (1974), 128-31; Ronald Miao, "Literary Criticism at the End of the Eastern Han," *Literature East & West,* 16 (1972), 1016-26; E. R. Hughes, "A Discussion about Literature by Emperor Wen of the Wei Dynasty (third century A.D.," Appendix I of *The Art of Letters: Lu Chi's "Wen fu,"* *A.D. 302* (Princeton: Princeton Univ. Press, 1951), pp. 231-34.

For an informative study of the background to Ts'ao P'i's work, in addition to the Holzman article cited immediately above, see Burton Watson, "Literary Theory in the Eastern Han," in *Yoshikawa hakase taikyū kinen Chūgoku bungaku ronshū . . . (Studies in Chinese Literature Dedicated to Dr. Yoshikawa Kōjirō on His Sixty-fifth Birthday)* (Tokyo: Chikuma Shob, 1968), pp. 1-13 (separate pagination).

[6] For text, see *Wen hsüan* 17.1a-10a. This work appears in complete Western-language translations by five different scholars. Those by the first two are especially recommended: Achilles Fang, "Rhymeprose on Literature: The *Wen-fu* of Lu Chi (A.D. 261-303)," *HJAS,* 14 (1951), 527-66; rpt. in *Studies in Chinese Literature,* ed. John L. Bishop (Cambridge: Harvard Univ. Press, 1966), pp. 3-42; Chen Shih-hsiang, "Essay on Literature," in *Literature as Light against Darkness,* National Peking University Semi-centennial Papers, 11 (Peking: College of Arts, 1948), pp. 46-71; a later version appears in *Essay on Literature, Written by the Third-Century Chinese Poet Lu Chi, Translated by Shih-hsiang Chen in the Year* MCMXLVIII *(Revised 1952)* (Portland, Maine: Anthoensen Press, 1953), pp. xix-xxx; rpt. in *Anthology of Chinese Literature, From*

Earliest Times to the Fourteenth Century, ed. Cyril Birch (1965; rpt. Harmondsworth, Middlesex: Penguin Books, 1967), pp. 222-32; E. R. Hughes, *The Art of Letters,* pp. 94-108 (cf. review by Achilles Fang, *HJAS,* 14 [1951], 615-36); Georges Margouliès, *Le "Fou" dans le Wen-siuan: étude et textes* (Paris: Paul Geuthner, 1926), pp. 82-97 (cf. Erwin von Zach, "Zu G. Margouliès' Uebersetzung des Wen-fu," *TP,* 25 [1928], 360-64); a considerably revised version appears in the author's *Anthologie raisonnée de la littérature chinoise* (Paris: Payot, 1948), pp. 419-25; B. M. Alexéiev's Russian rendition appears in the *Bulletin de l'Académie des Sciences de l'URSS* (Classe des sciences littéraires et linguistiques), 3.4 (1944), 143-64.

Note also the following four Western-language studies of the "Wen fu": Chen Shih-hsiang, "Lu Chi's Life and the Correct Date of His 'Essay on Literature,'" and "Some Discussion of the Translation," in *Literature as Light against Darkness,* pp. 1-21, 22-45; Chou Ju-ch'ang, "An Introduction to Lu Chi's *Wen Fu,*" *Studia Serica,* 9 (1950), 42-65; Sister Mary Gregory Knoerle, "The Poetic Theories of Lu Chi, with a Brief Comparison with Horace's 'Ars Poetica,'" *Journal of Aesthetics and Art Criticism,* 25.2 (Winter 1966), 137-43.

[7] For text, see Ch'en Yen-chieh, *Shih-p'in chu (Poetry Gradings Annotated)* (1927; rpt. Taipei: T'ai-wan K'ai-ming shu-tien, 1960). The three prefaces and two of the three sections of gradings in the work are translated in full by John Timothy Wixted, "A Translation of the *Classification of Poets (Shih-p'in)* by Chung Hung (469-518)," Appendix A of "The Literary Criticism of Yüan Hao-wen (1190-1257)," Diss. Oxford 1976, pp. 462-91 (q.v. for an earlier version of the translations offered in this study).

Western-language studies of the *Shih-p'in* include the following: Hellmut Wilhelm, "A Note on Chung Hung and His *Shih-p'in,*" in *Wen-lin: Studies in the Chinese Humanities,* ed. Chow Tse-tsung (Madison: Univ. of Wisconsin Press, 1968), pp. 111-20; E Bruce Brooks, "A Geometry of the Shr pīn," in ibid., pp. 121-50; Cha Chu Whan, "On Enquiries for Ideal Poetry: An Instance of Chung Hung," *Tamkang Review,* 6.2 & 7.1 (Oct. 1975-Apr. 1976), 43-54; Yeh Chia-ying and Jan W. Walls, "Theory, Standards, and Practice of Criticizing Poetry in Chung Hung's *Shih-p'in,*" in *Studies in Chinese Poetry and Poetics,* Vol. 1, ed. Ronald C. Miao (San Francisco: Chinese Materials Center, 1978), 43-79; John Timothy Wixted, "The Nature of Evaluation in the *Shih-p'in* (Gradings of Poets) by Chung Hung (A.D. 469-518)," in *Theories of the Arts in China,* ed. Susan Bush and Christian Murck (Princeton: Princeton Univ. Press, 1983).

For Japanese-language translation and annotation to the *Shih-p'in,* see Takagi Masakazu *Shō Kō, Shihin (Chung*

Hung, Poetry Gradings) (Tokyo: Tōkai Daigaku Shup-pankai, 1978); Kōzen Hiroshi, "Shihin" in *Bun-gaku ronshū* (*A Collection of Discussions of Literature*), by Arai Ken and Kōzen Hiroshi (Tokyo: Asahi Shimbunsha, 1972), pp. 1-260 (hereafter cited as Kō‚ zen); and Takamatsu Kōmei (Takaaki) *Shihin shōkai . . .* (*Detailed Explication of Poetry Gradings*) (Hiro-saki: Chūgoku Bungakkai, 1959).

[8] For text, see *Wen hsüan,* Hsü 1a-3a. The preface is discussed and translated by James R. Hightower, "The *Wen hsüan* and Genre Theory," *HJAS,* 20 (1957), 512-33; rpt. in *Studies in Chinese Literature,* pp. 142-63. An abridged form of the Hightower article (including the complete translation) appears as the "Introduction" to Erwin von Zach, *Die Chinesische Anthologie: Über-setzungen aus dem* Wen hsüan, ed. Ilse Martin Fang (Cambridge: Harvard Univ. Press, 1958), pp. xiii-xvii. Additional translations appear by David R. Knechtges, tr., *Wen xuan or Selections of Refined Literature by Xiao Tong (501-531), Volume One: Rhapsodies on Metropolises and Capitals* (Princeton: Princeton Univ. Press, 1982); Margouliès, *Le "Fou" dans le Wen-siuan,* pp. 22-30; Basil Alexéiev, *La Littérature chinoise: Six conférences au Collège de France et au Musée Guimet* (Paris: Paul Geuthner, 1937), pp. 31-33 (partial).

[9] As noted by Konishi Jin'ichi, "The Genesis of the *Kokinshū* Style," tr. Helen C. McCullough, *HJAS,* 38.1 (June 1978), p. 66: "Among the anthologies of Six Dynasties verse known to the early Heian Japanese were the *Wen hsüan* and *Ku-chin shih-yüan ying-hua,* both compiled by Prince Chao-ming (Hsiao T'ung; 501-31), and the *Yü-t'ai hsin-yung,* compiled by Hsü Ling (507-83). . . . The *Wen hsüan,* in particular, enjoyed the very highest esteem, and no man unable to quote from it was considered educated. Fujiwara no Fuyutsugu (775-826), the grandfather of Emperor Montoku, is said to have committed the entire anthology to memory."

[10] For text and translation, see James Robert Hightower, "Some Characteristics of Parallel Prose," in *Studia Serica Bernhard Karlgren Dedicata,* ed. Søren Egerod and Else Glahn (Copenhagen: Ejnar Munksgaard, 1959), pp. 77-87; rpt. in *Studies in Chinese Literature,* pp. 125-135.

[11] For text, see *Wen-hsin tiao-lung hsin-shu fu t'ung-chien* (*Index du Wen sin tiao lung, avec texte critique*), ed. Wang Li-ch'i (1952; rpt. Taipei: Ch'eng-wen ch'u-pan-she, 1968). The work appears in a complete trans-lation by Vincent Yu-cheng Shih, *The Literary Mind and the Carving of Dragons* (New York: Columbia Univ. Press, 1959), and in a partial translation (five chapters) by Yang Hsien-yi and Gladys Yang, "Carv-ing a Dragon at the Core of Literature," *Chinese Lit-erature,* (June 1962), pp. 58-71.

Western-language studies of the work include the fol-lowing: Vincent Y. C. Shih, "Classicism in Liu Hsieh's 'Wen-hsin tiao-lung,'" *Asiatische Studien/Études Asia-tiques,* 7 (1953), pp. 122-34; Liu Shou-sung, "Liu Hsieh on Writing," *Chinese Literature,* (June 1962), pp. 72-81; Donald A. Gibbs, "Literary Theory in the *Wen-hsin tiao-lung,* Sixth Century Chinese Treatise on the Genesis of Literature and Conscious Artistry," Diss. Univ. of Washington 1970; Donald A. Gibbs, "Liu Hsieh, Author of the *Wen-hsin tiao-lung,*" *MS,* 29 (1970-71), 117-41; Ferenc Tökei, *Genre Theory in China in the 3rd-6th Centuries* (Budapest: Akadémiai Kiadó, 1971), pp. 81-177; Chi Ch'iu-lang, "Liu Hsieh as a Classicist and His Concepts of Tradition and Change," *Tamkang Review,* 4.1 (Apr. 1973), pp. 89-108; Vincent Y. C. Shih, "Liu Hsieh's Conception of Organic Unity," *Tamkang Review,* 4.2 (Oct. 1973), 1-10; James J. Y. Liu, *Chinese Theories of Literature,* passim.

Discussion of the title of this work and how it should be translated into English is found in James R. High-tower's review of Vincent Shih's translation, *HJAS,* 22 (1959), 284-86; in Achilles Fang's unsigned review of the same work, *The Times Literary Supplement* (Lon-don), 4 Dec. 1959, p. 713; in Gibbs, "Literary Theory in the *Wen-hsin tiao-lung,*" pp. 84-85; and in James J. Y. Liu, *Chinese Theories of Literature,* pp. 146-47. These and numerous additional renderings of the title are listed in Wixted, "Nature of Evaluation in the *Shih-p'in,*" n. 2.

[12] From the early-eighth until the mid-sixteenth cen-tury, Liu Hsieh's work goes virtually unmentioned in Chinese texts, except, for example, its being praised by Huang T'ing-chien (1045-1105) together with the *Shih-t'ung* (*Generalities on History*) by Liu Chih-chi (661-721), which latter work had been greatly influ-enced by the *Wen-hsin tiao-lung.* See Mekada Makoto, *Bungaku geijutsu ronsh* (*A Collection of Discussions of Literature and the Arts*) (Tokyo: Heibonsha, 1974), pp. 504-5, and Kōzen Hiroshi, *Bunshin chōryū* (*The Heart of Literature: Elaborations*) (the second part of a double volume, the first part being by Ikkai Tomo-yoshi, *Tō Emmei* (Tokyo: Chikuma Shobō, 1968), pp. 479-80.

In Japan, although passages of the work are cited in Kūkai's influential work, and although the title of the work is listed in the *Nihonkoku genzaisho mokuroku* (*Catalog of Works Extant in Japan*), completed in the period 889-97, no Japanese edition of the work ap-peared until 1731.

For a study and translation (of three of the six sec-tions) of the *Bunkyō hifuron,* see Richard Wainwright Bodman, "Poetics and Prosody in Early Mediaeval China: A Study and Translation of Kūkai's *Bunkyō hifuron,*" Diss. Cornell 1978. For Japanese studies of the work, see the titles he cites (pp. 501-2), as well as the useful text of the work edited by Chou Wei-te, *Wen-ching mi-fu lun* . . . (Peking: Jen-min wen-hsüeh ch'u-pan-she, 1975).

[13] This and other citations from the Chinese preface to the *Kokinshū* are from an unpublished translation by Leonard Grzanka (cited with permission); see n. 24.

[14] "Yüeh-chi," *Li chi* (Shih-san-ching chu-su ed. [1815; rpt. Taipei: I-wen yin-shu-kuan yin-hang, n.d.]), 37.4a, 38.12b. Translation by Donald Gibbs, "Literary Theory in Early China," unpublished paper presented to the University Seminar on Traditional China, Columbia Univ., 19 Feb. 1974, p. 10 (cited with permission). Cf. the translations by James Legge, *Li Chi: Book of Rites,* ed. Ch'u Chai and Winberg Chai (New Hyde Park, N.Y.: University Books, 1967 [rpt. of the Oxford 1885 two-vol. edition entitled *The Li Ki*]), II, 93, 112; and Chow Tse-tsung, "The Early History of the Chinese Word *Shih* (Poetry)," in *Wen-lin,* ed. Chow Tse-tsung, p. 158.

[15] Translation by Gibbs, "M. H. Abrams' Four Artistic Co-ordinates," p. 678 (with modifications). For another translation of this passage (different from those cited in n. 3), along with citation of numerous earlier classical texts wherein some form of "Poetry is the outcome of intent" is stated, see Chow Tse-tsung, "Early History of the Chinese Word *Shih,*" pp. 152-53, 155-58. For the earlier source for the rest of the quotation, note the following passage in the "Yüeh chi" chapter of the *Li chi* (39.23a-b): "Hence, singing means the prolonged expression of the words; there is the utterance of the words, and when the simple utterance is not sufficient, the prolonged expression of them. When that prolonged expression is not sufficient, there come the sigh and exclamation. When these are insufficient, unconsciously there come the motions of the hands and the stamping of the feet" (tr. Legge, *Li Chi,* II, 131).

[16] Translation by Gibbs, "M. H. Abrams' Four Artistic Co-ordinates," p. 678.

[17] The source of this tradition is found in the *Li chi:* 11.27a-30a (cf. Legge, *Li Chi,* I, 216; or Legge, *She King,* pp. 23-24).

[18] See *Li chi* 37.4b (cf. Legge, *Li Chi,* II, 93).

[19] *I ching,* Trigram 22; cf. *The I Ching or Book of Changes,* tr. Richard Wilhelm, rendered into English from the German by Cary F. Baynes (1950; 2nd ed., New York: Pantheon Books, 1961), p. 97.

"Yüan tao," *Wen-hsin tiao-lung,* Chap. 1. Translated into English, with a helpful commentary, by Gibbs, "Literary Theory in the *Wen-hsin tiao-lung,*" pp. 42-57, 179-93. Cf. the translations (complete) by Vincent

Shih, *The Literary Mind,* pp. 8-13, and Hughes, *The Art of Letters,* pp. 236-40; and the translations (partial) by Alexéiev, *La Littérature chinoise,* pp. 24-27; L. Z. Ejdlin, "The Academician V. M. Alexeev as a Historian of Chinese Literature," tr. Francis Woodman Cleaves, *HJAS,* 10 (1947), 51; and James J. Y. Liu, *Chinese Theories of Literature,* pp. 21-25, 146-48.

[20] For discussion of this crucial term in Chinese critical theory, see David Pollard, "Ch'i in Chinese Literary Theory," in *Chinese Approaches to Literature from Confucius to Liang Ch'i-ch'ao,* ed. Adele Austin Rickett (Princeton: Princeton Univ. Press, 1978), pp. 43-66; James J. Y. Liu, *Chinese Theories of Literature,* pp. 12, 70-72; and Yeh and Walls, "Theory, Standards, and Practice," pp. 61-62.

[21] "Great Preface" excerpt, as translated by Gibbs, "Literary Theory in Early China," p. 15.

[22] *Shih-p'in chu,* p. 1 (for the above three excerpts); cf. Takagi, pp. 31-35; K zen, pp. 22-25; and Takamatsu, pp. 1-2. For discussion of the relation between critical theory and early Chinese poetry, see Chen Shih-hsiang, "In Search of the Beginnings of Chinese Literary Criticism," in *Semitic and Oriental Studies, A Volume Presented to William Popper on the Occasion of His Seventy-fifth Birthday,* University of California Publications in Semitic Philology, 11 (Berkeley and Los Angeles: Univ. of California Press, 1951), pp. 45-63; Chow Tse-tsung, "The Early History of the Chinese Word *Shih,*" pp. 151-209; Chow Tse-tsung, "Ancient Chinese Views on Literature, the *Tao,* and Their Relationship," *Chinese Literature: Essays, Articles, Reviews,* 1.1 (Jan. 1979), pp. 3-29; and James J. Y. Liu, "Metaphysical Theories," Chap. 2, *Chinese Theories of Literature,* esp. pp. 16-26. For a clear summary of the metaphysical dimension to some of the texts referred to in the present study, see the beginning of the "Critical Introduction" by Pauline Yu, *The Poetry of Wang Wei* (Bloomington: Indiana Univ. Press, 1980), pp. 2-8.

[23] Although Confucius does not use these exact examples, in one famous *Analects* passage (*Lun yü* 17:8) he does state that the study of the *Shih ching* can teach one how to serve one's father and how to serve one's sovereign. For citation and discussion of the *Lun yü* passages that deal with literature, see the following: Donald Holzman, "Confucius and Ancient Chinese Literary Criticism," in *Chinese Approaches to Literature from Confucius to Liang Ch'i-ch'ao,* pp. 21-41; Vincent Y. C. Shih, "Literature and Art in 'The Analects,'" tr. C. Y. Hsu, *Renditions,* 8 (Autumn 1977), pp. 5-38; Ma Yau-woon, "Confucius as a Literary Critic: A Comparison with the Early Greeks," in *Essays in Chinese Studies Dedicated to Professor Jao Tsung-i* (Hong Kong, 1970), pp. 13-45; Hsin Kwan-chue, "Confucius on Art and Poetry," *Chinese Culture,* 16.3 (Sept.

1975), 31-62; Zau Sinmay, "Confucius on Poetry," *T'ien Hsia Monthly,* 7.2 (Sept. 1938), pp. 137-50; James J. Y. Liu, *Chinese Theories of Literature,* pp. 104, 107-111, 118.

[24] This and other citations from the Japanese preface to the *Kokinshū* are from an unpublished translation by Laurel Rasplica Rodd (cited with permission). Her complete translation of the *Kokinshū* (with the collaboration of Mary Catherine Henkenius), together with the complete *kanajo* and *manajo* translations referred to in this note and in n. 13, will be published in a forthcoming volume by the Princeton University Press.

[25] "The Two Prefaces to the Kokinshū," *AM,* NS 7 (1959), 40-51. Ceadel's article contains much useful information, notably his listing of arguments for and against the prior authorship of one or the other of the prefaces, as well as his bibliographical references to Japanese studies of the subject. Among the latter, note the articles by Ozawa Masao: "*Kokinshū* jo to *Shihin*," *Heian bungaku kenkyū,* 19 (Dec. 1956), 6-13, and "*Kokinshū* no jo to *Monzen* no jo," *Kokugo koku-bungaku hō,* 5 (1955), 1-9.

[26] See ta Hy zabur, "Rikuchō shiron to *Kokinshū* jo," *Nihon Chūgoku Gakkai hō,* 2 (1950), 128, for a listing of references to Chinese sources made by Tsurayuki.

[27] Whereas the *kanajo* paragraph ends with a nodding reference to pragmatic ends, the *manajo* passage is couched centrally in such terms: "On each fine day of a beautiful season, the emperors of antiquity would summon their ministers and have the officials taking part in the banquet offer up Japanese verse. The feelings between sovereign and subject could be seen by this, and the qualities of virtue and stupidity were then distinguished one from the other. This is how one may accord with the desires of the people, and select talent from among the courtiers."

[28] *Shih-p'in chu,* pp. 4-5; cf. Takagi, pp. 72-78; Kōzen, pp. 49-53; and Takamatsu, pp. 13-15.

[29] For the putative poets being referred to here, see this passage as quoted in Wixted, "Nature of Evaluation in the *Shih-p'in*," sect. 4 (where the attributions are based on the commentaries cited in n. 28 above).

[30] For informed Western-language discussion of these terms, see the following: Hightower, "*Wen hsüan* and Genre Theory," p. 519; Knechtges, *Wen xuan,* I, note to lines 29-36 of the "Preface" translation; Joseph Roe Allen III, "Chih Yü's *Discussion of Different Types of Literature:* A Translation and Brief Comment," in *Two Studies in Chinese Literary Criticism,* by Joseph Roe Allen III and Timothy S. Phelan, *Parerga,* 3 (Seattle, 1976), pp. 9-11; C. H. Wang, *The Bell and the Drum:*

Shih Ching as Formulaic Poetry in an Oral Tradition (Berkeley and Los Angeles: Univ. of California Press, 1974), pp. 3-4; Chen Shih-hsiang, "The *Shih-ching:* Its Generic Significance in Chinese Literary History and Poetics," *CYYY,* 39.1 (Jan. 1969); rpt. in *Studies in Chinese Literary Genres,* ed. Cyril Birch (Berkeley and Los Angeles: Univ. of California Press, 1974), pp. 8-41, esp. pp. 14-25; William McNaughton, "The Composite Image: *Shy Jing* Poetics," *JAOS,* 83 (1963), 101-3 (an abridgement appears in the author's *The Book of Songs* [New York: Twayne Publishers, 1971], pp. 105-6); Pauline Yu, "Metaphor and Chinese Poetry," *Chinese Literature: Essays, Articles, Reviews,* 3.2 (July 1981), 213-17.

For an excellent discussion of the term *feng,* see Donald Gibbs, "Notes on the Wind: The Term 'Feng' in Chinese Literary Criticism," in *Transition and Permanence: Chinese History and Culture, A Festschrift in Honor of Dr. Hsiao Kung-ch'üan,* ed. David C. Buxbaum and Frederick W. Mote (Hong Kong: Cathay Press, 1972), pp. 285-93. For helpful translations of four early Chinese critical texts that discuss the development in the meaning of the word *fu* (including a translation of *Wen-hsin tiao-lung,* Chap. 8, "Elucidating the *Fu*"), see Burton Watson, "Early Critical Statements on the Fu Form," Appendix I of *Chinese Rhyme-Prose: Poems in the Fu Form from the Han and Six Dynasties Periods* (New York: Columbia Univ. Press, 1971), pp. 111-22. For useful translated examples of *fu, pi,* and *hsing* in Chinese poetry, see Brooks, "Geometry of the Shr Pĭn," pp. 136-38. Note also Ying-hsiung Chou, "The Linguistic and Mythical Structure of *Hsing* as a Combinational Model," in *Chinese-Western Comparative Literature: Theory and Strategy,* ed. J. Deeney (Hong Kong: The Chinese Univ. Press, 1981), pp. 51-78.

One should comment on the statement by Robert H. Brower and Earl Miner that "we need not take too seriously the 'Six Genres' (*Rikugi*) of Japanese poetry mentioned by Tsurayuki in the Preface to the *Kokinshū,* Tsurayuki's six categories were an obvious attempt to produce equivalents for the six genres distinguished in China since the time of the *Classic of Songs (Shih Ching),* and they were not only meaningless in terms of Japanese poetic practice but also, like the pronouncements of our Renaissance critics, conveniently ignored by the poets" (*Japanese Court Poetry* [Stanford: Stanford Univ. Press, 1961], p. 178). The *rikugi,* it should be pointed out, are not genres but critical principles; and they were first formulated in the *Rites of Chou* (see n. 32). Makoto Ueda in his *Literary and Art Theories in Japan* (Cleveland: The Press of Western Reserve Univ., 1967, p. 9) states that "Tsurayuki uses the term 'form' for classifying poems into six categories," which too is quite misleading (cf. n. 34). Note also in this regard the article by Matsuda Takeo, "*Kokinshū* rikugisetsu no riyō kachi" ("The Usefulness of the Six

Principles' Statement in the *Kokinshū*"), *Heian bungaku kenkyū,* 19 (Dec. 1956), 14-19.

[31] *Shih-p'in chu,* p. 4; cf. Takagi, pp. 67-72; Kōzen, pp. 44-49; and Takamatsu, pp. 11-13.

[32] *Chou li* (Shih-san-ching chu-su ed. [1815; rpt. Taipei: I-wen yin-shu-kuan yin-hang, n.d.]) 23.13a; translation by Édouard Biot, *Le Tcheou li, ou Rites des Tcheou,* 2 vols. (1851; rpt. Taipei: Ch'eng-wen ch'u-pan-she, 1969), II, 50. C. H. Wang, *The Bell and the Drum,* p. 3.

[33] "Great Preface" excerpts, as translated by Gibbs, "Literary Theory in Early China," pp. 14-15. In reference to the Suasive, see Gibbs, "Notes on the Wind."

[34] As Hightowr notes ("*Wen hsüan* and Genre Theory," p. 519) in reference to the citation of the six terms in the *Wen hsüan* preface: "Three of the six items (*feng, ya, sung*) are the names of the chief divisions of the present *Classic of Songs,* and while there is no general agreement about their significance there, they are certainly not the names of tropes. *Fu, pi,* and *hsing* are variously interpreted and inconsistently applied by the commentators on the *Classic of Songs.*" See Pauline Yu, "Metaphor and Chinese Poetry," pp. 215-16, for the most systematic attempt to harmonize selected later interpretations of *fu, pi,* and *hsing.*

[35] Cf. the *kanajo:* "Hitomaro is dead, but poetry is still with us. Times may change, joy and sorrow come and go, but the words of these poems are eternal, endless as the green willow threads, unchanging as the needles of the pine, long as the trailing vines, permanent as birds' tracks."

[36] Translation by Holzman, "Literary Criticism in China in the Early Third Century," p. 131. Note the similar passage in a letter written by Ts'ao P'i's older brother, Ts'ao Chih: "There are only two ways of attaining immortality: the better way is to establish one's virtue and become famous; the next best method is to write books" (tr. Holzman, ibid., p. 122).

[37] From the *manajo;* cf. the *kanajo:* "Ono no Komachi is a modern Princess Sotō ri."

[38] From the *manajo.*

[39] *Shih-p'in chu,* p. 17; cf. Takagi, p. 171; Kōzen, p. 133; and Takamatsu, pp. 38-40.

[40] *Shih-p'in chu,* p. 25; cf. Takagi, pp. 252-54; Kōzen, pp. 170-71; and Takamatsu, pp. 66-67. The work of most poets treated in the *Shih-p'in* is ascribed a literary lineage deriving either directly from the *Shih ching* or the *Ch'u tz'u* (Songs of the South), or indirectly from one or the other through a family tree of inher-

itances. A chart of these literary filiations is provided by Brooks, "Geometry of the Shr Pĭn," p. 140 (as well as by Takagi, p. 15; Kōzen, p. 16; and Takamatsu, pp. 161-62). The following provide Western-language discussion of the subject: Brooks, passim; Wilhelm, "A Note on Chung Hung and His *Shih-p'in*," pp. 115-16; Yeh and Walls, "Theory, Standards, and Practice," pp. 45-48; and Wixted, "Nature of Evaluation in the *Shih-p'in*," sect. 5. The *Kokinshū* prefaces, one might note, offer but an echo to Chung Hung's elaborate scheme.

[41] Cf. the *kanajo:* "She is full of sentiment but weak."

[42] From the *manajo;* cf. the *kanajo:* "Ōtomo no Kuronushi's songs are rustic in form" (see also the excerpt cited below, at n. 52).

[43] From the *kanajo.*

[44] *Shih-p'in chu,* p. 29; cf. Takagi, pp. 286-87; Kōzen, p. 192; and Takamatsu, pp. 77-78.

[45] *Shih-p'in chu,* p. 8; cf. Takagi, pp. 115-16; Kōzen, pp. 71-73; and Takamatsu, pp. 83-85.

[46] *Shih-p'in chu,* p. 2; cf. Takagi, pp. 40-42; Kōzen, pp. 28-30; and Takamatsu, pp. 2-4.

[47] Early classical texts like the *Tso chuan,* the *Analects,* and *Mencius* generally speak of "substance" and "artistry" in terms of *chih* and *wen:* see the discussion of *Analects* passage 6.18 in the works cited in n. 23; for the *Tso chuan* and *Mencius* texts, see Chow Tse-tsung, "Early History of the Chinese Word *Shih,*" p. 156. Although the contrastive use of *shih* and *hua* for "substance" and "beauty" of expression appears in the *Wen hsüan* (3.34b), the source for the pairing is the *Lao-tzu* (*Tao-te ching* 38):

> Those who are the first to know have the
>   flowers (appearance) of Tao but are the
>   beginning of ignorance.
> For this reason the great man dwells in the
>   thick (substantial), and does not rest
>   with the thin (superficial).
> He dwells on the fruit (reality), and does not
>   rest with the flower (appearance).
> Therefore he rejects the one, and accepts the
>   other.

(Tr. Wing-tsit Chan, *A Source Book in Chinese Philosophy* [Princeton: Princeton Univ. Press, 1963], p. 158.)

[48] Note the following *Shih-p'in* passage:

> Among gentry and commoners nowadays, the fashion
> of verse-writing has reached a feverish pitch. No

sooner can a child manage to dress himself, than he begins school, hellbent on the pursuit. The upshot of this is that everyone, with mediocre rhymes and a mix of styles, has pretences to being a poet.

Slicked down, fatty sons from noble families, embarrassed lest their compositions not come up to par, spend all day fiddling with revisions and half the night crooning. In their estimation, their verses are outstanding; but a consensus of opinion finds them flat and pedestrian.

(*Shih-p'in chu*, p. 5; cf. Takagi, pp. 78-82; Kōzen, pp. 53-55; and Takamatsu, pp. 15-17.)

[49] Although inspired by the example of the *Shih-p'in*, Tsurayuki's list differs from its model in that it omits reference to the *Analects* quotation (17.8) which immediately follows the long passage by Chung Hung cited above: "Poetry teaches the art of sociability; it shows how to regulate feelings of resentment" (tr. James Legge, *Confucian Analects,* in *The Chinese Classics,* I, 323). The *Analects* citation modifies the expressive thrust of the original statement by Chung Hung.

Both Tsurayuki and Chung Hung couch their arguments in terms of the affective (and hence pragmatic) benefit that the expression of feeling has on the one giving such expression. Thus, both speak of poetry in terms that are genetic (i.e. the occasions that prompt it) and affective (i.e., the effect on the author, at least), as well as expressive.

[50] See the comments of James J. Y. Liu, "Pragmatic Theories," Chap. 6 of *Chinese Theories of Literature,* pp. 106-16; cf. the review by J. T. Wixted, *MS,* 33 (1977-78), 466-71.

[51] *Shih-p'in chu,* p. 26; cf. Takagi, pp. 263-64; Kōzen, pp. 173-75; and Takamatsu, pp. 67-68.

[52] Note the two additional examples cited earlier on p. 232.

[53] It is probably best to think of such statements, so popular in the Chinese critical tradition, as poetically expressed approximations—concrete in language but vague in reference—of traits perceived in a writer's work. Note the discussion of this by the following: Maureen Robertson, "' . . . To Convey What Is Precious': Ssu-k'ung T'u's Poetics and The Erh-shih ssu Shih P'in," in *Transition and Permanence,* pp. 332-33; Yeh and Walls, "Theory, Standards, and Practice," pp. 67-71; and Wixted, "Nature of Evaluation in the *Shih-p'in,*" sect. 5.

Helen Craig McCullough (essay date 1985)

SOURCE: "*Kokinshu* as Literary Entity" in *Brocade by Night: "Kokin Wakashu" and the Court Style in Japanese Classical Poetry,* Stanford University Press, 1985, pp. 421-93.

[*In the following excerpt taken from her important critical work on the* Kokinshu, *McCullough reviews all the books that comprise the anthology, particularly their topics, transitions, and arrangement.*]

Introduction

Tsurayuki and his colleagues undoubtedly viewed their imperial commission as a mandate to advance beyond the modest accomplishments of their immediate predecessors, the compilers of *Kudai waka* and *Shinsen man-'yōshū* . As we have seen, they brought together far more poems by far more authors, covered a wider range of topics and themes, and worked diligently to achieve a better balance between the Chinese and Japanese poetic traditions in order to establish the waka as the literary peer of the shi. They also confronted, with unprecedented vigor and inventiveness, the difficulties created by the brevity of the tanka as a vehicle for the new aesthetic.

Contemporary opinion, which was strongly influenced by Six Dynasties attitudes, conceived of the ideal *hare no uta* as a witty, essentially impersonal expression of familiar courtly sentiments, composed, perhaps, for a specific social or other occasion, but, like the Chinese composition below, capable of independent existence as a work of literature.

> Du Shenyan. Harmonizing with Wei Chengqing's "Going to Princess Yiyang's Mountain Lake"
>
> The path twists: lofty peaks press near;
> The bridge detours: crumbling banks bar
>   passage.
> Jade waters move wine flavor;
> Stalactites substitute for rice aroma.
> Binding the fog: green twigs are supple;
> Pulling the wind: purple vines hang long.
> Now we say feasting pleasure has waned,
> Go off toward the rear lake embankment.
>   QTS, p. 426

Unlike Du Shenyan's poem, however, numerous waka esteemed by early Heian taste, such as the allegorical poems below, required at least a word or two of explanation in order to be appreciated.

> KKS 282. Fujiwara Sekio. *Composed when he had been away from court for a long time at a mountain retreat*

. . . They will doubtless fall
without having seen the light
   of the shining sun—
the colored leaves enclosed by rocks
far back in the mountain depths.

KKS 364. Fujiwara Yoruka (?-?). *Composed when
she presented herself on the occasion of the birth of
the Crown Prince*

   . . . Ever will it shine,
undimmed by a clouded hour—
   the sun emergent
from the lofty eminence
of Kasuga-no-yama.

And there was a more serious, because more pervasive, problem stemming from the practice of borrowing Six Dynasties techniques like Du's. Admittedly
shallow, "Harmonizing with Wei Chengqing's 'Going to Princess Yiyang's Mountain Lake'" nevertheless offers a degree of structural and imagistic novelty by mere virtue of its length. We may find it a
briefly amusing exercise in witty reasoning. But a
thirty-one-syllable poem based on the same technique
may prove too slight to engage our attention at all.
Although the tanka below might be called an exemplary combination of wit and beauty, the author has
found room for only a single mitate, a trite one presented in a form so conventional that there is little
but the *makura kotoba—hisakata no*—to distinguish
it from innumerable others of its kind. How might the
compilers of an imperial anthology include many such
poems without committing the unpardonable sin of
boring their august patron, to say nothing of lesser
readers?

KKS 334. Anonymous. *Topic unknown*

   . . . We cannot detect
the flowering plum tree's blossoms,
   for white flakes of snow
flutter to earth everywhere,
obscuring the lofty skies.

It was apparent that some kind of supportive environment was needed. Whether or not Tsurayuki and the
others were slow to acknowledge the fact, as the manajo
seems to intimate, they did so in the end. And although
we might infer from a hasty survey of the category
names in Table 1, Chapter One, that they merely fell
back on well-known subject-matter classifications, presumably with a view to facilitating potentially interesting comparisons between poems on related topics and
themes, they in fact devised and applied an elaborate
set of editorial principles. The result was a complex
structure that not only presented individual poems in
intriguing contexts, but also constituted in itself an
original aesthetic achievement.[1]

Basic Editorial Principles

The compilers' ninth-century predecessors had attempted in various ways to deal with similar problems.
The *Ise monogatari* author had embedded peoms in
prose narratives, some of considerable length. Others
had combined waka with seasonal paintings on folding
screens, often in contexts with romantic narrative overtones inviting speculation about the figures presented,
as in the case of Tsurayuki's winter-plover tanka (HT
339). *Uta awase* organizers had paired poems on topics general (the four seasons, love) and specific (the
cuckoo, maidenflowers, chrysanthemums, love before
meeting), thus reinforcing literary appeal with challenges to the competitive instinct. Ōe no Chisato, in
Kudai waka, had adopted Chinese subject-matter categories and tacitly called on the reader to guess the
sources of his Chinese lines and examine the ways in
which he had treated them. The *Shinsen man'yōshū*
compiler had sorted poems into categories and, to some
extent, into subcategories (for example, by distinguishing between two kinds of love, omoi and koi), had
paid some attention to seasonal progression (for example, by assembling a group of "departing spring"
poems), had made a tentative start toward pairing
through diction, as in the two poems below (each of
which occupies the eleventh place in its book), had
paired waka with kanshi, and, in a final bid for the
reader's attention, had implicitly invited comment on
his critical acumen by dividing poems into superior
and inferior categories.

SSMYS 1 Spring 11, KKS 46. Anonymous

   . . . If we might transfer
plum-blossom scent to a sleeve
   and detain it there,
we would have a memento
though springtime were to pass.

SSMYS 2 Spring 11. Anonymous

   . . . If there were always
field lands dyed in deepest green
   for us to behold,
we would have a memento
though springtime were to go.

For the **Kokinshū** compilers, who were required to deal
with larger numbers of poems, authors, and topics, and
who had no intention of introducing shi or kanshi into
their collection, such potential models were necessarily of limited utility. Nevertheless, they furnished many
hints and, except for the privately oriented *Ise monogatari,* functioned as validating precedents.[2] In particular, acquaintance with *Shinsen man'yōshū* —or with
its parent, the Empress's Contest—taken in conjunction with the other contest and screen-poem activity of
the day, paved the way for the determination that Love

should figure as the largest category in the anthology. The decision was conservative in its return to native values, revolutionary in its readiness to grant the traditional Japanese poetic mainstream equality with imported subjects and themes. Although the Empress's Contest and *Shinsen man'yōshū* had recognized love as a formal topic, they had included only about one-fourth as many love as seasonal poems, and *Kudai waka* had omitted the topic altogether.

At the same time, Tsurayuki and the others endorsed the contemporary assumption that formal public poems on public topics deserved priority over similar poems on private topics—even to the extent of arbitrarily classifying a love poem under Spring, as they did with Komachi's KKS 113. Their 342 seasonal poems, the *hare no uta* par excellence in the collection, were assigned to the position of greatest prominence at the beginning (Books One-Six); and the 360 Love poems (Books Eleven-Fifteen) became the mainstay of the second half of the anthology. The minor subject-matter categories were positioned in descending order of publicness. Book Seven was allotted to Felicitations, poems composed for or otherwise associated with formal social occasions of an auspicious nature; Book Eight to Parting, a Chinese-inspired category considered relatively public because of the association between such poems and farewell parties for departing bureaucrats; and Book Nine to Travel, logically associated with Parting but more private. The five Love books were followed by Laments (Book Sixteen), which included both elegies and poems composed by the dying, and by Miscellaneous (Books Seventeen and Eighteen), a category including many poems in the expressing-feelings mode, such as the one below.

> KKS 961. Ono no Takamura. *Composed after his exile to Oki Province*

> . . . Did I ever think
> to find myself reeling in
> a fisherman's line
> away from all my old friends,
> cheerless in a distant land?

A symmetrical design was thus created, with Love balancing the seasons, and with the three small books in the first half of the anthology balancing the three in the second half.

At the end of each of these sections the compilers placed a group of poems that posed implicit challenges to the reader, and that, for reasons to be discussed later, failed to meet the aesthetic standards applied elsewhere in the anthology: Names of Things (Book Ten) and Eccentric Poems (most of Book Nineteen). Finally, in a kind of appendix (Book Twenty), they brought together a collection of songs used for court and Shinto ceremonies.

We may perceive in this structure not only dedication to principles of progression and association, but also consistent attention to balance—to harmonious opposition between the public and the private, and between the *hare no uta* of the two great subject-matter aggregations and the nonstandard waka of Books Ten and Nineteen. To examine individual books is to observe many instances of compromise. For example, Tsurayuki and the others, charged with "preserving the memory of the past," felt impelled to find room under Miscellaneous for famous waka like Narihira's KKS 884, even though such works were more public and impersonal (in content and tone, if not in kotobagaki) than many Love poems.

> KKS 884. Ariwara Narihira. *Once Narihira accompanied Prince Koretaka on an excursion. Back at their lodgings, the Prince's party drank and talked all through the night. When the eleven-day-old moon was about to set, the Prince, somewhat befuddled, prepared to retire, and Narihira composed this poem.*

> . . . Must the moon vanish
> in such great haste, leaving us
> still unsatisfied?
> Retreat, O rim of the hills,
> and refuse to let it set.

But the principles of progression, association, and balance had been formulated with more than one end in view. By presenting a richly imagistic procession of the seasons, and by tracing the bittersweet course of a paradigmatic love affair, the compilers sought to echo the elegant, poignant beauty of the individual poems; by including Names of Things and Eccentric Poems, and by playfully inviting the reader to search for the sometimes elusive connecting links between poems or groups of poems, they intended to parallel the wit that constituted the second element in the **Kokinshū** style; by endowing the anthology with a logical structure, they hoped to increase its usefulness as a reference work. They consequently followed their guidelines as consistently and in as much detail as possible, using such specific tactics as association by season or other kinds of chronology, by author, by event, by locale, by imagery, by content, by theme, and especially by diction in the broadest sense.

Books One-Six: The Seasons

Turning now to the anthology itself, we may view KKS 1 in a perspective somewhat different from Masaoka Shiki's. First and most obviously, the poem's subject matter, bridging two years, made it an ideal selection to lead off a chronologically arranged group of seasonal poems. When we note, in addition, that the author of every initial poem in every other **Kokinshū** book was either anonymous or dead at the time of compilation, we begin to understand why Motokata's maligned composition was not only included, but given precedence over Tsurayuki's better KKS 2, composed on the first day of spring.³ Considerations of smooth seasonal progression and of balance apparently prevailed.

KKS 1. Ariwara Motokata. *Composed on a day when spring arrived during the old year*

. . . Springtime has arrived
while the old year lingers on.
   What then of the year?
Are we to talk of "last year"?
Or are we to say "this year"?

KKS 2. Ki no Tsurayuki. *Composed on the first day of spring*

. . . On this first spring day
might warm breezes be melting
   the frozen waters
I scooped up, cupping my hands
and letting my sleeves soak through?

It is probably no accident that Tsurayuki's poem, with its Chinese allusion, its artful review of the seasons, its engo, and its excellent aural pattern, was placed precisely where it showed to best advantage, between the shallow wit of Motokata's waka and the simple, song-like, anonymous KKS 3:

KKS 3. Anonymous. *Topic unknown*

. . . Where are we to seek
the layered haze of springtime
   while snow still falls
in the hills of Yoshino,
the hills of fair Yoshino?

The technique employed in the sequence—a precursor of the medieval practice of constructing poetic sequences made up of *ji* ("background") and *mon* ("design") compositions—is one that recurs with some frequency in **Kokinshū**. In the scattering-blossoms group below, for example, the originality of Sosei's conception stands in sharp contrast to Sōku's two hackneyed treatments.

KKS 75. Sōku. *On seeing cherry blossoms scattering at the Urin'in*

. . . Although it is spring
where the cherry tree's blossoms
   take leave of the boughs,
the ever falling snowflakes
are unlikely to dissolve.

KKS 76. Sosei. *On seeing scattered cherry blossoms*

. . . Does anyone know
the dwelling place of the wind,
   scatterer of flowers?
Tell me that I may go there
and deliver a complaint.

KKS 77. Sōku. *On cherry blossoms at the Urin'in*

. . . You cherry blossoms,
I would like to scatter, too,
   for human beings
are but dismal spectacles
once their brief blooming is done.

Likewise, two good Felicitations waka by Henjō and Narihira, KKS 348 and KKS 349, seem even better when compared with the mediocrity of their neighbors. Emperor Kōkō's KKS 347 merely presents a thirty-one-syllable prose statement, and Koreoka's KKS 350 is competent but trite.

KKS 347. Emperor Kōkō. *A poem composed by the Ninna Emperor for His Majesty's celebration in honor of Archbiship Henjō's seventieth year*

. . . If only I might
manage somehow to survive,
   savoring pleasures
such as these, to witness your
eight thousand generations!

KKS 348. Archbishop Henjō. *While the Ninna Emperor was a Prince, he sent his grandmother a silver-trimmed staff to commemorate her eightieth year. When Henjō saw the staff, he composed this on the grandmother's behalf.*

. . . Might it have been cut
by one of the mighty gods?
   With its assistance,
I can climb the hill of age
for a thousand happy years.

KKS 349. Ariwara Narihira. *Composed when there was a fortieth-year celebration for the Horikawa Chancellor [Mototsune] at the Kujō Mansion*

. . . Scatter at random,
O blossoms of the cherry,
   and cloud the heavens,
that you may conceal the path
old age is said to follow.

KKS 350. Ki no Koreoka (?-?). *Composed on the day when Prince Sadatoki held a celebration at Ōi in honor of his aunt's fortieth year*⁴

. . . Like the countless years
of her life—such is the sum

of the pearly drops
in the cascade rushing down
Kameyama's mighty rocks.

In the same way, Tadanine's finely lyrical KKS 625 is
enhanced by emerging unexpectedly from a huddle of
wordplay poems:

KKS 623. Ono no Komachi. *Topic unknown*

. . . There is no seaweed
to be gathered in this bay.
   Does he not know it—
the fisher who comes and comes
until his legs grow weary?

KKS 624. Minamoto Muneyuki (d. 939). *Topic
unknown*

. . . If this night goes by
with no meeting between us,
   shall I, for a time
lengthy as a day in spring,
think you completely heartless?

KKS 625. Mibu no Tadamine. *Topic unknown*

. . . The hours before dawn
seem saddest of all to me
   since that leave-taking
when I saw in the heavens
the pale moon's indifferent face.

KKS 626. Ariwara Motokata. *Topic unknown*

. . . As a breaking wave
must glimpse the shore and return,
   so must I go back
frustrated and embittered
without having met my love.

KKS 627. Anonymous. *Topic unknown*

. . . That people should talk
before we have even met—
   might it be because
gossip resembles a wave
rising before the wind blows?

KKS 628. Mibu no Tadamine. *Topic unknown*

. . . How painful to have
this groundless reputation
   as though I were kin
to the River of Scandal
flowing in Michinoku.

KKS 629. Miharu Arisuke (?-?). *Topic unknown*

. . . Pointless though they be,
empty rumors have risen
   like Tatsuta's stream.
Shall I now abandon hope
of a successful crossing?

Besides serving as a foil for Tsurayuki's KKS 2, KKS
3 introduces the first Spring topic, which might be
identified as "lingering traces of winter in the new
year"—and in so doing, illustrates another ordering
device sometimes employed by the compilers, that of
authorship. There is a persistent tendency for the anonymous poems in a group to precede those by known
authors, whose works are then given in roughly chronological order. The "young greens" topic, for example,
consists of three poems by anonymous authors (KKS
18-20), one by Emperor Kōkō (KKS 21), and one by
Tsurayuki (KKS 22). . . .

In the opening pages of Book One, the authorship pattern is obscured by the introduction of the warbler, an
image conventionally associated with the transitional
period between winter and spring because of the bird's
presumed inability to distinguish between snow and plum
blossoms. KKS 4, a poem by a Period Two author, hints
that the warbler will soon appear; KKS 5 (anonymous)
and KKS 6 (Sosei) show him as present. The bird's
elegant confusion in KKS 6 serves as a link to a new
topic introduced in KKS 7, a man's similar confusion,
and that poem is consequently anonymous. The last two
"lingering snow" poems, KKS 8 and KKS 9, are by
Yasuhide (Period Two) and Tsurayuki (Period Three).

At this point in the Spring section, the weather has
settled sufficiently for the reintroduction of the warbler, which henceforth becomes a unifying image for
the season, flitting in and out while the characteristic
terrestrial phenomena of the first three months—young
greens, new willow leaves, plum blossoms, cherry blossoms, wisteria, and kerria—make their appearance in
chronological order, with primary attention devoted to
the two most important, cherry blossoms and plum
blossoms. As has been noted, almost 45 percent of
Book Two (KKS 90-118) is devoted to a final major
topic, hana—an inartistic disposition occasioned by the
necessity of including substantial numbers of existing
hana poems, and by the difficulty of placing these
undifferentiated blossoms within the seasonal pattern.

For the three major flower divisions, in particular, there
are numerous subdivisions: plum scent, elegant confusion, scattering petals, and others. Individual poems
are further linked through subordinate images, diction,
grammatical constructions, rhetorical techniques, and
the like. Of the four plum-blossom poems below, for
example, the first two have in common the word *sode*
("sleeve") and the use of a short, emphatic declarative
sentence followed by a question. The second and third
share the word *yado* ("house"), scented garments, and

the short declarative sentence; the third and fourth, scented garments, cause-and-effect reasoning, and a suggestion of romance. The four together constitute an elegant-confusion group, with bewilderment experienced first by the warbler, next by the speaker (in two poems), and finally by a third person. They are further bonded by tonal harmony, by the technique of indirect praise, and by the close union between man and nature established in each.

KKS 32. Anonymous. *Topic unknown*

. . . My sleeve is fragrant
just because I plucked a spray.
    Does the warbler think,
"I have found a plum in bloom,"
that he comes here with his song?

KKS 33. Anonymous. *Topic unknown*

. . . More than the color
it is the fragrance I find
    a source of delight.
Whose sleeve might have brushed against
the plum tree beside my house?

KKS 34. Anonymous. *Topic unknown*

. . . I will never plant
a flowering plum near my house:
    it is too vexing
to find myself mistaking this
for the scent of one I await.

KKS 35. Anonymous. *Topic unknown*

. . . I stopped but briefly
beside the plum tree in bloom—
    yet since then, I find,
the fragrance of my garments
calls forth someone's reproaches.

In some cases, the juxtaposition of two poems creates an explicit or implicit conversational exchange:

KKS 62. Anonymous. *Composed when someone called during the height of the cherry-blossom season after having stayed away a long time*

. . . They are called fickle,
these blossoms of the cherry,
    yet they have waited
for a person whose visits
come but seldom in the year.

KKS 63. Ariwara Narihira. *Reply*

. . . Had I not come today,
they would have fallen tomorrow

like drifting snowflakes.
Though they have not yet melted,
they are scarcely true flowers.

KKS 70. Anonymous. *Topic unknown*

. . . If, when we said, "Wait,"
they held fast to the branches,
    never scattering,
what could anyone prefer
to blossoms of the cherry?

KKS 71. Anonymous. *Topic unknown*

. . . It is just because
they scatter without a trace
    that cherry blossoms
delight us so, for in this world
lingering means ugliness.

The Spring books end with a block of eight poems lamenting the season's final passing. The size of that group and the prominence of its authors—Mitsune (three poems), Tsurayuki, Fukayabu, Motokata, Okikaze, and Narihira—demonstrate the importance attached to the theme by the compilers and, at the same time, remind us of the substantial nature of the contribution made by Tsurayuki and his colleagues to the Spring category as a whole. Fittingly, Mitsune utters the last word:

KKS 134. Ōshikōchi Mitsune. *An end-of-spring poem from the Teijiin Contest*

. . . Even were we not
disconsolate that today
    spring should take its leave,
might we simply walk away
from flowers blooming overhead?

Similar ordering principles characterize the treatment of Autumn, the other main seasonal category, which balances Spring but exceeds it slightly in size, thus paralleling the relationship between Love and the seasons. Book Four starts with a trio of "beginning autumn" waka using wind imagery—the first by Toshiyuki (deceased at the time of compilation), the second, a showy piece in the new style, by Tsurayuki, and the third, a songlike composition, by an anonymous author.

KKS 169. Fujiwara Toshiyuki. *Composed on the first day of autumn*

. . . Nothing meets the eye
to demonstrate beyond doubt
    that autumn has come—
yet suddenly we are struck
just by the sound of the wind.

KKS 170. Ki no Tsurayuki. *Composed when he accompanied some courtiers on an excursion to the Kamo River beach on the first day of autumn*

. . . How cool the wind feels
blowing across the river!
    Perhaps autumn, too,
is taking shape with the waves
as they ripple toward the shore.

KKS 171. Anonymous. *Topic unknown*

. . . First breeze of autumn—
fresh and fine as the lining
    it has uncovered
blowing against the bottom
of my dear husband's robe!

Another anonymous composition in the same vein, KKS 172, serves as a connection to a Star Festival sequence of eleven poems presenting the successive stages of the meeting between the Weaver Maid and the Ox-Driver . . . . The link is established through wind imagery.

KKS 172. Anonymous. *Topic unknown*

. . . Only yesterday
they transplanted the seedlings.
    When then did it start—
this blowing of autumn wind
rustling the rice-plant leaves?

KKS 173. Anonymous. *Topic unknown*

. . . Ever since the day
when the first autumn wind blew,
    not a day has passed
but I have stood on the beach
of the heavenly river.

The related topic of autumn sadness, treated in the group of poems following the parting of the star lovers, leads in turn first to melancholy autumn nights and then to enjoyment of the autumn moon, a topic signifying the arrival of the season's midpoint, the Fifteenth of the Eighth Month. The well-established position of autumn as a poetic subject is reflected in the large number of Eighth Month topics that follow: insects, wild geese, deer, bush clover, maidenflowers, and others. Sometimes the transitions between topics or between individual poems within groups are made through aural imagery, as in the examples below.

KKS 205. Anonymous. *Topic unknown*

. . . When cicadas sing
beside a mountain dwelling
    in the gathering dusk,

not a soul comes to visit—
unless we might count the wind.

KKS 206. Ariwara Motokata. *On the first wild goose*

. . . First of the wild geese:
though it is not the person
    I have waited for,
how splendid it seems to hear
the calling voice this morning!

KKS 213. Ōshikōchi Mitsune. *On hearing wild geese call*

. . . Ranged in procession
like a string of gloomy thoughts,
    the winging wild geese
give voice to mournful complaints
as night succeeds autumn night.

KKS 214. Mibu no Tadamine. *A poem from the contest at Prince Koresada's house*

. . . Of the year's seasons,
autumn is the loneliest
    at a mountain house.
How often I lie awake,
roused by the cry of the stag.

Sometimes the transitions rest on linguistic or rhetorical similarities, as in the next pair, both of which personify insects and use the phrase *aki no yo no* ("of autumn night[s]").

KKS 196. Fujiwara Tadafusa (?-?). *On a night when he heard crickets at someone's house*

. . . Do not wail, crickets,
in disconsolate accents.
    Though your sorrows be
long-lasting as autumn nights,
my own woes are longer still.

KKS 197. Fukiwara Toshiyuki. *A poem from the contest at Prince Koresada's house*

. . . Might it be because
they have fallen prey, like me,
    to melancholy
that those insects still lament
though the autumn night is done?

Sometimes the transitions depend on temporal progression. Thus poems about early migrants precede others in the wild-goose group, and poems about flowers in bloom precede those on scattering in the bush-clover group. And sometimes they work through thematic association. In the first two maidenflower poems below, the common element is the travel status of the speaker; in the second and third, it is spending the night in the fields.

KKS 227. Furu no Imamichi. *On seeing maiden-flowers at Otokoyama [Man Mountain] when he went to Nara to visit Archbishop Henjō*

. . . I travel along
casting reproachful glances
    at the maidenflowers.
What made them decide to grow
on a mountain named for a man?

KKS 228. Fujiwara Toshiyuki. *A poem from the contest at Prince Koresada's house*

. . . Though not journeying.
I will seek shelter tonight
    in an autumn field,
drawn by the intimacy
of the maidenflower's name.

KKS 229. Ono no Yoshiki (d. 902). *Topic unknown*

. . . If I stay the night
in a field brimming over
    with maidenflowers,
might I, although innocent,
be branded a ladies' man?

The major Autumn topic, brilliant foliage, is divided into two parts, colored leaves on the trees and scattering foliage, separated by the aesthetically effective interposition of a series of poems about white chrysanthemums. Within the group, links are established in the usual ways. Fujiwara Sekio's allegorical KKS 282, for example, has been paired with a poem entirely different in theme and tone, but very similar in structure and diction.[5]

KKS 281. Anonymous. *Topic unknown*

. . ."Gaze even at night,"
the shining moon tells us,
    "on the colored leaves
of the Saoyama oaks,
for they are soon to scatter."

KKS 282. Fujiwara Sekio. *Composed when he had been away from court for a long time at a mountain retreat*

. . . They will doubtless fall
without having seen the light
    of the shining sun—
the colored leaves enclosed by rocks
far back in the mountain depths.

The first two of the four momiji poems below are closely connected by theme, by a common place name,

and by cause-and-effect reasoning; the second and third by rain and wind imagery; and the third and fourth by wind.

KKS 283. Anonymous. *Topic unknown*

. . . Were one to cross it,
the brocade might break in two—
    colored autumn leaves
floating in random patterns
on the Tatsuta River.

KKS 284. Anonymous. *Topic unknown*

. . . Late autumn showers
must be falling at Mimuro,
    the divine mountain,
for colored leaves are floating
on the Tatsuta River.

KKS 285. Anonymous. *Topic unknown*

. . . O gale from the hills,
do not blow them all away—
    those many-hued leaves
at which I gaze for solace,
recalling their autumn show.

KKS 286. Anonymous. *Topic unknown*

. . . How wretched am I,
no more master of my fate
    than colored foliage
scattering from the branches,
helpless on the autumn wind.

As with Spring, Autumn ends with a sizable group of end-of-season poems by major figures—in this case, Sosei, Okikaze, Tsurayuki (two poems), and Mitsune. Again, the final composition is from Mitsune's brush:

KKS 313. Ōshikōchi Mitsune. *Composed on the last day of the Ninth Month*

. . . Autumn has set forth,
offering many-hued leaves
    like fragments of cloth.
If I knew what path to take,
I would go and seek it out.

The relationship of the Summer and Winter books to the Spring and Autumn ones resembles that of the smaller categories like Felicitations and Laments to the seasons and Love. They deal with topics outside the poetic mainstream, included for the sake of comprehensiveness. The short Book Three (Summer) contains few poems by named authors other than the compilers and three or four of their contemporaries. It begins with an anonymous composition, KKS 135, in which wisteria, a transitional flowering plant found also under Spring, is associated with the cuckoo, the **Kokinshū** summer topic par excellence. As with Spring and Autumn, the second poem, KKS 136, is by a named author, but—perhaps in witness to Summer's subordinate role—one of minor importance; and the third, KKS 137, as we may now expect, is anonymous. KKS 135 and KKS 136 both contain spring images, and each asks a question. KKS 137 is linked to KKS 136 by personification and to KKS 138, which ends the initial group, by thematic similarity and word repetition.

KKS 135. Anonymous. *Topic unknown*

. . . Cascades of flowers
bloom on the wisteria
  by my garden lake.
When might the mountain cuckoo
come with his melodious song?

KKS 136. Ki no Toshisada. *Seeing a cherry tree blooming in the Fourth Month*

. . . Was it unwilling
that some of our praise should go
  to all the others—
this tree blooming by itself
after the passing of spring?

KKS 137. Anonymous. *Topic unknown*

. . . You mountain cuckoo
awaiting the arrival
  of the Fifth Month:
flap your wings and sing today.
Last year's voice will do quite well.

KKS 138. Ise. *Topic unknown*

. . . If the Fifth Month comes,
we may have more than enough,
  cuckoo, of your song.
I would like to hear your voice
before the season begins.

The principle of progression governs the basic structure of the cuckoo block. The speakers await the bird's coming, delight in its first song, and react to its presence in various ways as the summer advances. Small groups of poems on subordinate topics, such as the wakeful listener, the cuckoo's association with the nether regions, and the shortness of summer nights, appear occasionally. Since the reservoir of eligible poems was small, the links in such cases are not always strong. For example, KKS 153, the first of two wakeful-listener poems, seems to be related to its predecessor, KKS 152, only through the author's common membership in the Ki family; and KKS 154, the second, to its successor, KKS 155, primarily through a common source, the Empress's Contest.

Similar problems of linkage confronted the compilers toward the end of Book Three. Two waka on two otherwise unrepresented topics, KKS 165-66, were apparently considered too good, or possibly too well known, to omit; and it was also necessary to work in suitable end-of-season poems. The sequence below was the one adopted.

KKS 164. Oshikōchi Mitsune. *On hearing a cuckoo singing*

. . . Since you are not I,
cuckoo, why need you lament
  as you go through life
in this world that seems to me
only a source of sorrow?

KKS 165. Archbishop Henjō. *Seeing dew on a lotus*

. . . How puzzling it seems
that lotus leaves untainted
  by impurity
should nonetheless deceive us,
displaying dewdrops as gems.

KKS 166. Kiyowara Fukayabu. *Composed toward dawn on a beautiful moonlit night*

. . . Now that dawn has come
while the evening lingers
  on this summer night,
in what cloudy hostelry
might the moon have gone to rest?

KKS 167. Ōshikōchi Mitsune. *Composed and sent off as a substitute, through reluctance to comply with a neighbor's request for some of his wild pinks*

. . . I have guarded them
even against specks of dust
  since first they blossomed—
those wild pinks, "flowers of the bed"
where I lie down with my wife.

KKS 168. Ōshikōchi Mitsune. *Composed on the last day of the Sixth Month*

. . . Are there cool breezes
blowing on a single side
  of the celestial path
where summer and autumn meet,
going their opposite ways?

In the case of KKS 165, the solution was to match the poem with another composition written from a Buddhist point of view, KKS 164; in that of KKS 166, the link with KKS 165 was probably intended to be forged through grammatical similarity.[6] KKS 166 associates with the next poem, KKS 167, through the notion of sleeping. The main image in KKS 167 is the wild pink (*nadeshiko*), which begins to bloom in summer, and which, as shown in the poem, is sometimes called *tokonatsu,* a name partially homophonous with *natsu* ("summer"). It is, however, best known as one of the Seven Plants of Autumn, and KKS 167 is consequently an appropriate choice to precede Mitsune's KKS 168, which ends the book, and which can be associated with it through common authorship and the word *natsu.* The wind imagery in KKS 168 prepares the reader for Toshiyuki's KKS 169, the first Autumn poem.

. . . . .

Book Six (Winter) begins with waka by an anonymous author, by Muneyuki, a Period Three figure with six poems in the anthology, and by a second anonymous author. The images in the first—fallen leaves and *shigure* (late autumn/early winter showers)—link it closely to Autumn, and specifically to the last poem in Book Five, KKS 313, where momiji is the central image. The link to KKS 315 is through the common notion of withering, and KKS 315 is connected to KKS 316 not only by cause-and-effect reasoning, but also by tonal similarity: the second poem, by its explicit mention of freezing weather, develops the withering theme of the first. As a group, the three demonstrate temporal progression from the transitional early rains through increasingly colder weather, paving the way for KKS 317, the first composition on the book's central topic, snow.

KKS 314. Anonymous. *Topic unknown*

. . . Taking warp and weft
from the wintry showers falling
    in the Godless Month,
the Tatsuta River weaves
a fabric of rich brocade.

KKS 315. Minamoto Muneyuki. *Composed as a winter poem*

. . . It is in winter
that a mountain hermitage
    grows lonelier still,
for humans cease to visit
and grasses wither and die.

KKS 316. Anonymous. *Topic unknown*

. . . Because the bright rays
of the celestial moon
    stream down chill and clear,
the waters where their light falls
have become the first to freeze.

KKS 317. Anonymous. *Topic unknown*

. . . As night settles in,
the cold finds its way through sleeves.
    Snow will be falling
at fair Yoshino, falling
in the hills of Yoshino.

The first and largest group of snow poems, consisting of six by anonymous authors (KKS 317-22) and ten by the compilers and their contemporaries (KKS 323-32), traces the progress of winter from preliminary flurries of quickly melting flakes to the height of the season, when drifts pile high in the mountains. The second, a group of late-winter poems (KKS 333-37)—two by anonymous authors, one by the Period One figure Ono no Takamura, and two by Tsurayuki and Tomonori—anticipates the coming of spring and comments on the resemblance between snow and early plum blossoms. Within both, there are links of the kind we have noticed for the other seasons. The two early-winter poems below, for example, share themes and images.

KKS 319. Anonymous. *Topic unknown*

. . . The falling snowflakes
must be melting as they strike:
    the sound grows louder
from the boisterous waters
flowing in the mountain stream.

KKS 320. Anonymous. *Topic unknown*

. . . Brown leaves come drifting
in the current of this stream:
    waters from snow-melt
must be increasing these days
in the heart of the mountains.

In the quartet below, KKS 327 is associated with KKS 326 through mountain imagery and the Empress's Contest, and with KKS 328 through mountain imagery, the same contest, common authorship, and the theme of reclusion. KKS 328 is linked to KKS 329 by emotional harmony.

KKS 326. Fujiwara Okikaze. *A poem from the Empress's Contest during the reign of the Kanpyō Emperor [Uda]*

. . . Gazing at snowflakes
as they blow in near the shore,
    we wonder if waves
might not indeed pass over
Sue-no-matsu Mountain.

KKS 327. Mibu no Tadamine. *A poem from the Empress's Contest during the reign of the Kanpyō*

Emperor

. . . Not even so much
as a message reaches us
   from one who entered
the hills of fair Yoshino,
finding his way through white drifts.

KKS 328. Mibu no Tadamine. *A poem from the
Empress's Contest during the reign of the Kanpyō
Emperor*

. . . At the mountain house
where all is overwhelmed by
   masses of white snow,
might even he who dwells there
feel overwhelmed by misery?

KKS 329. Ōshikōchi Mitsune. *Composed as he
watched falling snow*

. . . My heart is forlorn,
overburdened with misery.
   Might it be because
I am like a trackless road,
deserted when snow descends?

Five year-end poems (KKS 338-42) serve both as a
conclusion to Winter and as a summation of the seasons. Although the group may seem to lack coherence,
the placement of the poems is not random. KKS 338
and KKS 339, by Period Three poets, present similar
feelings of unhappiness evoked by the passing of time.
KKS 339 is connected imagistically, through snow, to
KKS 340, an anonymous poem on a related but separate theme. KKS 340 shares a common grammatical
feature—the suffix *keri,* indicating surprised discovery—with KKS 341, a composition by a Period Three
author. Tsurayuki's KKS 342 would appear to belong
with KKS 339, but was probably placed at the end of
the book to establish a connection through its kotobagaki with the superior-inferior relationship central to
the following Felicitations book, and also to demonstrate by its authorship the importance of the seasonal
books as a whole. In view of the compilers' interest in
symmetry, it may be pertinent to note that the survey
of the past, present, and future in KKS 341, the second
poem from the end, parallels Tsurayuki's review of
three seasons in KKS 2, the second poem from the
beginning.

KKS 338. Ōshikōchi Mitsune. *Composed on the
last day of the Twelfth Month, while the author was
waiting for a person who had gone off somewhere*

. . . The thing I await
is not the new year's coming,
   yet it happens now
without so much as a note

from the one who went away.

KKS 339. Ariwara Motokata. *Composed at year-
end*

. . . As each year in turn
gives way to its successor,
   the new one brings in
still greater descent of snow,
still steeper descent into age.

KKS 340. Anonymous. *A poem from the Empress's
Contest during the reign of the Kanpyō Emperor*

. . . When snow has fallen
and the year draws to a close,
   ah, then it is clear
that the pine tree is a tree
whose color never changes.

KKS 341. Harumichi Tsuraki (d. 920). *Composed
at year-end*

. . . Swift is their passage
as the flow of the Asuka,
   "Tomorrow River"—
the long months I spend saying,
"yesterday," "today," "tomorrow."

KKS 342. Ki no Tsurayuki. *Composed and submitted
by imperial command*

. . . My heart fills with gloom
as I watch the year depart,
   for shadows descend
even on the face I see
reflected in the mirror.

Books Seven-Nine: Felicitations, Parting, Travel

Most of the next book, Felicitations (KKS 343-64),
consists of poems in which speakers of lower status
wish long life to an Emperor or other personage. Many
were composed for longevity celebrations, events that
in the Heian period usually commemorated a decennial
milestone in an individual's life. The formal elements
of such occasions—a banquet, dances, the recitation of
poems, and so forth—are conjectured to have been
patterned after Chinese models, and it is likely that
most of the early poems composed for them were
kanshi.[7] No **Kokinshū** Felicitations waka by a known
author antedates Period Two. There was, however, a
native tradition of auspicious waka, traceable as far
back as *Kojiki* and *Nihon shoki,* and closely allied to
belief in word magic, as is demonstrated in the exchange below, between a Fujiwara nobleman and Emperor Daigo, which took place during a celebration on
the hundredth day after the birth of an imperial son.[8]
"Moon" is a metaphor for the child.

. . . For a hundred years
from this night on which we count
    every day a year,
we shall rejoice to behold
the light of the shining moon.

. . . If the word-spirit
lives in your auspicious speech,
    we shall indeed gaze
on the moon shining undimmed
though a hundred years elapse.

It was natural that the compilers should include Felicitations as part of their demonstration of the waka's fitness to replace the kanshi on formal occasions, and that Tsurayuki should have taken care to establish the credentials of the category, both in the kanajo and in his chōka, "A Long Poem Submitte d As a Prefatory Catalogue When He Presented Old Poems" (KKS 1002). In the kanajo, he first points out, "In the beginning . . . men found comfort in composing poems in which they expressed wishes for a lord's long life . . . through comparisons with pebbles." Later, during his description of the compilation process, he adds, "Selections were made from among . . . poems in which masters were revered and friends congratulated with mentions of cranes and turtles." In KKS 1002, he says, "It has been composed/through all the generations/since the divine age/of the mighty gods: poetry/called into being . . . /when, in annual custom,/men utter prayers/for our sovereign's long life,/speaking words of praise."

However, the number of available waka on the subject seems to have been small. Book Seven contains only twenty-two poems, of which eight (KKS 351, KKS 357-63) are actually seasonal compositions from four-seasons folding screens produced for longevity celebrations. A ninth (KKS 348), expressing thanks for a birthday present, is also peripheral to the main theme of the book. Of the other thirteen, four (KKS 343-46) offer anonymous good wishes to anonymous people, one (KKS 364) extends felicitations on the occasion of a child's birth, and the rest commemorate longevity observances held for Henjō (KKS 347), the Regent Moto-tsune (KKS 349), a lady of uncertain identity (KKS 350), an imperial Prince, Motoyasu (KKS 352-54), and two obscure figures named Fujiwara Miyoshi and Yo-shimine Tsunenari (KKS 355-56).

The poems are arranged in rough chronological order by author, proceeding from the anonymous quartet through Period Two to Period Three, with attention to seasonal progression within the large screen-poem group, where the main images are, successively, young greens, cherry blossoms, the cuckoo, autumn winds, colored leaves, and snow. A less immediately apparent unifying principle has also been followed. With few exceptions, the poems in the book are closely associated with the three most prominent figures of the day, Retired Emperor Uda, Emperor Daigo, and Fujiwara Tokihira, and especially with their immediate ancestors, Emperor K k and Fujiwara Mototsune. The relationships may be summarized as follows.

KKS 347: written by Emperor Kōkō, father of Emperor Uda and grandfather of Emperor Daigo

KKS 348: written on behalf of Emperor Kōkō's grandmother to be presented to the Emperor

KKS 349: written for Mototsune, cousin of Emperor Kōkō, father-in-law of Emperors Uda and Daigo, and father of Tokihira

KKS 350: written for a lady conjectured to have been Mototsune's daughter[9]

KKS 351: written for Empress Kōshi, Mototsune's sister

KKS 352-54: written for Emperor Kōkō's brother

KKS 357-63: written for Emperor Daigo's maternal uncle

KKS 364: written for Emperor Daigo's son, the future Emperor Murakami, whose mother was Mototsune's daughter and Tokihira's sister

Of the six waka not accounted for in the list, the four anonymous ones, KKS 343-46, appear to have been old songs, selected both to set the tone of the book and to comply with the imperial directive to present "old poems missing from *Man'yōshū*." Within that group, which is headed by the ancestor of the present Japanese national anthem,[10] the first two poems are linked by pebble/sand imagery, the second and third by shore imagery, and the third and fourth by the word *yachiyo* ("eight thousand years").

KKS 343. Anonymous. *Topic unknown*

. . . May our lord endure
for a thousand, eight thousand
    long generations—
may he live until pebbles
grow into mossy boulders.

KKS 344. Anonymous. *Topic unknown*

. . . By counting the grains
of fair sand on the seashore,
    I will find the sum
of the great number of years
you are destined to enjoy.

KKS 345. Anonymous. *Topic unknown*

. . . The plovers dwelling
at Sashide-no-iso
  by Shio-no-yama
cry *yachiyo,* wishing our lord
a reign of eight thousand years.

KKS 346. Anonymous. *Topic unknown*

. . . We will add my years
to your span of eight thousand
  and set them aside.
Let them remind you of me
when the time comes to use them.

The pebbles in KKS 343 and the turtles and cranes in KKS 355 recall the kanajo's references to congratulatory poems. It may not be too fanciful to suggest that the otherwise puzzling inclusion of KKS 355, honoring the minor figure Fujiwara Miyoshi, was considered necessary to give representation to two of the three main symbols of longevity, none of which appears elsewhere in Book Seven, and to surmise further that KKS 356, composed for the equally unimportant Yoshimine Tsunenari, was added to represent the third.

KKS 355. Ariwara Shigeharu (d. 905?). *Composed for a celebration in honor of Fujiwara Miyoshi's sixtieth year*

. . . Even turtles and cranes
meet unknown fates at the end
  of a thousand years.
Please leave the length of your life
to one whose heart is greedy.

KKS 356. Sosei. *Composed on behalf of Yoshimine Tsunenari's daughter for a celebration in honor of her father's fortieth year*

. . . This pine represents
prayers for your eternal life.
  May I always dwell
in the shadow of the tree
that endures a thousand years.

The thematic unity of Book Seven is greatly strengthened by the composition selected for the final position—KKS 364, by the Assistant Handmaid Fujiwara Yoruka (?-?). Tsurayuki and his colleagues could not have guessed that KKS 343, the first poem in the book, would some day become the national anthem, but it must have been apparent to them that with KKS 364 they were returning smoothly to their point of departure. Moreover, the pairing of KKS 364 with KKS 363, a waka by Tsurayuki (who once again appears in a strategic location), contributes powerfully to the total effect of what is in essence a formal, book-long tribute

to the ruling powers. Tsurayuki's reference to the Yoshino mountains, an area long associated with the imperial house, leads into Yoruka's mention of Mount Kasuga, the famous site of the Fujiwara tutelary shrine, and to her theme, the glory of the imperial family and its special relationship to the Fujiwara; his snow/flower mitate parallels her sun/Prince and Kasuga/Fujiwara metaphors; and his snowstorm paves the way for the dramatic contrast of her rising sun, symbolic of the divine majesty and eternal prosperity of Amaterasu's line.

KKS 363. Ki no Tsurayuki. *A poem written on a four-seasons screen behind the guest of honor when the Principal Handmaid celebrated the fortieth year of the Major Captain of the Right. Winter.*

. . . When white flakes of snow
flutter thick and fast toward earth,
  flowers indeed scatter
before the gale sweeping down
from fair Yoshino's mountains.

KKS 364. Fujiwara Yoruka. *Composed when she presented herself on the occasion of the birth of the Crown Prince*

. . . Ever will it shine,
undimmed by a clouded hour—
  the sun emergent
from the lofty eminence
of Kasuga-no-yama.

. . . . .

Book Eight (KKS 365-405) brings together poems on male friendship and parting, two interrelated topics so important in Chinese poetry that they could not conceivably have been disregarded by the **Kokinshū** compilers. Tsurayuki's mention of the first in the kanajo, "[Poets of the past] yearned for friends at the sound of waiting-insects," suggests that he and his colleagues may have considered the possibility of creating a separate category to accommodate it. But there was no Japanese precedent for such a step, and it is more likely that they planned from the start to combine the two, as Tsurayuki does by implication in his chōka, KKS 1002, where he writes, "[Poetry is composed] when tears are shed by people / who must part too soon." The relative weakness of Confucianism in Japan, the strength of the love-poem tradition, and the compilers' determination to assert native values must all have contributed to the further decision that Parting should not exclude poems on separation between the sexes.

Book Eight is divisible into two parts. The poems in the first, more public in tone than those in the second, usually deal with situations in which government officials are about to set out on trips entailing sustained absences, to the sorrow of those close to them; most of those in the second record briefer or less significant partings.

The initial poem, KKS 365, seems to owe its position to two circumstances. First, it combines an attractive sound pattern with two kakekotoba, thus illustrating the compilers' notion of a properly balanced treatment of the topic; second, the speaker is the traveler himself, rather than someone seeing him off, as was more usual, and the poem consequently can be combined neatly with the old waka that follow. Read in isolation, KKS 365 might be regarded as a jesting composition addressed to male companions at a farewell party, but in context it becomes part of a three-poem exchange between a man and a woman. KKS 368, the plaint of a grieving mother, ends what might be called a prologue, four poems bound together by Man'yō-style lyricism.

KKS 365. Ariwara Yukihira. *Topic unknown*

. . . I must leave you now,
to journey to Inaba,
  where pines top the peaks,
but I will return at once
if you say you pine for me.

KKS 366. Anonymous. *Topic unknown*

. . . How long must I wait
to see again the traveler
  who leaves this morning,
journeying where wild bees hum
in autumn bush-clover fields?

KKS 367. Anonymous. *Topic unknown*

. . . Though I part from you,
journeying to boundless
  lands beyond the clouds,
you shall accompany me
in the fastness of my heart.

KKS 368. *Composed by the mother of Ono no Chifuru when Chifuru went to take up his duties as Vice-Governor of Michinoku*

. . . Please do not deny,
you men of the barrier,
  passage to this heart
sent by a loving mother
as guardian for her son.

There follows a group of six waka (KKS 369-74) by named Period Two and Period Three authors, which are all by and for men, and which introduce the chief topic of Book Eight, the departure of an official for the provinces. As with the pair below, they tend to express

similar sentiments in similar ways.

KKS 371. Ki no Tsurayuki. *Composed at a farewell party*

. . . I mourn your absence
even as we say farewell.
  How then might I feel
after you have journeyed forth
to lands beyond the white clouds?

KKS 372. Ariwara Shigeharu. *Composed when a friend left for the provinces*

. . . Might it be because
I think of the great distance
  soon to divide us—
this longing I feel for you
while we are still face to face?

Perhaps to break the monotony, a trio of poems by women follows KKS 374. The private tone of the first one, KKS 375, links it to the introductory quartet at the start of the book, but the speaker, unlike the *Man-'yōshū* wife whose husband shares her grief, is a *Kokinshū*-style neglected woman with Chinese affinities. Utsuku, the author of KKS 376, is a lonely lady using Chinese-inspired wordplay to lament her plight; and the anonymous author of KKS 377 bases her poem on Six Dynasties reasoning. Chinese associations thus establish this as a group standing in contrast to the earlier one of approximately the same size.

KKS 375. Anonymous. *Topic unknown*

. . . I will not inquire
when you might be setting forth,
  though if you leave me
I will vanish from the earth
like a drop of morning dew.

KKS 376. Utsuku (?-?). *Sent to Fujiwara Kimitoshi when the author left for Hitachi*

. . . I cannot rely
on regular attentions
  from Kimitoshi,
and so I have decided
to journey to Hitachi.

KKS 377. Anonymous. *A poem composed and sent out by a lady when Ki no Munesada, who was preparing to journey eastward, took his leave toward dawn after having spent the night at someone's house*

. . . We cannot tell now,
but let us try a small test:
  if we both survive,

will it be I who forget
or you who fail to visit?

A second group of male Parting poems (KKS 378-84) seems to differ from the first only in that none of the departing travelers is mentioned by name in the kotobagaki. But since two of the seven compositions are addressed to "close friends," and since none is identified as a banquet piece, the compilers may have considered the group more private in nature than the first, an attitude that would account for their relative positions. "Close friend" does not appear in any of the earlier kotobagaki.

The first part ends with another group of seven poems (KKS 385-91). In a sense, the group forms a pair with the preceding one: the number of poems in each is the same, and whereas the earlier one names none of the travelers, this names them all. (The first long group contains six poems and names some but not all of the travelers.) But its content is relatively diverse. The first two poems are formal farewells composed at a party for a man traveling to Tsukushi on official business, and the next three concern a man who is going to the same area for private reasons. Of these three, one was written by the traveler, one by a male friend, and one by a female entertainer named Shirome. Shirome's waka, a unique fusion of the Japanese lovers'-parting theme with the Chinese friendship theme, might be said to resolve the tension between the two earlier groups involving women.

> KKS 387. Shirome (?-?). *Composed at Yamazaki, at a farewell party for Minamoto Sane, who was going to Tsukushi to bathe in the hot springs*

> . . . If life were to last
> however long we saw fit,
>   would we be likely
> to suffer such deep distress
> just because of a parting?

The placement of the last two poems in this part, KKS 390 and KKS 391, appears designed to demonstrate the attributes of the Parting poem proper, and thus to return to the note sounded at the outset with Yukihira's KKS 365. As frequently happens, a work by Tsurayuki occupies the penultimate position. Modern readers may find it of minor interest. Nevertheless, it deals with the topic in the approved manner, expressing muted unhappiness, playing on the name of the place, and creating accomplished aural effects with k's, n's, a's, and o's. That Tsurayuki himself rated it highly is shown by its presence in *Shinsen waka*.

> KKS 390. Ki no Tsurayuki. *Composed at Ōsaka Barrier when he went to see off Fujiwara Koreoka, who was leaving to serve as Vice-Governor of Musashi*

> . . . So now after all
> you go across and leave us!
>   The Hill of Meeting
> has turned out to be a name
> that merely feeds empty hope.

KKS 391, doubtless one of many eligible candidates for the last position, was probably chosen in part because the author was Fujiwara Kanesuke, a young court noble who became Tsurayuki's patron around the beginning of the tenth century, and in part because it forms a smooth link, through Shirayama ("White Mountain"), between Tsurayuki's poem, written in the mountains between the capital and Ōtsu, and Henjō's KKS 392, the first waka in the second part.

> KKS 391. Fujiwara Kanesuke (877-933). *Composed at a farewell party for Ōe no Chifuru, who was leaving for Koshi.*

> . . . Though I know little
> of White Mountain in Koshi
>   where you are going,
> I shall follow behind you,
> seeking your tracks in the snow.

> KKS 392. Archbishop Henjō. *Composed as someone was preparing to return home at dusk after having come to worship at Kazan*

> . . . Would that in the dusk
> our brush-woven fence might seem
>   a range of mountains:
> then he would stay here, saying,
> "I cannot cross them at night."

KKS 392 is the first of five poems written by monks when parting with visitors who were returning home after brief pious or sightseeing excursions. The next three waka commemorate an even less consequential separation: Tsurayuki and Mitsune, having been summoned to attend upon an Imperial Prince, exchange farewells with him as they leave (KKS 397-99). These are followed by four anonymous poems on unspecified topics, which form a unit with solid imagistic and linguistic connections:

> KKS 400. Anonymous. *Topic unknown*

> . . . I shall wrap them up
> as a memento of you
>   and take them away—
> these clear beads that strike my sleeve
> as we part, alas, too soon.

> KKS 401. Anonymous. *Topic unknown*

> . . . They will never dry
> until the day we meet—

these sleeves drenched with tears
shed because my love for you
exceeds all bound and measure.

KKS 402. Anonymous. *Topic unknown*

. . . Since you have chosen,
gentle spring drizzle, to fall,
   please turn the sky black
that I may keep him with me
and assign the blame to you.

KKS 403. Anonymous. *Topic unknown*

. . . Whatever the cost,
I must keep him from leaving.
   Scatter, you cherry blossoms,
until he can no longer
know which is the way to go.

Finally, two poems lead into Travel by discussing partings after chance meetings on the road. The first is
Tsurayuki's admirable KKS 404. The second, Tomonori's KKS 405, serves as the last word on the Parting
topic and, by echoing the positive tone of Yukihira's
KKS 365, returns the reader to the point of origin.

KKS 405. Ki no Tomonori. *Composed at parting,
after he had addressed a few words to someone in
a carriage encountered on the road*

. . . Although we part now,
following our different ways,
   we will meet again
like an under-belt's two ends
circling to come together.

. . . . .

Nostalgia for home, the preeminent courtly travel sentiment, constitutes the theme of the first Travel waka,
KKS 406, the author of which, Abe no Nakamaro (698-
770), is the earliest known **Kokinshū** poet and the only
one to write from a foreign land. Typical in one sense
and unique in another, the poem was a suitable choice
to lead off the minuscule Book Nine, which contains
only sixteen poems. With it the compilers paired a
similar expression of homesickness by the Period One
poet Ono no Takamura, who must have seemed to them
almost equally remote in time and space. Nakamaro
wrote at the beginning of a long sea voyage home,
Takamura at the beginning of a long sea voyage into
exile.

KKS 406. Abe no Nakamaro. *Composed on seeing
the moon in China*

. . . When I gaze far out
across the plain of heaven,

I see the same moon
that came up over the hill
of Mikasa at Kasuga.

KKS 407. Ono no Takamura. *Sent to someone in
the capital as he boarded ship after having been
sentenced to exile in Oki Province*

. . . Carry word to them,
seafolk in your fishing boat,
   that I have rowed forth
onto the spreading sea plain
bound for many an island.

Like Takamura's KKS 407, the next four poems (KKS
408-11) describe water-associated outward journeys.
KKS 412, linked to KKS 411 by bird imagery, forms
a return-journey pair with KKS 413, which is linked
by mountain imagery to KKS 414, the first of three
poems concerning outward journeys without watery
associations. The compilers thus repeat, on a smaller
scale, their tactic of breaking up groups of similar
poems, observed previously in the treatment of the
autumn-leaf and bureaucratic-parting themes.

Book Nine ends with a series of five poems about
short private excursions (KKS 417-21), a disposition
recalling the structure of Book Eight. As in the two
examples below, the tone of all is jesting.

KKS 418. Ariwara Narihira. *Once when Narihira
was on a hunting trip with Prince Koretaka, the
party dismounted on the bank of a stream called
Amanogawa [River of Heaven]. As they were drinking there, the Prince commanded Narihira to offer
him a wine cup with a poem expressing sentiments
appropriate for a hunter arriving at the River of
Heaven.*

. . . Having hunted all day,
let us borrow a lodging
   from the Weaver Maid,
for we have come to the shore
of the River of Heaven.

KKS 421. Sosei. *Composed at Offering Hill when
Retired Emperor Uda traveled to Nara*

. . . I must make cloth strips
by cutting up my patched sleeves—
   but perhaps the gods,
surfeited with autumn leaves,
may just give them back again.

Although Sosei's KKS 421 is a good poem, it cannot
be said to express orthodox travel feelings, and so seems
at first glance a strange choice for the conspicuous
position it occupies. Granted that the compilers apparently found Travel poems hard to come by, we might

have expected them to prefer a poem like Mitsune's KKS 416 below. Their selection of KKS 421, like their decision to allocate the whole last third of Book Nine to poems aiming at courtly wit, can best be understood if we postulate a desire to provide a tonal link to Book Ten, which, as will be noted in more detail later, brings together a collection of versified puns.

> KKS 416. Ōshikōchi Mitsune. *Composed on the way to Kai Province*

> . . . During this long trip
> I have lain time after time
> with grass for pillow,
> brushing away the first-frost
> that forms when the nights grow cold.

Books Eleven-Fifteen: Love

The five Love books trace the history of an imaginary romance from beginning to end, through stages identifiable as (1) one-sided attachment prior to intimacy (categorized by Japanese scholars as *awanu koi,* "not-meeting love"), (2) strong mutual attachment with frequent nocturnal meetings (*au koi,* "meeting love"), and (3) mutual attachment declining on one side, with erratic meetings ending in final separation (*aite awanu koi,* "meeting and not-meeting love"). As we have seen, the idea of a structured collection of Love poems was not new: the *Man'yōshū* editors had made a start toward seasonal and imagistic ordering; the early Heian contests had sometimes used *awanu koi* and *au koi* as topics (*dai*); and *Shinsen man'yōshū* had attempted to establish a distinction between omoi and koi. But there was no precedent for the *Kokinshū* compilers' comprehensive chronological treatment, for the complexity and consistency of their subgroupings, or for the care with which they fitted the whole into a larger framework, balancing the seasonal books by presenting the course of a love affair as a human parallel to the environmental cycle of new growth, full bloom, and decay, and preserving tonal harmony by emphasizing the unhappy aspects and transitory nature of sexual attraction.[11]

Awanu koi, the concern of the first subdivision (KKS 469-633, Books Eleven and Twelve and more than half of Thirteen), emerges as the best-represented *Kokinshū* Love theme. Tsurayuki and the others assembled a total of 165 poems, most of which dealt with lovesick men and the diverse, inconsistent, predominantly melancholy states to which they were prone: inability to think clearly, daydreaming, pessimism, optimism, frustration, self-reproach, yearning to find solace in dreams, fear of scandal, reckless indifference to gossip, and so on. Since most upper-class Heian couples were probably strangers, or nearly so, when they spent the first night together, it would be natural to think that real-life *awanu koi* was at best a lukewarm emotion, and that a poem

like KKS 551 below would normally indicate a relatively advanced stage in a relationship. However, the compilers have assigned KKS 551 to stage one; and examination of the structure of the stage-one group indicates that they have done so with a specific decorum in mind.

> KKS 551. Anonymous. *Topic unknown*

> . . . Burdened by this love,
> must I perish like the snow,
> which in its falling
> parts the sedge and cloaks its roots
> far back in the distant hills?

In organizing this group of poems, the compilers modified their usual practice of interweaving anonymous and known authors on the basis of chronology and topic. They followed that procedure in the eighteen-poem section of Book Thirteen with which the subdivision ends, but—possibly in response to the problems posed by exceptionally large numbers of anonymous poems, or possibly in a quest for novelty—they allocated Book Eleven almost wholly to anonymous authors and Book Twelve to named ones. With uncharacteristic disregard for symmetry, however, they inserted a group of named authors into the first part of Book Eleven. Although the initial poem in Book Eleven, KKS 469, is anonymous, the next is by Sosei.

> KKS 469. Anonymous. *Topic unknown*

> . . . This love has cast me
> into confusion as sweet
> as sweet flags growing
> in the Fifth Month, in the time
> when cuckoos come forth to sing.[12]

> KKS 470. Sosei. *Topic unknown*

> . . . Though I but know you
> through others, love has made me
> like chrysanthemum dew,
> rising by night and by day
> fading into nothingness.

Sosei's composition elucidates the character and significance of its predecessor. The anonymous poet's mental turmoil, we are to understand, arises not from intimate involvement with his mistress, but from romantic infatuation with a stranger. And that this is to be regarded as the paradigmatic stage-one situation is made explicit in eleven more waka by named authors, of which the two below are representative.[13]

> KKS 474. Ariwara Motokata. *Topic unknown*

> . . . Over and over,
> like white waves from the offing,

my fond thoughts return
to an absolute stranger
who has carried off my heart.

KKS 476. Ariwara Narihira. *On the day of an ar-
chery meet at the riding grounds of the Body-guards
of the Right, Narihira glimpsed a lady's face through
the silk curtains of a carriage opposite. He sent her
this poem.*

. . . How very foolish!
Shall I spend all of today
 lost in pensive thought,
my heart bewitched by someone
neither seen nor yet unseen?

It is not certain that all anonymous *Kokinshū* stage-
one authors meant to depict men in such straits. KKS
493 and KKS 498 below, for example, might well have
been intended to reflect intimate relationships. But the
compilers, eager to distance *Kokinshū* from what the
kanajo called the "trivial words" of the bona fide lover,
apparently considered it necessary to seek out or compose poems in which the stage-one speaker was unmistakably identified as a man head-over-heels in love
with a woman known to him only from hearsay, through
a chance glimpse, or by some other accident—a supremely literary, because patently implausible, situation. Only then, it seems, were they content to follow
their basic structural plan by filling the remainder of
Book Eleven with anonymous compositions like KKS
551, which were susceptible to interpretation as treatments of the same theme.

KKS 493. Anonymous. *Topic unknown*

. . . Others have told me
quiet pools are to be found
 in the swiftest stream.
Why, then, is this love of mine
all unrelieved turbulence?

KKS 498. Anonymous. *Topic unknown*

. . . Distraught by passion,
how can I not weep aloud
 as the warbler cries
perched on the uppermost branch
of the plum in my garden?

The subject of the stage-two group—romance at its
happiest—was one that the compilers were unlikely to
wish to emphasize, since it not only lacked substantial
Chinese and Japanese literary associations, but also
conflicted with the basic tone of the anthology. They
limited it to sixty-eight waka (KKS 634-701), many of
them focusing on the minor difficulties besetting the
relationship. The man laments the shortness of nights
spent with his mistress, grieves over dawn partings,

complains about time spent between meetings, professes
an inability to control his passion, and so on. The
woman, who was a remote figure in stage one but
shares the stage here, worries about gossip, meets her
lover in dreams, waits for visits, and echoes the man's
distress at daybreak. Although the presence of numerous anonymous compositions makes generalization
risky, approximately 50 percent of the stage-two poems, like the example below, can be constructed as
expressions of feminine emotions.

KKS 692. Anonymous. *Topic unknown*

. . . Were I to send word,
"The moon is fine, and the night
 is also pleasant,"
it would be like saying, "Come."
It is not that I do not wait.

Stage three concentrates on the woman whose lover is
gradually losing interest and drifting away. In a manner reminiscent of the seasonal books—where, for
example, harbingers of spring alternate with late snow-
falls—the downward course of the affair is interrupted
by short-lived signs of reconciliation, but the roles of
the sexes have been effectively reversed. Although the
man appears from time to time, protesting his devotion
or expressing a reluctance to say a final farewell, he
tends to recede into the background. It is the distraught
woman with whose feelings we are now principally
concerned. She begins to doubt the man, becomes aware
of infidelities, views the future with misgivings, tries
to forget, feels resentment, mourns, blames herself,
hopes against hope, and, as in the poem below, attempts to resign herself to the situation.

KKS 799. Sosei. *Topic unknown*

. . . What am I to do
with someone who would leave me
 despite my deep love?
I must simply think of you
as flowers that scatter too soon.

Taken out of context, KKS 799 might be construed as
a man's comment on a woman, but there is little doubt
that Heian readers regarded the speaker as a woman,
or that Sosei intended them to do so. Of 127 poems in
stage three (KKS 702-828), nineteen are by named
women, several by known male authors assuming transparent feminine personas as in *Yu tai xin yong,* and a
very large number, of which KKS 739 below is representative, by anonymous writers speaking as women.
By making approximately 95 percent of the speakers
in stage one men and approximately 80 percent of those
in stage three women, the compilers have established
a rough balance between the sexes (equally mixed in
stage two). Or to put it differently, the two main groups
embody, respectively, Japanese and Six Dynasties ap-

proaches to love, with the romantic Heian man, in a significant assertion of independence, enjoying a slight numerical priority over the Chinese lonely lady.

KKS 739. Anonymous. *Topic unknown*

> . . . Rest a while, at least,
> when I beg you not to leave,
> for if you rush off,
> I will ask the bridge in front
> to bring your horse to his knees.

Two groups of waka, one in stage one and the other in stage three, conspicuously depart from the above authorial norms. The second (KKS 747-53), which is the less problematic, begins with Narihira's famous *tsuki ya aranu*. The poem's theme—the misery of the lover separated by an impenetrable barrier from a former mistress—is repeated, with some modification, in compositions by two important court nobles, Tokihira's brother Nakahira and Emperor Daigo's maternal relative Kanesuke, which are followed by compositions by Mitsune, Motokata, an anonymous author, and Tomo-nori; and the seven together form a block interrupting a long sequence of feminine complaints about desertion. Although we may find the precise location of these poems puzzling, it is not difficult to understand why they were included under stage three: the theme was at least marginally appropriate for the subdivision; Narihira's poem clearly could not be omitted from the anthology; and almost all the other authors were men with a special claim to the compilers' attention.

But most of the poems in the stage-one group (KKS 552-59), which divides a series of laments by forlorn male lovers, seem simply out of place. For example, Komachi appears to allude to an established relationship in KKS 552 below, and Sosei and Toshiyuki appear to assume stage-three lonely lady personas in KKS 555 and KKS 559.

KKS 552. Ono no Komachi. *Topic unknown*

> . . . Did you come to me
> because I dropped off to sleep
> tormented by love?
> If I had known I dreamed,
> I would not have awakened.

KKS 555. Sosei. *Topic unknown*

> . . . Now that the cold breath
> of the autumn wind strikes deep,
> I hope against hope
> to see an indifferent man,
> night after darkening night.

KKS 559. Fujiwara Toshiyuki. *A poem from the*

Empress's Contest during the reign of the Kanpyō Emperor

> . . . Does my beloved
> avoid the eyes of others
> even on dream paths
> visited by night as waves
> visit Suminoe shore?

And what are we to make of the flirtatious exchange in KKS 556-57?

KKS 556. Abe no Kiyoyuki. *Suggested by the monk Shinsei's sermon during a memorial service at the Lower Izumo Temple; sent to Ono no Komachi*

> . . . They are only tears
> shed for one I cannot see—
> those fair white jewels
> that will not stay in my sleeve
> when I seek to wrap them up.

KKS 557. Ono no Komachi. *Reply*

> . . . Tears that do no more
> than turn into beads on sleeves
> are formal indeed.
> Mine flow in a surging stream,
> try though I may to halt them.

The best explanation seems to be that the compilers decided to insert KKS 747-53 with an eye to breaking up a potentially monotonous series of similar poems, and that they then assembled and inserted KKS 552-59, doing probable violence to authorial intent, for purposes of symmetry. By including the Kiyoyuki-Komachi exchange, they arrived at a total number of feminine speakers exactly equal to the number of male speakers in the later group.

That kind of sequence-breaking, which we have already observed in other subject-matter categories, recurs on a smaller scale in other Love contexts, such as the following, where a dream poem divides a group focusing on tears.

KKS 572. Ki no Tsurayuki. *A poem from the Empress's Contest during the reign of the Kanpyō Emperor*

> . . . Did I not pour forth
> these tears of longing for you,
> the breast of my robe
> would take on the red color
> of the flame that consumes me.

KKS 573. Ki no Tsurayuki. *Topic unknown*

> . . . As the years pass by,

so its ceaseless flow rolls on—
    the river of tears
whose bubbles never congeal
before winter's icy breath.

KKS 574. Ki no Tsurayuki. *Topic unknown*

. . . Might dew have settled
on the dream paths I followed
    throughout the long night?
My sleeves, drenched before I slept,
even now remain undried.

KKS 575. Sosei. *Topic unknown*

. . . How reluctantly
I arise in the morning
    following a night
when I have at least glimpsed you
in an evanescent dream!

KKS 576. Fujiwara Tadafusa. *Topic unknown*

. . . If these tears I shed
were simply a false display,
    I would not use stealth
to wring moisture from the sleeve
of my silken Chinese robe.

KKS 577. Ōe no Chisato. *Topic unknown*

. . . Although I soaked them,
weeping and wailing aloud,
    to those who may ask
I will answer that my sleeves
were drenched by the springtime rains.

There are other familiar organizing strategies in the Love books as a whole. One of the commonest is imagistic association, as in KKS 498-99 (birds) below.

KKS 498. Anonymous. *Topic unknown*

. . . Distraught by passion
how can I not weep aloud
    as the warbler cries
perched on the uppermost branch
of the plum in my garden?

KKS 499. Anonymous. *Topic unknown*

. . . Do you, O cuckoo
from the foot-wearying hills,
    seek in vain to sleep,
your heart, like mine, never free
of longing for a loved one?

Here the spring warbler precedes the summer cuckoo. Similar attention to seasonal progression occurs in other instances, notably in this ten-poem sequence:

KKS 542. Anonymous. *Topic unknown*

. . . I pray that your heart
may lose its coldness toward me
    and melt completely,
even as ice vanishes
with the coming of springtime.

KKS 543. Anonymous. *Topic unknown*

. . . When a new day dawns,
like a wailing cicada
    I spend it in tears,
and by night my smoldering heart
emulates the firefly's glow.

KKS 544. Anonymous. *Topic unknown*

. . . That summer insects
should thus immolate themselves
    is simply because
they are enthralled by the flame
as I am enthralled by you.

KKS 545. Anonymous. *Topic unknown*

. . . On this sleeve of mine,
harder than ever to dry
    when evening draws in,
the dew of autumn comes down
to add its bit of moisture.

KKS 546. Anonymous. *Topic unknown*

. . . There is no season
in which we can find respite
    from love's sad yearnings,
but how strangely our passion
deepens in the autumn dusk!

KKS 547. Anonymous. *Topic unknown*

. . . Mine is not a love
as plain to see as rice ears
    in the autumn fields,
but never is there a time
when you are not in my heart.

KKS 548. Anonymous. *Topic unknown*

. . . Shall I forget you
even for an interval
    brief as the radiance
of lightning illumining
rice ears in autumnal fields?

KKS 549. Anonymous. *Topic unknown*

. . . Why should I suffer
from this urge to concealment?
   What is to keep me
from flaunting my devotion
as miscanthus flaunts its plumes?

KKS 550. Anonymous. *Topic unknown*

   . . . For me these are days
when miseries multiply—
   when my heart shatters
as layers of foamy snow
crumble beneath their own weight.

KKS 551. Anonymous. *Topic unknown*

   . . . Burdened by this love,
must I perish like the snow,
   which in its falling
parts the sedge and cloaks its roots
far back in the distant hills?

The principle of progression frequently operates elsewhere as well—for example, in gossip poems, which speak of groundless rumors in stage one, lament the inevitability of justified talk in stage two, and fear irreparable harm to the relationship in stage three; and in stage-two poems where concern shifts from the night of meeting to the moment of parting to the next day.

Sometimes pairs of poems present conversational exchanges, either explicitly, as in KKS 556-57 above, or implicitly, as in KKS 659-60 below.

KKS 659. Anonymous. *Topic unknown*

   . . . Burning with passion,
I shrink before the high dike
   of other men's eyes.
My heart is set on the stream,
but how am I to reach it?

KKS 660. Anonymous. *Topic unknown*

   . . . How might it happen
that the dike of others' eyes
   suffices to dam
a passion as turbulent
as a rapid's seething flow?

Sometimes the use of a place name is the common element:

KKS 695. Anonymous. *Topic unknown*

   . . . Ah, if I might see
without an instant's delay
   the flower I yearn for—
a wild pink of Yamato,

blooming by a mountain fence!

KKS 696. Anonymous. *Topic unknown*

   . . . I am not thinking
anything (like "Anything"
   in the land of Tsu)
except "I long to meet you
'Forever' (in Yamashiro)."[14]

KKS 697. Ki no Tsurayuki. *Topic unknown*

   . . . I long for a way
to meet you as constantly
   as in far Cathay
people dress in gorgeous robes
foreign to Yamato's isles.

In many cases, two poems appear to be joined through diction or grammar. KKS 763 and KKS 764 both end with noun-particle-verb constructions using the suffix *ramu*, indicative of speculation about the cause of a perceived phenomenon; *shimo* ("frost") in KKS 693 repeats the particles *shi mo* in KKS 692; *koto ni* ("especially," suppressed in the translation) in KKS 587 is probably to be taken as punning on koto in KKS 586.[15]

KKS 763. Anonymous. *Topic unknown*

   . . . That year-end showers
fall so soon upon my sleeve—
   might it be because
satiety has called forth
the autumn of your passion?

KKS 764. Anonymous. *Topic unknown*

   . . . My passion is not
shallow as a mountain spring.
   Why, then, must that man
never show himself to me
save as a fleeting image?

KKS 692. Anonymous. *Topic unknown*

   . . . Were I to send word,
"The moon is fine, and the night
   is also pleasant,"
it would be like saying, "Come."
It is not that I do not wait.

KKS 693. Anonymous. *Topic unknown*

   . . . Should you fail to come,
I will avoid the bedroom
   and remain outside,
even though frost may gather
on my deep purple hair-cord.

KKS 586. Mibu no Tadamine. *Topic unknown*

. . . Why should I languish
in vain longing for someone
  merely at the sound
of a koto being played
while the autumn wind whispers?

KKS 587. Ki no Tsurayuki. *Topic unknown*

. . . Whenever rain falls
my love for her increases,
  rising as rises
swamp water at Yodo marsh,
where harvesters glean wild rice.

As Book Fifteen draws to a close, a six-poem sequence establishes a firm connection between autumn (the classic symbol of evanescence) and the dissolution of romantic ties.

KKS 819. Anonymous. *Topic unknown*

. . . What grief to see you
growing ever more remote,
  as when a wild goose
takes leave of the reedy shore
and wings its way toward the sky.

KKS 820. Anonymous. *Topic unknown*

. . . Still more saddening
than the leaves of trees changing
  in year-end drizzles—
the encounter of old vows
with the autumn of your love.

KKS 821. Anonymous. *Topic unknown*

. . . At Musashino
where the chill wind of autumn
  has blown ceaselessly,
every leaf on every plant
has lost its former color.

KKS 822. Ono no Komachi. *Topic unknown*

. . . Because I trusted
someone who grew tired of me,
  my life, alas, must be
as empty as a rice ear
blasted by harsh autumn winds.

KKS 823. Taira Sadafun. *Topic unknown*

. . . Having resented,
I merely resent anew
  that as autumn winds
turn back a kudzu vine's leaves,

so you turn back from your vows.

KKS 824. Anonymous. *Topic unknown*

. . . I thought of *aki*
as autumn, no kin to me,
  but now I hear it
as satiety, naming
the flirt who cast me aside.

Two more compositions, both ending with the phrase *toshi zo henikeru* ("years have gone by"), attest to the irrevocable nature of the couple's estrangement; and the final word is pronounced in a conversational exchange using water imagery (KKS 827-28). Tomonori's distraught speaker in KKS 827 compares himself (or, more likely, herself) to a bubble, the prime Buddhist symbol of transitoriness; the anonymous author of KKS 828, playing on a river name, replies with a Buddhist rebuke, reminiscent in its pessimistic tone of the last seasonal poem, KKS 342: "Nothing is more ephemeral than love. What did you expect?"

KKS 827. Ki no Tomonori. *Topic unknown*

. . . Consumed by misery,
I long to vanish as swiftly
  as a floating bubble.
Were the bubble to flow on,
what might its future become?

KKS 828. Anonymous. *Topic unknown*

. . . Let us accept it.
Love's course can but remind us
  of the Yoshino,
the river falling between
Husband Mountain and Wife Hill.

KKS 342. Ki no Tsurayuki. *Composed and submitted by imperial command*

. . . My heart fills with gloom
as I watch the year depart,
  for shadows descend
even on the face I see
reflected in the mirror.

Books Sixteen-Eighteen: Laments, Miscellaneous

The river imagery and religious overtones of KKS 827 and KKS 828 lead into the next book, Laments (KKS 829-62), which begins with a poem about the River of Crossings, a hazard faced by the souls of the dead in the nether regions:

KKS 829. Ono no Takamura. *Composed upon the death of a woman he had loved*

. . . I wish my teardrops
might descend like driving rain,
   for she would come home
if flood waters were to rise
in the River of Crossings.

Like other initial poems in the anthology, KKS 829 is both typical and atypical of its category. The compilers, obliged to include Laments for the sake of comprehensiveness, made it their business to demonstrate that waka about death need not be too personal and specific to qualify as *hare no uta*. On the one hand, they controlled the range of subject matter and style in the thirty-four poems they admitted, supplying 41 percent of the total themselves, their largest joint contribution to any *Kokinshū* category; on the other, they minimized personalism by placing the most formal compositions at the front. Takamura's poem was probably chosen to begin Book Sixteen because it distanced the experience of bereavement by using Six Dynasties reasoning, exaggeration, and a blatantly artificial conception. The kotobagaki tells us that the author was mourning a woman he had loved, but the language of the waka is so general that it might refer to a casual acquaintance. (There are no pronouns in the original.)

Other poems near the front of the book, such as KKS 830 and KKS 832 below, also dilute grief with elaborate conceits.

KKS 830. Sosei. *Composed on the night when the remains of the Former Chancellor [Yoshifusa] were taken to the vicinity of Shirakawa [White River]*

. . . Anguished tears of blood
descend in seething torrents:
   White River, it seems,
was a name doomed to vanish
with the passing of our lord.

KKS 832. Kamutsuke Mineo (?-?). *Composed after the burial of the Horikawa Chancellor [Mototsune] at Fukakusayama [Mountain of Rich Grasses]*

. . . If you have feelings,
flowering cherries in the fields
   at Fukakusa,
will you not just this one year
put forth charcoal-colored blooms?

Some merely rephrase Buddhist aphorisms:

KKS 833. Ki no Tomonori. *Sent to the house when Fujiwara Toshiyuki no Ason died*

. . . He appears to me
when I wake and when I sleep.
   Ah, but after all
this transient world itself

is only an empty dream.

KKS 834. Ki no Tsurayuki. *Written upon the death of someone he had known well*

. . . I should have called it
no more than a fleeting dream,
   yet it seemed to me
to possess reality—
this world in which we exist.

What makes Takamura's poem atypical, then, is not its tone or style but its subject matter. Presumably as a deliberate policy, the compilers have failed to include a single poem on the death of a child, one of the cruelest of bereavements; and Takamura's is the only one of the thirty-four in which a spouse or lover is mourned. Of the other elegies in the book, one concerns a sister, six speak of parents, and most of the remainder commemorate the deaths of important personages, friends, and acquaintances.[16] The deaths are, in short, almost all of a kind to be borne with relative equanimity.

Tsurayuki and his colleagues have adjusted structure to subject matter with remarkable care in this book. It comprises four major parts. The first three contain poems composed, respectively, during the period immediately following the individual's death (KKS 829-39), during the formal mourning period (KKS 840-47), and after the mourning period (KKS 848-56), and the fourth consists of six deathbed poems (KKS 857-62). Although the reader might anticipate the most poignant expressions of loss in part one, the first three poems after Takamura's (KKS 830-32) prove to be highly formal compositions on the deaths of public figures. KKS 833 is a condolatory poem, and the next two, KKS 834 and KKS 835, concern friends of the authors. KKS 836, on a sister, forms a pair in authorship and style with KKS 835. Both focus not on the deceased, but on the concept of death:

KKS 835. Mibu no Tadamine. *On a friend's death*

. . . Why should we say "dream"
only of that which we see
   while we lie asleep?
This fugitive world itself
is scarcely reality.

KKS 836. Mibu no Tadamine. *On his older sister's death*

. . . Even a swift stream
may become a standing pool
   when we dam it up,
but no weir exists to block
someone going from this world.

KKS 837 is another condolatory poem, and KKS 838

and KKS 839, by Tsurayuki and Tadamine, commemorate the passing of their colleague Tomonori. KKS 838 and KKS 839 have probably been placed at the end of the group because they are slightly less formal and abstract than the other nine.

KKS 838. Ki no Tsurayuki. *Composed when Ki no Tomonori died*

. . . Though I cannot tell
whether my transient life
    may end tomorrow,
all my thoughts today belong
to sorrow for another.

KKS 839. Mibu no Tadamine. *Composed when Ki no Tomonori died*

. . . Why of all seasons
did he take his leave of us
    in these autumn days
when loneliness chills our hearts
even at the sight of the living?

Of the eight poems involving the mourning period, the first five concern the deaths of parents, and so might be expected to convey a deeper sense of loss than most of those in part one. But the compilers have lessened the impact by selecting only poems written after the first access of grief, by including a condolatory verse (KKS 843), and by preferring formal, impersonal works similar in tone to those in part one. The poets' principal concern in most of the five has been to exhibit originality in the use of tear imagery. For example:

KKS 841. Mibu no Tadamine. *Written while in mourning for his father*

. . . This unraveled thread
from a wisteria robe
    now becomes a cord
on which to string the jewels
of a mourner's bitter tears.

KKS 843. Mibu no Tadamine. *Written when he went to condole with someone who was in mourning*

. . . That your tears should fall
thus ceaselessly as raindrops—
    might it be because
your sleeves, dyed in charcoal hues,
somehow share the stuff of clouds?

The last three poems in this part, all written during or shortly after years of national mourning, might seem to be out of order, since they are more public in nature than their five predecessors. It appears, however, that the compilers meant them to serve as a link to part three, where almost without exception the deceased

are again prominent figures, friends, and acquaintances, rather than close relatives, but where the style is less formal and ornate than in part one. All three are free of conspicuous artifice:

KKS 845. Ono no Takamura. *Composed while view--ng blossoms near a pond during a year of national mourning*

. . . Unbid, his image
rises clear in memory's eye
    when I see the flowers
in bright, quiet reflection
on the surface of the pond.

KKS 846. Fun'ya no Yasuhide. *Composed on the death anniversary of the Fukakusa Emperor [Ninmyō]*

. . . Today marks a year
since the shining sun darkened,
    hiding its radiance
in a haze-shrouded valley
overgrown with tall grasses.

KKS 847. Archbishop Henjō. *During the reign of the Fukakusa Emperor, the author was in constant attendance on the throne as Head Chamberlain. When the Emperor died, he abandoned court life, went to Mount Hiei, and became a monk. He wrote this poem in the following year, when everyone had stopped wearing mourning and he had begun to hear of rejoicings over promotions and other such things.*

. . . Everyone, they say,
has made the change from mourning
    into gay attire.
Will you not, O mossy sleeve,
at least give up your moisture?

Part three complements part one. The two resemble one another in basic respects—they are nearly the same size, both focus on public figures, friends, and acquaintances, and each contains one poem about a close relative—but part three establishes a separate identity through the greater particularity of its conceptions. No Heian reader could have mistaken the subject of the waka below for anyone but Minamoto Tōru, the man who shaped his famous garden lake to resemble Shiogama Bay in northeastern Japan.

KKS 852. Ki no Tsurayuki. *Composed on seeing the re-creation of Shiogama when he went to the home of the Kawara Minister of the Left after the Minister's death*

. . . How lonely it looks—
the vast expanse of garden

with no smoke rising
above Shiogama shore
now that the master is gone.

Poems like the two below also point to relatively specific persons and situations.

KKS 848. Minamoto Yoshiari (845-97). *Passing the
residence of the Kawara Minister during the autumn
of the Minister's death, he observed that the leaves
had not yet taken on a deeper color. He composed
this poem and sent it inside.*

. . . Ah, how suddenly
all is desolate and sad!
   Not even the leaves
wear their accustomed colors
at the masterless dwelling.

KKS 850. Ki no Mochiyuki. *Someone who had
planted a cherry tree had died just as the tree was
about to bloom. Mochiyuki composed this poem
when he saw the blossoms.*

. . . Human life, alas,
has proved more transitory
   than cherry blossoms.
I had not thought of wondering
which of them I might mourn first.

In all three compositions, the poets complain that the
times are out of joint: smoke is not rising from the salt
fires at Shiogama; leaves are not changing color in
autumn; men are not outlasting cherry blossoms. And
the compilers have responded by disrupting the natural
order in another respect. In one group of four successive poems, they present autumn leaves, the cuckoo,
cherry blossoms, and plum blossoms (KKS 848-51); in
a second, only slightly less tight grouping, miscanthus,
cuckoo, and hana (KKS 853, KKS 855-56). Such deliberate, sustained reversals of normal seasonal progression occur nowhere else in the anthology.

The mention of flowers connects KKS 856 to KKS
857, the first of the six deathbed poems in part four,
which also uses spring imagery. KKS 857 in turn forms
a pair with KKS 858 by virtue of authorship and style:
the two are by the only women represented in this part,
and both make affecting, straightforward lyrical statements.

KKS 857. *The Princely Minister of Ceremonial
[Atsuyoshi] had begun to live with the Kan'in Fifth
Princess, but before long the Princess died. The
Prince found a note tied to one of her curtain-dais
streamers, took it down, and saw a poem in her
handwriting.*

. . . If in truth your love

is too ardent to permit
   of forgetfulness,
please feel pity when you see
haze trailing in the mountains.

KKS 858. Anonymous. *A man's wife suddenly fell
ill while he was away in the provinces. When she
had grown fatally weak, she composed this poem
and died.*

. . . It grieves my spirit
to take leave without hearing
   the sound of your voice,
yet what will it be for you
to sleep in an empty bed?

After a pair of Buddhist reflections on ephemerality
(KKS 859-60), Laments ends with two nice blends of
reasoning and emotion by Narihira and his son Shigeharu. Shigeharu's poem, the last in the book, functions
as a bleak rejoinder to KKS 829, the first.

KKS 862. Ariwara Shigeharu. *The author suddenly
fell ill while on his way to visit a friend in Kai
Province. Realizing that he was dying, he gave
someone this poem to take to his mother in the
capital.*

. . ."Only a short trip
to Kai Province and back,"
   so I thought as I left—
yet it was the departure
from which there is no return.

As we would anticipate, the two Miscellaneous books,
Seventeen and Eighteen (70 and 68 poems, KKS 863-
932, KKS 933-1000), contain numerous poems not
readily classifiable under more specific rubrics. For
example:

KKS 865. Anonymous. *Topic unknown*

. . . In what might I wrap
the great happiness I feel?
   Had I foreseen it,
I would have said, "Make wide sleeves
on this robe of Chinese silk."

KKS 997. Fun'ya no Arisue. *Composed and pre-
sented during the reign of the Jōgan Emperor
[Seiwa], when His Majesty asked about the date of
'Man'yōshū'*

. . . It is an old work
from that famous capital
   bearing the same name
as *nara* oaks whose leaves gleam
rain-wet in the Godless Month.

There are also two distinct groups of waka, centering respectively on the moon and water, which might have been expected to appear in a separate category comparable to Chisato's Wind and Moon, but which nevertheless could be considered miscellaneous in Xiao Tong's sense. On the other hand, most of the remaining compositions (approximately three-fifths of the total) seem, like the two below, to be obvious candidates for Expressing Feelings (*jukkai*). Tsurayuki and his colleagues, we perceive, have not only rejected a tripartite division like Chisato's, but also ignored the conventional distinction between Miscellaneous and Expressing Feelings.

KKS 948. Anonymous. *Topic unknown*

. . . Has life on this earth
given rise to human grief
  since antiquity,
or am I the only one
who finds it so hard to bear?

KKS 993. Fujiwara Tadafusa. *Composed when the men in the Crown Prince's Attendants' Office received wine, at a time during the reign of the Kanpyō Emperor when Tadafusa had been named third-ranking officer in an embassy to China*

. . . Nowadays I find
that during the lengthy nights
  I rise as first-frost
rises on slender bamboo
and sit with much on my mind.

A partial explanation is probably to be sought in the compilers' disinclination to draw attention to the jukkai category, which, although too well established to be excluded altogether, stood on the boundary between the *hare no uta* and the inadmissibly personal statement. To subsume the category under Miscellaneous was to make it less personal. Another, more exclusively structural consideration must also have been involved. The creation of three separate categories would have violated the symmetry of the **Kokinshū** master design, which envisioned three, and only three, post-Love books, including Laments, to balance the three post-seasonal books. It was thus desirable for more than one reason that the poems be presented in two books, both labeled Miscellaneous.

The compilers decided to mass approximately half of their thirty or so truly miscellaneous poems in each of two locations, the first at the beginning of Book Seventeen, to confirm the appropriateness of the title, and the last in a complementary position toward the end of Book Eighteen. They assigned the thirty moon and water poems to Book Seventeen and the bulk of the jukkai compositions to Book Eighteen. To fill out Book Seventeen, and perhaps to provide a change of pace,

they then divided moon from water by inserting old age, which although properly a jukkai theme could defensibly be distinguished from the main concerns of Book Eighteen: the troubles stemming from social relationships, career problems, and other external circumstances. In that manner, they were also able to create two books containing almost identical numbers of poems.

Carrying the principle of balance a step further, Tsurayuki and the others pursued a conscious policy of making the tone and style of Book Seventeen as buoyant and formal as possible in order to establish a contrast with, and attenuate, the pessimistic personalism inherent in the main subject matter of Book Eighteen. In the fourteen-poem miscellaneous group with which Book Seventeen begins (KKS 863-76), there are witty treatments of such pleasant matters as the meeting of the Weaver Maid and the Ox-Driver, parties, individual good fortune, auspicious court events, and amusing incidents. Tone and theme, rather than topic, seem to have determined the placement of several of the poems, such as the two below, of which the first would probably have been assigned to Autumn and the second to Parting if the authors had emphasized the frustration of the lovers and the sorrow of separation, rather than the joy of meeting.

KKS 863. Anonymous. *Topic unknown*

. . . Dew sprinkling my robe:
might it be spray from the oar
  of a boat crossing
where the banks come together
on the River of Heaven?

KKS 864. Anonymous. *Topic unknown*

. . . With what reluctance
we say goodbye on a night
  when a ring of friends
sits in fellowship precious
as robes of Chinese brocade!

Almost all the moon poems (KKS 877-85) either offer praise, make courtly comments suitable to social situations, or construct clever conceits; and most of the water poems (KKS 910-30) play with words, feign elegant confusion, question, reason, and otherwise exemplify the *hare no uta* at its most formal. For example:

KKS 881. Ki no Tsurayuki. *On seeing the moon reflected in a pond*

. . . There could not be two,
so I had believed—and yet
  here is a bright moon
not at the rim of the hills

but rising from watery depths.

KKS 882. Anonymous. *Topic unknown*

. . . Swift runs the channel
in the River of Heaven
    where clouds take their course,
and thus the moon flows onward,
its bright rays never pausing.

KKS 918. Ki no Tsurayuki. *Composed on encoun-
tering rain at Tamino Island when he had gone
down to Naniwa*

. . . To escape the rain,
I have gone to Tamino,
    Isle of Straw Raincoats,
but its name, I have observed,
does nothing to keep me dry.

KKS 919. Ki no Tsurayuki. *Composed when the
Priestly Retired Emperor commanded him to present
a poem on the topic "cranes standing on a sand-
bank" during an excursion to the Western River*

. . . We might mistake them
for waves blown in by the wind
    and lingering there—
that flock of reed-dwelling cranes
standing beside the river.

In making selections for the large old-age block (KKS
886-909)—a potentially disruptive element because of
its subject matter—the compilers limited overt expressions of melancholy to seven or eight compositions. In
the first four poems, the speaker looks back to a happy
past; in the next four, and in several later ones, he
recognizes his condition without complaint; in others,
he discusses the longevity of pine trees rather than his
own advanced years; and in one, quoted below, he
goes so far as to congratulate himself on being old.

KKS 903. Fujiwara Toshiyuki. *Composed during
the [reign of Emperor Uda], when His Majesty gave
wine to the men in the Courtiers' Hall and presided
over a concert*

. . . Why did I repine
because old age had claimed me?
    Had I not grown old,
how might I have been present
to join in this day's pleasure?

Book Seventeen ends with three screen poems. The
first was probably included, in spite of its melancholy
tone, because its topic and provenance permitted a
smooth transition between a preceding waterfall group
(KKS 922-29) and Tsurayuki's KKS 931. Tsurayuki,
who again occupies a penultimate position, makes a

strong, positive statement, reaffirming the basic tone
of the book:

KKS 930. Sanjō no Machi. *Composed during the
reign of the Tamura Emperor [Montoku], when His
Majesty looked at a screen painting in the Table
Room and said to the ladies-in-waiting, "The waterfall is charming. Compose some poems about it."*

. . . Might it be the same
as the cataract of grief
    dammed fast in my heart?
Though we see water falling,
no sound reaches our ears.

KKS 931. Ki no Tsurayuki. *On flowers in a screen
painting*

. . . Eternal colors!
Might it perhaps be that spring
    has remained on earth,
never leaving since the time
when they first began to bloom?

The last poem, KKS 932, is linked to Tsurayuki's by
provenance and seasonal progression, and to KKS 933,
the first poem in Book Eighteen, by theme and tone:

KKS 932. Sakanoue Korenori. *A poem composed
and written on a folding screen to accompany a
picture*

. . . This autumn sadness
evokes tears reminiscent
    of crying wild geese
crossing where hill paddy rice
is reaped and hung down to dry.

KKS 933. Anonymous. *Topic unknown*

. . . In this world of ours
what is there of constancy?
    Yesterday's deep pool
in the River of Tomorrow
today becomes a rapid.

Consciousness of ephermerality, implicit in KKS 932
and explicit in KKS 933, contributes to the gloomy
ambience of Book Eighteen. It may be observed, for
example, in the two poems below, as well as in numerous others.

KKS 942. Anonymous. *Topic unknown*

. . . Might this world be real,
or might it be but a dream?
    Whether it be dream
or reality I know not,
for we are here and not here.

KKS 943. Anonymous. *Topic unknown*

. . . For one in this world
life means being here today
    and gone tomorrow.
Might we call it saddening,
or shall we call it bitter?

But the typical Book Eighteen speaker is concerned with more immediate personal problems. He leads a miserable life in society, ponders means of escape, considers the advantages of reclusion, worries about his aptitude for the eremitic life, longs to seek refuge in the mountains, bewails such specific misfortunes as exile, dismissal from office, and estrangement from friends, and at last becomes either a recluse or, as in the poem below, a homeless wanderer.

KKS 989. Anonymous. *Topic unknown*

. . . Fate seems to decree
that my wandering must soon
    lose all direction—
I who have no more roots now
than dust floating in the wind.

As a group, the waka in Book Eighteen are more personal than any others in the anthology. A kotobagaki like the one below warns us, however, against the assumption that their sentiments spring directly from individual experience. Like the Love poems in Books Eleven-Fifteen, these are conventional treatments of conventional themes.

KKS 955. Mononobe Yoshina (?-?). *A poem in which no syllable is repeated*

. . . I think of going
into mountains to escape
    the trials of the world,
but the person in my thoughts
becomes a chain to hold me.

Perhaps to point up the fact that Expressing Feelings, properly treated, could claim a legitimate place alongside other *hare no uta* topics, the compilers have ended Book Eighteen with three formal waka presented to the throne. The first two are tactful complaints about bureaucratic disappointments; the third is probably to be taken as an oblique reminder of the author's earlier position as an imperial favorite.

KKS 998. Ōe no Chisato. *Presented when he submitted poems during the reign of the Kanpyō Emperor*

. . . May its accents reach
to the realm above the clouds—
    the sorrowful voice

of the crane among the reeds,
left alone behind his mates.

KKS 999. Fujiwara Kachien. *Presented when he submitted poems during the reign of the Kanpyō Emperor*

. . . Would that like spring haze
it might take visible form
    for our lord to see—
this longing, locked in my heart,
of which others know nothing.

KKS 1000. Ise. *Composed and set down at the end when she presented poems in response to an imperial command*

. . . I long for a way
to recapture bygone times,
    to see the palace
of which I but hear rumors
noisy as a rushing stream.

Within the major groupings of both Miscellaneous books, poems are joined in the customary ways. Just as there is temporal progression (albeit imperfect) in Book Eighteen from early unhappiness to thoughts of reclusion to actual divorce from society, so the old-age group in Book Seventeen deals first with the speaker's past, then with his present, and finally with his future (i.e., with the prospect of imminent death). The last old-age composition is associated imagistically with the first water poem:

KKS 910. Anonymous. *Topic unknown*

. . . Though I cling to life,
I resemble floating foam
    where sea currents meet:
the froth exists, but for it
there is no sheltering shore.

KKS 911. Anonymous. *Topic unknown*

. . . Awaji Island,
encircled by a garland
    of fair white breakers
such as the sea god uses
when he decorates his head!

As usual, many other links are accomplished through imagery. KKS 911 is linked to KKS 912 by islands and waves:

KKS 912. Anonymous. *Topic unknown*

. . . As from the broad sea
waves come rolling in toward shore,
    over and over,

so would I gaze, time after time,
on fair Tamatsu Island.

In the pair below, the common element is tears.

KKS 940. Anonymous. *Topic unknown*

. . . The dew that appears
on each leafy utterance
    of the word called "ah"—
what is it but fallen tears
shed in memory of the past?

KKS 941. Anonymous. *Topic unknown*

. . . I do not tell them
of each sorrow and travail
    life burdens me with—
and yet my tears, I perceive,
are always the first to know.

The last two waka of the initial Miscellaneous group
are bound together by seasonal progression:

KKS 875. Kengei. *Composed when some women
looked at him and laughed*

. . . I may look to you
like a tree rotting unseen
    deep in the mountains,
but if I should will it so,
blossoms would flower in my heart.

KKS 876. Ki no Tomonori. *Once when he had gone
to someone else's house to avoid an unlucky direction, his host lent him a robe to wear. He composed
this poem as he prepared to return the garment on
the following morning.*

. . . Light was the night robe
as a cicada's frail wings,
    yet heavy indeed
hangs the sumptuous fragrance
perfuming all it has touched.

Other connections are established through place, as in
the first pair below, through authorship, as in the second, or through both, as in the third (where the authors
are brothers).

KKS 928. Mibu no Tadamine. *Composed while
viewing Otowa Falls on Mount Hiei*

. . . Not a strand of black!
It must have passed through long years
    into ripe old age—
the upper stream of this fall
seething in headlong descent.

KKS 929. Oshikōchi Mitsune. *On the same waterfall*

. . . That fleecy white cloud,
steadfast to a single place
    despite blowing winds—
what might it be but water
descending through the ages!

KKS 969. Ariwara Narihira. *When Ki no Toshisada
was appointed Vice-Governor of Awa, Narihira
planned a farewell dinner for him. The hour grew
late, but Toshisada, busy with last-minute errands,
failed to appear. Narihira sent him this poem.*

. . . Now that I have learned
how painful it is to wait,
    I will be faithful
in my visits to houses
where people may expect me.

KKS 970. Ariwara Narihira. *In the days when Narihira attended Prince Koretaka, the Prince be-came
a monk and went to live at Ono. Narihira set out to
call on him there in the First Month. Since Ono
was at the foot of Mount Hiei, the snow was very
deep, but he managed to struggle to the hermitage,
where he found the Prince looking bored and forlorn. After returning to the capital, he sent the
Prince this poem.*

. . . When for an instant
I forget, it seems a dream.
    Did I imagine
I would make my way through snow
in order to see my lord?

KKS 922. Ariwara Yukihira. *Composed at Nunohiki
Falls*

. . . I will gather up
the transparent beads scattered
    by the waterfall
and borrow them when sadness
has consumed my store of tears.

KKS 923. Ariwara Narihira. *Composed when a
group of people were reciting poems at the foot of
Nunohiki Falls*

. . . There must be a man
unstringing them at the top—
    those transparent beads
scattering incessantly.
Alas for my narrow sleeves!

*Books Ten and Nineteen: Names of Things, Miscella-
neous Forms*

The next book, Miscellaneous Forms, shares a number

of characteristics with Book Ten, Names of Things. Each follows a series of books compiled on the basis of subject matter but is not itself so compiled, each appeals to the reader's competitive instinct, and each deviates from the usual ***Kokinshū*** aesthetic standards.

Book Ten, the shorter and less interesting of the two, comprises forty-seven poems arranged in four groups, roughly classifiable as birds and insects, plants, places, and artifacts. Almost all are examples of the "hidden topic" (*kakushidai*) waka, a composition in which the object is the clever concealment of a specified word or words. Sometimes, as with KKS 426 below, there is a connection between the kakushidai and the poem's subject matter; more often, as with KKS 428, there is none.[17]

KKS 426. Anonymous. *Ume [plum]*

. . . Although they diffuse
a fragrance we shall long for,
    the blossoms, alas,
show little disposition
to linger before our eyes.

KKS 428. Ki no Tsurayuki. *Sumomo no hana [damson blossoms]*

. . . Now that so little
remains to us of springtime,
    even the warbler
seems to gaze off into space,
lost in melancholy thought.

The poet may conceal more than one word, as in the first two compositions below, or distribute syllables in a designated pattern, as in the third.

KKS 454. Ki no Menoto (?-?). *Sasa, matsu, biwa, baseoba [bamboo grass, pine, loquat, banana leaf]*

. . . Though I have shown him
the true state of my feelings,
    the days have slipped by
while I have waited calmly,
expecting to see him soon.

KKS 455. Hyōe (?-?). *Nashi, natsume, kurumi [pear, jujube, walnut]*

. . . This is quite pointless.
Cease your constant lamenting.
    It is not as though
you were leaving the body
that has come through the crisis.

KKS 468. Archbishop Shōhō (ca. 832?-909). *Composed when someone told him to recite a sea-sonal poem beginning and ending with the sylla-bles ha*

and ru *and playing on nagame [pensive gaze]*

. . . Intending to feast
my eyes to satiety,
    I wandered among
the blossoms, and now my heart
threatens to scatter with them.

And in the variation known as *oriku,* illustrated below, the five initial syllables spell out the topic word.[18]

KKS 439. Ki no Tsurayuki. *Composed on the occasion of a Suzakuin maiden-flower contest, with one of the five syllables of ominaeshi [maidenflower] beginning each of the five lines*

. . . No human can tell
the full sum of the autumns
    he has lived to see—
the belling stag frequenting
Ogurayama's high peak.

That such literary games were already popular in the mid-ninth century is suggested by the existence of poems like Yasuhide's KKS 445 and Narihira's KKS 410 below. That their vogue persisted is apparent from the preponderance of Period Three authors in Book Ten, from Retired Emperor Uda's sponsorship of a Names of Things contest around 905, and from the decision to establish a *mono no na* category in ***Kokinshū***. That the compilers personally welcomed them as vehicles for the display of virtuosity can be inferred from the inclusion here of generous samples of their own work.[19]

KKS 445. Fun'ya no Yasuhide. *Composed by command of the Nijō Empress [Kōshi] when she was still known as the Mother of the Crown Prince. Topic: medo [a plant resembling bush clover] into which artificial flowers made of wood shavings had been thrust.*

. . . It is not, it seems,
a flowering tree—and yet
    it puts forth blossoms!
May there also be a time
when this aged stock bears fruit.

KKS 410. Ariwara Narihira. *Once Narihira was traveling toward the east with one or two friends. When the party reached a place in Mikawa Province called Eight Bridges, they dismounted to sit under the trees, attracted by the sight of some irises blooming beside the stream. Narihira composed this poem, his object being to express sentiments appropriate for a traveler, while beginning each line with the proper syllable from the word* kakitsubata *[iris].*

. . . I have a dear wife

familiar to me as skirts
  of a well-worn robe,
and thus these distant travels
darken my heart with sorrow.

An occasional kakushidai or oriku poem succeeds in satisfying the aesthetic criteria by which the compilers have appraised other **Kokinshū** waka. Narihira's KKS 410 appears under Travel, and the composition below would not seem out of place in Autumn.

KKS 432. Anonymous. *Yamagaki no ki* [*mountain persimmon tree*]

. . . Autumn has arrived:
now as the breezes blow cold,
  will not the crickets
utter their plaints night by night
from the plaited brushwood fence?

For the most part, however, the content of Book Ten has been measured with an indulgent yardstick. KKS 455 above, negligible as literature, has gained admission merely because the author has produced an intelligible statement concealing three designated words; and similar considerations have prevailed in many other cases. Book Ten is put forward not as serious literature but as a diversion, a species of *kyōgen,* a lighthearted invitation to the reader to forget *mono no aware,* admire displays of mental agility, and amuse himself by trying to find hidden words without recourse to the kotobagaki.

. . . . .

In Book Nineteen, the compilers have brought together waka on assorted subjects, composed in assorted poetic forms and arranged in three categories identified as tanka, sedōka, and haikaika. The "tanka" section, which appears to have been mislabeled by an early copyist, consists of five chōka and a hanka (KKS 1001-6); the sedōka of four repeating poems (KKS 1007-10); and the haikaika of fifty-eight poems resembling ordinary **Kokinshū** tanka in external form but distinctive in content (KKS 1011-68).

Because dictionaries define haikai as "jest," early scholars assumed that humorous authorial intent was the defining characteristic of the fifty-eight **Kokinshū** haikaika. In support of their position, we might cite such poems as KKS 1023 and KKS 1062:

KKS 1023. Anonymous. *Topic unknown*

. . . Beyond enduring,
this passion that attacks me
  from pillow and foot:
I get up and seat myself
in the middle of the bed.

KKS 1062. Ariwara Motokata. *Topic unknown*

. . . What distressful thoughts
must afflict the anguished mind
  of the poor old world,
made an object of hatred
by such multitudes of men!

But if the compilers had wished to isolate humorous poems, they would presumably have assigned waka like the following to Book Nineteen, rather than to Miscellaneous.

KKS 873. Minamoto Tōru. *Composed on the morning after the Gosechi dances, when he had found a jewel from a hair ornament and had gone looking for the owner*

. . ."Who is your owner?"
To my query the white jewel
  returned no answer.
Might it be permissible
to fall in love with them all?

KKS 874. Fujiwara Toshiyuki. *During the reign of the Kanpyō Emperor, the men in the Courtiers' Hall told someone to take a jar to the Empress's apartments with a request for leftover wine. Her Majesty's Chamberlains laughed and took the jar to their mistress, but no answer was made. Toshiyuki sent this poem to one of the Chamberlains after the messenger had returned with his report.*

. . . Where might he be now—
the little wine-jar turtle?
  He has paddled out
far into the open sea
through Koyorogi's rocky surf.

KKS 923. Ariwara Narihira. *Composed when a group of people were reciting poems at the foot of Nunohiki Falls*

. . . There must be a man
unstringing them at the top—
  those transparent beads
scattering incessantly.
Alas for my narrow sleeves!

They also would probably have excluded poems like the three haikaika below, which are unlikely to have been written to provoke mirth.

KKS 1018. Anonymous. *Topic unknown*

. . . The mists of autumn
now clear away, now gather,
  and thus the beauty
of maidenflowers in bloom

now appears, now vanishes.

KKS 1030. Ono no Komachi. *Topic unknown*

. . . On those moonless nights
when I long in vain for him,
   love robs me of sleep
and my agitated heart
burns like a crackling fire.

KKS 1067. Ōshikōchi Mitsune. *Composed when the Priestly Retired Emperor, on a visit to the Western River, ordered poems on the topic "monkeys crying in mountain valleys"*

. . . Desist, O monkeys,
from melancholy laments.
   Is this not a day
when rich honor is bestowed
on all your mountain valleys?

When we note, in addition, that two **Kokinshū** haikaika, KKS 1020 and KKS 1031, appear as formal seasonal compositions in the Empress's Contest, and that the organization of the fifty-eight haikaika in Book Nineteen parallels the overall **Kokinshū** structure in major respects, progressing from the seasons through love to miscellaneous, it seems reasonable to agree with modern scholars who regard the poems not as informal jokes, but as flawed attempts at *hare no uta*.[20]

Why, we might ask, did Tsurayuki and his colleagues not discard these waka, as they discarded other compositions from the Empress's Contest and elsewhere that they deemed inferior? A partial explanation may be found in the unquestionable superiority of a poem like Mitsune's KKS 1067 to verses such as the two below from *Shinsen man'yōshū*.[21] The compilers may simply have considered KKS 1067 and the others in Book Nineteen too good to ignore altogether.

SSMYS 2. Autumn 8. Anonymous

. . . I have never heard
that they make their way back to
   the heavens above,
yet one mistakes them for stars—
those autumn chrysanthemums.

SSMYS 2. Love 1. Anonymous

. . . To feel this yearning
on a single occasion
   would be hard enough,
yet my heart will soon be torn
into a thousand pieces.

The availability of this large group of poems also suggested the possibility of creating a counterpart to Book Ten, and so of recognizing the popularity of the kakushidai poem without damage to the anthology's overall structure. And, as a final consideration, incorporating the haikaika helped solve the problem of where to put the tiny chōka and sedōka sections, which were necessary for the sake of completeness but could not stand alone.

The resultant collection, like Book Ten, provided a change of pace and offered an implicit challenge. As befitted its prominence at the end of the anthology proper, the bid to engage and divert was a strong one. In Book Ten, the answers to the puzzles are plainly stated in the kotobagaki, and the puzzles themselves are of only momentary interest. In Book Nineteen, the reader receives an invitation to bring the full range of his critical faculties to bear. What is the difference between these poems and their seasonal, Love, and Miscellaneous relatives? In what specific respects does each fall short of the compilers' standards? Since such questions are pertinent to our concerns, let us review a few sample cases.

Sometimes the defect is apparent. Seeking a novel treatment of the star lovers theme, Kanesuke, the author of KKS 1014 below, has shifted the focus from the Weaver Maid, where we would expect it, to the Ox-Driver. His conception is amusing and original, as the compilers have recognized in including the poem, but it lacks the deft touch needed to reconcile it with the romantic tone appropriate to a Tanabata composition. The contrast with KKS 175, a model of its kind, is instructive. By using the intensely evocative word momiji, the anonymous poet suffuses his lines with the beauty of autumn leaves; by resorting to the colloquial-sounding, faintly ridiculous *hagi* ("shins"), Kanesuke moves outside the limits of the permissible, not only for his topic, but for the *hare no uta* in general. Hagi, which cannot be made compatible with an ambience of elegance and grace, appears nowhere else in the anthology.

KKS 1014. Fujiwara Kanesuke. *Written on the Sixth of the Seventh Month in anticipation of the Seventh*

. . . Might he be crossing
the heavenly stream today,
   showing with bared shins
his consuming impatience
to be with his beloved?

KKS 175. Anonymous. *Topic unknown*

. . . Is it for a bridge
of many-hued leaves to span
   the heavenly stream
that the Weaver Maid awaits
the arrival of autumn?

KKS 1027, a poem with a noticeable utagaki flavor,

provides another example of an original conception defeated by questionable diction. Its author, too, has sacrificed beauty in the pursuit of wit. She seems to have hoped to create the requisite balance by introducing the pillow word *ashihiki no,* which was thought to confer an aura of archaic dignity, but a ludicrous effect results from the juxtaposition of that term with the colloquial *sōzu* ("scarecrow"). There is no other scarecrow in **Kokinshū.**

KKS 1027. Anonymous. *Topic unknown*

   . . . Ah, what a trial!
Even *you* make bold, it seems,
    to run after me—
you scarecrow in a paddy
among the foot-wearying hills.

KKS 1027 also suffers from the absence of an attractive sound pattern, a shortcoming it shares with many other haikaika. KKS 1040 below, for example, presents an acceptably conventional conception, and there is no fault in the vocabulary. The author achieves a degree of wit by means of his *ōnusa* ("sacred wand") conceit, which is probably an allusion to the well-known exchange between Narihira and an anonymous lady (KKS 706-7). But *ōnusa* is not a sensuous image, and no beauty is provided by the language, which fails utterly to achieve the rhythmic, subtly patterned flow of a superior *hare no uta* like Tsurayuki's HT 801.

KKS 1040. Anonymous. *Topic unknown*

   . . . If you assured me
that you cared only for me,
    I would be able
to place all my trust in you—
but your heart is a sacred wand.

HT 801. Ki no Tsurayuki

   . . . No chill in the wind
blowing beneath cherry trees
    where blossoms scatter,
yet we see a fall of snow
unknown to the firmament.

Although the second poem below, KKS 1046, also lacks a clearly discernible sound pattern, its placement suggests that the compilers questioned it primarily because of its mitate. The author of the preceding waka, KKS 1045, cannot be criticized for an indifference to auditory effect (note the repetition of syllables beginning with g and t), but the poem is robbed of beauty by the comparison of the woman to a horse—particularly unfortunate because the Heian animal, scruffy and stocky, in no way resembled the clean-limbed thoroughbred that a modern reader might picture. The compilers, by pairing the two poems, imply that the

simile is equally at fault in KKS 1046 (probably because it carries dusty, bedraggled overtones).

KKS 1045. Anonymous. *Topic unknown*

   . . . Do you regard me—
the person you cast aside—
    as a horse in spring
ready to be sent away
to forage in the meadows?

KKS 1046. Anonymous. *Topic unknown*

   . . . Does your coldness mean
that you are discarding me
    as though I were only
an old nest, last year's lodging,
abandoned by a warbler?

Formal imbalance seems to be the problem in other cases. In KKS 1035, for example, the emphasis is not on the speaker's feelings, the putative subject of the composition, which must have been intended as a love poem, but on the jo—on the summer robes thin as cicadas' frail wings—which could be said to occupy four of the five lines. (The verbs in the fourth line do double duty.) For contrast, let us consider KKS 715, a poem from Love (4) with a similar theme. *Natsukoromo* ("summer robes") is there used as a *makura kotoba,* adding elegant overtones without distracting attention from the main statement. The cicada imagery associates directly with the speaker's sadness, reinforces the theme of transitoriness (by association with autumn, the main cicada season in poetry), and links unobtrusively, through thin wings, with *usuku* (a form of *usushi,* "thin") in line 4. KKS 1035 is heavy-handed by comparison.

KKS 1035. Ōshikōchi Mitsune. *Topic unknown*

   . . . Habituation
leads, does it not, to close ties,
    even as wrinkles
mold well-worn summer garments
thin as cicadas' frail wings?

KKS 715. Ki no Tomonori. *A poem from the Empress's Contest during the reign of the Kanpyō Emperor*

   . . . How it saddens me
to hear the cicada's voice
    heralding a time
when your affection for me
will seem thin as summer robes.

Some haikaika authors stumble when they attempt originality in the use of personification. We may surmise that Motokata's basic aim in KKS 1062 below was not to arouse laughter, but simply to use personification in an unexpected way, and thus to add a touch of novelty to the conventional theme of the world as a vale of tears. But the compilers, in pairing his poem with one attributing rational thought processes to the years, indicated that there were limits to the acceptable use of the device. Elegant and amusing when applied to birds and flowers, personification relegated a poem to eccentric status when applied to the world and time.

KKS 1062. Ariwara Motokata. *Topic unknown*

. . . What distressful thoughts
must afflict the anguished mind
    of the poor old world,
made an object of hatred
by such multitudes of men!

KKS 1063. Anonymous. *Topic unknown*

. . . What was I doing,
that now I am an old man
    with nothing achieved?
And what embarrassing thoughts
might have passed through the years'
        minds?

KKS 1063 can be said to suffer from tonal imbalance as well. In the first three lines, the poet utters a despairing cry; in the last two, he impresses us as flippant. A similar flaw seems to have doomed KKS 1047. Unlike most of the other poems we have examined, it possesses a sound pattern and imagery of the requisite grace, but they are not sufficient to bridge the gulf between the romantic atmosphere of the last three lines and the brisk, prosaic approach of the first two, with their overtones of sweaty summer heat.

KKS 1047. Anonymous. *Topic unknown*

. . . Feigning great good sense,
I followed summer custom,
    but still I sleep alone
now when leaves of bamboo grass
whisper on cold frosty nights.

An inappropriate use of imagery was another cause of demotion. Although Komachi's KKS 1030 has been praised in the West,[22] the compilers must have felt that it overstepped the fine line between decorum and exaggeration. It was permissible to compare smoldering passion to the hidden fires in Mount Fuji, but a heart could not snap, crackle, and pop.

Sometimes it is difficult to follow the compilers' reasoning. KKS 1018, for example, seems a competent treatment of a conventional topic, deficient in aural interest but nevertheless combining reasoning with attractive imagery. We are obliged to conjecture that

Tsurayuki and his colleagues did not consider the conception a sufficiently interesting substitute for the usual approach, which was to play on the flower's name as Mitsune has done in KKS 233.

KKS 1018. Anonymous. *Topic unknown*

. . . The mists of autumn
now clear away, now gather,
    and thus the beauty
of maidenflowers in bloom
now appears, now vanishes.

KKS 233. Ōshikōchi Mitsune. *A poem composed and presented at a Suzakuin maidenflower contest*

. . . Yearning for a mate,
the stag utters plaintive cries.
    Is he not aware
that in the field where he dwells
the blossoms are maidenflowers?

Similarly, there appears to be no fault in Mitsune's penultimate KKS 1067, which impresses the reader as a model of its kind—witty, expressing auspicious sentiments appropriate to the occasion, and distinguished by great aural appeal. The compilers may have felt that *mashira* ("monkey"), in spite of its contribution to the sound pattern, departed unacceptably from the assigned topic, which used the word *saru* for monkey, or, alternatively, that *mashira* erred on the side of colloquialism.[23]

Despite such problematic cases, exaggeration in the broadest sense (i.e., imbalance or breach of decorum resulting from the pursuit of novelty) appears to have been the common element in most haikai poems. Almost all of the flaws we have identified might be subsumed under that heading. So, too, might the shortcomings of Muneyana's KKS 1020, mentioned earlier, where the poet, desirous of punning on *fujibakama* ("wisteria-trousers"), makes the blatantly arbitrary claim that crickets produce the sound *tsuzuri sase* ("patch and sew"). And so might those of KKS 1031 below. The subject matter of KKS 1031 is ambiguous, a defect from the compilers' standpoint, but the poem's fatal weakness is that the author has reached for originality by using the verb *tsumu* ("pick," "pinch") in a manner incompatible with courtly elegance.

KKS 1031. Fujiwara Okikaze. *A poem from the Empress's Contest during the reign of the Kanpyō Emperor*

. . . I wish I could be
a young herb in a meadow
    where springtime haze trails,
for then perhaps that person
might feel tempted to pick me.

The haikai section can be called a faithful mirror of contemporary social and cultural realities. On the one hand, ninth-century Heian aristocrats were acutely conscious of the greatness of Chinese civilization; on the other, they were demonstrating a growing desire to assert native values. The authors who strained too hard for wit were emulating what they regarded as the most advanced Chinese literary fashion; the compilers who faulted them were responding to a new emphasis on grace, elegance, and beauty, apparent in literature, in all the fine and applied arts, and in almost every other aspect of upper-class daily life. Even more clearly than the rest of the anthology, Book Nineteen reveals that the Chinese-inspired notion of balance between form and content had come in practice to mean a harmonious blend of Chinese wit and Japanese beauty, and that a poem deficient in beauty could not rank as a successful formal composition. The book is, in short, not only a witty challenge to would-be literary critics, as was suggested earlier, but also, like *Kokinshū* itself, an assertion of national pride and confidence.

As a structural entity, Book Nineteen exhibits familiar patterns of association and progression. Some of them, such as subject-matter groupings and rhetorical pairings, have been mentioned above, as have correspondences to Book Ten within the overall arrangement of the anthology. One of the latter, the deviation from *Kokinshū* aesthetic norms, can now be characterized in more specific terms. A review of sample compositions has shown the nature of that deviation to be the same in both cases—namely, a consistent tendency on the part of the authors to stress wit at the expense of grace. It is characteristic of the compilers' taste for paradox that the wit counts as a virtue in Book Ten and a fault in Book Nineteen.

Book Twenty: Songs

By adding the appendix-like Book Twenty, a selection of thirty-two song lyrics (KKS 1069-1100), Tsurayuki and his colleagues accomplished three ends. They equaled the number of books in *Man'yōshū* and *Keikokushū,* the major predecessors of their anthology; they made room for a type of waka probably considered worthy of inclusion both because it could be roughly equated with the *yue fu* and because it embraced eastern folk songs like the ones in Book Fourteen of *Man'yōshū;* and they provided a structural and tonal counterpart to the prefaces, thus completing their organizational pattern.

Unlike the other nineteen maki, Book Twenty appears at first to lack a general title. The first five of its thirty-two poems are grouped as Folk Music Office Songs (*ōutadokoro no ōn'uta*), the next thirteen as Sacred Songs (*kami asobi no uta*), and the last fourteen as Eastern Songs (*azuma uta*). Actually, however, all three groups consist of selections from the repertoire of the Folk Music Office,[24] and we may consequently regard Folk Music Office Songs as both a general title and a heading for the first group.

That small group consists of miscellaneous songs for ceremonial occasions, brought together, it seems, partly on the basis of shared antiquity and partly with other structural considerations in mind. The first two, for example, follow the principle of seasonal progression, the third and fourth are linked by diurnal progression, and the fourth and fifth share mountain imagery.

Kami asobi no uta, the heading attached to the second group, is another name for *kagura uta,* songs used in "sacred music" performances at Shinto shrines and the Heian court.[25] The customary structure of such events is adumbrated in KKS 1074-81. The first six *uta* derive from the kagura category known as *torimono* ("things taken"), songs so called from the auspicious objects successively flourished as a god was welcomed during the initial stages of a program. The compilers have recognized the special religious importance of sakaki branches by including two sakaki *torimono:*

KKS 1074. *A torimono song*

. . . How luxuriant
in the presence of the gods—
   the sakaki leaves
growing where a sacred fence
encloses the mountain shrine.

KKS 1075. *A torimono song*

. . . Like the sakaki,
flourishing with leaves unscathed
   by recurrent frosts,
even so will they prosper,
those attendants of the gods.

After the torimono, which accounted for a large segment of the total performance, it was usual to present a song to Karakami, a palace guardian deity. The compilers have substituted one in honor of the goddess Amaterasu:

KKS 1080. *A song for the Sun Goddess*

. . . Rein in your young horse
at Hinokuma River,
   at Hinokuma,
and let him drink there a while
that I may at least see your back.

A standard kagura performance ended with another substantial round of singing and dancing, designed to entertain and then to see off the divine visitor. It is represented by a single song:

KKS 1081. *A song in modulated key*

. . . Plum blossom rain hats!
Those are the hats the warblers
    stich up for themselves,
finding willow filaments
and twisting them into thread.

The last five songs in this group (KKS 1082-86) prove to derive not from the kagura repertoire, as would have been expected, but from the Great Thanksgiving Service (*daijōsai*), a Shinto ceremony staged at the start of a new reign, with the Emperor as its central figure.[26] Some daijōsai uta, like KKS 1083 for Emperor Seiwa below, treat folk concerns; others, like KKS 1084, concentrate on the sovereign (here Emperor Yōzei). All include place names associated with their places of origin.

KKS 1083. *A song in modulated key*

. . . I would feel sorry,
sorry (ah, Sarayama
    in Mimasaka!)
if gossip tarnished my name.
Never, never must it be.

KKS 1084. *A song in modulated key*

. . . We shall serve our lord
for countless generations,
    ceaselessly as flows
the barrier's Fuji River
in the province of Mino.

With one exception, the songs in the third group are identified as *azuma uta* from specific eastern provinces. Folk Music Office songs from the east were often presented as adjuncts to kagura performances, notably at the special festivals (*rinjisai*) of two major shrines near the capital, Kamo and Iwashimizu. The compilers have arranged their examples by province, with subdivisions of the usual kind. KKS 1093 and KKS 1094, for instance, are linked by ocean imagery, KKS 1088 and KKS 1089 by a common place name. The last poem in the group—and the only one in Book Twenty by a named author—is a song composed for the Kamo Special Festival by Toshiyuki:

KKS 1100. Fujiwara Toshiyuki. *A song for the Kamo Winter Festival*

. . . Through ten thousand years,
never will their color change—
    the fair young pine trees
fresh and green at the great shrine
of the mighty Kamo gods.

Several questions suggest themselves. Why has KKS 1080 replaced the orthodox song in honor of Karakami?

Why are daijōsai songs listed under the heading *kami asobi no uta*? Why are *azuma uta* emphasized and other types of regional songs virtually ignored? Why does a collection of folk songs end with a work by a famous contemporary poet? The answers are probably to be sought both in the compilers' sense of mission and in their concern for form.

As noted in Chapter Five, Tsurayuki attempts in part one of the kanajo to describe the characteristics, uses, and history of Japanese poetry in such a way as to place the waka on an equal footing with the shi and kanshi. The second part of the preface, although it may be regarded as primarily an account of the anthology's immediate origins, demonstrates the same attitude when it praises the reigning sovereign, boasts that it is he who has commissioned **Kokinshū,** asserts that the collection will guarantee the survival of the waka (thus maintaining it to be worthy of preservation as serious literature), and rejoices that the compilers "have been born in this era and . . . have lived to see poetry receive official recognition." The apparent anomalies in Book Twenty can be said to arise from similar concerns. By inserting KKS 1080, the compilers have not only honored the progenitor of the imperial line, but also linked their anthology to the puissant goddess; by including daijōsai songs associated with Period Two and Period Three sovereigns, they have paralleled the kanajo praise of Emperor Daigo; by placing the daijōsai group immediately after the kagura songs, where it acquires a borrowed aura of holiness, they have further complimented the ruling house.

The *Man'yōshū* precedent provides one probable reason for the emphasis on *azuma uta*. Assuming that Tsurayuki and his colleagues wished to keep Book Twenty small so as to balance it against the preface(s), they may have slighted other types of folk songs in order to include an ample representation of the one singled out by their predecessors. We should also bear in mind, however, that there was a close connection between the *azuma uta* and the Kamo Special Festival, an event said to have been founded by Emperor Uda.[27] If the tradition is correct, to call attention to such songs was to pay indirect homage to one of the men most responsible for the return of the waka to public life.

Finally, Toshiyuki's poem, KKS 1100, was a uniquely felicitous choice for the key position at the end of the anthology. Because it had been composed for the first Kamo Special Festival,[28] it repeated the obeisance to Retired Emperor Uda. Stylistically, it returned the reader to the **Kokinshū** norm, bridging the gap between the compilers' basic standards and the relative naïveté of the Book Twenty songs. Tonally, it was a ringing assertion of native beliefs, values, and attitudes—a return to the magico-religious roots of Japanese literature, and to Man'yō-style optimism, proclaiming even time, the invincible antagonist, to be powerless against the mighty gods. And no Heian reader would have missed the implicit comparison of the fair young pine trees to **Kokinshū** itself. In this, their last poetic statement, the compilers echo Tsurayuki's triumphant pronouncement at the end of the kanajo: "Time may pass and circumstances may change, pleasures and sorrows may succeed one another, but these poems will endure."

Notes

[1] The discussion below draws frequently on Matsuda, *Kokinshū no kōzō,* which is the most comprehensive treatment of the subject. See also Arai; Konishi, "Association and Progression"; and Kikuchi, *Kokinteki sekai.*

[2] Although *Ise monogatari* as such was not an acceptable model for an official poetry collection, it or similar works may have helped to inspire the inclusion of the kotobagaki, the introductory remarks that function in *Kokinshū* as brief notations of the circumstances under which the waka were composed. The origins of the individual comments cannot be traced today, but it seems likely that the compilers provided some from their own brushes—including many instances of the commonest one, *dai shirazu,* "topic unknown," which often seems to mean "circumstances of composition unknown"—and that they obtained others from the sources they used. For a discussion of the possible relationship between one group of *Kokinshū* kotobagaki and a group of almost identical prose passages in *Ise monogatari,* see McCullough, *Tales of Ise,* pp. 60-61. The verbatim reproduction of sources, taken in conjunction with the Heian predilection for flexible nomenclature, may also help to explain the varying forms in which authors' names appear in the anthology. (See McCullough, *Kokin Wakashū.*) The notion of editorial consistency in this respect, which has been imposed in the present volume, was as foreign to Tsurayuki and his colleagues as to their *Man'yōshū* predecessors.

[3] Reasoning from analogy, scholars conjecture that Motokata must have been dead by the time *Kokinshū* was completed. However, his dates remain unknown.

[4] Prince Sadatoki (874-929) was Emperor Seiwa's son by a daughter of Fujiwara Mototsune.

[5] The translations obscure the correspondences between the first 3 lines: the colored leaves on the oak trees at Saoyama will probably scatter (KKS 281); the colored leaves enclosed by rocks in the deep mountains will probably scatter (KKS 282).

[6] Mitsune expresses the conventional Buddhist belief that this world is a place of sorrows; Henjō probably alludes to a passage in the *Lotus Sutra,* "These songs of the Buddha . . . are as untainted with worldly things

as the lotus flower in the water." (Translation from Katō et al., *Three-Fold Lotus Sutra,* pp. 246-47.) KKS 165 and 166 both ask questions in feigned puzzlement: "Why should it deceitfully seek to make us take dewdrops for gems?" (KKS 165); "Where in the clouds might the moon be sheltering?" (KKS 166).

[7] This was the case, for example, at an event commemorated in *Kaifūsō* (KFS 64).

[8] *Ōkagami,* p. 47 (translated in McCullough, *Ōkagami,* p. 76).

[9] See Matsuda, *Kokinshū no kōzō,* p. 342, for a discussion of her identity.

[10] The first line of the anthem reads *kimi ga yo wa* ("[May] our lord's reign [endure]"), a variation that appears to date from the medieval period. See Ozawa, *Kokin wakashū,* p. 168.

[11] There seems to have been nothing comparable in early Chinese literature. It might be noted, however, that the principle of progression was employed in Vidyākāra's *Subhāṣtaratnakoṣa,* an 11th-century anthology of Sanskrit court poetry. See Ingalls, p. 192.

[12] In attempting to call attention to the wordplay, the translation of KKS 469 falsifies the tone. See Chap. 5, n. 79.

[13] There are actually 13 poems in the group beginning with KKS 470, counting an anonymous lady's reply to a composition by Narihira.

[14] There are puns on *naniwa* (place name; "anything") and *towa* (place name Toba with medial voicing; "eternally," "forever").

[15] *Koto ni masaru* can mean "exceeds the koto."

[16] The relationship of the deceased to the poet is unclear in a few cases, such as KKS 850, 855, and 856.

[17] The syllables *wa* and *ha* are developments from an original single syllable.

[18] Still more complex forms flourished later in the Heian period, but it is uncertain whether they were known in Tsurayuki's day. See *Waka bungaku daijiten,* p. 139: *oriku kutsukamuri no uta;* and McCullough and McCullough, p. 77, n. 46.

[19] Tsurayuki, Tomonori, and Tadamine, with 6, 5, and 2 poems respectively, account for more than 27 percent of the compositions in Book Ten. Only Mitsune is unrepresented.

[20] See Kikuchi, "*Kokinshū* haikaika ron"; and Kikuchi,

Kokinteki sekai, pp. 204-18, to both of which the discussion below is generally indebted. The title haikaika has yet to be satisfactorily explained. The translation Eccentric Poems is based on the conjecture that the compilers used the term to mean deviation from a norm. Alternatively, Tsurayuki and the others may have intended it to be taken as license to smile at the authors' shortcomings; or, like "tanka," it may represent a misinformed later addition.

[21] See the discussion in Chap. 4, p. 268.

[22] Brower and Miner, *Japanese Court Poetry,* pp. 205-6.

[23] The second suggestion is an old one. See Matsuda, *Shinshaku,* 2: 933.

[24] An administrative entity created around the end of the 8th century to gather, preserve, edit, perform, and teach native folk songs, as opposed to imported musical forms, which were under the jurisdiction of the Bureau of Elegant Music (*gagakuryo*).

[25] See McCullough and McCullough, pp. 410-11, for a discussion.

[26] For details, see McCullough and McCullough, pp. 374-78.

[27] See Tachibana, *Ōkagami,* pp. 51-52 (translated in McCullough, *Ōkagami,* pp. 295-96).

[28] *Ōkagami,* p. 253 (translated in McCullough, *Ōkagami,* p. 216).

Abbreviations

Citations of poetry contests in the form "B.1" refer to the numbers in Appendix B. For the editions used and full publication data, see the Works Cited section, pp. 561-67.

BKSRS *Bunka shūreishū*

BS *Bo shi chang qing ji*

CC *Chu ci*

FDK *Fudoki kayō*

GR Hanawa Hokinoichi, comp., *[Shinkō] Gunsho ruijū*

GS Uchida Sennosuke, ed., *Gyokutai shin'ei*

GSS *Gosenshū*

HH Hagitani Boku, *Heianchō uta awase taisei*

HT Ki no Tsurayuki, *Tosa nikki* (ed. Hagitani Boku)

KBKK Sugawara Michizane, *Kanke bunsō, kanke kōshū*

KeiKS *Keikokushū*

KFS *Kaifūsō*

KJK *Kojiki kayō*

KKS *Kokin wakashū* (ed. Saeki Umetomo)

KT Kuroita Katsumi, ed., *Kokushi taikei*

KW *Kudai waka,* in *[Kōchū] Kokka taikei*

MYS *Man'yōshū* (ed. Takagi Ichinosuke et al.)

NKBT Takagi Ichinosuke et al., *Nihon koten bungaku taikei*

NS *Nihon shoki kayō*

QHSJN Ding Fubao, ed., *Quan han sanguo jin nanbei chao shi*

QTS *Quan tang shi*

RUS *Ryōunshū*

SIS *Shūishū*

SJ *Shi jing.* The numbers cited are those in Karlgren, *Book of Odes*

SKKS *Shinkokinshū*

SSMYS *Shinsen man'yōshū* (Takano Taira)

SW *Shinsen waka*

TN Ki no Tsurayuki, *Tosa nikki* (ed. Suzuki Tomotarō et al.)

WX Xiao Tong, ed., *Wen xuan*

YFSJ Guo Maoqian, ed., *Yue fu shi ji*

YTXY Xu Ling, comp., *Yu tai xin yong*

ZKT Matsushita Daisaburō, *Zoku kokka taikan*

Edwin A. Cranston (essay date 1988)

SOURCE: "A Web in the Air," *Monumenta Nipponica: Studies in Japanese Culture,* Vol. 43, No.3, Autumn, 1988, pp. 332-52.

[*In the following excerpt, Cranston evaluates McCullough's translation of the* Kokinshu *and directly compares some of her versions of particular poems with those of other translators.*]

. . . People who have practiced translation, especially poetic translation, tend to have strong opinions on the subject; others couldn't care less. I belong to the former category. Miller, pp. 758-59, makes it clear that he regards literary scholarship and translation as sciences. I do not. Not at least in the sense 'science' has acquired since it came to be applied to the exact natural sciences, rather than to knowledge in general. 'The results of science,' Miller says, p. 758, 'whatever the field or discipline, are significant only to the extent that they prove themselves capable of being replicated.' I am sure that is true. But it is not true of literature, or of writing about literature, and emphatically it is not applicable to the translation of poetry. The mind of the scholar/translator, in its interpretive mode (when not dealing with mere fact), confronts the mind of the poet with imponderable consequences. No one could predict, no one could *replicate* Stephen Owen's. *Omen of the World,*[42] to take a recent example. The essence of humanistic activity is precisely that it cannot be replicated. Not, that is, without simply copying what someone else has done.

I suspect that proponents of 'scientific' translation would prefer prose glosses, as literal as can be made. If so, they miss the whole challenge of recreating a poem. Admittedly, the enterprise has a special status, is dubious as a strictly *scientific* activity, and is fraught with aesthetic hazard. Fortunately, it's also fun. It's something extra the art historians and other historians, the linguists and other scientists don't have. For some of us, it does indeed provide adequate reason to learn a language: translation, the interface of two languages, remains the heart of the matter. Anyway, crusty critics who prefer their toast unbuttered will always be around to remind us of our self-indulgent ways. They serve an essential function: translators need a bad conscience.

McCullough puts forward her own views on translation in her 'Translator's Preface' (*Anthology,* p. vi). Hers is essentially an either-or position: 'A waka may be treated as a point of departure for a very different poem in another language, or an effort may be made to reproduce content, form, and tone as faithfully as possible.' She regards herself (*pace* Miller) as having followed the second method. Alas, she does not admit the real problem: an 'effort' *must* be made to produce a 'poem', or there will be no fidelity to her three criteria. Every translator who aims for more than a prose gloss will be compelled to produce a poem. Trying to be 'faithful' (which doesn't mean that the result won't be 'very different') should provide the 'net'—not a safety net, but the net of the tennis-match metaphor—

that gives the game its rules; or the mold that the vigor of the poem tries to break and fly out of. The writer of a sonnet experiences tensions at least as great. As Joseph Brodsky has said, writing poetry provides a unique pleasure that once tasted cannot be forgone.[43] So does poetic translation. And the reason is the same: the experience pushes you into 'solutions'—words, thoughts, patterns—that are exhilarating, unpredictable. Impossible to replicate.

Arthur Waley had words of wisdom on this subject: the type of translation desirable depends on what is being translated.[44] Obvious, but true. People who are drawn to material-culture studies are naturally drawn to certain kinds of texts; those who are drawn primarily to poetry *per se,* to other kinds—*waka* among them. Both tend to extrapolate their preferences. My preference is for *waka,* a short poem highly susceptible to what might be called metamorphic translation. This poem creates itself anew in the crucible of the translator's mind more readily than most. Here I must part company with Waley, who considered it 'of all poetries the most completely untranslatable'.[45] I would rather say, one of the most rewarding. But I do agree with his dictum that 'whether the translator's style is contemporary or archaic does not matter.'[46] What matters is that it work.

What would work for *waka? Waka* has a syllabic form, and that is a place to start. Over time, that syllabic rhythm will imprint itself in the translator's mind, and his translations come to mimic it. Short-long-short-long-long. That pulse, that sinuosity, is the 'groove' into which to pour Waley's 'quicksilver'.[47] But the syntax of the Japanese will fight against that of English, setting up a polar tension in this little tube. Out of that tension will come the best translations. And the imperative to run true to form will cut across literalistic fidelities, wherein lies the bad conscience referred to above. The choices shouldn't be too easy. But, since all this activity is a form of play, not too difficult, either.

Let's get down to cases. I shall start with a translation I have admired for many years, one by Donald Keene. The poet is Saigyō.

SSKS 12:1199

    . . . Living all alone
    In this space between the rocks
    Far from the city,
    Here, where no one can see me,
    I shall give myself to grief.[48]

I cannot imagine how this could be improved. It has the stamp of authentic taste and that simple inevitability that is the rarest of achievements. It also scans precisely, 5-7-5-7-7.

Here is another, by E. Bruce Brooks, whose little article 'A Yakamochi Sampler' has much to teach about taste, restraint, and natural flow in translation.

MYS 8:1567, Ōtomo no Yakamochi

. . . Hidden in the clouds
the geese call, passing over
    the fields of autumn
whose ripening crop of grain
is no more full than my love[49]

If Brooks (who consistently scans with exactitude) and Keene show one possibility, Brower and Miner have long established another:

KKS 15:747, Narihira

. . . What now is real?
This moon, this spring, are altered
    From their former being—
While this alone, my mortal body, remains
As ever changed by love beyond all change.[50]

On the scale of things, this must be accounted 'a very different poem'. It is a reading, expansive, conceptual, exuberantly Byronic, of Narihira's fragment of sad puzzlement.

McCullough's own practice has been illustrated in a number of examples already quoted. Her poems scan, and many read exceptionally well. It is impossible to know how much credit must be given to Stephen D. Carter, to whom McCullough acknowledges an indebtedness in her 'Translator's Preface' (*Anthology,* p. vi), but I think it would be remiss not to mention his name. McCullough has provided in the 'wit, refinement, and conservatism' by which she epitomizes the 'mature *Kokinshū* style' (*Brocade,* p. 207) the most apt description of her own manner. The following illustrates this style at its best:

KKS 11:484, Anonymous

. . . For love of someone
as remote as the heavens,
    I muse in the dusk,
my thoughts vagrant as dark clouds
forming their fleeting banners.

This version is excellent in the way that it scans (characteristically in an exact 5-7-5-7-7), flows, and beautifully restates the original. But it came about from dissolving the original and letting it reform: the miracle of metamorphosis. In the process the order of exposition and images has altered. 'Vagrant as dark clouds', strongly harmonic in sound and image, does not 'translate' anything, but transmutes the first two lines. 'Forming their fleeting banners', the real stroke of this version, interprets one word—*hatate.* Is this too 'a very different poem'? It is a poem, and that is what matters.

McCullough's might truly be called 'classical translations'—they sit firmly in their form. But she does allow herself elbow-room, as in the following, for a line that lives:

KKS 3:166, Kiyowara no Fukayabu

. . . Now that dawn has come
while the evening lingers
    on this summer night,
in what cloudy hostelry
might the moon have gone to rest?

'Hostelry' is of course derived from the verb *yadoru* ('to lodge').

The following permits itself even more latitude.

KKS 11:528, Anonymous

. . . Because of this love
my body has been transformed
    into a shadow,
but not, alas, the shadow
that follows your every step.

This is a clever translation, one that indulges in rendering one word, *kage* ('shadow'), twice. Those who think such licence improper will be displeased, but a poet might be pleased to be so rendered.

Rhythms are seductive, and 5-7-5-7-7 can be as seductive for the translator as 4-6 *p'ien-wen* was for Tsura-yuki and his Chinese models. The following is a case in point.

KKS 12:574, Tsurayuki

. . . Might dew have settled
on the dream paths I followed
    throughout the long night?
My sleeves, drenched before I slept,
even now remain undried.

'Before I slept' is an interpretation handy for the scansion requirements but not called for otherwise. Overfidelity to form can make for dull reading if it goes on too long; the perfect, smooth eggshell sometimes cries to be broken.

So let's open things up a little, and let out whatever creature lurks inside. First, two more of McCullough's 'classical' translations:

MYS 6:925, Yamabe no Akahito

. . . When night settles in,

black as leopard-flower seeds,
  a plover's ceaseless cry
sounds where *hisaki* trees grow
along the clean river beach.

This version (*Brocade,* p. 108) is so honest that it ruins the rhythm of the fourth line by refusing to English an obscure botanical item. But the *makurakotoba* proved irresistible. *Nubatama,* probably not less obscure than *hisaki,* is out on the prowl as 'leopard-flower seeds', one of the things Kenkyūsha's *Wa-ei* says *hiōgi* (whose black berries *nubatama* may have been) is the Japanese name of (the other being 'blackberry lily'). Suggestive of swart night, a black panther, the image is wildly inappropriate in its associations—and yet so right. It crops up again in another Man'yō poem translated by McCullough (*Brocade,* p. 147):

MYS 8:1646, Oharida no Azumamaro

  . . . How sad it would be
were it to melt tomorrow!
  Let us drench ourselves
in the snow that has fallen
on this seed-black evening.

Ho hum, the leopard seems to be put off by the snow, leaving only the seeds. Nothing particularly wrong with the translation, though. But how well I recall the sudden release I experienced on a late, dark night when I turned the page to the following, by my student, the poet Carl Kay:[51]

HHHHOOOOOOOOOOOOOOOOOOOOOOOOOOOWHHHHE
EEEEEEEEEEEEEEEEEEEEEEEE
Snow!

                              SNOW!

                lets you and I go play in the
snow
                we cant wait for tomorrow we
gotta do it NOW

    anthracite night anthracite night in the
anthracite night like leopards
    like leopards like leopards running like
leopards like leopards LEAPING

            and landing

                                blackberries
blackberries blackberries

CHHHHHHHHHHHHHHHHHHHHHHHHHHMEAAHHH
HHHHHHHHHHHHHHHHHH

wooooooooooooooooooooooooooooooohaaaaaaaaaaaaaaaa

you nice and wet   are

nice and wet   I'm

A quite different poem? Or the late flowering of a leopard seed from the carboniferous forest of the mind, buried under the drifts of fallen years? Come, poet-translators, don't be afraid. The leopards won't bite—they're too happy leaping in the snow.

Mention of wild animals brings to mind McCullough's explanation of how *kakekotoba* work (*Brocade,* p. 221): 'It is as though one were to say in English, "The animal appeared to be a bare-faced lie had been told."' Precisely. She has provided a model that in fact will work in translation, although she seems not to entertain that possibility. Let's try a few 'bare-faced' translations. One has already been given, but I'll repeat it here, as my menagerie is still lean:

KKS 1:20, Tsurayuki

  . . . A catalpa bow
Bent and strung to spring rain
  Falls at last today:
If it rains tomorrow too,
We'll be picking the young greens.

                              [EAC]

McCullough's version runs:

  Today there fell rains
of spring, season recalling
  tautened birchwood bows.
If they but fall tomorrow,
we will be picking young greens.

Here are a couple of others:

SW 62; MYS 10:2211, Anonymous

  . . . Once I had loosened
And retied my sister's sash
  I stood up to go
High across Tatsuta Mountain
The fall leaves had grown brighter.

                              [EAC]

Here the translation provides an expanded counterpart for the *kakekotoba* (*tatsu* ['get up to go'] / *Tatsu*ta Mountain) rather than rendering it directly.

McCullough, *Anthology,* p. 307:

  Autumn foliage
takes on deeper colors now
  at Mount Tatsuta,
whose name recalls how I leave,

having loosed and tied her sash.

This is fine, too, except that 'leave' makes an unintended (and unwanted?) *engo*. But the 'whose name recalls' technique for handling this kind of *jo* goes better, I feel, in *chōka* than in the compactness of *tanka*.

KKS 5:263, Mibu no Tadamine

> . . . Once the rain begins,
> Dress for the *Wet* Mountain now
>   Wears fall leaves so bright
> Even they who come and go
> Shimmer to their very sleeves.

[EAC]

Again, the effect has been rendered, rather than the exact word.

McCullough, *Anthology,* p. 66:

> At Kasatoriyama—
> Umbrella-Wielding in rain—
>   the brilliant colors
> of autumnal foliage
> set travelers' sleeves aglow.

The first *waka* translations I recall reading by Helen McCullough were those in her 1968 *Tales of Ise.* Many were of **Kokinshū** poems translated again in the work under review. It may be of some interest to compare versions and see how her practice has altered.

KKS 1:8, Fun'ya no Yasuhide

> . . . As I rejoice
> In the sunlight of spring
> I regret only
> That my hair has grown
> White as this snow.
> In *Tales of Ise*

[ToI]

> Rare is the fortune
> of one who basks in the sun
>   on this springtime day,
> yet how can I not lament
> that snow should whiten my head?
> In *Kokin Wakashā*

[KW]

The unpretentious simplicity of the earlier version will probably appeal more to some readers. Obviously, rhythmic considerations have yet to enter in. For all its simplicity, the first version is not necessarily any closer to the original, which remains a *tertium quid.*

KKS 1:27, Henjō

> . . . Pale green
> Twisted threads
> Piercing beads
> Of white dew—
> Willows in spring.

[ToI]

> It twists together
> leafy threads of tender green
>   and fashions jewels
> by piercing clear, white dewdrops—
> the willow tree in springtime.

[KW]

The first version, in the imagistic tradition, is haiku-like, and effective in its way. Loyalty to the image will inevitably clash with the imperative to work out a connected statement in a set form.

KKS 5:292, Henjō

> . . . Faithlessly
> The tree
> Chosen to shelter
> A man hard-pressed
> Sheds its scarlet leaves.

[ToI]

> Autumn foliage
> has scattered from the branches,
>   leaving no shelter
> where the lonely recluse
> comes looking for a haven.

[KW]

Again, a modern minimalism and freedom have been sacrificed for a classical form.

KKS 12:554, Komachi

> . . . When longing for him
> Tortures me beyond endurance,
>   I reverse my robe—
> Garb of night, black as
>   leopard-flower berries—
> And wear it inside out.

[ToI]

> When longing for you
> torments me beyond my strength,
>   I reverse my robe,
> raiment of seed-black night,
> and put it on inside out.

[KW]

The adjustments here are quite interesting. 'Him' has changed to 'you', illustrating one of the many ambigu_ ities of this poetry. The second line had been tautened and strengthened, the third left as it was, except for indentation and punctuation. The long explanatory fourth line has been curtailed and improved by leaving out the leopards. It is worth observing that the translator has not cared to insert a definite article in the revised line to achieve a perfect syllable count. Evidence that other criteria can override syllable count is always welcome. 'And wear it inside out' in line five is right, although a syllable short; 'and put it on . . . ' is weak and puttery, seven syllables and all.

KKS 12:557, Komachi

. . . Tears that but form gems on sleeves,
Must come, I think,
From an insincere heart,
For mine, though I seek to repress them,
Gush forth in torrents.

[ToI]

  Tears that do no more
than turn into beads on sleeves
  are formal indeed.
Mine flow in a surging stream,
try though I may to halt them.

[KW]

The first version is prosy, and the second an improvement in that regard, although still a bit stiff in the joints. 'Formal' is an interesting translation of *oroka* ('foolish'). Perhaps a third attempt is in order.

  Shallow tears are they
That falling on a person's sleeves
  Form in little beads;
I cannot even dam the flood,
For mine are a gushing stream.

(EAC)

KKS 14:708, Anonymous

. . . Captured by the gale,
The smoke from the salt-fires
Of the fisher folk at Suma
Has drifted off
In an unforeseen direction.

[ToI]

  Yielding to the gale,
it has drifted to a place
  I never dreamed of—
the smoke rising from salt fires
tended by Suma seafolk.

[KW]

Here the second try has resulted in a real poem, and a fine one. The rhythm, pacing, and the s-alliteration of the last lines make it 'work'. The gasp of realization in the *-keri* ending is reflected in the strong middle line of the translation.

In her *Tales of Ise* McCullough used some of the most impressive of the Brower-Miner translations from *Japanese Court Poetry,* perhaps feeling it was futile to try to improve on them. With new confidence, she now provides her own versions of such poems as the following:

KKS 13:656, Komachi

  . . . In waking daylight,
Then, oh then it can be understood,
  But when I see myself
Shrinking from those hostile eyes
Even in my dreams: this is misery itself.

[Brower-Miner]

  In the waking world
you must, I suppose, take care,
  but how it pains me
that you should keep out of sight
even in the realm of dreams.

[McCullough]

McCullough's translation follows the standard commentaries in understanding Komachi to be referring to her lover, but the Brower-Miner reading is not ruled out by anything in the original, and is psychologically more interesting.

KKS 15:797, Komachi

  . . . Find mutability
In that being which alters without fading
  In its outward hue—
In the color, looks, and the deceptive flower
Of the heart of what this world calls man!

[Brower-Miner]

  So much have I learned:
the blossom that fades away,
  its color unseen,
is the flower in the heart
of one who lives in this world.

[McCullough]

McCullough has done something quite fine with this beautiful Komachi poem. Her restraint reads very well opposite the Brower-Miner flamboyance, and is touching and personal in a way that the 'philosophical' version cannot match. The first line is especially praiseworthy, bringing across as it does the effect of the *ni zo arikeru* (whereas Brower and Miner have again chosen an abstraction).

KKS 18:938, Komachi

   . . . Misery holds me fixed,
And I would eagerly cut loose these roots
   To become a floating plant—
I should yield myself up utterly
If the inviting stream might be relied upon.
                           [Brower-Miner]

   In this forlorn state
I find life dreary indeed:
   if a stream beckoned,
I would gladly cut my roots
and float away like duckweed.

                           [McCullough]

McCullough's version avoids the fault of over-interpretation ('if the . . . stream might be relied upon') characteristic of this particular type of Brower-Miner translation, and her astringency creates a lower-keyed and more wistful effect. Her first two lines are rather 'explanatory', however. Neither version approaches the intricate complexity of the original.

KKS 19:1030, Komachi

   . . . On such a night as this
When the lack of moonlight shades your way
   to me,
   I wake from sleep my passion blazing,
My breast a fire raging, exploding flame
While within me my heart chars.
                           [Brower-Miner]

   On those moonless nights
when I long in vain for him,
   love robs me of sleep
and my agitated heart
burns like a crackling fire.

                           [McCullough]

Brower and Miner's all-stops-out translation of this poem is a hard act to follow, to say the least. Every fire image is exploited to the full, and after the translators have laid claim to 'blazing . . . raging . . . exploding . . . chars', what is there left to work with? Their Komachi sets the world on fire. McCullough's is quieter, more passive; her fire burns only within her, in the last line. It is another case of more from less: not a tumultuous sexual inferno (on a hot tin roof?), but a lonely woman suffering in the dark from desire. How long it took to come up with the perfect last line is a question I would like to ask. Until that fell into place it must have been impossible to proceed. 'Within me my heart chars' needed an answer. It found one. *Kokoro yakeori* with its crackling k's also found its metamorphosis.[52]

For some reason, McCullough refrained from using the

most spectacular of the Brower-Miner versions in her *Ise.* Still, a comparison will be of interest:

KKS 15:747, Narihira

   . . . What now is real?
This moon, this spring, are altered
   From their former being—
While this alone, my mortal body, remains
As ever changed by love beyond all change.
                           [Brower-Miner]

   Is this not the moon?
And is this not the springtime,
   the springtime of old?
Only this body of mine
the same body as before . . .

                           [McCullough]

The difference between the famous Brower-Miner formulation of this poem and McCullough's (and probably any other) is betrayed in the opening question. It is perverse not to focus on the moon, wither the poet bends his gaze. But since the poem is difficult only in regard to what it means, not what it says, why not follow the words? There is a distinction after all between *aranu* ('not exist') and *naranu* ('is not'). Narihira uses one of each, for his own paradoxical purposes. Let's allow him his paradox, and not be so ready to pluck out his mystery:

   Is there no moon?
And is this springtime not the spring
   Of times gone by?
My self alone remaining
Still the self it was before. . . .

                           (EAC)

The questions may be rhetorical, or they may be real. In the state of passionate confusion it is hard to be sure. We should leave them open, and imply no answer.

Since I do for the most part admire McCullough's translations, let me pick out a few more I think are particularly good:

KKS 3:145, Anonymous

   . . . O cuckoo singing
amid the summer mountains:
   if you have feelings,
do not harrow with your voice
one whose heart already aches.

KKS 5:283, Anonymous

   . . . Were one to cross it,

the brocade might break in two—
  colored autumn leaves
floating in random patterns
on the Tatsuta River.

KKS 11:519, Anonymous

  . . . How painful it is
to cherish a secret love—
  but whom shall I tell
of my yearnings for someone
who never dreams that I care?

Ōe no Chisato (*Brocade*, p. 255)

  . . . The sun of autumn
approaches the mountain rim.
  Walk along, red horse,
that my mother may see me
before night's shadows descend.

KKS 4:193, Chisato

  . . . Autumn does not come
for me alone among men—
  yet I am burdened
with a thousand vague sorrows
when I gaze upon the moon.

KKS 13:661, Ki no Tomonori

  . . . I shall not show it
as a safflower flaunts its red—
  not though I perish
of a love kept as secret
as streams in a hidden marsh.

All these please me by their liquid flow, their rhythm, pacing, elegant or otherwise appropriate tone, and the way they run smoothly into the *tanka* form. *Kokoro* and *kotoba* in balance, they are truly classical translations. Many others in these volumes are as good.

Others please me less. 'Minding of rock-creeping vines' for *tsuno sahau,* line one of MYS 2:135 (*Brocade*, p. 105) minds me uncomfortably of J. L. Pierson.[53] The end of the translation of this poem ('wept into my sleeve / . . . / cried until the tears soaked through') is a touch too lachrimose for my taste. This is a bit too much for the simple *tōrite nurenu* ('were all wet through [with tears]'). Perhaps 'snuffle the snot in my nose' (*Brocade*, p. 111) is too Anglo-Saxon even for Okura's *hana bishibishi ni* (MYS 5:892, line 12). In MYS 12:3034 *kiri* is 'mist', not 'smoke', despite the speaker's flames (*Brocade*, p. 124).

KKS 13:644, Narihira

  . . . Grieved that last night's dream

should have ended so soon,
  I try to doze off—
and now with what poignancy
its evanescence strikes home!

What interpretation lies behind the last two lines? The poem is supposed to be about a frustrated attempt to recapture the fragile moment of bliss by means of a dream. Anyway, 'strikes home' is too centered, sharp, and powerful for the vague feeling state involved.

KKS 9:411, Narihira

  . . . If you are in truth
what your name seems to make you,
  I will put to you,
capital-bird, this question:
do things go well with my love?

The translation scans, but, alas: let's try to see if we can get it closer:

  Well, let me ask you,
If you bear this as your name,
  Capital Bird:
Is the one for whom I long
Still there, or is she not?

                    [EAC]

Ari ya nashi ya to. More specifically, 'Is she alive, or is she not?' Is she is, or is she ain't?

KKS 16:861, Narihira

  . . . Upon this pathway,
I have long heard others say,
  man sets forth at last—
yet I had not thought to go
so very soon as today.

This reads well, but fails in its responsibility to *kinō kyō*, the nugget of the poem. (It leaves out *kinō* altogether.) The orthodox interpretation of *kinō kyō* is as a unitary expression meaning 'these days'. This vitiates the poem, in my opinion. In any case, the words should be kept together. An unorthodox reading:

  It is a road
That we go on at the end—
  Oh, I had heard that,
But I never realized,
Yesterday, today.

                    [EAC]

KKS 14:724, Minamoto no Tōru

  . . . Do you not know it?
You alone can set my heart
  astir with feelings

confused as moss-fern patterns
on cloth from Michinoku.

The first line of the translation is itself whole cloth, and quite unnecessarily so:

Random-patterned cloth
From Shinobu in the Northland—
     Pray because of whom
Will the turmoil now begin?
Surely not because of me!

                              [EAC]

KKS 19:1036, Tadamine

. . . Please do not object
if I come to visit you:
     it would be painful
were others to discover
how you deny me your bed.

The poem is based upon a *jo* presenting the image of a water plant called *nenunawa* (now called *junsai*, 'water shield'), impinging on the echoic *nenu na wa* . . . ('a name for not sleeping [with you]'). (The novelist Tanizaki describes this plant, and comments on both names, in his *Yume no Ukihashi*.)[54] McCullough's translation has let the *jo* sink to the bottom—it is nowhere in sight. The poem calls for a little more *dokyō*:

In hidden marshes
Bedded under water grows
     The slumbrous roperoot:
Rootless must the rumor be
That I've never bedded you.

                              [EAC]

KKS 4:244, Sosei

. . . Can it be fitting
that none but I should stand here
     to feel emotion?
Wild pinks blowing where crickets
chirr in the gathering dusk!

'To feel emotion' fits the syllable count, but it is a curiously 'explanatory' rendering of *aware to omowamu*. 'Can it be fitting' is also wide of the mark. This is not an inquiry about propriety, but a cry for a kindred spirit. There is a feeling of a hammered-together translation here. And *yūkage* ≠ *yūgure*!

Am I then alone
In knowing what it is to sigh
     Over these wild pinks
Flowering where crickets chirr
In the evening light?

                              [EAC]

It is fairly amazing that two complete English translations of the **Kokinshū** should have appeared almost simultaneously. Whatever the respective translators may feel, the reader can only benefit from alternate versions of this classic anthology. Laurel Rasplica Rodd and Mary Catherine Henkenius have shown themselves more experimental than McCullough in their approach to translation. As the examples below will illustrate, they dispense with punctuation and substitute open spaces for pauses and breaks in the flow of prosody. The pauses are sometimes of their own making—they seem to be asking the reader to rest and meditate a while before proceeding. The effect takes getting used to, and perhaps I still have some way to go in that regard. Unquestionably, they are trying to reach the inner essence of the poem; with what success can be debated.

KKS 15:797, Komachi

. . . that which fades within
without changing its color
     is the hidden bloom
of the heart of man   in
this world of disillusion

                              [Rodd-Henkenius]

So much have I learned:
the blossom that fades away,
     its color unseen,
is the flower in the heart
of one who lives in this world.

                              [McCullough]

I admire the McCullough version in ways already mentioned. Yet Rodd-Henkenius show themselves to be more sensitive to the *inner* fading that the poem is about. Which having said, I am led to wonder what game, if any, Rodd-Henkenius are playing with 'within/without'. None, I suspect—'without' probably carries no double load. If it did, there would be a paradox: an outward color fading, yet not fading. If it does not, the placement of the two words is fortuitous, and a bit unfortunate. 'Of disillusion' is the kind of overly explanatory addition that, in principle, is best to avoid. It will be noted that Rodd-Henkenius also more or less adhere to 5-7-5-7-7, although to achieve it here, the 'rest' in the fourth line must be counted as one beat. There is considerable inconsistency in their practice in this latter regard.

KKS 1:1, Ariwara no Motokata

. . . spring is here before
year's end   when New Year's Day has
     not yet come around
what should we call it   is it
still last year or is it this

                              [Rodd-Henkenius]

Springtime has arrived
while the old year lingers on.
   What then of the year?
Are we to talk of 'last year'?
Or are we to say 'this year'?

               [McCullough]

Here is the notorious first poem of the *Kokinshū*, so roundly denounced by Masaoka Shiki.[55] Indeed, it would be hard to make a defense of the *Kokinshū* on the basis of this poem alone. . . . As for the translations, McCullough surely has the better version, the layout of her final lines matching that of the original.

KKS 20:1078, Anonymous

   . . . from Adachi in
far Michinoku comes this
  spindle bow   as its
tips draw together   silently
come to me   now and always

              [Rodd-Henkenius]

   If I should draw you,
as men draw *mayumi* bows
  from Michinoku,
pray yield to me forever—
but secretly, secretly.

              [McCullough]

Of these two versions, I rather prefer Rodd-Henkenius, although it fails to render the seductive bed-time song of *shinobi shinobi*. The open spaces here create tensions that work quite well. And McCullough for some reason omits Adachi. But both versions interpose an 'as' when none is needed. This kind of zeugma-based *jo* can be rendered clean of simile:

   From famed Adachi
In far Michinoku come
  Bows of spindlewood:
When I draw you, bend to me,
Softly, softly, always bend!

              [EAC]

KKS 15:782, Komachi

   . . . it's over   I know
for I've grown old and tiresome
  as the chill autumn
rains   even his words of love
fade and wither like the leaves

             [Rodd-Henkenius]

   Even your pledges,
leaves of words, have lost their green
  now that falling tears
dim my youth as drizzling rains
transform autumnal foliage.

             [McCullough]

Were it not for the overdose of self-pity in the first two lines, I would prefer the Rodd-Henkenius version here. 'it's over I know' is a valiant attempt to do something echoic and otherwise effective with *ima wa tote*. But both versions fail again by stubbornly recasting Komachi's statement into an overt simile. It is not:

   Now that I am old
And fallen into years
  Of wintry rain,
The very foliage of your words
Is but a wrack of withered leaves.

              [EAC]

KKS 12:605, Tsurayuki

   . . . days pass into months
and still I have not touched my
  true white bow   at night
drawn taut   I tremble   rising
resting   unable to sleep

             [Rodd-Henkenius]

   Sleepless in the night,
I rise and sink down again,
  my thoughts lingering
on the white spindlewood bow,
untouched after all these years.

             [McCullough]

This is my favorite poem by Tsurayuki, and the one that tells me clear as clear that he was more than a skillful technician and an aristocratic arbiter of taste. I can think of no more powerfully erotic poem in the courtly tradition. The *jo* here has a seductive force that goes beyond mere technique, and strikes the underlayers of libido. The Rodd-Henkenius version is particularly masterful, its spacing creating almost unbearable tensions. The McCullough version is also full of passion, more plaintive and less breathless. Poems based on *jo* are the most fun to work with: there is an alternative universe in them waiting to be touched into life. The translators have been unable to resist. Neither could Tsurayuki. Nor can I:

   Hands have not touched,
Months and days gone by, white
  Spindletree bow:
Drawn taut, I quiver in the night,
Rising, sinking, far from sleep.

             [EAC]

Notes

   . . . [42] Stephen Owen, *Traditional Chinese Poetry and Poetics: Omen of the World,* University of Wisconsin

Press, 1985.

Owen's essays on Chinese poetry in this volume are exceptionally rich in insights into the poetic process, and into how poems 'work'.

[43] 'One who writes a poem writes it because the language prompts, or simply dictates, the next line. Beginning a poem, the poet as a rule doesn't know the way it is going to come out; and at times he is very surprised by the way it turns out, since it often turns out better than he expected, often his thought carries further than he reckoned. And that is the moment when the future of language invades the present. . . . The one who writes a poem writes it above all because verse writing is an extraordinary accelerator of consciousness, of thinking, of comprehending the universe. Having experienced this acceleration once, one is no longer capable of abandoning the chance to repeat this experience. . . . '

Nobel Lecture, Stockholm, 1987, as excerpted in 'The Poets' Theatre Presents an Evening with Joseph Brodsky', 15 February 1988, Cambridge, Mass.

[44] Arthur Waley, 'Notes on Translation (1958)' in Ivan Morris, ed., *Madly Singing in the Mountains: An Appreciation and Anthology of Arthur Waley,* Harper & Row, New York, 1970, p. 152.

[45] Waley, 'The Originality of Japanese Civilization', in *Madly Singing,* p. 134.

Waley, like Reckert . . . , mentions the *coplas* of southern Spain in connection with *waka.*

[46] Waley, 'Notes on Translation', p. 162.

[47] 'An *uta* runs into its mould like quicksilver into a groove.' Waley, 'The Originality of Japanese Civilization', p. 334.

[48] Donald Keene, ed., *Anthology of Japanese Literature,* Tuttle, Rutland, Vermont, & Tokyo, 1955, p. 196.

[49] E. Bruce Brooks, 'A Yakamochi Sampler', in *East-West Review,* 3:1 (Winter 1966-1967), p. 83.

[50] *Japanese Court Poetry,* p. 193.

[51] Carl Kay, 'The Translation of Classical Japanese Poetry', Senior Thesis, Department of East Asian Languages and Civilizations, Harvard University, 1978, p. 91.

Kay 'offer[s] "anthracite night" as an English phrase that approximates the kind of magical incantational effect that [*nubatama no*] might have had in the age of

kotodama' (p. 90). He remarks that his translation is 'a bit looser [than Pierson's]' (p. 91).

For the record, Pierson's translation is as follows:

'(1/2) In the snow of this night (black as a nubafruit), / (3) come let us all get wet!/ (4/5) For the next morning, if it disappears, how regrettable it would be.'

J. L. Pierson, tr., *The Manyôsû,* Brill, Leiden, 1954, 8, p. 252.

Pierson's numbers in parentheses refer to corresponding lines in the original.

[52] McCullough is amusing at the expense of her own achievement when, explaining why the *Kokinshū* compilers may have thought it best to include Komachi's poem with the *haikaika* . . . , or 'Eccentric Poems', she says, 'It was permissible to compare smoldering passion to the hidden fires in Mount Fuji, but a heart could not snap, crackle, and pop' (*Brocade,* p. 488).

[53] Pierson favors this formula for rendering metaphorical *makurakotoba* in his *Man'yōshū* translations, for example, *Manyôsû,* 2, p. 78.

[54] Tanizaki Jun'ichiro, *Yume no Ukihashi,* in *Tanizaki Jun'ichirō Shū* (*Gendai Nihon no Bungaku* 7), Gakushū Kenkyūsha, 1976, p. 374.

[55] In McCullough's quotation from the Brower article referred to . . . above: 'The poem is so silly that it fails to rise even to the level of vulgar wit, as if one were to say, "This child of mixed blood, born between a Japanese and a foreigner—are we to call it "Japanese," or should we call it "foreigner"?' (*Brocade,* p. 4).

FURTHER READING

Cranston, Edwin A. "The Dark Path: Images of Longing in Japanese Love Poetry." *Harvard Journal of Asiatic Studies,* 35 (1975): 60-100.

Reviews dozens of examples of Japanese love poetry and its prevailing imagery.

Harper, T. J. "Norinaga on the Translation of *Waka:* His Preface to *A Kokinshu Telescope.*" In *The Distant Isle: Studies and Translations of Japanese Literature in Honor of Robert H. Brower,* pp. 205-30, edited by Thomas Hare, Robert Borgen, and Sharalyn Orbaugh. Ann Arbor: Center for Japanese Studies, The University of Michigan, 1996.

Reprints and discusses Motoori Norinaga's preface (much of it in Japanese) to his *A Kokinshu Telescope,* which deals with problems in translating Japanese poetry.

Keene, Donald. *Seeds in the Heart: Japanese Literature from Earliest Times to the Late Sixteenth Century.* New York: Henry Holt and Company, 1993, 1,280 p.

    History of Japanese literature which includes an overview of the *Kokinshu* and a chapter on collections of waka that preceded the *Kokinshu.*

Konishi, Jin'ichi. *A History of Japanese Literature: Volume Two: The Early Middle Ages,* edited by Earl Miner, translated by Aileen Gatten. Princeton, N. J.: Princeton University Press, 1986, 464 p.

    History of Japanese literature which includes discussion and analysis of waka and the *Kokinshu* style.

McCullough, Helen Craig. *Tales of Ise: Lyrical Episodes from Tenth-Century Japan.* Stanford: Stanford University Press, 1968, 277 p.

    Translation of *Tales of Ise,* a classic Japanese poetry anthology roughly contemporaneous to the *Kokinshu.*

Rodd, Laurel Rasplica. An introduction to *Kokinshu: A Collection of Poems Ancient and Modern,* translated by Laurel Rasplica Rodd with Mary Catherine Henkenius. Princeton: Princeton University Press, 1984, pp. 3-34.

    Discusses the historical value of the work, how it came to be compiled, its rules and arrangement, and the importance of context in appreciating the poems included.

Tertullian

c. 155-60 - c. 245

(Full name Quintus Septimus Florens Tertullianus.) Roman theologian and apologist.

INTRODUCTION

Considered the father of Western Christian literature, Tertullian was among the most influential of the early Latin theologians. A moralist and polemicist who began his literary career as an eloquent defender of Christianity, Tertullian later abandoned Catholicism in favor of the fervent, puritanical faith known as Montanism. Despite this fact, he is generally recognized as a steadfast proponent of the purity of Christian doctrine and as a tireless enemy of heresy and paganism. His works are thought to have indelibly shaped Latin ecclesiastical literature in the early third century and they continue to retain their vitality and cogency in the contemporary era.

Biographical Information

Many of the details of Tertullian's life are open to speculation and have been reconstructed by scholars using cues from his literary works and from the works of later commentators, particularly St. Jerome. Tertullian was born in the ancient city of Carthage sometime between 155 and 160 A. D., and is believed to have been the son of a Roman centurion stationed in North Africa. Educated in grammar, rhetoric, philosophy, and the law in his youth, Tertullian traveled to Rome as a young man to further his studies. He most likely practiced law there for a time. In Rome he discovered Christianity, and after his return to Carthage in approximately 195 converted to that faith. It was during the final years of the second century that he began to compose his earliest Christian apologetic works, as well as other writings of moral and ascetic theology. By the first decade of the third century Tertullian had risen to became an important and influential member of the African Church, and he increasingly devoted himself to his literary activities. He composed a series of attacks on pagan philosophy and unorthodox Christianity, along with numerous tracts on Christian issues and related subjects. Sometime before 210, Tertullian, having become more and more displeased with the stolidity of many Christians and clergymen, converted to Montanism, a sectarian movement begun by the prophet Montanus and defined by its strident and ascetic moralism. Following his second conversion, Tertullian wrote many of his most vehement pronouncements on the morality of his contem-

poraries and moved far afield from the orthodox Christianity he had earlier championed. Tertullian wrote his final treatises by or before 222, though he was said to have lived to an advanced age by St. Jerome, perhaps stretching two decades or more from the date of his last works.

Major Works

Scholars have divided Tertullian's thirty-one extant writings into three general categories: apologetic treatises, polemical-dogmatic works, and moral and ascetical writings. This last group is generally also split by critics who differentiate between Tertullian's writing prior to and after his conversion to Montanism. The first category of apologetic works includes Tertullian's early *Ad nationes* (c. 197; translated as *To the Heathens*) and *Apologeticum* (c. 197; *Apology*). The former represents his initial condemnation of paganism and defense of the Christian faith, while the latter focuses more specifically on Roman political prejudices against Christians. Other apologetic writings are: *De testimo-*

nio animae (c. 198-206; *The Testimony of the Soul*), in which Tertullian argues that pagans often demonstrate their belief in the unity of God; *Ad Scapulam* (c. 212), an open letter addressed to the Christian-hating proconsul of Africa, Scapula; and *Adversus Judaeos* (c. 198-206; translated as *Against the Jews*), which argues that Jewish ideas regarding punishment and retribution should give way to Christ-like forgiveness.

Tertullian's polemical and dogmatic writings roughly span the middle portion of his literary career, from 200 to 213. *De praescriptione haereticorum* (c. 200; *On the Prescription of Heretics*), one of his most significant works in this mode, demonstrates Tertullian's considerable knowledge of Roman law and contends that only doctrine derived from the apostolic Church should be construed as true, and that Gnostic teachings may be refuted as heresy. By far Tertullian's longest work, the *Adversus Marcionem* (c. 207; *Against Marcion*) was originally composed in five books. In it he explains the true nature of God and Christ and the natural affinity of the Old and New Testaments, and later attacks the New Testament of his close contemporary Marcion. *Adversus Praxean* (c. 213; *Against Praxeas*) contains Tertullian's description of the Church doctrine of the Trinity, while *De baptismo* (c. 198; *On Baptism*) provides details about the authentic Church baptism, condemning heretical forms of the rite. The remainder of Tertullian's polemical writings, *Adversus Hermogenem* (c. 200), *Adversus Valentinianos* (c. 207-08), *Scorpiace* (c. 203-13), *De carne Christi* (c. 210), and *De anima* (c. 210), refute specific Gnostic beliefs or their individual proponents.

In the third category of Tertullian's writings are grouped his several practical, moral, and ascetical treatises, many of which were written in the latter portion of his literary career, during the time of his greatest adherence to the Montanist faith. His Catholic, moral works include: *De oratione* (c. 198), a treatise giving instructions on prayer, specifically on the "Our Father"; *De patientia* (c. 200), which discusses the virtue of patience; and *De paenitentia* (c. 203), a treatise on the proper penance to be performed after committing a Sin. One of Tertullian's pre-Montanist practical and ascetical treatises, *Ad martyres* (c. 197) reflects his attempt to mitigate the suffering of imprisoned Christians. Other practical works include: *De spectaculis* (c. 197), an injunction against the immorality of pagan theatre; *De cultu feminarum* (c. 200), a condemnation of contemporary feminine dress and adornments; and *Ad uxorem* (c. 206; translated as *To His Wife*), in which he asks that his spouse not remarry after his death. Tertullian revisited many of these same themes in his Montanist writings, often stating his opinions much more stridently. *De exhortatione castitatis* (c. 208) and *De monogamia* (c. 217) both condemn the practice of second marriage. *De virginibus velandis* (c. 207) states that virgins should

wear veils whenever they appear in public; *De corona* (c. 211) attacks the pagan custom of crowning soldiers and rejects the possibility of Christian service in the military; *De idololatria* (c. 211) strictly forbids the practice of idolatry; and *De pallio* (c. 213-22) includes his personal remarks on the efficacy of the cloak as opposed to the Roman toga. Tertullian's Montanist moral treatises oppose the ideal of Christian flight from persecution (*De fuga in persecutione*, c. 212) and defend Montanist fasting practices (*De ieiunio adversus psychicos*, c. 213-22). *De pudicitia* (c. 217-22) demonstrates a radical change from Tertullian's earlier thought by denying the Church's power to forgive sins.

Textual History

Tertullian's extant writings have survived into the modern era primarily through five manuscripts, along with additional fragmentary document evidence. The *Corpus Trecense* was originally codified around 523 and is today available through a twelfth-century text. The original *Corpus Masburense* is thought to have been compiled before 494 and exists in a manuscript dating from 1550. Also compiled before 494, the *Corpus Agobardinum* includes twenty-one of Tertullian's works—the primary text of this corpus is the *Codex Parisinus latinus* (1622, referred to as the *Agobardinus*). A fourth manuscript, the *Corpus Cluniacense*, is the largest, containing twenty-seven treatises and can be traced to the middle of the sixth century. The *Codex Ottobonianus latinus* provides further textual evidence and includes excerpts from *De pudicitia, De paenitentia, De patientia,* and *De spectaculis*. A manuscript fragment of the *De spectaculis* dating from the ninth century seems to imply the existence of another corpus. As for the lost works of Tertullian, many references to these appear throughout the extant treatises and in the writings of later commentators. Scholars have been able to include several treatises Tertullian composed in Greek along with his seven-book *De ecstasi*, which dealt with the pronouncements of Montanist prophets, among Tertullian's lost works.

Critical Reception

Largely condemned for his Montanist apostasy by writers in the early Christian and Medieval eras, Tertullian has since the nineteenth century been recognized for his immense contribution as the progenitor of Latin ecclesiastical literature. Modern critical interest in Tertullian's writings has, in addition to the ongoing process of translation and exegesis from Medieval Latin texts, focused on several common themes relating to the apologist's style, intention, and views on Christianity. While scholars universally agree that Tertullian's style, whether in the original Latin or in translation, is marred by obscurity and dislocution, most have acknowledged that the difficulty of his writings is matched by the brilliance of his insights and the acuteness of his knowledge. Other topics of particular interest to scholars have been Tertullian's view of the authentic Church and his battles against heresy, his much-publicized and often-misinterpreted distaste for philosophy, the relation of his writings to those of early Latin scripture and his understanding of those texts, and the development of his own thought in the Catholic and Montanist phases of his career. In relation to this last point, several commentators have attempted to date precisely the composition of Tertullian's treatises in order to trace the effects of Montanism on his view of contemporary Christianity and of the Church. Scholars have frequently taken an interest in Tertullian's famous paradox, which states, "And the Son of God died; it is by all means to be believed, because it is absurd. And He was buried and rose again; the fact is certain, because it is impossible." Many commentators have seen this statement as an encapsulation of Tertullian's rhetorical method and as a touchstone for his complex theology.

PRINCIPAL WORKS

Ad martyres (theological treatise) c. 197

Ad nationes [*To the Heathens*] (theological treatise) c. 197

Apologeticum [*Apology*] (theological treatise) c. 197

De spectaculis (theological treatise) c. 197

Adversus Judaeos [*Against the Jews*] (theological treatise) c. 198-206

De testimonio animae [*The Testimony of the Soul*] (theological treatise) c. 198-206

De baptismo [*On Baptism*] (theological treatise) c. 198

De oratione (theological treatise) c. 198

Adversus Hermogenem (theological treatise) c. 200

De cultu feminarum (theological treatise) c. 200

De patientia (theological treatise) c. 200

De praescriptione haereticorum [*On the Prescription of Heretics*] (theological treatise) c. 200

De paenitentia (theological treatise) c. 203

Scorpiace (theological treatise) c. 203-13

Ad uxorem [*To His Wife*] (treatise) c. 206

Adversus Valentinianos (theological treatise) c. 207-08

Adversus Marcionem [*Against Marcion*] (theological treatise) c. 207

De virginibus velandis (treatise) c. 207

De exhortatione castitatis (treatise) c. 208

De anima (theological treatise) c. 210

De carne Christi (theological treatise) c. 210

De resurrectione carnis (theological treatise) c. 210

De corona (theological treatise) c. 211

De idololatria (theological treatise) c. 211

De fuga in persecutione (theological treatise) c. 212

Ad Scapulam (theological treatise) c. 212

De ieiunio adversus psychicos (theological treatise) c. 213-22

De pallio (treatise) c. 213-22

Adversus Praxean [*Against Praxeas*] (theological treatise) c. 213

De pudicitia (theological treatise) c. 217-22

De monogamia (treatise) c. 217

---

*PRINCIPAL ENGLISH TRANSLATIONS

On the Testimony of the Soul and On the 'Prescription' of Heretics [translated by T. H. Bindley] 1914

Tertullian's Treatises Concerning Prayer, Concerning Baptism [translated by Alex Souter] 1919

Against Praxeas [translated by Alex Souter] 1920

Concerning the Resurrection of the Flesh [translated by Alex Souter] 1922

Apology, De spectaculis [translated by T. R. Glover] 1931

Tertullian's Treatise against Praxeas [translated by E. Evans] 1948

Apologetical Works [translated by Rudolph Arbesmann] 1950

On the Soul [translated by E. A. Quain] 1950

The Testimony of the Soul [translated by R. Arbesmann] 1950

Tertullian: Treatises on Marriage and Remarriage [translated by William P. Le Saint] 1951

Tertullian's Tract on Prayer [translated by E. Evans] 1953

Tertullian's Homily on the Incarnation [translated by E. Evans] 1956

Tertullian: The Treatise against Hermogenes [translated by J. H. Waszink] 1956

Disciplinary, Moral, and Ascetical Works [translated by Rudolph Arbesmann] 1959

Tertullian: Treatises on Penance [translated by William P. Le Saint] 1959

Tertullian's Treatise on the Resurrection [translated by E. Evans] 1960

Tertullian: Apologeticum [translated by C. Becker] 1961

Tertullian's Homily on Baptism [translated by E. Evans] 1968

De idololatria [translated by J. H. Waszink and J. C. M. van Winden] 1987

*All of Tertullian's extant works have been translated into English and appear in *Ante-Nicene Christian Library* (edited by F. Oehler; translated by P. Holmes and S. Thelwall, 1868-70; also published as *Ante-Nicene Fathers* in 1884 and reprinted in 1957).

CRITICISM

Edgar J. Goodspeed (essay date 1942)

SOURCE: "Tertullian," in *A History of Early Christian Literature,* University of Chicago Press, 1942, pp. 210-26.

[*In the following excerpt, Goodspeed surveys Tertullian's writings and briefly summarizes the main characteristics of his literary style.*]

In the latter part of the first century the writing of Latin literature was already passing into the hands of provincials, men from North Africa and Spain, like Seneca, Martial, and Quintilian. The district about Carthage was particularly active in literary lines, and it is not strange that it was there that the Bible began to be translated into Latin. It was there, and not in Rome, that Latin Christianity had its beginning and that it soon began to express itself vigorously in Latin books.

The first great figure in Latin Christianity was Tertullian, or Quintus Septimius Florens Tertullianus, to give him his full name. He was born in Carthage, about A.D. 155-60, of good family, and seems, from what he says in his writings, to have visited Athens and Rome in early life, studying to be a lawyer and entering fully into the excesses of heathen life in those centers. At Rome he seems to have practiced law and taught rhetoric, with marked success. There, it appears, he was converted, and he returned to Carthage a Christian. Jerome says he became a presbyter in the church there. At any rate, he threw himself into the Christian cause with tremendous vigor, especially in the crises which persecution now and then brought on for the church. These attacks called forth the notable apologetic pieces which were among his earliest writings, but a wealth of other books, practical, doctrinal, and polemic, soon followed.

The heroic behavior of Christian martyrs deeply impressed Tertullian. He may have had glimpses of it in the first year of Commodus, A.D. 180, when twelve Christians—seven men and five women—from the neighboring town of Scilli suffered martyrdom in Carthage. The simple story of their trial and fate is the earliest of Latin martyrdoms.

In A.D. 197-98 there was another outbreak against the African Christians. Their habit of holding aloof from public shows, which were both pagan and brutal in character, kept them away from the public celebration of the victory of the emperor, Septimius Severus, over his rivals, and precipitated a fresh persecution. Tertullian came to the defense of his harassed brethren with the fiery vehemence and fervor that always characterized him. In a work addressed **To the Heathen** (**Ad Nationes,** two books) he vigorously protested against the laws condemning Christians simply as such and without first examining their behavior and manner of life. He protests also against the calumnies heaped upon them and the charges of incest, child murder, and disloyalty to the empire that were made against them. He refers to the ancient pagan practice of exposing undesired children and throws back the charges upon those who made them.

A second book of this same year, A.D. 197, was his great **Apology** (**Apologeticus**). It was addressed to the Roman governors of provinces and presents a similar argument, though in a more restrained and legal tone. He repels again the stock charges of child-slaying, incest, and cannibalism and admits that Christians do not worship the old gods but holds that they are not disloyal to the empire; though they cannot call the emperor God, they respect and revere him and are good Romans. Here Tertullian points out that persecution simply advances Christianity: "We multiply every time we are mowed down by you; the blood of Christians is seed"—the most famous of all his famous observations.

These writings were preceded in the same year, 197, by a short address *To the Martyrs* already in prison, encouraging them and cheering them on. But the *Address to the Heathen* and the *Apology* form Tertullian's main contribution to Christian defense literature, and they are powerful reinforcements of it.

Upon the death of Severus, fourteen years later, A.D. 211, and the accession of Caracalla, persecution began again, and once more, in 212-13, Tertullian wrote a short but vigorous apology addressed *To Scapula,* the proconsul of Africa, warning him, in view of well-known Roman precedents favorable to Christians, not to proceed against them.

Trenchant and timely as were his writings in the apologetic field, his practical, doctrinal, and polemic works were no less so. No ancient list of his writings has come down to us, but in the oldest manuscript we have of Tertullian, the Codex Agobardinus, given by Agobard, bishop of Lyons, who died in A.D. 840, to a church there, there is a list of twenty-one of his works, which that manuscript originally contained. From other sources, however, this list can be increased to forty-three, and possibly even to forty-five.

The majority of these were practical in character, dealing with Christian morality and true Christian behavior in situations of certain kinds or in relation to special groups and matters. Tertullian defends the Christian soldier who refuses to wear the chaplet or wreath on his head, regarding it as a heathenish practice (*On the Chaplet*). He condemns public games, shows, and theatrical and gladiatorial exhibitions as brutal, immoral, and interwoven with pagan rites (*On Idolatry*). He also wrote *On Veiling Virgins, On the Adornment of Women, On Baptism, On Patience, On Prayer, On Modesty,* and *On Repentance.*

In the doctrinal field Tertullian was not markedly creative, for he owed much to Irenaeus and Melito. He was also much influenced by Stoic philosophy and by what he had been taught by the church at Rome, where he was converted. Yet his work *Against Praxeas* is a notable defense of the doctrine of the Trinity, particularly against the followers of the Roman Sabellius, who flourished late in the second and early in the third century and held Monarchian and modalistic views. Praxeas in his solicitude for the divine unity identified Father, Son, and Holy Spirit, so that it was the Father

himself who was born of a virgin and suffered on the cross. Tertullian wrote also *On the Flesh of Christ, On the Resurrection of the Flesh,* and *On the Soul*—a work which Harnack calls the first book on Christian psychology.

Closely related to these were his polemic writings, attacking the positions of heretics and schismatics. In his book *On Prescription of Heretics,* which Hort called a most plausible and most mischievous book,[1] he argues that, after exhausting reasoning with such people, one must simply say, "What we hold is the belief of the church, handed down from the apostles, from bishop to bishop, in all the historic centers of Christianity, so it must be true, and there is no more to be said." This shows that when he wrote this book, at least, Tertullian was a strong adherent of the Catholic movement, which Irenaeus reflected. He was, in fact, much influenced in his polemic writings by Irenaeus, and Tertullian and Irenaeus are the first Catholic Fathers.

This appeal to the great apostolic churches, as faithful depositories of Christian tradition, naturally directed North African Christians to Rome, the only church in the West of apostolic foundation:

> Since you are close upon Italy, you have Rome, from which there comes even into your hands the very authority [of the apostles]. How happy is its church, upon which apostles poured forth all their doctrine, along with their blood! Where Peter endures a passion like his Lord's! Where Paul wins his crown in a death like John's! Where the apostle John was first plunged unhurt into boiling oil, and then returned to his island exile!.... The Law and the prophets she unites with the writings of evangelists and apostles, from which she drinks in her faith [chap. 36].

This is very much what Irenaeus says in his *Refutation* (iii. 3. 2, 3) about the position of the Roman church, which he in Lyons looked up to from Gaul, just as Tertullian looked up to it from Africa.

But Tertullian's greatest polemic work was that *Against Marcion,* in five books, written over and over again, until his work upon it spread over ten or twelve years of his life, from about 200 to 212. This elaborate work gives us our principal information about Marcion, and especially about his effort to put a Christian scripture consisting of the Gospel of Luke and ten letters of Paul in place of the Jewish scriptures which then made up most of the Bible of Christian churches. Other polemic writings were *Against the Jews, Against Hermogenes,* and *Against the Valentinians.*

We have grouped Tertullian's writings as apologetic, practical, doctrinal, and polemic. But there is also a value in surveying them in the order in which they were written, for they reveal the gradual shift in his religious views, which carried him in the course of ten years from the bosom of the Catholic church into that of the Montanist sect. He was a strong Puritan in feeling and, whatever direction he took, was pretty sure to go to extremes. His devotion to the Catholic movement and his aversion to heretics are very marked in the **Prescription of Heretics,** which he wrote in his first period, when he was a thoroughgoing Catholic. It covers the years 197 to 202. He had become a Christian probably by A.D. 195, perhaps a little earlier. In 197, as we have seen, he wrote his principal apologetic books, **To the Martyrs, To the Heathen,** the **Apologeticus,** and also the **Testimony of the Soul,** which he thought essentially Christian by nature and itself a witness to Christianity.

In the course of the next five years, 198-202, he wrote twelve other books and treatises: **On Shows** (two editions), **On the Dress of Women, On Baptism, On Repentance, On Patience, On Prayer, To His Wife** (against remarriage of women), **On Idolatry, On Prescription of Heretics, Against Marcion** (two editions), **Against Hermogenes,** and **Against the Jews.**

The edict of Severus in 202, forbidding anyone to become a Christian, marks a shift in Tertullian's attitude. He now begins to see truth and value in the Montanists' position—their Puritan morality, in contrast with the growing laxity of the Roman church; their spiritual emphasis, in contrast with the political cast that was coming over Roman Christianity. For five years Tertullian works to build these Montanist values into his Catholic Christianity. He is still a Catholic, but he sees the worth of Montanism, too, and strives to realize them both and to unite them.

In this period of tension he probably wrote three works now lost: *On Ecstasy,* in seven books, dealing with Montanism; *On the Hope of the Faithful* including the millennial expectations, which he shared; and *On Paradise*—these probably in 202-3 to 204-5. The **Exhortation to Chastity** and the book **On Veiling Virgins** also belong to this time, 204-5 to 206-7.

But by 207-8 the tension had become unbearable, and Tertullian with other Montanists left the church. He now produced a third edition of the first four books **Against Marcion,** his longest work, 207-8. He also wrote now **Against the Valentinians** and *Against the Followers of Apelles,* the Marcionite leader, a work now lost. These belong to 207-8. In 210 he wrote **On the Cloak** (which he wore instead of the toga), in 211 **On the Chaplet,** and in 211-12, **On Flight in Persecution,** holding it inadmissible.

In the following five years, 208-13, he wrote also the books **On the Flesh of Christ, On the Testimony of the Soul, On the Soul, On the Resurrection,** and the fifth and final book **Against Marcion,** completing his

discussion of Marcion's proposed scripture, Luke and Paul. In Books i and ii, Tertullian had dealt with Marcion's doctrine that the Creator and the Father of Jesus were different beings; in Book iii he argued that the Christian movement does not contradict the prophets but fulfils them; in Books iv and v he uses Marcion's own scripture, Luke and Paul, to establish this.

About 212 he wrote his short apology to the proconsul, **To Scapula,** and in 212 or 213 his **Scorpiace,** warning against the scorpion sting of heresy and encouraging to martyrdom, which some Gnostics taught was unnecessary. In the course of the next five years he wrote **Against Praxeas** his defense of the Trinity, and soon after 217-18 his book **On Monogamy,** protesting against second marriages, and his work **On Fasting.** And finally, not long before 222-23, he wrote the work **On Modesty,** bitterly assailing the action of Calixtus, bishop of Rome, in declaring that the sins of adultery and fornication, though committed after baptism, could be forgiven by the church; it had previously been held that while God could forgive them, along with murder and idolatry, the church could not. Tertullian's invective against this action stands in sharp contrast to his rhapsody upon the Roman church, in his **Prescription of Heretics,** chapter 36, written twenty years before, in 198-202/3:

> The Pontifex Maximus, that is the bishop of bishops, issues an edict: I remit, to such as have discharged the requirements of repentence (or penitence), the sins both of adultery and of fornication. O edict which cannot be inscribed "Good deed!" [chap. 1].

All three of these last works of Tertullian, in fact (**Monogamy, Fasting,** and **Modesty**), are bitter in their denunciation of the laxity that was pervading the Roman church under Zephyrinus and Calixtus. He felt strongly that it had forfeited the spiritual heritage of Christianity. "You have quenched the spirit," he cried, "You have driven away the Comforter (Paraclete)."

At the time of Tertullian's death, soon after A.D. 222-23, he had left the Montanists and organized a little sect of his own, for Augustine, almost two hundred years later, found a group of Tertullianists still meeting independently in Carthage and brought them back into the church.

Some of Tertullian's writings, like the one **On Veiling Virgins,** he wrote first in Greek. Whether he was the author of the *Martyrdom of Perpetua and Felicitas,* women of Carthage who suffered in the persecution of A.D. 202-3, is not certain; it is extant in both Greek and Latin and is a work of moving simplicity. Perpetua was a woman of position, while Felicitas was a slave. The account is written from a Montanist point of view. Jerome also mentions a book *On the Difficulties of Marriage* addressed "to a philosophic friend," which may have been written early in life and possibly even in a lighter vein, for Jerome speaks of him as "playing" (*lusit*) with the subject.

Of the works of Tertullian, thirty-one have been preserved, and the names of more than a dozen others can be gathered from references to them in Tertullian himself, in Jerome, or in the table of contents of the Codex Agobardinus. The Greek form of the book *On Baptism* dealt also with the question of heretical baptism and was evidently a different book from the Latin work of that name. Other lost writings are the *Hope of the Faithful, Paradise, Against the Followers of Apelles,* the *Origin of the Soul, Fate, Ecstasy,* the *Garments of Aaron, To a Philosophic Friend, Flesh and Soul, Submission of Soul,* and the *Superstition of the World.* The Greek forms of the works *On Shows* and *On the Veiling of Virgins* have also been lost. He may also have written *On Clean and Unclean Animals* and *On Circumcision,* as Jerome intimates (*Epist.* 36:1).

Tertullian is always the advocate; there is nothing judicial about his attitude; he sees only one side. His style is impetuous, dramatic, direct, varied, often richly illustrated, sometimes full of apostrophe and exclamation, gifted, but uncontrolled, except by overwhelming conviction. It reveals unmistakably one of the most powerful personalities of the early church, whose works have for the most part survived even though he had withdrawn from the Catholic church years before his death.

The Latin version of the Bible was just coming into being in North Africa in Tertullian's day, and he was well versed in scripture, probably both Greek and Latin. Like Irenaeus, he had a New Testament, and these two are the first Christian Fathers of whom this can be said. Tertullian's included the Four Gospels, the Acts, and thirteen letters of Paul, besides I Peter, I John and Jude, the Revelation of John, and at first the *Shepherd* of Hermas, though later in life he repudiated that book with great scorn, for what he considered its moral laxity.[2]

Tertullian also knew early Christian literature very well, especially Justin, Tatian, Melito, Irenaeus, and Clement. His own influence was very marked upon Minucius Felix and upon Cyprian, his great literary successor in North Africa, the bishop of Carthage from A.D. 250 to 258. Jerome reports that he once met an aged man who in his youth had known one of Cyprian's assistants, who said that Cyprian made it a rule to read something of Tertullian's every day and would often say when he wanted to consult Tertullian, "Give me the Master." . . .

Notes

[1] F. J. A. Hort, *Six Lectures on the Ante-Nicene Fa-*

thers (London, 1895), p. 103.

[2] *On Modesty* x. 20.

William P. Le Saint (essay date 1951)

SOURCE: "To His Wife: Introduction," "An Exhortation to Chastity: Introduction," and "Monogamy: Introduction," in *Tertullian: Treatises on Marriage and Remarriage: To His Wife, An Exhortation to Chastity, Monogamy,* translated by William P. Le Saint, The Newman Press, 1951, pp. 3-9, 39-41, 67-9.

[*In the following excerpt, Le Saint examines Tertullian's three treatises on marriage—Ad uxorem, De exhortatione castitatis, and De monogamia—maintaining that these works demonstrate "the gradual deterioration of his thought from Catholic orthodoxy to . . . fanatical Montanism."*]

The three treatises on marriage, [**Ad Uxorem, De exhortatione castitatis,** and **De monogamia**] . . . , though not generally classified among Tertullian's major compositions, are works of considerable interest and importance. Patrologists and students of the history of dogma have long recognized their value as aids in tracing the gradual deterioration of his thought from Catholic orthodoxy to the harsh extremes of fanatical Montanism.[1] The professional theologian finds here source material which, with certain judicious reservations, can be used in support of the argument from tradition for theses on such vital subjects as the sacramental nature of marriage, the Church's jurisdiction over the marriage of Christians, the indissolubility of the contract-bond. Specialists in other fields are acquainted with passages in these works touching on questions of ecclesiastical discipline, moral problems, and liturgical practices which do much to clarify and illustrate the Church's code and cult at a very early period in Christian antiquity.

It is probably safe to say that for the general reader, perhaps even for most specialists, there is greater interest in single chapters, in individual paragraphs and sentences, than there is in the central thesis which these treatises develop and defend. In a true sense the parts here are of greater significance than the whole. For the theme of all three compositions is one which seems to have little pertinence today. Tertullian is concerned with the subject of second marriage. May a Christian man or woman remarry after the death of a consort? In the treatise addressed **To His Wife** he advises against it, although he admits that to remarry is no sin.[2] In the **Exhortation to Chastity** his earlier counsel has already become an uncompromising command, while in the work on **Monogamy** he speaks of all second marriage as adultery, and attacks, with savage violence, the "sensualists" and "enemies of the Paraclete" who justify it by appeals to Holy Scripture and especially to the authority of St. Paul. Thus, what should be a matter of personal preference or personal ideals is made a matter of conscience; ascetical is confused with moral theology, discipline with doctrine; and a way of life which in some circumstances is of value to some individuals becomes a strict and essential obligation imposed upon all Christians. It is well to remind ourselves that such warped and exaggerated views were not the views of Catholics. They were heretical errors and were condemned by the Church as heretical, along with similar excesses in the direction of an unnatural rigidism propounded by Marcionites, Manicheans, Priscillianists, and other avowed enemies of sex and marriage.

This is not to say that the early Church looked favorably upon second marriage. Her attitude was the attitude of St. Paul,[3] one of toleration, not encouragement. In the face of a carnal world, it seemed much more consistent with her mission to encourage temperance, moderation, self-control, abnegation, asceticism; and if her asceticism seems misguided and severe by modern standards, we may be helped to understand it by reflecting that it was, at least in part, a reaction of disgust at the degrading licentiousness of her pagan surroundings. A detailed history of this question need not be given here. For the purpose of an introductory note it is sufficient to say that the general sentiment of the early Church was in favor of the legitimacy and against the propriety of second marriage;[4] the Montanist error lay in denying both propriety and legitimacy.

It is evident, then, that to know Tertullian the Montanist it is necessary to know his treatises on marriage. In fact, they epitomize the changing course, just as they reflect the changing temper, of his whole Christian life; for he wrote the *Ad uxorem* as a Catholic, the *De exhortatione castitatis* during a period which patrologists call one of semi-Montanism, and the *De monogamia* after his final, definite break with the Church. Of course, other points were at issue between Catholics and Montanists besides the dispute over second marriage. They were divided on such questions as the obligation of accepting ecstatic revelations as authentic manifestations of the Holy Spirit; the nature, number, and severity of the fasts to be imposed upon the Christian community; the sinfulness of flight during times of persecution; the priesthood of the laity; the Church's use of her power to forgive sins. We cannot say, then, that Tertullian's views on second marriage were decisive in making him a Montanist, but there can be no doubt that they contributed materially to his defection from the Church. Both St. Augustine[5] and St. Jerome,[6] in speaking of his heresy, state specifically that it consisted in a denial of the legitimacy of second marriage, an error which,

they insist, is manifestly opposed to the teaching of St. Paul.

To His Wife

The treatise *Ad uxorem* is easily the best of Tertullian's three works on marriage. It is divided into two parts. In the first, he urges his wife to remain a widow if he should die before her. She is free to remarry, should she so wish, but she ought to consider the weighty reasons which advise against it. In brief, and roughly in order these reasons are: 1) marriage is good, but continence is better; 2) the polygamy of the Patriarchs is no argument in favor of multiple marriage; 3) St. Paul clearly shows his disapproval of second marriage; 4) it is concupiscence, manifested in a variety of ways, which impels people to marry a second time—and Christians should resist concupiscence; 5) the example of the saints encourages us to lead a life of continence; 6) even some pagans esteem and practice chastity; 7) when God separates husband and wife by the death of one or the other, He indicates His will that they remain single; 8) the Church shows her mind on the subject by not admitting digamists to the episcopacy.

These are Tertullian's principal arguments; along with them he uses many others which are subordinate and subsidiary. They are almost all repeated, in one form or another, but with much less moderation, in the *De exhortatione castitatis* and the *De monogamia.* Tertullian's policy in controversy is one of unremitting attack, with whatever weapons he has at hand—good or bad. As a result, while he is always vigorous, he is not always convincing,[7] and even readers who might be sympathetic to the thesis he here advances can hardly be favorably impressed by all of the arguments he uses in attempting to establish it. There are paralogisms on every page, and interpretations of Scripture which are either naive misapprehensions or tendentious distortions of its sense. It has been said that Tertullian was a good logician but a poor casuist.[8] This is a perspicacious appraisal, yet readers who examine the case he makes out against second marriage will see much more reason to concur with the latter estimate of his abilities than with the former.

The second half of the treatise deals with the subject of mixed marriage[9] and, in its essentials, it is as relevant today as it was eighteen hundred years ago. Tertullian begs his wife, if she does remarry, to make certain that she marries *in the Lord,* that is to say, that she marries another Christian. He shows that this is according to the teaching of the Apostle and points out, in a number of graphic illustrations, the difficulties and dangers which are involved in marriage with a person not of the faith. This section of his work, in spite of its almost inevitable exaggerations, is one of great interest and value. "Perhaps no monument of ecclesiastical antiquity portrays so well or so completely the whole manner of domestic life among ancient Christians."[10] The second section of the *Ad uxorem* contains passages of real beauty and concludes with an appreciation of Christian marriage which is unsurpassed in patristic literature.

It must be admitted, however, that Tertullian is a very difficult author to read—in English as well as in Latin—and it is possible that some who know nothing of his work, apart from a few popular phrases, may be disappointed when they come to grips, for the first time, with his paragraphs. The treatise *Ad uxorem* is fairly typical of his style. He is, paradoxically, at once concise and involved, brilliant and obscure.[11] There are passages here, as in almost all his works, which, except in paraphrase, produce no effect on the mind beyond what an eminent classicist once called "sheer paralysis."[12] Tertullian has a gift for words rather than sentences and it is much easier to appreciate his sallies than it is to follow his arguments. Perhaps this is why he is so often quoted and so infrequently quoted at length. He is, in spite of his defects, a truly great writer; there will be few to quarrel with the judgment of almost all present-day patrologists that he is the greatest in the West before Augustine.

The extant writings of Tertullian were composed during a period of literary activity which lasted for about twenty-five years, from c. 197 to c. 222 A. D. It is generally agreed that the *Ad uxorem* is to be dated some time between the years 200 and 206 A. D. Harnack argues[13] that it was probably written when Tertullian and his wife were still in the prime of life, since it was evidently composed before his lapse into Montanism, and this took place, as we know, when he reached middle age.[14] Moreover, he addresses his wife in terms which show that he must have had some reason for thinking that she would be able, without too much difficulty, to marry again after his death. There seems to be little point in attempting to date the composition more definitely than this. We can be fairly certain that it was not written long after the year 200 A. D. Tertullian was born between 150 and 160 A. D. Thus, if he composed the treatise in the year 200 A. D., it would have been written when he was about forty or fifty years of age. This might still be called the prime of life, which, happily, is not too restricted, either in meaning or duration. However, it does approach pretty close to what we must think of as a *terminus post quem non* in speaking of middle age, even middle age in the life of a man who, as St. Jerome says, *fertur vixisse usque ad decrepitam aetatem*.[15] . . .

. . . . .

[*An Exhortation to Chastity*]

There is very little controversy nowadays[1] over the problem of dating the *De exhortatione castitatis*.[2] It was written, apparently, between the years 204 and 212 A.D., at a time when Tertullian, although obviously in sympathy with Montanism, was not as yet a member of the sect nor a declared opponent of the traditional teaching of the Church on any significant point of doctrine or discipline. On the subject of second marriage his attitude is not essentially different from what it was a few years before in the first part of the *Ad uxorem*. Some new arguments are proposed and some old ones expanded, but his answer to the problem remains the same: Christians should not remarry. Tertullian is more intransigent, more opinionated in the way he argues his case, but he has not yet come to consider the rejection of second marriage an *articulus stantis vel cadentis Ecclesiae*.

In a number of significant passages the *De exhortatione castitatis* illustrates Tertullian's growing tendency to endorse other Montanist ideas. Thus, for example, he quotes (10) with approval the words of the Montanist visionary, Prisca, as the words of a "holy prophetess"; and, when he speaks of the Church and the priesthood, his language suggests (7) that he has in mind, as an ideal, the internal, unorganized church of the Spirit rather than the visible, hierarchical church of Christ. Yet nowhere does he attack the Church with the bitterness which is so marked a characteristic of the *De monogamia,* nor does he identify himself with the sectaries by the use of such expressions as *nostri* and *vestri, penes nos* and *penes vos* or *eos,* expressions of partisanship which are of frequent occurrence in all of his later compositions and which help to identify them as Montanist.

The treatise is addressed to a friend, evidently a fellow Catholic, who has recently lost his wife. Tertullian urges him not to remarry. In developing his exhortation he stresses an argument against second marriage based on what he considers the clear indication of God's will that such unions should be avoided. God tolerates second marriage, but the very fact that He merely *tolerates* it proves that His positive will excludes what His permissive will allows. All the evidence of Sacred Scripture, both in the Old and the New Testament, shows that the practice is to be rejected. The Apostle himself, speaking in the name of the Lord, reprobates it when he asserts, equivalently, that it is the lesser of two evils.

In the course of his argument, especially in his exegesis (9) of Matt. 5. 28 and 1 Cor. 7. 1, 32 f., Tertullian is led to speak of marriage itself in terms which are somewhat less than enthusiastic. He does not dare to condemn a way of life which God Himself has blessed, but he does appear to regret its necessity.[3] His attitude here is that of a man who accepts the will of God but who does not like it. He seems to feel that there is something essentially unclean in any union of the sexes. Such unions may be legalized by external forms but they remain, in themselves, ugly and degrading; they are "good" only by extrinsic denomination. According to this twisted viewpoint, marriage is nothing but legitimate debauchery; it is a legitimate abuse rather than a legitimate use; or, to express his thought more exactly, the distinction between "use" and "abuse" is meaningless when there is question of the sex relationship, since this is not something which is good in itself, or even indifferent. It is, at best, a bad means justified by a good end.

It must be pointed out that such a position is quite inconsistent with much that he wrote on the subject of marriage in other places. There are passages in the **Ad uxorem** which reveal an attitude towards marriage, especially Christian marriage, which is certainly more than one of grim acceptance or sour toleration.[4] Some of the most vigorous pages in his **Adversus Marcionem** are devoted to the refutation of ideas similar to those which he himself defends in the present treatise.[5] And in the **De anima** he declares explicitly that we are to revere nature and not to be ashamed of it; the married state is blessed, not cursed by God and there is nothing immodest except excess.[6] D'Alès puts the matter briefly and well when he writes: "Tertullien a beaucoup écrit sur le mariage, et sur aucun sujet il ne s'est tant contredit."[7] . . .

. . . . .

[*Monogamy*]

The **De monogamia** is one of Tertullian's most notable contributions to the cause of militant Montanism. The arguments developed in the treatise are substantially the same as those which he used in the **Ad uxorem** and the **De exhortatione castitatis** to oppose the practice of successive polygamy; the great difference is in the way they are presented. Before, he wrote as a private individual expressing a private conviction; now he writes as the representative of a group, expounding sectarian dogma. Before, he was a counselor, seeking to persuade; now he is a zealot, determined to destroy. His language throughout the treatise is fierce and fanatical. Catholics he characterizes as "sensualists"; although "members of God's household, they are given to wantonness"; they "find their joy in things of the flesh," for "such things as are of the Spirit, please them not." He indicates a new allegiance and at the same time affirms an old conviction when he declares that "we who are deservedly called the 'spiritual' because of the spiritual charisms we have received . . . admit but one marriage, as we recognize but one God."[1]

There are a number of passages in this treatise which make it clear that Tertullian's extreme views on the illegitimacy of second marriage, expressed so vigorously in earlier writings, had by this time been con-

demned as heretical,[2] and that his adversaries had appealed to the authority of St. Paul to justify their position and his condemnation.[3] This opposition sufficiently accounts for the polemical tone of the treatise—if it be necessary to account for anything so typical of Tertullian as a controversial attitude. Accordingly, we need not assume that the **De monogamia** was written to answer the charges of some one particular antagonist. Rolffs' conjecture that it was intended as a rebuttal of an anti-Montanist tract of Hippolytus (preserved, supposedly, by Epiphanius, *Haer.* 48. 1-13)[4] cannot be proved and has been generally rejected.[5]

Whatever the occasion of the work, it is quite evident from what has been said above, that it was composed after Tertullian had joined forces with the Montanist party at Carthage.[6] We are thus enabled to date it some time after 212/213 A.D., since it was at this time that he wrote the **De fuga in persecutione,** the treatise which marks his definite break with the Church. It is also reasonably certain that it was composed before the **De ieiunio,**[7] which, in turn, is prior to the **De pudicitia,**[8] apparently Tertullian's last extant work. The **De pudicitia** was written between the years 217 and 222 A.D. Hence, on this evidence, we may say with fair probability that the **De monogamia** was composed between 212 and 222 A.D. Further precision, however, is possible. Tertullian himself tells us that he wrote one hundred and sixty years after St. Paul addressed his first epistle to the Corinthians.[9] Since modern authorities date this epistle in the year 57 A.D., we arrive at 217 A.D. as the most likely date of the **De monogamia.**

The treatise is constructed according to an orderly and easily discernible plan. Tertullian declares in his introduction that Montanism represents a mean between two extremes, heretical repudiation of marriage and Catholic licentiousness in repeating it (1). The doctrine of monogamy, announced authoritatively by the Paraclete, is not an innovation (2-3). It is supported by evidence found in the Old Testament (4-7), the Gospels (8-9), and the Epistles of St. Paul (10-14). To speak of it as harsh and heretical is absurd (15); and the popular arguments advanced to support the practice of second marriage are utterly trivial (16). Finally, Christians ought to be inspired to a love of continence by the example of so many men and women, in and out of the Church, whose lives were models of chastity (17).

Montanism warped Tertullian's judgment and ruined his life, but it did not impair his literary style. In fact, after he threw off the restraining influence of the Church, he began to write with greater passion, with a bolder and more combative eloquence than ever before.[10] The **De monogamia** is a party pamphlet and it follows the party line; yet it is also the work of a brilliant controversialist fighting for a cause very near his own heart. The result is an impressive piece of special pleading, aggressive, abusive, but perfectly sincere. Tertullian is often a sophist, but he is never a hypocrite. He reveals in this treatise all the exasperating self-confidence of the professional reformer and self-appointed custodian of public morals, but his rigorism is joined with a genius for strong language not always found among the puritanical. Perhaps there has never been so slashing a style put at the service of so narrow and illiberal a system. It is one of the great tragedies of the early Church that a man of Tertullian's remarkable talents should have rebelled against the prudent moderation imposed by Catholic orthodoxy, to give himself over with whole-hearted devotion to the propagation of bigotry.[11] . . .

Notes

To His Wife

[1] See, for example, J. Tixeront, *History of Dogmas* (tr. from the 5th French ed. by H. L. B., St. Louis 1910) 1. 323.

[2] *Ad ux.* 1. 7. For a useful synopsis of Tertullian's views on marriage and remarriage, cf. H. Preisker, *Christentum und Ehe in den ersten drei Jahrhunderten* (Berlin 1927) 187-200.

[3] Cf. Rom. 7. 2 f.; 1 Cor. 7. 8 f., 39 f.; 1 Tim. 5. 14.

[4] The Eastern Church judged second marriage more severely than did the Church in the West. Athenagoras (*Suppl.* 33), writing on the Christian ideal of chastity in marriage, declares that the man who takes a second wife after the death of his first is a 'cloaked adulterer.' Clement of Alexandria (*Strom.* 3. 12. 82. 4) considers that such unions are a mark of imperfection, while Origen (*Hom. in Luc.* 17) says that digamists will be saved in the name of Christ, but will not be among those who are crowned by Him. The earliest statement in the Western Church is that of the *Pastor Hermae* (*mand.* 4.4), to the effect that one who remarries does not sin 'but, if he dwells by himself, he acquires great honor to himself with the Lord.' It is to this doctrine of the *Pastor Hermae* that Tertullian alludes when, in the Montanist treatise *De pudicitia* (10), he speaks of the 'scripture of the Shepherd, which is the only one that favors adulterers and which has not found place in the divine canon.' For a comparative study of the views on this subject which prevailed in the East and West, cf. G. H. Joyce, *Christian Marriage* (2nd ed. London 1948) 584-600; on the teaching of Athenagoras, see K. v. Preysing, 'Ehezweck und zweite Ehe bei Athenagoras,' *Theol. Quartalschrift* 110 (1929) 115 ff. The early history of the whole question is well summarized by F. Meyrick, 'Marriage,' DCA [Dictionary of Christian Antiquities] 2. 1103 f.; see also A. Knecht, *Handbuch des katholischen Eherechts* (Freiburg i. Br.

1928) 750-53. The most detailed study of successive polygamy, from the viewpoint of dogmatic theology, is still that of J. Perrone, *De matrimonio Christiano* (Rome 1858) 3. 74-111; for a less complete, though more modern treatment, see C. Boyer, *Synopsis praelectionum de sacramento matrimonii* (Rome 1947) 58-60. Official pronouncements of the Church on the subject may be found in ES [Enchiridion symbolorum, 21st ed., ed. by H. Denziger, C. Bannwart, J. B. Umberg] 55, 424, 465, 541. It is the Church's teaching here that even *tertia et ulteriora matrimonia* may be contracted without sin. This reflects the doctrine of St. Jerome and St. Augustine. St. Jerome writes (*Epist.* 49.8): '*Non damno bigamos et trigamos et, si dici potest, octogamos*'; and St. Augustine (*De bono vid.* 12): '*De tertiis et quartis et de ultra pluribus nuptiis solent homines movere quaestionem. Unde et breviter respondeam: nec ullas nuptias audeo damnare, nec eis verecundiam numero-sitatis auferre.*'—On the history of the special discipline for clerics, cf. J. M. Ludlow, 'Digamy,' DCA 1.552 f.; and below, n. 65.

[5] *De bono vid.* 4.6; *De haer. ad Quodvultdeum* 86. In the latter passage Tertullian is said to have become a heretic *quia transiens ad Cataphrygas . . . coepit etiam secundas nuptias contra apostolicam doctrinam tamquam stupra damnare.*

[6] *Comm. in Epist. ad Titum* 1.6

[7] This is in disaccord with the opinion of Vincent of Lerins who, in a famous description of Tertullian's ability as a writer, says (*Comm.* 24): *Iam porro orationis suae laudes quis exsequi valeat, quae tanta nescio qua rationum necessitate conferta est, ut ad consensum sui, quos suadere non potuerit, impellat: cuius quot paene verba, tot sententiae sunt; quot sensus, tot victoriae?*

[8] J. Tixeront, *A Handbook of Patrology* (tr. from the 4th French ed. by S. A. Raemers, St. Louis 1944) 110. His judgment is that Tertullian is an 'implacable logician,' though he 'has the defects of his qualities' and 'his logic runs to paradox.' See also O. Bardenhewer, *Geschichte der altkirchlichen Literatur* 2 (2nd ed. Freiburg i. Br. 1914) 383 f.; P. de Labriolle, *History and Literature of Christianity from Tertullian to Boethius* (tr. from the French by H. Wilson, London-New York 1924) 94-96.

[9] On the problem of mixed marriages in the ancient Church see J. Köhne, *Die Ehen zwischen Christen und Heiden in den ersten christlichen Jahrhunderten* (Paderborn 1931); the same, 'Uber die Mischehen in den ersten christlichen Zeiten,' *Theol. und Glaube* 23 (1931) 333-50.

[10] The statement is made by J. Fessler, *Institutiones Patrologiae* (ed. B. Jungmann, Innsbruck 1890) 1.272.

[11] Tertullian's style has not always been as highly esteemed by Latinists as it is today. A celebrated German philologist of the 18th century, David Ruhnken, states flatly: *'Tertullianum latinitatis certe pessimum auctorem esse aio et confirmo'* (quoted by E. F. Leopold, *Zeitsch. f. hist. Theol.* 8 [1838] 33).

[12] T. R. Glover, *Tertullian: Apologia, De Spectaculis* (LCL, London 1931) xxvi. J. H. Waszink believes that with Tertullian, as with Aristotle, paraphrases of the text 'serve the purpose of correct understanding better than literal translations'; cf. *Quinti Septimi Florentis Tertulliani: De anima* (Amsterdam 1947) ix. It is the opinion of so competent a critic as A. Souter that Tertullian is the most difficult of all Latin prose writers; cf. *Tertullian: Concerning Prayer and Baptism* (SPCK [Society for Promoting Christian Knowledge], London 1919) xi.

[13] A. Harnack, *Die Chronologie der altchristlichen Litteratur bis Eusebius* 2 (Leipzig 1904) 273.

[14] Cf. St. Jerome, *De viris illustribus* 53.

[15] *Ibid.* . . .

. . . . .

An Exhortation to Chastity

[1] References to earlier literature on the subject may be found in O. Bardenhewer, *op. cit.,* 2. 395. For a study of the date of the *De exhortatione castitatis* in its relationship to the *Ad uxorem* and the *De monogamia,* see G. N. Bonwetsch, *Die Schriften Tertullians nach der Zeit ihrer Abfassung untersucht* (Bonn 1878) 57-61. The dates given here, 204 and 212 A.D., represent *termini ante* and *post quem non,* according to a consensus of estimates given by various modern patrologists.

[2] The word *castitas* may be taken as synonymous with *continentia,* here in the title and throughout the treatise. See TLL [Thesaurus Linguae latinae] 3.542.

[3] St. Jerome (*Adv. Iov.* 1.13) refers to a work *De molestiis nuptiarum,* now lost, written when Tertullian was still a young man. For some interesting comments on Tertullian's attitude to women, marriage and the family, cf. Monceaux, *op. cit.* 1.387. He writes: 'Ce grand ennemi du mariage était marié, naturellement.'

[4] *Ad ux.* 1.2 f.; 2.8.

[5] Cf. *Adv. Marc.* 1.29; 5.7, 15; also Preisker, *op. cit.* 197. Compare, too, *De res. carn.* 5, and *De carne Chr.* 4. On the difference between the basic principles of Montanist and Marcionite asceticism, see P. de Labriolle, *La crise Montaniste* 396. It may be said, in general, that the Montanists warned against marriage because of their belief in the proximity of the parousia; the Marcionites rejected it absolutely because of their belief that it was established by the creator-god of the Old Testament and, accordingly, must be considered as something evil in itself.

[6] *De an.* 27.4. In 11.4 of the same treatise Tertullian speaks of the 'ecstatic vision' of Adam, 'wherein he prophesied that great sacrament in Christ and in the Church.'

[7] d'Alès, *op. cit.* 370. . . .

. . . . .

Monogamy

[1] The quotations in this paragraph are all taken from ch. 1. Other, more specific accusations are found in later chapters; they include a vicious attack on the private life of one of the Catholic bishops (12).

[2] See, for example, 2: *Mongamiae disciplinam in haeresim exprobant.* Also, 15: *Quae haeresis, si secundas nuptias, ut illicitas, iuxta adulterium iudicamus?* This point is further discussed by A. Hauck, *Tertullian's Leben und Schriften* (Erlangen 1877) 397; de Labriolle, *La crise montaniste,* 383.

[3] Cf. 10 and 11. In the *Ad uxorem* and the *De exhortatione castitatis* Tertullian neglected to answer adequately the serious difficulty against his position found in 1 Cor. 7.39: 'A woman is bound as long as her husband is alive, but, if her husband dies, she is free. Let her marry whom she pleases. . . . ' It was this text, apparently, which his adversaries quoted against him, and he studies it at great length in the present treatise.

[4] E. Rolffs, *Urkunden aus dem antimontanistischen Kampfe des Abendlandes (Texte und Unters.* 12.4, Leipzig 1895) 50-109.

[5] Harnack, *Die Chronologie der altchrist. Litt.* 2.287, is in sympathy with Rolffs' theory, but he admits that it cannot be proved. It is opposed by Bardenhewer, *op. cit.* 2.422, de Labriolle, *op. cit.* 383, and Monceaux, *op. cit.* 428.

[6] St. Jerome writes (*De vir. ill.* 53) that Tertullian became a Montanist because of the 'envy and insults of the Roman clergy' and adds that after his lapse he composed a number of treatises in which he dealt with the new prophecy—*specialiter autem adversus Ecclesiam texuit volumina de pudicitia, de persecutione, de ieiuniis, de monogamia, de exstasi.* It is impossible to say just how well organized Montanism was at Carthage before Tertullian gave his support to the movement.

[7] In the first chapter of the *De ieiunio* Tertullian speaks

of a work of his 'already composed in defense of monogamy.'

[8] There are frequent references in the *De pudicitia* to the illegitimacy of second marriage. The whole treatise should be read in conjunction with the *De monogamia* to obtain a complete picture of Tertulian's views on the subject.

[9] Ch. 3.

[10] De Labriolle, *op. cit.* 392, says of the *De monogamia:* 'Jamais Tertullien n'a été aussi vif, aussi nerveux, aussi pressant que dans cet ouvrage.'

[11] Tertullian's personality and its influence on the great decisions of his life has been the subject of a recent analysis by B. Nisters, *Tertullian: Seine Persönlichkeit und sein Schicksal* (Münster i. W. 1950). On Tertullian's place in the rigorist movement of his age, and on rigorism as a persistent phenomenon in Church history, see R. Knox, *Enthusiasm* (Oxford 1950), especially 25-49. For estimates of Tertullian's character which are more favorable than those usually encountered, cf. the excellent paper by J. Tixeront, 'Tertullien moraliste,' *Mélanges de patrologie et d'histoire des dogmes* (2nd ed. Paris 1921) 117-152; and C. De Lisle Shortt, *The Influence of Philosophy on the Mind of Tertullian* (London n.d.) 98-105. . . .

William P. Le Saint (essay date 1959)

SOURCE: "On Penitence: Introduction" and "On Purity: Introduction" in *Tertullian: Treatises on Penance: On Penitence and On Purity,* translated by William P. Le Saint, The Newman Press, 1959, pp. 3-13, 41-52.

[*In the following excerpt, Le Saint discusses and compares Tertullian's two treatises on the subject of Christian penitence—*De pudicitia *and* De paenitentia.]

Orthodox Christianity regards the doctrine of the divine forgiveness of sins as an essential article of faith. The nature of this forgiveness, its manner and measure, its causes and its effects, have all been subjects of controversy, but whoever accepts the Apostles' Creed as an expression of elementary Christian doctrine professes his belief in the basic truth that in some sense, in some way and under certain conditions God does pardon the sins of men. This belief has its foundation in Scripture[1] and finds its historical expression in the traditional teaching of the Church. The great interest of Tertullian's treatises on repentance derives from the influence which they exercised on the development of this tradition in the West, and from the contribution which they make to our understanding of the Church's ministerial forgiveness of sins at a period quite close to the apostolic or sub-apostolic age. By common con-

sent of competent critics they are the two most important documents of ancient Christian literature for the study of one of the most difficult questions in the history of dogma: the doctrine and discipline of ecclesiastical penance during the first centuries of our era. Bernhard Poschmann, a writer whose authority in all that concerns the early history of penitential theology is unexcelled, has stated that the judgement which one forms of the theory and practice of penance in Christian antiquity will be determined, in large measure, by the interpretation which one puts upon the **De paenitentia** and **De pudicitia** of Tertullian.[2]

The penitential system of the early Church was founded on her belief that she had received from Christ a power to remit and to retain sin.[3] The earliest post-canonical evidence that this power was exercised in the forgiveness of sins committed after Baptism is preserved in the *Pastor Hermae,* an apocryphal apocalyptic tract written, at least in part, to refute the opinions of 'certain teachers' who insisted that there was no ecclesiastical penance but that of Baptism.[4] Further, evidence from the same period is furnished by more or less explicit and detailed statements in Irenaeus, Clement of Alexandria and certain Church Orders composed at this time, particularly the Syriac *Didascalia* and the so-called *Apostolic Tradition* of Hippolytus; there are, moreover, pertinent notices in Eusebius on the practice of Dionysius of Corinth (*c.* 171 A.D.) and the penance of Natalius at Rome (*c.* 200 A.D.); the subject is treated more completely by Origen in a number of interesting and instructive passages; the witness of Cyprian at the middle of the third century is, of course, formal and frequent.[5]

It is clear, then, that the teaching of Tertullian on the ecclesiastical forgiveness of sins does not exist in a literary vacuum. The evidence which his writings afford on the doctrine and discipline of the Church *circa* 200 A.D. may be summarized as follows. There is a well-known ritual of penance in the Church called *exomologesis,* established as a means of assisting members of the Church to obtain pardon for sins committed after Baptism. This ritual includes confession of one's sins and the performance of public penance by way of deprecation and satisfaction. It terminates directly in the restoration of the sinner to peace and communion with the Church, and, at least indirectly, in the forgiveness of his sins in the sight of God. The whole process is directed by ecclesiastical authority, and the pardon conceded at its close is granted by the bishop. Teltullian has no interest in ascribing the efficacy of *exomologesis* to any particular act or acts within the whole complexus. He is content that at the end of the process the sinner is reconciled not only to the Church but also to God Himself.[6]

This description of Tertullian's teaching is drawn from both the **De paenitentia** and the **De pudicitia.** As will be seen, they are works quite different in spirit, written for different purposes at different periods of his life, but the picture which they present of the orthodox Christian theory and practice of penance is essentially the same. The *De paenitentia* is a work of Tertullian's Catholic period, a kind of sermon addressed to the faithful on the subject of repentance and forgiveness, largely expository and hortatory in character, tolerant in tone. The *De pudicitia* was composed after Tertullian's lapse into Montanism. It is a violent, argumentative party pamphlet, directed against a particular piece of Church legislation on penance which Tertullian and his faction of rigid fanatics considered intolerably lax. It is significant that, in spite of these divergencies, the only substantial difference between the two treatises in what concerns the nature and administration of *exomologesis* is this: in the *De paenitentia* Tertullian places no restriction of any kind on the Church's power to forgive sins; in the *De pudicitia* he introduces the Montanist distinction between remissible and irremissible sins, conceding a power to the bishop to forgive the former but restricting forgiveness of the latter to God alone.

The interpretation of many passages in both treatises has been and remains controversial. This is true especially of those texts which bear on the existence of private penance in the early Church, the distinction between mortal and venial sins, the effect of episcopal absolution, the role of the faithful, particularly the martyrs, in the forgiveness of sins, the concept of compensatory satisfaction. The problem, however, which has been most discussed and about which the sharpest difference of opinion exists has to do with the crucial question of whether or not the Church granted pardon to the capital sins of apostasy, murder and adultery before the middle of the third century. Many theologians and historians of dogma assert that the *De paeni tentia* and *De pudicitia* of Tertullian clearly prove that it was not the practice of the early Church to pardon serious sins; others insist, just as positively, that these treatises prove the exact opposite.[7] These and other controversial questions will be considered in the notes, in connection with the translation and interpretation of passages pertinent to each particular problem. No attempt can be made to settle long-standing disputes in footnotes to a text, but it is hoped that a complete and objective canvassing of the opposing arguments will be of some help to the interested reader in forming his own opinion as to the merits of rival positions.

The extreme difficulty and obscurity of Tertullian's style and language are responsible, in no small measure, for the development of the controversies here referred to. It is indeed unfortunate that subjects of such great interest and importance should be set forth in phrases which often seem designed to conceal rather than to reveal their author's thought. Serious students, however, will find that, in spite of their obscurity, the treatises are invaluable not only as source books for the theology of penance but also for the light which they throw on many other questions relating to the life and faith of the early Church. Tertullian is notoriously the most difficult of all Latin prose writers, yet he always means *something,* and the effort which one makes to pierce through to his meaning can be an enjoyable as well as a rewarding experience. The literary value of the *De paenitentia* and *De pudicitia* may seem negligible, but their theological and historical significance is unsurpassed. They are books to be studied, not merely read. Tertullian was one of the most learned men of his age,[8] and no one who is interested in the study of antiquity, whether secular or religious, will find any of his writings disappointing or dull.

Since the importance of these treatises is theological rather than literary or artistic, it has seemed best to translate them quite literally, even though this results in a version which reflects the distortions of Tertullian's style as well as the ambiguity of his thought, and even though one feels that with Tertullian, as with St. Paul, no literal translation can ever give the full meaning of all that he intends to say. A paraphrase of his thought would be easier to read and understand than a close reproduction of its original expression, but there is always the danger that in a free translation, particularly of controversial matter, the text will be amplified by interpretations and interpolations which are tendentious. In the interest of clarity and intelligibility difficult passages will be discussed in the notes; in the interest of impartiality the text will be translated as literally as possible.

All translators of Tertullian have found it necessary to apologize for the awkward English which is the result of their efforts to produce a faithful version of his vigorous and imaginative but highly irregular prose. His whole habit of thought and manner of expression, even his method of argumentation, are utterly foreign and strange to us. Such expressions as 'to drink the sheep of a second penance' (*De pud.* 10.12), and 'dregs of milk which contain the virus of lust' (*De pud.* 6.15) produce little effect upon the modern reader beyond a desire to emend the text. The ancients themselves found him difficult and obscure. Lactantius says he is *parum facilis, minus comptus, multum obscurus* (*Div. Inst.* 5.1.23) and Jerome describes him as *creber in sententiis sed difficilis in loquendo* (*Epist.* 58.10). Tertullian is a writer of marvelous fertility and inventiveness, yet these very qualities contribute to the incoherence which is so marked a characteristic of his style. His sentences are quite often poorly constructed, a jumble of ideas which pour out in unnatural combinations of words and phrases, strange metaphors, neologisms, cryptic allusions, paradoxes and paralogisms, antitheses, multiple parentheses—a rich but disordered miscellany complicated by asyndeton, ellipsis and the use of every form of brachylogy known to grammarians. Efforts to modernize Tertullian inevitably end in failure. Perhaps the best apology a translator can make for his work is that a polished version would not be faithful to a rough original; if his English does not read smoothly, it may be pleaded in extenuation that the Latin doesn't either.[9] . . .

On Penitence[10]

The *De paenitentia,* as has been said, was written by Tertullian while he was yet a Catholic. It contains a brief explanation of what Christians understand by the virtue of penitence, discourses on the importance of this virtue and shows how it is to be practiced in the Church. It is not, however, and it was not intended to be, a systematic study of the penitential theory and practice of Christian antiquity. The purpose of the treatise is moral and ascetical, not didactic; the emphasis, throughout, is on the importance and necessity of penitence rather than on its nature or external forms. Quite probably it was originally a sermon which Tertullian preached to the people at Carthage;[11] it is direct and personal in its approach, often admonitory, resembling closely a type of composition which ancient rhetoricians described as 'paraenetic.'[12] Most patrologists are of the opinion that it was addressed to catechumens, but there are good reasons for holding with Rauschen that it was also intended as an instruction and exhortation for the baptized.[13]

The work falls naturally into three parts. In the first (cc. 1-4) Tertullian speaks of penance as a virtue. Pagans have no concept of what this virtue means. For them *paenitentia* is no more than an unpleasant emotion caused by a past act; it may even follow upon an act which was good in itself (c. 1). Christians, however, understand that it is sin which makes repentance necessary and gives it meaning. Repentance supposes the reprobation of one's evil deeds and an amendment of life; it is motivated by fear of God; it is required by the divine justice; it effects the forgiveness of sins and, thus, has salvation as its fruit (c. 2). Repentance is demanded for all sins, external and internal alike (c. 3). God Himself commands it and He has also promised to reward it (c. 4).

Chapters 5 and 6 deal more specifically with the penitence of those who have not yet been baptized. Conversion to a new life is essential in repentance, and once this conversion has been signed and sealed by Baptism it must never be 'unsealed' or repudiated by a return to sin (c. 5). The obligation of penitence presses most urgently upon the catechumens. The thought of their future Baptism must not encourage them to sin, rashly confiding in the pardon which they are about to receive. Forgiveness is certainly the effect of Baptism, but we are baptized *because* we have ceased to sin, not *in order that* we may cease to do so. Our freedom from punishment will be bought at the price of the penance we practice; if this penance does not include a sincere conversion, it is false coin and God will reject it (c. 6).

Chapters 7-12 have to do with the important question of post-baptismal penitence. Sins committed by persons who are not yet members of the Church are forgiven by *paenitentia prima;* this includes conversion and the reception of Baptism. If anyone should be so unfortunate as to sin after he has been baptized, God, in His mercy, allows him a *paenitentia secunda* for the forgiveness of his offense. This second penitence must not be neglected—and it may not be repeated (c. 7). The possibility of a second forgiveness is proved by a number of passages in the New Testament, particularly by the parables of the lost drachma, the lost sheep and the prodigal son (c. 8). *Paenitentia secunda* requires the performance of those external penitential acts which constitute the well-known discipline of *exomologesis* (c. 9). The performance of public penance is humiliating and most men try to avoid it, but if they neglect it, they cannot be saved (c. 10). It is proper that one should suffer when one has sinned (c. 11), yet the pain which *exomologesis* causes the sinner is as nothing to the punishment of hell which it enables him to escape (12).

This third section of the treatise has been much discussed and variously interpreted. It poses two principal problems, distinct but closely related: (1) Is the *paeni-tentia secunda* described here essentially an ecclesiastical process, terminated by ecclesiastical absolution, or is it a private personal matter between the sinner and God, terminated by an absolution[14] granted by God and by Him alone? (2) If it is terminated by an ecclesiastical absolution, does this reconcile the sinner to God or only to the Church? These questions will be treated at some length in notes on the text, but it may be said here, briefly, that the positions which seem to be most easily defended are these: (1) The *paenitentia secunda* of which Tertullian speaks in this treatise is necessarily externalized by *exomologesis,* and *exomologesis* is an ecclesiastical process which ends with ecclesiastical absolution. (2) This absolution reconciles the sinner directly and immediately to the Church but indirectly and mediately to God Himself. These propositions are established with good probability from evidence in the *De paenitentia* itself; they are proved conclusively if this is combined with evidence supplied by the *De pudicitia.* The problem of whether or not the *peccata capitalia* were excluded from ecclesiastical absolution belongs to a discussion of the *De pudicitia* and will be examined in connection with the analysis of that treatise. It may be noted here, however, that there is nothing in the *De paenitentia* which indicates that the Church refused to pardon serious sins, and a number of passages which prove rather conclusively that she granted it.

It seems best to date the **De paenitentia** some time between 200 and 206 A.D. (Monceaux) or 198 and 202/3 A.D. (Harnack). It was certainly written before 207, the year in which Tertullian began to express some sympathy with Montanist ideas. There is not the slightest trace of any such sympathy in this treatise. In fact, as will be seen, Tertullian finds it necessary in the **De pudicitia** to repudiate the earlier tolerance which he showed in dealing with the subject of penitence, presumably tolerance of the sort manifested in the **De paenitentia.** Noeldechen believes that the work was composed early in the year 204 A.D., arguing (1) that the reference in c. 12.2 to recent volcanic disturbances is to be understood as an allusion to the eruption of Vesuvius in 203 A.D., (2) that the death of Plautian in January 204 A.D. occasioned Tertullian's remark on the nature of pagan repentance in c. 1.4, (3) that the special attention given to the ambitious conduct of office seekers, c. 11.4, indicates that Tertullian wrote shortly after the close of the year, the season during which it was customary for politicians to solicit the electorate.[15] The only one of these arguments which can be taken seriously is the first, and even this is rejected by Harnack, who considers it arbitrary to suppose that a reference to Vesuvius is intended when Vesuvius is not mentioned by name or otherwise identified.[16] . . .

. . . . .

The **De pudicitia**[1] is one of Tertullian's most violent Montanist treatises—a passionate, bigoted and yet utterly sincere attack on the doctrine and discipline of the orthodox Church. Tertullian felt and professed a deep love for the Church of Christ. He was convinced that it was not he who had left the Church; rather it was the Church that had left him! This she did, he believed, when she refused to accept the utterances of Montanist prophets as the authentic word of God, and when she refused to impose upon her members the austere moral discipline inculcated by the new 'revelations' of the Paraclete. In his various Montanist writings Tertullian protests against the Church's toleration of second marriage, her attitude towards flight during times of persecution, her relatively mild legislation in the matter of fasting and other external penitential practices. All of his Montanist tracts are characterized by a warped and exaggerated asceticism; in all of them Tertullian's indignation is impressive, even when his position is impossible and his arguments absurd.

The **De pudicitia,** possibly the last of Tertullian's extant works, criticizes the policy which the Church follows in granting pardon to serious sins. In none of his writings does he show a fiercer temper. He is without pity in his condemnation of human frailty, completely unashamed in his demands for harshness and intoler-

ance. From beginning to end he is the true fanatic; he is impatient of all opposition; his mind is closed to every viewpoint but his own; he is convinced that he stands at Armageddon and battles for the Lord. The modern reader can feel nothing but sorrow that so great and devoted a talent should have served so bigoted a cause.

The treatise was occasioned by the peremptory edict of a Catholic bishop decreeing that members of the Church who committed adultery were not to be permanently excluded from the Church but were to be readmitted to communion after the performance of public penance. This decree Tertullian condemns as subversive of that perfect purity which is demanded of the Christian. Any indulgence granted to sins of the flesh he regards as a profanation of the body of Christ and an invitation to further sin. His arguments are almost exclusively scriptural. He insists that the sacred text, rightly understood, clearly proves that the Church must not forgive sins of adultery and fornication. He draws on a bewilderingly large number of texts from both the Old and the New Testament to establish this thesis, revealing throughout the whole treatise a familiarity with the Bible which is truly amazing. One hardly knows which is the more remarkable—his readiness in quoting Scripture or his genius for distorting it.

The argument is developed in chapters 5 to 20. Chapters 1 to 4 are introductory, and chapters 21 and 22 an epilogue. Tertullian begins his treatise with a statement on the excellence of chastity and a complaint that this virtue has suffered harm as the result of a recent episcopal directive allowing pardon to adultery and fornication. Tertullian acknowledges that he himself, before he was enlightened by the new prophecy, found no fault with the practice of forgiving serious sins, but he rejoices that he now has a finer appreciation of purity and is a better and a holier man than he was before (c. 1). If his opponents say that Scripture proves the kindness and mercy of God, he will answer that it also proves His severity and justice. This apparent contradiction is resolved if we remember that sins are of two kinds: some are remissible and others irremissible. Penance is required for all sins; if it is done for remissible sins, the Church grants pardon at its close; if it is done for irremissible sins, no such ecclesiastical pardon is allowed. Thus God shows His mercy in the first instance and His justice in the second (c. 2). When penance is done for irremissible sins it is not done in vain, since pardon will be granted in heaven even though it is not allowed on earth. This conflicts with the opinion of his adversaries, who insist that forgiveness of such sins is the fruit of an absolution which the Church gives here below (c. 3). There is no essential difference between adultery and fornication as far as carnal defilement is concerned. Public penance is required for both these sins, but the Church may not forgive them. If a Christian should be guilty of unnatural vice, he is not only refused absolution but is even excluded from the performance of exomologesis (c. 4).

Tertullian finds his first scriptural argument in the Decalogue. God prohibits idolatry, adultery and murder, in that order. This proves the gravity of adultery, and shows how inconsistent his opponents are when they forgive sins of impurity while refusing to forgive murder and idolatry (c. 5). The law of the Old Testament has not been abrogated but it has been perfected in Christ, who condemns not only external sins of the flesh but even lustful desires. Examples of immorality under the old dispensation are no excuse for laxness under the law of Christ (c. 6). The parables of the lost sheep, the lost drachma and the prodigal son may seem to justify the Church in her practice of forgiving the serious sins of her subjects. This, however, perverts the meaning of the parables since, if we study them carefully, we shall see that Christ is there promising pardon to pagans, not to Christians. Hence the parables of mercy prove that all sins may be forgiven to pagans in the *paenitentia prima* of Baptism, but not to Christians in the *paenitentia secunda* of exomologesis (cc. 7-9). It is incorrect to say, as his opponents do, that Christ's mercy is meant more for Christians than it is for pagans, since pagans sin in ignorance and, therefore, have less need of mercy. This may be consistent with the teaching of Hermas, the shepherd of adulterers, but it is not consistent with the teaching of the Gospels (c. 10). Nor does the fact that Christ personally forgave serious sins prove that the Church may do so (c. 11).

The teaching and example of the apostles may be added to the lessons of the Gospel. When the apostles were assembled in the council at Jerusalem they laid no burdens upon the faithful but the obligation of abstaining from sacrifices, fornications and blood, that is to say, from idolatry, adultery and murder. These, then, are the sins which they consider irremissible (c. 12). The letters of St. Paul, particularly *First* and *Second Corinthians,* are cited by the laxists as proving that pardon may be granted to a Christian guilty of adultery. It can be shown, however, that the sinner whom Paul forgives in his second letter is not the incestuous man whom he condemned in his first. Moreover, the whole tenor of Paul's epistles is inconsistent with the notion that he would ever tolerate the forgiveness of adultery by the Church (cc. 13-17).

Scripture not only condemns adultery but teaches explicitly that it is to be punished by excommunication, and by an excommunication which lasts not just for a short time but for life. If impurity is forgiven, it is forgiven by *paenitentia prima* to those who have not yet become members of the Church. There is also, however, a *paenitentia secunda* for those who sin after Baptism. If they have been guilty of lesser or remissible sins, pardon is granted them by the bishop; if

they have been guilty of greater or irremissible sins, pardon is granted by God alone (c. 1). St. John, in the Apocalypse, permits no pardon to Christians guilty of adultery; rather he condemns them to 'the pool of fire,' with no indication that they will be pardoned; and in his (first) epistle he speaks quite clearly of a *sin unto death,* that is to say, an irremissible sin (c. 19). So, too, Barnabas, in his *Epistle to the Hebrews,* teaches that second penance was never promised by the apostles to Christians guilty of adultery or fornication (c. 20).[2]

In conclusion, Tertullian concedes that the Church has a power to forgive sins, but he insists that the exercise of this power is restricted by a new revelation of the Paraclete. His opponents claim that the Church's power to forgive sin derives from the fact that Christ gave to St. Peter the keys of the kingdom of heaven and promised that whatsoever he loosed on earth would be loosed also in heaven. This power, however, belonged to Peter personally, and it now belongs to the church of the Spirit, not to the hierarchical church. Therefore it is possessed by those only who have the Spirit, and it is not possessed *ex officio* by the bishops as successors of the apostles (c. 21). Finally, this power must not be allowed to the martyrs. Martyrdom will efface one's own sins but not the sins of others. If the martyrs are permitted to forgive adultery, they must be allowed to forgive apostates and murderers also, apostates in particular, since apostasy is so much more excusable than adultery (c. 22).

It will be seen from this rapid survey that the distinction between remissible and irremissible sins is essential to the argument of the *De pudicitia.* We must remember that when Tertullian makes this distinction he means 'remissible or irremissible by the Church,' not 'remissible or irremissible by God,' since he states explicitly that sins which the Church may not forgive, God actually does forgive (3.3, 5; 18.18). The distinction is new in Tertullian's penitential theology; at least, it is not mentioned or implied in the *De paenitentia* or any other of his pre-Montanist writings. Its importance is sufficiently indicated by the fact that it is responsible for, or closely identified with, all of the principal controversies which have arisen over the interpretation of this treatise.

The three most crucial questions in dispute are these: (1) Which sins did Tertullian consider to be of such objective gravity that they were excluded from ecclesiastical absolution? (2) Who was the author of the edict which occasioned the composition of the *De pudicitia?* (3) Is there any convincing evidence in this treatise that at the beginning of the third century the Church refused to pardon the sins of murder and apostasy and that she was just beginning to pardon sins of adultery and fornication?
The first of these problems is complicated by a lack of

precision in Tertullian's division of sins. He uses a number of different expressions to describe sins which are of greater (*maxima, capitalia, mortalia, exitiosa, maiora, gravia*) or lesser (*mediocria, modica, leviora, peccata cotidianae incursionis*) guilt, and it is not always possible to determine the exact meaning or extension of these terms. Then, too, he does not always clearly indicate which sins are to be subjected to public penance and which may be forgiven without it. Finally, he gives different lists of serious sins in different places, and his attitude towards these sins does not always seem to be completely consistent.

The safest conclusions which emerge from a study of passages pertinent to Tertullian's classification of sins[3] appear to be these. (1) There is some evidence, though it is by no means conclusive, that Tertullian recognized two distinct classes of sins, corresponding roughly to the modern division of mortal and venial sins. It is not certain, however, that he uses *maiora, mortalia, capitalia,* etc., as synonyms, or that all of the sins which he speaks of as *remissibilia* would be venial in the sense in which we use the word today. In terms of forgiveness, Tertullian says that some sins are *remissibilia* and others are not; in terms of gravity, he says that some sins are of greater and others of lesser guilt. Though he teaches, as a Montanist, that all sins of lesser guilt are remissible, he does not teach that all sins of greater guilt are irremissible. (2) It is not clear from the *De pudicitia* that Tertullian recognized the existence of an intermediate class of sins between the *levia* and the *maxima* which were forgiven by private penance. (3) The catalogue of crimes in 19.25 is intended as a typical and not an exhaustive inventory of serious sins. It corresponds rather closely with other lists given elsewhere in the writings of Tertullian. In all such lists the capital sins of idolatry (apostasy), murder and adultery are conspicuous, but they are not the only sins which Tertullian regards as mortal. The matter may be summed up thus. Both as Catholic and Montanist Tertullian recognized a distinction between sins of greater and those of lesser gravity. It cannot be proved that in his Catholic period he considered *any* grave sin irremissible, nor can it be proved that in his Montanist period he considered *all* grave sins irremissible.

The problem of determining the authorship of the edict which occasioned the composition of the *De pudicitia* has been studied frequently and needs no more than a brief synopsis here. Three principal views have been proposed. Older editors and commentators attributed the decree to Zephyrinus, bishop of Rome from 198 to 217. With the discovery of the Philosophoumena of Hippolytus in 1850, scholars all but unanimously accepted Callistus (bishop of Rome 217-222) as the author, since they considered that the charge of laxity in forgiving sins of impurity which Hippolytus makes against Callistus (*Philosoph.* 9.12) must be understood

as referring to his issuance of the edict of toleration which Tertullian condemns in *De pud.* 1.6. Other passages in the *De pudicitia* which are thought to prove the Roman provenance of the edict will be found in cc. 13.7 and 21.5, 9. In recent years, however, scholars have been abandoning the idea that the decree was issued by a bishop of Rome. K. Adam, P. Galtier, B. Poschmann and other authorities on the history of penance argue quite convincingly that it was promulgated by an African bishop, probably Agrippinus of Carthage. This view has, at present, a certain ascendancy, although it is not universally received and the decree continues to be referred to in the literature as the 'Edict of Callistus.'[4]

The evidence from the *De pudicitia* that before the year 200 the Church did not grant absolution to the sins of murder and apostasy (idolatry), and that it was only about this time that she began to forgive adultery and fornication may be summarized thus. Tertullian repeatedly insists that his opponents are inconsistent in granting absolution to adultery, while refusing it to murder and apostasy.[5] It is inconceivable that he could have used such an argument if the Church actually did grant pardon to these sins at this time. That adultery was not forgiven before the third century seems clear from the very fact that an edict was issued *circa* 215 decreeing its forgiveness. Then, too, it is difficult to account for the bitterness of Tertullian's language in the *De pudicitia,* if the bishop whose legislation he condemns were simply continuing an earlier tradition of tolerance.

Against this position and these arguments various lines of attack have developed. Some theologians attempt to settle the matter dogmatically, contending that ecclesiastical absolution is a necessary means of salvation for those who have sinned seriously after Baptism, and that, therefore, the Church, at no time in her history, could have withheld absolution from those who were properly disposed to receive it. The argument proceeds *a non posse ad non esse;* if a thing is impossible, it never happened! The Church may not refuse to pardon serious sins; therefore there can be no evidence in the *De pudicitia* that she did refuse to pardon them. There are a number of sound theological objections to this argument, but even apart from them, most students will be unwilling to accept it because of an understandable reluctance to settle historical questions on *a priori* grounds.[6]

Not a few writers concede that the *De pudicitia* proves the existence of a rigid but slowly relaxing penitential discipline *at the time* and *in the place* where the treatise was written. They insist, however, that while it furnishes evidence for the practice of a particular church in Africa, it may not be cited as proving that the universal Church, or even the Church of Rome, refused to pardon serious sins before the beginning of the third century. It will be observed that, according to this interpretation, Tertullian in the *De pudicitia* protests against a practice which was just beginning in the African Church, not one which had always existed but which he thought should be changed because of a new revelation. The author of the peremptory edict is the innovator; Tertullian himself is not. Thus, on the evidence of the *De pudicitia,* it is admitted that the African church did refuse to pardon murder and apostasy and was just beginning to pardon the sin of adultery at the time Tertullian wrote this treatise.

Not all students will admit that this is a correct interpretation of the text of the *De pudicitia,* nor do they see that it comes to grips with a fundamental problem in Tertullian's teaching on ecclesiastical penance. This problem is created by the apparent contradiction between the teaching of the *De paenitentia* and the *De pudicitia* on the forgiveness of serious sins. In the former treatise Tertullian says that all sins may be and are forgiven by the Church; in the latter he insists that adultery *must not* be forgiven and he asserts that murder and apostasy *are not* forgiven by the Church. Various solutions of this problem have been proposed, none of them completely satisfactory. The following explanation, although it admittedly leaves some subordinate questions unanswered, seems to be most consistent with the evidence furnished by both treatises.

In the *De paenitentia* Tertullian taught that all sins, no matter how grave, may be forgiven by *paenitentia secunda*. In the *De pudicitia,* under the influence of Montanist rigorism, he repudiates this teaching when he says that adultery must not be forgiven by the Church. Thus the *De pudicitia* does not prove that the orthodox Church, even the local church in Africa, refused to pardon adultery before the promulgation of the peremptory edict. This edict may well have been issued precisely in order to check the growing rigidism of a party of puritans in some particular locality.[7] Tertullian never protests that the edict is an innovation; rather he admits that he himself has changed his viewpoint on the subject of ecclesiastical absolution after his enlightenment by the new prophecy. The innovator is not the bishop who implements a tradition of tolerance by his formal decree of indulgence, but Tertullian who protests against it.[8]

The evidence of the *De pudicitia* that murder and apostasy were not forgiven by the Church at this time is more difficult to deal with. Some students, as noted above, simply concede that the local church which Tertullian has in mind did refuse forgiveness to these sins. This explanation, however, does not do full justice to the evidence of the *De paenitentia* that the Church grants pardon to all sins, with no distinction made as to their gravity. Others contend that in the *De paenitentia* Tertullian teaches that *God* forgives all sins, not that the *Church* does. This is an easy solution but

it, too, seems to ignore the evidence of the *De paenitentia* that it is exomologesis, the ecclesiastical *paenitentia secunda,* which effects the forgiveness of all sins, no matter how serious. B. Poschmann suggests that when Tertullian says that the Church refuses pardon to murderers and apostates, he means that she does not grant them peace and communion during their lifetime, but only at the hour of their death. Thus there is a sense in which it can be said that these sins are not remitted (*De pudicitia*), even though they are remissible (*De paenitentia*).[9] Positive arguments that murder and apostasy were forgiven in the Church before the middle of the third century have been developed by Galtier and others, particularly from evidence in the *Acta Petri,* Cyprian, Dionysius of Alexandria, Hippolytus, *Pastor Hermae,* Clement of Alexandria and early Church councils.[10]

It is impossible to say exactly when the *De pudicitia* was written. The dates 217/22 are frequently given, but they depend on the theory that Callistus was author of the edict against which the *De pudicitia* was a protest and, hence, they have no more certainty than has this theory. Patrologists generally place it, along with the *De monogamia* and the *De ieiunio,* among Tertullian's latest works.[11] The *De monogamia* was composed about 217, and some authorities are of the opinion that it precedes the *De pudicitia.* This sequence, however, can neither be proved nor disproved. In the absence of any more definite evidence we must be content to say, simply, that the treatise was composed some time after 212/13, since it was at this time that Tertullian broke with the Church and allied himself with the Montanist party at Carthage. . . .

Notes

On Penitence

[1] For a more detailed study of this subject, particularly with reference to the teaching of the New Testament, see E. Redlich, *The Forgiveness of Sins* (Edinburgh 1937).

[2] Poschmann III 20.

[3] The words of Christ which are cited in justification of this claim occur in Matt.16.19; 18.15-18; John 20.19-23.

[4] For the more recent literature on the penitential doctrine and discipline of the *Pastor Hermae,* see J. Quasten, *Patrology* (Westminster 1950) 1.104 f.

[5] Evidence for the existence of post-baptismal ecclesiastical penitence before the year A.D. 250 has been collected and studied by O. Watkins, *A History of Penance* (London 1920) 1.3-222; A. D'Alès, *L'édit de Calliste* (Paris 1914); B. Poschmann, *Paenitentia se-*

cunda. Die kirchliche Busse im ältesten Christentum bis Cyprian und Origenes (Bonn 1940). P. Galtier, *Aux origines du sacrement de pénitence* (Rome 1951), gives particular attention to New Testament texts and to the literature of the sub-apostolic period. For Cyprian, see A. D'Alès, *La théologie de saint Cyprien* (Paris 1922); K. Rahner, 'Die Busslehre des hl. Cyprian von Karthago,' ZKT 74 (1952) 252-76; M. Bévenot, 'The Sacrament of Penance and St. Cyprian's *De lapsis*,' TS 16 (1955) 175-213. For Origen, E. Latko, *Origen's Concept of Penance* (Quebec 1949) and K. Rahner, 'La doctrine d'Origène sur la pénitence,' RSR 37 (1950) 47-97, 252-86, 422-56.

[6] The best recent studies on Tertullian's theology of penance are those of C. Daly, 'The Sacrament of Penance in Tertullian,' IER 69 (1947) 693-707, 815-21; 70 (1948) 730-46, 832-48; 73 (1950) 159-69, and K. Rahner, 'Zur Theologie der Busse bei Tertullian, *Abhandlungen über Theologie und Kirche. Festschrift f. K. Adam, hrsg. v. M. Reding* (Düsseldorf 1943) 139-67. See, also, the bibliographies in Quasten, *op. cit.* 2.301 f., 314 f., 335.

[7] The following may be listed as representatives of the viewpoint that Tertullian's treatises on penance prove that it was not the practice of the early Church to forgive serious sins: J. Sirmundus, *Historia paenitentiae publicae* (Paris 1651) 1-9; F. Funk, 'Zur altchristlichen Bussdisciplin,' *Kirchengeschichtliche Abhandlungen und Untersuchungen* 1 (1896) 151-81; A. Harnack, *History of Dogma* (tr. from the 3rd German ed. by N. Buchanan, London 1896) 2.108-12; L. Duchesne, *His-toire ancienne de l'Église* (Paris 1916) 1.518-20. The contrary opinion has been defended by J. Morinus, *Commentarius historicus de disciplina in admini-stratione sacramenti paenitentiae* (Anvers 1682) 670-85; P. Monceaux, *Histoire littéraire de l'Afrique chrétienne* (Paris 1902) 1.432; G. Esser, *Die Buss-schriften Tertullians de paenitentia und das Indulgenzedikt des Papstes Kallistus* (Bonn 1905). D. Petavius, *De vetere in ecclesia ratione poenitentiae diatriba. Dogmata theologica* 8 (Paris 1867) 182, favors the first opinion; however, in a later work, *Diatriba de poenitentia et reconciliatione veteris ecclesiae mo-ribus recepta, ibid.* 451, he states that, *re altius et accuratius perspecta,* he has come to the conclusion that it was never the practice of the universal Church to refuse pardon to capital sins. References to other representatives of these two schools may be found in Poschmann I 283 f.

[8] Tertullian reveals a thorough familiarity with Latin and Greek letters; he has read widely in medical literature; in philosophy and law he has a specialist's learning. The judgement of antiquity is summed up in the famous eulogy of Vincent of Lerins, *Commonitorium* 24: *Quid enim hoc viro doctius? Quid in divinis atque humanis rebus exercitatius? Nempe omnem philosophiam et cunctas philosophorum sectas, auctores,*

assertatores sectarum, omnesque eorum disciplinas, omnem historiarum atque studiorum varietatem mira quadam mentis capacitate complexus est.

[9] E. Norden voices the common opinion of classical literary critics when he says that 'Tertullian is, without doubt, the most difficult of all authors who wrote in Latin.' *Die antike Kunstprosa* (2nd ed. Leipzig 1909) 2.606. For complete bibliographies on his language and style, see Quasten, *op. cit.* 2.250 f. and J. Waszink, *Tertullianus. De anima. Edited with Introduction and Commentary* (Amsterdam 1947) 601-603 and 610-20.

[10] The word 'penitence' has been chosen for the English title of this treatise since it avoids the controversial connotations which attach to the terms 'repentance' and 'penance' and since it most closely approximates the various senses of *paenitentia* which Tertullian supposes or explains in the course of his composition. The persons whom he addressed had a definite notion, carried over from classical Latin and from their ordinary speech, of what *paenitentia* meant. At the beginning of his discourse Tertullian insists that for the Christian this concept is not enough. To the pagan *paenitentia* signifies nothing more that a feeling of regret for something which he did in the past. To the Christian, however, it means sorrow for sin and conversion to a new way of life. It includes a fear of God's punishments, the performance of painful actions by way of satisfaction and, in terms of its relationship to ecclesiastical ritual, it means Baptism (*paenitentia prima*) and exomologesis (*paenitentia secunda*). Thus it encompasses everything which at any time and in any way is required of the sinner who seeks the forgiveness of God. There is no one word in any modern language which will convey all of these meanings and, for this reason, Teeuwen is of the opinion that the title should always be given in Latin in order to avoid misconceptions and misrepresentation; cf. St. W. J. Teeuwen, 'De voce *paenitentia* apud Tertullianum,' *Mnemosyne* 55 (1927) 410. That *paenitentia* means more than repentance in the sense of *mutatio mentis* and *conversio* is clear from Tertullian's use of the word with such verbs as *amplexari* (4.2), *invadere* (2.13; 4.2), *capessere* (6.1), *cogere* (2.10), *adsumere* (6.1), *adhibere* (2.12), *adimplere* (6.4), *includere* (6.1), *suscipere* (5.1), *fungi* (5.2). It is interesting that in the first edition of his translation (Kempten 1870) Kellner entitles the treatise *Über die Busse;* in the Cologne edition of 1882 he has *Über die Bekehrung;* and in the Kempten-Munich edition of 1912 the title is again *Über die Busse.*—For the spelling *paenitentia* rather than *poenitentia,* see Teeuwen, *op. cit.* 419. Other uses of the word and its derivatives in early Christian writers may be seen in A. Blaise-H. Chirat, *Dictionnaire latin-français des auteurs chrétiens* (Strasbourg 1954) 588 f.

[11] On Tertullian's use of the sermon form in many of

his compositions, see Monceaux, *op. cit.* 1.366. Other references to Tertullian as a preacher are given by G. Diercks, *Tertullianus. De oratione* (Bussum 1947) xcix f., and E. Dekkers, *Tertullianus en de Geschiedenes der Liturgie* (Brussels-Amsterdam 1947) 39 f.

[12] Cf. St. Pacian's treatise, *Parainesis sive exhortatorius libellus ad poenitentiam.*

[13] Rauschen's opinion is discussed below, *De paen.* note 110.

[14] Tertullian uses a great variety of words and images in speaking of the salutary effect of *paenitentia:* we find, for example, *venia, reconciliatio, restitutio, pax, communio, salus, remedium, iasis, curatio, emendatio, planca, merx, ianua, reaedificatio, reformatio, redintegratio, oblitteratio, indulgentia, ignoscentia, expiatio, satisfactio, compensatio.* Related verbs are: *absolvere, revocare, sanare, mederi, reviviscere, purgare, mundare, emendare, expungere, dispungere, donare, in ecclesiam recipere, redigere, reddere.*

[15] E. Noeldechen, *Die Abfassungszeit der Schriften Tertullians.* TU 5 (Leipzig 1888) 59-62.

[16] A. Harnack, *Die Chronologie der altchristlichen Litteratur* (Leipzig 1904) 2.271 f. For other literature on this subject, see O. Bardenhewer, *Geschichte der altkirchlichen Literatur* (Freiburg 1914) 2.417. . . .

. . . . .

On Purity

[1] This work is generally referred to in English as the treatise on *Modesty,* the title given it in Thelwall's translation. In modern usage, however, the word 'modesty' does not correspond exactly to *pudicitia* as Tertullian understands the term in this treatise. He is concerned, throughout, with the defense of a virtue which is violated by sins of adultery and fornication. This is the virtue of purity or chastity, not precisely and certainly not primarily the virtue of modesty. What we call 'modesty' today is a safeguard of what Tertullian calls *pudicitia;* compare *De cultu fem.* 2, where he declares that the virtue of purity (*pudicitia*) is necessary for salvation, and that this virtue will be preserved by the avoidance of extremes (i.e. by modesty) in dress and ornamentation. In *Apol.* 50.12 he states that the pagan persecutors, in condemning a Christian girl *ad lenonem potius quam ad leonem,* acknowledge that Christians consider the violation of chastity (*pudicitia*) a more dreadful punishment than death; cf. below, note 31. In *Apol.* 35.5 he distinguishes *modestia, verecundia* and *pudicitia,* paralleling these virtues with *probitas, sobrietas* and *castitas* in the preceding paragraph. See, also, Novatian's treatise *De bono pudicitiae,* a work which deals very definitely with the virtue of

chastity and, at the same time, closely imitates, in a number of passages, the *De pudicitia* of Tertullian. That *pudicitia,* in other early Christian writers as well as in classical Latin, quite frequently means sexual purity, may easily be seen from the dictionaries. Tertullian's concept of *pudicitia* is illustrated, also, by his use of the word *impudicitia* in this present treatise; cf. 6.14; 14.17; 15.4; 16.22; 18.1, 11. In all of these places, and particularly in 14.27 and 18.11, 'impurity' is closer to his meaning than is 'immodesty.' As early a commentator as J. Pamelius, *Tertulliani opera* (Cologne 1617) 716, found difficulty with the title of this treatise. He remarks that the contents of the work would be more clearly indicated if it were called *Adversus paenitentiam* rather than *De pudicitia,* but he suggests that the latter title was chosen because, in attacking adultery and fornication as he does in his book, Tertullian is really writing in defense of purity (*pudi-citia*).

[2] It will be observed that throughout this section of his work Tertullian's argument is largely one of rebuttal. His opponents appeal to definite passages in Scripture which they insist justify their forgiveness of serious sins, e.g. the parables of mercy, the example of Christ, the teaching and example of the apostles. These arguments he examines in order and attempts to refute either by substituting his own interpretation of the passages in question or by setting over against them other passages which appear to destroy their force.

[3] For *peccata gravia,* cf. 3.13; 19.20; 21.14; 19.28; 21.2; 18.17; 19.25. For *peccata levia,* 1.19; 2.10; 7.20; 18.17; 19.22-24. For *peccata irremissibilia,* 2.12, 14, 15; 16.5; 9.20; 13.19.

[4] See the bibliography in Quasten, *op. cit.* 2.314 f.

[5] Cf. *De pud.* 5.8, 15; 6.7 f.; 9.20; 12.5, 11; 19.15.

[6] The dogmatic argument is found in a number of the older manuals of theology; see, for example, D. Palmieri, *De poenitentia* (Rome 1879) 93 f. It is defended, also, by J. Stufler in a series of articles in the *Zeitschrift für katholische Theologie,* 1907 to 1914; cf. in particular, 'Die Bussisziplin in der abendländischen Kirche bis Kallistus,' ZKT 31 (1907) 433-73. The best evaluation of the dogmatic argument is that of J. Umberg, 'Absolutionspflicht und altchristl. Bussdisziplin,' *Scholastik* II (1927) 321 ff.

[7] That such parties of rigorists existed in Africa is clear from St. Cyprian, *Epist.* 55.21: *Et quidem apud antecessores nostros quidam de episcopis istic in provincia nostra dandam pacem moechis non puta-verunt et in totum paenitentiae locum contra adulteria clauserunt.*

[8] This is the view of Galtier I 201-6, Daly, *op. cit.*

70.845-48 and many others. Mortimer, however, *op. cit.* II, asserts, 'it is not true that Tertullian nowhere says he is combating an innovation,' and B. Botte, in his review of Daly's study, BTAM 6 (1950-53) 104 f., remarks that the problem is not to be solved by insisting that Tertullian's position in the *De pudicitia* represents a break with an earlier tradition which he had supported in the *De paenitentia.* Perhaps it is safest to say that rigorism and tolerance were in conflict from the beginning of the Church's history, and that Tertullian, who in his early years as a Christian favored a policy of moderation and leniency in dealing with sinners, eventually came to reject this policy and insist upon severity, not so much because he considered tolerance an innovation but because he considered that it was forbidden by the new revelation of the Paraclete.

[9] Poschmann I 330; cf., also, D'Alès III 203 f.

[10] Galtier I 209-20.

[11] Cf. Noeldechen, *op. cit.* 150-54; Harnack, *Chronologie* 286. . . .

Abbreviations

AC F.J. Dölger, Antike und Christentum. Münster i. W.

ACW Ancient Christian Writers, edit. J. Quasten and J. C. Plumpe. Westminster, Md.

ANF Ante-Nicene Fathers. Buffalo and New York

BALAC Bulletin d'ancienne littérature et d'archéologie chrétienne. Paris

BLE Bulletin de littérature ecclésiastique. Toulouse

BTAM Bulletin de théologie ancienne et médiévale. Louvain

DACL Dictionnaire d'archéologie chrétienne et de liturgie. Paris

DB Enchiridion symbolorum, 21st ed., ed. by H. Denzinger, C. Bannwart, J. B. Umberg

DCA Dictionary of Christian Antiquities, edit. W. Smith and S. Cheetham. Hartford

DCB Dictionary of Christian Biography, edit. W. Smith and H. Wace. London

DTC Dictionnaire de théologie catholique. Paris

ERE Encyclopedia of Religion and Ethics, edit. J. Hastings. New York and Edinburgh

ETL Ephemerides Theologicae Lovanienses. Louvain

HTR Harvard Theological Review. Cambridge, Mass.

IER Irish Ecclesiastical Record. Dublin

ITQ Irish Theological Quarterly. Dublin

JBL Journal of Biblical Literature. Philadelphia

JTS Journal of Theological Studies. London

LF Library of the Fathers. Oxford

LMB Le musée belge. Louvain

MSR Mélanges de science religieuse. Lille

NRT Nouvelle revue théologique. Tournai

PJ Philosophisches Jahrbuch der Görresgesellschaft. Fulda

RAC Reallexikon für Antike und Christentum, edit. Th. Klauser. Leipzig

RB Revue biblique. Paris

RE Realenzyklopädie der classischen Altertumswissenschaft, edit. E. Pauly, G. Wissowa. Stuttgart

RHE Revue d'histoire ecclésiastique. Louvain

RJ Enchiridion Patristicum, 11th ed., ed. by M. Rouët de Journel

RSR Recherches de science religieuse. Paris

SE Sacris Erudiri. Brugge

TG Theologie und Glaube. Paderborn

TLL Thesaurus linguae latinae. Leipzig

TQ Theologische Quartalschrift. Tübingen

TS Theological Studies. Woodstock, Md.

VC Vigiliae Christianae. Amsterdam

ZKT Zeitschrift für katholische Theologie. Innsbruck

ZNW Zeitschrift für die neutestamentliche Wissenschaft und die Kunde der älteren Kirche. Giessen

D'Alès I A. D'Alès, *La théologie de Tertullien* (Paris 1905)

D'Alès II A. D'Alès, *De paenitentia* (Paris 1926)

D'Alès III A. D'Alès, *L'édit de Calliste* (Paris 1914)

Borleffs I J. W. Ph. Borleffs, 'Observationes criticae in Tertulliani De paenitentia libellum,' *Mnemosyne* 60 (1932) 254-316

Borleffs II J. W. Ph. Borleffs, 'Un nouveau manuscrit de Tertullien,' VC 5 (1951) 65-79

Galtier I P. Galtier, *De paenitentia* (Rome 1950)

Galtier II P. Galtier, *L'Église et la rémission des péchés aux premiers siècles* (Paris 1932)

Galtier III P. Galtier, *Aux origines du sacrement de pénitence* (Rome 1951)

Hoppe I H. Hoppe, *Syntax und Stil des Tertullian* (Leipzig 1903)

Hoppe II H. Hoppe, *Beiträge zur Sprache und Kritik Tertullians* (Lund 1932)

Poschmann I B. Poschmann, *Paenitentia secunda. Die kirchliche Busse im ältesten Christentum bis Cyprian und Origenes* (Bonn 1940)

Poschmann II B. Poschmann, *Der Ablass im Licht der Bussgeschichte* (Bonn 1948)

Poschmann III B. Poschmann, *Busse und Letzte Ölung* (Handbuch der Dogmengeschichte, edit. M. Schmaus, J. Geiselmann, H. Rahner 4.3, Freiburg 1951)

Teeuwen I St. W. J. Teeuwen, *Sprachlicher Bedeutungswandel bei Tertullian* (Studien zur Geschichte und Kultur des Altertums 14.1, Paderborn 1926)

Teeuwen II St. W. J. Teeuwen, 'De voce *paenitentia* apud Tertullianum,' *Mnemosyne* 55 (1927) 410-19

Timothy D. Barnes (essay date 1969)

SOURCE: "Tertullian's *Scorpiace*," *The Journal of Theological Studies,* Vol. XX, 1969, pp. 105-32.

[*In the following essay, Barnes argues that Tertullian's* Scorpiace *was composed in 203-04, rather than during his post-207 Montanist period, as many scholars have contended.*]

Modern scholarship has been unjustly selective in its treatment of Tertullian. Some of his works, most notably the **Apologeticum** and **De Pallio,** receive lavish attention and repeated investigation; and even a lost treatise is capable of provoking lengthy speculations.[2] Yet other works, ultimately of no less importance, suffer almost total neglect. The consequences have been serious, for the general understanding of Tertullian no less than for the interpretation of the neglected treatises. Although the two most recent studies devoted specifically to its elucidation were published in 1927 and 1886,[3] the **Scorpiace** is habitually misdated by nearly a decade—and that under the influence of those two fundamental errors which, above all else, have so far prevented an accurate delineation of Tertullian's intellectual development.

The first error is to confuse Montanism with enthusiasm.[4] Even if Montanists manifested enthusiasm, Montanism possessed a definite and definable theological content. It is wrong to assume that Tertullian must already have embraced Montanist doctrines before he could write in a rigoristic or enthusiastic vein.[5] Rather, it was his natural propensity to rigorism which led him to Montanism.[6] The second error is to assume that no more than three outbreaks of persecution occurred in Africa during Tertullian's literary career: the first in 197, the occasion of the **Ad Nationes** and **Apologeticum;** the second in 202/3—the so-called 'persecution of Septimius Severus'; and the third in 211-13 (or 211/12), often styled 'the persecution of Scapula'. On this assumption are founded almost all recent attempts to determine the chronology of Tertullian's writings.[7] But it seems never to have been examined critically—let alone justified.

The standard date of the **Scorpiace** is 211-13.[8] It is deduced as follows. The **Scorpiace** was written at a time of persecution and in Tertullian's Montanist period. Tertullian's Montanist period began *c.* 207/8 . . . and during it there was only one outbreak of persecution, namely 'the persecution of Scapula'. 'Therefore, the **Scorpiace** dates from 211-13.[10] A different date was proposed long ago by H. Kellner. He argued that its placid tenor and theological orthodoxy preclude such a late date. Consequently, he supposed that the persecution during which it was composed was 'the Severan persecution', identified the festivities alluded to . . . as the *decennalia* of Severus, and assigned the **Scorpiace** to the middle of 203.[12]

Not many scholars have adopted Kellner's view that the **Scorpiace** is an early work of Tertullian.[13] The majority follow A. Harnack and P. de Labriolle in rejecting it, on two grounds. First, they hold its theological orthodoxy irrelevant to the date of the **Scorpiace,** and adduce the **Ad Scapulam** as a parallel. Securely dated to the late summer or autumn of 212 (3. 3),[14] it lacks all traces of Montanism and reads very much like a précis of the **Apologeticum** of nearly fifteen years earlier. Secondly, the **Scorpiace** contains an apparent reference (5. 1) to the second book of the **Adversus Marcionem,** which was not written before 207/8 (cf. i. 15. 1).[15]

The reasons given for rejecting Kellner's date are inadequate. Silence about the Christians' internal quarrels was necessary if Tertullian was to make out a good case to the proconsul Scapula. The willingness, or rather the eagerness, of all Christians to die for their faith and the untainted purity of their lives were apologetic commonplaces, whose effect was destroyed if the pleader turned to castigate Gnostics or Marcionites.[16] Admittedly, Justin had done just that.[17] But Tertullian, the superior orator, would not commit the same mistake.[18] A similar reticence was neither necessary nor desirable when Tertullian was attacking faint-hearted Gnostics for a purely Christian audience. The *Scorpiace* should be compared, not with the *Ad Scapulam,* but with two other treatises. The title of the *Adversus Valentinianos* proclaims its purpose, and the *De Anima* was intended to refute the psychological basis of several Gnostic philosophies. Yet the former styles a notorious Montanist pamphleteer 'Proculus noster' (*Val.* 5. 1),[19] and the latter describes a service celebrated in a Montanist conventicle (*An.* 9. 4).[20] As for the reference to the *Adversus Marcionem,* it is important to note Tertullian's exact words:

> longum est ut deum meum bonum ostendam, quod iam a nobis didicerunt Marcionitae (*Scorp.* 5. 1).

The extant *Adversus Marcionem* is the latest of three distinct works directed against Marcion's theology (*Marc.* i. 1. 1/2). The second closely preceded the third and was on the same scale as the five extant books. But the first was a much briefer tract, whose date is unknown.[21] Since no refutation of Marcion, however perfunctory, could avoid the proof of God's goodness,[22] the allusion in the *Scorpiace* can as easily be to the earliest as to the latest of the three treatises. It thus provides no evidence for its date.

The arguments so far advanced are not conclusive. The standard date of 211-13 is completely indefensible. But Kellner's date of 203 is deduced from the false premiss that the years 202/3 saw a sudden outbreak of persecution throughout the Roman Empire which was the result of an imperial edict.[23] The *Scor-piace* requires a full re-examination. Sections I-V of this article will establish that its theology and language indicate that it was written before Tertullian became a Montanist. Sections VI-VII will propose a precise date (late 203 or early 204), and VIII will adumbrate some consequences of its acceptance. For the problem has been posed incorrectly. Both Kellner and Harnack thought that the issue was a straight choice: the *Scorpiace* belonged to either 'the Severan persecution' or 'the persecution of Scapula'. But other dates are possible. Indeed, 221/2 has actually been proposed, though not supported by arguments or used to challenge the accepted chronological framework for Tertullian.[24]

I. The Argument

Tertullian habitually conformed to the precepts of an-

cient rhetorical theory, even when discussing philosophical or doctrinal subjects.[25] The *Scorpiace* is no exception, and is susceptible of the same sort of analysis as the *Apologeticum.*[26] What follows is not the only possible analysis. Some might prefer to distinguish two separate lines of argument: proof of the necessity of martyrdom (2-4; 8. 1-15. 6), and proof of its goodness (5-7). That would not affect the conclusions which will be drawn. None the less, the analysis offered here makes the general structure simpler and better articulated.

1. *Exordium,* including *narratio* (1. 6-8).

The scorpion is a dangerous beast.[27] Yet against its sting there are both natural antidotes and, for the Christian, faith.[28] But faith is attacked by a different sort of scorpion. When persecution rages the Gnostics, the Valentinians, and the faint-hearted attack simple Christians. Men are dying without cause, they say: for Christ died that we might not. Watchful faith can crush this scorpion. But now is a time of persecution, we are being hunted down, the poison is having its effect. An antidote, therefore, is needed: to provide one is my purpose in writing.[29]

2. 1/2 *Propositio.*

The goodness of martyrdom is entailed by its necessity. It is ordained by God, and what is ordained by God is good.

2. 2-14. 3 *Confirmatio,* including *reprehensio.*

(1) In the books of the Law God forbade (2. 2-14) and punished (3) idolatry. His purpose was to encourage martyrdom (4. 1).

> First objection: some invent another God who does not desire martyrdom, or reject our God who does, or else, if they cannot deny God, deny his will (4. 2).

> Reply: I have refuted such doctrines elsewhere. Here it suffices to note that the God who forbids idolatry is the God of Israel. We must obey him, and it is idolatry to suggest that there is another God (4. 3-5).

> Second objection: the goodness of God's will is called in question (5. 1).

> Reply:

> (i) God must be believed to be good; therefore his will too is good (5. 1-2).

> (ii) What God wills, i.e. martyrdom, is good because

it is the opposite of idolatry which is evil (5. 3-5).

(iii) Men's reluctance to be martyrs does not prove martyrdom to be evil (5. 5):

(*a*) Medical analogy: just as men try to avoid the surgery which will save their lives, so also they perversely shun martyrdom, which is God's medicine (5. 6-13);

(*b*) Athletic analogy:

(1) Martyrdom may be viewed as a contest set before us by God. In it we can escape and conquer the devil. Thus again God is helping us (6. 1-2);

(2) Competitors in earthly contests take injuries without complaining: the prizes to be won by martyrdom are far more glorious than in those (6. 2-11).

Third objection: it is said that God is a murderer (7. 1).

Reply: God does kill—but in order that the victim may live (7. 1-7).[30]

(II) Restatement of the issue (8. 1) and further proofs:

(*a*) In the Old Testament those who were moved by the spirit of God suffered martyrdom (8. 1-8);

(*b*) Christ ordained martyrdom for his followers (9; 11)—and he meant martyrdom here on earth, not in heaven as the Valentinians think (10);

(*c*) so too did the apostles Peter, John, and Paul (12-14).

15. *Peroratio.*[31]

The apostles' message is still valid: they proved its validity by their martyrdoms. If Prodicus or Valentinus had told them that Christians need not confess their faith on earth, lest God seem to be demanding human sacrifice or Christ seeking redemption for himself by men's deaths, they would have said 'Get thee behind me, Satan.' Men today should say the same. But Prodicus and Valentinus will harm no one—unless he has failed to drink this antidote to their poison.

II. The Essence Of Montanism

The rise of Montanism has provoked widely differing interpretations. A brief selection will illustrate their variety, even among English scholars. One sees in Montanism a return to the lost simplicity of Christianity's earliest days,[32] another 'Christianity perverted by fear of learning and speculation'.[33] A third holds it

to be a revival of that Phrygian fanaticism which of old inspired the orgiastic cult of Cybele and Attis.[34] Yet another, censoriously surveying nineteen centuries of aberration from Catholic Truth, refuses to take the phenomenon too seriously, and ascribes it to the peculiar geography of Phrygia.[35] A recent theory offers a sociological explanation: Montanism is to be regarded as 'a revolt, the prophetic and eschatological religion of the native countryside against the Hellenized Christianity of the towns'.[36] The most recent view, however, reverts to the preoccupations of an earlier age and blames Montanism on a familiar scapegoat: it was caused (or at least decisively influenced) by the local communities of Jews.[37]

Quot homines tot sententiae. To judge between them, or to perform the sadly neglected task of sifting fact from hostile and unfounded rumour, need not be attempted here.[38] It is necessary only to ascertain the distinguishing features of Montanism. How did the Montanist differ from any other Christian? To this question the ancients gave a unanimous answer: a Montanist was one who believed that the Holy Spirit had spoken through Montanus, Prisc(ill)a, and Maximilla.

A contemporary of Montanus, writing in Asia soon after, has left a detailed account of the origins of Montanism.[39] The devil took possession of Montanus, who began to utter ecstatic prophecies, and soon also of two women (i.e. Prisc(ill)a and Maximilla). After frequent deliberations on their prophecies, the churches in Asia pronounced them to be not of divine origin but profane, and the Montanists were excommunicated. About the same time, Irenaeus severely castigated those whose fear of false prophecy led them to deny the possibility of genuine prophecy within the church.[40]

In the earliest days the Spirit spoke not only through the chosen prophet and prophetesses, but also through their followers.[41] The *Passio Perpetuae* pleads for the public reading of worthy new examples of faith as well as the old, and proclaims that the Holy Spirit still speaks to men, in the new prophecies and visions promised long ago by God.[42] As a Montanist, Tertullian held the overriding sin of the Catholics to be that they quarrel with the Paraclete, deny the New Prophecy, refuse to receive the Spirit.[43] He wrote long tracts, now lost, on the subject of ecstatic possession,[44] and described how a woman in Carthage used to become ecstatic and converse with angels, sometimes even with God (*An.* 9. 4).[45] Later, as such prophecies ceased, Montanism crystallized into an institutional church.[46] But its adherents felt that the point at issue between themselves and the Catholics had not changed. Towards 400 a Montanist, desirous of converting the aristocratic Marcella, sent her a list of *testimonia* from St. John's Gospel to show that Jesus had promised to send the Paraclete. Jerome replied that the promise had been redeemed long ago when the Paraclete came to Jesus' original disciples, and appealed to the Acts of the Apostles.[47]

The cataloguers of heresies took the same view. Hippolytus observed on two separate occasions that the Montanists agreed with the orthodox on the creation of the universe and on questions relating to the Christ. Their disagreement consisted in regarding the prophecies of Montanus, Priscilla, and Maximilla as genuine. Hence their innovations in practical matters like fasting: they believed that the prophetesses had commanded them.[48] Epiphanius introduces the Phrygian heretics by stating that they accept both the Old and New Testaments and the resurrection of the dead, but err in vaunting their possession of the prophet Montanus and the two prophetesses. He concedes that their interpretation of the Trinity is orthodox: it is by 'taking notice of spirits of error and the promptings of demons' that they have cut themselves off from the church.[49] Similarly, Filastrius remarks that the Montanists accept the Prophets and the Law, believe in the Father, the Son, and the Holy Spirit, and expect the resurrection of the body, just as the church ordains. But they proclaim certain prophets of their own, whom neither the real Prophets nor the Christ foretold.[50]

Late writers alone accuse the Montanists of purely doctrinal heresy.[51] According to the anonymous author of the *Dialogus Montanistae et Orthodoxi,* followed by Didymus of Alexandria, they are guilty of three main errors: though the other two both concern their belief that Montanus, Priscilla, and Maximilla possessed genuine prophetic gifts, the most heinous of the three is to hold that the three *hypostaseis* are one person.[52] The charge is patently unfair and anachronistic. It is substantiated only by the quotation and tendentious exposition of an oracular saying of Montanus: 'I am the Father, the Son, and the Spirit.'[53] Apart from the dialogue, Didymus, and a very few others, all the ancients agreed that the Montanists' errors all either consist in or derive from their acceptance as genuine of the prophecies of Montanus, Prisc(ill)a, and Maxi-milla.

III. Tertullian as a Montanist

Jerome aptly summed up the manifestations of Tertullian's lapse into Montanism:

> ad Montani dogma delapsus in multis libris novae prophetiae meminit (*De Viris Illustribus,* 53).

He thus stated the main criterion for deciding which of Tertullian's works are Montanist in inspiration. But a slight amplification is desirable. . . . For present purposes five [occurrences (one or more) in Tertullian's treatises of certain words or phrases which are distinctive of Montanist beliefs][54] will be considered:[55]

1. The naming of Montanus, Prisc(ill)a,[56] or Maxi-milla;

2. Reference to the New Prophecy;

3. The designation of the Holy Spirit as the 'Paracletus';[57]

4. Abuse of the catholics as 'psychici';

5. 'Nos/vos' or 'noster/vester' used either explicitly or by implication to contrast Montanists with catholics. . . .

All the distinctive signs of Tertullian's Montanism are absent from the *Scorpiace.*[58] But their absence has almost always been adjudged insufficient to preclude a late date. Something positive is therefore needed. Is there nothing in the *Scorpiace* which a convinced Montanist could not have written? One passage at least seems to be of such a nature. Tertullian argues that, when Jesus said to his disciples 'Blessed are ye when men shall revile you and persecute you, etc.',[60] he was laying down a rule of conduct for all Christians:

> quamquam etsi omnem hanc persecutionem con-dicionalem in solos tunc apostolos destinasset, utique per illos cum toto sacramento, cum propagine no-minis, cum traduce spiritus sancti in nos quoque spectasset etiam persecutionis obeundae disciplina ut in hereditarios discipulos et apostolici seminis frutices (*Scorp.* 9. 3).[61]

Tertullian here states that communion with the Holy Spirit has been passed on from the original apostles to successive generations of their followers. He thus adheres to the position of the *De Praescriptione Haereticorum:*

> et perinde ecclesias apud unamquamque civitatem condiderunt, a quibus traducem fidei et semina doctrinae ceterae exinde ecclesiae mutuatae sunt et cottidie mutuantur ut ecclesiae fiant (20. 5);

> perinde utique et ceterae exhibent quos ab apostolis in episcopatum constitutos apostolici seminis traduces habeant (32. 3).

The central thesis of the *De Praescriptione Haereticorum* is that God's truth was revealed by Jesus to his disciples and that they in turn handed knowledge of it on to the churches which they founded.[62] The *Scorpiace* reiterates this doctrine, in a form which leaves no place for the New Prophecy of Montanus, Prisc(ill)a, and Maximilla.[63] Can Tertullian possibly have written the phrase 'cum traduce spiritus sancti' as a Montanist? It implicitly denies the legitimacy of prophecy outside the church; it implies that the Paraclete came to the apostles soon after the Ascension;[64] it effectively repudiates the central tenet of the Montanist's creed.

The implications of another passage are almost as strong. Tertullian exhorts his reader

> etsi adhuc clausum putas caelum, memento claves eius hic dominum Petro et per eum ecclesiae reliquisse, quas hic unusquisque interrogatus atque confessus feret secum (*Scorp.* 10. 8).

It has usually seemed possible to take these as the words of a Montanist.[65] But a comparison with the *De Praescriptione Haereticorum* and the *De Pudicitia* suggests otherwise.[66] In the latter, which is Montanist to the core, Tertullian angrily rejects his catholic opponents' appeal to Matt. 16: 18/19:

> de tua nunc sententia quaero, unde hoc ius ecclesiae usurpes. si quia dixerit Petro dominus: *super hanc petram aedificabo ecclesiam meam, tibi dedi claves regni caelestis,* vel: *quaecumque alligaveris vel solveris in terra, erunt alligata vel soluta in caelis,* idcirco praesumis et ad te derivasse solvendi et alligandi potestatem, id est ad omnem ecclesiam Petri propinquam? qualis es, evertens atque commutans manifestam domini intentionem personaliter hoc Petro conferentem? *super te,* inquit, *aedificabo ecclesiam meam,* et: *dabo tibi claves,* non ecclesiae, et: *quaecumque solveris vel alligaveris,* non quae solverint vel alligaverint (*Pud.* 21. 9/10).

In the former work, however, Tertullian probably accepted a different interpretation:

> latuit aliquid Petrum, aedificandae ecclesiae petram dictum, claves regni caelorum consecutum et solvendi et alligandi in caelis et in terris potestatem? (*Praes. Haer.* 22. 4)

The *Scorpiace* asserts, while the *De Pudicitia* denies, that the 'keys of heaven' passed from Peter to the church. Even if the *De Praescriptione Haereticorum* is not explicit on the occurrence of such a transfer, the relevance of the *De Pudicitia* is plain. Some attempt to gloss over the difficulty by pointing out, correctly enough, that in the *Scorpiace* Peter does not possess 'the power of the keys' in the technical sense of being entrusted with the absolute right of forgiving sins, but that he is merely the representative of the church.[67] But it is hard to believe that Tertullian could have chosen the precise words of the passage quoted (*Scorp.* 10. 8), if he was already a Montanist.

IV. Flight from Persecution

When persecution threatened in the second and third centuries, how was the Christian to comport himself? Clearly, he must be prepared to bear witness to and suffer for his faith rather than deny it. The Gnostics might maintain that it was not here on earth but in the timeless beyond that the witness was to be borne. But both orthodox and Montanist repudiated this doctrine. Hence the argument of the *Scorpiace* has seemed to be irrelevant to date.[68] Yet there was a third possibility, besides confession and denial: flight until danger was past—a course which commended itself to many a bishop.[69]

In the *De Patientia* and *Ad Uxorem* Tertullian allowed flight from persecution. In the former he speaks of it as normal:

> si fuga urgeat, incommoda fugae caro militat; si et carcer praeveniat, caro in vinculis, etc. (*Pat.* 13. 6).

In the latter he justifies the practice: even if not laudable, it is permissible—and at all events better than apostasy under torture (*Ux.* i. 3. 4). Later, however, in works which are demonstrably Montanist, he professed the deepest contempt for such cowardice. In the *De Corona Militis* he observes that rejection of the prophecies of the Holy Spirit inevitably entails avoidance of martyrdom: a man who rejects the prophecies appeals to the scriptures, packs his bag, and flees from city to city (1. 4/5). And he devoted a whole treatise to the problem.

The opening of the *De Fuga in Persecutione* states its subject:

> quaesisti proxime, Fabi frater, fugiendum necne sit in persecutione, quod nescio quid annuntiaretur (1. 1).

And Tertullian soon reveals what audience he is addressing:

> procuranda autem examinatio penes vos, <qui>, si forte Paracletum non recipiendo, deductorem omnis veritatis, merito adhuc etiam aliis quaestionibus obnixi estis (1. 1).

Thus the *De Fuga* is apparently written to convince those who are not Montanists that they ought not to flee from persecution.

Tertullian argues that persecution is sent by God to test men's faith (1. 2-3. 2): it is therefore good and not to be shunned (4). He then deals with two objections: that flight is better than apostasy (5), and was enjoined by Jesus (6-8). Next he argues from the conduct of the apostles (9), counters the claim that 'he who flees will fight again' (10), and castigates the clergy (11). Fabius thus has his answer (12. 1). But, Tertullian adds, buying off persecution is no better than flight (12. 1-14. 2)—and, since the way is narrow, a man needs the Paraclete (14. 3). The central argument is thus independent of Tertullian's Montanist beliefs. The Paraclete is named only at the very beginning and very end (1. 1; 14. 3). Elsewhere Tertullian uses 'spiritus', and then in a sense susceptible of an orthodox interpretation (as 6. 4). And his employment of Montanist oracles is circumspect and allusive (9. 4; cf. 11. 2). It follows that the *De Fuga* is not quite what it seems. It is not just a discussion of how a Christian is to behave in time of persecution: it is a Montanist *pro-trepticus*. For the conduct which is obligatory for every Christian (1. 2-14. 2) is in practice possible only for those who accept the guidance of the Paraclete (14. 3).

The historical situation and the theological presuppositions of the *De Fuga in Persecutione* and the *Scorpiace* are vastly different. In the *Scorpiace* the issue is whether the Christian has to bear witness when arrested; in the *De Fuga* whether to avoid arrest. Yet the two are not complementary. For, although one is directed against the Gnostic and the other against the catholic position, and both are addressed to the same audience (the ordinary Christians of Carthage), they give different advice. The *Scorpiace* seems to imply the possibility of flight: if its author and readers are being hunted like hares (1. 11), might they not run away like hares? The *De Fuga* explicitly repudiates not only flight but escape from persecution by bribery—'nummaria fuga' (12. 1); and it states that only those possessed by the Paraclete will have the courage to do what is required of them. There is an obvious explanation for these differences: the *Scorpiace* was written several years before the *De Fuga in Persecutione,* and before Tertullian became a Montanist.[70]

V. Language and Style

The language and style of the *Scorpiace* have on occasion been judged to put its composition close in time to that of the *De Fuga in Persecutione* and the *De Anima.* The judgement has been based on striking similarities of phrase or on the *Scorpiace's* possession of characteristics of Tertullian's late style.[71] The two types of argument demand separate consideration.

The *Scorpiace* (10. 8) shares with the *De Anima* (55. 5) the metaphor of the key(s) of heaven, and with the *De Fuga* a number of coincidences of phrase.[72] With some authors this might amount to proof of contemporaneity. But in the case of Tertullian there is an abundance of counter-examples: some turns of phrase and combinations of choice *exempla* so appealed to their author that he repeated them after an interval of several years. Thus the *Apologeticum* characterizes the Emperor Hadrian in a brilliant (and accurate) epigram: 'omnium curiositatum explorator' (5. 7). Later, probably almost a full decade later,[73] Tertullian adapted the phrase to describe a Father of the church: 'Irenaeus, omnium doctrinarum curiosissimus explorator' (*Val.* 5. 1). Again, much of the material in the *Apologeticum*

was used practically unchanged fifteen years later in the *Ad Scapulam.*[74] In the earlier work Tertullian proclaimed the loyalty of Christians to the emperor:

> unde Cassii et Nigri et Albini? . . . de Romanis, nisi fallor, id est de non Christianis. atque adeo omnes illi, sub ipsa impietatis eruptione, et sacra faciebant pro salute imperatoris et genium eius deierabant, alii foris, alii intus, et utique publicorum hostium nomen Christianis dabant (*Apol.* 35. 9/10).

In the later the claim is reiterated:

> sic et circa maiestatem imperatoris infamamur; tamen numquam Albiniani, nec Nigriani, vel Cassiani inveniri potuerunt Christiani, sed idem ipsi qui per genios eorum in pridie usque iuraverant, qui pro salute eorum hostias et fecerant et voverant, qui Christianos saepe damnaverant, hostes eorum sunt reperti (*Scap.* 2. 5).

And Tertullian displays his recondite knowledge of certain primitive Roman deities no less than four times:[75]

> taceo deos Forculum a foribus et Cardeam a cardinibus et liminum Limentinum, sive qui alii inter vicinos apud vos numinum ianitorum adorantur (*Nat.* ii. 15. 5);

> certi enim esse debemus, si quos latet per ignorantiam litteraturae saecularis, etiam ostiorum deos apud Romanos, Cardeam a cardinibus appellatam et Forculum a foribus et Limentinum a limine et ipsum Ianum a ianua (*Idol.* 15. 5);

> quas mihi potestates ianitrices adfirmas iuxta Romanam superstitionem, †Barnum[76] quendam et Forculum et Limentinum? (*Scorp.* 10. 6)

> at enim Christianus nec ianuam suam laureis infamabit, si norit, quantos deos etiam ostiis diabolus adfinxerit, Ianum a ianua, Limentinum a limine, Forculum et Carnam a foribus atque cardinibus (*Cor.* 13. 9).[77]

Whatever the date of the *Scorpiace* and the *De Idololatria,* the four works span at least eleven years: the *Ad Nationes* was written in 197,[78] and the *De Corona Militis,* a Montanist work, hardly earlier than 208.[79]

Thus mere coincidences of phrase between two of Tertullian's treatises, however striking, are a poor guide for chronology. And the *Scorpiace* itself is linked to the *Apologeticum,* no less than to the *De Anima* and *De Fuga in Persecutione.* The pair both describe Nero as the first persecutor with an appeal to Tacitus:[80]

> consulite commentarios vestros, illic reperietis pri-

mum Neronem in hanc sectam cum maxime Romae orientem Caesariano gladio ferocisse (*Apol.* 5. 3);

vitas Caesarum legimus: orientem fidem Romae primus Nero cruentavit (*Scorp.* 15. 3).

They also produce the same list of examples of human sacrifice:

infantes penes Africam Saturno immolabatur palam usque ad proconsulatum Tiberii . . . sed et nunc in occulto perseveratur hoc sacrum facinus . . . maior aetas apud Gallos Mercurio prosecabatur. remitto fabulas Tauricas theatris suis. sed et in illa religiosissima urbe Aeneadarum piorum est Iuppiter quidam, quem ludis suis humano sanguine proluunt (*Apol.* 9. 2-5);

sed enim Scytharum Dianam aut Gallorum Mercurium aut Afrorum Saturnum hominum victima placari apud saeculum licuit, et Latio ad hodiernum Iovi media in urbe humanus sanguis ingustatur (*Scorp.* 7. 6).

Style appears to offer a firmer basis for argument. Even if the number of precisely dated treatises is very small, the professedly Montanist works and the ***Ad Scapulam*** possess certain common features which distinguish them as a class from the demonstrably early and orthodox works. Tertullian's late style is marked by a slightly increasing use of anaphora and by the greatly increasing frequency of the word 'et'. Not only does 'et' often come in after other conjunctions, but Tertullian shows ever greater preference for syndeton with 'et' and distaste for asyndeton.[81] Such characteristics are all manifestations of a single trend towards a more rhythmical prose with more alliteration and rhyme. It is perhaps ironical that as Tertullian sank deeper into Montanism and thus (one might expect) became more estranged from the values of pagan civilization, his style became ever more mannered and artistic.[82] But his development has a wider relevance. His use of 'et', so far from being consistent or unchanging, is the most variable aspect of his style. Tertullian is, therefore, a standing refutation of those who would decide questions of literary attribution by 'scientific' statistics based on the principle that an author's use of common conjunctions must remain relatively constant.[83]

Where does the ***Scorpiace*** fit into the development of Tertullian's style? One passage either exemplifies or foreshadows his late use of 'et':

carceres illic et vincula et flagella et saxa et gladii et impetus Iudaeorum et coetus nationum et tribunorum elogia et regum auditoria et proconsulum tribunalia et Caesaris nomen interpretem non habent (15. 2).[84]

But it would be wrong to take this as proof of a late date. For the ***De Praescriptione Haereticorum*** exhibits the same phenomenon:

ubi metus in deum, ibi gravitas honesta et diligentia attonita et cura sollicita et adlectio explorata et communicatio deliberata et promotio emerita et subiectio religiosa et apparitio devota et processio modesta et ecclesia unita et dei omnia (43. 5).

In both works the example quoted is practically unique. It is perhaps more significant that the ***Scorpiace*** writes 'Teletos scilicet et Anicetos et Abascantos Valentini' (10. 1). Writing about 212 Tertullian would surely have preferred the order 'Valentini scilicet Teletos et Anicetos, Abascantos'—a use of 'et' characteristic of the works of his Montanist period, but rarely found anywhere in Latin literature outside Tertullian.[85] Furthermore, the ***Scorpiace***'s comparatively infrequent employment of 'et' for 'etiam'[86] and after other conjunctions[87] ranks it with the early works, as does its preference for asyndetic over syndetic combinations.[88]

To argue from its style alone that the ***Scorpiace*** must be an early work would hardly be legitimate. Nevertheless, if stylistic affinities are to count for anything, they too unequivocally indicate that the ***Scorpiace*** was composed before Tertullian became a Montanist.

VI. Some Imaginary Arguments

An over-zealous searcher for historical allusions in the ***Scorpiace*** once produced proof that its date was either 212 (his first guess) or 213 (the second).[89] He found allusions to Caracalla or Scapula (1. 10), to Caracalla's murder of Geta (8. 3), to his killing of Geta's partisans (3. 4/5) and to the *constitutio Antoniniana* (15. 3). The last allusion would probably now be held to imply a date no earlier than 214 or 215.[90] But no matter: the method of proof was questionable, and immediately drew forth sharp rebuke.[91] Nevertheless, the four alleged allusions must be examined.

First, Caracalla or Scapula as persecutor:

et nunc in praesentia rerum est medius ardor, ipsa canicula persecutionis, ab ipso scilicet cynocephalo (1. 10).

The allusion to the baboon could hardly be more obscure. But why imagine a reference to Caracalla, or Scapula, or, as some older commentators held,[92] to Severus or Plautianus? It is more plausible to see a reference to the devil.[93] That would explain the sarcastic 'scilicet' and the emphatic 'ipso': Tertullian is again (as in 1. 6-8) rehearsing the arguments of the Gnostics whom he is about to refute.[94] There may also be a pun. The dog-headed ape comes after the dog-star of persecution, and is appropriate to the metaphors of hot weather. For both baboons and the devil were associated with Egypt and Ethiopia.[95]

Secondly, Caracalla's murder of his brother:

> a primordio enim iustitia vim patitur. statim ut
> coli deus coepit, invidiam religio sortita est. qui
> deo placuerat occiditur, et quidem a fratre (8. 2/
> 3).

Cain's murder of Abel not only fits perfectly into its context but is also an obvious example for Tertullian to use here, with his predilection for arguments based on an object's origin or original qualities.[96] In fact, he names Cain on four other occasions—all of them earlier than the death of Geta on 26 December 211.[97]

Third, the deaths of Geta's sympathizers:

> itaque (sc. after making the golden calf) tria milia
> hominum a parentibus proximis caesa, quia tam
> proximum parentem deum offenderant . . . In Arith-
> mis cum divertisset Israel apud Sethim, abeunt libidi-
> natum ad filias Moab, invitantur ad idola, . . . ob
> hanc quoque idololatriam moechiae sororem viginti
> tria milia domesticis obtruncata gladiis divi-nae irae
> litaverunt (3. 4/5).

Tertullian adduces these two examples as proof that God always punishes idolatry and supersition: what more natural than the selection of these two striking episodes?[98]

Fourthly, the *constitutio Antoniniana:*

> tunc Paulus civitatis Romanae consequitur nati-
> vitatem, cum illic martyrii renascitur generositate
> (15. 3).

The Roman citizenship in question is surely Paul's. For it was only as a result of his possession of it that he was sent to Rome for trial.[99] Thus the sentence quoted may be· paraphrased: 'Paul reaped the reward of being born a Roman citizen, when he was reborn by his martyrdom in Rome.'[100]

Another theory claims to find literary derivation: the first chapter of the **Scorpiace** was inspired by the fourth book of Clement of Alexandria's *Stromateis,* the statements about the Gnostics being a mere literary device for introducing Tertullian's discussion, not the description of a historical situation.[101] If true, that need not affect the date of the **Scorpiace:** it might instead bring welcome precision to the chronology of Clement's life.[102] But the theory is baseless. The supposed literary derivation consists merely of factually similar reports of the Gnostics' reaction to persecution. Since their behaviour at such times tended always to be as Clement and Tertullian describe it,[103] the two need be no more than independent observers of the same phenomenon.

VII. *Pythicus Agon*

> adhuc Carthaginem singulae civitates gratulando
> inquietant donatam Pythico agone post stadii senec-
> tutem. ita ab aevo dignissimum creditum est studi-
> orum experimentum committere, artes corporum et
> vocum de praestantia expendere, praemio indice,
> spectaculo iudice, sententia voluptate (*Scorp.* 6. 2/
> 3).

Tertullian's sarcasm is plain. The stadium has become unfashionable, displaced from popular favour by the *Pythicus agon.* This was a musical contest with dancing and singing ('artes corporum et vocum') and, when Tertullian wrote, embassies were still arriving in Carthage to offer the congratulations of other African cities on its establishment. Can the allusion be dated?

The Carthaginian Pythia are attested by two inscriptions. One is too mutilated to permit any secure deduction about their nature;[104] the other commemorates the victory of a musical performer.[105] That was only to be expected. The Pythian games at Delphi, legend asserted, began with musical contests, athletics being added at a later stage.[106] And the countless Pythia which sprang up through the centuries in Hellenistic and Roman cities modelled themselves on the Delphian.[107]

It is hard, therefore, to divorce the *Pythicus agon* from the building of the odeum in Carthage, which was specifically designed for musical performances.[108] Three pieces of evidence set its construction *c.* 200. First, the archaeological remains have been excavated.[109] Secondly, an unfortunate experience of Apuleius soon after 160 may be relevant. One of his speeches, to the provincial *concilium* of Africa, was rained off and had to be postponed to the following day.[110] Odea, in contrast to theatres, were always roofed.[111] Thirdly, Tertullian reports a spectacular discovery during the digging of the foundations. A Punic cemetery was uncovered containing bones, which, though 500 years old, had hardly begun to decay (*Res. Mort.* 42. 8).

In the years around 200, one occasion seems far more likely than any other to have seen the construction of the odeum and the institution of the *Pythicus agon:* the visit of Septimius Severus to Carthage. Analogy supports the synchronism. The best-documented parallel is Hadrian in the east two generations earlier: there city after city seized on the opportunity afforded by the imperial presence to found new games or to refound old ones.[112] The habit did not die: games were founded in the east in honour of Severus' presence between 197 and 202,[113] and again as Caracalla proceeded to his Parthian war in 214/15.[114] In Africa cities sought and received benefits from Severus.[115] Carthage received the 'ius Italicum' (which meant exemption from direct taxation) and the grant was celebrated on the imperial coinage.[116] Tertullian represents the *Pythicus agon* too as a privilege granted to Carthage ('donatam'). Surely both grants were obtained from the emperor in person during his visit.

Can the visit be dated accurately? The movements of Severus are well known until 202. Proclaimed emperor at Carnuntum on 9 April 193, he marched on Rome and entered it in early June. Almost at once he set out for the east, where he remained until 196. Then he returned westwards to defeat Clodius Albinus at Lugdunum on 19 February 197, and departed again for the orient later that year, remaining there till 202. In 202 he returned to Rome to celebrate his *decennalia,* probably in June.[117] Now, however, the evidence fades out. It is certain that Severus was in Rome for the *ludi saeculares* in 204 (at the end of May),[118] and that he left the capital for the last time to go to Britain in 208.[119] Where is the African visit to be fitted in? Literary evidence is no help. Philostratus is the only extant author to mention it.[120] It is absent from the fragmentary text of Cassius Dio, and the author of the *Historia Augusta* lost interest in his good and detailed source for the reign of Severus as soon as he got the emperor to Egypt (in 199).[121] There remains the more ambiguous testimony of coins and inscriptions.

Some numismatists have inferred from the coins that the imperial visit to Africa belongs to 206/7.[122] But the coins celebrate imperial favours to Carthage on issues of 203 and 204.[123] More important, the *familia rationis castrensis* erected two dedications to Severus at Lambaesis in 203.[124] Therefore, since this body habitually accompanied the emperor, the emperor and his entourage were in Numidia at some time in 203.[125] Severus went to Lepcis, and perhaps conducted a brief campaign against the nomads of Tripolitania:[126] consequently, his stay in Africa presumably included a winter.[127] But which date is preferable, 202/3 or 203/4? Opinions differ.[128] The coins appear to favour 203/4.[129] But it was in 202 that the inhabitants of Lepcis assumed the title of 'Septimiani' and commissioned dedications to the emperor and his elder son 'ob eximiam ac divinam in se indulgentiam'.[130] That implies that Lepcis was granted the 'ius Italicum' in 202,[131] and that the imperial house stayed there for the winter of 202/3.[132]

What of Carthage? Perhaps Severus visited the city once only, at the end of his stay in Africa. The emperor was lavish in his generosity to Lepcis as his *patria:* besides granting fiscal privilege, he imported Greek architects and sculptors to rebuild a large part of the city in extravagant magnificence.[133] Such devotion to Lepcis could be advertised widely by a simple expedient: Severus could make it his port of disembarkation in Africa. Cities vied for the honour of being

the first in a province to receive a mere governor. In his *De Officio Proconsulis* Ulpian advised proconsuls to enter their provinces by the normal route: the provincials considered it a matter of great importance. The people of Asia, he records, obtained a rescript from Caracalla making it obligatory for the proconsul of Asia to land at Ephesus.[134] Hence the apparent conflict of evidence of the date of Severus' tour of Africa can easily be resolved. As follows:

> late summer/autumn 202—Severus sails to Lepcis; spring 203—he travels from Lepcis (via Theveste) to Lambaesis; mid-203—journey from Lambaesis (via Cirta) to Carthage and return to Italy.[135]

If this reasoning is admitted as correct, a precise date can be deduced for the **Scorpiace.** If the *Pythicus agon* was instituted to celebrate Severus' visit to Carthage in the summer of 203, the **Scorpiace** was written at the end of 203 or early in 204: neither so long after the visit that embassies of congratulation had stopped arriving, nor so soon afterwards that their arrival was not worthy of remark.

VIII. Conclusions

There have been three stages in the argument. Two arrive at firm conclusions, while the third is more speculative. First, its argument and theology exclude a date for the **Scorpiace** later than Tertullian's conversion to Montanism (sections I-IV). Second, its language and style indicate that it belongs among his early works (V). Third, an allusion to the *Pythicus agon* seems to permit the deduction of a precise date, viz. late 203 or early 204 (VI-VII). On the last point, caution is necessary. Unavoidably, reliance has been placed on the fallible instruments of historical analogy and conjecture. None the less, in default of disproof, let the date of 203/4 stand as a working hypothesis. What consequences follow?

Several of the fixed points are removed from the standard chronology of Tertullian, which has been founded on three erroneous assumptions. One assumption is that Tertullian became a priest and, for a spell, largely occupied himself writing sermons: hence his treatises in this genre could all be grouped together and dated either *c.* 197 or soon after 200.[136] Though it has the support of Jerome, the view that Tertullian was a priest is false.[137] A second assumption used to be that the **De Pudicitia** attacked Callistus, Bishop of Rome *c.* 220.[138] This identification of Tertullian's adversary is now rightly discarded by most scholars—but the date deduced from it is still sometimes accorded the status of fact.[139] The third and most pernicious assumption has been that all Tertullian's writings which were composed at a time of persecution belonged to one of three specific outbreaks (197, 202/3, 211-13). If the **Scorpiace** was written late in 203 or early in 204, the assumption is proved false. What justification will remain, therefore, for continuing to assign the **Ad Martyras** and **De Spectaculis** precisely to 197 or 202, the **De Corona Militis** to 211, or the **De Fuga in Persecutione** to 212?[140]

Once these fixed points disappear, previous reconstructions of the chronology of Tertullian can be replaced by something fundamentally new which lacks their defects. There will be an important corollary for the understanding of Tertullian. A new order for his writings cannot fail to force a revaluation of his intellectual development. A recent and vivid vignette of Tertullian contains the following two sentences:

> Tertullian's hatred for the Roman Empire seems to have grown over the years. In **De Idololatria** (*circa* 211) he does not trouble to affirm the formal loyalty which characterizes the **Apology** fourteen years before.[141]

The statements in the **De Idololatria** appear in a different light when the treatise is dated correctly. There is no trace of Montanism in it;[142] stylistically it belongs with other early works;[143] and one passage even seems to put its composition before that of the **Apologeticum**.[144]

The misdating of Tertullian's works derives in large part from a misinterpretation of the nature of persecution in the Roman Empire, especially in the age of the Severi. Ecclesiastical historians have mostly followed Eusebius in supposing that the persecutions of the first decade of the third century were practically confined to the years 202 and 203 and were the direct result of imperial action. They have also improved on Eusebius by identifying this imperial action as an edict of Septimius Severus concerning the Christians which is reported by the *Historia Augusta*.[145] But the edict is demonstrably fictitious, and the ecclesiastical historians have neglected accurate chronology.[146] For Egypt, there is unimpeachable evidence to refute Eusebius and show persecution continuing at least until 205 or 206.[147] If the **Scorpiace** was written in late 203 or early 204, a similar argument becomes available for persecution in Africa. Thus the **Scorpiace** is relevant to one of the central problems which confront any student of the ancient world, or of Christianity: how to penetrate behind the interpretation of Eusebius to the realities of early Christian history. Eusebius regarded the persecution of Christians as an abnormal state of affairs,[148] and connected its varying incidence with the reigns of different emperors.[149] Hence he supposed Severus the direct instigator of the persecution in Alexandria which involved Origen.[150] Hence too, perhaps, he wrongly assigned the death of Polycarp to the reign of Marcus Aurelius, for him a reign of persecution, instead of that of Antoninus Pius.[151] The implications of such errors are profound. In matters large or small, to scrutinize

Eusebius critically, not to trust him blindly[152]—that is the way of truth.

APPENDIX

> illic constitues et synagogas Iudaeorum, fontes persecutionum, apud quas apostoli flagella perpessi sunt, et populos nationum cum suo quidem circo, ubi facile conclamant: usque quo genus tertium? (*Scorp.* 10. 10)

Some still cite this famous utterance as proof that the Jews were prominent in fomenting the persecution of Christians in the Carthage of Tertullian's day.[153] But that is to ignore, not merely the immediate context ('apud quas apostoli flagella perpessi sunt')[154], but also a general characteristic of the writer. Tertullian is maintaining, against the Gnostics, that the Christian must be prepared to suffer for his faith here on earth, not just in heaven. The point is driven home by a *reductio ad absurdum*. The Gnostic view entails that persecution and hatred will be encountered in heaven: hence the Gnostic must imagine that the Jews who persecuted the apostles and the mob howling in the amphitheatre will be there, not here on earth. That is obviously false, and entails the falsity of the Gnostic position. Tertullian's choice of examples is careful and deliberate. The second is the contemporary fact, the first is the earliest persecution of the Christians. Ter-tullian is employing a favourite mode of argument: he focuses attention on the origins of persecution. For he held that what was true of an object's origin was necessarily always true of the object itself:

> omne genus ad originem suam censeatur necesse est (*Praes. Haer.* 20. 7).[155]

Notes

[1] I am very grateful for the kind assistance and criticisms of Professor H. Chadwick and Dr. F. G. B. Millar.

[2] Viz. *Ad amicum philosophum,* known only from Jerome, *Ep.* xxii. 22; *Adversus Jovinianum,* i. 13: P. Frassinetti, 'Gli scritti matrimoniali di Seneca e Tertulliano', *Rendiconti Istituto Lombardo,* Classe di Lettere, lxxxviii (1955), pp. 151-88; C. Tibiletti, 'Un opusculo perduto di Tertulliano: Ad amicum philosophum', *Atti Torino,* Ser. ii, xcv (1960-1), pp. 122-66.

[3] Respectively, E. Buonaiuti, 'L' "Antiscorpionico" di Tertulliano', *Richerche religiose,* iii (1927), pp. 146-52; E. Noeldechen, 'Das Odeum Karthagos und Tertullian's Scorpiace. 212', *Zeitschr. für kirchl. Wissenschaft und kirchl. Leben,* vii (1886), pp. 87-98.
[4] For justification of this term, R. A. Knox, *Enthusi-*

asm (1950), pp. 1 ff.

[5] Compare two verdicts on the *De Idololatria:* P. Monceaux, *Rev. phil.*[2] xxii (1898), p. 89, found it 'tout montaniste d'inspiration', and dated it to 211/12; A. Harnack, *Die Chronologie der altchristlichen Litteratur bis Eusebius,* ii (1904), p. 273, retorted 'Rigorismus ist nicht Montanismus', and dated it *c.* 200.

[6] H. von Campenhausen, *Theologische Blätter,* viii (1929), col. 198.

[7] That is, since the discovery of the best recension of the *Acts of the Scillitan Martyrs,* and their consequent redating from 200-2 to 180. Complete documentation would be pointless: dissent alone I have tried to register in full.

[8] See the catalogue of proposed dates (lamentably incomplete) at R. Braun, *'Deus Christianorum'. Recherches sur le vocabulaire doctrinal de Tertullien* (*Publ. Fac. des Lettres d'Alger,* xli, 1962), p. 574. Most recently, W. H. C. Frend, *Rivista di storia e letteratura religiosa,* iv (1968), pp. 8/9, uses the *Scorpiace* as evidence for the conduct of Jews in Carthage *c.* 212. . . .

[10] e.g., G. N. Bonwetsch, *Die Schriften Tertullians nach der Zeit ihrer Abfassung* (1878), p. 52—though admitting 203 as also possible. . . .

[12] H. Kellner, *Der Katholik*[2], xlii (1879), p. 567; *Wetzer und Welte's Kirchenlexicon*[2], xi (1899), col. 1401; H. Kellner-G. Esser, *Tertullians ausgewählte Schriften ins deutsche übersetzt,* ii (*Bibliothek der Kirchenväter,* xxiv, 1915), pp. 21 ff.

[13] At the time of writing I am aware only of E. Altendorf, *Einheit und Heiligkeit der Kirche* (*Arbeiten zur Kirchengeschichte,* xx, 1932), p. 38 n. 19, quoting a verbal opinion of H. von Soden; E. von Petersdorff, *Daemonologie,* i (1956), p. 416 n. 1528; and K. Aland, *Kirche und Staat: Festschrift für Bischof D. Hermann Kunst* (1967), p. 30, who refers in passing and without amplification to 'die Frühschrift Scorpiace'. Braun, op. cit., p. 574, fails to register a single adherent of the early date.

[14] Cf. B. E. Thomasson, *Die Statthalter der römischen Provinzen Nordafrikas von Augustus bis Diocletianus,* ii (1960), pp. 112/13.

[15] Harnack, op. cit., p. 284 n. 3; P. de Labriolle, *La Crise montaniste* (1913), pp. 445/6.

[16] Willingness to die: Justin, *Apol.* i. 8, 57; ii. 4; Athenagoras, *Legatio,* 3; Tatian, *Or. ad Graecos,* 4; Tertullian, *Apol.* 1. 12; *Scap.* 1. 1; etc. Purity of life: Justin, *Apol.* i. 14; ii. 2; Athenagoras, *Legatio,* 10;

Tatian, *Or. ad Graecos,* 33; Theophilus, *Ad Autolycum,* iii. 13 ff.; Tertullian, *Apol.* 3. 3; *Scap.* 2. 3; etc.

[17] *Apol.* i. 16; 26.

[18] *Apol.* 44. 3 makes it true by definition that no Christian can ever commit any ordinary crime.

[19] For Proculus, see Eusebius, *H.E.* ii. 25. 6; [Tertullian], *Adv. omn. haer.* 7. 2; Pacianus, *Ep.* i. 2 (*P.L.* xiii, col. 1053); Jerome, *De Viris Illustribus,* 59.

[20] J. H. Waszink, *Tertulliani De Anima* (1947), pp. 167 ff.

[21] G. Quispel, *De Bronnen van Tertullianus' Adversus Marcionem* (1943), p. 3, plausibly dates it after the *De praescriptione Haereticorum*—but the date of that cannot be determined with any precision.

[22] Note Irenaeus, *Adv. Haer.* i. 25. 1: the salient fact about Marcion is his blasphemy in making God the author of evil.

[23] Kellner, op. cit. (1899), col. 1401: 'die Schrift gehört entschieden in die Zeit einer schweren, grossen, lange dauernden und allgemeinen Verfolgung, also in die Zeit der severianischen'. . . .

[24] P. de Labriolle, *Histoire de la littérature latine chrétienne* (1920), ad fin., Tableau N° 2, cf. p. 137. The date is professedly taken from Monceaux—who put the *Scorpiace* in 211 or 212 (op. cit., p. 92).

[25] Demonstrated in detail in an unpublished study by R. D. Sider, *Structure and Method of Argument in the Writings of Tertullian* (Oxford D.Phil. thesis, 1965).

[26] On which, most recently, R. Braun, *Hommages à J. Bayet* (1964), pp. 114-21.

[27] Tertullian opens with a stylized set-piece (cf. *Marc.* i. 1. 3). One may compare several orations of Dio of Prusa: the first, for example, begins with a story about Timotheus the flute-player and Alexander the Great. . . .

[28] Cf. Galen, . . . 1. 13 (*Corp. Med. Gr.* v. 4. 2, p. 392 = vi, pp. 754/5 Kühn). . . .

[29] Galen gives the recipes for several antidotes against the scorpion's sting (*De Antidotis,* ii. 12 = xiv, pp. 175 ff. Kühn). Another metaphor was available. Cf. 1. 2: *aliquid et magia circumligat; Pap. Gr. Mag.* vii, ll. 193 ff. . . .

[30] A. Vaccari, *Scritti di erudizione e di filologia,* ii (1958), pp. 7-11, contends that the quotation 'Sophia iugulavit filios suos' comes, not from Prov. 9: 2, but

from Ecclus. 4: 11. For Tertullian's introduction 'voce Solomonis' (7. 1), he compares Clement, *Stromateis,* vii. 105. 1.

[31] 15. 1-5 serve a double function: as part of the peroration, and as a continuation of the argument of 12-14.

[32] J. de Soyres, *Montanism and the Primitive Church* (1878), p. 107.

[33] H. M. Gwatkin, *Early Church History,* ii² (1912), p. 73.

[34] H. H. Milman, *History of Latin Christianity,* i⁴ (1867), p. 47.

[35] Knox, op. cit., pp. 25, 29.

[36] W. H. C. Frend, *Martyrdom and Persecution in the Early Church* (1965), pp. 290-4, esp. 294.

[37] J. M. Ford, *J.E.H.* xvii (1966), pp. 145-58.

[38] There is a good general survey of the sources for Montanism by K. Aland, 'Bemerkungen zum Montanismus und zur frühchristlichen Eschatologie', *Kirchengeschichtliche Entwürfe* (1960), pp. 105-48. One example will illustrate what still needs to be done. Frend, op. cit., p. 290, thinks it probable that Montanus was a castrated priest of Cybele, while E. Evans, *Tertullian's Treatise against Praxeas* (1948), p. 75, states it as an unimpeachable fact. On what grounds? That Jerome, *Ep.* xli. 4, calls him 'abscisum et semivirum'. This is evidence, not for Montanus, but for Jerome's propensity to reckless and unfounded invective: see D. S. Wiesen, *St. Jerome as a Satirist* (1964), pp. 166 ff., esp. 177.

[39] Quoted by Eusebius, *H.E.* v. 16.

[40] *Adv. Haer.* iii. 11. 9.

[41] Eusebius, *H.E.* v. 16. 14.

[42] *Pass. Perp.* 1. 1, 1. 4. On the date and reliability of the document, see now *J.T.S.,* N.S. xix (1968), pp. 521-5.

[43] *Prax.* 1. 1 ff.; etc. Cf. below, pp. 113-15.

[44] Jerome, *De Viris Illustribus,* 24, 40, 53.

[45] Such conversations were, of course, no prerogative of the Montanists; but the connotations of the passage are clear (Waszink, op. cit., pp. 167/8; 484/5).

[46] Ambrosiaster, *Comm. in Ep. i ad Tim. 3. 2.* (*P.L.* xvii, col. 470/496); Jerome, *Ep.* xli. 3. Which is rel-

evant to the nature of Montanism: see J. G. Davies, *J.T.S.,* N.S. vi (1955), pp. 90-4.

[47] Jerome, *Ep.* xli. 1.

[48] *Philosophoumena,* viii. 19; x. 25.

[49] *Panarion,* xlviii. 1. 3/4.

[50] *Divers. Haeres.* xlix. 1/2 (*C.S.E.L.* xxxviii, p. 26; *C.C.L.* ix, p. 238).

[51] Listed by Aland, op. cit., p. 117 n. 94; cf. pp. 111/12.

[52] *Dialogus Montanistae et Orthodoxi:* G. Ficker, *Zeitschr. für Kirchengesch.* xxvi (1905), pp. 452 ff.; P. de Labriolle, *Les sources de l'histoire du Montanisme* (1913), pp. 97 ff.; Didymus, *De Trinitate,* iii. 41 (*P.G.* xxxix, cols. 983 ff.). For the dependence of the latter, see G. Bardy, *Didyme l'aveugle* (1910), pp. 237/8. P. de Labriolle, *Bull. d'anc. litt. et d'arch. chrét.* iii (1913), p. 286, explained the apparent plagiarism by supposing the *Dialogus* an early work of Didymus himself.

[53] This oracle has sometimes been gravely misunderstood in yet another way. A. Hilgenfeld, *Ketzergeschichte des Urchristentums* (1884), p. 592, gave the true interpretation: 'Montanus wollte . . . nur in Namen des Vaters, des Sohnes und des Paraklet reden.' Yet Knox, op. cit., p. 37, seems to take Montanus to claim that he himself was the Paraclete.

[54] Cf. Labriolle, *La Crise montaniste,* pp. 354 ff.

[55] A comprehensive treatment could not ignore other signs of Montanism, especially 'agnitio spiritalium charismatum' (*Mon.* 1. 2; etc.): cf. A. Hilgenfeld, *Die Glossolalie in der alten Kirche* (1850), pp. 115 ff.

[56] Cf. Labriolle, op. cit., p. 23 n. 1.

[57] I exclude, of course, *Praes. Haer.* 8. 14/15: there, and there alone in Tertullian, John 16: 13 is given an orthodox interpretation.

[58] Even this obvious truth has on occasion been denied. A. Réville, *Revue des deux mondes²,* liv (1864), p. 178, classed the *Scorpiace* as one of the treatises which 'appartiennent visiblement à la période du montanisme déclaré'. . . .

[60] Matt. 5: 11; Luke 6: 22.

[61] Cf. in general W. Bender, *Die Lehre über den Heiligen Geist bei Tertullian* (*Münchener Theol. Stud.* xviii, 1961).

[62] Cf. R. F. Refoulé, *Tertullien: Traité de la Prescrip-*

tion contre les Hérétiques (*Sources chrétiennes,* xlvi, 1957), pp. 45 ff., 82 ff.

[63] Compare *Marc.* iv. 5. 2/3. As a Montanist, Tertullian still held that the apostolic succession was a mark of true doctrine. What he had ceased to believe was that it was a vehicle for the transmission of the Holy Spirit.

[64] As *Praes. Haer.* 20. 4; cf. Irenaeus, *Adv. Haer.* iii. 11. 9.

[65] Thus K. Adam, *Theol. Quartalschrift,* xciv (1912), p. 205; Waszink, op. cit., p. 6*. I have not seen J. Ludwig, *Die Primatworte Mt. 16. 18, 19 in der altkirchlichen Exegese* (*Neutestamentliche Abhand.* xix. 4, 1952). But the passage had already been adduced as an indication of the *Scorpiace*'s early date by Kellner, op. cit., col. 1401.

[66] Altendorf, op. cit., pp. 37/8.

[67] So Adam, op. cit., p. 205. Cf. Altendorf, op. cit., p. 38.

[68] A. Orbe, *Los primeros herejes ante la persecución* (*Analecta Gregoriana,* lxxxiii, 1956), esp. pp. 50 ff., 90 ff. (assuming the date to be 213).

[69] See the evidence assembled by H. Leclercq, *Dict. d'arch. chrét.* v (1923), cols. 2660 ff. For the modern Catholic view, note G. Bardy, *Dict. de théol. cath.* xv (1946), col. 138, on the *De Fuga:* 'il condamne, avec une exagération manifeste, la fuite en temps de persécution.'

[70] The order is often implausibly reversed: e.g., Buonaiuti, op. cit., p. 146.

[71] E. Noeldechen, 'Die Abfassungszeit der Schriften Tertullians', *T.U.* v. 2 (1888), pp. 1-164, at pp. 91-4, 111-14; Waszink, op. cit., p. 6*; G. Säflund, *De Pallio und die stilistische Entwicklung Tertullians* (*Skr. utg. av Svenska Inst. i Rom,* viii, 1955), p. 72.

[72] Listed by Noeldechen, op. cit., pp. 111-13.

[73] Cf. above, p. 114. The earliest precisely datable sign of Tertullian's Montanism falls in 207/8 (*Marc.* i. 29. 4. cf. 15. 1).

[74] The *Ad Scapulam* was written in late 212 . . . ; the *Apologeticum* in 197 or very soon after (A. Harnack, *Zeitschr. für Kirchengesch.* ii (1878), pp. 574 ff.).

[75] The names come from Varro, *Nat.* ii. 1. 8. Cf. R. Agahd, *Jahrbücher für classische Philologie,* Supp. xxiv (1898), pp. 1-220, esp. pp. 185/6.

[76] 'Barnus' is nowhere else attested: *Thes. ling. lat.* ii, col. 1755.

[77] For the sake of consistency I have quoted from *C.C.L.* i/ii. W. Otto, *Thes. ling. lat., Onomasticon,* ii, cols. 200/1, argued convincingly that Tertullian himself always used the form 'Carna', which was later corrupted except at *Cor.* 13. 9.

[78] Cf. C. Becker, *Tertullians Apologeticum. Werden und Leistung* (1954), pp. 33-5.

[79] *Cor.* 1. 1 records an imperial donative to the soldiers. Usually assumed to be for the accession of Caracalla and Geta in February 211, it could instead be for their joint consulates in 208 (cf. G. Barbieri, *Diz. epig.* iv, cols. 859/60).

[80] Not Suetonius: *J.R.S.* lviii (1968), p. 35.

[81] Säflund, op. cit., pp. 60 ff.

[82] Cf. E. Norden, *Die antike Kunstprosa*² (1909), pp. 606 ff.

[83] As A. Q. Morton, *Journal of the Royal Statistical Society,* Ser. A. cxxviii (1965), pp. 169-224; *Essays in Memory of G. H. C. Macgregor* (1965), pp. 209 ff.; etc. Morton has already been subjected to devastating criticism by G. Herdan, *Journal of the Royal Statistical Society,* Ser. A. cxxviii (1965), pp. 229-31—to which he was unable to contrive a relevant reply (ibid., p. 233).

[84] Quoted by Säflund, op. cit., p. 72, as coming from one of 'den Schriften aus der Zeit des grossen Verfolgung des Jahres 211/12'.

[85] E. Löfstedt, *Zur Sprache Tertullians* (1920), pp. 29-33.

[86] See Säflund's statistics, op. cit., p. 60.

[87] Cf. Säflund, op. cit., p. 64. For the *Scorpiace* and the *De Fuga in Persecutione,* I make the occurrences of 'nam et', 'sed et', 'sic et', and 'ita et' at the beginning of a sentence come to approximately 1 and 2 per 1,000 words respectively.

[88] Cf. Säflund, op. cit., pp. 65 ff. For the *Scorpiace* I leave this as a largely subjective judgement: complications are imported by the long quotations and expositions of scripture.

[89] E. Noeldechen, op. cit. (1886), pp. 95-8; op. cit. (1888), pp. 13, 112, 114; *Historisches Taschenbuch*⁶, vii (1888), pp. 188-90.

[90] F. Millar, *J.E.A.* xlvii (1962), pp. 124-31, argues for autumn 214 as the date of the *constitutio.* Later discus-

sions have neither reinstated the traditional date of 212 nor established a third date as the correct one.

[91] G. Kr(üger), *Literarisches Centralblatt für Deutschland,* 1889, col. 459, protested that Noeldechen's methods 'die Citrone ausquetschen, bis weniger als Nichts vom Saft darin bleibt'. Noeldechen was undeterred: see his article 'Zeitgeschichtliche Anspielungen in den Schriften Tertullians', *Zeitschrift für wissenschaftliche Theologie,* xxxii (1889), pp. 411-29.

[92] Pamelius and Junius (reported by F. Oehler, *Tertulliani quae supersunt omnia,* i (1853), p. 498).

[93] So *Thes. ling. lat.* iv, col. 1590, following Rigaltius and Oehler, but not citing any sort of parallel: Rigaltius had observed simply 'diabolo, canina invidia genus humanum vexante'. That is insufficient. The devil could, of course, take any shape: *Martyrium Petri et Pauli,* 14 (*Acta Apostolorum Apocrypha,* ed. R. A. Lipsius and M. Bonnet (1891-1903), i, p. 132); *Acta Petri et Pauli,* 35 (ibid., p. 194); *Acta Thomae,* 44 (ibid. ii. 2, p. 161); Athanasius, *Vita Antonii,* 6-9; etc.

[94] Cf. Origen, *Contra Celsum,* vi. 30 (on the seven archontic daemons which Celsus ascribed to the Christians). . . . But the devil as a dog is comparatively common—witness Goethe's *Faust.*

[95] Baboons: Pliny, *Nat. Hist.* vi. 184, 190. The devil: F. J. Dölger, *Die Sonne der Gerechtigkeit und der Schwarze* (*Liturgiegeschichtliche Forschungen,* ii, 1918), pp. 52 ff.

[96] . . . H. Pétré, *L'exemplum chez Tertullien* (n.d., publ. 1941), pp. 97/8.

[97] *Marc.* ii. 25. 3 ff.; *Orat.* 7. 3; *Pat.* 5. 16; *Val.* 29. 1/ 2. The date of Geta's death: *J.T.S.,* N.S. xix (1968), pp. 522-5.

[98] From Exod. 32; Numb. 25. Cf. Pétré, op. cit., pp. 101-3.

[99] Acts 22: 25 ff. On the legal issue, see P. D. A. Garnsey, *J.R.S.* lvi (1966), pp. 182 ff.

[100] For 'nativitas', see H. Rönsch, *Itala und Vulgata*[2] (1875), p. 52; H. Hoppe, *Syntax und Stil des Tertullian* (1903), p. 122. 'Nativitatem consequi' seems very bold—even for Tertullian.

[101] Buonaiuti, op. cit., pp. 149/50, 152. In particular, he contends that Tertullian has copied Clement's reports of the denigration of martyrdom by Heracleon and Basilides (*Stromateis,* iv. 71/2, 81).

[102] Cf. H. Chadwick, *Early Christian Thought and the Classical Tradition* (1966), p. 31: 'the only certain date in his biography is that he wrote the first book of the *Stromateis* between 193 and 211.'

[103] W. H. C. Frend, 'The Gnostic Sects and the Roman Empire', *J.E.H.* v (1954), pp. 25-37.

[104] *Arch.-epigr. Mitt. aus Oesterreich-Ungarn,* viii (1884), pp. 219/20, no. 49 (Perinthus: third century). . . . [The] man it honours could well be a musician: cf. F. W. Hasluck, *Cyzicus* (1910), pp. 210 ff., for the cult.

[105] *I.L.S.* 5233 (Ostia: third century). Dessau noted 'citharoedus puto vel tibicen'.

[106] Pausanias, x. 7. 2 ff.

[107] The best collections of evidence are still those of J. H. Krause, *Die Gymnastik und Agonistik der Hellenen* (1841), pp. 791 ff.; *Die Pythien, Nemeen und Isthmien* (1841), pp. 53 ff. See also some of the inscriptions discussed by L. Robert, *Anatolian Studies presented to W. H. Buckler* (1939), pp. 237 ff.; *Hellenica* xi/xii (1960), pp. 350 ff.

[108] A. Audollent, *Carthage romaine* (1901), p. 258; P. Lenschau, P-W, x, cols. 2206/7. The only epigraphic evidence for the odeum seems to be the obscure and fragmentary *I.L.T.* 983.

[109] P. Gauckler, *Rev. arch.*[3] xli (1902), pp. 383 ff. The underlying Punic necropolis (*Res. Mort.* 42. 8) was also found.

[110] *Florida,* 16 (p. 26 Helm). The date was perhaps 163 precisely. For *Florida,* 9 (p. 15) names Severianus, 17 (p. 31) Scipio Orfitus as proconsul of Africa. Their proconsular years were, respectively, 162/3 and 163/4: R. Syme, *Rev. ét. anc.* lxi (1959), pp. 316 ff.

[111] Daremberg-Saglio, *Dict. des ant.* iv, cols. 150 ff.

[112] W. Weber, *Untersuchungen zur Geschichte des Kaisers Hadrianus* (1907), pp. 123 ff.; 211 ff.

[113] Hartmann, P-W, ii. A, cols. 961-4.

[114] F. W. Drexler, *Caracallas Zug nach dem Orient und der letzte Partherkrieg* (Diss. Halle, 1880).

[115] T. R. S. Broughton, *The Romanization of Africa Proconsularis* (1929), pp. 153/4; R. M. Haywood, *Trans. Amer. Phil. Ass.* lxxi (1940), pp. 175 ff.; T. D. Barnes, *Historia,* xvi (1967), pp. 105/6.

[116] *Dig.* 50. 15. 8. 11; . . . Cf. I. Mundle, *Historia,* x (1961), pp. 228-37.

[117] Evidence and modern discussions are fully cited by

J. Hasebroek, *Untersuchungen zur Geschichte des Kaisers Septimius Severus* (1921), pp. 16-128; F. Millar, *A Study of Cassius Dio* (1964), pp. 139-45.

[118] *C.I.L.* vi. 32326/7.

[119] Dio, lxxvii (lxxvi). 11; *B.M.C., Roman Empire,* v, pp. 270-2, 350-3.

[120] *Vit. soph.* ii. 20. 2 (p. 103 Kayser). . . .

[121] R. Syme, *Ammianus and the Historia Augusta* (1968), p. 34. The ignorant Herodian states outright that Severus never left Italy between 202 and 208 (iii. 10. 1/2; 13. 1; 14. 2).

[122] H. Mattingly, *B.M.C., Roman Empire,* v, p. clix, arguing from various coins described on pp. 262-7, 347-9.

[123] Ibid., pp. 208/9 (imperial titulature of A.D. 201-6); 218 (201-10); 248 (204); 332 (202-10); 334/5 (203); 341-3 (204).

[124] *C.I.L.* viii. 2702, 18250. For other evidence, also relevant but not so conclusive, see G. J. Murphy, *The Reign of the Emperor L. Septimius Severus from the Evidence of the Inscriptions* (1945), pp. 33/4; M. Leglay, *C.R.A.I.* 1956, pp. 303/4.

[125] O. Hirschfeld, *Die kaiserlichen Verwaltungsbeamten*[2] (1905), pp. 315/16.

[126] Cf. Aurelius Victor, *Caes.* 20. 19: quin etiam Tripoli, cuius Lepti oppido oriebatur, bellicosae gentes submotae procul.

[127] Cf. Philostratus, *Vit. soph.* ii. 20. 2 . . .

[128] 202/3: J. Guey, *Rev. afric.* xciv (1950), pp. 55 ff.; Millar, op. cit., p. 145. 203/4; Hasebroek, op. cit., pp. 133-5; Murphy, op. cit., p. 33; Mundle, op. cit., p. 234; Barnes, op. cit., p. 103 n. 128.

[129] But see Guey, op. cit., p. 63, for Hasebroek's reliance on unverified types.

[130] *I.R.T.* 393; 423. In contrast, *I.R.T.* 412 (of the same year) lacks the epithet 'Septimiani'.

[131] Recorded at *Dig.* 50. 15. 8. 11.

[132] So Guey, op. cit., pp. 62/3. He also argues from *I.R.T.* 292—which is inconclusive.

[133] J. B. Ward-Perkins, *J.R.S.* xxxviii (1948), pp. 59 ff.; M. F. Squarciapino, *Leptis Magna* (1966), pp. 95 ff.

[134] *Dig.* 1. 16. 4. 5; cf. *Jahreshefte des öst. arch. Inst.* xlv (1960), Beiblatt, cols. 83/4, no. 8.

[135] Severus may have been back in Rome before the end of 203 in order to distribute his fourth *liberalitas.* But cf. G. Barbieri, *Diz. epig.* iv, pp. 858/9.

[136] K. Adam, *Der Katholik*[4], xxxvii (1908), p. 433, assigns works belonging to Tertullian's 'katechetische Tätigkeit innerhalb der christlichen Gemeinde' to 197 or earlier; Monceaux, op. cit., p. 87, declares 'à la deuxième période (de 200 environ à 206), appartiennent les ouvrages où . . . Tertullien parle en prêtre'.

[137] Jerome, *De Viris Illustribus,* 53. Disproved finally by H. Koch, *Theologische Studien und Kritiken,* ciii (1931), pp. 108-14.

[138] See B. Altaner, *Theologische Revue,* xxxviii (1939), pp. 129-38; reprinted at *Kleine Patristiche Schriften* (*T.U.* lxxxiii, 1967), pp. 540-53. The words 'ad omnem ecclesiam Petri propinquam' (*Pud.* 21. 9 . . .) are clearly incompatible with the view that Tertullian is attacking a bishop of Rome. A. Harnack therefore emended 'omnem' to 'Romanam' (*Sitzungsber. der preuss. Akad. Berlin,* Phil.-hist. Klasse, 1927, p. 148).

[139] e.g., J. Quasten, *Patrology,* ii (1953), pp. 247, 312/13; B. Altaner-A. Stuiber, *Patrologie*[7] (1967), pp. 148, 159.

[140] The dates are those of the handbooks: Schanz-Hosius, *Gesch. der röm. Litt.* iii[3] (1922), pp. 283/4, 296, 298; Quasten, op. cit., pp. 292/3, 309/10; Altaner-Stuiber, op. cit., pp. 156-9. There is some wavering on the *De Spectaculis.* Schanz-Hosius and Quasten pose the problem as a straight choice between 197 and 202. Others follow Monceaux, op. cit., p. 87, in putting it *c.* 200 at the supposed start of Tertullian's preaching career (e.g., Frend, *Martyrdom and Persecution* (1965), p. 342 n. 148). Altaner-Stuiber seem to avoid the issue by giving the date as 197-200.

[141] Frend, op. cit., p. 372. However, Frend now holds the *De Idololatria* 'scritto probabilmente nel periodo premontanista di Tertulliano' (*Rivista di storia e letteratura religiosa,* iv (1968), p. 6). But he offers no reason for his change of mind.

[142] Harnack, *Chronologie,* ii, p. 273 . . .

[143] Säflund, op. cit., p. 60, has calculated the frequency of 'et' for etiam'. For the combinations 'nam et', 'sed et', 'sic et', and 'ita et' at the beginning of a sentence, I make the frequency approximately 1.3 per thousand words (. . . ; Säflund, op. cit., p. 64).

[144] Viz. *Idol.* 15. 10/11 > *Apol.* 35.4. See R. Heinze, *Bericht über die Verhandlungen der königl. sächs. Ges.*

der Wiss. Leipzig, Phil.-hist. Klasse, lxii (1910), p. 441; Becker, op. cit., pp. 349/50.

[145] *H.A., Severus* 17. 1. Again, any attempt at full documentation of modern opinions would be pointless. But there is a clear line of derivation between the earliest and a very recent account of the persecutions in the reign of Severus. Eusebius . . . made Aquila prefect of Egypt in 203 (*H.E.* vi. 2. 2, 2. 12, 3. 3; cf. A. Stein, *Die Präfekten von Ägypten* (1950), pp. 111/ 12). Frend writes 'The Severan persecution was the first co-ordinated world-wide movement against the Christians. . . . Apart from the years 202-3, and the situation which had developed . . . in Carthage, the reigns of Septimius Severus and his son Caracalla (211-17) were tolerant' (op. cit. (1965), pp. 312, 323), and makes Subatianus Aquila prefect of Egypt from 'early in 202' (ibid., p. 342 n. 149). For the prefecture of Aquila, that is simply to defy the evidence of known papyri: viz. *Sammelbuch* 4639 (published in 1910); *P. Giss.* 48 (1910); *P. Oxy.* 1111 (1911); *P.S.I.* 199 (1914); *Sammelbuch* 9393 = *P. Mil. Vog.* 237 (1957); and now *B.G.U.* 2024 (1966).

[146] K. H. Schwarte, *Historia,* xii (1963), pp. 185-208; J. R. Rea, *La Parola del Passato,* xxii (1967,) pp. 48-54; T. D. Barnes, *J.T.S.,* N.S. xix (1968), pp. 526/7; *J.R.S.* lviii (1968), pp. 40/1. R. Freudenberger, *Wiener Studien,* lxxxi (1968), pp. 206-17, adds nothing of importance, and betrays no awareness of the crucial chronological issue or of the relevant papyri (see p. 209 n. 15).

[147] *J.T.S.,* N.S. xix (1968), pp. 526/7.

[148] Note *H.E.* v. 21. 1/2.

[149] Eusebius ascribes all the persecutions of Christians before 250 to one of three causes. If persecution occurred during the reign of a bad emperor, it was clearly due to his depravity (*H.E.* ii. 25, iii. 17, vi. 1, vi. 28). But if the emperor was good, the cause must be popular agitation (iii. 32/3, iv. 12/13, iv. 15. 1, v. 1) or the machinations of sinister individuals (iii. 32, iv. 3, iv. 17, v. 21).

[150] *H.E.* vi. 1, 2. 2 ff.

[151] Cf. *J.T.S.,* N.S. xviii (1967), pp. 434-7; xix (1968), pp. 512-14.

[152] As H. Grégoire, *Les persécutions dans l'empire romain*[2] (1964), pp. 108 ff. n. 25; Frend, op. cit., p. 295 n. 1. The former assigns the martyrdom of Polycarp to 177, the latter to 165-8, simply because neither will believe that Eusebius has placed it in the wrong reign. Frend has justly observed elsewhere that 'broadly speaking, the issue is whether one trusts Eusebius or not' (*Oikoumene* (1964), p. 500). Grégoire does just that,

consistently—and follows Eusebius, *H.E.* iv. 15. 48, in synchronizing the deaths of Polycarp and Pionius (op. cit., p. 111). Frend, however, for once declines to follow Eusebius, and correctly assigns the martyrdom of Pionius to 250 (op. cit. (1965), pp. 316, 410-12; cf. T. D. Barnes, *J.T.S.,* N.S. xix (1968), pp. 529-31). But if Eusebius misplaces Pionius by eighty years, why assume (with Frend) that he cannot have misplaced Polycarp by a decade?

[153] Frend, op. cit. (1965), p. 334; op. cit. (1968), pp. 8/ 9. Against, F. Millar, *J.R.S.,* lvi (1966), p. 234.

[154] As Frend, op. cit. (1968), p. 8: 'è ovvio che Tertulliano pensava a ciò che avveniva qua e là in Cartagine. Egli era un giornalista, non un antiquario, e il riferimento agli apostoli si trova lì per enfasi.' That is to say, the relative clause means—precisely nothing.

[155] For another important example of the technique, cf. *J.R.S.* lviii (1968), pp. 34/5.

Stephen Gero (essay date 1970)

SOURCE: *"Miles Gloriosus:* The Christian and Military Service according to Tertullian," *Church History,* Vol. 39, No. 3, September, 1970, pp. 285-98.

[*In the following essay, Gero investigates significant changes in Tertullian's attitude toward Christian military service, arguing that "Tertullian at first condoned Christian service in the army, but later, when he recognized its dangers . . . firmly and totally came to oppose it."*]

The aim of this paper is to throw some light on Tertullian's attitude to military service. His statements on this subject are highly useful for a more accurate understanding of his own changing views on the empire and the duties of citizenship. They are also important evidence for marking a crucial stage in the pre-Constantinian evolution of the relations of church and state. It will be seen that the whole question of Christians serving in the Roman army became relevant only in the late second century; Tertullian is one of the earliest literary witnesses for this momentous development. Therefore, on both counts, the texts deserve close scrutiny.

A detailed exposition of this history of the early Christian attitude to war cannot be given here; the reader is directed to the ample scholarly literature dealing with the subject.[1] However, a brief account of some very relevant aspects of the outlook of the apostolic and sub-apostolic church will be sketched out to help situate Tertullian in the spectrum of early Christian thought. When, in the course of this summary, questions will arise that more properly belong to the field of New

Testament exegesis, bibliographic leads will be provided, without the extended discussion they would merit in a more comprehensive treatment.

It should be noted that for the specific purposes of this paper we need not be delayed by the question of war and violence, righteous or otherwise, in the Old Testament. Tertullian clearly states that the old law has been superseded by the *nova lex* of evangelical peace. For him the bellicosity of the old dispensation is no longer normative.[2]

It is well-known that Jesus in the canonical gospels, in spite of the radical tone and implications of his precepts, is not anywhere represented as explicitly dealing with the morality of the military profession. Here is not the place to speculate on those reasons for this silence that are bound up with the theological programme of the gospels. At any rate, it is generally admitted that the gospel records manifest a certain quietistic indifference to the concrete social questions of the day, though of course they specify a most demanding set of ethical imperatives for the individual. The extent of the influence of eschatology on dominical sayings, the vexed questions of "Interimsethik" and the Messianic consciousness all enter into the problem; but anyone familiar with the state of New Testament scholarship will realize that we could not hope to make even a beginning within the limits of this paper.[3]

Nevertheless, it is true that, in Luke 3:14, John the Baptist does not command the soldiers who come to him to lay down their arms, but only to observe righteousness; in the incidents of the faithful centurion, the conversion of Cornelius, and the jailkeeper of Philippi[4] there is no trace of condemnation of the profession of these individuals. Pressing the point a little, these instances could amount to an implicit legitimation of the military calling. In Luke-Acts especially, the pro-Roman apologetic thrust of which is well known, one naturally expects no denigration of the military forces of the empire; the writer's presentation of the *pax romana* as conducive to the spread of the gospel entails, if not the justification, at least the acceptance of that coercive power whereby tranquillity was maintained.[5]

The fact that there are two different strains of thought *vis-à-vis* the state in the New Testament, epitomized in Romans 13 and Revelation 13 respectively, is also a commonplace of New Testament scholarship.[6] To a certain extent these are not mutually exclusive, for an apocalyptic timetable does not necessarily involve disloyalty to the powers that be.[7] Yet it is undeniable that there is a tension between the attitude of Romans, I Peter, and the pastoral epistles which sanctifies the secular authorities as instruments of a just and benevolent deity, and that apocalyptic vision[8] which sees the empire as the embodiment of demonic evil.[9] We must

leave aside some of the exegetical ramifications of the subject.[10] We only have to recognize the persistence of the two schools of political thinking, so to speak, and that the unresolved tension[11] does appear in Tertullian.

A more immediately important observation is that the "Pauline-Petrine" tradition of loyalty does not involve active participation in the life of the *polis*. Paul reproves those who go before pagan judges;[12] hence it is quite unlikely that he would have sanctioned for the faithful any form of military service, which would have broken down the valued cultural autonomy of the Christian community even more than mere litigation in law courts. The obligations of loyalty are exhausted in obedience to the magistrates and inoffensive moral behavior.[13]

As was already pointed out, the apocalyptic strain in early Christianity was not necessarily more subversive than Pauline loyalism. The tendency to separatism, to be sure, would have been stronger, with an especially vivid abhorrence of the army, the evil instrument *par excellence* of the diabolic power of the empire.

The profession of loyalty, beginning with Clement of Rome, and throughout the second-century apologies, is a constant theme, reiterating the Pauline *iure divino* declarations. The apocalyptic tradition is of course also perpetuated in the writings of Papias, Irenaeus, Hippolytus, and Commodian. But, as we have said, the whole history cannot be traced here.[14] These Fathers usually accompanied their statements with vigorous assertions of the absolute peacefulness of the faithful: armies are not needed on account of the Christians. The attitude of the early Fathers shows that almost joyous irresponsibility and that pervasive idealism which characterize groups far removed from contact with the experience of actual political power and decision-making.[15]

The indirect evidence of "military" language can be exaggerated beyond due bounds. The use of a certain set of verbal images does not imply necessary approbation. It is quite possible to take over symbols not only in a favorable or neutral sense but also with a "combative" intent. Perhaps an example from a different field will be helpful. Christian art appropriated the pagan symbols of the good shepherd (*Philanthropia*) and the lighthouse (hope), amplifying but not annulling their pristine meaning. However, it seems that the adoption of Dionysiac floral symbolism (the true vine) implied a conscious devaluation of the original orgiastic associations.[16]

At any rate, it seems to me that military language in the New Testament and the early Fathers[17] was probably more prompted by an apocalyptic-spiritual allegorization of the Old Testament than by concrete admiration of the military institutions of the empire. Psychological interpretations of the early Christians as warriors *manqués* of course cannot be ruled out, but I do not regard myself competent to pursue such a line of research. What is certain, however, is that the influence of the army was amazingly pervasive by the end of the second century, not the least in the matter of language.[18] "Military" terminology was not confined to Christians, but was current in the cults of Bacchus, Venus, Isis, and of course, *par excellence,* in Mithraism. As Ramsay MacMullen points out, "The prestige and convenience of military organization . . . put its stamp on other groups quite unconnected with the army."[19] In the civil bureaucracy "the lowliest scribbler wore a military belt, was called a *miles,* and after the completion of his *militia, veteranus.*"[20] It is thus likely that military terminology as it became current also became trite. Perhaps *militia Christi* did not have quite the emotive value we might think it possessed.[21]

To cut short the discussion of the general issues of this early period, I can do no better than quote von Campenhausen's statement: "For little enclaves of a fairly humble status in the peaceful interior of a well-ordered empire, where there was practically no conscription,[22] it was easy to avoid anything to do with the army. . . . Christians were still outside the field of political responsibility. . . . Till about A.D. 175 there were, as far as one can tell, no Christian soldiers,[23] and therefore no *actual* questions about military service arose."[24] I agree with von Campenhausen, as against Cadoux,[25] that these early sources, especially the New Testament, do not address themselves to the specific problem, and hence can be expected to yield no answer. The apostolic church did not legislate on behalf of those outside her pale. For her own members the problem was irrelevant.

The New Testament speaks with no certain voice on the question of military service. Both Tertullian and his later opponents could draw ammunition from it. It should be recognized that Tertullian's Christian legalism is not a necessary outcome of the position of the apostolic church and the New Testament, in this particular matter of military service at least.

Until the decade of 170-180 there is no literary or epigraphic evidence for Christian soldiers in the army. If there were any, they were so few as to attract no notice whatsoever. They would certainly have been soldier-converts, not baptized Christians who volunteered. The enlistment period was twenty-five years[26] or more and the penalties for desertion severe. It seems unlikely that Christian civilians—many of whom in any case were ineligible Jews, slaves and women—would have enlisted in this early period. However, it seems that the situation changed drastically in Tertullian's time. To understand the reasons for this, we have to review the pertinent social developments of the era of the early Severan rulers.[27]

A period of civil anarchy followed the murder of Commodus.[28] The Senate temporarily exercised the power of government, but its impotence in face of the military gangsterism of the Praetorians became soon manifest. Septimius Severus, successor of the ineffectual Pertinax and the buffoon Didius Julianus, though paying occasional politic deference to the Senate and the people of Rome,[29] early recognized that retention of his rule depended on the good will of the army. Dio Cassius' version of Severus' death-bed advice to his sons Geta and Caracalla, "Agree, enrich the soldiers and you can despise everybody else,"[30] is perhaps apocryphal, but expresses well the spirit of both Severus' own policy and that of Caracalla.

Septimius Severus decided to found the power of the state on quasi-military rural communities, resulting in an amalgamation between peasant settlements and garrisons. Soldiers were allowed to form *collegia;* marriages of soldiers were regularized, and their families allowed to live within the camp precincts. Frontier troops were given land of their own to cultivate;[31] purely local service became more common.[32]

Though he did not follow the first part of his father's advice,[33] Caracalla showed even more favoritism than Severus to the military. The regular pay of soldiers, already increased by Severus, he raised by a further fifty per cent, in addition to frequent *donativa.* Dio quotes his extravagant expressions of praise for soldiers. His whole reign was devoted to military campaigns. Dio records that Caracalla declared, "No one but I ought to have money so that I can give it to the soldiers."[34] Though his troops could not protect him from assasination, their loyalty honored him in death by extorting his deification from the murderers.[35]

The policy of Severus and Caracalla certainly issued in increased respectability for the military profession and its closer approximation to civilian life. There were, as we saw, many new inducements for embracing a soldier's life. The empire became militarized to a great degree. As MacMullen points out, "The emperor . . . drew closer to his troops, and the balance of power and prestige inclined under Septimius Severus toward army officers."[36] When one notes that the reigns of Septimius Severus and Caracalla (193-217) roughly coincide with the period of Tertullian's literary activity, it seems plausible that Tertullian's own attitude to the military profession, and the outlook of the whole Christian community, would have been profoundly affected by these important social developments. There seems to be evidence for this in Tertullian's writings.

In the *Apologeticum* of 197, Tertullian, as we shall see below, recognizes the presence of Christian soldiers in the army, and uses it as an argument in favor of his coreligionists. Fifteen years later, when he wrote *de Corona* and *de Idololatria,* the pro-military policy of the Severi already had such great success that even baptized Christians were joining the army. The whole development provoked his strongest opposition, and prompted him to produce detailed moral arguments against the permissibility of military service for Christians. It seems that rather than charging his very definite change of attitude to Montanism, one should recognize the sudden influx of Christians into the military profession, with its new opportunities for advancement and greater respectability, as a contributing, if indeed not the main, factor. In view of the earlier remarks on "military" terminology in Christian writings, I think we can safely dismiss the frequent martial metaphors of Tertullian as peripheral to this intensely practical problem of whether or not Christians should serve in the Roman army. Three passages in Tertullian's writings epitomize his attitude to military service. These will now be taken up in some detail.[37]

I. *Apol.* 42, 3 (157, 10-13)

> Nauigamus et nos uobiscum et uobiscum militamus et rustricamur et mercamur; proinde miscemus artes, operas nostras publicamus usui uestro.

> (We sail together with you, we go to war, we till the ground, we conduct business together with you. We blend our skills with yours; our efforts are at your service.)

The *Apologeticum* belongs to the earlier phase of Tertullian's literary activity. The work is frankly apologetic, is directed to the pagan magistrates, and uses all the devices of the art of suasion. In this chapter Tertullian is bent on refuting the charge of social uselessness "Neque enim Brochmanae aut Indorum gymnosophistae sumus, siluicolae et exules uitae."2 (Apol. 42, 1) In demolishing the accusation, Tertullian gives a list of the various activities in which Christians willingly participate—"vobiscum militamus" is part of a series. His earlier statement in ch. 37 ("impleuimus . . . castella . . . castra ipsa")[38] has a similar flavor. Tertullian enumerates all the places where Christians can be found; since he only excludes the pagan temples, forts and camps are quite naturally part of his list. Of course the assertion as such need not be taken literally; in the same breath he claims that nearly all the inhabitants of the cities of the empire are Christians.[39]

The ambiguity in the exact significance of *militanus* should be noted. The two meanings of *militare* are (1) literally, *militiam exercere* (2) figuratively, *servire, obsequi, operam dare*.[40] It is not at all certain which alternative is appropriate in this passage. If one notes that the parallel members of the construction: *nauigamus, rusticamur,* and *mercamur* all refer to everyday activities, carried on both in peacetime and in time of war, the translation "we do service together with you" gains some support. In favor of the literal meaning is the already quoted passage in ch. 37, that

Christians are in "*castella* [and] *castra ipsa.*" *Castellum* and *castra* are technical military terms. More decisive is Tertullian's reference to Christians in the army of Marcus Aurelius during the Quadi campaign.[41]

Thus there is some reason for both interpretations, with the evidence inclining perhaps more toward the literal meaning. However, the statement has to be interpreted in light of the declaration of ch. 37 "' . . . apud istam disciplinam magis occidi licet quam occidere'."[42] Perhaps Tertullian used *militare* with studied ambiguity.

It should of course be noted that the term does not necessarily imply the reprehensible concomitant of violence which he elsewhere rejects. As MacMullen puts it, "Many a recruit need never have struck a blow in anger, outside a tavern."[43] Soldiers carried out many functions which today would be more proper to policemen or contractors.[44] That a person joined the army did not *ex post facto* imply that he was but a hired killer.

All the arguments Tertullian uses are within the apologetic tradition; he is familiar with the work of his predecessors.[45] In particular, the statement that Christians do accept their fair share of the civic burdens appears also in Justin Martyr,[46] and perhaps goes back to the commonplaces of Hellenistic Jewish apologetic.[47] What is significant here is that Tertullian, in utilizing the standard apologetic approach, alludes, but only in passing and not systematically,[48] to the occasional presence of Christians in the army. In 197 military service had not yet become a crucial moral issue for him.

To illustrate the great influence that literary form and putative destination had upon the ideology of his works, it will be instructive to compare the tract *de Pallio* with Tertullian's apologetic treatises. If one accepts Quasten's conjecture that *de Pallio* was written in 193, the work belongs in his early Catholic period.[49] This short tract was written very much along the lines of a Cynic distribe[50] and sets forth the author's radical rejection of society *à la* Diogenes. It is in sharp contrast to the tone of the *Apologeticum*,[51] where indeed it would have been self-defeating for Tertullian to strike a Cynic pose. However if, as it is more likely, the "triple rule" refers to 209-211, the joint *imperium* of Severus and his sons, *de Pallio* belongs to the period of *de Corona* and *Ad Scapulam*. If this dating is correct, the difference in tone between *de Pallio* and the apologetic *Ad Scapulam* (212) is all the more striking. In this latter plea to the African perfect Tertullian sets forth an impeccably orthodox exposition of Romans 13, and betrays no trace of the brusque anti-social sentiments of *de Pallio*. To be sure, he threatens the migistrates with divine vengeance, but as far as his attitude to the state is concerned, he speaks much more *sotto voce.*

II. The next crucial text is chapter 11 of *de Corona.*[52] This treatise was written to glorify a flagrant act of military disobedience on the part of a Christian soldier (ch. 1). Most of the work is of no interest to us here, taken up as it is with a rather artificial antiquarian discussion on the use of wreath and crowns. But in ch. 11 Tertullian succinctly summarizes his changed outlook to military service. As we said before, there seems to be some evidence that his *volte-face,* if it be called that, was motivated by the sudden influx of Christians into the army, made a very attractive career through the Severan reforms. At any rate, here Tertullian speaks with no uncertain voice, and both the relative disinterest in the subject of military service and the ambiguity of intention, that we found in the **Apologeticum** disappear.

Recognizing that the question of triumphal crowns is only incidental to the wider problem, Tertullian adduces several arguments for denying the very legitimacy of military service. It should be noted that the ethical question is posed only for Christians. The pre-Constantinian church, both by choice and by necessity, did not concern herself with the private morality of pagans, except to the extent that this affected the well-being of the Christian community.

Tertullian takes his stand on denying the possibility of divided loyalties, expanding the dominical dictum about serving two masters.[53] "Credimusne humanum sacramentum diuino superduci licere, et in alium dominum respondere post Christum . . . ?"[54] Then he invokes the Christian obligation not to shed blood, "Licebit in gladio conuersari, Domino pronuntiante gladio periturum qui gladio fuerit usus?"[55] Next he points out the radical implications of the cultural separatism incumbent on the believer. The Christian should not go to law courts, and should not avenge even his own private wrongs; hence *a fortiori* he must not be a soldier, a man of violence.

His final argument hinges on the illicit acts of idolatry which the soldier is forced to do in the course of his service, such as guard duty at pagan temples, and eating forbidden meat ("Et cenabit illic, ubi apostolo non placet?"[56]) It is most interesting that Tertullian does not give a very prominent place in his argument to these acts of idolatry; in particular he makes no reference to emperor-worship. Some have argued[57] that the real motivation for the early Christian opposition to military service was the danger of the compulsory idolatry which was greater than in civilian life, rather than mere abhorrence of bloodshed. In this passage at least, Tertullian does not give much support to this position. Von Campenhausen, after quoting one of Tertullian's many arguments, from **de Idololatria,**[58] states: "Here he is not thinking primarily of killing and bloodshed

by soldiers. What Tertullian feared was the denial of Christ and the taint of pagan worship, which seemed inevitable in view of the strictness of military discipline and the role played by pagan religion in the whole ceremonial and life of the army."[59] Admittedly in **de Idololatria** 19 the question of idol-worship is emphasized more than in **de Corona** 11; but it should be remembered that the treatise brings under the ban of idolatry, very broadly conceived, practically every human activity. The military profession is condemned along with the pursuit of art, literature, astrology, civil magistracy, etc. Tertullian condemns even the signing of contracts, which were under the aegis of pagan deities, as idolatry. Therefore his opposition to military service on account of its idolatrous associations is here in no way exceptional, but is rather demanded by the structure and logic of the treatise.

More generally, the quite liberal religious policy of the Roman army has been demonstrated. Though, to be sure, higher officers had to conduct the statutory ceremonies in the *Feriale,* there was no discouragement of the private pursuit of other worship.[60] In this period the Christian in the army was not really exposed to a greater danger of idolatry than in civilian life. The question of idolatry in the army did become more acute in the latter part of the third century;[61] but I think this has to be viewed in the context of the post-Aurelian *renovatio* and its demands for stringent and visible loyalty.

But let us return to **de Corona.** Tertullian gives the very earliest literary evidence for the phenomenon of already-baptized Christians volunteering for the army—indeed a most significant development. ("Ipsum de castris lucis in castra tenebrarum nomen deferre transgressionis est.")[62] Tertullian inflexibly opposes such apostasy; he is slightly more sympathetic to the predicament of soldier converts, recognizing the examples of the soldiers baptized by John, and of the centurion Cornelius. Yet, theoretically, when a soldier becomes a Christian, he should immediately abandon his calling ". . . suscepta fide atque signata,[63] aut deserendum statim sit, ut a multis actum, aut omnibus modis cauillandum, ne quid aduersus deum committatur quae nec extra militiam permittuntur, aut nouissime perpetiendum pro deo, quod aeque fides pagana condixit."[64]

Tertullian seems to say that if the soldier does not immediately abandon his profession, he would have to resort to such acts of subterfuge which are not permitted even to lay believers (*extra militiam*), and that he must be willing to suffer for the faith just as Christian civilians (*fides pagana*). Many, of course, as Tertullian says, did follow the radical solution, as the acts of military martyrs attest (though none of these *Acta* date back to this early period[65]). But his polemic shows the prevalence of a less courageous stand also. Tertullian rejects any accommodation or plea of necessity. "Non admittit status fidei allegationem necessitatis. Nulla est necessitas delinquendi, quibus una est necessitas non delinquendi."[66] To continue the polemic against crowns, he postulates the "contrary-to-fact" condition of lawful military service, and proceeds to bludgeon further his opponents. But his opinion is summed up in "omni ope expulero militiam."[67]

In the next chapter Tertullian rises to real heights of eloquence in describing the horrors of war. "Triumphi laurea foliis struitur, an cadaueribus? lemniscis ornatur, an bustis? unguentis delibuitur an lacrimis coniugum et matrum?"[68] Then he continues with a truly important theme, later taken up by Jerome and Augustine, "fortasse quorumdam et Christianorum; et *apud barbaros enim Christus.*"[69] Loyalty to Christ unites Roman and barbarian.

III. *De Corona* 11 is Tertullian's mature and logical position, consistent with his ethical rigorism. Chapter 19 of *de Idololatria* reinforces his stand, but in no way modifies it. We already had some occasion to comment on the spirit of this treatise.[70] The argument in ch. 19 is more concise and more theoretical than *de Corona* 11, and seems in some ways to presuppose the fuller treatment in *de Corona.* This would be a factor in favor of dating this treatise after *de Corona.* But the dating is not really essential. In expression, subject matter and tone it certainly seems to belong in the same group as *de Corona,* which was written after 211.[71] The passage gives extremely interesting points about the arguments used by the laxer party. Apparently some felt that the position of ordinary soldiers was not reprehensible since, unlike officers, they did not have to conduct sacrifices or order capital punishment ("caligata[72] uel inferior quaeque, cui non sit necessitas immolationum uel capitalium iudociorum."[73]). With remorseless logic Tertullian demolishes this pitiful argument, by using the grand theme of the whole treatise, the *non licet* of divided loyalties "Non conuenit sacramento diuino et humano, signo Christi et signo diaboli,[74] castris lucis et castris tenebrarum;[75] non potest una anima duobus deberi, deo et Caesari[76]."[77] He pours deserved scorn on the fantastic appeals to the *virga* (rod) of Moses, the *fibulum* (buckle) of Aaron, and the *lorum* (belt) of John the Baptist. Since these items were part of the Roman soldier's equipment, Tertullian's adversaries invoked these biblical figures to legitimate their military profession. Tertullian also lightly dismisses the more relevant examples of Joshua and his host. He can justifiably do so in context of his argument; for, according to Tertullian, even the instance of the soldiers who came to John the Baptist and "forman obseruationis acceperant"[78] is not normative: the Lord, in disarming Peter, unbelted[79] every soldier ("omnem postea militem dominus in Petro exarmando discinxit").[80]

Finally, the conclusions of this paper will be briefly recapitulated. The apostolic and sub-apostolic period was not faced with the problem of actual military service, and hence did not provide guidelines for the changed situation of the late second century. The social and military reforms of the Severan dynasty made the military professions much more appealing than before; this resulted in baptized Christians joining the army, perhaps in considerable numbers. Tertullian's earlier statements in the *Apologeticum* are brief and ambiguous; they do not amount to more than a mere acknowledgment of the presence of Christian soldiers in the ranks. Tertullian uses this fact as an apologetic argument, but, in line with the earlier literature, does not yet view military service as a crucial moral problem. The sudden influx of Christians into the army awakened him to the potential dangers of a permissive attitude. His mature position of inflexible opposition to military service is embodied in *de Corona* and *de Idololatria,* written about fifteen years after the *Apologeticum.* His negative attitude fits well into the framework of his rigoristic moral theology, and bears the familiar trademarks of pitiless logic and utter disdain for the hesitation and compromises of *infirma caro.*[81]

If the interpretation of this paper is correct, Tertullian at first condoned Christian service in the army, but later, when he recognized its dangers and its fundamental incompatibility, in his mind, with loyalty to Christ, firmly and totally came to oppose it. He set himself completely against Christian participation in that integration of the military and civil institutions wherein the Severan rulers saw the means both for maintaining their rule and for renewing the military strength of the empire. His condemnation was in the end ineffective, contending against an important trend in the evolution of Roman society. The church in North Africa could not sell her soul, so to speak, to Constantine; she had already sold it much earlier, to Septimius Severus and to Caracalla.

Notes

[1] See the review article of J. Fontaine, "Christians and Military Service in the Early Church," in *Concilium,* 7 (1965), 107-119. Few of the treatments of the subject attain the objectivity of R. H. Bainton's "The Early Church and War," *Harvard Theological Review,* 39 (1946), 189-211. A. Harnack's *Militia Christi* (Tübingen: Mohr, 1905) is especially valuable for giving a collection of original texts from the Fathers and the Acts of Martyrs (pp. 93-122). I feel uncomfortable with some of Harnack's generalizations, (e.g. p. 3, "In jenen Religionen, in denen die religiösen und die politischen Ziele so gut wie ganz zusammenfallen, sind alle 'religiosi' auch 'milites' und der Kreig ist die *ultima ratio* der Religion; er ist immer 'heiliger' Kreig.") Harnack's thoughts on the subject are summarized in *Mission und Ausbreitung* . . . , (Leipzig, 1924), 4. Auflage, Band 2, pp. 571-84. Important, though rather

disconcertingly "anti-pacifist," is E. A. Ryan's "The Rejection of Military Service by the Early Christians," *Theological Studies,* 13 (1952), 1-29. The monograph of C. J. Cadoux, *The Early Christian Attitude to War* (London: Headley, 1919), assembles much scholarly information; his conclusions are occasionally vitiated by a doctrinaire pacifism and an anti-Catholic bias (see e.g. p. 150). J. Hornus' exhaustive study, *Evangile et Labarum* (Geneva, 1960), while a storehouse of rich documentation, is too tractarian in tone, and is in places methodologically unsound (as in uncritical use of *Acta*). Sometimes his learning is marshalled to support bizarre theories. (See e.g., his *outré* exegesis of the third canon of the Council of Arles, pp. 128-29). H. Leclerq's older article "Militarisme" in *Dict. d'Archéologie Chrétienne,* tome XI, cols. 1108-1181 is most useful for the epigraphic material. We shall also have occasion to refer to H. von Campenhausen's *Tradition and Life in the Church* (Philadelphia: Fortress, 1963), esp. ch. 7, "Military Service in the Early Church," pp. 160-170.

[2] *Aduersus Iudaeos* III, ch. 10 (1346, 72-76), "The old law vindicated itself by the vengeance of the sword . . . the new law pointed to clemency, and changed the former savagery of swords and lances into tranquility." It should be noted that the latter part of the treatise (ch. 9-14) is perhaps spurious. J. Quasten, *Initiation. . . .* (Paris: Cerf, 1958), vol. 2, pp. 316-317.

[3] See e.g. N. Perrin, *Rediscovering the Teaching of Jesus* (N.Y.: Harper and Row, 1967); W. G. Kümmel, *Promise and Fulfillment* (Naperville, 1957); A. N. Wilder *Eschatology and Ethics in the Teaching of Jesus,* 3rd edition (N.Y., 1954).

[4] Police duties were not distinguished from strictly military ones. Cadoux, *op. cit.,* p. 20.

[5] See Feine-Behm-Kümmel, *Introduction to the New Testament,* 14th edition (N.Y.: Abingdon Press, 1966), pp. 101-102, 114-117.

[6] F. X. Murphy, *Politics and the Early Christian* (New York, 1967), pp. 50-56; F. Dvornik, *Early Christian and Byzantine Political Philosophy* (Washington, 1966), vol. 1, pp. 50-56. Both these works give encyclopedic but far from authoritative treatments of the subject. Also, see O. Cullmann, *The Early Church* (London: S.C.M., 1956), p. 122; O. Cullmann, *Dieu et César* (Paris-Neuchâtel: Delachaux et Niestlé, 1956), chaps. 2, 3; H. von Campenhausen, *op. cit.,* pp. 148-54.

[7] Harnack, *Militia Christi,* p. 50, "Die Eschatologie wurde . . . zu einem quietistischen und konservierenden Prinzip."

[8] We pass over the question of the authorship of II Thessalonians. The eschatological element has been used to deny Pauline authorship; but of course this involves some circular reasoning. See Feine-Behm-Kümmel, *op. cit.,* pp. 185-190.

[9] Cullmann's resolution of the contradiction in terms of his theory of time and a "half-realized" *Regnum Christi* is quite attractive. The end is already accomplished since the coming of Christ, though the framework of the world still remains. Therefore the Christian neither completely rejects nor completely accepts the world. (Cullmann, *Dieu et César,* pp. 6-7).

[10] As for instance the sharp controversy about the meaning of "exousiai" in Romans 13, on whether the word denotes angelic or human powers. Cullmann, *The Early Church,* p. 121; von Campenhausen, *op. cit.,* p. 146; R. Kittel, *Theo. Dict. of the N.T.* (Grand Rapids: Eerdmans, 1964), Vol. 1, articles *basileus-basileia,* pp. 564-593.

C. F. Sleeper in "Political Responsibility according to I Peter," *Novum Testamentum,* 10 (1969), 270ff. sustains the thesis that the ethics of I Peter are eschatologically motivated. Bo Reicke in the Anchor commentary on the epistle develops the more standard viewpoint that the ethics merely manifest the social conservatism of the Christian community.

[11] As H. Rahner says in *Kirche und Staat im frühen Christentum* (München: Käsel-Verlag, 1961), p. 22, the early Christians were in a "schwingenden Mitte zwischen Ja und Nein der Kirche zum Staat."

[12] I Cor. 6:1. It is interesting that Paul gives an "eschatological" reason (6:3, "Do you not know that we shall judge angels").

[13] I. Pet. 2:16-17.

[14] Murphy, *op. cit.,* provides a recent and fairly reliable survey.

[15] This is of course only a suggestion, which cannot be explored here in detail. See Justin, I Apol. 1:14, 27:1-3.

[16] For a discussion of these interesting but highly uncertain matters see e.g., C. R. Morey, *Early Christian Art* (Princeton, 1953); P. Du Bourget, *Early Christian Painting* (N.Y., 1965); W. Weidlé, *The Baptism of Art* (London, 1946); A. Grabar, *Christian Iconography* (Princeton, 1968).

[17] See the florilegium in Harnack, *Militia Christi,* pp. 93-114.

[18] R. MacMullen, *Soldier and Civilian in the Later Roman Empire,* (Cambridge, Mass.: Harvard, 1963), pp. 165-69. This is an important and highly original

study.

[19] MacMullen, *op. cit.,* pp. 163-64.

[20] MacMullen, *op. cit.,* p. 164.

[21] For all these reasons I think that R. Klein in *Tertullian und das Römische Reich* (Heidelberg: C. Winter, 1968), pp. 121-122, overestimates the significance of Tertullian's military language. We shall have occasion to refer to this work of Klein further.

[22] See Harnack, *Militia Christi,* p. 48, footnote 1, for documentation. The conscript situation of the *Acta Maximiliani* could only arise in the late third century (See Harnack, *op. cit.,* pp. 114-117 for text).

[23] The date 175 is uncertain. Ryan (*op. cit.,* p. 8) proposes 170; Bainton (*op. cit.,* p. 192), has 173. The problem depends on the dating of Celsus' testimony and of the episode of the *Legio Fulminata.* At any rate there is no evidence before the decade of 170-180.

[24] von Campenhausen, *op. cit.,* pp. 161-162.

[25] Cadoux, p. 20. It should be noted that Cadoux carefully qualifies his opinion.

[26] Ryan, *op. cit.,* p. 19.

[27] *Cambridge Ancient History,* Vol. XII (Cambridge, 1939); J. Gagé, *Les Classes Sociales dans l'Empire Romain* (Paris, 1964). The chief primary sources for this period are Dio Cassius, Herodian and the *Historia Augusta.*

[28] Commodus distributed his favors indescriminately to soldiers and gladiators. Herodian, I:6-17 *passim* (Loeb ed., 1969, pp. 28-123).

[29] C.A.H. Vol. XII, pp. 1-6. Dio, LXXV: 2, 3.

[30] Dio LXXVII:15, 2 "homoneite, tous strati ōtas ploutizete, tōn all ōn pantōn kataphroneite." (Loeb ed., Vol. IX, pp. 270-272.)

[31] Foreshadowing the system of *limitanei* under the tetrarchy, and the soldier holdings in the Byzantine Empire during the Macedonian dynasty.

[32] See Herodian III:8, 3-5. (Loeb ed., p. 309) for the whole policy of Severus.

[33] He had his brother brutally murdered. Dio. LXXVIII, 2 (Loed ed., pp. 280-282).

[34] Dio. LXVIII:10, 4. (Loeb ed., p. 298) "oudena anthrōpōn plēn emou argurion echein dein, hina auto tois stratiōtais charizōmai."

[35] Dio, LXXIX:9, 3. (Loeb, p. 372).

[36] MacMullen. *op. cit.,* p. 176. MacMullen suggests the fascinating theory that the development of rigid hierarchical structure in the late Roman Empire was due not so much to eastern influences as to the all-pervasive presence of the army.

MacMullen's book, authoritative and original though it is, understandably tends to de-emphasize the distinctions between soldier and civilian, since the author is in fact writing to dispel notions of strict separation.

It should be noted that the policy of Severus and Caracalla greatly strengthened but did not in itself create the trend.

[37] All the works cited in footnote 1 that deal with the early Christian attitude to war discuss Tertullian's contribution, although very briefly in some cases. E. g., Bainton, *op. cit.,* p. 202; Ryan, *op. cit.,* pp. 17-19; Harnack, *Militia Christi,* pp. 32-40, 58-69; Cadoux, *op cit.,* esp. pp. 113-119. There is also relevant material in monographs on Tertullian. Quotations from Tertullian will be made according to *Corpus Christianorum* (Turnholt: Brepols, 1954), vol. II, page and line numbers in parentheses. C. Guignebert in his massive work, *Tertullien, Etude sur ses sentiments a l'égard de l'Empire et de la société civile* (Paris, 1901), is in general so critical of his subject that he lacks the modicum of empathy needed for a deeper understanding. His treatment of Tertullian's attitude to military service (pp. 189-200) is superficial and disorganized. The following is a characteristically flippant statement of Guignebert: "The Christian, as Tertullian conceives him, owes the Emperor a more or less Platonic affection, but he owes the empire neither his love or his blood." (p. 200). A. d'Alès, *La Théologie de Tertullien* (Paris: Beauchesne, 1905), pp. 414-422, is not especially useful. The recent book of R. Klein, *Tertullian und das römische Reich* (Heidelberg: C. Winter, 1968), devotes a substantial appendix (pp. 102-124) to "Tertullians Stellung zum Kriegsdienst." We shall frequently refer to Klein's work. I have not been able to find any articles in the periodical literature exclusively devoted to the subject of Tertullian and military service.

[38] Apol. 37, 4 (148, 21-22). Cf. Clement, Protrepticus 10:100 on the ubiquity of Christians.

[39] Apol. 37, 8. (143, 36-38).

[40] *Thesaurus Linguae Latinae,* Vol. VIII, Pars 2, (Leipzig: Teubner, 1966), cols. 965-971. This monumental work takes account of both classical and nonclassical usage (including Christian Latin).

[41] Apol. 5, 6 (96, 26-27). " . . . illam Germanicam sitim

Christianorum forte militum precationibus impetrato imbri discussam contestatur."

[42] Apol. 37, 5 (148, 26-27).

[43] MacMullen, *op. cit.,* p. 1.

[44] I quote an extract from the records of a legion stationed in Egypt as an interesting example: "*Titus Flavius Valens* . . .

Assigned to papyrus manufacture, year . . . January 15. Returned, same year . . . Assigned to mint, year . . . Returned same year, January 17. Assigned to . . . year . . . of the Emperor Domitian, A(pril) 13 . . . Assigned to granary at Mercurium . . . Returned same year, July 14. . . . " (N. Lewis and M. Reinhold, *Roman Civilization* [N.Y., 1955], Vol. II, p. 510).

[45] As Klein points out (*op. cit.,* p. 26) " . . . findet sich bei ihm nahezu alle Gedanken der griechischen Apologeten wieder, jedoch viel klarer, gestraffter, und wesentlich aggressiver." See J. Lortz, *Tertullian als Apologet,* 2. Band (Münster [Westf]: Aschendroff, 1927), Kap. 13.

[46] I Apol., chs. 12, 17.

[47] E.g. Philo, *Leg.* 356.

[48] As Klein remarks (*op. cit.,* p. 106), "Die wenigen Andeutungen [of the Apologeticum] geben kein vollstandiges Bild."

[49] If "praesentis imperii triplex uirtus" (*Pal.* 2, 7, [737, 79-80]) refers to the simultaneous rule of Didius Julianus, Niger, and Severus. Quasten, *op. cit.,* vol. 2, p. 374 G. Säflund's arguments for a late date (after 220) are unconvincing. (*De Pallio und die stilistische Entwicklung Tertullians* [Lund: Gleerup, 1955]).

[50] In *Pal.* 5, 4 (748, 38-43) "non milito" is part of a listing of those civic functions which he, in the guise of the Cynic, rejects. I think this is a purely formal phrase; it is certainly not couched in terms of an imperative for the whole Christian community.

[51] I consider Klein's attempt (op. cit., pp. 87-101) to see in *de Pallio* the expression of pure patriotism, true *romanitas,* and to assimilate the treatise to the more irenic *Apologeticum,* completely unconvincing. Incidentally, I find Klein's expression "das neue *Reichsvolk*" rather ominous. D. van Berchem ("Le *de pallio* de Tertullien et le conflict de christianisme et de l'Empire," *Museum Helveticum,* t. 1 [1944], 100-144) views the work as a *défi* to the Empire, "pas d'ature chose qu'un manifeste contre Rome" p. 109). In the main I think van Berchem is correct, though he underestimates the Cynic element in the work. See P. Wendland, *Philo*

und die kynisch-stoische Diatribe (Berlin, 1895); A. Oltrarame, *Les origines de la diatribe romaine* (Lausanne, 1926); J. Geffcken, *Kynika und Verwandtes* (Heidelberg, 1909). Klein's arguments should always be seen in the context of his central thesis, namely that Tertullian strove for a reconciliation of the church and the state, and that he had a "grosse Zukunftsvision eines verchristlichen Römerreiches" (*op. cit.,* p. 106). Klein is acutely aware that he is advocating very much a minority position; the reader of his book should also keep this in mind.

[52] The text in C.C. should be supplemented by J. Fontaine's annotated edition, *Q. Septimi Florentis Tertulliani De Corona* (*Tertullien sur la Couronne*), (Paris: Presses Universitaires, 1966). The work definitely dates from after 211.

[53] Matt. 6:24, Luke 16:13.

[54] Cor. 11, 1 (1056, 4-6).

[55] Cor. 11, 2 (1056, 9-11). It should be noted that for the purposes of the argument, Tertullian ignores the diversity of duties in the army, and assimilates them all *sub gladio* (Guignebert [*op. cit.,* p. 193, footnote 4] rightly dismisses the laudatory remarks about the sword in *De Resurrectione Carnis* 16 as irrelevant rhetoric.)

[56] Cor. 11, 3 (1056, 16-17). The reference is to I Cor. 8:10.

[57] E.g. Ryan, *op. cit.,* pp. 10-11 and Leclerq in his article in D.A.C. This position seems to be especially popular in Catholic works, with the significant addition of H. von Campenhausen.

[58] von Campenhausen, *op. cit.,* p. 163. Both here, and in the German edition, the quotation is mistakenly footnoted as being taken from Cor. 11, whereas it is from Idol. 19. Klein (*op. cit.,* p. 110), in citing von Campenhausen, does not correct the error.

[59] von Campenhausen, *op. cit.,* p. 163.

[60] A. D. Nock, "The Roman Army and the Roman Religious Year," *Harvard Theological Review,* 45 (1952), 187-252. For the text of the *Feriale Duranum,* see *Yale Classical Studies,* 7 (1940), 1-222; Lewis and Reinhold, *op. cit.,* pp. 567-568. Still authoritative for religious practices in the Roman army is A. von Domaszewski, "Die Religion des römischen Heeres," in *Westdeutsche Zeitschrift für Geschichte und Kunst,* B. 14 (1895), 1-121. Domaszewski presents essential epigraphic and monumental data. For emperor worship in general, see L. Cerfaux and J. Tondriau, *Un concurrent de christianisme, le oulte des souverains* (Tournai, 1957), esp. pp. 339-409. The authors maintain that the emperor cult was not the main cause of the persecu-

tions, but rather Christianity's other-worldly aspirations, which passed beyond the confines of the empire (p. 392).

[61] Cadoux, *op. cit.,* p. 151.

[62] Cor. 11, 4 (1057, 26-27).

[63] Technical terms for the immersion and chrismation at baptism. Cf. Augustine, *peccat. merit.,* I, 25, 36 "suscipere baptismum"; Hippolytus, *Apostolic Tradition,* ch. 22.

[64] Cor. 11, 4 (1047, 32-36). *Fides pagana* means "the religion of the civilians." *Paganus* did not take on the sense of "pagan" before the fourth century. Chr. Mohrmann, "Encore une fois paganus," *Vigiliae Christianae* 6 (1952), 109-121.

[65] See e.g., *Acta Marcelli* (298 A.D.) in Harnack, *Militia Christi,* pp. 117-119.

[66] Cor. 11, 6 (1057, 43-45).

[67] Cor. 12, 1 (1058, 3). The last clause in 11, 6, an admittedly difficult passage, does not seem to support Klein's interpretation of a really different "third alternative." Klein thinks (*op. cit.,* p., 114) that Tertullian said that soldiers should try to avoid contamination with idolatry, and yet stay in the service. "Das mag für die Mehrzal der Soldaten gegolten haben und darin ist sicherlich die *Verbindungslinie zum Apologeticum* zu fassen." Klein is forcing all the evidence into the Procrustean bed of his theory (see footnote 51). To my mind at least, Tertullian's "I banish us from military life" is quite unequivocal.

[68] Cor. 12, 4 (1059, 27-30). Tertullian's indebtedness to Stoic thought here (B. Schöpf, *Das Tötungsrecht bei den frühchristlichen Schriftstellern bis zum Zeit Konstantins* [Regensburg, 1953], pp. 200-202) does not invalidate the genuineness of feeling and the grandeur of expression.

[69] Cor. 12, 4 (1059, 30-31).

[70] See above, p. 14.

[71] Harnack does not offer any really cogent reasons for advancing the date to 198-202/203. He admits that "sechszehn schriften in 5 Jahren erscheint etwas viel" (*Chronologie . . . bis Eusebius* [Leipzig: Hinrichs, 1904], II. Band, p. 273, p. 295). Harnack, quite rightly, objects to Monceaux' identification of the rigorism of *de Idolatria* with Montanism. The reference in ch. 13 definitely dates *de Idolatria* after *de Spectaculis.* There seems to be no way to establish the dating of the work with any certainty. The majority of scholars (including Quasten) incline toward dating it after *de*

Corona.

[72] The *caliga* was the heavy soldier's boot; hence came to denote the common soldier.

[73] Idol. 19, 1 (1120, 13-14).

[74] *Signum* is a military standard. Tertullian is probably thinking of the cruciform *vexillae.* Cf. Apol. 16, 8.

[75] Could this expression be an echo of *de Corona* 15, where the Mithraist *miles* is initiated *in castris vere tenebrarum?*

[76] A bold identification of the Emperor with the *mammona* of Matt. 6:24.

[77] Idol. 19, 2 (1120, 14-17). In the magnificient confrontation of *castra lucis and castra diabolis,* Tertullian shows the influence of the apocalyptis-dualistic strain of early Christian thinking.

[78] Idol. 19, 3 (1120, 22). Guignebert (*op. cit.,* p. 191) attributes the statement in Luke 3:14 to Jesus!

[79] In the *Acta Marcelli* the martyr signifies his rejection of military service by throwing off his belt (" . . . reiecto etiam cingulo militari coram signis legionis . . ."). Harnack, *Militia Christi,* p. 117.

[80] Idol. 19, 3 (1120, 23-24). Quite a cogent argument except for the fact that it does not take into account the case of Cornelius. I don't see any justification for Klein's assertion that Idol. 19 is not concerned with the service of Christians in the Roman army but is rather directed against the "general brutalization of military life and warfare." (*op. cit.,* p. 110) Tertullian is not given to vague philosophizing; he is severely purposeful, and directs his arguments to specific opponents—in this case those Christian soldiers who inexcusably lingered *in castra tenebrarum.*

[81] I don't quite see in what way Tertullian "switched the points" (" . . . er hat . . . die Weichen für die zukünftige Entwicklung gestellt," Klein, *op. cit.,* p. 124). I find it difficult to regard Tertullian, as Klein does, as a Eusebius *avant la lettre.*

H. B. Timothy (essay date 1973)

SOURCE: "Tertullian of Carthage," in *The Early Christian Apologists and Greek Philosophy,* Van Gorcum & Comp. B. V., 1973, pp. 40-58.

[In the following essay, Timothy explores the sustained antipathy toward Greek philosophy in the writings and

thought of Tertullian.]

Tertullian is a man clearly with a quarrel on his hands. Dispensing with preliminaries he throws down the challenge to his opponents with these words:

> "Our contest lies against these things, the institutions of our ancestors, the authority of tradition"—by which he means, as the context shows, the tradition of paganism—"the laws of our governors and the reasonings of the wise."

The last-named come in particularly for the full brunt of his attack, for out of their own conjectures they have ingeniously composed their physical philosophy. Their systems which existed in a crude form in the apostolic times, though found of late in a somewhat polished form, are still essentially the same. If there is any basis for comparison between them and the Christians, it consists in what they have borrowed from Christianity and not Christianity from them, for "which of the poets or the sophists", asks Tertullian, "has not drunk at the fountain of the prophets?"

They have perverted what they found in scripture by altering what pleased them to suit their own designs, because being still in obscurity they lacked the means required for proper understanding of the scriptures. Some of them likewise have altered and corrupted the "newly given revelation" into a philosophic system, striking off from the one way many inexplicable ways. They have transformed the simplicity of the truth which they were too proud to believe and what was certain they, with their fastidious admixtures, have infected with uncertainty. Whatever in their own systems corresponds with prophetic wisdom they either ascribe to some other source or apply in some other sense. Thus truth is jeopardized, for they pretend either that truth is aided by falsehood or that falsehood derives support from truth which has wellnigh been excluded by the poisons with which they have contaminated it.

Having in some detail explained the techniques employed by the philosophers to this end Tertullian proceeds to lay down what he considers to be the effective remedy.

There must be a separation of the sentiments entertained by Christians in common with philosophy from the arguments the philosophers employ by recalling all questions to the inspired standard of God. Whatever noxious vapours exhaled by philosophy obscure the clear and wholesome atmosphere of truth require to be cleared away by shattering the arguments drawn from the principles of things and by setting over against them the maxims of heavenly wisdom, that the pitfalls whereby philosophy ensnares the heathen may be removed and the methods repressed that heresy makes use of to shake the faith of Christians.

The philosophers in general are comparable to Thales of Miletus who, while star-gazing, fell into a well. They are stupidly curious about natural phenomena while ever oblivious of the creator and ruler of all; they cannot be counted really wise since, where their discovery began, they wandered away from the beginning of wisdom which is the fear of God. What passes with them for investigation of the scriptures ends up as the metamorphosis of the latter into what their own minds have produced.

The very variety of the philosophic schools is further evidence of their service to untruth, more diversity than unanimity being discoverable among them: even in their agreement can be discovered diversity. Where, then, does truth come in when by the variety of its mutually antagonistic sects philosophy is itself divided into manifold heresies? These mockers and corrupters of the truth which they merely affect to hold care for nothing but vainglory: they philosophize in purple and, while holding to the name and honour that go with wisdom, forsake their principles. Their curious researches may have unearthed some elements of truth but these they changed into the products of their own minds as their vain desires increased, so that the truth they found has degenerated, and from one or two drops of the same they produce a perfect flood of argument. Speaking of his experience of the loquacious city of Athens, of the straining of philosophy after that facility of language which, rather than teaching, is mere talk, the apostle Paul sounded a warning against "subtle words and philosophy" signifying worldly learning which, he saw, would prove injurious to the truth.

By this same token, Tertullian continues, all heresies stand condemned because they consist of the resources of subtle speech and the rules of philosophy which is the material of this world's wisdom, the rash interpreter of the nature and dispensation of God, the origin of the aeons and who can tell what infinite forms, and the trinity of man in the system of Basilides, and Marcion's better god with all his tranquillity. Down with the teaching of Zeno which has contributed to equating matter with God and that of Heraclitus with his doctrine involving a god of fire. The unpardonable offence of the philosophers is the part that they have played in aiding and abetting the heretics who associate with them as well as with magicians, mountebanks and astrologers: they are the patriarchs of heresy and along with other representatives of cultured paganism transmitters of heathen superstition. The same subject-matter is discussed repeatedly by heretics and philosophers alike, the same arguments are involved: "What is the source of evil? Why is it allowed? What is the origin of man: how does he come into existence?—and the question raised recently by Valentinus, "How did God originate?" and the answer that he gives, "From invention and abortion." "O unhappy Aristotle", cries

Tertullian, "who invented for these men the dialectic art of building up and pulling down . . . embarrassing even to itself, detracting everything and treating actually of nothing, whence are derived those "fables and endless genealogies", those "unprofitable questions", and "words that spread like a cancer." The apostle Paul, placing a restriction on all such things, expressly names philosophy.

Because of their desire for knowledge the heretics misinterpret Pauls' advice to "prove all things", and the dominical text likewise, "Seek and ye shall find." The advice to seek, says Tertullian, was needless enough for the apostles who had the Holy Spirit to instruct them, but even less so for us who have received the testimony of both the apostles and the Spirit and who, therefore have no need of additional research. One must seek doubtless till he find and believe when he has found. All that remains thereafter is to hold fast what one has believed, provided one also believes this, that there is no more to be believed, so nothing further to be sought after having found and believed what was taught by Christ who commands us to seek no further. Once one has believed his seeking is at an end for he has through believing found what he was looking for. If one must go on seeking so long as the possibility exists of finding anything, either he does not yet believe, because so far he has not found what he seeks, or having found it he has lost it or ceased to believe in it. Such seeking indicates the absence of fixed tenets, therefore, the absence of belief. Once anyone has laid hold of Jesus Christ, in short, and entered into enjoyment of the Gospel, he has no use for curious investigation or disputation: faith in Christ is all that he requires.

The answer to the question whether God required any material for the creation of the world is forthcoming not from the philosophers but from the prophets, from Wisdom itself, God's counsellor. The school of heaven is the school for Christians. Let the latter restrict themselves to what lies in their own field: let their seeking be confined to what can be investigated without impairing the rule of faith, to know nothing opposed to which is to know everything and with regard to which the rule of reason is applicable, under the three heads: Matter, Time, and Limit, with the questions, What?, When? and How long? related thereto respectively. There must be no interpretation which ignores this principle. Where after all is the need for such intellectual curiosity when the most ordinary person has direct access to the essential knowledge of God? "There is not a Christian workman", Tertullian confidently asserts, "but discovers God and manifests him and hence assigns to him all those attributes which go to make up a divine being, though as Plato affirms it is far from easy to find out the maker of the universe and hard, when he is found, to make him known to all. It is better to remain in ignorance lest one should arrive at

knowledge of what one ought not to know. As to what Christians ought to know, that has been provided for. Whoever has the fear of God, provided he has attained to the knowledge and truth of God will, even though ignorant of all else, possess complete and perfect wisdom. If it is a question of revelation, it is better to be in ignorance of something because God has not revealed it than to know it according to human wisdom because man has been so bold as to assume it. "I praise the faith that has believed", Tertullian confesses, "in the duty of complying with the rule before learning the reason for it" and with one of his not infrequent rhetorical flourishes, he says, apostrophizing the soul, "I summon thee not as when, formed in schools, trained up in libraries, nurtured in the academies and porticos of Attica, thou pourest forth thy wisdom. I address thee, simple and unpolished, and uncultured and untaught, such as they have who have thee only, that very thing of the road, the street and the workshop, unsullied and entire. I want thine inexperience since in thy meagre experience no one feels any confidence. I ask of thee what thou bringest into man, which thou knowest from thyself or from thine author, whoever he may be."

Next to be dealt with are the crimes laid by Tertullian at the door of the philosophers with reference to God, creation, and the destiny of the soul, in connection with which we learn that the authority of the physical philosophers is alleged as the *mancipium* or special property of wisdom, in particular where the mystery of matter is concerned, though "the renowned Mercurius Trismegistus", we are told, who was master of all physical philosophy was unable to arrive at a solution, but then, neither the prophets nor the apostles nor even Christ had any knowledge concerning it.

The aim of the Stoics is to demonstrate, points out Tertullian, that matter, the material from which everything was created by the Lord, was unborn and unmade, having neither beginning nor end, and to establish the divine nature of the material elements. In this, of course, they are not alone, for the professors of wisdom in general from whose genius the spirit of every heresy derives have called the world's unworthy elements divine, according to their various schools of thought. Thales assumed the basic world-stuff to be water: Heraclitus, fire: Anaximenes, air: Anaximander, all the heavenly bodies: Plato, the stars and Zeno, air and ether. This is the error censured by Paul in his letter to the Galatians where he speaks of that "physical and natural speculation which holds the elements to be God." The fault, I suppose, of the divine doctrine, Tertullian says ironically, lies in its springing from Judaea rather than from Greece: it is evident that Christ erred in that, instead of sophists he sent out fishermen to preach. The ordinary man may be in error but is better off for erring simply than the physical philosophers who err speculatively. God had offenders in the wise and prudent who would not seek after him, though he was discoverable in his many mighty works, or who philosophized about him rashly and thereby furnished the heretics with their arts, not expounding God as they found him, but preferring to dispute about his quality, his nature, and even his abode. The worst of their aberrations is the trouble to which they go to prove the divine indifference or impassibility. It was from Epicurus that Marcion derived the foremost term of his philosophy, and the Gnostics would have men contemplate the "lonely goodness" of God. How, Tertullian demands, could a previously uncommunicative deity begin suddenly to communicate himself? How is salvation, an activity of goodness, to be reconciled with celestial neutrality? Nothing is so suited as salvation to the character of God whose nature would negate itself, if he should cease to act, as we are taught by God, not by the philosophers.

In addition, through assailing the veracity of the senses which are the stamp of man's rationality, God's dispensation has been impeached by the heretics. Valentinus draws a distinction between the bodily sense-organs and the intellectual faculties, a dualism responsible for the Gnostic aeons and genealogies. If, counters Tertullian, a dualism is involved, it has to do solely with the objects of sense-perception, not with the locus of soul and mind or sense and intellect. But why, he expostulates, adopt such methods in any case for torturing simple knowledge and for crucifying truth. You overthrow the whole condition of human life, he protests, railing at the Academy: you turn the order of nature in its entirety upside down: you veil the good providence of God himself by calling in question the trustworthiness of human sense-perception.

The philosophers have sought also to repudiate the resurrection of the body and for this the Stoics and the Epicureans are to be held responsible, though their teaching on the subject is not subscribed to by all the philosophic schools, since Pythagoras, Empedocles and Plato uphold the opposite point of view. That the latter, though not entering, at least knocked at the door of truth, Tertullian is willing to allow, but that is as far by way of compromise or conciliation as he is prepared to go.

His mantle, he tells us, has been adopted into a new and nobler philosophy, yet its original material has a tendency in many places to shine through. He sings avowedly a new song but the strains of the old song he was trained to can not infrequently be heard. "I must needs use a name", he says, "to express the essence of which that being consists who is called God and who is accounted the Great Supreme, not from his name but owing to his essence." God is one, he reasons, otherwise he does not exist, "because we more properly believe that what is not as it ought to be has no existence." He acknowledges that Christianity has unam-

biguously declared the principle of the uniqueness and the unity of God, but he bases the principle on a philosophical assumption and it is by logical deduction that he arrives at the proof of it. Reason forbids, he argues, belief in more gods than one, for God must by definition be a being to whom there is no equal, since he is the Great-Supreme. That being to whom nothing is equal must moreover be unique. It therefore follows that God is one. He debates the relationship of substance to attribute and speaks of reasoning from species to genus and vice versa.

It is, however, with regard to certain tenets of the Stoic philosophy, in which as a Roman lawyer he was trained, that the persisting influence of his intellectual heritage, the forces that had stamped themselves, in a sense, ineradicably on his mind and outlook, may be most clearly seen.

He considers sin in every form irrational and the world a prison house, a thought with which he would console the imprisoned martyrs and reconcile them to their fate. He says, with a touch of Stoic self-sufficiency, "My only business is with myself" and adds with something of the Stoic's proud indifference, "I have, apart from that, no other care save not to care." With reference to Peter's experience recorded in Acts X,9f., he sees in the "vessel coming down, like a huge sheet lowered by the four corners to the earth" and containing "all quadrupeds and creeping things of the earth and wild birds", a vision of universal community. He has also reminiscences of Stoic fatalism. It was, in Tertullian's opinion, necessary that there should have been heresies. The scriptures themselves were fashioned by the will of God to furnish material for heretics. It was no less necessary that evil should exist and that the Lord should be betrayed.

Recurrence for Tertullian, as for the Stoics, lies at the heart of all creation. "Whatever", he writes, "you chance on has been already in existence and whatever you have lost returns unfailingly . . . All things after passing out of sight revert to their former state . . . they come to an end for the very purpose of coming into existence once again."

On the subject of man's mortality he echoes the familiar Stoic attitude. "There is one thing only that much concerns us in this life and that is getting quickly out of it: there is nothing to be feared after death, if there is nothing to be felt."

In several respects he is not far removed from Stoic pantheism. He gives expression to the sentiment in several places throughout his works that all things are full of their maker and occupied by him. Rather than think of the natural elements as not worthy of God, he prefers to regard them as divine, in spite of his having on this very point severely criticised the pagan philosophers, and likens the Son, the Logos, to a ray emitted by the Creator by whose active agency all things, he says, consist, though here the aim may be to safeguard the idea of God's transcendence and unity.

His anthropology has also an unmistakably Stoic ring. There are, quite literally, an outer and inner man. The latter is the soul which is born of the divine afflatus, but, as regards its form is an exact replica of the body: both are in fact bodies, for example, the soul has eyes and ears wherewith to see God and hear His voice.

Calling in question the distinction drawn by the dialecticians between the natural and the supernatural, he insists that everything without exception falls into the former category, for nature, he argues, if it is anything, is a reasonable work of God. "We are worshippers", he declares, "of one God of whose existence and character nature teaches all mankind, who will never be concealed, will never be absent, will always be known and heard . . . , who has for his witness all this that we are and wherein we exist, whereby proof is afforded of his being and unity". Even in matters of faith it is pointless to expect men to arrive at knowledge of the deity by the unaided light of reason, because those even who believe depend on some token of the latter in works worthy of God. There is, accordingly, for faith a basic unity of reason and of natural revelation. God must first be known from nature and thereafter authenticated by instruction, from nature through His works and by instruction through the revelation he has given in the scriptures, with the aid of discipline. Scripture, nature and discipline combine to reinforce awareness of God, each in its own way ministering to His purpose. Scripture establishes God's law, nature attests it, while discipline exacts it, and whatever is out of harmony with these three can have no claim to be of God. If scripture is uncertain, nature is manifest, and with regard to nature's witness scripture can be in no uncertainty. If as regards the latter there is any dubiety, discipline indicates what has been ratified by God.

The resurrection of the dead is testified to by "the whole revolving order of things", and affords an illustration of the divine energies displayed as much in nature as in God's spoken word. God wrote it in His mighty works before He wrote it in the scriptures, with the intention of sending prophecy (or scripture) as a supplementary instructor.

The Greeks used the term, . . . [logos] which is correctly understood as signifying "word", but the older meaning, "reason" signifies the thought or consciousness of God. A statement already made is recalled to the effect that God made the cosmos and everything it contains by his Word and Reason and Power. The wise men of the Greeks agree that the Logos or Word and Reason are responsible for the creation of the world.

Zeno lays it down that he who fashioned all things should be called creator, though he also designates him Fate, God, the soul of Jupiter and the necessity of things. Cleanthes gathers up all these various designations under the name of spirit. To the Word and Reason and Power by means of which, as we proclaim, says Tertullian, God created everything, we also ascribe spirit, as their appropriate substance, the Word dwelling in the latter when it speaks forth, Reason being present when it commands and Power presiding when it carries things into effect. By his exorcising, healing and life-restoring miracles, by his stilling of the storm and his walking on the sea, Christ is proved to be God's Logos, the same who was doing and who had done all things, the primal, first-begotten Word.

The Son's authority was not restricted to things that pertained to the world's creation, for at all times he held converse with men, from Adam to the patriarchs and the prophets, in visions, dreams, dark sayings and the like, laying from the beginning the foundation of what he intended to follow out to the end. For the sake of those who later in history were to witness the Incarnation he rehearsed his destined role so as to smooth the path of faith, or to make belief in the Incarnation easier for them when it eventually took place.

God's overall perfection springs from his eternity and his rationality. Everything in him is bound to be rational as it is natural, and since nothing can be accounted good but what is rationally good, reason will be a necessary attribute of his goodness. He has provided, disposed and arranged everything by reason, and according to reason everything he has willed should be handled and understood. Reason will thus be found to lend support to tradition, custom and faith. It is the rudder without which those who are ignorant of God steer their whole course through life, knowing not how to avoid the tempest which is threatening the world.

Before the world was made, and prior to the generation of the Son, God existed . . . in and for himself, since nothing else extrinsic to himself was in existence. Even then, however, God was not alone, for he had his Reason with him . . . Reason was first in him.

God is the source also of the generalized primordial law that rules the universe and from which all other manifestations of the law of God derive. Within the latter like the leaves and branches present (potentially) at the embryonic stage of a tree's development, were comprised all the precepts of the posterior law which in due time germinated when disclosed. There existed before Moses an unwritten law which in a natural way was understood habitually and habitually observed and was not given primarily at Horeb or at Sinai in the desert but first existed in Paradise and at given periods passed through successive stages of reformation or improvement (for the patriarchs, for the Jews, and later for the Gentiles), in keeping with the circumstances of the times, with a view to man's salvation.

The role delegated to the Paraclete in the Christian economy is the direction of discipline, the unfolding of the scriptures, the reformation of intellect and making progress toward better things; for nothing is without its progressive stages of development. The creation, little by little, advances to fruition. First, there is the grain; then, from the grain, the shoot; and, from the shoot, the shrub. Branches and leaves follow. Presently the full-grown tree expands to view and finally emerge the flourish and the mellow fruit from it. So it is with goodness, for the God of creation and the God of goodness are the same. The latter was to begin with in an elementary state, motivated by the natural fear of God. From there, through the Law and the prophets, it advanced to infancy; thence, through the Gospel, to the fervour of its youth; and now, through the Paraclete, it is coming to a settled state of maturity.

The argument for Christian practices is strengthened when they are upheld by nature, "the first ruler of all", the authority of which, on the ground of the *consensus gentium* is one of the chief factors setting the standard for Christians. Any practice, per contra, that is opposed to nature sets those indulging in it at variance with the rest of their fellow-men, or with humanity at large.

As for the soul, rationality impressed on it from the first moment of its creation by its author who is himself essentially rational is its natural condition. The soul has knowledge of itself without which it would have been incapable of fulfilling its true function. It is in keeping with the fitness of things in a special way that man should have been equipped with such a soul as to be in a unique sense the rational animal. "O testimony of the soul by nature Christian", exclaims Tertullian. Though in bondage to the body, led astray by depravities, weakened by lusts and by passions, and in slavery to false gods, the soul, notwithstanding, whenever it comes to itself, as when roused from sleep or illness or the like, and whenever it acquires something of its natural soundness, speaks of God. Every soul by its own right proclaims what Christians may not utter above their breath.

The testimonies of the soul are one with those of nature and of reason; they are simple as they are true, and commonplace as they are simple; universal as they are commonplace, natural as they are universal, and divine as they are natural. One has only to reflect upon the majesty of nature from which the soul derives its authority. Nature is the mistress, her disciple is the soul, but all that is taught and all that is learned comes from Him who teaches the mistress, that is to say, from God.

The soul was before prophecy and its endowment from the beginning was the inborn knowledge of God which amongst the Egyptians, the Assyrians, and the inhabitants of Pontus, is the same, seeing that their souls call the God of the Jews their God. Goodness, originally divine, inborn and natural resides in the soul of man and makes the soul akin to God whose image or form in man, received originally from the divine afflatus has been lost as a result of human sin. The likeness of God in man persists, however, as the earnest of his eternal destiny, for what comes from God cannot be so much extinguished as obscured. Obscured it can be, because it is not God; extinguished it cannot be, because its being derives from Him. It continues to manifest itself, being indestructible, in that native attribute of goodness, man's freedom and power of will.

At Christ's coming the Creator who is law, reason and world-soul initiated a process of recapitulation whereby the human race is renewed and illuminated and in which Jesus figures as the enlightener and trainer of mankind, the master teaching them how to escape to safety, and preparing by degrees the means of healing for the inflamed condition induced by Adam's sin.

Men cannot plead ignorance of God or Providence, for the world is itself inscribed with the signature of its maker and in each man's conscience the inscription may be read.

Because it is good originally and remembers its origin, God is assented to from within the soul of man, by such expressions as "Good God", "God knows" etc. It is thus that in prophetic forecasts the soul's divinity bursts forth. Every land has its own language but the subjects that speech deals with are common to them all, and man is the one name belonging to every nation upon earth. God is everywhere, goodness is everywhere, the soul's witness is world-wide.

Nature is a source in many of the knowledge of the immortality of the soul, and of the knowledge of God in all, as is the conscience of a nation when it attests the one, supreme divinity, and other intelligent or rational beings like ourselves when they acknowledge God as judge. What commends common-sense is its simplicity, its sharing the same sentiments and opinions and the fact that its pronouncements are open and accessible to each and everyone. It may not like the divine reason which can often be at variance with superficial appearances lie at the very heart of things, but, for all that, it is divine.

Some of Tertullian's statements quoted at the beginning of this chapter have already afforded some indication as to how he felt about Greek culture in general. His reaction is on the whole denunciatory and at times abusive in the extreme. He seems to take special pleasure in the prospect of deified emperors and governors of provinces who persecuted the Christians, philosophers who scouted the idea of a hereafter, not to mention other, more colourful representatives of the pagan way of life, enveloped in fires more fierce than those wherewith, in the days of their power and pride of life, their wrath waxed hot against the followers of Christ, or tossing in the fiery billows of the judgment after death; yet even in his castigation of institutions embodying that pagan way of life he cannot refrain here and there from being philosophical.

Believe your books, if you must, he counsels his pagan audience, but so much more believe those that are divine and which agree with the light of nature in the witness of the soul. Choose which you find to be, he tells them, the more faithful friend of truth. Your books may be distrusted but neither God nor nature lie; or consider the result, he says of what goes on at the racecourse—disfiguration, among other things, of the human countenance which is no different from the disfiguration of the image of God himself. Such excesses accompanying participation in the public sports, games, shows, etc. are totally opposed to nature, to reason and to God, and all that is so opposed deserves to be branded as monstrous among men.

With the object of upholding the integrity of human sense-experience, and in proof of its wholesome influence he points with approbation to the cultural and civilizing accomplishments of which the sense-impressions are the source—*"tot artes, tot ingenia, tot studia, negotia, officia, commercia, remedia, consilia, solatia, victus, cultus ornatusque omnia"*. The body or man's physical constitution is the medium, he contends, for the procreation of the arts, the mind's pursuits and powers, and the soul's activities. There is thus no reason to exclude the physical from the eternal life of heaven. It therefore follows that the doctrine of the resurrection of the body is acceptable as a reasonable belief.

This conclusion is reinforced by a brief excursus into physiological psychology. Thinking is physically conditioned. The faculty, which rules in the sensory perceptual field of human experience is situated in the brain or in the space between the eyebrows or wherever else the philosophers see fit to locate it. The physical is, therefore, the locus in which the thought processes occur. The soul, so long as it is embodied, is never separate from the flesh, while the flesh does nothing without the soul.

Even the virtues which the Christian extols are not produced on soil foreign to the cultivated life. Modesty, the pre-condition of all good dispositions, is, like every worthy human quality, the outcome of breeding and educational influences. The flower of manners, it is a rare thing, not perfected easily, yet tenuous if life, if nature, training, and self-discipline play their part. Neglect of study on the other hand leads to lapse in discipline, which is regrettable. The soul's substance is not benefitted by education but its conduct and discipline are; such nurture does nothing to increase the soul, but adds to its grace and embellishment.

Tertullian deplores the fact that many Christians are uneducated, that still more falter in their faith, that some again are lacking in intellectual stability and in need of instruction, direction and strengthening. There are those also of a somewhat perverse inclination—the uneducated mostly—who take wrong meanings out of words, while the majority are startled at the slightest mention of the Trinitarian formula or any allusion to common-sense. Certain people are well satisfied with simply having believed carrying in their minds through ignorance a faith which they have never put to the test and the foundation of which is mere probability, so unlike those "who have agonized into the same light of truth from the same womb of a common ignorance". Yet we see something of the other side of Tertullian, when, in a self-revealing moment, he confesses openly that, new disciple that he is, and a follower of the apostle Paul, he believes nothing in the meantime but that nothing should rashly be believed and that whatever is believed without enquiry into its source is believed rashly; but to continue the former strain, the heretics, he says, with the philosophers and others laugh and jeer at the things Christians believe and this should be enough to challenge the latter to avail themselves of their rhetoric as well as their philosophy.

It is not that the adjuncts to civilized existence are unconditionally bad, for nature teaches, as is known universally, that God is the creator of the universe, that the universe is good, and that it belongs to man by the free gift of his maker who has blessed the whole of his creation for wholesome and good uses. Not cultured living in itself but the excesses attending it, is what is being condemned. Christ came in the flesh not to enlighten feardriven boors and savages . . . but men already civilized, yet under illusions from their culture, so that they might arrive through him at the knowledge of the truth.

The whole creation fashioned with a rivalry among its several parts demonstrates the regulation of the universe by an over-ruling reason. "Will a single floweret from the hedgerow", asks Tertullian, " . . . a single little shellfish from any sea, . . . a single stray feather of a moorfowl, to say nothing of a peacock, inform you that the creator was a poor craftsman?" "Imitate, if you can", he says elsewhere, "the bee's cells, the ant's hills, the spider's webs, the silkworm's threads. Endure, if you know how, the creatures that take possession of your bed and house, the blister beetle's poisonous injections, the fly's spikes, the gnat's sheath and sting. Take a turn finally round yourself; survey man inside out. Even this handiwork of our God will please you, inasmuch as your own Lord, that better

God, loved it so well." Nothing in fact occurs without the will of God, whether it be for the shielding or for the shaking of faith.

This somewhat rhapsodic train of thought is apparently no answer to the question which breaks in upon it at this point: "What of evil things?" God made these things, but not of his own will and pleasure, is Tertullian's reply; that would have been unworthy and unseemly of him as well as being at variance with the universal fitness of things. The fault really lies in matter which, admittedly, may be evil and yet good things are created out of it.

But the questioner is not satisfied insisting, "What about the text: 'It is I who create evil.'?" and Tertullian replies by explaining that two kinds of evil are involved— *mala culpae,* evils of sin of which the devil is the cause; and *mala poenae,* penal evils the author of which is God. The former are morally bad, whereas the latter resulting from the operation of divine justice on human sin which is the consequence of the schism that arose initially from the first anti-rational action on man's part in an otherwise good world, may seem to be evil in the eyes of those who suffer them, but are not actually so, since they are providentially and remedially arranged.

"Then, what of evil in the larger, cosmic sense?", reiterates the questioner. The two kinds of evil, answers Tertullian, come into it again. There is that which, owing to the evil spirit's intervention, supervenes upon the soul, and a natural, antecedent evil which arises of itself—we might prefer to say "primordially" or "nonderivatively"—our nature being corrupted by another nature owning a god and father of its own.

Tertullian thus asserts the basic unity of all being and in support of his assertion invokes the sacramental principle.

What, in your estimate, he says, addressing the heretics, is the utter disgrace of my God, in fact is the sacrament of man's salvation. The Son has been seen and heard and met in the Incarnation . . . uniting God and man in himself, God in mighty deeds, in weak ones man, so that he might give to man as much as he takes from God.

God held converse with man that man might learn to act like God; God dealt on equal terms with man that man might learn to deal on equal terms with him; God was made little that man might be made great.

Take it all in all, whatever happens happens for Tertullian in the best of all possible worlds—except for the philosophers for some of whom he shows a degree of preference by the labels he attaches to each of them— " . . . the nobility of Plato, the force of Zeno, the level-

headedness of Aristotle, the stupidity of Epicurus, the sadness of Heraclitus, and the madness of Empedocles", but for all of them, apparently, without exception he has this final parting shot:

> What has Athens to do with Jerusalem; what concord is there between the Academy and the Church? The Christian's instruction comes from the porch of Solomon who taught that the Lord should be sought in simplicity of heart. Away with all efforts to produce a mottled Stoic-Platonic-dialectic Christianity! Where is there any likeness between the Christian and the philosopher; between the disciple of Greece and the disciple of heaven; between the man whose object is fame and the man whose object is life; between the talker and the doer; between him who builds up and him who pulls down; between the friend and the foe of error; between one who corrupts the truth and one who restores and teaches it?

A. A. R. Bastiaensen (essay date 1977)

SOURCE: "Tertullian's Argumentation in *De praescriptione haereticorum* 20, 1ff.," *Vigiliae Chris-tianae,* Vol. 31, No. 1, March, 1977, pp. 35-46.

[*In the following essay, Bastiaensen probes Tertullian's rhetorical strategies in his writings against heresy.*]

Tertullian's **De praescriptione haereticorum** does not cease to arouse the interest of the scholarly world. Not to mention other problems, up to this day the dispute continues about the important term *praescriptio:* has it a juridical background, as Mr. Michaélidès maintains, in accordance with many previous commentators,[1] or is it a more general term of argumentation and discussion, as Mr. Fredouille thinks?[2] In view of this and other disagreements we may foresee for some time to come the continuing of the discussions on Tertullian's treatise. In those discussions inevitably will keep coming up questions concerning the interpretation of chapter 20ff., as this section of the work, in particular the end of chapter 21, still has not yielded all its secrets. In the next pages a cautious attempt will be made to outline the course of the argumentation from 20,1 onward and, within this cadre, to establish more specifically the exact meaning of the last paragraphs of chapter 21.[3]

Tertullian starts by alluding to a number of doctrinal points concerning God, the Son and the Son's mission. It is a repetition *per summa capita* of chapter 13, where the *regula fidei* of the orthodox church had been described. This *regula* contains the essential elements of the catholic faith: the existence of only one God, the mission of the Son, who preached the faith and announced the kingdom of heaven, who was put to death and rose from the grave, who sent the Spirit, and who one day will come to bestow on the elected eternal life and the promised heavenly things. The main points of this *regula,* then, are reproduced here but, the context now being a context of discussion, their truth is left in suspension not to contravene the rules of logic: *Christus Iesus, dominus noster, permittat dicere interim, quisquis est, cuiuscumque dei filius, cuiuscumque materiae homo et deus, cuiuscumque fidei praeceptor, cuiuscumque mercedis repromissor.* It must be noted, for that matter, that in chapter 20ff. concrete doctrinal points as such are not the object of Tertullian's demonstration. In accordance with the general plan of his work he seeks the justification of the catholic faith by tracing it back to its origin, not by discussing its contents. The allusions of 20,1, therefore, are more or less accidental, provoked by the recollection of the *regula fidei* from chapter 13, but couched in such a way as to demonstrate the author's impartiality at the start of his argumentation.

In 20,2 this argumentation begins properly. It starts with an exposé of mainly historical character, presenting the facts the demonstration has to rely on. In broad outline the exposé (20,2-9) is as follows:

> Christ entrusted the doctrine of faith, inhering in his mission, to the apostles; the apostles, in their turn, promulgated it in the face of the Jewish and heathen world by founding communities and assigning them as depositaries of this doctrine, the apostolic churches. These churches have handed and still do hand it over to new communities, which by receiving it became and become apostolic churches themselves. So, all churches are, in fact, one apostolic church; they form a brotherhood and live in communion with one another on the basis of the one faith handed down from the apostles.

These facts being established, Tertullian proceeds to draw up a twofold claim, which claim, in its turn, will prepare the way for the proof that only the catholic faith is in possession of the truth. We use the word 'claim' to render Tertullian's *praescriptio-praescribere:* (21,1) *Hinc igitur dirigimus praescriptionem: si dominus Christus Iesus apostolos misit ad praedicandum, alios non esse recipiendos praedicatores quam Christus instituit . . . ;* (21,3) *quid autem praedicaverint . . . praescribam non aliter probari debere nisi per easdem ecclesias quas ipsi apostoli condiderunt.* Whether the use of *praescriptio-praescribere* has a juridical background or not,[4] it is clear both from the general sense of the term and, with regard to this passage, from the prohibitive character of the subordinate clauses (*non esse recipiendos; . . . non aliter probari debere*) that the idea of 'necessity', 'inevitability' is foremost in Tertullian's mind. Not in a moral sense, as an 'obligation' imposed on human free will, but as an unavoidable logical step, a thesis, a claim, which nothing can prevent to arise from the historical facts.

The claim is a twofold one, bearing on the apostles as the only authorized preachers of the faith and on the apostolic churches as its only authorized depositaries. The double application does not prevent Tertullian from seeing it as one single claim, as appears from 22,1, where he gives the heretics an opportunity to attack *hanc praescriptionem.* Indeed, as we shall see further, the heretics' attack on *hanc praescriptionem* (from 22,2 onward) is a twofold one, on the apostles and on the apostolic churches; in other words, it corresponds exactly to the twofold claim. As Tertullian uses the singular: *hanc praescriptionem,* he apparently sees the claim as one in spite of its twofold application.[5]

The substance, then, of 21,1-3 might be rendered as follows:

> Hence we draw up this claim: as preachers of the doctrine of faith only the apostles can be held true; as witnesses to what they preached only the apostolic churches can be held true.

Next follows the crucial passage (21,4-22,1), which in the original text reads:[6] (21,4) *Si haec ita sunt, constat perinde omnem doctrinam, quae cum illis ecclesiis apostolicis matricibus et originalibus fidei conspiret, veritati deputandam, id sine dubio tenentem, quod ecclesiae ab apostolis, apostoli a Christo, Christus a deo accepit,* (21,5) *omnem vero doctrinam de mendacio praeiudicandam quae sapiat contra veritatem ecclesiarum et apostolorum Christi et dei.* (21,6) *Superest ergo uti demonstremus, an haec nostra doctrina cuius regulam supra edidimus de apostolorum traditione censeatur et ex hoc ipso ceterae[7] de mendacio veniant.* (21,7) *Communicamus cum ecclesiis apostolicis, quod nulla doctrina diversa: hoc est testimonium veritatis.* (22,1) *Sed quoniam tam expedita probatio est ut si statim proferatur nihil iam sit retractandum, ac si prolata non sit a nobis, locum interim demus diversae parti, si quid putant ad infirmandam hanc praescriptionem movere se posse.*

The interpretation of the first two paragraphs of this passage seems to offer no problems. The author states that the claim of 21,1-3, establishing the apostles and the apostolic churches as the only intermediaries in the handing down of the faith, provides us with a touchstone to divide between true and false doctrines. This is about what he says:

> If the claim drawn up above is correct, then the logical conclusion must be: such doctrinal systems as agree with the convictions of the apostolic churches must be considered to be in the right; they undoubtedly contain that which was revealed by God and transmitted through Christ and the apostles. On the other hand, any system holding convictions against the doctrine of the apostolic churches—doctrine proved by its transmission from God through Christ and the apostles—must

be prejudged to stem from falsehood.

Then follows the last step in the argumentation, the application of the touchstone, demonstrating the truth of catholic doctrine. After a preliminary observation in 21,6, the proof is formulated in 21,7. But, on the face of it, the passage 21,6-7 is rather obscure. It needs a close examination, in which the next paragraph (22,1), too, must be included, as it is intimately connected with 21,6-7. Even a look at 22,2ff. and the ensuing chapters will be necessary, for this section results from and, consequently, throws light upon, the argumentation in chapter 21.

We start with a paraphrase of Tertullian's text, as we understand it, accompanying the different paragraphs with a few words of comment. Next, to justify our interpretation, details of the text will receive particular attention.

21,6. The way to divide between true and false doctrines having been found (21,4-5), Tertullian states he is in a position now to demonstrate that truth is on the side of catholic doctrine:

> The result from the foregoing is the possibility for us to demonstrate that our system—the doctrinal contents of which we have given above[8]—really does go back to the apostles and *eo ipso* the other systems do come forth from falsehood.

21,7. Finally, then, the demonstration. Applying his touchstone Tertullian proves in a few words that catholic doctrine is right:

> We are in communion with the apostolic churches (which implies that we share their convictions); this communion is lacking in all the other systems; so, in contrast with them, we are in possession of the truth.

22,1. This proof, the author says, is so clinching that the only way for the heretics to escape defeat is to try and cut at the proof's support, at the claim, that is, which in a former stage of the argumentation had established the authority of the apostles and the apostolic churches:

> This demonstration is such an efficient one that it makes further reasoning superfluous; let us, therefore, as if we had not produced it, give an opportunity to the opposite side to express whatever point they feel capable of raising to invalidate our claim.

22,2ff. Consequently, from 22,2 onward, Tertullian makes the heretics raise objections against the claim of 21,1-3. This claim being twofold: 1) only the apostles can be considered as legitimate preachers of the faith,

2) only the apostolic churches are depositaries of the contents of their preaching, the author has the heretics make a twofold attack—only, of course, to be rebutted by him. In 22,2-27,1 they cast doubts on the apostles' knowledge of the entire doctrine of the faith (22,2-25,1) and on their willingness to hand it over without restriction (25,1-27,1), in 27,1-37,1 on the capability of the churches to receive and to preserve in its original purity the preaching of the apostles.[9]

These objections proving null and void, the conclusion remains that the claim establishing the authority of the apostles and the apostolic churches is fully operative. This, then, secures the validity of the thesis that communion with the apostolic churches is the mark of truth. And, as a result, the last step, too, is legitimate: the agreement with the apostolic churches puts the catholics in the right, whereas the heretics, on account of their disagreement, are left in the wrong.

It remains for us to elucidate some details in the text of 21,6ff.

First of all, we must account for our interpretation of *superest* in *Superest . . . uti demonstremus* ('the result . . . is the possibility for us to demonstrate'). In point of fact, the impersonal use of *superesse* with a consecutive nuance is frequent in deductive argumentation. This particular nuance proceeds from the idea of exclusion the expression *superest* implies. Often the logical process of exclusion is explicit: so in Tertullian **Adversus Hermogenem** 16,4: *Exclusa itaque materia . . . superest uti deum omnia ex nihilo fecisse constet;* **Adversus Marcionem** 4,10,6: *Atque ita discutiendum cuius hominis filius* (Christus) *accipi debeat, patris an matris. Si ex deo patre est, utique non ex homine; si non est ex homine < patre >, superest ut ex homine sit matre; si ex homine < matre >, iam apparet quia ex virgine;*[10] see also *De anima* 21,3; *De pudicitia* 13,23-25; **Adversus Marcionem** 2,10,1; 3,20,7, and elsewhere. But the idea of exclusion may also recede into the background, leaving the consecutive nuance master of the field. The following texts may be quoted in which this process is on its way, or has altogether come, to completion. In **Adversus Marcionem** 4,15,7 Tertullian rejects Marcion's thesis about the two Gods, the God of the Old and the God of the New Covenant: *nec erit iam discrimini locus, quo duo dei funt, sublatoque discrimine supererit unum deum renuntiari.* In *De resurrectione mortuorum* 6,6 the author draws a comparison between the sculptor Phidias modelling a statue of Jupiter from ivory and God modelling man from clay: 'must we conclude', he says, 'that we find more attractive the creation of a god by man than the creation of man by God?': *Phidiae manus Iovem Olympium ex ebore molitae adorantur . . . ; deus vivus et deus verus quamcumque materiae vilitatem nonne de sua operatione purgasset et ab omni infirmitate sanasset? An hoc supererit ut honestius homo deum quam hom-*

inem deus finxerit? In ***Adversus Marcionem*** 4,28,7 the paradoxical consequences are put forward of Marcion's thesis that Christ has nothing to do with the God of the Old Covenant, the 'Creator': 'if Christ disapproves of the Creator's severity towards those who blaspheme his Spirit and deny his Christ, then, in due consequence, the Spirit of that God may be blasphemed and his Christ denied with impunity': *Aut si et per haec (Christus) severitatem eius (= Creatoris) infuscat, non remissuri blasphemiam et occisuri etiam in gehennam, superest ut et illius diversi dei impune et Spiritus blasphemetur et Christus negetur et nihil intersit de cultu eius deve contemptu et, sicut de contemptu nulla poena, ita et de cultu nulla speranda sit merces.* In ***De monogamia*** 3,2 Tertullian infers from the Apostle's preference for celibacy that married people, too, should consider living in continence: *Bonum, inquit, homini mulierem non contingere. Ergo malum est contingere. Nihil enim bono contrarium nisi malum. Ideoque superesse ut et qui habeant uxores sic sint quasi non habentes, quo magis qui non habent habere non debeant.* Taking these texts into account,[11] the conclusion seems justified that in the text of ***De praescriptione,*** too, the consecutive purport is predominant: *superest uti demonstremus* is equivalent to *sequitur uti demonstremus.*

Translations such as 'It remains that we demonstrate',[12] in my opinion, miss the point in that they announce the demonstration as something new, something not naturally proceeding from the foregoing. In Tertullian's *superest uti demonstremus* no foreign element is hinted at; on the contrary, the demonstration is announced as a logical consequence of the thesis drawn up in the two preceding paragraphs.

Another point to discuss is the turn of phrase *demonstremus an . . . censeatur.* Instead of a more regular construction, like the accusative with infinitive, Tertullian uses the conjunction *an* with a dependent interrogative sentence. From the point of view of classical grammar this might seem startling, but in Tertullian's usage it is by no means uncommon. The strong affirmative value of this construction with *an* is due to the fact that *an* in Tertullian often assumes the significance of *nonne.* This use of *an* is found in independent phrases, where *an* often asks for the reader's assent in exactly the same way as classical *nonne* does. We may refer to ***De praescriptione*** 8,10: *an qui scit se intus fuisse et foras actum, is potius pulsabit et ostium novit?;* ***Adversus Marcionem*** 3,18,7: *Moyses . . . cur aereum serpentem ligno impositum pendentis habitu in spectaculum salutare proposuit? An et hic dominicae crucis vim intentabat?*[13] But in subordinate clauses also this affirmative *an* appears. So in ***Adversus Marcionem*** 1,10,2: *maior popularitas generis humani . . . deum Moysei . . . norunt; etiam tantam idolatria dominationem obumbrante, seorsum tamen illum quasi proprio nomine 'deum' perhibent et 'deum deorum' et 'si deus dederit' et 'quod deo placet' et 'deo*

commendo'. Vide an noverint quem omnia posse testantur. Nec hoc ullis Moysei libris debent. 'Evidently they know him', as Mr. Evans' translation has it.[14] Likewise ***De resurrectione mortuorum*** 36,1ff.: *Videamus nunc an et Saducaeorum versutiam elidens (Christus) nostram magis sententiam erexerit . . . Habes igitur dominum confirmantem adversus haereticos Iudaeorum quod et nunc negatur apud Saducaeos christianorum, solidam resurrectionem.* 'Did not Christ, by refuting the Sadducees' subtleties, confirm our opinion?' And very near to our passage ***De patientia*** 5,3: *Consideremus igitur de inpatientia, an sicut patientia in deo, ita adversaria eius in adversario nostro nata atque comperta sit,* which amounts to saying: 'As patience cannot but be God's attribute, so impatience cannot but be the devil's.' Other instances can be found in ***Ad nationes*** 1,14,3; ***De pudicitia*** 6,6; ***Adversus Marcionem*** 4,25,11, etc. We are faced, therefore, with a particular feature of Tertullian's language, in which the author, by means of an interrogative clause, provokes the reader's agreement with what is his strong personal conviction. It is an emotionally conditioned and forcefully expressed affirmation, characteristic of Tertullian's passionate style.

There is a textual problem in the second half of 21,6. In the version of the *Agobardinus,* the highest-ranking manuscript, the phrase reads: *Superest ergo uti demonstremus an haec nostra doctrina . . . de apostolorum traditione censeatur et ex hoc ipso ceterae de mendacio veniant.* The other manuscripts have a second *an* inserted before *ceterae.* Their reading is adopted by most of the editors, but Rauschen, Martin and Kroymann follow the *Agobardinus.*[15] One can see the latters' point. As appears from 21,4-5, the words *ceterae de mendacio veniant* are to such a degree the logical consequence, better still the counterpart, of *haec nostra doctrina . . . de apostolorum traditione censeatur,* that a second *an* must be considered useless and, in view of the insertion *ex hoc ipso,* even positively awkward. *Ex hoc ipso* does not mean 'in the same way', but 'in consequence of this'; the demonstration, therefore, bears, not on a twofold, but on a single object, the apostolic origin of the catholic faith, which necessarily implies the spurious character of the other systems. Yet, on the face of it, the object is a composite one, and a copyist could easily feel called upon to supplement the supposedly wanting conjunction. I take it, therefore, that Rauschen *et al.* rightly choose the text of the *Agobardinus.*

The expression *de apostolorum traditione censeatur* points to the past, to the period, that is, in which the apostles handed down to the churches what they themselves had learnt from Christ. *Apostolorum traditio* denotes the act and moment in which the apostles entrusted the faith to the churches:[16] at that moment the truth of christian doctrine entered history. *Censeri* in the meaning of 'to take its origin', 'to proceed' is particular to Tertullian's vocabulary, as has been amply demonstrated by Professor Waszink.[17] In our passage the parallelism with *de mendacio veniant* is illustrative. For both *apostolorum traditio* as referring to the past and *censeri* in the sense of *oriri* we may quote **Adversus Marcionem** 1,21,4, where Tertullian defends against Marcion the identity between the God of the New Testament and the God of the Old, the 'Creator'. At the time of the apostles, he says, that identity never was questioned. *Quodsi post apostolorum tempora adulterium veritas passa est circa dei regulam, ergo iam apostolica traditio nihil passa est in tempore suo circa dei regulam, et non alia agnoscenda erit traditio apostolorum quam quae hodie apud ipsorum ecclesias editur. Nullam autem apostolici census ecclesiam invenias quae non in Creatore christianizet.* As for *apostolica (apostolorum) traditio,* there is a slight difference with our passage in that *traditio,* here, instead of the act of handing down the doctrine, denotes more this doctrine itself, but the reference to the past is clear enough: *in tempore suo.* In *apostolici census ecclesiam* the substantive *census* (= origin) obviously corresponds to *censeri.*

In 21,7 the short sentence *Communicamus cum ecclesiis apostolicis, quod nulla doctrina diversa* constitutes the proof, announced in the preceding paragraph. It is a critical phrase, and it is the more deplorable that the translations proposed by the various editors and commentators are in striking disagreement. Most authors supply *est* in the subordinate clause and take *doctrina* in the sense of 'teaching', 'doctrine', 'contents of the faith', 'point of doctrine'. So Holmes, who translates: 'We hold communion with the apostolic churches, because our doctrine is in no respect different from theirs.'[18] Kellner-Esser and Christine Mohrmann,[19] on the other hand, add a verb like *facit* and, understanding *doctrina* as 'a doctrinal system', 'a religious opinion and its adherents', they render: 'We hold communion with the apostolic churches, which is not the case with any of the divergent opinions (*i.e.* the heresies).'

This last translation seems to me decidedly preferable. As has been pointed out above,[20] doctrine as such, the contents of the faith, is not at the heart of Tertullian's demonstration. The only place in his work where it receives full attention is chapter 13, as the author gives the *regula fidei* of the orthodox church. In 20,1, at the start of his argumentation, he alludes, as we have seen, to some points of this *regula,* but only in passing, not as an essential part of his reasoning. This reasoning runs along historical and factual lines, prescinding from any doctrinal discussion and concentrating only on the origins of the catholic and the heretical systems. True, in 21,6 the *regula fidei* is mentioned again, but once more in passing and in a significant context: *haec nostra doctrina cuius regulam supra edidimus.* Evidently the relative clause *cuius regulam supra edidimus* refers to the description of christian doctrine, the *regula fidei,*

of chapter 13. In consequence *doctrina* cannot mean 'the contents of the faith', but must have the sense of 'a doctrinal system', 'a belief': 'our belief the contents of which we have given above'. To this *nostra doctrina,* then, in 21,6 corresponds *nulla doctrina diversa* in 21,7.[21] The confrontation, opposing in 21,6 the catholic and the heretical beliefs (*haec nostra doctrina* v. *ceterae doctrinae*), continues in 21,7: (*nos*) *communicamus* v. (*nulla*) *doctrina diversa.* In Holmes's translation this confrontation is ignored, which, in my opinion, makes his rendering come dangerously near to a meaningless phrase.

Communicamus cum ecclesiis apostolicis also needs a word of explanation. Tertullian says: 'We live in communion with, we belong to the brotherhood of the apostolic churches.' The expression, probably, refers to 20,8-9, where the characteristics of this brotherhood are described: *Probant unitatem* (ecclesiarum) *communicatio pacis et appellatio fraternitatis et contesseratio hospitalitatis. Quae iura non alia ratio regit quam eiusdem sacramenti una traditio.* Now, one might argue that the author overstates his case: as it is a question of belief, only a sharing of convictions is required. But in Tertullian's eyes the common christian belief works out in the social and charitable functionings of christian life. Sincere brotherhood presupposes unity of faith: *eiusdem sacramenti una traditio.* He only shares the doctrine of the apostolic churches, who is tied to them by bonds of friendship and mutual obligation. As the heretics have severed these bonds, they have lost contact with the churches' faith and, consequently, with the faith of the apostles: they cannot possibly possess the truth.

Our last remark concerns the kind of retrograde step the reasoning makes in 22,1. The author, in a curious move, more or less disregards the proof he has given, irrefutable as it is, and from now one, for many chapters to follow, concentrates on the attacks the heretics make against the claim, *i.e.* against the proof's presupposition. The proof itself, obviously, is not foremost in Tertullian's mind; it is, of course, an essential element in the discussion, and as such it has received proper attention, but, all in all, it is disposed of without much circumstance. The claim, on the contrary, is the author's real concern; he spends the remaining part of his treatise chiefly to establishing its validity (chapter 22-37). In this context the expression *hanc praescriptionem* in 22,1, perhaps, deserves some attention. It has been set forth above that it refers to the claim drawn up in 21,1-3.[22] Now, the use of the pronoun *hanc* suggests that the proof deduced from, and subsequent in the text to, the claim has not really been present in the author's mind. On the contrary, he was preoccupied by the heretics' questioning of the proof's guarantee, the authority of the apostles and the churches. It is this questioning which he intends to deal with, convinced that, once this resistance is shattered, victory over heresy is all but won.

Notes

[1] D. Michaélidès, *Foi, Écritures et Tradition, ou Les 'Praescriptiones' chez Tertullien*, Collection Théologie 76 (Paris 1969) *passim;* a rich bibliography, on pp. 154-162, presents the older works.

[2] J.-Cl. Fredouille, *Tertullien et la conversion de la culture antique* (Paris 1972) 195-234. In the course of his exposé Mr. Fredouille also discusses the related problem of the exact title of Tertullian's treatise: instead of the traditional *De praescriptione haereticorum* he proposes *De praescriptionibus adversus haereses omnes:* see 228ff.

[3] In Refoulé's edition 21,6-7; cfr. R. Refoulé, *Quinti Septimi Florentis Tertulliani Opera* I, Corpus Christianorum, series Latina 1 (Turnholti 1954) 203. In Kroymann 21,6-7 constitutes the first part of 22,1; the second half of 22,1 coincides with Refoulé's 22,1; cfr. Aem.Kroymann, *Quinti Septimi Florentis Tertulliani Opera* II, Corpus Scriptorum Ecclesiasticorum Latinorum 70 (Vindobonae et Lipsiae 1942) 25. The difference certainly has something to do with a divergence of interpretation: is *superest ergo uti demonstremus* (21,6; 22,1 in Kroymann) a conclusion resulting from, and therefore linked with, the foregoing, or is it the beginning of a new phase in the argumentation? Kroymann's arrangement of the text presupposes the second opinion. In my view, as will appear further on, Refoulé's arrangement is preferable.

[4] See introduction of this paper.

[5] In 35,1 and 44,3 the plural *praescriptiones* appears. Whichever the reason for the plural in these passages, it remains that in chapter 21-22 the singular is a matter of fact. Whether there is a difference of meaning between the singular and the plural, remains for us undecided.

[6] We follow the division of the text adopted by Refoulé: see note 3.

[7] Reading of the *Agobardinus,* the best manuscript, against *an ceterae* of the other witnesses: for the justification of our choice, see below. Other textual uncertainties in the passage do not seem to be of any consequence for the interpretation.

[8] In chapter 13, where the *regula fidei* is formulated; see p. 35 f.

[9] In chapter 27 and 28 the author specifically has in mind the orthodox churches, which took possession of the apostles' preaching in incorrupt form; from 29,1 to 35,1, with a reverse of the medal, the heretics are in-tended: they came too late for the inheritance, or else their inheritance proved a sham; in chapter 35 and 36 the emphasis is again on the churches, which are truly apostolic, whereas the heresies are degenerations. Against several commentators we hold with Michaélidès that in chapter 27 to 37 Tertullian still refers to the claim of chapter 21 and does not introduce new claims (*praescriptio novitatis, praescriptio longi temporis,* etc.). His reasoning, probably, is less complicate than some would have it (see Michaélidès, *o.c.,* 45 and 55-70, with further references).

[10] We follow the reading proposed by Kroymann and adopted by Refoulé in *Tertulliani Opera* I, 563; Moreschini only adopts the conjecture *matre* (C. Moreschini, *Tertulliani Adversus Marcionem* [Milano-Varese 1971] 184); Evans rejects the insertion of both *patre* and *matre* (E. Evans, *Tertullian. Adversus Marcionem. Books 4 and 5* [Oxford 1972] 298). Whichever the right reading, it remains that *superest* is clearly a pivotal word in the argumentation: 'the only possible conclusion is . . . '

[11] We are indebted, for tracing them, to Claesson's precious lexicon: G. Claesson, *Index Tertullianeus. Q-Z* (Paris 1975) 1590. After Tertullian this use of *superest* lives on: many instances in Lactantius' *Divinae institutiones:* see 1,23,1. 11,44; 3,3,7f.; 7,8,1, and elsewhere. A consultation of lexica on philosophical writing prior to Tertullian (Lucretius, Cicero, Seneca) did not yield anything conclusive.

[12] P. Holmes, in *The Ante-Nicene Fathers* III (New York 1903) 252, followed by J. Quasten, *Patrology.* II. *The Ante-Nicene Literature after Irenaeus* (Utrecht-Antwerp 1953) 271. Likwise de Labriolle: 'Reste donc à démontrer' (P. de Labriolle-R. Refoulé, *Tertullien. Traité de la prescription contre les hérétiques,* Sources Chrétiennes 46 [Paris 1957] 115) and Kellner-Esser: 'Wir müssen also nur noch den Beweis liefern' (A. Kellner-G. Esser, *Tertullians apologetische, dogmatische und montanistische Schriften,* Bibliothek der Kirchenväter 24 [Kempten-München 1915] 327).

[13] For other instances of this use of *an* in independent sentences, see G. Thörnell, *Studia Tertullianea* II (Uppsala 1920) 2, n. 1.

[14] E. Evans, *Tertullian. Adversus Marcionem. Books 1 to 3* (Oxford 1972) 27.

[15] G. Rauschen, *Tertulliani Liber de praescriptione haereticorum,* Florilegium Patristicum 4 (Bonnae 1906) 32; likewise in the second edition, procured by J. Martin (Bonnae 1930) 21 (Rauschen's text is adhered to by de Labriolle: P.de Labriolle, *Tertullien. De praescriptione haereticorum* [Paris 1907] 44, but in Refoulé's new edition of de Labriolle's work the reading with *an* is adopted: de Labriolle-Refoulé, *o.c.,* 115); Aem.

Kroymann, *Tertulliani Opera* II, 25. For the manuscript evidence and the other editions, see Refoulé, *Tertulliani Opera* I, 203.

[16] One might even ask if *apostolorum traditio* does not mean 'the handing over (by Christ) to the apostles', but, probably, Tertullian refers to what happened between the apostles and the churches. As for the general sense, there is no difference between the two interpretations.

[17] J. H. Waszink, *Quinti Septimi Florentis Tertulliani De anima* (Amsterdam 1947) 282.

[18] In *The Ante-Nicene Fathers* III, 252f.; the translation is copied by Quasten, *Patrology,* 271. Likewise de Labriolle: 'parce que notre doctrine ne diffère en rien de la leur' (de Labriolle-Refoulé, *o.c.,* 115), adopted by Michaélidès, *o.c.,* 55 and Fredouille, *o.c.,* 226.

[19] See Kellner-Esser, *o.c.,* 327; Christine Mohrmann, *Tertullianus. Apologeticum en andere geschriften uit Tertullianus' voor-montanistischen tijd,* Monumenta Christiana I,3 (Utrecht-Brussel, 1951) 156.

[20] See p. 35f.

[21] Similar is the meaning of *doctrina* in 21,4-5: *omnem doctrinam quae cum . . . ecclesiis apostolicis . . . conspiret . . . , id . . . tenentem quod ecclesiae ab apostolis, apostoli a Christo, Christus a deo accepit; omnem . . . doctrinam . . . quae sapiat contra veritatem ecclesiarum;* in the whole passage not points of doctrine are meant, but the systems that contain them.

[22] See p. 39; for the use of the singular, see p. 37.

John F. Jansen (essay date 1982)

SOURCE: "Tertullian and the New Testament," in *The Second Century: A Journal of Early Christian Studies,* Vol. 2, No. 4, Winter, 1982, pp. 191-207.

[In the following essay, Jansen studies Tertullian's views on and interpretation of the New Testament.]

Various aspects of Tertullian's use of the Bible have received scholarly attention. One excellent study has been devoted to Tertullian and the Old Testament.[1] The present essay[2] deals with Tertullian and the New Testament.

I

Tertullian and the Canon of the New Testament

By Tertullian's time the basic scope of the New Testament had taken shape in the West. Tertullian has citations or clear allusions to all of the New Testament books except James, 2 Peter, 2 and 3 John.[3] However, citation as such does not necessarily answer the question of canon. We are still in a fluid period—witness the Muratorian Canon list. The word "canon" is not yet employed to designate a fixed body of Holy Scripture, and the Latin equivalent, *regula,* points to a fixed summary of apostolic faith rather than to writings. In Tertullian the world *instrumentum* most nearly includes what we would call "canon."[4] For example, in **Modesty** 10.12 Tertullian asks sarcastically whether the Shepherd of Hermas "deserved to be included in the sacred canon" (*diuino instrumento meruisset incidi*).

As we would expect, Tertullian's validation of the four gospels as "canonical" comes in his refutation of Marcion's unnamed and truncated "Gospel":

> I lay it down to begin with that the documents of the gospel [*euangelicum instrumentum*] have the apostles for their authors, and that this task of promulgating the gospel was imposed upon them by our Lord himself. If they also have for their authors apostolic men [*apostolicos*], yet these stand not alone, but as companions of apostles or followers of apostles. . . . (**Adv. Marc.** IV.2.1)

This makes for a certain priority, he goes on. As apostles Matthew and John introduce or instill (*insinuant*) faith to us, "while from among apostolic men Luke and Mark give it renewal [*instaurant*]." Nonetheless, all four gospels are authoritative Scripture.

If Luke's Gospel is authoritative, so is his Acts. Tertullian attacks Marcion for rejecting Acts (**Adv. Marc.** V.1.5, **Prasescr. haer.** 23.2).

For Tertullian, as for Marcion, Paul is "the" apostle. But he asks why Marcion does not accept the Pastorals when he does accept Philemon:

> This epistle alone has so profited by its brevity as to escape Marcion's falsifying hands. As however he has accepted this letter to a single person, I do not see why he has rejected two written to Timothy and one to Titus about the church system. I suppose he had a whim to meddle even with the number of the epistles. (**Adv. Marc.** V.21.1)

1 Peter, 1 John, and Revelation are authoritative because they were written by apostles.[5] But what of the Epistle to the Hebrews? Tertullian believes the epistle was written by Barnabas, thus by an "apostolic man." Does this mean that he considered the book "canonical"? Some[6] hold that his validation of Hebrews is the same as that of the Lukan writings. It seems to me, however, that this is not so:

> The Scriptures composed by the apostles themselves

are the principal determinants of that discipline which, like a priest, guards the perfect sanctity of the temple of God. . . . I would like, however, over and above this, to add the testimony of one of the postles' companions which aptly confirms as a secondary authority of the masters [i.e. the apostles: *idoneium confirmandi de proximo iure disciplinam magistrorum*]. For there is also extant a book entitled To the Hebrews, written by Barnabas, a man well accredited by God since Paul associates him with himself in the observance of continence. (***Pud.*** 20.1-2)

Is this "proximate" or "next best" authority the same as that given Mark and Luke, who are also "apostolic men"? I do not believe this is the case because those evangelists are included in the *evangelicum instrumentum,* while the latter word is not used with reference to Hebrews. Tertullian makes supportive use of the epistle.

Such supportive use can be seen as parallel to Tertullian's supportive appeal to *Enoch* to corroborate certain prophetic texts. It is hardly accidental that those who hold that Tertullian gives "canonical" status to Hebrews say the same thing about *Enoch.*[7] To be sure, he often cites *Enoch* (e.g. *Idol.* 4.5; *Cult. fem.* I.3.1, *Res. mort.* 32.1) and in the last named even introduces a citation with *habes scriptum.* But what does this mean? The older translation of Holmes in the *Ante Nicene Fathers* rendered this: "you have it declared in Scripture." But *scriptum* is not yet *scriptum est* or *scriptura* and not all *scriptura* is Holy Scripture. After all, Tertullian has said that Hermas, the *scriptura Pastoris,* does not belong in the sacred canon (***Pud.*** 10.12). So Evans renders the phrase, "you have it written." Von Campenhausen says the most one can say:

> Tertullian would certainly have liked to add Enoch to the Old and Hebrews to the New Testament; but he contents himself with commending the testimony of these works and with justifying his own appeal to them. He is not striving for any 'reform' of the Bible.[8]

Very different is the case with the *Shepherd* of Hermas. The Muratorian Canon recommended the Shepherd as edifying literature but not as Scripture to be read in public assembly "nor (be counted) among the prophets, whose number is complete or among the apostles." Not so Tertullian. In an earlier writing he had already made a belittling reference to it (***Orat.*** 16.1), but in his later writings he castigates the book as one "which alone is favorable to adulterers" and one which had been judged "apocryphal and false by all the councils of the churches" (***Pud.*** 10.12). Le Saint observes that "Tertullian is the first Christian Latin writer to use the word 'apocryphal' as a designation of non-canonical or spurious books

of the New Testament."[9]

A good example of Tertullian's rejection of apocryphal books is his comment on the *Acts of Paul:*

> But if certain *Acts of Paul,* which are falsely so named, claim the example of Thecla for allowing women to teach and to baptize, let men know that in Asia the presbyter who compiled that document [*scripturam*], thinking to add of his own to Paul's reputation, was found out, and though he professed he had done it for love of Paul, was deposed from his position. (Bapt. 17.5)

This is not to say that Tertullian cannot make apologetic and supportive use of documents we now know to be apocryphal. It simply means he does not give such writings canonical status. An example is the *Acts of Pilate* (a tradition Eusebius, in *Hist. eccl.* II.2.2, also took to be authentic):

> All these facts [of cross and resurrection] were reported to Tiberius, the reigning emperor, by Pilate who was by now a Christian himself, so far as his conscience was concerned. (***Apol.*** 21.24)

More important for the question of canon is what the "new prophecy" of Montanism meant for Tertullian. For the moment we defer what he has to say about the Paraclete's illumination of Scripture. Here we are concerned with those few times when Tertullian actually cites the new prophecy. The question is that raised earlier with reference to *Enoch* and Hebrews—does Tertullian cite these Montanist sayings supportively or as themselves scriptural? Does the prophecy supplement or merely illumine Scripture? Of the several citations[10] one deserves particular attention. In his ***Exhortation to Chastity*** is a passage on the blessings of continence that concludes with two Old Testament quotations and continues: "In line with this [*ita enim*] the Apostle also says that 'to be wise according to the flesh is death, but to be wise according to the spirit is life eternal.'" This is followed by a citation from the new prophecy:

> *Item per sanctam prophetidem Priscam ita euangelizatur, quod 'sanctus minister sanctimoniam nouerit ministrare.' 'Purificantia' enim 'cum cor dat,' ait, 'et uisiones uident et ponentes faciem deorsum etiam uoces audiunt salutares, tam manifestas quam et occultas.'* (***Exhort. cast.*** 10.5)

Le Saint renders: "In like manner the holy prophetess Prisca declares that every holy minister will know how to administer things that are holy. 'For,' she says, 'continence effects harmony of soul, and the pure see visions and, bowing down, hear voices speaking clearly words salutary and secret.'" However, Stegman,[11] following Karpp,[12] holds that here a Montanist saying is given equal scriptural status because *item* places the saying alongside the prophetic and apostolic texts, and *euangelizatur* carries the same force as canonical proclamation.

Without minimizing the importance of the new prophecy for Tertullian, I cannot see that the use made of Montanist sayings here is more than illustrative and supportive. The new prophecy does not add to the biblical revelation but rather supports and illustrates the biblical texts. One can compare the passage just cited with one in the treatise on **Resurrection,** which may be the earliest witness to Tertullian's shift to Montanism. There he has to vindicate the resurrection of the flesh against those opponents who hold that flesh is unworthy of restoration and resurrection. Tertullian gives a long list of biblical references, beginning with the creation story, to show the dignity of that flesh "which God with his own hands constructed in God's image" (**Res. mort.** 9.1). The trouble with the opponents is that they retain only those scriptures in which the flesh is sullied; they should retain also those scriptures in which flesh is adorned (*inlustatur*)—and another series of biblical texts follow. The conclusion comes in 11.1. Those who deny the dignity of the flesh are themselves bound to the flesh because they despise that discipline that points to the resurrection of the flesh. "Concerning those the Paraclete also says very well [*luculenter*] by Prisca the prophetess, 'Lumps of flesh they are, and the flesh they hate." (**Res. mort.** 11.2). The saying serves to corroborate and tie together the preceding argument from Scripture. Indeed, the treatise closes with a passage declaring that the new prophecy dispels the ambiguities of Scripture and thus makes everything clear.

Moreover, if the new prophecy were intended to supplement or add to the biblical canon we would expect more use of these sayings. A. F. Walls says: "The Montanist, like the catholic, drew his faith and inspiration from the prophetic and apostolic Scriptures. This may explain why Tertullian's extant Montanist writings can yield only a bare half-dozen oracles of the New Prophecy."[13]

Withal, to affirm the books of the New Testament insofar as these books have been received means that one must do battle against those who delete or distort them. In large measure this is the burden of the books against Marcion and of his **Prescription against Heretics:**

> One man perverts Scripture with this hand, another with this exegesis. If Valentinus seems to have used the whole Bible, he laid violent hands on the truth with just as much cunning as Marcion. Marcion openly and nakedly used the knife, not the pen, massacring Scripture to suit his own material. Valentinus spared the text, since he did not invent scriptures to suit his matter, but matter to suit the

> Scriptures. Yet he took more away, and added more, by taking away the proper meanings of particular words and by adding fantastic arrangements. (**Praescr. haer.** 38.7-10)

Against all such efforts to tamper with the New Testament, Tertullian points the warning of Revelation 22:18f. ("if any one adds to them, God will add to him the plagues described in this book, and if any one takes away from the words of the book of this prophecy, God will take away his share in the tree of life"):

> I worship the fullness of the Scripture [*adoro scripturae plenitudinem*] by means of which He reveals to us both the Maker and the things made; but in the Gospel I find in addition Him who is both the Minister and the Intermediary of the Maker—the Word. But whether it was from underlying matter that all things were made [as claimed by Hermogenes], I have as yet read nowhere. That Scripture has it is for Hermogenes' workshop to show us. If it is not in Scripture [*Si non est scriptum*], let him fear the 'Woe' that was meant for all those 'who add or take away.' (**Adv. Hermog.** 22.5)

II

Tertullian and the Text of the New Testament

How early are the Latin versions of the New Testament? Scholars have debated whether Tertullian's numerous citations reflect early Latin versions or represent his own translation, or both.[14] Danielou is confident that "Quotations in the works of Tertullian and Cyprian point clearly to the existence of Latin translations of the Old Testament at the end of the second century," and he is confident that the same is true for the New Testament. "In view of the fact that there were few Christians and that these spoke only Latin, it is obvious that there must have been a Latin translation of the New Testament at a very early stage."[15] In all probability Tertullian's citations of the New Testament sometimes represent his own translation and at other times reflect the fluid character of the early Latin versions.

This raises many interesting questions which cannot be explored here—such as his preference for *sermo* over *verbum* in the Johannine prologue.[16] Here we limit our discussion to one variant reading with which Tertullian is familiar and which he uses polemically.

The accepted reading of John 1:13 in the later Valgate, as in all of our Greek manuscripts, is the plural: "who *were born,* not of blood nor of the will of the flesh nor of the will of man, but of God." However, several ancient witnesses, mostly Latin, read the text in the singular: "who *was born,* not of blood nor of the will of the flesh nor of the will of man but of God."[17] This makes the verse a Christological statement that suggests the virgin birth. It would appear that the singular reading is known by Irenaeus. At any rate, Tertullian not only knows this reading but vindicates it over against the Valentinians, who used the plural to support their doctrine.

> What then is the meaning of 'Was born not of blood nor of the will of the flesh nor of the will of man, but of God' [*sed ex deo natus est*]? This text will be of more use to me than to them [the Valentinians], when I have refuted those who falsify it. For they maintain that it was thus written, 'Were born [*nati sunt*] not of blood, nor of the will of the flesh or of a man, but of God,' as though it referred to the above-mentioned believers in his name: and from it they try to prove that there exists that mystic seed of the elect and spiritual which they baptize for themselves. But how can it mean this, when those who believe in the name of the Lord are all of them by the common law of human kind born of blood and of the will of the flesh and of a man, as also is Valentinus himself? Consequently, the singular is correct . . . [*adeo singulariter, ut de domino, scriptus est: 'sed ex deo natus est . . .'*]. (**Carne Chr.** 19.1-2)

Tertullian goes on to insist that although Christ was not born of the will of the flesh, his flesh is real flesh. "We understand, then, a denial that the Lord's nativity was the result of coition . . . but no denial that it was by a partaking of the womb" (19.4). In short, the reading that textual criticism commends to us Tertullian knew only as being in the hands of the heretics. That was reason enough to disavow it.

III

Tertullian and the Authority of the New Testament

For Tertullian the New Testament, as the Old, is *scriptura, divina literatura, sancti commentarii, sacrosanctus stilus,* etc. We have noted above that *instrumentum* and *paratura* most nearly express what we mean by canon, though it can also refer to particular books or to a number of books as well as to Scripture in its entirety. *Instrumentum* also suggests that Tertullian understands the authority of Scripture as law.[18] Indeed, from the beginning God's revelation has been that of Law. Long before God gave his law to Moses, he had already given it in Paradise.

> For in this law given to Adam we recognize in embryo all the precepts which afterwards sprouted forth when given through Moses; that is, 'Thou shalt love the Lord thy God from all thy whole heart and out of thy whole soul; Thou shalt love thy neighbour

as thyself. . . . (**Adv. Jud.** 2.3)[19]

But with Christ the old Law has been fulfilled and displaced by the new Law:

> . . . there was to supervene a time whereat the precepts of the ancient Law and of the old ceremonies would cease, and the promise of the new law [*nouae legis promissio*], and the recognition of spiritual sacrifices, and the promise of the New Testament [*nouvi testamenti pollicitatio*] supervene. . . . that the promised new law is now in operation [*quam legem nouam promissam nunc operari*]. . . . And, primarily, we must lay it down that the ancient Law and the prophets could not have ceased, unless He were come who was constantly announced, through the same Law and through the same prophets, as to come. (**Adv. Jud.** 6.1-4)

If Old Testament ceremonies have been abrogated by the Gospel, this does not mean a lessening but rather a more stringent discipline of the new Law. In one of the later treatises from his Montanist period, we read:

> Having considered the example given us by the Patriarchs, let us now go on to study the law documented in the Scriptures [*instrumenta legalium scripturarum*], so that we may thus examine, in due order, the whole of the sacred canon [*ut per ordinem de omni nostra paratura retractemus*]. There are some who occasionally assert that they are not subject to the Law, the Law which Christ did not destroy but fulfilled. . . . We declare that the Law is abrogated in the sense that the burdens which it imposed no longer rest upon us, the burdens, according to the Apostles, which 'not even our fathers were able to bear.' However, such of its precepts as have to do with righteousness not only continue in force but have even been extended, so that our 'justice may abound more than that of the Scribes and Pharisees.' If this holds true of justice, it also holds true of chastity. (**Mon.** 7.1,2)

Scripture, nature, and discipline establish the law of Christ.

> The defence of our opinion is as follows, according to Scripture, nature, and discipline. Scripture establishes the law, nature testifies to it and discipline demands it. [*Scriptura legem condit, natura contestatur, disciplina exigit*]. . . . Therefore let it be a rule for you, that you will find God's will in Scripture, nature, and discipline. . . . (**Virg. vel.** 16.1-2)

Scripture is thus the constitutive principle, nature its corroborating witness, and discipline the practical appropriation of the new Law.[20] On the one hand Tertullian speaks of a *nova disciplina* because in these latter days the Paraclete has enjoined on believers a more rigorous discipline: "But now, in these latter times

He has restricted what He allowed before and revoked the indulgence which He had then permitted" (***Exhort. cast.*** 6.2). On the other hand Tertullian claims that the changes are consonant with what Scripture has always said.

If Scripture is God's revealed truth, how can there be so many divergent and irreconcilable interpretations of Christian faith? If Shakespeare's Antonio can say,

> Mark you this, Bassanio,
> The devil can cite Scripture to his purpose,

Tertullian can say the same: "Who interprets the meaning of those passages which make for heresy? The devil, of course, whose business it is to pervert truth. . . . " (***Praescr. haer.*** 40.1.) That is why we need the Rule of Faith, a *regula* that cannot be equated with a particular baptismal creed nor with the whole of Scripture. The Rule of Faith appears to be a doctrinal summary of apostolic faith and serves as a correct and authoritative interpretation of Scripture.[21] In practice this means that Scripture belongs to the Church and can be rightly understood only in the Church.

> If therefore truth must be adjudged to us 'as many as walk according to this rule' which the Church has handed down from the apostles, the apostles from Christ, and Christ from God, the principle which we propounded is established, the principles which ruled that heretics are not to be allowed to enter an appeal to Scripture. . . . (***Praescr. haer.*** 37.1)

He continues:

> Corruption of the Scriptures and of their interpretation is to be expected wherever difference in doctrine is discovered [*Illic igitur et scripturarum et expositionum adulteratio deputanda est ubi doctrinae est ubi doctrinae diuersitas inuenitur*]. . . . Just as their corruption of doctrine would not have been successful without their corruption of its literature [*Sicut illis non potuisset succedere corruptela doctrinae sine corruptela instrumentorum eius*], so our doctrinal integrity would have failed us without the integrity of the sources by which doctrine is dealt with. (***Praescr. haer.*** 38.1-3)

Since truth always precedes error, this rule of faith which derives from Christ himself is prior to all heresies. The "novelty" of heresy is a constant theme in Tertullian's controversial works:

> Who are you? When did you arrive, and where from? You are not my people; what are you doing on my land? By what right are you cutting down my timber, Marcion? By whose leave are you diverting my waters, Valentinus? By what authority are you moving my boundaries, Apelles? This property bel-

ongs to me. . . . I am heir to the apostles. As they provided in their will, as they bequeathed it in trust and confirmed it under oath, so, on their terms, I hold it. (***Praescr. haer.*** 37.3-5)

The same argument marks Tertullian's works against Marcion and Hermogenes.[22] Since heretics are not in the Church, they have no right to the Scriptures. "Therefore I take my stand above all on this point; they are not to be admitted to any discussion of Scripture at all" (***Praescr. haer.*** 15.3). Titus 3:10 is sufficient warrant for not having anything to do with those who are factious. "Besides, arguments about Scripture achieve nothing but a stomachache or a headache" (***Praescr. haer.*** 6.2). [In practice Tertullian belies this assertion, for his works against the heretics are above all arguments drawn from Scripture.]

Scripture is fruitless without the Rule of Faith. Scriptural arguments are fruitless not only with reference to heretics but with reference to well-meaning people in the Church. Too often people have allowed the dominical word, "Seek and you shall find," to become an occasion for useless speculation—and this the heretics will always use to deceive the faithful. The words "Seek and you shall find" are for those who did not know Jesus as the Christ; they are not meant for us who have been taught by the apostles "as they were taught by the Holy Spirit." "Thy faith hath saved thee,' it says, not thy biblical learning [*non exercitatio scripturarum*]. Faith is established by the Rule . . ." (***Praescr. haer.*** 14.3,5). That is to say, the authority of Scripture is the authority of that faith which has been given to the Church.

From the relation between Scripture and tradition we turn once more to the relation between Scripture and Spirit. To what extent did the new prophecy affect Tertullian's view of Scripture? When discussing the question of canon, we asked whether the new prophecy supplemented or added to Scripture. Now we ask whether the new prophecy displaced or superseded Scripture.

Consider a passage from the treatise on ***Idolatry:*** "Need I, with my poor memory, suggest anything more? Need I quote more from Scripture? When the Holy Spirit has spoken, that is surely enough" (***Idol.*** 4.5). Writing in 1924, Roberts saw in this passage a marked change in Tertullian's view of Scripture. In the earlier writings, he said, Scripture proofs were so important (e.g. ***Spec.***) that Tertullian would wrest a passage to support his theme, while now "the voice of the Spirit is sufficient without the support of the written word."[23] This position is not persuasive. In the first place, although some date the work on ***Idolatry*** within the period of Montanist influence, many others date it much earlier. Secondly, the context argues against Roberts' conclusion. Tertullian begins with the explicit condemnation of idolatry in the decalogue and follows with warning passages from Isaiah and the Psalms (including also two warnings from *Enoch*). Only after these citations does he ask whether he needs to quote more Scripture. When he says, "The Holy Spirit has spoken," the inference is plain that the Spirit has spoken sufficiently in Scripture. The passage does not speak to the question of Montanist influence.[24]

The conclusion of the treatise on *Resurrection,* as we have noted above, does not suggest that the new prophecy supplements or displaces Scripture; it illumines Scripture and resolves its ambiguities. Tertullian often quotes Jesus' word: "I have yet many things to say to you, but you cannot bear them now. When the Spirit of truth comes, he will guide you into all truth . . . for he will take what is mine and declare it to you" (John 16:12). Tertullian asks "whether or not it is possible that the Paraclete has revealed anything at all which is an innovation opposed to the Catholic tradition [*an capiat Paracletum aliquid tale docuisse quod aut nouum deputari possit aduersus catholicam traditionem*] or which imposes moral obligations upon us inconsistent with the 'light burden' referred to by the Lord" (*Mon. 2.1*). To be sure, he goes on, citing John 16:12, "The Holy Spirit will reveal such things as may be considered innovations (*illum quae et noua existimari possint*), since they were not revealed before . . ." (2.2). But what seems innovation is not really so because the Spirit only brings to mind what Christ taught and, therefore, what is already implicit in Scripture—a claim Tertullian often has to prove by very tortuous exegesis.

Karpp is right when he says that the new prophecy "rührt an die Grenzen der Lehre und des Kanons, aber überschreitet sie nicht."[25] Of course Montanist rigor affects the interpretation of particular texts, but its primary influence is on discipline, not on the authority of Scripture or Tradition.

IV

Tertullian and the Interpretation of the New Testament

Considerable research has been devoted to Tertullian's hermeneutic.[26] Here we point to some aspects that find expression in his interpretation of the New Testament.

The Wholeness and Unity of Scripture.

In a passage cited above Tertullian said that he adores "the fullness of Scripture" (*Adv. Hermog.* 22.5). That fullness, of course, embraces Old and New Testament, and the burden of the first three books against Marcion is to show that the Old Testament is the sub-structure of the New. After some initial skirmishing Tertullian proposes to "take up the real battle, fighting hand to hand" because the "front line" at which the battle must

be fought is over "the Creator's scriptures" (*Adv. Marc.* III.5.1). Marcion cannot understand the Gospel or the Apostle because he has rejected the Old Testament. "I shall adduce the Gospel as a supplement to the Old Testament" (*euangelium ut supplementum instrumenti ueteris adhibebo—Adv. Hermog.* 20.4).

The wholeness and unity of Scripture are seen not only in the bond between the testaments but also in the harmony of the New Testament writings. Whatever their differences, the four Gospels reflect a harmony in essentials. "It matters not that the arrangement of their narrative varies, so long as there is agreement in the essentials of faith . . ." (*Adv. Marc.* IV.2.2). The Fourth Gospel may be very different from the Synoptics, but Praxeas cannot claim its support for his heresy that the Son is identical with the Father. The Fourth Gospel may not have such prayers as "My God, my God, why hast thou forsaken me?" or "Father, into thy hands I commit my spirit," but when the Johannine Jesus says that he is "ascending to my Father and your Father," there is a unity of Scripture that cannot be gainsaid (*Adv. Prax.* 25.2).

What is true of the Gospels is true of the whole New Testament:

> Fortunately the apostles are at one in what concerns the canons of faith and discipline. For 'whether it be I or they,' he says, 'thus do we preach.' It is a matter of importance, then, to the Christian religion as such, that one should not believe John granted anything which Paul refused. Whoever regards this consistency of the Holy Spirit will be guided by Him to an understanding of His words. (*Pud.* 19.3-4)

Take, for example, Paul's confrontation with Peter at Antioch. It may be that Paul's zeal was more pronounced in this early period than his later readiness to become all things to all men—but this does not signify a difference with Peter in doctrine but only in conduct.[27]

Scripture Interprets Scripture

Tertullian knows, of course, that the unity of Scripture does not mean that every passage is equally plain. Accordingly, since the Scripture cannot be inconsistent or contradictory, what is clear must interpret and illumine what is not so clear. For example, in response to those who deny an actual resurrection of the body because some passages use the language of resurrection figuratively, Tertullian says:

> In the first place, what will become of all those other passages of divine scripture which so openly attest a corporeal resurrection as to admit of no suspicion of a figurative signification? . . . things

uncertain should be prejudged by things certain, and things obscure by things manifest. . . . (***Res.mort.*** 21.1-2)

This is a constant principle. Praxeas had distorted John's meaning because he had based everything on a single text ("Do you not believe that I am in the Father and the Father in me?"). "On account of Philip's one remark and the Lord's reply" Tertullian makes "a complete study of John's Gospel, so that so many things clearly stated both before it and after it may not be overturned by one remark, which ought to be interpreted in accordance with them all and even in contradiction with its own meaning" [*etiam aduersus suos sensus interpretandus*] (***Adv. Prax.*** 26.1). Note how Tertullian responds to those Sensualists (*Psychici*) who say that adultery is forgiveable by equating Paul's forgiveness of the offending brother in 2 Corinthians 2:5 with the incestuous man whom Paul had condemned in 1 Corinthians 5:4f. With Montanist rigor Tertullian offers a host of passages to show that Paul is consistent in his view and cannot have contradicted himself. To his opponents he says:

> Surrender at last to such numerous texts as these that one passage to which you cling. The few are eclipsed by the many, the uncertain by the certain, the obscure by the clear. [*Pauca multa, dubia certis, obscura manifestis adumbrantur.*] Even if it were certain that the Apostle had pardoned the fornication of that Corinthian, yet this would be but another instance of something which he did on one occasion only, against his own regular practice and in view of the circumstances of the time. (***Pud.*** 17.18)

Heretics like Praxeas do the opposite—they force their interpretation on an obscure passage and use that to color the whole.[28] Tertullian's principle is sound; one wishes that he had abided by it himself.

The "Simplicitas" of Scripture

We should seek the plain and literal meaning wherever possible, avoiding those allegories that the heretics spin out of the Bible. The Valentinians with their allegories are not different from the pagan Eleusinian mysteries (***Adv. Val.*** 1.3f.). Christians should seek "the marrow of Scripture" (*medullam scripturarum*). To do so, they cannot do better than to join the school of Christ, whose disciples were the students to whom the Lord made known the veiled import of his own language [*cui potius figuram uocis suae declarasset*]" (***Scorp*** 12.1). Especially important is the way we deal with the figurative language of the parables. To be sure, Jesus spoke in parables, but he also spoke plainly and without figurative speech to his disciples. So we must interpret the figurative language of the parables by the plain teaching of doctrine. "We, however, do not take the parables as sources of doctrine, but rather take doctrine as a norm of interpreting the parables" (***Pud.*** 9.1). To ask why a hundred sheep, or why ten drachmas, or why the woman's broom in Luke 15—these are details that will only "seduce me from truth through the subtleties of an artificial exegesis." [*et coactarum expositionum subtilitate plerumque deducunt a ueritate*] (***Pud.*** 9.2). And yet concern for the literal sense must not forget that figurative language in Scripture has its own appropriate place. Marcion distorted the Old Testament because he took figurative language literally (***Adv. Marc.*** III.5.4). Attention must be paid to context, syntax, punctuation, and vocabulary.

Although Tertullian affirms the *simplicitas* of Scripture, some texts are not simple. We take two examples. The first is a text the meaning of which led Tertullian to a change of mind. It is not related to such issues as second repentance, flight in persecution, or second marriage—issues in which changes can be attributed to the new discipline of Montanism. It is simply a problem text on which many besides Tertullian have changed their mind— "baptism for the dead" in 1 Corinthians 15:29. In *Resurrection* 48.11 we read:

> And again, if some are baptized for the dead, we shall enquire whether this is with good reason. Certainly he suggests that they had instituted that custom on the assumption by which they supposed that vicarious baptism [*vicarium baptisma*] would be of benefit even to another flesh toward the hope of resurrection. . . .

Against Marcion, Tertullian writes:

> 'What,' he asks, 'shall they do who are baptized for the dead, if the dead rise not?' . . . Abstain then from at once blaming the apostle as either having recently invented this or given it his approval. . . . We see him in another context setting a limit, of one baptism. Consequently, to be baptized for the dead is to be baptized for bodies: for I have shown that what was dead is the body. What shall they do who are baptized for bodies, if bodies do not rise? (***Adv. Marc.*** V.10.1-2)

While these remarks are somewhat ambiguous, I take it that in ***Resurrection*** he says that the Corinthians practiced a vicarious baptism,[29] while in ***Adversus Marcionem*** he takes the phrase more figuratively so that "for the dead" means "for dead bodies"—not of others but of those who have been buried with Christ into a "baptism into death."[30] A second example suggests how the new prophecy of Montanism can lead Terrtullian away from the plain meaning of Scripture. Commenting on Peter at the Mount of Transfiguration, he asks what the evangelist means when describing Peter as "not knowing what he said":

> Was it by a mere mistake? or was it for the reason by which we, in our argument for the new prophecy, claim that ecstasy or being beside oneself is a concomitant of grace? For when a man is in the spirit, especially when he has sight of the glory of God, or when God is speaking of him, he must of necessity fall out of his senses, because in fact he is overshadowed by the power of God—on which there is disagreement between us and the natural men [*de quo cum inter nos et psychicos*]. Meanwhile it is easy to prove that Peter was beside himself. (*Adv. Marc.* IV.22.4-5)

Here certainly is one instance where Montanist influence has dictated his interpretation. Doubtless the passage would be further illuminated if we had the lost books *On Ecstasy,* but the discussion of ectasy in *On the Soul* provides sufficient background for Tertullian's interpretation.[31]

What Is Not Specifically Permitted Is Forbidden

Whether this can be called a rule of interpretation is debatable since it occurs in a limited number of texts. It may also be that the argument from silence reflects the influence of Roman law.[32] In any case, one can say that this interpretive practice becomes increasingly prominent in the later writings.

Already in *De spectaculis* 3.1 the question is raised whether Scripture has anything to say about Christian participation in the pagan games and shows. Tertullian does not have much patience with those who "demand a testimony from holy Scripture, when faced with giving up the spectacles, and declare the matter an open question, because such a renunciation is neither specifically nor in so many words enjoined upon the servants of God." Yet what is not explicit may be implicit in the first Psalm; Scripture need not spell something out to speak to it.

The treatise *Against Hermogenes* belongs to the earlier period also. Here Tertullian counters Hermogenes' denial of a *creatio ex nihilo* simply because Scripture does not state this explicitly. "Scripture could quite well omit to add that He [God] had made them out of nothing, but it should have said by all means that he had made them out of matter, if He had made them so . . ." (*Adv. Hermog.* 21.3).
The silences of Scripture may be equivalent to command. In *Idolatry,* for example, Tertullian asks what

implications might be found in the fact that the Ark contained unclean animals. Opponents of rigorist discipline saw in this a witness to God's mercy. Tertullian is willing to grant this argument in part: "We shall not be disturbed if, after the type of the Ark, the raven and the kite, the wolf, the dog and the serpent, are found in the Church." But notice: "If the Ark is the type, at any rate no idolater is found in it. No animal is the figure of the idolater. *What was not in the Ark can have no place in the Church.*" (*Idol.* 24.24).

In *De corona militis* this argument becomes more pointed. How shall we establish the validity of an unwritten Christian tradition not to wear crowns?

> To be sure, it is very easy to ask: 'Where in Scripture are we forbidden to wear a crown? But, can you show me a text which says we should be crowned? When men demand the support of a scriptural text for a view they do not hold, they ought to be willing to subject their own stand to the same test of holy writ. . . . [They say] 'Whatever is not forbidden is, without question allowed.' Rather do I say, *'Whatever is not specifically permitted is forbidden'* [italics mine] [*Immo prohibetur quod non ultro est permissum].* (*Cor. mil.* 4.2)

Probably the work on *Chastity* belongs to this same period, a time when he was becoming increasingly rigorous in discipline but had not yet gone beyond his earlier writings with reference to second marriage. Considering the question whether Scripture is explicit on this matter, he says:

> Neither in the Gospel nor in the epistles of Paul himself will you find any permission for second marriage based on commandment of God. This fact, then, confirms the conclusion that marriage is to be contracted only once, since we must acknowledge that *a thing is forbidden by God when* [italics mine] there is no evidence that He permits it. (*Exhort. cast.* 4.2)

The treatise *On Monogamy* carries this further. Here we read that the Paraclete has forbidden second marriage (2.1). Even if Scripture be interpreted to have allowed a second marriage before the present dispensation of the Spirit, "I might also argue that what is merely permitted is not an absolute good" (*Mon.* 3.3). To demonstrate that the Paraclete's new teaching is but the unfolding of what has always been God's will, Tertullian presses the argument from scriptural silence beyond any of his earlier efforts. In Genesis, for example, even after the first fratricidal murder, there was no crime of bigamy. To be sure, Lamech was a bigamist, but "there was no second Lamech to imitate the first in marrying two wives. *What Scripture does not mention it de-*

nies" [*Negat scriptura quod non notat*] (**Mon.** 4.4). And, as for the Ark, "Not even unclean birds could enter in company with two females" (4.5)! All this "has the force of a law [*quae utique lex est*]" (5.1). As we would expect, these Old Testament references are followed by a long list of New Testament texts that seek to prove Tertullian's discipline.

One reason why we cannot define precisely his principles of interepreting Scripture is because we can never divorce his exegetical method from the controversies in which he was engaged. He is preeminently the controversialist rather than the exegete. It is not without significance that in all of his writings Tertullian has only one short commentary on Scripture, **De oratione**, and that work is more a homily which begins with an exposition of the Lord's Prayer.

Notes

[1] J.E.L. Van der Geest, *Le Christ et L'Ancien Testament chez Tertullien* (Nijmegen: Dekker & van de Vogt, 1972).

[2] This essay is a revision of a paper presented on April 9, 1981, to the Southwest Seminar on the Development of Early Catholic Christianity. Chapter and section references are from *Tertvlliani Opera in Corpvs Christianorvn,* Series Latina, Pars I,II (Tvrnholti: Typographi Brepols Editores Pontificii, 1954). For the most part the translations are taken from those editions noted in T. D. Barnes, *Tertullian, A Historical and Literary Study* (Oxford: Clarendon Press, 1971), pp. 286-291.

[3] The index of the *Series Latina* edition of Tertullian's works lists four allusions to James and eight to 2 Peter, but these are not demonstrable. H. Roensch, *Das Neue Testament Tertulliens* (Leipzig, 1871) is still a valuable reconstruction of Tertullian's citations. He deals with the suggested allusions to James and 2 Peter and finds them wanting.

[4] *Instrumentum* and *paratura* are used synonymously when applied to the "canon" of Scripture. Cf. R. Braun, *Deus Christianorum: Recherches sur le vocabulaire doctrinal de Tertullien* (Paris: Presses Universitaires de France, 1962) 463-473. Cf. also van der Geest, *op. cit.,* pp. 16-24.

[5] E.g. about 1 John, " . . . abortive Marcionites whom the apostle John pronounced antichrists" (*Adv. Marc.* III.8.1); about Revelation, "Now the apostle John in the Apocalypse describes a sharp two-edged sword" (*Adv. Marc.* III.14.3); about 1 Peter, "concerning moderation of toilet and adornment there is the evident authority of Peter, who with the same voice, because with the same Spirit, as Paul. . . . " (*Orat.*

20.2).

[6] Ellen Flesseman-van Leer, *Tradition and Scripture in the Early Church* (Assen: Van Gorcum and Comp., G. A. Heck, and Dr. J. Prakke, 1953) 174, "In this way also the authority and canonicity of the epistle of Barnabas (today called the Epistle to the Hebrews) is proved. . . . "

[7] *Ibid.,* " . . . Tertullian cannot appeal to the authority of the churches when he defends the canonicity of the book of Enoch . . ." So also A. D'Alès, *La Théólogie de Tertullien* (Paris: Gabriel Beauchesne & C., 1905) 225, "En dehors du canon, il vénère et cite plusiers fois, comme Écriture inspirée, le livre d'Hénoch."

[8] H. Von Campenhausen, *The Formation of the Christian Bible* (Philadelphia: Fortress Press, 1972) 276.

[9] In *Ancient Christian Writers,* no. 28 (Westminster: Newman Press, 1959), note 607 on *Purity [Modesty],* p. 278.

[10] Tertullian mentions Montanus, Prisca, and Maximilla together in *Iei.* 12.4 and in *Adv. Prax.* 1.5; Montanus is mentioned in *Iei.* 12.4, while Prisca is mentioned in *Exhort. cast.* 10.5 and in *Resurr. mort.* 11.2. More often he refers to the "new prophecy." There are six actual citations from the new prophecy: *Exhort. cast.* 10.4, *Resurr. mort.* 11.2, *Fug.* 9.4 (two citations), *Pud.* 21.7.

[11] Claire A. B. Stegman, *The Development of Tertullian's Doctrine of Spiritus Sanctus* (an unpublished Ph.D. dissertation, Southern Methodist University, 1978) 160.

[12] H. Karpp, *Schrift und Geist bei Tertullian* (Gütersloh: C. Bertelsmann Verlag, 1955), p. 61. However, Stegman does not express Karpp's earlier caution on p. 6, that Tertullian's view of the Spirit "rührt an die Grenzen der Lehre und des Kanons, *aber überschreitet sie nicht*" (italics mine).

[13] A. F. Walls, "The Montanist 'Catholic Epistle' and its New Testament Prototype," in *Studia Evangelica,* vol. 3, *Texte und Untersuchungen zur Geschichte der altchristlichen Literatur,* vol. 88 (Berlin: Akademie-Verlag, 1964) 443.

[14] Cf. T. P. O'Malley, *Tertullian and the Bible* (Nijmegen/Utrecht: Dekker & van de Vogt, 1967) 4-8.

[15] J. Daniélou, *The Origins of Latin Christianity* (Philadelphia: Westminster Press, 1977) 5,7.

[16] Cf. the tabulation of "sermo" and "verbum" in Braun, *op. cit.,* p.267, and Marjorie O'Rourke Boyle,

"Sermo: Reopening the Conversation on Translating Jn. 1,1" *Vigiliae Christianae* 31 (1977) 161-168.

[17] Cf. B. M. Metzger, *A Textual Commentary on the Greek New Testament* (New York: United Bible Societies, 1971) 196f. for a brief analysis of the manuscript data. Of recent versions, only the Jerusalem Bible decides for the singular "who was born. . . . "

[18] Cf. G. L. Bray, *Holiness and the Will of God: Perspectives on the Theology of Tertullian* (Atlanta: John Knox Press, 1979), ch. 4.

[19] Danielou, *op. cit.,* affirms the authenticity of the first eight chapters of *Adversus Judaeos.* So does J. Quasten, *Patrology,* vol. 2 (Westminster: Newman Press, 1953).

[20] Bray, *op. cit.,* pp. 111-123, has a good discussion of this trilogy of *scriptura, natura, disciplina.*

[21] For a discussion of the Rule of Faith, compare Flesseman-van Leer, *op. cit.,* with J. H. Waszink, "Tertullian's Principles and Methods of Exegesis," in *Early Christian Literature and the Classical Intellectual Tradition,* ed. W. R. Schoedel and R. L. Wilken (Théologie historique 53; Paris: Beauchesne, 1979). Waszink criticizes O'Malley's suggestion that in Tertullian the Rule of Faith is much more important than Scripture, and also Flesseman-van Leer, who comes close to equating the Rule of Faith with Scripture in its entirety.

[22] E.g. *Adv. Marc.* IV.4.1, "Only such a reckoning of dates, as will assume that authority belongs to that which is found to be older, and will prejudge as corrupt that which is convicted of having come later." In *Adv. Hermong* 1.1, "When dealing with heretics . . . we follow the practice of laying down against them a peremptory rule based on the lateness [of their documents]."

[23] R. E. Roberts, *The Theology of Tertullian* (London: Epworth Press, 1924) 19.

[24] So also S. L. Greenslade in *Early Latin Theology,* vol. 5 of Library of Christian Classics (Philadelphia: Westminster Press, 1956) 86.

[25] Karpp, *op. cit.,* p. 6.

[26] In addition to works cited above, cf. O. Kuss, "Zur Hermeneutik Tertullians," in *Schriftauslegung,* ed. J. Ernst (München: Verlag Ferdinand Schöningh, 1972); K. Holl, "Tertullian als Schriftsteller," in *Gesammelte Aufsätze zur Kirchengeschichte,* III (Tübingen: J. C. B. Mohr, 1928); R. P. C. Hanson, "Notes on Tertullian's Interpretation of Scripture,"

in *Journal of Theological Studies,* n.s. 12 (1961) 273-279; R. D. Sider *Ancient Rhetoric and the Art of Tertullian* (London: Oxford University Press, 1971).

[27] " . . . in respect to the unity of their preaching, as we have read earlier in this epistle, they had joined their right hands, and by the very act of having divided their spheres of work had signified their agreement in the fellowship of the gospel: as he says in another place, 'Whether it were I or they, so we preach'" (*Adv. Marc.* I.20.4). Again: "Even so, how can their [the heretics'] point that Peter was reproved by Paul prove that Paul introduced a new form of Gospel, different from that which Peter and the rest put out before him? . . . But if Peter was reproved for dissociating himself from the Gentiles out of respect of persons after he had once eaten with them, that was surely a fault of conduct, not of preaching" (*Praescr. haer.* 23.5-9).

[28] Modalists lean everything on a very few passages (Isa. 45:5; John 10:30; 14:8,10,11) and "they wish the whole appurtenance of both testaments to yield, though the smaller number ought to be understood in accordance with the greater [*cedere cum oporteat secundum plura intellegi pauciora*]. But this is characteristic of all heretics" (*Adv. Prax.* 20.2).

[29] Cf. B. M. Foschini, *"Those Who Are Baptized For the Dead," 1 Cor. 15:29, An Exegetical and Historical Dissertation* (Worcester: Heffernan Press, 1951). On p. 41 he points to *Adv. Marc.* IV.11.8, where Tertullian says that Marcion's god "refuses baptism except to the celibate or the eunuch, keeping it back until death or divorce." Foschini recognizes that this may simply imply a tendency to postpone baptism (as later in the time of Constantine), but it may also refer to baptism for the dead "practiced by ignorant Catholics as well as by heretics (including Marcionites?)."

[30] *Ibid.,* p. 64ff. Foschini links the second interpretation with that of Chrysostom.

[31] Cf. also Waszink's commentary, *De Anima,* edited with introduction and commentary (Amsterdam: J. M. Meulenhoof, 1947), p. 481f. for a discussion of Tertullian's concept of ecstasy.

[32] So Bray, *op. cit.,* p. 148.

Karen Jo Torjesen (essay date 1989)

SOURCE: "Tertullian's 'Political Ecclesiology' and Women's Leadership," in *Studia Patristica, Vol. XXI: Papers Presented to the Tenth International Conference on Patristic Studies Held in Oxford 1987; Sec-*

ond Century: Tertullian, the West, Clement of Alexandria and Origen, Athanasius, edited by Elizabeth A. Livingstone, Peeters Press, 1989, pp. 277-82.

[*In the following essay, Torjesen examines Tertullian's scathing denunciation of women's leadership in the Church, noting that he saw the Church as a public and political body and, therefore, not the proper domain of women.*]

The thesis of this communication is that Tertullian's attitude towards women's leadership is a consequence of his concept of the church as a body politic. First, I would like to refresh your memory of Tertullian's views on women's leadership and then briefly outline his political ecclesiology. This will prepares us for the analysis of three passages on women's leadership where we will see how Tertullian's condemnation of women's leadership is determined by his political ecclesiology.

Women of the congregations familiar to Tertullian assumed a wide variety of activities, teaching, baptizing, exorcising and healing. The leader of the Cainite congregation was a woman and a theologian. Her arguments regarding the nature of baptism occupy Tertullian's rhetorical and exegetical skills for long stretches of his treatise on Baptism[1]. Women of other congregations were teaching and debating (*contendere,* entering into theological discussion)[2]. Women whose teaching activites focused on catechizing probably assumed the responsibility for baptizing their catechumens[3].

Tertullian's attitude toward women exercising these ministries is well documented by virtue of his own seething rhetoric. On women exercising the ministry of teaching he says:

> And the women of these heretics, how wanton they are! For they are bold enough to teach, to dispute, to enact exorcism, to undertake cures—maybe even to baptize[4].

> It is not permitted to a woman to speak in church. Neither may she teach, baptize, offer, nor claim for herself any function proper to a man, least of all the sacerdotal office[5].

Nor on the topic of women baptizing is Tertullian's sense of outraged propriety abated:

> But the impudence of that woman who assumed the right to teach, she is evidently not going to arrogate to her the right to baptize as well—unless perhaps some new serpent appears, like that original one, so that as that woman abolished baptism, some other should on her own authority confer it[6].

There are several paradoxes in Tertullian's thought with regard to women—women may not teach, baptize or exorcise or heal, but they belong to the clergy; women may not speak in church, either to discuss or to ask questions, but they may prophesy; under special circumstances even the laity may baptize or offer the eucharist, but under no conditions could a woman do these things. These paradoxes can be resolved if we examine Tertullian's rhetoric in the passages on women and interpret them in the light of his novel understanding of the church as a political body.

Church as Body Politic

Tertullian's description of the Christian community dramatically marks the transition from a concept of the church modelled on the household to a concept of the church modelled on the body politic. From Tertullian's perspective the church was a legal body (*corpus* or *societas*) unified by a common law (*lex fidei*) and a common discipline (*disciplina*)[7]. Tertullian conceives this society as analogous to Roman society, divided, like it, into distinct classes or ranks which are distinguished from one another in terms of honor and authority. The clergy (*ordo ecclesiasticus*) form a rank similar to the *ordo senatorius;* the laity form the *ordo plebius.*

The clergy as the *ordo ecclesiasticus* represent and manifest the honor and authority of the church; therefore it is imperative that they exemplify the moral discipline of the church[8]. By virtue of their rank they, like their counterparts the senators, possess certain rights, the right to baptize (*ius dandi baptismi*), the right to teach (*ius docendi*), the right to offer the eucharist (*ius offrendi*) and the right to restore to fellowship after penance (*ius delicta donandi*)[9]. Tertullian shows that he is sensitive to the fact that what had once been ministries have become, in fact, legal rights and privileges when he says that the clergy are not to exercise their rank as though they were part of an *imperium*[10].

De Praescriptione Haereticorum 41

Tertullian's scathing condemnation of women's ministries among groups that he designated as heretical was part of a larger denunciation of the ecclesiastical conduct of those groups. They were "without gravity, without authority, and without discipline". By which he means, there were not clear enough distinctions between catechumens and baptized, between clergy and laity, or between pagan visitors and believers. There was evidently a heated dispute between church groups that were beginning to adopt institutional structures resembling those of Roman society and government and those who persisted in the older organizational pattern modelled on the household[11]. These latter defended the lack of a rigidly maintained hierarchy between clergy and laity and between catechumens and baptized by claiming it expressed the simplicity of Christ. Tertullian called their simplicity "the destruction of discipline[12]. On the other hand these groups called the concern for hierarchy (or what Tertullian calls discipline) pandering (*lenocinium*), meaning that the concern for showing the proper honors to the proper rank was nothing other than vain attempts at flattery.

These groups which Tertullian attacks have church offices ranked like those of Tertullian's churches and similar rites of ordination by which persons were installed into those offices. What Tertullian seems to be criticizing is the lack of social distance between those of different ranks, the lack of formality (authority and gravity) in maintaining these distinctions. The most intriguing question is what is Tertullian using as a standard for comparison, if the organizational structure of both groups is the same. I would like to suggest that Tertullian's standard is the dignity, gravity and formality with which public affairs are conducted, the tone, or mood found in the municipal assemblies or curia. Against this standard, the "heretical groups" who still espouse the household as the pattern for church life appear to Tertullian as lacking gravity, authority and discipline.

It is in this context that Tertullian attacks women's ministries, "The very women of these heretics, how wanton they are! For they are bold enough to teach, to dispute, to enact exorcism, to undertake cures—it may be even to baptize"[13]. The sexual connotation of the English word wanton is not inappropriate. The latin term *pocaces* means bold, shameless, and impudent. When applied to women, it is applied when they are outside of their proper sphere—the domestic[14]. Their very presence in the male sphere—the public sphere—means that they are unchaste, unchaste because they have left their proper sphere. Thus the women who are teaching, disputing, exorcising and healing are wanton in Tertullian's thinking because they have left their appropriate sphere. This is echoed again in the sentiment they are bold and audacious enough to teach.

De Baptismo 17

In Tertullian's treatise on Baptism he addresses a very formidable opponent, a woman theologian, leader of the Cainite sect, whose intellectual powers had persuaded many from congregations known to Tertullian to subscribe to her teachings. After defending the validity of water baptism Tertullian in closing turns to the question of who has the right to baptize. The right lies first and foremost with the bishop; because baptism is one of his specific functions, it is a right; however, also of presbyters, dea-

cons and even of the laity. Nevertheless the bishop has the preeminent right over baptism. For the sake of the "honor" (dignity) of the church, the authority of the bishop must be respected in all cases where minor clergy or laity are administering baptism.

The term Tertullian uses to designate the right of clergy or laity to exercise a ministry of the church is a legal term—*ius*. The laity by virtue of their baptism possess the right to baptize, as they also possess the right to teach and to offer the eucharist. However, although the laity may exercise all of these ministries, women may exercise none of them. Tertullian, among the opening salvos of his attack on his theological adversary, says that women do not even possess the right to teach sound doctrine, much less to create heresies. Here the term he uses is *ius docendi*. As he concludes his treatise he returns to her again and calls her a wanton (*petulantia*) woman who has *usurped* the right to teach.

In Tertullian's new vision of the church as a political body, the church's ministries have become legal rights to be exercised only by full members of the political body. Since women could not be citizens of the state, either by holding office, participating in debate or exercising any public functions, then it was self-evident for Tertullian that neither could they do so in the body politic of the church. The right to minister—teach, baptize, etc.—was not a right restricted to the clergy; they were the rights of all the citizens who were members of the body politic. However, women could not be members of the body politic. In "On the Veiling of Virgins" Tertullian spells this out.

> It is not permitted to a woman to speak in the church, nor to baptize, nor to offer, nor to claim to herself a lot in any male function[15].

Women's performance of public activities (i.e. exercising the *ius docendi, ius baptizandi,* etc.) meant that they had abandoned the domestic sphere, so again Tertullian describes such women as wanton (*petulantia*). And when they exercise any public ministry, they are usurping rights that do not belong to them because they are women; legal rights can belong only to men[16].

De Virginibus Velandis

In Tertullian's mind the church had become irrevocably a public sphere. Women who came to church had, in effect, left the household and entered a public male sphere. Not only their comportment, but also their dress and grooming must reflect a respect for the public-male character of this space. Nowhere is the trauma of this transition from household space to public space more poignant than in Tertullian's passionate treatise on the veiling of virgins. "Young women", he scolds, "you wear your veils out on the streets (*in vicis*), so you should wear them in the church (*in ecclesiis*); you wear them when you are among strangers (*extraneos*), then wear them among your brothers (*fratres*). If you won't wear your veils in church, then I challenge you to go around in public without them"[17]. But that is just the point, the church had been a private sphere, like a household; it was a place where women could come and go openly and freely as they did in the domestic sphere. What Tertullian is insisting on, is that the church is *not* a private sphere, it is in fact no different than the market place. The rules of propriety for women that apply in the streets have now been brought into the inner—once domestic—sanctum of the church.

For Tertullian the sense of the church as a public place is so profound that he launches on what must have been a thankless and perhaps futile campaign. The virgins who were part of the ecclesiastical order, part of the clergy, sat in special seats reserved for them as did the presbyters, widows and bishop. Their number and their commitment to a life of chastity was for the rest of the church one of its proudest emblems. These virgins were not veiled, to signify their unmarried state. These young women, unveiled, dedicated to God, were like a public and visible offering to God by the church and a cause for praise and glory[18]. Tertullian calls this practice a "liberty" granted by the church to honor the virgin and her choice. As Tertullian formulates it she is honored by being granted the right (*ius*) not to wear a veil. Tertullian is bitterly opposed to this practice, and more even interesting than his denunciations are the motives behind them.

His biting description of the practice is quite instructive, "for after being brought forward into the midst of the church and elated by the public announcement of their good deed, and laden by the brethren with every honour and charitable bounty" these virgins on public display will no doubt become sexually active. It is the public character of their presence in the church that most offends Tertullian; it is not even so much their unveiledness that makes their presence a "public" presence, rather it is their being publicly honored (like holders of public office). He argues that to grant a virgin dedicated to God the right not to wear a veil and to honor her with this right is the same as honoring her with the right to hold male offices or rank (chap. ix). In conclusion he states flatly, "nothing in the way of public honor is permitted to a virgin"[19].

As before, so also in this context, for women to assume public roles was equivalent to unchastity. In the end, as he tells it, virgins who receive public honors will eventually become pregnant, add to their guilt by attempting abortions and contriving to conceal their motherhood. Public presence is the very opposite of chastity, a virgin "must necessarily be imperilled by the public exhibition of herself"[20].

Notes

[1] *De Bapt.* I, 17.

[2] *De Prae. Haer.* 41.

[3] Several scholars have interpreted such passages referring to women leaders teaching and baptizing to mean that women involved in the process of evangelizing and catechizing also baptized their converts. See Elisabeth Schussler Fiorenza, *In Memory of Her* (New York, 1983), p. 173; H. Achelis and J. Fleming, *Die syrische Didascalia uebersetzt und erklart* (TU, 25,2; Leipzig, 1904).

[4] *De Praes.* 41.

[5] *De Virg. Vel.* 9.1.

[6] *De Bap.* 17.

[7] On the church as *corpus* or *societas* see E. Herrmann, *Ecclesia in Re Publica* (Frankfurt, 1980), p. 42; A. Beck, *Römisches Recht bei Tertullian and Cyprian* (Halle, 1930), p. 58; on *lex fidei*, Beck, p. 51; on *disciplina* see Beck, p. 54.

[8] *Ex. Cast.* 7, *De Mon.* 12.

[9] On *ius dandi baptismi* see *Ex cast.* 7; on *ius docendi* see *De Bapt.* 1; on *ius offrendi* see *Ex Cast.* 7; on *ius delicta donandi* see *De Pud.* 21.

[10] *De Mon.* 12.

[11] E. Schussler Fiorenza identifes the evolution of the household model of church organization, see pp. 285-334. She believes that genderization of church offices took place at this point. Since both materfamilias and paterfamilias exercised leadership roles in the household, I do not see the genderization of leadership taking place until the political model of leadership is adopted.

[12] *Ex Cast.* 7.

[13] *De Praes.* 41.

[14] The virtue of chastity is measured by three factors: appearing in public places, clothing and make-up and sexual activities. Thus appearing in public places was sufficient cause to warrant the accusation of wanton; see "Treatise on Chastity", in M. R. Lefkowitz and M. B. Fant, *Women's Life in Greece*

and Rome (Baltimore, 1985), p. 104.

[15] *De Vir. Vel.* 9.

[16] In Greek and Roman political theory women could not participate in public life, i.e. holding office, giving speeches or voting. See Aristotle, *Politics*, III.1; Philo, *Special Laws,* III.169, Elshtain, J. Elshtain, *Public Man, Private Woman* (Princeton, 1981), pp. 19-54.

[17] *De Vir. Vel.* 13.

[18] *De Vir. Vel.* 14.

[19] *De Vir. Vel.* 15.

[20] *De Vir. Vel.* 17.

David Rankin (essay date 1995)

SOURCE: "Conclusions: The Church according to Tertullian" in *Tertullian and the Church*, Cambridge University Press, 1995, pp. 111-16.

[*In the following excerpt, Rankin comments on Tertullian's view of the authentic Church and the imagery he uses to describe it.*]

Occasional references to an 'ecclesia in caelis' can be found in Tertullian's writings. Yet, for the most part, Tertullian sees the true church as an historical, empirical reality the authentication for which can be found at least partly in the present age. This reality is partly determined by the nature and the circumstances of the church's foundation by the apostles, and partly by its Spirit-driven activity in the present time, but, above all, by its present nature, consistent with its promise as the eschatological community, as both the Body of Christ and the Bride of Christ.[1] This church in the power of the Spirit, which power enables it to become now what it is in promise, is not yet the Kingdom of God, but its anticipation in history.[2] In this Tertullian differs from both Origen and Clement of Alexandria, for example, for whom the present reality is but an imperfect shadow of some heavenly, as yet unrealised ideal. Tertullian is consistent in his understanding of the historical and empirical nature of this church, and, in this sense, no significant difference is discernible in his ecclesiology in the transition from Catholic to New Prophet. What do change, however, are the criteria by which for him the reality and the authentication of the true church are evaluated; that is, what it is for this church to be faithful to its essential and authentic nature.

Some of the images employed by Tertullian to depict the church are drawn from secular life, though most do have biblical and other Christian connections. 'Castra', though reflecting the influence of both the Old Testament and the book of Revelation, was an obvious image for those who lived in the increasingly militarised world of the Severans. The employment of 'navis', though it might reflect the influence of the Gospels—the 'little boat' on which the first disciples experienced some of their most significant encounters with the power of Jesus—would also be an obvious one in a province dependent on the sea for its contact with the rest of the Roman world. 'Schola' and 'secta' are the images most obviously reflecting a non-biblical milieu. Drawn from the world of pagan philosophy and education, they were employed by Tertullian both to provide useful points of recognition for pagans and to proclaim the moral and ideological superiority of Christianity over its pagan rivals. Tertullian's depiction of the church-as-mother—used consistently throughout his career—though not original with him, is given such a new treatment in his ecclesiology that it yet lays claim as a quasi-original 'Tertullianism'! None before him had so decisively employed the image as one which established the church as possessing a personalised identity separate from her members. In nothing else, save perhaps in his trinitarian language and his emphasis on the essential holiness of the church, was Tertullian to exercise such a lasting influence on later Christian thought.

Tertullian's presentation of the church as the Body of Christ is reflected in his employment of the images 'corpus', 'Christus', 'Spiritus' and 'trinity'. While he could use the first mentioned in the secular sense of an 'association' and at times in a particularly formal and routine manner, his use of all four images suggests most strongly that he understood the image of the church as the Body of Christ in a more than metaphorical sense. There is with him an unmistakable identification between the true church and the person of Christ which comes perilously close to seeing the church as an extension of the Incarnation itself. And yet such an identification would be by no means absolute for Tertullian and is possible only where the Spirit is demonstrably present in the midst of the church. The use of the image of the Body of Christ reinforces Tertullian's emphasis on the necessary unity of the church, which church, being the Body of Christ, cannot be divided against itself and can only be that which in reality it is called to be. Tertullian employs the images of 'virgin' and 'Bride of Christ'—and often together—in a manner which corresponds very closely to New Testament and early patristic usage. These images emphasise the necessary holiness of the church and in a thoroughly eschatological way. The church is not to become at the End the virgin Bride of Christ; she is that in the present-time, and can be none other now than that which she is to be at the End. The images are not unconnected . . . to that of the church as the Body of Christ.

Had Tertullian lived to see the development of the now familiar ecclesiological formularies, he would almost certainly have approved of the affirmation of the church as 'one, holy, catholic and apostolic'. Throughout both major periods of his Christian life he constantly stressed the necessary unity of the church, from the communion of the various congregations spread throughout the known world, to that 'oneness' and 'peace' within a single congregation.[3] For Tertullian the scriptural bases for this essential unity are found at Ephesians 4,4-6 and in Paul's criticism of division in 1 Corinthians, passim. The images which are employed by him most often to illustrate this 'unity'—particularly at the local congregational level—are those related to that of the Body of Christ; though at least one of these . . . could also be employed by Tertullian in a more secular sense. Whether this unity was essential to the authentication of the true church, or was merely a useful though non-essential indicator, is not clear.

The catholicity of the church, which at this time was an attribute primarily associated with that of its unity, was also very important, at least in Tertullian's early thought; it receives no explicit mention later on. Given the widespread suspicion of the New Prophecy movement, even in his own day, it may not have been prudent for Tertullian to lay too much stress on this aspect of his ecclesiology. None of the particular images employed by him speak directly to it, though he undoubtedly understood its scriptural bases to lie both in the Great Commission at Matthew 28,19f. and in Acts. Catholicity seems for him not to have been essential to the authenticity of the true church, but rather a useful indicator of that church's unity and apostolicity.

The holiness of the church in Tertullian's thought is, however, another matter. It is crucial to his understanding of the essential nature of the authentic church; this is particularly so in the later period, though it is far from absent earlier; it is an attribute without which the church cannot be the true church, and is surpassed in importance in this regard possibly only by that of apostolicity. Its scriptural bases are found in 1 Corinthians 5, 1 Timothy 1, 19f., Ephesians 5 and 2 Corinthians 11. Tertullian's understanding of this holiness is also profoundly influenced by the eschatological framework of his thought, by his consequent understanding of the demands of sanctification and of 'holiness' generally, and by the natural rigour of his own personality. At least four of the major images employed by Tertullian represent this particular aspect of his ecclesiology—those of 'ark', 'camp', 'bride (of Christ)', and 'virgin'.

Three of these—the first, the third and the fourth—draw their inspiration from the Bible. The second is drawn principally from the secular world. This particular attribute of the true church is given most emphasis in his later writings, but is also present in the earlier period when concern for the purity and exclusiveness of doctrine is found in the foreground of his thought. It denotes for him one of the crucial aspects of the 'primitive' church, which church should be the model for his own time. The holiness of the church, however, lies not in the process of its historical development, nor in some ideal to be sought though perhaps never achieved, but in what it is by the grace of God. A less than holy church is, for Tertullian, not logically possible. Anything less than holy cannot authentically be the church. It is not that the church should be or could be holy; it is holy. It is already, in the present-time, the virgin Bride of Christ. It can seek only to conform to its own inherent nature.

It is the attribute of apostolicity which denotes for Tertullian the second plank of the essential nature of the one, true church. It is not only because thereby—in the Stoic sense—it can be 'traced back' to its (earthly) origins, but rather because it can thereby be traced back to a divine authentication. God sent his Christ, Christ anointed and sent out his apostles, and they in turn founded the church. This is what sets the church above and apart from all other human institutions. In theory those others could well be united, catholic, perhaps even holy (though probably not), but they could never trace their origins back to the apostles appointed by Christ. Apostolicity remained for Tertullian the key to the nature of the true church; it was only the manner in which this attribute was to be demonstrated which was to change in his transition from Catholic to New Prophet.

At *De Pudicitia* 21, 1 Tertullian seeks to distinguish between 'doctrinam apostolorum et potestatem'. Both were important to his concept of the church and Tertullian never denied oversight of the former to the bishops. Yet when he was faced with the administration of penitential discipline, with the forgiveness of grievous sinners and their possible readmission to communion, and with the question of who possessed the authority to 'act' in the name of God, the question of 'power' (potestas) became of primary importance. While doctrinal orthodoxy can be traced by way of episcopal succession back to the tradition established by the apostles themselves, disciplinary 'power' had to be authenticated in the contemporary church by proven possession of that same Spirit which had indwelt Christ, his apostles and the prophets.

Schweizer comments that 'God's Spirit marks out in freedom the pattern that church order afterwards recognises; it is therefore functional, regulative, serving, but not constitutive, and that is what is decisive'.[4] Tertullian's observation in **De Pudicitia** 21,17 that the true church is that of the Spirit, and not that which is constituted by a number of bishops, reflects this same sentiment. And yet Moltmann's assertion that 'the church has never existed in a historically demonstrable ideal, a form in which faith and experience coincided'[5] is one to which Tertullian could not give assent if it meant agreeing that such coincidence is never possible in the present age. Tertullian was an 'heir of the Apostles' and the church was truly both the 'Body of Christ' and the 'virgin Bride of Christ'. In these particular aspects of Tertullian's thought lie the answers to many of the questions concerning his 'high' ecclesiology—his apparent identification of the visible church with that 'in caelis', for example—and his understanding of what constituted the essential attributes or notes of the one, authentic church founded by the apostles of Christ.

Notes

[1] Moltmann, *The church*, p. 20.

[2] Ibid,. p. 196.

[3] *De Baptismo* 17.

[4] Schweizer, *Church order in the New Testament* (London, 1961) p. 205.

[5] Moltmann, *The church*, p.21.

Eric Osborn (essay date 1997)

SOURCE: "Simplicity and Perfection" in *Tertullian, First Theologian of the West,* Cambridge University Press, 1997, pp. 1-26.

[*In the following excerpt, Osborn observes the essential importance of simplicity, founded on the perfection of Christ, in Tertullian's thought.*]

'We also are religious and our religion is simple', objected the Roman proconsul to the martyr Speratus, at his trial near Carthage on 17 July 180. 'If you will listen calmly', replied Speratus, 'I shall tell you the mystery of simplicity.'[1] Tertullian was not the only African who liked paradox.[2] Speratus claims simplicity for Christians rather than pagans. He counters the accusation that Christians are secret and sinister, by asserting that their secret is simplicity. He draws on the New Testament account of the mystery of salvation. The writer to the Ephesians had been concerned to tell the nations of the unsearchable riches of Christ and to bring to light

'the economy of the mystery which has been hidden from all ages in the God who created all things' (Eph. 3.9). The church declares to heavenly powers the manifold . . . wisdom of God (Eph. 3.10), which is the divine mystery. The end of salvation, the vision of Christ and the church present a great mystery (Eph. 5.32).

Tertullian's lust for simplicity, supported by superlatives, persists throughout his work and is a good place to begin a study of his thought. A fine exposition, which begins 'Tertullien déconcerte', goes on to insist that Tertullian took a simple and total choice when he became a Christian and that his complexity comes from his earlier intellectual formation; whether a study of his thought begins from either simplicity or complexity, it will discover a profound unity.[3]

A man of keen and violent disposition (*acris et vehementis ingenii'*),[4] much of Tertullian's lively talk is concerned with clarifying what others have confused. Like Paul, he reiterates that he wants to know nothing but Christ crucified. Christ revealed himself, not as a tradition, but as truth (*virg.* 1.1). Truth is simple (*ap.* 23.7f.), but philosophers have mixed with it their own opinions (*ap.* 47.4) and sunk to a perversity (*Marc.* 5.19.8) which tortures truth ('unde ista tormenta cruciandae simplicitatis et suspendendae vertiatis?' *an.* 18.7). The soul testifies in its simplicity (*test.* 1.6) and its evidence is simple and divine (*test.* 5.1). Truth leads to beauty so female dress should be marked by simplicity (*cult.* 1.2.4 et passim). When Valentinians accuse ordinary Christians of simplicity, he replies 'although simple, we nevertheless know everthing' (*Val.* 3.5). He writes (*res.* 2.11) to strengthen the faith of simple believers, employing his rhetorical skill on their behalf against heretics (*res.* 5.1).

The Simple Beginning

The divine economy of salvation is reflected in Christian baptism, which points to past and future. Life begins at baptism; here Tertullian shows his yearning for what is simple, in 'the sacrament of our Christian water, which washes away the sins of our original blindness and frees us for eternal life' (*bapt.* 1.1.). Yet simplicity never displaces reason. Those who do not examine the reasons behind simple baptism, and who stay with an unexamined faith, are vulnerable through their ignorance (*ibid.*). The wrong kind of simplicity needs instruction, guidance and protection (*res.* 2.11).[5] Tertullian rejects the naïveté of those who want a proof-text which forbids their attendance at the games (*spect.* 3.1) and the artless heresy which abolishes all discipline (*praescr.* 41.3). A heretical viper[6] has turned many away from baptism, through that common perversity which rejects anything simple. 'Nothing, absolutely nothing, hardens human minds as much as the obvious simplicity of what God does, and the contrasting greatness of what he thereby achieves. The unadorned fact, that with such radical simplicity, without pomp, without any special preparation, and indeed, at no cost, a man is lowered into water, is dipped, while a few words are spoken, and then emerges, not much (if at all) cleaner, makes it all the more incredible that he gains eternal life in this way' (*bapt.* 2.1). In striking contrast, idol worship uses every possible embroidery of ritual and every additional expense.

Fussy, wretched incredulity denies God's primary properties of simplicity and power, which should be received with wonder and faith. God is found by the simple in heart (*praescr.* 7.10) and he appeared to Elijah openly and simply (*apertus et simplex, pat.* 15.6). God is too simple to have worked a Docetist deception (*carn.* 5.10). For the unbeliever, there is nothing in such plain acts as baptism and the pretended effects are impossible: which illustrates how God uses foolish things to confound worldly wisdom and does easily what men find most difficult.

The subtlety of God's simplicity is linked with his wisdom and power, which derive stimulus from their opposites of folly and impossibility, 'since every virtue receives its cause from those things by which it is provoked' (*bapt.* 2.3). So strife becomes a second theme of Tertullian's thought.[7] He links it with Pauline paradox, and it is fundamental to the Stoicism which looked back to Heraclitus whom Justin saw as a Christian before Christ. Simplicity and weakness belong to God as his omnipotent rejection of earthly power and wisdom. Christians who follow this divine simplicity are little fishes (*bapt.* 1.3) who cannot live apart from the water of baptism. Here their faith is contracted to the one word . . . which stands for Jesus Christ, son of God, saviour.[8]

Repetition underlines simplicity and Tertullian employs it to reinforce his claims. More than this, his key words (goodness, reason and discipline) link together diverse things which are derived from one simple divine origin. Goodness explains every part of the creative act (*Marc.* 2.4.5). Reason is founded in God who is ever rational, and provides grounds for Tertullian's every argument (including his paradoxes) and for his constant attacks upon his opponents (*paen.* 1). *Ratio* is his favourite word. Discipline governs all details of conduct. The constant refrain of these themes provides unity in his writing.

Christians are plain people because they accept the world as God's creation. This means that they do not run of into seclusion, but live like others; they eat, dress, bathe, work, trade, sail, fight, farm and practise a craft. They do not observe the common religious rites; but they are no less human or reasonable for that (*ap.* 42.4). Their simple lives are matched in modesty by simple dress (*cult.* 2.13.3). They follow the New Testament aesthetic of 'putting on' Christ.

Simplicity, in Tertullian, sometimes exacts its price and affects his arguments. The sudden enunciation of God's name is, for most, not the testimony of a soul which is naturally Christian, but the testimony of a soul which is not very Christian. The appeal to lines of episcopal succession is controversial rather than an end to controversy and, in any case, Tertullian always wants to obey conscience rather than bishop. In his case the two rarely agree.[9] Above all, Tertullian seems to fail in his account of divine justice and love. In his rejection of Marcion, he claims that only retributive justice can discourage sin.[10]

These matters will be dealt with again later. The points to note at this stage are three. First, we must expect that a passion for simplicity might induce errors. Theology, like philosophy, is a complex matter and those who cut corners suffer accidents.[11] Second, those who turn every corner arrive nowhere. Debate differs from argument. The orator who silences his opponent rarely uses adequate argument. Against the plea for fear as an essential deterrent against sin, Marcion simply shook his head and said 'Absit'; he was silent but not convinced. Third, theologians and other exponents of rational argument commonly make a few bad mistakes. By far the best example is Augustine, who dominated a culture for a thousand years, and whose argument for the liquidation of schismatics through the severity of love[12] is only matched, for unconvincing barbarity, by his accounts of predestination and original sin. These three dangers make an exploration of Tertullian's arguments obligatory.

Intricate Apologetic

Tertullian's defence of simplicity will always have a twist of paradox, and qualifications of fundamental force. There are his own deep conflicts. How complicated was he? One writer[13] produced a book to probe the disorder of his personality, another composed a large tome to show the perversity of his ethics.[14] Many have followed the verdict that he is a troubled fideist.[15]

More disconcerting is the praise of his admirers. Even a sober scholar could write: 'Roman restraint, legal clarity and military discipline were transmuted into an intellectual and moral force in the ardent, aspiring mind and heart of Tertullian.'[16] Enthusiasm gallops away with another:

Ardent in temperament, endowed with an intelligence as subtle and original as it was aggressive and audacious, he added to his natural gifts a profound erudition, which far from impeding only gave weight to the movements of his alert and robust mind . . . Harassed from without, the African Church was also torn from within by an accumulation of evils; apostasies, heresies, and schisms abounded. Up through the confusion were thrust Tertullian's mighty shoulders, casting off the enemies of the Gospel on every side. He was not formed for defensive warfare.[17]

It is regrettable that some scholars want to award prizes rather than to understand what is alien to them.

A recent and restrained assessment, which touches lightly on the ideas of Tertullian in favour of his history and his literary achievement, calls him a 'Christian Sophist'.[18] This is helpful, but uncomfortably ambiguous, since Tertullian spent much time attacking and repudiating what is commonly regarded as sophistry.

How complex is Tertullian? There is no lack of intricate argument, however forcefully it may be presented; worse still, in the interests of simplicity and speed, steps are often omitted and details which have appeared earlier are not repeated. We might call this 'Tertullian's Trick'; because often, when we think we have found a fallacy and caught him out, we find that he has answered our objection elsewhere. A good orator does not repeat detail. For his interpreters today, this should be less of a difficulty after fifty years of philosophical analysis; but some still look for systems and the fun of deconstructing them. Many manage to ignore the truth that conclusions are ambiguous without the argument which leads to them. In order to understand an author we must remember the cards he has already played.

To a remarkable extent, Tertullian respected conventional rhetorical forms which made his work more accessible to his contemporaries.[19] Tertullian faced a complex situation, where the culture of Greece and Rome, the religion of Israel and the new faith in Jesus came together in a mixture of conflict and agreement. Each component had internal diversity within which Tertullian had to choose. A critical eclecticism was characteristic of all parties. The importance of Tertullian for cultural history is immense, and he may rightly be called the 'first theologian of the West', provided this does not limit his influence to the West or obscure his massive debt to Irenaeus.[20] Justin had anticipated him, by his move to Rome, and it is remarkable how much had been achieved. But Justin still writes in Greek and his ideas are difficult because undeveloped. His interest is that of an originator whose ideas are taken up and developed by others who add, alter and diverge. As a result, his own meaning is frequently uncertain.

Tertullian's achievement was not merely cultural and linguistic, but above all intellectual. For, 'despite his obvious originality, he displays those characteristics which are to be found throughout Latin Christianity: a realism which knows nothing of the Platonist devaluation of matter; a subjectivity, which gives special prominence to inner experience; and a pessimism which lays more stress on the experience of sin than on transfiguration'.[21]

Tertullian believed in change. Plato gave place to Heraclitus and the Stoics. The way up is the way down. All things change and all things renew themselves. Nothing ends except to begin again (*res.* 12). While Clement, for all his delight in Heraclitus, looked beyond the world of material things to Plato's intellectual realities (*strom.* 6.1), Tertullian saw reality in flesh and matter, and found truth in an unending series of paradoxes.

He began as an apologist and apologetic displays the contingency of theology and philosophy.[22] It begins from a faith to which objections are made by opponents or experiences of widely diverse kinds. . . . Romans will not like his higher loyalty to Christ, radical Christians will not like his political conformism, some will find him too indulgent and others will find him too ascetic; either they will not dance when they hear the pipes or they will not lament with those who mourn. When the Baptist neither eats nor drinks, he is demonic and when Jesus eats and drinks he is a glutton and a winebibber (Matt. 11.16-19).

However consistent the position of the apologist is, it will not appear consistent until there has been careful analysis and then it may look too complex.

> They live in countries of their own, but simply as sojourners; they share the life of citizens, they endure the lot of foreigners; every foreign land is to them a fatherland, and every fatherland a foreign land. They marry like the rest of the world. They breed children, but they do not cast their offspring adrift. They eat together but do not sleep together. They exist in the flesh, but they live not after the flesh. They spend their existence upon earth, but their citizenship is in heaven. They obey the established laws, and in their own lives they surpass the laws . . . The Jews war against them as aliens, and the Greeks persecute them.[23]

To meet apparent inconsistencies, like Tertullian's denigration and exaltation of marriage and philosophy, apologetic needs linking argument (for which it may not have enough time) as well as a few general concepts (economy of salvation, logos) which maintain a scattered presence.[24] Tertullian goes further, so that these concepts embrace fundamental questions of theology. The remarkable thing is that, for all his vehemence, his ideas do hold together. He had a deep, abiding concern. As a Stoic, he began with an unde-fined consciousness of God.[25] As a Christian, he filled that concept with the gospel, the story of salvation which ran from creation to apocalypse. The golden thread which runs through his thought is the recapitu-lation of all things in Christ.

Apologetic presents an extreme case of the tensions faced by all philosophy and theology. Today, theolo-gians are reluctant to distinguish historical from sys-tematic theology because every theology is marked by its historical situation and specific questions. This move is mirrored in a wider reaction against the sci-entific positivism which was the last gesture of En-lightenment epistemology. In a wide-ranging review of the human sciences, we find one common feature: 'a willingness to emphasise the local and contingent, a desire to underline the extent to which our own concepts and attitudes have been shaped by particular historical circumstances, and a correspondingly strong dislike—amounting almost to hatred in the case of Wittgenstein—of all overarching theories and singu-lar schemes of explanation'.[26] An apologist, like Tertullian, is more likely to be understood in such an intellectual climate. For we have all learnt that within the most carefully argued and tidy system, there are polarities and contradictions which cannot be ignored. What Gödel showed for mathematics (that there is no self-sufficient, consistent autonomy) seems true of all rational systems.

What did Tertullian write? His many writings show the range of his apologetic.[27] In 197, he exhorts the martyrs (*mart.*), confronting the major challenge to faith which was the suffering of God's faithful people and defending the faith before a persecuting state (*nat., ap.*). Between 198 and 206, he argues that faith is natural (*test.*), he confronts the Jewish attack (*Jud.*)—the gospel had come to Carthage through Jewish Chris-tians. The threat of heresy is met with a general re-sponse and a statement of the essential rule of Chris-tian faith (*praescr.*). One well-argued alternative, the dualism of Hermogenes (*Herm.*) is dissected, analysed and refuted. The public behaviour of Christians is rigorously directed away from attendance at games (*spect.*), frequency of marriage (*ux.*) and fine clothing (*cult.*). Prayer (*or.*) and baptism (*bapt.*) explain mat-ters of devotion and worship. Patience (*pat.*) is a private virtue while penitence (*paen.*) has both pri-vate and public consequences.

During his middle period (207-8) when signs of Montanist[28] influence begin to appear, substantial works are directed against heretical dualism. The work **Against Marcion** (*Marc.*)[29] owes its present form to this period, but builds on earlier work. Valentinians are attacked both in the short work which bears their

name (*Val.*) and in the anti-docetic works which de-fend the flesh (*carn., res.*). Chastity (*cast.*) and mod-est dress (*virg.*) continue the ascetic strain of ethics while the hostility of the state to Christians is further considered (*cor., scorp.*) and a particular oppressor is challenged (*Scap.*). Idolatry is condemned as false and the source of all evil (*idol.*) and the nature of the soul is examined (*an.*).

During the final period of his writing (213-22), Tertullian is plainly at odds with catholic, 'psychic' (unspiritual)[30] Christianity. Rigorous ethical demands are expressed in the rejection of flight during perse-cution (*fug.*) and remarriage (*mon.*), and the commen-dation of fasting (*iei.*) and modesty (*pud.*). His attack on Praxeas defends the distinction of persons within the trinity and the distinction of substances within the incarnate Christ (*Prax.*). Yet the chains of secular culture retain their subordinate place below the 'bet-ter philosophy' (*pall.*).

Tertullian's one central idea (the economy of salva-tion perfected in Christ) runs from his **Apologeticum** to the better philosophy (*pall.*) and his theology of trinity and incarnation (*Prax.*). This provides internal unity to his thought, within all complexity. It is the constant factor. Montanism is the result, not the cause, of Tertullian's concern for the perfection of the di-vine economy.

Tertullian has two external controls on the complexi-ties of apologetic and theology: brevity and paradox. Brevity had been claimed as a Christian virtue from the beginning (1 Tim. 1.3f.). Justin (*1 apol.* 14) took the brevity of Christ's sayings as proof he was not a sophist, and Irenaeus contrasted the short word of the gospel with the long-winded law. Sextus (*sent.* 430) linked brevity with the knowledge of God. For Tertullian, truth and brevity (*Marc.* 2.28.3), certainty and brevity (*an.* 2.7) go together. The Lord's Prayer is a compendium of the whole gospel (*or.* 9.1). Con-ciseness is a welcome necessity; prolixity is a bore (*virg.* 4.4). On this theme scripture, especially the Wisdom literature, and Stoic tradition coincided.[31] We have already noted some reasons for brevity. As an orator and a preacher, Tertullian leaves a lot out, so that he will not lose his audience. As a Stoic and a follower of Paul, he accepts paradox as a common means of ordering truth. Indeed there is a primal paradox. 'Truth and hatred of truth come into our world together. As soon as truth appears, it is the enemy' (*ap.* 7.3).

We return to his simplicity. Tertullian was himself, not a Christian Cicero. Seneca is often one of us (*saepe noster*); we are never his. A Christian builds his faith on his own foundation, not that of another (*an.* 26.1). Christ was not mistaken when he solemnly entrusted the proclamation of his gospel to simple fishermen instead of skilful sophists (*an.* 3.3). As his follower, Tertullian rejoices in the mere name of Christian and the message of the little fishes: 'Jesus Christ, son of God, saviour'. A simple criterion governs the Christian's logic. Confronted by exuberance of words and ideas, he applies a constant criterion of truth. In contrast, Marcion loves uncertainty, and prefers it to the certainty of the rule of faith. 'Now if to your plea, which itself remains uncertain, there be applied further proofs derived from uncertainties, we shall be caught up in such a chain of questions, which depend on our discussion of these equally uncertain proofs and whose uncertainty will endanger faith, so that we shall slide into those insoluble questions which the apostle dislikes' (*Marc.* 1.9.7). In opposition Tertullian insists 'I shall therefore insist, with complete confidence that he is no God who is today uncertain, because until now he has been unknown; because as soon as it is agreed that God exists, from this very fact it follows that he never has been unknown, and therefore never uncertain' (*Marc.* 1.9.10).

Divine Unicity[32]

The first question of early Christian theology was: is there one God, good and true, who is creator of this world of sin and evil? For Tertullian, God's own simple unity is ultimate. 'God is not God if he be not one' (*Marc.* 1.3.1). He holds the universe in his hand like a bird's nest. Heaven is his throne and earth is his footstool (*Marc.* 2.25.2). However, because he is found through faith in Jesus, he does not conform to ultimate Neoplatonic simplicity. We shall see that, for Tertullian as for other second-century theologians, the way to one God is through the son and the spirit.[33]

Marcion is equally convinced about God's unicity, which he places above the duality of creation and redemption, and claims: 'One single work is sufficient for our god; he has liberated man by his supreme and most excellent goodness, which is of greater value than all destructive insects' (*Marc.* 1.17.1).[34] But Marcion, says Tertullian, is a great muddler and his higher god has produced nothing which might give ground for believing in his existence. How can he be superior when he can show no work to compare with, for example, the human being produced by the inferior god? The question 'does this god exist?' is answered from what he has done and the question 'what is this god like?' is determined by the quality of his work. Marcion's uncreative god does not pass the first test, so the second does not apply.

In the alleged interests of unity, Marcion multiplies. He may begin from two gods, but he finishes with many more and his account is far from simple.

> So you have three substances of deity in the higher regions, and in the lower regions four. When to these are added their own Christs—one who has appeared in the time of Tiberius, another who is promised by the creator—Marcion is obviously being robbed by those persons who assume that he postulates two gods, when he implies that there are nine, even if he does not know it. (*Marc.* 1.15.6)

Here Tertullian is drawing his own polemical conclusions from Marcion's views and does not help his case; but there is more than caricature because, once mediators are introduced, multiplication sets in.[35]

There are also historical confusions for Marcion. His god turned up at his destined time, because of certain astrological complexities, which Marcionites enjoy, even if the stars were made by the lesser god; for the greater god may have been held back by the rising moon, or some witchery, or by the position of Saturn or Mars (*Marc.* 1.18.1). Whatever the delay, he glided down in the fifteenth year of Tiberius, to be a saving spirit. Yet the pest-laden wind of his salvation did not begin to blow until some year in the reign of Antoninus Pius. This delay implies difference and confusion. For from Tiberius to Antoninus Pius, 115 years and 6½ months elapsed; the god whom Marcion then introduced cannot be the god whom Christ revealed, for the interim between Christ and Marcion rules out identity.

Beyond this confusion lie Marcion's great dichotomies—the antitheses of law and gospel, creation and salvation—which run from beginning to end (*Marc.* 1.19.4). Marcion's god could not have been revealed by Christ who came before Marcion introduced the division between two gods. Yet Marcion claims that he restored a rule of faith which had been corrupted, over all those intervening years; Tertullian wonders at the patience of Christ who waited so long for Marcion to deliver him (*Marc.* 1.20.1).

This argument suggests again the cost of simplicity and the apparent naïveté of Tertullian in the interests of apologetic. By itself, the argument has no force whatever. Marcion claimed that he was a reformer who went back to the original gospel and apostle.[36] However, Tertullian makes the argument respectable by referring to Paul (in Galatians) who was not commending another god and another Christ, but attributing the annulment of the old dispensation to the creator himself who (through Isaiah and Jeremiah) had declared the intention that he would do something new and make a new covenant. Later, by exact examination of the prophets (*Marc.* 3), Luke's Gospel (*Marc.* 4) and Paul (*Marc.* 5), he shows that the evidence for Marcion's primitive gospel is not to be found.[37] Tertullian further states that the first Christians were certain about God the creator and about his Christ, while they argued about almost everything else, and that certainty continues in all apostolic churches. This argument is sound, since Marcionites could not point to a particular ancient church which followed their teaching (*Marc.* 1.21.3).

Divine simplicity has no vulgar fractions. God is eternal, rational and perfect; his salvation is universal, whereas Marcion's God leaves out Jews and Christians because they belong to the creator. More importantly, because he saves only souls and not bodies, the strange god never provides more than a 'semi-salvation'. Surely a god of perfect goodness could save the whole of man? 'Wholly damned by the creator, he should have been wholly restored by the god of sovereign goodness' (*Marc.* 1.24.4). Marcion's god cannot do anything to protect his believers from the malignant power of the creator, as it works through everything from thunder, war and plague to creeping, crawling insects. 'Just how do you think you are emancipated from his kingdom when his flies still creep over your face? . . . You profess a God who is purely and simply good; however you cannot prove the perfect goodness of him who does not perfectly set you free' (*Marc.* 1.24.7).

There are now perverse and muddled objections made against the almighty God, lord and founder of the universe,[38] who 'has been known from the beginning, has never hidden himself, has shone in constant splendor, even before Romulus and long before Tiberius' (*Marc.* 2.2.1) The riches of his wisdom and knowledge are deep, his judgements are unsearchable and his ways past finding out (Rom. 11.34); therefore his simplicity will not be evident to the natural man, who cannot receive the things of the spirit. 'And so God is supremely great just when man thinks he is small, God is supremely best just when man thinks him not good, he is especially one when man thinks there are two gods or more' (*Marc.* 2.2.6). Innocence and understanding have gone, for man 'has lost the grace of paradise, and that intimacy with God, by which, had he obeyed, he would have known all the things of God' (*Marc.* 2.2.6).

Indeed, simplicity marked creation, for all came from and was marked by the one goodness of God (*Marc.* 2.4.6). The gift of freedom was part of this goodness and it was never revoked. Otherwise Marcion would protest 'What sort of lord is this ineffective, instable, faithless being who rescinds his own decisions?' (*Marc.* 2.7.3) None of these negative epithets should ever be applied to the unmixed goodness of God.

The same simplicity marks his providence which dispenses light and darkness, good and evil. But how can this fail to compromise his simple goodness? Because the evil which he dispenses is a punishment for sin and therefore good (*Marc.* 2.14.3).

Is there a simple gospel? Such simplicity may be hard to see; but it is there to be found, as indeed in the different Gospels of the apostles, John and Matthew, and of the apostolic men, Luke and Mark. All follow the same rule of one creator God and his Christ, born of a virgin, fulfilling law and prophets. 'It does not matter if there be some variation in the arrangement of their narratives, provided that there is agreement in the substance of the faith' (*Marc.* 4.2.2). Marcion's mutilated Gospel subverts the substance of the gospel. It bears no name, for he stopped short of inventing a title. No written work should be recognized if it cannot hold its head erect, offer some consistency and promise some credibility by naming a title and an author.

Truth is to be distinguished by its simplicity, with which proud men fuss and fiddle, so mixing it with falsehood that nothing certain remains. 'When they had found a simple and straightforward God, they began to disagree about him, not as he had been revealed to them, but in order to debate about his properties, his nature, his place' (*ap.* 47.5). Some say he is physical, others incorporeal, some that he is made of atoms, others that he consists of numbers. Some claim he governs the world, perhaps from inside or perhaps from outside, others declare that he is idle. Such confusion is not primitive but contrived, not ancient wisdom but modern muddle. There is nothing as old as the truth of the scriptures which philosophers have perverted in every possible way.

Yet Christians wear the cloak of the philosopher, because of its simplicity and because they have found the better philosophy (*pall.* 6). The toga may offer higher status in the community; but it is an elaborate thing of many folds (*pall.* 1.1). While everything changes, not all change is good. Primitive simplicity is challenged by luxury. It was a bad day when Alexander, on fire with his triumph over the Persians, exchanged his armour for a pair of puffed-up, Persian trousers, made of silk. When philosophers move into purple, what is to stop them from wearing golden slippers (*pall.* 4.7)? What could be less philosophical than that?

The change to the philosopher's cloak is justified by its simplicity as a garment, in contrast to the many folds of the toga which are a cumbersome nuisance (*pall.* 5.1). The cloak is the most convenient garment and saves time in dressing (*pall.* 5.3). Further, it designates independence and freedom from the duties of forum, elections, senate, platforms and every other part of public life. It wears out no seats, attacks no laws, argues no pleas, is worn by no judge, soldier or king. 'I have seceded from the community. My sole business is with myself and my one care is not to care.' When accused of laziness, it replies, 'No one is born for another, and he dies for himself alone' (*pall.* 5.4). Simplicity of detachment is achieved because the philosophers' cloak has become Christian and found the better philosophy (*pall.* 6.2) in Jesus Christ, son of God and saviour. So the law of change is justified. We cannot avoid change; we should ensure that it is change to the good.[39]

Perfection in Dishonour: 'Jesus Christ, Son of God, Saviour'

The answer to the question about one God, good and true, was: 'Yes there is one God, if he not only created the world, but also acted to renew it in Jesus Christ.' God's utter disgrace was the pledge of mankind's salvation. God came to man's level, so that man might reach God's level. God became small that man might become great (*Marc.* 2.27.7).

Simplicity was not empty. All was summed up in Christ. Following Paul, Tertullian (*pud.* 14 et passim) knew nothing but Christ and him crucified. This was the sole hope (*unica spes*) of the world, the necessary dishonour (*necessarium dedecus*) of faith (*carn.* 5.3). In a word, God is one God, when the son hands over the kingdom to the father.

Behind the fish ('Jesus Christ, son of God, saviour')[40] lay the even simpler confession of Jesus as Messiah or Christ (Matt. 27.17, 22; John 1.41; Acts 9.22; 1 John 5.1). When the gospel moved from its Jewish context into the Greek world, this title meant less and 'Christ' became a surname for Jesus. The basic confession then became 'Jesus Christ is Lord' (parallel to the 'Emperor is Lord' of the imperial cult)[41] or 'Jesus Christ is son of God'. Christians had their own answer to pagan and Jewish acclamations, such as 'one is Zeus-Serapis', 'great is Diana of the Ephesians', or even 'Hear O Israel . . . . This simple formula was used as a confession of faith at baptism, being expanded first into a twofold faith in father and son, then into a threefold faith in father, son and spirit, and receiving various supplements. The simplicity of the fish remained. There was one lord, one faith, one baptism.

'Jesus Christ, son of God, saviour' points to the economy of salvation and the recapitulation of all things in Christ, who is Christus Victor.[42] Recapitulation is chiefly linked with Irenaeus;[43] but it also dominates the New Testament and the theology of Ignatius, Justin, Clement of Alexandria, Tertullian and Athanasius. It includes three sets of motifs: Christ corrects and perfects all that is; as Christus Victor he is the climax of the economy of saving history; and as the perfection of being, goodness and truth, he gives life to the dying, righteousness to sinners and truth to those in error.

Tertullian describes the work of salvation as continuous with creation.[44] The human race is summed up, 'that is to refer back to the beginning or to revise from the beginning' (*Marc.* 5.17.1), reformed (*Marc.* 3.9.5) and restored (*pat.* 15.1).[45] Redemption through a ransom paid (*fug.* 12.2f.) leads to liberty (*carn.* 14.3).[46] Christ as mediator (*sequester, res.* 51.2) is clothed with

humanity (*Prax.* 12.3) and reconciles (*Marc.* 5.19.5) man to God.[47] The sacrifice of Christ, the paschal lamb, is offered by the great high priest (*Jud.* 14.8). His voluntary death is a propitiation but not a vicarious satisfaction for sin.[48] As teacher, Christ brings illumination through saving discipline (*ap.* 47.11; *pat.* 12.4) and a better philosophy (*pall.* 6.2).[49] As divine physician, he heals sinners (*scorp.* 5.8).[50] By his descent to hell, he has restored (*an.* 55.1f.) patriarchs and prophets.

Finally, by the trophy of the cross, he has triumphed over death, the last enemy (*Marc.* 4.20.5). His victory is not that of the warrior Messiah for whom the Jews had looked (*Jud.* 9.1-20), but is the spiritual overthrow of the armies of wickedness (*Marc.* 4.20-4). This salvation was also a new creation (*iei.* 14.2; *Marc.* 5.12.6).[51]

The saving victory of Jesus began as his fulfilment of Jewish prophecies, within the saving history . . . . Why did the gospel come so late in human history? The answer lay in the plan of God's saving economy or dispensation which prepared the way for and found its climax in the victory of Christ who overthrew the powers of darkness. For apocalyptic dwelt on cosmic triumph as well as on fulfilment of prophetic hope. Jesus reigned as the son of God over all created things and every power in heaven and on earth. Devils fled in fear before his name.

To Jews, therefore, Tertullian's answer is direct. There is only one question: whether Christ, announced by the prophets as the object of universal faith, has, or has not, come (*Jud.* 7.1). The proof is plain in the rapid, universal spread of the gospel.[52] It is evident that[53] no gate or city is closed to him, his sound is gone out into all the earth, gates of brass are opened and he reigns over all.

> But Christ's name reaches out everywhere, is believed everywhere, is worshipped by all the nations we have listed, rules everywhere, is everywhere adored, is bestowed equally everywhere upon all; in his presence no king receives more favour, no barbarian receives less joy; no dignities or families merit special distinction; to all he is equal, to all king, to all judge, to all 'God and lord'. Nor might you hesitate to believe what we assert, since you see it actually happening. (*Jud.* 7.9-8.1).

Christ is the bull who, in fulfilment of Joseph's blessing,[54] tosses the nations to the ends of the earth, on the horns of his cross, which was also foretold in the outstretched hands of Moses (Exod. 17.8-16). How else can we explain the peculiar position of Moses, as he sat with arms outstretched, rather than kneeling or prostrate on the earth, unless it be that the name of Jesus was his theme? Jesus would one day engage the devil in single combat and conquer by the sign of the cross (*Jud.* 10.1). He is the God who reigns from the tree,[55] who came once in humility and will come again with glory (*Jud.* 10.12). Death reigned from Adam to Christ who concluded the rule of death by dying on the tree of the cross. The government is on his shoulder. No other king rules in this way. 'But only the new king of the new ages, Christ Jesus, has carried on his shoulder the dominion and majesty of his new glory, which is the cross' (*Marc.* 3.19.3).

The victory of Christ is strongly affirmed in demilitarized military terms. For he who straps his sword on his thigh is fairer than the children of men and grace pours from his lips. He who so rides in majesty, rides in meekness and righteousness, which are not the 'proper business of battles' (Ps. 45.2-4). His strange warfare of the word invades every nation, bringing all to faith, and ruling by his victory over death (*Marc.* 3.14.6).

Christ conquers as a human being, when his obedience triumphs over the same devil before whom Adam fell (*Marc.* 2.8.3). This second conflict was all the more painful to the devil because he had won the first contest, and was all the sweeter to the man who, by a victory, recovered his salvation, a more glorious paradise and the fruit of the tree of life (*Marc.* 2.10.6).

'O Christ even in your novelties you are old!' (*Marc.* 4.21.5) Incidents in the mission of the disciples (the feeding of the multitude, the confession of Peter, being ashamed of Christ) show him to be the Christ of the creator (*Marc.* 4.21.5). All Christ's words and deeds, even his resurrection, point back to the prophets (*Marc.* 4.43.9). All that Christ did was part of a continuous saving economy, which God began immediately after the fall of Adam. His goodness now took the form of justice, severity and even, as the Marcionites claim, cruelty. 'Thus God's goodness was prior and according to nature, his severity came later and for a reason. The one was innate, the other accidental; the one his own, the other adapted; the one freely flowing, the other admitted as an expedient' (*Marc.* 2.11.2). There is unbroken continuity in God's goodness which, since the fall, has had an opposition with which to contend. Spontaneous goodness is replaced by justice which is the agent (*procuratio*) of goodness. Goodness needed a new means to contend with its adversary and fear of punishment was the only effective way (*Marc.* 2.13.2).

While he reforms rather than destroys, and restores rather than abolishes (*Marc.* 2.29.3), there is change and correction. In the place of an eye for an eye and a tooth for a tooth, he offers a cheek for a cheek, with the difference that it is the second cheek of the victim rather than the cheek of the aggressor which is struck (*Marc.* 4.16.4); this kind of imaginative paradox is typical of Tertullian. This brilliant example is emblematic of the recapitulation which both fulfils and corrects.

Recapitulation is both retrospective and prospective, both fulfilment of the past and promise of the future. Because of his preoccupation with Marcion, Tertullian seems more concerned with fulfilment than with promise. Furthermore, the miracle of new life through baptism did not do as much as he hoped. Clement of Alexandria and Irenaeus celebrate more vividly the present glory of new life in Christ. In this difference some have seen the contrast between Greek and Latin Christianity.[56] Yet the disciples of the new covenant receive a new way to pray from the new grace of a renewing God (*or.* 1) and Christians believe in one God in a new way (*Prax.* 3).[57]

The economy would not have been complete until he, to whom it had all been directed, had come. The mass of fulfilled prophecy is too great for anyone to deny. In him we find the sure mercies of David. It is he, not David, who is a witness, prince and commander to the nations, and on whom all nations now call (*Marc.* 3.20.10). His new word is decisive and brief,[58] a compendium which offers relief from the burdensome details of the law. Isaiah foretold new things and Jeremiah a new covenant (*Marc.* 4.1.6). Finally, to those who, in the face of all this evidence, deny the kingdom of Christ, there remains the second coming which will not be in humility, but in power and glory (*Marc.* 3.7.8).

Marcion is wasting his complicated time when he tries to separate the strange, simple goodness of Christ from the alleged evil of the creator (*Marc.* 1.2.3). The first Christians disagreed about almost everything else; but they did not waver from undivided faith in the creator and his Christ (*Marc.* 1.21.3). Even Marcion allows Christ to appear on the mountain with Moses and Elijah, the first who formed God's people and established the old covenant, the second who reformed God's people and consummated[59] the new covenant (*Marc.* 4.22.1). 'He, who made, is best able to remake,[60] seeing that it is a far greater work to make than to remake, to give a beginning than to give it back again' (*res.* 11.10). The wonder of the gospel should not obscure the marvel of creation.

Problems of Recapitulation

The summing up of all things in Christ, who is Christus Victor, shaped the theology of the first three centuries. It has persisted since then, in varying form, whether it be in the Eucharist of eastern and western churches or in hymns like *Vexilla regis prodeunt* and *Ein' feste Burg* or in the Easter liturgy of every tradition. Its place in the Latin Mass, in the Greek *Christos Niketes* and in the Lutheran tradition[61] is equally secure. It found its strongest statement in Athanasius' *De Incarnatione* and its difficulties are most apparent in the conclusion of this work.

> For as when the sun is up darkness no longer prevails, but if there is any left anywhere it is driven away; so now, when the Divine Manifestation of the Word of God is come, the darkness of the idols prevails no longer, but every part of the whole earth is everywhere illuminated by his teaching . . . and men, looking to the true God, the Word of the Father, abandon idols, and themselves come to a clear knowledge of the true God.

> Now this is the proof that Christ is God, the Word and Power of God. For, human things ceasing, and the Word of Christ remaining, it is plain to all that the things which are ceasing are temporary, but that He who remains is God and the true Son of God, the Only-begotten Word. (*de inc.* 55, Bindley trans.)

The triumphal claims of this passage concerning the destruction of evil do not fit reality then or now. There does not appear to have been a change of government. Indeed, from the beginning there were difficulties with recapitulation. Death, despite the sting of martyrdom, may have been destroyed; but sin was still clearly present. Christians were not displaying the climax of divine and human history, for mediocrity spread widely in the early church. Laodiceans were neither hot nor cold, but drastically indigestible (Rev. 3.15f.).[62] Tertullian speaks of *mediocritas nostra* (*paen.* 6.1) and develops a doctrine of original sin.[63]

From such disappointment, two types of perfectionism emerged—apocalyptic and Gnostic. Irenaeus and Tertullian both viewed with sympathy the New Prophecy of the followers of Montanus. Clement of Alexandria gave critical recognition to some elements of Valentinianism. Irenaeus had wonderful millenarian expectations. If all was summed up in Christ, what remained had to be sensational—a thousand branches on every vine and a thousand grapes on every twig. Lions normally eat only the best of animal steaks.[64] Yet in the last days, says Irenaeus, we know from the scriptures that lions will eat straw. They cannot eat the lambs with whom they lie down. If the straw is so good as to be attractive to lions, we shall truly feast on what is provided for us.

The perfectionist movement known as Gnosticism was not confined to Christianity. The desire to sur-

pass (*supergredi*) others is always widespread; to the question 'What must I do to be saved?' is added the question 'What must I do to be a better Jew or Christian, than my neighbour?' Gnosticism is a complex movement. Tertullian saw that its final strength and weakness lay in its claim to surpass reason. Like all theosophy, Gnosticism presents philosophy without argument, which is like opera without music, Shakespeare without words and ballet without movement. Complex argument can be replaced by pretentious narrative. The Gnostic reply is always that his critic is shallow (not profound) or even intellectually and morally depraved.[65] The relevance of Gnosticism for Tertullian is first, its reaction against mediocrity in favour of perfection and second, its movement from argument to story. Unlike Clement of Alexandria, he neither appreciated its abstract tendency nor offered a higher competitive gnosis.

Perfectionism had emerged as a problem very early in Christian history. The Letter to the Ephesians affirmed strongly that all has been summed up in Christ and that the church is the eschatological miracle which rises from earth to heaven. There is no way in which this miracle can be surpassed. The believer must simply hold to the one faith within the one body, walk in the light and stand firm in the whole armour of God.

Apologists claimed evidence for finality in the moral excellence of Christian lives and in the spread of the gospel. Such moral excellence was the ground for Justin's conversion, and Tertullian made much of it. He pointed to the chastity and integrity of Christians, the courage of the martyrs and the mutual love of the community. This claim caused his discontent with the church universal. He remained within the community of the church at Carthage;[66] but he certainly expressed dissent. When his bishop offered absolution for the sins of adultery and fornication, Tertullian was outraged, because this controverted his claim that Christians were eschatological paragons of virtue. Tertullian wrote off the majority of Christians as psychics or carnal, in contrast to the spiritual Christians of whom he was one.

The spread of the gospel was a second proof of recapitulation. We are of yesterday, Tertullian said, but we fill the forums and the towns. We are in every country, growing from seed which is the blood of martyrs. The world, too, is a better place; marshes are drained and roads are better.[67] Theodicy could point to a future consummation in Christ's return and to the present and visible fruits of his triumph. When Christians faced persecution the latter were precious signs. Even persecution, said Justin, showed that the demons (or pagan gods) were fearful. It was different when Christians had gained political power. Christians soon realized that they were not at the *eschaton.*

Perfection in God

In a Christian empire theodicy ceased to be the first question, until Augustine faced the end of empire in his *City of God,* and explained why Christians could not expect to win any but the final and decisive test.

While recapitulation of all things in Christ, which dominated the theology of Tertullian, Irenaeus and the early Athanasius, gave way in the fourth century, to christology and trinity, the questions could never be held apart. The first question and answer were 'Is there one God?' and 'Only if the creator has acted to redeem the world in Christ.' The second question 'How can one God be both father and son?' is necessary if God is to be credible. The divine economy has to be within God; it cannot be the detachable plan of a changeable being. The economy of the mystery had been hidden from all ages *in* the God who made all things (*Eph.* 3.9).

Christology moved to the centre. How could God be both father and son? Recapitulation might remove distinctions in God. Tertullian spoke of the entire dishonour of his God; but he attacked the monarchianism of Praxeas for crucifying the father, and proposed a doctrine of trinity. The christological debates were inevitable. Before they finished, recapitulation no longer had to do with history and Christus Victor, but with the trinity which summed up the divine being.

This was not, as some have thought, a mistake. The history of the councils of the fourth century is no more elevating than the history of councils in any century: 'After Constantine, there is not much that is not humiliating—the long period of dogmatic squabbling while the Empire was falling to pieces; the destruction or loss of most of the irreplaceable treasures of antiquity; the progressive barbarisation of Europe; we need not follow the melancholy record.'[68] Arius did miss the point of the whole early tradition, that faith in one God is only possible if that God redeems the world which he first made; but his lack of perception sparked off a genuine advance. For faith in divine redemption can never rely on fulfilled prophecy, external plan or natural evidences, but only on the being of God.

This profound move is apparent in the theology of Gregory Nazianzus.[69] After the fall of Adam, God corrected and sustained, in diverse ways, the fallen race (*orat.* 38.13.36.325). When it became clear that a stronger medicine was needed, the incarnation provided the peak of God's saving work. The key to salvation is that Christ is God (*orat.* 33.16f.36.236). God is father, son and holy spirit. The full deity of

the son must be preserved (*orat.* 33.17.36.236). In the incarnation there is condescension (*orat.* 37.2.36.284f.) and recapitulation (*orat.* 2.23f. 35.284f.). God sums up and contains all (*orat.* 38.7.36.317). 'A few drops of blood recreate the whole world and draw men together into a unity' (*orat.* 45.29.36.664). The new Adam is a suffering God (*orat.* 30.1.36.36.104) who overcomes human sin. For Gregory, even where the economy is given pre-eminence, the summing up which is its centre is the triune God. Indeed it is recapitulation which makes God one and perfects human knowledge of the divine.

Tertullian anticipates this move from recapitulation to incarnation and trinity. Christus Victor reflected the prophetic apocalyptic tradition. . . . This was for Tertullian, the *unica spes,* the *necessarium dedecus,* the *sacramentum oikonomiae.* In the end, the mass of prophetic fulfilment is replaced by this one claim, and by faith in the triune God.

Simplicity and recapitulation, which dominated early Christian theology, including that of Tertullian, found their place in one God, father, son and spirit. Tertullian's ideas persist into the fourth century and indeed into the twentieth century, where a metaphysical poem ends:

> A condition of complete simplicity
> (Costing not less than everything)
> And all shall be well and
> All manner of thing shall be well
> When the tongues of flame are in-folded
> Into the crowned knot of fire
> And the fire and the rose are one.[70]

Notes

[1] Speratus speaks in reply to the proconsul's claim, 'Et nos religiosi sumus et simplex est nostra religio.' Speratus says, 'Si tranquillas praebueris aures tuas, dico mysterium simplicitatis.' *Passio sanctorum Scillitanorum,* 3f. See *Acta Martyrum,* ed. H. Musurillo, *The acts of the Christian martyrs* (Oxford, 1972), 86.

[2] This term is commonly used of Tertullian in the sense of apparent contradiction (Cicero: 'admirabilia contraque opinionem omnium' (*Paradoxa Stoicorum,* 4)), rather than in the more complex logical sense (Zeno, Russell). See J. van Heyenroot, Logical Paradoxes, in P. Edwards (ed.), *Encyclopedia of Philosophy,* vol. v (New York, 1967), 45-51. The two senses will sometimes over-lap.

[3] 'This unity lies behind the pseudo-paradoxes and pseudo-contradictions.' J.-C. Fredouille, *Tertullien et la conversion de la culture antique* (Paris, 1972), 485.

[4] Jerome, *vir. illust.* 57.

[5] In this bad sense, the greater part of the faithful are *simplices* (*ne dixerim imprudentes et idiotae*) who, having moved from many gods to one God, panic at the exposition of the trinity (*Prax.* 3.1). The same people are uncertain about the value of martyrdom, find their doubts exploited by Gnostics (*scorp.* 1.5), and cannot answer objections against the maduess of dying for God (*scorp.* 1.7).

[6] The Cainite heresy which honoured Cain because he resisted the evil God of the Old Testament. Tertullian's snakes prefer dry places.

[7] See discussion of paradox in ch. 3 and of opposites in ch. 4.

[8] To this formula we shall return in the second part of this chapter.

[9] Charles Munier, La tradition apostolique chez Tertullien, in Collected studies series CS341, Autorité épiscopale et sollicitude pastorale, *L'année canonique,* 33 (Paris, 1979), 175-92 (192).

[10] See below, ch. 5. Despite initial simplicity, Tertullian develops a complex argument here.

[11] Gerhard Ebeling often set out his lectures in numbered chapters, sections, paragraphs and even propositions. When he once came to chapter 4, section 3, paragraph 5, proposition 2, he paused and said with a smile, 'Entschuldigen Sie, bitte, wenn ich alles zu einfach mache!'

[12] *On the Epistle of John,* 7.8. See my, *Ethical patterns in early Christian thought* (Cambridge, 1976), 179-81.

[13] B. Nisters, *Tertullian, seine Persönlichkeit und sein Schicksal* (Münster, 1950).

[14] C. Rambaux, *Tertullien face aux morales des trois premiers siècles* (Paris, 1979).

[15] See following chapters for discussion of A. Labhardt, Tertullien et la philosophie ou la recherche d'une 'position pure', *MH,* 7 (1950), 159-80.

[16] H. von Campenhausen, *The fathers of the Latin church* (London, 1964), 6.

[17] B. B. Warfield, *Studies in Tertullian and Augustine* (Oxford, 1930), 3f.

[18] T. D. Barnes, *Tertullian, A historical and literary study,* 2nd edn (Oxford, 1985), 211-32.

[19] See R. D. Sider, *Ancient rhetoric and the art of Tertullian* (Oxford, 1971), and the work of C. Munier, J.-C. Fredouille and H. Steiner who sees this valuable area of study as 'wohl erschöpft'.

[20] Note the necessary qualification of G. L. Prestige, *God in patristic thought* (London, 1936), 97: 'He was very far, indeed, from being merely the father of Latin theology. His ultimate influence on Greek theological speculation was probably very considerable.'

[21] J. Daniélou, *Latin Christianity,* 341.

[22] See D. Allen, Motives, rationales, and religious beliefs, *APQ,* 3 (1966), 112ff., for a useful account of the logic of objection and rebuttal.

[23] *Ad Diognetum,* 5.

[24] A recent writer calls this 'polemical Christianity'. (A. J. Guerra, Polemical Christianity: Tertullian's search for certainty, *The Second Century* (1990), 108). He points out that Tertullian draws on five kinds of support for his position (scripture, reason, moral excellence, spiritual witness and tradition) and that he uses different combinations when he attacks different enemies.

[25] In modern jargon, 'a God-shaped blank'.

[26] Quentin Skinner, *The return of grand theory to the human sciences* (Cambridge, 1985), 12.

[27] On the chronology of Tertullian's works, I accept the argument and conclusions of R. Braun, *Deus Christianorum,* 563-77.

[28] See below, ch. 10.

[29] See below, ch. 5.

[30] The term is taken from Paul (1 Cor. 2.14; 15.44-6) . . . .

[31] J.-C. Fredouille, *Tertullien et la conversion de la culture antique,* 33, notes Zeno (D.L. 7.59), Cicero, Seneca (*ep.* 38), Tacitus and Marcus Aurelius (*med.* 4.51).

[32] This word, popular among French theologians, is useful to express Tertullian's claim concerning the unity and uniqueness of God.

[33] Clement of Alexandria solved this problem with his thematic statement [about] negative theology. . . (*strom.* 5.11.71). See also G. L. Prestige's account of Tertullian's 'organic monotheism', *God in patristic thought,* 98f.

[34] Which, for Marcion, deny the perfect goodness of their maker.

[35] See below, ch. 5 for the problem of polemic and ch. 9 for a discussion of Valentinianism and the bureaucratic fallacy.

[36] Tertullian's argument is used today, at a popular level, by Orthodox against Roman Catholics and by Roman Catholics against Protestants.

[37] This is an example of Tertullian's Trick: omitting steps which he mentions elsewhere.

[38] 'deus omnipotens, dominus et conditor universitatis'.

[39] This is the point where Tertullian and Stoics differ markedly from Alexandrians and Platonists.

[40] See F.J. Dölger, . . . [Der] heilige Fisch in den antiken Religionen und im Christentum (Münster, 1922).

[41] *mart. Pol.* 8.2.

[42] Because the concept of salvation easily becomes too subjective, 'victor' is often to be preferred as a translation . . . (*TWNT* VII, 1,005-24). In the Old Testament, salvation points to the rescue of those oppressed by military power or injustice; because of human limitations, God emerges as the ultimate deliverer. In the New Testament, the same notion of rescue is found in God's relation to the whole human race. In the classical world, saviours could be gods, men who helped or healed, philosophers, statesmen or rulers. Hadrian is frequently celebrated as the saviour of a town or a person. On a wider scale, the emperor brought in, as saviour, the golden age. Philo gives the title of saviour to God who delivers his people, preserves the world, and liberates the soul from passion (*sobr.* 55; *immut.* 129; *somn.* 1.112; *leg. all.* 11.105).

The message of the angels to the shepherds (Luke 2.10f.) links the titles 'saviour' and 'lord'. In the Fourth Gospel, the son is seen as the saviour of the world (John 3.17; cf. 1 John. 4.14). In the New Testament, the title of 'saviour' is found less frequently than the verb 'save' and the noun 'salvation'. This may be a reaction against Jewish expectations of a national deliverer (*TWNT* VII, 1,021). The Pastoral Epistles find the title important for the rejection of heretical claims.

[43] G. Aulen, *Christus Victor* (London, 1953), 32-51.

[44] A. Viciano, *Cristo salvador y liberador del hombre*

(Pamplona, 1986), 269-350.

[45] *Ibid.,* 118-23.

[46] *Ibid.,* 126-9.

[47] *Ibid.,* 129-33.

[48] *Ibid.,* 133-8 and 318-20.

[49] *Ibid.,* 138-40.

[50] *Ibid.,* 141-3.

[51] *Ibid.,* 341-50.

[52] 'Die Kirchengeschichte ist eine Siegesgeschichte des Christenthums'. G. Leonhardi, *Die apologetischen Grundgedanken Tertullians* (Leipzig, 1882), 7. It was indeed the universal character of Christianity which brought it into conflict with the state.

[53] Tertullian misquotes Isa. 45.1, reading *Kurios* for Cyrus.

[54] Deut. 33.17. Moses gives this blessing to Joseph.

[55] Ps. 96.10 is often so quoted in early Christian writing; no adequate reason has been found for the reading. See E. F. Osborn, *Justin Martyr* (Tübingen, 1973), 103-5, and J. H. Charlesworth, Christian and Jewish self-definition in light of the Christian additions to the Apocryphal writings, in E. P. Sanders *et al.* (eds.), *Jewish and Christian self-definition,* vol. 11, *Aspects of Judaism in the Graeco-Roman period* (London, 1981), 27-55.

[56] See Daniélou, *Latin Christianity,* 341.

[57] And as for Novalis, Easter is 'ein Weltverjüngungsfest'.

[58] See The short word, in Osborn, *Beginning of Christian philosophy,* 206-40.

[59] Elijah is an eschatological figure who came as John the Baptist.

[60] As so often, Augustine takes up Tertullian's ideas, 'qui fecit, refecit'. *Ep.* 231.6. He discards Tertullian's exaggeration of creation's superiority over recreation. Tertullian reverses the priority in *Prax.*

[61] Aulen, *Christus Victor.*

[62] Today it is claimed that 'unambitious mediocrity is of course part of the Anglo-Saxon tradition' (Iris Murdoch, *The sovereignty of good* (London, 1970), 50), and the arguments against enthusiasm in National Socialism and Islamic Fundamentalism are overwhelm-

ing.

[63] See below, ch. 8.

[64] They would not be interested in the contemporary Cheeseburger.

[65] The issue is more complex. See the discussion on Valentinianism, ch. 9, below.

[66] See David Rankin, *Tertullian and the church* (Cambridge, 1995), 41-51.

[67] To 'disseminate' with Post-modernists, the camels are running on time.

[68] W. R. Inge, *The Platonic tradition in English religious thought* (London, 1926), III.

[69] See E. F. Osborn, Theology and economy in Gregory the Theologian, in H. C. Brennecke, E. L. Grasmück and C. Markschies (eds.), *Logos, FS for L. Abramowski* (Berlin, 1993), 361-83.

[70] T. S. Eliot, *Four Quartets* (London, 1944), 44 Note also p. 33:

> Here the impossible union
> Of spheres of existence is actual,
> Here the past and future
> Are conquered, and reconciled.

Tertullian's Works

an.	*de anima*
ap.	*apologeticum*
bapt.	*de baptismo*
carn.	*de carne Christi*
cast.	*de exhortatione castitatis*
cor.	*de corona*
cult.	*de cultu feminarum, libri II*
fug.	*de fuga in persecutione*
Herm.	*adversus Hermogenem*
idol.	*de idololatria*
iei.	*de ieiunio*
Jud.	*adversus Judaeos*
Marc.	*adversus Marcionem, libri V*
mart.	*ad martyras*
mon.	*de monogamia*
nat.	*ad nationes, libri II*
or.	*de oratione*
paen.	*de paenitentia*
pall.	*de pallio*
pat.	*de patientia*
praescr.	*de praescriptione haereticorum*
Prax.	*adversus Praxean*
pud.	*de pudicitia*
res.	*de resurrectione mortuorum*
Scap.	*ad Scapulam*
scorp.	*scorpiace*
spect.	*de spectaculis*
test.	*de testimonio animae*
ux.	*ad uxorem, libri II*
Val.	*adversus Valentinianos*
virg.	*de virginibus velandis*

FURTHER READING

Ayers. Robert H. "Language, Logic, and Reason in Tertullian." In *Language, Logic, and Reason in the Church Fathers: A Study of Tertullian, Augustine, and Aquinas.* Hildesheim and New York: Georg Olms Verlag, 1979, pp. 7-60.

Analyzes Tertullian's attitude toward reason and philosophy, arguing that his thought exhibits a basic consistency and appeal to rationality.

Barnes, Timothy David. *Tertullian: A Historical and Literary Study.* Oxford: Clarendon Press, 1971, 320 p.

Attempts to reconstruct Tertullian's life from extant biographical material and his own writings.

Bray, Gerald. "The Legal Concept of *Ratio* in Tertullian."

Vigiliae Christianae 31, No. 2 (June 1977): 94-116.
   Explores Tertullian's use of the word *ratio* in a philosophic sense, arguing against the contention that "Tertullian assimilated *ratio* to God in imitation of the Stoics."

Daly, Cahal B. *Tertullian the Puritan and His Influence: An Essay in Historical Theology.* Dublin: Four Courts Press, 1993, 221 p.
   Studies Tertullian's theology of the Church in the context of the history of Christian penance.

de Labriolle, Pierre. "The First Christian Fathers in the Latin Tongue: Tertullian." In *History and Literature of Christianity from Tertullian to Boethius.* London: Routledge & Kegan Paul, Ltd., 1924, pp. 50-105.
   Examines Tertullian's life ans style, offering an in-depth study of his extant works.

Mason, A. J. "Tertullian and Purgatory." *The Journal of Theological Studies* III (1902): 598-601.
   Considers Tertullian's view of purgatory as described briefly in his *De anima.*

Moffatt, James. "Aristotle and Tertullian." *The Journal of Theological Studies* XVII, No. 66 (January 1916): 170-71.
   Observes "a curious affinity between Tertullian's famous paradox and a passage in Aristotle's *Rhetoric.*"

O'Malley, T. P. *Tertullian and the Bible: Language—Imagery—Exegesis.* Utrecht: Dekker & Van de Vegt, 1967, 186 p.
   In-depth analysis of Tertullian's writings on and knowledge of the Latin *Bible.*

Power, Victor. "Tertullian: Father of Clerical Animosity toward the Theatre." *Educational Theatre Journal* XXIII, No. 1 (March 1971): 36-50.
   Discussess the influence of Tertullian's treatise *De spectaculis* on later Christian attitudes toward the morality of theater-going.

Sider, Robert Dick. *Ancient Rhetoric and the Art of Tertullian.* London: Oxford University Press, 1971, 139 p.
   Probes the rhetorical style and method of Tertullian's treatises.

Souter, Alex. "A Tenth-Century Fragment of Tertullian's *Apology.*" *The Journal of Theological Studies* VIII (1907): 297-300.
   Notes variations in two texts (one fragmentary) of Tertullian's *Apologeticum.*

Waszink, J. H. "Observations on Tertullian's Treatise Against Hermogenes." *Vigiliae Christianae* IX (1955): 129-47.
   Examines the sources of the doctrine of Hermogenes and of Tertullian's refutation of that doctrine in his

CLASSICAL AND MEDIEVAL LITERATURE CRITICISM

INDEXES

Literary Criticism Series
Cumulative Author Index

Literary Criticism Series
Cumulative Topic Index

CMLC Cumulative Nationality Index

CMLC Cumulative Title Index

CMLC Cumulative Critic Index

How to Use This Index

The main references

```
Calvino, Italo
  1923–1985 ....... CLC 5, 8, 11, 22, 33, 39,
                                    73; SSC 3
```

list all author entries in the following Gale Literary Criticism series:

BLC = *Black Literature Criticism*
CLC = *Contemporary Literary Criticism*
CLR = *Children's Literature Review*
CMLC = *Classical and Medieval Literature Criticism*
DA = *DISCovering Authors*
DAB = *DISCovering Authors: British*
DAC = *DISCovering Authors: Canadian*
DAM = *DISCovering Authors: Modules*
　　　DRAM: *Dramatists Module;* *MST*: *Most-Studied Authors Module;*
　　　MULT: *Multicultural Authors Module;* *NOV*: *Novelists Module;*
　　　POET: *Poets Module;* *POP*: *Popular Fiction and Genre Authors Module*
DC = *Drama Criticism*
HLC = *Hispanic Literature Criticism*
LC = *Literature Criticism from 1400 to 1800*
NCLC = *Nineteenth-Century Literature Criticism*
PC = *Poetry Criticism*
SSC = *Short Story Criticism*
TCLC = *Twentieth-Century Literary Criticism*
WLC = *World Literature Criticism, 1500 to the Present*

The cross-references

```
See also CANR 23; CA 85-88;
  obituary CA116
```

list all author entries in the following Gale biographical and literary sources:

AAYA = *Authors & Artists for Young Adults*
AITN = *Authors in the News*
BEST = *Bestsellers*
BW = *Black Writers*
CA = *Contemporary Authors*
CAAS = *Contemporary Authors Autobiography Series*
CABS = *Contemporary Authors Bibliographical Series*
CANR = *Contemporary Authors New Revision Series*
CAP = *Contemporary Authors Permanent Series*
CDALB = *Concise Dictionary of American Literary Biography*
CDBLB = *Concise Dictionary of British Literary Biography*
DLB = *Dictionary of Literary Biography*
DLBD = *Dictionary of Literary Biography Documentary Series*
DLBY = *Dictionary of Literary Biography Yearbook*
HW = *Hispanic Writers*
JRDA = *Junior DISCovering Authors*
MAICYA = *Major Authors and Illustrators for Children and Young Adults*
MTCW = *Major 20th-Century Writers*
NNAL = *Native North American Literature*
SAAS = *Something about the Author Autobiography Series*
SATA = *Something about the Author*
YABC = *Yesterday's Authors of Books for Children*

Literary Criticism Series
Cumulative Author Index

5, 61; CDBLB 1914-1945; DLB 10, 20;
MTCW
Audiberti, Jacques 1900-1965 **CLC 38; DAM**
DRAM
See also CA 25-28R
Audubon, John James 1785-1851 **NCLC 47**
Auel, Jean M(arie) 1936- CLC 31, 107; **DAM**
POP
See also AAYA 7; BEST 90:4; CA 103; CANR
21, 64; INT CANR-21; SATA 91
Auerbach, Erich 1892-1957 **TCLC 43**
See also CA 118; 155
Augier, Emile 1820-1889 **NCLC 31**
See also DLB 192
August, John
See De Voto, Bernard (Augustine)
Augustine, St. 354-430 **CMLC 6; DAB**
Aurelius
See Bourne, Randolph S(illiman)
Aurobindo, Sri
See Ghose, Aurabinda
Austen, Jane 1775-1817 **NCLC 1, 13, 19, 33,**
51; DA; DAB; DAC; DAM MST, NOV;
WLC
See also AAYA 19; CDBLB 1789-1832; DLB
116
Auster, Paul 1947- **CLC 47**
See also CA 69-72; CANR 23, 52
Austin, Frank
See Faust, Frederick (Schiller)
Austin, Mary (Hunter) 1868-1934 **TCLC 25**
See also CA 109; DLB 9, 78
Autran Dourado, Waldomiro
See Dourado, (Waldomiro Freitas) Autran
Averroes 1126-1198 **CMLC 7**
See also DLB 115
Avicenna 980-1037 **CMLC 16**
See also DLB 115
Avison, Margaret 1918- CLC 2, 4, 97; **DAC;**
DAM POET
See also CA 17-20R; DLB 53; MTCW
Axton, David
See Koontz, Dean R(ay)
Ayckbourn, Alan 1939- CLC 5, 8, 18, 33, 74;
DAB; DAM DRAM
See also CA 21-24R; CANR 31, 59; DLB 13;
MTCW
Aydy, Catherine
See Tennant, Emma (Christina)
Ayme, Marcel (Andre) 1902-1967 **CLC 11**
See also CA 89-92; CANR 67; CLR 25; DLB
72; SATA 91
Ayrton, Michael 1921-1975 **CLC 7**
See also CA 5-8R; 61-64; CANR 9, 21
Azorin **CLC 11**
See also Martinez Ruiz, Jose
Azuela, Mariano 1873-1952 **TCLC 3; DAM**
MULT; HLC
See also CA 104; 131; HW; MTCW
Baastad, Babbis Friis
See Friis-Baastad, Babbis Ellinor
Bab
See Gilbert, W(illiam) S(chwenck)
Babbis, Eleanor
See Friis-Baastad, Babbis Ellinor
Babel, Isaac
See Babel, Isaak (Emmanuilovich)
Babel, Isaak (Emmanuilovich) 1894-1941(?)
TCLC 2, 13; SSC 16
See also CA 104; 155
Babits, Mihaly 1883-1941 **TCLC 14**
See also CA 114
Babur 1483-1530 **LC 18**

Bacchelli, Riccardo 1891-1985 **CLC 19**
See also CA 29-32R; 117
Bach, Richard (David) 1936- CLC 14; **DAM**
NOV, POP
See also AITN 1; BEST 89:2; CA 9-12R; CANR
18; MTCW; SATA 13
Bachman, Richard
See King, Stephen (Edwin)
Bachmann, Ingeborg 1926-1973 **CLC 69**
See also CA 93-96; 45-48; CANR 69; DLB 85
Bacon, Francis 1561-1626 **LC 18, 32**
See also CDBLB Before 1660; DLB 151
Bacon, Roger 1214(?)-1292 **CMLC 14**
See also DLB 115
Bacovia, George **TCLC 24**
See also Vasiliu, Gheorghe
Badanes, Jerome 1937- **CLC 59**
Bagehot, Walter 1826-1877 **NCLC 10**
See also DLB 55
Bagnold, Enid 1889-1981 CLC 25; **DAM**
DRAM
See also CA 5-8R; 103; CANR 5, 40; DLB 13,
160, 191; MAICYA; SATA 1, 25
Bagritsky, Eduard 1895-1934 **TCLC 60**
Bagrjana, Elisaveta
See Belcheva, Elisaveta
Bagryana, Elisaveta **CLC 10**
See also Belcheva, Elisaveta
See also DLB 147
Bailey, Paul 1937- **CLC 45**
See also CA 21-24R; CANR 16, 62; DLB 14
Baillie, Joanna 1762-1851 **NCLC 71**
See also DLB 93
Bainbridge, Beryl (Margaret) 1933-CLC 4, 5,
8, 10, 14, 18, 22, 62; **DAM NOV**
See also CA 21-24R; CANR 24, 55; DLB 14;
MTCW
Baker, Elliott 1922- **CLC 8**
See also CA 45-48; CANR 2, 63
Baker, Jean H. **TCLC 3, 10**
See also Russell, George William
Baker, Nicholson 1957- CLC 61; **DAM POP**
See also CA 135; CANR 63
Baker, Ray Stannard 1870-1946 **TCLC 47**
See also CA 118
Baker, Russell (Wayne) 1925- **CLC 31**
See also BEST 89:4; CA 57-60; CANR 11, 41,
59; MTCW
Bakhtin, M.
See Bakhtin, Mikhail Mikhailovich
Bakhtin, M. M.
See Bakhtin, Mikhail Mikhailovich
Bakhtin, Mikhail
See Bakhtin, Mikhail Mikhailovich
Bakhtin, Mikhail Mikhailovich 1895-1975
CLC 83
See also CA 128; 113
Bakshi, Ralph 1938(?)- **CLC 26**
See also CA 112; 138
Bakunin, Mikhail (Alexandrovich) 1814-1876
NCLC 25, 58
Baldwin, James (Arthur) 1924-1987CLC 1, 2,
3, 4, 5, 8, 13, 15, 17, 42, 50, 67, 90; **BLC 1;**
DA; DAB; DAC; DAM MST, MULT, NOV,
POP; DC 1; SSC 10; WLC
See also AAYA 4; BW 1; CA 1-4R; 124; CABS
1; CANR 3, 24; CDALB 1941-1968; DLB
2, 7, 33; DLBY 87; MTCW; SATA 9; SATA-
Obit 54
Ballard, J(ames) G(raham) 1930-CLC 3, 6, 14,
36; **DAM NOV, POP; SSC 1**
See also AAYA 3; CA 5-8R; CANR 15, 39, 65;
DLB 14; MTCW; SATA 93

Balmont, Konstantin (Dmitriyevich) 1867-1943
TCLC 11
See also CA 109; 155
Balzac, Honore de 1799-1850NCLC 5, 35, 53;
DA; DAB; DAC; DAM MST, NOV; SSC
5; WLC
See also DLB 119
Bambara, Toni Cade 1939-1995 CLC 19, 88;
BLC 1; DA; DAC; DAM MST, MULT;
WLCS
See also AAYA 5; BW 2; CA 29-32R; 150;
CANR 24, 49; DLB 38; MTCW
Bamdad, A.
See Shamlu, Ahmad
Banat, D. R.
See Bradbury, Ray (Douglas)
Bancroft, Laura
See Baum, L(yman) Frank
Banim, John 1798-1842 **NCLC 13**
See also DLB 116, 158, 159
Banim, Michael 1796-1874 **NCLC 13**
See also DLB 158, 159
Banjo, The
See Paterson, A(ndrew) B(arton)
Banks, Iain
See Banks, Iain M(enzies)
Banks, Iain M(enzies) 1954- **CLC 34**
See also CA 123; 128; CANR 61; DLB 194;
INT 128
Banks, Lynne Reid **CLC 23**
See also Reid Banks, Lynne
See also AAYA 6
Banks, Russell 1940- **CLC 37, 72**
See also CA 65-68; CAAS 15; CANR 19, 52;
DLB 130
Banville, John 1945- **CLC 46**
See also CA 117; 128; DLB 14; INT 128
Banville, Theodore (Faullain) de 1832-1891
NCLC 9
Baraka, Amiri 1934-CLC 1, 2, 3, 5, 10, 14, 33;
BLC 1; DA; DAC; DAM MST, MULT,
POET, POP; DC 6; PC 4; WLCS
See also Jones, LeRoi
See also BW 2; CA 21-24R; CABS 3; CANR
27, 38, 61; CDALB 1941-1968; DLB 5, 7,
16, 38; DLBD 8; MTCW
Barbauld, Anna Laetitia 1743-1825NCLC 50
See also DLB 107, 109, 142, 158
Barbellion, W. N. P. **TCLC 24**
See also Cummings, Bruce F(rederick)
Barbera, Jack (Vincent) 1945- **CLC 44**
See also CA 110; CANR 45
Barbey d'Aurevilly, Jules Amedee 1808-1889
NCLC 1; SSC 17
See also DLB 119
Barbusse, Henri 1873-1935 **TCLC 5**
See also CA 105; 154; DLB 65
Barclay, Bill
See Moorcock, Michael (John)
Barclay, William Ewert
See Moorcock, Michael (John)
Barea, Arturo 1897-1957 **TCLC 14**
See also CA 111
Barfoot, Joan 1946- **CLC 18**
See also CA 105
Baring, Maurice 1874-1945 **TCLC 8**
See also CA 105; DLB 34
Barker, Clive 1952- CLC 52; **DAM POP**
See also AAYA 10; BEST 90:3; CA 121; 129;
INT 129; MTCW
Barker, George Granville 1913-1991 CLC 8,
48; **DAM POET**
See also CA 9-12R; 135; CANR 7, 38; DLB

20; MTCW

Barker, Harley Granville
See Granville-Barker, Harley
See also DLB 10

Barker, Howard 1946- **CLC 37**
See also CA 102; DLB 13

Barker, Pat(ricia) 1943- **CLC 32, 94**
See also CA 117; 122; CANR 50; INT 122

Barlow, Joel 1754-1812 **NCLC 23**
See also DLB 37

Barnard, Mary (Ethel) 1909- **CLC 48**
See also CA 21-22; CAP 2

Barnes, Djuna 1892-1982 CLC 3, 4, 8, 11, 29;
SSC 3
See also CA 9-12R; 107; CANR 16, 55; DLB
4, 9, 45; MTCW

Barnes, Julian (Patrick) 1946- CLC 42; DAB
See also CA 102; CANR 19, 54; DLB 194;
DLBY 93

Barnes, Peter 1931- **CLC 5, 56**
See also CA 65-68; CAAS 12; CANR 33, 34,
64; DLB 13; MTCW

Baroja (y Nessi), Pio 1872-1956TCLC 8; HLC
See also CA 104

Baron, David
See Pinter, Harold

Baron Corvo
See Rolfe, Frederick (William Serafino Austin
Lewis Mary)

Barondess, Sue K(aufman) 1926-1977 CLC 8
See also Kaufman, Sue
See also CA 1-4R; 69-72; CANR 1

Baron de Teive
See Pessoa, Fernando (Antonio Nogueira)

Barres, (Auguste-) Maurice 1862-1923 TCLC
47
See also CA 164; DLB 123

Barreto, Afonso Henrique de Lima
See Lima Barreto, Afonso Henrique de

Barrett, (Roger) Syd 1946- **CLC 35**

Barrett, William (Christopher) 1913-1992
CLC 27
See also CA 13-16R; 139; CANR 11, 67; INT
CANR-11

Barrie, J(ames) M(atthew) 1860-1937 TCLC
2; DAB; DAM DRAM
See also CA 104; 136; CDBLB 1890-1914;
CLR 16; DLB 10, 141, 156; MAICYA;
YABC 1

Barrington, Michael
See Moorcock, Michael (John)

Barrol, Grady
See Bograd, Larry

Barry, Mike
See Malzberg, Barry N(athaniel)

Barry, Philip 1896-1949 **TCLC 11**
See also CA 109; DLB 7

Bart, Andre Schwarz
See Schwarz-Bart, Andre

Barth, John (Simmons) 1930-CLC 1, 2, 3, 5, 7,
9, 10, 14, 27, 51, 89; DAM NOV; SSC 10
See also AITN 1, 2; CA 1-4R; CABS 1; CANR
5, 23, 49, 64; DLB 2; MTCW

Barthelme, Donald 1931-1989CLC 1, 2, 3, 5, 6,
8, 13, 23, 46, 59; DAM NOV; SSC 2
See also CA 21-24R; 129; CANR 20, 58; DLB
2; DLBY 80, 89; MTCW; SATA 7; SATA-
Obit 62

Barthelme, Frederick 1943- **CLC 36**
See also CA 114; 122; DLBY 85; INT 122

Barthes, Roland (Gerard) 1915-1980 CLC 24,
83
See also CA 130; 97-100; CANR 66; MTCW

Barzun, Jacques (Martin) 1907- **CLC 51**
See also CA 61-64; CANR 22

Bashevis, Isaac
See Singer, Isaac Bashevis

Bashkirtseff, Marie 1859-1884 **NCLC 27**

Basho
See Matsuo Basho

Bass, Kingsley B., Jr.
See Bullins, Ed

Bass, Rick 1958- **CLC 79**
See also CA 126; CANR 53

Bassani, Giorgio 1916- **CLC 9**
See also CA 65-68; CANR 33; DLB 128, 177;
MTCW

Bastos, Augusto (Antonio) Roa
See Roa Bastos, Augusto (Antonio)

Bataille, Georges 1897-1962 **CLC 29**
See also CA 101; 89-92

Bates, H(erbert) E(rnest) 1905-1974 CLC 46;
DAB; DAM POP; SSC 10
See also CA 93-96; 45-48; CANR 34; DLB 162,
191; MTCW

Bauchart
See Camus, Albert

Baudelaire, Charles 1821-1867 NCLC 6, 29,
55; DA; DAB; DAC; DAM MST, POET;
PC 1; SSC 18; WLC

Baudrillard, Jean 1929- **CLC 60**

Baum, L(yman) Frank 1856-1919 **TCLC 7**
See also CA 108; 133; CLR 15; DLB 22; JRDA;
MAICYA; MTCW; SATA 18

Baum, Louis F.
See Baum, L(yman) Frank

Baumbach, Jonathan 1933- **CLC 6, 23**
See also CA 13-16R; CAAS 5; CANR 12, 66;
DLBY 80; INT CANR-12; MTCW

Bausch, Richard (Carl) 1945- **CLC 51**
See also CA 101; CAAS 14; CANR 43, 61; DLB
130

Baxter, Charles (Morley) 1947- CLC 45, 78;
DAM POP
See also CA 57-60; CANR 40, 64; DLB 130

Baxter, George Owen
See Faust, Frederick (Schiller)

Baxter, James K(eir) 1926-1972 **CLC 14**
See also CA 77-80

Baxter, John
See Hunt, E(verette) Howard, (Jr.)

Bayer, Sylvia
See Glassco, John

Baynton, Barbara 1857-1929 **TCLC 57**

Beagle, Peter S(oyer) 1939- **CLC 7, 104**
See also CA 9-12R; CANR 4, 51; DLBY 80;
INT CANR-4; SATA 60

Bean, Normal
See Burroughs, Edgar Rice

Beard, Charles A(ustin) 1874-1948 TCLC 15
See also CA 115; DLB 17; SATA 18

Beardsley, Aubrey 1872-1898 **NCLC 6**

Beattie, Ann 1947-CLC 8, 13, 18, 40, 63; DAM
NOV, POP; SSC 11
See also BEST 90:2; CA 81-84; CANR 53;
DLBY 82; MTCW

Beattie, James 1735-1803 **NCLC 25**
See also DLB 109

Beauchamp, Kathleen Mansfield 1888-1923
See Mansfield, Katherine
See also CA 104; 134; DA; DAC; DAM MST

Beaumarchais, Pierre-Augustin Caron de 1732-
1799 **DC 4**
See also DAM DRAM

Beaumont, Francis 1584(?)-1616 LC 33; DC 6
See also CDBLB Before 1660; DLB 58, 121

**Beauvoir, Simone (Lucie Ernestine Marie
Bertrand) de** 1908-1986CLC 1, 2, 4, 8, 14,
31, 44, 50, 71; DA; DAB; DAC; DAM MST,
NOV; WLC
See also CA 9-12R; 118; CANR 28, 61; DLB
72; DLBY 86; MTCW

Becker, Carl (Lotus) 1873-1945 **TCLC 63**
See also CA 157; DLB 17

Becker, Jurek 1937-1997 **CLC 7, 19**
See also CA 85-88; 157; CANR 60; DLB 75

Becker, Walter 1950- **CLC 26**

Beckett, Samuel (Barclay) 1906-1989 CLC 1,
2, 3, 4, 6, 9, 10, 11, 14, 18, 29, 57, 59, 83;
DA; DAB; DAC; DAM DRAM, MST,
NOV; SSC 16; WLC
See also CA 5-8R; 130; CANR 33, 61; CDBLB
1945-1960; DLB 13, 15; DLBY 90; MTCW

Beckford, William 1760-1844 **NCLC 16**
See also DLB 39

Beckman, Gunnel 1910- **CLC 26**
See also CA 33-36R; CANR 15; CLR 25;
MAICYA; SAAS 9; SATA 6

Becque, Henri 1837-1899 **NCLC 3**
See also DLB 192

Beddoes, Thomas Lovell 1803-1849 NCLC 3
See also DLB 96

Bede c. 673-735 **CMLC 20**
See also DLB 146

Bedford, Donald F.
See Fearing, Kenneth (Flexner)

Beecher, Catharine Esther 1800-1878 NCLC
30
See also DLB 1

Beecher, John 1904-1980 **CLC 6**
See also AITN 1; CA 5-8R; 105; CANR 8

Beer, Johann 1655-1700 **LC 5**
See also DLB 168

Beer, Patricia 1924- **CLC 58**
See also CA 61-64; CANR 13, 46; DLB 40

Beerbohm, Max
See Beerbohm, (Henry) Max(imilian)

Beerbohm, (Henry) Max(imilian) 1872-1956
TCLC 1, 24
See also CA 104; 154; DLB 34, 100

Beer-Hofmann, Richard 1866-1945 TCLC 60
See also CA 160; DLB 81

Begiebing, Robert J(ohn) 1946- **CLC 70**
See also CA 122; CANR 40

Behan, Brendan 1923-1964 CLC 1, 8, 11, 15,
79; DAM DRAM
See also CA 73-76; CANR 33; CDBLB 1945-
1960; DLB 13; MTCW

Behn, Aphra 1640(?)-1689LC 1, 30; DA; DAB;
DAC; DAM DRAM, MST, NOV, POET;
DC 4; PC 13; WLC
See also DLB 39, 80, 131

Behrman, S(amuel) N(athaniel) 1893-1973
CLC 40
See also CA 13-16; 45-48; CAP 1; DLB 7, 44

Belasco, David 1853-1931 **TCLC 3**
See also CA 104; DLB 7

Belcheva, Elisaveta 1893- **CLC 10**
See also Bagryana, Elisaveta

Beldone, Phil "Cheech"
See Ellison, Harlan (Jay)

Beleno
See Azuela, Mariano

Belinski, Vissarion Grigoryevich 1811-1848
NCLC 5
See also DLB 198

Belitt, Ben 1911- **CLC 22**
See also CA 13-16R; CAAS 4; CANR 7; DLB
5

Bethlen, T. D.
  See Silverberg, Robert
Beti, Mongo   CLC 27; BLC 1; DAM MULT
  See also Biyidi, Alexandre
Betjeman, John 1906-1984 CLC 2, 6, 10, 34,
    43; DAB; DAM MST, POET
  See also CA 9-12R; 112; CANR 33, 56; CDBLB
    1945-1960; DLB 20; DLBY 84; MTCW
Bettelheim, Bruno 1903-1990   CLC 79
  See also CA 81-84; 131; CANR 23, 61; MTCW
Betti, Ugo 1892-1953   TCLC 5
  See also CA 104; 155
Betts, Doris (Waugh) 1932-   CLC 3, 6, 28
  See also CA 13-16R; CANR 9, 66; DLBY 82;
    INT CANR-9
Bevan, Alistair
  See Roberts, Keith (John Kingston)
Bey, Pilaff
  See Douglas, (George) Norman
Bialik, Chaim Nachman 1873-1934 TCLC 25
Bickerstaff, Isaac
  See Swift, Jonathan
Bidart, Frank 1939-   CLC 33
  See also CA 140
Bienek, Horst 1930-   CLC 7, 11
  See also CA 73-76; DLB 75
Bierce, Ambrose (Gwinett) 1842-1914(?)
    TCLC 1, 7, 44; DA; DAC; DAM MST; SSC
    9; WLC
  See also CA 104; 139; CDALB 1865-1917;
    DLB 11, 12, 23, 71, 74, 186
Biggers, Earl Derr 1884-1933   TCLC 65
  See also CA 108; 153
Billings, Josh
  See Shaw, Henry Wheeler
Billington, (Lady) Rachel (Mary) 1942- CLC
    43
  See also AITN 2; CA 33-36R; CANR 44
Binyon, T(imothy) J(ohn) 1936-   CLC 34
  See also CA 111; CANR 28
Bioy Casares, Adolfo 1914-1984 CLC 4, 8, 13,
    88; DAM MULT; HLC; SSC 17
  See also CA 29-32R; CANR 19, 43, 66; DLB
    113; HW; MTCW
Bird, Cordwainer
  See Ellison, Harlan (Jay)
Bird, Robert Montgomery 1806-1854 NCLC 1
Birney, (Alfred) Earle 1904-1995 CLC 1, 4, 6,
    11; DAC; DAM MST, POET
  See also CA 1-4R; CANR 5, 20; DLB 88;
    MTCW
Bishop, Elizabeth 1911-1979 CLC 1, 4, 9, 13,
    15, 32; DA; DAC; DAM MST, POET; PC
    3
  See also CA 5-8R; 89-92; CABS 2; CANR 26,
    61; CDALB 1968-1988; DLB 5, 169;
    MTCW; SATA-Obit 24
Bishop, John 1935-   CLC 10
  See also CA 105
Bissett, Bill 1939-   CLC 18; PC 14
  See also CA 69-72; CAAS 19; CANR 15; DLB
    53; MTCW
Bitov, Andrei (Georgievich) 1937-   CLC 57
  See also CA 142
Biyidi, Alexandre 1932-
  See Beti, Mongo
  See also BW 1; CA 114; 124; MTCW
Bjarme, Brynjolf
  See Ibsen, Henrik (Johan)
Bjoernson, Bjoernstjerne (Martinius) 1832-
    1910   TCLC 7, 37
  See also CA 104
Black, Robert

See Holdstock, Robert P.
Blackburn, Paul 1926-1971   CLC 9, 43
  See also CA 81-84; 33-36R; CANR 34; DLB
    16; DLBY 81
Black Elk 1863-1950 TCLC 33; DAM MULT
  See also CA 144; NNAL
Black Hobart
  See Sanders, (James) Ed(ward)
Blacklin, Malcolm
  See Chambers, Aidan
Blackmore, R(ichard) D(oddridge) 1825-1900
    TCLC 27
  See also CA 120; DLB 18
Blackmur, R(ichard) P(almer) 1904-1965
    CLC 2, 24
  See also CA 11-12; 25-28R; CAP 1; DLB 63
Black Tarantula
  See Acker, Kathy
Blackwood, Algernon (Henry) 1869-1951
    TCLC 5
  See also CA 105; 150; DLB 153, 156, 178
Blackwood, Caroline 1931-1996 CLC 6, 9, 100
  See also CA 85-88; 151; CANR 32, 61, 65; DLB
    14; MTCW
Blade, Alexander
  See Hamilton, Edmond; Silverberg, Robert
Blaga, Lucian 1895-1961   CLC 75
  See also CA 157
Blair, Eric (Arthur) 1903-1950
  See Orwell, George
  See also CA 104; 132; DA; DAB; DAC; DAM
    MST, NOV; MTCW; SATA 29
Blais, Marie-Claire 1939- CLC 2, 4, 6, 13, 22;
    DAC; DAM MST
  See also CA 21-24R; CAAS 4; CANR 38; DLB
    53; MTCW
Blaise, Clark 1940-   CLC 29
  See also AITN 2; CA 53-56; CAAS 3; CANR
    5, 66; DLB 53
Blake, Fairley
  See De Voto, Bernard (Augustine)
Blake, Nicholas
  See Day Lewis, C(ecil)
  See also DLB 77
Blake, William 1757-1827 NCLC 13, 37, 57;
    DA; DAB; DAC; DAM MST, POET; PC
    12; WLC
  See also CDBLB 1789-1832; CLR 52; DLB 93,
    163; MAICYA; SATA 30
Blasco Ibanez, Vicente 1867-1928   TCLC 12;
    DAM NOV
  See also CA 110; 131; HW; MTCW
Blatty, William Peter 1928- CLC 2; DAM POP
  See also CA 5-8R; CANR 9
Bleeck, Oliver
  See Thomas, Ross (Elmore)
Blessing, Lee 1949-   CLC 54
Blish, James (Benjamin) 1921-1975 CLC 14
  See also CA 1-4R; 57-60; CANR 3; DLB 8;
    MTCW; SATA 66
Bliss, Reginald
  See Wells, H(erbert) G(eorge)
Blixen, Karen (Christentze Dinesen) 1885-1962
  See Dinesen, Isak
  See also CA 25-28; CANR 22, 50; CAP 2;
    MTCW; SATA 44
Bloch, Robert (Albert) 1917-1994   CLC 33
  See also CA 5-8R; 146; CAAS 20; CANR 5;
    DLB 44; INT CANR-5; SATA 12; SATA-Obit
    82
Blok, Alexander (Alexandrovich) 1880-1921
    TCLC 5; PC 21
  See also CA 104

Blom, Jan
  See Breytenbach, Breyten
Bloom, Harold 1930-   CLC 24, 103
  See also CA 13-16R; CANR 39; DLB 67
Bloomfield, Aurelius
  See Bourne, Randolph S(illiman)
Blount, Roy (Alton), Jr. 1941-   CLC 38
  See also CA 53-56; CANR 10, 28, 61; INT
    CANR-28; MTCW
Bloy, Leon 1846-1917   TCLC 22
  See also CA 121; DLB 123
Blume, Judy (Sussman) 1938-   CLC 12, 30;
    DAM NOV, POP
  See also AAYA 3; CA 29-32R; CANR 13, 37,
    66; CLR 2, 15; DLB 52; JRDA; MAICYA;
    MTCW; SATA 2, 31, 79
Blunden, Edmund (Charles) 1896-1974 CLC
    2, 56
  See also CA 17-18; 45-48; CANR 54; CAP 2;
    DLB 20, 100, 155; MTCW
Bly, Robert (Elwood) 1926- CLC 1, 2, 5, 10, 15,
    38; DAM POET
  See also CA 5-8R; CANR 41; DLB 5; MTCW
Boas, Franz 1858-1942   TCLC 56
  See also CA 115
Bobette
  See Simenon, Georges (Jacques Christian)
Boccaccio, Giovanni 1313-1375   CMLC 13;
    SSC 10
Bochco, Steven 1943-   CLC 35
  See also AAYA 11; CA 124; 138
Bodel, Jean 1167(?)-1210   CMLC 28
Bodenheim, Maxwell 1892-1954   TCLC 44
  See also CA 110; DLB 9, 45
Bodker, Cecil 1927-   CLC 21
  See also CA 73-76; CANR 13, 44; CLR 23;
    MAICYA; SATA 14
Boell, Heinrich (Theodor) 1917-1985 CLC 2,
    3, 6, 9, 11, 15, 27, 32, 72; DA; DAB; DAC;
    DAM MST, NOV; SSC 23; WLC
  See also CA 21-24R; 116; CANR 24; DLB 69;
    DLBY 85; MTCW
Boerne, Alfred
  See Doeblin, Alfred
Boethius 480(?)-524(?)   CMLC 15
  See also DLB 115
Bogan, Louise 1897-1970 CLC 4, 39, 46, 93;
    DAM POET; PC 12
  See also CA 73-76; 25-28R; CANR 33; DLB
    45, 169; MTCW
Bogarde, Dirk   CLC 19
  See also Van Den Bogarde, Derek Jules Gaspard
    Ulric Niven
  See also DLB 14
Bogosian, Eric 1953-   CLC 45
  See also CA 138
Bograd, Larry 1953-   CLC 35
  See also CA 93-96; CANR 57; SAAS 21; SATA
    33, 89
Boiardo, Matteo Maria 1441-1494   LC 6
Boileau-Despreaux, Nicolas 1636-1711 LC 3
Bojer, Johan 1872-1959   TCLC 64
Boland, Eavan (Aisling) 1944- CLC 40, 67,
    113; DAM POET
  See also CA 143; CANR 61; DLB 40
Boll, Heinrich
  See Boell, Heinrich (Theodor)
Bolt, Lee
  See Faust, Frederick (Schiller)
Bolt, Robert (Oxton) 1924-1995 CLC 14; DAM
    DRAM
  See also CA 17-20R; 147; CANR 35, 67; DLB
    13; MTCW

MTCW

Callimachus c. 305B.C.-c. 240B.C. **CMLC 18**
See also DLB 176

Calvin, John 1509-1564 **LC 37**

Calvino, Italo 1923-1985 **CLC 5, 8, 11, 22, 33, 39, 73; DAM NOV; SSC 3**
See also CA 85-88; 116; CANR 23, 61; DLB 196; MTCW

Cameron, Carey 1952- **CLC 59**
See also CA 135

Cameron, Peter 1959- **CLC 44**
See also CA 125; CANR 50

Campana, Dino 1885-1932 **TCLC 20**
See also CA 117; DLB 114

Campanella, Tommaso 1568-1639 **LC 32**

Campbell, John W(ood, Jr.) 1910-1971 **CLC 32**
See also CA 21-22; 29-32R; CANR 34; CAP 2; DLB 8; MTCW

Campbell, Joseph 1904-1987 **CLC 69**
See also AAYA 3; BEST 89:2; CA 1-4R; 124; CANR 3, 28, 61; MTCW

Campbell, Maria 1940- **CLC 85; DAC**
See also CA 102; CANR 54; NNAL

Campbell, (John) Ramsey 1946-**CLC 42; SSC 19**
See also CA 57-60; CANR 7; INT CANR-7

Campbell, (Ignatius) Roy (Dunnachie) 1901-1957 **TCLC 5**
See also CA 104; 155; DLB 20

Campbell, Thomas 1777-1844 **NCLC 19**
See also DLB 93; 144

Campbell, Wilfred **TCLC 9**
See also Campbell, William

Campbell, William 1858(?)-1918
See Campbell, Wilfred
See also CA 106; DLB 92

Campion, Jane **CLC 95**
See also CA 138

Campos, Alvaro de
See Pessoa, Fernando (Antonio Nogueira)

Camus, Albert 1913-1960**CLC 1, 2, 4, 9, 11, 14, 32, 63, 69; DA; DAB; DAC; DAM DRAM, MST, NOV; DC 2; SSC 9; WLC**
See also CA 89-92; DLB 72; MTCW

Canby, Vincent 1924- **CLC 13**
See also CA 81-84

Cancale
See Desnos, Robert

Canetti, Elias 1905-1994**CLC 3, 14, 25, 75, 86**
See also CA 21-24R; 146; CANR 23, 61; DLB 85, 124; MTCW

Canin, Ethan 1960- **CLC 55**
See also CA 131; 135

Cannon, Curt
See Hunter, Evan

Cao, Lan 1961- **CLC 109**
See also CA 165

Cape, Judith
See Page, P(atricia) K(athleen)

Capek, Karel 1890-1938 **TCLC 6, 37; DA; DAB; DAC; DAM DRAM, MST, NOV; DC 1; WLC**
See also CA 104; 140

Capote, Truman 1924-1984**CLC 1, 3, 8, 13, 19, 34, 38, 58; DA; DAB; DAC; DAM MST, NOV, POP; SSC 2; WLC**
See also CA 5-8R; CANR 18, 62; CDALB 1941-1968; DLB 2, 185; DLBY 80, 84; MTCW; SATA 91

Capra, Frank 1897-1991 **CLC 16**
See also CA 61-64; 135

Caputo, Philip 1941- **CLC 32**

See also CA 73-76; CANR 40

Caragiale, Ion Luca 1852-1912 **TCLC 76**
See also CA 157

Card, Orson Scott 1951-**CLC 44, 47, 50; DAM POP**
See also AAYA 11; CA 102; CANR 27, 47; INT CANR-27; MTCW; SATA 83

Cardenal, Ernesto 1925- **CLC 31; DAM MULT, POET; HLC; PC 22**
See also CA 49-52; CANR 2, 32, 66; HW; MTCW

Cardozo, Benjamin N(athan) 1870-1938 **TCLC 65**
See also CA 117; 164

Carducci, Giosue (Alessandro Giuseppe) 1835-1907 **TCLC 32**
See also CA 163

Carew, Thomas 1595(?)-1640 **LC 13**
See also DLB 126

Carey, Ernestine Gilbreth 1908- **CLC 17**
See also CA 5-8R; SATA 2

Carey, Peter 1943- **CLC 40, 55, 96**
See also CA 123; 127; CANR 53; INT 127; MTCW; SATA 94

Carleton, William 1794-1869 **NCLC 3**
See also DLB 159

Carlisle, Henry (Coffin) 1926- **CLC 33**
See also CA 13-16R; CANR 15

Carlsen, Chris
See Holdstock, Robert P.

Carlson, Ron(ald F.) 1947- **CLC 54**
See also CA 105; CANR 27

Carlyle, Thomas 1795-1881 **NCLC 70; DA; DAB; DAC; DAM MST**
See also CDBLB 1789-1832; DLB 55; 144

Carman, (William) Bliss 1861-1929 **TCLC 7; DAC**
See also CA 104; 152; DLB 92

Carnegie, Dale 1888-1955 **TCLC 53**

Carossa, Hans 1878-1956 **TCLC 48**
See also DLB 66

Carpenter, Don(ald Richard) 1931-1995 **CLC 41**
See also CA 45-48; 149; CANR 1

Carpentier (y Valmont), Alejo 1904-1980**CLC 8, 11, 38, 110; DAM MULT; HLC**
See also CA 65-68; 97-100; CANR 11; DLB 113; HW

Carr, Caleb 1955(?)- **CLC 86**
See also CA 147

Carr, Emily 1871-1945 **TCLC 32**
See also CA 159; DLB 68

Carr, John Dickson 1906-1977 **CLC 3**
See also Fairbairn, Roger
See also CA 49-52; 69-72; CANR 3, 33, 60; MTCW

Carr, Philippa
See Hibbert, Eleanor Alice Burford

Carr, Virginia Spencer 1929- **CLC 34**
See also CA 61-64; DLB 111

Carrere, Emmanuel 1957- **CLC 89**

Carrier, Roch 1937- **CLC 13, 78; DAC; DAM MST**
See also CA 130; CANR 61; DLB 53

Carroll, James P. 1943(?)- **CLC 38**
See also CA 81-84

Carroll, Jim 1951- **CLC 35**
See also AAYA 17; CA 45-48; CANR 42

Carroll, Lewis **NCLC 2, 53; PC 18; WLC**
See also Dodgson, Charles Lutwidge
See also CDBLB 1832-1890; CLR 2, 18; DLB 18, 163, 178; JRDA

Carroll, Paul Vincent 1900-1968 **CLC 10**

See also CA 9-12R; 25-28R; DLB 10

Carruth, Hayden 1921- **CLC 4, 7, 10, 18, 84; PC 10**
See also CA 9-12R; CANR 4, 38, 59; DLB 5, 165; INT CANR-4; MTCW; SATA 47

Carson, Rachel Louise 1907-1964 **CLC 71; DAM POP**
See also CA 77-80; CANR 35; MTCW; SATA 23

Carter, Angela (Olive) 1940-1992 **CLC 5, 41, 76; SSC 13**
See also CA 53-56; 136; CANR 12, 36, 61; DLB 14; MTCW; SATA 66; SATA-Obit 70

Carter, Nick
See Smith, Martin Cruz

Carver, Raymond 1938-1988 **CLC 22, 36, 53, 55; DAM NOV; SSC 8**
See also CA 33-36R; 126; CANR 17, 34, 61; DLB 130; DLBY 84, 88; MTCW

Cary, Elizabeth, Lady Falkland 1585-1639 **LC 30**

Cary, (Arthur) Joyce (Lunel) 1888-1957 **TCLC 1, 29**
See also CA 104; 164; CDBLB 1914-1945; DLB 15, 100

Casanova de Seingalt, Giovanni Jacopo 1725-1798 **LC 13**

Casares, Adolfo Bioy
See Bioy Casares, Adolfo

Casely-Hayford, J(oseph) E(phraim) 1866-1930 **TCLC 24; BLC 1; DAM MULT**
See also BW 2; CA 123; 152

Casey, John (Dudley) 1939- **CLC 59**
See also BEST 90:2; CA 69-72; CANR 23

Casey, Michael 1947- **CLC 2**
See also CA 65-68; DLB 5

Casey, Patrick
See Thurman, Wallace (Henry)

Casey, Warren (Peter) 1935-1988 **CLC 12**
See also CA 101; 127; INT 101

Casona, Alejandro **CLC 49**
See also Alvarez, Alejandro Rodriguez

Cassavetes, John 1929-1989 **CLC 20**
See also CA 85-88; 127

Cassian, Nina 1924- **PC 17**

Cassill, R(onald) V(erlin) 1919- **CLC 4, 23**
See also CA 9-12R; CAAS 1; CANR 7, 45; DLB 6

Cassirer, Ernst 1874-1945 **TCLC 61**
See also CA 157

Cassity, (Allen) Turner 1929- **CLC 6, 42**
See also CA 17-20R; CAAS 8; CANR 11; DLB 105

Castaneda, Carlos 1931(?)- **CLC 12**
See also CA 25-28R; CANR 32, 66; HW; MTCW

Castedo, Elena 1937- **CLC 65**
See also CA 132

Castedo-Ellerman, Elena
See Castedo, Elena

Castellanos, Rosario 1925-1974**CLC 66; DAM MULT; HLC**
See also CA 131; 53-56; CANR 58; DLB 113; HW

Castelvetro, Lodovico 1505-1571 **LC 12**

Castiglione, Baldassare 1478-1529 **LC 12**

Castle, Robert
See Hamilton, Edmond

Castro, Guillen de 1569-1631 **LC 19**

Castro, Rosalia de 1837-1885 **NCLC 3; DAM MULT**

Cather, Willa
See Cather, Willa Sibert

Cather, Willa Sibert 1873-1947 **TCLC 1, 11, 31; DA; DAB; DAC; DAM MST, NOV; SSC 2; WLC**
See also AAYA 24; CA 104; 128; CDALB 1865-1917; DLB 9, 54, 78; DLBD 1; MTCW; SATA 30

Catherine, Saint 1347-1380 **CMLC 27**

Cato, Marcus Porcius 234B.C.-149B.C. **CMLC 21**

Catton, (Charles) Bruce 1899-1978 **CLC 35**
See also AITN 1; CA 5-8R; 81-84; CANR 7; DLB 17; SATA 2; SATA-Obit 24

Catullus c. 84B.C.-c. 54B.C. **CMLC 18**

Cauldwell, Frank
See King, Francis (Henry)

Caunitz, William J. 1933-1996 **CLC 34**
See also BEST 89:3; CA 125; 130; 152; INT 130

Causley, Charles (Stanley) 1917- **CLC 7**
See also CA 9-12R; CANR 5, 35; CLR 30; DLB 27; MTCW; SATA 3, 66

Caute, (John) David 1936- **CLC 29; DAM NOV**
See also CA 1-4R; CAAS 4; CANR 1, 33, 64; DLB 14

Cavafy, C(onstantine) P(eter) 1863-1933 **TCLC 2, 7; DAM POET**
See also Kavafis, Konstantinos Petrou
See also CA 148

Cavallo, Evelyn
See Spark, Muriel (Sarah)

Cavanna, Betty **CLC 12**
See also Harrison, Elizabeth Cavanna
See also JRDA; MAICYA; SAAS 4; SATA 1, 30

Cavendish, Margaret Lucas 1623-1673 **LC 30**
See also DLB 131

Caxton, William 1421(?)-1491(?) **LC 17**
See also DLB 170

Cayer, D. M.
See Duffy, Maureen

Cayrol, Jean 1911- **CLC 11**
See also CA 89-92; DLB 83

Cela, Camilo Jose 1916- **CLC 4, 13, 59; DAM MULT; HLC**
See also BEST 90:2; CA 21-24R; CAAS 10; CANR 21, 32; DLBY 89; HW; MTCW

Celan, Paul **CLC 10, 19, 53, 82; PC 10**
See also Antschel, Paul
See also DLB 69

Celine, Louis-Ferdinand **CLC 1, 3, 4, 7, 9, 15, 47**
See also Destouches, Louis-Ferdinand
See also DLB 72

Cellini, Benvenuto 1500-1571 **LC 7**

Cendrars, Blaise 1887-1961 **CLC 18, 106**
See also Sauser-Hall, Frederic

Cernuda (y Bidon), Luis 1902-1963 **CLC 54; DAM POET**
See also CA 131; 89-92; DLB 134; HW

Cervantes (Saavedra), Miguel de 1547-1616 **LC 6, 23; DA; DAB; DAC; DAM MST, NOV; SSC 12; WLC**

Cesaire, Aime (Fernand) 1913- **CLC 19, 32, 112; BLC 1; DAM MULT, POET**
See also BW 2; CA 65-68; CANR 24, 43; MTCW

Chabon, Michael 1963- **CLC 55**
See also CA 139; CANR 57

Chabrol, Claude 1930- **CLC 16**
See also CA 110

Challans, Mary 1905-1983
See Renault, Mary

See also CA 81-84; 111; SATA 23; SATA-Obit 36

Challis, George
See Faust, Frederick (Schiller)

Chambers, Aidan 1934- **CLC 35**
See also CA 25-28R; CANR 12, 31, 58; JRDA; MAICYA; SAAS 12; SATA 1, 69

Chambers, James 1948-
See Cliff, Jimmy
See also CA 124

Chambers, Jessie
See Lawrence, D(avid) H(erbert Richards)

Chambers, Robert W(illiam) 1865-1933 **TCLC 41**
See also CA 165

Chandler, Raymond (Thornton) 1888-1959 **TCLC 1, 7; SSC 23**
See also AAYA 25; CA 104; 129; CANR 60; CDALB 1929-1941; DLBD 6; MTCW

Chang, Eileen 1920-1995 **SSC 28**
See also CA 166

Chang, Jung 1952- **CLC 71**
See also CA 142

Chang Ai-Ling
See Chang, Eileen

Channing, William Ellery 1780-1842 **NCLC 17**
See also DLB 1, 59

Chaplin, Charles Spencer 1889-1977 **CLC 16**
See also Chaplin, Charlie
See also CA 81-84; 73-76

Chaplin, Charlie
See Chaplin, Charles Spencer
See also DLB 44

Chapman, George 1559(?)-1634 **LC 22; DAM DRAM**
See also DLB 62, 121

Chapman, Graham 1941-1989 **CLC 21**
See also Monty Python
See also CA 116; 129; CANR 35

Chapman, John Jay 1862-1933 **TCLC 7**
See also CA 104

Chapman, Lee
See Bradley, Marion Zimmer

Chapman, Walker
See Silverberg, Robert

Chappell, Fred (Davis) 1936- **CLC 40, 78**
See also CA 5-8R; CAAS 4; CANR 8, 33, 67; DLB 6, 105

Char, Rene(-Emile) 1907-1988 **CLC 9, 11, 14, 55; DAM POET**
See also CA 13-16R; 124; CANR 32; MTCW

Charby, Jay
See Ellison, Harlan (Jay)

Chardin, Pierre Teilhard de
See Teilhard de Chardin, (Marie Joseph) Pierre

Charles I 1600-1649 **LC 13**

Charriere, Isabelle de 1740-1805 **NCLC 66**

Charyn, Jerome 1937- **CLC 5, 8, 18**
See also CA 5-8R; CAAS 1; CANR 7, 61; DLBY 83; MTCW

Chase, Mary (Coyle) 1907-1981 **DC 1**
See also CA 77-80; 105; SATA 17; SATA-Obit 29

Chase, Mary Ellen 1887-1973 **CLC 2**
See also CA 13-16; 41-44R; CAP 1; SATA 10

Chase, Nicholas
See Hyde, Anthony

Chateaubriand, Francois Rene de 1768-1848 **NCLC 3**
See also DLB 119

Chatterje, Sarat Chandra 1876-1936(?)
See Chatterji, Saratchandra

See also CA 109

Chatterji, Bankim Chandra 1838-1894 **NCLC 19**

Chatterji, Saratchandra **TCLC 13**
See also Chatterje, Sarat Chandra

Chatterton, Thomas 1752-1770 **LC 3; DAM POET**
See also DLB 109

Chatwin, (Charles) Bruce 1940-1989 **CLC 28, 57, 59; DAM POP**
See also AAYA 4; BEST 90:1; CA 85-88; 127; DLB 194

Chaucer, Daniel
See Ford, Ford Madox

Chaucer, Geoffrey 1340(?)-1400 **LC 17; DA; DAB; DAC; DAM MST, POET; PC 19; WLCS**
See also CDBLB Before 1660; DLB 146

Chaviaras, Strates 1935-
See Haviaras, Stratis
See also CA 105

Chayefsky, Paddy **CLC 23**
See also Chayefsky, Sidney
See also DLB 7, 44; DLBY 81

Chayefsky, Sidney 1923-1981
See Chayefsky, Paddy
See also CA 9-12R; 104; CANR 18; DAM DRAM

Chedid, Andree 1920- **CLC 47**
See also CA 145

Cheever, John 1912-1982 **CLC 3, 7, 8, 11, 15, 25, 64; DA; DAB; DAC; DAM MST, NOV, POP; SSC 1; WLC**
See also CA 5-8R; 106; CABS 1; CANR 5, 27; CDALB 1941-1968; DLB 2, 102; DLBY 80, 82; INT CANR-5; MTCW

Cheever, Susan 1943- **CLC 18, 48**
See also CA 103; CANR 27, 51; DLBY 82; INT CANR-27

Chekhonte, Antosha
See Chekhov, Anton (Pavlovich)

Chekhov, Anton (Pavlovich) 1860-1904 **TCLC 3, 10, 31, 55; DA; DAB; DAC; DAM DRAM, MST; DC 9; SSC 2, 28; WLC**
See also CA 104; 124; SATA 90

Chernyshevsky, Nikolay Gavrilovich 1828-1889 **NCLC 1**

Cherry, Carolyn Janice 1942-
See Cherryh, C. J.
See also CA 65-68; CANR 10

Cherryh, C. J. **CLC 35**
See also Cherry, Carolyn Janice
See also AAYA 24; DLBY 80; SATA 93

Chesnutt, Charles W(addell) 1858-1932 **TCLC 5, 39; BLC 1; DAM MULT; SSC 7**
See also BW 1; CA 106; 125; DLB 12, 50, 78; MTCW

Chester, Alfred 1929(?)-1971 **CLC 49**
See also CA 33-36R; DLB 130

Chesterton, G(ilbert) K(eith) 1874-1936 **TCLC 1, 6, 64; DAM NOV, POET; SSC 1**
See also CA 104; 132; CDBLB 1914-1945; DLB 10, 19, 34, 70, 98, 149, 178; MTCW; SATA 27

Chiang, Pin-chin 1904-1986
See Ding Ling
See also CA 118

Ch'ien Chung-shu 1910- **CLC 22**
See also CA 130; MTCW

Child, L. Maria
See Child, Lydia Maria

Child, Lydia Maria 1802-1880 **NCLC 6**
See also DLB 1, 74; SATA 67

Cohen-Solal, Annie 19(?)-   CLC 50
Colegate, Isabel 1931-   CLC 36
    See also CA 17-20R; CANR 8, 22; DLB 14;
    INT CANR-22; MTCW
Coleman, Emmett
    See Reed, Ishmael
Coleridge, M. E.
    See Coleridge, Mary E(lizabeth)
Coleridge, Mary E(lizabeth) 1861-1907TCLC
    73
    See also CA 116; 166; DLB 19, 98
Coleridge, Samuel Taylor 1772-1834NCLC 9,
    54; DA; DAB; DAC; DAM MST, POET;
    PC 11; WLC
    See also CDBLB 1789-1832; DLB 93, 107
Coleridge, Sara 1802-1852   NCLC 31
    See also DLB 199
Coles, Don 1928-   CLC 46
    See also CA 115; CANR 38
Coles, Robert (Martin) 1929-   CLC 108
    See also CA 45-48; CANR 3, 32, 66; INT
    CANR-32; SATA 23
Colette, (Sidonie-Gabrielle) 1873-1954 TCLC
    1, 5, 16; DAM NOV; SSC 10
    See also CA 104; 131; DLB 65; MTCW
Collett, (Jacobine) Camilla (Wergeland) 1813-
    1895 NCLC 22
Collier, Christopher 1930-   CLC 30
    See also AAYA 13; CA 33-36R; CANR 13, 33;
    JRDA; MAICYA; SATA 16, 70
Collier, James L(incoln) 1928- CLC 30; DAM
    POP
    See also AAYA 13; CA 9-12R; CANR 4, 33,
    60; CLR 3; JRDA; MAICYA; SAAS 21;
    SATA 8, 70
Collier, Jeremy 1650-1726   LC 6
Collier, John 1901-1980   SSC 19
    See also CA 65-68; 97-100; CANR 10; DLB
    77
Collingwood, R(obin) G(eorge) 1889(?)-1943
    TCLC 67
    See also CA 117; 155
Collins, Hunt
    See Hunter, Evan
Collins, Linda 1931-   CLC 44
    See also CA 125
Collins, (William) Wilkie 1824-1889 NCLC 1,
    18
    See also CDBLB 1832-1890; DLB 18, 70, 159
Collins, William 1721-1759   LC 4, 40; DAM
    POET
    See also DLB 109
Collodi, Carlo 1826-1890   NCLC 54
    See also Lorenzini, Carlo
    See also CLR 5
Colman, George 1732-1794
    See Glassco, John
Colt, Winchester Remington
    See Hubbard, L(afayette) Ron(ald)
Colter, Cyrus 1910-   CLC 58
    See also BW 1; CA 65-68; CANR 10, 66; DLB
    33
Colton, James
    See Hansen, Joseph
Colum, Padraic 1881-1972   CLC 28
    See also CA 73-76; 33-36R; CANR 35; CLR
    36; MAICYA; MTCW; SATA 15
Colvin, James
    See Moorcock, Michael (John)
Colwin, Laurie (E.) 1944-1992 CLC 5, 13, 23,
    84
    See also CA 89-92; 139; CANR 20, 46; DLBY
    80; MTCW

Comfort, Alex(ander) 1920-CLC 7; DAM POP
    See also CA 1-4R; CANR 1, 45
Comfort, Montgomery
    See Campbell, (John) Ramsey
Compton-Burnett, I(vy) 1884(?)-1969 CLC 1,
    3, 10, 15, 34; DAM NOV
    See also CA 1-4R; 25-28R; CANR 4; DLB 36;
    MTCW
Comstock, Anthony 1844-1915   TCLC 13
    See also CA 110
Comte, Auguste 1798-1857   NCLC 54
Conan Doyle, Arthur
    See Doyle, Arthur Conan
Conde, Maryse 1937-   CLC 52, 92; BLCS;
    DAM MULT
    See also Boucolon, Maryse
    See also BW 2
Condillac, Etienne Bonnot de 1714-1780 L C
    26
Condon, Richard (Thomas) 1915-1996CLC 4,
    6, 8, 10, 45, 100; DAM NOV
    See also BEST 90:3; CA 1-4R; 151; CAAS 1;
    CANR 2, 23; INT CANR-23; MTCW
Confucius 551B.C.-479B.C.   CMLC 19; DA;
    DAB; DAC; DAM MST; WLCS
Congreve, William 1670-1729 LC 5, 21; DA;
    DAB; DAC; DAM DRAM, MST, POET;
    DC 2; WLC
    See also CDBLB 1660-1789; DLB 39, 84
Connell, Evan S(helby), Jr. 1924-CLC 4, 6, 45;
    DAM NOV
    See also AAYA 7; CA 1-4R; CAAS 2; CANR
    2, 39; DLB 2; DLBY 81; MTCW
Connelly, Marc(us Cook) 1890-1980   CLC 7
    See also CA 85-88; 102; CANR 30; DLB 7;
    DLBY 80; SATA-Obit 25
Connor, Ralph   TCLC 31
    See also Gordon, Charles William
    See also DLB 92
Conrad, Joseph 1857-1924TCLC 1, 6, 13, 25,
    43, 57; DA; DAB; DAC; DAM MST, NOV;
    SSC 9; WLC
    See also CA 104; 131; CANR 60; CDBLB
    1890-1914; DLB 10, 34, 98, 156; MTCW;
    SATA 27
Conrad, Robert Arnold
    See Hart, Moss
Conroy, Donald Pat(rick) 1945-   CLC 30, 74;
    DAM NOV, POP
    See also AAYA 8; AITN 1; CA 85-88; CANR
    24, 53; DLB 6; MTCW
Conroy, Pat
    See Conroy, Donald Pat(rick)
Constant (de Rebecque), (Henri) Benjamin
    1767-1830 NCLC 6
    See also DLB 119
Conybeare, Charles Augustus
    See Eliot, T(homas) S(tearns)
Cook, Michael 1933-   CLC 58
    See also CA 93-96; CANR 68; DLB 53
Cook, Robin 1940-   CLC 14; DAM POP
    See also BEST 90:2; CA 108; 111; CANR 41;
    INT 111
Cook, Roy
    See Silverberg, Robert
Cooke, Elizabeth 1948-   CLC 55
    See also CA 129
Cooke, John Esten 1830-1886   NCLC 5
    See also DLB 3
Cooke, John Estes
    See Baum, L(yman) Frank
Cooke, M. E.
    See Creasey, John

Cooke, Margaret
    See Creasey, John
Cook-Lynn, Elizabeth 1930-   CLC 93; DAM
    MULT
    See also CA 133; DLB 175; NNAL
Cooney, Ray   CLC 62
Cooper, Douglas 1960-   CLC 86
Cooper, Henry St. John
    See Creasey, John
Cooper, J(oan) California   CLC 56; DAM
    MULT
    See also AAYA 12; BW 1; CA 125; CANR 55
Cooper, James Fenimore 1789-1851 NCLC 1,
    27, 54
    See also AAYA 22; CDALB 1640-1865; DLB
    3; SATA 19
Coover, Robert (Lowell) 1932-   CLC 3, 7, 15,
    32, 46, 87; DAM NOV; SSC 15
    See also CA 45-48; CANR 3, 37, 58; DLB 2;
    DLBY 81; MTCW
Copeland, Stewart (Armstrong) 1952-CLC 26
Copernicus, Nicolaus 1473-1543   LC 45
Coppard, A(lfred) E(dgar) 1878-1957 TCLC
    5; SSC 21
    See also CA 114; DLB 162; YABC 1
Coppee, Francois 1842-1908   TCLC 25
Coppola, Francis Ford 1939-   CLC 16
    See also CA 77-80; CANR 40; DLB 44
Corbiere, Tristan 1845-1875   NCLC 43
Corcoran, Barbara 1911-   CLC 17
    See also AAYA 14; CA 21-24R; CAAS 2;
    CANR 11, 28, 48; CLR 50; DLB 52; JRDA;
    SAAS 20; SATA 3, 77
Cordelier, Maurice
    See Giraudoux, (Hippolyte) Jean
Corelli, Marie 1855-1924   TCLC 51
    See also Mackay, Mary
    See also DLB 34, 156
Corman, Cid 1924-   CLC 9
    See also Corman, Sidney
    See also CAAS 2; DLB 5, 193
Corman, Sidney 1924-
    See Corman, Cid
    See also CA 85-88; CANR 44; DAM POET
Cormier, Robert (Edmund) 1925-CLC 12, 30;
    DA; DAB; DAC; DAM MST, NOV
    See also AAYA 3, 19; CA 1-4R; CANR 5, 23;
    CDALB 1968-1988; CLR 12; DLB 52; INT
    CANR-23; JRDA; MAICYA; MTCW; SATA
    10, 45, 83
Corn, Alfred (DeWitt III) 1943-   CLC 33
    See also CA 104; CAAS 25; CANR 44; DLB
    120; DLBY 80
Corneille, Pierre 1606-1684   LC 28; DAB;
    DAM MST
Cornwell, David (John Moore) 1931- CLC 9,
    15; DAM POP
    See also le Carre, John
    See also CA 5-8R; CANR 13, 33, 59; MTCW
Corso, (Nunzio) Gregory 1930-   CLC 1, 11
    See also CA 5-8R; CANR 41; DLB 5, 16;
    MTCW
Cortazar, Julio 1914-1984CLC 2, 3, 5, 10, 13,
    15, 33, 34, 92; DAM MULT, NOV; HLC;
    SSC 7
    See also CA 21-24R; CANR 12, 32; DLB 113;
    HW; MTCW
CORTES, HERNAN 1484-1547   LC 31
Corwin, Cecil
    See Kornbluth, C(yril) M.
Cosic, Dobrica 1921-   CLC 14
    See also CA 122; 138; DLB 181
Costain, Thomas B(ertram) 1885-1965   CLC

30
See also CA 5-8R; 25-28R; DLB 9

Costantini, Humberto 1924(?)-1987   **CLC 49**
See also CA 131; 122; HW

Costello, Elvis 1955-   **CLC 21**

Cotes, Cecil V.
See Duncan, Sara Jeannette

Cotter, Joseph Seamon Sr. 1861-1949 **TCLC 28; BLC 1; DAM MULT**
See also BW 1; CA 124; DLB 50

Couch, Arthur Thomas Quiller
See Quiller-Couch, SirArthur (Thomas)

Coulton, James
See Hansen, Joseph

Couperus, Louis (Marie Anne) 1863-1923 **TCLC 15**
See also CA 115

Coupland, Douglas 1961-**CLC 85; DAC; DAM POP**
See also CA 142; CANR 57

Court, Wesli
See Turco, Lewis (Putnam)

Courtenay, Bryce 1933-   **CLC 59**
See also CA 138

Courtney, Robert
See Ellison, Harlan (Jay)

Cousteau, Jacques-Yves 1910-1997 **CLC 30**
See also CA 65-68; 159; CANR 15, 67; MTCW; SATA 38, 98

Cowan, Peter (Walkinshaw) 1914-   **SSC 28**
See also CA 21-24R; CANR 9, 25, 50

Coward, Noel (Peirce) 1899-1973**CLC 1, 9, 29, 51; DAM DRAM**
See also AITN 1; CA 17-18; 41-44R; CANR 35; CAP 2; CDBLB 1914-1945; DLB 10; MTCW

Cowley, Abraham 1618-1667   **LC 43**
See also DLB 131, 151

Cowley, Malcolm 1898-1989   **CLC 39**
See also CA 5-8R; 128; CANR 3, 55; DLB 4, 48; DLBY 81, 89; MTCW

Cowper, William 1731-1800 **NCLC 8; DAM POET**
See also DLB 104, 109

Cox, William Trevor 1928-   **CLC 9, 14, 71; DAM NOV**
See also Trevor, William
See also CA 9-12R; CANR 4, 37, 55; DLB 14; INT CANR-37; MTCW

Coyne, P. J.
See Masters, Hilary

Cozzens, James Gould 1903-1978**CLC 1, 4, 11, 92**
See also CA 9-12R; 81-84; CANR 19; CDALB 1941-1968; DLB 9; DLBD 2; DLBY 84, 97; MTCW

Crabbe, George 1754-1832   **NCLC 26**
See also DLB 93

Craddock, Charles Egbert
See Murfree, Mary Noailles

Craig, A. A.
See Anderson, Poul (William)

Craik, Dinah Maria (Mulock) 1826-1887 **NCLC 38**
See also DLB 35, 163; MAICYA; SATA 34

Cram, Ralph Adams 1863-1942   **TCLC 45**
See also CA 160

Crane, (Harold) Hart 1899-1932 **TCLC 2, 5, 80; DA; DAB; DAC; DAM MST, POET; PC 3; WLC**
See also CA 104; 127; CDALB 1917-1929; DLB 4, 48; MTCW

Crane, R(onald) S(almon) 1886-1967 **CLC 27**

See also CA 85-88; DLB 63

Crane, Stephen (Townley) 1871-1900   **TCLC 11, 17, 32; DA; DAB; DAC; DAM MST, NOV, POET; SSC 7; WLC**
See also AAYA 21; CA 109; 140; CDALB 1865-1917; DLB 12, 54, 78; YABC 2

Crase, Douglas 1944-   **CLC 58**
See also CA 106

Crashaw, Richard 1612(?)-1649   **LC 24**
See also DLB 126

Craven, Margaret 1901-1980   **CLC 17; DAC**
See also CA 103

Crawford, F(rancis) Marion 1854-1909**TCLC 10**
See also CA 107; DLB 71

Crawford, Isabella Valancy 1850-1887 **NCLC 12**
See also DLB 92

Crayon, Geoffrey
See Irving, Washington

Creasey, John 1908-1973   **CLC 11**
See also CA 5-8R; 41-44R; CANR 8, 59; DLB 77; MTCW

Crebillon, Claude Prosper Jolyot de (fils) 1707-1777   **LC 28**

Credo
See Creasey, John

Credo, Alvaro J. de
See Prado (Calvo), Pedro

Creeley, Robert (White) 1926- **CLC 1, 2, 4, 8, 11, 15, 36, 78; DAM POET**
See also CA 1-4R; CAAS 10; CANR 23, 43; DLB 5, 16, 169; MTCW

Crews, Harry (Eugene) 1935- **CLC 6, 23, 49**
See also AITN 1; CA 25-28R; CANR 20, 57; DLB 6, 143, 185; MTCW

Crichton, (John) Michael 1942- **CLC 2, 6, 54, 90; DAM NOV, POP**
See also AAYA 10; AITN 2; CA 25-28R; CANR 13, 40, 54; DLBY 81; INT CANR-13; JRDA; MTCW; SATA 9, 88

Crispin, Edmund   **CLC 22**
See also Montgomery, (Robert) Bruce
See also DLB 87

Cristofer, Michael 1945(?)-   **CLC 28; DAM DRAM**
See also CA 110; 152; DLB 7

Croce, Benedetto 1866-1952   **TCLC 37**
See also CA 120; 155

Crockett, David 1786-1836   **NCLC 8**
See also DLB 3, 11

Crockett, Davy
See Crockett, David

Crofts, Freeman Wills 1879-1957   **TCLC 55**
See also CA 115; DLB 77

Croker, John Wilson 1780-1857   **NCLC 10**
See also DLB 110

Crommelynck, Fernand 1885-1970   **CLC 75**
See also CA 89-92

Cromwell, Oliver 1599-1658   **LC 43**

Cronin, A(rchibald) J(oseph) 1896-1981 **CLC 32**
See also CA 1-4R; 102; CANR 5; DLB 191; SATA 47; SATA-Obit 25

Cross, Amanda
See Heilbrun, Carolyn G(old)

Crothers, Rachel 1878(?)-1958   **TCLC 19**
See also CA 113; DLB 7

Croves, Hal
See Traven, B.

Crow Dog, Mary (Ellen) (?)-   **CLC 93**
See also Brave Bird, Mary
See also CA 154

Crowfield, Christopher
See Stowe, Harriet (Elizabeth) Beecher

Crowley, Aleister   **TCLC 7**
See also Crowley, Edward Alexander

Crowley, Edward Alexander 1875-1947
See Crowley, Aleister
See also CA 104

Crowley, John 1942-   **CLC 57**
See also CA 61-64; CANR 43; DLBY 82; SATA 65

Crud
See Crumb, R(obert)

Crumarums
See Crumb, R(obert)

Crumb, R(obert) 1943-   **CLC 17**
See also CA 106

Crumbum
See Crumb, R(obert)

Crumski
See Crumb, R(obert)

Crum the Bum
See Crumb, R(obert)

Crunk
See Crumb, R(obert)

Crustt
See Crumb, R(obert)

Cryer, Gretchen (Kiger) 1935-   **CLC 21**
See also CA 114; 123

Csath, Geza 1887-1919   **TCLC 13**
See also CA 111

Cudlip, David 1933-   **CLC 34**

Cullen, Countee 1903-1946 **TCLC 4, 37; BLC 1; DA; DAC; DAM MST, MULT, POET; PC 20; WLCS**
See also BW 1; CA 108; 124; CDALB 1917-1929; DLB 4, 48, 51; MTCW; SATA 18

Cum, R.
See Crumb, R(obert)

Cummings, Bruce F(rederick) 1889-1919
See Barbellion, W. N. P.
See also CA 123

Cummings, E(dward) E(stlin) 1894-1962**CLC 1, 3, 8, 12, 15, 68; DA; DAB; DAC; DAM MST, POET; PC 5; WLC 2**
See also CA 73-76; CANR 31; CDALB 1929-1941; DLB 4, 48; MTCW

Cunha, Euclides (Rodrigues Pimenta) da 1866-1909 **TCLC 24**
See also CA 123

Cunningham, E. V.
See Fast, Howard (Melvin)

Cunningham, J(ames) V(incent) 1911-1985 **CLC 3, 31**
See also CA 1-4R; 115; CANR 1; DLB 5

Cunningham, Julia (Woolfolk) 1916- **CLC 12**
See also CA 9-12R; CANR 4, 19, 36; JRDA; MAICYA; SAAS 2; SATA 1, 26

Cunningham, Michael 1952-   **CLC 34**
See also CA 136

Cunninghame Graham, R(obert) B(ontine) 1852-1936 **TCLC 19**
See also Graham, R(obert) B(ontine) Cunninghame
See also CA 119; DLB 98

Currie, Ellen 19(?)-   **CLC 44**

Curtin, Philip
See Lowndes, Marie Adelaide (Belloc)

Curtis, Price
See Ellison, Harlan (Jay)

Cutrate, Joe
See Spiegelman, Art

Cynewulf c. 770-c. 840   **CMLC 23**

Czaczkes, Shmuel Yosef

See Faust, Frederick (Schiller)

Evans, Marian
See Eliot, George

Evans, Mary Ann
See Eliot, George

Evarts, Esther
See Benson, Sally

Everett, Percival L. 1956-   **CLC 57**
See also BW 2; CA 129

Everson, R(onald) G(ilmour) 1903- **CLC 27**
See also CA 17-20R; DLB 88

Everson, William (Oliver) 1912-1994 **CLC 1,
5, 14**
See also CA 9-12R; 145; CANR 20; DLB 5,
16; MTCW

Evtushenko, Evgenii Aleksandrovich
See Yevtushenko, Yevgeny (Alexandrovich)

Ewart, Gavin (Buchanan) 1916-1995 **CLC 13,
46**
See also CA 89-92; 150; CANR 17, 46; DLB
40; MTCW

Ewers, Hanns Heinz 1871-1943   **TCLC 12**
See also CA 109; 149

Ewing, Frederick R.
See Sturgeon, Theodore (Hamilton)

Exley, Frederick (Earl) 1929-1992 **CLC 6, 11**
See also AITN 2; CA 81-84; 138; DLB 143;
DLBY 81

Eynhardt, Guillermo
See Quiroga, Horacio (Sylvestre)

Ezekiel, Nissim 1924-   **CLC 61**
See also CA 61-64

Ezekiel, Tish O'Dowd 1943-   **CLC 34**
See also CA 129

Fadeyev, A.
See Bulgya, Alexander Alexandrovich

Fadeyev, Alexander   **TCLC 53**
See also Bulgya, Alexander Alexandrovich

Fagen, Donald 1948-   **CLC 26**

Fainzilberg, Ilya Arnoldovich 1897-1937
See Ilf, Ilya
See also CA 120; 165

Fair, Ronald L. 1932-   **CLC 18**
See also BW 1; CA 69-72; CANR 25; DLB 33

Fairbairn, Roger
See Carr, John Dickson

Fairbairns, Zoe (Ann) 1948-   **CLC 32**
See also CA 103; CANR 21

Falco, Gian
See Papini, Giovanni

Falconer, James
See Kirkup, James

Falconer, Kenneth
See Kornbluth, C(yril) M.

Falkland, Samuel
See Heijermans, Herman

Fallaci, Oriana 1930-   **CLC 11, 110**
See also CA 77-80; CANR 15, 58; MTCW

Faludy, George 1913-   **CLC 42**
See also CA 21-24R

Faludy, Gyoergy
See Faludy, George

Fanon, Frantz 1925-1961   **CLC 74; BLC 2;
DAM MULT**
See also BW 1; CA 116; 89-92

Fanshawe, Ann 1625-1680   **LC 11**

Fante, John (Thomas) 1911-1983   **CLC 60**
See also CA 69-72; 109; CANR 23; DLB 130;
DLBY 83

Farah, Nuruddin 1945-**CLC 53; BLC 2; DAM
MULT**
See also BW 2; CA 106; DLB 125

Fargue, Leon-Paul 1876(?)-1947   **TCLC 11**

See also CA 109

Farigoule, Louis
See Romains, Jules

Farina, Richard 1936(?)-1966   **CLC 9**
See also CA 81-84; 25-28R

Farley, Walter (Lorimer) 1915-1989 **CLC 17**
See also CA 17-20R; CANR 8, 29; DLB 22;
JRDA; MAICYA; SATA 2, 43

Farmer, Philip Jose 1918-   **CLC 1, 19**
See also CA 1-4R; CANR 4, 35; DLB 8;
MTCW; SATA 93

Farquhar, George 1677-1707   **LC 21; DAM
DRAM**
See also DLB 84

Farrell, J(ames) G(ordon) 1935-1979 . **CLC 6**
See also CA 73-76; 89-92; CANR 36; DLB 14;
MTCW

Farrell, James T(homas) 1904-1979**CLC 1, 4,
8, 11, 66; SSC 28**
See also CA 5-8R; 89-92; CANR 9, 61; DLB 4,
9, 86; DLBD 2; MTCW

Farren, Richard J.
See Betjeman, John

Farren, Richard M.
See Betjeman, John

Fassbinder, Rainer Werner 1946-1982**CLC 20**
See also CA 93-96; 106; CANR 31

Fast, Howard (Melvin) 1914- **CLC 23; DAM
NOV**
See also AAYA 16; CA 1-4R; CAAS 18; CANR
1, 33, 54; DLB 9; INT CANR-33; SATA 7

Faulcon, Robert
See Holdstock, Robert P.

Faulkner, William (Cuthbert) 1897-1962 **CLC
1, 3, 6, 8, 9, 11, 14, 18, 28, 52, 68; DA; DAB;
DAC; DAM MST, NOV; SSC 1; WLC**
See also AAYA 7; CA 81-84; CANR 33;
CDALB 1929-1941; DLB 9, 11, 44, 102;
DLBD 2; DLBY 86, 97; MTCW

Fauset, Jessie Redmon 1884(?)-1961 **CLC 19,
54; BLC 2; DAM MULT**
See also BW 1; CA 109; DLB 51

Faust, Frederick (Schiller) 1892-1944(?)
TCLC 49; DAM POP
See also CA 108; 152

Faust, Irvin 1924-   **CLC 8**
See also CA 33-36R; CANR 28, 67; DLB 2,
28; DLBY 80

Fawkes, Guy
See Benchley, Robert (Charles)

Fearing, Kenneth (Flexner) 1902-1961 **CLC
51**
See also CA 93-96; CANR 59; DLB 9

Fecamps, Elise
See Creasey, John

Federman, Raymond 1928-   **CLC 6, 47**
See also CA 17-20R; CAAS 8; CANR 10, 43;
DLBY 80

Federspiel, J(uerg) F. 1931-   **CLC 42**
See also CA 146

Feiffer, Jules (Ralph) 1929-   **CLC 2, 8, 64;
DAM DRAM**
See also AAYA 3; CA 17-20R; CANR 30, 59;
DLB 7, 44; INT CANR-30; MTCW; SATA
8, 61

Feige, Hermann Albert Otto Maximilian
See Traven, B.

Feinberg, David B. 1956-1994   **CLC 59**
See also CA 135; 147

Feinstein, Elaine 1930-   **CLC 36**
See also CA 69-72; CAAS 1; CANR 31, 68;
DLB 14, 40; MTCW

Feldman, Irving (Mordecai) 1928-   **CLC 7**

See also CA 1-4R; CANR 1; DLB 169

Felix-Tchicaya, Gerald
See Tchicaya, Gerald Felix

Fellini, Federico 1920-1993   **CLC 16, 85**
See also CA 65-68; 143; CANR 33

Felsen, Henry Gregor 1916-   **CLC 17**
See also CA 1-4R; CANR 1; SAAS 2; SATA 1

Fenno, Jack
See Calisher, Hortense

Fenton, James Martin 1949-   **CLC 32**
See also CA 102; DLB 40

Ferber, Edna 1887-1968   **CLC 18, 93**
See also AITN 1; CA 5-8R; 25-28R; CANR 68;
DLB 9, 28, 86; MTCW; SATA 7

Ferguson, Helen
See Kavan, Anna

Ferguson, Samuel 1810-1886   **NCLC 33**
See also DLB 32

Fergusson, Robert 1750-1774   **LC 29**
See also DLB 109

Ferling, Lawrence
See Ferlinghetti, Lawrence (Monsanto)

Ferlinghetti, Lawrence (Monsanto) 1919(?)-
CLC 2, 6, 10, 27, 111; DAM POET; PC 1
See also CA 5-8R; CANR 3, 41; CDALB 1941-
1968; DLB 5, 16; MTCW

Fernandez, Vicente Garcia Huidobro
See Huidobro Fernandez, Vicente Garcia

Ferrer, Gabriel (Francisco Victor) Miro
See Miro (Ferrer), Gabriel (Francisco Victor)

Ferrier, Susan (Edmonstone) 1782-1854
NCLC 8
See also DLB 116

Ferrigno, Robert 1948(?)-   **CLC 65**
See also CA 140

Ferron, Jacques 1921-1985   **CLC 94; DAC**
See also CA 117; 129; DLB 60

Feuchtwanger, Lion 1884-1958   **TCLC 3**
See also CA 104; DLB 66

Feuillet, Octave 1821-1890   **NCLC 45**
See also DLB 192

Feydeau, Georges (Leon Jules Marie) 1862-
1921   **TCLC 22; DAM DRAM**
See also CA 113; 152; DLB 192

Fichte, Johann Gottlieb 1762-1814 **NCLC 62**
See also DLB 90

Ficino, Marsilio 1433-1499   **LC 12**

Fiedeler, Hans
See Doeblin, Alfred

Fiedler, Leslie A(aron) 1917- **CLC 4, 13, 24**
See also CA 9-12R; CANR 7, 63; DLB 28, 67;
MTCW

Field, Andrew 1938-   **CLC 44**
See also CA 97-100; CANR 25

Field, Eugene 1850-1895   **NCLC 3**
See also DLB 23, 42, 140; DLBD 13; MAICYA;
SATA 16

Field, Gans T.
See Wellman, Manly Wade

Field, Michael 1915-1971   **TCLC 43**
See also CA 29-32R

Field, Peter
See Hobson, Laura Z(ametkin)

Fielding, Henry 1707-1754 **LC 1; DA; DAB;
DAC; DAM DRAM, MST, NOV; WLC**
See also CDBLB 1660-1789; DLB 39, 84, 101

Fielding, Sarah 1710-1768   **LC 1, 44**
See also DLB 39

Fields, W. C. 1880-1946   **TCLC 80**
See also DLB 44

Fierstein, Harvey (Forbes) 1954-   **CLC 33;
DAM DRAM, POP**
See also CA 123; 129

Figes, Eva 1932- **CLC 31**
See also CA 53-56; CANR 4, 44; DLB 14

Finch, Anne 1661-1720 **LC 3; PC 21**
See also DLB 95

Finch, Robert (Duer Claydon) 1900- **CLC 18**
See also CA 57-60; CANR 9, 24, 49; DLB 88

Findley, Timothy 1930- **CLC 27, 102; DAC; DAM MST**
See also CA 25-28R; CANR 12, 42, 69; DLB 53

Fink, William
See Mencken, H(enry) L(ouis)

Firbank, Louis 1942-
See Reed, Lou
See also CA 117

Firbank, (Arthur Annesley) Ronald 1886-1926 **TCLC 1**
See also CA 104; DLB 36

Fisher, M(ary) F(rances) K(ennedy) 1908-1992 **CLC 76, 87**
See also CA 77-80; 138; CANR 44

Fisher, Roy 1930- **CLC 25**
See also CA 81-84; CAAS 10; CANR 16; DLB 40

Fisher, Rudolph 1897-1934 **TCLC 11; BLC 2; DAM MULT; SSC 25**
See also BW 1; CA 107; 124; DLB 51, 102

Fisher, Vardis (Alvero) 1895-1968 **CLC 7**
See also CA 5-8R; 25-28R; CANR 68; DLB 9

Fiske, Tarleton
See Bloch, Robert (Albert)

Fitch, Clarke
See Sinclair, Upton (Beall)

Fitch, John IV
See Cormier, Robert (Edmund)

Fitzgerald, Captain Hugh
See Baum, L(yman) Frank

FitzGerald, Edward 1809-1883 **NCLC 9**
See also DLB 32

Fitzgerald, F(rancis) Scott (Key) 1896-1940 **TCLC 1, 6, 14, 28, 55; DA; DAB; DAC; DAM MST, NOV; SSC 6, 31; WLC**
See also AAYA 24; AITN 1; CA 110; 123; CDALB 1917-1929; DLB 4, 9, 86; DLBD 1, 15, 16; DLBY 81, 96; MTCW

Fitzgerald, Penelope 1916- **CLC 19, 51, 61**
See also CA 85-88; CAAS 10; CANR 56; DLB 14, 194

Fitzgerald, Robert (Stuart) 1910-1985 **CLC 39**
See also CA 1-4R; 114; CANR 1; DLBY 80

FitzGerald, Robert D(avid) 1902-1987 **CLC 19**
See also CA 17-20R

Fitzgerald, Zelda (Sayre) 1900-1948 **TCLC 52**
See also CA 117; 126; DLBY 84

Flanagan, Thomas (James Bonner) 1923- **CLC 25, 52**
See also CA 108; CANR 55; DLBY 80; INT 108; MTCW

Flaubert, Gustave 1821-1880 **NCLC 2, 10, 19, 62, 66; DA; DAB; DAC; DAM MST, NOV; SSC 11; WLC**
See also DLB 119

Flecker, Herman Elroy
See Flecker, (Herman) James Elroy

Flecker, (Herman) James Elroy 1884-1915 **TCLC 43**
See also CA 109; 150; DLB 10, 19

Fleming, Ian (Lancaster) 1908-1964 **CLC 3, 30; DAM POP**
See also CA 5-8R; CANR 59; CDBLB 1945-1960; DLB 87; MTCW; SATA 9

Fleming, Thomas (James) 1927- **CLC 37**
See also CA 5-8R; CANR 10; INT CANR-10;

SATA 8

Fletcher, John 1579-1625 **LC 33; DC 6**
See also CDBLB Before 1660; DLB 58

Fletcher, John Gould 1886-1950 **TCLC 35**
See also CA 107; DLB 4, 45

Fleur, Paul
See Pohl, Frederik

Flooglebuckle, Al
See Spiegelman, Art

Flying Officer X
See Bates, H(erbert) E(rnest)

Fo, Dario 1926- **CLC 32, 109; DAM DRAM**
See also CA 116; 128; CANR 68; DLBY 97; MTCW

Fogarty, Jonathan Titulescu Esq.
See Farrell, James T(homas)

Folke, Will
See Bloch, Robert (Albert)

Follett, Ken(neth Martin) 1949- **CLC 18; DAM NOV, POP**
See also AAYA 6; BEST 89:4; CA 81-84; CANR 13, 33, 54; DLB 87; DLBY 81; INT CANR-33; MTCW

Fontane, Theodor 1819-1898 **NCLC 26**
See also DLB 129

Foote, Horton 1916- **CLC 51, 91; DAM DRAM**
See also CA 73-76; CANR 34, 51; DLB 26; INT CANR-34

Foote, Shelby 1916- **CLC 75; DAM NOV, POP**
See also CA 5-8R; CANR 3, 45; DLB 2, 17

Forbes, Esther 1891-1967 **CLC 12**
See also AAYA 17; CA 13-14; 25-28R; CAP 1; CLR 27; DLB 22; JRDA; MAICYA; SATA 2

Forche, Carolyn (Louise) 1950- **CLC 25, 83, 86; DAM POET; PC 10**
See also CA 109; 117; CANR 50; DLB 5, 193; INT 117

Ford, Elbur
See Hibbert, Eleanor Alice Burford

Ford, Ford Madox 1873-1939 **TCLC 1, 15, 39, 57; DAM NOV**
See also CA 104; 132; CDBLB 1914-1945; DLB 162; MTCW

Ford, Henry 1863-1947 **TCLC 73**
See also CA 115; 148

Ford, John 1586-(?) **DC 8**
See also CDBLB Before 1660; DAM DRAM; DLB 58

Ford, John 1895-1973 **CLC 16**
See also CA 45-48

Ford, Richard 1944- **CLC 46, 99**
See also CA 69-72; CANR 11, 47

Ford, Webster
See Masters, Edgar Lee

Foreman, Richard 1937- **CLC 50**
See also CA 65-68; CANR 32, 63

Forester, C(ecil) S(cott) 1899-1966 **CLC 35**
See also CA 73-76; 25-28R; DLB 191; SATA 13

Forez
See Mauriac, Francois (Charles)

Forman, James Douglas 1932- **CLC 21**
See also AAYA 17; CA 9-12R; CANR 4, 19, 42; JRDA; MAICYA; SATA 8, 70

Fornes, Maria Irene 1930- **CLC 39, 61**
See also CA 25-28R; CANR 28; DLB 7; HW; INT CANR-28; MTCW

Forrest, Leon (Richard) 1937-1997 **CLC 4; BLCS**
See also BW 2; CA 89-92; 162; CAAS 7; CANR 25, 52; DLB 33

Forster, E(dward) M(organ) 1879-1970 **CLC 1, 2, 3, 4, 9, 10, 13, 15, 22, 45, 77; DA; DAB;**

DAC; DAM MST, NOV; SSC 27; WLC
See also AAYA 2; CA 13-14; 25-28R; CANR 45; CAP 1; CDBLB 1914-1945; DLB 34, 98, 162, 178, 195; DLBD 10; MTCW; SATA 57

Forster, John 1812-1876 **NCLC 11**
See also DLB 144, 184

Forsyth, Frederick 1938- **CLC 2, 5, 36; DAM NOV, POP**
See also BEST 89:4; CA 85-88; CANR 38, 62; DLB 87; MTCW

Forten, Charlotte L. **TCLC 16; BLC 2**
See also Grimke, Charlotte L(ottie) Forten
See also DLB 50

Foscolo, Ugo 1778-1827 **NCLC 8**

Fosse, Bob **CLC 20**
See also Fosse, Robert Louis

Fosse, Robert Louis 1927-1987
See Fosse, Bob
See also CA 110; 123

Foster, Stephen Collins 1826-1864 **NCLC 26**

Foucault, Michel 1926-1984 **CLC 31, 34, 69**
See also CA 105; 113; CANR 34; MTCW

Fouque, Friedrich (Heinrich Karl) de la Motte 1777-1843 **NCLC 2**
See also DLB 90

Fourier, Charles 1772-1837 **NCLC 51**

Fournier, Henri Alban 1886-1914
See Alain-Fournier
See also CA 104

Fournier, Pierre 1916- **CLC 11**
See also Gascar, Pierre
See also CA 89-92; CANR 16, 40

Fowles, John 1926- **CLC 1, 2, 3, 4, 6, 9, 10, 15, 33, 87; DAB; DAC; DAM MST**
See also CA 5-8R; CANR 25; CDBLB 1960 to Present; DLB 14, 139; MTCW; SATA 22

Fox, Paula 1923- **CLC 2, 8**
See also AAYA 3; CA 73-76; CANR 20, 36, 62; CLR 1, 44; DLB 52; JRDA; MAICYA; MTCW; SATA 17, 60

Fox, William Price (Jr.) 1926- **CLC 22**
See also CA 17-20R; CAAS 19; CANR 11; DLB 2; DLBY 81

Foxe, John 1516(?)-1587 **LC 14**
See also DLB 132

Frame, Janet 1924- **CLC 2, 3, 6, 22, 66, 96; SSC 29**
See also Clutha, Janet Paterson Frame

France, Anatole **TCLC 9**
See also Thibault, Jacques Anatole Francois
See also DLB 123

Francis, Claude 19(?)- **CLC 50**

Francis, Dick 1920- **CLC 2, 22, 42, 102; DAM POP**
See also AAYA 5, 21; BEST 89:3; CA 5-8R; CANR 9, 42, 68; CDBLB 1960 to Present; DLB 87; INT CANR-9; MTCW

Francis, Robert (Churchill) 1901-1987 **CLC 15**
See also CA 1-4R; 123; CANR 1

Frank, Anne(lies Marie) 1929-1945 **TCLC 17; DA; DAB; DAC; DAM MST; WLC**
See also AAYA 12; CA 113; 133; CANR 68; MTCW; SATA 87; SATA-Brief 42

Frank, Bruno 1887-1945 **TCLC 81**
See also DLB 118

Frank, Elizabeth 1945- **CLC 39**
See also CA 121; 126; INT 126

Frankl, Viktor E(mil) 1905-1997 **CLC 93**
See also CA 65-68; 161

Franklin, Benjamin
See Hasek, Jaroslav (Matej Frantisek)

Franklin, Benjamin 1706-1790 **LC 25; DA;**

DAB; DAC; DAM MST; WLCS
See also CDALB 1640-1865; DLB 24, 43, 73

Franklin, (Stella Maria Sarah) Miles (Lampe)
1879-1954   TCLC 7
See also CA 104; 164

Fraser, (Lady) Antonia (Pakenham) 1932-
CLC 32, 107
See also CA 85-88; CANR 44, 65; MTCW;
SATA-Brief 32

Fraser, George MacDonald 1925-   CLC 7
See also CA 45-48; CANR 2, 48

Fraser, Sylvia 1935-   CLC 64
See also CA 45-48; CANR 1, 16, 60

Frayn, Michael 1933- CLC 3, 7, 31, 47; DAM
DRAM, NOV
See also CA 5-8R; CANR 30, 69; DLB 13, 14,
194; MTCW

Fraze, Candida (Merrill) 1945-   CLC 50
See also CA 126

Frazer, J(ames) G(eorge) 1854-1941 TCLC 32
See also CA 118

Frazer, Robert Caine
See Creasey, John

Frazer, Sir James George
See Frazer, J(ames) G(eorge)

Frazier, Charles 1950-   CLC 109
See also CA 161

Frazier, Ian 1951-   CLC 46
See also CA 130; CANR 54

Frederic, Harold 1856-1898   NCLC 10
See also DLB 12, 23; DLBD 13

Frederick, John
See Faust, Frederick (Schiller)

Frederick the Great 1712-1786   LC 14

Fredro, Aleksander 1793-1876   NCLC 8

Freeling, Nicolas 1927-   CLC 38
See also CA 49-52; CAAS 12; CANR 1, 17,
50; DLB 87

Freeman, Douglas Southall 1886-1953 TCLC
11
See also CA 109; DLB 17

Freeman, Judith 1946-   CLC 55
See also CA 148

Freeman, Mary Eleanor Wilkins 1852-1930
TCLC 9; SSC 1
See also CA 106; DLB 12, 78

Freeman, R(ichard) Austin 1862-1943 TCLC
21
See also CA 113; DLB 70

French, Albert 1943-   CLC 86

French, Marilyn 1929- CLC 10, 18, 60; DAM
DRAM, NOV, POP
See also CA 69-72; CANR 3, 31; INT CANR-
31; MTCW

French, Paul
See Asimov, Isaac

Freneau, Philip Morin 1752-1832   NCLC 1
See also DLB 37, 43

Freud, Sigmund 1856-1939   TCLC 52
See also CA 115; 133; CANR 69; MTCW

Friedan, Betty (Naomi) 1921-   CLC 74
See also CA 65-68; CANR 18, 45; MTCW

Friedlander, Saul 1932-   CLC 90
See also CA 117; 130

Friedman, B(ernard) H(arper) 1926- CLC 7
See also CA 1-4R; CANR 3, 48

Friedman, Bruce Jay 1930-   CLC 3, 5, 56
See also CA 9-12R; CANR 25, 52; DLB 2, 28;
INT CANR-25

Friel, Brian 1929-   CLC 5, 42, 59; DC 8
See also CA 21-24R; CANR 33, 69; DLB 13;
MTCW

Friis-Baastad, Babbis Ellinor 1921-1970 CLC

12
See also CA 17-20R; 134; SATA 7

Frisch, Max (Rudolf) 1911-1991 CLC 3, 9, 14,
18, 32, 44; DAM DRAM, NOV
See also CA 85-88; 134; CANR 32; DLB 69,
124; MTCW

Fromentin, Eugene (Samuel Auguste) 1820-
1876   NCLC 10
See also DLB 123

Frost, Frederick
See Faust, Frederick (Schiller)

Frost, Robert (Lee) 1874-1963 CLC 1, 3, 4, 9,
10, 13, 15, 26, 34, 44; DA; DAB; DAC;
DAM MST, POET; PC 1; WLC
See also AAYA 21; CA 89-92; CANR 33;
CDALB 1917-1929; DLB 54; DLBD 7;
MTCW; SATA 14

Froude, James Anthony 1818-1894 NCLC 43
See also DLB 18, 57, 144

Froy, Herald
See Waterhouse, Keith (Spencer)

Fry, Christopher 1907- CLC 2, 10, 14; DAM
DRAM
See also CA 17-20R; CAAS 23; CANR 9, 30;
DLB 13; MTCW; SATA 66

Frye, (Herman) Northrop 1912-1991 CLC 24,
70
See also CA 5-8R; 133; CANR 8, 37; DLB 67,
68; MTCW

Fuchs, Daniel 1909-1993   CLC 8, 22
See also CA 81-84; 142; CAAS 5; CANR 40;
DLB 9, 26, 28; DLBY 93

Fuchs, Daniel 1934-   CLC 34
See also CA 37-40R; CANR 14, 48

Fuentes, Carlos 1928- CLC 3, 8, 10, 13, 22, 41,
60, 113; DA; DAB; DAC; DAM MST,
MULT, NOV; HLC; SSC 24; WLC
See also AAYA 4; AITN 2; CA 69-72; CANR
10, 32, 68; DLB 113; HW; MTCW

Fuentes, Gregorio Lopez y
See Lopez y Fuentes, Gregorio

Fugard, (Harold) Athol 1932- CLC 5, 9, 14, 25,
40, 80; DAM DRAM; DC 3
See also AAYA 17; CA 85-88; CANR 32, 54;
MTCW

Fugard, Sheila 1932-   CLC 48
See also CA 125

Fuller, Charles (H., Jr.) 1939- CLC 25; BLC 2;
DAM DRAM, MULT; DC 1
See also BW 2; CA 108; 112; DLB 38; INT 112;
MTCW

Fuller, John (Leopold) 1937-   CLC 62
See also CA 21-24R; CANR 9, 44; DLB 40

Fuller, Margaret   NCLC 5, 50
See also Ossoli, Sarah Margaret (Fuller
marchesa d')

Fuller, Roy (Broadbent) 1912-1991 CLC 4, 28
See also CA 5-8R; 135; CAAS 10; CANR 53;
DLB 15, 20; SATA 87

Fulton, Alice 1952-   CLC 52
See also CA 116; CANR 57; DLB 193

Furphy, Joseph 1843-1912   TCLC 25
See also CA 163

Fussell, Paul 1924-   CLC 74
See also BEST 90:1; CA 17-20R; CANR 8, 21,
35, 69; INT CANR-21; MTCW

Futabatei, Shimei 1864-1909   TCLC 44
See also CA 162; DLB 180

Futrelle, Jacques 1875-1912   TCLC 19
See also CA 113; 155

Gaboriau, Emile 1835-1873   NCLC 14

Gadda, Carlo Emilio 1893-1973   CLC 11
See also CA 89-92; DLB 177

Gaddis, William 1922- CLC 1, 3, 6, 8, 10, 19,
43, 86
See also CA 17-20R; CANR 21, 48; DLB 2;
MTCW

Gage, Walter
See Inge, William (Motter)

Gaines, Ernest J(ames) 1933- CLC 3, 11, 18,
86; BLC 2; DAM MULT
See also AAYA 18; AITN 1; BW 2; CA 9-12R;
CANR 6, 24, 42; CDALB 1968-1988; DLB
2, 33, 152; DLBY 80; MTCW; SATA 86

Gaitskill, Mary 1954-   CLC 69
See also CA 128; CANR 61

Galdos, Benito Perez
See Perez Galdos, Benito

Gale, Zona 1874-1938 TCLC 7; DAM DRAM
See also CA 105; 153; DLB 9, 78

Galeano, Eduardo (Hughes) 1940-   CLC 72
See also CA 29-32R; CANR 13, 32; HW

Galiano, Juan Valera y Alcala
See Valera y Alcala-Galiano, Juan

Galilei, Galileo 1546-1642   LC 45

Gallagher, Tess 1943-   CLC 18, 63; DAM
POET; PC 9
See also CA 106; DLB 120

Gallant, Mavis 1922-   CLC 7, 18, 38; DAC;
DAM MST; SSC 5
See also CA 69-72; CANR 29, 69; DLB 53;
MTCW

Gallant, Roy A(rthur) 1924-   CLC 17
See also CA 5-8R; CANR 4, 29, 54; CLR 30;
MAICYA; SATA 4, 68

Gallico, Paul (William) 1897-1976   CLC 2
See also AITN 1; CA 5-8R; 69-72; CANR 23;
DLB 9, 171; MAICYA; SATA 13

Gallo, Max Louis 1932-   CLC 95
See also CA 85-88

Gallois, Lucien
See Desnos, Robert

Gallup, Ralph
See Whitemore, Hugh (John)

Galsworthy, John 1867-1933 TCLC 1, 45; DA;
DAB; DAC; DAM DRAM, MST, NOV;
SSC 22; WLC 2
See also CA 104; 141; CDBLB 1890-1914;
DLB 10, 34, 98, 162; DLBD 16

Galt, John 1779-1839   NCLC 1
See also DLB 99, 116, 159

Galvin, James 1951-   CLC 38
See also CA 108; CANR 26

Gamboa, Federico 1864-1939   TCLC 36

Gandhi, M. K.
See Gandhi, Mohandas Karamchand

Gandhi, Mahatma
See Gandhi, Mohandas Karamchand

Gandhi, Mohandas Karamchand 1869-1948
TCLC 59; DAM MULT
See also CA 121; 132; MTCW

Gann, Ernest Kellogg 1910-1991   CLC 23
See also AITN 1; CA 1-4R; 136; CANR 1

Garcia, Cristina 1958-   CLC 76
See also CA 141

Garcia Lorca, Federico 1898-1936 TCLC 1, 7,
49; DA; DAB; DAC; DAM DRAM, MST,
MULT, POET; DC 2; HLC; PC 3; WLC
See also CA 104; 131; DLB 108; HW; MTCW

Garcia Marquez, Gabriel (Jose) 1928- CLC 2,
3, 8, 10, 15, 27, 47, 55, 68; DA; DAB; DAC;
DAM MST, MULT, NOV, POP; HLC; SSC
8; WLC
See also AAYA 3; BEST 89:1, 90:4; CA 33-
36R; CANR 10, 28, 50; DLB 113; HW;
MTCW

See Laxness, Halldor
See also CA 103; 164
Guenter, Erich
See Eich, Guenter
Guest, Barbara 1920-   **CLC 34**
See also CA 25-28R; CANR 11, 44; DLB 5,
193
Guest, Judith (Ann) 1936-   **CLC 8, 30; DAM
NOV, POP**
See also AAYA 7; CA 77-80; CANR 15; INT
CANR-15; MTCW
Guevara, Che   **CLC 87; HLC**
See also Guevara (Serna), Ernesto
Guevara (Serna), Ernesto 1928-1967
See Guevara, Che
See also CA 127; 111; CANR 56; DAM MULT;
HW
Guild, Nicholas M. 1944-   **CLC 33**
See also CA 93-96
Guillemin, Jacques
See Sartre, Jean-Paul
Guillen, Jorge 1893-1984   **CLC 11; DAM
MULT, POET**
See also CA 89-92; 112; DLB 108; HW
Guillen, Nicolas (Cristobal) 1902-1989   **CLC
48, 79; BLC 2; DAM MST, MULT, POET;
HLC; PC 23**
See also BW 2; CA 116; 125; 129; HW
Guillevic, (Eugene) 1907-   **CLC 33**
See also CA 93-96
Guillois
See Desnos, Robert
Guillois, Valentin
See Desnos, Robert
Guiney, Louise Imogen 1861-1920   **TCLC 41**
See also CA 160; DLB 54
Guiraldes, Ricardo (Guillermo) 1886-1927
TCLC 39
See also CA 131; HW; MTCW
Gumilev, Nikolai (Stepanovich) 1886-1921
TCLC 60
See also CA 165
Gunesekera, Romesh 1954-   **CLC 91**
See also CA 159
Gunn, Bill   **CLC 5**
See also Gunn, William Harrison
See also DLB 38
Gunn, Thom(son William) 1929-**CLC 3, 6, 18,
32, 81; DAM POET**
See also CA 17-20R; CANR 9, 33; CDBLB
1960 to Present; DLB 27; INT CANR-33;
MTCW
Gunn, William Harrison 1934(?)-1989
See Gunn, Bill
See also AITN 1; BW 1; CA 13-16R; 128;
CANR 12, 25
Gunnars, Kristjana 1948-   **CLC 69**
See also CA 113; DLB 60
Gurdjieff, G(eorgei) I(vanovich) 1877(?)-1949
TCLC 71
See also CA 157
Gurganus, Allan 1947-   **CLC 70; DAM POP**
See also BEST 90:1; CA 135
Gurney, A(lbert) R(amsdell), Jr. 1930-   **CLC
32, 50, 54; DAM DRAM**
See also CA 77-80; CANR 32, 64
Gurney, Ivor (Bertie) 1890-1937   **TCLC 33**
Gurney, Peter
See Gurney, A(lbert) R(amsdell), Jr.
Guro, Elena 1877-1913   **TCLC 56**
Gustafson, James M(oody) 1925-   **CLC 100**
See also CA 25-28R; CANR 37
Gustafson, Ralph (Barker) 1909-   **CLC 36**

See also CA 21-24R; CANR 8, 45; DLB 88
Gut, Gom
See Simenon, Georges (Jacques Christian)
Guterson, David 1956-   **CLC 91**
See also CA 132
Guthrie, A(lfred) B(ertram), Jr. 1901-1991
CLC 23
See also CA 57-60; 134; CANR 24; DLB 6;
SATA 62; SATA-Obit 67
Guthrie, Isobel
See Grieve, C(hristopher) M(urray)
Guthrie, Woodrow Wilson 1912-1967
See Guthrie, Woody
See also CA 113; 93-96
Guthrie, Woody   **CLC 35**
See also Guthrie, Woodrow Wilson
Guy, Rosa (Cuthbert) 1928-   **CLC 26**
See also AAYA 4; BW 2; CA 17-20R; CANR
14, 34; CLR 13; DLB 33; JRDA; MAICYA;
SATA 14, 62
Gwendolyn
See Bennett, (Enoch) Arnold
H. D.   **CLC 3, 8, 14, 31, 34, 73; PC 5**
See also Doolittle, Hilda
H. de V.
See Buchan, John
Haavikko, Paavo Juhani 1931-   **CLC 18, 34**
See also CA 106
Habbema, Koos
See Heijermans, Herman
Habermas, Juergen 1929-   **CLC 104**
See also CA 109
Habermas, Jurgen
See Habermas, Juergen
Hacker, Marilyn 1942- **CLC 5, 9, 23, 72, 91;
DAM POET**
See also CA 77-80; CANR 68; DLB 120
Haeckel, Ernst Heinrich (Philipp August) 1834-
1919 **TCLC 83**
See also CA 157
Haggard, H(enry) Rider 1856-1925 **TCLC 11**
See also CA 108; 148; DLB 70, 156, 174, 178;
SATA 16
Hagiosy, L.
See Larbaud, Valery (Nicolas)
Hagiwara Sakutaro 1886-1942 **TCLC 60; PC
18**
Haig, Fenil
See Ford, Ford Madox
Haig-Brown, Roderick (Langmere) 1908-1976
CLC 21
See also CA 5-8R; 69-72; CANR 4, 38; CLR
31; DLB 88; MAICYA; SATA 12
Hailey, Arthur 1920-**CLC 5; DAM NOV, POP**
See also AITN 2; BEST 90:3; CA 1-4R; CANR
2, 36; DLB 88; DLBY 82; MTCW
Hailey, Elizabeth Forsythe 1938-   **CLC 40**
See also CA 93-96; CAAS 1; CANR 15, 48;
INT CANR-15
Haines, John (Meade) 1924-   **CLC 58**
See also CA 17-20R; CANR 13, 34; DLB 5
Hakluyt, Richard 1552-1616   **LC 31**
Haldeman, Joe (William) 1943-   **CLC 61**
See also CA 53-56; CAAS 25; CANR 6; DLB
8; INT CANR-6
Haley, Alex(ander Murray Palmer) 1921-1992
**CLC 8, 12, 76; BLC 2; DA; DAB; DAC;
DAM MST, MULT, POP**
See also BW 2; CA 77-80; 136; CANR 61; DLB
38; MTCW
Haliburton, Thomas Chandler 1796-1865
NCLC 15
See also DLB 11, 99

Hall, Donald (Andrew, Jr.) 1928-   **CLC 1, 13,
37, 59; DAM POET**
See also CA 5-8R; CAAS 7; CANR 2, 44, 64;
DLB 5; SATA 23, 97
Hall, Frederic Sauser
See Sauser-Hall, Frederic
Hall, James
See Kuttner, Henry
Hall, James Norman 1887-1951   **TCLC 23**
See also CA 123; SATA 21
Hall, (Marguerite) Radclyffe 1886-1943
TCLC 12
See also CA 110; 150
Hall, Rodney 1935-   **CLC 51**
See also CA 109; CANR 69
Halleck, Fitz-Greene 1790-1867   **NCLC 47**
See also DLB 3
Halliday, Michael
See Creasey, John
Halpern, Daniel 1945-   **CLC 14**
See also CA 33-36R
Hamburger, Michael (Peter Leopold) 1924-
CLC 5, 14
See also CA 5-8R; CAAS 4; CANR 2, 47; DLB
27
Hamill, Pete 1935-   **CLC 10**
See also CA 25-28R; CANR 18
Hamilton, Alexander 1755(?)-1804   **NCLC 49**
See also DLB 37
Hamilton, Clive
See Lewis, C(live) S(taples)
Hamilton, Edmond 1904-1977   **CLC 1**
See also CA 1-4R; CANR 3; DLB 8
Hamilton, Eugene (Jacob) Lee
See Lee-Hamilton, Eugene (Jacob)
Hamilton, Franklin
See Silverberg, Robert
Hamilton, Gail
See Corcoran, Barbara
Hamilton, Mollie
See Kaye, M(ary) M(argaret)
Hamilton, (Anthony Walter) Patrick 1904-1962
CLC 51
See also CA 113; DLB 10
Hamilton, Virginia 1936-   **CLC 26; DAM
MULT**
See also AAYA 2, 21; BW 2; CA 25-28R;
CANR 20, 37; CLR 1, 11, 40; DLB 33, 52;
INT CANR-20; JRDA; MAICYA; MTCW;
SATA 4, 56, 79
Hammett, (Samuel) Dashiell 1894-1961 **CLC
3, 5, 10, 19, 47; SSC 17**
See also AITN 1; CA 81-84; CANR 42; CDALB
1929-1941; DLBD 6; DLBY 96; MTCW
Hammon, Jupiter 1711(?)-1800(?)   **NCLC 5;
BLC 2; DAM MULT, POET; PC 16**
See also DLB 31, 50
Hammond, Keith
See Kuttner, Henry
Hamner, Earl (Henry), Jr. 1923-   **CLC 12**
See also AITN 1; CA 73-76; DLB 6
Hampton, Christopher 1946- **CLC 4**
See also CA 25-28R; DLB 13; MTCW
Hamsun, Knut   **TCLC 2, 14, 49**
See also Pedersen, Knut
Handke, Peter 1942-**CLC 5, 8, 10, 15, 38; DAM
DRAM, NOV**
See also CA 77-80; CANR 33; DLB 85, 124;
MTCW
Hanley, James 1901-1985   **CLC 3, 5, 8, 13**
See also CA 73-76; 117; CANR 36; DLB 191;
MTCW
Hannah, Barry 1942-   **CLC 23, 38, 90**

See also CA 108; 110; CANR 43, 68; DLB 6;
    INT 110; MTCW
Hannon, Ezra
    See Hunter, Evan
Hansberry, Lorraine (Vivian) 1930-1965**CLC
    17, 62; BLC 2; DA; DAB; DAC; DAM
    DRAM, MST, MULT; DC 2**
    See also AAYA 25; BW 1; CA 109; 25-28R;
    CABS 3; CANR 58; CDALB 1941-1968;
    DLB 7, 38; MTCW
Hansen, Joseph 1923-   **CLC 38**
    See also CA 29-32R; CAAS 17; CANR 16, 44,
    66; INT CANR-16
Hansen, Martin A. 1909-1955   **TCLC 32**
Hanson, Kenneth O(stlin) 1922-   **CLC 13**
    See also CA 53-56; CANR 7
Hardwick, Elizabeth 1916-   **CLC 13; DAM
    NOV**
    See also CA 5-8R; CANR 3, 32; DLB 6; MTCW
Hardy, Thomas 1840-1928**TCLC 4, 10, 18, 32,
    48, 53, 72; DA; DAB; DAC; DAM MST,
    NOV, POET; PC 8; SSC 2; WLC**
    See also CA 104; 123; CDBLB 1890-1914;
    DLB 18, 19, 135; MTCW
Hare, David 1947-   **CLC 29, 58**
    See also CA 97-100; CANR 39; DLB 13;
    MTCW
Harewood, John
    See Van Druten, John (William)
Harford, Henry
    See Hudson, W(illiam) H(enry)
Hargrave, Leonie
    See Disch, Thomas M(ichael)
Harjo, Joy 1951-   **CLC 83; DAM MULT**
    See also CA 114; CANR 35, 67; DLB 120, 175;
    NNAL
Harlan, Louis R(udolph) 1922-   **CLC 34**
    See also CA 21-24R; CANR 25, 55
Harling, Robert 1951(?)-   **CLC 53**
    See also CA 147
Harmon, William (Ruth) 1938-   **CLC 38**
    See also CA 33-36R; CANR 14, 32, 35; SATA
    65
Harper, F. E. W.
    See Harper, Frances Ellen Watkins
Harper, Frances E. W.
    See Harper, Frances Ellen Watkins
Harper, Frances E. Watkins
    See Harper, Frances Ellen Watkins
Harper, Frances Ellen
    See Harper, Frances Ellen Watkins
Harper, Frances Ellen Watkins 1825-1911
    **TCLC 14; BLC 2; DAM MULT, POET;
    PC 21**
    See also BW 1; CA 111; 125; DLB 50
Harper, Michael S(teven) 1938-   **CLC 7, 22**
    See also BW 1; CA 33-36R; CANR 24; DLB
    41
Harper, Mrs. F. E. W.
    See Harper, Frances Ellen Watkins
Harris, Christie (Lucy) Irwin 1907-   **CLC 12**
    See also CA 5-8R; CANR 6; CLR 47; DLB 88;
    JRDA; MAICYA; SAAS 10; SATA 6, 74
Harris, Frank 1856-1931   **TCLC 24**
    See also CA 109; 150; DLB 156, 197
Harris, George Washington 1814-1869**NCLC
    23**
    See also DLB 3, 11
Harris, Joel Chandler 1848-1908   **TCLC 2;
    SSC 19**
    See also CA 104; 137; CLR 49; DLB 11, 23,
    42, 78, 91; MAICYA; YABC 1
Harris, John (Wyndham Parkes Lucas) Beynon

1903-1969
    See Wyndham, John
    See also CA 102; 89-92
Harris, MacDonald   **CLC 9**
    See also Heiney, Donald (William)
Harris, Mark 1922-   **CLC 19**
    See also CA 5-8R; CAAS 3; CANR 2, 55; DLB
    2; DLBY 80
Harris, (Theodore) Wilson 1921-   **CLC 25**
    See also BW 2; CA 65-68; CAAS 16; CANR
    11, 27, 69; DLB 117; MTCW
Harrison, Elizabeth Cavanna 1909-
    See Cavanna, Betty
    See also CA 9-12R; CANR 6, 27
Harrison, Harry (Max) 1925-   **CLC 42**
    See also CA 1-4R; CANR 5, 21; DLB 8; SATA
    4
Harrison, James (Thomas) 1937-   **CLC 6, 14,
    33, 66; SSC 19**
    See also CA 13-16R; CANR 8, 51; DLBY 82;
    INT CANR-8
Harrison, Jim
    See Harrison, James (Thomas)
Harrison, Kathryn 1961-   **CLC 70**
    See also CA 144; CANR 68
Harrison, Tony 1937-   **CLC 43**
    See also CA 65-68; CANR 44; DLB 40; MTCW
Harriss, Will(ard Irvin) 1922-   **CLC 34**
    See also CA 111
Harson, Sley
    See Ellison, Harlan (Jay)
Hart, Ellis
    See Ellison, Harlan (Jay)
Hart, Josephine 1942(?)- **CLC 70; DAM POP**
    See also CA 138
Hart, Moss 1904-1961 **CLC 66; DAM DRAM**
    See also CA 109; 89-92; DLB 7
Harte, (Francis) Bret(t) 1836(?)-1902**TCLC 1,
    25; DA; DAC; DAM MST; SSC 8; WLC**
    See also CA 104; 140; CDALB 1865-1917;
    DLB 12, 64, 74, 79, 186; SATA 26
Hartley, L(eslie) P(oles) 1895-1972 **CLC 2, 22**
    See also CA 45-48; 37-40R; CANR 33; DLB
    15, 139; MTCW
Hartman, Geoffrey H. 1929-   **CLC 27**
    See also CA 117; 125; DLB 67
Hartmann, Sadakichi 1867-1944   **TCLC 73**
    See also CA 157; DLB 54
Hartmann von Aue c. 1160-c. 1205 **CMLC 15**
    See also DLB 138
Hartmann von Aue 1170-1210   **CMLC 15**
Haruf, Kent 1943-   **CLC 34**
    See also CA 149
Harwood, Ronald 1934-   **CLC 32; DAM
    DRAM, MST**
    See also CA 1-4R; CANR 4, 55; DLB 13
Hasegawa Tatsunosuke
    See Futabatei, Shimei
Hasek, Jaroslav (Matej Frantisek) 1883-1923
    TCLC 4
    See also CA 104; 129; MTCW
Hass, Robert 1941-   **CLC 18, 39, 99; PC 16**
    See also CA 111; CANR 30, 50; DLB 105;
    SATA 94
Hastings, Hudson
    See Kuttner, Henry
Hastings, Selina   **CLC 44**
Hathorne, John 1641-1717   **LC 38**
Hatteras, Amelia
    See Mencken, H(enry) L(ouis)
Hatteras, Owen   **TCLC 18**
    See also Mencken, H(enry) L(ouis); Nathan,
    George Jean

Hauptmann, Gerhart (Johann Robert) 1862-
    1946   **TCLC 4; DAM DRAM**
    See also CA 104; 153; DLB 66, 118
Havel, Vaclav 1936-   **CLC 25, 58, 65; DAM
    DRAM; DC 6**
    See also CA 104; CANR 36, 63; MTCW
Haviaras, Stratis   **CLC 33**
    See also Chaviaras, Strates
Hawes, Stephen 1475(?)-1523(?)   **LC 17**
    See also DLB 132
Hawkes, John (Clendennin Burne, Jr.) 1925-
    CLC 1, 2, 3, 4, 7, 9, 14, 15, 27, 49
    See also CA 1-4R; CANR 2, 47, 64; DLB 2, 7;
    DLBY 80; MTCW
Hawking, S. W.
    See Hawking, Stephen W(illiam)
Hawking, Stephen W(illiam) 1942- **CLC 63,
    105**
    See also AAYA 13; BEST 89:1; CA 126; 129;
    CANR 48
Hawkins, Anthony Hope
    See Hope, Anthony
Hawthorne, Julian 1846-1934   **TCLC 25**
    See also CA 165
Hawthorne, Nathaniel 1804-1864   **NCLC 39;
    DA; DAB; DAC; DAM MST, NOV; SSC
    3, 29; WLC**
    See also AAYA 18; CDALB 1640-1865; DLB
    1, 74; YABC 2
Haxton, Josephine Ayres 1921-
    See Douglas, Ellen
    See also CA 115; CANR 41
Hayaseca y Eizaguirre, Jorge
    See Echegaray (y Eizaguirre), Jose (Maria
    Waldo)
Hayashi, Fumiko 1904-1951   **TCLC 27**
    See also CA 161; DLB 180
Haycraft, Anna
    See Ellis, Alice Thomas
    See also CA 122
Hayden, Robert E(arl) 1913-1980   **CLC 5, 9,
    14, 37; BLC 2; DA; DAC; DAM MST,
    MULT, POET; PC 6**
    See also BW 1; CA 69-72; 97-100; CABS 2;
    CANR 24; CDALB 1941-1968; DLB 5, 76;
    MTCW; SATA 19; SATA-Obit 26
Hayford, J(oseph) E(phraim) Casely
    See Casely-Hayford, J(oseph) E(phraim)
Hayman, Ronald 1932-   **CLC 44**
    See also CA 25-28R; CANR 18, 50; DLB 155
Haywood, Eliza 1693(?)-1756   **LC 44**
    See also DLB 39
Haywood, Eliza (Fowler) 1693(?)-1756 **LC 1,
    44**
Hazlitt, William 1778-1830   **NCLC 29**
    See also DLB 110, 158
Hazzard, Shirley 1931-   **CLC 18**
    See also CA 9-12R; CANR 4; DLBY 82;
    MTCW
Head, Bessie 1937-1986 **CLC 25, 67; BLC 2;
    DAM MULT**
    See also BW 2; CA 29-32R; 119; CANR 25;
    DLB 117; MTCW
Headon, (Nicky) Topper 1956(?)-   **CLC 30**
Heaney, Seamus (Justin) 1939- **CLC 5, 7, 14,
    25, 37, 74, 91; DAB; DAM POET; PC 18;
    WLCS**
    See also CA 85-88; CANR 25, 48; CDBLB
    1960 to Present; DLB 40; DLBY 95; MTCW
Hearn, (Patricio) Lafcadio (Tessima Carlos)
    1850-1904   **TCLC 9**
    See also CA 105; 166; DLB 12, 78
Hearne, Vicki 1946-   **CLC 56**

See also CA 139

Hearon, Shelby 1931-   **CLC 63**
See also AITN 2; CA 25-28R; CANR 18, 48

Heat-Moon, William Least   **CLC 29**
See also Trogdon, William (Lewis)
See also AAYA 9

Hebbel, Friedrich 1813-1863 **NCLC 43; DAM
  DRAM**
See also DLB 129

Hebert, Anne 1916-**CLC 4, 13, 29; DAC; DAM
  MST, POET**
See also CA 85-88; CANR 69; DLB 68; MTCW

Hecht, Anthony (Evan) 1923- **CLC 8, 13, 19;
  DAM POET**
See also CA 9-12R; CANR 6; DLB 5, 169

Hecht, Ben 1894-1964   **CLC 8**
See also CA 85-88; DLB 7, 9, 25, 26, 28, 86

Hedayat, Sadeq 1903-1951   **TCLC 21**
See also CA 120

Hegel, Georg Wilhelm Friedrich 1770-1831
  NCLC 46
See also DLB 90

Heidegger, Martin 1889-1976   **CLC 24**
See also CA 81-84; 65-68; CANR 34; MTCW

Heidenstam, (Carl Gustaf) Verner von 1859-
  1940   **TCLC 5**
See also CA 104

Heifner, Jack 1946-   **CLC 11**
See also CA 105; CANR 47

Heijermans, Herman 1864-1924   **TCLC 24**
See also CA 123

Heilbrun, Carolyn G(old) 1926-   **CLC 25**
See also CA 45-48; CANR 1, 28, 58

Heine, Heinrich 1797-1856   **NCLC 4, 54**
See also DLB 90

Heinemann, Larry (Curtiss) 1944-   **CLC 50**
See also CA 110; CAAS 21; CANR 31; DLBD
  9; INT CANR-31

Heiney, Donald (William) 1921-1993
See Harris, MacDonald
See also CA 1-4R; 142; CANR 3, 58

Heinlein, Robert A(nson) 1907-1988**CLC 1, 3,
  8, 14, 26, 55; DAM POP**
See also AAYA 17; CA 1-4R; 125; CANR 1,
  20, 53; DLB 8; JRDA; MAICYA; MTCW;
  SATA 9, 69; SATA-Obit 56

Helforth, John
See Doolittle, Hilda

Hellenhofferu, Vojtech Kapristian z
See Hasek, Jaroslav (Matej Frantisek)

Heller, Joseph 1923-**CLC 1, 3, 5, 8, 11, 36, 63;
  DA; DAB; DAC; DAM MST, NOV, POP;
  WLC**
See also AAYA 24; AITN 1; CA 5-8R; CABS
  1; CANR 8, 42, 66; DLB 2, 28; DLBY 80;
  INT CANR-8; MTCW

Hellman, Lillian (Florence) 1906-1984**CLC 2,
  4, 8, 14, 18, 34, 44, 52; DAM DRAM; DC 1**
See also AITN 1, 2; CA 13-16R; 112; CANR
  33; DLB 7; DLBY 84; MTCW

Helprin, Mark 1947-**CLC 7, 10, 22, 32; DAM
  NOV, POP**
See also CA 81-84; CANR 47, 64; DLBY 85;
  MTCW

Helvetius, Claude-Adrien 1715-1771   **LC 26**

Helyar, Jane Penelope Josephine 1933-
See Poole, Josephine
See also CA 21-24R; CANR 10, 26; SATA 82

Hemans, Felicia 1793-1835   **NCLC 71**
See also DLB 96

Hemingway, Ernest (Miller) 1899-1961 **CLC
  1, 3, 6, 8, 10, 13, 19, 30, 34, 39, 41, 44, 50,
  61, 80; DA; DAB; DAC; DAM MST, NOV;**

SSC 25; WLC
See also AAYA 19; CA 77-80; CANR 34;
  CDALB 1917-1929; DLB 4, 9, 102; DLBD
  1, 15, 16; DLBY 81, 87, 96; MTCW

Hempel, Amy 1951-   **CLC 39**
See also CA 118; 137

Henderson, F. C.
See Mencken, H(enry) L(ouis)

Henderson, Sylvia
See Ashton-Warner, Sylvia (Constance)

Henderson, Zenna (Chlarson) 1917-1983 **SSC
  29**
See also CA 1-4R; 133; CANR 1; DLB 8; SATA
  5

Henley, Beth   **CLC 23; DC 6**
See also Henley, Elizabeth Becker
See also CABS 3; DLBY 86

Henley, Elizabeth Becker 1952-
See Henley, Beth
See also CA 107; CANR 32; DAM DRAM,
  MST; MTCW

Henley, William Ernest 1849-1903   **TCLC 8**
See also CA 105; DLB 19

Hennissart, Martha
See Lathen, Emma
See also CA 85-88; CANR 64

Henry, O.   **TCLC 1, 19; SSC 5; WLC**
See also Porter, William Sydney

Henry, Patrick 1736-1799   **LC 25**

Henryson, Robert 1430(?)-1506(?)   **LC 20**
See also DLB 146

Henry VIII 1491-1547   **LC 10**

Henschke, Alfred
See Klabund

Hentoff, Nat(han Irving) 1925-   **CLC 26**
See also AAYA 4; CA 1-4R; CAAS 6; CANR
  5, 25; CLR 1, 52; INT CANR-25; JRDA;
  MAICYA; SATA 42, 69; SATA-Brief 27

Heppenstall, (John) Rayner 1911-1981   **CLC
  10**
See also CA 1-4R; 103; CANR 29

Heraclitus c. 540B.C.-c. 450B.C.   **CMLC 22**
See also DLB 176

Herbert, Frank (Patrick) 1920-1986 **CLC 12,
  23, 35, 44, 85; DAM POP**
See also AAYA 21; CA 53-56; 118; CANR 5,
  43; DLB 8; INT CANR-5; MTCW; SATA 9,
  37; SATA-Obit 47

Herbert, George 1593-1633   **LC 24; DAB;
  DAM POET; PC 4**
See also CDBLB Before 1660; DLB 126

Herbert, Zbigniew 1924-   **CLC 9, 43; DAM
  POET**
See also CA 89-92; CANR 36; MTCW

Herbst, Josephine (Frey) 1897-1969   **CLC 34**
See also CA 5-8R; 25-28R; DLB 9

Hergesheimer, Joseph 1880-1954   **TCLC 11**
See also CA 109; DLB 102, 9

Herlihy, James Leo 1927-1993   **CLC 6**
See also CA 1-4R; 143; CANR 2

Hermogenes fl. c. 175-   **CMLC 6**

Hernandez, Jose 1834-1886   **NCLC 17**

Herodotus c. 484B.C.-429B.C.   **CMLC 17**
See also DLB 176

Herrick, Robert 1591-1674 **LC 13; DA; DAB;
  DAC; DAM MST, POP; PC 9**
See also DLB 126

Herring, Guilles
See Somerville, Edith

Herriot, James 1916-1995**CLC 12; DAM POP**
See also Wight, James Alfred
See also AAYA 1; CA 148; CANR 40; SATA
  86

Herrmann, Dorothy 1941-   **CLC 44**
See also CA 107

Herrmann, Taffy
See Herrmann, Dorothy

Hersey, John (Richard) 1914-1993**CLC 1, 2, 7,
  9, 40, 81, 97; DAM POP**
See also CA 17-20R; 140; CANR 33; DLB 6,
  185; MTCW; SATA 25; SATA-Obit 76

Herzen, Aleksandr Ivanovich 1812-1870
  NCLC 10, 61

Herzl, Theodor 1860-1904   **TCLC 36**

Herzog, Werner 1942-   **CLC 16**
See also CA 89-92

Hesiod c. 8th cent. B.C.-   **CMLC 5**
See also DLB 176

Hesse, Hermann 1877-1962**CLC 1, 2, 3, 6, 11,
  17, 25, 69; DA; DAB; DAC; DAM MST,
  NOV; SSC 9; WLC**
See also CA 17-18; CAP 2; DLB 66; MTCW;
  SATA 50

Hewes, Cady
See De Voto, Bernard (Augustine)

Heyen, William 1940-   **CLC 13, 18**
See also CA 33-36R; CAAS 9; DLB 5

Heyerdahl, Thor 1914-   **CLC 26**
See also CA 5-8R; CANR 5, 22, 66; MTCW;
  SATA 2, 52

Heym, Georg (Theodor Franz Arthur) 1887-
  1912   **TCLC 9**
See also CA 106

Heym, Stefan 1913-   **CLC 41**
See also CA 9-12R; CANR 4; DLB 69

Heyse, Paul (Johann Ludwig von) 1830-1914
  TCLC 8
See also CA 104; DLB 129

Heyward, (Edwin) DuBose 1885-1940 **TCLC
  59**
See also CA 108; 157; DLB 7, 9, 45; SATA 21

Hibbert, Eleanor Alice Burford 1906-1993
  CLC 7; DAM POP
See also BEST 90:4; CA 17-20R; 140; CANR
  9, 28, 59; SATA 2; SATA-Obit 74

Hichens, Robert (Smythe) 1864-1950   **TCLC
  64**
See also CA 162; DLB 153

Higgins, George V(incent) 1939-**CLC 4, 7, 10,
  18**
See also CA 77-80; CAAS 5; CANR 17, 51;
  DLB 2; DLBY 81; INT CANR-17; MTCW

Higginson, Thomas Wentworth 1823-1911
  TCLC 36
See also CA 162; DLB 1, 64

Highet, Helen
See MacInnes, Helen (Clark)

Highsmith, (Mary) Patricia 1921-1995**CLC 2,
  4, 14, 42, 102; DAM NOV, POP**
See also CA 1-4R; 147; CANR 1, 20, 48, 62;
  MTCW

Highwater, Jamake (Mamake) 1942(?)- **CLC
  12**
See also AAYA 7; CA 65-68; CAAS 7; CANR
  10, 34; CLR 17; DLB 52; DLBY 85; JRDA;
  MAICYA; SATA 32, 69; SATA-Brief 30

Highway, Tomson 1951-**CLC 92; DAC; DAM
  MULT**
See also CA 151; NNAL

Higuchi, Ichiyo 1872-1896   **NCLC 49**

Hijuelos, Oscar 1951- **CLC 65; DAM MULT,
  POP; HLC**
See also AAYA 25; BEST 90:1; CA 123; CANR
  50; DLB 145; HW

Hikmet, Nazim 1902(?)-1963   **CLC 40**
See also CA 141; 93-96

Hildegard von Bingen 1098-1179 **CMLC 20**
See also DLB 148

Hildesheimer, Wolfgang 1916-1991 **CLC 49**
See also CA 101; 135; DLB 69, 124

Hill, Geoffrey (William) 1932- **CLC 5, 8, 18, 45; DAM POET**
See also CA 81-84; CANR 21; CDBLB 1960 to Present; DLB 40; MTCW

Hill, George Roy 1921- **CLC 26**
See also CA 110; 122

Hill, John
See Koontz, Dean R(ay)

Hill, Susan (Elizabeth) 1942- **CLC 4, 113; DAB; DAM MST, NOV**
See also CA 33-36R; CANR 29, 69; DLB 14, 139; MTCW

Hillerman, Tony 1925- **CLC 62; DAM POP**
See also AAYA 6; BEST 89:1; CA 29-32R; CANR 21, 42, 65; SATA 6

Hillesum, Etty 1914-1943 **TCLC 49**
See also CA 137

Hilliard, Noel (Harvey) 1929- **CLC 15**
See also CA 9-12R; CANR 7, 69

Hillis, Rick 1956- **CLC 66**
See also CA 134

Hilton, James 1900-1954 **TCLC 21**
See also CA 108; DLB 34, 77; SATA 34

Himes, Chester (Bomar) 1909-1984 **CLC 2, 4, 7, 18, 58, 108; BLC 2; DAM MULT**
See also BW 2; CA 25-28R; 114; CANR 22; DLB 2, 76, 143; MTCW

Hinde, Thomas **CLC 6, 11**
See also Chitty, Thomas Willes

Hindin, Nathan
See Bloch, Robert (Albert)

Hine, (William) Daryl 1936- **CLC 15**
See also CA 1-4R; CAAS 15; CANR 1, 20; DLB 60

Hinkson, Katharine Tynan
See Tynan, Katharine

Hinton, S(usan) E(loise) 1950- **CLC 30, 111; DA; DAB; DAC; DAM MST, NOV**
See also AAYA 2; CA 81-84; CANR 32, 62; CLR 3, 23; JRDA; MAICYA; MTCW; SATA 19, 58

Hippius, Zinaida **TCLC 9**
See also Gippius, Zinaida (Nikolayevna)

Hiraoka, Kimitake 1925-1970
See Mishima, Yukio
See also CA 97-100; 29-32R; DAM DRAM; MTCW

Hirsch, E(ric) D(onald), Jr. 1928- **CLC 79**
See also CA 25-28R; CANR 27, 51; DLB 67; INT CANR-27; MTCW

Hirsch, Edward 1950- **CLC 31, 50**
See also CA 104; CANR 20, 42; DLB 120

Hitchcock, Alfred (Joseph) 1899-1980**CLC 16**
See also AAYA 22; CA 159; 97-100; SATA 27; SATA-Obit 24

Hitler, Adolf 1889-1945 **TCLC 53**
See also CA 117; 147

Hoagland, Edward 1932- **CLC 28**
See also CA 1-4R; CANR 2, 31, 57; DLB 6; SATA 51

Hoban, Russell (Conwell) 1925- **CLC 7, 25; DAM NOV**
See also CA 5-8R; CANR 23, 37, 66; CLR 3; DLB 52; MAICYA; MTCW; SATA 1, 40, 78

Hobbes, Thomas 1588-1679 **LC 36**
See also DLB 151

Hobbs, Perry
See Blackmur, R(ichard) P(almer)

Hobson, Laura Z(ametkin) 1900-1986 **CLC 7,**
25
See also CA 17-20R; 118; CANR 55; DLB 28; SATA 52

Hochhuth, Rolf 1931- **CLC 4, 11, 18; DAM DRAM**
See also CA 5-8R; CANR 33; DLB 124; MTCW

Hochman, Sandra 1936- **CLC 3, 8**
See also CA 5-8R; DLB 5

Hochwaelder, Fritz 1911-1986 **CLC 36; DAM DRAM**
See also CA 29-32R; 120; CANR 42; MTCW

Hochwalder, Fritz
See Hochwaelder, Fritz

Hocking, Mary (Eunice) 1921- **CLC 13**
See also CA 101; CANR 18, 40

Hodgins, Jack 1938- **CLC 23**
See also CA 93-96; DLB 60

Hodgson, William Hope 1877(?)-1918 **TCLC 13**
See also CA 111; 164; DLB 70, 153, 156, 178

Hoeg, Peter 1957- **CLC 95**
See also CA 151

Hoffman, Alice 1952- **CLC 51; DAM NOV**
See also CA 77-80; CANR 34, 66; MTCW

Hoffman, Daniel (Gerard) 1923-**CLC 6, 13, 23**
See also CA 1-4R; CANR 4; DLB 5

Hoffman, Stanley 1944- **CLC 5**
See also CA 77-80

Hoffman, William M(oses) 1939- **CLC 40**
See also CA 57-60; CANR 11

Hoffmann, E(rnst) T(heodor) A(madeus) 1776-1822 **NCLC 2; SSC 13**
See also DLB 90; SATA 27

Hofmann, Gert 1931- **CLC 54**
See also CA 128

Hofmannsthal, Hugo von 1874-1929**TCLC 11; DAM DRAM; DC 4**
See also CA 106; 153; DLB 81, 118

Hogan, Linda 1947- **CLC 73; DAM MULT**
See also CA 120; CANR 45, 69; DLB 175; NNAL

Hogarth, Charles
See Creasey, John

Hogarth, Emmett
See Polonsky, Abraham (Lincoln)

Hogg, James 1770-1835 **NCLC 4**
See also DLB 93, 116, 159

Holbach, Paul Henri Thiry Baron 1723-1789 **LC 14**

Holberg, Ludvig 1684-1754 **LC 6**

Holden, Ursula 1921- **CLC 18**
See also CA 101; CAAS 8; CANR 22

Holderlin, (Johann Christian) Friedrich 1770-1843 **NCLC 16; PC 4**

Holdstock, Robert
See Holdstock, Robert P.

Holdstock, Robert P. 1948- **CLC 39**
See also CA 131

Holland, Isabelle 1920- **CLC 21**
See also AAYA 11; CA 21-24R; CANR 10, 25, 47; JRDA; MAICYA; SATA 8, 70

Holland, Marcus
See Caldwell, (Janet Miriam) Taylor (Holland)

Hollander, John 1929- **CLC 2, 5, 8, 14**
See also CA 1-4R; CANR 1, 52; DLB 5; SATA 13

Hollander, Paul
See Silverberg, Robert

Holleran, Andrew 1943(?)- **CLC 38**
See also CA 144

Hollinghurst, Alan 1954- **CLC 55, 91**
See also CA 114

Hollis, Jim
See Summers, Hollis (Spurgeon, Jr.)

Holly, Buddy 1936-1959 **TCLC 65**

Holmes, Gordon
See Shiel, M(atthew) P(hipps)

Holmes, John
See Souster, (Holmes) Raymond

Holmes, John Clellon 1926-1988 **CLC 56**
See also CA 9-12R; 125; CANR 4; DLB 16

Holmes, Oliver Wendell, Jr. 1841-1935 **TCLC 77**
See also CA 114

Holmes, Oliver Wendell 1809-1894 **NCLC 14**
See also CDALB 1640-1865; DLB 1, 189; SATA 34

Holmes, Raymond
See Souster, (Holmes) Raymond

Holt, Victoria
See Hibbert, Eleanor Alice Burford

Holub, Miroslav 1923- **CLC 4**
See also CA 21-24R; CANR 10

Homer c. 8th cent. B.C.- **CMLC 1, 16; DA; DAB; DAC; DAM MST, POET; PC 23; WLCS**
See also DLB 176

Hongo, Garrett Kaoru 1951- **PC 23**
See also CA 133; CAAS 22; DLB 120

Honig, Edwin 1919- **CLC 33**
See also CA 5-8R; CAAS 8; CANR 4, 45; DLB 5

Hood, Hugh (John Blagdon) 1928-**CLC 15, 28**
See also CA 49-52; CAAS 17; CANR 1, 33; DLB 53

Hood, Thomas 1799-1845 **NCLC 16**
See also DLB 96

Hooker, (Peter) Jeremy 1941- **CLC 43**
See also CA 77-80; CANR 22; DLB 40

Hooks, bell **CLC 94; BLCS**
See also Watkins, Gloria

Hope, A(lec) D(erwent) 1907- **CLC 3, 51**
See also CA 21-24R; CANR 33; MTCW

Hope, Anthony 1863-1933 **TCLC 83**
See also CA 157; DLB 153, 156

Hope, Brian
See Creasey, John

Hope, Christopher (David Tully) 1944- **CLC 52**
See also CA 106; CANR 47; SATA 62

Hopkins, Gerard Manley 1844-1889 **NCLC 17; DA; DAB; DAC; DAM MST, POET; PC 15; WLC**
See also CDBLB 1890-1914; DLB 35, 57

Hopkins, John (Richard) 1931- **CLC 4**
See also CA 85-88

Hopkins, Pauline Elizabeth 1859-1930 **TCLC 28; BLC 2; DAM MULT**
See also BW 2; CA 141; DLB 50

Hopkinson, Francis 1737-1791 **LC 25**
See also DLB 31

Hopley-Woolrich, Cornell George 1903-1968
See Woolrich, Cornell
See also CA 13-14; CANR 58; CAP 1

Horatio
See Proust, (Valentin-Louis-George-Eugene-) Marcel

Horgan, Paul (George Vincent O'Shaughnessy) 1903-1995 **CLC 9, 53; DAM NOV**
See also CA 13-16R; 147; CANR 9, 35; DLB 102; DLBY 85; INT CANR-9; MTCW; SATA 13; SATA-Obit 84

Horn, Peter
See Kuttner, Henry

Hornem, Horace Esq.
See Byron, George Gordon (Noel)

Horney, Karen (Clementine Theodore Danielsen) 1885-1952   **TCLC 71**
See also CA 114; 165

Hornung, E(rnest) W(illiam) 1866-1921   **TCLC 59**
See also CA 108; 160; DLB 70

Horovitz, Israel (Arthur) 1939-**CLC 56; DAM DRAM**
See also CA 33-36R; CANR 46, 59; DLB 7

Horvath, Odon von
See Horvath, Oedoen von
See also DLB 85, 124

Horvath, Oedoen von 1901-1938   **TCLC 45**
See also Horvath, Odon von
See also CA 118

Horwitz, Julius 1920-1986   **CLC 14**
See also CA 9-12R; 119; CANR 12

Hospital, Janette Turner 1942-   **CLC 42**
See also CA 108; CANR 48

Hostos, E. M. de
See Hostos (y Bonilla), Eugenio Maria de

Hostos, Eugenio M. de
See Hostos (y Bonilla), Eugenio Maria de

Hostos, Eugenio Maria
See Hostos (y Bonilla), Eugenio Maria de

Hostos (y Bonilla), Eugenio Maria de 1839-1903   **TCLC 24**
See also CA 123; 131; HW

Houdini
See Lovecraft, H(oward) P(hillips)

Hougan, Carolyn 1943-   **CLC 34**
See also CA 139

Household, Geoffrey (Edward West) 1900-1988   **CLC 11**
See also CA 77-80; 126; CANR 58; DLB 87; SATA 14; SATA-Obit 59

Housman, A(lfred) E(dward) 1859-1936   **TCLC 1, 10; DA; DAB; DAC; DAM MST, POET; PC 2; WLCS**
See also CA 104; 125; DLB 19; MTCW

Housman, Laurence 1865-1959   **TCLC 7**
See also CA 106; 155; DLB 10; SATA 25

Howard, Elizabeth Jane 1923-   **CLC 7, 29**
See also CA 5-8R; CANR 8, 62

Howard, Maureen 1930-   **CLC 5, 14, 46**
See also CA 53-56; CANR 31; DLBY 83; INT CANR-31; MTCW

Howard, Richard 1929-   **CLC 7, 10, 47**
See also AITN 1; CA 85-88; CANR 25; DLB 5; INT CANR-25

Howard, Robert E(rvin) 1906-1936   **TCLC 8**
See also CA 105; 157

Howard, Warren F.
See Pohl, Frederik

Howe, Fanny 1940-   **CLC 47**
See also CA 117; CAAS 27; SATA-Brief 52

Howe, Irving 1920-1993   **CLC 85**
See also CA 9-12R; 141; CANR 21, 50; DLB 67; MTCW

Howe, Julia Ward 1819-1910   **TCLC 21**
See also CA 117; DLB 1, 189

Howe, Susan 1937-   **CLC 72**
See also CA 160; DLB 120

Howe, Tina 1937-   **CLC 48**
See also CA 109

Howell, James 1594(?)-1666   **LC 13**
See also DLB 151

Howells, W. D.
See Howells, William Dean

Howells, William D.
See Howells, William Dean

Howells, William Dean 1837-1920**TCLC 7, 17, 41**

See also CA 104; 134; CDALB 1865-1917; DLB 12, 64, 74, 79, 189

Howes, Barbara 1914-1996   **CLC 15**
See also CA 9-12R; 151; CAAS 3; CANR 53; SATA 5

Hrabal, Bohumil 1914-1997   **CLC 13, 67**
See also CA 106; 156; CAAS 12; CANR 57

Hroswitha of Gandersheim c. 935-c. 1002   **CMLC 29**
See also DLB 148

Hsun, Lu
See Lu Hsun

Hubbard, L(afayette) Ron(ald) 1911-1986   **CLC 43; DAM POP**
See also CA 77-80; 118; CANR 52

Huch, Ricarda (Octavia) 1864-1947 **TCLC 13**
See also CA 111; DLB 66

Huddle, David 1942-   **CLC 49**
See also CA 57-60; CAAS 20; DLB 130

Hudson, Jeffrey
See Crichton, (John) Michael

Hudson, W(illiam) H(enry) 1841-1922 **TCLC 29**
See also CA 115; DLB 98, 153, 174; SATA 35

Hueffer, Ford Madox
See Ford, Ford Madox

Hughart, Barry 1934-   **CLC 39**
See also CA 137

Hughes, Colin
See Creasey, John

Hughes, David (John) 1930-   **CLC 48**
See also CA 116; 129; DLB 14

Hughes, Edward James
See Hughes, Ted
See also DAM MST, POET

Hughes, (James) Langston 1902-1967 **CLC 1, 5, 10, 15, 35, 44, 108; BLC 2; DA; DAB; DAC; DAM DRAM, MST, MULT, POET; DC 3; PC 1; SSC 6; WLC**
See also AAYA 12; BW 1; CA 1-4R; 25-28R; CANR 1, 34; CDALB 1929-1941; CLR 17; DLB 4, 7, 48, 51, 86; JRDA; MAICYA; MTCW; SATA 4, 33

Hughes, Richard (Arthur Warren) 1900-1976   **CLC 1, 11; DAM NOV**
See also CA 5-8R; 65-68; CANR 4; DLB 15, 161; MTCW; SATA 8; SATA-Obit 25

Hughes, Ted 1930- **CLC 2, 4, 9, 14, 37; DAB; DAC; PC 7**
See also Hughes, Edward James
See also CA 1-4R; CANR 1, 33, 66; CLR 3; DLB 40, 161; MAICYA; MTCW; SATA 49; SATA-Brief 27

Hugo, Richard F(ranklin) 1923-1982 **CLC 6, 18, 32; DAM POET**
See also CA 49-52; 108; CANR 3; DLB 5

Hugo, Victor (Marie) 1802-1885 **NCLC 3, 10, 21; DA; DAB; DAC; DAM DRAM, MST, NOV, POET; PC 17; WLC**
See also DLB 119, 192; SATA 47

Huidobro, Vicente
See Huidobro Fernandez, Vicente Garcia

Huidobro Fernandez, Vicente Garcia 1893-1948   **TCLC 31**
See also CA 131; HW

Hulme, Keri 1947-   **CLC 39**
See also CA 125; CANR 69; INT 125

Hulme, T(homas) E(rnest) 1883-1917 **TCLC 21**
See also CA 117; DLB 19

Hume, David 1711-1776   **LC 7**
See also DLB 104

Humphrey, William 1924-1997   **CLC 45**

See also CA 77-80; 160; CANR 68; DLB 6

Humphreys, Emyr Owen 1919-   **CLC 47**
See also CA 5-8R; CANR 3, 24; DLB 15

Humphreys, Josephine 1945-   **CLC 34, 57**
See also CA 121; 127; INT 127

Huneker, James Gibbons 1857-1921 **TCLC 65**
See also DLB 71

Hungerford, Pixie
See Brinsmead, H(esba) F(ay)

Hunt, E(verette) Howard, (Jr.) 1918- **CLC 3**
See also AITN 1; CA 45-48; CANR 2, 47

Hunt, Kyle
See Creasey, John

Hunt, (James Henry) Leigh 1784-1859 **NCLC 70; DAM POET**
See also DLB 96, 110, 144

Hunt, (James Henry) Leigh 1784-1859 **NCLC 1; DAM POET**

Hunt, Marsha 1946-   **CLC 70**
See also BW 2; CA 143

Hunt, Violet 1866(?)-1942   **TCLC 53**
See also DLB 162, 197

Hunter, E. Waldo
See Sturgeon, Theodore (Hamilton)

Hunter, Evan 1926- **CLC 11, 31; DAM POP**
See also CA 5-8R; CANR 5, 38, 62; DLBY 82; INT CANR-5; MTCW; SATA 25

Hunter, Kristin (Eggleston) 1931-   **CLC 35**
See also AITN 1; BW 1; CA 13-16R; CANR 13; CLR 3; DLB 33; INT CANR-13; MAICYA; SAAS 10; SATA 12

Hunter, Mollie 1922-   **CLC 21**
See also McIlwraith, Maureen Mollie Hunter
See also AAYA 13; CANR 37; CLR 25; DLB 161; JRDA; MAICYA; SAAS 7; SATA 54

Hunter, Robert (?)-1734   **LC 7**

Hurston, Zora Neale 1903-1960**CLC 7, 30, 61; BLC 2; DA; DAC; DAM MST, MULT, NOV; SSC 4; WLCS**
See also AAYA 15; BW 1; CA 85-88; CANR 61; DLB 51, 86; MTCW

Huston, John (Marcellus) 1906-1987 **CLC 20**
See also CA 73-76; 123; CANR 34; DLB 26

Hustvedt, Siri 1955-   **CLC 76**
See also CA 137

Hutten, Ulrich von 1488-1523   **LC 16**
See also DLB 179

Huxley, Aldous (Leonard) 1894-1963 **CLC 1, 3, 4, 5, 8, 11, 18, 35, 79; DA; DAB; DAC; DAM MST, NOV; WLC**
See also AAYA 11; CA 85-88; CANR 44; CDBLB 1914-1945; DLB 36, 100, 162, 195; MTCW; SATA 63

Huxley, T(homas) H(enry) 1825-1895 **NCLC 67**
See also DLB 57

Huysmans, Joris-Karl 1848-1907 **TCLC 7, 69**
See also CA 104; 165; DLB 123

Hwang, David Henry 1957-   **CLC 55; DAM DRAM; DC 4**
See also CA 127; 132; INT 132

Hyde, Anthony 1946-   **CLC 42**
See also CA 136

Hyde, Margaret O(ldroyd) 1917-   **CLC 21**
See also CA 1-4R; CANR 1, 36; CLR 23; JRDA; MAICYA; SAAS 8; SATA 1, 42, 76

Hynes, James 1956(?)-   **CLC 65**
See also CA 164

Ian, Janis 1951-   **CLC 21**
See also CA 105

Ibanez, Vicente Blasco
See Blasco Ibanez, Vicente

Ibarguengoitia, Jorge 1928-1983   **CLC 37**

Korolenko, Vladimir G.
See Korolenko, Vladimir Galaktionovich
Korolenko, Vladimir Galaktionovich 1853-
1921   **TCLC 22**
See also CA 121
Korzybski, Alfred (Habdank Skarbek) 1879-
1950   **TCLC 61**
See also CA 123; 160
Kosinski, Jerzy (Nikodem) 1933-1991 **CLC 1,
2, 3, 6, 10, 15, 53, 70; DAM NOV**
See also CA 17-20R; 134; CANR 9, 46; DLB
2; DLBY 82; MTCW
Kostelanetz, Richard (Cory) 1940- **CLC 28**
See also CA 13-16R; CAAS 8; CANR 38
Kostrowitzki, Wilhelm Apollinaris de 1880-
1918
See Apollinaire, Guillaume
See also CA 104
Kotlowitz, Robert 1924-   **CLC 4**
See also CA 33-36R; CANR 36
Kotzebue, August (Friedrich Ferdinand) von
1761-1819 **NCLC 25**
See also DLB 94
Kotzwinkle, William 1938-   **CLC 5, 14, 35**
See also CA 45-48; CANR 3, 44; CLR 6; DLB
173; MAICYA; SATA 24, 70
Kowna, Stancy
See Szymborska, Wislawa
Kozol, Jonathan 1936-   **CLC 17**
See also CA 61-64; CANR 16, 45
Kozoll, Michael 1940(?)-   **CLC 35**
Kramer, Kathryn 19(?)-   **CLC 34**
Kramer, Larry 1935-**CLC 42; DAM POP; DC
8**
See also CA 124; 126; CANR 60
Krasicki, Ignacy 1735-1801   **NCLC 8**
Krasinski, Zygmunt 1812-1859   **NCLC 4**
Kraus, Karl 1874-1936   **TCLC 5**
See also CA 104; DLB 118
Kreve (Mickevicius), Vincas 1882-1954**TCLC
27**
Kristeva, Julia 1941-   **CLC 77**
See also CA 154
Kristofferson, Kris 1936-   **CLC 26**
See also CA 104
Krizanc, John 1956-   **CLC 57**
Krleza, Miroslav 1893-1981   **CLC 8**
See also CA 97-100; 105; CANR 50; DLB 147
Kroetsch, Robert 1927- **CLC 5, 23, 57; DAC;
DAM POET**
See also CA 17-20R; CANR 8, 38; DLB 53;
MTCW
Kroetz, Franz
See Kroetz, Franz Xaver
Kroetz, Franz Xaver 1946-   **CLC 41**
See also CA 130
Kroker, Arthur (W.) 1945-   **CLC 77**
See also CA 161
Kropotkin, Peter (Aleksieevich) 1842-1921
TCLC 36
See also CA 119
Krotkov, Yuri 1917-   **CLC 19**
See also CA 102
Krumb
See Crumb, R(obert)
Krumgold, Joseph (Quincy) 1908-1980 **CLC
12**
See also CA 9-12R; 101; CANR 7; MAICYA;
SATA 1, 48; SATA-Obit 23
Krumwitz
See Crumb, R(obert)
Krutch, Joseph Wood 1893-1970   **CLC 24**
See also CA 1-4R; 25-28R; CANR 4; DLB 63

Krutzch, Gus
See Eliot, T(homas) S(tearns)
Krylov, Ivan Andreevich 1768(?)-1844 **NCLC
1**
See also DLB 150
Kubin, Alfred (Leopold Isidor) 1877-1959
TCLC 23
See also CA 112; 149; DLB 81
Kubrick, Stanley 1928-   **CLC 16**
See also CA 81-84; CANR 33; DLB 26
Kumin, Maxine (Winokur) 1925- **CLC 5, 13,
28; DAM POET; PC 15**
See also AITN 2; CA 1-4R; CAAS 8; CANR 1,
21, 69; DLB 5; MTCW; SATA 12
Kundera, Milan 1929- **CLC 4, 9, 19, 32, 68;
DAM NOV; SSC 24**
See also AAYA 2; CA 85-88; CANR 19, 52;
MTCW
Kunene, Mazisi (Raymond) 1930-   **CLC 85**
See also BW 1; CA 125; DLB 117
Kunitz, Stanley (Jasspon) 1905-**CLC 6, 11, 14;
PC 19**
See also CA 41-44R; CANR 26, 57; DLB 48;
INT CANR-26; MTCW
Kunze, Reiner 1933-   **CLC 10**
See also CA 93-96; DLB 75
Kuprin, Aleksandr Ivanovich 1870-1938
TCLC 5
See also CA 104
Kureishi, Hanif 1954(?)-   **CLC 64**
See also CA 139; DLB 194
Kurosawa, Akira 1910-**CLC 16; DAM MULT**
See also AAYA 11; CA 101; CANR 46
Kushner, Tony 1957(?)-**CLC 81; DAM DRAM**
See also CA 144
Kuttner, Henry 1915-1958   **TCLC 10**
See also Vance, Jack
See also CA 107; 157; DLB 8
Kuzma, Greg 1944-   **CLC 7**
See also CA 33-36R
Kuzmin, Mikhail 1872(?)-1936   **TCLC 40**
Kyd, Thomas 1558-1594**LC 22; DAM DRAM;
DC 3**
See also DLB 62
Kyprianos, Iossif
See Samarakis, Antonis
La Bruyere, Jean de 1645-1696   **LC 17**
Lacan, Jacques (Marie Emile) 1901-1981
CLC 75
See also CA 121; 104
Laclos, Pierre Ambroise Francois Choderlos de
1741-1803   **NCLC 4**
La Colere, Francois
See Aragon, Louis
Lacolere, Francois
See Aragon, Louis
La Deshabilleuse
See Simenon, Georges (Jacques Christian)
Lady Gregory
See Gregory, Isabella Augusta (Persse)
Lady of Quality, A
See Bagnold, Enid
**La Fayette, Marie (Madelaine Pioche de la
Vergne Comtes** 1634-1693   **LC 2**
Lafayette, Rene
See Hubbard, L(afayette) Ron(ald)
Laforgue, Jules 1860-1887**NCLC 5, 53; PC 14;
SSC 20**
Lagerkvist, Paer (Fabian) 1891-1974 **CLC 7,
10, 13, 54; DAM DRAM, NOV**
See also Lagerkvist, Par
See also CA 85-88; 49-52; MTCW
Lagerkvist, Par   **SSC 12**

See also Lagerkvist, Paer (Fabian)
Lagerloef, Selma (Ottiliana Lovisa) 1858-1940
TCLC 4, 36
See also Lagerlof, Selma (Ottiliana Lovisa)
See also CA 108; SATA 15
Lagerlof, Selma (Ottiliana Lovisa)
See Lagerloef, Selma (Ottiliana Lovisa)
See also CLR 7; SATA 15
La Guma, (Justin) Alex(ander) 1925-1985
CLC 19; BLCS; DAM NOV
See also BW 1; CA 49-52; 118; CANR 25; DLB
117; MTCW
Laidlaw, A. K.
See Grieve, C(hristopher) M(urray)
Lainez, Manuel Mujica
See Mujica Lainez, Manuel
See also HW
Laing, R(onald) D(avid) 1927-1989 **CLC 95**
See also CA 107; 129; CANR 34; MTCW
Lamartine, Alphonse (Marie Louis Prat) de
1790-1869 **NCLC 11; DAM POET; PC 16**
Lamb, Charles 1775-1834   **NCLC 10; DA;
DAB; DAC; DAM MST; WLC**
See also CDBLB 1789-1832; DLB 93, 107, 163;
SATA 17
Lamb, Lady Caroline 1785-1828   **NCLC 38**
See also DLB 116
Lamming, George (William) 1927- **CLC 2, 4,
66; BLC 2; DAM MULT**
See also BW 2; CA 85-88; CANR 26; DLB 125;
MTCW
L'Amour, Louis (Dearborn) 1908-1988 **CLC
25, 55; DAM NOV, POP**
See also AAYA 16; AITN 2; BEST 89:2; CA 1-
4R; 125; CANR 3, 25, 40; DLBY 80; MTCW
Lampedusa, Giuseppe (Tomasi) di 1896-1957
TCLC 13
See also Tomasi di Lampedusa, Giuseppe
See also CA 164; DLB 177
Lampman, Archibald 1861-1899   **NCLC 25**
See also DLB 92
Lancaster, Bruce 1896-1963   **CLC 36**
See also CA 9-10; CAP 1; SATA 9
Lanchester, John   **CLC 99**
Landau, Mark Alexandrovich
See Aldanov, Mark (Alexandrovich)
Landau-Aldanov, Mark Alexandrovich
See Aldanov, Mark (Alexandrovich)
Landis, Jerry
See Simon, Paul (Frederick)
Landis, John 1950-   **CLC 26**
See also CA 112; 122
Landolfi, Tommaso 1908-1979   **CLC 11, 49**
See also CA 127; 117; DLB 177
Landon, Letitia Elizabeth 1802-1838 **NCLC
15**
See also DLB 96
Landor, Walter Savage 1775-1864 **NCLC 14**
See also DLB 93, 107
Landwirth, Heinz 1927-
See Lind, Jakov
See also CA 9-12R; CANR 7
Lane, Patrick 1939-   **CLC 25; DAM POET**
See also CA 97-100; CANR 54; DLB 53; INT
97-100
Lang, Andrew 1844-1912   **TCLC 16**
See also CA 114; 137; DLB 98, 141, 184;
MAICYA; SATA 16
Lang, Fritz 1890-1976   **CLC 20, 103**
See also CA 77-80; 69-72; CANR 30
Lange, John
See Crichton, (John) Michael
Langer, Elinor 1939-   **CLC 34**

See also CA 121

Langland, William 1330(?)-1400(?)   **LC 19;**
    DA; DAB; DAC; DAM MST, POET
    See also DLB 146

Langstaff, Launcelot
    See Irving, Washington

Lanier, Sidney 1842-1881   **NCLC 6; DAM**
    POET
    See also DLB 64; DLBD 13; MAICYA; SATA
    18

Lanyer, Aemilia 1569-1645   **LC 10, 30**
    See also DLB 121

Lao Tzu   **CMLC 7**

Lapine, James (Elliot) 1949-   **CLC 39**
    See also CA 123; 130; CANR 54; INT 130

Larbaud, Valery (Nicolas) 1881-1957 **TCLC 9**
    See also CA 106; 152

Lardner, Ring
    See Lardner, Ring(gold) W(ilmer)

Lardner, Ring W., Jr.
    See Lardner, Ring(gold) W(ilmer)

Lardner, Ring(gold) W(ilmer) 1885-1933
    TCLC 2, 14
    See also CA 104; 131; CDALB 1917-1929;
    DLB 11, 25, 86; DLBD 16; MTCW

Laredo, Betty
    See Codrescu, Andrei

Larkin, Maia
    See Wojciechowska, Maia (Teresa)

Larkin, Philip (Arthur) 1922-1985**CLC 3, 5, 8,**
    9, 13, 18, 33, 39, 64; DAB; DAM MST,
    POET; PC 21
    See also CA 5-8R; 117; CANR 24, 62; CDBLB
    1960 to Present; DLB 27; MTCW

Larra (y Sanchez de Castro), Mariano Jose de
    1809-1837   **NCLC 17**

Larsen, Eric 1941-   **CLC 55**
    See also CA 132

Larsen, Nella 1891-1964   **CLC 37; BLC 2;**
    DAM MULT
    See also BW 1; CA 125; DLB 51

Larson, Charles R(aymond) 1938-   **CLC 31**
    See also CA 53-56; CANR 4

Larson, Jonathan 1961-1996   **CLC 99**
    See also CA 156

Las Casas, Bartolome de 1474-1566   **LC 31**

Lasch, Christopher 1932-1994   **CLC 102**
    See also CA 73-76; 144; CANR 25; MTCW

Lasker-Schueler, Else 1869-1945   **TCLC 57**
    See also DLB 66, 124

Laski, Harold 1893-1950   **TCLC 79**

Latham, Jean Lee 1902-1995   **CLC 12**
    See also AITN 1; CA 5-8R; CANR 7; CLR 50;
    MAICYA; SATA 2, 68

Latham, Mavis
    See Clark, Mavis Thorpe

Lathen, Emma   **CLC 2**
    See also Hennissart, Martha; Latsis, Mary J(ane)

Lathrop, Francis
    See Leiber, Fritz (Reuter, Jr.)

Latsis, Mary J(ane) 1927(?)-1997
    See Lathen, Emma
    See also CA 85-88; 162

Lattimore, Richmond (Alexander) 1906-1984
    CLC 3
    See also CA 1-4R; 112; CANR 1

Laughlin, James 1914-1997   **CLC 49**
    See also CA 21-24R; 162; CAAS 22; CANR 9,
    47; DLB 48; DLBY 96, 97

Laurence, (Jean) Margaret (Wemyss) 1926-
    1987   **CLC 3, 6, 13, 50, 62; DAC; DAM**
    MST; SSC 7
    See also CA 5-8R; 121; CANR 33; DLB 53;

MTCW; SATA-Obit 50

Laurent, Antoine 1952-   **CLC 50**

Lauscher, Hermann
    See Hesse, Hermann

Lautreamont, Comte de 1846-1870 **NCLC 12;**
    SSC 14

Laverty, Donald
    See Blish, James (Benjamin)

Lavin, Mary 1912-1996 **CLC 4, 18, 99; SSC 4**
    See also CA 9-12R; 151; CANR 33; DLB 15;
    MTCW

Lavond, Paul Dennis
    See Kornbluth, C(yril) M.; Pohl, Frederik

Lawler, Raymond Evenor 1922-   **CLC 58**
    See also CA 103

Lawrence, D(avid) H(erbert Richards) 1885-
    1930**TCLC 2, 9, 16, 33, 48, 61; DA; DAB;**
    DAC; DAM MST, NOV, POET; SSC 4, 19;
    WLC
    See also CA 104; 121; CDBLB 1914-1945;
    DLB 10, 19, 36, 98, 162, 195; MTCW

Lawrence, T(homas) E(dward) 1888-1935
    TCLC 18
    See also Dale, Colin
    See also CA 115; DLB 195

Lawrence of Arabia
    See Lawrence, T(homas) E(dward)

Lawson, Henry (Archibald Hertzberg) 1867-
    1922   **TCLC 27; SSC 18**
    See also CA 120

Lawton, Dennis
    See Faust, Frederick (Schiller)

Laxness, Halldor   **CLC 25**
    See also Gudjonsson, Halldor Kiljan

Layamon fl. c. 1200-   **CMLC 10**
    See also DLB 146

Laye, Camara 1928-1980   **CLC 4, 38; BLC 2;**
    DAM MULT
    See also BW 1; CA 85-88; 97-100; CANR 25;
    MTCW

Layton, Irving (Peter) 1912-**CLC 2, 15; DAC;**
    DAM MST, POET
    See also CA 1-4R; CANR 2, 33, 43, 66; DLB
    88; MTCW

Lazarus, Emma 1849-1887   **NCLC 8**

Lazarus, Felix
    See Cable, George Washington

Lazarus, Henry
    See Slavitt, David R(ytman)

Lea, Joan
    See Neufeld, John (Arthur)

Leacock, Stephen (Butler) 1869-1944**TCLC 2;**
    DAC; DAM MST
    See also CA 104; 141; DLB 92

Lear, Edward 1812-1888   **NCLC 3**
    See also CLR 1; DLB 32, 163, 166; MAICYA;
    SATA 18

Lear, Norman (Milton) 1922-   **CLC 12**
    See also CA 73-76

Leautaud, Paul 1872-1956   **TCLC 83**
    See also DLB 65

Leavis, F(rank) R(aymond) 1895-1978**CLC 24**
    See also CA 21-24R; 77-80; CANR 44; MTCW

Leavitt, David 1961-   **CLC 34; DAM POP**
    See also CA 116; 122; CANR 50, 62; DLB 130;
    INT 122

Leblanc, Maurice (Marie Emile) 1864-1941
    TCLC 49
    See also CA 110

Lebowitz, Fran(ces Ann) 1951(?)- **CLC 11, 36**
    See also CA 81-84; CANR 14, 60; INT CANR-
    14; MTCW

Lebrecht, Peter

See Tieck, (Johann) Ludwig

le Carre, John   **CLC 3, 5, 9, 15, 28**
    See also Cornwell, David (John Moore)
    See also BEST 89:4; CDBLB 1960 to Present;
    DLB 87

Le Clezio, J(ean) M(arie) G(ustave) 1940-
    CLC 31
    See also CA 116; 128; DLB 83

Leconte de Lisle, Charles-Marie-Rene 1818-
    1894   **NCLC 29**

Le Coq, Monsieur
    See Simenon, Georges (Jacques Christian)

Leduc, Violette 1907-1972   **CLC 22**
    See also CA 13-14; 33-36R; CANR 69; CAP 1

Ledwidge, Francis 1887(?)-1917   **TCLC 23**
    See also CA 123; DLB 20

Lee, Andrea 1953-   **CLC 36; BLC 2; DAM**
    MULT
    See also BW 1; CA 125

Lee, Andrew
    See Auchincloss, Louis (Stanton)

Lee, Chang-rae 1965-   **CLC 91**
    See also CA 148

Lee, Don L.   **CLC 2**
    See also Madhubuti, Haki R.

Lee, George W(ashington) 1894-1976**CLC 52;**
    BLC 2; DAM MULT
    See also BW 1; CA 125; DLB 51

Lee, (Nelle) Harper 1926-   **CLC 12, 60; DA;**
    DAB; DAC; DAM MST, NOV; WLC
    See also AAYA 13; CA 13-16R; CANR 51;
    CDALB 1941-1968; DLB 6; MTCW; SATA
    11

Lee, Helen Elaine 1959(?)-   **CLC 86**
    See also CA 148

Lee, Julian
    See Latham, Jean Lee

Lee, Larry
    See Lee, Lawrence

Lee, Laurie 1914-1997   **CLC 90; DAB; DAM**
    POP
    See also CA 77-80; 158; CANR 33; DLB 27;
    MTCW

Lee, Lawrence 1941-1990   **CLC 34**
    See also CA 131; CANR 43

Lee, Manfred B(ennington) 1905-1971**CLC 11**
    See also Queen, Ellery
    See also CA 1-4R; 29-32R; CANR 2; DLB 137

Lee, Shelton Jackson 1957(?)-   **CLC 105;**
    BLCS; DAM MULT
    See also Lee, Spike
    See also BW 2; CA 125; CANR 42

Lee, Spike
    See Lee, Shelton Jackson
    See also AAYA 4

Lee, Stan 1922-   **CLC 17**
    See also AAYA 5; CA 108; 111; INT 111

Lee, Tanith 1947-   **CLC 46**
    See also AAYA 15; CA 37-40R; CANR 53;
    SATA 8, 88

Lee, Vernon   **TCLC 5**
    See also Paget, Violet
    See also DLB 57, 153, 156, 174, 178

Lee, William
    See Burroughs, William S(eward)

Lee, Willy
    See Burroughs, William S(eward)

Lee-Hamilton, Eugene (Jacob) 1845-1907
    TCLC 22
    See also CA 117

Leet, Judith 1935-   **CLC 11**

Le Fanu, Joseph Sheridan 1814-1873**NCLC 9,**
    58; DAM POP; SSC 14

See Lezama Lima, Jose

Lima Barreto, Afonso Henrique de 1881-1922
TCLC 23
See also CA 117

Limonov, Edward 1944-   **CLC 67**
See also CA 137

Lin, Frank
See Atherton, Gertrude (Franklin Horn)

Lincoln, Abraham 1809-1865   **NCLC 18**

Lind, Jakov   **CLC 1, 2, 4, 27, 82**
See also Landwirth, Heinz
See also CAAS 4

Lindbergh, Anne (Spencer) Morrow 1906-
CLC 82; DAM NOV
See also CA 17-20R; CANR 16; MTCW; SATA
33

Lindsay, David 1878-1945   **TCLC 15**
See also CA 113

Lindsay, (Nicholas) Vachel 1879-1931 **TCLC
17; DA; DAC; DAM MST, POET; PC 23;
WLC**
See also CA 114; 135; CDALB 1865-1917;
DLB 54; SATA 40

Linke-Poot
See Doeblin, Alfred

Linney, Romulus 1930-   **CLC 51**
See also CA 1-4R; CANR 40, 44

Linton, Eliza Lynn 1822-1898   **NCLC 41**
See also DLB 18

Li Po 701-763   **CMLC 2**

Lipsius, Justus 1547-1606   **LC 16**

Lipsyte, Robert (Michael) 1938-**CLC 21; DA;
DAC; DAM MST, NOV**
See also AAYA 7; CA 17-20R; CANR 8, 57;
CLR 23; JRDA; MAICYA; SATA 5, 68

Lish, Gordon (Jay) 1934-   **CLC 45; SSC 18**
See also CA 113; 117; DLB 130; INT 117

Lispector, Clarice 1925-1977   **CLC 43**
See also CA 139; 116; DLB 113

Littell, Robert 1935(?)-   **CLC 42**
See also CA 109; 112; CANR 64

Little, Malcolm 1925-1965
See Malcolm X
See also BW 1; CA 125; 111; DA; DAB; DAC;
DAM MST, MULT; MTCW

Littlewit, Humphrey Gent.
See Lovecraft, H(oward) P(hillips)

Litwos
See Sienkiewicz, Henryk (Adam Alexander
Pius)

Liu, E 1857-1909   **TCLC 15**
See also CA 115

Lively, Penelope (Margaret) 1933-   **CLC 32,
50; DAM NOV**
See also CA 41-44R; CANR 29, 67; CLR 7;
DLB 14, 161; JRDA; MAICYA; MTCW;
SATA 7, 60

Livesay, Dorothy (Kathleen) 1909-**CLC 4, 15,
79; DAC; DAM MST, POET**
See also AITN 2; CA 25-28R; CAAS 8; CANR
36, 67; DLB 68; MTCW

Livy c. 59B.C.-c. 17   **CMLC 11**

Lizardi, Jose Joaquin Fernandez de 1776-1827
NCLC 30

Llewellyn, Richard
See Llewellyn Lloyd, Richard Dafydd Vivian
See also DLB 15

Llewellyn Lloyd, Richard Dafydd Vivian 1906-
1983 **CLC 7, 80**
See also Llewellyn, Richard
See also CA 53-56; 111; CANR 7; SATA 11;
SATA-Obit 37

Llosa, (Jorge) Mario (Pedro) Vargas

See Vargas Llosa, (Jorge) Mario (Pedro)

Lloyd, Manda
See Mander, (Mary) Jane

Lloyd Webber, Andrew 1948-
See Webber, Andrew Lloyd
See also AAYA 1; CA 116; 149; DAM DRAM;
SATA 56

Llull, Ramon c. 1235-c. 1316   **CMLC 12**

Locke, Alain (Le Roy) 1886-1954   **TCLC 43;
BLCS**
See also BW 1; CA 106; 124; DLB 51

Locke, John 1632-1704   **LC 7, 35**
See also DLB 101

Locke-Elliott, Sumner
See Elliott, Sumner Locke

Lockhart, John Gibson 1794-1854   **NCLC 6**
See also DLB 110, 116, 144

Lodge, David (John) 1935-**CLC 36; DAM POP**
See also BEST 90:1; CA 17-20R; CANR 19,
53; DLB 14, 194; INT CANR-19; MTCW

Lodge, Thomas 1558-1625   **LC 41**
See also DLB 172

Lodge, Thomas 1558-1625   **LC 41**

Loennbohm, Armas Eino Leopold 1878-1926
See Leino, Eino
See also CA 123

Loewinsohn, Ron(ald William) 1937- **CLC 52**
See also CA 25-28R

Logan, Jake
See Smith, Martin Cruz

Logan, John (Burton) 1923-1987   **CLC 5**
See also CA 77-80; 124; CANR 45; DLB 5

Lo Kuan-chung 1330(?)-1400(?)   **LC 12**

Lombard, Nap
See Johnson, Pamela Hansford

London, Jack   TCLC 9, 15, 39; SSC 4; WLC
See also London, John Griffith
See also AAYA 13; AITN 2; CDALB 1865-
1917; DLB 8, 12, 78; SATA 18

London, John Griffith 1876-1916
See London, Jack
See also CA 110; 119; DA; DAB; DAC; DAM
MST, NOV; JRDA; MAICYA; MTCW

Long, Emmett
See Leonard, Elmore (John, Jr.)

Longbaugh, Harry
See Goldman, William (W.)

Longfellow, Henry Wadsworth 1807-1882
**NCLC 2, 45; DA; DAB; DAC; DAM MST,
POET; WLCS**
See also CDALB 1640-1865; DLB 1, 59; SATA
19

Longinus c. 1st cent. -   **CMLC 27**
See also DLB 176

Longley, Michael 1939-   **CLC 29**
See also CA 102; DLB 40

Longus fl. c. 2nd cent. -   **CMLC 7**

Longway, A. Hugh
See Lang, Andrew

Lonnrot, Elias 1802-1884   **NCLC 53**

Lopate, Phillip 1943-   **CLC 29**
See also CA 97-100; DLBY 80; INT 97-100

Lopez Portillo (y Pacheco), Jose 1920-**CLC 46**
See also CA 129; HW

Lopez y Fuentes, Gregorio 1897(?)-1966 **CLC
32**
See also CA 131; HW

Lorca, Federico Garcia
See Garcia Lorca, Federico

Lord, Bette Bao 1938-   **CLC 23**
See also BEST 90:3; CA 107; CANR 41; INT
107; SATA 58

Lord Auch

See Bataille, Georges

Lord Byron
See Byron, George Gordon (Noel)

Lorde, Audre (Geraldine) 1934-1992 **CLC 18,
71; BLC 2; DAM MULT, POET; PC 12**
See also BW 1; CA 25-28R; 142; CANR 16,
26, 46; DLB 41; MTCW

Lord Houghton
See Milnes, Richard Monckton

Lord Jeffrey
See Jeffrey, Francis

Lorenzini, Carlo 1826-1890
See Collodi, Carlo
See also MAICYA; SATA 29

Lorenzo, Heberto Padilla
See Padilla (Lorenzo), Heberto

Loris
See Hofmannsthal, Hugo von

Loti, Pierre   **TCLC 11**
See also Viaud, (Louis Marie) Julien
See also DLB 123

Louie, David Wong 1954-   **CLC 70**
See also CA 139

Louis, Father M.
See Merton, Thomas

Lovecraft, H(oward) P(hillips) 1890-1937
TCLC 4, 22; DAM POP; SSC 3
See also AAYA 14; CA 104; 133; MTCW

Lovelace, Earl 1935-   **CLC 51**
See also BW 2; CA 77-80; CANR 41; DLB 125;
MTCW

Lovelace, Richard 1618-1657   **LC 24**
See also DLB 131

Lowell, Amy 1874-1925   **TCLC 1, 8; DAM
POET; PC 13**
See also CA 104; 151; DLB 54, 140

Lowell, James Russell 1819-1891   **NCLC 2**
See also CDALB 1640-1865; DLB 1, 11, 64,
79, 189

Lowell, Robert (Traill Spence, Jr.) 1917-1977
**CLC 1, 2, 3, 4, 5, 8, 9, 11, 15, 37; DA; DAB;
DAC; DAM MST, NOV; PC 3; WLC**
See also CA 9-12R; 73-76; CABS 2; CANR 26,
60; DLB 5, 169; MTCW

Lowndes, Marie Adelaide (Belloc) 1868-1947
TCLC 12
See also CA 107; DLB 70

Lowry, (Clarence) Malcolm 1909-1957 **TCLC
6, 40; SSC 31**
See also CA 105; 131; CANR 62; CDBLB
1945-1960; DLB 15; MTCW

Lowry, Mina Gertrude 1882-1966
See Loy, Mina
See also CA 113

Loxsmith, John
See Brunner, John (Kilian Houston)

Loy, Mina   CLC 28; DAM POET; PC 16
See also Lowry, Mina Gertrude
See also DLB 4, 54

Loyson-Bridet
See Schwob, (Mayer Andre) Marcel

Lucas, Craig 1951-   **CLC 64**
See also CA 137

Lucas, E(dward) V(errall) 1868-1938 **TCLC
73**
See also DLB 98, 149, 153; SATA 20

Lucas, George 1944-   **CLC 16**
See also AAYA 1, 23; CA 77-80; CANR 30;
SATA 56

Lucas, Hans
See Godard, Jean-Luc

Lucas, Victoria
See Plath, Sylvia

Maitland, Frederic 1850-1906 **TCLC 65**
Maitland, Sara (Louise) 1950- **CLC 49**
See also CA 69-72; CANR 13, 59
Major, Clarence 1936- **CLC 3, 19, 48; BLC 2; DAM MULT**
See also BW 2; CA 21-24R; CAAS 6; CANR 13, 25, 53; DLB 33
Major, Kevin (Gerald) 1949- **CLC 26; DAC**
See also AAYA 16; CA 97-100; CANR 21, 38; CLR 11; DLB 60; INT CANR-21; JRDA; MAICYA; SATA 32, 82
Maki, James
See Ozu, Yasujiro
Malabaila, Damiano
See Levi, Primo
Malamud, Bernard 1914-1986 **CLC 1, 2, 3, 5, 8, 9, 11, 18, 27, 44, 78, 85; DA; DAB; DAC; DAM MST, NOV, POP; SSC 15; WLC**
See also AAYA 16; CA 5-8R; 118; CABS 1; CANR 28, 62; CDALB 1941-1968; DLB 2, 28, 152; DLBY 80, 86; MTCW
Malan, Herman
See Bosman, Herman Charles; Bosman, Herman Charles
Malaparte, Curzio 1898-1957 **TCLC 52**
Malcolm, Dan
See Silverberg, Robert
Malcolm X **CLC 82; BLC 2; WLCS**
See also Little, Malcolm
Malherbe, Francois de 1555-1628 **LC 5**
Mallarme, Stephane 1842-1898 **NCLC 4, 41; DAM POET; PC 4**
Mallet-Joris, Francoise 1930- **CLC 11**
See also CA 65-68; CANR 17; DLB 83
Malley, Ern
See McAuley, James Phillip
Mallowan, Agatha Christie
See Christie, Agatha (Mary Clarissa)
Maloff, Saul 1922- **CLC 5**
See also CA 33-36R
Malone, Louis
See MacNeice, (Frederick) Louis
Malone, Michael (Christopher) 1942- **CLC 43**
See also CA 77-80; CANR 14, 32, 57
Malory, (Sir) Thomas 1410(?)-1471(?) **LC 11; DA; DAB; DAC; DAM MST; WLCS**
See also CDBLB Before 1660; DLB 146; SATA 59; SATA-Brief 33
Malouf, (George Joseph) David 1934- **CLC 28, 86**
See also CA 124; CANR 50
Malraux, (Georges-)Andre 1901-1976 **CLC 1, 4, 9, 13, 15, 57; DAM NOV**
See also CA 21-22; 69-72; CANR 34, 58; CAP 2; DLB 72; MTCW
Malzberg, Barry N(athaniel) 1939- **CLC 7**
See also CA 61-64; CAAS 4; CANR 16; DLB 8
Mamet, David (Alan) 1947- **CLC 9, 15, 34, 46, 91; DAM DRAM; DC 4**
See also AAYA 3; CA 81-84; CABS 3; CANR 15, 41, 67; DLB 7; MTCW
Mamoulian, Rouben (Zachary) 1897-1987 **CLC 16**
See also CA 25-28R; 124
Mandelstam, Osip (Emilievich) 1891(?)-1938(?) **TCLC 2, 6; PC 14**
See also CA 104; 150
Mander, (Mary) Jane 1877-1949 **TCLC 31**
See also CA 162
Mandeville, John fl. 1350- **CMLC 19**
See also DLB 146
Mandiargues, Andre Pieyre de **CLC 41**
See also Pieyre de Mandiargues, Andre

See also DLB 83
Mandrake, Ethel Belle
See Thurman, Wallace (Henry)
Mangan, James Clarence 1803-1849 **NCLC 27**
Maniere, J.-E.
See Giraudoux, (Hippolyte) Jean
Manley, (Mary) Delariviere 1672(?)-1724 **LC 1**
See also DLB 39, 80
Mann, Abel
See Creasey, John
Mann, Emily 1952- **DC 7**
See also CA 130; CANR 55
Mann, (Luiz) Heinrich 1871-1950 **TCLC 9**
See also CA 106; 164; DLB 66
Mann, (Paul) Thomas 1875-1955 **TCLC 2, 8, 14, 21, 35, 44, 60; DA; DAB; DAC; DAM MST, NOV; SSC 5; WLC**
See also CA 104; 128; DLB 66; MTCW
Mannheim, Karl 1893-1947 **TCLC 65**
Manning, David
See Faust, Frederick (Schiller)
Manning, Frederic 1887(?)-1935 **TCLC 25**
See also CA 124
Manning, Olivia 1915-1980 **CLC 5, 19**
See also CA 5-8R; 101; CANR 29; MTCW
Mano, D. Keith 1942- **CLC 2, 10**
See also CA 25-28R; CAAS 6; CANR 26, 57; DLB 6
Mansfield, Katherine **TCLC 2, 8, 39; DAB; SSC 9, 23; WLC**
See also Beauchamp, Kathleen Mansfield
See also DLB 162
Manso, Peter 1940- **CLC 39**
See also CA 29-32R; CANR 44
Mantecon, Juan Jimenez
See Jimenez (Mantecon), Juan Ramon
Manton, Peter
See Creasey, John
Man Without a Spleen, A
See Chekhov, Anton (Pavlovich)
Manzoni, Alessandro 1785-1873 **NCLC 29**
Mapu, Abraham (ben Jekutiel) 1808-1867 **NCLC 18**
Mara, Sally
See Queneau, Raymond
Marat, Jean Paul 1743-1793 **LC 10**
Marcel, Gabriel Honore 1889-1973 **CLC 15**
See also CA 102; 45-48; MTCW
Marchbanks, Samuel
See Davies, (William) Robertson
Marchi, Giacomo
See Bassani, Giorgio
Margulies, Donald **CLC 76**
Marie de France c. 12th cent. - **CMLC 8; PC 22**
Marie de l'Incarnation 1599-1672 **LC 10**
Marier, Captain Victor
See Griffith, D(avid Lewelyn) W(ark)
Mariner, Scott
See Pohl, Frederik
Marinetti, Filippo Tommaso 1876-1944 **TCLC 10**
See also CA 107; DLB 114
Marivaux, Pierre Carlet de Chamblain de 1688-1763 **LC 4; DC 7**
Markandaya, Kamala **CLC 8, 38**
See also Taylor, Kamala (Purnaiya)
Markfield, Wallace 1926- **CLC 8**
See also CA 69-72; CAAS 3; DLB 2, 28
Markham, Edwin 1852-1940 **TCLC 47**
See also CA 160; DLB 54, 186
Markham, Robert

See Amis, Kingsley (William)
Marks, J
See Highwater, Jamake (Mamake)
Marks-Highwater, J
See Highwater, Jamake (Mamake)
Markson, David M(errill) 1927- **CLC 67**
See also CA 49-52; CANR 1
Marley, Bob **CLC 17**
See also Marley, Robert Nesta
Marley, Robert Nesta 1945-1981
See Marley, Bob
See also CA 107; 103
Marlowe, Christopher 1564-1593 **LC 22; DA; DAB; DAC; DAM DRAM, MST; DC 1; WLC**
See also CDBLB Before 1660; DLB 62
Marlowe, Stephen 1928-
See Queen, Ellery
See also CA 13-16R; CANR 6, 55
Marmontel, Jean-Francois 1723-1799 **LC 2**
Marquand, John P(hillips) 1893-1960 **CLC 2, 10**
See also CA 85-88; DLB 9, 102
Marques, Rene 1919-1979 **CLC 96; DAM MULT; HLC**
See also CA 97-100; 85-88; DLB 113; HW
Marquez, Gabriel (Jose) Garcia
See Garcia Marquez, Gabriel (Jose)
Marquis, Don(ald Robert Perry) 1878-1937 **TCLC 7**
See also CA 104; 166; DLB 11, 25
Marric, J. J.
See Creasey, John
Marryat, Frederick 1792-1848 **NCLC 3**
See also DLB 21, 163
Marsden, James
See Creasey, John
Marsh, (Edith) Ngaio 1899-1982 **CLC 7, 53; DAM POP**
See also CA 9-12R; CANR 6, 58; DLB 77; MTCW
Marshall, Garry 1934- **CLC 17**
See also AAYA 3; CA 111; SATA 60
Marshall, Paule 1929- **CLC 27, 72; BLC 3; DAM MULT; SSC 3**
See also BW 2; CA 77-80; CANR 25; DLB 157; MTCW
Marsten, Richard
See Hunter, Evan
Marston, John 1576-1634 **LC 33; DAM DRAM**
See also DLB 58, 172
Martha, Henry
See Harris, Mark
Marti, Jose 1853-1895 **NCLC 63; DAM MULT; HLC**
Martial c. 40-c. 104 **PC 10**
Martin, Ken
See Hubbard, L(afayette) Ron(ald)
Martin, Richard
See Creasey, John
Martin, Steve 1945- **CLC 30**
See also CA 97-100; CANR 30; MTCW
Martin, Valerie 1948- **CLC 89**
See also BEST 90:2; CA 85-88; CANR 49
Martin, Violet Florence 1862-1915 **TCLC 51**
Martin, Webber
See Silverberg, Robert
Martindale, Patrick Victor
See White, Patrick (Victor Martindale)
Martin du Gard, Roger 1881-1958 **TCLC 24**
See also CA 118; DLB 65
Martineau, Harriet 1802-1876 **NCLC 26**
See also DLB 21, 55, 159, 163, 166, 190; YABC

McFadden, David 1940-   **CLC 48**
See also CA 104; DLB 60; INT 104
McFarland, Dennis 1950-   **CLC 65**
See also CA 165
McGahern, John 1934- **CLC 5, 9, 48; SSC 17**
See also CA 17-20R; CANR 29, 68; DLB 14;
MTCW
McGinley, Patrick (Anthony) 1937-   **CLC 41**
See also CA 120; 127; CANR 56; INT 127
McGinley, Phyllis 1905-1978   **CLC 14**
See also CA 9-12R; 77-80; CANR 19; DLB 11,
48; SATA 2, 44; SATA-Obit 24
McGinniss, Joe 1942-   **CLC 32**
See also AITN 2; BEST 89:2; CA 25-28R;
CANR 26; DLB 185; INT CANR-26
McGivern, Maureen Daly
See Daly, Maureen
McGrath, Patrick 1950-   **CLC 55**
See also CA 136; CANR 65
McGrath, Thomas (Matthew) 1916-1990**CLC
28, 59; DAM POET**
See also CA 9-12R; 132; CANR 6, 33; MTCW;
SATA 41; SATA-Obit 66
McGuane, Thomas (Francis III) 1939-**CLC 3,
7, 18, 45**
See also AITN 2; CA 49-52; CANR 5, 24, 49;
DLB 2; DLBY 80; INT CANR-24; MTCW
McGuckian, Medbh 1950-   **CLC 48; DAM
POET**
See also CA 143; DLB 40
McHale, Tom 1942(?)-1982   **CLC 3, 5**
See also AITN 1; CA 77-80; 106
McIlvanney, William 1936-   **CLC 42**
See also CA 25-28R; CANR 61; DLB 14
McIlwraith, Maureen Mollie Hunter
See Hunter, Mollie
See also SATA 2
McInerney, Jay 1955-**CLC 34, 112; DAM POP**
See also AAYA 18; CA 116; 123; CANR 45,
68; INT 123
McIntyre, Vonda N(eel) 1948-   **CLC 18**
See also CA 81-84; CANR 17, 34, 69; MTCW
McKay, ClaudeTCLC **7, 41; BLC 3; DAB; PC
2**
See also McKay, Festus Claudius
See also DLB 4, 45, 51, 117
McKay, Festus Claudius 1889-1948
See McKay, Claude
See also BW 1; CA 104; 124; DA; DAC; DAM
MST, MULT, NOV, POET; MTCW; WLC
McKuen, Rod 1933-   **CLC 1, 3**
See also AITN 1; CA 41-44R; CANR 40
McLoughlin, R. B.
See Mencken, H(enry) L(ouis)
McLuhan, (Herbert) Marshall 1911-1980
CLC 37, 83
See also CA 9-12R; 102; CANR 12, 34, 61;
DLB 88; INT CANR-12; MTCW
McMillan, Terry (L.) 1951- **CLC 50, 61, 112;
BLCS; DAM MULT, NOV, POP**
See also AAYA 21; BW 2; CA 140; CANR 60
McMurtry, Larry (Jeff) 1936-**CLC 2, 3, 7, 11,
27, 44; DAM NOV, POP**
See also AAYA 15; AITN 2; BEST 89:2; CA 5-
8R; CANR 19, 43, 64; CDALB 1968-1988;
DLB 2, 143; DLBY 80, 87; MTCW
McNally, T. M. 1961-   .CLC 82
McNally, Terrence 1939-   **CLC 4, 7, 41, 91;
DAM DRAM**
See also CA 45-48; CANR 2, 56; DLB 7
McNamer, Deirdre 1950-   **CLC 70**
McNeile, Herman Cyril 1888-1937
See Sapper

See also DLB 77
McNickle, (William) D'Arcy 1904-1977   **CLC
89; DAM MULT**
See also CA 9-12R; 85-88; CANR 5, 45; DLB
175; NNAL; SATA-Obit 22
McPhee, John (Angus) 1931-   **CLC 36**
See also BEST 90:1; CA 65-68; CANR 20, 46,
64, 69; DLB 185; MTCW
McPherson, James Alan 1943-   **CLC 19, 77;
BLCS**
See also BW 1; CA 25-28R; CAAS 17; CANR
24; DLB 38; MTCW
McPherson, William (Alexander) 1933- **CLC
34**
See also CA 69-72; CANR 28; INT CANR-28
Mead, Margaret 1901-1978   **CLC 37**
See also AITN 1; CA 1-4R; 81-84; CANR 4;
MTCW; SATA-Obit 20
Meaker, Marijane (Agnes) 1927-
See Kerr, M. E.
See also CA 107; CANR 37, 63; INT 107;
JRDA; MAICYA; MTCW; SATA 20, 61
Medoff, Mark (Howard) 1940-   **CLC 6, 23;
DAM DRAM**
See also AITN 1; CA 53-56; CANR 5; DLB 7;
INT CANR-5
Medvedev, P. N.
See Bakhtin, Mikhail Mikhailovich
Meged, Aharon
See Megged, Aharon
Meged, Aron
See Megged, Aharon
Megged, Aharon 1920-   **CLC 9**
See also CA 49-52; CAAS 13; CANR 1
Mehta, Ved (Parkash) 1934-   **CLC 37**
See also CA 1-4R; CANR 2, 23, 69; MTCW
Melanter
See Blackmore, R(ichard) D(oddridge)
Melies, Georges 1861-1938   **TCLC 81**
Melikow, Loris
See Hofmannsthal, Hugo von
Melmoth, Sebastian
See Wilde, Oscar (Fingal O'Flahertie Wills)
Meltzer, Milton 1915-   **CLC 26**
See also AAYA 8; CA 13-16R; CANR 38; CLR
13; DLB 61; JRDA; MAICYA; SAAS 1;
SATA 1, 50, 80
Melville, Herman 1819-1891 **NCLC 3, 12, 29,
45, 49; DA; DAB; DAC; DAM MST, NOV;
SSC 1, 17; WLC**
See also AAYA 25; CDALB 1640-1865; DLB
3, 74; SATA 59
Menander c. 342B.C.-c. 292B.C.   **CMLC 9;
DAM DRAM; DC 3**
See also DLB 176
Mencken, H(enry) L(ouis) 1880-1956   **TCLC
13**
See also CA 105; 125; CDALB 1917-1929;
DLB 11, 29, 63, 137; MTCW
Mendelsohn, Jane 1965(?)-   **CLC 99**
See also CA 154
Mercer, David 1928-1980**CLC 5; DAM DRAM**
See also CA 9-12R; 102; CANR 23; DLB 13;
MTCW
Merchant, Paul
See Ellison, Harlan (Jay)
Meredith, George 1828-1909   **TCLC 17, 43;
DAM POET**
See also CA 117; 153; CDBLB 1832-1890;
DLB 18, 35, 57, 159
Meredith, William (Morris) 1919- **CLC 4, 13,
22, 55; DAM POET**
See also CA 9-12R; CAAS 14; CANR 6, 40;

DLB 5
Merezhkovsky, Dmitry Sergeyevich 1865-1941
TCLC 29
Merimee, Prosper 1803-1870**NCLC 6, 65; SSC
7**
See also DLB 119, 192
Merkin, Daphne 1954-   **CLC 44**
See also CA 123
Merlin, Arthur
See Blish, James (Benjamin)
Merrill, James (Ingram) 1926-1995 **CLC 2, 3,
6, 8, 13, 18, 34, 91; DAM POET**
See also CA 13-16R; 147; CANR 10, 49, 63;
DLB 5, 165; DLBY 85; INT CANR-10;
MTCW
Merriman, Alex
See Silverberg, Robert
Merriman, Brian 1747-1805   **NCLC 70**
Merritt, E. B.
See Waddington, Miriam
Merton, Thomas 1915-1968   **CLC 1, 3, 11, 34,
83; PC 10**
See also CA 5-8R; 25-28R; CANR 22, 53; DLB
48; DLBY 81; MTCW
Merwin, W(illiam) S(tanley) 1927- **CLC 1, 2,
3, 5, 8, 13, 18, 45, 88; DAM POET**
See also CA 13-16R; CANR 15, 51; DLB 5,
169; INT CANR-15; MTCW
Metcalf, John 1938-   **CLC 37**
See also CA 113; DLB 60
Metcalf, Suzanne
See Baum, L(yman) Frank
Mew, Charlotte (Mary) 1870-1928   **TCLC 8**
See also CA 105; DLB 19, 135
Mewshaw, Michael 1943-   **CLC 9**
See also CA 53-56; CANR 7, 47; DLBY 80
Meyer, June
See Jordan, June
Meyer, Lynn
See Slavitt, David R(ytman)
Meyer-Meyrink, Gustav 1868-1932
See Meyrink, Gustav
See also CA 117
Meyers, Jeffrey 1939-   **CLC 39**
See also CA 73-76; CANR 54; DLB 111
Meynell, Alice (Christina Gertrude Thompson)
1847-1922   **TCLC 6**
See also CA 104; DLB 19, 98
Meyrink, Gustav   **TCLC 21**
See also Meyer-Meyrink, Gustav
See also DLB 81
Michaels, Leonard 1933- **CLC 6, 25; SSC 16**
See also CA 61-64; CANR 21, 62; DLB 130;
MTCW
Michaux, Henri 1899-1984   **CLC 8, 19**
See also CA 85-88; 114
Micheaux, Oscar 1884-1951   **TCLC 76**
See also DLB 50
Michelangelo 1475-1564   **LC 12**
Michelet, Jules 1798-1874   **NCLC 31**
Michener, James A(lbert) 1907(?)-1997 **CLC
1, 5, 11, 29, 60, 109; DAM NOV, POP**
See also AITN 1; BEST 90:1; CA 5-8R; 161;
CANR 21, 45, 68; DLB 6; MTCW
Mickiewicz, Adam 1798-1855   **NCLC 3**
Middleton, Christopher 1926-   **CLC 13**
See also CA 13-16R; CANR 29, 54; DLB 40
Middleton, Richard (Barham) 1882-1911
TCLC 56
See also DLB 156
Middleton, Stanley 1919-   **CLC 7, 38**
See also CA 25-28R; CAAS 23; CANR 21, 46;
DLB 14

90; DAB; DAC; DAM MST
See also CA 1-4R; CANR 1, 25, 42, 63; MTCW
Moore, Edward
See Muir, Edwin
Moore, George Augustus 1852-1933 **TCLC 7; SSC 19**
See also CA 104; DLB 10, 18, 57, 135
Moore, Lorrie   **CLC 39, 45, 68**
See also Moore, Marie Lorena
Moore, Marianne (Craig) 1887-1972**CLC 1, 2, 4, 8, 10, 13, 19, 47; DA; DAB; DAC; DAM MST, POET; PC 4; WLCS**
See also CA 1-4R; 33-36R; CANR 3, 61; CDALB 1929-1941; DLB 45; DLBD 7; MTCW; SATA 20
Moore, Marie Lorena 1957-
See Moore, Lorrie
See also CA 116; CANR 39
Moore, Thomas 1779-1852   **NCLC 6**
See also DLB 96, 144
Morand, Paul 1888-1976   **CLC 41; SSC 22**
See also CA 69-72; DLB 65
Morante, Elsa 1918-1985   **CLC 8, 47**
See also CA 85-88; 117; CANR 35; DLB 177; MTCW
Moravia, Alberto 1907-1990 **CLC 2, 7, 11, 27, 46; SSC 26**
See also Pincherle, Alberto
See also DLB 177
More, Hannah 1745-1833   **NCLC 27**
See also DLB 107, 109, 116, 158
More, Henry 1614-1687   **LC 9**
See also DLB 126
More, Sir Thomas 1478-1535   **LC 10, 32**
Moreas, Jean   **TCLC 18**
See also Papadiamantopoulos, Johannes
Morgan, Berry 1919-   **CLC 6**
See also CA 49-52; DLB 6
Morgan, Claire
See Highsmith, (Mary) Patricia
Morgan, Edwin (George) 1920-   **CLC 31**
See also CA 5-8R; CANR 3, 43; DLB 27
Morgan, (George) Frederick 1922-   **CLC 23**
See also CA 17-20R; CANR 21
Morgan, Harriet
See Mencken, H(enry) L(ouis)
Morgan, Jane
See Cooper, James Fenimore
Morgan, Janet 1945-   **CLC 39**
See also CA 65-68
Morgan, Lady 1776(?)-1859   **NCLC 29**
See also DLB 116, 158
Morgan, Robin (Evonne) 1941-   **CLC 2**
See also CA 69-72; CANR 29, 68; MTCW; SATA 80
Morgan, Scott
See Kuttner, Henry
Morgan, Seth 1949(?)-1990   **CLC 65**
See also CA 132
Morgenstern, Christian 1871-1914   **TCLC 8**
See also CA 105
Morgenstern, S.
See Goldman, William (W.)
Moricz, Zsigmond 1879-1942   **TCLC 33**
See also CA 165
Morike, Eduard (Friedrich) 1804-1875**NCLC 10**
See also DLB 133
Moritz, Karl Philipp 1756-1793   **LC 2**
See also DLB 94
Morland, Peter Henry
See Faust, Frederick (Schiller)
Morren, Theophil

See Hofmannsthal, Hugo von
Morris, Bill 1952-   **CLC 76**
Morris, Julian
See West, Morris L(anglo)
Morris, Steveland Judkins 1950(?)-
See Wonder, Stevie
See also CA 111
Morris, William 1834-1896   **NCLC 4**
See also CDBLB 1832-1890; DLB 18, 35, 57, 156, 178, 184
Morris, Wright 1910-   **CLC 1, 3, 7, 18, 37**
See also CA 9-12R; CANR 21; DLB 2; DLBY 81; MTCW
Morrison, Arthur 1863-1945   **TCLC 72**
See also CA 120; 157; DLB 70, 135, 197
Morrison, Chloe Anthony Wofford
See Morrison, Toni
Morrison, James Douglas 1943-1971
See Morrison, Jim
See also CA 73-76; CANR 40
Morrison, Jim   **CLC 17**
See also Morrison, James Douglas
Morrison, Toni 1931-**CLC 4, 10, 22, 55, 81, 87; BLC 3; DA; DAB; DAC; DAM MST, MULT, NOV, POP**
See also AAYA 1, 22; BW 2; CA 29-32R; CANR 27, 42, 67; CDALB 1968-1988; DLB 6, 33, 143; DLBY 81; MTCW; SATA 57
Morrison, Van 1945-   **CLC 21**
See also CA 116
Morrissy, Mary 1958-   **CLC 99**
Mortimer, John (Clifford) 1923- **CLC 28, 43; DAM DRAM, POP**
See also CA 13-16R; CANR 21, 69; CDBLB 1960 to Present; DLB 13; INT CANR-21; MTCW
Mortimer, Penelope (Ruth) 1918-   **CLC 5**
See also CA 57-60; CANR 45
Morton, Anthony
See Creasey, John
Mosca, Gaetano 1858-1941   **TCLC 75**
Mosher, Howard Frank 1943-   **CLC 62**
See also CA 139; CANR 65
Mosley, Nicholas 1923-   **CLC 43, 70**
See also CA 69-72; CANR 41, 60; DLB 14
Mosley, Walter 1952- **CLC 97; BLCS; DAM MULT, POP**
See also AAYA 17; BW 2; CA 142; CANR 57
Moss, Howard 1922-1987 **CLC 7, 14, 45, 50; DAM POET**
See also CA 1-4R; 123; CANR 1, 44; DLB 5
Mossgiel, Rab
See Burns, Robert
Motion, Andrew (Peter) 1952-   **CLC 47**
See also CA 146; DLB 40
Motley, Willard (Francis) 1909-1965 **CLC 18**
See also BW 1; CA 117; 106; DLB 76, 143
Motoori, Norinaga 1730-1801   **NCLC 45**
Mott, Michael (Charles Alston) 1930-**CLC 15, 34**
See also CA 5-8R; CAAS 7; CANR 7, 29
Mountain Wolf Woman 1884-1960   **CLC 92**
See also CA 144; NNAL
Moure, Erin 1955-   **CLC 88**
See also CA 113; DLB 60
Mowat, Farley (McGill) 1921- **CLC 26; DAC; DAM MST**
See also AAYA 1; CA 1-4R; CANR 4, 24, 42, 68; CLR 20; DLB 68; INT CANAR-24; JRDA; MAICYA; MTCW; SATA 3, 55
Moyers, Bill 1934-   **CLC 74**
See also AITN 2; CA 61-64; CANR 31, 52
Mphahlele, Es'kia

See Mphahlele, Ezekiel
See also DLB 125
Mphahlele, Ezekiel 1919-1983 **CLC 25; BLC 3; DAM MULT**
See also Mphahlele, Es'kia
See also BW 2; CA 81-84; CANR 26
Mqhayi, S(amuel) E(dward) K(rune Loliwe) 1875-1945 **TCLC 25; BLC 3; DAM MULT**
See also CA 153
Mrozek, Slawomir 1930-   **CLC 3, 13**
See also CA 13-16R; CAAS 10; CANR 29; MTCW
Mrs. Belloc-Lowndes
See Lowndes, Marie Adelaide (Belloc)
Mtwa, Percy (?)-   **CLC 47**
Mueller, Lisel 1924-   **CLC 13, 51**
See also CA 93-96; DLB 105
Muir, Edwin 1887-1959   **TCLC 2**
See also CA 104; DLB 20, 100, 191
Muir, John 1838-1914   **TCLC 28**
See also CA 165; DLB 186
Mujica Lainez, Manuel 1910-1984   **CLC 31**
See also Lainez, Manuel Mujica
See also CA 81-84; 112; CANR 32; HW
Mukherjee, Bharati 1940-**CLC 53; DAM NOV**
See also BEST 89:2; CA 107; CANR 45; DLB 60; MTCW
Muldoon, Paul 1951-**CLC 32, 72; DAM POET**
See also CA 113; 129; CANR 52; DLB 40; INT 129
Mulisch, Harry 1927-   **CLC 42**
See also CA 9-12R; CANR 6, 26, 56
Mull, Martin 1943-   **CLC 17**
See also CA 105
Mulock, Dinah Maria
See Craik, Dinah Maria (Mulock)
Munford, Robert 1737(?)-1783   **LC 5**
See also DLB 31
Mungo, Raymond 1946-   **CLC 72**
See also CA 49-52; CANR 2
Munro, Alice 1931-   **CLC 6, 10, 19, 50, 95; DAC; DAM MST, NOV; SSC 3; WLCS**
See also AITN 2; CA 33-36R; CANR 33, 53; DLB 53; MTCW; SATA 29
Munro, H(ector) H(ugh) 1870-1916
See Saki
See also CA 104; 130; CDBLB 1890-1914; DA; DAB; DAC; DAM MST, NOV; DLB 34, 162; MTCW; WLC
Murasaki, Lady   **CMLC 1**
Murdoch, (Jean) Iris 1919-**CLC 1, 2, 3, 4, 6, 8, 11, 15, 22, 31, 51; DAB; DAC; DAM MST, NOV**
See also CA 13-16R; CANR 8, 43, 68; CDBLB 1960 to Present; DLB 14, 194; INT CANR-8; MTCW
Murfree, Mary Noailles 1850-1922   **SSC 22**
See also CA 122; DLB 12, 74
Murnau, Friedrich Wilhelm
See Plumpe, Friedrich Wilhelm
Murphy, Richard 1927-   **CLC 41**
See also CA 29-32R; DLB 40
Murphy, Sylvia 1937-   **CLC 34**
See also CA 121
Murphy, Thomas (Bernard) 1935-   **CLC 51**
See also CA 101
Murray, Albert L. 1916-   **CLC 73**
See also BW 2; CA 49-52; CANR 26, 52; DLB 38
Murray, Judith Sargent 1751-1820 **NCLC 63**
See also DLB 37, 200
Murray, Les(lie) A(llan) 1938-**CLC 40; DAM POET**

See also CA 21-24R; CANR 11, 27, 56
Murry, J. Middleton
  See Murry, John Middleton
Murry, John Middleton 1889-1957 **TCLC 16**
  See also CA 118; DLB 149
Musgrave, Susan 1951-   **CLC 13, 54**
  See also CA 69-72; CANR 45
Musil, Robert (Edler von) 1880-1942 **TCLC
  12, 68; SSC 18**
  See also CA 109; CANR 55; DLB 81, 124
Muske, Carol 1945-   **CLC 90**
  See also Muske-Dukes, Carol (Anne)
Muske-Dukes, Carol (Anne) 1945-
  See Muske, Carol
  See also CA 65-68; CANR 32
Musset, (Louis Charles) Alfred de 1810-1857
  NCLC 7
  See also DLB 192
My Brother's Brother
  See Chekhov, Anton (Pavlovich)
Myers, L(eopold) H(amilton) 1881-1944
  TCLC 59
  See also CA 157; DLB 15
Myers, Walter Dean 1937-   **CLC 35; BLC 3;
  DAM MULT, NOV**
  See also AAYA 4, 23; BW 2; CA 33-36R;
  CANR 20, 42, 67; CLR 4, 16, 35; DLB 33;
  INT CANR-20; JRDA; MAICYA; SAAS 2;
  SATA 41, 71; SATA-Brief 27
Myers, Walter M.
  See Myers, Walter Dean
Myles, Symon
  See Follett, Ken(neth Martin)
Nabokov, Vladimir (Vladimirovich) 1899-1977
  **CLC 1, 2, 3, 6, 8, 11, 15, 23, 44, 46, 64;
  DA; DAB; DAC; DAM MST, NOV; SSC
  11; WLC**
  See also CA 5-8R; 69-72; CANR 20; CDALB
  1941-1968; DLB 2; DLBD 3; DLBY 80, 91;
  MTCW
Nagai Kafu 1879-1959   **TCLC 51**
  See also Nagai Sokichi
  See also DLB 180
Nagai Sokichi 1879-1959
  See Nagai Kafu
  See also CA 117
Nagy, Laszlo 1925-1978   **CLC 7**
  See also CA 129; 112
Naidu, Sarojini 1879-1943   **TCLC 80**
Naipaul, Shiva(dhar Srinivasa) 1945-1985
  CLC 32, 39; DAM NOV
  See also CA 110; 112; 116; CANR 33; DLB
  157; DLBY 85; MTCW
Naipaul, V(idiadhar) S(urajprasad) 1932-
  **CLC 4, 7, 9, 13, 18, 37, 105; DAB; DAC;
  DAM MST, NOV**
  See also CA 1-4R; CANR 1, 33, 51; CDBLB
  1960 to Present; DLB 125; DLBY 85;
  MTCW
Nakos, Lilika 1899(?)-   **CLC 29**
Narayan, R(asipuram) K(rishnaswami) 1906-
  CLC 7, 28, 47; DAM NOV; SSC 25
  See also CA 81-84; CANR 33, 61; MTCW;
  SATA 62
Nash, (Frediric) Ogden 1902-1971   **CLC 23;
  DAM POET; PC 21**
  See also CA 13-14; 29-32R; CANR 34, 61; CAP
  1; DLB 11; MAICYA; MTCW; SATA 2, 46
Nashe, Thomas 1567-1601(?)   **LC 41**
  See also DLB 167
Nashe, Thomas 1567-1601   **LC 41**
Nathan, Daniel
  See Dannay, Frederic

Nathan, George Jean 1882-1958   **TCLC 18**
  See also Hatteras, Owen
  See also CA 114; DLB 137
Natsume, Kinnosuke 1867-1916
  See Natsume, Soseki
  See also CA 104
Natsume, Soseki 1867-1916   **TCLC 2, 10**
  See also Natsume, Kinnosuke
  See also DLB 180
Natti, (Mary) Lee 1919-
  See Kingman, Lee
  See also CA 5-8R; CANR 2
Naylor, Gloria 1950-**CLC 28, 52; BLC 3; DA;
  DAC; DAM MST, MULT, NOV, POP;
  WLCS**
  See also AAYA 6; BW 2; CA 107; CANR 27,
  51; DLB 173; MTCW
Neihardt, John Gneisenau 1881-1973 **CLC 32**
  See also CA 13-14; CANR 65; CAP 1; DLB 9,
  54
Nekrasov, Nikolai Alekseevich 1821-1878
  NCLC 11
Nelligan, Emile 1879-1941   **TCLC 14**
  See also CA 114; DLB 92
Nelson, Willie 1933-   **CLC 17**
  See also CA 107
Nemerov, Howard (Stanley) 1920-1991**CLC 2,
  6, 9, 36; DAM POET**
  See also CA 1-4R; 134; CABS 2; CANR 1, 27,
  53; DLB 5, 6; DLBY 83; INT CANR-27;
  MTCW
Neruda, Pablo 1904-1973**CLC 1, 2, 5, 7, 9, 28,
  62; DA; DAB; DAC; DAM MST, MULT,
  POET; HLC; PC 4; WLC**
  See also CA 19-20; 45-48; CAP 2; HW; MTCW
Nerval, Gerard de 1808-1855**NCLC 1, 67; PC
  13; SSC 18**
Nervo, (Jose) Amado (Ruiz de) 1870-1919
  TCLC 11
  See also CA 109; 131; HW
Nessi, Pio Baroja y
  See Baroja (y Nessi), Pio
Nestroy, Johann 1801-1862   **NCLC 42**
  See also DLB 133
Netterville, Luke
  See O'Grady, Standish (James)
Neufeld, John (Arthur) 1938-   **CLC 17**
  See also AAYA 11; CA 25-28R; CANR 11, 37,
  56; CLR 52; MAICYA; SAAS 3; SATA 6,
  81
Neville, Emily Cheney 1919-   **CLC 12**
  See also CA 5-8R; CANR 3, 37; JRDA;
  MAICYA; SAAS 2; SATA 1
Newbound, Bernard Slade 1930-
  See Slade, Bernard
  See also CA 81-84; CANR 49; DAM DRAM
Newby, P(ercy) H(oward) 1918-1997 **CLC 2,
  13; DAM NOV**
  See also CA 5-8R; 161; CANR 32, 67; DLB
  15; MTCW
Newlove, Donald 1928-   **CLC 6**
  See also CA 29-32R; CANR 25
Newlove, John (Herbert) 1938-   **CLC 14**
  See also CA 21-24R; CANR 9, 25
Newman, Charles 1938-   **CLC 2, 8**
  See also CA 21-24R
Newman, Edwin (Harold) 1919-   **CLC 14**
  See also AITN 1; CA 69-72; CANR 5
Newman, John Henry 1801-1890   **NCLC 38**
  See also DLB 18, 32, 55
Newton, Suzanne 1936-   **CLC 35**
  See also CA 41-44R; CANR 14; JRDA; SATA
  5, 77

Nexo, Martin Andersen 1869-1954 **TCLC 43**
Nezval, Vitezslav 1900-1958   **TCLC 44**
  See also CA 123
Ng, Fae Myenne 1957(?)-   **CLC 81**
  See also CA 146
Ngema, Mbongeni 1955-   **CLC 57**
  See also BW 2; CA 143
Ngugi, James T(hiong'o)   **CLC 3, 7, 13**
  See also Ngugi wa Thiong'o
Ngugi wa Thiong'o 1938-   **CLC 36; BLC 3;
  DAM MULT, NOV**
  See also Ngugi, James T(hiong'o)
  See also BW 2; CA 81-84; CANR 27, 58; DLB
  125; MTCW
Nichol, B(arrie) P(hillip) 1944-1988 **CLC 18**
  See also CA 53-56; DLB 53; SATA 66
Nichols, John (Treadwell) 1940-   **CLC 38**
  See also CA 9-12R; CAAS 2; CANR 6; DLBY
  82
Nichols, Leigh
  See Koontz, Dean R(ay)
Nichols, Peter (Richard) 1927- **CLC 5, 36, 65**
  See also CA 104; CANR 33; DLB 13; MTCW
Nicolas, F. R. E.
  See Freeling, Nicolas
Niedecker, Lorine 1903-1970   **CLC 10, 42;
  DAM POET**
  See also CA 25-28; CAP 2; DLB 48
Nietzsche, Friedrich (Wilhelm) 1844-1900
  TCLC 10, 18, 55
  See also CA 107; 121; DLB 129
Nievo, Ippolito 1831-1861   **NCLC 22**
Nightingale, Anne Redmon 1943-
  See Redmon, Anne
  See also CA 103
Nik. T. O.
  See Annensky, Innokenty (Fyodorovich)
Nin, Anais 1903-1977 **CLC 1, 4, 8, 11, 14, 60;
  DAM NOV, POP; SSC 10**
  See also AITN 2; CA 13-16R; 69-72; CANR
  22, 53; DLB 2, 4, 152; MTCW
Nishida, Kitaro 1870-1945   **TCLC 83**
Nishiwaki, Junzaburo 1894-1982   **PC 15**
  See also CA 107
Nissenson, Hugh 1933-   **CLC 4, 9**
  See also CA 17-20R; CANR 27; DLB 28
Niven, Larry   **CLC 8**
  See also Niven, Laurence Van Cott
  See also DLB 8
Niven, Laurence Van Cott 1938-
  See Niven, Larry
  See also CA 21-24R; CAAS 12; CANR 14, 44,
  66; DAM POP; MTCW; SATA 95
Nixon, Agnes Eckhardt 1927-   **CLC 21**
  See also CA 110
Nizan, Paul 1905-1940   **TCLC 40**
  See also CA 161; DLB 72
Nkosi, Lewis 1936-   **CLC 45; BLC 3; DAM
  MULT**
  See also BW 1; CA 65-68; CANR 27; DLB 157
Nodier, (Jean) Charles (Emmanuel) 1780-1844
  NCLC 19
  See also DLB 119
Noguchi, Yone 1875-1947   **TCLC 80**
Nolan, Christopher 1965-   **CLC 58**
  See also CA 111
Noon, Jeff 1957-   **CLC 91**
  See also CA 148
Norden, Charles
  See Durrell, Lawrence (George)
Nordhoff, Charles (Bernard) 1887-1947
  TCLC 23
  See also CA 108; DLB 9; SATA 23

Norfolk, Lawrence 1963-   **CLC 76**
  See also CA 144
Norman, Marsha 1947-**CLC 28; DAM DRAM;**
    DC 8
  See also CA 105; CABS 3; CANR 41; DLBY
    84
Normyx
  See Douglas, (George) Norman
Norris, Frank 1870-1902   **SSC 28**
  See also Norris, (Benjamin) Frank(lin, Jr.)
  See also CDALB 1865-1917; DLB 12, 71, 186
Norris, (Benjamin) Frank(lin, Jr.) 1870-1902
    TCLC 24
  See also Norris, Frank
  See also CA 110; 160
Norris, Leslie 1921-   **CLC 14**
  See also CA 11-12; CANR 14; CAP 1; DLB 27
North, Andrew
  See Norton, Andre
North, Anthony
  See Koontz, Dean R(ay)
North, Captain George
  See Stevenson, Robert Louis (Balfour)
North, Milou
  See Erdrich, Louise
Northrup, B. A.
  See Hubbard, L(afayette) Ron(ald)
North Staffs
  See Hulme, T(homas) E(rnest)
Norton, Alice Mary
  See Norton, Andre
  See also MAICYA; SATA 1, 43
Norton, Andre 1912-   **CLC 12**
  See also Norton, Alice Mary
  See also AAYA 14; CA 1-4R; CANR 68; CLR
    50; DLB 8, 52; JRDA; MTCW; SATA 91
Norton, Caroline 1808-1877   **NCLC 47**
  See also DLB 21, 159, 199
Norway, Nevil Shute 1899-1960
  See Shute, Nevil
  See also CA 102; 93-96
Norwid, Cyprian Kamil 1821-1883 **NCLC 17**
Nosille, Nabrah
  See Ellison, Harlan (Jay)
Nossack, Hans Erich 1901-1978   **CLC 6**
  See also CA 93-96; 85-88; DLB 69
Nostradamus 1503-1566   **LC 27**
Nosu, Chuji
  See Ozu, Yasujiro
Notenburg, Eleanora (Genrikhovna) von
  See Guro, Elena
Nova, Craig 1945-   **CLC 7, 31**
  See also CA 45-48; CANR 2, 53
Novak, Joseph
  See Kosinski, Jerzy (Nikodem)
Novalis 1772-1801   **NCLC 13**
  See also DLB 90
Novis, Emile
  See Weil, Simone (Adolphine)
Nowlan, Alden (Albert) 1933-1983   **CLC 15;**
    DAC; DAM MST
  See also CA 9-12R; CANR 5; DLB 53
Noyes, Alfred 1880-1958   **TCLC 7**
  See also CA 104; DLB 20
Nunn, Kem   **CLC 34**
  See also CA 159
Nye, Robert 1939-   **CLC 13, 42; DAM NOV**
  See also CA 33-36R; CANR 29, 67; DLB 14;
    MTCW; SATA 6
Nyro, Laura 1947-   **CLC 17**
Oates, Joyce Carol 1938-**CLC 1, 2, 3, 6, 9, 11,**
    15, 19, 33, 52, 108; DA; DAB; DAC; DAM
    MST, NOV, POP; SSC 6; WLC

  See also AAYA 15; AITN 1; BEST 89:2; CA 5-
    8R; CANR 25, 45; CDALB 1968-1988; DLB
    2, 5, 130; DLBY 81; INT CANR-25; MTCW
O'Brien, Darcy 1939-   **CLC 11**
  See also CA 21-24R; CANR 8, 59
O'Brien, E. G.
  See Clarke, Arthur C(harles)
O'Brien, Edna 1936-   **CLC 3, 5, 8, 13, 36, 65;**
    DAM NOV; SSC 10
  See also CA 1-4R; CANR 6, 41, 65; CDBLB
    1960 to Present; DLB 14; MTCW
O'Brien, Fitz-James 1828-1862   **NCLC 21**
  See also DLB 74
O'Brien, Flann   **CLC 1, 4, 5, 7, 10, 47**
  See also O Nuallain, Brian
O'Brien, Richard 1942-   **CLC 17**
  See also CA 124
O'Brien, (William) Tim(othy) 1946-   **CLC 7,**
    19, 40, 103; DAM POP
  See also AAYA 16; CA 85-88; CANR 40, 58;
    DLB 152; DLBD 9; DLBY 80
Obstfelder, Sigbjoern 1866-1900   **TCLC 23**
  See also CA 123
O'Casey, Sean 1880-1964 **CLC 1, 5, 9, 11, 15,**
    88; DAB; DAC; DAM DRAM, MST;
    WLCS
  See also CA 89-92; CANR 62; CDBLB 1914-
    1945; DLB 10; MTCW
O'Cathasaigh, Sean
  See O'Casey, Sean
Ochs, Phil 1940-1976   **CLC 17**
  See also CA 65-68
O'Connor, Edwin (Greene) 1918-1968**CLC 14**
  See also CA 93-96; 25-28R
O'Connor, (Mary) Flannery 1925-1964 **CLC**
    1, 2, 3, 6, 10, 13, 15, 21, 66, 104; DA; DAB;
    DAC; DAM MST, NOV; SSC 1, 23; WLC
  See also AAYA 7; CA 1-4R; CANR 3, 41;
    CDALB 1941-1968; DLB 2, 152; DLBD 12;
    DLBY 80; MTCW
O'Connor, Frank   **CLC 23; SSC 5**
  See also O'Donovan, Michael John
  See also DLB 162
O'Dell, Scott 1898-1989   **CLC 30**
  See also AAYA 3; CA 61-64; 129; CANR 12,
    30; CLR 1, 16; DLB 52; JRDA; MAICYA;
    SATA 12, 60
Odets, Clifford 1906-1963**CLC 2, 28, 98; DAM**
    DRAM; DC 6
  See also CA 85-88; CANR 62; DLB 7, 26;
    MTCW
O'Doherty, Brian 1934-   **CLC 76**
  See also CA 105
O'Donnell, K. M.
  See Malzberg, Barry N(athaniel)
O'Donnell, Lawrence
  See Kuttner, Henry
O'Donovan, Michael John 1903-1966 **CLC 14**
  See also O'Connor, Frank
  See also CA 93-96
Oe, Kenzaburo 1935-   **CLC 10, 36, 86; DAM**
    NOV; SSC 20
  See also CA 97-100; CANR 36, 50; DLB 182;
    DLBY 94; MTCW
O'Faolain, Julia 1932-   **CLC 6, 19, 47, 108**
  See also CA 81-84; CAAS 2; CANR 12, 61;
    DLB 14; MTCW
O'Faolain, Sean 1900-1991 **CLC 1, 7, 14, 32,**
    70; SSC 13
  See also CA 61-64; 134; CANR 12, 66; DLB
    15, 162; MTCW
O'Flaherty, Liam 1896-1984**CLC 5, 34; SSC 6**
  See also CA 101; 113; CANR 35; DLB 36, 162;

    DLBY 84; MTCW
Ogilvy, Gavin
  See Barrie, J(ames) M(atthew)
O'Grady, Standish (James) 1846-1928 **TCLC**
    5
  See also CA 104; 157
O'Grady, Timothy 1951-   **CLC 59**
  See also CA 138
O'Hara, Frank 1926-1966   **CLC 2, 5, 13, 78;**
    DAM POET
  See also CA 9-12R; 25-28R; CANR 33; DLB
    5, 16, 193; MTCW
O'Hara, John (Henry) 1905-1970**CLC 1, 2, 3,**
    6, 11, 42; DAM NOV; SSC 15
  See also CA 5-8R; 25-28R; CANR 31, 60;
    CDALB 1929-1941; DLB 9, 86; DLBD 2;
    MTCW
O Hehir, Diana 1922-   **CLC 41**
  See also CA 93-96
Okigbo, Christopher (Ifenayichukwu) 1932-
    1967   **CLC 25, 84; BLC 3; DAM MULT,**
    POET; PC 7
  See also BW 1; CA 77-80; DLB 125; MTCW
Okri, Ben 1959-   **CLC 87**
  See also BW 2; CA 130; 138; CANR 65; DLB
    157; INT 138
Olds, Sharon 1942-   **CLC 32, 39, 85; DAM**
    POET; PC 22
  See also CA 101; CANR 18, 41, 66; DLB 120
Oldstyle, Jonathan
  See Irving, Washington
Olesha, Yuri (Karlovich) 1899-1960   **CLC 8**
  See also CA 85-88
Oliphant, Laurence 1829(?)-1888   **NCLC 47**
  See also DLB 18, 166
Oliphant, Margaret (Oliphant Wilson) 1828-
    1897   **NCLC 11, 61; SSC 25**
  See also DLB 18, 159, 190
Oliver, Mary 1935-   **CLC 19, 34, 98**
  See also CA 21-24R; CANR 9, 43; DLB 5, 193
Olivier, Laurence (Kerr) 1907-1989   **CLC 20**
  See also CA 111; 150; 129
Olsen, Tillie 1913-**CLC 4, 13; DA; DAB; DAC;**
    DAM MST; SSC 11
  See also CA 1-4R; CANR 1, 43; DLB 28; DLBY
    80; MTCW
Olson, Charles (John) 1910-1970 **CLC 1, 2, 5,**
    6, 9, 11, 29; DAM POET; PC 19
  See also CA 13-16; 25-28R; CABS 2; CANR
    35, 61; CAP 1; DLB 5, 16, 193; MTCW
Olson, Toby 1937-   **CLC 28**
  See also CA 65-68; CANR 9, 31
Olyesha, Yuri
  See Olesha, Yuri (Karlovich)
Ondaatje, (Philip) Michael 1943- **CLC 14, 29,**
    51, 76; DAB; DAC; DAM MST
  See also CA 77-80; CANR 42; DLB 60
Oneal, Elizabeth 1934-
  See Oneal, Zibby
  See also CA 106; CANR 28; MAICYA; SATA
    30, 82
Oneal, Zibby   **CLC 30**
  See also Oneal, Elizabeth
  See also AAYA 5; CLR 13; JRDA
O'Neill, Eugene (Gladstone) 1888-1953**TCLC**
    1, 6, 27, 49; DA; DAB; DAC; DAM DRAM,
    MST; WLC
  See also AITN 1; CA 110; 132; CDALB 1929-
    1941; DLB 7; MTCW
Onetti, Juan Carlos 1909-1994   **CLC 7, 10;**
    DAM MULT, NOV; SSC 23
  See also CA 85-88; 145; CANR 32, 63; DLB
    113; HW; MTCW

O Nuallain, Brian 1911-1966
See O'Brien, Flann
See also CA 21-22; 25-28R; CAP 2
Ophuls, Max 1902-1957   **TCLC 79**
See also CA 113
Opie, Amelia 1769-1853   **NCLC 65**
See also DLB 116, 159
Oppen, George 1908-1984   **CLC 7, 13, 34**
See also CA 13-16R; 113; CANR 8; DLB 5, 165
Oppenheim, E(dward) Phillips 1866-1946
    TCLC 45
See also CA 111; DLB 70
Opuls, Max
See Ophuls, Max
Origen c. 185-c. 254   **CMLC 19**
Orlovitz, Gil 1918-1973   **CLC 22**
See also CA 77-80; 45-48; DLB 2, 5
Orris
See Ingelow, Jean
Ortega y Gasset, Jose 1883-1955   **TCLC 9;**
    DAM MULT; HLC
See also CA 106; 130; HW; MTCW
Ortese, Anna Maria 1914-   **CLC 89**
See also DLB 177
Ortiz, Simon J(oseph) 1941-   **CLC 45; DAM**
    MULT, POET; PC 17
See also CA 134; CANR 69; DLB 120, 175; NNAL
Orton, Joe   **CLC 4, 13, 43; DC 3**
See also Orton, John Kingsley
See also CDBLB 1960 to Present; DLB 13
Orton, John Kingsley 1933-1967
See Orton, Joe
See also CA 85-88; CANR 35, 66; DAM DRAM; MTCW
Orwell, George   **TCLC 2, 6, 15, 31, 51; DAB;**
    WLC
See also Blair, Eric (Arthur)
See also CDBLB 1945-1960; DLB 15, 98, 195
Osborne, David
See Silverberg, Robert
Osborne, George
See Silverberg, Robert
Osborne, John (James) 1929-1994**CLC 1, 2, 5,**
    11, 45; DA; DAB; DAC; DAM DRAM,
    MST; WLC
See also CA 13-16R; 147; CANR 21, 56; CDBLB 1945-1960; DLB 13; MTCW
Osborne, Lawrence 1958-   **CLC 50**
Oshima, Nagisa 1932-   **CLC 20**
See also CA 116; 121
Oskison, John Milton 1874-1947   **TCLC 35;**
    DAM MULT
See also CA 144; DLB 175; NNAL
Ossian c. 3rd cent. -   **CMLC 28**
See also Macpherson, James
Ossoli, Sarah Margaret (Fuller marchesa d')
    1810-1850
See Fuller, Margaret
See also SATA 25
Ostrovsky, Alexander 1823-1886**NCLC 30, 57**
Otero, Blas de 1916-1979   **CLC 11**
See also CA 89-92; DLB 134
Otto, Whitney 1955-   **CLC 70**
See also CA 140
Ouida   **TCLC 43**
See also De La Ramee, (Marie) Louise
See also DLB 18, 156
Ousmane, Sembene 1923-   **CLC 66; BLC 3**
See also BW 1; CA 117; 125; MTCW
Ovid 43B.C.-18(?) **CMLC 7; DAM POET; PC**
    2

Owen, Hugh
See Faust, Frederick (Schiller)
Owen, Wilfred (Edward Salter) 1893-1918
    TCLC 5, 27; DA; DAB; DAC; DAM MST,
    POET; PC 19; WLC
See also CA 104; 141; CDBLB 1914-1945; DLB 20
Owens, Rochelle 1936-   **CLC 8**
See also CA 17-20R; CAAS 2; CANR 39
Oz, Amos 1939-**CLC 5, 8, 11, 27, 33, 54; DAM**
    NOV
See also CA 53-56; CANR 27, 47, 65; MTCW
Ozick, Cynthia 1928- **CLC 3, 7, 28, 62; DAM**
    NOV, POP; SSC 15
See also BEST 90:1; CA 17-20R; CANR 23, 58; DLB 28, 152; DLBY 82; INT CANR-23; MTCW
Ozu, Yasujiro 1903-1963   **CLC 16**
See also CA 112
Pacheco, C.
See Pessoa, Fernando (Antonio Nogueira)
Pa Chin   **CLC 18**
See also Li Fei-kan
Pack, Robert 1929-   **CLC 13**
See also CA 1-4R; CANR 3, 44; DLB 5
Padgett, Lewis
See Kuttner, Henry
Padilla (Lorenzo), Heberto 1932-   **CLC 38**
See also AITN 1; CA 123; 131; HW
Page, Jimmy 1944-   **CLC 12**
Page, Louise 1955-   **CLC 40**
See also CA 140
Page, P(atricia) K(athleen) 1916- **CLC 7, 18;**
    DAC; DAM MST; PC 12
See also CA 53-56; CANR 4, 22, 65; DLB 68; MTCW
Page, Thomas Nelson 1853-1922   **SSC 23**
See also CA 118; DLB 12, 78; DLBD 13
Pagels, Elaine Hiesey 1943-   **CLC 104**
See also CA 45-48; CANR 2, 24, 51
Paget, Violet 1856-1935
See Lee, Vernon
See also CA 104; 166
Paget-Lowe, Henry
See Lovecraft, H(oward) P(hillips)
Paglia, Camille (Anna) 1947-   **CLC 68**
See also CA 140
Paige, Richard
See Koontz, Dean R(ay)
Paine, Thomas 1737-1809   **NCLC 62**
See also CDALB 1640-1865; DLB 31, 43, 73, 158
Pakenham, Antonia
See Fraser, (Lady) Antonia (Pakenham)
Palamas, Kostes 1859-1943   **TCLC 5**
See also CA 105
Palazzeschi, Aldo 1885-1974   **CLC 11**
See also CA 89-92; 53-56; DLB 114
Paley, Grace 1922- **CLC 4, 6, 37; DAM POP;**
    SSC 8
See also CA 25-28R; CANR 13, 46; DLB 28; INT CANR-13; MTCW
Palin, Michael (Edward) 1943-   **CLC 21**
See also Monty Python
See also CA 107; CANR 35; SATA 67
Palliser, Charles 1947-   **CLC 65**
See also CA 136
Palma, Ricardo 1833-1919   **TCLC 29**
Pancake, Breece Dexter 1952-1979
See Pancake, Breece D'J
See also CA 123; 109
Pancake, Breece D'J   **CLC 29**
See also Pancake, Breece Dexter

See also DLB 130
Panko, Rudy
See Gogol, Nikolai (Vasilyevich)
Papadiamantis, Alexandros 1851-1911 **TCLC**
    29
Papadiamantopoulos, Johannes 1856-1910
See Moreas, Jean
See also CA 117
Papini, Giovanni 1881-1956   **TCLC 22**
See also CA 121
Paracelsus 1493-1541   **LC 14**
See also DLB 179
Parasol, Peter
See Stevens, Wallace
Pardo Bazán, Emilia 1851-1921   **SSC 30**
Pareto, Vilfredo 1848-1923   **TCLC 69**
Parfenie, Maria
See Codrescu, Andrei
Parini, Jay (Lee) 1948-   **CLC 54**
See also CA 97-100; CAAS 16; CANR 32
Park, Jordan
See Kornbluth, C(yril) M.; Pohl, Frederik
Park, Robert E(zra) 1864-1944   **TCLC 73**
See also CA 122; 165
Parker, Bert
See Ellison, Harlan (Jay)
Parker, Dorothy (Rothschild) 1893-1967 **CLC**
    15, 68; DAM POET; SSC 2
See also CA 19-20; 25-28R; CAP 2; DLB 11, 45, 86; MTCW
Parker, Robert B(rown) 1932- **CLC 27; DAM**
    NOV, POP
See also BEST 89:4; CA 49-52; CANR 1, 26, 52; INT CANR-26; MTCW
Parkin, Frank 1940-   **CLC 43**
See also CA 147
Parkman, Francis, Jr. 1823-1893   **NCLC 12**
See also DLB 1, 30, 186
Parks, Gordon (Alexander Buchanan) 1912-
    CLC 1, 16; BLC 3; DAM MULT
See also AITN 2; BW 2; CA 41-44R; CANR 26, 66; DLB 33; SATA 8
Parmenides c. 515B.C.-c. 450B.C.   **CMLC 22**
See also DLB 176
Parnell, Thomas 1679-1718   **LC 3**
See also DLB 94
Parra, Nicanor 1914-   **CLC 2, 102; DAM**
    MULT; HLC
See also CA 85-88; CANR 32; HW; MTCW
Parrish, Mary Frances
See Fisher, M(ary) F(rances) K(ennedy)
Parson
See Coleridge, Samuel Taylor
Parson Lot
See Kingsley, Charles
Partridge, Anthony
See Oppenheim, E(dward) Phillips
Pascal, Blaise 1623-1662   **LC 35**
Pascoli, Giovanni 1855-1912   **TCLC 45**
Pasolini, Pier Paolo 1922-1975   **CLC 20, 37,**
    106; PC 17
See also CA 93-96; 61-64; CANR 63; DLB 128, 177; MTCW
Pasquini
See Silone, Ignazio
Pastan, Linda (Olenik) 1932- **CLC 27; DAM**
    POET
See also CA 61-64; CANR 18, 40, 61; DLB 5
Pasternak, Boris (Leonidovich) 1890-1960
    CLC 7, 10, 18, 63; DA; DAB; DAC; DAM
    MST, NOV, POET; PC 6; SSC 31; WLC
See also CA 127; 116; MTCW
Patchen, Kenneth 1911-1972   **CLC 1, 2, 18;**

See also CA 118

Pinero, Arthur Wing 1855-1934   **TCLC 32; DAM DRAM**
See also CA 110; 153; DLB 10

Pinero, Miguel (Antonio Gomez) 1946-1988 **CLC 4, 55**
See also CA 61-64; 125; CANR 29; HW

Pinget, Robert 1919-1997   **CLC 7, 13, 37**
See also CA 85-88; 160; DLB 83

Pink Floyd
See Barrett, (Roger) Syd; Gilmour, David; Mason, Nick; Waters, Roger; Wright, Rick

Pinkney, Edward 1802-1828   **NCLC 31**

Pinkwater, Daniel Manus 1941-   **CLC 35**
See also Pinkwater, Manus
See also AAYA 1; CA 29-32R; CANR 12, 38; CLR 4; JRDA; MAICYA; SAAS 3; SATA 46, 76

Pinkwater, Manus
See Pinkwater, Daniel Manus
See also SATA 8

Pinsky, Robert 1940-**CLC 9, 19, 38, 94; DAM POET**
See also CA 29-32R; CAAS 4; CANR 58; DLBY 82

Pinta, Harold
See Pinter, Harold

Pinter, Harold 1930-**CLC 1, 3, 6, 9, 11, 15, 27, 58, 73; DA; DAB; DAC; DAM DRAM, MST; WLC**
See also CA 5-8R; CANR 33, 65; CDBLB 1960 to Present; DLB 13; MTCW

Piozzi, Hester Lynch (Thrale) 1741-1821 **NCLC 57**
See also DLB 104, 142

Pirandello, Luigi 1867-1936**TCLC 4, 29; DA; DAB; DAC; DAM DRAM, MST; DC 5; SSC 22; WLC**
See also CA 104; 153

Pirsig, Robert M(aynard) 1928-**CLC 4, 6, 73; DAM POP**
See also CA 53-56; CANR 42; MTCW; SATA 39

Pisarev, Dmitry Ivanovich 1840-1868 **NCLC 25**

Pix, Mary (Griffith) 1666-1709   **LC 8**
See also DLB 80

Pixerecourt, (Rene Charles) Guilbert de 1773-1844 **NCLC 39**
See also DLB 192

Plaatje, Sol(omon) T(shekisho) 1876-1932 **TCLC 73; BLCS**
See also BW 2; CA 141

Plaidy, Jean
See Hibbert, Eleanor Alice Burford

Planche, James Robinson 1796-1880**NCLC 42**

Plant, Robert 1948-   **CLC 12**

Plante, David (Robert) 1940-   **CLC 7, 23, 38; DAM NOV**
See also CA 37-40R; CANR 12, 36, 58; DLBY 83; INT CANR-12; MTCW

Plath, Sylvia 1932-1963   **CLC 1, 2, 3, 5, 9, 11, 14, 17, 50, 51, 62, 111; DA; DAB; DAC; DAM MST, POET; PC 1; WLC**
See also AAYA 13; CA 19-20; CANR 34; CAP 2; CDALB 1941-1968; DLB 5, 6, 152; MTCW; SATA 96

Plato 428(?)B.C.-348(?)B.C.   **CMLC 8; DA; DAB; DAC; DAM MST; WLCS**
See also DLB 176

Platonov, Andrei   **TCLC 14**
See also Klimentov, Andrei Platonovich

Platt, Kin 1911-   **CLC 26**

See also AAYA 11; CA 17-20R; CANR 11; JRDA; SAAS 17; SATA 21, 86

Plautus c. 251B.C.-184B.C.   **CMLC 24; DC 6**

Plick et Plock
See Simenon, Georges (Jacques Christian)

Plimpton, George (Ames) 1927-   **CLC 36**
See also AITN 1; CA 21-24R; CANR 32; DLB 185; MTCW; SATA 10

Pliny the Elder c. 23-79   **CMLC 23**

Plomer, William Charles Franklin 1903-1973 **CLC 4, 8**
See also CA 21-22; CANR 34; CAP 2; DLB 20, 162, 191; MTCW; SATA 24

Plowman, Piers
See Kavanagh, Patrick (Joseph)

Plum, J.
See Wodehouse, P(elham) G(renville)

Plumly, Stanley (Ross) 1939-   **CLC 33**
See also CA 108; 110; DLB 5, 193; INT 110

Plumpe, Friedrich Wilhelm 1888-1931 **TCLC 53**
See also CA 112

Po Chu-i 772-846   **CMLC 24**

Poe, Edgar Allan 1809-1849 **NCLC 1, 16, 55; DA; DAB; DAC; DAM MST, POET; PC 1; SSC 1, 22; WLC**
See also AAYA 14; CDALB 1640-1865; DLB 3, 59, 73, 74; SATA 23

Poet of Titchfield Street, The
See Pound, Ezra (Weston Loomis)

Pohl, Frederik 1919-   **CLC 18; SSC 25**
See also AAYA 24; CA 61-64; CAAS 1; CANR 11, 37; DLB 8; INT CANR-11; MTCW; SATA 24

Poirier, Louis 1910-
See Gracq, Julien
See also CA 122; 126

Poitier, Sidney 1927-   **CLC 26**
See also BW 1; CA 117

Polanski, Roman 1933-   **CLC 16**
See also CA 77-80

Poliakoff, Stephen 1952-   **CLC 38**
See also CA 106; DLB 13

Police, The
See Copeland, Stewart (Armstrong); Summers, Andrew James; Sumner, Gordon Matthew

Polidori, John William 1795-1821 **NCLC 51**
See also DLB 116

Pollitt, Katha 1949-   **CLC 28**
See also CA 120; 122; CANR 66; MTCW

Pollock, (Mary) Sharon 1936-   **CLC 50; DAC; DAM DRAM, MST**
See also CA 141; DLB 60

Polo, Marco 1254-1324   **CMLC 15**

Polonsky, Abraham (Lincoln) 1910-   **CLC 92**
See also CA 104; DLB 26; INT 104

Polybius c. 200B.C.-c. 118B.C.   **CMLC 17**
See also DLB 176

Pomerance, Bernard 1940-   **CLC 13; DAM DRAM**
See also CA 101; CANR 49

Ponge, Francis (Jean Gaston Alfred) 1899-1988 **CLC 6, 18; DAM POET**
See also CA 85-88; 126; CANR 40

Pontoppidan, Henrik 1857-1943   **TCLC 29**

Poole, Josephine   **CLC 17**
See also Helyar, Jane Penelope Josephine
See also SAAS 2; SATA 5

Popa, Vasko 1922-1991   **CLC 19**
See also CA 112; 148; DLB 181

Pope, Alexander 1688-1744   **LC 3; DA; DAB; DAC; DAM MST, POET; WLC**
See also CDBLB 1660-1789; DLB 95, 101

Porter, Connie (Rose) 1959(?)-   **CLC 70**
See also BW 2; CA 142; SATA 81

Porter, Gene(va Grace) Stratton 1863(?)-1924 **TCLC 21**
See also CA 112

Porter, Katherine Anne 1890-1980**CLC 1, 3, 7, 10, 13, 15, 27, 101; DA; DAB; DAC; DAM MST, NOV; SSC 4, 31**
See also AITN 2; CA 1-4R; 101; CANR 1, 65; DLB 4, 9, 102; DLBD 12; DLBY 80; MTCW; SATA 39; SATA-Obit 23

Porter, Peter (Neville Frederick) 1929-**CLC 5, 13, 33**
See also CA 85-88; DLB 40

Porter, William Sydney 1862-1910
See Henry, O.
See also CA 104; 131; CDALB 1865-1917; DA; DAB; DAC; DAM MST; DLB 12, 78, 79; MTCW; YABC 2

Portillo (y Pacheco), Jose Lopez
See Lopez Portillo (y Pacheco), Jose

Post, Melville Davisson 1869-1930 **TCLC 39**
See also CA 110

Potok, Chaim 1929-   **CLC 2, 7, 14, 26, 112; DAM NOV**
See also AAYA 15; AITN 1, 2; CA 17-20R; CANR 19, 35, 64; DLB 28, 152; INT CANR-19; MTCW; SATA 33

Potter, (Helen) Beatrix 1866-1943
See Webb, (Martha) Beatrice (Potter)
See also MAICYA

Potter, Dennis (Christopher George) 1935-1994 **CLC 58, 86**
See also CA 107; 145; CANR 33, 61; MTCW

Pound, Ezra (Weston Loomis) 1885-1972**CLC 1, 2, 3, 4, 5, 7, 10, 13, 18, 34, 48, 50, 112; DA; DAB; DAC; DAM MST, POET; PC 4; WLC**
See also CA 5-8R; 37-40R; CANR 40; CDALB 1917-1929; DLB 4, 45, 63; DLBD 15; MTCW

Povod, Reinaldo 1959-1994   **CLC 44**
See also CA 136; 146

Powell, Adam Clayton, Jr. 1908-1972**CLC 89; BLC 3; DAM MULT**
See also BW 1; CA 102; 33-36R

Powell, Anthony (Dymoke) 1905-**CLC 1, 3, 7, 9, 10, 31**
See also CA 1-4R; CANR 1, 32, 62; CDBLB 1945-1960; DLB 15; MTCW

Powell, Dawn 1897-1965   **CLC 66**
See also CA 5-8R; DLBY 97

Powell, Padgett 1952-   **CLC 34**
See also CA 126; CANR 63

Power, Susan 1961-   **CLC 91**

Powers, J(ames) F(arl) 1917-**CLC 1, 4, 8, 57; SSC 4**
See also CA 1-4R; CANR 2, 61; DLB 130; MTCW

Powers, John J(ames) 1945-
See Powers, John R.
See also CA 69-72

Powers, John R.   **CLC 66**
See also Powers, John J(ames)

Powers, Richard (S.) 1957-   **CLC 93**
See also CA 148

Pownall, David 1938-   **CLC 10**
See also CA 89-92; CAAS 18; CANR 49; DLB 14

Powys, John Cowper 1872-1963**CLC 7, 9, 15, 46**
See also CA 85-88; DLB 15; MTCW

Powys, T(heodore) F(rancis) 1875-1953

TCLC 9
See also CA 106; DLB 36, 162
Prado (Calvo), Pedro 1886-1952   **TCLC 75**
See also CA 131; HW
Prager, Emily 1952-   **CLC 56**
Pratt, E(dwin) J(ohn) 1883(?)-1964   **CLC 19; DAC; DAM POET**
See also CA 141; 93-96; DLB 92
Premchand   **TCLC 21**
See also Srivastava, Dhanpat Rai
Preussler, Otfried 1923-   **CLC 17**
See also CA 77-80; SATA 24
Prevert, Jacques (Henri Marie) 1900-1977 **CLC 15**
See also CA 77-80; 69-72; CANR 29, 61; MTCW; SATA-Obit 30
Prevost, Abbe (Antoine Francois) 1697-1763 **LC 1**
Price, (Edward) Reynolds 1933-**CLC 3, 6, 13, 43, 50, 63; DAM NOV; SSC 22**
See also CA 1-4R; CANR 1, 37, 57; DLB 2; INT CANR-37
Price, Richard 1949-   **CLC 6, 12**
See also CA 49-52; CANR 3; DLBY 81
Prichard, Katharine Susannah 1883-1969 **CLC 46**
See also CA 11-12; CANR 33; CAP 1; MTCW; SATA 66
Priestley, J(ohn) B(oynton) 1894-1984**CLC 2, 5, 9, 34; DAM DRAM, NOV**
See also CA 9-12R; 113; CANR 33; CDBLB 1914-1945; DLB 10, 34, 77, 100, 139; DLBY 84; MTCW
Prince 1958(?)-   **CLC 35**
Prince, F(rank) T(empleton) 1912-   **CLC 22**
See also CA 101; CANR 43; DLB 20
Prince Kropotkin
See Kropotkin, Peter (Aleksieevich)
Prior, Matthew 1664-1721   **LC 4**
See also DLB 95
Prishvin, Mikhail 1873-1954   **TCLC 75**
Pritchard, William H(arrison) 1932- **CLC 34**
See also CA 65-68; CANR 23; DLB 111
Pritchett, V(ictor) S(awdon) 1900-1997 **CLC 5, 13, 15, 41; DAM NOV; SSC 14**
See also CA 61-64; 157; CANR 31, 63; DLB 15, 139; MTCW
Private 19022
See Manning, Frederic
Probst, Mark 1925-   **CLC 59**
See also CA 130
Prokosch, Frederic 1908-1989   **CLC 4, 48**
See also CA 73-76; 128; DLB 48
Prophet, The
See Dreiser, Theodore (Herman Albert)
Prose, Francine 1947-   **CLC 45**
See also CA 109; 112; CANR 46
Proudhon
See Cunha, Euclides (Rodrigues Pimenta) da
Proulx, Annie
See Proulx, E(dna) Annie
Proulx, E(dna) Annie 1935-   **CLC 81; DAM POP**
See also CA 145; CANR 65
Proust, (Valentin-Louis-George-Eugene-) Marcel 1871-1922 **TCLC 7, 13, 33; DA; DAB; DAC; DAM MST, NOV; WLC**
See also CA 104; 120; DLB 65; MTCW
Prowler, Harley
See Masters, Edgar Lee
Prus, Boleslaw 1845-1912   **TCLC 48**
Pryor, Richard (Franklin Lenox Thomas) 1940- **CLC 26**

See also CA 122
Przybyszewski, Stanislaw 1868-1927**TCLC 36**
See also CA 160; DLB 66
Pteleon
See Grieve, C(hristopher) M(urray)
See also DAM POET
Puckett, Lute
See Masters, Edgar Lee
Puig, Manuel 1932-1990 **CLC 3, 5, 10, 28, 65; DAM MULT; HLC**
See also CA 45-48; CANR 2, 32, 63; DLB 113; HW; MTCW
Pulitzer, Joseph 1847-1911   **TCLC 76**
See also CA 114; DLB 23
Purdy, A(lfred) W(ellington) 1918- **CLC 3, 6, 14, 50; DAC; DAM MST, POET**
See also CA 81-84; CAAS 17; CANR 42, 66; DLB 88
Purdy, James (Amos) 1923- **CLC 2, 4, 10, 28, 52**
See also CA 33-36R; CAAS 1; CANR 19, 51; DLB 2; INT CANR-19; MTCW
Pure, Simon
See Swinnerton, Frank Arthur
Pushkin, Alexander (Sergeyevich) 1799-1837 **NCLC 3, 27; DA; DAB; DAC; DAM DRAM, MST, POET; PC 10; SSC 27; WLC**
See also SATA 61
P'u Sung-ling 1640-1715   **LC 3; SSC 31**
Putnam, Arthur Lee
See Alger, Horatio, Jr.
Puzo, Mario 1920-**CLC 1, 2, 6, 36, 107; DAM NOV, POP**
See also CA 65-68; CANR 4, 42, 65; DLB 6; MTCW
Pygge, Edward
See Barnes, Julian (Patrick)
Pyle, Ernest Taylor 1900-1945
See Pyle, Ernie
See also CA 115; 160
Pyle, Ernie 1900-1945   **TCLC 75**
See also Pyle, Ernest Taylor
See also DLB 29
Pyle, Howard 1853-1911   **TCLC 81**
See also CA 109; 137; CLR 22; DLB 42, 188; DLBD 13; MAICYA; SATA 16
Pym, Barbara (Mary Crampton) 1913-1980 **CLC 13, 19, 37, 111**
See also CA 13-14; 97-100; CANR 13, 34; CAP 1; DLB 14; DLBY 87; MTCW
Pynchon, Thomas (Ruggles, Jr.) 1937-**CLC 2, 3, 6, 9, 11, 18, 33, 62, 72; DA; DAB; DAC; DAM MST, NOV, POP; SSC 14; WLC**
See also BEST 90:2; CA 17-20R; CANR 22, 46; DLB 2, 173; MTCW
Pythagoras c. 570B.C.-c. 500B.C.   **CMLC 22**
See also DLB 176
Q
See Quiller-Couch, SirArthur (Thomas)
Qian Zhongshu
See Ch'ien Chung-shu
Qroll
See Dagerman, Stig (Halvard)
Quarrington, Paul (Lewis) 1953-   **CLC 65**
See also CA 129; CANR 62
Quasimodo, Salvatore 1901-1968   **CLC 10**
See also CA 13-16; 25-28R; CAP 1; DLB 114; MTCW
Quay, Stephen 1947-   **CLC 95**
Quay, Timothy 1947-   **CLC 95**
Queen, Ellery   **CLC 3, 11**
See also Dannay, Frederic; Davidson, Avram;

Lee, Manfred B(ennington); Marlowe, Stephen; Sturgeon, Theodore (Hamilton); Vance, John Holbrook
Queen, Ellery, Jr.
See Dannay, Frederic; Lee, Manfred B(ennington)
Queneau, Raymond 1903-1976 **CLC 2, 5, 10, 42**
See also CA 77-80; 69-72; CANR 32; DLB 72; MTCW
Quevedo, Francisco de 1580-1645   **LC 23**
Quiller-Couch, SirArthur (Thomas) 1863-1944 **TCLC 53**
See also CA 118; 166; DLB 135, 153, 190
Quin, Ann (Marie) 1936-1973   **CLC 6**
See also CA 9-12R; 45-48; DLB 14
Quinn, Martin
See Smith, Martin Cruz
Quinn, Peter 1947-   **CLC 91**
Quinn, Simon
See Smith, Martin Cruz
Quiroga, Horacio (Sylvestre) 1878-1937 **TCLC 20; DAM MULT; HLC**
See also CA 117; 131; HW; MTCW
Quoirez, Francoise 1935-   **CLC 9**
See also Sagan, Francoise
See also CA 49-52; CANR 6, 39; MTCW
Raabe, Wilhelm 1831-1910   **TCLC 45**
See also DLB 129
Rabe, David (William) 1940-   **CLC 4, 8, 33; DAM DRAM**
See also CA 85-88; CABS 3; CANR 59; DLB 7
Rabelais, Francois 1483-1553**LC 5; DA; DAB; DAC; DAM MST; WLC**
Rabinovitch, Sholem 1859-1916
See Aleichem, Sholom
See also CA 104
Rachilde 1860-1953   **TCLC 67**
See also DLB 123, 192
Racine, Jean 1639-1699   **LC 28; DAB; DAM MST**
Radcliffe, Ann (Ward) 1764-1823**NCLC 6, 55**
See also DLB 39, 178
Radiguet, Raymond 1903-1923   **TCLC 29**
See also CA 162; DLB 65
Radnoti, Miklos 1909-1944   **TCLC 16**
See also CA 118
Rado, James 1939-   **CLC 17**
See also CA 105
Radvanyi, Netty 1900-1983
See Seghers, Anna
See also CA 85-88; 110
Rae, Ben
See Griffiths, Trevor
Raeburn, John (Hay) 1941-   **CLC 34**
See also CA 57-60
Ragni, Gerome 1942-1991   **CLC 17**
See also CA 105; 134
Rahv, Philip 1908-1973   **CLC 24**
See also Greenberg, Ivan
See also DLB 137
Raimund, Ferdinand Jakob 1790-1836 **NCLC 69**
See also DLB 90
Raine, Craig 1944-   **CLC 32, 103**
See also CA 108; CANR 29, 51; DLB 40
Raine, Kathleen (Jessie) 1908-   **CLC 7, 45**
See also CA 85-88; CANR 46; DLB 20; MTCW
Rainis, Janis 1865-1929   **TCLC 29**
Rakosi, Carl 1903-   **CLC 47**
See also Rawley, Callman
See also CAAS 5; DLB 193
Raleigh, Richard

Author Index

Richardson, Dorothy Miller 1873-1957 **TCLC 3**
  See also CA 104; DLB 36
Richardson, Ethel Florence (Lindesay) 1870-1946
  See Richardson, Henry Handel
  See also CA 105
Richardson, Henry Handel   **TCLC 4**
  See also Richardson, Ethel Florence (Lindesay)
  See also DLB 197
Richardson, John 1796-1852 **NCLC 55; DAC**
  See also DLB 99
Richardson, Samuel 1689-1761 **LC 1, 44; DA; DAB; DAC; DAM MST, NOV; WLC**
  See also CDBLB 1660-1789; DLB 39
Richler, Mordecai 1931- **CLC 3, 5, 9, 13, 18, 46, 70; DAC; DAM MST, NOV**
  See also AITN 1; CA 65-68; CANR 31, 62; CLR 17; DLB 53; MAICYA; MTCW; SATA 44, 98; SATA-Brief 27
Richter, Conrad (Michael) 1890-1968 **CLC 30**
  See also AAYA 21; CA 5-8R; 25-28R; CANR 23; DLB 9; MTCW; SATA 3
Ricostranza, Tom
  See Ellis, Trey
Riddell, Charlotte 1832-1906   **TCLC 40**
  See also CA 165; DLB 156
Riding, Laura   **CLC 3, 7**
  See also Jackson, Laura (Riding)
Riefenstahl, Berta Helene Amalia 1902-
  See Riefenstahl, Leni
  See also CA 108
Riefenstahl, Leni   **CLC 16**
  See also Riefenstahl, Berta Helene Amalia
Riffe, Ernest
  See Bergman, (Ernst) Ingmar
Riggs, (Rolla) Lynn 1899-1954   **TCLC 56; DAM MULT**
  See also CA 144; DLB 175; NNAL
Riis, Jacob A(ugust) 1849-1914   **TCLC 80**
  See also CA 113; DLB 23
Riley, James Whitcomb 1849-1916 **TCLC 51; DAM POET**
  See also CA 118; 137; MAICYA; SATA 17
Riley, Tex
  See Creasey, John
Rilke, Rainer Maria 1875-1926 **TCLC 1, 6, 19; DAM POET; PC 2**
  See also CA 104; 132; CANR 62; DLB 81; MTCW
Rimbaud, (Jean Nicolas) Arthur 1854-1891 **NCLC 4, 35; DA; DAB; DAC; DAM MST, POET; PC 3; WLC**
Rinehart, Mary Roberts 1876-1958 **TCLC 52**
  See also CA 108; 166
Ringmaster, The
  See Mencken, H(enry) L(ouis)
Ringwood, Gwen(dolyn Margaret) Pharis 1910-1984   **CLC 48**
  See also CA 148; 112; DLB 88
Rio, Michel 19(?)-   **CLC 43**
Ritsos, Giannes
  See Ritsos, Yannis
Ritsos, Yannis 1909-1990   **CLC 6, 13, 31**
  See also CA 77-80; 133; CANR 39, 61; MTCW
Ritter, Erika 1948(?)-   **CLC 52**
Rivera, Jose Eustasio 1889-1928   **TCLC 35**
  See also CA 162; HW
Rivers, Conrad Kent 1933-1968   **CLC 1**
  See also BW 1; CA 85-88; DLB 41
Rivers, Elfrida
  See Bradley, Marion Zimmer
Riverside, John

  See Heinlein, Robert A(nson)
Rizal, Jose 1861-1896   **NCLC 27**
Roa Bastos, Augusto (Antonio) 1917- **CLC 45; DAM MULT; HLC**
  See also CA 131; DLB 113; HW
Robbe-Grillet, Alain 1922- **CLC 1, 2, 4, 6, 8, 10, 14, 43**
  See also CA 9-12R; CANR 33, 65; DLB 83; MTCW
Robbins, Harold 1916-1997   **CLC 5; DAM NOV**
  See also CA 73-76; 162; CANR 26, 54; MTCW
Robbins, Thomas Eugene 1936-
  See Robbins, Tom
  See also CA 81-84; CANR 29, 59; DAM NOV, POP; MTCW
Robbins, Tom   **CLC 9, 32, 64**
  See also Robbins, Thomas Eugene
  See also BEST 90:3; DLBY 80
Robbins, Trina 1938-   **CLC 21**
  See also CA 128
Roberts, Charles G(eorge) D(ouglas) 1860-1943 **TCLC 8**
  See also CA 105; CLR 33; DLB 92; SATA 88; SATA-Brief 29
Roberts, Elizabeth Madox 1886-1941 **TCLC 68**
  See also CA 111; 166; DLB 9, 54, 102; SATA 33; SATA-Brief 27
Roberts, Kate 1891-1985   **CLC 15**
  See also CA 107; 116
Roberts, Keith (John Kingston) 1935- **CLC 14**
  See also CA 25-28R; CANR 46
Roberts, Kenneth (Lewis) 1885-1957 **TCLC 23**
  See also CA 109; DLB 9
Roberts, Michele (B.) 1949-   **CLC 48**
  See also CA 115; CANR 58
Robertson, Ellis
  See Ellison, Harlan (Jay); Silverberg, Robert
Robertson, Thomas William 1829-1871 **NCLC 35; DAM DRAM**
Robeson, Kenneth
  See Dent, Lester
Robinson, Edwin Arlington 1869-1935 **TCLC 5; DA; DAC; DAM MST, POET; PC 1**
  See also CA 104; 133; CDALB 1865-1917; DLB 54; MTCW
Robinson, Henry Crabb 1775-1867 **NCLC 15**
  See also DLB 107
Robinson, Jill 1936-   **CLC 10**
  See also CA 102; INT 102
Robinson, Kim Stanley 1952-   **CLC 34**
  See also CA 126
Robinson, Lloyd
  See Silverberg, Robert
Robinson, Marilynne 1944-   **CLC 25**
  See also CA 116
Robinson, Smokey   **CLC 21**
  See also Robinson, William, Jr.
Robinson, William, Jr. 1940-
  See Robinson, Smokey
  See also CA 116
Robison, Mary 1949-   **CLC 42, 98**
  See also CA 113; 116; DLB 130; INT 116
Rod, Edouard 1857-1910   **TCLC 52**
Roddenberry, Eugene Wesley 1921-1991
  See Roddenberry, Gene
  See also CA 110; 135; CANR 37; SATA 45; SATA-Obit 69
Roddenberry, Gene   **CLC 17**
  See also Roddenberry, Eugene Wesley
  See also AAYA 5; SATA-Obit 69
Rodgers, Mary 1931-   **CLC 12**

  See also CA 49-52; CANR 8, 55; CLR 20; INT CANR-8; JRDA; MAICYA; SATA 8
Rodgers, W(illiam) R(obert) 1909-1969 **CLC 7**
  See also CA 85-88; DLB 20
Rodman, Eric
  See Silverberg, Robert
Rodman, Howard 1920(?)-1985   **CLC 65**
  See also CA 118
Rodman, Maia
  See Wojciechowska, Maia (Teresa)
Rodriguez, Claudio 1934-   **CLC 10**
  See also DLB 134
Roelvaag, O(le) E(dvart) 1876-1931 **TCLC 17**
  See also CA 117; DLB 9
Roethke, Theodore (Huebner) 1908-1963 **CLC 1, 3, 8, 11, 19, 46, 101; DAM POET; PC 15**
  See also CA 81-84; CABS 2; CDALB 1941-1968; DLB 5; MTCW
Rogers, Samuel 1763-1855   **NCLC 69**
  See also DLB 93
Rogers, Thomas Hunton 1927-   **CLC 57**
  See also CA 89-92; INT 89-92
Rogers, Will(iam Penn Adair) 1879-1935 **TCLC 8, 71; DAM MULT**
  See also CA 105; 144; DLB 11; NNAL
Rogin, Gilbert 1929-   **CLC 18**
  See also CA 65-68; CANR 15
Rohan, Koda   **TCLC 22**
  See also Koda Shigeyuki
Rohlfs, Anna Katharine Green
  See Green, Anna Katharine
Rohmer, Eric   **CLC 16**
  See also Scherer, Jean-Marie Maurice
Rohmer, Sax   **TCLC 28**
  See also Ward, Arthur Henry Sarsfield
  See also DLB 70
Roiphe, Anne (Richardson) 1935-   **CLC 3, 9**
  See also CA 89-92; CANR 45; DLBY 80; INT 89-92
Rojas, Fernando de 1465-1541   **LC 23**
Rolfe, Frederick (William Serafino Austin Lewis Mary) 1860-1913   **TCLC 12**
  See also CA 107; DLB 34, 156
Rolland, Romain 1866-1944   **TCLC 23**
  See also CA 118; DLB 65
Rolle, Richard c. 1300-c. 1349   **CMLC 21**
  See also DLB 146
Rolvaag, O(le) E(dvart)
  See Roelvaag, O(le) E(dvart)
Romain Arnaud, Saint
  See Aragon, Louis
Romains, Jules 1885-1972   **CLC 7**
  See also CA 85-88; CANR 34; DLB 65; MTCW
Romero, Jose Ruben 1890-1952   **TCLC 14**
  See also CA 114; 131; HW
Ronsard, Pierre de 1524-1585   **LC 6; PC 11**
Rooke, Leon 1934-   **CLC 25, 34; DAM POP**
  See also CA 25-28R; CANR 23, 53
Roosevelt, Theodore 1858-1919   **TCLC 69**
  See also CA 115; DLB 47, 186
Roper, William 1498-1578   **LC 10**
Roquelaure, A. N.
  See Rice, Anne
Rosa, Joao Guimaraes 1908-1967   **CLC 23**
  See also CA 89-92; DLB 113
Rose, Wendy 1948- **CLC 85; DAM MULT; PC 13**
  See also CA 53-56; CANR 5, 51; DLB 175; NNAL; SATA 12
Rosen, R. D.
  See Rosen, Richard (Dean)
Rosen, Richard (Dean) 1949-   **CLC 39**
  See also CA 77-80; CANR 62; INT CANR-30

NOV; WLC
See also CA 108; 132; CLR 10; DLB 72;
MAICYA; MTCW; SATA 20

St. John, David
See Hunt, E(verette) Howard, (Jr.)

Saint-John Perse
See Leger, (Marie-Rene Auguste) Alexis Saint-
Leger

Saintsbury, George (Edward Bateman) 1845-
1933   **TCLC 31**
See also CA 160; DLB 57, 149

Sait Faik   **TCLC 23**
See also Abasiyanik, Sait Faik

Saki   **TCLC 3; SSC 12**
See also Munro, H(ector) H(ugh)

Sala, George Augustus   **NCLC 46**

Salama, Hannu 1936-   **CLC 18**

Salamanca, J(ack) R(ichard) 1922- **CLC 4, 15**
See also CA 25-28R

Sale, J. Kirkpatrick
See Sale, Kirkpatrick

Sale, Kirkpatrick 1937-   **CLC 68**
See also CA 13-16R; CANR 10

Salinas, Luis Omar 1937-   **CLC 90; DAM**
MULT; HLC
See also CA 131; DLB 82; HW

Salinas (y Serrano), Pedro 1891(?)-1951
TCLC 17
See also CA 117; DLB 134

Salinger, J(erome) D(avid) 1919- **CLC 1, 3, 8,**
12, 55, 56; DA; DAB; DAC; DAM MST,
NOV, POP; SSC 2, 28; WLC
See also AAYA 2; CA 5-8R; CANR 39; CDALB
1941-1968; CLR 18; DLB 2, 102, 173;
MAICYA; MTCW; SATA 67

Salisbury, John
See Caute, (John) David

Salter, James 1925-   **CLC 7, 52, 59**
See also CA 73-76; DLB 130

Saltus, Edgar (Everton) 1855-1921 **TCLC 8**
See also CA 105

Saltykov, Mikhail Evgrafovich 1826-1889
NCLC 16

Samarakis, Antonis 1919-   **CLC 5**
See also CA 25-28R; CAAS 16; CANR 36

Sanchez, Florencio 1875-1910   **TCLC 37**
See also CA 153; HW

Sanchez, Luis Rafael 1936-   **CLC 23**
See also CA 128; DLB 145; HW

Sanchez, Sonia 1934-   **CLC 5; BLC 3; DAM**
MULT; PC 9
See also BW 2; CA 33-36R; CANR 24, 49; CLR
18; DLB 41; DLBD 8; MAICYA; MTCW;
SATA 22

Sand, George 1804-1876 **NCLC 2, 42, 57; DA;**
DAB; DAC; DAM MST, NOV; WLC
See also DLB 119, 192

Sandburg, Carl (August) 1878-1967 **CLC 1, 4,**
10, 15, 35; DA; DAB; DAC; DAM MST,
POET; PC 2; WLC
See also AAYA 24; CA 5-8R; 25-28R; CANR
35; CDALB 1865-1917; DLB 17, 54;
MAICYA; MTCW; SATA 8

Sandburg, Charles
See Sandburg, Carl (August)

Sandburg, Charles A.
See Sandburg, Carl (August)

Sanders, (James) Ed(ward) 1939-   **CLC 53**
See also CA 13-16R; CAAS 21; CANR 13, 44;
DLB 16

Sanders, Lawrence 1920-1998 **CLC 41; DAM**
POP
See also BEST 89:4; CA 81-84; 165; CANR

33, 62; MTCW

Sanders, Noah
See Blount, Roy (Alton), Jr.

Sanders, Winston P.
See Anderson, Poul (William)

Sandoz, Mari(e Susette) 1896-1966   **CLC 28**
See also CA 1-4R; 25-28R; CANR 17, 64; DLB
9; MTCW; SATA 5

Saner, Reg(inald Anthony) 1931-   **CLC 9**
See also CA 65-68

Sannazaro, Jacopo 1456(?)-1530   **LC 8**

Sansom, William 1912-1976 **CLC 2, 6; DAM**
NOV; SSC 21
See also CA 5-8R; 65-68; CANR 42; DLB 139;
MTCW

Santayana, George 1863-1952   **TCLC 40**
See also CA 115; DLB 54, 71; DLBD 13

Santiago, Danny   **CLC 33**
See also James, Daniel (Lewis)
See also DLB 122

Santmyer, Helen Hoover 1895-1986   **CLC 33**
See also CA 1-4R; 118; CANR 15, 33; DLBY
84; MTCW

Santoka, Taneda 1882-1940   **TCLC 72**

Santos, Bienvenido N(uqui) 1911-1996 **CLC**
22; DAM MULT
See also CA 101; 151; CANR 19, 46

Sapper   **TCLC 44**
See also McNeile, Herman Cyril

Sapphire 1950-   **CLC 99**

Sappho fl. 6th cent. B.C.-   **CMLC 3; DAM**
POET; PC 5
See also DLB 176

Sarduy, Severo 1937-1993   **CLC 6, 97**
See also CA 89-92; 142; CANR 58; DLB 113;
HW

Sargeson, Frank 1903-1982   **CLC 31**
See also CA 25-28R; 106; CANR 38

Sarmiento, Felix Ruben Garcia
See Dario, Ruben

Saroyan, William 1908-1981 **CLC 1, 8, 10, 29,**
34, 56; DA; DAB; DAC; DAM DRAM,
MST, NOV; SSC 21; WLC
See also CA 5-8R; 103; CANR 30; DLB 7, 9,
86; DLBY 81; MTCW; SATA 23; SATA-Obit
24

Sarraute, Nathalie 1900- **CLC 1, 2, 4, 8, 10, 31,**
80
See also CA 9-12R; CANR 23, 66; DLB 83;
MTCW

Sarton, (Eleanor) May 1912-1995 **CLC 4, 14,**
49, 91; DAM POET
See also CA 1-4R; 149; CANR 1, 34, 55; DLB
48; DLBY 81; INT CANR-34; MTCW;
SATA 36; SATA-Obit 86

Sartre, Jean-Paul 1905-1980 **CLC 1, 4, 7, 9, 13,**
18, 24, 44, 50, 52; DA; DAB; DAC; DAM
DRAM, MST, NOV; DC 3; WLC
See also CA 9-12R; 97-100; CANR 21; DLB
72; MTCW

Sassoon, Siegfried (Lorraine) 1886-1967 **CLC**
36; DAB; DAM MST, NOV, POET; PC 12
See also CA 104; 25-28R; CANR 36; DLB 20,
191; MTCW

Satterfield, Charles
See Pohl, Frederik

Saul, John (W. III) 1942- **CLC 46; DAM NOV,**
POP
See also AAYA 10; BEST 90:4; CA 81-84;
CANR 16, 40; SATA 98

Saunders, Caleb
See Heinlein, Robert A(nson)

Saura (Atares), Carlos 1932-   **CLC 20**

See also CA 114; 131; HW

Sauser-Hall, Frederic 1887-1961   **CLC 18**
See also Cendrars, Blaise
See also CA 102; 93-96; CANR 36, 62; MTCW

Saussure, Ferdinand de 1857-1913 **TCLC 49**

Savage, Catharine
See Brosman, Catharine Savage

Savage, Thomas 1915-   **CLC 40**
See also CA 126; 132; CAAS 15; INT 132

Savan, Glenn 19(?)-   **CLC 50**

Sayers, Dorothy L(eigh) 1893-1957 **TCLC 2,**
15; DAM POP
See also CA 104; 119; CANR 60; CDBLB 1914-
1945; DLB 10, 36, 77, 100; MTCW

Sayers, Valerie 1952-   **CLC 50**
See also CA 134; CANR 61

Sayles, John (Thomas) 1950- **CLC 7, 10, 14**
See also CA 57-60; CANR 41; DLB 44

Scammell, Michael 1935-   **CLC 34**
See also CA 156

Scannell, Vernon 1922-   **CLC 49**
See also CA 5-8R; CANR 8, 24, 57; DLB 27;
SATA 59

Scarlett, Susan
See Streatfeild, (Mary) Noel

Schaeffer, Susan Fromberg 1941- **CLC 6, 11,**
22
See also CA 49-52; CANR 18, 65; DLB 28;
MTCW; SATA 22

Schary, Jill
See Robinson, Jill

Schell, Jonathan 1943-   **CLC 35**
See also CA 73-76; CANR 12

Schelling, Friedrich Wilhelm Joseph von 1775-
1854   **CLC 30**
See also DLB 90

Schendel, Arthur van 1874-1946   **TCLC 56**

Scherer, Jean-Marie Maurice 1920-
See Rohmer, Eric
See also CA 110

Schevill, James (Erwin) 1920-   **CLC 7**
See also CA 5-8R; CAAS 12

Schiller, Friedrich 1759-1805 **NCLC 39, 69;**
DAM DRAM
See also DLB 94

Schisgal, Murray (Joseph) 1926-   **CLC 6**
See also CA 21-24R; CANR 48

Schlee, Ann 1934-   **CLC 35**
See also CA 101; CANR 29; SATA 44; SATA-
Brief 36

Schlegel, August Wilhelm von 1767-1845
NCLC 15
See also DLB 94

Schlegel, Friedrich 1772-1829   **NCLC 45**
See also DLB 90

Schlegel, Johann Elias (von) 1719(?)-1749 **L C**
5

Schlesinger, Arthur M(eier), Jr. 1917- **CLC 84**
See also AITN 1; CA 1-4R; CANR 1, 28, 58;
DLB 17; INT CANR-28; MTCW; SATA 61

Schmidt, Arno (Otto) 1914-1979   **CLC 56**
See also CA 128; 109; DLB 69

Schmitz, Aron Hector 1861-1928
See Svevo, Italo
See also CA 104; 122; MTCW

Schnackenberg, Gjertrud 1953-   **CLC 40**
See also CA 116; DLB 120

Schneider, Leonard Alfred 1925-1966
See Bruce, Lenny
See also CA 89-92

Schnitzler, Arthur 1862-1931 **TCLC 4; SSC 15**
See also CA 104; DLB 81, 118

Schoenberg, Arnold 1874-1951   **TCLC 75**

Somers, Jane
    See Lessing, Doris (May)
Somerville, Edith 1858-1949   **TCLC 51**
    See also DLB 135
Somerville & Ross
    See Martin, Violet Florence; Somerville, Edith
Sommer, Scott 1951-   **CLC 25**
    See also CA 106
Sondheim, Stephen (Joshua) 1930- **CLC 30,**
    39; DAM DRAM
    See also AAYA 11; CA 103; CANR 47, 68
Song, Cathy 1955-   **PC 21**
    See also CA 154; DLB 169
Sontag, Susan 1933-CLC **1, 2, 10, 13, 31, 105;**
    DAM POP
    See also CA 17-20R; CANR 25, 51; DLB 2,
    67; MTCW
Sophocles 496(?)B.C.-406(?)B.C.   **CMLC 2;**
    DA; DAB; DAC; DAM DRAM, MST; DC
    1; WLCS
    See also DLB 176
Sordello 1189-1269   **CMLC 15**
Sorel, Julia
    See Drexler, Rosalyn
Sorrentino, Gilbert 1929-CLC **3, 7, 14, 22, 40**
    See also CA 77-80; CANR 14, 33; DLB 5, 173;
    DLBY 80; INT CANR-14
Soto, Gary 1952- **CLC 32, 80; DAM MULT;**
    HLC
    See also AAYA 10; CA 119; 125; CANR 50;
    CLR 38; DLB 82; HW; INT 125; JRDA;
    SATA 80
Soupault, Philippe 1897-1990   **CLC 68**
    See also CA 116; 147; 131
Souster, (Holmes) Raymond 1921- CLC **5, 14;**
    DAC; DAM POET
    See also CA 13-16R; CAAS 14; CANR 13, 29,
    53; DLB 88; SATA 63
Southern, Terry 1924(?)-1995   **CLC 7**
    See also CA 1-4R; 150; CANR 1, 55; DLB 2
Southey, Robert 1774-1843   **NCLC 8**
    See also DLB 93, 107, 142; SATA 54
Southworth, Emma Dorothy Eliza Nevitte
    1819-1899   **NCLC 26**
Souza, Ernest
    See Scott, Evelyn
Soyinka, Wole 1934-CLC **3, 5, 14, 36, 44; BLC**
    3; DA; DAB; DAC; DAM DRAM, MST,
    MULT; DC 2; WLC
    See also BW 2; CA 13-16R; CANR 27, 39; DLB
    125; MTCW
Spackman, W(illiam) M(ode) 1905-1990 **CLC**
    46
    See also CA 81-84; 132
Spacks, Barry (Bernard) 1931-   **CLC 14**
    See also CA 154; CANR 33; DLB 105
Spanidou, Irini 1946-   **CLC 44**
Spark, Muriel (Sarah) 1918-CLC **2, 3, 5, 8, 13,**
    18, 40, 94; DAB; DAC; DAM MST, NOV;
    SSC 10
    See also CA 5-8R; CANR 12, 36; CDBLB 1945-
    1960; DLB 15, 139; INT CANR-12; MTCW
Spaulding, Douglas
    See Bradbury, Ray (Douglas)
Spaulding, Leonard
    See Bradbury, Ray (Douglas)
Spence, J. A. D.
    See Eliot, T(homas) S(tearns)
Spencer, Elizabeth 1921-   **CLC 22**
    See also CA 13-16R; CANR 32, 65; DLB 6;
    MTCW; SATA 14
Spencer, Leonard G.
    See Silverberg, Robert

Spencer, Scott 1945-   **CLC 30**
    See also CA 113; CANR 51; DLBY 86
Spender, Stephen (Harold) 1909-1995 **CLC 1,**
    2, 5, 10, 41, 91; DAM POET
    See also CA 9-12R; 149; CANR 31, 54; CDBLB
    1945-1960; DLB 20; MTCW
Spengler, Oswald (Arnold Gottfried) 1880-1936
    TCLC 25
    See also CA 118
Spenser, Edmund 1552(?)-1599 **LC 5, 39; DA;**
    DAB; DAC; DAM MST, POET; PC 8;
    WLC
    See also CDBLB Before 1660; DLB 167
Spicer, Jack 1925-1965   **CLC 8, 18, 72; DAM**
    POET
    See also CA 85-88; DLB 5, 16, 193
Spiegelman, Art 1948-   **CLC 76**
    See also AAYA 10; CA 125; CANR 41, 55
Spielberg, Peter 1929-   **CLC 6**
    See also CA 5-8R; CANR 4, 48; DLBY 81
Spielberg, Steven 1947-   **CLC 20**
    See also AAYA 8, 24; CA 77-80; CANR 32;
    SATA 32
Spillane, Frank Morrison 1918-
    See Spillane, Mickey
    See also CA 25-28R; CANR 28, 63; MTCW;
    SATA 66
Spillane, Mickey   **CLC 3, 13**
    See also Spillane, Frank Morrison
Spinoza, Benedictus de 1632-1677   **LC 9**
Spinrad, Norman (Richard) 1940-   **CLC 46**
    See also CA 37-40R; CAAS 19; CANR 20; DLB
    8; INT CANR-20
Spitteler, Carl (Friedrich Georg) 1845-1924
    TCLC 12
    See also CA 109; DLB 129
Spivack, Kathleen (Romola Drucker) 1938-
    CLC 6
    See also CA 49-52
Spoto, Donald 1941-   **CLC 39**
    See also CA 65-68; CANR 11, 57
Springsteen, Bruce (F.) 1949-   **CLC 17**
    See also CA 111
Spurling, Hilary 1940-   **CLC 34**
    See also CA 104; CANR 25, 52
Spyker, John Howland
    See Elman, Richard (Martin)
Squires, (James) Radcliffe 1917-1993 **CLC 51**
    See also CA 1-4R; 140; CANR 6, 21
Srivastava, Dhanpat Rai 1880(?)-1936
    See Premchand
    See also CA 118
Stacy, Donald
    See Pohl, Frederik
Stael, Germaine de 1766-1817
    See Stael-Holstein, Anne Louise Germaine
        Necker Baronn
    See also DLB 119
Stael-Holstein, Anne Louise Germaine Necker
    Baronn 1766-1817   **NCLC 3**
    See also Stael, Germaine de
    See also DLB 192
Stafford, Jean 1915-1979CLC **4, 7, 19, 68; SSC**
    26
    See also CA 1-4R; 85-88; CANR 3, 65; DLB 2,
    173; MTCW; SATA-Obit 22
Stafford, William (Edgar) 1914-1993 **CLC 4,**
    7, 29; DAM POET
    See also CA 5-8R; 142; CAAS 3; CANR 5, 22;
    DLB 5; INT CANR-22
Stagnelius, Eric Johan 1793-1823   **NCLC 61**
Staines, Trevor
    See Brunner, John (Kilian Houston)

Stairs, Gordon
    See Austin, Mary (Hunter)
Stannard, Martin 1947-   **CLC 44**
    See also CA 142; DLB 155
Stanton, Elizabeth Cady 1815-1902 **TCLC 73**
    See also DLB 79
Stanton, Maura 1946-   **CLC 9**
    See also CA 89-92; CANR 15; DLB 120
Stanton, Schuyler
    See Baum, L(yman) Frank
Stapledon, (William) Olaf 1886-1950   **TCLC**
    22
    See also CA 111; 162; DLB 15
Starbuck, George (Edwin) 1931-1996CLC **53;**
    DAM POET
    See also CA 21-24R; 153; CANR 23
Stark, Richard
    See Westlake, Donald E(dwin)
Staunton, Schuyler
    See Baum, L(yman) Frank
Stead, Christina (Ellen) 1902-1983 CLC **2, 5,**
    8, 32, 80
    See also CA 13-16R; 109; CANR 33, 40;
    MTCW
Stead, William Thomas 1849-1912 **TCLC 48**
Steele, Richard 1672-1729   **LC 18**
    See also CDBLB 1660-1789; DLB 84, 101
Steele, Timothy (Reid) 1948-   **CLC 45**
    See also CA 93-96; CANR 16, 50; DLB 120
Steffens, (Joseph) Lincoln 1866-1936 **TCLC**
    20
    See also CA 117
Stegner, Wallace (Earle) 1909-1993CLC **9, 49,**
    81; DAM NOV; SSC 27
    See also AITN 1; BEST 90:3; CA 1-4R; 141;
    CAAS 9; CANR 1, 21, 46; DLB 9; DLBY
    93; MTCW
Stein, Gertrude 1874-1946 TCLC **1, 6, 28, 48;**
    DA; DAB; DAC; DAM MST, NOV, POET;
    PC 18; WLC
    See also CA 104; 132; CDALB 1917-1929;
    DLB 4, 54, 86; DLBD 15; MTCW
Steinbeck, John (Ernst) 1902-1968CLC **1, 5, 9,**
    13, 21, 34, 45, 75; DA; DAB; DAC; DAM
    DRAM, MST, NOV; SSC 11; WLC
    See also AAYA 12; CA 1-4R; 25-28R; CANR
    1, 35; CDALB 1929-1941; DLB 7, 9; DLBD
    2; MTCW; SATA 9
Steinem, Gloria 1934-   **CLC 63**
    See also CA 53-56; CANR 28, 51; MTCW
Steiner, George 1929-   **CLC 24; DAM NOV**
    See also CA 73-76; CANR 31, 67; DLB 67;
    MTCW; SATA 62
Steiner, K. Leslie
    See Delany, Samuel R(ay, Jr.)
Steiner, Rudolf 1861-1925   **TCLC 13**
    See also CA 107
Stendhal 1783-1842 NCLC **23, 46; DA; DAB;**
    DAC; DAM MST, NOV; SSC 27; WLC
    See also DLB 119
Stephen, Adeline Virginia
    See Woolf, (Adeline) Virginia
Stephen, SirLeslie 1832-1904   **TCLC 23**
    See also CA 123; DLB 57, 144, 190
Stephen, Sir Leslie
    See Stephen, SirLeslie
Stephen, Virginia
    See Woolf, (Adeline) Virginia
Stephens, James 1882(?)-1950   **TCLC 4**
    See also CA 104; DLB 19, 153, 162
Stephens, Reed
    See Donaldson, Stephen R.
Steptoe, Lydia

See also AAYA 10; CA 5-8R; 139; CANR 37; CLR 1, 37; JRDA; MAICYA; SATA 6, 44, 78; SATA-Obit 73

Sutro, Alfred 1863-1933 **TCLC 6**
See also CA 105; DLB 10

Sutton, Henry
See Slavitt, David R(ytman)

Svevo, Italo 1861-1928 **TCLC 2, 35; SSC 25**
See also Schmitz, Aron Hector

Swados, Elizabeth (A.) 1951- **CLC 12**
See also CA 97-100; CANR 49; INT 97-100

Swados, Harvey 1920-1972 **CLC 5**
See also CA 5-8R; 37-40R; CANR 6; DLB 2

Swan, Gladys 1934- **CLC 69**
See also CA 101; CANR 17, 39

Swarthout, Glendon (Fred) 1918-1992**CLC 35**
See also CA 1-4R; 139; CANR 1, 47; SATA 26

Sweet, Sarah C.
See Jewett, (Theodora) Sarah Orne

Swenson, May 1919-1989 **CLC 4, 14, 61, 106; DA; DAB; DAC; DAM MST, POET; PC 14**
See also CA 5-8R; 130; CANR 36, 61; DLB 5; MTCW; SATA 15

Swift, Augustus
See Lovecraft, H(oward) P(hillips)

Swift, Graham (Colin) 1949- **CLC 41, 88**
See also CA 117; 122; CANR 46; DLB 194

Swift, Jonathan 1667-1745 **LC 1; DA; DAB; DAC; DAM MST, NOV, POET; PC 9; WLC**
See also CDBLB 1660-1789; DLB 39, 95, 101; SATA 19

Swinburne, Algernon Charles 1837-1909 **TCLC 8, 36; DA; DAB; DAC; DAM MST, POET; WLC**
See also CA 105; 140; CDBLB 1832-1890; DLB 35, 57

Swinfen, Ann **CLC 34**

Swinnerton, Frank Arthur 1884-1982**CLC 31**
See also CA 108; DLB 34

Swithen, John
See King, Stephen (Edwin)

Sylvia
See Ashton-Warner, Sylvia (Constance)

Symmes, Robert Edward
See Duncan, Robert (Edward)

Symonds, John Addington 1840-1893 **NCLC 34**
See also DLB 57, 144

Symons, Arthur 1865-1945 **TCLC 11**
See also CA 107; DLB 19, 57, 149

Symons, Julian (Gustave) 1912-1994 **CLC 2, 14, 32**
See also CA 49-52; 147; CAAS 3; CANR 3, 33, 59; DLB 87, 155; DLBY 92; MTCW

Synge, (Edmund) J(ohn) M(illington) 1871-1909 **TCLC 6, 37; DAM DRAM; DC 2**
See also CA 104; 141; CDBLB 1890-1914; DLB 10, 19

Syruc, J.
See Milosz, Czeslaw

Szirtes, George 1948- **CLC 46**
See also CA 109; CANR 27, 61

Szymborska, Wislawa 1923- **CLC 99**
See also CA 154; DLBY 96

T. O., Nik
See Annensky, Innokenty (Fyodorovich)

Tabori, George 1914- **CLC 19**
See also CA 49-52; CANR 4, 69

Tagore, Rabindranath 1861-1941**TCLC 3, 53; DAM DRAM, POET; PC 8**
See also CA 104; 120; MTCW

Taine, Hippolyte Adolphe 1828-1893 **NCLC 15**

Talese, Gay 1932- **CLC 37**
See also AITN 1; CA 1-4R; CANR 9, 58; DLB 185; INT CANR-9; MTCW

Tallent, Elizabeth (Ann) 1954- **CLC 45**
See also CA 117; DLB 130

Tally, Ted 1952- **CLC 42**
See also CA 120; 124; INT 124

Tamayo y Baus, Manuel 1829-1898 **NCLC 1**

Tammsaare, A(nton) H(ansen) 1878-1940 **TCLC 27**
See also CA 164

Tam'si, Tchicaya U
See Tchicaya, Gerald Felix

Tan, Amy (Ruth) 1952-**CLC 59; DAM MULT, NOV, POP**
See also AAYA 9; BEST 89:3; CA 136; CANR 54; DLB 173; SATA 75

Tandem, Felix
See Spitteler, Carl (Friedrich Georg)

Tanizaki, Jun'ichiro 1886-1965**CLC 8, 14, 28; SSC 21**
See also CA 93-96; 25-28R; DLB 180

Tanner, William
See Amis, Kingsley (William)

Tao Lao
See Storni, Alfonsina

Tarassoff, Lev
See Troyat, Henri

Tarbell, Ida M(inerva) 1857-1944 **TCLC 40**
See also CA 122; DLB 47

Tarkington, (Newton) Booth 1869-1946**TCLC 9**
See also CA 110; 143; DLB 9, 102; SATA 17

Tarkovsky, Andrei (Arsenyevich) 1932-1986 **CLC 75**
See also CA 127

Tartt, Donna 1964(?)- **CLC 76**
See also CA 142

Tasso, Torquato 1544-1595 **LC 5**

Tate, (John Orley) Allen 1899-1979 **CLC 2, 4, 6, 9, 11, 14, 24**
See also CA 5-8R; 85-88; CANR 32; DLB 4, 45, 63; MTCW

Tate, Ellalice
See Hibbert, Eleanor Alice Burford

Tate, James (Vincent) 1943- **CLC 2, 6, 25**
See also CA 21-24R; CANR 29, 57; DLB 5, 169

Tavel, Ronald 1940- **CLC 6**
See also CA 21-24R; CANR 33

Taylor, C(ecil) P(hilip) 1929-1981 **CLC 27**
See also CA 25-28R; 105; CANR 47

Taylor, Edward 1642(?)-1729 **LC 11; DA; DAB; DAC; DAM MST, POET**
See also DLB 24

Taylor, Eleanor Ross 1920- **CLC 5**
See also CA 81-84

Taylor, Elizabeth 1912-1975 **CLC 2, 4, 29**
See also CA 13-16R; CANR 9; DLB 139; MTCW; SATA 13

Taylor, Frederick Winslow 1856-1915 **TCLC 76**

Taylor, Henry (Splawn) 1942- **CLC 44**
See also CA 33-36R; CAAS 7; CANR 31; DLB 5

Taylor, Kamala (Purnaiya) 1924-
See Markandaya, Kamala
See also CA 77-80

Taylor, Mildred D. **CLC 21**
See also AAYA 10; BW 1; CA 85-88; CANR 25; CLR 9; DLB 52; JRDA; MAICYA; SAAS

5; SATA 15, 70

Taylor, Peter (Hillsman) 1917-1994 **CLC 1, 4, 18, 37, 44, 50, 71; SSC 10**
See also CA 13-16R; 147; CANR 9, 50; DLBY 81, 94; INT CANR-9; MTCW

Taylor, Robert Lewis 1912- **CLC 14**
See also CA 1-4R; CANR 3, 64; SATA 10

Tchekhov, Anton
See Chekhov, Anton (Pavlovich)

Tchicaya, Gerald Felix 1931-1988 **CLC 101**
See also CA 129; 125

Tchicaya U Tam'si
See Tchicaya, Gerald Felix

Teasdale, Sara 1884-1933 **TCLC 4**
See also CA 104; 163; DLB 45; SATA 32

Tegner, Esaias 1782-1846 **NCLC 2**

Teilhard de Chardin, (Marie Joseph) Pierre 1881-1955 **TCLC 9**
See also CA 105

Temple, Ann
See Mortimer, Penelope (Ruth)

Tennant, Emma (Christina) 1937- **CLC 13, 52**
See also CA 65-68; CAAS 9; CANR 10, 38, 59; DLB 14

Tenneshaw, S. M.
See Silverberg, Robert

Tennyson, Alfred 1809-1892 **NCLC 30, 65; DA; DAB; DAC; DAM MST, POET; PC 6; WLC**
See also CDBLB 1832-1890; DLB 32

Teran, Lisa St. Aubin de **CLC 36**
See also St. Aubin de Teran, Lisa

Terence 195(?)B.C.-159B.C. **CMLC 14; DC 7**

Teresa de Jesus, St. 1515-1582 **LC 18**

Terkel, Louis 1912-
See Terkel, Studs
See also CA 57-60; CANR 18, 45, 67; MTCW

Terkel, Studs **CLC 38**
See also Terkel, Louis
See also AITN 1

Terry, C. V.
See Slaughter, Frank G(ill)

Terry, Megan 1932- **CLC 19**
See also CA 77-80; CABS 3; CANR 43; DLB 7

Tertullian c. 155-c. 245 **CMLC 29**

Tertz, Abram
See Sinyavsky, Andrei (Donatevich)

Tesich, Steve 1943(?)-1996 **CLC 40, 69**
See also CA 105; 152; DLBY 83

Teternikov, Fyodor Kuzmich 1863-1927
See Sologub, Fyodor
See also CA 104

Tevis, Walter 1928-1984 **CLC 42**
See also CA 113

Tey, Josephine **TCLC 14**
See also Mackintosh, Elizabeth
See also DLB 77

Thackeray, William Makepeace 1811-1863 **NCLC 5, 14, 22, 43; DA; DAB; DAC; DAM MST, NOV; WLC**
See also CDBLB 1832-1890; DLB 21, 55, 159, 163; SATA 23

Thakura, Ravindranatha
See Tagore, Rabindranath

Tharoor, Shashi 1956- **CLC 70**
See also CA 141

Thelwell, Michael Miles 1939- **CLC 22**
See also BW 2; CA 101

Theobald, Lewis, Jr.
See Lovecraft, H(oward) P(hillips)

Theodorescu, Ion N. 1880-1967
See Arghezi, Tudor
See also CA 116

DAB; DAC; DAM MST, NOV; WLCS 2
See also AAYA 7; AITN 1; CA 5-8R; CAAS 4;
CANR 8, 40, 65; DLB 83; DLBY 87; INT
CANR-8; MTCW; SATA 56

Wiggins, Marianne 1947-   **CLC 57**
See also BEST 89:3; CA 130; CANR 60

Wight, James Alfred 1916-1995
See Herriot, James
See also CA 77-80; SATA 55; SATA-Brief 44

Wilbur, Richard (Purdy) 1921-**CLC 3, 6, 9, 14,**
53, 110; DA; DAB; DAC; DAM MST,
POET
See also CA 1-4R; CABS 2; CANR 2, 29; DLB
5, 169; INT CANR-29; MTCW; SATA 9

Wild, Peter 1940-   **CLC 14**
See also CA 37-40R; DLB 5

Wilde, Oscar (Fingal O'Flahertie Wills)
1854(?)-1900 **TCLC 1, 8, 23, 41; DA; DAB;**
DAC; DAM DRAM, MST, NOV; SSC 11;
WLC
See also CA 104; 119; CDBLB 1890-1914;
DLB 10, 19, 34, 57, 141, 156, 190; SATA 24

Wilder, Billy   **CLC 20**
See also Wilder, Samuel
See also DLB 26

Wilder, Samuel 1906-
See Wilder, Billy
See also CA 89-92

Wilder, Thornton (Niven) 1897-1975**CLC 1, 5,**
6, 10, 15, 35, 82; DA; DAB; DAC; DAM
DRAM, MST, NOV; DC 1; WLC
See also AITN 2; CA 13-16R; 61-64; CANR
40; DLB 4, 7, 9; DLBY 97; MTCW

Wilding, Michael 1942-   **CLC 73**
See also CA 104; CANR 24, 49

Wiley, Richard 1944-   **CLC 44**
See also CA 121; 129

Wilhelm, Kate   **CLC 7**
See also Wilhelm, Katie Gertrude
See also AAYA 20; CAAS 5; DLB 8; INT
CANR-17

Wilhelm, Katie Gertrude 1928-
See Wilhelm, Kate
See also CA 37-40R; CANR 17, 36, 60; MTCW

Wilkins, Mary
See Freeman, Mary Eleanor Wilkins

Willard, Nancy 1936-   **CLC 7, 37**
See also CA 89-92; CANR 10, 39, 68; CLR 5;
DLB 5, 52; MAICYA; MTCW; SATA 37, 71;
SATA-Brief 30

Williams, C(harles) K(enneth) 1936- **CLC 33,**
56; DAM POET
See also CA 37-40R; CAAS 26; CANR 57; DLB
5

Williams, Charles
See Collier, James L(incoln)

Williams, Charles (Walter Stansby) 1886-1945
TCLC 1, 11
See also CA 104; 163; DLB 100, 153

Williams, (George) Emlyn 1905-1987**CLC 15;**
DAM DRAM
See also CA 104; 123; CANR 36; DLB 10, 77;
MTCW

Williams, Hank 1923-1953   **TCLC 81**

Williams, Hugo 1942-   **CLC 42**
See also CA 17-20R; CANR 45; DLB 40

Williams, J. Walker
See Wodehouse, P(elham) G(renville)

Williams, John A(lfred) 1925-**CLC 5, 13; BLC**
3; DAM MULT
See also BW 2; CA 53-56; CAAS 3; CANR 6,
26, 51; DLB 2, 33; INT CANR-6

Williams, Jonathan (Chamberlain) 1929-

CLC 13
See also CA 9-12R; CAAS 12; CANR 8; DLB
5

Williams, Joy 1944-   **CLC 31**
See also CA 41-44R; CANR 22, 48

Williams, Norman 1952-   **CLC 39**
See also CA 118

Williams, Sherley Anne 1944-**CLC 89; BLC 3;**
DAM MULT, POET
See also BW 2; CA 73-76; CANR 25; DLB 41;
INT CANR-25; SATA 78

Williams, Shirley
See Williams, Sherley Anne

Williams, Tennessee 1911-1983**CLC 1, 2, 5, 7,**
8, 11, 15, 19, 30, 39, 45, 71, 111; DA; DAB;
DAC; DAM DRAM, MST; DC 4; WLC
See also AITN 1, 2; CA 5-8R; 108; CABS 3;
CANR 31; CDALB 1941-1968; DLB 7;
DLBD 4; DLBY 83; MTCW

Williams, Thomas (Alonzo) 1926-1990**CLC 14**
See also CA 1-4R; 132; CANR 2

Williams, William C.
See Williams, William Carlos

Williams, William Carlos 1883-1963**CLC 1, 2,**
5, 9, 13, 22, 42, 67; DA; DAB; DAC; DAM
MST, POET; PC 7; SSC 31
See also CA 89-92; CANR 34; CDALB 1917-
1929; DLB 4, 16, 54, 86; MTCW

Williamson, David (Keith) 1942-   **CLC 56**
See also CA 103; CANR 41

Williamson, Ellen Douglas 1905-1984
See Douglas, Ellen
See also CA 17-20R; 114; CANR 39

Williamson, Jack   **CLC 29**
See also Williamson, John Stewart
See also CAAS 8; DLB 8

Williamson, John Stewart 1908-
See Williamson, Jack
See also CA 17-20R; CANR 23

Willie, Frederick
See Lovecraft, H(oward) P(hillips)

Willingham, Calder (Baynard, Jr.) 1922-1995
CLC 5, 51
See also CA 5-8R; 147; CANR 3; DLB 2, 44;
MTCW

Willis, Charles
See Clarke, Arthur C(harles)

Willy
See Colette, (Sidonie-Gabrielle)

Willy, Colette
See Colette, (Sidonie-Gabrielle)

Wilson, A(ndrew) N(orman) 1950-   **CLC 33**
See also CA 112; 122; DLB 14, 155, 194

Wilson, Angus (Frank Johnstone) 1913-1991
CLC 2, 3, 5, 25, 34; SSC 21
See also CA 5-8R; 134; CANR 21; DLB 15,
139, 155; MTCW

Wilson, August 1945-**CLC 39, 50, 63; BLC 3;**
DA; DAB; DAC; DAM DRAM, MST,
MULT; DC 2; WLCS
See also AAYA 16; BW 2; CA 115; 122; CANR
42, 54; MTCW

Wilson, Brian 1942-   **CLC 12**

Wilson, Colin 1931-   **CLC 3, 14**
See also CA 1-4R; CAAS 5; CANR 1, 22, 33;
DLB 14, 194; MTCW

Wilson, Dirk
See Pohl, Frederik

Wilson, Edmund 1895-1972 **CLC 1, 2, 3, 8, 24**
See also CA 1-4R; 37-40R; CANR 1, 46; DLB
63; MTCW

Wilson, Ethel Davis (Bryant) 1888(?)-1980
CLC 13; DAC; DAM POET

See also CA 102; DLB 68; MTCW

Wilson, John 1785-1854   **NCLC 5**

Wilson, John (Anthony) Burgess 1917-1993
See Burgess, Anthony
See also CA 1-4R; 143; CANR 2, 46; DAC;
DAM NOV; MTCW

Wilson, Lanford 1937- **CLC 7, 14, 36; DAM**
DRAM
See also CA 17-20R; CABS 3; CANR 45; DLB
7

Wilson, Robert M. 1944-   **CLC 7, 9**
See also CA 49-52; CANR 2, 41; MTCW

Wilson, Robert McLiam 1964-   **CLC 59**
See also CA 132

Wilson, Sloan 1920-   **CLC 32**
See also CA 1-4R; CANR 1, 44

Wilson, Snoo 1948-   **CLC 33**
See also CA 69-72

Wilson, William S(mith) 1932-   **CLC 49**
See also CA 81-84

Wilson, (Thomas) Woodrow 1856-1924**TCLC**
79
See also CA 166; DLB 47

Winchilsea, Anne (Kingsmill) Finch Counte
1661-1720
See Finch, Anne

Windham, Basil
See Wodehouse, P(elham) G(renville)

Wingrove, David (John) 1954-   **CLC 68**
See also CA 133

Wintergreen, Jane
See Duncan, Sara Jeannette

Winters, Janet Lewis   **CLC 41**
See also Lewis, Janet
See also DLBY 87

Winters, (Arthur) Yvor 1900-1968 **CLC 4, 8,**
32
See also CA 11-12; 25-28R; CAP 1; DLB 48;
MTCW

Winterson, Jeanette 1959-**CLC 64; DAM POP**
See also CA 136; CANR 58

Winthrop, John 1588-1649   **LC 31**
See also DLB 24, 30

Wiseman, Frederick 1930-   **CLC 20**
See also CA 159

Wister, Owen 1860-1938   **TCLC 21**
See also CA 108; 162; DLB 9, 78, 186; SATA
62

Witkacy
See Witkiewicz, Stanislaw Ignacy

Witkiewicz, Stanislaw Ignacy 1885-1939
TCLC 8
See also CA 105; 162

Wittgenstein, Ludwig (Josef Johann) 1889-1951
TCLC 59
See also CA 113; 164

Wittig, Monique 1935(?)-   **CLC 22**
See also CA 116; 135; DLB 83

Wittlin, Jozef 1896-1976   **CLC 25**
See also CA 49-52; 65-68; CANR 3

Wodehouse, P(elham) G(renville) 1881-1975
CLC 1, 2, 5, 10, 22; DAB; DAC; DAM
NOV; SSC 2
See also AITN 2; CA 45-48; 57-60; CANR 3,
33; CDBLB 1914-1945; DLB 34, 162;
MTCW; SATA 22

Woiwode, L.
See Woiwode, Larry (Alfred)

Woiwode, Larry (Alfred) 1941-   **CLC 6, 10**
See also CA 73-76; CANR 16; DLB 6; INT
CANR-16

Wojciechowska, Maia (Teresa) 1927- **CLC 26**
See also AAYA 8; CA 9-12R; CANR 4, 41; CLR

Author Index

Literary Criticism Series
Cumulative Topic Index

This index lists all topic entries in Gale's *Classical and Medieval Literature Criticism, Contemporary Literary Criticism, Literature Criticism from 1400 to 1800, Nineteenth-Century Literature Criticism,* and *Twentieth-Century Literary Criticism.*

Topic Index

CMLC Cumulative Nationality Index

CMLC Cumulative Title Index

Title Index

Title Index

Title Index

493

Title Index

Title Index

CMLC Cumulative Critic Index

Critic Index

Critic Index

Critic Index

Critic Index

Critic Index

Critic Index

ISBN 0-7876-2408-X

90000